COLLINS GEM

FRENCH DICTIONARY

FRENCH • ENGLISH
ENGLISH • FRENCH

HarperCollins*Publishers*

Dictionnaires Le Robert
Paris

first published in this edition 1979
second edition 1988
third edition 1993

© **William Collins Sons & Co. Ltd. 1979, 1988**
© **HarperCollins Publishers 1993**

ISBN 0 00 458977-7

contributors / avec la collaboration de
Claude Nimmo, Lorna Sinclair,
Philippe Patry, Hélène Lewis,
Elisabeth Campbell, Renée Birks,
Jean-François Allain, Christine Penman

editorial staff / secrétariat de rédaction
Joyce Littlejohn, Catherine Love,
Lesley Robertson, Stephen Clarke,
Angela Campbell, Vivian Marr

DICTIONNAIRES LE ROBERT
12, avenue d'Italie
75013 PARIS

ISBN: 2-85036-136-4
Dépôt légal: avril 1993

A catalogue record for this book is
available from the British Library

Typeset by Morton Word Processing Ltd, Scarborough

Printed in Great Britain by
HarperCollins Manufacturing, Glasgow

TABLE DE MATIÈRES

CONTENTS

INTRODUCTION

Nous sommes très heureux que vous ayez décidé d'acheter le dictionnaire anglais Gem de Collins et espérons que vous aimerez l'utiliser et que vous en tirerez profit au lycée, à la maison, en vacances ou au travail.

Cette introduction a pour but de vous donner quelques conseils sur la meilleure façon d'utiliser au mieux votre dictionnaire, en vous référant non seulement à son importante nomenclature mais aussi aux informations contenues dans chaque entrée. Ceci vous aidera à lire et à comprendre, mais aussi à communiquer et à vous exprimer en anglais contemporain.

Le dictionnaire anglais Gem de Collins commence par la liste des abréviations utilisées dans le texte et par la transcription des sons par des symboles phonétiques. A la fin vous trouverez des tables de verbes français ainsi que la liste des verbes irréguliers en anglais, suivis d'une section finale sur les nombres et sur les expressions de temps.

COMMENT UTILISER VOTRE DICTIONNAIRE GEM COLLINS

Ce dictionnaire offre une masse d'informations et use de divers formes et tailles de caractères, symboles, abréviations, parenthèses et crochets. Les conventions et symboles utilisés sont expliqués dans les sections qui suivent.

Entrées

Les mots que vous cherchez dans le dictionnaire (les 'entrées') sont classés par ordre alphabétique. Ils sont imprimés en **caractères gras** pour pouvoir être repérés rapidement. Les deux entrées figurant en haut de page indiquent le premier et le dernier mot qui apparaissent sur la page en question.

Des informations sur l'usage ou sur la forme de certaines entrées sont données entre parenthèses, après la transcription phonétique. Ces indications apparaissent sous forme abrégée et en italiques (ex *(fam)*, *(COMM)*).

Dans les cas appropriés, les mots apparentés aux entrées sont regroupés sous la même entrée (**ronger, rongeur; accept, acceptance**) et apparaissent en caractères gras, légèrement plus petits que ceux de l'entrée.

Les expressions courantes dans lesquelles apparaît l'entrée sont indiquées par des caractères romains gras différents (ex **avoir du retard**).

Transcription phonétique

La transcription phonétique de chaque entrée (indiquant sa prononciation) est indiquée entre crochets immédiatement après l'entrée (ex **fumer** [fyme]; **knead** [ni:d]). Une liste de ces symboles figure à la page x.

Traductions

Les traductions des entrées apparaissent en caractères ordinaires et, lorsque plusieurs sens ou usages coexistent, ces traductions sont séparées par un point-virgule. Vous trouverez souvent entre parenthèses d'autres mots en italiques qui précèdent les traductions. Ces mots fournissent souvent certains des contextes dans lesquels l'entrée est susceptible d'être utilisée (ex **rough** (*voice*) ou (*weather*)) ou offrent des synonymes (ex **rough** (*violent*)).

'Mots-clés'

Une importance particulière est accordée à certains mots français et anglais qui sont considérés comme des "mots-clés" dans chacune des langues. Cela peut être dû à leur utilisation très fréquente ou au fait qu'ils ont divers types d'usages (ex **vouloir, plus**; **get, that**). Une combinaison de losanges et de chiffres vous aident à distinguer différentes catégories grammaticales et différents sens. D'autres renseignements utiles apparaissent en italiques et entre parenthèses dans la langue de l'utilisateur.

Données grammaticales

Les catégories grammaticales sont données sous forme abrégée et en italiques après la transcription phonétique des entrées (ex *vt, adv, conj*).

Les genres des noms français sont indiqués de la manière suivante: *nm* pour un nom masculin et *nf* pour un nom féminin. Le féminin et le pluriel irréguliers de certains noms sont également indiqués (**directeur, trice; cheval, aux**).

Le masculin et le féminin des adjectif sont indiqués lorsque ces deux formes sont différentes (ex **noir, e**). Lorsque l'adjectif a un féminin ou un pluriel irrégulier, ces formes sont clairement indiquées (ex **net, nette**). Les pluriels irréguliers des noms, et les formes irrégu- liers des verbes anglais sont indiqués entre paren- thèses, avant la catégorie grammaticale (ex **man** ... (*pl* **men**) *n*; **give** (*pt* **gave**, *pp* **given**) *vt*).

INTRODUCTION

We are delighted you have decided to buy the Collins Gem French Dictionary and hope you will enjoy and benefit from using it at school, at home, on holiday or at work.

This introduction gives you a few tips on how to get the most out of your dictionary — not simply from its comprehensive wordlist but also from the information provided in each entry. This will help you to read and understand modern French, as well as communicate and express yourself in the language.

The Collins Gem French Dictionary begins by listing the abbrevia- tions used in the text and illustrating the sounds shown by the phonetic symbols. You will find French verb tables and English irregular verbs at the back, followed by a final section on numbers and time expressions.

USING YOUR COLLINS GEM DICTIONARY

A wealth of information is presented in the dictionary, using various typefaces, sizes of type, symbols, abbreviations and brackets. The conventions and symbols used are explained in the following sec- tions.

Headwords
The words you look up in a dictionary — "headwords" — are listed alphabetically. They are printed in **bold type** for rapid identifica- tion. The two words appearing at the top of each page indicate the first and last word dealt with on the page in question.

Information about the usage or form of certain headwords is given in brackets after the phonetic spelling. This usually appears in abbreviated form and in italics (e.g. (*fam*), (*COMM*)).

Where appropriate, words related to headwords are grouped in the same entry (**ronger, rongeur; accept, acceptance**) in a slightly smaller bold type than the headword.

Common expressions in which the headword appears are shown in a different bold roman type (e.g. **avoir du retard**).

Phonetic spellings

The phonetic spelling of each headword (indicating its pronunciation) is given in square brackets immediately after the headword (e.g. **fumer** |fyme|; **knead** |ni:d|). A list of these symbols is given on page x.

Translations

Headword translations are given in ordinary type and, where more than one meaning or usage exists, these are separated by a semicolon. You will often find other words in italics in brackets before the translations. These offer suggested contexts in which the headword might appear (e.g. **rough** (*voice*) or (*weather*)) or provide synonyms (e.g. **rough** (*violent*)).

"Key" words

Special status is given to certain French and English words which are considered as "key" words in each language. They may, for example, occur very frequently or have several types of usage (e.g. **vouloir, plus; get, that**). A combination of lozenges and numbers helps you to distinguish different parts of speech and different meanings. Further helpful information is provided in brackets and in italics in the relevant language for the user.

Grammatical information

Parts of speech are given in abbreviated form in italics after the phonetic spellings of headwords (e.g. *vt, adv, conj*).

Genders of French nouns are indicated as follows: *nm* for a masculine and *nf* for a feminine noun. Feminine and irregular plural forms of nouns are also shown (**directeur, trice; cheval, aux**).

Adjectives are given in both masculine and feminine forms where these forms are different (e.g. **noir, e**). Clear information is provided where adjectives have an irregular feminine or plural form (e.g. **net, nette**).

ABRÉVIATIONS

ABBREVIATIONS

abréviation	**ab(b)r**	abbreviation
adjectif, locution adjective	**adj**	adjective, adjectival phrase
adverbe, locution adverbiale	**adv**	adverb, adverbial phrase
administration	**ADMIN**	administration
agriculture	**AGR**	agriculture
anatomie	**ANAT**	anatomy
architecture	**ARCHIT**	architecture
article défini	**art déf**	definite article
article indéfini	**art indéf**	indefinite article
l'automobile	**AUT(O)**	the motor car and motoring
aviation, voyages aériens	**AVIAT**	flying, air travel
biologie	**BIO(L)**	biology
botanique	**BOT**	botany
anglais de Grande-Bretagne	**BRIT**	British English
conjonction	**conj**	conjunction
commerce, finance, banque	**COMM**	commerce, finance, banking
comparatif	**compar**	comparative
informatique	**COMPUT**	computing
construction	**CONSTR**	building
nom utilisé comme adjectif	**cpd**	compound element
cuisine, art culinaire	**CULIN**	cookery
article défini	**def art**	definite article
déterminant: article, adjectif démonstratif ou indéfini etc	**dét**	determiner: article, demonstrative etc
diminutif	**dimin**	diminutive
économie	**ECON**	economics
électricité, électronique	**ELEC**	electricity, electronics
exclamation, interjection	**excl**	exclamation, interjection
féminin	**f**	feminine
langue familière (! emploi vulgaire)	**fam (!)**	colloquial usage (! particularly offensive)
emploi figuré	**fig**	figurative use
(verbe anglais) dont la particule est inséparable du verbe	**fus**	(phrasal verb) where the particle cannot be separated from main verb
généralement	**gén, gen**	generally
géographie, géologie	**GEO**	geography, geology
géométrie	**GEOM**	geometry
impersonnel	**impers**	impersonal
article indéfini	**indef art**	indefinite article
langue familière (! emploi vulgaire)	**inf(!)**	colloquial usage (! particularly offensive)
infinitif	**infin**	infinitive
informatique	**INFORM**	computing
invariable	**inv**	invariable
irrégulier	**irreg**	irregular

ABRÉVIATIONS

ABBREVIATIONS

domaine juridique	**JUR**	law
grammaire, linguistique	**LING**	grammar, linguistics
masculin	**m**	masculine
mathématiques, algèbre	**MATH**	mathematics, calculus
médecine	**MÉD MED**	medical term, medicine
masculin ou féminin, suivant le sexe	**m/f**	masculine or feminine depending on sex
domaine militaire, armée	**MIL**	military matters
musique	**MUS**	music
nom	**n**	noun
navigation, nautisme	**NAVIG, NAUT**	sailing, navigation
adjectif ou nom numérique	**num**	numeral adjective or noun
	o.s.	oneself
péjoratif	**péj, pej**	derogatory, pejorative
photographie	**PHOT(O)**	photography
physiologie	**PHYSIOL**	physiology
pluriel	**pl**	plural
politique	**POL**	politics
participe passé	**pp**	past participle
préposition	**prép, prep**	preposition
pronom	**pron**	pronoun
psychologie, psychiatrie	**PSYCH**	psychology, psychiatry
temps du passé	**pt**	past tense
quelque chose	**qch**	
quelqu'un	**qn**	
religions, domaine ecclésiastique	**REL**	religions, church service
	sb	somebody
enseignement, système scolaire et universitaire	**SCOL**	schooling, schools and universities
singulier	**sg**	singular
	sth	something
subjonctif	**sub**	subjunctive
sujet (grammatical)	**su(b)j**	(grammatical) subject
superlatif	**superl**	superlative
techniques, technologie	**TECH**	technical term, technology
télécommunications	**TEL**	telecommunications
télévision	**TV**	television
typographie	**TYP(O)**	typography, printing
anglais des USA	**US**	American English
verbe	**vb**	verb
verbe intransitive	**vi**	intransitive verb
verbe transitive	**vt**	transitive verb
zoologie	**ZOOL**	zoology
marque déposée	**®**	registered trademark
indique une équivalence culturelle	**≈**	introduces a cultural equivalent

TRANSCRIPTION PHONÉTIQUE

CONSONNES

CONSONANTS

NB. **p**, **b**, **t**, **d**, **k**, **g** sont suivis d'une aspiration en anglais.

NB. **p**, **b**, **t**, **d**, **k**, **g** are not aspirated in French.

poupée *bombe*	p	*puppy*
bombe	b	*baby*
tente *thermal*	t	*tent*
dinde	d	*daddy*
coq qui képi	k	*cork kiss chord*
gag bague	g	*gag guess*
sale ce nation	s	*so rice kiss*
zéro rose	z	*cousin buzz*
tache chat	ʃ	*sheep sugar*
gilet juge	ʒ	*pleasure beige*
	tʃ	*church*
	dʒ	*judge general*
fer phare	f	*farm raffle*
valve	v	*very rev*
	θ	*thin maths*
	ð	*that other*
lent salle	l	*little ball*
rare rentrer	ʀ	
	r	*rat rare*
maman femme	m	*mummy comb*
non nonne	n	*no ran*
agneau vigne	ɲ	
	ŋ	*singing bank*
hop!	h	*hat reheat*
yeux paille pied	j	*yet*
nouer oui	w	*wall bewail*
huile lui	ɥ	
	x	*loch*

DIVERS

MISCELLANEOUS

pour l'anglais: le r final se prononce en liaison devant une voyelle	*	in French wordlist: no liason
pour l'anglais: précède la syllabe accentuée	'	in French transcription: no liaison

PHONETIC TRANSCRIPTION

VOYELLES

NB. La mise en équivalence de certains sons n'indique qu'une ressemblance approximative.

VOWELS

NB. The pairing of some vowel sounds only indicates approximate equivalence.

ici vie lyre	i iː	heel bead
	ɪ	hit pity
jouer été	e	
lait jouet merci	ɛ	set tent
plat amour	a æ	bat apple
bas pâte	ɑ ɑː	after car calm
	ʌ	fun cousin
le premier	ə	over above
beurre peur	œ	
peu deux	ø ɜː	urn fern work
or homme	ɔ	wash pot
mot eau gauche	o ɔː	born cork
genou roue	u	full soot
	uː	boon lewd
rue urne	y	

DIPHTONGUES

DIPHTHONGS

ɪə	beer tier
ɛə	tear fair there
eɪ	date place day
aɪ	life buy cry
au	owl foul now
əu	low no
ɔɪ	boil boy oily
uə	poor tour

NASALES

NASAL VOWELS

matin plein	ɛ̃
brun	œ̃
sang an dans	ɑ̃
non pont	õ

x

A *abr* = **autoroute**

a *vb voir* **avoir**

MOT-CLÉ

à [a] (*à* + *le* = **au**, *à* + *les* = **aux**) *prép* **1** (*endroit, situation*) at, in; **être ~ Paris/au Portugal** to be in Paris/Portugal; **être ~ la maison/l'école** to be at home/at school; **~ la campagne** to be in the country; **c'est à 10 km/~ 20 minutes (d'ici)** it's 10 km/20 minutes away

2 (*direction*) to; **aller ~ Paris/au Portugal** to go to Paris/Portugal; **aller ~ la maison/~ l'école** to go home/to school; **~ la campagne** to the country

3 (*temps*): **~ 3 heures/minuit** at 3 o'clock/midnight; **au printemps/mois de juin** in the spring/the month of June

4 (*attribution, appartenance*) to; **le livre est ~ Paul/~ lui/~ nous** this book is Paul's/his/ours; **donner qch ~ qn** to give sth to sb

5 (*moyen*) with; **se chauffer au gaz** to have gas heating; **~ bicyclette** on a *ou* by bicycle; **~ la main/machine** by hand/machine

6 (*provenance*): **boire ~ la bouteille** to drink from the bottle

7 (*caractérisation, manière*): **l'homme aux yeux bleus** the man with the blue eyes; **~ la russe** the Russian way

8 (*but, destination*): **tasse ~ café** coffee cup; **maison ~ vendre** house for sale

9 (*rapport, évaluation, distribution*): **100 km/unités ~ l'heure** 100 km/units per *ou* an hour; **payé ~ l'heure** paid by the hour; **cinq ~ six** five to six

abaisser [abese] *vt* to lower, bring down; (*manette*) to pull down; (*fig*) to debase; to humiliate; **s'~** *vi* to go down; (*fig*) to demean o.s.

abandon [abɑ̃dɔ̃] *nm* abandoning; giving up; withdrawal; **être à l'~** to be in a state of neglect

abandonner [abɑ̃dɔne] *vt* (*personne*) to abandon; (*projet, activité*) to abandon, give up; (*SPORT*) to retire *ou* withdraw from; (*céder*) to surrender; **s'~** *vi* to let o.s. go; **s'~ à** (*paresse, plaisirs*) to give o.s. up to

abasourdir [abazurdir] *vt* to stun, stagger

abat-jour [abaʒur] *nm inv* lampshade

abats [aba] *nmpl* (*de bœuf, porc*) offal *sg*; (*de volaille*) giblets

abattement [abatmɑ̃] *nm* (*déduction*) reduction; **~ fiscal** = tax allowance

abattoir [abatwar] *nm* slaughterhouse

abattre [abatʀ(ə)] *vt* (*arbre*) to cut down, fell; (*mur, maison*) to pull down; (*avion, personne*) to shoot down; (*animal*) to shoot, kill; (*fig*) to wear out, tire out; to demoralize; **s'~** *vi* to crash down; **s'~ sur** to beat down on; to rain down on

abbaye [abei] *nf* abbey

abbé [abe] *nm* priest; (*d'une abbaye*) abbot

abcès [apsɛ] *nm* abscess

abdiquer [abdike] *vi* to abdicate ◆ *vt* to renounce, give up

abeille [abɛj] *nf* bee

aberrant, e [abɛʀɑ̃, -ɑ̃t] *adj* absurd

abêtir [abetiʀ] *vt* to make morons of (*ou* a moron of)

abîme [abim] *nm* abyss, gulf

abîmer [abime] *vt* to spoil, damage; **s'~** *vi* to get spoilt *ou* damaged

ablation [ablɑsjɔ̃] *nf* removal

aboi [abwa] *nmpl*: aux ~ at bay

abolir [abɔliʀ] *vt* to abolish

abondance [abɔ̃dɑ̃s] *nf* abundance; *(richesse)* affluence

abondant, e [abɔ̃dɑ̃, -ɑ̃t] *adj* plentiful, abundant, copious

abonder [abɔ̃de] *vi* to abound, be plentiful; ~ **dans le sens de qn** to concur with sb

abonné, e [abɔne] *nm/f* subscriber; season ticket holder

abonnement [abɔnmɑ̃] *nm* subscription; *(transports, concerts)* season ticket

abonner [abɔne] *vt*: s'~ **à** to subscribe to, take out a subscription to

abord [abɔʀ] *nm*: être d'un ~ facile to be approachable; ~s *nmpl (environs)* surroundings; au premier ~ at first sight, initially; d'~ first

abordable [abɔʀdabl(ə)] *adj* approachable; reasonably priced

aborder [abɔʀde] *vi* to land ♦ *vt (sujet, difficulté)* to tackle; *(personne)* to approach; *(rivage etc)* to reach; *(NAVIG: attaquer)* to board

aboutir [abutiʀ] *vi (négociations etc)* to succeed; ~ **à/dans/sur** to end up at/in/on

aboyer [abwaje] *vi* to bark

abrégé [abʀeʒe] *nm* summary

abréger [abʀeʒe] *vt* to shorten

abreuver [abʀœve] *vt (fig)*: ~ **qn de** to shower or swamp sb with; s'~ *vi* to drink; **abreuvoir** *nm* watering place

abréviation [abʀevjasjɔ̃] *nf* abbreviation

abri [abʀi] *nm* shelter; à l'~ under cover; à l'~ **de** sheltered from; *(fig)* safe from

abricot [abʀiko] *nm* apricot

abriter [abʀite] *vt* to shelter; *(loger)* to accommodate; s'~ *vi* to shelter, take cover

abroger [abʀɔʒe] *vt* to repeal

abrupt, e [abʀypt] *adj* sheer, steep; *(ton)* abrupt

abrutir [abʀytiʀ] *vt* to daze; to exhaust; to stupefy

absence [apsɑ̃s] *nf* absence; *(MÉD)* blackout; mental blank

absent, e [apsɑ̃, -ɑ̃t] *adj* absent; *(distrait: air)* vacant, faraway ♦ *nm/f* absentee; s'~er *vi* to take time off work; *(sortir)* to leave, go out

absolu, e [apsɔly] *adj* absolute; *(caractère)* rigid, uncompromising; **absolument** *adv* absolutely

absorber [apsɔʀbe] *vt* to absorb; *(gén MÉD: manger, boire)* to take

absoudre [apsudʀ(ə)] *vt* to absolve

abstenir [apstəniʀ]: s'~ *vi (POL)* to abstain; s'~ **de qch/de faire** to refrain from sth/from doing

abstraction [apstʀaksjɔ̃] *nf* abstraction; **faire** ~ **de** to set ou leave aside

abstrait, e [apstʀɛ, -ɛt] *adj* abstract

absurde [apsyʀd(ə)] *adj* absurd

abus [aby] *nm* abuse; ~ **de confiance** breach of trust

abuser [abyze] *vi* to go too far, overstep the mark ♦ *vt* to deceive, mislead; s'~ *vi* to be mistaken; ~ **de** to misuse; *(violer, duper)* to take advantage of; **abusif, ive** *adj* exorbitant; excessive; improper

acabit [akabi] *nm*: **de cet** ~ of that type

académie [akademi] *nf* academy; *(ART: nu)* nude; *(SCOL: circonscription)* = regional education authority

acajou [akaʒu] *nm* mahogany

acariâtre [akaʀjɑtʀ(ə)] *adj* cantankerous

accablant, e [akɑblɑ̃, ɑ̃t] *adj (témoignage, preuve)* overwhelming

accablement [akɑblɑmɑ̃] *nm* despondency

accabler [akɑble] *vt* to overwhelm, overcome; *(suj: témoignage)* to condemn, damn; ~ **qn d'injures** to heap ou shower abuse on sb

accalmie [akalmi] *nf* lull

accaparer [akapaʀe] *vt* to monopolize; *(suj: travail etc)* to take up (all) the time ou attention of

accéder [aksede]: ~ **à** *vt (lieu)*

reach; (fig) to accede to, attain; (accorder: requête) to grant, accede to

accélérateur [akseleratœr] nm accelerator

accélération [akselerasjɔ̃] nf acceleration

accélérer [akselere] vt to speed up ♦ vi to accelerate

accent [aksɑ̃] nm accent; (inflexions expressives) tone (of voice); (PHONETIQUE, fig) stress; mettre l'~ sur (fig) to stress; ~ aigu/grave acute/grave accent

accentuer [aksɑ̃tɥe] vt (LING) to accent; (fig) to accentuate, emphasize; s'~ vi to become more marked ou pronounced

acceptation [akseptasjɔ̃] nf acceptance

accepter [aksepte] vt to accept; (tolérer) ~ que qn fasse to agree to sb doing; ~ de faire to agree to do

accès [aksɛ] nm (à un lieu) access; (MED) attack; fit, bout; (: outbreak ♦ nmpl (routes etc) means of access, approaches; d'~ facile easily accessible; ~ de colère fit of anger

accessible [aksesibl(ə)] adj accessible; (livre, sujet): ~ à qn within the reach of sb; (sensible): ~ à open to

accessoire [akseswar] adj secondary; incidental ♦ nm accessory; (THEATRE) prop

accident [aksidɑ̃] nm accident; par ~ by chance; ~ de la route road accident; ~ du travail industrial injury ou accident; ~ é, e (relief, terrain) uneven; hilly

acclamer [aklame] vt to cheer, acclaim

accolade [akɔlad] nf (amicale) embrace; (signe) brace

accommodant, e [akɔmɔdɑ̃, -ɑ̃t] adj accommodating; easy-going

accommoder [akɔmɔde] vt (CULIN) to prepare; (points de vue) to reconcile; s'~ de to put up with; to make do with

accompagnateur, trice [akɔ̃paɲatœr, -tris] nm/f (MUS) accompanist; (de voyage: guide) guide; (: d'enfants) accompanying adult; (de voyage organisé) courier

accompagner [akɔ̃paɲe] vt to accompany, go ou come with; (MUS) to accompany

accompli, e [akɔ̃pli] adj accomplished

accomplir [akɔ̃plir] vt (tâche, projet) to carry out; (souhait) to fulfil; s'~ vi to be fulfilled

accord [akɔr] nm agreement; (entre des styles, tons etc) harmony; (MUS) chord; d'~! OK!; se mettre d'~ to come to an agreement; être d'~ to agree

accordéon [akɔrdeɔ̃] nm (MUS) accordion

accorder [akɔrde] vt (faveur, délai) to grant; (harmoniser) to match; (MUS) to tune; s'~ vt to get on together; to agree

accoster [akɔste] vt (NAVIG) to draw alongside ♦ vi to berth

accotement [akɔtmɑ̃] nm verge (BRIT), shoulder

accouchement [akuʃmɑ̃] nm delivery, (child)birth; labour

accoucher [akuʃe] vi to give birth, have a baby; (être en travail) to be in labour ♦ vt to deliver; ~ d'un garçon to give birth to a boy

accouder [akude]: s'~ vi to rest one's elbows on/against; **accoudoir** nm armrest

accoupler [akuple] vt to couple; (pour la reproduction) to mate; s'~ vt to mate

accourir [akurir] vi to rush ou run up

accoutrement [akutrəmɑ̃] (péj) nm (tenue) outfit

accoutumance [akutymɑ̃s] nf (gén) adaptation; (MED) addiction

accoutumé, e [akutyme] adj (habituel) customary, usual

accoutumer [akutyme] vt: s'~ à to get accustomed ou used to

accréditer [akʀedite] vt (nouvelle) to substantiate

accroc [akʀo] nm (déchirure) tear; (fig) hitch, snag

accrochage [akʀɔʃaʒ] nm (AUTO) collision

accrocher [akʀɔʃe] vt (suspendre): ~ qch à to hang sth (up) on; (attacher: remorque): ~ qch à to hitch sth (up) to; (heurter) to catch; to catch on; to hit; (déchirer): ~ qch (à) to catch sth (on); (MIL) to engage; (fig) to catch, attract; s'~ (se disputer) to have a clash ou brush; s'~ à (rester pris à) to catch on; (agripper, fig) to hang on ou cling to

accroître [akʀwatʀ(ə)] vt to increase; s'~ to increase

accroupir [akʀupiʀ]: s'~ vi to squat, crouch (down)

accru, e [akʀy] pp de accroître

accueil [akœj] nm welcome; comité d'~ reception committee

accueillir [akœjiʀ] vt to welcome; (loger) to accommodate

acculer [akyle] vt: ~ qn à ou contre to drive sb back against

accumuler [akymyle] vt to accumulate, amass; s'~ vi to accumulate, to pile up

accusation [akyzasjɔ̃] nf (gén) accusation; (JUR) charge; (partie): l'~ the prosecution; mettre en ~ to indict

accusé, e [akyze] nm/f accused; defendant; ~ de réception acknowledgement of receipt

accuser [akyze] vt to accuse; (fig) to emphasize, bring out; to show; ~ qn de to accuse sb of; (JUR) to charge sb with; ~ qch de (rendre responsable) to blame sth for; ~ réception de to acknowledge receipt of

acerbe [asɛʀb(ə)] adj caustic, acid

acéré, e [aseʀe] adj sharp

achalandé, e [aʃalɑ̃de] adj: bien ~ well-stocked; well-patronized

acharné, e [aʃaʀne] adj (lutte, adversaire) fierce, bitter; (travail) re-

lentless, unremitting

acharner [aʃaʀne]: s'~ vi to go at fiercely; s'~ contre to set o.s. against; to dog; s'~ à faire to try doggedly to do; to persist in doing

achat [aʃa] nm buying no pl; purchase; faire des ~s to do some shopping

acheminer [aʃmine] vt (courrier) to forward, dispatch; (troupes) to convey, transport; (train) to route; s'~ vers to head for

acheter [aʃte] vt to buy, purchase; (soudoyer) to buy; ~ qch à (marchand) to buy ou purchase sth from; (ami etc: offrir) to buy sth for; **acheteur, euse** nm/f buyer; shopper; (COMM) buyer

achever [aʃve] vt to complete, finish; (blessé) to finish off; s'~ vi to end

acide [asid] adj sour, sharp; (CHIMIE) acid(ic) ♦ nm acid

acier [asje] nm steel; **aciérie** nf steelworks sg

acné [akne] nf acne

acolyte [akɔlit] (péj) nm associate

acompte [akɔ̃t] nm deposit; (versement régulier) instalment; (sur somme due) payment on account

à-côté [akote] nm side-issue; (argent) extra

à-coup [aku] nm (du moteur) (hic)cough; (fig) jolt; par ~s by fits and starts

acoustique [akustik] nf (d'une salle) acoustics pl

acquéreur [akeʀœʀ] nm buyer, purchaser

acquérir [akeʀiʀ] vt to acquire

acquis, e [aki, -iz] pp de acquérir ♦ nm (accumulated) experience; être ~ à (plan, idée) to fully agree with; son aide nous est ~e we can count on her help

acquit [aki] vb voir acquérir ♦ nm (quittance) receipt; par ~ de conscience to set one's mind at rest

acquitter [akite] vt (JUR) to acquit; (facture) to pay, settle; s'~ de to discharge, fulfil

âcre [ɑkʀ(ə)] adj acrid, pungent

acrobate [akʀɔbat] nm/f acrobat

acte [akt(ə)] nm act, action; (THÉÂTRE) act; ~s nmpl (compte-rendu) proceedings; prendre ~ de to note, take note of; faire ~ de candidature to apply; faire ~ de présence to put in an appearance; ~ de naissance birth certificate

acteur [aktœʀ] nm actor

actif, ive [aktif, -iv] adj active ♦ nm (COMM) assets pl; (fig): avoir à son ~ to have to one's credit; population active working population

action [aksjɔ̃] nf (gen) action; (COMM) share; une bonne ~ a good deed; ~naire nm/f shareholder; ~ner vt to work; to activate; to operate

activer [aktive] vt to speed up; s'~ vi to bustle about; to hurry up

activité [aktivite] nf activity

actrice [aktʀis] nf actress

actualiser [aktɥalize] vt to actualize; to bring up to date

actualité [aktɥalite] nf (d'un problème) topicality; (événements): l'~ current events; les ~s nfpl (CINÉMA, TV) the news

actuel, le [aktɥɛl] adj (présent) present; (d'actualité) topical; **actuellement** adv at present; at the present time

acuité [akɥite] nf acuteness

adaptateur [adaptatœʀ] nm (ÉLEC) adapter

adapter [adapte] vt to adapt; s'~ (à) (suj: personne) to adapt (to); ~ qch à (approprier) to adapt sth to (fit); ~ qch sur/dans/à (fixer) to fit sth on/into/on

additif [aditif] nm additive

addition [adisjɔ̃] nf addition; (au café) bill; ~ner vt to add (up)

adepte [adept] nm/f follower

adéquat, e [adekwa, -at] adj appropriate, suitable

adhérent, e [adeʀɑ̃, -ɑ̃t] nm/f (de club) member

adhérer [adeʀe]: ~ à vi (coller) to adhere ou stick to; (se rallier à) to join; to support; **adhésif, ive** adj adhesive, sticky ♦ nm adhesive; **adhésion** nf joining; membership; support

adieu, x [adjø] excl goodbye ♦ nm farewell; dire ~ à qn to say goodbye ou farewell to sb

adjectif [adʒɛktif] nm adjective

adjoindre [adʒwɛ̃dʀ(ə)] vt: ~ qch à (attacher) to add sth to; s'~ vt (collaborateur etc) to take on, appoint; **adjoint, e** nm/f assistant; **adjoint au maire** deputy mayor; **directeur adjoint** assistant manager

adjudant [adʒydɑ̃] nm (MIL) warrant officer

adjudication [adʒydikasjɔ̃] nf sale by auction; (pour travaux) invitation to tender (BRIT) ou bid (US)

adjuger [adʒyʒe] vt (prix, récompense) to award; (lors d'une vente) to auction (off); s'~ vt to take for o.s.

adjurer [adʒyʀe] vt: ~ qn de faire to implore ou beg sb to do

admettre [admɛtʀ(ə)] vt (laisser entrer) to admit; (candidat: SCOL) to pass; (tolérer) to allow, accept; (reconnaître) to admit, acknowledge

administrateur, trice [administʀatœʀ, -tʀis] nm/f (COMM) director; (ADMIN) administrator; ~ judiciaire receiver

administration [administʀasjɔ̃] nf administration; l'A~ ≈ the Civil Service

administrer [administʀe] vt (biens, remède, sacrement etc) to administer; (gérer) to manage, run

admirable [admiʀabl(ə)] adj admirable, wonderful

admirateur, trice [admiʀatœʀ, -tʀis] nm/f admirer

admiration [admiʀasjɔ̃] nf admiration

admirer [admiʀe] vt to admire

admis, e pp de **admettre**

admissible [admisibl(ə)] adj (candidat) eligible; (comportement) ad missible, acceptable

admission [admisjɔ̃] *nf* admission; acknowledgement; **demande d'~** application for membership

adolescence [adɔlesɑ̃s] *nf* adolescence

adolescent, e [adɔlesɑ̃, -ɑ̃t] *nm/f* adolescent, teenager

adonner [adɔne]: **s'~ à** *vt* (*sport*) to devote o.s. to; (*boisson*) to give o.s. over to

adopter [adɔpte] *vt* to adopt; (*projet de loi etc*) to pass; **adoptif, ive** *adj* (*parents*) adoptive; (*fils, patrie*) adopted

adorer [adɔʀe] *vt* to adore; (*REL*) to worship

adosser [adose] *vt*: **~ qch à** *ou* **contre** to stand sth against; **s'~ à** *ou* **contre** to lean with one's back against

adoucir [adusiʀ] *vt* (*goût, température*) to make milder; (*avec du sucre*) to sweeten; (*peau, voix*) to soften; (*caractère*) to mellow

adresse [adʀɛs] *nf* (*voir* **adroit**) skill, dexterity; (*domicile*) address; **à l'~ de** (*pour*) for the benefit of

adresser [adʀese] *vt* (*lettre: expédier*) to send; (*: écrire l'adresse sur*) to address; (*injure, compliments*) to address; **s'~ à** (*parler à*) to speak to, address; (*s'informer auprès de*) to go and see; (*: bureau*) to enquire at; (*suj: livre, conseil*) to be aimed at; **~ la parole à** to speak to, address

adroit, e [adʀwa, -wat] *adj* skilful, skilled

adulte [adylt(ə)] *nm/f* adult, grown-up ♦ *adj* (*chien, arbre*) fully-grown, mature; (*attitude*) adult, grown-up

adultère [adyltɛʀ] *nm* (*acte*) adultery

advenir [advəniʀ] *vi* to happen

adverbe [advɛʀb(ə)] *nm* adverb

adversaire [advɛʀsɛʀ] *nm/f* (*SPORT, gén*) opponent, adversary; (*MIL*) adversary, enemy

adverse [advɛʀs(ə)] *adj* opposing

aération [aeʀɑsjɔ̃] *nf* airing; ventilation

aérer [aeʀe] *vt* to air; (*fig*) to lighten

aérien, ne [aeʀjɛ̃, -ɛn] *adj* (*AVIAT*) air *cpd*, aerial; (*câble, métro*) overhead; (*fig*) light

aéro... [aeʀo] *préfixe*: **~bic** *nm* aerobics *sg*; **~gare** *nf* airport (buildings); (*en ville*) air terminal; **~glisseur** *nm* hovercraft; **~naval, e** *adj* air and sea *cpd*; **~phagie** [aeʀofaʒi] *nf* (*MED*) wind, aerophagia (*TECH*); **~port** *nm* airport; **~porté, e** *adj* airborne, airlifted; **~sol** *nm* aerosol

affable [afabl(ə)] *adj* affable

affaiblir [afeblir] *vt* to weaken; **s'~ vi** to weaken

affaire [afɛʀ] *nf* (*problème, question*) matter; (*criminelle, judiciaire*) case; (*scandaleuse etc*) affair; (*entreprise*) business; (*marché, transaction*) deal; business *no pl*; (*occasion intéressante*) bargain; **~s** *nfpl* (*intérêts publics et privés*) affairs; (*activité commerciale*) business *sg*; (*effets personnels*) things, belongings; **ce sont mes ~s** (*cela me concerne*) that's my business; **ceci fera l'~** this will do (nicely); **avoir ~ à** to be faced with; to be dealing with; **les A~s étrangères** Foreign Affairs; **s'affairer** *vi* to busy o.s., bustle about

affaisser [afese]: **s'~** *vi* (*terrain, immeuble*) to subside, sink; (*personne*) to collapse

affaler [afale]: **s'~** *vi* to collapse *ou* slump into/onto

affamé, e [afame] *adj* starving

affecter [afɛkte] *vt* to affect; (*telle ou telle forme etc*) to take on; **~ qch à** to allocate *ou* allot sth to; **~ qn à** to appoint sb to; (*diplomate*) to post sb to

affectif, ive [afɛktif, -iv] *adj* emotional

affection [afɛksjɔ̃] *nf* affection; (*mal*) ailment; **~ner** *vt* to be fond of

affectueux, euse [afɛktɥø, -øz] *adj* affectionate

afférent, e [aferɑ̃, -ɑ̃t] *adj*: ~ à pertaining *ou* relating to

affermir [afɛrmir] *vt* to consolidate, strengthen

affichage [afiʃaʒ] *nm* billposting; (*électronique*) display

affiche [afiʃ] *nf* poster; (*officielle*) notice; (*THÉÂTRE*) bill; **tenir l'~** to run

afficher [afiʃe] *vt* (*affiche*) to put up; (*réunion*) to put up a notice about; (*électroniquement*) to display; (*fig*) to exhibit, display

affilée [afile]: **d'~** *adv* at a stretch

affiler [afile] *vt* to sharpen

affilier [afilje]: **s'~ à** *vt* (*club, société*) to join

affiner [afine] *vt* to refine

affirmatif, ive [afirmatif, -iv] *adj* affirmative

affirmation [afirmasjɔ̃] *nf* assertion

affirmer [afirme] *vt* (*prétendre*) to maintain, assert; (*autorité etc*) to assert

affligé, e [afliʒe] *adj* distressed, grieved; **~ de** (*maladie, tare*) afflicted with

affliger [afliʒe] *vt* (*peiner*) to distress, grieve

affluence [aflyɑ̃s] *nf* crowds *pl*; **heures d'~** rush hours; **jours d'~** busiest days

affluent [aflyɑ̃] *nm* tributary

affluer [aflye] *vi* (*secours, biens*) to flood in, pour in; (*sang*) to rush, flow

affolement [afɔlmɑ̃] *nm* panic

affoler [afɔle] *vt* to throw into a panic; **s'~** *vi* to panic

affranchir [afrɑ̃ʃir] *vt* to put a stamp *ou* stamps on; (*à la machine*) to frank (*BRIT*), meter (*US*); (*fig*) to free, liberate; **affranchissement** *nm* postage

affréter [afrete] *vt* to charter

affreux, euse [afrø, -øz] *adj* dreadful, awful

affront [afrɔ̃] *nm* affront

affrontement [afrɔ̃tmɑ̃] *nm* clash, confrontation

affronter [afrɔ̃te] *vt* to confront, face

affubler [afyble] (*péj*) *vt*: ~ **qn de** to rig *ou* deck sb out in; (*surnom*) to attach to sb

affût [afy] *nm*: **à l'~ (de)** (*gibier*) lying in wait (for); (*fig*) on the lookout (for)

affûter [afyte] *vt* to sharpen, grind

afin [afɛ̃]: ~ **que** *conj* so that, in order that; ~ **de faire** in order to do, so as to do

africain, e [afrikɛ̃, -ɛn] *adj, nm/f* African

Afrique [afrik] *nf*: **l'~** Africa; **l'~ du Sud** South Africa

âge [ɑʒ] *nm* age; **quel ~ as-tu?** how old are you?; **prendre de l'~** to be getting on (in years); **l'~ ingrat** the awkward age; **l'~ mûr** maturity; **âgé, e** *adj* old, elderly; **âgé de 10 ans** 10 years old

agence [aʒɑ̃s] *nf* agency, office; (*succursale*) branch; ~ **de voyages** travel agency; ~ **immobilière** estate (*BRIT*) *ou* real estate (*US*) agent's (office); ~ **matrimoniale** marriage bureau

agencer [aʒɑ̃se] *vt* to put together; to arrange, lay out

agenda [aʒɛ̃da] *nm* diary

agenouiller [aʒnuje]: **s'~** *vi* to kneel (down)

agent [aʒɑ̃] *nm* (*aussi*: ~ **de police**) policeman; (*ADMIN*) official, officer; (*fig*: *élément, facteur*) agent; ~ **d'assurances** insurance broker; ~ **de change** stockbroker

agglomération [aglɔmerɑsjɔ̃] *nf* town; built-up area; **l'~ parisienne** the urban area of Paris

aggloméré [aglɔmere] *nm* (*bois*) chipboard; (*pierre*) conglomerate

agglomérer [aglɔmere] *vt* to pile up; (*TECH*: *bois, pierre*) to compress

aggraver [agrave] *vt* to worsen, aggravate; (*JUR*: *peine*) to increase; **s'~** *vi* to worsen

agile [aʒil] *adj* agile, nimble

agir [aʒiʀ] vi to act; **il s'agit de** it's a matter ou question of; it is about; (*il importe que*): **il s'agit de faire** we (ou you etc) must do

agitation [aʒitɑsjɔ̃] nf (hustle and bustle) agitation, excitement; (*politique*) unrest, agitation

agité, e [aʒite] adj fidgety, restless; agitated, perturbed; (*mer*) rough

agiter [aʒite] vt (bouteille, chiffon) to shake; (bras, mains) to wave; (*préoccuper, exciter*) to perturb

agneau, x [aɲo] nm lamb

agonie [agɔni] nf mortal agony, death pangs pl; (fig) death throes pl

agrafe [agʀaf] nf (de vêtement) hook, fastener; (de bureau) staple; **agrafer** vt to fasten; to staple; **agrafeuse** nf stapler

agraire [agʀɛʀ] adj land cpd

agrandir [agʀɑ̃diʀ] vt to enlarge; (magasin, domaine) to extend, enlarge; **s'~** vi to be extended; to be enlarged; **agrandissement** nm (PHOTO) enlargement

agréable [agʀeabl(ə)] adj pleasant, nice

agréé, e [agʀee] adj: **concessionnaire ~** registered dealer

agréer [agʀee] vt (requête) to accept; **~ à** to please, suit; **veuillez ~ ...** (formule épistolaire) yours faithfully

agrégation [agʀegɑsjɔ̃] nf highest teaching diploma in France; **agrégé, e** nm/f holder of the agrégation

agrément [agʀemɑ̃] nm (accord) consent, approval; (attraits) charm, attractiveness; (plaisir) pleasure

agrémenter [agʀemɑ̃te] vt to embellish, adorn

agresser [agʀese] vt to attack

agresseur [agʀesœʀ] nm aggressor, attacker; (POL, MIL) aggressor

agressif, ive [agʀesif, -iv] adj aggressive

agricole [agʀikɔl] adj agricultural

agriculteur [agʀikyltœʀ] nm farmer

agriculture [agʀikyltyʀ] nf agriculture; farming

agripper [agʀipe] vt to grab, clutch; (pour arracher) to snatch, grab; **s'~ à** to cling (on) to, clutch, grip

agrumes [agʀym] nmpl citrus fruit(s)

aguerrir [ageʀiʀ] vt to harden

aguets [agɛ] nmpl: **être aux ~** to be on the look out

aguicher [agiʃe] vt to entice

ahuri, e [ayʀi] adj (stupéfait) flabbergasted; (idiot) dim-witted

ai vb voir **avoir**

aide [ɛd] nm/f assistant; carer ♦ nf assistance, help; (secours financier) aid; **à l'~ de** (avec) with the help ou aid of; **appeler (qn) à l'~** to call for help (from sb); **~ judiciaire** nf legal aid; **~ sociale** nf (assistance) state aid; **~-mémoire** nm inv memoranda pages pl; (key facts) handbook; **~-soignant, e** nm/f auxiliary nurse

aider [ɛde] vt to help; **s'~ de** (se servir de) to use, make use of; **~ à qch** (faciliter) to help (towards) sth

aie etc vb voir **avoir**

aïe [aj] excl ouch

aïeul, e [ajœl] nm/f grandparent, grandfather(mother); forebear

aïeux [ajø] nmpl grandparents; forebears, forefathers

aigle [ɛgl(ə)] nm eagle

aigre [ɛgʀ(ə)] adj sour, sharp; (fig) sharp, cutting; **aigreur** nf sourness; sharpness; **aigreurs d'estomac** heartburn sg; **aigrir** vt (personne) to embitter; (caractère) to sour

aigu, ë [egy] adj (objet, arête, douleur, intelligence) sharp; (son, voix) high-pitched, shrill; (note) high (-pitched)

aiguille [egɥij] nf needle; (de montre) hand; **~ à tricoter** knitting needle

aiguiller [egɥije] vt (orienter) to direct; **aiguilleur du ciel** [egɥijœʀ] nm air-traffic controller

aiguillon [egɥijɔ̃] nm (d'abeille) sting; **~ner** vt to spur ou goad on

aiguiser [egize] vt to sharpen; (fig)

to stimulate; to excite

ail [aj] *nm* garlic

aile [ɛl] *nf* wing; **aileron** *nm* (*de requin*) fin; **ailier** *nm* winger

aille *etc vb voir* **aller**

ailleurs [ajœʀ] *adv* elsewhere, somewhere else; **partout/nulle part ~** everywhere/nowhere else; **d'~** (*du reste*) moreover, besides; **par ~** (*d'autre part*) moreover, furthermore

aimable [ɛmabl(ə)] *adj* kind, nice

aimant [ɛmɑ̃] *nm* magnet

aimer [eme] *vt* to love; (*d'amitié, affection, par goût*) to like; (*souhait*): **j'~ais ...** I would like ...; **bien ~ qn/qch** to like sb/sth; **j'aime mieux ou autant vous dire que** I may as well tell you that; **j'~ais autant y aller maintenant** I'd rather go now; **j'~ais mieux faire** I'd much rather do

aine [ɛn] *nf* groin

aîné, e [ene] *adj* elder, older; (*le plus âgé*) eldest, oldest ♦ *nm/f* oldest child *ou* one, oldest boy *ou* son/girl *ou* daughter; **aînesse** *nf*: **droit d'aînesse** birthright

ainsi [ɛ̃si] *adv* (*de cette façon*) like this, in this way, thus; (*ce faisant*) thus ♦ *conj* thus, so; **~ que** (*comme*) (just) as; (*et aussi*) as well as; **pour ~ dire** so to speak; **et ~ de suite** and so on

air [ɛʀ] *nm* air; (*mélodie*) tune; (*expression*) look, air; **prendre l'~** to get some (fresh) air; (*avion*) to take off; **avoir l'~** (*sembler*) to look, appear; **avoir l'~ de** to look like; **avoir l'~ de faire** to look as though one is doing, appear to be doing

aire [ɛʀ] *nf* (*zone, fig, MATH*) area

aisance [ɛzɑ̃s] *nf* ease; (*richesse*) affluence

aise [ɛz] *nf* comfort ♦ *adj*: **être bien ~ que** to be delighted that; **être à l'~ *ou* à son ~** to be comfortable; (*pas embarrassé*) to be at ease; (*financièrement*) to be comfortably off; **se mettre à l'~** to make o.s. comfortable; **être mal à l'~ *ou* à**

son **~** to be uncomfortable; to be ill at ease; **en faire à son ~** to do as one likes; **aisé, e** *adj* easy; (*assez riche*) well-to-do, well-off

aisselle [ɛsɛl] *nf* armpit

ait *vb voir* **avoir**

ajonc [aʒɔ̃] *nm* gorse *no pl*

ajourner [aʒuʀne] *vt* (*réunion*) to adjourn; (*décision*) to defer, postpone

ajouter [aʒute] *vt* to add; **~ foi à** to lend *ou* give credence to

ajusté, e [aʒyste] *adj*: **bien ~** (*robe etc*) close-fitting

ajuster [aʒyste] *vt* (*régler*) to adjust; (*vêtement*) to alter; (*coup de fusil*) to aim; (*cible*) to aim at; (*TECH, gén: adapter*): **~ qch à** to fit sth to

alarme [alaʀm(ə)] *nf* alarm; **donner l'~** to give *ou* raise the alarm; **alarmer** *vt* to alarm; **s'~r** *vi* to become alarmed

album [albɔm] *nm* album

albumine [albymin] *nf* albumin; **avoir *ou* faire de l'~** to suffer from albuminuria

alcool [alkɔl] *nm*: **l'~** alcohol; **un ~** a spirit, a brandy; **~ à brûler** methylated spirits (*BRIT*), wood alcohol (*US*); **~ à 90°** surgical spirit; **~ique** *adj, nm/f* alcoholic; **~isme** *nm* alcoholism; **alco(o)test** ® *nm* Breathalyser ®; (*test*) breath-test

aléas [alea] *nmpl* hazards; **aléatoire** *adj* uncertain; (*INFORM*) random

alentour [alɑ̃tuʀ] *adv* around (about); **~s** *nmpl* (*environs*) surroundings; **aux ~s de** in the vicinity *ou* neighbourhood of, around about; (*temps*) around about

alerte [alɛʀt(ə)] *adj* agile, nimble; brisk, lively ♦ *nf* alert; warning; **alerter** *vt* to alert

algèbre [alʒɛbʀ(ə)] *nf* algebra

Alger [alʒe] *n* Algiers

Algérie [alʒeʀi] *nf*: **l'~** Algeria; **algérien, ne** *adj* Algerian ♦ *nm/f*: **A~, ne** Algerian

algue [alg(ə)] *nf* (*gén*) seaweed *no pl*; (*BOT*) alga

alibi [alibi] *nm* alibi

aliéné, e [aljene] *nm/f* insane person,

lunatic (péj)

aligner [aliɲe] vt to align, line up; (idées, chiffres) to string together; (adapter): ~ qch sur to bring sth into alignment with; s'~ (soldats etc) to line up; s'~ sur (POL) to align o.s. on

aliment [alimɑ̃] nm food

alimentation [alimɑ̃tɑsjɔ̃] nf feeding; supplying; (commerce) food trade; (produits) groceries pl; (régime) diet; (INFORM) feed

alimenter [alimɑ̃te] vt to feed; (TECH): ~ (en) to supply (with); to feed (with); (fig) to sustain, keep going

alinéa [alinea] nm paragraph

aliter [alite]: s'~ vi to take to one's bed

allaiter [alete] vt to (breast-)feed, nurse; (suj: animal) to suckle

allant [alɑ̃] nm drive, go

allécher [aleʃe] vt: ~ qn to make sb's mouth water; to tempt ou entice sb

allée [ale] nf (de jardin) path; (en ville) avenue, drive; ~s et venues comings and goings

alléger [aleʒe] vt (voiture) to make lighter; (chargement) to lighten; (souffrance) to alleviate, soothe

allègre [alɛgʀ(ə)] adj lively, cheerful

alléguer [alege] vt to put forward (as proof ou an excuse)

Allemagne [aləmaɲ] nf: l'~ Germany; **allemand, e** adj, nm/f German ♦ nm (LING) German

aller [ale] nm (trajet) outward journey; (billet: aussi: ~ simple) single (BRIT) ou one-way (US) ticket ♦ vi (gén) to go; ~ à (convenir) to suit; (suj: forme, pointure etc) to fit; ~ avec (couleurs, style etc) to go (well) with; je vais y ~/me fâcher I'm going to go/to get angry; ~ voir to go and see, go to see; allez! come on!; allons! come now!; comment allez-vous? how are you?; **comment ça va?** how are you?;

(affaires etc) how are things?; **il va bien/mal** he's well/not well, he's fine/ill; **ça va bien/mal** (affaires etc) it's going well/not going well; ~ **mieux** to be better; **cela va sans dire** that goes without saying; **il y va de leur vie** their lives are at stake; **s'en** ~ (partir) to be off, go, leave; (disparaître) to go away; ~ **(et) retour** return journey (BRIT); round trip; (billet) return (ticket) (BRIT), round trip ticket (US)

allergique [alɛʀʒik] adj: ~ à allergic to

alliage [aljaʒ] nm alloy

alliance [aljɑ̃s] nf (MIL, POL) alliance; (mariage) marriage; (bague) wedding ring

allier [alje] vt (métaux) to ally; (POL, gén) to ally; (fig) to combine; s'~ to become allies; to combine

allô [alo] excl hullo, hallo

allocation [alɔkɑsjɔ̃] nf allowance; ~ **(de) chômage** unemployment benefit; ~ **(de) logement** rent allowance; ~s **familiales** ≈ child benefit

allocution [alɔkysjɔ̃] nf short speech

allonger [alɔ̃ʒe] vt to lengthen, make longer; (étendre: bras, jambe) to stretch (out); s'~ vi to get longer; (se coucher) to lie down, stretch out; ~ **le pas** to hasten one's step(s)

allouer [alwe] vt to allocate, allot

allumage [alymaʒ] nm (AUTO) ignition

allume-cigare [alymsigaʀ] nm inv cigar lighter

allumer [alyme] vt (lampe, phare, radio) to put ou switch on; (pièce) to put ou switch the light(s) on in; (feu) to light; s'~ vi (lumière, lampe) to come ou go on

allumette [alymɛt] nf match

allure [alyʀ] nf (vitesse) speed, pace; (démarche) walk; (maintien) bearing; (aspect, air) look; **avoir de l'**~ to have style; **à toute** ~ at top speed

allusion [alyzjɔ̃] nf allusion; (sousentendu) hint; **faire** ~ **à** to allude to refer to; to hint at

aloi [alwa] *nm*: de bon ~ of genuine worth *ou* quality

MOT-CLÉ
---

alors [alɔʀ] *adv* **1** (*à ce moment-là*) then, at that time; **il habitait ~ à Paris** he lived in Paris at that time **2** (*par conséquent*) then; **tu as fini? ~ je m'en vais** have you finished? I'm going then; et ~? so what?

~ **que** *conj* **1** (*au moment où*) when, as; **il est arrivé alors que je partais** he arrived as I was leaving **2** (*pendant que*) while, when; **~ qu'il était à Paris, il a visité ...** while *ou* when he was in Paris, he visited ...

3 (*tandis que*) whereas, while; **~ que son frère travaillait dur, lui se reposait** while his brother was working hard, HE would rest

---

alouette [alwɛt] *nf* (sky)lark

alourdir [aluʀdiʀ] *vt* to weigh down, make heavy

alpage [alpaʒ] *nm* pasture

Alpes [alp(ə)] *nfpl*: **les ~** the Alps

alphabet [alfabɛ] *nm* alphabet; (*livre*) ABC (book); **alphabétiser** *vt* to teach to read and write; to eliminate illiteracy in

alpinisme [alpinism(ə)] *nm* mountaineering, climbing; **alpiniste** *nm/f* mountaineer, climber

Alsace [alzas] *nf* Alsace; **alsacien, ne** *adj*, *nm/f* Alsatian

altercation [altɛʀkasjɔ̃] *nf* altercation

altérer [alteʀe] *vt* to falsify; to distort; to debase; to impair

alternateur [altɛʀnatœʀ] *nm* alternator

alternatif, ive [altɛʀnatif, -iv] *adj* alternating; **alternative** *nf* (*choix*) alternative; **alternativement** *adv* alternately

Altesse [altɛs] *nf* Highness

altitude [altityd] *nf* altitude, height

alto [alto] *nm* (*instrument*) viola

altruisme [altʀɥism(ə)] *nm* altruism

aluminium [alyminjɔm] *nm* aluminium (*BRIT*), aluminum (*US*)

amabilité [amabilite] *nf* kindness, amiability

amadouer [amadwe] *vt* to coax, cajole; to mollify, soothe

amaigrir [amegʀiʀ] *vt* to make thin(ner)

amalgame [amalgam] *nm* (*alliage pour les dents*) amalgam

amande [amɑ̃d] *nf* (*de l'amandier*) almond; (*de noyau de fruit*) kernel; **amandier** *nm* almond (tree)

amant [amɑ̃] *nm* lover

amarrer [amaʀe] *vt* (*NAVIG*) to moor; (*gén*) to make fast

amas [amɑ] *nm* heap, pile

amasser [amɑse] *vt* to amass

amateur [amatœʀ] *nm* amateur; en ~ (*péj*) amateurishly; ~ **de musique/sport** *etc* music/sport *etc* lover

amazone [amazon] *nf*: en ~ side-saddle

ambages [ɑ̃baʒ]: **sans ~** *adv* plainly

ambassade [ɑ̃basad] *nf* embassy; (*mission*): en ~ on a mission; **ambassadeur, drice** *nm/f* ambassador(dress)

ambiance [ɑ̃bjɑ̃s] *nf* atmosphere

ambiant, e [ɑ̃bjɑ̃, -ɑ̃t] *adj* (*air, milieu*) surrounding; (*température*) ambient

ambigu, ë [ɑ̃bigy] *adj* ambiguous

ambitieux, euse [ɑ̃bisjø, -øz] *adj* ambitious

ambition [ɑ̃bisjɔ̃] *nf* ambition

ambulance [ɑ̃bylɑ̃s] *nf* ambulance; **ambulancier, ière** *nm/f* ambulance man(woman) (*BRIT*), paramedic (*US*)

ambulant, e [ɑ̃bylɑ̃, -ɑ̃t] *adj* travelling, itinerant

âme [ɑm] *nf* soul

améliorer [ameljɔʀe] *vt* to improve; **s'~** *vi* to improve, get better

aménagements [amenaʒmɑ̃] *nmpl* developments; ~ **fiscaux** tax adjustments

aménager [amenaʒe] *vt* (*agencer, transformer*) to fit out; to lay out; (: *quartier, territoire*) to develop; (*installer*) to fix up, put in; **ferme aménagée** converted farmhouse

amende [amɑ̃d] *nf* fine; **mettre à l'~** to penalize; **faire ~ honorable** to make amends

amender [amɑ̃de] *vt* (*loi*) to amend; **s'~** *vi* to mend one's ways

amener [amne] *vt* to bring; (*causer*) to bring about; (*baisser: drapeau, voiles*) to strike; **s'~** *vi* to show up (*fam*), turn up

amenuiser [amənɥize]: **s'~** *vi* to grow slimmer, lessen; to dwindle

amer, amère [amɛʀ] *adj* bitter

américain, e [ameʀikɛ̃, -ɛn] *adj, nm/f* American

Amérique [ameʀik] *nf* America; l'~ **centrale/latine** Central/Latin America; l'~ **du Nord/du Sud** North/South America

amerrir [ameʀiʀ] *vi* to land (on the sea)

amertume [amɛʀtym] *nf* bitterness

ameublement [amœbləmɑ̃] *nm* furnishing; (*meubles*) furniture

ameuter [amøte] *vt* (*badauds*) to draw a crowd of; (*peuple*) to rouse

ami, e [ami] *nm/f* friend; (*amant/maitresse*) boyfriend/girlfriend ♦ *adj*: **pays/groupe ~** friendly country/group; **être ~ de l'ordre** to be a lover of order; **un ~ des arts** a patron of the arts

amiable [amjabl(ə)]: **à l'~** *adv* (*JUR*) out of court; (*gén*) amicably

amiante [amjɑ̃t] *nm* asbestos

amical, e, aux [amikal, -o] *adj* friendly; **amicale** *nf* (*club*) association; **amicalement** *adv* in a friendly way; (*formule épistolaire*) regards

amidon [amidɔ̃] *nm* starch

amincir [amɛ̃siʀ] *vt* (*objet*) to thin (down); **s'~** *vi* to get thinner ou slimmer; **~ qn** to make sb thinner ou slimmer

amincissant, e *adj*: **régime ~**

(slimming) diet; **crème ~e** slenderizing cream

amiral, aux [amiʀal, -o] *nm* admiral

amitié [amitje] *nf* friendship; **prendre en ~** to befriend; **faire ou présenter ses ~s à qn** to send sb one's best wishes

ammoniac [amɔnjak] *nm*: (**gaz**) **~ ammonia**

ammoniaque [amɔnjak] *nf* ammonia (water)

amoindrir [amwɛ̃dʀiʀ] *vt* to reduce

amollir [amɔliʀ] *vt* to soften

amonceler [amɔ̃sle] *vt* to pile ou heap up; **s'~** *vi* to pile ou heap up; (*fig*) to accumulate

amont [amɔ̃]: **en ~** *adv* upstream; (*sur une pente*) uphill

amorce [amɔʀs] *nf* (*sur un hameçon*) bait; (*explosif*) cap; primer; priming; (*fig: début*) beginning(s), start

amorphe [amɔʀf(ə)] *adj* passive, lifeless

amortir [amɔʀtiʀ] *vt* (*atténuer: choc*) to absorb, cushion; (*bruit, douleur*) to deaden; (*COMM: dette*) to pay off; (: *mise de fonds, matériel*) to write off; **~ un abonnement** to make a season ticket pay (for itself); **amortisseur** *nm* shock absorber

amour [amuʀ] *nm* love; (*liaison*) love affair, love; **faire l'~** to make love: **s'amouracher de** (*péj*) *vt* to become infatuated with; **amoureux, euse** *adj* (*regard, tempérament*) amorous; (*vie, problèmes*) love *cpd*; (*personne*): **amoureux (de qn)** in love (with sb) ♦ *nmpl* courting couple(s); **amour-propre** *nm* self-esteem, pride

amovible [amɔvibl(ə)] *adj* removable, detachable

ampère [ɑ̃pɛʀ] *nm* amp(ere)

amphithéâtre [ɑ̃fiteɑtʀ(ə)] *nm* amphitheatre; (*d'université*) lecture hall ou theatre

ample [ɑ̃pl(ə)] *adj* (*vêtement*) roomy, ample; (*gestes, mouvement*) broad; (*ressources*) ample; **ampleur**

nf (*importance*) scale, size; extent

amplificateur [ɑ̃plifikatœr] *nm* amplifier

amplifier [ɑ̃plifje] *vt* (*son, oscillation*) to amplify; (*fig*) to expand, increase

ampoule [ɑ̃pul] *nf* (*électrique*) bulb; (*de médicament*) phial; (*aux mains, pieds*) blister; **ampoulé, e** [ɑ̃pule] (*péj*) *adj* pompous, bombastic

amputer [ɑ̃pyte] *vt* (*MED*) to amputate; (*fig*) to cut ou reduce drastically

amusant, e [amyzɑ̃, -ɑ̃t] *adj* (*divertissant, spirituel*) entertaining, amusing; (*comique*) funny, amusing

amuse-gueule [amyzgœl] *nm inv* appetizer, snack

amusement [amyzmɑ̃] *nm* amusement; (*jeu etc*) pastime, diversion

amuser [amyze] *vt* (*divertir*) to entertain, amuse; (*égayer, faire rire*) to amuse; (*détourner l'attention de*) to distract; **s'~** *vi* (*jouer*) to amuse o.s., play; (*se divertir*) to enjoy o.s., have fun; (*fig*) to mess around

amygdale [amidal] *nf* tonsil

an [ɑ̃] *nm* year; **le jour de l'~, le premier de l'~, le nouvel ~** New Year's Day

analogique [analɔʒik] *adj* analogical; (*INFORM, montre*) analogue

analogue [analɔg] *adj*: **~ (à)** analogous (to), similar (to)

analphabète [analfabɛt] *nmf* illiterate

analyse [analiz] *nf* analysis; (*MED*) test; **analyser** *vt* to analyse; to test

ananas [anana] *nm* pineapple

anarchie [anarʃi] *nf* anarchy

anathème [anatɛm] *nm*: **jeter l'~ sur** to curse

anatomie [anatɔmi] *nf* anatomy

ancêtre [ɑ̃sɛtr(ə)] *nmf* ancestor

anchois [ɑ̃ʃwa] *nm* anchovy

ancien, ne [ɑ̃sjɛ̃, -jɛn] *adj* old; (*de jadis, de l'antiquité*) ancient; (*précédent, ex-*) former, old ♦ *nmf* (*dans une tribu*) elder; **anciennement** *adv* formerly; **ancienneté** *nf* oldness; an-

tiquity; (*ADMIN*) (length of) service; seniority

ancre [ɑ̃kr(ə)] *nf* anchor; **jeter/lever l'~** to cast/weigh anchor; **à l'~** at anchor; **ancrer** [ɑ̃kre] *vt* (*CONSTR: câble etc*) to anchor; (*fig*) to fix firmly; **s'~r** *vi* (*NAVIG*) to (cast) anchor

Andorre [ɑ̃dɔr] *nf* Andorra

andouille [ɑ̃duj] *nf* (*CULIN*) sausage made of chitterlings; (*fam*) clot, nit

âne [ɑn] *nm* donkey, ass; (*péj*) dunce

anéantir [aneɑ̃tir] *vt* to annihilate, wipe out; (*fig*) to obliterate, destroy; to overwhelm

anémie [anemi] *nf* anaemia; **anémique** *adj* anaemic

ânerie [ɑnri] *nf* stupidity; stupid ou idiotic comment *etc*

anesthésie [anɛstezi] *nf* anaesthesia; **faire une ~ locale/générale à qn** to give sb a local/general anaesthetic

ange [ɑ̃ʒ] *nm* angel; **être aux ~s** to be over the moon

angélus [ɑ̃ʒelys] *nm* angelus; evening bells *pl*

angine [ɑ̃ʒin] *nf* throat infection; **~ de poitrine** angina

anglais, e [ɑ̃glɛ, -ɛz] *adj* English ♦ *nm/f*: **A~, e** Englishman(woman) ♦ *nm* (*LING*) English; **les A~** the English; **filer à l'~e** to take French leave

angle [ɑ̃gl(ə)] *nm* angle; (*coin*) corner; **~ droit** right angle

Angleterre [ɑ̃glətɛr] *nf*: **l'~** England

anglo... [ɑ̃glɔ] *préfixe* Anglo-, anglo(-); **~phone** *adj* English-speaking

angoissé, e [ɑ̃gwase] *adj* (*personne*) full of anxieties ou hang-ups (*fam*)

angoisser [ɑ̃gwase] *vt* to harrow, cause anguish to ♦ *vi* to worry, fret

anguille [ɑ̃gij] *nf* eel

anicroche [anikrɔʃ] *nf* hitch, snag

animal, e, aux [animal, -o] *adj, nm* animal

animateur, trice [animatœr, -tris] *nm/f* (*de télévision*) host; (*de groupe*) leader, organizer

animation [animasjɔ̃] *nf* (*voir animé*) busyness; liveliness; (*CINEMA: technique*) animation

animé, e [anime] *adj* (*lieu*) busy, lively; (*conversation, réunion*) lively, animated; (*opposé à in~*) animate

animer [anime] *vt* (*ville, soirée*) to liven up; (*mettre en mouvement*) to drive

anis [ani] *nm* (*CULIN*) aniseed; (*BOT*) anise

ankyloser [ɑ̃kiloze]: **s'~** *vi* to get stiff

anneau, x [ano] *nm* (*de rideau, bague*) ring; (*de chaîne*) link

année [ane] *nf* year

annexe [anɛks(ə)] *adj* (*problème*) related; (*document*) appended; (*salle*) adjoining ♦ *nf* (*bâtiment*) annex(e); (*de document, ouvrage*) annex, appendix; (*jointe à une lettre*) enclosure

anniversaire [anivɛrsɛr] *nm* birthday; (*d'un événement, bâtiment*) anniversary

annonce [anɔ̃s] *nf* announcement; (*signe, indice*) sign; (*aussi: ~ publicitaire*) advertisement; **les petites ~s** the classified advertisements, the small ads

annoncer [anɔ̃se] *vt* to announce; (*être le signe de*) to herald; **s'~ bien/difficile** to look promising/difficult; **annonceur, euse** *nm/f* (*TV, RADIO: speaker*) announcer; (*publicitaire*) advertiser

annuaire [anɥɛr] *nm* yearbook, annual; **~ téléphonique** (telephone) directory, phone book

annuel, le [anɥɛl] *adj* annual, yearly

annuité [anɥite] *nf* annual instalment

annuler [anɥle] *vt* (*rendez-vous, voyage*) to cancel, call off; (*mariage*) to annul; (*jugement*) to quash (*BRIT*), repeal (*US*); (*résultats*) to declare void; (*MATH, PHYSIQUE*) to cancel out

anodin, e [anɔdɛ̃, -in] *adj* harmless; insignificant, trivial

anonyme [anɔnim] *adj* anonymous; (*fig*) impersonal

ANPE *sigle f* (= *Agence nationale pour l'emploi*) national employment agency

anse [ɑ̃s] *nf* (*de panier, tasse*) handle; (*GÉO*) cove

antan [ɑ̃tɑ̃]: **d'~** *adj* of long ago

antarctique [ɑ̃taʀktik] *adj* Antarctic ♦ *nm*: **l'A~** the Antarctic

antécédents [ɑ̃tesedɑ̃] *nmpl* (*MÉD etc*) past history *sg*

antenne [ɑ̃tɛn] *nf* (*de radio*) aerial; (*d'insecte*) antenna, feeler; (*poste avancé*) outpost; (*petite succursale*) sub-branch; **passer à l'~** to go on the air; **prendre l'~** to tune in; **2 heures d'~** 2 hours' broadcasting time

antérieur, e [ɑ̃teʀjœʀ] *adj* (*d'avant*) previous, earlier; (*de devant*) front

anti... [ɑ̃ti] *préfixe* anti...; **~alcoolique** *adj* anti-alcohol; **~atomique** *adj*: **abri ~atomique** fallout shelter; **~biotique** *nm* antibiotic; **~brouillard** *nm*: **phare ~brouillard** fog lamp

anticipation [ɑ̃tisipasjɔ̃] *nf*: **livre/film d'~** science fiction book/film

anticipé, e [ɑ̃tisipe] *adj*: **avec mes remerciements ~s** thanking you in advance *ou* anticipation

anticiper [ɑ̃tisipe] *vt* (*événement, coup*) to anticipate, foresee

anti: ~conceptionnel, le *adj* contraceptive; **~corps** *nm* antibody; **~dote** *nm* antidote

antigel [ɑ̃tiʒɛl] *nm* antifreeze

antihistaminique [ɑ̃tiistaminik] *nm* antihistamine

Antilles [ɑ̃tij] *nfpl*: **les ~** the West Indies

antilope [ɑ̃tilɔp] *nf* antelope

anti: ~mite(s) *adj, nm*. (*produit*) ~ mothproofer; moth repellent; **~parasite** *adj* (*RADIO, TV*): **dispositif ~** suppressor; **~pathique** *adj* unpleasant, disagreeable; **~pelliculaire** *adj* anti-dandruff

antipodes [ɑ̃tipɔd] *nmpl* (*GÉO*): **les**

~ the antipodes; (*fig*): être aux ~ de to be the opposite extreme of

antiquaire [ɑ̃tikɛʀ] *nm/f* antique dealer

antique [ɑ̃tik] *adj* antique; (*très vieux*) ancient, antiquated

antiquité [ɑ̃tikite] *nf* (*objet*) antique; **l'A~** Antiquity; **magasin d'~s** antique shop

anti: ~rabique *adj* rabies *cpd*; **~rouille** *adj inv* anti-rust *cpd*; **traitement ~rouille** rustproofing; **~sémite** *adj* anti-Semitic; **~septique** *adj, nm* antiseptic; **~vol** *adj inv* (*dispositif*) ~vol anti-theft device

antre [ɑ̃tʀ(ə)] *nm* den, lair

anxieux, euse [ɑ̃ksjø, -øz] *adj* anxious, worried

AOC *sigle f* (= appellation d'origine contrôlée) label guaranteeing the quality of wine

août [u] *nm* August

apaiser [apeze] *vt* (*colère, douleur*) to soothe; (*faim*) to appease; (*personne*) to calm (down), pacify; **s'~** *vi* (*tempête, bruit*) to die down, subside

apanage [apanaʒ] *nm*: être l'~ de to be the privilege *ou* prerogative of

aparté [apaʀte] *nm* (*THEATRE*) aside; (*entretien*) private conversation

apathique [apatik] *adj* apathetic

apatride [apatʀid] *nm/f* stateless person

apercevoir [apɛʀsəvwaʀ] *vt* to see; **s'~ de** *vt* to notice; **s'~ que** to notice that

aperçu [apɛʀsy] *nm* (*vue d'ensemble*) general survey; (*intuition*) insight

apéritif [apeʀitif] *nm* (*boisson*) aperitif; (*réunion*) drinks *pl*

à-peu-près [apøpʀɛ] (*péj*) *nm inv* vague approximation

apeuré, e [apœʀe] *adj* frightened, scared

aphone [afɔn] *adj* voiceless

aphte [aft(ə)] *nm* mouth ulcer

apiculture [apikyltyʀ] *nf* beekeeping, apiculture

apitoyer [apitwaje] *vt* to move to pity; **s'~** (**sur**) to feel pity (for)

aplanir [aplaniʀ] *vt* to level; (*fig*) to smooth away, iron out

aplatir [aplatiʀ] *vt* to flatten; **s'~** *vi* to become flatter; to be flattened; (*fig*) to lie flat on the ground

aplomb [aplɔ̃] *nm* (*équilibre*) balance, equilibrium; (*fig*) self-assurance; nerve; **d'~** steady; (*CONSTR*) plumb

apogée [apɔʒe] *nm* (*fig*) peak, apogee

apologie [apɔlɔʒi] *nf* vindication, praise

apostrophe [apɔstʀɔf] *nf* (*signe*) apostrophe

apostropher [apɔstʀɔfe] *vt* (*interpeller*) to shout at, address sharply

apothéose [apɔteoz] *nf* (*point culminant*) pinnacle of achievement; (*MUS*) grand finale

apôtre [apotʀ(ə)] *nm* apostle

apparaître [apaʀɛtʀ(ə)] *vi* to appear

apparat [apaʀa] *nm*: **tenue/dîner d'~** ceremonial dress/dinner

appareil [apaʀɛj] *nm* (*outil, machine*) piece of apparatus, device; appliance; (*politique, syndical*) machinery; (*avion*) (aero)plane, aircraft *inv*; (*téléphonique*) phone; (*dentier*) brace (*BRIT*), braces (*US*); **qui est à l'~?** who's speaking?; **dans le plus simple ~** in one's birthday suit; **~r** [apaʀeje] *vi* (*NAVIG*) to cast off, get under way ♦ *vt* (*assortir*) to match up; **~(-photo)** [apaʀɛj(fɔto)] *nm* camera

apparemment [apaʀamɑ̃] *adv* apparently

apparence [apaʀɑ̃s] *nf* appearance

apparent, e [apaʀɑ̃, -ɑ̃t] *adj* visible; obvious; (*superficiel*) apparent

apparenté, e [apaʀɑ̃te] *adj*: **~ à** related to; (*fig*) similar to

apparition [apaʀisjɔ̃] *nf* appearance; (*surnaturelle*) apparition

appartement [apaʀtəmɑ̃] *nm* flat (*BRIT*), apartment (*US*)

appartenir [apaʀtəniʀ]: **~ à** *vt* to

belong to; **il lui appartient de** it is up to him to, it is his duty to

apparu, e pp de **apparaître**

appât [apɑ] nm (PÊCHE) bait; (fig) lure, bait

appauvrir [apovʀiʀ] vt to impoverish

appel [apɛl] nm (cal); (nominal) roll call; (: SCOL) register; (MIL: recrutement) call-up; **faire ~ à** (invoquer) to appeal to; (avoir recours à) to call on; (nécessiter) to call for, require; **faire ~** (JUR) to appeal; **faire l'~** to call the roll; to call the register; **sans ~** (fig) final, irrevocable; **~ d'offres** (COMM) invitation to tender; **faire un ~ de phares** to flash one's headlights; **~ (téléphonique)** (tele)phone call

appelé [aple] nm (MIL) conscript

appeler [aple] vt to call; (faire venir: médecin etc) to call, send for; (fig: nécessiter) to call for, demand; **s'~:** **elle s'appelle Gabrielle** her name is Gabrielle, she's called Gabrielle; **comment ça s'appelle?** what is it called?; **être appelé à** (fig) to be destined to; **~ qn à comparaître** (JUR) to summon sb to appear; **en ~ à** to appeal to

appendice [apɛ̃dis] nm appendix; **appendicite** nf appendicitis

appentis [apɑ̃ti] nm lean-to

appesantir [apzɑ̃tiʀ]: **s'~** vi to grow heavier; **s'~ sur** (fig) to dwell on

appétissant, e [apetisɑ̃, -ɑ̃t] adj appetizing, mouth-watering

appétit [apeti] nm appetite; **bon ~!** enjoy your meal!

applaudir [aplodiʀ] vt to applaud ♦ vi to applaud, clap; **applaudissements** nmpl applause sg, clapping sg

application [aplikasjɔ̃] nf application

applique [aplik] nf wall lamp

appliquer [aplike] vt to apply; (loi) to enforce; **s'~** vi (élève etc) to apply o.s.

appoint [apwɛ̃] nm (extra) contribution ou help; **avoir/faire l'~** (en payant) to have/give the right change ou money; **chauffage d'~** extra

heating

appointements [apwɛ̃tmɑ̃] nmpl salary sg

appontement [apɔ̃tmɑ̃] nm landing stage, wharf

apport [apɔʀ] nm supply; contribution

apporter [apɔʀte] vt to bring

apposer [apoze] vt to append; to affix

appréciable [apʀesjabl(ə)] adj appreciable

apprécier [apʀesje] vt to appreciate; (évaluer) to estimate, assess

appréhender [apʀeɑ̃de] vt (craindre) to dread; (arrêter) to apprehend

apprendre [apʀɑ̃dʀ(ə)] vt to learn; (événement, résultats) to learn of, hear of; **~ qch à qn** (informer) to tell sb (of) sth; (enseigner) to teach sb sth; **~ à faire qch** to learn to do sth; **~ à qn à faire qch** to teach sb to do sth); **apprenti, e** nm/f apprentice; (fig) novice, beginner; **apprentissage** nm learning; (COMM, SCOL: période) apprenticeship

apprêté, e [apʀete] adj (fig) affected

apprêter [apʀete] vt to dress, finish

appris, e pp de **apprendre**

apprivoiser [apʀivwaze] vt to tame

approbation [apʀobasjɔ̃] nf approval

approche [apʀɔʃ] nf approaching; approach

approcher [apʀɔʃe] vi to approach, come near ♦ vt to approach; (rapprocher): **~ qch (de qch)** to bring ou put sth near (to sth); **s'~ de** to approach, go ou come near to; **~ de** (quantité, moment) to approach

approfondir [apʀofɔ̃diʀ] vt to deepen; (question) to go further into

approprié, e [apʀɔpʀije] adj: **~ (à)** appropriate (to), suited to

approprier [apʀɔpʀije]: **s'~** vt to appropriate, take over

approuver [apʀuve] vt to agree with; (autoriser: loi, projet) to ap prove, pass; (*trouver louable*) to approve of

approvisionner [apʀɔvizjɔne] *vt* to supply; (*compte bancaire*) to pay funds into; **s'~ en** to stock up with

approximatif, ive [apʀɔksimatif, -iv] *adj* approximate, rough; vague

appui [apɥi] *nm* support; **prendre ~ sur** to lean on; to rest on; **l'~ de la fenêtre** the windowsill, the window ledge; **appui(e)-tête** *nm inv* headrest

appuyer [apɥije] *vt* (*poser*): ~ **qch sur/contre** to lean *ou* rest sth on/ against; (*soutenir: personne, demande*) to support, back (up): ~ **sur** (*bouton, frein*) to press, push; (*mot, détail*) to stress, emphasize; (*suj: chose: peser sur*) to rest (heavily) on, press against; **s'~ sur** to lean on; to rely on; ~ **à droite** to bear (to the) right

âpre [apʀ(ə)] *adj* acrid, pungent; (*fig*) harsh; bitter; ~ **au gain** grasping

après [apʀe] *prép* after ♦ *adv* afterwards; **2 heures ~** 2 hours later; ~ **qu'il est** *ou* **soit parti** after he left; ~ **avoir fait** after having done; **d'~** (*selon*) according to; ~ **coup** after the event, afterwards; ~ **tout** (*au fond*) after all; **et (puis) ~?** so what?; **après-demain** the day after tomorrow; **après-guerre** *nm* post-war years *pl*; **après-midi** *nm ou nf (inv)* afternoon

à-propos [apʀɔpo] *nm* (*d'une remarque*) aptness; **faire preuve d'~** to show presence of mind

apte [apt(ə)] *adj* capable; (*MIL*) fit

aquarelle [akwaʀɛl] *nf* (*tableau*) watercolour; (*genre*) watercolours *pl*

aquarium [akwaʀjɔm] *nm* aquarium

arabe [aʀab] *adj* Arabic; (*désert, cheval*) Arabian; (*nation, peuple*) Arab ♦ *nm/f*: **A~** Arab ♦ *nm* (*LING*) Arabic

Arabie [aʀabi] *nf*: **l'~** (*Saoudite*) Saudi Arabia

arachide [aʀaʃid] *nf* (*plante*) groundnut (plant); (*graine*) peanut, ground-

nut

araignée [aʀɛɲe] *nf* spider

arbitraire [aʀbitʀɛʀ] *adj* arbitrary

arbitre [aʀbitʀ(ə)] *nm* (*SPORT*) referee; (: *TENNIS, CRICKET*) umpire; (*fig*) arbiter, judge; (*JUR*) arbitrator; **arbitrer** *vt* to referee; to umpire; to arbitrate

arborer [aʀbɔʀe] *vt* to bear, display

arbre [aʀbʀ(ə)] *nm* tree; (*TECH*) shaft; ~ **de transmission** (*AUTO*) driveshaft; ~ **généalogique** family tree

arbuste [aʀbyst(ə)] *nm* small shrub

arc [aʀk] *nm* (*arme*) bow; (*GEOM*) arc; (*ARCHIT*) arch; **en ~ de cercle** semi-circular

arcade [aʀkad] *nf* arch(way); ~**s** *nfpl* (*série*) arcade *sg*, arches

arcanes [aʀkan] *nmpl* mysteries

arc-boutant [aʀkbutã] *nm* flying buttress

arceau, x [aʀso] *nm* (*métallique etc*) hoop

arc-en-ciel [aʀkãsjɛl] *nm* rainbow

arche [aʀʃ(ə)] *nf* arch; ~ **de Noé** Noah's Ark

archéologie [aʀkeɔlɔʒi] *nf* archeology; **archéologue** *nm/f* archeologist

archet [aʀʃɛ] *nm* bow

archevêque [aʀʃəvɛk] *nm* archbishop

archipel [aʀʃipɛl] *nm* archipelago

architecte [aʀʃitɛkt(ə)] *nm* architect

architecture [aʀʃitɛktyʀ] *nf* architecture

archive [aʀʃiv] *nf* file; ~**s** *nfpl* (*collection*) archives

arctique [aʀktik] *adj* Arctic ♦ *nm*: **l'A~** the Arctic

ardemment [aʀdamã] *adv* ardently, fervently

ardent, e [aʀdã, -ãt] *adj* (*soleil*) blazing; (*fièvre*) raging; (*amour*) ardent, passionate; (*prière*) fervent

ardoise [aʀdwaz] *nf* slate

ardt *abr* = **arrondissement**

ardu, e [aʀdy] *adj* (*travail*) arduous; (*problème*) difficult; (*pente*) steep

arène [aʀɛn] *nf* arena; ~**s** *nfpl* (*am-*

phithéâtre) bull-ring sg

arête [aʀɛt] nf (*de poisson*) bone; (*d'une montagne*) ridge; (*GEOM etc*) edge

argent [aʀʒɑ̃] nm (*métal*) silver; (*monnaie*) money; ~ **de poche** pocket money; ~ **liquide** ready money, (ready) cash; **argenterie** nf silverware; silver plate

argentin, e [aʀʒɑ̃tɛ̃, -in] adj (*son*) silvery; (*d'Argentine*) Argentinian, Argentine

Argentine [aʀʒɑ̃tin] nf: **l'~** Argentina, the Argentine

argile [aʀʒil] nf clay

argot [aʀgo] nm slang; **argotique** adj slang cpd; slangy

arguer [aʀgɥe]: ~ **de** vt to put forward as a pretext ou reason

argument [aʀgymɑ̃] nm argument

argumentaire [aʀgymɑ̃tɛʀ] nm sales leaflet

argumenter [aʀgymɑ̃te] vi to argue

argus [aʀgys] nm guide to second-hand car etc prices

aristocratique [aʀistɔkʀatik] adj aristocratic

arithmétique [aʀitmetik] adj arithmetic(al) ♦ nf arithmetic

armateur [aʀmatœʀ] nm shipowner

armature [aʀmatyʀ] nf framework; (*de tente etc*) frame

arme [aʀm(ə)] nf weapon; (*section de l'armée*) arm; ~**s** nfpl (*armement*) weapons, arms; (*blason*) (coat of) arms; ~ **à feu** firearm

armée [aʀme] nf army; ~ **de l'air** Air Force; ~ **de terre** Army

armement [aʀməmɑ̃] nm (*matériel*) arms pl, weapons pl; (: *d'un pays*) arms pl, armament

armer [aʀme] vt to arm; (*arme à feu*) to cock; (*appareil-photo*) to wind on; ~ **qch de** to fit sth with; to reinforce sth with

armistice [aʀmistis] nm armistice; **l'A~** ≈ Remembrance (BRIT) ou Veterans (US) Day

armoire [aʀmwaʀ] nf (tall) cupboard; (*penderie*) wardrobe (BRIT),

closet (US)

armoiries [aʀmwaʀi] nfpl coat sg of arms

armure [aʀmyʀ] nf armour no pl, suit of armour; **armurier** [aʀmyʀje] nm gunsmith; armourer

arnaquer [aʀnake] vt to swindle

aromates [aʀɔmat] nmpl seasoning sg, herbs (and spices)

aromatisé, e [aʀɔmatize] adj flavoured

arôme [aʀom] nm aroma; fragrance

arpenter [aʀpɑ̃te] vt (*salle, couloir*) to pace up and down

arpenteur [aʀpɑ̃tœʀ] nm surveyor

arqué, e [aʀke] adj bandy; arched

arrache-pied [aʀaʃpje]: **d'~** adv relentlessly

arracher [aʀaʃe] vt to pull out; (*page etc*) to tear off, tear out; (*légumes, herbe*) to pull up; (*bras etc*) to tear off; **s'~** vt (*article recherché*) to fight over; ~ **qch à qn** to snatch sth from sb; (*fig*) to wring sth out of sb

arraisonner [aʀɛzɔne] vt (*bateau*) to board and search

arrangeant, e [aʀɑ̃ʒɑ̃, -ɑ̃t] adj accommodating, obliging

arrangement [aʀɑ̃ʒmɑ̃] nm agreement, arrangement

arranger [aʀɑ̃ʒe] vt (*gén*) to arrange; (*réparer*) to fix, put right; (*régler*) to settle, sort out; (*convenir à*) to suit, be convenient for; **s'~** vi (*se mettre d'accord*) to come to an agreement; **ça va s'~** it'll sort itself out

arrestation [aʀɛstasjɔ̃] nf arrest

arrêt [aʀɛ] nm stopping; (*de bus etc*) stop; (*JUR*) judgment, decision; **rester ou tomber en** ~ **devant** to stop short in front of; **sans** ~ non-stop; continually; ~ **de mort** death sentence; ~ **de travail** stoppage (of work)

arrêté [aʀete] nm order, decree

arrêter [aʀete] vt to stop; (*chauffage etc*) to turn off, switch off; (*fixer: date etc*) to appoint, decide on; (*cri-*

minel, suspect) to arrest; **s'~** *vi* to stop; **~ de faire** to stop doing

arrhes [ar] *nfpl* deposit *sg*

arrière [arjɛr] *nm* back; *(SPORT)* fullback ♦ *adj inv:* **siège/roue ~** back *ou* rear seat/wheel; **à l'~** behind, at the back; **en ~** behind; *(tomber, aller)* backwards; **arriéré, e** *adj* *(d'argent)* arrears *pl;* **~-goût** *nm* aftertaste; **~-grand-mère** *nf* great-grandmother; **~-grand-père** *nm* great-grandfather; **~-pays** *nm inv* hinterland; **~-pensée** *nf* ulterior motive; mental reservation; **~-plan** *nm* background; **~-saison** *nf* late autumn; **~-train** *nm* hindquarters *pl*

arrimer [arime] *vt* to stow; to secure

arrivage [arivaʒ] *nm* arrival

arrivée [arive] *nf* arrival; *(ligne d'~)* finish; **~ d'air** air inlet

arriver [arive] *vi* to arrive; *(survenir)* to happen, occur; **il arrive à Paris à 8h** he gets to *ou* arrives in Paris at 8; **~ à** *(atteindre)* to reach; **~ à faire qch** to succeed in doing sth; **il arrive que** it happens that; **il lui arrive de faire** he sometimes does; **arriviste** *nm/f* go-getter

arrogance [arɔgɑ̃s] *nf* arrogance; **arrogant, e** [arɔgɑ̃, -ɑ̃t] *adj* arrogant

arroger [arɔʒe]: **s'~** *vt* to assume *(without right)*

arrondir [arɔ̃dir] *vt* (*forme, objet*) to round; *(somme)* to round off; **s'~** *vi* to become round(ed)

arrondissement [arɔ̃dismɑ̃] *nm* *(ADMIN)* ≈ district

arroser [aroze] *vt* to water; *(victoire)* to celebrate (over a drink); *(CULIN)* to baste; **arrosoir** *nm* watering can

arsenal, aux [arsənal, -o] *nm* *(NAVIG)* naval dockyard; *(MIL)* arsenal; *(fig)* gear, paraphernalia

art [ar] *nm* art; **~s ménagers** home economics *sg*

artère [artɛr] *nf* *(ANAT)* artery; *(rue)* main road

arthrite [artrit] *nf* arthritis

artichaut [artiʃo] *nm* artichoke

article [artikl(ə)] *nm* article; *(COMM)* item, article; **à l'~ de la mort** at the point of death; **~ de fond** *(PRESSE)* feature article

articulation [artikylɑsjɔ̃] *nf* articulation; *(ANAT)* joint

articuler [artikyle] *vt* to articulate

artifice [artifis] *nm* device, trick

artificiel, le [artifisjɛl] *adj* artificial

artificieux, euse [artifisjø, -øz] *adj* guileful, deceitful

artisan [artizɑ̃] *nm* artisan, (self-employed) craftsman; **artisanal, e, aux** *adj* of *ou* made by craftsmen; *(péj)* cottage industry *cpd,* unsophisticated; **artisanat** *nm* arts and crafts *pl*

artiste [artist(ə)] *nm/f* artist; *(de variétés)* entertainer; performer; **artistique** *adj* artistic

as[1] [a] *vb voir* **avoir**

as[2] [as] *nm* ace

ascendance [asɑ̃dɑ̃s] *nf* *(origine)* ancestry

ascendant, e [asɑ̃dɑ̃, -ɑ̃t] *adj* upward ♦ *nm* influence

ascenseur [asɑ̃sœr] *nm* lift *(BRIT),* elevator *(US)*

ascension [asɑ̃sjɔ̃] *nf* ascent; climb; **l'A~** *(REL)* the Ascension

aseptiser [asɛptize] *vt* to sterilize; to disinfect

asiatique [azjatik] *adj, nm/f* Asiatic, Asian

Asie [azi] *nf:* **l'~** Asia

asile [azil] *nm* *(refuge)* refuge, sanctuary; *(POL):* **droit d'~** (political) asylum; *(pour malades etc)* home

aspect [aspɛ] *nm* appearance, look; *(fig)* aspect, side; **à l'~ de** at the sight of

asperge [aspɛrʒ(ə)] *nf* asparagus *no pl*

asperger [aspɛrʒe] *vt* to spray, sprinkle

aspérité [asperite] *nf* excrescence, protruding bit (of rock *etc*)

asphalte [asfalt(ə)] *nm* asphalt

asphyxier [asfiksje] *vt* to suffocate, asphyxiate; *(fig)* to stifle

aspirateur [aspiratœR] *nm* vacuum cleaner

aspirer [aspire] *vt* *(air)* to inhale; *(liquide)* to suck (up); *(suj: appareil)* to suck up; ~ à to aspire to

aspirine [aspiRin] *nf* aspirin

assagir [asaʒiR] *vt* to quieten down; s'~ *vi* to quieten down, sober down

assaillir [asajiR] *vt* to assail, attack

assainir [aseniR] *vt* to clean up; to purify

assaisonner [asezɔne] *vt* to season

assassin [asasɛ̃] *nm* murderer; assassin; ~**er** [asasine] *vt* to murder; *(esp POL)* to assassinate

assaut [aso] *nm* assault, attack; **prendre d'~** to storm, assault; **donner l'~** to attack; **faire ~ de** *(rivaliser)* to vie with each other in

assécher [asefe] *vt* to drain

assemblée [asãble] *nf* *(réunion)* meeting; *(public, assistance)* gathering; assembled people; *(POL)* assembly

assembler [asãble] *vt* *(joindre, monter)* to assemble, put together; *(amasser)* to gather (together), collect (together); s'~ *vi* to gather

assener [asene] *vt:* ~ **un coup à qn** to deal sb a blow

asséner [asene] *vt* = **assener**

assentiment [asãtimã] *nm* assent, consent; approval

asseoir [aswaR] *vt* *(malade, bébé)* to sit up; to sit down; *(autorité, réputation)* to establish; s'~ *vi* to sit (o.s.) down

assermenté, e [asɛRmãte] *adj* sworn, on oath

asservir [asɛRviR] *vt* to subjugate, enslave

assez [ase] *adv* *(suffisamment)* enough, sufficiently; *(passablement)* rather, quite, fairly; ~ **de pain/ livres** enough *ou* sufficient bread/ books; **vous en avez** ~? have you got enough?

assidu, e [asidy] *adj* assiduous,

painstaking; regular; **assiduités** *nfpl* assiduous attentions

assied *etc vb voir* **asseoir**

assiéger [asjeʒe] *vt* to besiege

assiérai *etc vb voir* **asseoir**

assiette [asjɛt] *nf* plate; *(contenu)* plate(ful); ~ à **dessert** dessert plate; ~ **anglaise** assorted cold meats; ~ **creuse** (soup) dish, soup plate; ~ **de l'impôt** basis of (tax) assessment; ~ **plate** (dinner) plate

assigner [asiɲe] *vt:* ~ **qch à** *(poste, part, travail)* to assign sth to; *(limites)* to set sth to; *(cause, effet)* to ascribe sth to; ~ **qn à** to assign sb to

assimiler [asimile] *vt* to assimilate, absorb; *(comparer)*: ~ **qch/qn à** to liken *ou* compare sth/sb to; s'~ *vi* *(s'intégrer)* to be assimilated *ou* absorbed

assis, e [asi, -iz] *pp de* **asseoir** ♦ *adj* sitting (down), seated; **assise** *nf* *(fig)* basis, foundation; ~**es** *nfpl* *(JUR)* assizes; *(congrès)* (annual) conference

assistance [asistãs] *nf* *(public)* audience; *(aide)* assistance

assistant, e [asistã, -ãt] *nm/f* assistant; *(d'université)* probationary lecturer; ~**e sociale** social worker

assisté, e [asiste] *adj* *(AUTO)* power assisted

assister [asiste] *vt* to assist; ~ à *(scène, événement)* to witness; *(conférence, séminaire)* to attend, be at; *(spectacle, match)* to be at, see

association [asɔsjasjɔ̃] *nf* association

associé, e [asɔsje] *nm/f* associate; partner

associer [asɔsje] *vt* to associate; s'~ *vi* to join together ♦ *vt* *(collaborateur)* to take on (as a partner); s'~ à **qn pour faire** to join (forces) with sb to do; s'~ à to be combined with; *(opinions, joie de qn)* to share in; ~ **qn à** *(profits)* to give sb a share of; *(affaire)* to make sb a partner in; *(joie, triomphe)* to include sb in; ~ **qch à** *(joindre, allier)* to combine sth with

assoiffé, e [aswafe] adj thirsty

assombrir [asɔ̃bʀiʀ] vt to darken; (fig) to fill with gloom

assommer [asɔme] vt to batter to death; (étourdir, abrutir) to knock out; to stun

Assomption [asɔ̃psjɔ̃] nf: l'~ the Assumption

assorti, e [asɔʀti] adj matched, matching; (varié) assorted; ~ à matching

assortiment [asɔʀtimɑ̃] nm assortment, selection

assortir [asɔʀtiʀ] vt to match; s'~ de to be accompanied by; ~ qch à to match with; ~ qch à to accompany sth with

assoupi, e [asupi] adj dozing, sleeping; (fig) numbed; dulled; stilled

assouplir [asupliʀ] vt to make supple; (fig) to relax

assourdir [asuʀdiʀ] vt (bruit) to deaden, muffle; (suj: bruit) to deafen

assouvir [asuviʀ] vt to satisfy, appease

assujettir [asyʒetiʀ] vt to subject

assumer [asyme] vt (fonction, emploi) to assume, take on

assurance [asyʀɑ̃s] nf (certitude) assurance; (confiance en soi) (self-)confidence; (contrat) insurance (policy); (secteur commercial) insurance; ~ maladie health insurance; ~ tous risques (AUTO) comprehensive insurance; ~s sociales ≈ National Insurance (BRIT), ≈ Social Security (US); ~-vie nf life assurance ou insurance

assuré, e [asyʀe] adj (certain) : ~ de confident of ♦ nm/f insured (person); **assurément** adv assuredly, most certainly

assurer [asyʀe] vt to insure; (stabiliser) to steady; to stabilize; (victoire etc) to ensure; (frontières, pouvoir) to make secure; (service, garde) to provide; to operate; s'~ (contre) (COMM) to insure o.s. against; s'~ de/que (vérifier) to make sure of/

that; s'~ (de) (aide de qn) to secure; ~ qch à qn (garantir) to secure sth for sb; (certifier) to assure sb of sth; ~ à qn que to assure sb that; ~ qn de to assure sb of

asthme [asm(ə)] nm asthma

asticot [astiko] nm maggot

astiquer [astike] vt to polish, shine

astre [astʀ(ə)] nm star

astreignant, e [astʀɛɲɑ̃, -ɑ̃t] adj demanding

astreindre [astʀɛ̃dʀ(ə)] vt: ~ qn à qch to force sth upon sb; ~ qn à faire to compel ou force sb to do

astrologie [astʀɔlɔʒi] nf astrology

astronaute [astʀonot] nm/f astronaut

astronomie [astʀonɔmi] nf astronomy

astuce [astys] nf shrewdness, astuteness; (truc) trick, clever way; (plaisanterie) wisecrack; **astucieux, euse** adj clever

atelier [atalje] nm workshop; (de peintre) studio

athée [ate] adj atheistic ♦ nm/f atheist

Athènes [atɛn] n Athens

athlète [atlɛt] nm/f (SPORT) athlete; **athlétisme** nm athletics sg

atlantique [atlɑ̃tik] adj Atlantic ♦ nm: l'(océan) A~ the Atlantic (Ocean)

atlas [atlɑs] nm atlas

atmosphère [atmɔsfɛʀ] nf atmosphere

atome [atom] nm atom; **atomique** adj atomic, nuclear; (nombre, masse) atomic

atomiseur [atɔmizœʀ] nm atomizer

atone [aton] adj lifeless

atours [atuʀ] nmpl attire sg, finery sg

atout [atu] nm trump; (fig) asset; trump card

âtre [ɑtʀ(ə)] nm hearth

atroce [atʀɔs] adj atrocious

attabler [atable] : s'~ vi to sit down at (the) table

attachant, e [ataʃɑ̃, -ɑ̃t] adj engaging, lovable, likeable

attache [ataʃ] *nf* clip, fastener; (*fig*) tie

attacher [ataʃe] *vt* to tie up; (*étiquette*) to attach, tie on; (*souliers*) to do up ♦ *vi* (*poêle, riz*) to stick; s'~ à (*par affection*) to become attached to; s'~ à **faire** to endeavour to do; ~ **qch** à to tie *ou* attach sth to

attaque [atak] *nf* attack; (*cérébrale*) stroke; (*d'épilepsie*) fit

attaquer [atake] *vt* to attack; (*en justice*) to bring an action against, sue; (*travail*) to tackle, set about ♦ *vi* to attack

attardé, e [ataʀde] *adj* (*passants*) late; (*enfant*) backward; (*conceptions*) old-fashioned

attarder [ataʀde]: s'~ *vi* to linger, to stay on

atteindre [atɛ̃dʀ(ə)] *vt* to reach; (*blesser*) to hit; (*émouvoir*) to affect

atteint, e [atɛ̃, -ɛ̃t] *adj* (*MED*): être ~ de to be suffering from; attack; **hors d'~e** out of reach; **porter ~e** à to strike a blow at; to undermine

atteler [atle] *vt* (*cheval, bœufs*) to hitch up; (*wagons*) to couple; s'~ à (*travail*) to buckle down to

attelle [atɛl] *nf* splint

attenant, e [atnɑ̃, -ɑ̃t] *adj*: ~ (à) adjoining

attendant [atɑ̃dɑ̃] *adv*: en ~ meanwhile, in the meantime

attendre [atɑ̃dʀ(ə)] *vt* (*gén*) to wait for; (*être destiné ou réservé à*) to await, be in store for ♦ *vi* to wait; s'~ à (ce que) to expect (that); ~ un enfant to be expecting a baby; ~ de faire/d'être to wait until one does/is; ~ que to wait until; ~ qch de to expect sth of; en attendant meanwhile, in the meantime; be that as it may

attendrir [atɑ̃dʀiʀ] *vt* to move (to pity); (*viande*) to tenderize

attendu, e [atɑ̃dy] *adj* (*visiteur*) expected; ~ que considering that, since

attentat [atɑ̃ta] *nm* assassination at-

tempt; ~ **à la bombe** bomb attack; ~ **à la pudeur** indecent exposure *no pl*; indecent assault *no pl*

attente [atɑ̃t] *nf* wait; (*espérance*) expectation

attenter [atɑ̃te]: ~ à *vt* (*liberté*) to violate; ~ **à la vie de qn** to make an attempt on sb's life

attentif, ive [atɑ̃tif, -iv] *adj* (*auditeur*) attentive; (*travail*) scrupulous; careful; ~ **à** mindful of; careful to

attention [atɑ̃sjɔ̃] *nf* attention; (*prévenance*) attention, thoughtfulness *no pl*; **à l'~ de** for the attention of; **faire ~ (à)** to be careful (of); **faire ~ (à ce) que** to be *ou* make sure that; ~! careful!, watch out!; **attentionné, e** *adj* thoughtful, considerate

atténuer [atenɥe] *vt* to alleviate, ease; to lessen

atterrer [ateʀe] *vt* to dismay, appal

atterrir [ateʀiʀ] *vi* to land; **atterrissage** *nm* landing

attestation [atɛstasjɔ̃] *nf* certificate

attester [atɛste] *vt* to testify to

attirail [atiʀaj] *nm* gear; (*péj*) paraphernalia

attirant, e [atiʀɑ̃, -ɑ̃t] *adj* attractive, appealing

attirer [atiʀe] *vt* to attract; (*appâter*) to lure, entice; ~ **qn dans un coin/vers soi** to draw sb into a corner/towards one; ~ **l'attention de qn (sur)** to attract sb's attention (to); to draw sb's attention (to); s'~ **des ennuis** to bring trouble upon o.s., get into trouble

attiser [atize] *vt* (*feu*) to poke (up)

attitré, e [atitʀe] *adj* qualified; accredited; appointed

attitude [atityd] *nf* attitude; (*position du corps*) bearing

attouchements [atuʃmɑ̃] *nmpl* touching *sg*; (*sexuels*) fondling *sg*

attraction [atʀaksjɔ̃] *nf* (*gén*) attraction; (*de cabaret, cirque*) attraction

attrait [atʀɛ] *nm* appeal, attraction; lure

attrape-nigaud [atʀapnigo] *nm* con

attraper [atʀape] *vt* to catch;

(habitude, amende) to get, pick up; *(fam: duper)* to con

attrayant, e [atʀejɑ̃, -ɑ̃t] *adj* attractive

attribuer [atʀibɥe] *vt (prix)* to award; *(rôle, tâche)* to allocate, assign; *(imputer)*: **~ qch à** to attribute sth to; **s'~** *vt (s'approprier)* to claim for o.s.

attribut [atʀiby] *nm* attribute; *(LING)* complement

attrister [atʀiste] *vt* to sadden

attroupement [atʀupmɑ̃] *nm* crowd, mob

attrouper [atʀupe]: **s'~** *vi* to gather

au [o] *prép* +*dét* = **à** +**le**

aubade [obad] *nf* dawn serenade

aubaine [obɛn] *nf* godsend; *(financière)* windfall

aube [ob] *nf* dawn, daybreak; **à l'~** at dawn *ou* daybreak

aubépine [obepin] *nf* hawthorn

auberge [obɛʀʒ(ə)] *nf* inn; **~ de jeunesse** youth hostel

aubergine [obɛʀʒin] *nf* aubergine

aubergiste [obɛʀʒist(ə)] *nm/f* innkeeper, hotel-keeper

aucun, e [okœ̃, -yn] *dét* no, *tournure négative* +any; *(positif)* any ♦ *pron* none, *tournure négative* +any; any(one); **sans ~ doute** without any doubt; **plus qu'~ autre** more than any other; **~ des deux** neither of the two; **~ d'entre eux** none of them; **d'~s** *(certains)* some; **aucunement** *adv* in no way, not in the least

audace [odas] *nf* daring, boldness; *(péj)* audacity; **audacieux, euse** *adj* daring, bold

au-delà [odla] *adv* beyond ♦ *nm*: **l'~** the hereafter; **~ de** beyond

au-dessous [odsu] *adv* underneath; below; **~ de** under(neath), below; *(limite, somme etc)* below, under; *(dignité, condition)* below

au-dessus [odsy] *adv* above; **~ de** above

au-devant [odvɑ̃]: **~ de** *prép (personne, danger)* to go (out) and meet; *(souhaits de qn)* to anticipate

audience [odjɑ̃s] *nf* audience; *(JUR: séance)* hearing

audio-visuel, le [odjovizɥɛl] *adj* audio-visual

auditeur, trice [oditœʀ, -tʀis] *nm/f* listener

audition [odisjɔ̃] *nf (ouïe, écoute)* hearing; *(JUR: de témoins)* examination; *(MUS, THÉÂTRE: épreuve)* audition

auditoire [oditwaʀ] *nm* audience

auge [oʒ] *nf* trough

augmentation [ɔgmɑ̃tasjɔ̃] *nf*: **~ (de salaire)** rise (in salary) *(BRIT)*, (pay) raise *(US)*

augmenter [ɔgmɑ̃te] *vt (gén)* to increase; *(salaire, prix)* to increase, raise, put up; *(employé)* to increase the salary of ♦ *vi* to increase

augure [ɔgyʀ] *nm* soothsayer, oracle; **de bon/mauvais ~** of good/ill omen; **~r** [ɔgyʀe] *vt*: **~r bien de** to augur well for

aujourd'hui [oʒuʀdɥi] *adv* today

aumône [omon] *nf inv* alms *sg*; **faire l'~ (à qn)** to give alms (to sb)

aumônier [omonje] *nm* chaplain

auparavant [opaʀavɑ̃] *adv* before(hand)

auprès [opʀɛ]: **~ de** *prép* next to, close to; *(recourir, s'adresser)* to; *(en comparaison de)* compared with

auquel [okɛl] *prép* +*pron* = **à** +**lequel**

aurai *etc vb voir* avoir

auréole [oʀeɔl] *nf* halo; *(tache)* ring

auriculaire [oʀikylɛʀ] *nm* little finger

aurons *etc vb voir* avoir

aurore [oʀoʀ] *nf* dawn, daybreak

ausculter [oskylte] *vt* to sound

aussi [osi] *adv (également)* also, too; *(de comparaison)* as ♦ *conj* therefore, consequently; **~ fort que** as strong as; **moi ~** me too; **~ bien que** *(de même que)* as well as

aussitôt [osito] *adv* straight away, immediately; **~ que** as soon as

austère [ɔstɛʀ] *adj* austere; stern

austral, e [ɔstʀal] *adj* southern

Australie [ɔstrali] nf: l'~ Australia; **australien, ne** adj, nm/f Australian

autant [otɑ̃] adv so much; (comparatif): ~ **(que)** as much (as); (nombre) as many (as); ~ **(de)** so much (ou many); as much (ou many); ~ **partir** we (ou you etc) may as well leave; ~ **dire que** ... one might as well say that ...; pour ~ for all that; **pour** ~ **que** assuming, as long as; **d'**~ **plus/mieux (que)** all the more/the better (since)

autel [otɛl] nm altar

auteur [otœr] nm author

authentique [otɑ̃tik] adj authentic, genuine

auto [oto] nf car

auto-: ~**biographie** nf autobiography; ~**bus** nm bus; ~**car** nm coach

autochtone [otɔkton] nm/f native

auto-: ~**collant, e** adj self-adhesive; (enveloppe) self-seal ♦ nm sticker; ~**couchettes** adj: **train** ~ **car** sleeper train; ~**cuiseur** nm pressure cooker; ~**défense** nf self-defence; **groupe d'**~ **vigilante committee**; ~**didacte** nm/f self-taught person; ~**école** nf driving school; ~**gestion** nf self-management; ~**graphe** nm autograph

automate [otomat] nm (machine) (automatic) machine

automatique [otomatik] adj automatic ♦ nm: l'~ direct dialling; **automatiser** vt to automate

automne [otɔn] nm autumn (BRIT), fall (US)

automobile [otomobil] adj motor cpd ♦ nf (motor) car; l'~ motoring; the car industry; **automobiliste** nm/f motorist

autonome [otonom] adj autonomous; **autonomie** nf autonomy; (POL) self-government, autonomy

autopsie [otopsi] nf post-mortem (examination), autopsy

autoradio [otoradjo] nm car radio

autorisation [otorizasjõ] nf permission, authorization; (papiers) permit

autorisé, e [otorize] adj (opinion, sources) authoritative

autoriser [otorize] vt to give permission for, authorize; (fig) to allow (of), sanction

autoritaire [otoritɛr] adj authoritarian

autorité [otorite] nf authority; **faire** ~ to be authoritative

autoroute [otorut] nf motorway (BRIT), highway (US)

auto-stop [otostop] nm: **faire de l'**~ to hitch-hike; **auto-stoppeur, euse** nm/f hitch-hiker

autour [otur] adv around; ~ **de** around; **tout** ~ all around

---

MOT-CLÉ

autre [otr(ə)] adj **1** (différent) other, different; **je préférerais un** ~ **verre** I'd prefer another ou a different glass

2 (supplémentaire) other; **je voudrais un** ~ **verre d'eau** I'd like another glass of water

3: ~ **chose** something else; ~ **part** somewhere else; **d'**~ **part** on the other hand

♦ pron: **un** ~ another (one); **nous/vous** ~**s** us/you; **d'**~**s** others; **l'**~ the other (one); **les** ~**s** the others; (autrui) others; **l'un et l'**~ both of them; **se détester l'un l'**~**/les uns les** ~**s** to hate each other ou one another; **d'une semaine à l'**~ from one week to the next; (incessamment) any week now; **entre** ~**s** among other things

---

autrefois [otrəfwa] adv in the past

autrement [otrəmɑ̃] adv differently; in another way; (sinon) otherwise; ~ **dit** in other words

Autriche [otriʃ] nf: l'~ Austria; **autrichien, ne** adj, nm/f Austrian

autruche [otryʃ] nf ostrich

autrui [otrɥi] pron others

auvent [ovɑ̃] nm canopy

aux [o] prép +dét = **à** + **les**

auxiliaire [oksiljɛr] adj, nm/f auxiliary

auxquelles [okɛl] *prép* +*pron* = à +lesquelles

auxquels [okɛl] *prép* +*pron* à +lesquels

avachi, e [avaʃi] *adj* limp, flabby

aval [aval] *nm* (*accord*) endorsement, backing; (GEO:) **en ~** downstream, downriver; (*sur une pente*) downhill

avalanche [avalɑ̃ʃ] *nf* avalanche

avaler [avale] *vt* to swallow

avance [avɑ̃s] *nf* (*de troupes etc*) advance; progress; (*d'argent*) advance; (*oppose à retard*) lead; being ahead of schedule; **~s** *nfpl* (*ouvertures*) overtures; (*amoureuses*) advances; (être) en ~ (to be) early; (*sur un programme*) (to be) ahead of schedule; à l'~, d'~ in advance

avancé, e [avɑ̃se] *adj* advanced; well on, well under way

avancement [avɑ̃smɑ̃] *nm* (*professionnel*) promotion

avancer [avɑ̃se] *vi* to move forward, advance; (*projet, travail*) to make progress; (être en saillie) to overhang; to jut out; (*montre, réveil*) to be fast; to gain ♦ *vt* to move forward, advance; (*argent*) to advance; (*montre, pendule*) to put forward; **s'~** *vi* to move forward, advance; (*fig*) to commit o.s.; to overhang; to jut out

avant [avɑ̃] *prép* before ♦ *adv*: trop/plus ~ too far/further forward ♦ *adj inv*: **siège/roue ~** front seat/wheel ♦ *nm* (*d'un véhicule, bâtiment*) front; (SPORT: *joueur*) forward; **~ qu'il parte/de faire** before he leaves/doing; **~ tout** (*surtout*) above all; à l'~ (*dans un véhicule*) in (the) front; en ~ forward(s); en ~ de in front of

avantage [avɑ̃taʒ] *nm* advantage; **~s sociaux** fringe benefits; **avantager** *vt* (*favoriser*) to favour; (*embellir*) to flatter; **avantageux, euse** *adj* attractive; attractively priced

avant-: ~bras *nm inv* forearm; **~coureur** *adj*: signe **~coureur** advance indication *ou* sign; **~-**

dernier, ière *adj, nm/f* next to last, last but one; **~goût** *nm* foretaste; **~hier** *adv* the day before yesterday; **~première** *nf* (*de film*) preview; **~projet** *nm* (preliminary) draft; **~propos** *nm* foreword; **~veille** *nf*; l'~ two days before

avare [avaʀ] *adj* miserly, avaricious ♦ *nm/f* miser; **~ de** (*compliments etc*) sparing of

avarié, e [avaʀje] *adj* rotting

avaries [avaʀi] *nfpl* (NAVIG) damage *sg*

avec [avɛk] *prép* with; (à l'égard de) to(wards), with

avenant, e [avnɑ̃, -ɑ̃t] *adj* pleasant; à l'~ in keeping

avènement [avɛnmɑ̃] *nm* (*d'un roi*) accession, succession; (*d'un changement*) advent, coming

avenir [avniʀ] *nm* future; à l'~ in future; **politicien d'~** politician with prospects *ou* a future

Avent [avɑ̃] *nm*: l'~ Advent

aventure [avɑ̃tyʀ] *nf* adventure; (*amoureuse*) affair: **s'aventurer** *vi* to venture; **aventureux, euse** *adj* adventurous, venturesome; (*projet*) risky, chancy

avenue [avny] *nf* avenue

avérer [aveʀe]: **s'~** *vb* +*attrib* to prove *vb* be

averse [avɛʀs(ə)] *nf* shower

averti, e [avɛʀti] *adj* (well-)informed

avertir [avɛʀtiʀ] *vt*: **~ qn** (de qch/que) to warn sb (of sth/that); (*renseigner*) to inform sb (of sth/that); **avertissement** *nm* warning; **avertisseur** *nm* horn, siren

aveu x [avø] *nm* confession

aveugle [avœgl(ə)] *adj* blind; **aveuglément** *adv* blindly; **~r** *vt* to blind

aviateur, trice [avjatœʀ, -tʀis] *nm/f* aviator, pilot

aviation [avjasjɔ̃] *nf* aviation; (*sport*) flying; (MIL) air force

avide [avid] *adj* eager; (*péj*) greedy, grasping

avilir [aviliʀ] *vt* to debase

avion [avjɔ̃] *nm* (aero)plane (BRIT);

(air)plane (US); **aller (quelque part) en ~** to go (somewhere) by plane, fly (somewhere); **par ~** by airmail; **à réaction** jet (plane)

aviron [avirɔ̃] nm oar; (sport): **l'~** rowing

avis [avi] nm opinion; (notification) notice; **changer d'~** to change one's mind; **jusqu'à nouvel ~** until further notice

avisé, e [avize] adj sensible, wise

aviser [avize] vt (voir) to notice, catch sight of; (informer): **~ qn de que** to advise ou inform sb of/that ♦ vi to think about things, assess the situation; **s'~ de qch/que** to become suddenly aware of sth/that; **s'~ de faire** to take it into one's head to do

avocat, e [avɔka, -at] nm/f (JUR) barrister (BRIT), lawyer ♦ nm (CULIN) avocado (pear); **~ général** assistant public prosecutor

avoine [avwan] nf oats pl

┌─ **MOT-CLÉ** ─────────────

avoir [avwar] nm assets pl, resources pl; (COMM) credit ♦ vt
♦ vt **1** (posséder) to have; **elle a 2 enfants/une belle maison** she has (got) 2 children/a lovely house; **il a les yeux bleus** he has (got) blue eyes
2 (âge, dimensions) to be; **il a 3 ans** he is 3 (years old); **le mur a 3 mètres de haut** the wall is 3 metres high; voir aussi **faim peur** etc
3 (fam: duper) to do, have; **on vous a eu!** you've been done ou had!
4: en ~ contre qn to have a grudge against sb; **en ~ assez** to be fed up; **j'en ai pour une demi-heure** it'll take me half an hour
♦ vb aux **1** to have; **~ mangé/dormi** to have eaten/slept
2 (avoir +à +infinitif): **~ à faire qch** to have to do sth; **vous n'avez qu'à lui demander** you only have to ask him
♦ vb impers **1: il y a** (+ singulier) there is; (+ pluriel) there are; **qu'y-**

a-t-il?, **qu'est-ce qu'il y a?** what's the matter?, what is it?; **il doit y avoir une explication** there must be an explanation; **il n'y a qu'à ...** there's only got to ...
2 (temporel): **il y a 10 ans** 10 years ago; **il y a 10 ans/longtemps que je le sais** I've known it for 10 years/a long time; **il y a 10 ans qu'il est arrivé** it's 10 years since he arrived

└────────────────────

avoisiner [avwazine] vt to be near ou close to; (fig) to border ou verge on

avortement [avɔrtəmɑ̃] nm abortion

avorter [avɔrte] vi (MED) to have an abortion; (fig) to fail

avoué, e [avwe] adj avowed ♦ nm (JUR) ≈ solicitor

avouer [avwe] vt (crime, défaut) to confess to; **~ avoir fait/que** to admit ou confess to having done/that

avril [avril] nm April

axe [aks(ə)] nm axis; (de roue etc) axle; (fig) main line; **~ routier** main road, trunk road; **axer** vt: **axer qch sur** to centre sth on

ayons etc vb voir **avoir**

azote [azɔt] nm nitrogen

B

babines [babin] nfpl chops

babiole [babjɔl] nf (bibelot) trinket; (vétille) trifle

bâbord [babɔr] nm: **à ou par ~** to port, on the port side

baby-foot [babifut] nm table football

bac [bak] abr m = **baccalauréat;** ♦ nm (bateau) ferry; (récipient) tub; tray; tank

baccalauréat [bakalɔrea] nm high school diploma

bachelier, ière [baʃəlje, -jɛr] nm/f holder of the baccalauréat

bachoter [baʃɔte] (fam) vi to cram (for an exam)

bâcler [bakle] vt to botch up

badaud, e [bado, -od] nm/f idle onlooker, stroller

badigeonner [badiʒɔne] vt to distemper; to colourwash; (barbouiller) to daub

badin, e [badɛ̃, -in] adj playful

badiner [badine] vi: ~ avec qch to treat sth lightly

baffe [baf] nf slap, clout

bafouer [bafwe] vt to deride, ridicule

bafouiller [bafuje] vi, vt to stammer

bagage [bagaʒ] nm: ~s luggage sg; ~s à main hand-luggage

bagarre [bagaʀ] nf fight, brawl; **bagarrer: se bagarrer** vi to have a fight ou scuffle, fight

bagatelle [bagatɛl] nf trifle

bagne [baɲ] nm penal colony

bagnole [baɲɔl] (fam) nf car

bagout [bagu] nm: avoir du ~ to have the gift of the gab

bague [bag] nf ring; ~ de fiançailles engagement ring; ~ de serrage clip

baguette [bagɛt] nf stick; (cuisine chinoise) chopstick; (de chef d'orchestre) baton; (pain) stick of (French) bread; ~ magique magic wand

baie [bɛ] nf (GÉO) bay; (fruit) berry; ~ (vitrée) picture window

baignade [bɛɲad] nf bathing

baigner [bɛɲe] vt (bébé) to bath; ~ vi to have a swim, go swimming ou bathing; **baignoire** nf bath(tub)

bail [baj] (pl baux) nm lease

bâiller [baje] vi to yawn; (être ouvert) to gape

bâillon [bajɔ̃] nm gag; **bâillonner** vt to gag

bain [bɛ̃] nm bath; prendre un ~ to have a bath; se mettre dans le ~ (fig) to get into it ou things; ~ de foule walkabout; ~ de soleil: prendre un ~ de soleil to sunbathe; ~s de mer sea bathing sg; **bain-marie** nm: faire chauffer au bain-marie (boîte etc) to immerse in boiling water

baiser [beze] nm kiss ♦ vt (main, front) to kiss; (fam!) to screw (!)

baisse [bɛs] nf fall, drop; "~ sur la

viande" "meat prices down"

baisser [bese] vt lower; (radio, chauffage) to turn down; (AUTO: phares) to dip (BRIT), lower (US) ♦ vi to fall, drop, go down; **se** ~ vi to bend down

bal [bal] nm dance; (grande soirée) ball; ~ costumé fancy-dress ball

balader [balade] vt (trainer) to trail round; **se** ~ vi to go for a walk ou stroll; to go for a drive

baladeur [baladœʀ] nm personal stereo, Walkman (®)

balafre [balafʀ(ə)] nf gash, slash; (cicatrice) scar

balai [balɛ] nm broom, brush; **balai-brosse** nm (long-handled) scrubbing brush

balance [balɑ̃s] nf scales pl; (de précision) balance; (signe): la B~ Libra

balancer [balɑ̃se] vt to swing; (lancer) to fling, chuck; (renvoyer, jeter) to chuck out ♦ vi to swing; **se** ~ vi to swing; to rock; to sway; **se** ~ **de** (fam) not to care about; **balancier** nm (de pendule) pendulum; (perche) (balancing) pole; **balançoire** nf swing; (sur pivot) seesaw

balayer [baleje] vt (feuilles etc) to sweep up, brush up; (pièce) to sweep; (poussière) to sweep away; to sweep aside; (suj: radar) to scan; **balayeur, euse** nm/f roadsweeper; **balayeuse** nf (machine) roadsweeper

balbutier [balbysje] vi, vt to stammer

balcon [balkɔ̃] nm balcony; (THÉÂTRE) dress circle

baleine [balɛn] nf whale; (de parapluie, corset) rib; **baleinière** nf whaleboat

balise [baliz] nf (NAVIG) beacon; (marker) buoy; (AVIAT) runway light, beacon; (AUTO, SKI) sign, marker; **baliser** vt to mark out (with lights etc)

balivernes [balivɛʀn(ə)] nfpl nonsense sg

ballant, e [balɑ̃, -ɑ̃t] adj dangling

balle 28 bariolé

balle [bal] nf (de fusil) bullet; (de sport) ball; (paquet) bale; (fam: franc) franc; ~ **perdue** stray bullet

ballerine [balʀin] nf ballet dancer

ballet [balɛ] nm ballet

ballon [balɔ̃] nm (de sport) ball; (jouet, AVIAT) balloon; (de vin) glass; ~ **de football** football

ballot [balo] nm bundle; (péj) nitwit

ballottage [balɔtaʒ] nm (POL) second ballot

ballotter [balɔte] vi to roll around; to toss ♦ vt to shake about; to toss

balnéaire [balneɛʀ] adj seaside cpd

balourd, e [baluʀ, -uʀd(ə)] adj clumsy ♦ nm/f clodhopper

balustrade [balystʀad] nf railings pl, handrail

bambin [bɑ̃bɛ̃] nm little child

ban [bɑ̃] nm cheer; ~s nmpl (de mariage) banns; **mettre au ~ de** to outlaw from

banal, e [banal] adj banal, commonplace; (péj) trite

banane [banan] nf banana

banc [bɑ̃] nm seat, bench; (de poissons) shoal; ~ **d'essai** (fig) testing ground; ~ **de sable** sandbank

bancaire [bɑ̃kɛʀ] adj banking, bank cpd

bancal, e [bɑ̃kal] adj wobbly; bowlegged

bandage [bɑ̃daʒ] nm bandage

bande [bɑ̃d] nf (de tissu etc) strip; (MED) bandage; (motif) stripe; (magnétique etc) tape; (groupe) band; (: péj) bunch; **par la ~** in a roundabout way; **faire ~ à part** to keep to o.s.; ~ **dessinée** comic strip; ~ **sonore** sound track

bandeau, x [bɑ̃do] nm headband; (sur les yeux) blindfold; (MED) head bandage

bander [bɑ̃de] vt (blessure) to bandage; (muscle) to tense; ~ **les yeux à qn** to blindfold sb

banderole [bɑ̃dʀɔl] nf banner, streamer

bandit [bɑ̃di] nm bandit; **banditisme** nm violent crime, armed robberies pl

bandoulière [bɑ̃duljɛʀ] nf: **en ~** (slung ou worn) across the shoulder

banlieue [bɑ̃ljø] nf suburbs pl; **lignes/quartiers de ~** suburban lines/areas; **trains de ~** commuter trains

bannière [banjɛʀ] nf banner

bannir [baniʀ] vt to banish

banque [bɑ̃k] nf bank; (activités) banking; ~ **d'affaires** merchant bank; **~route** [bɑ̃kʀut] nf bankruptcy

banquet [bɑ̃kɛ] nm dinner; (d'apparat) banquet

banquette [bɑ̃kɛt] nf seat

banquier [bɑ̃kje] nm banker

banquise [bɑ̃kiz] nf ice field

baptême [batɛm] nm christening; baptism; ~ **de l'air** first flight

baquet [bakɛ] nm tub, bucket

bar [baʀ] nm bar

baraque [baʀak] nf shed; (fam) house; ~ **foraine** fairground stand

baraqué, e [baʀake] adj well-built, hefty

baraquements [baʀakmɑ̃] nmpl (for refugees, workers etc) huts

baratin [baʀatɛ̃] (fam) nm smooth talk, patter; **baratiner** vt to chat up

barbare [baʀbaʀ] adj barbaric

barbe [baʀb(ə)] nf beard; **quelle ~!** (fam) what a drag ou bore!; **à la ~ de qn** under sb's nose; ~ **à papa** candy-floss (BRIT), cotton candy (US)

barbelé [baʀbəle] nm barbed wire no pl

barboter [baʀbɔte] vi to paddle, dabble; **barboteuse** [baʀbɔtøz] nf rompers pl

barbouiller [baʀbuje] vt to daub; **avoir l'estomac barbouillé** to feel queasy

barbu, e [baʀby] adj bearded

barda [baʀda] (fam) nm kit, gear

barder [baʀde] (fam) vi: **ça va ~** sparks will fly, things are going to get hot

barème [baʀɛm] nm scale; table

baril [baʀil] nm barrel; keg

bariolé, e [baʀjɔle] adj gaudily-coloured

baromètre [baʀɔmɛtʀ(ə)] nm barometer

baron [baʀɔ̃] nm baron; **baronne** nf baroness

baroque [baʀɔk] adj (ART) baroque; (fig) weird

barque [baʀk(ə)] nf small boat

barquette [baʀkɛt] nf (pour repas) tray; (pour fruits) punnet

barrage [baʀaʒ] nm dam; (sur route) roadblock, barricade

barre [baʀ] nf bar; (NAVIG) helm; (écrite) line, stroke

barreau, x [baʀo] nm bar; (JUR): le ~ the Bar

barrer [baʀe] vt (route etc) to block; (mot) to cross out; (chèque) to cross (BRIT); (NAVIG) to steer; se ~ vi (fam) to clear off

barrette [baʀɛt] nf (pour cheveux) (hair) slide (BRIT) ou clip (US)

barricader [baʀikade] vt to barricade

barrière [baʀjɛʀ] nf fence; (obstacle) barrier; (porte) gate

barrique [baʀik] nf barrel, cask

bas, basse [bɑ, bɑs] adj low ♦ nm bottom, lower part; (vêtement) stocking ♦ adv low; (parler) softly; au ~ mot at the lowest estimate; en ~ down below; at (ou to) the bottom; (dans une maison) downstairs; en ~ de at the bottom of; mettre ~ to give birth; à ~ ...! down with ...!; ~ morceaux nmpl (viande) cheap cuts

basané, e [bazane] adj tanned, bronzed

bas-côté [bakote] nm (de route) verge (BRIT), shoulder (US)

bascule [baskyl] nf: (jeu de) ~ seesaw; (balance à) ~ scales pl; fauteuil à ~ rocking chair

basculer [baskyle] vi to fall over, topple (over); (benne) to tip up ♦ vt (aussi: faire ~) to tip out, tip up

base [bɑz] nf base; (POL) rank and file; (fondement, principe) basis; de ~ basic; à ~ de café etc coffee etc

-based; ~ de données database; **baser** vt to base; se ~ sur vt (preuves) to base one's argument on

bas-fond [bafɔ̃] nm (NAVIG) shallow; ~s nmpl (fig) dregs

basilic [bazilik] nm (CULIN) basil

basket [baskɛt] nm trainer (BRIT), sneaker (US); (aussi: ~-ball) basketball

basque [bask(ə)] adj, nm/f Basque

basse [bɑs] adj voir **bas** ♦ nf (MUS) bass; ~-**cour** nf farmyard

bassin [basɛ̃] nm (cuvette) bowl; (pièce d'eau) pond, pool; (de fontaine, GÉO) basin; (ANAT) pelvis; (portuaire) dock

bassine [basin] nf (ustensile) basin; (contenu) bowl(ful)

bas-ventre [bavɑ̃tʀ(ə)] nm (lower part of the) stomach

bat vb voir **battre**

bât [bɑ] nm packsaddle

bataille [bɑtaj] nf battle; fight

bâtard, e [bɑtaʀ, -aʀd(ə)] nm/f illegitimate child, bastard (pej)

bateau, x [bato] nm boat, ship; **bateau-mouche** nm passenger pleasure boat (on the Seine)

batelier, ière [batəlje, -jɛʀ] nm/f (de bac) ferryman(woman)

bâti, e [bɑti] adj: bien ~ well-built

batifoler [batifɔle] vi to frolic about

bâtiment [bɑtimɑ̃] nm building; (NAVIG) ship, vessel; (industrie) building trade

bâtir [bɑtiʀ] vt to build

bâtisse [bɑtis] nf building

bâton [bɑtɔ̃] nm stick; à ~s rompus informally

bats vb voir **battre**

battage [bataʒ] nm (publicité) (hard) plugging

battant [batɑ̃] nm (de cloche) clapper; (de volets) shutter, flap; (de porte) side; (fig: personne) fighter; porte à double ~ double door

battement [batmɑ̃] nm (de cœur) beat; (intervalle) interval (between classes, trains); 10 minutes de ~ 10 minutes to spare; ~ **de paupières** blinking *no pl* (of eyelids)

batterie [batʀi] *nf* (MIL, ELEC) battery; (MUS) drums *pl*, drum kit; ~ **de cuisine** pots and pans *pl*; kitchen utensils *pl*

batteur [batœʀ] *nm* (MUS) drummer; (appareil) whisk

battre [batʀ(ə)] *vt* to beat; (suj: pluie, vagues) to beat *ou* lash against; (blé) to thresh; (passer au peigne fin) to scour ♦ *vi* (cœur) to beat; (volets etc) to bang, rattle; ~ *vi* la mesure to beat time; ~ **en brèche** to demolish; ~ **son plein** to be at its height, be going full swing; ~ **des mains** to clap one's hands

battue [baty] *nf* (chasse) beat; (policière etc) search, hunt

baume [bom] *nm* balm

baux [bo] *nmpl de* **bail**

bavard, e [bavaʀ, -aʀd(ə)] *adj* (very) talkative; gossipy; **bavarder** *vi* to chatter; (indiscrètement) to gossip; to blab

bave [bav] *nf* dribble; (de chien etc) slobber; (d'escargot) slime; ~**r** *vi* to dribble; to slobber; **en** ~ **r** (fam) to have a hard time (of it); ~**tte** *nf* bib; **baveux, euse** *adj* (omelette) runny

bavure [bavyʀ] *nf* smudge; (fig) hitch; blunder

bayer [baje] *vi*: ~ **aux corneilles** to stand gaping

bazar [bazaʀ] *nm* general store; (fam) jumble; ~**der** (fam) *vt* to chuck out

B.C.B.G. *sigle adj* (= bon chic bon genre) preppy, smart and trendy

B.C.G. *sigle m* (= bacille Calmette-Guérin) BCG

bd. *abr* = **boulevard**

B.D. *sigle f* = **bande dessinée**

béant, e [beɑ̃, -ɑ̃t] *adj* gaping

béat, e [bea, -at] *adj* showing open-eyed wonder; blissful; **béatitude** *nf* bliss

beau(bel), belle [bo, bɛl] (*mpl* ~**x**) *adj* beautiful, lovely; (homme) handsome ♦ *adv*: **il fait** ~ the weather's fine; **un** ~ **jour** one (fine) day; **de plus belle** more than ever, even more; **on a** ~ **essayer** however hard we try; **bel et bien** well and truly; **faire le** ~ (chien) to sit up and beg

---

MOT-CLÉ

beaucoup [boku] *adv* **1 a lot; il boit** ~ he drinks a lot; **il ne boit pas** ~ he doesn't drink much *ou* a lot
2 (suivi de plus, trop etc) much, a lot, far; **il est** ~ **plus grand he is** much *ou* a lot *ou* far taller
3: ~ **de** (nombre) many, a lot of; (quantité) a lot of; ~ **d'étudiants/de touristes** a lot of *ou* many students/tourists; ~ **de courage** a lot of courage; **il n'a pas** ~ **d'argent** he hasn't got much *ou* a lot of money
4: **de** ~ by far

---

beau: ~**fils** *nm* son-in-law; (remariage) stepson; ~**frère** *nm* brother-in-law; ~**père** *nm* father-in-law; (remariage) step-father

beauté [bote] *nf* beauty; **de toute** ~ beautiful; **en** ~ brilliantly

beaux-arts [bozaʀ] *nmpl* fine arts

beaux-parents [bopaʀɑ̃] *nmpl* wife's (ou husband's) family, in-laws

bébé [bebe] *nm* baby

bec [bɛk] *nm* beak, bill; (de récipient) spout; lip; (fam) mouth; ~ **de gaz** (street) gaslamp; ~ **verseur** pouring lip

bécane [bekan] (fam) *nf* bike

bec-de-lièvre [bɛkdəljɛvʀ(ə)] *nm* harelip

bêche [bɛʃ] *nf* spade; **bêcher** *vt* to dig

bécoter [bekɔte]: **se** ~ *vi* to smooch

becqueter [bɛkte] (fam) *vt* to eat

bedaine [bədɛn] *nf* paunch

bedonnant, e [bədɔnɑ̃, -ɑ̃t] *adj* pot-bellied

bée [be] *adj*: **bouche** ~ gaping

beffroi [befʀwa] *nm* belfry

bégayer [begeje] vt, vi to stammer

bègue [bɛg] nm/f: être ~ to have a stammer

béguin [begɛ̃] nm: avoir le ~ de ou pour to have a crush on

beige [bɛʒ] adj beige

beignet [bɛɲɛ] nm fritter

bel [bɛl] adj voir beau

bêler [bele] vi to bleat

belette [bəlɛt] nf weasel

belge [bɛlʒ(ə)] adj, nm/f Belgian

Belgique [bɛlʒik] nf: la ~ Belgium

bélier [belje] nm ram; (signe): le B~ Aries

belle [bɛl] adj voir beau ♦ nf (SPORT) decider; ~-fille nf daughter-in-law; (remariage) step-daughter; ~-mère nf mother-in-law; stepmother; ~-sœur nf sister-in-law

belliqueux, euse [belikø, -øz] adj aggressive, warlike

belvédère [bɛlvedɛr] nm panoramic viewpoint (or small building there)

bémol [bemɔl] nm (MUS) flat

bénédiction [benediksjɔ̃] nf blessing

bénéfice [benefis] nm (COMM) profit; (avantage) benefit: **bénéficier de** vt to enjoy; to benefit by ou from; to get, be given; **bénéfique** adj beneficial

benêt [bənɛ] nm simpleton

bénévole [benevɔl] adj voluntary, unpaid

bénin, igne [benɛ̃, -iɲ] adj minor, mild; (tumeur) benign

bénir [benir] vt to bless; **bénit, e** adj consecrated; **eau bénite** holy water

benjamin, e [bɛ̃ʒamɛ̃, -in] nm/f youngest child

benne [bɛn] nf skip; (de téléphérique) (cable) car; ~ **basculante** tipper (BRIT), dump truck (US)

B.E.P.C. sigle m = brevet d'études du premier cycle

béquille [bekij] nf crutch; (de bicyclette) stand

berceau, x [bɛrso] nm cradle, crib

bercer [bɛrse] vt to rock, cradle; (suj: musique etc) to lull; ~ **qn de** (promesses etc) to delude sb with

berceuse nf lullaby

béret (basque) [berɛ(bask(ə))] nm beret

berge [bɛrʒ(ə)] nf bank

berger, ère [bɛrʒe, -ɛr] nm/f shepherd(ess)

berlingot [bɛrlɛ̃go] nm (emballage) carton (pyramid shaped)

berlue [bɛrly] nf: **j'ai la** ~ I must be seeing things

berner [bɛrne] vt to fool

besogne [bəzɔɲ] nf work no pl, job

besoin [bəzwɛ̃] nm need; (pauvreté): **le** ~ need, want; **faire ses** ~**s** to relieve o.s.; **avoir** ~ **de qch/faire qch** to need sth/to do sth; **au** ~ if need be

bestiaux [bɛstjo] nmpl cattle

bestiole [bɛstjɔl] nf (tiny) creature

bétail [betaj] nm livestock, cattle pl

bête [bɛt] nf animal; (bestiole) insect, creature ♦ adj stupid, silly; **il cherche la petite** ~ he's over-pernickety ou overfussy; ~ **noire** pet hate

bêtise [betiz] nf stupidity; stupid thing (to say ou do)

béton [betɔ̃] nm concrete; (en) ~ (alibi, argument) cast iron; ~ **armé** reinforced concrete; **bétonnière** nf cement mixer

betterave [bɛtrav] nf beetroot (BRIT), beet (US); ~ **sucrière** sugar beet

beugler [bøgle] vi to low; (radio etc) to blare ♦ vt (chanson) to bawl out

Beur [bœr] nm/f person of North African origin living in France

beurre [bœr] nm butter; **beurrer** vt to butter; **beurrier** [bœrje] nm butter dish

beuverie [bœvri] nf drinking session

bévue [bevy] nf blunder

Beyrouth [berut] n Beirut

bi... [bi] préfixe bi..., two-

biais [bjɛ] nm (moyen) device, expedient; (aspect) angle; **en** ~, **de** ~ (obliquement) at an angle; (fig) indirectly; **biaiser** vi (fig) to sidestep the issue

bibelot [biblo] *nm* trinket, curio

biberon [bibRɔ̃] *nm* (feeding) bottle; **nourrir au ~** to bottle-feed

bible [bibl(ə)] *nf* bible

biblio... *préfixe*: **~bus** *nm* mobile library van; **~phile** *nmf* booklover; **~thécaire** *nmf* librarian; **~thèque** *nf* library; (*meuble*) bookcase

bicarbonate [bikaʀbɔnat] *nm*: **~ (de soude)** bicarbonate of soda

biceps [bisɛps] *nm* biceps

biche [biʃ] *nf* doe

bichonner [biʃɔne] *vt* to groom

bicolore [bikɔlɔʀ] *adj* two-coloured

bicoque [bikɔk] *nf* (*péj*) shack

bicyclette [bisiklɛt] *nf* bicycle

bide [bid] *nm* (*fam*: *ventre*) belly; (*THEATRE*) flop

bidet [bidɛ] *nm* bidet

bidon [bidɔ̃] *nm* can ♦ *adj inv* (*fam*) phoney

bidonville [bidɔ̃vil] *nm* shanty town

bidule [bidyl] (*fam*) *nm* thingumajig

bielle [bjɛl] *nf* connecting rod

MOT-CLÉ

---

bien [bjɛ̃] *nm* **1** (*avantage, profit*): **faire du ~ à qn** to do sb good; **dire du ~ de** to speak well of; **c'est pour son ~** it's for his own good

2 (*possession, patrimoine*) possession, property; **son ~ le plus précieux** his most treasured possession; **avoir du ~** to have property; **~s (de consommation etc)** (consumer *etc*) goods

3 (*moral*): **le ~** good; **distinguer le ~ du mal** to tell good from evil

♦ *adv* **1** (*de façon satisfaisante*) well; **elle travaille/mange ~** she works/eats well; **croyant ~ faire**, **je/il ...** thinking I/he was doing the right thing, I/he ...; **c'est ~ fait!** it serves him (*ou her etc*) right!

2 (*valeur intensive*) quite; **~ jeune** quite young; **~ assez** quite enough; **~ mieux** (very) much better; **j'espère ~ y aller** I do hope to go; **je veux ~ le faire** (*concession*) I'm quite willing to do it; **il faut ~ le**

faire it has to be done

3: **~ du temps/des gens** quite a time/a number of people

♦ *adj inv* **1** (*en bonne forme, à l'aise*): **je me sens ~** I feel fine; **je ne me sens pas ~** I don't feel well; **on est ~ dans ce fauteuil** this chair is very comfortable

2 (*joli, beau*) good-looking; **tu es ~ dans cette robe** you look good in that dress

3 (*satisfaisant*) good; **elle est ~**, **cette maison/secrétaire** it's a good house/she's a good secretary

4 (*moralement*) right; (*: personne*) good, nice; (*respectable*) respectable; **ce n'est pas ~ de ...** it's not right to ...; **elle est ~**, **cette femme** she's a nice woman, she's a good sort; **des gens ~** respectable people

5 (*en bons termes*): **être ~ avec qn** to be on good terms with sb

♦ *préfixe*: **~aimé** *adj, nmf* beloved; **~être** *nm inv* well-being; **~faisance** *nf* charity; **~faisant, e** *adj* (*chose*) beneficial; **~fait** *nm* act of generosity, benefaction; (*de la science etc*) benefit; **~faiteur, trice** *nmf* benefactor/benefactress; **~fondé** *nm* soundness; **~fonds** *nm* property; **~heureux, euse** *adj* happy; (*REL*) blessed, blest; **~ que** *conj* (*al)though; **~ sûr** *adv* certainly

bienséant, e [bjɛ̃seɑ̃, ɑ̃t] *adj* seemly

bientôt [bjɛ̃to] *adv* soon; **à ~** see you soon

bienveillant, e [bjɛ̃vɛjɑ̃, ɑ̃t] *adj* kindly

bienvenu, e [bjɛ̃vny] *adj* welcome; **bienvenue** *nf*: **souhaiter la ~e à** to welcome; **~e à** welcome to

bière [bjɛʀ] *nf* (*boisson*) beer; (*cercueil*) bier; **~ (à la) pression** draught beer; **~ blonde** lager; **~ brune** brown ale

biffer [bife] *vt* to cross out

bifteck [biftɛk] *nm* steak

bifurquer [bifyʀke] vi (route) to fork; (véhicule) to turn off

bigarré, e [bigaʀe] adj multicoloured; (disparate) motley

bigorneau, x [bigɔʀno] nm winkle

bigot, e [bigo, -ɔt] (péj) adj bigoted

bigoudi [bigudi] nm curler

bijou, x [biʒu] nm jewel; **bijouterie** nf jeweller's (shop); jewellery; **bijoutier, ière** nm/f jeweller

bilan [bilɑ̃] nm (COMM) balance sheet(s); end of year statement; (fig (net) outcome; (: de victimes) toll; **faire le ~ de** to assess; to review; **déposer son ~** to file a bankruptcy statement

bile [bil] nf bile; **se faire de la ~** (fam) to worry o.s. sick

bilieux, euse [biljø, -jøz] adj bilious; (fig: colérique) testy

bilingue [bilɛ̃g] adj bilingual

billard [bijaʀ] nm billiards sg; billiard table; **c'est du ~** (fam) it's a cinch

bille [bij] nf (gén) ball; (du jeu de billes) marble; (de bois) log

billet [bije] nm (aussi: ~ de banque) (bank)note; (de cinéma, de bus) ticket; (courte lettre) note; ~ **circulaire** round-trip ticket

billetterie [bijetʀi] nf ticket office; (distributeur) ticket machine; (BANQUE) cash dispenser

billion [biljɔ̃] nm billion (BRIT), trillion (US)

billot [bijo] nm block

bimensuel, le [bimɑ̃sɥɛl] adj bimonthly

binette [binɛt] nf hoe

binocle [binɔkl(ə)] nm pince-nez

bio... préfixe bio...; ~**graphie** nf biography; ~**logie** nf biology; ~**logique** adj biological

Birmanie [biʀmani] nf Burma

bis¹, e [bi, biz] adj (couleur) greyish brown

bis² [bis] adv: **12 bis** 12a ou A ♦ excl, nm encore

bisannuel, le [bizanɥɛl] adj biennial

biscornu, e [biskɔʀny] adj twisted

biscotte [biskɔt] nf (breakfast) rusk

biscuit [biskɥi] nm biscuit; sponge cake

bise [biz] nf (baiser) kiss; (vent) North wind

bissextile [bisɛkstil] adj: **année ~** leap year

bistouri [bisturi] nm lancet

bistro(t) [bistʀo] nm bistro, café

bitume [bitym] nm asphalt

bizarre [bizaʀ] adj strange, odd

blafard, e [blafaʀ, -aʀd(ə)] adj wan

blague [blag] nf (propos) joke; (farce) trick; **sans ~!** no kidding!; **~ à tabac** tobacco pouch

blaguer [blage] vi to joke ♦ vt to tease

blaireau, x [blɛʀo] nm (ZOOL) badger; (brosse) shaving brush

blairer [blɛʀe] (fam) vt: **je ne peux pas le ~** I can't bear ou stand him

blâme [blam] nm blame; (sanction) reprimand

blâmer [blame] vt to blame

blanc, blanche [blɑ̃, blɑ̃ʃ] adj white; (non imprimé) blank; (innocent) pure ♦ nm/f white, white man(woman) ♦ nm (couleur) white; (espace non écrit) blank; (aussi: ~ d'œuf) (egg-)white; (: ~ de poulet) breast, white meat; (: vin ~) white wine; ~ **cassé** off-white; **chèque en ~** blank cheque; (à chauffer) white-hot; (tirer, charger) with blanks; **~-bec** nm greenhorn; **blanche** nf (MUS) minim (BRIT), halfnote (US); **blancheur** nf whiteness

blanchir [blɑ̃ʃiʀ] vt (gén) to whiten; (linge) to launder; (CULIN) to blanch; (fig: disculper) to clear ♦ vi to grow white; (cheveux) to go white **blanchisserie** nf laundry

blason [blazɔ̃] nm coat of arms

blazer [blazɛʀ] nm blazer

blé [ble] nm wheat; ~ **noir** (nm) buckwheat

bled [blɛd] (péj) nm hole

blême [blɛm] adj pale

blessé, e [blese] adj injured ♦ nm/f injured person; casualty

blesser [blese] vt to injure; (délibérément: MIL etc) to wound; (suj: souliers etc, offenser) to hurt; ~ to injure o.s.; se ~ **au pied** etc to injure one's foot etc

blessure [blesyʀ] nf injury; wound

bleu, e [blø] adj blue; (bifteck) very rare ♦ nm (couleur) blue; (novice) greenhorn; (contusion) bruise; (vêtement: aussi: ~s) overalls pl; ~ marine navy blue

bleuet [bløɛ] nm cornflower

bleuté, e [bløte] adj blue-shaded

blinder [blɛ̃de] vt to armour; (fig) to harden

bloc [blɔk] nm (de pierre etc) block; (de papier à lettres) pad; (ensemble) group, block; **serré à** ~ tightened right down; **en** ~ as a whole; wholesale; ~ **opératoire** operating ou theatre block; ~ **sanitaire** toilet block; ~**age** [blɔkaʒ] nm blocking; jamming; freezing; (PSYCH) hang-up

bloc-notes [blɔknɔt] nm note pad

blocus [blɔkys] nm blockade

blond, e [blɔ̃, -ɔd] adj fair; blond; (sable, blés) golden; ~ **cendré** ash blond

bloquer [blɔke] vt (passage) to block; (pièce mobile) to jam; (crédits, compte) to freeze

blottir [blɔtiʀ]: **se** ~ vi to huddle up

blouse [bluz] nf overall

blouson [bluzɔ̃] nm blouson jacket; ~ **noir** (fig) ≈ rocker

bluff [blœf] nm bluff

bluffer [blœfe] vi to bluff

bobard [bɔbaʀ] (fam) nm tall story

bobine [bɔbin] nf reel; (ELEC) coil

bocal, aux [bɔkal, -o] nm jar

bock [bɔk] nm glass of beer

bœuf [bœf, pl bø] nm ox, steer; (CULIN) beef

bof! [bɔf] (fam) excl don't care!; (pas terrible) nothing special

bohème [bɔɛm] adj happy-go-lucky, unconventional; **bohémien, ne** [bɔɛmjɛ̃, -jɛn] nm/f gipsy

boire [bwaʀ] vt to drink;

(s'imprégner de) to soak up; ~ **un coup** to have a drink

bois [bwa] nm wood; **de** ~, **en** ~ wooden

boisé, e [bwaze] adj woody, wooded

boisson [bwasɔ̃] nf drink; **pris de** ~ drunk, intoxicated

boîte [bwat] nf box; (entreprise) place, firm; **aliments en** ~ canned ou tinned (BRIT) foods; ~ **à gants** glove compartment; ~ **aux lettres** letter box; ~ **d'allumettes** box of matches; (vide) matchbox; ~ **(de conserves)** can ou tin (BRIT) (of food); ~ **de nuit** night club; ~ **de vitesses** gear box; ~ **postale** PO Box

boiter [bwate] vi to limp; (fig) to wobble; to be shaky

boîtier [bwatje] nm case

boive etc vb voir **boire**

bol [bɔl] nm bowl; **un** ~ **d'air** a breath of fresh air; **j'en ai ras le** ~ (fam) I'm fed up with this

bolide [bɔlid] nm racing car; **comme un** ~ at top speed, like a rocket

bombance [bɔ̃bɑ̃s] nf: **faire** ~ to have a feast, revel

bombarder [bɔ̃baʀde] vt to bomb; ~ **qn de** (cailloux, lettres) to bombard sb with; **bombardier** nm bomber

bombe [bɔ̃b] nf bomb; (atomiseur) (aerosol) spray

bomber [bɔ̃be] vi to bulge; (cambrer ♦ vt: **le torse** to swell out one's chest

---

MOT-CLÉ

bon, bonne [bɔ̃, bɔn] adj **1** (agréable, satisfaisant) good; **un** ~ **repas/restaurant** a good meal/restaurant; **être** ~ **en maths** to be good at maths
2 (charitable): **être** ~ **(envers)** to be good (to)
3 (correct) right; **le** ~ **numéro/moment** the right number/moment
4 (souhaits): ~ **anniversaire** happy

birthday; ~ **voyage** have a good trip; **bonne chance** good luck; **bonne année** happy New Year; **bonne nuit** good night

5 (*approprié*): ~ **à/pour** fit to/for

6: ~ **enfant** adj inv accommodating, easy-going; **bonne femme** (*péj*) woman; **de bonne heure** early; ~ **marché** cheap ♦ adv cheap; ~ **sens** witticism; ~ **sens** common sense; ~ **vivant** jovial chap; **bonnes œuvres** charitable works, charities

♦ **nm 1** (*billet*) voucher; (*aussi*: ~-**cadeau**) gift voucher; ~ **d'essence** petrol coupon; ~ **du Trésor** Treasury bond

2: **avoir du** ~ to have its good points; **pour le** ~ for good

♦ *adv*: **il fait** ~ it's ou the weather is fine; **sentir** ~ to smell good; **tenir** ~ to stand firm

♦ *excl* good!; **ah** ~? really?; *voir aussi* **bonne**

bonbon [bɔ̃bɔ̃] *nm* (boiled) sweet

bonbonne [bɔ̃bɔn] *nf* demijohn

bond [bɔ̃] *nm* leap; **faire un** ~ to leap in the air; ~**e** [bɔ̃d] *nf* bunghole

bondé, e [bɔ̃de] *adj* packed (full)

bondir [bɔ̃diʀ] *vi* to leap

bonheur [bɔnœʀ] *nm* happiness; **porter** ~ (à qn) to bring (sb) luck; **au petit** ~ haphazardly; **par** ~ fortunately

bonhomie [bɔnɔmi] *nf* goodnaturedness

bonhomme [bɔnɔm] (*pl* **bonshommes** [bɔ̃zɔm]) *nm* fellow; ~ **de neige** snowman

bonification [bɔnifikasjɔ̃] *nf* bonus

bonifier [bɔnifje] *vt* to improve

boniment [bɔnimɑ̃] *nm* patter *no pl*

bonjour [bɔ̃ʒuʀ] *excl* hello; good morning (*ou* afternoon)

bonne [bɔn] *adj voir* **bon** ♦ *nf* (*domestique*) maid; ~ **à tout faire** general help; ~ **d'enfant** nanny; ~**ment** *adv*: **tout** ~**ment** quite simply

bonnet [bɔnɛ] *nm* bonnet, hat; (*de soutien-gorge*) cup; ~ **d'âne** dunce's cap; ~ **de bain** bathing cap

bonneterie [bɔnɛtri] *nf* hosiery

bonshommes [bɔ̃zɔm] *nmpl de* bonhomme

bonsoir [bɔ̃swaʀ] *excl* good evening

bonté [bɔ̃te] *nf* kindness *no pl*

bonus [bɔnys] *nm* no-claims bonus

bord [bɔʀ] *nm* (*de table, verre, falaise*) edge; (*de rivière, lac*) bank; (*de route*) side; (*monter*) à ~ (to go) on board; **jeter par-dessus** ~ to throw overboard; **le commandant/les hommes du** ~ the ship's master/crew; **au** ~ **de la mer** at the seaside; **être au** ~ **des larmes** to be on the verge of tears

bordeaux [bɔʀdo] *nm* Bordeaux (wine) ♦ *adj inv* maroon

bordel [bɔʀdɛl] *nm* brothel; (*fam!*) bloody mess (*!*)

border [bɔʀde] *vt* (*être le long de*) to border; to line; (*garnir*): ~ **qch de** to line sth with; to trim sth with; (*qn dans son lit*) to tuck up

bordereau, x [bɔʀdəʀo] *nm* slip; statement

bordure [bɔʀdyʀ] *nf* border; **en** ~ **de** on the edge of

borgne [bɔʀɲ] *adj* one-eyed

borne [bɔʀn(ə)] *nf* boundary stone; (*aussi*: ~ **kilométrique**) kilometre-marker, ≈ milestone; ~**s** *nfpl* (*fig*) limits; **dépasser les** ~**s** to go too far

borné, e [bɔʀne] *adj* narrow; narrow-minded

borner [bɔʀne] *vt* to limit; to confine; **se** ~ **à faire** to content o.s. with doing; to limit o.s. to doing

Bosnie-Herzégovine [bɔzni-ɛʀtzegɔvin] *nf* Bosnia (and) Herzegovina

bosquet [bɔskɛ] *nm* grove

bosse [bɔs] *nf* (*de terrain etc*) bump; (*enflure*) lump; (*du bossu, du chameau*) hump; **avoir la** ~ **des maths** *etc* to have a gift for maths *etc*; **il a roulé sa** ~ he's been around

bosser [bɔse] (*fam*) *vi* to work; to slave (away)

bossu, e [bɔsy] nm/f hunchback

bot [bo] adj m: **pied** ~ club foot

botanique [bɔtanik] nf botany ♦ adj botanic(al)

botte [bɔt] nf (soulier) (high) boot; (gerbe): ~ **de paille** bundle of straw; ~ **de radis** bunch of radishes; ~s **de caoutchouc** wellington boots; ~r [bɔte] vt to put boots on; to kick; (fam): **ça me botte** I fancy that

bottin [bɔtɛ̃] nm directory

bottine [bɔtin] nf ankle boot

bouc [buk] nm goat; (barbe) goatee; ~ **émissaire** scapegoat

boucan [bukɑ̃] nm din, racket

bouche [buʃ] nf mouth; **le** ~ **à** ~ the kiss of life; ~ **d'égout** manhole; ~ **d'incendie** fire hydrant; ~ **de métro** métro entrance

bouché, e [buʃe] adj (temps, ciel) overcast; (péj: personne) thick

bouchée [buʃe] nf mouthful; ~s **à la reine** chicken vol-au-vents

boucher [buʃe] nm [buʃɛ, -ɛʁ] (boucher) butcher ♦ vt (pour colmater) to stop up; to fill up; (obstruer) to block (up); **se** ~ vi (tuyau etc) to block up, get blocked up; ~ **le nez** to hold one's nose; ~**rie** [buʃʁi] nf butcher's (shop); (fig) slaughter

bouche-trou [buʃtʁu] nm (fig) stop-gap

bouchon [buʃɔ̃] nm stopper; (en liège) cork; (fig: embouteillage) holdup; (PÊCHE) float; ~ **doseur** measuring cap

boucle [bukl(ə)] nf (forme, figure) loop; (objet) buckle; ~ (**de cheveux**) curl; ~ **d'oreilles** earring

bouclé, e [bukle] adj curly

boucler [bukle] vt (fermer: ceinture etc) to fasten; (: magasin) to shut; (terminer) to finish off; (: budget) to balance; (enfermer) to shut away; (: quartier) to seal off ♦ vi to curl

bouclier [buklije] nm shield

bouddhiste [budist(ə)] nm/f Buddhist

bouder [bude] vi to sulk ♦ vt to turn one's nose up at; to refuse to have anything to do with

boudin [budɛ̃] nm (CULIN) black pudding

boue [bu] nf mud

bouée [bwe] nf buoy; ~ (**de sauvetage**) lifebuoy

boueux, euse [bwø, -øz] adj muddy ♦ nm refuse collector

bouffe [buf] (fam) nf grub (fam), food

bouffée [bufe] nf puff; ~ **de fièvre/ de honte** flush of fever/shame

bouffer [bufe] (fam) vi to eat

bouffi, e [bufi] adj swollen

bouge [buʒ] nm (low) dive; hovel

bougeoir [buʒwaʁ] nm candlestick

bougeotte [buʒɔt] nf: **avoir la** ~ to have the fidgets

bouger [buʒe] vi to move; (dent etc) to be loose; (changer) to alter; (agir) to stir ♦ vt to move

bougie [buʒi] nf candle; (AUTO) spark(ing) plug

bougon, ne [bugɔ̃, -ɔn] adj grumpy

bougonner [bugɔne] vi, vt to grumble

bouillabaisse [bujabɛs] nf type of fish soup

bouillant, e [bujɑ̃, -ɑ̃t] adj (qui bout) boiling; (très chaud) boiling (hot)

bouillie [buji] nf gruel; (de bébé) cereal; **en** ~ (fig) crushed

bouillir [bujiʁ] vi, vt to boil

bouilloire [bujwaʁ] nf kettle

bouillon [bujɔ̃] nm (CULIN) stock no pl; ~**ner** [bujɔne] vi to bubble; (fig) to bubble up; to foam

bouillotte [bujɔt] nf hot-water bottle

boulanger, ère [bulɑ̃ʒe, -ɛʁ] nm/f baker

boulangerie [bulɑ̃ʒʁi] nf bakery

boule [bul] nf (gén) ball; (pour jouer) bowl; (de machine à écrire) golf-ball; **se mettre en** ~ (fig: fam) to fly off the handle, to blow one's top; ~ **de neige** snowball

bouleau, x [bulo] nm (silver) birch

boulet [bulɛ] nm (aussi: ~ **de canon**)

cannonball

boulette [bulɛt] *nf* ball

boulevard [bulvar] *nm* boulevard

bouleversement [bulvɛrsəmã] *nm* upheaval

bouleverser [bulvɛrse] *vt* (*émouvoir*) to overwhelm; (*causer du chagrin*) to distress; (*pays, vie*) to disrupt; (*papiers, objets*) to turn upside down

boulier [bulje] *nm* abacus

boulon [bulɔ̃] *nm* bolt

boulot, te [bulo, -ɔt] *adj* plump, tubby ♦ *nm* (*fam: travail*) work

boum [bum] *nm* bang ♦ *nf* party

bouquet [bukɛ] *nm* (*de fleurs*) bunch (of flowers), bouquet; (*de persil etc*) bunch; (*parfum*) bouquet

bouquin [bukɛ̃] (*fam*) *nm* book; **bouquiner** (*fam*) *vi* to read; to browse around (in a bookshop); **bouquiniste** *nmf* bookseller

bourbeux, euse [burbø, -øz] *adj* muddy

bourbier [burbje] *nm* (quag)mire

bourde [burd(ə)] *nf* (*erreur*) howler; (*gaffe*) blunder

bourdon [burdɔ̃] *nm* bumblebee

bourdonner [burdɔne] *vi* to buzz

bourg [bur] *nm* small market town

bourgeois, e [burʒwa, -waz] *adj* (*péj*) = (upper) middle class; **bourgeois; ~ie** [burʒwazi] *nf* = upper middle classes *pl*; bourgeoisie

bourgeon [burʒɔ̃] *nm* bud

Bourgogne [burgɔɲ] *nf*: la ~ Burgundy ♦ *nm*: b~ burgundy (wine)

bourguignon, ne [burgiɲɔ̃, -ɔn] *adj* of *ou* from Burgundy, Burgundian

bourlinguer [burlɛ̃ge] *vi* to knock about a lot, get around a lot

bourrade [burad] *nf* shove, thump

bourrage [buraʒ] *nm*: ~ de crâne brainwashing; (*SCOL*) cramming

bourrasque [burask(ə)] *nf* squall

bourratif, ive [buratif] (*fam*) *adj* filling, stodgy (*péj*)

bourré, e [bure] *adj* (*rempli*): ~ de crammed full of; (*fam: ivre*) plastered, tanked up (*BRIT*)

bourreau, x [buro] *nm* executioner; (*fig*) torturer; ~ de travail workaholic

bourrelet [burlɛ] *nm* draught excluder; (*de peau*) fold *ou* roll (of flesh)

bourrer [bure] *vt* (*pipe*) to fill; (*poêle*) to pack; (*valise*) to cram (full)

bourrique [burik] *nf* (*âne*) ass

bourru, e [bury] *adj* surly, gruff

bourse [burs(ə)] *nf* (*subvention*) grant; (*porte-monnaie*) purse; la B~ the Stock Exchange

boursoufler [bursufle] *vt* to puff up, bloat

bous *vb voir* **bouillir**

bousculade [buskylad] *nf* rush; crush; **bousculer** [buskyle] *vt* to knock over; to knock into; (*fig*) to push, rush

bouse [buz] *nf* dung *no pl*

boussole [busɔl] *nf* compass

bout [bu] *vb voir* **bouillir** ♦ *nm* bit; (*d'un bâton etc*) tip; (*d'une ficelle, table, rue, période*) end; au ~ de at the end of, after; pousser qn à ~ to push sb to the limit; venir à ~ de to manage to finish; à ~ portant at point-blank range; ~ filtre filter tip

boutade [butad] *nf* quip, sally

boute-en-train [butɑ̃trɛ̃] *nm inv* (*fig*) live wire

bouteille [butɛj] *nf* bottle; (*de gaz butane*) cylinder

boutique [butik] *nf* shop

bouton [butɔ̃] *nm* button; (*BOT*) bud; (*sur la peau*) spot; (*de porte*) knob; ~ de manchette cuff-link; ~ d'or buttercup; **boutonner** *vt* to button up; **boutonnière** *nf* buttonhole; **bouton-pression** *nm* press stud

bouture [butyr] *nf* cutting

bovins [bɔvɛ̃] *nmpl* cattle *pl*

bowling [bɔliŋ] *nm* (tenpin) bowling; (*salle*) bowling alley

box [bɔks] *nm* lock-up (garage); (*d'écurie*) loose-box

boxe [bɔks(ə)] *nf* boxing

boyau, x [bwajo] *nm* (*galerie*) pas-

sage(way); (narrow) gallery; ~x
nmpl (viscères) entrails, guts
B.P. abr = boîte postale
bracelet [braslɛ] nm bracelet;
bracelet-montre nm wristwatch
braconnier [brakɔnje] nm poacher
brader [brade] vt to sell off; ~ie
[bradri] nf cut-price shop ou stall
braguette [bragɛt] nf fly ou flies pl
(BRIT), zipper (US)
brailler [braje] vt to bawl, yell
braire [brɛr] vi to bray
braise [brɛz] nf embers pl
brancard [brɑ̃kar] nm (civière)
stretcher; **brancardier** nm stretcher-
bearer
branchages [brɑ̃ʃaʒ] nmpl boughs
branche [brɑ̃ʃ] nf branch
branché, e [brɑ̃ʃe] (fam) adj trendy
brancher [brɑ̃ʃe] vt to connect (up);
(en mettant la prise) to plug in
branle [brɑ̃l] nm: donner le ~ à,
mettre en ~ to set in motion
branle-bas [brɑ̃lba] nm inv commotion
braquer [brake] vi (AUTO) to turn
(the wheel) ♦ vt (revolver etc): ~
qch sur to aim sth at, point sth at;
(mettre en colère): ~ qn to put sb's
back up
bras [bra] nm arm ♦ nmpl (fig: travailleurs) labour sg, hands; à ~ rac-
courcis with fists flying; ~ droit
(fig) right hand man
brasier [brazje] nm blaze, inferno
bras-le-corps [bralkɔr]: à ~ adv
(a)round the waist
brassard [brasar] nm armband
brasse [bras] nf (nage) breast-
stroke; ~ papillon butterfly
brassée [brase] nf armful
brasser [brase] vt to mix; ~
l'argent/les affaires to handle a lot
of money/business
brasserie [brasri] nf (restaurant)
café-restaurant; (usine) brewery
brave [brav] adj (courageux) brave;
(bon, gentil) good, kind
braver [brave] vt to defy
bravo [bravo] excl bravo ♦ nm cheer

bravoure [bravur] nf bravery
break [brɛk] nm (AUTO) estate car
brebis [brəbi] nf ewe; ~ galeuse
black sheep
brèche [brɛʃ] nf breach, gap; être
sur la ~ (fig) to be on the go
bredouille [brəduj] adj empty-
handed
bredouiller [brəduje] vi, vt to mumble, stammer
bref, brève [brɛf, brɛv] adj short,
brief ♦ adv in short; d'un ton ~
sharply, curtly; en ~ in short, in
brief
Brésil [brezil] nm Brazil
Bretagne [brətaɲ] nf Brittany
bretelle [brətɛl] nf (de fusil etc)
sling; (de vêtement) strap;
(d'autoroute) slip road (BRIT),
entrance/exit ramp (US); ~s nfpl
(pour pantalon) braces (BRIT), sus-
penders (US)
breton, ne [brətɔ̃, -ɔn] adj, nm/f
Breton
breuvage [brœvaʒ] nm beverage,
drink
brève [brɛv] adj voir bref
brevet [brəvɛ] nm diploma, certificate; ~ d'études du premier cycle
school certificate (taken at age 16);
~ (d'invention) patent; **breveté, e**
adj patented; (diplôme) qualified
bribes [brib] nfpl bits, scraps;
snatches; par ~ piecemeal
bricolage [brikɔlaʒ] nm: le ~ do-it-
yourself
bricole [brikɔl] nf trifle; small job
bricoler [brikɔle] vi to do DIY jobs;
to potter about ♦ vt to fix up; to tinker with; **bricoleur, euse** nm/f handy-
man(woman), DIY enthusiast
bride [brid] nf bridle; (d'un bonnet)
string, tie; à ~ abattue flat out, hell
for leather; laisser la ~ sur le cou
à to give free rein to
bridé, e [bride] adj: yeux ~s slit
eyes
bridge [bridʒ(ə)] nm bridge
brièvement [brijɛvmɑ̃] adv briefly
brigade [brigad] nf (POLICE)

squad; (*MIL*) brigade; (*gén*) team
brigadier [brigadje] *nm* sergeant
brigandage [brigãdaʒ] *nm* robbery
briguer [brige] *vt* to aspire to
brillamment [brijamã] *adv* brilliantly
brillant, e [brijã, -ãt] *adj* brilliant; bright; (*luisant*) shiny, shining ♦ *nm* (*diamant*) brilliant
briller [brije] *vi* to shine
brimer [brime] *vt* to harass; to bully
brin [brɛ̃] *nm* (*de laine, ficelle etc*) strand; (*fig*): **un ~ de** a bit of; ~ **d'herbe** blade of grass; ~ **de muguet** sprig of lily of the valley
brindille [brɛ̃dij] *nf* twig
brio [brijo] *nm*: **avec ~** with panache
brioche [brijɔʃ] *nf* brioche (bun); (*fam*: *ventre*) paunch
brique [brik] *nf* brick ♦ *adj inv* brick red
briquer [brike] *vt* to polish up
briquet [brike] *nm* (cigarette) lighter
brise [briz] *nf* breeze
briser [brize] *vt* to break; **se ~** *vi* to break
britannique [britanik] *adj* British ♦ *nmf*: **B~** British person, Briton; **les B~s** the British
brocante [brɔkãt] *nf* junk, second-hand goods *pl*
brocanteur, euse [brɔkãtœr, -øz] *nmf* junkshop owner; junk dealer
broche [brɔʃ] *nf* brooch; (*CULIN*) spit; (*MÉD*) pin; **à la ~** spit-roasted
broché, e [brɔʃe] *adj* (*livre*) paper-backed
brochet [brɔʃɛ] *nm* pike *inv*
brochette [brɔʃɛt] *nf* skewer
brochure [brɔʃyr] *nf* pamphlet, brochure, booklet
broder [brɔde] *vt* to embroider ♦ *vi* to embroider the facts; **broderie** *nf* embroidery
broncher [brɔ̃ʃe] *vi*: **sans ~** without flinching; without turning a hair
bronches [brɔ̃ʃ] *nfpl* bronchial tubes; **bronchite** *nf* bronchitis

bronze [brɔ̃z] *nm* bronze
bronzer [brɔ̃ze] *vt* to tan ♦ *vi* to get a tan; **se ~** to sunbathe
brosse [brɔs] *nf* brush; **coiffé en ~** with a crewcut; ~ **à cheveux** hairbrush; ~ **à dents** toothbrush; ~ **à habits** clothesbrush; **brosser** *vt* (*nettoyer*) to brush; (*fig*: *tableau etc*) to paint; to draw; **se brosser les dents** to brush one's teeth
brouette [bruɛt] *nf* wheelbarrow
brouhaha [bruaa] *nm* hubbub
brouillard [brujar] *nm* fog
brouille [bruj] *nf* quarrel
brouiller [bruje] *vt* to mix up; to confuse; (*rendre trouble*) to cloud; (*désunir*: *amis*) to set at odds; **se ~** *vi* (*vue*) to cloud over; (*détails*) to become confused; (*gens*) to fall out
brouillon, ne [brujɔ̃, -ɔn] *adj* disorganised; unmethodical ♦ *nm* draft
broussailles [brusaj] *nfpl* undergrowth *sg*; **broussailleux, euse** *adj* bushy
brousse [brus] *nf*: **la ~** the bush
brouter [brute] *vt* to graze
broutille [brutij] *nf* trifle
broyer [brwaje] *vt* to crush; ~ **du noir** to be down in the dumps
bru [bry] *nf* daughter-in-law
brugnon [brynɔ̃] *nm* (*BOT*) nectarine
bruiner [bruine] *vb impers*: **il bruine** it's drizzling, there's a drizzle
bruire [bruir] *vi* to murmur; to rustle
bruit [brui] *nm*: **un ~** a noise, a sound; (*fig*: *rumeur*) a rumour; **le ~** noise; **sans ~** without a sound, noiselessly; ~ **de fond** background noise
bruitage [bruitaʒ] *nm* sound effects *pl*
brûlant, e [brylã, -ãt] *adj* burning; (*liquide*) boiling (hot); (*regard*) fiery
brûlé, e [bryle] *adj* (*fig*: *démasqué*) blown ♦ *nm*: **odeur de ~** smell of burning
brûle-pourpoint [brylpurpwɛ̃] : **à ~** *adv* point-blank
brûler [bryle] *vt* to burn; (*suj*: *eau*

bouillante) to scald; (*consommer: électricité, essence*) to use; (*feu rouge, signal*) to go through ♦ *vi* to burn; (*jeu*) to be warm; **se ~** to burn o.s.; to scald o.s.; **se ~ la cervelle** to blow one's brains out

brûlure [bʀylyʀ] *nf* (*lésion*) burn; (*sensation*) burning (sensation); **~s d'estomac** heartburn *sg*

brume [bʀym] *nf* mist

brun, e [bʀœ̃, -yn] *adj* brown; (*cheveux, personne*) dark; **brunir** *vi* to get a tan

brusque [bʀysk(ə)] *adj* abrupt; **brusquer** *vt* to rush

brut, e [bʀyt] *adj* raw, crude, rough; (*COMM*) gross; (*données*) raw; (*pétrole*) **~** crude (oil)

brutal, e, aux [bʀytal, -o] *adj* brutal; **brutaliser** *vt* to handle roughly, manhandle

Bruxelles [bʀysɛl] *n* Brussels

bruyamment [bʀɥijamɑ̃] *adv* noisily

bruyant, e [bʀɥijɑ̃, -ɑ̃t] *adj* noisy

bruyère [bʀɥijɛʀ] *nf* heather

bu, e *pp* de **boire**

buccal, e, aux [bykal, -o] *adj*: **par voie ~e** orally

bûche [byʃ] *nf* log; **prendre une ~** (*fig*) to come a cropper; **~ de Noël** Yule log; **~r** [byʃe] *nm* pyre; bonfire ♦ *vi* (*fam*) to swot (*BRIT*), slave (away) ♦ *vt* to swot up (*BRIT*), slave away at; **~ron** [byʃʀɔ̃] *nm* woodcutter

budget [bydʒɛ] *nm* budget

buée [bɥe] *nf* (*sur une vitre*) mist; (*de l'haleine*) steam

buffet [byfɛ] *nm* (*meuble*) sideboard; (*de réception*) buffet; **~ (de gare)** (*station*) buffet, snack bar

buffle [byfl(ə)] *nm* buffalo

buis [bɥi] *nm* box tree; (*bois*) box(wood)

buisson [bɥisɔ̃] *nm* bush

buissonnière [bɥisɔnjɛʀ] *adj*: **faire l'école ~** to skip school

bulbe [bylb(ə)] *nm* (*BOT, ANAT*) bulb; (*coupole*) onion-shaped dome

Bulgarie [bylgaʀi] *nf* Bulgaria

bulle [byl] *nf* bubble

bulletin [byltɛ̃] *nm* (*communiqué, journal*) bulletin; (*papier*) form; (*SCOL*) report; **~ d'informations** news bulletin; **~ de salaire** pay-slip; **~ (de vote)** ballot paper; **~ météorologique** weather report

bureau, x [byʀo] *nm* (*meuble*) desk; (*pièce, service*) office; **~ de change** (foreign) exchange office *ou* bureau; **~ de location** box office; **~ de poste** post office; **~ de tabac** tobacconist's (shop); **~ de vote** polling station; **bureaucratie** *nf* bureaucracy

burin [byʀɛ̃] *nm* cold chisel; (*ART*) burin

burlesque [byʀlɛsk(ə)] *adj* ridiculous; (*LITTÉRATURE*) burlesque

bus¹ [by] *vb voir* **boire**; **bus²** [bys] *nm* bus

busqué, e [byske] *adj* (*nez*) hook(ed)

buste [byst(ə)] *nm* (*ANAT*) chest; bust

but [by] *vb voir* **boire** ♦ *nm* (*cible*) target; (*fig*) goal; aim; (*FOOTBALL etc*) goal; **de ~ en blanc** point-blank; **avoir pour ~ de faire** to aim to do; **dans le ~ de** with the intention of

butane [bytan] *nm* butane; Calor gas (®)

buté, e [byte] *adj* stubborn, obstinate

buter [byte] *vi*: **~ contre/sur** to bump into; to stumble against ♦ *vt* to antagonize; **se ~** *vi* to get obstinate; to dig in one's heels

butin [bytɛ̃] *nm* booty, spoils *pl*; (*d'un vol*) loot

butte [byt] *nf* mound, hillock; **être en ~ à** to be exposed to

buvais *etc vb voir* **boire**

buvard [byvaʀ] *nm* blotter

buvette [byvɛt] *nf* bar

buveur, euse [byvœʀ, -øz] *nmf* drinker

C

c' [s] dét voir ce
CA sigle m = **chiffre d'affaires**
ça [sa] pron (pour désigner) this; (: plus loin) that; (comme sujet indéfini) it; ~ va? how are you?; (d'accord?) OK?, all right?; ~ alors! well really!; ~ fait 10 ans (que) it's 10 years (since); c'est ~ that's right
çà [sa] adv: ~ et là here and there
cabane [kaban] nf hut, cabin
cabaret [kabaʀɛ] nm night club
cabas [kaba] nm shopping bag
cabillaud [kabijo] nm cod inv
cabine [kabin] nf (de bateau) cabin; (de plage) (beach) hut; (de piscine etc) cubicle; (de camion, train) cab; (d'avion) cockpit; ~ d'essayage fitting room; ~ spatiale space capsule; ~ (téléphonique) call ou (tele)phone box
cabinet [kabinɛ] nm (petite pièce) closet; (de médecin) surgery (BRIT), office (US); (de notaire etc) office; (: clientèle) practice; (POL) Cabinet; ~s nmpl (w.-c.) toilet sg; ~ d'affaires business consultants' (bureau), business partnership; ~ de toilette toilet; ~ de travail study
câble [kɑbl(ə)] nm cable
cabrer [kabʀe]: se ~ vi (cheval) to rear up; (avion) to nose up; (fig) to revolt, rebel
cabriole [kabʀijɔl] nf caper; somersault
cacahuète [kakaɥɛt] nf peanut
cacao [kakao] nm cocoa (powder); (boisson) cocoa
cache [kaʃ] nm mask, card (for masking) ♦ nf hiding place
cache-cache [kaʃkaʃ] nm: jouer à ~ to play hide-and-seek
cachemire [kaʃmir] nm cashmere
cache-nez [kaʃne] nm inv scarf, muffler
cacher [kaʃe] vt to hide, conceal; se

~ vi to hide; to be hidden ou concealed; ~ qch à qn to hide ou conceal sth from sb; il ne s'en cache pas he makes no secret of it
cachet [kaʃɛ] nm (comprimé) tablet; (sceau: du roi) seal; (: de la poste) postmark; (rétribution) fee; (fig) style, character; **cacheter** vt to seal
cachette [kaʃɛt] nf hiding place; en ~ on the sly, secretly
cachot [kaʃo] nm dungeon
cachotterie [kaʃɔtri] nf: faire des ~s to be secretive
cactus [kaktys] nm cactus
cadavre [kadavʀ(ə)] nm corpse, (dead) body
caddie [kadi] nm (supermarket) trolley
caddy nm = **caddie**
cadeau, x [kado] nm present, gift; faire un ~ à qn to give sb a present ou gift; faire ~ de qch à qn to make a present of sth to sb, give sth as a present
cadenas [kadna] nm padlock
cadence [kadɑ̃s] nf (MUS) cadence; (: tempo) rhythm; (de travail etc) rate; en ~ rhythmically; in time
cadet, te [kadɛ, -ɛt] adj younger; (le plus jeune) youngest ♦ nm/f youngest child ou one, youngest boy ou son/girl ou daughter
cadran [kadrɑ̃] nm dial; ~ solaire sundial
cadre [kɑdʀ(ə)] nm frame; (environnement) surroundings pl; (limites) scope ♦ nm/f (ADMIN) managerial employee, executive; dans le ~ de (fig) within the framework ou context of; rayer qn des ~s to dismiss sb
cadrer [kadʀe] vi: ~ avec to tally ou correspond with ♦ vt to centre
caduc, uque [kadyk] adj obsolete; (BOT) deciduous
cafard [kafar] nm cockroach; avoir le ~ to be down in the dumps
café [kafe] nm coffee; (bistro) café ♦ adj inv coffee(-coloured); ~ au lait white coffee; ~ noir black coffee; ~ tabac tobacconist's or newsagent's

serving coffee and spirits; **cafetière**
nf (pot) coffee-pot

cafouillage [kafujaʒ] nm shambles
sg

cage [kaʒ] nf cage; ~ (des buts)
goal; ~ d'escalier (stair)well; ~
thoracique rib cage

cageot [kaʒo] nm crate

cagibi [kaʒibi] nm shed

cagneux, euse [kaɲø, -øz] adj
knock-kneed

cagnotte [kaɲɔt] nf kitty

cagoule [kagul] nf cowl; hood; (SKI
etc) cagoule

cahier [kaje] nm notebook; ~ de
brouillons roughbook, jotter; ~
d'exercices exercise book

cahot [kao] nm jolt, bump

caïd [kaid] nm big chief, boss

caille [kaj] nf quail

cailler [kaje] vi (lait) to curdle;
(sang) to clot

caillot [kajo] nm (blood) clot

caillou, x [kaju] nm (little) stone;
caillouteux, euse adj stony; pebbly

Caire [kɛʀ] nm: le ~ Cairo

caisse [kɛs] nf box; (où l'on met la
recette) cashbox; till; (où l'on paye)
cash desk (BRIT), check-out; (de
banque) cashier's desk; (TECH)
case, casing; ~ d'épargne savings
bank; ~ de retraite pension fund; ~
enregistreuse cash register; **cais-
sier, ière** nm/f cashier

cajoler [kaʒɔle] vt to wheedle, coax;
to surround with love

cake [kɛk] nm fruit cake

calandre [kalɑ̃dʀ(ə)] nf radiator grill

calanque [kalɑ̃k] nf rocky inlet

calcaire [kalkɛʀ] nm limestone ♦ adj
(eau) hard; (GEO) limestone cpd

calciné, e [kalsine] adj burnt to
ashes

calcul [kalkyl] nm calculation; le ~
(SCOL) arithmetic; ~ (biliaire)
(gall)stone; ~ (rénal) (kidney)
stone; **calculateur** nm calculator;
calculatrice nf calculator

calculer [kalkyle] vt to calculate,
work out; (combiner) to calculate

calculette [kalkylɛt] nf pocket calculator

cale [kal] nf (de bateau) hold; (en
bois) wedge; ~ sèche dry dock

calé, e [kale] (fam) adj clever,
bright

caleçon [kalsɔ̃] nm pair of under-
pants, trunks pl

calembour [kalɑ̃buʀ] nm pun

calendes [kalɑ̃d] nfpl: renvoyer
aux ~ grecques to postpone indefinitely

calendrier [kalɑ̃dʀije] nm calendar;
(fig) timetable

calepin [kalpɛ̃] nm notebook

caler [kale] vt to wedge; ~ (son
moteur/véhicule) to stall (one's
engine/vehicle)

calfeutrer [kalføtʀe] vt to (make)
draughtproof; se ~ vi to make o.s.
snug and comfortable

calibre [kalibʀ(ə)] nm (d'un fruit)
grade; (d'une arme) bore, calibre;
(fig) calibre

califourchon [kalifuʀʃɔ̃]: à ~ adv
astride

câlin, e [kɑlɛ̃, -in] adj cuddly, cud-
dlesome; tender

câliner [kɑline] vt to fondle, cuddle

calmant [kalmɑ̃] nm tranquillizer,
sedative; (pour la douleur) painkiller

calme [kalm(ə)] adj calm, quiet ♦
nm calm(ness), quietness

calmer [kalme] vt to calm (down);
(douleur, inquiétude) to ease, soothe;
se ~ vi to calm down

calomnie [kalɔmni] nf slander;
(écrite) libel; **calomnier** vt to slander; to libel

calorie [kalɔʀi] nf calorie

calorifuge [kalɔʀify ʒ] adj (heat-)
insulating, heat-retaining

calotte [kalɔt] nf (coiffure) skullcap;
(gifle) slap; **calotte glaciaire** nf
(GEO) icecap

calquer [kalke] vt to trace; (fig) to
copy exactly

calvaire [kalvɛʀ] nm (croix) wayside
cross, calvary; (souffrances) suffering

calvitie [kalvisi] nf baldness
camarade [kamaʀad] nm/f friend, pal; (POL) comrade; **camaraderie** nf friendship
cambouis [kãbwi] nm dirty oil ou grease
cambrer [kãbʀe] vt to arch
cambriolage [kãbʀijɔlaʒ] nm burglary; **cambrioler** [kãbʀijɔle] vt to burgle (BRIT), burglarize (US); **cambrioleur, euse** nm/f burglar
came [kam] nf: **arbre à ~s** camshaft
camelote [kamlɔt] nf rubbish, trash, junk
caméra [kameʀa] nf (CINÉMA, TV) camera; (d'amateur) cine-camera
caméscope nm camcorder
camion [kamjɔ̃] nm lorry (BRIT), truck; (plus petit, fermé) van; **~ de dépannage** breakdown (BRIT) ou tow (US) truck; **camion-citerne** nm tanker; **camionnette** nf (small) van; **camionneur** nm (entrepreneur) haulage contractor (BRIT), trucker (US); (chauffeur) lorry (BRIT) ou van driver; van driver
camisole [kamizɔl] nf: **~ (de force)** straitjacket
camomille [kamɔmij] nf camomile; (boisson) camomile tea
camoufler [kamufle] vt to camouflage; (fig) to conceal, cover up
camp [kã] nm camp; (fig) side
campagnard, e [kãpaɲaʀ, -aʀd(ə)] adj country cpd
campagne [kãpaɲ] nf country, countryside; (MIL, POL, COMM) campaign; **à la ~** in the country
camper [kãpe] vi to camp ♦ vt to sketch; **se ~ devant** to plant o.s. in front of; **campeur, euse** nm/f camper
camphre [kãfʀ(ə)] nm camphor
camping [kãpiŋ] nm camping; (terrain de) ~ campsite, camping site; **faire du ~** to go camping
Canada [kanada] nm: **le ~** Canada; **canadien, ne** adj, nm/f Canadian; **canadienne** nf (veste) fur-lined jack-

et
canaille [kanɑj] (péj) nf scoundrel
canal, aux [kanal, -o] nm canal; (naturel) channel; **canalisation** [kanalizasjɔ̃] nf (tuyau) pipe; **canaliser** [kanalize] vt to canalize; (fig) to channel
canapé [kanape] nm settee, sofa
canard [kanaʀ] nm duck
canari [kanaʀi] nm canary
cancans [kãkã] nmpl (malicious) gossip sg
cancer [kãseʀ] nm cancer; (signe): **le C~** Cancer; **~ de la peau** skin cancer
cancre [kãkʀ(ə)] nm dunce
candeur [kãdœʀ] nf ingenuousness, guilelessness
candidat, e [kãdida, -at] nm/f candidate; (à un poste) applicant, candidate; **candidature** nf (candidature): **poser sa candidature** to submit an application, apply
candide [kãdid] adj ingenuous, guileless
cane [kan] nf (female) duck
caneton [kantɔ̃] nm duckling
canette [kanɛt] nf (de bière) (fliptop) bottle
canevas [kanva] nm (COUTURE) canvas
caniche [kaniʃ] nm poodle
canicule [kanikyl] nf scorching heat
canif [kanif] nm penknife, pocket knife
canine [kanin] nf canine (tooth)
caniveau, x [kanivo] nm gutter
canne [kan] nf (walking) stick; **~ à pêche** fishing rod; **~ à sucre** sugar cane
cannelle [kanɛl] nf cinnamon
canoë [kanɔe] nm canoe; (sport) canoeing
canon [kanɔ̃] nm (arme) gun; (HISTOIRE) cannon; (d'une arme: tube) barrel; (fig) model; (MUS) canon; **~ rayé** rifled barrel
canot [kano] nm ding(h)y; **~ de sauvetage** lifeboat; **~ pneumatique** inflatable ding(h)y; **~age** nm row-

ing; **~ier** [kɑ̃tɔtje] nm boater

cantatrice [kɑ̃tatris] nf (opera) singer

cantine [kɑ̃tin] nf canteen

cantique [kɑ̃tik] nm hymn

canton [kɑ̃tɔ̃] nm district consisting of several communes; (en Suisse) canton

cantonade [kɑ̃tɔnad] : **à la ~** adv to everyone in general; from the rooftops

cantonner [kɑ̃tɔne] vt (MIL) to quarter, station; **se ~ dans** to confine o.s. to

cantonnier [kɑ̃tɔnje] nm roadmender

canular [kanylar] nm hoax

caoutchouc [kautʃu] nm rubber; **~ mousse** foam rubber

cap [kap] nm (GEO) cape; headland; (fig) hurdle; watershed; (NAVIG): **changer de ~** to change course; **mettre le ~ sur** to head ou steer for

C.A.P. sigle m (= Certificat d'aptitude professionnelle) vocational training certificate taken at secondary school

capable [kapabl(ə)] adj able, capable; **~ de qch/faire** capable of sth/doing

capacité [kapasite] nf (compétence) ability; (JUR, contenance) capacity; **~ (en droit)** basic legal qualification

cape [kap] nf cape, cloak; **rire sous ~** to laugh up one's sleeve

C.A.P.E.S. [kapes] sigle m (= Certificat d'aptitude pédagogique à l'enseignement secondaire) teaching diploma

capillaire [kapilɛr] adj (soins, lotion) hair cpd; (vaisseau etc) capillary

capitaine [kapiten] nm captain

capital, e, aux [kapital, -o] adj major; of paramount importance; fundamental ♦ nm capital; (fig) stock; asset; voir aussi **capitaux**; **~ (social)** authorized capital; **~e** nf (ville) capital; (lettre) capital (letter); **~iser** vt to amass, build up; **~isme** nm capitalism; **~iste** adj, nm/f capitalist;

capitaux [kapito] nmpl (fonds) capital sg

capitonné, e [kapitɔne] adj padded

caporal, aux [kapɔral, -o] nm lance corporal

capot [kapo] nm (AUTO) bonnet (BRIT), hood (US)

capote [kapɔt] nf (de voiture) hood (BRIT), top (US); (fam) condom

capoter [kapɔte] vi to overturn

câpre [kɑpr(ə)] nf caper

caprice [kapris] nm whim, caprice; passing fancy; **capricieux, euse** adj capricious; whimsical; temperamental

Capricorne [kaprikɔrn] nm: **le ~** Capricorn

capsule [kapsyl] nf (de bouteille) cap; (BOT etc, spatiale) capsule

capter [kapte] vt (ondes radio) to pick up; (eau) to harness; (fig) to win, capture

captivant, e adj captivating; fascinating

captivité [kaptivite] nf captivity

capturer [kaptyre] vt to capture

capuche [kapyʃ] nf hood

capuchon [kapyʃɔ̃] nm hood; (de stylo) cap, top

capucine [kapysin] nf (BOT) nasturtium

caquet [kake] nm: **rabattre le ~ à qn** to bring sb down a peg or two

caqueter [kakte] vi to cackle

car [kar] nm coach ♦ conj because, for

carabine [karabin] nf carbine, rifle

caractère [karaktɛr] nm (gén) character; avoir bon/mauvais **~** to be good/ill-natured; **en ~s gras** in bold type; **en petits ~s** in small print; **~s d'imprimerie** (block) capitals; **caractériel, le** adj (of) character ♦ nm/f emotionally disturbed child

caractérisé, e [karakterize] adj: **c'est une grippe ~e** it is a clear (-cut) case of flu

caractéristique [karakteristik] adj, nf characteristic

carafe [karaf] nf decanter; carafe

caraïbe [kaʀaib] adj Caribbean ♦ n: les C~s the Caribbean (Islands); la mer des C~s the Caribbean Sea

carambolage [kaʀɑ̃bɔlaʒ] nm multiple crash, pileup

caramel [kaʀamɛl] nm (bonbon) caramel, toffee; (substance) caramel

carapace [kaʀapas] nf shell

caravane [kaʀavan] nf caravan; **caravaning** nm caravanning; (emplacement) caravan site

carbone [kaʀbɔn] nm carbon; (feuille) carbon, sheet of carbon paper; (double) carbon (copy); **carbonique** [kaʀbɔnik] adj: **neige carbonique** dry ice; **carbonisé, e** [kaʀbɔnize] adj charred

carburant [kaʀbyʀɑ̃] nm (motor) fuel

carburateur [kaʀbyʀatœʀ] nm carburettor

carcan [kaʀkɑ̃] nm (fig) yoke, shackles pl

carcasse [kaʀkas] nf carcass; (de véhicule etc) shell

cardiaque [kaʀdjak] adj cardiac, heart cpd ♦ nmf heart patient

cardigan [kaʀdigɑ̃] nm cardigan

cardiologue [kaʀdjɔlɔg] nmf cardiologist, heart specialist

carême [kaʀɛm] nm: le C~ Lent

carence [kaʀɑ̃s] nf incompetence, inadequacy; (manque) deficiency

caresse [kaʀɛs] nf caress

caresser [kaʀese] vt to caress, fondle; (fig: projet) to toy with

cargaison [kaʀgɛzɔ̃] nf cargo, freight

cargo [kaʀgo] nm cargo boat, freighter

carie [kaʀi] nf: la ~ (dentaire) tooth decay; **une ~** a bad tooth

carillon [kaʀijɔ̃] nm (d'église) bells pl; (de pendule) chimes pl; (de porte) door chime ou bell

carlingue [kaʀlɛ̃g] nf cabin

carnassier, ière [kaʀnasje, -jɛʀ] adj carnivorous

carnaval [kaʀnaval] nm carnival

carnet [kaʀnɛ] nm (calepin) note-book; (de tickets, timbres etc) book; (d'école) school report; (journal intime) diary; **~ de chèques** cheque book

carotte [kaʀɔt] nf carrot

carpette [kaʀpɛt] nf rug

carré, e [kaʀe] adj square; (fig: franc) straightforward ♦ nm (de terrain, jardin) patch, plot; (MATH) square; **mètre/kilomètre ~** square metre/kilometre

carreau, x [kaʀo] nm (en faïence etc) (floor) tile; (wall) tile; (de fenêtre) (window) pane; (motif) check, square; (CARTES: couleur) diamonds pl; (: carte) diamond; **tissu à ~x** checked fabric

carrefour [kaʀfuʀ] nm crossroads sg

carrelage [kaʀlaʒ] nm tiling; (tiled) floor

carrelet [kaʀlɛ] nm (poisson) plaice

carrément [kaʀemɑ̃] adv straight out, bluntly; completely, altogether

carrière [kaʀjɛʀ] nf (de roches) quarry; (métier) career; **militaire de ~** professional soldier

carriole [kaʀjɔl] (péj) nf old cart

carrossable [kaʀɔsabl(ə)] adj suitable for (motor) vehicles

carrosse [kaʀɔs] nm (horse-drawn) coach

carrosserie [kaʀɔsʀi] nf body, coachwork no pl; (activité, commerce) coachbuilding

carrure [kaʀyʀ] nf build; (fig) stature, calibre

cartable [kaʀtabl(ə)] nm (d'écolier) satchel, (school)bag

carte [kaʀt(ə)] nf (de géographie) map; (marine, du ciel) chart; (de fichier, d'abonnement etc, à jouer) card; (au restaurant) menu; (aussi: **~ postale**) (post)card; (: **~ de visite**) (visiting) card; **à la ~** (au restaurant) à la carte; **~ bancaire** cash card; **~ de crédit** credit card; **~ d'identité** identity card; **~ de séjour** residence permit; **~ grise** (AUTO) ~ (car) registration book, logbook; **~ routière** road map; **~**

téléphonique phonecard

carter [kaʀtɛʀ] nm sump

carton [kaʀtɔ̃] nm (matériau) cardboard; (boite) (cardboard) box; (d'invitation) invitation card; **faire un ~** (au tir) to have a go at the rifle range; to score a hit; **~ (à dessin)** portfolio; **cartonné, e** adj (livre) hardback, cased; **carton-pâte** nm pasteboard

cartouche [kaʀtuʃ] nf cartridge; (de cigarettes) carton

cas [kɑ] nm case; **faire peu de ~/grand ~ de** to attach little/great importance to; **en aucun ~** no no account; **au ~ où** in case; **en ~ de** in case of, in the event of; **en ~ de besoin** if need be; **en tout ~** in any case, at any rate; **~ de conscience** matter of conscience

casanier, ière [kazanje, -jɛʀ] adj stay-at-home

cascade [kaskad] nf waterfall, cascade; (fig) stream, torrent

cascadeur, euse [kaskadœʀ, -øz] nm/f stuntman(girl)

case [kɑz] nf (hutte) hut; (compartiment) compartment; (pour le courrier) pigeonhole; (sur un formulaire, de mots croisés etc) box

caser [kɑze] vt (trouver de la place pour) to put (away); to put up; (fig) to find a job for; to marry off

caserne [kazɛʀn(ə)] nf barracks pl

cash [kaʃ] adv: **payer ~** to pay cash down

casier [kɑzje] nm (à journaux etc) rack; (de bureau) filing cabinet; (: à cases) set of pigeonholes; (case) compartment; pigeonhole; (: à clef) locker; **~ judiciaire** police record

casino [kazino] nm casino

casque [kask(ə)] nm helmet; (chez le coiffeur) (hair-)drier; (pour audition) (head-)phones pl, headset

casquette [kaskɛt] nf cap

cassant, e [kɑsɑ̃, -ɑ̃t] adj brittle; (fig) brusque, abrupt

cassation [kɑsasjɔ̃] nf: **cour de ~** final court of appeal

casse [kɑs] nf (pour voitures): **mettre à la ~** to scrap; (dégâts): **il y a eu de la ~** there were a lot of breakages; **~-cou** adj inv daredevil, reckless; **~-croûte** nm inv snack; **~-noisette(s)** nm inv nutcrackers pl; **~-noix** nm inv nutcrackers pl; **~-pieds** (fam) adj inv: **il est ~-pieds** he's a pain in the neck

casser [kɑse] vt to break; (ADMIN: gradé) to demote; (JUR) to quash; **se ~** vi to break

casserole [kasʀɔl] nf saucepan

casse-tête [kɑstɛt] nm inv (jeu) brain teaser; (difficultés) headache (fig)

cassette [kasɛt] nf (bande magnétique) cassette; (coffret) casket

casseur [kɑsœʀ] nm hooligan

cassis [kasis] nm blackcurrant

cassoulet [kasulɛ] nm bean and sausage hot-pot

cassure [kɑsyʀ] nf break, crack

castor [kastɔʀ] nm beaver

castrer [kastʀe] vt (mâle) to castrate; (: cheval) to geld; (femelle) to spay

catalogue [katalɔg] nm catalogue

cataloguer [katalɔge] vt to catalogue, to list; (péj) to put a label on

catalyseur [katalizœʀ] nm catalytic convertor

catalyseur [katalizœʀ] nm catalyst

cataplasme [kataplasm(ə)] nm poultice

cataracte [kataʀakt(ə)] nf cataract

catastrophe [katastʀɔf] nf catastrophe, disaster; **catastrophé, e** [katastʀɔfe] (fam) adj deeply saddened

catch [katʃ] nm (all-in) wrestling; **catcheur, euse** nm/f (all-in) wrestler

catéchisme [kateʃism(ə)] nm catechism

catégorie [kategɔʀi] nf category

catégorique [kategɔʀik] adj categorical

cathédrale [katedʀal] nf cathedral

catholique [katɔlik] adj, nm/f Catholic; (Roman) Catholic; **pas très ~** a bit shady ou fishy

catimini [katimini] : **en ~** adv on

the sly
cauchemar [koʃmaʀ] *nm* nightmare
cause [koz] *nf* cause; (*JUR*) lawsuit,
case; à ~ de because of, owing to;
pour ~ de on account of; owing to;
(et) pour ~ and for (a very) good
reason; être en ~ to be at stake; to
be involved: to be in question; mettre en ~ to implicate; to call into
question; remettre en ~ to challenge; ~r [koze] *vt* to cause ♦ *vi* to
talk, chat; ~rie [kozʀi] *nf* talk
caution [kosjɔ̃] *nf* guarantee, security; deposit; (*JUR*) bail (bond); (*fig*)
backing, support; payer la ~ de qn
to stand bail for sb; libéré sous ~
released on bail; ~ner [kosjɔne] *vt* to
guarantee; (*soutenir*) to support
cavalcade [kavalkad] *nf* (*fig*) stampede
cavalier, ière [kavalje, -jεʀ] *adj* (*désinvolte*) offhand ♦ *nm/f* rider; (au
bal) partner ♦ *nm* (*ÉCHECS*)
knight; faire ~ seul to go it alone
cave [kav] *nf* cellar ♦ *adj*: yeux ~s
sunken eyes
caveau, x [kavo] *nm* vault
caverne [kavεʀn(ə)] *nf* cave
C.C.P. *sigle m* = compte chèques
postaux
CD *sigle m* (= compact disc) CD
CD-ROM *sigle m* CD-ROM
CE *n abr* (= Communauté Europé-
enne) EC

---

ce, cette [sə, sεt] (*devant nm* cet +
voyelle ou h aspiré; *pl* ces) *dét*
(*proximité*) this; these *pl*; (*non-
proximité*) that; those *pl*; cette
maison(-ci/là) this/that house; cette
nuit (*qui vient*) tonight; (*passée*)
last night
♦ *pron* 1: c'est it's *ou* it is; c'est un
peintre he's *ou* he is a painter; ce
sont des peintres they're *ou* they are
painters; c'est le facteur *etc* (à
la porte) it's the postman; qui est-
ce? who is it?; (*en désignant*) who is
he/she?; qu'est-ce? what is it?

2: ~ qui, ~ que what; (*chose qui*):
il est idiot, ~ qui me chagrine
he's stupid, which saddens me; tout
~ qui bouge everything that *ou*
which moves; tout ~ que je sais all
I know; ~ dont j'ai parlé what I
talked about; ~ que c'est grand!
it's so big!; *voir aussi* -ci; est-ce
que; n'est-ce pas; c'est-à-dire

---

ceci [səsi] *pron* this
cécité [sesite] *nf* blindness
céder [sede] *vt* to give up ♦ *vi* (*pont,
barrage*) to give way; (*personne*) to
give in; ~ à to yield to, give in to
CEDEX [sedεks] *sigle m* (= courrier
d'entreprise à distribution exceptionnelle) postal service for bulk users
cédille [sedij] *nf* cedilla
cèdre [sεdʀ(ə)] *nm* cedar
CEI *sigle m* (= Communauté des États
Indépendants) CIS
ceinture [sɛ̃tyʀ] *nf* belt; (*taille*)
waist; (*fig*) ring; belt; circle; ~ de
sécurité safety *ou* seat belt; ~r *vt*
(*saisir*) to grasp (round the waist)
cela [s(ə)la] *pron* that; (*comme sujet
indéfini*) it; quand/où ~? when/
where (was that)?
célèbre [selεbʀ(ə)] *adj* famous
célébrer [selebʀe] *vt* to celebrate;
(*louer*) to extol
céleri [sεlʀi] *nm*: ~(-rave) celeriac;
~ (en branche) celery
célérité [seleʀite] *nf* speed, swiftness
célibat [seliba] *nm* celibacy; bache-
lorhood; spinsterhood; **célibataire**
[selibatεʀ] *adj* single, unmarried
celle(s) [sεl] *pron voir* celui
cellier [selje] *nm* storeroom
cellulaire [selylεʀ] *adj*: voiture *ou*
fourgon ~ prison *ou* police van
cellule [selyl] *nf* (*gén*) cell
cellulite [selylit] *nf* excess fat, cellulite

---

celui, celle [səlɥi, sεl] (*mpl* ceux,
fpl celles) *pron* 1: ~-ci/là, celle-ci/
là this one/that one; ceux-ci,

celles-ci these (ones); ceux-là, celles-là those (ones); ~ de mon frère my brother's; ~ du salon/du dessous the one in (ou from) the lounge/below

2: ~ qui bouge the one which ou that moves; (personne) the one who moves; ~ que je vois the one (which ou that) I see; the one (whom) I see; ~ dont je parle the one I'm talking about

3 (valeur indéfinie): ~ qui veut whoever wants

cendre [sɑ̃dʀ(ə)] nf ash; ~s nfpl (d'un foyer) ash(es), cinders; (volcaniques) ash sg; (d'un défunt) ashes; sous la ~ (CULIN) in (the) embers; cendrier nm ashtray

cène [sɛn] nf: la ~ (Holy) Communion

censé, e [sɑ̃se] adj: être ~ faire to be supposed to do

censeur [sɑ̃sœʀ] nm (SCOL) deputy-head (BRIT), vice-principal (US); (CINÉMA, POL) censor

censure [sɑ̃syʀ] nf censorship; ~r [sɑ̃syʀe] vt (CINÉMA, PRESSE) to censor; (POL) to censure

cent [sɑ̃] num a hundred, one hundred; centaine nf: une centaine (de) about a hundred, a hundred or so; plusieurs centaines (de) several hundred; des centaines (de) hundreds (of); centenaire adj hundred-year-old ♦ nm (anniversaire) centenary; centième num hundredth; centigrade nm centigrade; centilitre nm centilitre; centime nm centime; centimètre nm centimetre; (ruban) tape measure, measuring tape

central, e, aux [sɑ̃tʀal, -o] adj central ♦ nm: ~ (téléphonique) (telephone) exchange; centrale nf power station

centre [sɑ̃tʀ(ə)] nm centre; ~ commercial shopping centre; ~ d'apprentissage training college; centre-ville nm town centre, down-

town (area) (US)

centuple [sɑ̃typl(ə)] nm: le ~ de qch a hundred times sth; au ~ a hundredfold

cep [sɛp] nm (vine) stock

cèpe [sɛp] nm (edible) boletus

cependant [səpɑ̃dɑ̃] adv however

céramique [seʀamik] nf ceramics sg

cercle [sɛʀkl(ə)] nm circle; (objet) band, hoop; ~ vicieux vicious circle

cercueil [sɛʀkœj] nm coffin

céréale [seʀeal] nf cereal

cérémonie [seʀemɔni] nf ceremony; ~s nfpl (péj) fuss sg, to-do sg

cerf [sɛʀ] nm stag

cerfeuil [sɛʀfœj] nm chervil

cerf-volant [sɛʀvɔlɑ̃] nm kite

cerise [səʀiz] nf cherry; cerisier nm cherry (tree)

cerné, e [sɛʀne] adj: les yeux ~s with dark rings ou shadows under the eyes

cerner [sɛʀne] vt (MIL etc) to surround; (fig: problème) to delimit, define

certain, e [sɛʀtɛ̃, -ɛn] adj certain ♦ dét certain; d'un ~ âge past one's prime, not so young; un ~ temps (quite) some time; ~s some; certainement adv (probablement) most probably ou likely; (bien sûr) certainly, of course

certes [sɛʀt(ə)] adv admittedly; of course; indeed (yes)

certificat [sɛʀtifika] nm certificate

certitude [sɛʀtityd] nf certainty

cerveau, x [sɛʀvo] nm brain

cervelas [sɛʀvəla] nm saveloy

cervelle [sɛʀvɛl] nf (ANAT) brain

ces [se] dét voir ce

C.E.S. sigle m (= Collège d'enseignement secondaire) ≈ (junior) secondary school (BRIT)

cesse [sɛs]: sans ~ adv continually, constantly; continuously; il n'avait de ~ que he would not rest until

cesser [sese] vt to stop ♦ vi to stop; cease; ~ de faire to stop doing

cessez-le-feu nm inv ceasefire

c'est-à-dire [sɛtadiʀ] adv that is (to

cet, cette [sɛt] dét voir ce

ceux [sø] pron celui

CFC abr (= chlorofluorocarbon) npl CFC

C.F.D.T. sigle f = Confédération française démocratique du travail

C.G.T. sigle f = Confédération générale du travail

chacun, e [ʃakœ̃, -yn] pron each; (indéfini) everyone, everybody

chagrin [ʃagʀɛ̃] nm grief, sorrow; **chagriner** vt to grieve; to bother

chahut [ʃay] nm uproar; **chahuter** vt to rag, bait ♦ vi to make an uproar

chaîne [ʃɛn] nf chain; (RADIO, TV: stations) channel; **travail à la ~** production line work; **~ (de montage ou de fabrication)** production ou assembly line; **~ (de montagnes)** (mountain) range; **~ (haute-fidélité ou hi-fi)** hi-fi system; **~ (stéréo)** stereo (system)

chair [ʃɛʀ] nf flesh ♦ adj: (couleur) **~** flesh-coloured; **avoir la ~ de poule** to have goosepimples ou gooseflesh; **bien en ~** plump, wellpadded; **en ~ et en os** in the flesh

chaire [ʃɛʀ] nf (d'église) pulpit; (d'université) chair

chaise [ʃɛz] nf chair; **~ longue** deckchair

châle [ʃal] nm shawl

chaleur [ʃalœʀ] nf heat; (fig) warmth; fire, fervour; heat

chaleureux, euse [ʃalœʀø, -øz] adj warm

chaloupe [ʃalup] nf launch; (de sauvetage) lifeboat

chalumeau, x [ʃalymo] nm blowlamp, blowtorch

chalutier [ʃalytje] nm trawler

chamailler [ʃamaje]: **se ~** vi to squabble, bicker

chambouler [ʃãbule] vt to disrupt, turn upside down

chambre [ʃãbʀ(ə)] nf bedroom; (TECH) chamber; (POL) chamber, house; (JUR) court; (COMM) chamber; federation; **faire ~ à part** to

sleep in separate rooms; **~ à air** (de pneu) (inner) tube; **~ à coucher** bedroom; **~ à un lit/deux lits** (à l'hôtel) single-/twin-bedded room; **~ d'amis** spare ou guest room; **~ noire** (PHOTO) dark room

chambrer [ʃãbʀe] vt (vin) to bring to room temperature

chameau, x [ʃamo] nm camel

champ [ʃã] nm field; **prendre du ~** to draw back; **~ de bataille** battlefield; **~ de courses** racecourse; **~ de tir** rifle range

champagne [ʃãpaɲ] nm champagne

champêtre [ʃãpɛtʀ(ə)] adj country cpd, rural

champignon [ʃãpiɲɔ̃] nm mushroom; (terme générique) fungus; **~ de Paris** button mushroom

champion, ne [ʃãpjɔ̃, -jɔn] adj, nm/f champion; **championnat** nm championship

chance [ʃãs] nf: **la ~** luck; **~s** nfpl (probabilités) chances; **une ~** a stroke ou piece of luck ou good fortune; (occasion) a lucky break; **avoir de la ~** to be lucky

chanceler [ʃãsle] vi to totter

chancelier [ʃãsəlje] nm (allemand) chancellor

chanceux, euse [ʃãsø, -øz] adj lucky

chandail [ʃãdaj] nm (thick) sweater

chandelier [ʃãdəlje] nm candlestick

chandelle [ʃãdɛl] nf (tallow) candle; **dîner aux ~s** candlelight dinner

change [ʃãʒ] nm (COMM) exchange

changement [ʃãʒmã] nm change; **~ de vitesses** gears pl; gear change

changer [ʃãʒe] vt (modifier) to change, alter; (remplacer, COMM, rhabiller) to change ♦ vi to change, alter; **se ~** vi to change (o.s.); **~** (remplacer: adresse, nom, voiture etc) to change one's; (échanger, alterner: côté, place, train etc) to change +npl: **~ de couleur/direction** to change colour/direction; **~ d'idée** to change one's mind; **~ de vitesse** to change gear

chanson [ʃɑ̃sɔ̃] nf song

chant [ʃɑ̃] nm song; (art vocal) singing; (d'église) hymn; **~age** [ʃɑ̃taʒ] nm blackmail; **faire du ~** to use blackmail; **~er** [ʃɑ̃te] vi, vt to sing; **si cela lui chante** (fam) if he feels like it; **~eur, euse** [ʃɑ̃tœʀ, -øz] nm/f singer

chantier [ʃɑ̃tje] nm (building) site; (sur une route) roadworks pl; **mettre en ~** to put in hand; **~ naval** shipyard

chantilly [ʃɑ̃tiji] nf voir **crème**

chantonner [ʃɑ̃tɔne] vi, vt to sing to oneself, hum

chanvre [ʃɑ̃vʀ(ə)] nm hemp

chaparder [ʃapaʀde] vt to pinch

chapeau, x [ʃapo] nm hat; **~ mou** trilby

chapelet [ʃaplɛ] nm (REL) rosary

chapelle [ʃapɛl] nf chapel; **~ ardente** chapel of rest

chapelure [ʃaplyʀ] nf (dried) breadcrumbs pl

chapiteau, x [ʃapito] nm (de cirque) marquee, big top

chapitre [ʃapitʀ(ə)] nm chapter; (fig) subject, matter

chaque [ʃak] dét each, every; (indéfini) every

char [ʃaʀ] nm (à foin &c) cart, waggon; (de carnaval) float; **~ (d'assaut)** tank

charabia [ʃaʀabja] (péj) nm gibberish

charade [ʃaʀad] nf riddle; (mimée) charade

charbon [ʃaʀbɔ̃] nm coal; **~ de bois** charcoal

charcuterie [ʃaʀkytʀi] nf (magasin) pork butcher's shop and delicatessen; (produits) cooked pork meats pl; **charcutier, ière** nm/f pork butcher

chardon [ʃaʀdɔ̃] nm thistle

charge [ʃaʀʒ(ə)] nf (fardeau) load, burden; (explosif, ELEC, MIL, JUR) charge; (rôle, mission) responsibility; **~s** nfpl (du loyer) service charges; **à la ~ de** (dépendant de) dependent upon; (aux frais de)

chargeable to; **j'accepte, à ~ de revanche** I accept, provided I can do the same for you one day; **prendre en ~** to take charge of; (suj: véhicule) to take on; (dépenses) to take care of; **~s sociales** social security contributions; **~ment** [ʃaʀʒəmɑ̃] nm (objets) load

charger [ʃaʀʒe] vt (voiture, fusil, caméra) to load; (batterie) to charge ♦ vi (MIL etc) to charge; **se ~ de** vt to see to; **~ qn de (faire) qch** to put sb in charge of (doing) sth

chariot [ʃaʀjo] nm trolley; (charrette) waggon; (de machine à écrire) carriage

charité [ʃaʀite] nf charity; **faire la ~ à** to give (something) to

charmant, e [ʃaʀmɑ̃, -ɑ̃t] adj charming

charme [ʃaʀm(ə)] nm charm; **charmer** vt to charm

charnel, le [ʃaʀnɛl] adj carnal

charnière [ʃaʀnjɛʀ] nf hinge; (fig) turning-point

charnu, e [ʃaʀny] adj fleshy

charpente [ʃaʀpɑ̃t] nf frame(work); **charpentier** nm carpenter

charpie [ʃaʀpi] nf: **en ~** (fig) in shreds ou ribbons

charrette [ʃaʀɛt] nf cart

charrier [ʃaʀje] vt to carry (along); to cart, carry

charrue [ʃaʀy] nf plough (BRIT), plow (US)

chasse [ʃas] nf hunting; (au fusil) shooting; (poursuite) chase; (aussi: **~ d'eau**) flush; **la ~ est ouverte** the hunting season is open; **~ gardée** private hunting grounds pl; **prendre en ~** to give chase to; **tirer la ~ (d'eau)** to flush the toilet, pull the chain; **à courre** hunting

chassé-croisé [ʃasekʀwaze] nm (fig) mix-up where people miss each other in turn

chasse-neige [ʃasnɛʒ] nm inv snowplough (BRIT), snowplow (US)

chasser [ʃase] vt to hunt; (expulser) to chase away ou out, drive away

out; **chasseur, euse** nm/f hunter ♦
nm (avion) fighter; **chasseur de
têtes** nm (fig) headhunter

châssis [ʃɑsi] nm (AUTO) chassis;
(cadre) frame; (de jardin) cold
frame

chat [ʃa] nm cat

châtaigne [ʃɑtɛɲ] nf chestnut;
châtaignier nm chestnut (tree)

châtain [ʃɑtɛ̃] adj inv chestnut
(brown); chestnut-haired

château, x [ʃɑto] nm castle; ~
d'eau water tower; ~ **fort** stronghold, fortified castle

châtier [ʃɑtje] vt to punish; (fig:
style) to polish; **châtiment** nm punishment

chaton [ʃɑtɔ̃] nm (ZOOL) kitten

chatouiller [ʃatuje] vt to tickle;
(l'odorat, le palais) to titillate; **cha-
touilleux, euse** adj ticklish; (fig)
touchy, over-sensitive

chatoyer [ʃatwaje] vi to shimmer

châtrer [ʃɑtʀe] vt (mâle) to castrate; (: cheval) to geld; (femelle) to
spay

chatte [ʃat] nf (she-)cat

chaud, e [ʃo, -od] adj (gén) warm;
(très chaud) hot; (fig) hearty;
heated; **il fait ~** it's warm; it's hot;
avoir ~ to be warm; to be hot; **ça
me tient ~** it keeps me warm; **rester au ~** to stay in the warm

chaudière [ʃodjɛʀ] nf boiler

chaudron [ʃodʀɔ̃] nm cauldron

chauffage [ʃofaʒ] nm heating; ~
central central heating

chauffard [ʃofaʀ] nm (péj) reckless
driver; hit-and-run driver

chauffe-eau [ʃofo] nm inv water-
heater

chauffer [ʃofe] vt to heat ♦ vi to
heat up, warm up; (trop ~: moteur)
to overheat; **se ~** vi (se mettre en
train) to warm up; (au soleil) to
warm o.s.

chauffeur [ʃofœʀ] nm driver;
(privé) chauffeur

chaume [ʃom] nm (du toit) thatch

chaumière [ʃomjɛʀ] nf (thatched)

cottage

chaussée [ʃose] nf road(way)

chausse-pied [ʃospje] nm shoe-horn

chausser [ʃose] vt (bottes, skis) to
put on; (enfant) to put shoes on; ~
du 38/42 to take size 38/42

chaussette [ʃosɛt] nf sock

chausson [ʃosɔ̃] nm slipper; (de
bébé) bootee; ~ **(aux pommes)**
(apple) turnover

chaussure [ʃosyʀ] nf shoe; ~**s bas-
ses** flat shoes; ~**s de ski** ski boots

chauve [ʃov] adj bald

chauve-souris [ʃovsuʀi] nf bat

chauvin, e [ʃovɛ̃, -in] adj chauvinis-
tic

chaux [ʃo] nf lime; **blanchi à la ~**
whitewashed

chavirer [ʃaviʀe] vi to capsize

chef [ʃɛf] nm head, leader; (de cuisine) chef; **en ~** (MIL etc) in chief;
~ **d'accusation** charge; ~ **d'entreprise** company head; ~ **d'état** head
of state; ~ **de file** (de parti etc)
leader; ~ **de gare** station master; ~
d'orchestre conductor; ~**-d'œuvre**
[ʃɛdœvʀ(ə)] nm masterpiece; ~**-lieu**
[ʃɛfljø] nm county town

chemin [ʃəmɛ̃] nm path; (itinéraire,
direction, trajet) way; **en ~** on the
way; ~ **de fer** railway (BRIT), rail-
road (US); **par chemin de fer** by
rail

cheminée [ʃəmine] nf chimney; (à
l'intérieur) chimney piece, fireplace;
(de bateau) funnel

cheminement [ʃəminmã] nm progress; course

cheminot [ʃəmino] nm railwayman

chemise [ʃəmiz] nf shirt; (dossier)
folder; ~ **de nuit** nightdress

chemisier [ʃəmizje] nm blouse

chenal, aux [ʃənal, -o] nm channel

chêne [ʃɛn] nm oak (tree); (bois)
oak

chenil [ʃənil] nm kennels pl

chenille [ʃənij] nf (ZOOL) caterpillar; (AUTO) caterpillar track

chèque [ʃɛk] nm cheque (BRIT),
check (US); ~ **sans provision** bad

cheque; ~ **de voyage** traveller's cheque; **chéquier** *nm* cheque book

cher, ère [ʃɛʀ] *adj* (*aimé*) dear; (*coûteux*) expensive, dear ♦ *adv*: **cela coûte** ~ it's expensive

chercher [ʃɛʀʃe] *vt* to look for; (*gloire etc*) to seek; **aller** ~ to go for, go and fetch; ~ **à faire** to try to do; **chercheur, euse** [ʃɛʀʃœʀ, -øz] *nm/f* researcher, research worker

chère [ʃɛʀ] *adj voir* **cher** ♦ *nf*: **la bonne** ~ good food

chéri, e [ʃeʀi] *adj* beloved, dear; (**mon**) ~ darling

chérir [ʃeʀiʀ] *vt* to cherish

cherté [ʃɛʀte] *nf*: **la** ~ **de la vie** the high cost of living

chétif, ive [ʃetif, -iv] *adj* puny, stunted

cheval, aux [ʃəval, -o] *nm* horse; (*AUTO*): ~ (**vapeur**) horsepower *no pl*; **faire du** ~ to ride; **à** ~ on horseback; **à** ~ **sur** astride; (*fig*) overlapping; ~ **de course** racehorse

chevalet [ʃəvalɛ] *nm* easel

chevalier [ʃəvalje] *nm* knight

chevalière [ʃəvaljɛʀ] *nf* signet ring

chevalin, e [ʃəvalɛ̃, -in] *adj*: **boucherie** ~**e** horse-meat butcher's

chevaucher [ʃəvoʃe] *vi* (*aussi*: **se** ~) to overlap (each other) ♦ *vt* to be astride, straddle

chevaux [ʃəvo] *nmpl de* **cheval**

chevelu, e [ʃəvly] *adj* with a good head of hair, hairy (*péj*)

chevelure [ʃəvlyʀ] *nf* hair *no pl*

chevet [ʃəvɛ] *nm*: **au** ~ **de qn** at sb's bedside; **lampe de** ~ bedside lamp

cheveu, x [ʃəvø] *nm* hair; **x** *nmpl* (*chevelure*) hair *sg*; **avoir les** ~**x courts** to have short hair

cheville [ʃəvij] *nf* (*ANAT*) ankle; (*de bois*) peg; (*pour une vis*) plug

chèvre [ʃɛvʀ(ə)] *nf* (she-)goat

chevreau, x [ʃəvʀo] *nm* kid

chèvrefeuille [ʃɛvʀəfœj] *nm* honeysuckle

chevreuil [ʃəvʀœj] *nm* roe deer *inv*; (*CULIN*) venison

chevronné, e [ʃəvʀɔne] *adj* seasoned

MOT-CLÉ

chez [ʃe] *prép* **1** (*à la demeure de*) at; (: *direction*) to; ~ **qn** at/to sb's house *ou* place; ~ **moi** at home; (*direction*) home

2 (+*profession*): ~ **le boulanger/dentiste** at *or* to the baker's/dentist's

3 (*dans le caractère, l'œuvre de:*) in; ~ **les renards/Racine** in foxes/Racine

---

chez-soi [ʃeswa] *nm inv* home

chic [ʃik] *adj inv* chic, smart; (*généreux*) nice, decent ♦ *nm* stylishness; ~! great!; **avoir le** ~ **de** to have the knack of; ~**ane** [ʃikan] *nf*: (*querelle*) squabble

chicaner [ʃikane] *vi* (*ergoter*): ~ **sur** to quibble about

chiche [ʃiʃ] *adj* niggardly, mean ♦ *excl* (*au un défi*) you're on!

chichi [ʃiʃi] (*fam*) *nm* fuss

chicorée [ʃikɔʀe] *nf* (*café*) chicory; (*salade*) endive

chien [ʃjɛ̃] *nm* dog; **en** ~ **de fusil** curled up; ~ **de garde** guard dog

chiendent [ʃjɛ̃dɑ̃] *nm* couch grass

chienne [ʃjɛn] *nf* dog, bitch

chier [ʃje] (*fam!*) *vi* to crap (!)

chiffon [ʃifɔ̃] *nm* (*piece of*) rag; ~**ner** [ʃifɔne] *vt* to crumple; (*tracasser*) to concern; ~**nier** [ʃifɔnje] *nm* rag-and-bone man

chiffre [ʃifʀ(ə)] *nm* (*représentant un nombre*) figure; numeral; (*montant, total*) total, sum; **en** ~**s ronds** in round figures; ~ **d'affaires** turnover; **chiffrer** *vt* (*dépense*) to put a figure to, assess; (*message*) to (en)code, cipher

chignon [ʃiɲɔ̃] *nm* chignon, bun

Chili [ʃili] *nm*: **le** ~ Chile

chimie [ʃimi] *nf* chemistry; **chimique** *adj* chemical; **produits chimiques** chemicals

Chine [ʃin] *nf*: **la** ~ China

chinois, e [ʃinwa, -waz] *adj, nm/f* Chinese ♦ *nm* (*LING*) Chinese

chiot [ʃjo] *nm* pup(py)

chips [ʃips] *nfpl* crisps (*BRIT*), (potato) chips (*US*)

chiquenaude [ʃiknod] *nf* flick, flip

chirurgical, e, aux [ʃiʀyʀʒikal, -o] *adj* surgical

chirurgie [ʃiʀyʀʒi] *nf* surgery; ~ esthétique plastic surgery; **chirurgien, ne** *nm/f* surgeon

choc [ʃɔk] *nm* impact; shock; crash; (*moral*) shock; (*affrontement*) clash

chocolat [ʃɔkɔla] *nm* chocolate; (*boisson*) (hot) chocolate; ~ au lait milk chocolate

chœur [kœʀ] *nm* (*chorale*) choir; (*OPÉRA, THÉÂTRE*) chorus; **en ~** in chorus

choisir [ʃwaziʀ] *vt* to choose, select

choix [ʃwa] *nm* choice, selection; **avoir le ~** to have the choice; **premier ~** (*COMM*) class one; **de ~** choice, selected; **au ~** as you wish

chômage [ʃomaʒ] *nm* unemployment; **mettre au ~** to make redundant, put out of work; **être au ~** to be unemployed *ou* out of work; **chômeur, euse** *nm/f* unemployed person

chope [ʃɔp] *nf* tankard

choquer [ʃɔke] *vt* (*offenser*) to shock; (*commotionner*) to shake (up)

choriste [kɔʀist(ə)] *nm/f* choir member; (*OPÉRA*) chorus member

chorus [kɔʀys] *nm*: **faire ~ (avec)** to voice one's agreement (with)

chose [ʃoz] *nf* thing; **c'est peu de ~** it's nothing (really); it's not much

chou, x [ʃu] *nm* cabbage; **mon petit ~** (my) sweetheart; ~ **à la crème** cream bun (*made of choux pastry*)

chouchou, te [ʃuʃu, -ut] *nm/f* (*SCOL*) teacher's pet

choucroute [ʃukʀut] *nf* sauerkraut

chouette [ʃwɛt] *nf* owl ♦ *adj* (*fam*) great, smashing

chou-fleur [ʃuflœʀ] *nm* cauliflower

choyer [ʃwaje] *vt* to cherish; to pamper

chrétien, ne [kʀetjɛ̃, -ɛn] *adj, nm/f* Christian

Christ [kʀist] *nm*: **le ~** Christ; **christianisme** *nm* Christianity

chrome [kʀom] *nm* chromium; **chromé, e** *adj* chromium-plated

chronique [kʀɔnik] *adj* chronic ♦ *nf* (*de journal*) column, page; (*historique*) chronicle; (*RADIO, TV*): **la ~ sportive/théâtrale** the sports/theatre review; **la ~ locale** local news and gossip

chronologique [kʀɔnɔlɔʒik] *adj* chronological

chronomètre [kʀɔnɔmɛtʀ(ə)] *nm* stopwatch; **chronométrer** *vt* to time

chrysanthème [kʀizɑ̃tɛm] *nm* chrysanthemum

C.H.U. *sigle m* (= *centre hospitalier universitaire*) = (teaching) hospital

chuchoter [ʃyʃɔte] *vt, vi* to whisper

chuinter [ʃɥɛ̃te] *vi* to hiss

chut [ʃyt] *excl* sh!

chute [ʃyt] *nf* fall; (*de bois, papier: déchet*) scrap; **faire une ~ (de 10 m)** to fall (10 m); ~ **(d'eau)** waterfall; **la ~ des cheveux** hair loss; ~ **libre** free fall; ~**s de pluie/neige** rain/snowfalls

Chypre [ʃipʀ] Cyprus

-ci [si] *adv voir* **par** ♦ *dét*: **ce garçon-ci/-là** this/that boy; **ces femmes-ci/-là** these/those women

ci-après [siapʀɛ] *adv* hereafter

cible [sibl(ə)] *nf* target

ciboulette [sibulɛt] *nf* (small) chive

cicatrice [sikatʀis] *nf* scar

cicatriser [sikatʀize] *vt* to heal

ci-contre [sikɔ̃tʀ(ə)] *adv* opposite

ci-dessous [sidəsu] *adv* below

ci-dessus [sidəsy] *adv* above

cidre [sidʀ(ə)] *nm* cider

Cie *abr* (= *compagnie*) Co.

ciel [sjɛl] *nm* sky; (*REL*) heaven; **cieux** *nmpl* (*littéraire*) sky *sg*, skies; **à ~ ouvert** open-air; (*mine*) opencast

cierge [sjɛʀʒ(ə)] *nm* candle

cieux [sjø] *nmpl de* **ciel**

cigale [sigal] *nf* cicada

cigare [sigar] nm cigar

cigarette [sigaʀɛt] nf cigarette

ci-gît [siʒi] adv +vb here lies

cigogne [sigɔɲ] nf stork

ci-inclus, e [siɛ̃kly, -yz] adj, adv enclosed

ci-joint, e [siʒwɛ̃, -ɛ̃t] adj, adv enclosed

cil [sil] nm (eye)lash

cime [sim] nf top; (montagne) peak

ciment [simɑ̃] nm cement; ~ armé reinforced concrete

cimetière [simtjɛʀ] nm cemetery; (d'église) churchyard

cinéaste [sineast(ə)] nm/f film-maker

cinéma [sinema] nm cinema; ~tographique adj film cpd, cinema cpd

cinéphile [sinefil] nm/f cinema-goer

cinglant, e [sɛ̃glɑ̃, -ɑ̃t] adj (échec) crushing

cinglé, e [sɛ̃gle] (fam) adj crazy

cingler [sɛ̃gle] vt to lash; (fig) to sting

cinq [sɛ̃k] num five

cinquantaine [sɛ̃kɑ̃tɛn] nf: une ~ (de) about fifty; avoir la ~ (âge) to be around fifty

cinquante [sɛ̃kɑ̃t] num fifty; **cinquantenaire** adj, nm/f fifty-year-old

cinquième [sɛ̃kjɛm] num fifth

cintre [sɛ̃tʀ(ə)] nm coat-hanger

cintré, e [sɛ̃tʀe] adj (chemise) fitted

cirage [siʀaʒ] nm (shoe) polish

circonflexe [siʀkɔ̃flɛks(ə)] adj: accent ~ circumflex accent

circonscription [siʀkɔ̃skʀipsjɔ̃] nf district; ~ électorale (d'un député) constituency

circonscrire [siʀkɔ̃skʀiʀ] vt to define, delimit; (incendie) to contain

circonstance [siʀkɔ̃stɑ̃s] nf circumstance; (occasion) occasion

circonvenir [siʀkɔ̃vniʀ] vt to circumvent

circuit [siʀkɥi] nm (trajet) tour, (round) trip; (ELEC, TECH) circuit

circulaire [siʀkylɛʀ] adj, nf circular

circulation [siʀkylasjɔ̃] nf circulation; (AUTO): la ~ (the) traffic

circuler [siʀkyle] vi to drive (along);

to walk along; (train etc) to run; (sang, devises) to circulate; **faire ~** (nouvelle) to spread (about), circulate; (badauds) to move on

cire [siʀ] nf wax; **ciré** [siʀe] nm oilskin; **cirer** [siʀe] vt to wax, polish

cirque [siʀk(ə)] nm circus; (GEO) cirque; (fig) chaos, bedlam; carry-on

cisaille(s) [sizaj] nf(pl) (gardening) shears pl

ciseau, x [sizo] nm: ~ (à bois) chisel; ~x nmpl (paire de ~x) (pair of) scissors

ciseler [sizle] vt to chisel, carve

citadin, e [sitadɛ̃, -in] nm/f city dweller

citation [sitasjɔ̃] nf (d'auteur) quotation; (JUR) summons sg

cité [site] nf town; (plus grande) city; ~ universitaire students' residences pl

citer [site] vt (un auteur) to quote (from); (nommer) to name; (JUR) to summon

citerne [sitɛʀn(ə)] nf tank

citoyen, ne [sitwajɛ̃, -ɛn] nm/f citizen

citron [sitʀɔ̃] nm lemon; ~ vert lime; **citronnade** nf lemonade; **citronnier** nm lemon tree

citrouille [sitʀuj] nf pumpkin

civet [sivɛ] nm stew

civière [sivjɛʀ] nf stretcher

civil, e [sivil] adj (JUR, ADMIN, poli) civil; (non militaire) civilian; **en ~** in civilian clothes; **dans le ~** in civilian life

civilisation [sivilizasjɔ̃] nf civilization

civisme [sivism(ə)] nm publicspiritedness

clair, e [klɛʀ] adj light; (chambre) light, bright; (eau, son, fig) clear ♦ adv: **voir ~** to see clearly; **tirer qch au ~** to clear sth up, clarify sth; **mettre au ~** (notes etc) to tidy up; **le plus ~** de son temps the better part of his time; ~ **de lune** moonlight; **clairement** adv clearly

clairière [klɛʀjɛʀ] nf clearing

clairon [klɛʀɔ̃] nm bugle

claironner [klɛʀɔne] vt (fig) to trumpet, shout from the rooftops

clairsemé, e [klɛʀsəme] adj sparse

clairvoyant, e [klɛʀvwajɑ̃, -ɑ̃t] adj perceptive, clear-sighted

clandestin, e [klɑ̃dɛstɛ̃, -in] adj clandestine, covert; passager ~ stowaway

clapier [klapje] nm (rabbit) hutch

clapoter [klapɔte] vi to lap

claque [klak] nf (gifle) slap

claquer [klake] vi (drapeau) to flap; (porte) to bang, slam; (coup de feu) to ring out ♦ vt (porte) to slam, bang; (doigts) to snap; se ~ un muscle to pull ou strain a muscle

claquettes [klakɛt] nfpl tap-dancing sg

clarinette [klaʀinɛt] nf clarinet

clarté [klaʀte] nf lightness, brightness; (d'un son, de l'eau) clearness; (d'une explication) clarity

classe [klɑs] nf class; (SCOL: local) class(room); (: leçon, élèves) class; faire la ~ to be a ou the teacher; to teach; **~ment** [klɑsmɑ̃] nm (rang: SCOL; SPORT) placing; (: SPORT) placings pl; (liste: SCOL) class list (in order of merit); (: SPORT) placings pl; **~r** [klɑse] vt (idées, livres) to classify; (papiers) to file; (candidat, concurrent) to grade; (JUR: affaire) to close; se **~r premier/dernier** to come first/last; (SPORT) to finish first/last

classeur [klɑsœʀ] nm (cahier) file; (meuble) filing cabinet

classique [klasik] adj classical; (sobre: coupe etc) classic(al); (habituel) standard, classic

clause [kloz] nf clause

claustrer [klostʀe] vt to confine

clavecin [klavsɛ̃] nm harpsichord

clavicule [klavikyl] nf collarbone

clavier [klavje] nm keyboard

clé [kle] nf key; (MUS) clef; (de mécanicien) spanner (BRIT), wrench (US); **prix** ~s en main (d'une voiture) on-the-road price; ~ **anglaise** (monkey) wrench; ~ **de contact** ig-

nition key

clef [kle] nf = clé

clément, e [klemɑ̃, -ɑ̃t] adj (temps) mild; (indulgent) lenient

clerc [klɛʀ] nm: ~ **de notaire** solicitor's clerk

clergé [klɛʀʒe] nm clergy

cliché [kliʃe] nm (PHOTO) negative; print; (LING) cliché

client, e [klijɑ̃, -ɑ̃t] nm/f (acheteur) customer, client; (d'hôtel) guest, patron; (du docteur) patient; (de l'avocat) client; **clientèle** nf (du magasin) customers pl, clientèle; (du docteur, de l'avocat) practice

cligner [kliɲe] vi: ~ **des yeux** to blink (one's eyes); ~ **de l'œil** to wink; **clignotant** [kliɲɔtɑ̃] nm (AUTO) indicator; **clignoter** [kliɲɔte] vi (étoiles etc) to twinkle; (lumière) to flash; (: vaciller) to flicker

climat [klima] nm climate

climatisation [klimatizasjɔ̃] nf air conditioning; **climatisé, e** adj air-conditioned

clin d'œil [klɛ̃dœj] nm wink; en un ~ in a flash

clinique [klinik] nf nursing home

clinquant, e [klɛ̃kɑ̃, -ɑ̃t] adj flashy

cliqueter [klikte] vi to clash; to jangle, jingle; to chink

clochard, e [klɔʃaʀ, -aʀd(ə)] nm/f tramp

cloche [klɔʃ] nf (d'église) bell; (fam) clot; ~ **à fromage** cheese-cover

cloche-pied [klɔʃpje]: à ~ adv on one leg, hopping (along)

clocher [klɔʃe] nm church tower; (en pointe) steeple ♦ vi (fam) to be ou go wrong; de ~ (péj) parochial

cloison [klwazɔ̃] nf partition (wall)

cloître [klwatʀ(ə)] nm cloister

cloîtrer [klwatʀe] vt: se ~ to shut o.s. up ou away

cloque [klɔk] nf blister

clore [klɔʀ] vt to close; **clos, e** adj voir **maison**; **huis** ♦ nm (enclosed) field

clôture [klotyʀ] nf closure; (barrière) enclosure; **clôturer** vt (ter-

rain) to enclose; (*débats*) to close

clou [klu] *nm* nail; (*MÉD*) boil; ~**s** *nmpl* (*passage clouté*) pedestrian crossing; **pneus à ~s** studded tyres; **le ~ du spectacle** the highlight of the show; ~ **de girofle** clove; **clouer** *vt* to nail down *ou* up

clown [klun] *nm* clown

club [klœb] *nm* club

C.N.R.S. *sigle m* = **Centre nationale de la recherche scientifique**

coasser [kɔase] *vi* to croak

cobaye [kɔbaj] *nm* guinea-pig

coca [kɔka] *nm* Coke ®

cocaïne [kɔkain] *nf* cocaïne

cocasse [kɔkas] *adj* comical, funny

coccinelle [kɔksinɛl] *nf* ladybird (*BRIT*), ladybug (*US*)

cocher [kɔʃe] *nm* coachman ♦ *vt* to tick off; (*entailler*) to notch

cochère [kɔʃɛr] *adj f*: **porte ~** carriage entrance

cochon, ne [kɔʃɔ̃, -ɔn] *nm* pig ♦ *adj* (*fam*) dirty, smutty; **cochonnerie** (*fam*) *nf* filth; rubbish, trash

cocktail [kɔktɛl] *nm* cocktail; (*réception*) cocktail party

coco [kɔko] *nm voir* **noix**; (*fam*) bloke

cocorico [kɔkɔriko] *excl, nm* cock-a-doodle-do

cocotier [kɔkɔtje] *nm* coconut palm

cocotte [kɔkɔt] *nf* (*en fonte*) casserole; ~ (**minute**) pressure cooker; **ma ~** (*fam*) sweetie (pie)

cocu [kɔky] *nm* cuckold

code [kɔd] *nm* code ♦ *adj*: **phares ~s** dipped lights; **se mettre en ~(s)** to dip one's (head)lights; ~ **à barres** bar code; ~ **civil** Common Law; ~ **de la route** highway code; ~ **pénal** penal code; ~ **postal** (*numéro*) post (*BRIT*) *ou* zip (*US*) code

cœur [kœr] *nm* heart; (*CARTES: couleur*) hearts *pl*; (: *carte*) heart; **avoir du ~** to be kind-hearted; **avoir mal au ~** to feel sick; **en avoir le ~ net** to be clear in one's own mind (about it); **par ~** by heart; **de bon ~** willingly; **cela lui**

tient à ~ that's (very) close to his heart

coffre [kɔfr(ə)] *nm* (*meuble*) chest; (*d'auto*) boot (*BRIT*), trunk (*US*); **coffre(-fort)** *nm* safe

coffret [kɔfrɛ] *nm* casket

cognac [kɔɲak] *nm* brandy, cognac

cogner [kɔɲe] *vi* to knock

cohérent, e [kɔerɑ̃, -ɑ̃t] *adj* coherent, consistent

cohorte [kɔɔrt] *nf* troop

cohue [kɔy] *nf* crowd

coi, coite [kwa, kwat] *adj*: **rester ~** to remain silent

coiffe [kwaf] *nf* headdress

coiffé, e [kwafe] *adj*: **bien/mal ~** with tidy/untidy hair; ~ **en arrière** with one's hair brushed *ou* combed back

coiffer [kwafe] *vt* (*fig*) to cover, top; **se ~** *vi* to do one's hair; to put on one's hat; ~ **qn** to do sb's hair

coiffeur, euse [kwafœr, -øz] *nm/f* hairdresser; **coiffeuse** *nf* (*table*) dressing table

coiffure [kwafyr] *nf* (*cheveux*) hairstyle, hairdo; (*chapeau*) hat, headgear *no pl*; (*art*): **la ~** hairdressing

coin [kwɛ̃] *nm* corner; (*pour coincer*) wedge; **l'épicerie du ~** the local grocer; **dans le ~** (*aux alentours*) in the area, around about; (*localement*): **au ~ du feu** by the fireside; **regard en ~** sideways glance

coincé, e [kwɛ̃se] *adj* stuck, jammed; (*fig: inhibé*) inhibited, hung up (*fam*)

coincer [kwɛ̃se] *vt* to jam

coïncidence [kɔɛ̃sidɑ̃s] *nf* coincidence

coïncider [kɔɛ̃side] *vi* to coincide

col [kɔl] *nm* (*de chemise*) collar; (*encolure, cou*) neck; (*de montagne*) pass; ~ **de l'utérus** cervix; ~ **roulé** polo-neck

colère [kɔlɛr] *nf* anger; **une ~** a fit of anger; (**se mettre**) **en ~** (to get) angry; **coléreux, euse** *adj*, **colérique** *adj* quick-tempered, irascible

colifichet [kɔlifiʃɛ] *nm* trinket

colimaçon [kɔlimasɔ̃] nm: **escalier en ~** spiral staircase

colin [kɔlɛ̃] nm hake

colique [kɔlik] nf diarrhoea; colic (pains)

colis [kɔli] nm parcel

collaborateur, trice [kɔlabɔʀatœʀ, -tʀis] nm/f (aussi POL) collaborator; (d'une revue) contributor

collaborer [kɔlabɔʀe] vi to collaborate; **~ à** to collaborate on; (revue) to contribute to

collant, e [kɔlɑ̃, -ɑ̃t] adj sticky; (robe etc) clinging, skintight; (péj) clinging ♦ nm (bas) tights pl

collation [kɔlasjɔ̃] nf light meal

colle [kɔl] nf glue; (à papiers peints) (wallpaper) paste; (devinette) teaser, riddle; (SCOL: fam) detention

collecte [kɔlɛkt(ə)] nf collection

collectif, ive [kɔlɛktif, -iv] adj collective; (visite, billet) group cpd

collection [kɔlɛksjɔ̃] nf collection; (EDITION) series; **collectionner** vt (tableaux, timbres) to collect; **collectionneur, euse** nm/f collector

collectivité [kɔlɛktivite] nf group; **~s locales** nfpl (ADMIN) local authorities

collège [kɔlɛʒ] nm (école) (secondary) school; (assemblée) body; **collégien** nm schoolboy; **collégienne** nf schoolgirl

collègue [kɔlɛg] nm/f colleague

coller [kɔle] vt (papier, timbre) to stick (on); (affiche) to stick up; (enveloppe) to stick down; (morceaux) to stick ou glue together; (fam: mettre, fourrer) to stick, shove; (SCOL: fam) to keep in ♦ vi (être collant) to be sticky; (adhérer) to stick; **~ à** to stick to

collet [kɔlɛ] nm (piège) snare, noose; (cou): **prendre qn au ~** to grab sb by the throat; (fam) **monté** adj inv straight-laced

collier [kɔlje] nm (bijou) necklace; (de chien, TECH) collar; **~ (de barbe)** narrow beard along the line of the jaw

collimateur [kɔlimatœʀ] nm: **avoir qn/qch dans le ~** (fig) to have sb/sth in one's sights

colline [kɔlin] nf hill

collision [kɔlizjɔ̃] nf collision; crash; **entrer en ~ (avec)** to collide (with)

colmater [kɔlmate] vt (fuite) to seal off; (brèche) to plug, fill in

colombe [kɔlɔ̃b] nf dove

colon [kɔlɔ̃] nm settler

colonel [kɔlɔnɛl] nm colonel

colonie [kɔlɔni] nf colony; **~ (de vacances)** holiday camp (for children)

colonne [kɔlɔn] nf column; **se mettre en ~ par deux** to get into twos; **~ (vertébrale)** spine, spinal column

colorant [kɔlɔʀɑ̃] nm colouring

colorer [kɔlɔʀe] vt to colour

colorier [kɔlɔʀje] vt to colour (in)

coloris [kɔlɔʀi] nm colour, shade

colporter [kɔlpɔʀte] vt to hawk, peddle

colza [kɔlza] nm rape

coma [kɔma] nm coma

combat [kɔ̃ba] nm fight; fighting no pl; **~ de boxe** boxing match

combattant [kɔ̃batɑ̃] nm: **ancien ~** war veteran

combattre [kɔ̃batʀ(ə)] vt to fight; (épidémie, ignorance) to combat, fight against

combien [kɔ̃bjɛ̃] adv (quantité) how much; (nombre) how many; (exclamatif) how; **~ de** how much; how many; **~ de temps** how long; **~ coûte/pèse ceci?** how much does this cost/weigh?

combinaison [kɔ̃binɛzɔ̃] nf combination; (astuce) device, scheme; (de femme) slip; (d'aviateur) flying suit; (d'homme-grenouille) wetsuit; (bleu de travail) boiler suit (BRIT), coveralls pl (US)

combine [kɔ̃bin] nf trick; (péj) scheme, fiddle (BRIT)

combiné [kɔ̃bine] nm (aussi: **~ téléphonique**) receiver

combiner [kɔ̃bine] vt to combine; (plan, horaire) to work out, devise

comble [kɔ̃bl(ə)] *adj* (*salle*) packed (full) ♦ *nm* (*du bonheur, plaisir*) height; ♦ ~s *nmpl* (*CONSTR*) attic sg, loft sg; c'est le ~! that beats everything!

combler [kɔ̃ble] *vt* (*trou*) to fill in; (*besoin, lacune*) to fill; (*déficit*) to make good; (*satisfaire*) to fulfil

combustible [kɔ̃bystibl(ə)] *nm* fuel

comédie [kɔmedi] *nf* comedy; (*fig*) playacting *no pl*; ~ **musicale** musical; **comédien, ne** *nm/f* actor(tress)

comestible [kɔmɛstibl(ə)] *adj* edible

comique [kɔmik] *adj* (*drôle*) comical; (*THEATRE*) comic ♦ *nm* (*artiste*) comic, comedian

comité [kɔmite] *nm* committee; ~ **d'entreprise** works council

commandant [kɔmɑ̃dɑ̃] *nm* (*gén*) commander, commandant; (*NAVIG, AVIAT*) captain

commande [kɔmɑ̃d] *nf* (*COMM*) order; ~s *nfpl* (*AVIAT etc*) controls; **sur** ~ to order; ~ **à distance** remote control

commandement [kɔmɑ̃dmɑ̃] *nm* command; (*REL*) commandment

commander [kɔmɑ̃de] *vt* (*COMM*) to order; (*diriger, ordonner*) to command; ~ **à qn de faire** to command *ou* order sb to do

commando [kɔmɑ̃do] *nm* commando (squad)

MOT-CLÉ

comme [kɔm] *prép* **1** (*comparaison*) like; **tout** ~ **son père** just like his father; **fort** ~ **un bœuf** as strong as an ox; **joli** ~ **tout** ever so pretty
2 (*manière*) like; **faites-le** ~ **ça** do it like this, do it this way; ~ **ci**, ~ **ça** so-so, middling
3 (*en tant que*) as a; **donner** ~ **prix** to give as a prize; **travailler** ~ **secrétaire** to work as a secretary
♦ *conj* **1** (*ainsi que*) as; **elle écrit** ~ **elle parle** she writes as she talks; ~ **si** as if
2 (*au moment où, alors que*) as; **il est parti** ~ **j'arrivais** he left as I

arrived
3 (*parce que, puisque*) as; ~ **il était en retard, il ...** as he was late, he ...
♦ *adv*: ~ **il est fort!/c'est bon!** he's so strong/it's so good!

commémorer [kɔmemɔre] *vt* to commemorate

commencement [kɔmɑ̃smɑ̃] *nm* beginning, start, commencement

commencer [kɔmɑ̃se] *vt, vi* to begin, start, commence; ~ **à** *ou* **de faire** to begin *ou* start doing

comment [kɔmɑ̃] *adv* how ♦ *nm*: **le** ~ **et le pourquoi** the whys and wherefores; ~? (*que dites-vous*) pardon?

commentaire [kɔmɑ̃tɛr] *nm* comment; remark

commenter [kɔmɑ̃te] *vt* (*jugement, événement*) to comment (up)on; (*RADIO, TV*: *match, manifestation*) to cover

commérages [kɔmeraʒ] *nmpl* gossip *sg*

commerçant, e [kɔmɛrsɑ̃, -ɑ̃t] *nm/f* shopkeeper, trader

commerce [kɔmɛrs(ə)] *nm* (*activité*) trade, commerce; (*boutique*) business; **vendu dans le** ~ sold in the shops; **commercial, e, aux** *adj* commercial, trading; (*péj*) commercial; **commercialiser** *vt* to market

commère [kɔmɛr] *nf* gossip

commettre [kɔmɛtr(ə)] *vt* to commit

commis [kɔmi] *nm* (*de magasin*) (shop) assistant; (*de banque*) clerk; ~ **voyageur** commercial traveller

commissaire [kɔmisɛr] *nm* (*de police*) = (police) superintendent; ~-**priseur** *nm* auctioneer

commissariat [kɔmisarja] *nm* police station

commission [kɔmisjɔ̃] *nf* (*comité, pourcentage*) commission; (*message*) message; (*course*) errand; ~s *nfpl* (*achats*) shopping *sg*

commode [kɔmɔd] *adj* (*pratique*) convenient, handy; (*facile*) easy;

(*air, personne*) easy-going; (*personne*): **pas ~** awkward (to deal with) ♦ *nf* chest of drawers; **commodité** *nf* convenience

commotion [kɔmosjɔ̃] *nf*: ~ **(cérébrale)** concussion; **commotionné, e** *adj* shocked, shaken

commun, e [kɔmœ̃, -yn] *adj* common; (*pièce*) communal, shared; (*réunion, effort*) joint; **cela sort du ~** it's out of the ordinary; **le ~ des mortels** the common run of people; **en ~** (*faire*) jointly; **mettre en ~** to pool, share; *voir aussi* **communs**

communauté [kɔmynote] *nf* community; (*JUR*): **régime de la ~** communal estate settlement

commune [kɔmyn] *nf* (*ADMIN*) commune, ≈ district; (: *urbaine*) ≈ borough

communication [kɔmynikɑsjɔ̃] *nf* communication; ~ **(téléphonique)** (telephone) call

communier [kɔmynje] *vi* (*REL*) to receive communion; (*fig*) to be united; **communion** [kɔmynjɔ̃] *nf* communion

communiquer [kɔmynike] *vt* (*nouvelle, dossier*) to pass on, convey; (*maladie*) to pass on; (*peur etc*) to communicate; (*chaleur, mouvement*) to transmit ♦ *vi* to communicate; **se ~ à** (*se propager*) to spread

communisme [kɔmynism(ə)] *nm* communism; **communiste** *adj, nmf* communist

communs [kɔmœ̃] *nmpl* (*bâtiments*) outbuildings

commutateur [kɔmytatœr] *nm* (*ELEC*) (change-over) switch, commutator

compact, e [kɔ̃pakt] *adj* dense, compact

compagne [kɔ̃paɲ] *nf* companion

compagnie [kɔ̃paɲi] *nf* (*firme, MIL*) company; (*groupe*) gathering; **tenir ~ à qn** to keep sb company; **fausser ~ à qn** to give sb the slip, slip *ou* sneak away from sb; ~ **aérienne** airline (company)

compagnon [kɔ̃paɲɔ̃] *nm* companion

comparable [kɔ̃parabl(ə)] *adj*: ~ **(à)** comparable (to)

comparaison [kɔ̃parɛzɔ̃] *nf* comparison

comparaître [kɔ̃parɛtr(ə)] *vi*: ~ **(devant)** to appear (before)

comparer [kɔ̃pare] *vt* to compare; ~ **qch/qn à** *ou* **et** (*pour choisir*) to compare sth/sb with *ou* and; (*pour établir une similitude*) to compare sth/sb to

comparse [kɔ̃pars(ə)] (*péj*) *nmf* associate, stooge

compartiment [kɔ̃partimɑ̃] *nm* compartment

comparution [kɔ̃parysjɔ̃] *nf* appearance

compas [kɔ̃pa] *nm* (*GÉOM*) (pair of) compasses *pl*; (*NAVIG*) compass

compatible [kɔ̃patibl(ə)] *adj* compatible

compatir [kɔ̃patir] *vi*: ~ **(à)** to sympathize (with)

compatriote [kɔ̃patrijɔt] *nmf* compatriot

compenser [kɔ̃pɑ̃se] *vt* to compensate for, make up for

compère [kɔ̃pɛr] *nm* accomplice

compétence [kɔ̃petɑ̃s] *nf* competence

compétent, e [kɔ̃petɑ̃, -ɑ̃t] *adj* (*apte*) competent, capable

compétition [kɔ̃petisjɔ̃] *nf* (*gén*) competition; (*SPORT*): **épreuve** event; **la ~** competitive sport; **la ~ automobile** motor racing

complainte [kɔ̃plɛ̃t] *nf* lament

complaire [kɔ̃plɛr]: **se ~** *vi* to take pleasure in/in being among

complaisance [kɔ̃plɛzɑ̃s] *nf* kindness; **pavillon de ~** flag of convenience; **complaisant, e** [kɔ̃plɛzɑ̃, -ɑ̃t] *adj* (*aimable*) kind, obliging

complément [kɔ̃plemɑ̃] *nm* complement; remainder; ~ **d'information** (*ADMIN*) supplementary *ou* further information; **complémentaire** *adj* complementary; (*additionnel*) supplementary

complet, ète [kɔ̃plɛ, -ɛt] *adj* complete; *(plein: hôtel etc)* full ♦ *nm* *(aussi:* ~*veston)* suit; **complète-ment** *adv* completely; **compléter** *vt (porter à la quantité voulue)* to complete; *(augmenter)* to complement, supplement; to add to

complexe [kɔ̃plɛks(ə)] *adj, nm* complex; **complexé, e** *adj* mixed-up, hung-up

complication [kɔ̃plikasjɔ̃] *nf* complexity, intricacy; *(difficulté, ennui)* complication

complice [kɔ̃plis] *nm* accomplice

compliment [kɔ̃plimɑ̃] *nm* *(louange)* compliment; ~**s** *nmpl* *(fé-licitations)* congratulations

compliqué, e [kɔ̃plike] *adj* complicated, complex; *(personne)* complicated

complot [kɔ̃plo] *nm* plot

comportement [kɔ̃pɔrtəmã] *nm* behaviour

comporter [kɔ̃pɔrte] *vt* to consist of, comprise; *(être équipé de)* to have; *(impliquer)* to entail; **se** ~ *vi* to behave

composant [kɔ̃pozɑ̃] *nm* component

composante [kɔ̃pozɑ̃t] *nf* component

composé [kɔ̃poze] *nm* compound

composer [kɔ̃poze] *vt (musique, texte)* to compose; *(mélange, équipe)* to make up; *(faire partie de)* to make up ♦ *vi (transiger)* to come to terms; **se** ~ **de** to be composed of, be made up of; ~ **un numéro** to dial a number

compositeur, trice [kɔ̃pozitœr, -tris] *nm/f (MUS)* composer

composition [kɔ̃pozisjɔ̃] *nf* composition; *(SCOL)* test; **de bonne** ~ *(accommodant)* easy to deal with

composter [kɔ̃pɔste] *vt* to date-stamp; to punch

compote [kɔ̃pɔt] *nf* stewed fruit *no pl;* ~ **de pommes** stewed apples; **compotier** *nm* fruit dish *ou* bowl

compréhensible [kɔ̃preɑ̃sibl(ə)]

adj comprehensible; *(attitude)* understandable

compréhensif, ive [kɔ̃preɑ̃sif, -iv] *adj* understanding

comprendre [kɔ̃prɑ̃dr(ə)] *vt* to understand; *(se composer de)* to comprise, consist of

compresse [kɔ̃prɛs] *nf* compress

compression [kɔ̃presjɔ̃] *nf* compression; reduction

comprimé [kɔ̃prime] *nm* tablet

comprimer [kɔ̃prime] *vt* to compress; *(fig: crédit etc)* to reduce, cut down

compris, e [kɔ̃pri, -iz] *pp* de **comprendre** ♦ *adj (inclus)* included; ~ **entre** *(situé)* contained between; **la maison** ~**e/non** ~**e, y/ non** ~ **la maison** including/ excluding the house; **100 F tout** ~ 100 F all inclusive *ou* all-in

compromettre [kɔ̃prɔmetr(ə)] *vt* to compromise

compromis [kɔ̃prɔmi] *nm* compromise

comptabilité [kɔ̃tabilite] *nf (activité, technique)* accounting, accountancy; *(d'une société: comptes)* accounts *pl,* books *pl;* (: *service)* accounts office

comptable [kɔ̃tabl(ə)] *nm/f* accountant

comptant [kɔ̃tɑ̃] *adv:* **payer** ~ to pay cash; **acheter** ~ to buy for cash

compte [kɔ̃t] *nm* count, counting; *(total, montant)* count, (right) number; *(bancaire, facture)* account; ~**s** *nmpl (FINANCE)* accounts, books; *(fig)* explanation *sg;* **en fin de** ~ all things considered; **à bon** ~ at a favourable price; *(fig)* lightly; **avoir son** ~ (: *fam)* to have had it; **pour le** ~ **de** on behalf of; **pour son propre** ~ for one's own benefit; **pour le** ~ **de** to take account of; **travailler à son** ~ to work for oneself; **rendre** ~ *(à qn)* **de qch** to give (sb) an account of sth; *voir aussi* **rendre;** ~ **à rebours** countdown; ~ **chèques postaux** Post Office account; ~ **cou-**

rant current account

compte-gouttes [kɔ̃tgut] nm inv dropper

compter [kɔ̃te] vt to count; (facturer) to charge for; (avoir à son actif, comporter) to have; (prévoir) to allow, reckon; (penser, espérer): ~ réussir to expect to succeed ♦ vi to count; (être économe) to economize; (figurer): ~ parmi to be ou rank among; ~ sur to count (up)on; ~ avec qch/qn to reckon with ou take account of sth/sb; sans ~ besides which

compte rendu [kɔ̃t, kɔ̃] nm account, report; (de film, livre) review

compte-tours [kɔ̃ttur] nm inv rev(olution) counter

compteur [kɔ̃tœr] nm meter; ~ de vitesse speedometer

comptine [kɔ̃tin] nf nursery rhyme

comptoir [kɔ̃twar] nm (de magasin) counter

compulser [kɔ̃pylse] vt to consult

comte [kɔ̃t] nm count

comtesse [kɔ̃tɛs] nf countess

con, ne [kɔ̃, kɔn] (fam!) adj damned ou bloody (BRIT) stupid (!)

concéder [kɔ̃sede] vt to grant; (défaite, point) to concede

concentrer [kɔ̃sɑ̃tre] vt to concentrate; se ~ vi to concentrate

concept [kɔ̃sɛpt] nm concept

conception [kɔ̃sɛpsjɔ̃] nf conception; (d'une machine etc) design

concerner [kɔ̃sɛrne] vt to concern; en ce qui me concerne as far as I am concerned

concert [kɔ̃sɛr] nm concert; de ~ in unison; together

concerter [kɔ̃sɛrte] vt to devise; se ~ vi (collaborateurs etc) to put our (ou their etc) heads together

concessionnaire [kɔ̃sesjɔnɛr] nm/f agent, dealer

concevoir [kɔ̃səvwar] vt (idée, projet) to conceive (of); (méthode, plan d'appartement, décoration) to plan, design; (enfant) to conceive; bien/mal conçu well-/badly-designed

concierge [kɔ̃sjɛrʒ(ə)] nm/f caretaker; (d'hôtel) head porter

concile [kɔ̃sil] nm council

conciliabules [kɔ̃siljabyl] nmpl (private) discussions, confabulations

concilier [kɔ̃silje] vt to reconcile; se ~ vt to win over

concitoyen, ne [kɔ̃sitwajɛ̃, -jɛn] nm/f fellow citizen

concluant, e [kɔ̃klyɑ̃, -ɑ̃t] adj conclusive

conclure [kɔ̃klyr] vt to conclude

conclusion [kɔ̃klyzjɔ̃] nf conclusion

concois etc vb voir **concevoir**

concombre [kɔ̃kɔ̃br(ə)] nm cucumber

concorder [kɔ̃kɔrde] vi to tally, agree

concourir [kɔ̃kurir] vi (SPORT) to compete; ~ à (effet etc) to work towards

concours [kɔ̃kur] nm competition; (SCOL) competitive examination; (assistance) aid, help; ~ de circonstances combination of circumstances; ~ hippique horse show

concret, ète [kɔ̃krɛ, -ɛt] adj concrete

concrétiser [kɔ̃kretize] vt (plan, projet) to put in concrete form; se ~ vi to materialize

conçu, e [kɔ̃sy] pp de **concevoir**

concubinage [kɔ̃kybinaʒ] nm (JUR) cohabitation

concurrence [kɔ̃kyrɑ̃s] nf competition; jusqu'à ~ de up to

concurrent, e [kɔ̃kyrɑ̃, -ɑ̃t] nm/f (SPORT, ECON etc) competitor; (SCOL) candidate

condamner [kɔ̃dane] vt (blâmer) to condemn; (JUR) to sentence; (porte, ouverture) to fill in, block up; (malade) to give up (hope for); ~ qn à 2 ans de prison to sentence sb to 2 years' imprisonment

condensation [kɔ̃dɑ̃sasjɔ̃] nf condensation

condenser [kɔ̃dɑ̃se] vt to condense; se ~ vi to condense

condisciple [kɔ̃disipl(ə)] nm/f school

fellow, fellow student

condition [kɔ̃disjɔ̃] nf condition; ~s nfpl (tarif, prix) terms; (circonstances) conditions; **sans** ~ unconditional ♦ adv unconditionally; **à** ~ **de ou que** provided that; **conditionnel, le** adj conditional ♦ nm conditional (tense)

conditionnement [kɔ̃disjɔnmã] nm (emballage) packaging

conditionner [kɔ̃disjɔne] vt (déterminer) to determine; (COMM: produit) to package; (fig: personne) to condition; **air conditionné** air conditioning

condoléances [kɔ̃dɔleɑ̃s] nfpl condolences

conducteur, trice [kɔ̃dyktœʀ, -tʀis] nm/f driver ♦ nm (ELEC etc) conductor

conduire [kɔ̃dɥiʀ] vt to drive; (délégation, troupeau) to lead; **se** ~ vi to behave; ~ **vers/à** to lead towards/to; ~ **qn quelque part** to take sb somewhere; **to drive sb somewhere**

conduite [kɔ̃dɥit] nf (comportement) behaviour; (d'eau, de gaz) pipe; **sous la** ~ **de** led by; ~ **à gauche** left-hand drive; ~ **intérieure** saloon (car)

cône [kon] nm cone

confection [kɔ̃fɛksjɔ̃] nf (fabrication) making; (COUTURE): **la** ~ **the** clothing industry; **vêtement de** ~ ready-to-wear ou off-the-peg garment

confectionner [kɔ̃fɛksjɔne] vt to make

conférence [kɔ̃feʀɑ̃s] nf (exposé) lecture; (pourparlers) conference; ~ **de presse** press conference

confesser [kɔ̃fese] vt to confess; **se** ~ vi (REL) to go to confession

confession [kɔ̃fesjɔ̃] nf confession; (culte: catholique etc) denomination

confiance [kɔ̃fjɑ̃s] nf confidence, trust; faith; **avoir** ~ **en** to have confidence ou faith in, trust; **mettre qn en** ~ to win sb's trust; ~ **en soi** self-confidence

confiant, e [kɔ̃fjɑ̃, -ɑ̃t] adj confident; trusting

confidence [kɔ̃fidɑ̃s] nf confidence

confidentiel, le [kɔ̃fidɑ̃sjɛl] adj confidential

confier [kɔ̃fje] vt: ~ **à qn** (objet en dépôt, travail etc) to entrust to sb; (secret, pensée) to confide to sb; **se** ~ **à qn** to confide in sb

confiné, e [kɔ̃fine] adj enclosed; stale

confins [kɔ̃fɛ̃] nmpl: **aux** ~ **de** on the borders of

confirmation [kɔ̃fiʀmasjɔ̃] nf confirmation

confirmer [kɔ̃fiʀme] vt to confirm

confiserie [kɔ̃fizʀi] nf (magasin) confectioner's ou sweet shop; ~s (bonbons) confectionery sg; **confiseur, euse** nm/f confectioner

confisquer [kɔ̃fiske] vt to confiscate

confit, e [kɔ̃fi, -it] adj: **fruits** ~s crystallized fruits ♦ nm: ~ **d'oie** conserve of goose

confiture [kɔ̃fityʀ] nf jam; ~ **d'oranges** (orange) marmalade

conflit [kɔ̃fli] nm conflict

confondre [kɔ̃fɔ̃dʀ(ə)] vt (jumeaux, faits) to confuse, mix up; (témoin, menteur) to confound; **se** ~ vi to merge; **se** ~ **en excuses** to apologize profusely; **confondu, e** [kɔ̃fɔ̃dy] adj (stupéfait) speechless, overcome

conforme [kɔ̃fɔʀm(ə)] adj: ~ **à** in accordance with; in keeping with; true to

conformément [kɔ̃fɔʀmemã] adv: ~ **à** in accordance with

conformer [kɔ̃fɔʀme] vt: **se** ~ **à** to conform to

conformité [kɔ̃fɔʀmite] nf: **en** ~ **avec** in accordance with, in keeping with

confort [kɔ̃fɔʀ] nm comfort; **tout** ~ (COMM) with all modern conveniences; **confortable** adj comfortable

confrère [kɔ̃fʀɛʀ] nm colleague; fellow member; **confrérie** nf brotherhood

confronter [kɔ̃fʀɔ̃te] vt to confront; (textes) to compare, collate

confus, e [kɔ̃fy, -yz] *adj* (*vague*) confused; (*embarrassé*) embarrassed
confusion [kɔ̃fyzjɔ̃] *nf* (*voir confus*) confusion; embarrassment; (*voir confondre*) confusion, mixing up
congé [kɔ̃ʒe] *nm* (*vacances*) holiday; **en** ~ on holiday; off (work); **semaine de** ~ week off; **prendre son** ~ à to give in one's notice to; ~ **de maladie** sick leave; ~**s payés** paid holiday
congédier [kɔ̃ʒedje] *vt* to dismiss
congélateur [kɔ̃ʒelatœʀ] *nm* freezer, deep freeze
congeler [kɔ̃ʒle] *vt* to freeze
congestion [kɔ̃ʒɛstjɔ̃] *nf* congestion; ~ **cérébrale** stroke
congestionner [kɔ̃ʒɛstjɔne] *vt* to congest; (*MED*) to flush
congrès [kɔ̃gʀɛ] *nm* congress
congru, e [kɔ̃gʀy] *adj*: **la portion** ~**e** the smallest *ou* meanest share
conifère [kɔnifɛʀ] *nm* conifer
conjecture [kɔ̃ʒɛktyʀ] *nf* conjecture
conjoint, e [kɔ̃ʒwɛ̃, -wɛ̃t] *adj* joint ♦ *nm/f* spouse
conjonction [kɔ̃ʒɔ̃ksjɔ̃] *nf* (*LING*) conjunction
conjonctivite [kɔ̃ʒɔ̃ktivit] *nf* conjunctivitis
conjoncture [kɔ̃ʒɔ̃ktyʀ] *nf* circumstances *pl*; climate
conjugaison [kɔ̃ʒygɛzɔ̃] *nf* (*LING*) conjugation
conjuguer [kɔ̃ʒyge] *vt* (*LING*) to conjugate; (*efforts etc*) to combine
conjuration [kɔ̃ʒyʀasjɔ̃] *nf* conspiracy
conjurer [kɔ̃ʒyʀe] *vt* (*sort, maladie*) to avert; (*implorer*) to beseech, entreat
connaissance [kɔnɛsɑ̃s] *nf* (*savoir*) knowledge *no pl*; (*personne connue*) acquaintance; **être sans** ~ to be unconscious; **perdre/reprendre** ~ to lose/regain consciousness; **à ma/sa** ~ to (the best of) my/his knowledge; **avoir** ~ **de** to be aware of; **prendre** ~ **de** (*document etc*) to peruse; **en**

~ **de cause** with full knowledge of the facts
connaître [kɔnɛtʀ(ə)] *vt* to know; (*éprouver*) to experience; (*avoir*) to have; to enjoy; ~ **de nom/vue** to know by name/sight; **ils se sont connus à Genève** they (first) met in Geneva
connecté, e [kɔnɛkte] *adj* on line
connecter [kɔnɛkte] *vt* to connect
connerie [kɔnʀi] (*fam!*) *nf* stupid thing (to do *ou* say)
connu, e [kɔny] *adj* (*célèbre*) well-known
conquérir [kɔ̃keʀiʀ] *vt* to conquer, win; **conquête** *nf* conquest
consacrer [kɔ̃sakʀe] *vt* (*REL*) to consecrate; (*fig: usage etc*) to sanction, establish; (*employer*) to devote, dedicate
conscience [kɔ̃sjɑ̃s] *nf* conscience; **avoir/prendre** ~ **de** to be/become aware of; **perdre** ~ to lose consciousness; **avoir bonne/mauvaise** ~ to have a clear/guilty conscience; **consciencieux, euse** *adj* conscientious; **conscient, e** *adj* conscious
conscrit [kɔ̃skʀi] *nm* conscript
consécutif, -ive [kɔ̃sekytif, -iv] *adj* consecutive; ~ **à** following upon
conseil [kɔ̃sɛj] *nm* (*avis*) piece of advice, advice *no pl*; (*assemblée*) council; **prendre** ~ (**auprès de qn**) to take advice (from sb); ~ **d'administration** board (of directors); **le** ~ **des ministres** the Cabinet
conseiller, ère [kɔ̃seje, kɔ̃sejɛʀ] *nm/f* adviser ♦ *vt* (*personne*) to advise; (*méthode, action*) to recommend, advise; ~ **à qn de** to advise sb to
consentement [kɔ̃sɑ̃tmɑ̃] *nm* consent
consentir [kɔ̃sɑ̃tiʀ] *vt* to agree, consent
conséquence [kɔ̃sekɑ̃s] *nf* consequence; **en** ~ (*donc*) consequently; (*de façon appropriée*) accordingly; **ne pas tirer à** ~ to be unlikely to have any repercussions

conséquent, e [kɔ̃sekɑ̃, -ɑ̃t] *adj* logical, rational; (*fam: important*) substantial; **par ~** consequently

conservateur, trice [kɔ̃sɛʀvatœʀ, -tʀis] *nm/f* (*POL*) conservative; (*de musée*) curator

conservatoire [kɔ̃sɛʀvatwaʀ] *nm* academy; (*ECOLOGIE*) conservation area

conserve [kɔ̃sɛʀv] *nf* (*gén pl*) canned *ou* tinned (*BRIT*) food; **en ~** canned, tinned (*BRIT*)

conserver [kɔ̃sɛʀve] *vt* (*faculté*) to retain, keep; (*amis, livres*) to keep; (*préserver, aussi CULIN*) to preserve

considérable [kɔ̃sideʀabl(ə)] *adj* considerable, significant, extensive

considération [kɔ̃sideʀɑsjɔ̃] *nf* consideration; (*estime*) esteem

considérer [kɔ̃sideʀe] *vt* to consider; **~ qch comme** to regard sth as

consigne [kɔ̃siɲ] *nf* (*de gare*) left luggage (office) (*BRIT*), checkroom (*US*); (*ordre, instruction*) instructions *pl*; **~ (automatique)** left-luggage locker; **~r** [kɔ̃siɲe] *vt* (*note, pensée*) to record; (*punir*) to confine to barracks; to put in detention; (*COMM*) to put a deposit on

consistant, e [kɔ̃sistɑ̃, -ɑ̃t] *adj* thick; solid

consister [kɔ̃siste] *vi*: **~ en/dans/à faire** to consist of/in/in doing

consœur [kɔ̃sœʀ] *nf* (*lady*) colleague; fellow member

consoler [kɔ̃sɔle] *vt* to console

consolider [kɔ̃sɔlide] *vt* to strengthen; (*fig*) to consolidate

consommateur, trice [kɔ̃sɔmatœʀ, -tʀis] *nm/f* (*ECON*) consumer; (*dans un café*) customer

consommation [kɔ̃sɔmɑsjɔ̃] *nf* (*boisson*) drink; **~ aux 100 km** (*AUTO*) (fuel) consumption per 100 km

consommer [kɔ̃sɔme] *vt* (*suj: personne*) to eat *ou* drink, consume; (: *voiture, usine, poêle*) to use, consume ♦ *vi* (*dans un café*) to (have) a drink

consonne [kɔ̃sɔn] *nf* consonant

conspirer [kɔ̃spiʀe] *vi* to conspire

constamment [kɔ̃stamɑ̃] *adv* constantly

constant, e [kɔ̃stɑ̃, -ɑ̃t] *adj* constant; (*personne*) steadfast

constat [kɔ̃sta] *nm* (*d'huissier*) certified report; (*de police*) report; (*affirmation*) statement

constatation [kɔ̃statɑsjɔ̃] *nf* (*observation*) (observed) fact, observation; (*affirmation*) statement

constater [kɔ̃state] *vt* (*remarquer*) to note; (*ADMIN, JUR: attester*) to certify; (*dire*) to state

consterner [kɔ̃stɛʀne] *vt* to dismay

constipé, e [kɔ̃stipe] *adj* constipated

constitué, e [kɔ̃stitɥe] *adj*: **~ de** made up *ou* composed of

constituer [kɔ̃stitɥe] *vt* (*comité, équipe*) to set up; (*dossier, collection*) to put together; (*suj: éléments: composer*) to make up, constitute; (*représenter, être*) to constitute; **se ~ prisonnier** to give o.s. up

constitution [kɔ̃stitysjɔ̃] *nf* (*composition*) composition, make-up; (*santé, POL*) constitution

constructeur [kɔ̃stʀyktœʀ] *nm* manufacturer, builder

construction [kɔ̃stʀyksjɔ̃] *nf* construction, building

construire [kɔ̃stʀɥiʀ] *vt* to build, construct

consul [kɔ̃syl] *nm* consul; **consulat** *nm* consulate

consultation [kɔ̃syltɑsjɔ̃] *nf* consultation; **~s** *nfpl* (*POL*) talks; **heures de ~** (*MED*) surgery (*BRIT*) *ou* office (*US*) hours

consulter [kɔ̃sylte] *vt* to consult ♦ *vi* (*médecin*) to hold surgery (*BRIT*), be in (the office) (*US*)

consumer [kɔ̃syme] *vt* to consume; **se ~** *vi* to burn

contact [kɔ̃takt] *nm* contact; **au ~ de** (*air, peau*) on contact with; (*gens*) through contact with; **mettre/couper le ~** (*AUTO*) to switch on/off the ignition; **entrer en**

ou **prendre** ~ **avec** to get in touch
ou contact with; **contacter** vt to contact, get in touch with

contagieux, euse [kɔ̃taʒjø, -øz] adj
contagious; infectious

contaminer [kɔ̃tamine] vt to
contaminate

conte [kɔ̃t] nm tale; ~ **de fées** fairy
tale

contempler [kɔ̃tɑ̃ple] vt to contemplate, gaze at

contemporain, e [kɔ̃tɑ̃pɔRɛ̃, -ɛn]
adj, nm/f contemporary

contenance [kɔ̃tnɑ̃s] nf (d'un récipient) capacity; (attitude) bearing,
attitude; **perdre** ~ to lose one's composure

conteneur [kɔ̃tnœR] nm container

contenir [kɔ̃tniR] vt to contain;
(avoir une capacité de) to hold

content, e [kɔ̃tɑ̃, -ɑ̃t] adj pleased,
glad; ~ **de** pleased with; **contenter**
vt to satisfy, please; **se ~er de** to
content o.s. with

contentieux [kɔ̃tɑ̃sjø] nm (COMM)
litigation; litigation department

contenu [kɔ̃tny] nm (d'un bol) contents pl; (d'un texte) content

conter [kɔ̃te] vt to recount, relate

contestable [kɔ̃tɛstabl(ə)] adj questionable

contestation [kɔ̃tɛstɑsjɔ̃] nf (POL)
protest

conteste [kɔ̃tɛst(ə)]: **sans** ~ adv
unquestionably, indisputably

contester [kɔ̃tɛste] vt to question,
contest ♦ vi (POL, gén) to protest,
rebel (against established authority)

contexte [kɔ̃tɛkst(ə)] nm context

contigu, ë [kɔ̃tigy] adj: ~ **(à)** ad-
jacent (to)

continent [kɔ̃tinɑ̃] nm continent

continu, e [kɔ̃tiny] adj continuous;
(courant) ~ direct current, DC

continuel, le [kɔ̃tinɥɛl] adj (qui se
répète) constant, continual; (continuous

continuer [kɔ̃tinɥe] vt (travail, voyage etc) to continue (with), carry on
(with), go on (with); (prolonger)

alignement, rue) to continue ♦ vi
(pluie, vie, bruit) to continue, go on;
(voyageur) to go on; ~ **à** ou **de faire** to go on ou continue doing

contorsionner [kɔ̃tɔRsjɔne]: **se** ~
vi to contort o.s., writhe about

contour [kɔ̃tuR] nm outline, contour

contourner [kɔ̃tuRne] vt to go round

contraceptif, ive [kɔ̃tRasɛptif, -iv]
adj, nm contraceptive; **contraception** [kɔ̃tRasɛpsjɔ̃] nf contraception

contracté, e [kɔ̃tRakte] adj tense

contracter [kɔ̃tRakte] vt (muscle
etc) to tense, contract; (maladie,
dette, obligation) to contract; (assurance) to take out; **se** ~ vi (métal,
muscles) to contract

contractuel, le [kɔ̃tRaktɥɛl] nm/f
(agent) traffic warden

contradiction [kɔ̃tRadiksjɔ̃] nf contradiction; **contradictoire** adj contra-
dictory, conflicting

contraignant, e [kɔ̃tRɛɲɑ̃, ɑ̃t] adj
restricting

contraindre [kɔ̃tRɛ̃dR(ə)] vt: ~ **qn à
faire** to compel sb to do; **contraint, e** [kɔ̃tRɛ̃,
-ɛ̃t] adj (mine, air) constrained,
forced; **contrainte** nf constraint

contraire [kɔ̃tRɛR] adj, nm opposite;
~ **à** contrary to; **au** ~ on the contrary

contrarier [kɔ̃tRaRje] vt (personne)
to annoy, bother; (fig) to impede; to
thwart, frustrate; **contrariété**
[kɔ̃tRaRjete] nf annoyance

contraste [kɔ̃tRast(ə)] nm contrast

contrat [kɔ̃tRa] nm contract; ~ **de
travail** employment contract

contravention [kɔ̃tRavɑ̃sjɔ̃] nf
(amende) fine; (P.-V. pour stationnement interdit) parking ticket

contre [kɔ̃tR(ə)] prép against; (en
échange) in exchange) for; **par** ~
on the other hand

contrebande [kɔ̃tRəbɑ̃d] nf (trafic)
contraband, smuggling; (marchandise) contraband, smuggled goods pl;
faire la ~ **de** to smuggle

contrebas [kɔ̃tRəba]: **en** ~ adv
(down) below

contrebasse [kɔ̃trəbas] nf (double) bass

contre: ~**carrer** vt to thwart; ~**cœur:** à ~**cœur** adv (be-)grudgingly, reluctantly; ~**coup** nm repercussions pl; par ~**coup** as an indirect consequence; ~**dire** vt (personne) to contradict; (témoignage, assertion, faits) to refute

contrée [kɔ̃tre] nf region; land

contrefaçon [kɔ̃trəfasɔ̃] nf forgery

contrefaire [kɔ̃trəfɛr] vt (document, signature) to forge, counterfeit; (personne, démarche) to mimic; (dénaturer: sa voix etc) to disguise

contre-indication (pl contre-indications) nf (MED) contra-indication

contre-jour [kɔ̃trəʒur]: à ~ adv against the sunlight

contremaître [kɔ̃trəmɛtr(ə)] nm foreman

contrepartie [kɔ̃trəparti] nf compensation; en ~ in return

contre-pied [kɔ̃trəpje] nm: prendre le ~ de to take the opposing view of; to take the opposite course to

contre-plaqué [kɔ̃trəplake] nm plywood

contrepoids [kɔ̃trəpwa] nm counterweight, counterbalance

contrer [kɔ̃tre] vt to counter

contresens [kɔ̃trəsɑ̃s] nm misinterpretation; mistranslation; nonsense no pl; à ~ the wrong way

contretemps [kɔ̃trətɑ̃] nm hitch; à ~ (MUS) out of time; (fig) at an inopportune moment

contrevenir [kɔ̃trəvnir]: ~ à vt to contravene

contribuable [kɔ̃tribyabl(ə)] nm/f taxpayer

contribuer [kɔ̃tribɥe]: ~ à vt to contribute towards; **contribution** nf contribution; **contributions directes/indirectes** direct/indirect taxation; **mettre à contribution** to call upon

contrôle [kɔ̃trol] nm checking no pl, check; supervision; monitoring;

(test) test, examination; **perdre le ~ de** (véhicule) to lose control of; ~ **continu** (SCOL) continuous assessment; ~ **d'identité** identity check; **des naissances** birth control

contrôler [kɔ̃trole] vt (vérifier) to check; (surveiller) to supervise; to monitor, control; (maîtriser, COMM: firme) to control; **contrôleur, euse** nm/f (de train) (ticket) inspector; (de bus) conductor(tress)

contrordre [kɔ̃trɔrdr(ə)] nm: **sauf** ~ unless otherwise directed

controversé, e [kɔ̃trɔvɛrse] adj (personnage, question) controversial

contusion [kɔ̃tyzjɔ̃] nf bruise, contusion

convaincre [kɔ̃vɛ̃kr(ə)] vt: ~ **qn (de qch)** to convince sb (of sth); ~ **qn** (de faire) to persuade sb to; ~ **qn de** (JUR: délit) to convict sb of

convalescence [kɔ̃valesɑ̃s] nf convalescence

convenable [kɔ̃vnabl(ə)] adj suitable; (assez bon, respectable) decent

convenance [kɔ̃vnɑ̃s] nf: à ma/votre ~ to my/your liking; ~**s** nfpl (normes sociales) proprieties

convenir [kɔ̃vnir] vi to be suitable; ~ **à** to suit; **il convient de** it is advisable to; (bienséant) it is right ou proper to; ~ **de** (bien-fondé de qch) to admit (to), acknowledge; (date, somme etc) to agree upon; ~ **que** (admettre) to admit that; ~ **de faire** to agree to do

convention [kɔ̃vɑ̃sjɔ̃] nf convention; ~**s** nfpl (convenances) convention sg; ~ **collective** (ECON) collective agreement; **conventionné, e** adj (ADMIN) applying charges laid down by the state

convenu, e [kɔ̃vny] pp de **convenir** ♦ adj agreed

conversation [kɔ̃vɛrsasjɔ̃] nf conversation

convertir [kɔ̃vɛrtir] vt: ~ **qn (à)** to convert sb (to); **se** ~ **(à)** to be converted (to); ~ **qch en** to convert sth into

conviction [kɔ̃viksjɔ̃] nf conviction

convienne etc vb voir convenir

convier [kɔ̃vje] vt: ~ qn à (dîner etc) to (cordially) invite sb to

convive [kɔ̃viv] nm/f guest (at table)

convivial, e [kɔ̃vivjal] adj (IN-FORM) user-friendly

convocation [kɔ̃vɔkasjɔ̃] nf (document) notification to attend; summons sg

convoi [kɔ̃vwa] nm (de voitures, prisonniers) convoy; (train) train

convoiter [kɔ̃vwate] vt to covet

convoquer [kɔ̃vɔke] vt (assemblée) to convene; (subordonné) to summon; (candidat) to ask to attend; ~ qn (à) (réunion) to invite sb to (attend)

convoyeur [kɔ̃vwajœR] nm (NAVIG) escort ship; ~ de fonds security guard

coopération [kɔɔpeRasjɔ̃] nf cooperation; (ADMIN): la C~ ≈ Voluntary Service Overseas (BRIT), ≈ Peace Corps (US)

coopérer [kɔɔpeRe] vi: ~ (à) to cooperate (in)

coordonner [kɔɔRdɔne] vt to coordinate

copain [kɔpɛ̃] nm mate, pal

copeau, x [kɔpo] nm shaving

copie [kɔpi] nf copy; (SCOL) script, paper; exercise

copier [kɔpje] vt, vi to copy; ~ sur to copy from

copieur [kɔpjœR] nm (photo)copier

copieux, euse [kɔpjø, -øz] adj copious

copine [kɔpin] nf = copain

copropriété [kɔpRɔpRijete] nf coownership, joint ownership

coq [kɔk] nm cock, rooster; ~-à-l'âne [kɔkalɑn] nm inv abrupt change of subject

coque [kɔk] nf (de noix, mollusque) shell; (de bateau) hull; à la ~ (CULIN) (soft-)boiled

coquelicot [kɔkliko] nm poppy

coqueluche [kɔklyʃ] nf whooping-cough

coquet, te [kɔkɛ, -ɛt] adj flirtatious; appearance-conscious; pretty

coquetier [kɔktje] nm egg-cup

coquillage [kɔkijaʒ] nm (mollusque) shellfish inv; (coquille) shell

coquille [kɔkij] nf shell; (TYPO) misprint; ~ St Jacques scallop

coquin, e [kɔkɛ̃, -in] adj mischievous, roguish; (polisson) naughty

cor [kɔR] nm (MUS) horn; (MÉD): ~ (au pied) corn; réclamer à ~ et à cri to clamour for

corail, aux [kɔRaj, -o] nm coral no pl

Coran [kɔRɑ̃] nm: le ~ the Koran

corbeau, x [kɔRbo] nm crow

corbeille [kɔRbɛj] nf basket; ~ à papier waste paper basket ou bin

corbillard [kɔRbijaR] nm hearse

corde [kɔRd] nf rope; (de violon, raquette, d'arc) string; (ATH-LÉTISME, AUTO): la ~ the rails pl; usé jusqu'à la ~ threadbare; ~ à linge washing ou clothes line; ~ à sauter skipping rope; ~s vocales vocal cords; **cordée** [kɔRde] nf (d'alpinistes) rope, roped party

cordial, e, aux [kɔRdjal] adj (formule épistolaire) (kind) regards

cordon [kɔRdɔ̃] nm cord, string; ~ ombilical umbilical cord; ~ sanitaire/de police sanitary/police cordon

cordonnerie [kɔRdɔnRi] nf shoe repairer's (shop); **cordonnier** [kɔRdɔnje] nm shoe repairer

coriace [kɔRjas] adj tough

corne [kɔRn(ə)] nf horn; (de cerf) antler

corneille [kɔRnɛj] nf crow

cornemuse [kɔRnəmyz] nf bagpipes pl

cornet [kɔRnɛ] nm (paper) cone; (de glace) cornet, cone

corniche [kɔRniʃ] nf (de meuble, neigeuse) cornice; (route) coast road

cornichon [kɔRniʃɔ̃] nm gherkin

Cornouailles [kɔRnwaj] nf Cornwall

corporation [kɔRpɔRasjɔ̃] nf corporate body

corporel, le [kɔrpɔrɛl] *adj* bodily; (*punition*) corporal

corps [kɔr] *nm* body; **à son ~ défendant** against one's will; **à ~ perdu** headlong; **perdu ~ et biens** lost with all hands; **prendre ~** to take shape; **~ à ~** *adv* hand-to-hand ♦ *nm* clinch; **~ de garde** guardroom; **le ~ électoral** the electorate; **le ~ enseignant** the teaching profession

corpulent, e [kɔrpylɑ̃, -ɑ̃t] *adj* stout

correct, e [kɔrɛkt] *adj* correct; (*passable*) adequate

correction [kɔrɛksjɔ̃] *nf* (*voir corriger*) correction; (*voir correct*) correctness; (*rature, surcharge*) correction, emendation; (*coups*) thrashing

correctionnel, le [kɔrɛksjɔnɛl] *adj* (*JUR*): **tribunal ~** ≈ criminal court

correspondance [kɔrɛspɔ̃dɑ̃s] *nf* correspondence; (*de train, d'avion*) connection; **cours par ~** correspondence course; **vente par ~** mailorder business

correspondant, e [kɔrɛspɔ̃dɑ̃, -ɑ̃t] *nm/f* correspondent; (*TEL*) person phoning (*ou* being phoned)

correspondre [kɔrɛspɔ̃dr(ə)] *vi* to correspond, tally; **~ à** to correspond to; **~ avec qn** to correspond with sb

corrida [kɔrida] *nf* bullfight

corridor [kɔridɔr] *nm* corridor

corriger [kɔriʒe] *vt* (*devoir*) to correct; (*punir*) to thrash; **~ qn de** (*défaut*) to cure sb of

corrompre [kɔrɔ̃pr(ə)] *vt* to corrupt; (*acheter: témoin etc*) to bribe

corruption [kɔrypsjɔ̃] *nf* corruption; bribery

corsage [kɔrsaʒ] *nm* bodice; blouse

corse [kɔrs(ə)] *adj, nm/f* Corsican ♦ *nf*: **la C~** Corsica

corsé, e [kɔrse] *adj* vigorous; (*vin, goût*) full-flavoured; (*fig*) spicy; tricky

corset [kɔrsɛ] *nm* corset; bodice

cortège [kɔrtɛʒ] *nm* procession

corvée [kɔrve] *nf* chore, drudgery *no pl*

cosmétique [kɔsmetik] *nm* beauty care product

cossu, e [kɔsy] *adj* well-to-do

costaud, e [kɔsto, -od] *adj* strong, sturdy

costume [kɔstym] *nm* (*d'homme*) suit; (*de théâtre*) costume; **costumé, e** *adj* dressed up

cote [kɔt] *nf* (*en Bourse etc*) quotation; quoted value; (*d'un cheval*): **la ~** the odds *pl* on; (*d'un candidat etc*) rating; (*sur un croquis*) dimension; **~ d'alerte** danger *ou* flood level.

côte [kot] *nf* (*rivage*) coast(line); (*pente*) slope; (: *sur une route*) hill; (*ANAT*) rib; (*d'un tricot, tissu*) rib, ribbing *no pl*; **~ à ~** side by side; **la C~** (**d'Azur**) the (French) Riviera

côté [kote] *nm* (*gén*) side; (*direction*) way, direction; **de chaque ~** (**de**) on each side (of); **de tous les ~s** from all directions; **de quel ~ est-il parti?** which way did he go?; **de ce/de l'autre ~** this/the other way; **du ~ de** (*provenance*) from; (*direction*) towards; (*proximité*) near; **de ~** sideways; on one side; to one side; aside; **laisser/mettre de ~** to leave/put to one side; **à ~** (*right*) nearby; beside; next door; (*d'autre part*) besides; **à ~ de** beside; next to (this); **être aux ~s de** to be by the side of

coteau, x [kɔto] *nm* hill

côtelette [kotlɛt] *nf* chop

coter [kɔte] *vt* (*en Bourse*) to quote

côtier, ière [kotje, -jɛr] *adj* coastal

cotisation [kɔtizɔsjɔ̃] *nf* subscription, dues *pl*; (*pour une pension*) contributions *pl*

cotiser [kɔtize] *vi*: (**à**) to pay contributions (to); **se ~** *vi* to club together

coton [kɔtɔ̃] *nm* cotton; **~ hydrophile** cotton wool (*BRIT*), absorbent cotton (*US*)

côtoyer [kotwaje] *vt* to be close to; to rub shoulders with; to run alongside

cou [ku] nm neck

couchant [kuʃɑ̃] adj: **soleil** ~ setting sun

couche [kuʃ] nf (strate: gén, GÉO) layer; (de peinture, vernis) coat; (de bébé) nappy (BRIT), diaper (US); ~s nfpl (MÉD) confinement sg; ~ **d'ozone** ozone layer; ~s **sociales** social levels ou strata

couché, e [kuʃe] adj lying down; (au lit) in bed

couche-culotte [kuʃkylɔt] nf disposable nappy (BRIT) ou diaper (US) and waterproof pants in one

coucher [kuʃe] nm (du soleil) setting ♦ vt (personne) to put to bed; (: loger) to put up; (objet) to put on its side ♦ vi to sleep; se ~ vi (pour dormir) to go to bed; (pour se reposer) to lie down; (soleil) to set; ~ **de soleil** sunset

couchette [kuʃɛt] nf couchette; (de marin) bunk

coucou [kuku] nm cuckoo

coude [kud] nm (ANAT) elbow; (de tuyau, de la route) bend; ~ **à** ~ shoulder to shoulder, side by side

coudre [kudʀ(ə)] vt (bouton) to sew on; (robe) to sew (up) ♦ vi to sew

couenne [kwan] nf (de lard) rind

couette [kwɛt] nf duvet, quilt; ~s nfpl (cheveux) bunches

couffin [kufɛ̃] nm Moses basket

couler [kule] vi to flow, run; (fuir: stylo, récipient) to leak; (sombrer: bateau) to sink ♦ vt (cloche, sculpture) to cast; (bateau) to sink; (fig) to ruin, bring down

couleur [kulœʀ] nf colour (BRIT), color (US); (CARTES) suit; **film/télévision en** ~s colo(u)r film/television

couleuvre [kulœvʀ(ə)] nf grass snake

coulisse [kulis] nf: ~s nfpl (THÉÂTRE) wings; (fig): **dans les** ~s behind the scenes; **coulisser** vi to slide, run

couloir [kulwaʀ] nm corridor, passage; (de bus) gangway; (sur la route) bus lane; (SPORT: de piste) lane; (GÉO) gully; ~ **aérien/de navigation** air/shipping lane

coup [ku] nm (heurt, choc) knock; (affectif) blow, shock; (agressif) blow; (avec arme à feu) shot; (de l'horloge) chime; stroke; (SPORT) stroke; shot; blow; (fam: fois) time; ~ **de coude** nudge (with the elbow); ~ **de tonnerre** clap of thunder; ~ **de sonnette** ring of the bell; ~ **de crayon** stroke of the pencil; **donner un** ~ **de balai** to give the floor a sweep; **avoir le** ~ (fig) to have the knack; **boire un** ~ to have a drink; **être dans le** ~ to be in on it; **du** ~ ... so (you see) ...; **d'un seul** ~ (subitement) suddenly; (à la fois) at one go; in one blow; **du premier** ~ first time; **du même** ~ at the same time; **à** ~ **sûr** definitely, without fail; ~ **sur** ~ in quick succession; **sur le** ~ outright; **sous le** ~ **de** (surprise etc) under the influence of; ~ **de chance** stroke of luck; ~ **de couteau** stab (of a knife); ~ **d'envoi** kick-off; ~ **d'essai** first attempt; ~ **de feu** shot; ~ **de filet** (POLICE) haul; ~ **de frein** (sharp) braking no pl; ~ **de main**: **donner un** ~ **de main** à qn to give sb a (helping) hand; ~ **d'œil** glance; ~ **de pied** kick; ~ **de poing** punch; ~ **de soleil** sunburn no pl; ~ **de téléphone** phone call; ~ **de tête** (fig) (sudden) impulse; ~ **de théâtre** (fig) dramatic turn of events; ~ **de vent** gust of wind; **en coup de vent** in a tearing hurry; ~ **franc** free kick

coupable [kupabl] adj guilty ♦ nm/f (gén) culprit; (JUR) guilty party

coupe [kup] nf (verre) goblet; (à fruits) dish; (SPORT) cup; (de cheveux, de vêtement) cut; (graphique, plan) (cross) section; **être sous la** ~ **de** to be under the control of

coupe-papier [kuppapje] nm inv paper knife

couper [kupe] vt to cut; (retrancher)

to cut (out); (*route, courant*) to cut
off; (*appétit*) to take away; (*vin,
cidre*) to blend; (: *à table*) to dilute
♦ *vi* to cut; (*prendre* un *raccourci*)
to take a short-cut; se ~ *vi* (*se blesser*) to cut o.s.; ~ **la parole à qn** to
cut sb short

couple [kupl(ə)] *nm* couple

couplet [kuplɛ] *nm* verse

coupole [kupɔl] *nf* dome; cupola

coupon [kupɔ̃] *nm* (*ticket*) coupon;
(*de tissu*) remnant; roll; ~**-réponse**
nm reply coupon

coupure [kupyʀ] *nf* cut; (*billet de
banque*) note; (*de journal*) cutting;
~ **de courant** power cut

cour [kuʀ] *nf* (*de ferme, jardin*)
(court)yard; (*d'immeuble*) back
yard; (*JUR, royale*) court; faire la
~ **à qn** to court sb; ~ **d'assises**
court of assizes; ~ **martiale** court-
martial

courage [kuʀaʒ] *nm* courage, bravery; **courageux, euse** *adj* brave,
courageous

couramment [kuʀamɑ̃] *adv* com-
monly; (*parler*) fluently

courant, e [kuʀɑ̃, -ɑ̃t] *adj* (*fréquent*) common; (*COMM, gén: normal*) standard; (*en cours*) current
♦ *nm* current; (*fig*) movement; trend;
être au ~ (**de**) (*fait, nouvelle*) to
know (about); **mettre qn au** ~ (**de**)
(*nouveau travail etc*) to tell sb (about);
(*nouveau travail
etc*) to teach sb the basics (of); se
tenir au ~ (**de**) (*techniques etc*) to
keep o.s. up-to-date (on); **dans le**
~ (*pendant*) in the course of; **le 10**
~ (*COMM*) the 10th inst.; ~ **d'air**
draught; ~ **électrique** (electric)
current, power

courbature [kuʀbatyʀ] *nf* ache

courbe [kuʀb(ə)] *adj* curved ♦ *nf*
curve; ~**r** [kuʀbe] *vt* to bend

coureur, euse [kuʀœʀ, -øz] *nm/f*
(*SPORT*) runner (*ou* driver); (*péj*)
womanizer; manhunter; ~ **automobile** racing driver

courge [kuʀʒ(ə)] *nf* (*CULIN*) marrow; **courgette** [kuʀʒɛt] *nf* courgette

(*BRIT*), zucchini (*US*)

courir [kuʀiʀ] *vi* to run ♦ *vt*
(*SPORT: épreuve*) to compete in;
(*risque*) to run; (*danger*) to face; ~
les magasins to go round the shops;
le bruit court que the rumour is
going round that

couronne [kuʀɔn] *nf* crown; (*de
fleurs*) wreath, circlet

courons *etc vb voir* **courir**

courrier [kuʀje] *nm* mail, post;
(*lettres à écrire*) letters *pl*; avion
long/moyen ~ long-/medium-haul
plane

courroie [kuʀwa] *nf* strap; (*TECH*)
belt

courrons *etc vb voir* **courir**

cours [kuʀ] *nm* (*leçon*) lesson; class;
(*série de leçons, cheminement*)
course; (*écoulement*) flow; (*COMM*)
rate; price; **donner libre** ~ **à** to
give free expression to; **avoir** ~
(*monnaie*) to be legal tender; (*fig*) to
be current; (*SCOL*) to have a class
ou lecture; **en** ~ (*année*) current;
(*travaux*) in progress; **en** ~ **de route** on the way; **au** ~ **de** in the
course of, during; ~ **d'eau** water-
way; ~ **du soir** night school

course [kuʀs(ə)] *nf* running;
(*SPORT: épreuve*) race; (*d'un taxi,
autocar*) journey, trip; (*petite mission*) errand; ~**s** *nfpl* (*achats*) shopping *sg*; **faire des** ~**s** to do some
shopping

court, e [kuʀ, kuʀt(ə)] *adj* short
♦ *adv* short ♦ *nm*: ~ (**de tennis**) (tennis) court; **tourner** ~ to come to a
sudden end; **ça fait** ~ that's not
enough; **à** ~ **de** short of; **prendre
qn de** ~ to catch sb unawares; **tirer
à la** ~**e paille** to draw lots; ~**-
circuit** *nm* short-circuit

courtier, ère [kuʀtje, -jɛʀ] *nm/f* broker

courtiser [kuʀtize] *vt* to court, woo

courtois, e [kuʀtwa, -waz] *adj* courteous

couru, e [kuʀy] *pp de* **courir** ♦ *adj*:
c'est ~ it's a safe bet

cousais *etc* vb voir **coudre**

couscous [kuskus] nm couscous

cousin, e [kuzɛ̃, -in] nm/f cousin

coussin [kusɛ̃] nm cushion

cousu, e [kuzy] pp de **coudre**

coût [ku] nm cost; **le ~ de la vie** the cost of living

coûtant [kutã] adj m: **au prix ~** at cost price

couteau, x [kuto] nm knife; **~ à cran d'arrêt** flick-knife

coûter [kute] vt, vi to cost; **combien ça coûte?** how much is it?, what does it cost?; **coûte que coûte** at all costs; **coûteux, euse** adj costly, expensive

coutume [kutym] nf custom

couture [kutyʀ] nf sewing; dressmaking; (*points*) seam; **couturier** [kutyʀje] nm fashion designer; **couturière** [kutyʀjɛʀ] nf dressmaker

couvée [kuve] nf brood, clutch

couvent [kuvã] nm (*de sœurs*) convent; (*de frères*) monastery

couver [kuve] vt to hatch; (*maladie*) to be sickening for ♦ vi (*feu*) to smoulder; (*révolte*) to be brewing

couvercle [kuvɛʀkl(ə)] nm lid; (*de bombe aérosol etc, qui se visse*) cap, top

couvert, e [kuvɛʀ, -ɛʀt(ə)] pp de **couvrir** ♦ adj (*ciel*) overcast ♦ nm place setting; (*place à table*) place; (*au restaurant*) cover charge; **~s** nmpl (*ustensiles*) cutlery sg; **~ de** covered with ou in; **mettre le ~** to lay the table

couverture [kuvɛʀtyʀ] nf blanket; (*de bâtiment*) roofing; (*de livre, assurance, fig*) cover; (*presse*) coverage; **~ chauffante** electric blanket

couveuse [kuvøz] nf (*de maternité*) incubator

couvre-feu nm curfew

couvre-lit nm bedspread

couvrir [kuvʀiʀ] vt to cover; **se ~** vi (*ciel*) to cloud over; (*s'habiller*) to cover up; (*se coiffer*) to put on one's hat

crabe [kʀab] nm crab

cracher [kʀaʃe] vi, vt to spit

crachin [kʀaʃɛ̃] nm drizzle

craie [kʀɛ] nf chalk

craindre [kʀɛ̃dʀ(ə)] vt to fear, be afraid of; (*être sensible à: chaleur, froid*) to be easily damaged by

crainte [kʀɛ̃t] nf fear; **de ~ de/que** for fear of/that; **craintif, ive** adj timid

cramoisi, e [kʀamwazi] adj crimson

crampe [kʀãp] nf cramp

cramponner [kʀãpɔne] : **se ~** vi to hang ou cling on (to)

cran [kʀã] nm (*entaille*) notch; (*de courroie*) hole; (*courage*) guts pl; **~ d'arrêt** safety catch

crâne [kʀan] nm skull

crâner [kʀane] (*fam*) vi to show off

crapaud [kʀapo] nm toad

crapule [kʀapyl] nf villain

craquement [kʀakmã] nm crack, snap; (*du plancher*) creak, creaking no pl

craquer [kʀake] vi (*bois, plancher*) to creak; (*fil, branche*) to snap; (*couture*) to come apart; (*fig*) to break down ♦ vt (*allumette*) to strike

crasse [kʀas] nf grime, filth

cravache [kʀavaʃ] nf (*riding*) crop

cravate [kʀavat] nf tie

crawl [kʀol] nm crawl; **dos ~é** back-stroke

crayeux, euse [kʀɛjø, -øz] adj chalky

crayon [kʀɛjɔ̃] nm pencil; **~ à bille** ball-point pen; **~ de couleur** crayon, colouring pencil; **~ optique** light pen; **crayon-feutre** [kʀɛjɔ̃føtʀ(ə)] nm felt(-tip) pen

créancier, ière [kʀeãsje, -jɛʀ] nm/f creditor

création [kʀeasjɔ̃] nf creation

créature [kʀeatyʀ] nf creature

crèche [kʀɛʃ] nf (*de Noël*) crib; (*garderie*) crèche, day nursery

crédit [kʀedi] nm (*gén*) credit; **~s** nmpl (*fonds*) funds; **payer/acheter à ~** to pay/buy on credit ou on easy terms; **faire ~ à qn** to give sb credit; **créditer** vt: **créditer un compte**

(de) to credit an account (with)

crédule [kʀedyl] adj credulous, gullible

créer [kʀee] vt to create; (THÉÂTRE) to produce (for the first time)

crémaillère [kʀemajɛʀ] nf (RAIL) rack; **pendre la ~** to have a house-warming party

crématoire [kʀematwaʀ] adj: **four ~** crematorium

crème [kʀɛm] nf cream; (entremets) cream dessert ♦ adj inv cream (-coloured); **un (café) ~** a white coffee; (US) **~ à raser** shaving cream; **~ chantilly** whipped cream; **~ fouettée** = crème chantilly; **crémerie** nf dairy; **crémeux, euse** adj creamy

créneau, x [kʀeno] nm (de fortification) crenel(le); (fig) gap, slot; (AUTO): **faire un ~** to reverse into a parking space (alongside the kerb)

crêpe [kʀɛp] nf (galette) pancake ♦ nm (tissu) crepe; **crêpé, e** adj (cheveux) backcombed; **crêperie** nf pancake shop ou restaurant

crépir [kʀepiʀ] vt to roughcast

crépiter [kʀepite] vi to sputter, splutter; to crackle

crépu, e [kʀepy] adj frizzy, fuzzy

crépuscule [kʀepyskyl] nm twilight, dusk

cresson [kʀesɔ̃] nm watercress

crête [kʀɛt] nf (de coq) comb; (de vague, montagne) crest

creuser [kʀøze] vt (trou, tunnel) to dig; (sol) to dig a hole in; (bois) to hollow out; (fig) to go (deeply) into; **ça creuse** that gives you a real appetite; **se ~ (la cervelle)** to rack one's brains

creux, euse [kʀø, -øz] adj hollow ♦ nm hollow; (fig: sur graphique etc) trough; **heures creuses** slack periods; off-peak periods

crevaison [kʀəvɛzɔ̃] nf puncture

crevasse [kʀəvas] nf (dans le sol) crack, fissure; (de glacier) crevasse

crevé, e [kʀəve] adj (fam) (fatigué) all in, exhausted

crever [kʀəve] vt (papier) to tear, break; (tambour, ballon) to burst ♦ vi (pneu) to burst; (automobiliste) to have a puncture (BRIT) ou a flat (tire); (fam) to die; **cela lui a crevé un œil** it blinded him in one eye

crevette [kʀəvɛt] nf: **~ (rose)** prawn; **~ grise** shrimp

cri [kʀi] nm cry, shout; (d'animal: spécifique) cry, call; **c'est le dernier ~** (fig) it's the latest fashion

criant, e [kʀijɑ̃, -ɑ̃t] adj (injustice) glaring

criard, e [kʀijaʀ, -aʀd(ə)] adj (couleur) garish, loud; (voix) yelling

crible [kʀibl(ə)] nm riddle; **passer qch au ~** (fig) to go over sth with a fine-tooth comb

criblé, e [kʀible] adj: **~ de** riddled with; (de dettes) crippled with

cric [kʀik] nm (AUTO) jack

crier [kʀije] vi (pour appeler) to shout, cry (out); (de peur, de douleur etc) to scream, yell ♦ vt (ordre, injure) to shout (out), yell (out)

crime [kʀim] nm crime; (meurtre) murder; **criminel, le** nm/f criminal; murderer

crin [kʀɛ̃] nm hair no pl; (fibre) horsehair; **~ière** [kʀinjɛʀ] nf mane

crique [kʀik] nf creek, inlet

criquet [kʀikɛ] nm locust; grasshopper

crise [kʀiz] nf crisis; (MÉD) attack; fit; **~ cardiaque** heart attack; **~ de foie** bilious attack; **~ de nerfs** attack of nerves

crisper [kʀispe] vt to tense; (poings) to clench; **se ~** vi to tense; to clench; (personne) to get tense

crisser [kʀise] vi (neige) to crunch; (pneu) to screech

cristal, aux [kʀistal, -o] nm crystal; **~lin, e** adj crystal-clear

critère [kʀitɛʀ] nm criterion

critiquable [kʀitikabl(ə)] adj open to criticism

critique [kʀitik] adj critical ♦ nm/f (de théâtre, musique) critic ♦ nf criticism; (*THÉÂTRE etc: article*) review; ~r [kʀitike] *vt* (*dénigrer*) to criticize; (*évaluer, juger*) to assess, examine (critically)

croasser [kʀɔase] *vi* to caw

Croatie [kʀɔsl] *nf* Croatia

croc [kʀo] *nm* (*dent*) fang; (*de boucher*) hook

croc-en-jambe [kʀɔkɑ̃ʒɑ̃b] *nm*: faire un ~ à qn to trip sb up

croche [kʀɔʃ] *nf* (*MUS*) quaver (*BRIT*), eighth note (*US*); ~-pied [kʀɔʃpje] *nm* = croc-en-jambe

crochet [kʀɔʃe] *nm* (*détour*) detour; (*TRICOT: aiguille*) crochet hook; (: *technique*) crochet; **vivre aux ~s de qn** to live ou sponge off sb; **crocheter** *vt* (*serrure*) to pick

crochu, e [kʀɔʃy] *adj* hooked; clawlike

crocodile [kʀɔkɔdil] *nm* crocodile

crocus [kʀɔkys] *nm* crocus

croire [kʀwaʀ] *vt* to believe; **se ~ fort** to think one is strong; ~ **que** to believe ou think that; ~ **à**, ~ **en** to believe in

crois *vb voir* **croître**

croisade [kʀwazad] *nf* crusade

croisé, e [kʀwaze] *adj* (*veston*) double-breasted

croisement [kʀwazmɑ̃] *nm* (*carrefour*) crossroads *sg*; (*BIO*) crossing; crossbreed

croiser [kʀwaze] *vt* (*personne, voiture*) to pass; (*route*) to cross, cut across; (*BIO*) to cross ♦ *vi* (*NAVIG*) to cruise; **se ~** *vi* (*personnes, véhicules*) to pass each other; (*routes, lettres*) to cross; (*regards*) to meet; ~ **les jambes/bras** to cross one's legs/fold one's arms

croiseur [kʀwazœʀ] *nm* cruiser (*warship*)

croisière [kʀwazjɛʀ] *nf* cruise; **vitesse de ~** (*AUTO etc*) cruising speed

croissance [kʀwasɑ̃s] *nf* growth

croissant [kʀwasɑ̃] *nm* (*à manger*) croissant; (*motif*) crescent

croître [kʀwatʀ(ə)] *vi* to grow

croix [kʀwa] *nf* cross; **en ~** in the

form of a cross; **la C~ Rouge** the Red Cross

croque-monsieur [kʀɔkməsjø] *nm inv* toasted ham and cheese sandwich

croquer [kʀɔke] *vt* (*manger*) to crunch; to munch; (*dessiner*) to sketch ♦ *vi* to be crisp ou crunchy; **chocolat à ~** plain dessert chocolate

croquis [kʀɔki] *nm* sketch

crosse [kʀɔs] *nf* (*de fusil*) butt; (*de revolver*) grip

crotte [kʀɔt] *nf* droppings *pl*

crotté, e [kʀɔte] *adj* muddy, mucky

crottin [kʀɔtɛ̃] *nm* dung, manure

crouler [kʀule] *vi* (*s'effondrer*) to collapse; (*être délabré*) to be crumbling

croupe [kʀup] *nf* rump; **en ~** pillion

croupir [kʀupiʀ] *vi* to stagnate

croustillant, e [kʀustijɑ̃, -ɑ̃t] *adj* crisp; (*fig*) spicy

croûte [kʀut] *nf* crust; (*du fromage*) rind; (*MÉD*) scab; **en ~** (*CULIN*) in pastry

croûton [kʀutɔ̃] *nm* (*CULIN*) crouton; (*bout du pain*) crust, heel

croyable [kʀwajabl(ə)] *adj* credible

croyant, e [kʀwajɑ̃, -ɑ̃t] *nm/f* believer

C.R.S. *sigle fpl* (= *Compagnies républicaines de sécurité*) state security police force ♦ *sigle m* member of the C.R.S.

cru, e [kʀy] *pp de* **croire** ♦ *adj* (*non cuit*) raw; (*lumière, couleur*) harsh; (*paroles, description*) crude ♦ *nm* (*vignoble*) vineyard; (*vin*) wine

crû *pp de* **croître**

cruauté [kʀyote] *nf* cruelty

cruche [kʀyʃ] *nf* pitcher, jug

crucifix [kʀysifi] *nm* crucifix

crucifixion [kʀysifiksjɔ̃] *nf* crucifixion

crudités [kʀydite] *nfpl* (*CULIN*) salads

cruel, le [kʀyɛl] *adj* cruel

crus *etc vb voir* **croire**; **croître**

crûs *etc vb voir* **croître**

crustacés [kʀystase] *nmpl* shellfish

Cuba [kyba] *nf* Cuba

cube [kyb] *nm* cube; (*jouet*) brick;

mètre ~ cubic metre; **2 au ~ 2** cubed

cueillette [kœjɛt] nf picking; *(quantité)* crop, harvest

cueillir [kœjiʀ] vt *(fruits, fleurs)* to pick, gather; *(fig)* to catch

cuiller [kɥijɛʀ] nf spoon; ~ **à café** coffee spoon; *(CULIN)* ≈ teaspoonful; ~ **à soupe** soup-spoon; *(CULIN)* ≈ tablespoonful

cuillère [kɥijɛʀ] nf = **cuiller**

cuillerée [kɥijʀe] nf spoonful

cuir [kɥiʀ] nm leather; ~ **chevelu** scalp

cuire [kɥiʀ] vt *(aliments)* to cook; *(au four)* to bake; *(poterie)* to fire ♦ vi to cook; *(viande)* well done; **trop cuit** overdone

cuisant, e [kɥizɑ̃, -ɑ̃t] adj *(douleur)* stinging; *(fig: souvenir, échec)* bitter

cuisine [kɥizin] nf *(pièce)* kitchen; *(art culinaire)* cookery, cooking; *(nourriture)* cooking, food; **faire la ~** to cook

cuisiné, e [kɥizine] adj: **plat ~** ready-made meal or dish; **cuisiner** vt to cook; *(fam)* to grill ♦ vi to cook; **cuisinier, ière** nm/f cook; **cuisinière** nf *(poêle)* cooker

cuisse [kɥis] nf thigh; *(CULIN)* leg

cuisson [kɥisɔ̃] nf cooking; firing

cuit, e pp de **cuire**

cuivre [kɥivʀ(ə)] nm copper; **les ~s** *(MUS)* the brass

cul [ky] *(fam!)* nm arse (!)

culasse [kylas] nf *(AUTO)* cylinder-head; *(de fusil)* breech

culbute [kylbyt] nf somersault; *(accidentelle)* tumble, fall

culminant, e [kylminɑ̃, -ɑ̃t] adj: **point ~** highest point

culminer [kylmine] vi to reach its highest point; to tower

culot [kylo] nm *(effronterie)* cheek

culotte [kylɔt] nf *(de femme)* knickers pl *(BRIT)*, panties pl *(US)*; ~ **de cheval** riding breeches pl

culpabilité [kylpabilite] nf guilt

culte [kylt(ə)] nm *(religion)* religion; *(hommage, vénération)* worship; *(protestant)* service

cultivateur, trice [kyltivatœʀ, -tʀis] nm/f farmer

cultivé, e [kyltive] adj *(personne)* cultured, cultivated

cultiver [kyltive] vt to cultivate; *(légumes)* to grow, cultivate

culture [kyltyʀ] nf cultivation; growing; *(connaissances etc)* culture; ~ **physique** physical training; **culturisme** nm body-building

cumin [kymɛ̃] nm cumin; *(carvi)* caraway seeds pl

cumuler [kymyle] vt *(emplois, honneurs)* to hold concurrently; *(salaires)* to draw concurrently; *(JUR: droits)* to accumulate

cupide [kypid] adj greedy, grasping

cure [kyʀ] nf *(MED)* course of treatment; **n'avoir ~ de** to pay no attention to

curé [kyʀe] nm parish priest

cure-dent [kyʀdɑ̃] nm toothpick

cure-pipe [kyʀpip] nm pipe cleaner

curer [kyʀe] vt to clean out

curieux, euse [kyʀjø, -øz] adj *(étrange)* strange, curious; *(indiscret)* curious, inquisitive ♦ nmpl *(badauds)* onlookers; **curiosité** nf curiosity; *(site)* unusual feature

curriculum vitae [kyʀikylɔmvite] nm inv curriculum vitae

curseur [kyʀsœʀ] nm *(INFORM)* cursor

cuti-réaction [kytiʀeaksjɔ̃] nf *(MED)* skin-test

cuve [kyv] nf vat; *(à mazout etc)* tank; **cuvée** [kyve] nf vintage

cuvette [kyvɛt] nf *(récipient)* bowl, basin; *(GEO)* basin

C.V. sigle m *(AUTO)* = **cheval vapeur**; *(COMM)* = **curriculum vitae**

cyanure [sjanyʀ] nm cyanide

cyclable [siklablə] adj: **piste ~** cycle track

cycle [siklə] nm cycle

cyclisme [siklismə] nm cycling

cycliste [siklist(ə)] nm/f cyclist ♦ adj cycle cpd: **coureur ~** racing cyclist

cyclomoteur [siklɔmɔtœʀ] nm

moped

cyclone [siklon] nm hurricane

cygne [sip] nm swan

cylindre [silɛ̃dr(ə)] nm cylinder; **cylindrée** nf (AUTO) (cubic) capacity

cymbale [sɛ̃bal] nf cymbal

cynique [sinik] adj cynical

cystite [sistit] nf cystitis

D

d' [d] prép voir de

dactylo [daktilo] nf (aussi: ~graphe) typist; (: ~graphie) typing; **~graphier** vt to type (out)

dada [dada] nm hobby-horse

daigner [dɛɲe] vt to deign

daim [dɛ̃] nm (fallow) deer inv; (peau) buckskin; (imitation) suede

dalle [dal] nf paving stone; slab

daltonien, ne [daltɔnjɛ̃, -jɛn] adj colour-blind

dam [dam] nm: **au grand ~ de** much to the detriment (ou annoyance) of

dame [dam] nf lady; (CARTES, ECHECS) queen; **~s** nfpl (jeu) draughts sg (BRIT), checkers sg (US)

damner [dɑne] vt to damn

dancing [dɑ̃siŋ] nm dance hall

Danemark [danmark] nm Denmark

danger [dɑ̃ʒe] nm danger; **dangereux, euse** [dɑ̃ʒʀø, -øz] adj dangerous

danois, e [danwa, -waz] adj Danish ♦ nm/f: **D~, e** Dane ♦ nm (LING) Danish

dans [dɑ̃] prép 1 (position) in; (à l'intérieur de) inside; **c'est ~ le tiroir/le salon** it's in the drawer/lounge; **~ la boîte** in ou inside the box; **marcher ~ la ville** to walk about the town

2 (direction) into; **elle a couru ~ le salon** she ran into the lounge

3 (provenance) out of, from; **je l'ai**

pris ~ **le tiroir/salon** I took it out of ou from the drawer/lounge; **boire un verre ~** to drink out of ou from a glass

4 (temps) in; **~ 2 mois** in 2 months, in 2 months' time

5 (approximation) about; **~ les 20F** about 20F

danse [dɑ̃s] nf: **la ~** dancing; **une ~** a dance; **danser** vi, vt to dance; **danseur, euse** nm/f ballet dancer; (au bal etc) dancer; partner

dard [dar] nm sting (organ)

date [dat] nf date; **de longue ~** longstanding; **~ de naissance** date of birth; **~ limite** deadline; **dater** vt, vi to date; **dater de** to date from; **à dater de** (as) from

datte [dat] nf date; **dattier** nm date palm

dauphin [dofɛ̃] nm (ZOOL) dolphin

davantage [davɑ̃taʒ] adv more; (plus longtemps) longer; **~ de** more

de(d') (de +le = du, de +les = des) prép 1 (appartenance) of; **le toit ~ la maison** the roof of the house; **la voiture d'Elisabeth/~ mes parents** Elizabeth's/my parents' car

2 (provenance) from; **il vient ~ Londres** he comes from London; **elle est sortie du cinéma** she came out of the cinema

3 (caractérisation, mesure): **un mur ~ brique/bureau d'acajou** a brick wall/mahogany desk; **un billet ~ 50F** a 50F note; **une pièce ~ 2m ~ large** ou **large ~ 2m** a room 2m wide, a 2m-wide room; **un bébé ~ 10 mois** a 10-month-old baby; **12 mois ~ crédit/travail** 12 months' credit/work; **augmenter ~ 10F** to increase by 10F; **14 à 18 from 14 to 18

♦ dét 1 (phrases affirmatives) some (souvent omis); **du vin, ~ l'eau, des pommes** (some) wine, (some) water, (some) apples; **des enfants** sont venus some children came; **pendant des mois** for months **2** (phrases interrogatives et négatives) any; **a-t-il du vin?** has he got any wine?; **il n'a pas ~ pommes/ d'enfants** he hasn't (got) any apples/children, he has no apples/ children

dé [de] nm (à jouer) die ou dice; (aussi: **~ à coudre**) thimble

déambuler [deãbyle] vi to stroll about

débâcle [debɑkl(ə)] nf rout

déballer [debale] vt to unpack

débandade [debãdad] nf rout; scattering

débarbouiller [debaʀbuje] vt to wash; **se ~** vi to wash (one's face)

débarcadère [debaʀkadɛʀ] nm wharf

débardeur [debaʀdœʀ] nm (maillot) tank top

débarquer [debaʀke] vt to unload, land ♦ vi to disembark; (fig) to turn up

débarras [debaʀɑ] nm lumber room; junk cupboard; **bon ~!** good riddance!

débarrasser [debaʀɑse] vt to clear; **se ~ de** vt to get rid of; **~ qn de** (vêtements, paquets) to relieve sb of

débat [deba] nm discussion, debate

débattre [debatʀ(ə)] vt to discuss, debate; **se ~** vi to struggle

débaucher [deboʃe] vt (licencier) to lay off, dismiss; (entraîner) to lead astray, debauch

débile [debil] adj weak, feeble; (fam: idiot) dim-witted

débit [debi] nm (d'un liquide, fleuve) flow; (d'un magasin) turnover of goods; (élocution) delivery; (bancaire) debit; **~ de boissons** drinking establishment; **~ de tabac** tobacconist's; **~er** vt (compte) to debit; (liquide, gaz) to give out; (couper: bois, viande) to cut up; (péj: paroles etc) to churn out; **~eur, trice** nm/f debtor ♦ adj in debit; (compte) debit

cpd

déblayer [debleje] vt to clear

débloquer [debloke] vt (frein) to release; (prix, crédits) to free

déboires [debwaʀ] nmpl setbacks

déboiser [debwaze] vt to deforest

déboîter [debwate] vt (AUTO) to pull out; **se ~ le genou** etc to dislocate one's knee etc

débonnaire [debonɛʀ] adj easygoing, good-natured

débordé, e [debɔʀde] adj: **être ~ (de)** (travail, demandes) to be snowed under (with)

déborder [debɔʀde] vi to overflow; (lait etc) to boil over; **~ (de) qch** (dépasser) to extend beyond sth

débouché [debuʃe] nm (pour vendre) outlet; (perspective d'emploi) opening

déboucher [debuʃe] vt (évier, tuyau etc) to unblock; (bouteille) to uncork ♦ vi: **~ de** to emerge from; **~ sur** to come out onto; to open out onto

débourser [debuʀse] vt to pay out

debout [dəbu] adv: **être ~** (personne) to be standing, stand; (: levé, éveillé) to be up; (chose) to be upright; **être encore ~** (fig: en état) to be still going; **se mettre ~** to stand up; **se tenir ~** to stand; **~!** stand up!; (du lit) get up!; **cette histoire ne tient pas ~** this story doesn't hold water

déboutonner [debutɔne] vt to undo, unbutton

débraillé, e [debʀɑje] adj slovenly, untidy

débrancher [debʀɑʃe] vt to disconnect; (appareil électrique) to unplug

débrayage [debʀejaʒ] nm (AUTO) clutch; **débrayer** [debʀeje] vi (AUTO) to declutch; (cesser le travail) to stop work

débris [debʀi] nm (fragment) fragment ♦ nmpl (déchets) debris sg; debris sg

débrouillard, e [debʀujaʀ, -aʀd] adj smart, resourceful

débrouiller [debʀuje] vt to disentangle, untangle; **se ~** vi to manage

débusquer [debyske] *vt* to drive out (from cover)

début [deby] *nm* beginning, start; **~s** *nmpl* (*dans la vie*) beginnings; (*de carrière*) début *sg*

débutant, e [debytã, -ãt] *nm/f* beginner, novice

débuter [debyte] *vi* to begin, start; (*faire ses débuts*) to start out

deçà [dəsa] : **en ~ de** *prép* this side of

décacheter [dekaʃte] *vt* to unseal

décadence [dekadãs] *nf* decadence; decline

décaféiné, e [dekafeine] *adj* decaffeinated

décalage [dekala3] *nm* gap; discrepancy; **~ horaire** time difference (*between time zones*); time-lag

décaler [dekale] *vt* (*dans le temps: avancer*) to bring forward; (: *retarder*) to put back; (*changer de position*) to shift forward *ou* back

décalquer [dekalke] *vt* to trace; (*par pression*) to transfer

décamper [dekãpe] *vi* to clear out *ou* off

décaper [dekape] *vt* to strip; (*avec abrasif*) to scour; (*avec papier de verre*) to sand

décapiter [dekapite] *vt* to behead; (*par accident*) to decapitate

décapotable [dekapɔtabl(ə)] *adj* convertible

décapsuler [dekapsyle] *vt* to take the cap *ou* top off; **décapsuleur** *nm* bottle-opener

décédé, e [desede] *adj* deceased

décéder [desede] *vi* to die

déceler [desle] *vt* to discover, detect; to indicate, reveal

décembre [desãbr(ə)] *nm* December

décemment [desamã] *adv* decently

décennie [deseni] *nf* decade

décent, e [desã, -ãt] *adj* decent

déception [desɛpsjɔ̃] *nf* disappointment

décerner [desɛrne] *vt* to award

décès [desɛ] *nm* death, decease

décevoir [desvwar] *vt* to disappoint

déchaîner [deʃene] *vt* to unleash, arouse; **se ~** to be unleashed

déchanter [deʃãte] *vi* to become disillusioned

décharge [deʃar3(ə)] *nf* (*dépôt d'ordures*) rubbish tip *ou* dump; (*électrique*) electrical discharge; **à la ~ de** in defence of

décharger [deʃar3e] *vt* (*marchandise, véhicule*) to unload; (ELEC, *faire feu*) to discharge; **~ qn de** (*responsabilité*) to release sb from

décharné, e [deʃarne] *adj* emaciated

déchausser [deʃose] *vt* (*skis*) to take off; **se ~** *vi* to take off one's shoes; (*dent*) to come *ou* work loose

déchéance [deʃeãs] *nf* degeneration; decay, decline; fall

déchet [deʃɛ] *nm* (*de bois, tissu etc*) scrap; (*perte*: *gén* COMM) waste, wastage; **~s** *nmpl* (*ordures*) refuse *sg*, rubbish *sg*

déchiffrer [deʃifre] *vt* to decipher

déchiqueter [deʃikte] *vt* to tear *ou* pull to pieces

déchirant, e [deʃirã, -ãt] *adj* heartrending

déchirement [deʃirmã] *nm* (*chagrin*) wrench, heartbreak; (*gén pl*: *conflit*) rift, split

déchirer [deʃire] *vt* to tear; (*en morceaux*) to tear up; (*pour ouvrir*) to tear off; (*arracher*) to tear out; (*fig*) to rack; to tear (*apart*); **se ~** *vi* to tear, rip; **se ~ un muscle** to tear a muscle

déchirure [deʃiryr] *nf* (*accroc*) tear, rip; **~ musculaire** torn muscle

déchoir [deʃwar] *vi* (*personne*) to lower o.s., demean o.s.

déchu, e [deʃy] *adj* fallen; deposed

décidé, e [deside] *adj* (*personne, air*) determined; **c'est ~** it's decided

décidément [desidemã] *adv* undoubtedly; really

décider [deside] *vt*: **~ qch** to decide on sth; **se ~** (**à faire**) to decide (to do), make up one's mind (to do); **se ~ pour** to decide for *ou* in favour of;

~ **de faire/que** to decide to do/that;
~ **qn (à faire qch)** to persuade sb
(to do sth); ~ **de qch** to decide upon
sth; (*suj: chose*) to determine sth

décilitre [desilitʀ(ə)] *nm* decilitre

décimal, e, aux [desimal, -o] *adj*
decimal; **décimale** *nf* decimal

décimètre [desimɛtʀ(ə)] *nm* decimetre; **double** ~ (20 cm) ruler

décisif, ive [desizif, -iv] *adj* decisive

décision [desizjɔ̃] *nf* decision; (*fermeté*) decisiveness, decision

déclaration [deklaʀasjɔ̃] *nf* declaration; registration; (*discours: POL etc*) statement; (*d'impôts*) ≈ tax return; ~ **(de sinistre)** (insurance) claim

déclarer [deklaʀe] *vt* to declare; (*décès, naissance*) to register; se ~ *vi* (*feu, maladie*) to break out

déclasser [deklase] *vt* to relegate; to downgrade; to lower in status

déclencher [deklɑ̃ʃe] *vt* (*mécanisme etc*) to release; (*sonnerie*) to set off, activate; (*attaque, grève*) to launch; (*provoquer*) to trigger off; se ~ *vi* to release itself; to go off

déclic [deklik] *nm* trigger mechanism; (*bruit*) click

décliner [dekline] *vi* to decline ♦ *vt* (*invitation*) to decline; (*responsabilité*) to refuse to accept; (*nom, adresse*) to state

déclivité [deklivite] *nf* slope, incline

décocher [dekɔʃe] *vt* to throw; to shoot

décoiffer [dekwafe] *vi*: se ~ to take off one's hat

déçois *etc vb voir* **décevoir**

décollage [dekɔlaʒ] *nm* (*AVIAT*) takeoff

décoller [dekɔle] *vt* to unstick ♦ *vi* (*avion*) to take off; se ~ *vi* to come unstuck

décolleté, e [dekɔlte] *adj* low-cut; wearing a low-cut dress ♦ *nm* low neck(line); (*bare*) neck and shoulders; (*plongeant*) cleavage

décolorer [dekɔlɔʀe] *vt* (*tissu*) to fade; (*cheveux*) to bleach, lighten;

se ~ *vi* to fade

décombres [dekɔ̃bʀ(ə)] *nmpl* rubble *sg*, debris *sg*

décommander [dekɔmɑ̃de] *vt* to cancel; (*invités*) to put off; se ~ *vi* to cancel one's appointment *etc*, cry off

décomposé, e (*pourri*) decomposed; (*visage*) haggard, distorted

décompte [dekɔ̃t] *nm* deduction; (*facture*) detailed account

déconcerter [dekɔ̃sɛʀte] *vt* to disconcert, confound

déconfit, e [dekɔ̃fi, -it] *adj* crestfallen; **~ure** [dekɔ̃fityʀ] *nf* failure, defeat; collapse, ruin

décongeler [dekɔ̃ʒle] *vt* to thaw

déconner [dekɔne] *vi* (*fam*) to talk rubbish

déconseiller [dekɔ̃seje] *vt*: ~ **qch (à qn)** to advise (sb) against sth

déconsidérer [dekɔ̃sideʀe] *vt* to discredit

décontracté, e [dekɔ̃tʀakte] *adj* relaxed, laid-back (*fam*)

décontracter [dekɔ̃tʀakte] *vt* to relax; se ~ *vi* to relax

déconvenue [dekɔ̃vny] *nf* disappointment

décor [dekɔʀ] *nm* décor; (*paysage*) scenery; **~s** *nmpl* (*THEATRE*) scenery *sg*, décor *sg*; (*CINEMA*) set *sg*; **~ateur** [dekɔʀatœʀ] *nm* (*interior*) set designer; (*CINEMA*) set designer; **~ation** [dekɔʀasjɔ̃] *nf* decoration; **~er** [dekɔʀe] *vt* to decorate

décortiquer [dekɔʀtike] *vt* to shell; (*riz*) to hull; (*fig*) to dissect

découcher [dekuʃe] *vi* to spend the night away from home

découdre [dekudʀ(ə)] *vt* to unpick; se ~ *vi* to come unstitched; **en ~** (*fig*) to fight, do battle

découler [dekule] *vi*: ~ **de** to ensue *ou* follow from

découper [dekupe] *vt* (*papier, tissu etc*) to cut up; (*volaille, viande*) to carve; (*détacher: manche, article*) to cut out; se ~ **sur** (*ciel, fond*) to stand out against

décourager [dekuraʒe] vt to discourage; **se** ~ vi to lose heart, become discouraged

décousu, e [dekuzy] adj unstitched; (fig) disjointed, disconnected

découvert, e [dekuvɛʀ, -ɛʀt(ə)] adj (tête) bare, uncovered; (lieu) open, exposed ♦ nm (bancaire) overdraft; **découverte** nf discovery

découvrir [dekuvʀiʀ] vt to discover; (apercevoir) to see; (enlever ce qui couvre ou protège) to uncover; (montrer, dévoiler) to reveal; **se** ~ vi to take off one's hat; to take something off; (au lit) to uncover o.s.; (ciel) to clear

décret [dekʀɛ] nm decree; **décréter** vt to decree; to order; to declare

décrié, e [dekʀije] adj disparaged

décrire [dekʀiʀ] vt to describe

décrocher [dekʀɔʃe] vt (dépendre) to take down; (téléphone) to take off the hook; (: pour répondre): ~ (le téléphone) to lift the receiver; (fig: contrat etc) to get, land ♦ vi to drop out; to switch off

décroître [dekʀwatʀ(ə)] vi to decrease, decline

décrypter [dekʀipte] vt to decipher

déçu, e [desy] pp de **décevoir**

décupler [dekyple] vt, vi to increase tenfold

dédaigner [dedɛɲe] vt to despise, scorn; (négliger) to disregard, spurn; **dédaigneux, euse** [dedɛɲø, -øz] adj scornful, disdainful

dédain [dedɛ̃] nm scorn, disdain

dédale [dedal] nm maze

dedans [dədɑ̃] adv inside; (pas en plein air) indoors, inside ♦ nm inside; **au** ~ on the inside; inside; **en** ~ (vers l'intérieur) inwards; voir aussi **là**

dédicacer [dedikase] vt: ~ (à qn) to sign (for sb), autograph (for sb)

dédier [dedje] vt to dedicate

dédire [dediʀ]: **se** ~ vi to go back on one's word; to retract, recant

dédommager [dedɔmaʒe] vt: ~ qn

(de) to compensate sb (for); (fig) to repay sb (for)

dédouaner [dedwane] vt to clear through customs

dédoubler [deduble] vt (classe, effectifs) to split (into two); ~ **les** trains to run additional trains

déduire [dedɥiʀ] vt: ~ qch (de) (ôter) to deduct sth (from); (conclure) to deduce ou infer sth (from)

déesse [deɛs] nf goddess

défaillance [defajɑ̃s] nf (syncope) blackout; (fatigue) (sudden) weakness no pl; (technique) fault, failure; (morale etc) weakness; ~ **cardiaque** heart failure

défaillir [defajiʀ] vi to faint; to feel faint; (mémoire etc) to fail

défaire [defɛʀ] vt (installation) to take down, dismantle; (paquet etc, nœud, vêtement) to undo; **se** ~ vi to come undone; **se** ~ **de** (se débarrasser de) to get rid of; (se séparer de) to part with

défait, e [defɛ, -ɛt] adj (visage) haggard, ravaged; **défaite** nf defeat

défalquer [defalke] vt to deduct

défaut [defo] nm (moral) fault, failing, defect; (d'étoffe, métal) fault, flaw, defect; (manque, carence): ~ **de** lack of; shortage of; **en** ~ at fault; in the wrong; **faire** ~ (manquer) to be lacking; **à** ~ failing that; **à** ~ **de** for lack ou want of; **par** ~ (JUR) in his (ou her etc) absence

défavorable [defavɔʀabl(ə)] adj (avis, conditions, jury) unfavourable (BRIT), unfavorable (US)

défavoriser [defavɔʀize] vt to put at a disadvantage

défection [defɛksjɔ̃] nf defection, failure to give support ou assistance; failure to appear; **faire** ~ (d'un parti etc) to withdraw one's support, leave

défectueux, euse [defɛktɥø, -øz] adj faulty, defective

défendre [defɑ̃dʀ(ə)] vt to defend; (interdire) to forbid; **se** ~ vi to defend o.s.; ~ **à qn qch/de faire** to forbid sb sth/to do; **il se défend** (fig) he can hold his own; **se ~ de/contre** (se protéger) to protect o.s. from/against; **se ~ de** (se garder de) to refrain from; (nier): **se ~ de vouloir** to deny wanting

défense [defãs] nf defence; (d'éléphant etc) tusk; "~ de fumer/cracher" "no smoking/spitting"

déférer [defere] vt (JUR) to refer; **~ à** (requête, décision) to defer to

déferler [defɛrle] vi (vagues) to break; (fig) to surge

défi [defi] nm (provocation) challenge; (bravade) defiance

défiance [defjãs] nf mistrust, distrust

déficit [defisit] nm (COMM) deficit

défier [defje] vt (provoquer) to challenge; (fig) to defy, brave; **se ~ de** (se méfier de) to distrust

défigurer [defigyre] vt to disfigure

défilé [defile] nm (GEO) (narrow) gorge ou pass; (soldats) parade; (manifestants) procession, march

défiler [defile] vi (troupes) to march past; (sportifs) to parade; (manifestants) to march; (visiteurs) to pour, stream; **se ~ vi** (se dérober) to slip away, sneak off

définir [definir] vt to define

définitif, ive [definitif, -iv] adj (final) final; (pour longtemps) permanent, definitive; (sans appel) final, definite; **définitive** nf: **en définitive** eventually; (somme toute) when all is said and done

définitivement [definitivmã] adv definitively; permanently; definitely

déflagration [deflagrasjɔ̃] nf explosion

défoncer [defɔ̃se] vt (caisse) to stave in; (porte) to smash ou break down; (lit, fauteuil) to burst (the springs of); (terrain, route) to rip ou plough up

déformation [deformasjɔ̃] nf: **~ professionnelle** conditioning by one's job

déformer [deforme] vt to put out of

shape; (corps) to deform; (pensée, fait) to distort; **se ~ vi** to lose its shape

défouler [defule]: **se ~ vi** to unwind, let off steam

défraîchir [defreʃir]: **se ~ vi** to fade; to become worn

défrayer [defreje] vt: **~ qn** to pay sb's expenses; **la chronique** to be in the news

défricher [defriʃe] vt to clear (for cultivation)

défroquer [defroke] vi (aussi: se ~) to give up the cloth

défunt, e [defœ̃, -œ̃t] adj: **son ~ père** his late father ♦ nm/f deceased

dégagé, e [degaʒe] adj clear; (ton, air) casual, jaunty

dégagement [degaʒmã] nm: **voie de ~** slip road; **itinéraire de ~** alternative route (to relieve congestion)

dégager [degaʒe] vt (exhaler) to give off; (délivrer) to free, extricate; (désencombrer) to clear; (isoler: idée, aspect) to bring out; **se ~** (odeur) to be given off; (passage, ciel) to clear

dégarnir [degarnir] vt (vider) to empty, clear; **se ~ vi** (tempes, crâne) to go bald

dégâts [dega] nmpl damage sg

dégel [deʒel] nm thaw

dégeler [deʒle] vt to thaw (out); (fig) to unfreeze ♦ vi to thaw (out)

dégénérer [deʒenere] vi to degenerate; (empirer) to go from bad to worse

dégingandé, e [deʒɛ̃gãde] adj gangling

dégivrer [deʒivre] vt (frigo) to defrost; (vitres) to de-ice

déglutir [deglytir] vt, vi to swallow

dégonflé, e [degɔ̃fle] adj (pneu) flat

dégonfler [degɔ̃fle] vt (pneu, ballon) to let down, deflate; **se ~ vi** (fam) to chicken out

dégouliner [deguline] vi to trickle, drip

dégourdi, e [degurdi] adj smart, resourceful

dégourdir [degurdir] vt: se ~ (les jambes) to stretch one's legs (fig)

dégoût [degu] nm disgust, distaste

dégoûtant, e [degutã, -ãt] adj disgusting

dégoûté, e [degute] adj disgusted; ~ de sick of

dégoûter [degute] vt to disgust; ~ qn de qch to put sb off sth

dégoutter [degute] vi to drip

dégradé [degrade] nm (PEINTURE) gradation

dégrader [degrade] vt (MIL: officier) to degrade; (abîmer) to damage, deface; se ~ vi (relations, situation) to deteriorate

dégrafer [degrafe] vt to unclip, unhook

degré [dəgre] nm degree; (d'escalier) step; alcool à 90 ~s surgical spirit

dégressif, ive [degresif, -iv] adj on a decreasing scale

dégrèvement [degrɛvmɑ̃] nm tax relief

dégringoler [degrɛ̃gɔle] vi to tumble (down)

dégrossir [degrosir] vt (fig) to work out roughly; to knock the rough edges off

déguenillé, e [degnije] adj ragged, tattered

déguerpir [degɛrpir] vi to clear off

dégueulasse [degœlas] (fam) adj disgusting

déguisement [degizmɑ̃] nm disguise

déguiser [degize] vt to disguise; se ~ vi (se costumer) to dress up; (pour tromper) to disguise o.s.

déguster [degyste] vt (vins) to taste; (fromages etc) to sample; (savourer) to enjoy, savour

dehors [dəɔr] adv outside; (en plein air) outdoors ♦ nm outside ♦ nmpl (apparences) appearances; mettre ou jeter ~ (expulser) to throw out; au ~ outside; outwardly; au ~ de outside; en ~ (vers l'extérieur) out-

side; outwards; en ~ de (hormis) apart from

déjà [deʒa] adv already; (auparavant) before, already

déjeuner [deʒœne] vi to (have) lunch; (le matin) to have breakfast ♦ nm lunch; breakfast

déjouer [deʒwe] vt to elude; to foil

delà [dəla] adv: par ~, en ~ (de), au ~ (de) beyond

délabrer [delabre]: se ~ vi to fall into decay, become dilapidated

délacer [delase] vt to unlace

délai [delɛ] nm (attente) waiting period; (sursis) extension (of time); (temps accordé) time limit; à bref ~ shortly, very soon; at short notice; dans les ~s within the time limit

délaisser [delese] vt to abandon, desert

délasser [delase] vt (reposer) to relax; (divertir) to divert, entertain; se ~ vi to relax

délateur, trice [delatœr, -tris] nm/f informer

délavé, e [delave] adj faded

délayer [deleje] vt (CULIN) to mix (with water etc); (peinture) to thin down

delco [dɛlko] nm (AUTO) distributor

délecter [delɛkte]: se ~ vi to revel ou delight in

délégué, e [delege] nm/f delegate; representative

déléguer [delege] vt to delegate

délibéré, e [delibere] adj (conscient) deliberate; (déterminé) determined

délibérer [delibere] vi to deliberate

délicat, e [delika, -at] adj (plein de tact) tactful; (attentionné) thoughtful; (exigeant) fussy, particular; procédés peu ~ unscrupulous methods; **délicatement** adv delicately; (avec douceur) gently

délice [delis] nm delight

délicieux, euse [delisjø, -jøz] adj (au goût) delicious; (sensation, impression) delightful

délimiter [delimite] vt to delimit, demarcate; to determine; to define

délinquance [delēkɑ̃s] nf criminality; **délinquant, e** [delēkɑ̃, -ɑ̃t] adj, nm/f delinquent

délirer [delire] vi to be delirious; (fig) to be raving, be going wild

délit [deli] nm (criminal) offence; ~ d'initié (BOURSE) insider dealing ou trading

délivrer [delivre] vt (prisonnier) to (set) free, release; (passeport, certificat) to issue; ~ qn de (ennemis) to deliver ou free sb from; (fig) to relieve sb of; to rid sb of

déloger [deloʒe] vt (locataire) to turn out; (objet coincé, ennemi) to dislodge

deltaplane [deltaplan] nm hang-glider

déluge [delyʒ] nm (biblique) Flood

déluré, e [delyre] adj smart, resourceful; (péj) forward, pert

demain [dəmɛ̃] adv tomorrow

demande [dəmɑ̃d] nf (requête) request; (revendication) demand; (ADMIN, formulaire) application; (ECON): la ~ demand; "~s d'emploi" "situations wanted"; ~ de poste job application

demandé, e [dəmɑ̃de] adj (article etc): très ~ (very) much in demand

demander [dəmɑ̃de] vt to ask for; (date, heure etc) to ask; (nécessiter) to require, demand; se ~ to wonder; (sens purement réfléchi) to ask o.s.; ~ qch à qn to ask sb for sth; to ask sb sth; ~ à qn de faire to ask sb to do; on vous demande au téléphone you're wanted on the phone

demandeur, euse [dəmɑ̃dœr, -øz] nm/f: ~ d'emploi job-seeker; (job) applicant

démangeaison [demɑ̃ʒɛzɔ̃] nf itching

démanger [demɑ̃ʒe] vi to itch

démanteler [demɑ̃tle] vt to break up; to demolish

démaquillant [demakijɑ̃] nm make-up remover

démaquiller [demakije] vt: se ~ to

remove one's make-up

démarche [demarʃ(ə)] nf (allure) gait, walk; (intervention) step; approach; (fig: intellectuelle) thought processes pl; approach; faire des ~s auprès de qn to approach sb

démarcheur, euse [demarʃœr, -øz] nm/f (COMM) door-to-door salesman(woman)

démarquer [demarke] vt (prix) to mark down; (joueur) to stop marking

démarrage [demaraʒ] nm start

démarrer [demare] vi (conducteur) to start (up); (véhicule) to move off; (travaux) to get moving; **démarreur** nm (AUTO) starter

démêler [demele] vt to untangle

démêlés [demele] nmpl problems

déménagement [demenaʒmɑ̃] nm move, removal; **camion de ~** removal van

déménager [demenaʒe] vt (meubles) to (re)move ♦ vi to move (house); **déménageur** nm removal man; (entrepreneur) furniture remover

démener [demne]: se ~ vi to thrash about; (fig) to exert o.s.

dément, e [demɑ̃, -ɑ̃t] adj (fou) mad, crazy; (fam) brilliant, fantastic

démentiel, le [demɑ̃sjɛl] adj insane

démentir [demɑ̃tir] vt to refute; ~ que to deny that

démerder [demerde] (fam): se ~ vi to sort things out for o.s.

démesuré, e [demzyre] adj immoderate

démettre [demetr(ə)] vt: ~ qn de (fonction, poste) to dismiss sb from; se ~ (de ses fonctions) to resign (from) one's duties; se ~ l'épaule etc to dislocate one's shoulder etc

demeurant [dəmœrɑ̃]: au ~ adv for all that

demeure [dəmœr] nf residence; mettre qn en ~ de faire to enjoin ou order sb to do; à ~ permanently

demeurer [dəmœre] vi (habiter) to live; (séjourner) to stay; (rester) to remain

demi, e [dəmi] *adj* half ♦ *nm* (*bière*) ≈ half-pint (*0,25 litres*) ♦ *préfixe*: /~... half-, semi-, demi-: **trois heures/bouteilles et ~es** three and a half hours/bottles, three hours/ bottles and a half; **il est 2 heures/ midi et ~e** it's half past 2/12; **à ~** half-; **à la ~** (*heure*) on the half-hour; **~-cercle** *nm* semicircle; **en ~-cercle** semicircular ♦ *adv* in a half circle; **~-douzaine** *nf* half-dozen, half a dozen; **~-finale** *nf* semi-final; **~-frère** *nm* half-brother; **~heure** *nf* half-hour, half an hour; **~journée** *nf* half-day, half a day; **~litre** *nm* half-litre, half a litre; **~livre** *nf* half-pound, half a pound; **~mot** *adv*: **à ~-mot** without having to spell things out; **~-pension** *nf* (*à l'hôtel*) half-board; **~-place** *nf* half-fare

démis, e [demi, -iz] *adj* (*épaule etc*) dislocated

demi: **~-saison** *nf*: **vêtements de ~-saison** spring *ou* autumn clothing; **~-set** *adj inv* (*beurre, fromage*) slightly salted; **~-sœur** *nf* half-sister

démission [demisjɔ̃] *nf* resignation; **donner sa ~** to give *ou* hand in one's notice; **démissionner** *vi* (*de son poste*) to resign

demi-tarif [dəmitaʀif] *nm* half-price; (*TRANSPORTS*) half-fare

demi-tour [dəmituʀ] *nm* about-turn; **faire ~** to turn (and go) back; (*AUTO*) to do a U-turn

démocratie [demɔkʀasi] *nf* democracy; **démocratique** [demɔkʀatik] *adj* democratic

démodé, e [demɔde] *adj* old-fashioned

démographique [demɔgʀafik] *adj* demographic, population *cpd*

demoiselle [dəmwazɛl] *nf* (*jeune fille*) young lady; (*célibataire*) single lady, maiden lady; **~ d'honneur** bridesmaid

démolir [demɔliʀ] *vt* to demolish

démon [demɔ̃] *nm* (*enfant turbulent*) devil, demon; **le D~** the Devil

démonstration [demɔ̃stʀɑsjɔ̃] *nf* demonstration; (*aérienne, navale*) display

démonté, e [demɔ̃te] *adj* (*fig*) raging, wild

démonter [demɔ̃te] *vt* (*machine etc*) to take down, dismantle; **se ~** *vi* (*personne*) to lose countenance

démontrer [demɔ̃tʀe] *vt* to demonstrate

démordre [demɔʀdʀ(ə)] *vi*: **ne pas ~ de** to refuse to give up, stick to

démouler [demule] *vt* (*gâteau*) to turn out

démuni, e [demyni] *adj* (*sans argent*) impoverished

démunir [demyniʀ] *vt*: **~ qn de** to deprive sb of; **se ~ de** to part with, give up

dénatalité [denatalite] *nf* fall in the birth rate

dénaturer [denatyʀe] *vt* (*goût*) to alter; (*pensée, fait*) to distort

déniaiser [denjeze] *vt*: **~ qn** to teach sb about life

dénicher [denife] *vt* to unearth; to track *ou* hunt down

dénier [denje] *vt* to deny

dénigrer [denigʀe] *vt* to denigrate, run down

dénivellation [denivelɑsjɔ̃] *nf* = **dénivellement**

dénivellement [denivɛlmɑ̃] *nm* ramp; dip; difference in level

dénombrer [denɔ̃bʀe] *vt* (*compter*) to count; (*énumérer*) to enumerate, list

dénomination [denɔminɑsjɔ̃] *nf* designation, appellation

dénommer [denɔme] *vt* to name

dénoncer [denɔ̃se] *vt* to denounce; **se ~** *vi* to give o.s. up, come forward

dénouement [denumɑ̃] *nm* outcome

dénouer [denwe] *vt* to unknot, undo

dénoyauter [denwajote] *vt* to stone

denrée [dɑ̃ʀe] *nf*: **~s** (*alimentaires*) foodstuffs

dense [dɑ̃s] *adj* dense

densité [dɑ̃site] *nf* density

dent [dɑ̃] *nf* tooth; **en ~s de scie**

serrated; jagged; ~ **de lait/sagesse** milk/wisdom tooth; ~**aire** adj dental

dentelé, e [dɑ̃tle] adj jagged, indented

dentelle [dɑ̃tɛl] nf lace no pl

dentier [dɑ̃tje] nm denture

dentifrice [dɑ̃tifʀis] nm toothpaste

dentiste [dɑ̃tist(ə)] nm/f dentist

dénuder [denyde] vt to bare

dénué, e [denɥe] adj: ~ **de** devoid of; lacking in; **dénuement** [denymɑ̃] nm destitution

déodorant [deodoʀɑ̃] nm deodorant

dépannage [depanaʒ] nm: **service de** ~ (AUTO) breakdown service

dépanner [depane] vt (voiture, télévision) to fix, repair; (fig) to bail out, help out; **dépanneuse** nf breakdown lorry (BRIT), tow truck (US)

dépareillé, e [depaʀeje] adj (collection, service) incomplete; (objet) odd

déparer [depaʀe] vt to spoil, mar

départ [depaʀ] nm leaving no pl, departure; (SPORT) start; (sur un horaire) departure; **au** ~ at the start; à **son** ~ when he left

départager [depaʀtaʒe] vt to decide between

département [depaʀtəmɑ̃] nm department

départir [depaʀtiʀ] : **se** ~ **de** vt to abandon, depart from

dépassé, e [depɑse] adj superseded, outmoded; (affolé) panic-stricken

dépasser [depɑse] vt (véhicule, concurrent) to overtake; (endroit) to pass, go past; (somme, limite) to exceed; (fig: en beauté etc) to surpass, outshine; (être en saillie sur) to jut out above (ou in front of) ♦ vi (jupon) to show

dépaysé, e [depeize] adj disoriented

dépecer [depəse] vt to joint, cut up

dépêche [depɛʃ] nf dispatch

dépêcher [depeʃe] vt to dispatch; **se** ~ vi to hurry

dépeindre [depɛ̃dʀ(ə)] vt to depict

dépendre [depɑ̃dʀ(ə)]: ~ **de** vt to depend on; (financièrement etc) to be dependent on

dépens [depɑ̃] nmpl: **aux** ~ **de** at the expense of

dépense [depɑ̃s] nf spending no pl, expense, expenditure no pl; (fig) consumption; expenditure

dépenser [depɑ̃se] vt to spend; (gaz, eau) to use; (fig) to expend, use up; **se** ~ vi (se fatiguer) to exert o.s.

dépensier, ière [depɑ̃sje, -jɛʀ] adj: **il est** ~ he's a spendthrift

déperdition [depɛʀdisjɔ̃] nf loss

dépérir [depeʀiʀ] vi to waste away; to wither

dépêtrer [depetʀe] vt: **se** ~ **de** to extricate o.s. from

dépeupler [depœple] vt to depopulate; **se** ~ vi to be depopulated

dépilatoire [depilatwaʀ] adj depilatory, hair-removing

dépister [depiste] vt to detect; (voleur) to track down; (poursuivants) to throw off the scent

dépit [depi] nm vexation, frustration; **en** ~ **de** in spite of; ~ **du bon sens** contrary to all good sense; **dépité, e** adj vexed, frustrated

déplacé, e [deplase] adj (propos) out of place, uncalled-for

déplacement [deplasmɑ̃] nm (voyage) trip, travelling no pl

déplacer [deplase] vt (table, voiture) to move, shift; (employé) to transfer, move; (os, vertèbre etc) to displace; **se** ~ vi to move; (voyager) to travel

déplaire [deplɛʀ] vi: **ceci me déplaît** I don't like this, I dislike this; **se** ~ vr: **se** ~ **quelque part** to be unhappy somewhere; **déplaisant, e** adj disagreeable

dépliant [deplijɑ̃] nm leaflet

déplier [deplije] vt to unfold

déplorer [deplɔʀe] vt (regretter) to deplore

déployer [deplwaje] vt to open out, spread; to deploy; to display, exhibit

déporter [depɔʀte] vt (POL) to deport; (dévier) to carry off course

déposer [depoze] vt (aén: mettre, poser) to lay ou put down; (à la banque, à la consigne) to deposit; (passager) to drop (off), set down; (roi) to depose; (ADMIN: faire enregistrer) to file; to register; (JUR: (contre) to testify ou give evidence (against); se ~ to settle; **déposi-taire** nm/f (COMM) agent

dépôt [depo] nm (à la banque, sédiment) deposit; (entrepôt, réserve) warehouse, store; (gare) depot; (prison) cells pl

dépotoir [depotwar] nm dumping ground, rubbish dump

dépouille [depuj] nf (d'animal) skin, hide; (humaine): ~ (mortelle) mortal remains pl

dépouillé, e [depuje] adj (fig) bare, bald

dépouiller [depuje] vt (animal) to skin; (spolier) to deprive of one's possessions; (documents) to go through, peruse; ~ qn/qch de to strip sb/sth of; ~ le scrutin to count the votes

dépourvu, e [depurvy] adj: ~ de lacking in, without; au ~ unprepared

déprécier [depresje] vt to depreciate; se ~ vi to depreciate

dépression [depresjɔ̃] nf depression; ~ (nerveuse) (nervous) breakdown

déprimer [deprime] vt to depress

MOT-CLÉ

depuis [dəpɥi] prép 1 (point de départ dans le temps) since; **il habite Paris ~ 1983**/l'an dernier he has been living in Paris since 1983/last year; **~ quand le connaissez-vous?** how long have you known him?
2 (temps écoulé) for; **il habite Paris ~ 5 ans** he has been living in Paris for 5 years; **je le connais ~ 3 ans** I've known him for 3 years
3 (lieu): **il a plu ~ Metz** it's been raining since Metz; **elle a téléphoné ~ Valence** she rang from Valence
4 (quantité, rang) from; **~ les plus petits jusqu'aux plus grands** from the youngest to the oldest
♦ adv (temps) since (then); **je ne**

---

lui ai pas parlé ~ I haven't spoken to him since (then); **~ que** conj (ever) since; **~ qu'il m'a dit ça** (ever) since he said that to me

député, e [depyte] nm/f (POL) ≈ Member of Parliament (BRIT), ≈ Member of Congress (US)

députer [depyte] vt to delegate

déraciner [derasine] vt to uproot

dérailler [deraje] vi (train) to be derailed; **faire ~** to derail

déraisonner [derezɔne] vi to talk nonsense, rave

dérangement [derãʒmã] nm (gêne) trouble; (gastrique etc) disorder; (mécanique) breakdown; **en ~** (téléphone) out of order

déranger [derãʒe] vt (personne) to trouble, bother; to disturb; (projets) to disrupt, upset; (objets, vêtements) to disarrange; **se ~** vi to put o.s. out; to (take the trouble to) come ou go out; **est-ce que cela vous dérange si ...?** do you mind if ...?

déraper [derape] vi (voiture) to skid; (personne, semelles, couteau) to slip

déréglé, e [deregle] adj (mœurs) dissolute

dérégler [deregle] vt (mécanisme) to put out of order; (estomac) to upset

dérider [deride] vt to brighten up; **se ~** to brighten up

dérision [derizjɔ̃] nf: **tourner en ~** to deride

dérivatif [derivatif] nm distraction

dérive [deriv] nf (de dériveur) centre-board; **aller à la ~** (NAVIG, fig) to drift

dérivé, e [derive] adj (TECH) by-product; **~e** nf (MATH) derivative

dériver [derive] vt (MATH) to derive; (cours d'eau etc) to divert ♦ vi (bateau) to drift; **~ de** to derive from

dermatologue [dermatɔlɔg] nm/f dermatologist

dernier, ière [dernje, -jɛr] adj last;

(le plus récent) latest, last; **lundi/le mois** ~ last Monday/month; **du** ~ **chic** extremely smart; **les** ~**s honneurs** the last tribute; **en** ~ last; **ce** ~ **the latter**; **dernièrement** *adv* recently

dérobé, e [derobe] *adj (porte)* secret, hidden; **à la** ~**e** surreptitiously

dérober [derobe] *vt* to steal; **se** ~ *vi (s'esquiver)* to slip away; to shy away; **se** ~ **sous** *(s'effondrer)* to give way beneath; **se** ~ **à** *(justice, regards)* to hide from; *(obligation)* to shirk; ~ **qch à (la vue de) qn** to conceal *ou* hide sth from sb's (view)

dérogation [derogasjɔ̃] *nf* (special) dispensation

déroger [derɔʒe] : ~ **à** *vt* to go against, depart from

dérouiller [deruje] *vt*: **se** ~ **les jambes** to stretch one's legs *(fig)*

déroulement [derulmã] *nm (d'une opération etc)* progress

dérouler [derule] *vt (ficelle)* to unwind; *(papier)* to unroll; **se** ~ *vi (avoir lieu)* to take place; *(se passer)* to go on; to unfold

déroute [derut] *nf* rout; total collapse; ~**r** [derute] *vt (avion, train)* to reroute, divert; *(étonner)* to disconcert, throw (out)

derrière [derjɛr] *adv, prép* behind ♦ *nm (d'une maison)* back; *(postérieur)* behind, bottom; **les pattes de** ~ the back *ou* hind legs; **par** ~ from behind; *(fig)* behind one's back

des [de] *dét voir* **de** ♦ *prép* +*dét* = **de** +**les**

dès [dɛ] *prép* from; ~ **que** as soon as; ~ **son retour** as soon as he was *(ou* is) back; ~ **lors** from then on; ~ **lors que** from the moment (that)

désabusé, e [dezabyze] *adj* disillusioned

désaccord [dezakɔr] *nm* disagreement; ~**é, e** [dezakɔrde] *adj (MUS)* out of tune

désaffecté, e [dezafɛkte] *adj* disused

désagréable [dezagreabl(ə)] *adj*

unpleasant

désagréger [dezagreʒe] : **se** ~ *vi* to disintegrate, break up

désagrément [dezagremã] *nm* annoyance, trouble *no pl*

désaltérer [dezaltere] *vt*: **se** ~ to quench one's thirst

désamorcer [dezamɔrse] *vt* to defuse; to forestall

désapprobateur, trice [dezaprobatœr, -tris] *adj* disapproving

désapprouver [dezapruve] *vt* to disapprove of

désarçonner [dezarsɔne] *vt* to unseat, throw; *(fig)* to throw, puzzle

désarmant, e [dezarmã, -ãt] *adj* disarming

désarroi [dezarwa] *nm* disarray

désarticulé, e [dezartikyle] *adj (pantin, corps)* dislocated

désastre [dezastr(ə)] *nm* disaster

désavantage [dezavãtaʒ] *nm* disadvantage; *(inconvénient)* drawback, disadvantage; **désavantager** *vt* to put at a disadvantage

désavouer [dezavwe] *vt* to disown

désaxé, e [dezakse] *adj (fig)* unbalanced

descendre [desãdr(ə)] *vt (escalier, montagne)* to go *(ou* come) down; *(valise, paquet)* to take *ou* get down; *(étagère etc)* to lower; *(fam: abattre)* to shoot down ♦ *vi* to go *(ou* come) down; *(passager: s'arrêter)* to get out, alight; ~ **à pied/en voiture** to walk/drive down; ~ **de** *(famille)* to be descended from; ~ **du train** to get out of *ou* get off the train; ~ **d'un arbre** to climb down from a tree; ~ **de cheval** to dismount; ~ **à l'hôtel** to stay at a hotel

descente [desãt] *nf* descent, going down; *(chemin)* way down; *(SKI)* downhill (race); **au milieu de la** ~ halfway down; ~ **de lit** bedside rug; ~ **(de police)** (police) raid

description [dɛskripsjɔ̃] *nf* description

désemparé, e [dezãpare] *adj* bewildered, distraught

désemparer [dezɑ̃pare] vi: sans ~ without stopping

désemplir [dezɑ̃plir] vi: ne pas ~ to be always full

déséquilibre [dezekilibr(ə)] nm (position): en ~ unsteady; (fig: des forces, du budget) imbalance; **déséquilibré, e** [dezekilibre] nm/f (PSYCH) unbalanced person; **déséquilibrer** [dezekilibre] vt to throw off balance

désert, e [dezɛr, -ɛrt(ə)] adj deserted ♦ nm desert

déserter [dezɛrte] vi, vt to desert

désertique [dezɛrtik] adj desert cpd; (barren, empty

désespéré, e [dezɛspere] adj desperate

désespérer [dezɛspere] vt to drive to despair ♦ vi: ~ de to despair of

désespoir [dezɛspwar] nm despair; en ~ de cause in desperation

déshabillé [dezabije] nm négligée

déshabiller [dezabije] vt to undress; se ~ vi to undress (o.s.)

désherbant [dezɛrbɑ̃] nm weed-killer

déshériter [dezerite] vt to disinherit

déshérités [dezerite] nmpl: les ~ the underprivileged

déshonneur [dezɔnœr] nm dishonour

déshydraté, e [dezidrate] adj dehydrated

desiderata [deziderata] nmpl requirements

désigner [dezine] vt (montrer) to point out, indicate; (dénommer) to denote; (candidat etc) to name

désinfectant, e [dezɛ̃fɛktɑ̃, -ɑ̃t] adj, nm disinfectant; **désinfecter** [dezɛ̃fɛkte] vt to disinfect

désintégrer [dezɛ̃tegre] vt to disintegrate; se ~ vi to disintegrate

désintéressé, e [dezɛ̃terese] adj disinterested, unselfish

désintéresser [dezɛ̃terese] vt: se ~ (de) to lose interest in

désintoxication [dezɛ̃tɔksikasjɔ̃] nf: faire une cure de ~ to undergo treatment for alcoholism (ou drug addiction)

désinvolte [dezɛ̃vɔlt(ə)] adj casual, off-hand; **désinvolture** nf casualness

désir [dezir] nm wish; (fort, sensuel) desire

désirer [dezire] vt to want, wish for; (sexuellement) to desire; je désire ... (formule de politesse) I would like ...

désister [deziste]: se ~ vi to stand down, withdraw

désobéir [dezɔbeir] vi: ~ (à qn/qch) to disobey (sb/sth); **désobéissant, e** adj disobedient

désobligeant, e [dezɔbliʒɑ̃, -ɑ̃t] adj disagreeable

désodorisant [dezɔdɔrizɑ̃] nm air freshener, deodorizer

désœuvré, e [dezœvre] adj idle

désolé, e [dezɔle] adj (paysage) desolate; je suis ~ I'm sorry

désoler [dezɔle] vt to distress, grieve

désolidariser [desɔlidarize] vt: se ~ de ou d'avec to dissociate o.s. from

désopilant, e [dezɔpilɑ̃, -ɑ̃t] adj hilarious

désordonné, e [dezɔrdɔne] adj untidy

désordre [dezɔrdr(ə)] nm disorder(liness), untidiness; (anarchie) disorder; ~s nmpl (POL) disturbances, disorder sg; en ~ in a mess, untidy

désorienté, e [dezɔrjɑ̃te] adj disorientated

désormais [dezɔrmɛ] adv from now on

désosser [dezɔse] vt to bone

desquelles [dekɛl] prép +pron = de +lesquelles

desquels [dekɛl] prép +pron = de +lesquels

dessaisir [dessizir]: se ~ de vt to give up, part with

dessaler [desale] vt (eau de mer) to desalinate; (CULIN) to soak

desséché, e [desefe] adj dried up

dessécher [desefe] vt to dry out, parch; se ~ vi to dry out

dessein [desɛ̃] nm design; à ~ intentionally, deliberately

desserrer [deseʀe] vt (to loosen; (frein) to release

dessert [desɛʀ] nm dessert, pudding

desserte [desɛʀt(ə)] nf (table) side table; (transport): la ~ du village est assurée par autocar there is a coach service to the village

desservir [desɛʀviʀ] vt (ville, quartier) to serve; (nuire à) to go against, put at a disadvantage; (débarrasser): ~ (la table) to clear the table

dessin [desɛ̃] nm (œuvre, art) drawing; (motif) pattern, design; (contour) (out)line; ~ animé cartoon (film); ~ humoristique cartoon

dessinateur, trice [desinatœʀ, -tʀis] nm/f drawer; (de bandes dessinées) cartoonist; (industriel) draughtsman(woman) (BRIT), draftsman(woman) (US)

dessiner [desine] vt to draw; (concevoir) to design

dessous [dəsu] adv underneath, beneath ♦ nm underside ♦ nmpl (sousvêtements) underwear sg; en ~, par ~ underneath; below; au-dessous (de) below; (peu digne de) beneath; avoir le ~ to get the worst of it; **dessous-de-plat** nm inv tablemat

dessus [dəsy] adv on top; (collé, écrit) on it ♦ nm top; en ~ above; par ~ over it ♦ prép over; au-dessus (de) above; avoir le ~ to get the upper hand; **dessus-de-lit** nm inv bedspread

destin [destɛ̃] nm fate; (avenir) destiny

destinataire [dɛstinatɛʀ] nm/f (POSTES) addressee; (d'un colis) consignee

destination [dɛstinɑsjɔ̃] nf (lieu) destination; (usage) purpose; à ~ de bound for, travelling to

destinée [dɛstine] nf fate; (existence, avenir) destiny

destiner [dɛstine] vt: ~ qn à (poste, sort) to destine sb for; ~ qn/

qch à (prédestiner) to destine sb/sth to +verbe; (envisager de donner): ~ qch à qn to intend sb to have sth; (adresser) to intend sth for sb; to intend sth at sb; **être destiné à** (sort) to be destined to +verbe; (usage) to be meant for; (suj: sort) to be in store for

destituer [dɛstitɥe] vt to depose

désuet, ète [desɥɛ, -ɛt] adj outdated, outmoded; **désuétude** nf: **tomber en désuétude** to fall into disuse

détachant [detafɑ̃] nm stain remover

détachement [detafmɑ̃] nm detachment

détacher vt (enlever) to detach, remove; (délier) to untie; (ADMIN): ~ qn (auprès de ou à) to post sb (to); se ~ vi (tomber) to come off; to come out; (se défaire) to come undone; se ~ sur to stand out against; se ~ de (se désintéresser) to grow away from

détail [detaj] nm detail; (COMM): le ~ retail; en ~ in detail; au ~ (COMM) retail; separately

détaillant [detajɑ̃] nm retailer

détailler [detaje] vt (expliquer) to explain in detail; to detail; (examiner) to look over, examine

détartrant [detaʀtʀɑ̃] nm scale remover

détecter [detɛkte] vt to detect

détective [detɛktiv] nm (policier: en Grande Bretagne) detective; ~ (privé) private detective

déteindre [detɛ̃dʀ(ə)] vi (tissu) to fade; (fig): ~ sur to rub off on

dételer [dɛtle] vt to unharness

détendre [detɑ̃dʀ(ə)] vt (tissu) ~ to lose its tension; to relax

détenir [detniʀ] vt (fortune, objet, secret) to be in possession of; (prisonnier) to detain, hold; (record, pouvoir) to hold

détente [detɑ̃t] nf relaxation; (d'une arme) trigger

détention [detɑ̃sjɔ̃] nf possession;

detention; holding; ~ **préventive** (pre-trial) custody

détenu, e [detny] nm/f prisoner

détergent [detɛrʒɑ̃] nm detergent

détériorer [deterjɔre] vt to damage; **se** ~ vi to deteriorate

déterminé, e [detɛrmine] adj (résolu) determined; (précis) specific, definite

déterminer [detɛrmine] vt (fixer) to determine; (décider): ~ **qn à faire** to decide sb to do

déterrer [detɛre] vt to dig up

détestable [detɛstabl(ə)] adj foul, ghastly; detestable, odious

détester [detɛste] vt to hate, detest

détonation [detɔnasjɔ̃] nf detonation, bang, report (of a gun)

détonner [detɔne] vi (MUS) to go out of tune; (fig) to clash

détour [detur] nm detour; (tournant) bend, curve; **sans** ~ (fig) plainly

détourné, e [deturne] adj (moyen) roundabout

détournement [deturnəmɑ̃] nm: ~ **d'avion** hijacking; ~ **de mineur** corruption of a minor

détourner [deturne] vt to divert; (par la force) to hijack; (yeux, tête) to turn away; (de l'argent) to embezzle; **se** ~ vi to turn away

détracteur, trice [detraktœr, -tris] nm/f disparager, critic

détraquer [detrake] vt to put out of order; (estomac) to upset; **se** ~ vi to go wrong

détrempé, e [detrɑ̃pe] adj (sol) sodden, waterlogged

détresse [detrɛs] nf distress

détriment [detrimɑ̃] nm: **au** ~ **de** to the detriment of

détritus [detritys] nmpl rubbish sg, refuse sg

détroit [detrwa] nm strait

détromper [detrɔ̃pe] vt to disabuse

détrôner [detrone] vt to dethrone

détrousser [detruse] vt to rob

détruire [detrɥir] vt to destroy

dette [dɛt] nf debt

D.E.U.G. [dœg] sigle m

deuil [dœj] nm (perte) bereavement; (période) mourning; (chagrin) grief; **être en** ~ to be in mourning

deux [dø] num two; **les** ~ both; **ses** ~ **mains** both his hands, his two hands; ~ **points** colon sg; **deuxième** num second; **deuxièmement** adv secondly, in the second place; **deux-pièces** nm inv (tailleur) two-piece suit; (de bain) two-piece (swimsuit); (appartement) two-roomed flat (BRIT) ou apartment (US); **deux-roues** nm inv two-wheeled vehicle

devais etc vb voir **devoir**

dévaler [devale] vt to hurtle down

dévaliser [devalize] vt to rob, burgle

dévaloriser [devalɔrize] vt to depreciate; **se** ~ vi to depreciate

dévaluation [devalɥasjɔ̃] nf depreciation; (ECON: mesure) devaluation

devancer [dəvɑ̃se] vt to be ahead of; to get ahead of; to arrive before; (prévenir) to anticipate

devant [dəvɑ̃] adv in front; (à distance: en avant) ahead ♦ prép in front of; ahead of; (avec mouvement: passer) past; (fig) before, in front of; faced with; in view of ♦ nm front; **prendre les** ~s to make the first move; **les pattes de** ~ the front legs, the forelegs; **par** ~ (boutonner) at the front; (entrer) the front way; **aller au-devant de** qn to go out to meet sb; **aller au-devant de** (désirs de qn) to anticipate

devanture [dəvɑ̃tyr] nf (façade) (shop) front; (étalage) (shop) window

déveine [devɛn] nf rotten luck no pl

développement [devlɔpmɑ̃] nm development

développer [devlɔpe] vt to develop; **se** ~ vi to develop

devenir [dəvnir] vb +attrib to become; ~ **instituteur** to become a teacher; **que sont-ils devenus?** what has become of them?

dévergondé, e [devɛrgɔ̃de] adj wild, shameless

déverser [devɛʀse] vt (liquide) to pour (out); (ordures) to tip (out); se ~ dans (fleuve, mer) to flow into

dévêtir [devetiʀ] vt to undress; se ~ vi to undress

devez etc vb voir **devoir**

déviation [devjasjɔ̃] nf deviation; (AUTO) diversion (BRIT), detour (US)

dévider [devide] vt to unwind

devienne etc vb voir **devenir**

dévier [devje] vt (fleuve, circulation) to divert; (coup) to deflect ♦ vi to veer (off course)

devin [dəvɛ̃] nm soothsayer, seer

deviner [dəvine] vt to guess; (prévoir) to foresee; (apercevoir) to distinguish; **devinette** [dəvinɛt] nf riddle

devins etc vb voir **devenir**

devis [dəvi] nm estimate, quotation

dévisager [devizaʒe] vt to stare at

devise [dəviz] nf (formule) motto, watchword; (ECON: monnaie) currency; ~s nfpl (argent) currency sg

deviser [dəvize] vi to converse

dévisser [devise] vt to unscrew, undo; se ~ vi to come unscrewed

dévoiler [devwale] vt to unveil

devoir [dəvwaʀ] nm duty; (SCOL) homework no pl; (: en classe) exercise ♦ vt (argent, respect): ~ qch (à qn) to owe (sb) sth; (suivi de l'infinitif: obligation): **il doit le faire** he has to do it, he must do it; (: intention): **il doit partir demain** he is (due) to leave tomorrow; (: probabilité): **il doit être tard** it must be late

dévolu, e [devɔly] adj: ~ à allotted to ♦ nm: **jeter son ~ sur** to fix one's choice on

dévorer [devɔʀe] vt to devour; (suj: feu, soucis) to consume

dévot, e [devo, -ɔt] adj devout, pious

dévotion [devɔsjɔ̃] nf devoutness; **être à la ~ de qn** to be totally devoted to sb

dévoué, e [devwe] adj devoted

dévouer [devwe]: se ~ vi (se sacrifier) to sacrifice o.s. (for); (se consacrer): se ~ à to devote ou dedicate o.s. to

dévoyé, e [devwaje] adj delinquent

devrai etc vb voir **devoir**

diabète [djabɛt] nm diabetes sg; **diabétique** [djabetik] nm/f diabetic

diable [djɑbl(ə)] nm devil

diabolo [djabolo] nm (boisson) lemonade with fruit cordial

diacre [djakʀ(ə)] nm deacon

diagnostic [djagnɔstik] nm diagnosis sg

diagnostiquer [djagnɔstike] vt to diagnose

diagonal, e, aux [djagɔnal, -o] adj diagonal; ~e nf diagonal; **en ~e** diagonally; **lire en ~e** to skim through

diagramme [djagʀam] nm chart, graph

dialecte [djalɛkt(ə)] nm dialect

dialogue [djalɔg] nm dialogue

diamant [djamɑ̃] nm diamond; **diamantaire** nm diamond dealer

diamètre [djamɛtʀ(ə)] nm diameter

diapason [djapazɔ̃] nm tuning fork

diaphragme [djafʀagm(ə)] nm diaphragm

diaporama [djapɔʀama] nm slide show

diapositive [djapozitiv] nf transparency, slide

diarrhée [djaʀe] nf diarrhoea

dictateur [diktatœʀ] nm dictator; **dictature** nf dictatorship

dictée [dikte] nf dictation

dicter [dikte] vt to dictate

dictionnaire [diksjɔnɛʀ] nm dictionary

dicton [diktɔ̃] nm saying, dictum

dièse [djɛz] nm sharp

diesel [djezɛl] nm diesel ♦ adj inv diesel

diète [djɛt] nf (jeûne) starvation diet; (régime) diet

diététique [djetetik] adj: **magasin ~** health food shop

dieu, x [djø] nm god; D~ God; **mon D~!** good heavens!

diffamation [difamasjɔ̃] nf slander; (écrite) libel

différé [difeʀe] nm (TV): **en ~**

(pre-)recorded

différence [diferɑ̃s] nf difference; à la ~ de unlike; **différencier** [diferɑ̃sje] vt to differentiate; **différend** [diferɑ̃] nm difference (of opinion), disagreement

différent, e [diferɑ̃, -ɑ̃t] adj: ~ (de) different (from); ~s objets different ou various objects

différer [difere] vt to postpone, put off ♦ vi: ~ (de) to differ (from)

difficile [difisil] adj difficult; (exigeant) hard to please; **difficilement** adv with difficulty

difficulté [difikylte] nf difficulty; en ~ (bateau, alpiniste) in difficulties

difforme [diform(ə)] adj deformed, misshapen

diffuser [difyze] vt (chaleur, bruit) to diffuse; (émission, musique) to broadcast; (nouvelle, idée) to circulate; (COMM) to distribute

digérer [diʒere] vt to digest; (fig: accepter) to stomach, put up with; **digestif** nm (after-dinner) liqueur

digne [diɲ] adj dignified; ~ de worthy of; ~ de foi trustworthy

dignité [diɲite] nf dignity

digression [digresjɔ̃] nf digression

digue [dig] nf dike, dyke

dilapider [dilapide] vt to squander

dilemme [dilɛm] nm dilemma

diligence [diliʒɑ̃s] nf stagecoach; (empressement) despatch

diluer [dilɥe] vt to dilute

diluvien, ne [dilyvjɛ̃, -jɛn] adj: pluie ~ne torrential rain

dimanche [dimɑ̃ʃ] nm Sunday

dimension [dimɑ̃sjɔ̃] nf (grandeur) size; (côte, de l'espace) dimension

diminuer [diminɥe] vt to reduce, decrease; (ardeur etc) to lessen; (personne: physiquement) to undermine; (dénigrer) to belittle ♦ vi to decrease, diminish; **diminutif** nm (surnom) pet name; **diminution** nf decreasing, diminishing

dinde [dɛ̃d] nf turkey

dindon [dɛ̃dɔ̃] nm turkey

dîner [dine] nm dinner ♦ vi to have

dinner

dingue [dɛ̃g] (fam) adj crazy

diplomate [diplɔmat] adj diplomatic ♦ nm diplomat; (fig) diplomatist

diplomatie [diplɔmasi] nf diplomacy

diplôme [diplom] nm diploma; **diplômé, e** adj qualified

dire [diʀ] nm: au ~ de according to ♦ vt to say; (secret, mensonge) to tell; leurs ~s what they say; ~ l'heure/la vérité to tell the time/the truth; ~ qch à qn to tell sb sth; ~ à qn qu'il fasse ou de faire to tell sb to do; on dit que they say that; ceci dit that being said; (à ces mots) whereupon; si cela lui dit (plaire) if he fancies it; que dites-vous de (penser) what do you think of; on dirait que it looks (ou sounds etc) as if; dis/dites (donc) I say; (à propos) by the way

direct, e [diʀɛkt] adj direct ♦ nm (TV): en ~ live; **directement** adv directly

directeur, trice [diʀɛktœʀ, -tʀis] nmf (d'entreprise) director; (de service) manager(eress); (d'école) head (teacher) (BRIT), principal (US)

direction [diʀɛksjɔ̃] nf management; conducting; supervision; (AUTO) steering; (sens) direction; "toutes ~s" "all routes"

dirent vb voir **dire**

dirigeant, e [diʀiʒɑ̃, -ɑ̃t] adj managerial; ruling ♦ nmf (d'un parti etc) leader; (d'entreprise) manager

diriger [diʀiʒe] vt (entreprise) to manage, run; (véhicule) to steer; (orchestre) to conduct; (recherches, travaux) to supervise; (braquer: regard, arme): ~ sur to point ou level at; se ~ (s'orienter) to find one's way; se ~ vers ou sur to make ou head for

dirigisme [diʀiʒism(ə)] nm (ECON) state intervention, interventionism

dis etc vb voir **dire**

discernement [disɛʀnəmɑ̃] nm (bon sens) discernment, judgement

discerner [disɛʀne] vt to discern,

make out

discipline [disiplin] nf discipline;
 discipliner vt to discipline; to control
discontinu, e [diskɔ̃tiny] adj inter-
 mittent
discontinuer [diskɔ̃tinɥe] vi: sans
 ~ without stopping, without a break
disconvenir [diskɔ̃vnir] vi: ne pas
 ~ de qch/que not to deny sth/that
discordant, e [diskɔrdã, -ãt] adj
 discordant; conflicting
discothèque [diskɔtɛk] nf (disques)
 record collection; (: dans une bibliothèque) record library; (boîte de
 nuit) discothèque
discourir [diskurir] vi to discourse,
 hold forth
discours [diskur] nm speech
discret, ète [diskrɛ, -ɛt] adj discreet; (fig) unobtrusive; quiet
discrétion [diskresjɔ̃] nf discretion;
 être à la ~ de qn to be in sb's
 hands; (fig) unlimited; as much as
 one wants
discrimination [diskriminasjɔ̃] nf
 discrimination; sans ~ indiscriminately
disculper [diskylpe] vt to exonerate
discussion [diskysjɔ̃] nf discussion
discutable [diskytabl(ə)] adj debatable
discuté, e [diskyte] adj controversial
discuter [diskyte] vt (contester) to
 question, dispute; (débattre: prix) to
 discuss ♦ vi to talk; (ergoter) to argue; ~ de to discuss
dise etc vb voir **dire**
disette [dizɛt] nf food shortage
diseuse [dizøz] nf: ~ de bonne
 aventure fortuneteller
disgracieux, euse [disgrasjø, -jøz]
 adj ungainly, awkward
disjoindre [disʒwɛ̃dr(ə)] vt to take
 apart; se ~ vi to come apart
disjoncteur [disʒɔ̃ktœr] nm (ÉLEC)
 circuit breaker
disloquer [disloke] vt (chaise) to dismantle; se ~ vi (parti, empire) to
 break up; se ~ l'épaule to dislocate
 one's shoulder

disons vb voir **dire**
disparaître [disparɛtr(ə)] vi to disappear; (à la vue) to vanish, disappear; to be hidden ou concealed; (se
 perdre: traditions etc) to die out; faire ~ to remove; to get rid of
disparition [disparisjɔ̃] nf disappear-
 ance
disparu, e [dispary] nm/f missing
 person; (défunt) departed
dispensaire [dispɑ̃sɛr] nm community clinic
dispenser [dispɑ̃se] vt (donner) to
 lavish, bestow; (exempter): ~ qn de
 to exempt sb from; se ~ de vt to
 avoid; to get out of
disperser [disperse] vt to scatter;
 (fig: son attention) to dissipate
disponibilité [disponibilite] nf (AD-
 MIN): être en ~ to be on leave of
 absence; **disponible** [disponibl(ə)] adj
 available
dispos [dispo] adj m: (frais et) ~
 fresh (as a daisy)
disposé, e [dispoze] adj: bien/mal
 ~ (humeur) in a good/bad mood; ~
 à (prêt à) willing ou prepared to
disposer [dispoze] vt (arranger, placer) to arrange ♦ vi: vous pouvez
 ~ you may leave; ~ de to have (at
 one's disposal); to use; se ~ à faire to prepare to do, be about to do
dispositif [dispozitif] nm device;
 (fig) system, plan of action; set-up
disposition [dispozisjɔ̃] nf (arrangement) arrangement, layout; (humeur) mood; (tendance) tendency;
 ~s nfpl (mesures) steps, measures;
 (préparatifs) arrangements; (loi,
 testament) provisions; (aptitudes)
 bent sg, aptitude sg; à la ~ de qn at
 sb's disposal
disproportionné, e [disprɔpɔr-
 sjɔne] adj disproportionate, out of all
 proportion
dispute [dispyt] nf quarrel, argument
disputer [dispyte] vt (match) to
 play; (combat) to fight; (course) to
 run, fight; se ~ vi to quarrel; (fig)
 ~ qch
 à qn to fight with sb over sth

disquaire [diskɛr] nm/f record dealer

disqualifier [diskalifje] vt to disqualify

disque [disk(ə)] nm (MUS) record; (forme, pièce) disc; (SPORT) discus; ~ compact compact disc; ~ d'embrayage (AUTO) clutch plate

disquette [diskɛt] nf floppy disk, diskette

disséminer [diseminə] vt to scatter

disséquer [diseke] vt to dissect

dissertation [disɛrtasjɔ̃] nf (SCOL) essay

disserter [disɛrte] vi: ~ sur to discourse upon

dissimuler [disimyle] vt to conceal

dissiper [disipe] vt to dissipate; (fortune) to squander; se ~ vi (brouillard) to clear, disperse; (doutes) to melt away; (élève) to become unruly

dissolu, e [disɔly] adj dissolute

dissolvant [disɔlvɑ̃] nm solvent; ~ (gras) nail polish remover

dissonant, e [disɔnɑ̃, -ɑ̃t] adj discordant

dissoudre [disudr(ə)] vt to dissolve; se ~ vi to dissolve

dissuader [disɥade] vt: ~ qn de faire/de qch to dissuade sb from doing/from sth

dissuasion [disɥazjɔ̃] nf: force de ~ deterrent power

distance [distɑ̃s] nf distance; (fig: écart) gap; à ~ at ou from a distance; **distancer** vt to outdistance

distant, e [distɑ̃, -ɑ̃t] adj (réservé) distant; ~ de (lieu) far away from

distendre [distɑ̃dr(ə)] vt to distend; se ~ vi to distend

distiller [distile] vt to distil; **distillerie** nf distillery

distinct, e [distɛ̃(kt), distɛ̃kt(ə)] adj distinct; **distinctif, ive** adj distinctive

distingué, e [distɛ̃ge] adj distinguished

distinguer [distɛ̃ge] vt to distinguish

distraction [distraksjɔ̃] nf (manque d'attention) absent-mindedness; (oubli) lapse (in concentration); (dé-

tente) diversion, recreation; (passe-temps) distraction, entertainment

distraire [distrɛr] vt (déranger) to distract; (divertir) to entertain, divert; se ~ vi to amuse ou enjoy o.s.

distrait, e [distrɛ, -ɛt] adj absent-minded

distribuer [distribɥe] vt to distribute; to hand out; (CARTES) to deal (out); (courrier) to deliver; **distributeur** nm (COMM) distributor; (automatique) (vending) machine; (: de billets) (cash) dispenser; **distribution** nf distribution; (postale) delivery; (choix d'acteurs) casting, cast

dit, e [di, dit] pp de dire ♦ adj (fixé): le jour ~ the arranged day; (surnommé): X, ~ Pierrot X, known as Pierrot

dites vb voir dire

divaguer [divage] vi to ramble; to rave

divan [divɑ̃] nm divan

divers, e [divɛr, -ɛrs(ə)] adj (varié) diverse, varied; (différent) different, various ♦ dét (plusieurs) various, several; (frais) ~ sundries, miscellaneous (expenses)

divertir [divɛrtir] vt to amuse, entertain; se ~ vi to amuse ou enjoy o.s.

divin, e [divɛ̃, -in] adj divine

diviser [divize] vt (gén, MATH) to divide; (morceler, subdiviser) to divide (up), split (up); **division** nf division

divorce [divɔrs(ə)] nm divorce; **divorcé, e** nm/f divorcee; **divorcer** vi to get a divorce, get divorced; **divorcer de** ou **d'avec** qn to divorce sb

divulguer [divylge] vt to divulge, disclose

dix [dis] num ten; **dixième** num tenth

dizaine [dizɛn] nf (10) ten; (environ 10): une ~ (de) about ten, ten or so

do [do] nm (note) C; (en chantant la gamme) do(h)

dock [dɔk] nm dock

docker [dɔkɛr] nm docker

docte [dɔkt(ə)] adj learned

docteur [dɔktœr] nm doctor

doctorat [dɔktɔra] nm: ~ (d'Université) doctorate; ~ d'État ≈ Ph.D.

doctrine [dɔktʁin] nf doctrine

document [dɔkymɑ̃] nm document

documentaire [dɔkymɑ̃tɛʁ] adj, nm documentary

documentaliste [dɔkymɑ̃talist(ə)] nmf archivist; researcher

documentation [dɔkymɑ̃tasjɔ̃] nf documentation, literature; (PRESSE, TV: service) research

documenter [dɔkymɑ̃te] vt: se ~ (sur) to gather information (on)

dodeliner [dɔdline] vi: ~ de la tête to nod one's head gently

dodo [dodo] nm: aller faire ~ to go to beddy-byes

dodu, e [dɔdy] adj plump

dogue [dɔg] nm mastiff

doigt [dwa] nm finger; à deux ~s de within an inch of; un ~ de lait a drop of milk; ~ de pied toe

doigté [dwate] nm (MUS) fingering; (fig: habileté) diplomacy, tact (compétition) points for

doit etc vb voir **devoir**

doléances [dɔleɑ̃s] nfpl complaints; grievances

dollar [dɔlaʁ] nm dollar

D.O.M. [deɔɛm, dɔm] sigle m = département d'outre-mer

domaine [dɔmɛn] nm estate, property; (fig) domain, field

domestique [dɔmɛstik] adj domestic ♦ nmf servant, domestic

domicile [dɔmisil] nm home, place of residence; à ~ at home; **domicilié, e** adj: être domicilié à to have one's home in ou at

dominant, e [dɔminɑ̃, -ɑ̃t] adj dominant; predominant

dominateur, trice [dɔminatœʁ, -tʁis] adj dominating; domineering

dominer [dɔmine] vt to dominate; (passions etc) to control, master; (surpasser) to outclass, surpass ♦ vi to be in the dominant position; **se** ~ vi to control o.s.

domino [dɔmino] nm domino

dommage [dɔmaʒ] nm (préjudice)

harm, injury; (dégâts, pertes) damage no pl; c'est ~ de faire/que to do that; a shame ou pity to do/that; **dommages-intérêts** nmpl damages

dompter [dɔ̃te] vt to tame; **dompteur, euse** nmf trainer; liontamer

don [dɔ̃] nm (cadeau) gift; (charité) donation; (aptitude) gift, talent; avoir des ~s pour to have a gift ou talent for

donc [dɔ̃k] conj therefore, so; (après une digression) so, then

donjon [dɔ̃ʒɔ̃] nm keep

donné, e [dɔne] adj (convenu) given; (pas cher): c'est ~ it's a gift; étant ~ ... given ...; **donnée** nf (MATH, gén) datum

donner [dɔne] vt to give; (vieux habits etc) to give away; (spectacle) to put on; (film) to show; ~ qch à qn to give sb sth, give sth to sb; ~ sur (suj: fenêtre, chambre) to look (out) onto; ~ dans (piège etc) to fall into; **se** ~ à fond to give one's all; s'en ~ à cœur joie (fam) to have a great time

---

MOT-CLÉ

dont [dɔ̃] pron relatif **1** (appartenance: objets) whose, of which; (appartenance: êtres animés) whose; **la maison** ~ **le toit est rouge** the house the roof of which is red; the house whose roof is red; **je connais la sœur** ~ **le frère** the man whose sister I know

2 (parmi lesquel(le)s): **2 livres,** ~ **l'un est** ... 2 books, one of which is ...; **il y avait plusieurs personnes,** ~ **Gabrielle** there were several people, among them Gabrielle; **10 blessés,** ~ **2 grièvement** 10 injured, 2 of them seriously

3 (complément d'adjectif, de verbe): **le fils** ~ **il est si fier** the son he's so proud of; **ce** ~ **je parle** what I'm talking about

---

doré, e [dɔʁe] adj golden; (avec dorure) gilt, gilded

dorénavant [dɔʀenavɑ̃] adv henceforth

dorer [dɔʀe] vt (cadre) to gild; (faire) ~ (CULIN) to brown

dorloter [dɔʀlɔte] vt to pamper

dormir [dɔʀmiʀ] vi to sleep; (être endormi) to be asleep

dortoir [dɔʀtwaʀ] nm dormitory

dorure [dɔʀyʀ] nf gilding

dos [do] nm back; (de livre) spine; **"voir au ~"** "see over"; **de ~** from the back

dosage [dozaʒ] nm mixture

dose [doz] nf dose; **~r** [doze] vt to measure out; to mix in the correct proportions; (fig) to expend in the right amounts; to strike a balance between

dossard [dosaʀ] nm number (worn by competitor)

dossier [dosje] nm (renseignements, fichier) file; (de chaise) back; (PRESSE) feature

dot [dɔt] nf dowry

doter [dɔte] vt to equip

douane [dwan] nf (poste, bureau) customs pl; (taxes) (customs) duty; **douanier, ière** adj customs cpd ♦ nm customs officer

double [dubl(ə)] adj, adv double ♦ nm (2 fois plus): **le ~** (de) twice as much (ou many) (as); (autre exemplaire) duplicate, copy; (sosie) double; (TENNIS) doubles sg; **en ~** (exemplaire) in duplicate; **faire ~ emploi** to be redundant

doubler [duble] vt (multiplier par 2) to double; (vêtement) to line; (dépasser) to overtake, pass; (film) to dub; (acteur) to stand in for ♦ vi to double

doublure [dublyʀ] nf lining; (CINEMA) stand-in

douce [dus] adj voir doux; **douceâtre** adj sickly sweet; **doucement** adv gently; slowly; **doucereux, euse** adj (péj) sugary; **douceur** nf softness; sweetness; mildness; gentleness; **~urs** nfpl (friandises) sweets

douche [duʃ] nf shower; **~s** nfpl

(salle) shower room sg: **se doucher** vi to have ou take a shower

doudoune [dudun] nf padded jacket; boob (fam)

doué, e [dwe] adj gifted, talented; ~ **de** endowed with

douille [duj] nf (ÉLEC) socket; (de projectile) case

douillet, te [duje, -ɛt] adj cosy; (péj) soft

douleur [dulœʀ] nf pain; (chagrin) grief, distress; **douloureux, euse** adj painful

doute [dut] nm doubt; **sans ~** no doubt; (probablement) probably

douter [dute] vt to doubt; **~ de** (allié) to doubt, have (one's) doubts about; (résultat) to be doubtful of; **se ~ de qch/que** to suspect sth/that; **je m'en doutais** I suspected as much

douteux, euse [dutø, -øz] adj (incertain) doubtful; (discutable) dubious, questionable; (péj) dubious-looking

Douvres [duvʀ(ə)] n Dover

doux, douce [du, dus] adj soft; (sucré, agréable) sweet; (peu fort: moutarde, clément: climat) mild; (pas brusque) gentle

douzaine [duzɛn] nf (12) dozen; (environ 12): **une ~** (de) a dozen or so, twelve or so

douze [duz] num twelve; **douzième** num twelfth

doyen, ne [dwajɛ̃, -ɛn] nm/f (en âge, ancienneté) most senior member; (de faculté) dean

dragée [dʀaʒe] nf sugared almond; (MÉD) (sugar-coated) pill

dragon [dʀagɔ̃] nm dragon

draguer [dʀage] vt (rivière) to dredge; to drag; (fam) to try to pick up

dramatique [dʀamatik] adj dramatic; (tragique) tragic ♦ nf (TV) (television) drama

dramaturge [dʀamatyʀʒ(ə)] nm dramatist, playwright

drame [dʀam] nm (THÉÂTRE) drama

drap [dʀa] nm (de lit) sheet; (tissu) woollen fabric

drapeau, x [dʀapo] nm flag; sous les ~x with the colours, in the army

dresser [dʀese] vt (mettre vertical, monter) to put up, erect; (fig: liste, bilan, contrat) to draw up; (animal) to train; se ~ vi (falaise, obstacle) to stand; to tower (up); (personne) to draw o.s. up; ~ qn contre qn to set sb against sb; ~ l'oreille to prick up one's ears

drogue [dʀɔg] nf drug; la ~ drugs pl; **drogué, e** [dʀɔge] nm/f drug addict

droguer [dʀɔge] vt (victime) to drug; (malade) to give drugs to; se ~ vi (aux stupéfiants) to take drugs; (péj: de médicaments) to dose o.s. up

droguerie [dʀɔgʀi] nf hardware shop

droguiste [dʀɔgist(ə)] nm keeper (ou owner) of a hardware shop

droit, e [dʀwa, dʀwat] adj (non courbe) straight; (vertical) upright, straight; (fig: loyal) upright, straight(forward); (opposé à gauche) right, right-hand ♦ adv straight ♦ nm (prérogative) right; (taxe) duty, tax; (: d'inscription) fee; (JUR:) le ~ law; **avoir le ~ de** to be allowed to; **avoir ~ à** to be entitled to; **être en ~ de** to have a ou the right to; **être dans son ~** to be within one's rights; **à ~e** on the right; (direction) (to the) right; **~s d'auteur** royalties; **~s d'inscription** nmpl enrolment fee; (competition) entry fee; **droite** nf (POL): **la droite** the right (wing)

droitier, ière [dʀwatje, jɛʀ] nm/f right-handed person

droits nmpl voir droit

droiture [dʀwatyʀ] nf uprightness, straightness

drôle [dʀol] adj funny; **une ~ d'idée** a funny idea; **drôlement** adv (très) terribly, awfully

dromadaire [dʀɔmadɛʀ] nm drome-

dary

dru, e [dʀy] adj (cheveux) thick, bushy; (pluie) heavy

du [dy] dét voir de ♦ prép +dét = de +le

dû, due [dy] vb voir devoir ♦ adj (somme) owing, owed; (: venant à échéance) due; (causé par): ~ à due to ♦ nm due; (somme) dues pl

dubitatif, ive [dybitatif, -iv] adj doubtful, dubious

duc [dyk] nm duke; **duchesse** nf duchess

dûment [dymã] adv duly

Dunkerque [dœkɛʀk] n Dunkirk

duo [dyo] nm (MUS) duet

dupe [dyp] nf dupe ♦ adj: (ne pas) être ~ de (not) to be taken in by

duplex [dyplɛks] nm (appartement) split-level apartment, duplex

duplicata [dyplikata] nm duplicate

duquel [dykɛl] prép +pron = de +lequel

dur, e [dyʀ] adj (pierre, siège, travail, problème) hard; (lumière, voix, climat) harsh; (sévère) hard, harsh; (cruel) hard(-hearted); (porte, col) stiff; (viande) tough ♦ adv hard; **d'oreille** hard of hearing

durant [dyʀã] prép (au cours de) during; (pendant) for; **des mois ~** for months

durcir [dyʀsiʀ] vt, vi to harden; se ~ vi to harden

durée [dyʀe] nf length; (d'une pile etc) life; (déroulement: des opérations etc) duration

durement [dyʀmã] adv harshly

durer [dyʀe] vi to last

dureté [dyʀte] nf hardness; harshness; stiffness; toughness

durit [dyʀit] nf (®) nf (car radiator) hose

dus etc vb voir devoir

duvet [dyvɛ] nm down; (sac de couchage) down-filled sleeping bag

dynamique [dinamik] adj dynamic

dynamisme [dinamism] nm dynamism

dynamite [dinamit] nf dynamite

dynamiter [dinamite] vt to (blow up with) dynamite

dynamo [dinamo] nf dynamo

dysenterie [disɑ̃tʀi] nf dysentery

dyslexie [disleksi] nf dyslexia, word-blindness

E

eau, x [o] nf water; ~x nfpl (MED) waters; **prendre l'~** to leak, let in water; **tomber à l'~** (fig) to fall through; ~ **courante** running water; ~ **de Cologne** Eau de Cologne; ~ **de Javel** bleach; ~ **de toilette** toilet water; ~ **douce** fresh water; ~ **minérale** mineral water; ~ **plate** still water; ~ **salée** salt water; **eau-de-vie** nf brandy; **eau-forte** nf etching

ébahi, e [ebai] adj dumbfounded

ébattre [ebatʀ(ə)]: **s'~** vi to frolic

ébaucher [eboʃe] vt to sketch out, outline; **s'~** vi to take shape

ébène [ebɛn] nf ebony

ébéniste [ebenist(ə)] nm cabinet-maker

éberlué, e [ebɛʀlɥe] adj astounded

éblouir [ebluiʀ] vt to dazzle

éblouissement [ebluismɑ̃] nm (faiblesse) dizzy turn

éborgner [ebɔʀɲe] vt: ~ **qn** to blind sb in one eye

éboueur [ebwœʀ] nm dustman (BRIT), garbageman (US)

ébouillanter [ebujɑ̃te] vt to scald; (CULIN) to blanch

éboulement [ebulmɑ̃] nm rock fall

ébouler [ebule]: **s'~** vi to crumble, collapse

éboulis [ebuli] nmpl fallen rocks

ébouriffé, e [ebuʀife] adj tousled

ébranler [ebʀɑ̃le] vt to shake; (rendre instable: mur) to weaken; **s'~** vi (partir) to move off

ébrécher [ebʀeʃe] vt to chip

ébriété [ebʀijete] nf: **en état d'~** in a state of intoxication

ébrouer [ebʀue]: **s'~** vi to shake o.s.; (souffler) to snort

ébruiter [ebʀɥite] vt to spread, dis-

close

ébullition [ebylisjɔ̃] nf boiling point; **en ~** boiling; (fig) in an uproar

écaille [ekaj] nf (de poisson) scale; (de coquille) shell; (matière) tortoiseshell; ~**r** [ekaje] vt (poisson) to scale; (huître) to open; **s'~r** vi to flake ou peel (off)

écarlate [ekaʀlat] adj scarlet

écarquiller [ekaʀkije] vt: ~ **les yeux** to stare wide-eyed

écart [ekaʀ] nm gap; (embardée) swerve; sideways leap; (fig) departure, deviation; **à l'~** out of the way; **à l'~ de** away from

écarté, e [ekaʀte] adj (lieu) out-of-the-way, remote; (ouvert): **les jambes ~es** legs apart; **les bras ~s** arms outstretched

écarteler [ekaʀtəle] vt to quarter; (fig) to tear

écarter [ekaʀte] vt (séparer) to move apart, separate; (éloigner) to push back, move away; (ouvrir: bras, jambes) to spread, open; (: rideau) to draw (back); (éliminer: candidat, possibilité) to dismiss; **s'~** vi to part; to move away; **s'~ de** to wander from

écervelé, e [esɛʀvəle] adj scatterbrained, featherbrained

échafaud [eʃafo] nm scaffold

échafaudage [eʃafodaʒ] nm scaffolding

échafauder [eʃafode] vt (plan) to construct

échalote [eʃalɔt] nf shallot

échancrure [eʃɑ̃kʀyʀ] nf (de robe) scoop neckline; (de côte, arête rocheuse) indentation

échange [eʃɑ̃ʒ] nm exchange; **en ~ de** in exchange ou return for

échanger [eʃɑ̃ʒe] vt: ~ **qch (contre)** to exchange sth (for); **échangeur** nm (AUTO) interchange

échantillon [eʃɑ̃tijɔ̃] nm sample

échappement [eʃapmɑ̃] nm (AUTO) exhaust

échapper [eʃape]: ~ **à** vt (gardien) to escape (from); (punition, péril) to escape (from);

escape; s'~ vi to escape; ~ à qn (*détail*, *sens*) to escape sb; (*objet qu'on tient*) to slip out of sb's hands; laisser ~ (*cri etc*) to let out; l'~ belle to have a narrow escape

écharde [eʃaʀd(ə)] nf splinter (of wood)

écharpe [eʃaʀp(ə)] nf scarf; (*de maire*) sash; (*MED*) sling

échasse [eʃɑs] nf stilt

échauffer [eʃofe] vt (*métal, moteur*) to overheat; (*fig: exciter*) to fire, excite; s'~ vi (*SPORT*) to warm up; (*dans la discussion*) to become heated

échéance [eʃeɑ̃s] nf (*d'un paiement: date*) settlement date; (: *somme due*) financial commitment(s); (*fig*) deadline; à brève/longue ~ short/long-term ♦ adv in the short/long run

échéant [eʃeɑ̃] : le cas ~ adv if the case arises

échec [eʃɛk] nm failure; (*ÉCHECS*); ~ et mat/au roi checkmate/check; ~s nmpl (*jeu*) chess sg; tenir en ~ to hold in check; faire ~ à to foil ou thwart

échelle [eʃɛl] nf ladder; (*fig, d'une carte*) scale

échelon [eʃlɔ̃] nm (*d'échelle*) rung; (*ADMIN*) grade

échelonner [eʃlɔne] vt to space out

échevelé, e [eʃəvle] adj tousled, dishevelled; wild, frenzied

échine [eʃin] nf backbone, spine

échiquier [eʃikje] nm chessboard

écho [eko] nm echo; ~s nmpl (*potins*) gossip sg, rumours

échoir [eʃwaʀ] vi (*dette*) to fall due; (*délais*) to expire; ~ à to fall to

échouer [eʃwe] vi to fail; s'~ vi to run aground

échu, e [eʃy] pp de échoir

éclabousser [eklabuse] vt to splash

éclair [eklɛʀ] nm (*d'orage*) flash of lightning, lightning no pl; (*gâteau*) éclair

éclairage [eklɛʀaʒ] nm lighting;

éclaircie [eklɛʀsi] nf bright interval

éclaircir [eklɛʀsiʀ] vt to lighten; (*fig*)

to clear up; to clarify; (*CULIN*) to thin (down); s'~ vi to clear; s'~ la voix to clear one's throat; **éclaircissement** nm clearing up; clarification

éclairer [eklɛʀe] vt (*lieu*) to light (up); (*personne: avec une lampe etc*) to light the way for; (*fig*) to enlighten; to shed light on ♦ vi : ~ mal/bien to give a poor/good light; s'~ à l'électricité to have electric lighting

éclaireur, euse [eklɛʀœʀ, -øz] nm/f (*scout*) (boy) scout/(girl) guide ♦ nm (*MIL*) scout

éclat [ekla] nm (*de bombe, de verre*) fragment; (*du soleil, d'une couleur etc*) brightness, brilliance; (*d'une cérémonie*) splendour; (*scandale*): faire un ~ to cause a commotion; ~s de voix shouts; ~s de rire roar of laughter

éclatant, e [eklatɑ̃, -ɑ̃t] adj brilliant

éclater [eklate] vi (*pneu*) to burst; (*bombe*) to explode; (*guerre, épidémie*) to break out; (*groupe, parti*) to break up; ~ en sanglots/de rire to burst out sobbing/laughing

éclipser [eklipse] : s'~ vi to slip away

éclopé, e [eklɔpe] adj lame

éclore [eklɔʀ] vi (*œuf*) to hatch; (*fleur*) to open (out)

écluse [eklyz] nf lock

écœurant, e [ekœʀɑ̃, -ɑ̃t] adj (*gâteau etc*) sickly

écœurer [ekœʀe] vt: ~ qn to make sb feel sick

école [ekɔl] nf school; aller à l'~ to go to school; ~ normale teachers' training college; ~ publique ~ state school; **écolier, ière** nm/f schoolboy/girl

écologie [ekɔlɔʒi] nf ecology; environmental studies pl

écologique [ekɔlɔʒik] adj environment-friendly

éconduire [ekɔ̃dɥiʀ] vt to dismiss

économe [ekɔnɔm] adj thrifty ♦ nm/f (*de lycée etc*) bursar (BRIT), treasurer (US)

économie [ekɔnɔmi] nf economy; (gain: d'argent, de temps etc) saving; (science) economics sg; ~s nfpl (pécule) savings; **économique** adj (avantageux) economical; (ECON) economic; **économiser** [ekɔnɔmize] vt, vi to save

écoper [ekɔpe] vi to bale out; (fig) to cop it; ~ (de) to get

écorce [ekɔrs(ə)] nf bark; (de fruit) peel

écorcher [ekɔrʃe] vt (animal) to skin; (égratigner) to graze; **écorchure** nf graze

écossais, e [ekɔsɛ, -ɛz] adj Scottish ♦ nm/f: É~, e Scot

Écosse [ekɔs] nf: l'~ Scotland

écosser [ekɔse] vt to shell

écouler [ekule] vt to sell; to dispose of; s'~ vi (eau) to flow (out); (jours, temps) to pass (by)

écourter [ekurte] vt to curtail, cut short

écoute [ekut] nf (RADIO, TV): temps/heure d'~ listening (ou viewing) time/hour; **prendre** l'~ to tune in; **rester** à l'~ (de) to stay tuned in (to)

écouter [ekute] vt to listen to; **écoutes téléphoniques** phone tapping sg; **écouteur** nm (TEL) receiver; (RADIO) headphones pl, headset

écran [ekrɑ̃] nm screen

écrasant, e [ekrazɑ̃, -ɑ̃t] adj overwhelming

écraser [ekraze] vt to crush; (piéton) to run over; s'~ (au sol) to crash; s'~ **contre** to crash into

écrémer [ekreme] vt to skim

écrevisse [ekrəvis] nf crayfish inv

écrier [ekrije]: s'~ vi to exclaim

écrin [ekrɛ̃] nm case, box

écrire [ekrir] vt to write; s'~ to write to each other; ça s'écrit comment? how is it spelt?; **écrit** nm document; (examen) written paper; par écrit in writing

écriteau, x [ekrito] nm notice, sign

écriture [ekrityr] nf writing;

(COMM) entry; ~s nfpl accounts, books; l'É~, les É~s the Scriptures

écrivain [ekrivɛ̃] nm writer

écrou [ekru] nm nut

écrouer [ekrue] vt to imprison; to remand in custody

écrouler [ekrule]: s'~ vi to collapse

écru, e [ekry] adj (toile) raw, unbleached; (couleur) off-white, écru

ECU sigle m ECU

écueil [ekœj] nm reef; (fig) pitfall; stumbling block

écuelle [ekɥɛl] nf bowl

éculé, e [ekyle] adj (chaussure) down-at-heel; (fig: péj) hackneyed

écume [ekym] nf foam; (CULIN) scum; **écumer** vt (CULIN) to skim; (fig) to plunder

écureuil [ekyrœj] nm squirrel

écurie [ekyri] nf stable

écusson [ekysɔ̃] nm badge

écuyer, ère [ekɥije, -ɛr] nm/f rider

eczéma [ɛgzema] nm eczema

édenté, e [edɑ̃te] adj toothless

E.D.F. sigle f (= Electricité de France) national electricity company

édifice [edifis] nm edifice, building

édifier [edifje] vt to build, erect; (fig) to edify

édit [edi] nm edict

éditer [edite] vt (publier) to publish; (: disque) to produce; **éditeur, trice** nm/f editor; publisher; **édition** nf editing no pl; edition; (industrie du livre) publishing

édredon [edrədɔ̃] nm eiderdown

éducateur, trice [edykatœr, -tris] nm/f teacher; (in special school) instructor

éducatif, ive [edykatif, -iv] adj educational

éducation [edykasjɔ̃] nf education; (familiale) upbringing; (manières) (good) manners pl; ~ **physique** physical education

édulcorer [edylkɔre] vt to sweeten; (fig) to tone down

éduquer [edyke] vt to educate; (élever) to bring up; (faculté) to train

effacé, e [efase] adj unassuming

effacer [efase] vt to erase, rub out; **s'~** (inscription etc) to wear off; (pour laisser passer) to step aside

effarant, e [efarɑ̃, -ɑ̃t] adj alarming

effarer [efare] vt to alarm

effaroucher [efaʀuʃe] vt to frighten ou scare away; to alarm

effectif, ive [efɛktif, -iv] adj real; effective ♦ nm (MIL) strength; (SCOL) (pupil) numbers pl; **effectivement** adv effectively; (réellement) actually, really; (en effet) indeed

effectuer [efɛktɥe] vt (opération) to carry out; (déplacement, trajet) to make; (mouvement) to execute

efféminé, e [efemine] adj effeminate

effervescent, e [efɛʀvɛsɑ̃, -ɑ̃t] adj effervescent; (fig) agitated

effet [efɛ] nm (résultat, artifice) effect; (impression) impression; **~s** nmpl (vêtements etc) things; faire de l'~ (médicament, menace) to have an effect; en ~ indeed; to de serre greenhouse effect; gaz à effet de serre greenhouse gas

efficace [efikas] adj (personne) efficient; (action, médicament) effective

effilé, e [efile] adj slender; sharp; streamlined

effiler [efile] vt (tissu) to fray

effilocher [efilɔʃe]: **s'~** vi to fray

efflanqué, e [eflɑ̃ke] adj emaciated

effleurer [eflœʀe] vt to brush (against); (sujet) to touch upon; (suj: idée, pensée): **~ qn** to cross sb's mind

effluves [eflyv] nmpl exhalation(s)

effondrer [efɔ̃dʀe]: **s'~** vi to collapse

efforcer [efɔʀse]: **s'~** de vt to try hard to do, try hard to

effort [efɔʀ] nm effort

effraction [efʀaksjɔ̃] nf: **s'introduire par ~** dans to break into

effrayant, e [efʀɛjɑ̃, -ɑ̃t] adj frightening

effrayer [efʀeje] vt to frighten, scare

effréné, e [efʀene] adj wild

effriter [efʀite]: **s'~** vi to crumble

effroi [efʀwa] nm terror, dread no pl

effronté, e [efʀɔ̃te] adj insolent, brazen

effroyable [efʀwajabl(ə)] adj horrifying, appalling

effusion [efyzjɔ̃] nf effusion; **sans ~ de sang** without bloodshed

égal, e, aux [egal, -o] adj equal; (plan: surface) even, level; (constant: vitesse) steady; (équitable) even ♦ nm/f equal; **être ~ à** (prix, nombre) to be equal to; **ça lui est ~** it's all the same to him; he doesn't mind; **sans ~** matchless, unequalled; **à l'~ de** (comme) just like; **d'~ à ~** as equals; **~ement** adv equally; evenly; steadily; (aussi) too, as well; **~er** vt to equal; **~** vt (sol, salaires) to level (out); (chances) to equalize ♦ vi (SPORT) to equalize; **~ité** nf equality; evenness; steadiness; (MATH) identity; **être à ~ité** (de points) to be equal

égard [egaʀ] nm: **~s** nmpl consideration sg; **à cet ~** in this respect; **eu ~ à** in view of; **par ~ pour** out of consideration for; **sans ~ pour** without regard for; **à l'~ de** towards; concerning

égarement [egaʀmɑ̃] nm distraction; aberration

égarer [egaʀe] vt to mislay; (moralement) to lead astray; **s'~** vi to get lost, lose one's way; (objet) to go astray; (dans une discussion) to wander

égayer [egeje] vt (personne) to amuse; to cheer up; (récit, endroit) to brighten up, liven up

églantine [eglɑ̃tin] nf wild ou dog rose

église [egliz] nf church; **aller à l'~** to go to church

égoïsme [egoism(ə)] nm selfishness; **égoïste** adj selfish

égorger [egɔʀʒe] vt to cut the throat of

égosiller [egozije]: **s'~** vi to shout o.s. hoarse

égout [egu] nm sewer

égoutter [egute] vt (linge) to wring out; (vaisselle) to drain ♦ vi to drip; s'~ vi to drip; **égouttoir** nm draining board; (mobile) draining rack

égratigner [egratiɲe] vt to scratch; **égratignure** nf scratch

égrillard, e [egrijar, -ard(ə)] adj ribald

Égypte [eʒipt(ə)] nf: l'~ Egypt; **égyptien, ne** adj, nm/f Egyptian

eh [e] excl hey!; ~ bien well

éhonté, e [eɔte] adj shameless, brazen

éjecter [eʒɛkte] vt (TECH) to eject; (fam) to kick ou chuck out

élaborer [elabɔre] vt to elaborate; (projet, stratégie) to work out; (rapport) to draft

élaguer [elage] vt to prune

élan [elɑ̃] nm (ZOOL) elk, moose; (SPORT: avant le saut) run up; (d'objet en mouvement) momentum; (fig: de tendresse etc) surge; prendre de l'~ to gather speed

élancé, e [elɑ̃se] adj slender

élancement [elɑ̃smɑ̃] nm shooting pain

élancer [elɑ̃se]: s'~ vi to dash, hurl o.s.; (fig: arbre, clocher) to soar (upwards)

élargir [elarʒir] vt to widen; (vêtement) to let out; (JUR) to release; s'~ vi to widen; (vêtement) to stretch

élastique [elastik] adj elastic ♦ nm (de bureau) rubber band; (pour la couture) elastic no pl

électeur, trice [elɛktœr, -tris] nm/f elector, voter

élection [elɛksjɔ̃] nf election

électorat [elɛktɔra] nm electorate

électricien, ne [elɛktrisjɛ̃, -ɛn] nm/f electrician

électricité [elɛktrisite] nf electricity; allumer/éteindre l'~ to put on/off the light

électrique [elɛktrik] adj electric(al)

électrochoc [elɛktrɔʃɔk] nm electric shock treatment

électroménager [elɛktrɔmenaʒe]

adj, nm: appareils ~s, l'~ domestic (electrical) appliances

électronique [elɛktrɔnik] adj electronic ♦ nf electronics sg

électrophone [elɛktrɔfɔn] nm record player

élégant, e [elegɑ̃, -ɑ̃t] adj elegant; (solution) neat, elegant; (attitude, procédé) courteous, civilized

élément [elemɑ̃] nm element; (pièce) component, part; **élémentaire** adj elementary

éléphant [elefɑ̃] nm elephant

élevage [ɛlvaʒ] nm breeding; (de bovins) cattle rearing

élévation [elevasjɔ̃] nf (gén) elevation; (voir élever) raising; (voir s'élever) rise

élevé, e [ɛlve] adj (prix, sommet) high; (fig: noble) elevated; **bien/mal ~** well-/ill-mannered

élève [elɛv] nm/f pupil

élever [ɛlve] vt (enfant) to bring up, raise; (bétail, volaille) to breed; (abeilles) to keep; (hausser: taux, niveau) to raise; (fig: âme, esprit) to elevate; (édifier: monument) to put up, erect; s'~ vi (avion, alpiniste) to go up; (niveau, température, aussi: cri etc) to rise; (survenir: difficultés) to arise; s'~ à (suj: frais, dégâts) to amount to, add up to; s'~ contre qch to rise up against sth; ~ la voix to raise one's voice; **éleveur, euse** nm/f breeder

élimé, e [elime] adj threadbare

éliminatoire [eliminatwar] nf (SPORT) heat

éliminer [elimine] vt to eliminate

élire [elir] vt to elect

elle [ɛl] pron (sujet) she; (: chose) it; (complément) her; it; ~s they; them; ~-même herself; itself; ~s-mêmes themselves; voir aussi **il**

élocution [elɔkysjɔ̃] nf delivery; défaut d'~ speech impediment

éloge [elɔʒ] nm (gén no pl) praise; **élogieux, euse** adj laudatory, full of praise

éloigné, e [elwaɲe] adj distant, far-off; **éloignement** [elwaɲmɑ̃] *nm* removal; putting off; estrangement; (*fig*) distance

éloigner [elwaɲe] *vt* (*objet*) to move *ou* take sth away (from); (*personne*) to take sb away *ou* remove sth (from); (*échéance*) to put off, postpone; (*soupçons, danger*) to ward off; **s'~** (**de**) (*personne*) to go away (from); (*véhicule*) to move away (from); (*affectivement*) to become estranged (from)

élongation [elɔ̃gasjɔ̃] *nf* strained muscle

élu, e [ely] *pp de* **élire** ♦ *nm/f* (POL) elected representative

élucubrations [elykybʀasjɔ̃] *nfpl* wild imaginings

éluder [elyde] *vt* to evade

Elysée *nm:* (**le palais de**) **l'~** (**the**) **Elysee Palace** (*the French president's residence*)

émacié, e [emasje] *adj* emaciated

émail, aux [emaj, -o] *nm* enamel

émaillé, e [emaje] *adj* (*fig*): **~ de** dotted with

émanciper [emɑ̃sipe] *vt* to emancipate; **s'~** *vi* (*fig*) to become emancipated *ou* liberated

émaner [emane]: **~ de** *vt* to come from; (ADMIN) to proceed from

emballage [ɑ̃balaʒ] *nm* wrapping; packaging

emballer [ɑ̃bale] *vt* to wrap (up); (*dans un carton*) to pack (up); (*fig: fam*) to thrill (to bits); **s'~** *vi* (*moteur*) to race; (*cheval*) to bolt; (*fig: personne*) to get carried away

embarcadère [ɑ̃baʀkadɛʀ] *nm* wharf, pier

embarcation [ɑ̃baʀkasjɔ̃] *nf* (small) boat, (small) craft *inv*

embardée [ɑ̃baʀde] *nf:* **faire une ~** to swerve

embarquement [ɑ̃baʀkəmɑ̃] *nm* embarkation; loading; boarding

embarquer [ɑ̃baʀke] *vt* (*personne*) to embark; (*marchandise*) to load; (*fam*) to cart off; to nick ♦ *vi* (*pas-*

sager) to board; **s'~** *vi* to board; **s'~ dans** (*affaire, aventure*) to embark upon

embarras [ɑ̃baʀa] *nm* (*obstacle*) hindrance; (*confusion*) embarrassment

embarrassant, e [ɑ̃baʀasɑ̃, -ɑ̃t] *adj* embarrassing

embarrasser [ɑ̃baʀase] *vt* (*encombrer*) to clutter (up); (*gêner*) to hinder, hamper; (*fig*) to put in an awkward position

embauche [ɑ̃boʃ] *nf* hiring; **bureau d'~** labour office; **~r** [ɑ̃boʃe] *vt* to take on, hire

embaumer [ɑ̃bome] *vt* to embalm; to fill with its fragrance; **~ la lavande** to be fragrant with (the scent of) lavender

embellie [ɑ̃beli] *nf* brighter period

embellir [ɑ̃beliʀ] *vt* to make more attractive; (*une histoire*) to embellish ♦ *vi* to grow lovelier *ou* more attractive

embêtements [ɑ̃bɛtmɑ̃] *nmpl* trouble *sg*

embêter [ɑ̃bɛte] *vt* to bother; **s'~** *vi* (*s'ennuyer*) to be bored

emblée [ɑ̃ble]: **d'~** *adv* straightaway

emboîter [ɑ̃bwate] *vt* to fit together; **s'~** (**dans**) to fit (into); **~ le pas à** qn to follow in sb's footsteps

embonpoint [ɑ̃bɔ̃pwɛ̃] *nm* stoutness

embouchure [ɑ̃buʃyʀ] *nf* (GEO) mouth

embourber [ɑ̃buʀbe]: **s'~** *vi* to get stuck in the mud

embourgeoiser [ɑ̃buʀʒwazœ]: **s'~** *vi* to adopt a middle-class outlook

embouteillage [ɑ̃butɛjaʒ] *nm* traffic jam

emboutir [ɑ̃butiʀ] *vt* (*heurter*) to crash into, ram

embranchement [ɑ̃bʀɑ̃ʃmɑ̃] *nm* (*routier*) junction; (*classification*) branch

embraser [ɑ̃bʀaze]: **s'~** *vi* to flare up

embrasser [ɑ̃bʀase] *vt* to kiss; (*su-*

jet, période) to embrace, encompass; *(carrière, métier)* to enter upon
embrasure [ɑ̃bʀɑzyʀ] *nf:* dans l'~ de la porte in the door(way)
embrayage [ɑ̃bʀɛjaʒ] *nm* clutch
embrayer [ɑ̃bʀeje] *vi (AUTO)* to let in the clutch
embrigader [ɑ̃bʀigade] *vt* to recruit
embrocher [ɑ̃bʀɔʃe] *vt* to put on a spit
embrouiller [ɑ̃bʀuje] *vt (fils)* to tangle (up); *(fiches, idées, personne)* to muddle up; s'~ *vi (personne)* to get in a muddle
embruns [ɑ̃bʀœ̃] *nmpl* sea spray *sg*
embûches [ɑ̃byʃ] *nfpl* pitfalls, traps
embué, e [ɑ̃bɥe] *adj* misted up
embuscade [ɑ̃byskad] *nf* ambush
embêché, e [ɑ̃meʃe] *adj* tipsy, merry
émeraude [emʀod] *nf* emerald
émerger [emɛʀʒe] *vi* to emerge; *(faire saillie, aussi fig)* to stand out
émeri [emʀi] *nm:* toile ou papier ~ emery paper
émérite [emeʀit] *adj* highly skilled
émerveiller [emɛʀveje] *vt* to fill with wonder; s'~ de to marvel at
émetteur, trice [emetœʀ, -tʀis] *adj* transmitting; *(poste)* ~ transmitter
émettre [emetʀ(ə)] *vt (son, lumière)* to give out, emit; *(message etc: RADIO)* to transmit; *(billet, timbre, emprunt)* to issue; *(hypothèse, avis)* to voice, put forward ♦ *vi* to broadcast
émeus *etc* vb voir **émouvoir**
émeute [emøt] *nf* riot
émietter [emjete] *vt* to crumble
émigrer [emigʀe] *vi* to emigrate
éminence [eminɑ̃s] *nf* distinction; *(colline)* knoll, hill; Son E~ His Eminence; **éminent, e** [eminɑ̃, -ɑ̃t] *adj* distinguished
émission [emisjɔ̃] *nf* emission; transmission; issue; *(RADIO, TV)* programme, broadcast; ~s *fpl* emissions
emmagasiner [ɑ̃magazine] *vt* to (put into) store; *(fig)* to store up
emmanchure [ɑ̃mɑ̃ʃyʀ] *nf* armhole

emmêler [ɑ̃mele] *vt* to tangle (up); *(fig)* to muddle up; s'~ *vi* to get into a tangle
emménager [ɑ̃menaʒe] *vi* to move in; ~ dans to move into
emmener [ɑ̃mne] *vt* to take (with one); *(comme otage, capture)* to take away; ~ qn au cinéma to take sb to the cinema
emmerder [ɑ̃mɛʀde] *(fam!) vt* to bug, bother; s'~ *vi* to be bored stiff
emmitoufler [ɑ̃mitufle] *vt* to wrap up (warmly)
émoi [emwa] *nm* commotion; *(trouble)* agitation
émonder [emɔ̃de] *vt* to prune
émotif, ive [emɔtif, -iv] *adj* emotional
émotion [emosjɔ̃] *nf* emotion
émousser [emuse] *vt* to blunt; *(fig)* to dull
émouvoir [emuvwaʀ] *vt (troubler)* to stir, affect; *(toucher, attendrir)* to move; *(indigner)* to rouse; s'~ *vi* to be affected; to be moved; to be roused
empailler [ɑ̃paje] *vt* to stuff
empaler [ɑ̃pale] *vt* to impale
emparer [ɑ̃paʀe]: s'~ de *vt (objet)* to seize, grab; *(comme otage, MIL)* to seize; *(suj: peur etc)* to take hold of
empâter [ɑ̃pɑte]: s'~ *vi* to thicken out
empêchement [ɑ̃pɛʃmɑ̃] *nm* (unexpected) obstacle, hitch
empêcher [ɑ̃pɛʃe] *vt* to prevent; ~ qn de faire to prevent ou stop sb (from) doing; il n'empêche que nevertheless; il n'a pas pu s'~ de rire he couldn't help laughing
empereur [ɑ̃pʀœʀ] *nm* emperor
empeser [ɑ̃pəze] *vt* to starch
empester [ɑ̃peste] *vi* to stink, reek
empêtrer [ɑ̃petʀe] *vt:* s'~ dans *(fils etc)* to get tangled up in
emphase [ɑ̃faz] *nf* pomposity, bombast
empiéter [ɑ̃pjete] *vi:* ~ sur to encroach upon

empiffrer [ɑ̃pifʀe]: **s'~** (*péj*) *vi* to stuff o.s.

empiler [ɑ̃pile] *vt* to pile (up)

empire [ɑ̃piʀ] *nm* empire; (*fig*) influence

empirer [ɑ̃piʀe] *vi* to worsen, deteriorate

emplacement [ɑ̃plasmɑ̃] *nm* site

emplettes [ɑ̃plɛt] *nfpl* shopping *sg*

emplir [ɑ̃pliʀ] *vt* to fill; **s'~** (**de**) to fill (with)

emploi [ɑ̃plwa] *nm* use; (*COMM, ECON*) employment; (*poste*) job, situation; **~ du temps** timetable, schedule

employé, e [ɑ̃plwaje] *nm/f* employee; **~ de bureau** office employee *ou* clerk

employer [ɑ̃plwaje] *vt* (*outil, moyen, méthode, mot*) to use; (*ouvrier, main-d'œuvre*) to employ; **s'~ à faire** to apply *ou* devote o.s. to doing; **employeur, euse** *nm/f* employer

empocher [ɑ̃pɔʃe] *vt* to pocket

empoigner [ɑ̃pwaɲe] *vt* to grab

empoisonner [ɑ̃pwazɔne] *vt* to poison; (*empester: air, pièce*) to stink out; (*fam*): **~ qn** to drive sb mad

emporté, e [ɑ̃pɔʀte] *adj* quicktempered

emporter [ɑ̃pɔʀte] *vt* to take (with one); (*en dérobant ou enlevant, emmener: blessés, voyageurs*) to take away; (*entraîner*) to carry away; (*arracher*) to tear off; (*avantage, approbation*) to win; **s'~** (*de colère*) to lose one's temper; **l'~** (**sur**) to get the upper hand (of); (*méthode etc*) to prevail (over); **boissons à ~** take-away drinks

empreint, e [ɑ̃pʀɛ̃, -ɛ̃t] *adj*: **~ de** marked with; tinged with; **empreinte** *nf* (*de pied, main*) print; (*fig*) stamp, mark; **~e** (**digitale**) fingerprint

empressé, e [ɑ̃pʀese] *adj* attentive

empressement [ɑ̃pʀɛsmɑ̃] *nm* (*hâte*) eagerness

empresser [ɑ̃pʀese]: **s'~** *vi* to surround sb with attentions; **s'~ de faire** (*se hâter*) to hasten to do

emprise [ɑ̃pʀiz] *nf* hold, ascendancy

emprisonner [ɑ̃pʀizɔne] *vt* to imprison

emprunt [ɑ̃pʀœ̃] *nm* borrowing *no pl*, loan

emprunté, e [ɑ̃pʀœ̃te] *adj* (*fig*) ill-at-ease, awkward

emprunter [ɑ̃pʀœ̃te] *vt* to borrow; (*itinéraire*) to take, follow; (*style, manière*) to adopt, assume

ému, e [emy] *pp de* **émouvoir ♦** *adj* excited; touched; moved

émulsion [emylsjɔ̃] *nf* (*cosmétique*) (water-based) lotion

MOT-CLÉ

---

en [ɑ̃] *prép* **1** (*endroit, pays*) in; (*direction*) to; **habiter ~ France/ville** to live in France/town; **aller ~ France/ville** to go to France/town

2 (*moment, temps*) in; **~ été/juin** in summer/June

3 (*moyen*) by; **~ avion/taxi** by plane/taxi

4 (*composition*) made of; **c'est ~ verre** it's (made of) glass; **un collier ~ argent** a silver necklace

5 (*description, état*): **une femme** (**habillée**) **~ rouge** a woman (dressed) in red; **peindre qch ~ rouge** to paint sth red; **~ T/étoile** T/star-shaped; **~ chemise/chaussettes** in one's shirt sleeves/socks; **~ soldat** as a soldier; **cassé ~ plusieurs morceaux** broken into several pieces; **~ réparation** being repaired, under repair; **~ vacances** on holiday; **~ deuil** in mourning; **le même ~ plus grand** the same but *ou* only bigger

6 (*avec gérondif*) while; on; by; **~ dormant** while sleeping, as one sleeps; **~ sortant** on going out, as he *etc* went out; **sortir ~ courant** to run out

♦ *pron* **1** (*indéfini*): **j'~ ai/veux** I have/want some; **~ as-tu?** have you got any?; **je n'~ veux pas** I don't want any; **j'~ ai 2** I've got 2; **combien y ~ a-t-il?** how many (of them) are there?; **j'~ ai assez** I've got enough (of it ou them); **(j'en ai marre)** I've had enough

2 (provenance) from there; **j'en viens** I've come from there

3 (cause): **il ~ est malade/perd le sommeil** he is ill/can't sleep because of it

4 (complément de nom, d'adjectif, de verbe): **j'~ connais les dangers** I know its ou the dangers; **j'~ suis fier/ai besoin** I am proud of it/need it

E.N.A. [cna] sigle f (= École Nationale d'Administration) one of the Grandes Écoles

encadrer [ɑ̃kɑdʀe] vt (tableau, image) to frame; (fig: entourer) to surround; (personnel, soldats etc) to train

encaissé, e [ɑ̃kese] adj steep-sided; with steep banks

encaisser [ɑ̃kese] vt (chèque) to cash; (argent) to collect; (fig: coup, défaite) to take

encart [ɑ̃kaʀ] nm insert

encastrer [ɑ̃kastʀe] vt: **~ qch dans** (mur) to embed sth in(to); (boîtier) to fit sth into

encaustique [ɑ̃kostik] nf polish, wax

enceinte [ɑ̃sɛ̃t] adj f: **~ (de 6 mois)** (6 months) pregnant ♦ nf (mur) wall; (espace) enclosure

encens [ɑ̃sɑ̃] nm incense

encercler [ɑ̃sɛʀkle] vt to surround

enchaîner [ɑ̃ʃene] vt to chain up; (mouvements, séquences) to link (together) ♦ vi to carry on

enchanté, e [ɑ̃ʃɑ̃te] adj delighted; enchanted; **~ (de faire votre connaissance)** pleased to meet you

enchantement [ɑ̃ʃɑ̃tmɑ̃] nm delight; (magie) enchantment

enchâsser [ɑ̃ʃɑse] vt to set

enchère [ɑ̃ʃɛʀ] nf bid; **mettre/vendre aux ~s** to put up for (sale by)/sell by auction

enchevêtrer [ɑ̃ʃvetʀe] vt to tangle (up)

enclencher [ɑ̃klɑ̃ʃe] vt (mécanisme) to engage; **s'~** vi to engage

enclin, e [ɑ̃klɛ̃, -in] adj: **~ à** inclined ou prone to

enclos [ɑ̃klo] nm enclosure

enclume [ɑ̃klym] nf anvil

encoche [ɑ̃kɔʃ] nf notch

encoignure [ɑ̃kɔɲyʀ] nf corner

encolure [ɑ̃kɔlyʀ] nf (tour de cou) collar size; (col, cou) neck

encombrant, e [ɑ̃kɔ̃bʀɑ̃, -ɑ̃t] adj cumbersome, bulky

encombre [ɑ̃kɔ̃bʀ(ə)]: **sans ~** adv without mishap ou incident

encombrer [ɑ̃kɔ̃bʀe] vt to clutter (up); (gêner) to hamper; **s'~ de** (bagages etc) to load ou burden o.s. with

encontre [ɑ̃kɔ̃tʀ(ə)]: **à l'~ de** prép against, counter to

MOT-CLÉ

encore [ɑ̃kɔʀ] adv **1** (continuation) still; **il y travaille ~** he's still working on it; **pas ~** not yet

2 (de nouveau) again; **j'irai ~ demain** I'll go again tomorrow; **~ une fois** (once) again; **~ deux jours** two more days

3 (intensif) even, still; **~ plus fort/mieux** even louder/better, louder/better still

4 (restriction) even so ou then, only; **~ pourrais-je le faire si ...** even so, I might be able to do it if ...; **si ~** if only

encore que conj although

---

encourager [ɑ̃kuʀaʒe] vt to encourage

encourir [ɑ̃kuʀiʀ] vt to incur

encrasser [ɑ̃kʀase] vt to clog up; (AUTO: bougies) to soot up

encre [ɑ̃kʀ(ə)] nf ink; **~ de Chine** Indian ink; **encrier** nm inkwell

encroûter [ɑ̃kʀute]: **s'~** vi (fig) to get into a rut, get set in one's ways

encyclopédie [ɑ̃siklɔpedi] nf encyclopaedia

endetter [ɑ̃dete] vt to get into debt;

s'~ *vi* to get into debt

endiablé, e [ɑ̃djable] *adj* furious; boisterous

endiguer [ɑ̃dige] *vt* to dyke (up); (*fig*) to check, hold back

endimancher [ɑ̃dimɑ̃ʃe] *vt*: s'~ to put on one's Sunday best

endive [ɑ̃div] *nf* chicory *no pl*

endoctriner [ɑ̃dɔktrine] *vt* to indoctrinate

endommager [ɑ̃dɔmaʒe] *vt* to damage

endormi, e [ɑ̃dɔrmi] *adj* asleep

endormir [ɑ̃dɔrmir] *vt* to put to sleep; (*suj: chaleur etc*) to send to sleep; (MED: *dent, nerf*) to anaesthetize; (*fig: soupçons*) to allay; s'~ *vi* to fall asleep, go to sleep

endosser [ɑ̃dose] *vt* (*responsabilité*) to take, shoulder; (*chèque*) to endorse; (*uniforme, tenue*) to put on, don

endroit [ɑ̃drwa] *nm* place; (*opposé à l'envers*) right side; à l'~ the right way out; the right way up; à l'~ de regarding

enduire [ɑ̃dɥir] *vt* to coat

enduit [ɑ̃dɥi] *nm* coating

endurant, e [ɑ̃dyrɑ̃, -ɑ̃t] *adj* tough, hardy

endurcir [ɑ̃dyrsir] *vt* (*physiquement*) to toughen; (*moralement*) to harden; s'~ *vi* to become tougher; to become hardened

endurer [ɑ̃dyre] *vt* to endure, bear

énergie [enerʒi] *nf* (PHYSIQUE) energy; (TECH) power; (*morale*) vigour, spirit; **énergique** *adj* energetic; vigorous; (*mesures*) drastic, stringent

énergumène [energymɛn] *nm* rowdy character *ou* customer

énerver [enerve] *vt* to irritate, annoy; s'~ *vi* to get excited, get worked up

enfance [ɑ̃fɑ̃s] *nf* (*âge*) childhood; (*fig*) infancy; (*enfants*) children *pl*

enfant [ɑ̃fɑ̃] *nm/f* child; ~ de chœur *nm* (REL) altar boy; ~er *vi* to give birth ♦ *vt* to give birth to; ~illage

(*péj*) *nm* childish behaviour *no pl*; ~in, e *adj* childlike; child *cpd*

enfer [ɑ̃fɛr] *nm* hell

enfermer [ɑ̃fɛrme] *vt* to shut up; (à *clef, interner*) to lock up

enfiévré, e [ɑ̃fjevre] *adj* (*fig*) feverish

enfiler [ɑ̃file] *vt* (*vêtement*) to slip on, slip into; (*insérer*): ~ qch dans to stick sth into; (*rue, couloir*) to take; (*perles*) to string; (*aiguille*) to thread

enfin [ɑ̃fɛ̃] *adv* at last; (*en énumérant*) lastly; (*de restriction, résignation*) still; well; (*pour conclure*) in a word

enflammer [ɑ̃flame] *vt* to set fire to; (MED) to inflame; s'~ *vi* to catch fire; to become inflamed

enflé, e [ɑ̃fle] *adj* swollen

enfler [ɑ̃fle] *vi* to swell (up)

enfoncer [ɑ̃fɔ̃se] *vt* (*clou*) to drive in; (*faire pénétrer*): ~ qch dans to push (*ou* drive) sth into; (*forcer: porte*) to break open; (: *plancher*) to cause to cave in (*dans la vase etc*) to sink in; (*sol, surface*) to give way; s'~ *vi* to sink in; (*forêt, ville*) to disappear into

enfouir [ɑ̃fwir] *vt* (*dans le sol*) to bury; (*dans un tiroir etc*) to tuck away

enfourcher [ɑ̃furʃe] *vt* to mount

enfourner [ɑ̃furne] *vt* to put in the oven

enfreindre [ɑ̃frɛ̃dr(ə)] *vt* to infringe, break

enfuir [ɑ̃fɥir]: s'~ *vi* to run away *ou* off

enfumer [ɑ̃fyme] *vt* to smoke out

engageant, e [ɑ̃gaʒɑ̃, -ɑ̃t] *adj* attractive, appealing

engagement [ɑ̃gaʒmɑ̃] *nm* (*promesse, contrat, POL*) commitment; (MIL: *combat, POL*) engagement

engager [ɑ̃gaʒe] *vt* (*embaucher*) to take on, engage; (*commencer*) to start; (*lier*) to bind, commit; (*impliquer, entraîner*) to involve; (*investir*) to invest, lay out; (*faire intervenir* to engage; (*inciter*) to urge; (*faire pénétrer*) to insert; to turn s.o. on, get taken on; (*MIL*) to enlist; (*promettre, politiquement*) to commit o.s.; (*débuter*) to start (up); **s'~ à faire** to undertake to do; **s'~ dans** (*rue, passage*) to turn into; (*s'emboîter*) to engage into; (*fig: affaire, discussion*) to enter into, embark on

engelures [āʒlyʀ] *nfpl* chilblains

engendrer [āʒādʀe] *vt* to father

engin [āʒɛ̃] *nm* machine; instrument; vehicle; (*AVIAT*) aircraft *inv*; missile

englober [āglɔbe] *vt* to include

engloutir [āglutiʀ] *vt* to swallow up

engoncé, e [āgɔ̃se] *adj*: **~ dans** cramped in

engorger [āgɔʀʒe] *vt* to obstruct, block

engouement [āgumā] *nm* (sudden) passion

engouffrer [āgufʀe] *vt* to swallow up, devour; **s'~ dans** to rush into

engourdir [āguʀdiʀ] *vt* to numb; (*fig*) to dull, blunt; **s'~** *vi* to go numb

engrais [āgʀɛ] *nm* manure; **~ (chimique)** (chemical) fertilizer

engraisser [āgʀese] *vt* to fatten

engrenage [āgʀənaʒ] *nm* gears *pl*, gearing; (*fig*) chain

engueuler [āgœle] *vt* (*fam*) to bawl at

enhardir [āaʀdiʀ]: **s'~** *vi* to grow bolder

énigme [enigm(ə)] *nf* riddle

enivrer [ānivʀe] *vt*: **s'~** to get drunk; **s'~ de** (*fig*) to become intoxicated with

enjambée [āʒābe] *nf* stride

enjamber [āʒābe] *vt* to stride over; (*suj: pont etc*) to span, straddle

enjeu, x [āʒø] *nm* stakes *pl*

enjoindre [āʒwɛ̃dʀ(ə)] *vt* to enjoin, order

enjôler [āʒole] *vt* to coax, wheedle

enjoliver [āʒɔlive] *vt* to embellish

enjoliveur *nm* (*AUTO*) hub cap

enjoué, e [āʒwe] *adj* playful

enlacer [ālase] *vt* (*étreindre*) to embrace, hug

enlaidir [ālediʀ] *vt* to make ugly ♦ *vi* to become ugly

enlèvement [ālɛvmā] *nm* (*rapt*) abduction, kidnapping

enlever [āl(ə)ve] *vt* (*ôter: gén*) to remove; (: *vêtement, lunettes*) to take off; (*emporter: ordures etc*) to take away; (*prendre*): **~ qch à qn** to take sth (away) from sb; (*kidnapper*) to abduct, kidnap; (*obtenir: prix, contrat*) to win

enliser [ālize]: **s'~** *vi* to sink, get stuck

enluminure [ālyminyʀ] *nf* illumination

enneigé, e [āneʒe] *adj* snowy; snowed-up

ennemi, e [ɛnmi] *adj* hostile; (*MIL*) enemy *cpd* ♦ *nm/f* enemy

ennui [ānɥi] *nm* (*lassitude*) boredom; (*difficulté*) trouble *no pl*; **avoir des ~s** to have problems; **ennuyer** *vt* to bother; (*lasser*) to bore; **s'ennuyer** *vi* to be bored; **s'ennuyer de** (*regretter*) to miss; **ennuyeux, euse** *adj* boring, tedious; annoying

énoncé [enɔ̃se] *nm* terms *pl*; wording

énoncer [enɔ̃se] *vt* to say, express; (*conditions*) to set out, state

enorgueillir [ānɔʀgœjiʀ]: **s'~ de** to pride o.s. on; to boast

énorme [enɔʀm(ə)] *adj* enormous, huge; **énormément** *adv* enormously; **énormément de neige/gens** an enormous amount of snow/number of people

enquérir [ākeʀiʀ]: **s'~ de** *vt* to inquire about

enquête [ākɛt] *nf* (*de journaliste, de police*) investigation; (*judiciaire, administrative*) inquiry; (*sondage d'opinion*) survey; **enquêter** *vi* to investigate; to hold an inquiry; to conduct a survey

enquiers *etc vb voir* **enquérir**

enraciné, e [āʀasine] *adj* deep-rooted

enragé, e [ɑ̃ʀaʒe] adj (MÉD) rabid, with rabies; (fig) fanatical

enrageant, e [ɑ̃ʀaʒɑ̃, -ɑ̃t] adj infuriating

enrager [ɑ̃ʀaʒe] vi to be in a rage

enrayer [ɑ̃ʀeje] vt to check, stop; **s'~** vi (arme à feu) to jam

enregistrement [ɑ̃ʀʒistʀəmɑ̃] nm recording; (ADMIN) registration; **~ des bagages** (à l'aéroport) baggage check-in; **enregistrer** [ɑ̃ʀʒistʀe] vt (MUS etc, remarquer, noter) to record; (fig: mémoriser) to make a mental note of; (ADMIN) to register; (bagages: par train) to register; (: à l'aéroport) to check in

enrhumer [ɑ̃ʀyme]: **s'~** vi to catch a cold

enrichir [ɑ̃ʀiʃiʀ] vt to make rich(er); (fig) to enrich; **s'~** vi to get rich(er)

enrober [ɑ̃ʀɔbe] vt: **~ qch de** to coat sth with; (fig) to wrap sth up in

enrôler [ɑ̃ʀole] vt to enlist; **s'~ (dans)** to enlist (in)

enrouer [ɑ̃ʀwe]: **s'~** vi to go hoarse

enrouler [ɑ̃ʀule] vt (fil, corde) to wind (up); **s'~** vi to coil up; to wind; **~ qch autour de** to wind sth (a)round

ensanglanté, e [ɑ̃sɑ̃glɑ̃te] adj covered with blood

enseignant, e [ɑ̃sɛɲɑ̃, -ɑ̃t] nm/f teacher

enseigne [ɑ̃sɛɲ] nf sign; **à telle ~ que** so much so that; **~ lumineuse** neon sign

enseignement [ɑ̃sɛɲmɑ̃] nm teaching; (ADMIN) education

enseigner [ɑ̃sɛɲe] vt, vi to teach; **~ qch à qn/à qn que** to teach sb sth/sb that

ensemble [ɑ̃sɑ̃bl(ə)] adv together ♦ nm (assemblage, MATH) set; (totalité): **l'~ du/de la** the whole ou entire; (unité, harmonie) unity; **impression/idée d'~** overall ou general impression/idea; **dans l'~ (en gros)** on the whole

ensemencer [ɑ̃səmɑ̃se] vt to sow

ensevelir [ɑ̃səvliʀ] vt to bury

ensoleillé, e [ɑ̃sɔleje] adj sunny

ensommeillé, e [ɑ̃sɔmeje] adj drowsy

ensorceler [ɑ̃sɔʀsəle] vt to enchant, bewitch

ensuite [ɑ̃sɥit] adv then, next; (plus tard) afterwards, later; **~ de quoi** after which

ensuivre [ɑ̃sɥivʀ(ə)]: **s'~** vi to follow, ensue

entailler [ɑ̃tɑje] vt to notch; to cut

entamer [ɑ̃tame] vt (pain, bouteille) to start; (hostilités, pourparlers) to open; (fig: altérer) to make a dent in; to shake; to damage

entasser [ɑ̃tase] vt (empiler) to pile up, heap up; (tenir à l'étroit) to cram together; **s'~** vi to pile up; to cram

entendre [ɑ̃tɑ̃dʀ(ə)] vt to hear; (comprendre) to understand; (vouloir dire) to mean; (vouloir): **~ être obéi/que** to mean to be obeyed/that; **s'~** vi (sympathiser) to agree; **s'~ (à qch/à faire)** (être compétent) to be good at sth/doing; **j'ai entendu dire que** I've heard (it said) that

entendu, e [ɑ̃tɑ̃dy] adj (réglé) agreed; (au courant: air) knowing; **(c'est) ~** all right, agreed; **c'est ~ (concession)** all right, granted; **bien ~** of course

entente [ɑ̃tɑ̃t] nf understanding; (accord, traité) agreement; **à double ~ (sens)** with a double meaning

entériner [ɑ̃teʀine] vt to ratify, confirm

enterrement [ɑ̃tɛʀmɑ̃] nm (cérémonie) funeral, burial

enterrer [ɑ̃teʀe] vt to bury

entêtant, e [ɑ̃tɛtɑ̃, -ɑ̃t] adj heady

entêté, e [ɑ̃tete] adj stubborn

en-tête [ɑ̃tɛt] nm heading; **papier à ~** headed notepaper

entêter [ɑ̃tete]: **s'~** vi to persist (in doing)

enthousiasme [ɑ̃tuzjasm(ə)] nm enthusiasm; **~r** vt to fill with enthusiasm; **s'~r (pour qch)** to get enthusiastic (about sth)

enticher [ɑ̃tiʃe]: **s'~ de** vt to become infatuated with

entier, ère [ɑ̃tje, -jɛʀ] adj (non entamé, en totalité) whole; (total, complet) complete; (fig: caractère) unbending ♦ nm (MATH) whole; **en ~** totally; in its entirety; **lait ~** full-cream milk; **entièrement** adv entirely, wholly

entonner [ɑ̃tɔne] vt (chanson) to strike up

entonnoir [ɑ̃tɔnwaʀ] nm funnel

entorse [ɑ̃tɔʀs(ə)] nf (MED) sprain; (fig): **~ au reglement** infringement of the rule

entortiller [ɑ̃tɔʀtije] vt (envelopper) to wrap; (enrouler) to twist, wind; (duper) to deceive

entourage [ɑ̃tuʀaʒ] nm circle, family (circle); entourage; (ce qui enclot) surround

entourer [ɑ̃tuʀe] vt to surround; (apporter son soutien à) to rally round; **~ de** to surround with; (trait) to encircle with

entourloupettes [ɑ̃tuʀlupɛt] nfpl mean tricks

entracte [ɑ̃tʀakt(ə)] nm interval

entraide [ɑ̃tʀɛd] nf mutual aid; **s'~r** vi to help each other

entrain [ɑ̃tʀɛ̃] nm spirit; **avec/sans ~** spiritedly/half-heartedly

entraînement [ɑ̃tʀɛnmɑ̃] nm training; (TECH) drive

entraîner [ɑ̃tʀene] vt (tirer: wagons) to pull; (charrier) to carry ou drag along; (TECH) to drive; (emmener: personne) to take (off); (mener à l'assaut, influencer) to lead; (SPORT) to train; (impliquer) to entail; (causer) to lead to, bring about; **s'~** vi (SPORT) to train; **s'~ à qch/à faire** to train o.s. for sth/to do; **~ qn à faire** (inciter) to lead sb to do; **entraîneur, euse** nm/f (SPORT) coach, trainer ♦ nm (HIPPISME) trainer; **entraîneuse** nf (de bar) hostess

entraver [ɑ̃tʀave] vt (circulation) to hold up; (action, progrès) to hinder

entre [ɑ̃tʀ(ə)] prép between; (parmi) among(st); **l'un d'~ eux/nous** one of them/us; **~ eux** among(st) themselves

entre-: ~bâillé, e adj half-open, ajar; **~choquer: s'~** vi to knock ou bang together; **~côte** nf entrecôte ou rib steak; **~couper: ~ qch de** to intersperse with; **~croiser: s'~** vi to intertwine

entrée [ɑ̃tʀe] nf entrance; (accès: au cinéma etc) admission; (billet) (admission) ticket; (CULIN) first course; **d'~** from the outset; **en matière** introduction

entrefaites [ɑ̃tʀəfɛt]: **sur ces ~** adv at this juncture

entrefilet [ɑ̃tʀəfile] nm paragraph (short article)

entrejambes [ɑ̃tʀəʒɑ̃b] nm crotch

entrelacer [ɑ̃tʀəlase] vt to intertwine

entrelarder [ɑ̃tʀəlaʀde] vt to lard

entremêler [ɑ̃tʀəmele] vt: **~ qch de** to (inter)mingle sth with

entremets [ɑ̃tʀəmɛ] nm (cream) dessert

entremetteur, euse [ɑ̃tʀəmɛtœʀ, -øz] nm/f go-between

entremise [ɑ̃tʀəmiz] nf intervention; **par l'~ de** through

entreposer [ɑ̃tʀəpoze] vt to store, put into storage

entrepôt [ɑ̃tʀəpo] nm warehouse

entreprenant, e [ɑ̃tʀəpʀənɑ̃, -ɑ̃t] adj (actif) enterprising; (trop galant) forward

entreprendre [ɑ̃tʀəpʀɑ̃dʀ(ə)] vt (se lancer dans) to undertake; (commencer) to begin ou start (upon); (personne) to buttonhole; to tackle

entrepreneur [ɑ̃tʀəpʀənœʀ] nm: **~ (en bâtiment)** (building) contractor

entreprise [ɑ̃tʀəpʀiz] nf (société) firm, concern; (action) undertaking, venture

entrer [ɑ̃tʀe] vi to go (ou come) in, enter ♦ vt (INFORM) to enter, input; (faire) **~ qch dans** to get sth into; ~ **dans** (gén) to enter; (pièce) to go (ou come) into; enter; (club) to join; (heurter) to run into; (être une composante de) to go into; to form part of; ~ **à l'hôpital** to go into hospital; **faire** ~ (visiteur) to show in

entresol [ɑ̃trəsɔl] nm mezzanine

entre-temps [ɑ̃trətɑ̃] adv meanwhile

entretenir [ɑ̃trətnir] vt to maintain; (famille, maîtresse) to support, keep; **s'~ (de)** to converse (about); ~ **qn (de)** to speak to sb (about)

entretien [ɑ̃trətjɛ̃] nm maintenance; (discussion) discussion, talk; (audience) interview

entrevoir [ɑ̃trəvwar] vt (à peine) to make out; (brièvement) to catch a glimpse of

entrevue [ɑ̃trəvy] nf meeting; (audience) interview

entrouvert, e [ɑ̃truvɛr, -ɛrt(ə)] adj half-open

énumérer [enymere] vt to list, enumerate

envahir [ɑ̃vair] vt to invade; (suj: inquiétude, peur) to come over; **envahissant, e** (péj) adj (personne) interfering, intrusive

enveloppe [ɑ̃vlɔp] nf (de lettre) envelope; (TECH) casing; outer layer

envelopper [ɑ̃vlɔpe] vt to wrap; (fig) to envelop, shroud

envenimer [ɑ̃vnime] vt to aggravate

envergure [ɑ̃vɛrgyr] nf (fig) scope; calibre

enverrai etc vb voir **envoyer**

envers [ɑ̃vɛr] prép towards, to, ♦ nm other side; (d'une étoffe) wrong side; **à l'**~ upside down; back to front; (vêtement) inside out

envie [ɑ̃vi] nf (sentiment) envy; (souhait) desire, wish; **avoir ~ de** (faire) to feel like (doing); (plus fort) to want (to do); **avoir ~ que** to wish that; **ça lui fait** ~ he would like that; **envier** vt to envy; **envieux, euse** adj envious

environ [ɑ̃virɔ̃] adv: ~ **3 h/2 km** (around) about 3 o'clock/2 km; voir

aussi **environs**

environnement [ɑ̃virɔnmɑ̃] nm environment

environner [ɑ̃virɔne] vt to surround

environs [ɑ̃virɔ̃] nmpl surroundings

envisager [ɑ̃vizaʒe] vt (examiner, considérer) to view, contemplate; (avoir en vue) to envisage

envoi [ɑ̃vwa] nm (paquet) parcel, consignment

envoler [ɑ̃vɔle]: **s'~** vi (oiseau) to fly away ou off; (avion) to take off; (papier, feuille) to blow away; (fig) to vanish (into thin air)

envoûter [ɑ̃vute] vt to bewitch

envoyé, e [ɑ̃vwaje] nm/f (POL) envoy; (PRESSE) correspondent

envoyer [ɑ̃vwaje] vt to send; (lancer) to hurl, throw; ~ **chercher** to send for

épagneul, e [epaɲœl] nm/f spaniel

épais, se [epɛ, -ɛs] adj thick; **épaisseur** nf thickness

épancher [epɑ̃ʃe]: **s'~** vi to open one's heart

épanouir [epanwir]: **s'~** vi (fleur) to bloom, come out; (visage) to light up; (fig) to blossom; to open up

épargne [eparɲ(ə)] nf saving

épargner [eparɲe] vt to save; (ne pas tuer ou endommager) to spare ♦ vi to save; ~ **qch à qn** to spare sb sth

éparpiller [eparpije] vt to scatter; (pour répartir) to disperse; **s'~** vi to scatter; (fig) to dissipate one's efforts

épars, e [epar, -ars(ə)] adj scattered

épatant, e [epatɑ̃, -ɑ̃t] (fam) adj super

épater [epate] vt to amaze; to impress

épaule [epol] nf shoulder

épauler [epole] vt (aider) to back up, support; (arme) to raise (to one's shoulder) ♦ vi to (take) aim

épaulette [epolɛt] nf epaulette; (rembourrage) shoulder pad

épave [epav] nf wreck

épée [epe] nf sword

épeler [eple] vt to spell

éperdu, e [epɛʀdy] adj distraught, overcome; passionate; frantic

éperon [epʀɔ̃] nm spur

épi [epi] nm (de blé, d'orge) ear

épice [epis] nf spice

épicer [epise] vt to spice

épicerie [episʀi] nf grocer's shop; (denrées) groceries pl; (: fine delicatessen; **épicier, ière** nm/f grocer

épidémie [epidemi] nf epidemic

épier [epje] vt to spy on, watch closely; (occasion) to look out for

épilepsie [epilɛpsi] nf epilepsy

épiler [epile] vt (jambes) to remove the hair from; (sourcils) to pluck

épilogue [epilɔg] nm (fig) conclusion, dénouement; **~r** [epilɔge] vi: **~r sur** to hold forth on

épinards [epinaʀ] nmpl spinach sg

épine [epin] nf thorn, prickle; (d'oursin etc) spine; **~ dorsale** backbone

épingle [epɛ̃gl(ə)] nf pin; **~ de nourrice** safety pin; **~ de sûreté ou double** safety pin

épingler [epɛ̃gle] vt (badge, décoration): **~ qch sur** to pin sth on(to); (fam) to catch, nick

épique [epik] adj epic

épisode [epizɔd] nm episode; film/roman **à ~s** serial; **épisodique** adj occasional

éploré, e [eplɔʀe] adj tearful

épluche-légumes [eplyʃlegym] nm inv (potato) peeler

éplucher [eplyʃe] vt (fruit, légumes) to peel; (fig) to go over with a fine-tooth comb; **épluchures** nfpl peelings

éponge [epɔ̃ʒ] nf sponge; **~r** vt (liquide) to mop up; (surface) to sponge; (fig: déficit) to soak up; **s'~r le front** to mop one's brow

épopée [epɔpe] nf epic

époque [epɔk] nf (de l'histoire) age, era; (de l'année, la vie) time; **d'~** (meuble) period cpd

poumoner [epumɔne]: **s'~** vi to shout o.s. hoarse

épouse [epuz] nf wife

épouser [epuze] vt to marry; (fig: idées) to espouse; (: forme) to fit

épousseter [epuste] vt to dust

époustouflant, e [epustuflɑ̃, -ɑ̃t] adj staggering, mind-boggling

épouvantable [epuvɑ̃tabl(ə)] adj appalling, dreadful

épouvantail [epuvɑ̃taj] nm (à oiseaux) scarecrow

épouvante [epuvɑ̃t] nf terror; **film d'~** horror film; **épouvanter** vt to terrify

époux [epu] nm husband ♦ nmpl (married) couple

éprendre [epʀɑ̃dʀ(ə)]: **s'~ de** vt to fall in love with

épreuve [epʀœv] nf (d'examen) test; (malheur, difficulté) trial, ordeal; (PHOTO) print; (TYPO) proof; (SPORT) event; **à l'~ des balles** bulletproof; **à toute ~** unfailing; **mettre à l'~** to put to the test

épris, e [epʀi, -iz] pp de **éprendre**

éprouver [epʀuve] vt (tester) to test; (marquer, faire souffrir) to afflict, distress; (ressentir) to experience

éprouvette [epʀuvɛt] nf test tube

épuisé, e [epɥize] adj exhausted; (livre) out of print; **épuisement** [epɥizmɑ̃] nm exhaustion

épuiser [epɥize] vt (fatiguer) to exhaust, wear ou tire out; (stock, sujet) to exhaust; **s'~** vi to wear ou tire o.s. out, exhaust o.s.; (stock) to run out

épurer [epyʀe] vt (liquide) to purify; (parti etc) to purge; (langue, texte) to refine

équateur [ekwatœʀ] nm equator; **(la république de) l'E~** Ecuador

équation [ekwasjɔ̃] nf equation

équerre [ekɛʀ] nf (à dessin) (set) square; (pour fixer) brace; **en ~** at right angles; **à l'~, d'~** straight

équilibre [ekilibʀ(ə)] nm balance; (d'une balance) equilibrium; **garder/perdre l'~** to keep/lose one's balance; **être en ~** to be balanced; **équilibré, e** adj (fig) well-balanced, stable; **équilibrer** vt to balance; **s'~** vi (poids) to balance; (fig: défauts etc) to balance each other out

équipage [ekipaʒ] nm crew

équipe [ekip] nf team; (bande: parfois péj) bunch

équipé, e [ekipe] adj: **bien/mal ~** well-/poorly-equipped

équipée [ekipe] nf escapade

équipement [ekipmã] nm equipment; **~s** nmpl (installations) amenities, facilities

équiper [ekipe] vt to equip; (voiture, cuisine) to equip, fit out; **~ qn/qch de** to equip sb/sth with

équipier, ière [ekipje, -jɛʀ] nm/f team member

équitable [ekitabl(ə)] adj fair

équitation [ekitasjɔ̃] nf (horse-)riding

équivalent, e [ekivalã, -ãt] adj, nm equivalent

équivaloir [ekivalwaʀ]: **~ à** vt to be equivalent to

équivoque [ekivɔk] adj equivocal, ambiguous; (louche) dubious

érable [eʀabl(ə)] nm maple

érafler [eʀafle] vt to scratch; **éraflure** nf scratch

éraillé, e [eʀaje] adj (voix) rasping

ère [ɛʀ] nf era; **en l'an 1050 de notre ~** in the year 1050 A.D.

érection [eʀɛksjɔ̃] nf erection

éreinter [eʀɛ̃te] vt to exhaust, wear out

ériger [eʀiʒe] vt (monument) to erect

ermite [ɛʀmit] nm hermit

éroder [eʀɔde] vt to erode

érotique [eʀɔtik] adj erotic

errer [eʀe] vi to wander

erreur [eʀœʀ] nf mistake, error; (morale) error; **faire ~** to be mistaken; **par ~** by mistake; **~ judiciaire** miscarriage of justice

érudit, e [eʀydi, -it] nm/f scholar

éruption [eʀypsjɔ̃] nf eruption; (MED) rash

es vb voir **être**

ès [ɛs] prép: **licencié ~ lettres/ sciences** ≈ Bachelor of Arts/Science

escabeau, x [ɛskabo] nm (tabouret) stool; (échelle) stepladder

escadre [ɛskadʀ(ə)] nf (NAVIG) squadron; (AVIAT) wing

escadron [ɛskadʀɔ̃] nm squadron

escalade [ɛskalad] nf climbing no pl; (POL etc) escalation

escalader [ɛskalade] vt to climb

escale [ɛskal] nf (NAVIG) call; port of call; (AVIAT) stop(over); **faire ~ à** to put in at; to stop over at

escalier [ɛskalje] nm stairs pl; dans l'~ ou les **~s** on the stairs; **~ roulant** escalator

escamoter [ɛskamɔte] vt (esquiver) to get round, evade; (faire disparaître) to conjure away

escapade [ɛskapad] nf: **faire une ~** to go on a jaunt; to run away ou off

escargot [ɛskaʀɡo] nm snail

escarmouche [ɛskaʀmuʃ] nf skirmish

escarpé, e [ɛskaʀpe] adj steep

escient [ɛsjã] nm: **à bon ~** advisedly

esclaffer [ɛsklafe]: **s'~** vi to guffaw

esclandre [ɛsklɑ̃dʀ(ə)] nm scene, fracas

esclavage [ɛsklavaʒ] nm slavery

esclave [ɛsklav] nm/f slave

escompter [ɛskɔ̃te] vt (COMM) to discount; (espérer) to expect, reckon upon

escorte [ɛskɔʀt(ə)] nf escort

escrime [ɛskʀim] nf fencing

escrimer [ɛskʀime]: **s'~** vi to wear o.s. out doing

escroc [ɛskʀo] nm swindler, conman

escroquer [ɛskʀɔke] vt: **~ qn (de qch)/qch (à qn)** to swindle sb (out of sth)/sth (out of sb); **escroquerie** nf swindle

espace [ɛspas] nm space

espacer [ɛspase] vt to space out; **s'~** vi (visites etc) to become less frequent

espadon [ɛspadɔ̃] nm swordfish no pl

espadrille [ɛspadʀij] nf rope-soled sandal

Espagne [ɛspaɲ(ə)] nf: **l'~** Spain

espagnol, e adj Spanish ♦ nm/f: **Es**

pagnol, e Spaniard ♦ *nm* (LING) Spanish

espèce [espɛs] *nf* (BIO, BOT, ZOOL) species *inv*; (*gén*: *sorte*) sort, kind, type; (*péj*): ~ **de maladroit!** you clumsy oaf!; ~ **s** *nfpl* (COMM) cash *sg*; **en** ~ in cash; **en l'~** in the case in point

espérance [espɛrãs] *nf* hope; ~ **de vie** life expectancy

espérer [espere] *vt* to hope for; **j'espère (bien)** I hope so; ~ **que/faire** to hope that/to do; ~ **en** to trust in

espiègle [espjɛgl(ə)] *adj* mischievous

espion, ne [espjɔ̃, -ɔn] *nm/f* spy

espionnage [espjɔnaʒ] *nm* espionage, spying

espionner [espjɔne] *vt* to spy (up)on

esplanade [esplanad] *nf* esplanade

espoir [espwar] *nm* hope

esprit [espri] *nm* (pensée, intellect) mind; (humour, ironie) wit; (mentalité, d'une loi etc, fantôme etc) spirit; **faire de l'~** to try to be witty; **reprendre ses ~s** to come to; **perdre l'~** to lose one's mind

esquimau, de, x [eskimo, -od] *adj*, *nm/f* Eskimo ♦ *nm* ice lolly (BRIT), popsicle (US)

esquinter [eskɛ̃te] (*fam*) *vt* to mess up

esquisse [eskis] *nf* sketch

esquisser [eskise] *vt* to sketch; **s'~** *vi* (amélioration) to begin to be detectable; ~ **un sourire** to give a vague smile

esquiver [eskive] *vt* to dodge; **s'~** *vi* to slip away

essai [ese] *nm* testing; testing; (tentative) attempt, try; (RUGBY) try; (LITTÉRATURE) essay; ~ **s** *nmpl* (AUTO) trials; ~ **gratuit** (COMM) free trial; **à l'~** on a trial basis

essaim [esɛ̃] *nm* swarm

essayer [eseje] *vt* (gén) to try; (vêtement, chaussures) to try (on); (restaurant, méthode, voiture) to try (out) ♦ *vi* to try; ~ **de faire** to try ou attempt to do

essence [esɑ̃s] *nf* (de voiture) petrol

(BRIT), gas(oline) (US); (extrait de plante, PHILOSOPHIE) essence; (espèce: d'arbre) species

essentiel, le [esɑ̃sjɛl] *adj* essential; **c'est l'~** (ce qui importe) that's the main thing; **l'~ de** the main part of

essieu, x [esjø] *nm* axle

essor [esɔr] *nm* (de l'économie etc) rapid expansion

essorer [esɔre] *vt* (en tordant) to wring (out); (par la force centrifuge) to spin-dry; **essoreuse** *nf* mangle, wringer; spin-dryer

essouffler [esufle] *vt* to make breathless; **s'~** *vi* to get out of breath; (fig) to run out of steam

essuie-glace [esɥiglas] *nm inv* windscreen (BRIT) ou windshield (US) wiper

essuie-main [esɥimɛ̃] *nm* hand towel

essuyer [esɥije] *vt* to wipe; (fig: subir) to suffer; **s'~** (après le bain) to dry o.s.; ~ **la vaisselle** to dry up the dishes

est[1] [ɛ] *vb voir* **être**

est[2] [ɛst] *nm* east ♦ *adj inv* east; (région) east(ern); **à l'est** in the east; (direction) to the east, east(wards); **à l'est de** (to the) east of

est-ce que [ɛskə] *adv*: ~ **c'est cher/c'était bon?** is it expensive/was it good?; **quand est-ce qu'il part?** when does he leave?, when is he leaving?; *voir aussi* **que**

esthéticienne [estetisjɛn] *nf* beautician

esthétique [estetik] *adj* attractive; aesthetically pleasing

estimation [estimasjɔ̃] *nf* valuation; assessment

estime [estim] *nf* esteem, regard

estimer [estime] *vt* (respecter) to esteem; (expertiser) to value; (évaluer) to assess, estimate; (penser): ~ **que/être** to consider that/o.s. to be

estival, e, aux [estival, -o] *adj* summer *cpd*

estivant, e [estivã, -ãt] *nm/f* (summer) holiday-maker

estomac [estɔma] nm stomach

estomaqué, e [estɔmake] adj flabbergasted

estomper [estɔ̃pe] vt (fig) to blur, dim; **s'~** vi to soften; to become blurred

estrade [estrad] nf platform, rostrum

estragon [estragɔ̃] nm tarragon

estropier [estrɔpje] vt to cripple, maim; (fig) to twist, distort

et [e] conj and; **~ lui?** what about him?; **~ alors!** so what!

étable [etabl(ə)] nf cowshed

établi [etabli] nm (work)bench

établir [etablir] vt (papiers d'identité, facture) to make out; (liste, programme) to draw up; (entreprise, camp, gouvernement, artisan) to set up; (réputation, usage, fait, culpabilité) to establish; **s'~** vi (se faire: entente etc) to be established; **s'~** (à son compte) to set up in business; **s'~ à/près de** to settle in/near

établissement [etablismɑ̃] nm making out; drawing up; setting up, establishing; (entreprise, institution) establishment; **~ scolaire** school, educational establishment

étage [eta3] nm (d'immeuble) storey, floor; (de fusée) stage; (GEO: de culture, végétation) level; **à l'~** upstairs; **au 2ème** = on the 2nd (BRIT) ou 3rd (US) floor; **de bas ~** low-born

étagère [eta3er] nf (rayon) shelf; (meuble) shelves pl

étai [ete] nm stay, prop

étain [etɛ̃] nm tin; (ORFÈVRERIE) pewter no pl

étais etc vb voir **être**

étal [etal] nm stall

étalage [etala3] nm display; display window; **faire ~ de** to show off, parade

étaler [etale] vt (carte, nappe) to spread (out); (peinture, liquide) to spread; (échelonner: paiements, vacances) to spread, stagger;

(marchandises) to display; (richesses, connaissances) to parade; **s'~** vi (liquide) to spread out; (fam) to fall flat on one's face; **s'~ sur** (suj: paiements etc) to be spread out over

étalon [etalɔ̃] nm (mesure) standard; (cheval) stallion

étamer [etame] vt (casserole) to tin(plate); (glace) to silver

étanche [etɑ̃ʃ] adj (récipient) watertight; (montre, vêtement) waterproof

étancher [etɑ̃ʃe] vt: **~ sa soif** to quench one's thirst

étang [etɑ̃] nm pond

étant [etɑ̃] vb voir **être; donné**

étape [etap] nf stage; (lieu d'arrivée) stopping place; (: CYCLISME) staging point; **faire ~ à** to stop off at

état [eta] nm (POL, condition) state; (liste) inventory, statement; **en mauvais ~** in poor condition; **en ~ (de marche)** in (working) order; **remettre en ~** to repair; **hors d'~** out of order; **être en ~/hors d'~ de faire** to be in a/in no fit state to do; **en tout ~ de cause** in any event; **être dans tous ses ~s** to be in a state; **faire ~ de** (alléguer) to put forward; **en ~ d'arrestation** under arrest; **~ civil** civil status; **~ des lieux** inventory of fixtures; **étatiser** vt to bring under state control

état-major [etama3ɔr] nm (MIL) staff

États-Unis [etazyni] nmpl: **les ~** the United States

étau, x [eto] nm vice (BRIT), vise (US)

étayer [eteje] vt to prop ou shore up etc.

etc. adv etc.

et c(a)etera [etsetera] adv et cetera, and so on

été [ete] pp de **être ♦** nm summer

éteindre [etɛ̃dr(ə)] vt (lampe, lumière, radio) to turn ou switch off (cigarette, incendie, bougie) to put out, extinguish; (JUR: dette) to extinguish; **s'~** vi to go out; to go off (mourir) to pass away; **éteint, e** adj *(fig)* lacklustre, dull; *(volcan)* extinct

étendard [etɑ̃daʀ] *nm* standard

étendre [etɑ̃dʀ(ə)] *vt (pâte, liquide)* to spread; *(carte etc)* to spread out; *(linge)* to hang up; *(bras, jambes, par terre: blessé)* to stretch out; *(diluer)* to dilute, thin; *(fig: agrandir)* to extend; s'~ *vi (augmenter, se propager)* to spread; *(terrain, forêt etc)* to stretch; *(s'allonger)* to stretch out; *(se coucher)* to lie down; *(fig: expliquer)* to elaborate

étendu, e [etɑ̃dy] *adj* extensive; **étendue** *nf (d'eau, de sable)* stretch, expanse; *(importance)* extent

éternel, le [etɛʀnɛl] *adj* eternal

éterniser [etɛʀnize]: s'~ *vi* to last for ages; to stay for ages

éternité [etɛʀnite] *nf* eternity

éternuer [etɛʀnɥe] *vi* to sneeze

êtes *vb voir* être

éthique [etik] *adj* ethical

ethnie [ɛtni] *nf* ethnic group

éthylisme [etilism(ə)] *nm* alcoholism

étiez *vb voir* être

étinceler [etɛ̃sle] *vi* to sparkle

étincelle [etɛ̃sɛl] *nf* spark

étioler [etjɔle]: s'~ *vi* to wilt

étiqueter [etikte] *vt* to label

étiquette [etikɛt] *nf* label; *(protocole)* l'~ etiquette

étirer [etiʀe] *vt* to stretch; s'~ *vi (personne)* to stretch; *(convoi, route)* s'~ sur to stretch out over

étoffe [etɔf] *nf* material, fabric

étoffer [etɔfe] *vt* to fill out; s'etoffer *vi* to fill out

étoile [etwal] *nf* star; à la belle ~ in the open; ~ de mer starfish; ~ filante shooting star; **étoilé, e** *adj* starry

étole [etɔl] *nf* stole

étonnant, e [etɔnɑ̃, -ɑ̃t] *adj* amazing

étonner [etɔne] *vt* to surprise, amaze; s'~ que/de to be amazed that/at; cela m'~ait (que) *(j'en doute)* I'd be very surprised (if)

touffée [tufe]: à l'~ *adv (CULIN)*

steamed; braised

étouffer [etufe] *vt* to suffocate; *(bruit)* to muffle; *(scandale)* to hush up ♦ *vi* to suffocate; s'~ *vi (en mangeant etc)* to choke

étourderie [etuʀdəʀi] *nf* heedlessness *no pl*; thoughtless blunder

étourdi, e [etuʀdi] *adj (distrait)* scatterbrained, heedless

étourdir [etuʀdiʀ] *vt (assommer)* to stun, daze; *(griser)* to make dizzy ou giddy; **étourdissement** *nm* dizzy spell

étourneau, x [etuʀno] *nm* starling

étrange [etʀɑ̃ʒ] *adj* strange

étranger, ère [etʀɑ̃ʒe, -ɛʀ] *adj* foreign; *(pas de la famille, non familier)* strange ♦ *nm/f* foreigner; stranger ♦ *nm*: à l'~ abroad; de l'~ from abroad; ~ à *(fig)* unfamiliar to; irrelevant to

étranglement [etʀɑ̃gləmɑ̃] *nm (d'une vallée etc)* constriction

étrangler [etʀɑ̃gle] *vt* to strangle; s'~ *vi (en mangeant etc)* to choke

étrave [etʀav] *nf* stem

MOT-CLÉ

être [etʀ(ə)] *nm* being; ~ humain human being

♦ *vb* +attrib 1 *(état, description)* to be; il est instituteur he is ou he's a teacher; vous êtes grand/intelligent/fatigué you are ou you're tall/clever/tired

2 *(+à: appartenir)* to be; le livre est à Paul the book is Paul's ou belongs to Paul; c'est à moi/eux it is ou it's mine/theirs

3 *(+de: provenance)*: il est de Paris he is from Paris; *(: appartenance)*: il est des nôtres he is one of us

4 *(date)*: nous sommes le 10 janvier it's the 10th of January (today) ♦ *vi* to be; je ne serai pas ici demain I won't be here tomorrow

♦ *vb aux* 1 to have; to be; ~ arrivé/allé to have arrived/gone; il est parti he has left, he has gone

2 *(forme passive)* to be; ~ **fait par** to be made by; **il a été promu** he has been promoted

3 (+à: *obligation*): **c'est à réparer** it needs repairing; **c'est à essayer** it should be tried

♦ *vb impers* **1**: **il est** +*adjectif* it is +*adjective*; **il est impossible de le faire** it's impossible to do it

2 *(heure, date)*: **il est 10 heures, c'est 10 heures** it is *ou* it's 10 o'clock

3 *(emphatique)*: **c'est moi à faire**; **c'est à lui de le faire** it's up to me to do it

étreindre [etʀɛ̃dʀ(ə)] *vt* to clutch, grip; *(amoureusement, amicalement)* to embrace; **s'~** *vi* to embrace

étrenner [etʀene] *vt* to use *(ou* wear) for the first time; **étrennes** [etʀɛn] *nfpl* Christmas box *sg*

étrier [etʀije] *nm* stirrup

étriller [etʀije] *vt (cheval)* to curry; *(fam: battre)* to slaughter *(fig)*

étriqué, e [etʀike] *adj* skimpy

étroit, e [etʀwa, -wat] *adj* narrow; *(vêtement)* tight; *(fig: serré)* close, tight; **à l'~** cramped; ~ **d'esprit** narrow-minded

étude [etyd] *nf* studying; *(ouvrage, rapport)* study; *(de notaire: bureau)* office; (: *charge)* practice; *(SCOL: salle de travail)* study room; ~**s** *nfpl* studies; **être à l'~** *(projet etc)* to be under consideration; **faire des ~s (de droit/médecine)** to study (law/medicine)

étudiant, e [etydjɑ̃, -ɑ̃t] *nm/f* student

étudié, e [etydje] *adj (démarche)* studied; *(système)* carefully designed; *(prix)* keen

étudier [etydje] *vt, vi* to study

étui [etɥi] *nm* case

étuve [etyv] *nf* steamroom

étuvée [etyve]: **à l'~** *adv* braised

eu, eue [y] *pp de* **avoir**

euh [ø] *excl* er

Europe [øʀɔp] *nf*: **l'~** Europe; **euro-**

péen, ne *adj, nm/f* European

eus *etc vb voir* **avoir**

eux [ø] *pron (sujet)* they; *(objet)* them

évacuer [evakɥe] *vt* to evacuate

évader [evade]: **s'~** *vi* to escape

évangile [evɑ̃ʒil] *nm* gospel

évanouir [evanwiʀ]: **s'~** *vi* to faint *(disparaître)* to vanish, disappear

évanouissement [evanwismɑ̃] *nm (syncope)* fainting fit; *(dans un accident)* loss of consciousness

évaporer [evapɔʀe]: **s'~** *vi* to evaporate

évaser [evaze] *vt (tuyau)* to widen, open out; *(jupe, pantalon)* to flare

évasif, ive [evazif, -iv] *adj* evasive

évasion [evazjɔ̃] *nf* escape

évêché [eveʃe] *nm* bishopric, bishop's palace

éveil [evɛj] *nm* awakening; **être e** ~ to be alert

éveillé, e [eveje] *adj* awake; *(vif)* alert, sharp

éveiller [eveje] *vt* to (a)waken; **s'~** *vi* to (a)waken; *(fig)* to be aroused

événement [evɛnmɑ̃] *nm* event

éventail [evɑ̃taj] *nm* fan; *(choix)* range

éventaire [evɑ̃tɛʀ] *nm* stall, stand

éventer [evɑ̃te] *vt (secret)* to uncover; **s'~** *vi (parfum)* to go stale

éventrer [evɑ̃tʀe] *vt* to disembowel *(fig)* to tear *ou* rip open

éventualité [evɑ̃tɥalite] *nf* eventuality; possibility; **dans l'~ de** in the event of

éventuel, le [evɑ̃tɥel] *adj* possible

éventuellement *adv* possibly

évêque [evɛk] *nm* bishop

évertuer [evɛʀtɥe]: **s'~** *vi* to try very hard to do

éviction [eviksjɔ̃] *nf* ousting; *(de locataire)* eviction

évidemment [evidamɑ̃] *adv* obviously

évidence [evidɑ̃s] *nf* obviousness; obvious fact; **de toute ~** quite obviously *ou* evidently; **en ~** conspicuous; **mettre en ~** to highlight;

bring to the fore; **évident, e** [evidã,
-ãt] *adj* obvious, evident
évider [evide] *vt* to scoop out
évier [evje] *nm* (kitchen) sink
évincer [evɛ̃se] *vt* to oust
éviter [evite] *vt* to avoid; ~ **de
faire/que qch ne se passe** to avoid
doing/sth happening; ~ **qch à qn** to
spare sb sth
évolué, e [evɔlɥe] *adj* advanced
évoluer [evɔlɥe] *vi* (*enfant, maladie*)
to develop; (*situation, moralement*)
to evolve, develop; (*aller à: effet,
danseur etc*) to move about, circle;
évolution *nf* development; evolution
évoquer [evɔke] *vt* to call to mind,
evoke; (*mentionner*) to mention
ex... [ɛks] *préfixe* ex-
exact, e [ɛgzakt] *adj* (*précis*) exact,
accurate, precise; (*correct*) correct;
(*ponctuel*) punctual; **à l'heure ~e** the
right ou exact time; **exactement** *adv*
exactly, accurately, precisely; (*c'est cela même*) exactly
ex aequo [ɛgzeko] *adj* equally
placed
exagéré, e [ɛgzaʒeʁe] *adj* (*prix etc*)
excessive
exagérer [ɛgzaʒeʁe] *vt* to exaggerate
♦ *vi* (*abuser*) to go too far; to overstep the mark; (*déformer les faits*)
to exaggerate
exalter [ɛgzalte] *vt* (*enthousiasmer*)
to excite, elate; (*glorifier*) to exalt
examen [ɛgzamɛ̃] *nm* examination;
(*SCOL*) exam, examination; **à l'~**
under consideration; (*COMM*) on approval
examiner [ɛgzamine] *vt* to examine
exaspérant, e [ɛgzaspeʁã, -ãt] *adj*
exasperating
exaspérer [ɛgzaspeʁe] *vt* to exasperate; to exacerbate
exaucer [ɛgzose] *vt* (*vœu*) to grant
excédent [ɛksedã] *nm* surplus; **en
~ surplus; ~ de bagages** excess
luggage
excéder [ɛksede] *vt* (*dépasser*) to exceed; (*agacer*) to exasperate
excellence [ɛkselãs] *nf* (*titre*) Excel-

lency
excellent, e [ɛkselã, -ãt] *adj* excellent
excentrique [ɛksãtʁik] *adj* eccentric; (*quartier*) outlying
excepté, e [ɛksɛpte] *adj, prép:* **les
élèves ~s, ~ les élèves** except for
the pupils; ~ **si** except if
exception [ɛksɛpsjɔ̃] *nf* exception; **à
l'~ de** except for, with the exception
of; **d'~** (*mesure, loi*) special, exceptional; **exceptionnel, le** *adj* exceptional
excès [ɛksɛ] *nm* surplus ♦ *nmpl* ex-
cesses; **à l'~** to excess; ~ **de vitesse** speeding *no pl*; **excessif, ive** *adj*
excessive
excitant, e [ɛksitã, -ãt] *adj* exciting
♦ *nm* stimulant; **excitation**
[ɛksitasjɔ̃] *nf* (*état*) excitement
exciter [ɛksite] *vt* to excite; (*suj:
café etc*) to stimulate; **s'~** *vi* to get
excited
exclamation [ɛksklamasjɔ̃] *nf* exclamation
exclamer [ɛksklame]: **s'~** *vi* to exclaim
exclure [ɛksklyʁ] *vt* (*faire sortir*) to
expel; (*ne pas compter*) to exclude,
leave out; (*rendre impossible*) to exclude, rule out; **il est exclu que** it's
out of the question that ...; **il n'est
pas exclu que ...**, it's not impossible
that ...; **exclusif, ive** *adj* exclusive;
exclusion *nf* expulsion; **à l'exclusion de** with the exclusion ou except-
ing of; **exclusivité** *nf* (*COMM*) exclusive rights *pl*; **film passant en
exclusivité** a film showing only at
excursion [ɛkskyʁsjɔ̃] *nf* (*en autocar*) excursion, trip; (*à pied*) walk,
hike
excuse [ɛkskyz] *nf* excuse; ~**s** *nfpl*
(*regret*) apology *sg*, apologies
excuser [ɛkskyze] *vt* to excuse; **s'~
(de)** to apologize (for); **excusez-
moi** "I'm sorry"; (*pour attirer
l'attention*) "excuse me"
exécrable [ɛgzekʁabl(ə)] *adj* atrocious

exécrer [ɛgzekʀe] vt to loathe, abhor
exécuter [ɛgzekyte] vt (prisonnier) to execute; (tâche etc) to execute, carry out; (MUS: jouer) to perform, execute; (INFORM) to run; s'~ vi to comply; **exécutif, ive** adj, nm (POL) executive; **exécution** nf execution; carrying out; **mettre à exécution** to carry out
exemplaire [ɛgzɑ̃plɛʀ] nm copy
exemple [ɛgzɑ̃pl(ə)] nm example; **par ~** for instance, for example; **donner l'~** to set an example; **prendre ~ sur** to take as a model; **à l'~ de** just like
exempt, e [ɛgzɑ̃, -ɑ̃t] adj: ~ **de** (dispense de) exempt from; (sans) free from
exercer [ɛgzɛʀse] vt (pratiquer) to exercise, practise; (prérogative) to exercise; (influence, contrôle) to exert; (former) to exercise, train; s'~ vi (sportif, musicien) to practise; (se faire sentir: pression etc) to be exerted
exercice [ɛgzɛʀsis] nm (tâche, travail) exercise; l'~ exercise; (MIL) drill; **en ~** (juge) in office; (médecin) practising
exhaustif, ive [ɛgzostif, -iv] adj exhaustive
exhiber [ɛgzibe] vt (montrer: papiers, certificat) to present, produce; (péj) to display, flaunt; s'~ vi to parade; (suj: exhibitionniste) to expose o.s.
exhorter [ɛgzɔʀte] vt to urge
exigeant, e [ɛgziʒɑ̃, -ɑ̃t] adj demanding; (péj) hard to please
exigence [ɛgziʒɑ̃s] nf demand, requirement
exiger [ɛgziʒe] vt to demand, require
exigu, ë [ɛgzigy] adj (lieu) cramped, tiny
exil [ɛgzil] nm exile; **exiler** vt to exile; s'~er vi to go into exile
existence [ɛgzistɑ̃s] nf existence
exister [ɛgziste] vi to exist; **il existe un/des** there is a/are (some)
exonérer [ɛgzɔneʀe] vt: ~ **de** to exempt from

exorbitant, e [ɛgzɔʀbitɑ̃, -ɑ̃t] adj (somme, nombre) exorbitant
exorbité, e [ɛgzɔʀbite] adj: **yeux ~s** bulging eyes
exotique [ɛgzɔtik] adj exotic
expatrier [ɛkspatʀije] vt: s'~ to leave one's country
expectative [ɛkspɛktativ] nf: **être dans l'~** to be still waiting
expédient [ɛkspedjɑ̃] (péj) nm expedient; **vivre d'~s** to live by one's wits
expédier [ɛkspedje] vt (lettre, paquet) to send; (troupes) to dispatch; (péj: travail etc) to dispose of, dispatch; **expéditeur, trice** nm/f sender
expédition [ɛkspedisjɔ̃] nf sending; (scientifique, sportive, MIL) expedition
expérience [ɛkspeʀjɑ̃s] nf (de la vie) experience; (scientifique) experiment
expérimenté, e [ɛkspeʀimɑ̃te] adj experienced
expérimenter [ɛkspeʀimɑ̃te] vt to test out, experiment with
expert, e [ɛkspɛʀ, -ɛʀt(ə)] adj, nm expert; ~ **en assurances** insurance valuer; **expert-comptable** nm ≈ chartered accountant (BRIT), ≈ certified public accountant (US)
expertise [ɛkspɛʀtiz] nf valuation; assessment; valuer's (ou assessor's) report; (JUR) (forensic) examination
expertiser [ɛkspɛʀtize] vt (objet de valeur) to value; (voiture accidentée etc) to assess damage to
expier [ɛkspje] vt to expiate, atone for
expirer [ɛkspiʀe] vi (prendre fin, mourir) to expire; (respirer) to breathe out
explicatif, ive [ɛksplikatif, -iv] adj explanatory
explication [ɛksplikasjɔ̃] nf explanation; (discussion) discussion; argument; ~ **de texte** (SCOL) critical analysis
explicite [ɛksplisit] adj explicit

expliquer [ɛksplike] vt to explain; s'~ to explain (o.s.); (discuter) to discuss things; to have it out; **son erreur s'explique** one can understand his mistake

exploit [ɛksplwa] nm exploit, feat

exploitation [ɛksplwatasjɔ̃] nf exploitation; running; ~ **agricole** farming concern; **exploiter** [ɛksplwate] vt (mine) to exploit, work; (entreprise, ferme) to run, operate; (clients, ouvriers, erreur, don) to exploit

explorer [ɛksplɔʀe] vt to explore

exploser [ɛksploze] vi to explode, blow up; (engin explosif) to go off; (fig: joie, colère) to burst out, explode; **explosif, ive** adj, nm explosive; **explosion** nf explosion

exportateur, trice [ɛkspɔʀtatœʀ, -tʀis] adj export cpd, exporting ♦ nm exporter

exportation [ɛkspɔʀtasjɔ̃] nf exportation; export

exporter [ɛkspɔʀte] vt to export

exposant [ɛkspozɑ̃] nm exhibitor

exposé, e [ɛkspoze] nm ♦ adj: ~ **au sud** facing south; **bien** ~ well situated

exposer [ɛkspoze] vt (marchandise) to display; (peinture) to exhibit, show; (parler de) to explain, set out; (mettre en danger, orienter, PHOTO) to expose; **exposition** nf (manifestation) exhibition; (PHOTO) exposure

exprès¹ [ɛkspʀɛ] adv (délibérément) on purpose; (spécialement) specially

exprès², esse [ɛkspʀɛs] adj (ordre, défense) express, formal ♦ adj inv (PTT) express ♦ adv

express [ɛkspʀɛs] adj, nm: (café) ~ espresso (coffee); (train) ~ fast train

expressément [ɛkspʀesemɑ̃] adv expressly; specifically

expression [ɛkspʀesjɔ̃] nf expression

exprimer [ɛkspʀime] vt (sentiment, idée) to express; (jus, liquide) to press out; s'~ vi (personne) to express o.s.

exproprier [ɛkspʀɔpʀije] vt to buy up by compulsory purchase, expropriate

expulser [ɛkspylse] vt to expel; (locataire) to evict; (SPORT) to send off

exquis, e [ɛkski, -iz] adj exquisite; delightful

exsangue [ɛksɑ̃g] adj bloodless, drained of blood

extase [ɛkstɑz] nf ecstasy; **s'extasier** vi to go into raptures over

extension [ɛkstɑ̃sjɔ̃] nf (d'un muscle, ressort) stretching; (fig) extension; expansion

exténuer [ɛkstenɥe] vt to exhaust

extérieur, e [ɛksteʀjœʀ] adj (porte, mur etc) outer, outside; (au dehors: escalier, w.-c) outside; (commerce) foreign; (influences) external; (apparent: calme, gaieté etc) surface cpd ♦ nm (d'une maison, d'un récipient etc) outside, exterior; (apparence) exterior; (d'un groupe social): l'~ the outside world; à l'~ outside; (à l'étranger) abroad; **extérieurement** adv on the outside; (en apparence) on the surface

exterminer [ɛkstɛʀmine] vt to exterminate, wipe out

externat [ɛkstɛʀna] nm day school

externe [ɛkstɛʀn(ə)] adj external, outer ♦ nm/f (MED) non-resident medical student (BRIT), extern (US); (SCOL) day pupil

extincteur [ɛkstɛ̃ktœʀ] nm (fire) extinguisher

extinction [ɛkstɛ̃ksjɔ̃] nf: ~ **de voix** loss of voice

extorquer [ɛkstɔʀke] vt to extort

extra [ɛkstʀa] adj inv first-rate; top-quality ♦ nm inv extra help

extrader [ɛkstʀade] vt to extradite

extraire [ɛkstʀɛʀ] vt to extract; **extrait** nm extract

extraordinaire [ɛkstʀaɔʀdinɛʀ] adj extraordinary; (POL: mesures etc) special

extravagant, e [ɛkstʀavagɑ̃, -ɑ̃t] adj extravagant; wild

extraverti, e [ɛkstʀavɛʀti] adj extro-vert

extrême [ɛkstʀɛm] adj, nm extreme; **extrêmement** adv extremely; **extrême-onction** nf last rites pl; **Extrême-Orient** nm Far East

extrémité [ɛkstʀemite] nf end; (situation) straits pl, plight; (geste désespéré) extreme action; ~s nfpl (pieds et mains) extremities; à la dernière ~ on the point of death

exutoire [ɛgzytwaʀ] nm outlet, release

F

F abr = franc

fa [fa] nm inv (MUS) F; (en chantant la gamme) fa

fable [fabl(ə)] nf fable

fabricant [fabʀikɑ̃] nm manufacturer

fabrication [fabʀikasjɔ̃] nf manufacture

fabrique [fabʀik] nf factory

fabriquer [fabʀike] vt to make; (industriellement) to manufacture; (fig): **qu'est-ce qu'il fabrique?** what is he doing?

fabulation [fabylasjɔ̃] nf fantasizing

fac [fak] (fam) abr f (SCOL) = faculté

façade [fasad] nf front, façade

face [fas] nf face; (fig: aspect) side ♦ adj: **le côté ~** heads; **perdre la ~** to lose face; **en ~ de** opposite; (fig) in front of; **de ~** from the front; face on; **~ à** facing; (fig) faced with, in the face of; **faire ~ à** to face; **~ à ~** facing each other ♦ nm inv encounter

facétieux, euse [fasesjø, -øz] adj mischievous

fâché, e [fɑʃe] adj angry; (désolé) sorry

fâcher [fɑʃe] vt to anger; **se ~** vi to get angry; **se ~ avec** (se brouiller) to fall out with

fâcheux, euse [fɑʃø, -øz] adj unfortunate, regrettable

facile [fasil] adj easy; (accommodant) easy-going; **~ment** adv easily; **facilité** nf easiness; (disposition) aptitude; **facilités** nfpl (possibilities) facilities; **facilités de paiement** easy terms; **faciliter** vt to make easier

façon [fasɔ̃] nf (manière) way; (d'une robe etc) making-up; cut; **~s** nfpl (péj) fuss sg; **de quelle ~?** (in) what way?; **de ~ à/à ce que** so as to/that; **de toute ~** anyway, in any case; **~ner** [fasɔne] vt (fabriquer) to manufacture; (travailler: matière) to shape, fashion; (fig) to mould, shape

facteur, trice [faktœʀ, -tʀis] nm/f postman(woman) (BRIT) (Brit), mailman(woman) (US) ♦ nm (MATH, fig: élément) factor; **~ de pianos** piano maker

factice [faktis] adj artificial

faction [faksjɔ̃] nf faction; (MIL) guard ou sentry (duty); watch

facture [faktyʀ] nf (à payer: gén) bill; (: COMM) invoice; (d'un artisan, artiste) technique, workmanship; **facturer** vt to invoice

facultatif, ive [fakyltatif, -iv] adj optional; (arrêt de bus) request cpd

faculté [fakylte] nf (intellectuelle, d'université) faculty; (pouvoir, possibilité) power

fade [fad] adj insipid

fagot [fago] nm bundle of sticks

faible [fɛbl(ə)] adj weak; (voix, lumière, vent) faint; (rendement, intensité, revenu etc) low ♦ nm weak point; (pour quelqu'un) weakness, soft spot; **~ d'esprit** feeble-minded; **faiblesse** nf weakness; **faiblir** vi to weaken; (lumière) to dim; (vent) to drop

faïence [fajɑ̃s] nf earthenware no pl; piece of earthenware

faignant, e [fɛɲɑ̃, -ɑ̃t] nm/f = fainéant, e

faille [faj] vb voir **falloir** ♦ nf (GÉO) fault; (fig) flaw, weakness

faillir [fajiʀ] vi: **j'ai failli tomber** I almost ou very nearly fell

faillite [fajit] *nf* bankruptcy

faim [fɛ̃] *nf* hunger; **avoir** ~ to be hungry; **rester sur sa** ~ (*aussi fig*) to be left wanting more

fainéant, e [fenɛɑ̃, -ɑ̃t] *nm/f* idler, loafer

MOT-CLÉ

---

faire [fɛʀ] *vt* 1 (*fabriquer, être l'auteur de*) to make; ~ **du vin/une offre/un film** to make wine/an offer/a film; ~ **du bruit** to make a noise

2 (*effectuer: travail, opération*) to do; **que faites-vous?** (*quel métier etc*) what do you do?; (*quelle activité: au moment de la question*) what are you doing?; ~ **la lessive** to do the washing

3 (*études*) to do; (*sport, musique*) to play; ~ **du droit/du français** to do law/French; ~ **du rugby/piano** to play rugby/the piano

4 (*simuler*): ~ **le malade/l'ignorant** to act the invalid/the fool

5 (*transformer, avoir un effet sur*): ~ **de qn un frustré/avocat** to make sb frustrated/a lawyer; **ça ne me fait rien** (*m'est égal*) I don't care *ou* mind; (*me laisse froid*) it has no effect on me; **ça ne fait rien** it doesn't matter; ~ **que** (*impliquer*) to mean that

6 (*calculs, prix, mesures*): **2 et 2 font 4** 2 and 2 are *ou* make 4; **ça fait 10 m/15F** it's 10 m/15F; **je vous le fais 10F** I'll let you have it for 10F

7: **qu'a-t-il fait de sa valise?** what has he done with his case?

8: **ne** ~ **que** (*sans cesse*) all he (ever) does is criticize; (*seulement*) he's only criticizing

9 (*dire*) to say; **vraiment?** fit-il really? he said

10 (*maladie*) to have; ~ **du diabète** to have diabetes *sg*

♦ *vb* 1 (*agir, s'y prendre*) to act, do; **il faut** ~ **vite** we (*ou you etc*) must act quickly; **comment a-t-il fait pour?** how did he manage to?; **fai-**

tes comme chez vous make yourself at home

2 (*paraître*) to look; ~ **vieux/démodé** to look old/old-fashioned; **ça fait bien** it looks good

♦ *vb substitut* to do; **ne le casse pas comme je l'ai fait** don't break it as I did; **je peux le voir? - faites!** can I see it? - please do!

♦ *vb impers* 1: **il fait beau** *etc* the weather is fine *etc*; *voir aussi* **jour froid** *etc*

2 (*temps écoulé, durée*): **ça fait 2 ans qu'il est parti** it's 2 years since he left; **ça fait 2 ans qu'il y est** he's been there for 2 years

♦ *vb semi-aux* 1: ~ +*infinitif* (*action directe*) to make; ~ **tomber/bouger qch** to make sth fall/move; ~ **démarrer un moteur/chauffer de l'eau** to start up an engine/heat some water; **cela fait dormir** it makes you sleep; ~ **travailler les enfants** to make the children work *ou* get the children to work

2 (*indirectement, par un intermédiaire*): ~ **réparer qch** to get *ou* have sth repaired; ~ **punir les enfants** to have the children punished; **se** ~ *vi* 1 (*vin, fromage*) to mature

2: **cela se fait beaucoup/ne se fait pas** it's done a lot/not done

3: **se** ~ +*nom ou pron* to make o.s. a skirt; **se** ~ **des amis** to make friends; **se** ~ **du souci** to worry; **il ne s'en fait pas** he doesn't worry

4: **se** ~ +*adj* (*devenir*) to be getting old; (*délibérément*): **se** ~ **beau** to do o.s. up

5: **se** ~ **à** (*s'habituer*) to get used to; **je n'arrive pas à me** ~ **à la nourriture/au climat** I can't get used to the food/climate

6: **se** ~ +*infinitif* to have one's eyes tested/have an operation; ~ **couper les cheveux** to get one's hair cut; **il va se** ~ **tuer/punir** he's going to get himself killed/get punished; **il s'est fait**

aider he got somebody to help him; **il s'est fait aider par Simon** he got Simon to help him; **se ~ ~ un vêtement** to get a garment made for o.s.

7 (impersonnel): **comment se fait-il/faisait-il que?** how is it/was it that?

faire-part [fɛʀpaʀ] nm inv announcement (of birth, marriage etc)

faisable [fəzabl(ə)] adj feasible

faisan, e [fəzɑ̃, -an] nm/f pheasant

faisandé, e [fəzɑ̃de] adj high (bad)

faisceau, x [fɛso] nm (de lumière etc) beam; (de branches etc) bundle

faisons vb voir **faire**

fait, e [fɛ, fɛt] adj (mûr: fromage, melon) ripe ♦ nm (événement) event, occurrence; (réalité, donnée) fact; **c'en est ~ de** that's the end of; **être le ~ de** (causé par) to be the work of; **être au ~** (de) to be informed (of); **au ~** (à propos) by the way; **en venir au ~** to get to the point; **de ~** (opposé à: de droit) de facto ♦ adv in fact; **du ~ de ceci/qu'il a menti** because of ou on account of this/his having lied; **de ce ~** for this reason; **en ~** in fact; **en ~ de repas** by way of a meal; **prendre ~ et cause pour qn** to support sb, side with sb; **prendre qn sur le ~** to catch sb in the act; **~ divers** news item; **~s et gestes de qn** sb's actions ou doings

faîte [fɛt] nm top; (fig) pinnacle, height

faites vb voir **faire**

faitout [fɛtu] nm = **fait-tout**

fait-tout [fɛtu] nm inv stewpot

falaise [falɛz] nf cliff

fallacieux, euse [falasjø, -øz] adj fallacious; deceptive; illusory

falloir [falwaʀ] vb impers: **il va ~ 100 F** we'll ou I'll need 100 F; **s'en ~: il s'en est fallu de 100 F/5 minutes** we (ou they) were 100 F short/5 minutes late (ou early); **il s'en faut de beaucoup qu'il soit** he is

far from being; **il s'en est fallu de peu que cela n'arrive** it very nearly happened; **ou peu s'en faut** or as good as; **il doit ~ du temps** that must take time; **il me faudrait 100 F** I would need 100 F; **il vous faut tourner à gauche après l'église** you have to turn left past the church; **nous avons ce qu'il (nous) faut** we have what we need; **il faut qu'il parte/a fallu qu'il parte** (obligation) he has to ou must leave/had to leave; **il a fallu le faire** it had to be done

falsifier [falsifje] vt to falsify; to doctor

famé, e [fame] adj: **mal ~** disreputable, of ill repute

famélique [famelik] adj half-starved

fameux, euse [famø, -øz] adj (illustre) famous; (bon: repas, plat etc) first-rate, first-class; (valeur intensive) real, downright

familial, e, aux [familjal, -o] adj family cpd; **familiale** nf (AUTO) estate car (BRIT), station wagon (US)

familiarité [familjaʀite] nf familiarity; familiarity; **~s** nfpl (privautés) familiarities

familier, ère [familje, -ɛʀ] adj (connu, impertinent) familiar; (dénotant une certaine intimité) informal, friendly; (LING) informal, colloquial ♦ nm regular (visitor)

famille [famij] nf family; **il a de la ~ à Paris** he has relatives in Paris

famine [famin] nf famine

fanatique [fanatik] adj fanatical ♦ nm/f fanatic; **fanatisme** nm fanaticism

faner [fane]: **se ~** vi to fade

fanfare [fɑ̃faʀ] nf (orchestre) brass band; (musique) fanfare

fanfaron, ne [fɑ̃faʀɔ̃, -ɔn] nm/f braggart

fange [fɑ̃ʒ] nf mire

fanion [fanjɔ̃] nm pennant

fantaisie [fɑ̃tezi] nf (spontanéité) fancy, imagination; (caprice) whim; extravagance ♦ adj: **bijou/pain de**

~ costume jewellery/fancy bread;

fantaisiste *adj* (*péj*) unorthodox, eccentric ♦ *nm/f* (*de music-hall*) variety artist *ou* entertainer

fantasme [fɑ̃tasm(ə)] *nm* fantasy

fantasque [fɑ̃task] *adj* whimsical, capricious; fantastic

fantastique [fɑ̃tastik] *adj* fantastic

fantôme [fɑ̃tom] *nm* ghost, phantom

faon [fɑ̃] *nm* fawn

farce [faʀs(ə)] *nf* (*viande*) stuffing; (*blague*) (practical) joke; (*THEATRE*) farce; **farcir** *vt* (*viande*) to stuff

fard [faʀ] *nm* make-up

fardeau, x [faʀdo] *nm* burden

farder [faʀde] *vt* to make up

farfelu, e [faʀfəly] *adj* hare-brained

farine [faʀin] *nf* flour; **farineux, euse** *adj* (*sauce, pomme*) floury ♦ *nmpl* (*aliments*) starchy foods

farouche [faʀuʃ] *adj* shy, timid; savage, wild; fierce

fart [faʀ(t)] *nm* (ski) wax

fascicule [fasikyl] *nm* volume

fasciner [fasine] *vt* to fascinate

fascisme [faʃism(ə)] *nm* fascism

fasse *etc vb voir* **faire**

faste [fast(ə)] *nm* splendour ♦ *adj*: **c'est un jour** ~ it's this (*ou* our *etc*) lucky day

fastidieux, euse [fastidjø, -øz] *adj* tedious, tiresome

fastueux, euse [fastɥø, -øz] *adj* sumptuous, luxurious

fatal, e [fatal] *adj* fatal; (*inévitable*) inevitable; **fatalité** *nf* fate; fateful coincidence; inevitability

fatidique [fatidik] *adj* fateful

fatigant, e [fatigɑ̃, -ɑ̃t] *adj* tiring; (*agaçant*) tiresome

fatigue [fatig] *nf* tiredness, fatigue

fatigué, e [fatige] *adj* tired

fatiguer [fatige] *vt* to tire, make tired; (*TECH*) to put a strain on, strain; (*fig: importuner*) to wear out ♦ *vi* (*moteur*) to labour, strain; **se** ~ to get tired; to tire o.s. (out)

fatras [fatʀa] *nm* jumble, hotchpotch

fatuité [fatɥite] *nf* conceitedness, smugness

faubourg [fobuʀ] *nm* suburb

fauché, e [foʃe] (*fam*) *adj* broke

faucher [foʃe] *vt* (*herbe*) to cut; (*champs, blés*) to reap; (*fig*) to cut down; to mow down

faucille [fosij] *nf* sickle

faucon [fokɔ̃] *nm* falcon, hawk

faudra *vb voir* **falloir**

faufiler [fofile] *vt* to tack, baste; **se** ~ **vi**: **se** ~ **dans** to edge one's way into; **se** ~ **parmi/entre** to thread one's way among/between

faune [fon] *nf* (*ZOOL*) wildlife, fauna

faussaire [fosɛʀ] *nm/f* forger

fausse [fos] *adj voir* **faux**

faussement [fosmɑ̃] *adv* (*accuser*) wrongly, wrongfully; (*croire*) falsely

fausser [fose] *vt* (*objet*) to bend, buckle; (*fig*) to distort

fausseté [foste] *nf* wrongness; falseness

faut *vb voir* **falloir**

faute [fot] *nf* (*erreur*) mistake, error; (*péché, manquement*) misdemeanour; (*FOOTBALL etc*) offence; (*TENNIS*) fault; **c'est de sa/ma** ~ it's his/my fault; **être en** ~ to be in the wrong; ~ **de** (*temps, argent*) for *ou* through lack of; **sans** ~ without fail; ~ **de frappe** typing error; ~ **professionnelle** professional misconduct *no pl*

fauteuil [fotœj] *nm* armchair; ~ **d'orchestre** seat in the front stalls; ~ **roulant** wheelchair

fauteur [fotœʀ] *nm*: ~ **de troubles** trouble-maker

fautif, ive [fotif, -iv] *adj* (*incorrect*) incorrect, inaccurate; (*responsable*) at fault, in the wrong; (*coupable*) guilty

fauve [fov] *nm* wildcat ♦ *adj* (*couleur*) fawn

faux¹ [fo] *nf* scythe

faux², fausse [fo, fos] *adj* (*inexact*) wrong; (*piano, voix*) out of tune; (*falsifié*) fake; forged; (*sournois, postiche*) false ♦ *adv* (*MUS*) out of tune ♦ *nm* (*copie*) fake, forgery; (*opposé au vrai*): **le faux** falsehood; **faire faux bond à qn** to stand sb up; **fausse alerte** false alarm; **fausse couche** miscarriage; **faux frais** *nmpl* extras, incidental expenses; **faux pas** tripping *no pl*; (*fig*) faux pas; **faux témoignage** (*délit*) perjury; **faux-filet** *nm* sirloin; **fauxfuyant** *nm* equivocation; **fauxmonnayeur** *nm* counterfeiter, forger

faveur [favœʀ] *nf* favour; **traitement de ~** preferential treatment; **à la ~ de** under cover of; thanks to; **en ~ de** in favour of

favorable [favɔʀabl(ə)] *adj* favourable

favori, te [favɔʀi, -it] *adj, nm/f* favourite; **~s** *nmpl* (*barbe*) sideboards (*BRIT*), sideburns

favoriser [favɔʀize] *vt* to favour

fax [faks] *nm* fax

fébrile [febʀil] *adj* feverish, febrile

fécond, e [fekɔ̃, -ɔ̃d] *adj* fertile; **~er** *vt* to fertilize; **~ité** *nf* fertility

fécule [fekyl] *nf* potato flour

féculent [fekylɑ̃] *nm* starchy food

fédéral, e, aux [fedeʀal, -o] *adj* federal

fée [fe] *nf* fairy; **~rie** *nf* enchantment; **~rique** *adj* magical, fairytale *cpd*

feignant, e [fɛɲɑ̃, -ɑ̃t] *nm/f* = fainéant, e

feindre [fɛ̃dʀ(ə)] *vt* to feign ♦ *vi* to dissemble; **~ de faire** to pretend to do

feinte [fɛ̃t] *nf* (*SPORT*) dummy

fêler [fele] *vt* to crack

félicitations [felisitasjɔ̃] *nfpl* congratulations

féliciter [felisite] *vt:* **~ qn (de)** to congratulate sb (on); **se ~ (de)** to congratulate o.s. (on)

félin, e [felɛ̃, -in] *adj* feline ♦ *nm* (big) cat

fêlure [felyʀ] *nf* crack

femelle [fəmɛl] *adj, nf* female

féminin, e [feminɛ̃, -in] *adj* feminine; (*sexe*) female; (*équipe, vêtements etc*) women's ♦ *nm* (*LING*) feminine; **féministe** *adj* feminist

femme [fam] *nf* woman; (*épouse*) wife; **~ au foyer ou** *nf* housewife; **~ de chambre** cleaning lady; **~ de ménage** = femme de chambre

fémur [femyʀ] *nm* femur, thighbone

fendre [fɑ̃dʀ(ə)] *vt* (*couper en deux*) to split; (*fissurer*) to crack; (*fig: traverser*) to cut through; to cleave through; **se ~** *vi* to crack

fenêtre [fənɛtʀ(ə)] *nf* window

fenouil [fənuj] *nm* fennel

fente [fɑ̃t] *nf* (*fissure*) crack; (*de boîte à lettres etc*) slit

féodal, e, aux [feɔdal, -o] *adj* feudal

fer [fɛʀ] *nm* iron; (*de cheval*) shoe; **~ à cheval** horseshoe; **~ (à repasser)** iron; **~ forgé** wrought iron

ferai *etc* *vb voir* faire

fer-blanc [fɛʀblɑ̃] *nm* tin(plate)

férié, e [feʀje] *adj:* **jour ~** public holiday

ferions *etc* *vb voir* faire

ferme [fɛʀm(ə)] *adj* firm ♦ *adv* (*travailler etc*) hard ♦ *nf* (*exploitation*) farm; (*maison*) farmhouse

fermé, e [fɛʀme] *adj* closed, shut; (*gaz, eau etc*) off; (*fig: personne*) uncommunicative; (*milieu*) exclusive

fermenter [fɛʀmɑ̃te] *vi* to ferment

fermer [fɛʀme] *vt* to close, shut; (*cesser l'exploitation de*) to close down, shut down; (*eau, lumière, électricité, robinet*) to put off, turn off; (*aéroport, route*) to close ♦ *vi* to close, shut; to close down, shut down; **se ~** *vi* (*yeux*) to close, shut; (*fleur, blessure*) to close up

fermeté [fɛʀməte] *nf* firmness

fermeture [fɛʀmətyʀ] *nf* closing; shutting; closing *ou* shutting down; putting *ou* turning off; (*dispositif*) catch; fastening, fastener; **~ à glissière** = fermeture éclair; **~ éclair** zip (fastener) (*BRIT*), zipper (*US*)

fermier, ière [fɛʀmje] *nm* farmer; **fermière** *nf* woman farmer; farmer's wife

fermoir [fɛʀmwaʀ] *nm* clasp

féroce [feʀɔs] *adj* ferocious, fierce

ferons vb voir **faire**

ferraille [fɛʀɑj] nf scrap iron; **mettre à la ~** to scrap

ferré, e [fɛʀe] adj hobnailed; steel-tipped; (fam): **en ~ well up on, hot at; **ferrer** [fɛʀe] vt (cheval) to shoe

ferronnerie [fɛʀɔnʀi] nf ironwork

ferroviaire [fɛʀɔvjɛʀ] adj rail(way) cpd (BRIT), rail(road) cpd (US)

ferry(boat) [feʀe(bot)] nm ferry

fertile [fɛʀtil] adj fertile; **~ en incidents** eventful, packed with incidents

féru, e [feʀy] adj: **~ de** with a keen interest in

férule [feʀyl] nf: **être sous la ~ de qn** to be under sb's (iron) rule

fervent, e [fɛʀvɑ̃, -ɑ̃t] adj fervent

fesse [fɛs] nf buttock; **fessée** nf spanking

festin [fɛstɛ̃] nm feast

festival [fɛstival] nm festival

festoyer [fɛstwaje] vi to feast

fêtard [fɛtaʀ] (péj) nm high liver, merry-maker

fête [fɛt] nf (religieuse) feast; (publique) holiday; (en famille etc) celebration; (kermesse) fête, fair, festival; (du nom) feast day, name day; **faire la ~** to live it up; **faire ~ à qn** to give sb a warm welcome; **les ~s (de fin d'année)** the festive season; **la salle/le comité des ~s** the village hall/festival committee; **~ foraine** (fun) fair; **la F~ Nationale** the national holiday; **fêter** vt to celebrate; (personne) to have a celebration for

fétu [fety] nm: **~ de paille** wisp of straw

feu, x [fø] nm (gén) fire; (signal lumineux) light; (de cuisinière) ring; (sensation de brûlure) burning (sensation) ♦ adj inv: **~ son père** his late father; **~x** nmpl (éclat, lumière) fire sg; (AUTO) (traffic) lights; **au ~!** (incendie) fire!; **à ~ doux/vif** over a slow/brisk heat; **à petit ~** over a gentle heat; (fig) slowly; **faire ~** to fire; **prendre ~** to catch fire; **mettre le ~ à** to set

fire to; **faire du ~** to make a fire; **avez-vous du ~?** (pour cigarette) have you (got) a light?; **~ arrière** rear light; **~ d'artifice** firework; (spectacle) fireworks pl; **~ de joie** bonfire; **~ rouge/vert/orange** red/green/amber (BRIT) ou yellow (US) light; **~x de brouillard** fog-lamps; **~x de croisement** dipped (BRIT) ou dimmed (US) headlights; **~x de position** sidelights; **~x de route** headlights

feuillage [fœjaʒ] nm foliage, leaves pl

feuille [fœj] nf (d'arbre) leaf; (de papier) sheet; **~ d'impôts** tax form; **~ de maladie** medical expenses claim form; **~ de paie** pay slip; **~ de vigne** (BOT) vine leaf; (sur statue) fig leaf; **~ volante** loose sheet

feuillet [fœjɛ] nm leaf

feuilleté, e [fœjte] adj (CULIN) flaky; (verre) laminated

feuilleter [fœjte] vt (livre) to leaf through

feuilleton [fœjtɔ̃] nm serial

feuillu, e [fœjy] adj leafy ♦ nm broad-leaved tree

feutre [føtʀ(ə)] nm felt; (chapeau) felt hat; (aussi: stylo-~) felt-tip pen; **feutré, e** adj feltlike; (pas, voix) muffled

fève [fɛv] nf broad bean

février [fevʀije] nm February

fi [fi] excl: **faire ~ de** to snap one's fingers at

fiable [fjabl] adj reliable

fiacre [fjakʀ(ə)] nm (hackney) cab ou carriage

fiançailles [fjɑ̃sɑj] nfpl engagement sg

fiancé, e [fjɑ̃se] nm/f fiancé(fiancée) ♦ adj: **être ~ (à)** to be engaged (to)

fiancer [fjɑ̃se]: **se ~** vi to become engaged

fibre [fibʀ(ə)] nf fibre; **~ de verre** fibreglass, glass fibre

ficeler [fisle] vt to tie up

ficelle [fisɛl] nf string no pl; piece of

length of string

fiche [fiʃ] nf (pour fichier) (index) card; (formulaire) form; (ELEC) plug

ficher [fiʃe] vt (dans un fichier) to file; (POLICE) to put on file; (planter) to stick, drive; (fam) to do; to give; to stick ou shove; se ~ de (fam) to make fun of; not to care about; fiche-(moi) le camp (fam) clear off; fiche-moi la paix leave me alone

fichier [fiʃje] nm file; card index

fichu, e [fiʃy] pp de **ficher** (fam) ♦ adj (fam: intensif: irréparable) bust, done for; (: intensif) wretched, darned ♦ nm (foulard) (head)scarf; **mal ~** (fam) feeling lousy; useless

fictif, ive [fiktif, -iv] adj fictitious

fiction [fiksjɔ̃] nf fiction; (fait imaginé) invention

fidèle [fidɛl] adj faithful ♦ nm/f (REL) les ~s the faithful pl; (à l'église) the congregation sg

fief [fjɛf] nm fief; (fig) preserve, stronghold

fier¹ [fje]: se fier à vt to trust

fier², fière [fjɛʀ] adj proud; **fierté** nf pride

fièvre [fjɛvʀ(ə)] nf fever; **avoir de la ~/39 de ~** to have a high temperature/a temperature of 39°C; **fiévreux, euse** adj feverish

figer [fiʒe] vt to congeal; (fig: personne) to freeze, root to the spot; se ~ vi to congeal; to freeze; (institutions etc) to become set, stop evolving

figue [fig] nf fig; **figuier** nm fig tree

figurant, e [figyʀɑ̃, -ɑ̃t] nm/f (THÉÂTRE) walk-on; (CINÉMA) extra

figure [figyʀ] nf (visage) face; (image, trace, forme, personnage) figure; (illustration) picture, diagram; **faire ~ de** to look like

figuré, e [figyʀe] adj (sens) figurative

figurer [figyʀe] vi to appear ♦ vt to represent; se ~ que to imagine that

fil [fil] nm (brin, fig: d'une histoire) thread; (du téléphone) cable, wire; (textile ou lin) linen; (d'un couteau) edge; **au ~ des années** with the passing of the years; **au ~ de l'eau** with the stream ou current; **coup de ~** phone call; ~ **à coudre** (sewing) thread; ~ **à pêche** fishing line; ~ **à plomb** plumbline; ~ **de fer** wire; ~ **de fer barbelé** barbed wire; ~ **électrique** electric wire

filament [filamɑ̃] nm (ELEC) filament; (de liquide) trickle, thread

filandreux, euse [filɑ̃dʀø, -øz] adj stringy

filasse [filas] adj inv white blond

filature [filatyʀ] nf (fabrique) mill; (policière) shadowing no pl, tailing

file [fil] nf line; (AUTO) lane; **en ~ indienne** in single file; **à la ~** (d'affilée) in succession; ~ **(d'attente) queue** (BRIT), line (US)

filer [file] vt (tissu, toile) to spin; (prendre en filature) to shadow, tail; (fam: donner): ~ **qch à qn** to slip sb sth ♦ vi (bas, liquide, pâte) to run; (aller vite) to fly past; (fam: partir) to make off; ~ **doux** to toe the line

filet [file] nm net; (CULIN) fillet; (d'eau, de sang) trickle; ~ **(à provisions)** string bag

filiale [filjal] nf (COMM) subsidiary

filière [filjɛʀ] nf: **passer par la ~** to go through the (administrative) channels; **suivre la ~** (dans sa carrière) to work one's way up (through the hierarchy)

filiforme [filifɔʀm(ə)] adj spindly; threadlike

filigrane [filigʀan] nm (d'un billet, timbre) watermark; **en ~** (fig) showing just beneath the surface

fille [fij] nf girl; (opposé à fils) daughter; **vieille ~** old maid; **fillette** nf (little) girl

filleul, e [fijœl] nm/f godchild, godson/daughter

film [film] nm (pour photo) (roll of)

film; (œuvre) film, picture, movie; (couche) film; ~ **d'animation** animated film; ~ **policier** thriller

filon [filɔ̃] nm vein, lode; (fig) lucrative line, money spinner

fils [fis] nm son; ~ **à papa** daddy's boy

filtre [filtʀ(ə)] nm filter; ~ **à air** (AUTO) air filter; **filtrer** vt to filter; (fig: candidats, visiteurs) to screen ♦ vi to filter (through)

fin¹ [fɛ̃] nf end; **fins** nfpl (but) ends; **prendre ~** to come to an end; **mettre ~ à** to put an end to; **à la fin** in the end, eventually; **sans fin** endless ♦ adv endlessly

fin², e [fɛ̃, fin] adj (papier, couche, fil) thin; (cheveux, poudre, pointe, visage) fine; (taille) neat, slim; (esprit, remarque) subtle; (ouïe) sharp ou keen eyes/ears; **vin fin** fine wine; **fin gourmet** gourmet; **fin prêt** quite ready; **fines herbes** mixed herbs

final, e [final] adj final ♦ nm (MUS) finale; **finale** nf; **quarts de finale** quarter finals; **8èmes/16èmes de finale** 2nd/1st round (in knock-out competition); **finalement** adv finally, in the end; (après tout) after all

finance [finɑ̃s] nf finance; ~**s** nfpl (situation) finances; (activités) finance sg; **moyennant ~** for a fee; **financer** vt to finance; **financier, ière** adj financial

finaud, e [fino, -od] adj wily

fine [fin] nf (alcool) liqueur brandy

finesse [fines] nf thinness; fineness; neatness, slimness; subtlety; shrewdness

fini, e [fini] adj finished; (MATH) finite; (intensif): **un menteur ~ a** liar through and through ♦ nm (d'un objet manufacturé) finish

finir [finiʀ] vt to finish ♦ vi to finish, end; ~ **quelque part/par faire** to end up somewhere/doing; ~ **de faire** to finish doing; (cesser)

to stop doing; **il finit par m'agacer** he's beginning to get on my nerves; ~ **en pointe/tragédie** to end in a point/in tragedy; **en ~ avec** to have done with; **il va mal** ~ he will come to a bad end

finition [finisjɔ̃] nf finishing; finish

finlandais, e [fɛ̃lɑ̃dɛ, -ɛz] adj Finnish ♦ nm/f: **F~, e** Finn

Finlande [fɛ̃lɑ̃d] nf: **la ~** Finland

fiole [fjɔl] nf phial

fioriture [fjɔʀityʀ] nf embellishment, flourish

firme [fiʀm(ə)] nf firm

fis vb voir **faire**

fisc [fisk] nm tax authorities pl; ~**al, e, aux** adj tax cpd, fiscal; ~**ité** nf tax system; (charges) taxation

fissure [fisyʀ] nf crack; ~**r** [fisyʀe] : **se ~r** vi to crack

fiston [fistɔ̃] (fam) nm son, lad

fit vb voir **faire**

fixation [fiksasjɔ̃] nf fixing; fastening; setting; (de ski) binding; (PSYCH) fixation

fixe [fiks(ə)] adj fixed; (emploi) steady, regular ♦ nm (salaire) basic salary; **à heure ~** at a set time; **menu à ~** set menu

fixé, e [fikse] adj: **être ~ (sur)** (savoir à quoi s'en tenir) to have made up one's mind (about); to know for certain (about)

fixer [fikse] vt (attacher): ~ **qch (à/ sur)** to fix ou fasten sth (to/onto); (déterminer) to fix, set; (CHIMIE, PHOTO) to fix; (regarder) to stare at; **se ~** vi (s'établir) to settle down; **se ~ sur** (suj: attention) to focus on

flacon [flakɔ̃] nm bottle

flageller [flaʒele] vt to flog, scourge

flageoler [flaʒɔle] vi (jambes) to sag

flageolet [flaʒɔlɛ] nm (MUS) flageolet; (CULIN) dwarf kidney bean

flagrant, e [flagʀɑ̃, -ɑ̃t] adj flagrant, blatant; **en ~ délit** in the act

flair [flɛʀ] nm sense of smell; (fig) intuition; **flairer** vt (humer) to sniff (at); (détecter) to scent

flamand, e [flamɑ̃, -ɑ̃d] adj Flemish

♦ *nm* (LING) Flemish ♦ *nmf*: F~, e Fleming; les F~s the Flemish

flamant [flamɑ̃] *nm* flamingo

flambant [flɑ̃bɑ̃] *adv*: ~ neuf brand new

flambé, e [flɑ̃be] *adj* (CULIN) flambé

flambeau, x [flɑ̃bo] *nm* (flaming) torch

flambée [flɑ̃be] *nf* blaze; (*fig*) flaring-up, explosion

flamber [flɑ̃be] *vi* to blaze (up)

flamboyer [flɑ̃bwaje] *vi* to blaze (up), to flame

flamme [flam] *nf* flame; (*fig*) fire, fervour; en ~s on fire, ablaze

flan [flɑ̃] *nm* (CULIN) custard tart ou pie

flanc [flɑ̃] *nm* side; (MIL) flank; prêter le ~ à (*fig*) to lay o.s. open to

flancher [flɑ̃ʃe] *vi* to fail, pack up; to quit

flanelle [flanɛl] *nf* flannel

flâner [flɑne] *vi* to stroll; **flânerie** *nf* stroll

flanquer [flɑ̃ke] *vt* to flank; (*fam*: *mettre*) to chuck, shove; (: *jeter*): ~ par terre/à la porte to fling to the ground/chuck out

flaque [flak] *nf* (*d'eau*) puddle; (*d'huile, de sang etc*) pool

flash [flaʃ] (*pl* flashes) *nm* (PHOTO) flash; ~ (d'information) newsflash

flasque [flask(ə)] *adj* flabby

flatter [flate] *vt* to flatter; se ~ de qch to pride o.s. on sth; **flatterie** *nf* flattery *no pl*; **flatteur, euse** *adj* flattering ♦ *nm/f* flatterer

fléau, x [fleo] *nm* scourge

flèche [flɛʃ] *nf* arrow; (*de clocher*) spire; (*de grue*) jib; monter en ~ (*fig*) to soar, rocket; partir en ~ to be off like a shot; **fléchette** *nf* dart; **fléchettes** *nfpl* (*jeu*) darts *sg*

fléchir [fleʃiʀ] *vt* (*corps, genou*) to bend; (*fig*) to sway, weaken ♦ *vi* (*poutre*) to sag, bend; (*fig*) to weaken, flag; to yield

flemmard, e [flemaʀ, -aʀd(ə)] *nm/f*

lazybones *sg*, loafer

flétrir [fletʀiʀ] *vt* to wither; se ~ *vi* to wither

fleur [flœʀ] *nf* flower; (*d'un arbre*) blossom; en ~ (*arbre*) in blossom; à ~ de terre just above the ground

fleurer [flœʀe] *vt*: ~ la lavande to have the scent of lavender

fleuri, e [flœʀi] *adj* in flower ou bloom; surrounded by flowers; (*fig*) flowery; florid

fleurir [flœʀiʀ] *vi* (*rose*) to flower; (*arbre*) to blossom; (*fig*) to flourish ♦ *vt* (*tombe*) to put flowers on; (*chambre*) to decorate with flowers

fleuriste [flœʀist(ə)] *nm/f* florist

fleuron [flœʀɔ̃] *nm* jewel

fleuve [flœv] *nm* river

flexible [flɛksibl(ə)] *adj* flexible

flexion [flɛksjɔ̃] *nf* flexing, bending

flic [flik] (*fam*) *nm* cop

flipper [flipœʀ] *nm* pinball (machine)

flirter [flœʀte] *vi* to flirt

flocon [flɔkɔ̃] *nm* flake

floraison [flɔʀɛzɔ̃] *nf* flowering; blossoming; flourishing

flore [flɔʀ] *nf* flora

florissant, e [flɔʀisɑ̃] *vb voir* fleurir ♦ *adj* (*économie, santé*) flourishing

flot [flo] *nm* flood, stream; ~s *mpl* (*de la mer*) waves; être à ~ (NAVIG) to be afloat; (*fig*) to be on an even keel; entrer à ~s to stream ou pour in

flotte [flɔt] *nf* (NAVIG) fleet; (*fam*) water; rain

flottement [flɔtmɑ̃] *nm* (*fig*) wavering, hesitation

flotter [flɔte] *vi* to float; (*nuage, odeur*) to drift; (*drapeau*) to fly; (*vêtements*) to hang loose; (*monnaie*) to float ♦ *vt* to float; faire ~ to float; **flotteur** *nm* float

flou, e [flu] *adj* fuzzy, blurred; (*fig*) woolly, vague

flouer [flue] *vt* to swindle

fluctuation [flyktɥasjɔ̃] *nf* fluctuation

fluet, te [flɥɛ, -ɛt] *adj* thin, slight

fluide [flɥid] *adj* fluid; (*circulation etc*) flowing freely ♦ *nm* fluid; (*force*) (mysterious) power

fluor [flyɔʀ] nm fluorine

fluorescent, e [flyɔʀesɑ̃, -ɑ̃t] adj fluorescent

flûte [flyt] nf flute; (verre) flute glass; (pain) long loaf; ~! drat it!; ~ à bec recorder

flux [fly] nm incoming tide; (écoulement) flow; **le ~ et le reflux** the ebb and flow

FM sigle f (= fréquence modulée) FM

foc [fɔk] nm jib

foi [fwa] nf faith; **sous la ~ du serment** under ou on oath; **ajouter ~** à to lend credence to; **digne de ~** reliable; **sur la ~ de** on the word ou strength of; **être de bonne/mauvaise ~** to be sincere/insincere; **ma ~ ...** well ...

foie [fwa] nm liver

foin [fwɛ̃] nm hay; **faire du ~** (fig: fam) to kick up a row

foire [fwaʀ] nf fair; (fête foraine) (fun) fair; **faire la ~** (fig: fam) to whoop it up; (exposition) trade fair

fois [fwa] nf time; **une/deux ~** once/twice; **2 ~ 2** 2 times 2; **quatre ~ plus grand (que)** four times as big (as); **une ~** (passé) once; (futur) sometime; **une ~ pour toutes** once and for all; **une ~ que once;** des ~ (parfois) sometimes; **à la ~** (ensemble) at once

foison [fwazɔ̃] nf: **une ~ de** an abundance of; **à ~** in plenty

foisonner [fwazɔne] vi to abound

fol [fɔl] adj voir **fou**

folâtrer [fɔlɑtʀe] vi to frolic (about)

folie [fɔli] nf (d'une décision, d'un acte) madness, folly; (état) madness, insanity; (acte) folly; **la ~ des grandeurs** delusions of grandeur; **faire des ~s** (en dépenses) to be extravagant

folklorique [fɔlklɔʀik] adj folk cpd; (fam) weird

folle [fɔl] adj, nf voir **fou; follement** adv (très) madly, wildly

foncé, e [fɔ̃se] adj dark

foncer [fɔ̃se] vi to go darker; (fam:

aller vite) to tear ou belt along; ~ **sur** to charge at

foncier, ère [fɔ̃sje, -ɛʀ] adj (honnêteté etc) basic, fundamental; (malhonnêteté) deep-rooted; (COMM) real estate cpd

fonction [fɔ̃ksjɔ̃] nf (rôle, MATH, LING) function; (emploi, poste) post, position; ~s nfpl (professionnelles) duties; **entrer en ~s** to take up one's post ou duties; **to take up office; voiture de ~** company car; **être ~ de** (dépendre de) to depend on; **en ~ de** (par rapport à) according to; **faire ~ de** to serve as; **la ~ publique** the state ou civil (BRIT) service; **fonctionnaire** [fɔ̃ksjɔnɛʀ] nm/f state employee, local authority employee; (dans l'administration) ≈ civil servant; **fonctionner** [fɔ̃ksjɔne] vi to work, function; (entreprise) to operate, function

fond [fɔ̃] nm (d'un récipient, trou) bottom; (d'une salle, scène) back; (d'un tableau, décor) background; (opposé à la forme) content; (SPORT): **le ~** long distance (running); **sans ~** bottomless; **au ~ de** at the bottom of; at the back of; **à ~** (connaître, soutenir) thoroughly; (appuyer, visser) right down ou home; **à ~ (de train)** (fam) full tilt; **dans le ~, au ~** (en somme) basically, really; **de ~ en comble** from top to bottom; **voir aussi fonds;** ~ **de teint** (make-up) foundation; ~ **sonore** background noise; background music

fondamental, e, aux [fɔ̃damɑ̃tal, -o] adj fundamental

fondant, e [fɔ̃dɑ̃, -ɑ̃t] adj (neige) melting; (poire) that melts in the mouth

fondateur, trice [fɔ̃datœʀ, -tʀis] nm/f founder

fondation [fɔ̃dasjɔ̃] nf founding; (établissement) foundation; ~s nfpl (d'une maison) foundations

fondé, e [fɔ̃de] adj (accusation etc) well-founded ♦ nm: ~ **de pouvoir** authorized representative; **être ~ à**

to have grounds for *ou* good reason to
fondement [fɔdmɑ̃] *nm* (*derrière*)
behind; ~s *nmpl* (*base*) foundations;
sans ~ (*rumeur etc*) groundless, unfounded
fonder [fɔde] *vt* to found; (*fig*) to
base; se ~ sur (*suj: personne*) to
base o.s. on
fonderie [fɔdʀi] *nf* smelting works *sg*
fondre [fɔdʀ(ə)] *vt* (*aussi: faire* ~)
to melt; (*dans l'eau*) to dissolve;
(*fig: mélanger*) to merge, blend ♦ *vi*
to melt; to dissolve; (*fig*) to melt
away; (*se précipiter*): ~ sur to
swoop down on; ~ en larmes to
burst into tears
fonds [fɔ̃] *nm* (*de bibliothèque*) collection; (*COMM*): ~ (*de commer-
ce*) business ♦ *nmpl* (*argent*) funds;
à ~ perdus with little or no hope of
getting the money back
fondu, e [fɔdy] *adj* (*beurre, neige*)
melted; (*métal*) molten; **fondue** *nf*
(*CULIN*) fondue
font *vb voir* **faire**
fontaine [fɔten] *nf* fountain;
(*source*) spring
fonte [fɔt] *nf* melting; (*métal*) cast
iron; **la** ~ **des neiges** (the spring)
thaw
foot [fut] (*fam*) *nm* football
football [futbol] *nm* football, soccer;
footballeur *nm* footballer
footing [futiŋ] *nm* jogging; **faire du**
~ to go jogging
for [fɔʀ] *nm*: **dans son** ~ **intérieur**
in one's heart of hearts
forain, e [fɔʀɛ̃, -ɛn] *adj* fairground
cpd ♦ *nm* stallholder; fairground entertainer
forçat [fɔʀsa] *nm* convict
force [fɔʀs(ə)] *nf* strength; (*puissance: surnaturelle etc*) power;
(*PHYSIQUE, MÉCANIQUE*) force;
~s *nfpl* (*physiques*) strength *sg*;
(*MIL*) forces; à ~ de by dint
of insisting; ~ **de** (*ou I etc*) kept on
insisting; **de** ~ forcibly, by force;
être de ~ **à faire** to be up to doing;
de première ~ first class; **les** ~s

de l'ordre the police
forcé, e [fɔʀse] *adj* forced; unin-
tended; inevitable
forcément [fɔʀsemɑ̃] *adv* necessarily; inevitably; (*bien sûr*) of
course
forcené, e [fɔʀsəne] *nm/f* maniac
forcer [fɔʀse] *vt* (*porte, serrure,
plante*) to force; (*moteur, voix*) to
strain ♦ *vi* (*SPORT*) to overtax o.s.;
~ **la dose** to overdo it; ~ **l'allure** to
increase the pace; **se** ~ (**pour faire**) to force o.s. (to do)
forcir [fɔʀsiʀ] *vi* (*grossir*) to broaden
out; (*vent*) to freshen
forer [fɔʀe] *vt* to drill, bore
forestier, ère [fɔʀɛstje, -ɛʀ] *adj* forest *cpd*
forêt [fɔʀɛ] *nf* forest
forfait [fɔʀfɛ] *nm* (*COMM*) fixed *ou*
set price; all-in deal *ou* price;
(*crime*) infamy; **déclarer** ~ to withdraw; **travailler à** ~ to work for a
lump sum; ~**aire** *adj* inclusive; set
forge [fɔʀʒ(ə)] *nf* forge, smithy
forger [fɔʀʒe] *vt* to forge; (*fig: personnalité*) to form; (*: prétexte*) to
contrive, make up
forgeron [fɔʀʒəʀɔ̃] *nm* (black)smith
formaliser [fɔʀmalize] *vt*: **se** ~ *vi* to
take offence (at)
formalité [fɔʀmalite] *nf* (*ADMIN,
JUR*) formality; (*acte sans importance*): **simple** ~ mere formality
format [fɔʀma] *nm* size
formater [fɔʀmate] *vt* (*disque*) to
format
formation [fɔʀmasjɔ̃] *nf* forming;
training; (*MUS*) group; (*MIL,
AVIAT, GÉO*) formation; ~ **permanente** continuing education; ~ **professionnelle** vocational training
forme [fɔʀm(ə)] *nf* (*gén*) form; (*d'un
objet*) shape, form; ~s *nfpl* (*bonnes
manières*) proprieties; (*d'une
femme*) figure *sg*; **en** ~ **de poire**
pear-shaped; **être en** ~ (*SPORT
etc*) to be on form; **en bonne et due**
~ **in due form**
formel, le [fɔʀmɛl] *adj* (*preuve, dé-*

cision) definite, positive; (*logique*) formal; **formellement** *adv* (*absolument*) positively

former [fɔʀme] *vt* to form; (*éduquer*) to train; **se ~** *vi* to form

formidable [fɔʀmidabl(ə)] *adj* tremendous

formulaire [fɔʀmylɛʀ] *nm* form

formule [fɔʀmyl] *nf* (*gén*) formula; (*formulaire*) form; **~ de politesse** polite phrase; letter ending

formuler [fɔʀmyle] *vt* (*émettre: réponse, vœux*) to formulate; (*expliciter: sa pensée*) to express

fort, e [fɔʀ, fɔʀt(ə)] *adj* strong; (*intensité, rendement*) high, great; (*corpulent*) stout; (*doué*) good, able ♦ *adv* (*serrer, frapper*) hard; (*sonner*) loud(ly); (*beaucoup*) greatly, very much; (*très*) very ♦ *nm* (*édifice*) fort; (*point fort*) strong point, forte; **se faire ~ de ...** to claim one can ...; **au plus ~ de** (*au milieu de*) in the thick of; at the height of; **~e tête** rebel

fortifiant [fɔʀtifjɑ̃] *nm* tonic

fortifier [fɔʀtifje] *vt* to strengthen, fortify; (*MIL*) to fortify

fortiori [fɔʀtjɔʀi]: **à ~** *adv* all the more so

fortuit, e [fɔʀtɥi, -it] *adj* fortuitous, chance *cpd*

fortune [fɔʀtyn] *nf* fortune; **faire ~** to make one's fortune; **de ~** makeshift; chance *cpd*

fortuné, e [fɔʀtyne] *adj* wealthy

fosse [fos] *nf* (*grand trou*) pit; (*tombe*) grave; **~ (d'orchestre)** (orchestra) pit

fossé [fose] *nm* ditch; (*fig*) gulf, gap

fossette [fosɛt] *nf* dimple

fossile [fosil] *nm* fossil

fossoyeur [foswajœʀ] *nm* gravedigger

fou(fol, folle [fu, fɔl] *adj* (*dérégle etc*) wild, erratic; (*fam: extrême, très grand*) terrific, tremendous ♦ *nm/f* madman(woman) ♦ *nm* (*du roi*) jester; **être fou de** to be mad *ou* crazy about; **avoir le fou**

rire to have the giggles; **faire le fou** to act the fool

foudre [fudʀ(ə)] *nf*: **la ~** lightning

foudroyant, e [fudʀwajɑ̃, -ɑ̃t] *adj* lightning *cpd*, stunning; (*maladie, poison*) violent

foudroyer [fudʀwaje] *vt* to strike down; **être foudroyé** to be struck by lightning; **~ qn du regard** to glare at sb

fouet [fwɛ] *nm* whip; (*CULIN*) whisk; **de plein ~** (*se heurter*) head on; **fouetter** *vt* to whip; to whisk

fougère [fuʒɛʀ] *nf* fern

fougue [fug] *nf* ardour, spirit

fouille [fuj] *nf* search; **~s** *nfpl* (*archéologiques*) excavations

fouiller [fuje] *vt* to search; (*creuser*) to dig ♦ *vi* to rummage

fouillis [fuji] *nm* jumble, muddle

fouiner [fwine] (*péj*) *vi*: **~ dans** to nose around *ou* about in

foulard [fulaʀ] *nm* scarf

foule [ful] *nf* crowd; **les ~s** the masses; **la ~** crowds *pl*; **une ~ de** masses of

foulée [fule] *nf* stride

fouler [fule] *vt* to press; (*sol*) to tread upon; **se ~** *vi* (*fam*) to overexert o.s.; **se ~ la cheville** to sprain one's ankle; **~ aux pieds** to trample underfoot; **foulure** [fulyʀ] *nf* sprain

four [fuʀ] *nm* oven; (*de potier*) kiln; (*THEATRE: échec*) flop

fourbe [fuʀb(ə)] *adj* deceitful

fourbu, e [fuʀby] *adj* exhausted

fourche [fuʀʃ(ə)] *nf* pitchfork; (*de bicyclette*) fork

fourchette [fuʀʃɛt] *nf* fork; (*STATISTIQUE*) bracket, margin

fourgon [fuʀgɔ̃] *nm* van; (*RAIL*) wag(g)on

fourmi [fuʀmi] *nf* ant; **~s** *nfpl* (*fig*) pins and needles; **fourmilière** *nf* anthill

fourmiller [fuʀmije] *vi* to swarm

fournaise [fuʀnɛz] *nf* blaze; (*fig*) furnace, oven

fourneau, x [fuʀno] *nm* stove

fournée [fuʀne] *nf* batch

fourni, e [furni] adj (barbe, cheveux) thick; (magasin): **bien ~ (en)** well stocked (with)

fournir [furnir] vt to supply; (preuve, exemple) to provide; supply; (effort) to put in; **fournisseur, euse** nm/f supplier

fourniture [furnityr] nf supply(ing); **~s** nfpl (provisions) supplies

fourrage [fura3] nm fodder

fourrager¹, ère [fura3e, -ɛr] adj fodder cpd

fourrager² vi: **fourrager dans/ parmi** (fouiller) to rummage through /among

fourré, e [fure] adj (bonbon etc) filled; (manteau etc) fur-lined ♦ nm thicket

fourreau, x [furo] nm sheath

fourrer [fure] (fam) vt to stick, shove; **se ~ dans/sous** to get into/ under

fourre-tout [furtu] nm inv (sac) holdall; (péj) junk room (ou cupboard); (fig) rag-bag

fourrière [furjɛr] nf pound

fourrure [furyr] nf fur; (sur l'animal) coat

fourvoyer [furvwaje]: **se ~** vi to go astray, stray

foutre [futr(ə)] (fam!) vt = **ficher**; **foutu, e** (fam!) adj = **fichu, e**

foyer [fwaje] nm (de cheminée) hearth; (famille) family; (maison) home; (de jeunes etc) (social) club; hostel; (salon) foyer; (OPTIQUE, PHOTO) focus sg; **lunettes à double ~** bi-focal glasses

fracas [fraka] nm din; crash; roar

fracasser [frakase] vt to smash

fraction [fraksjɔ̃] nf fraction; **fractionner** vt to divide (up), split (up)

fracture [fraktyr] nf fracture; **~ du crâne** fractured skull; **~r** [fraktyre] vt (coffre, serrure) to break open; (os, membre) to fracture

fragile [fraʒil] adj fragile, delicate; (fig) frail; **fragilité** nf fragility

fragment [fragmã] nm (d'un objet) fragment, piece; (d'un texte) passage, extract

fraîche [frɛʃ] adj voir **frais**

fraîcheur [frɛʃœr] nf coolness; freshness

fraîchir vi to get cooler; (vent) to freshen

frais, fraîche [frɛ, frɛʃ] adj fresh; (froid) cool ♦ adv (récemment) newly, fresh(ly) ♦ nm: **mettre au ~** to put in a cool place ♦ nmpl (débours) expenses; (COMM) costs; (facturés) charges; **il fait ~** it's cool; **servir ~** serve chilled; **prendre le ~** to take a breath of cool air; **faire des ~** to spend; **to go to a lot of expense; faire les ~ de** to bear the brunt of; **~ de scolarité** school fees (BRIT), tuition (US); **~ généraux** overheads

fraise [frɛz] nf strawberry; (TECH) countersink (bit); (de dentiste) drill; **~ des bois** wild strawberry

framboise [frãbwaz] nf raspberry

franc, franche [frã, frãʃ] adj (personne) frank, straightforward; (visage) open; (: net: refus, couleur) clear; (: coupure) clean; (intensif) downright; (exempt): **~ de port** postage paid ♦ adv: **parler ~** to be frank ou candid ♦ nm franc

français, e [frãsɛ, -ɛz] adj French ♦ nm/f: **F~, e** Frenchman(woman) ♦ nm (LING) French; **les F~** the French

France [frãs] nf: **la ~** France

franche [frãʃ] adj voir **franc; franchement** adv frankly; clearly; (tout à fait) downright

franchir [frãʃir] vt (obstacle) to clear, get over; (seuil, ligne, rivière) to cross; (distance) to cover

franchise [frãʃiz] nf frankness; (douanière, d'impôt) exemption; (ASSURANCES) excess

franciser [frãsize] vt to gallicize, Frenchify

franc-maçon [frãmasɔ̃] nm freemason

franco [frãko] adv (COMM): **~ (de port)** postage paid

francophone [frãkɔfɔn] adj French-speaking; **francophonie**

French-speaking communities

franc-parler [frɑ̃parle] nm inv outspokenness

franc-tireur [frɑ̃tirœr] nm (MIL) irregular; (fig) freelance

frange [frɑ̃ʒ] nf fringe

frangipane [frɑ̃ʒipan] nf almond paste

franquette [frɑ̃kɛt] : à la bonne ~ adv without any fuss

frappe [frap] nf (de pianiste, machine à écrire) touch; (BOXE) punch

frappé, e [frape] adj iced

frapper [frape] vt to hit, strike; (étonner) to strike; (monnaie) to strike, stamp; se ~ vi (s'inquiéter) to get worked up; ~ dans ses mains to clap one's hands; ~ du poing sur to bang one's fist on; frappé de stupeur dumbfounded

frasques [frask(ə)] nfpl escapades

fraternel, le [fratɛrnɛl] adj brotherly, fraternal

fraternité [fratɛrnite] nf brotherhood

fraude [frod] nf fraud; (SCOL) cheating; passer qch en ~ to smuggle sth in (ou out); ~ fiscale tax evasion; **frauder** vi, vt to cheat; **frauduleux, euse** adj fraudulent

frayer [freje] vt to open up, clear ♦ vi to spawn; (fréquenter): ~ avec to mix with

frayeur [frejœr] nf fright

fredonner [frədɔne] vt to hum

freezer [frizœr] nm freezing compartment

frein [frɛ̃] nm brake; ~ à main handbrake; ~s à disques/tambour disc/drum brakes

freiner [frene] vi to brake ♦ vt (progrès etc) to check

frelaté, e [frəlate] adj adulterated; (fig) tainted

frêle [frɛl] adj frail, fragile

frelon [frəlɔ̃] nm hornet

frémir [fremir] vi to tremble, shudder; to shiver; to quiver

frêne [frɛn] nm ash

frénétique [frenetik] adj frenzied,

frenetic

fréquemment [frekamɑ̃] adv frequently

fréquent, e [frekɑ̃, -ɑ̃t] adj frequent

fréquentation [frekɑ̃tasjɔ̃] nf frequenting; seeing; ~s nfpl (relations) company sg

fréquenté, e [frekɑ̃te] adj: très ~ (very) busy; mal ~ patronized by disreputable elements

fréquenter [frekɑ̃te] vt (lieu) to frequent; (personne) to see; se ~ to see each other

frère [frɛr] nm brother

fresque [frɛsk(ə)] nf (ART) fresco

fret [frɛ] nm freight

frétiller [fretije] vi to wriggle; to quiver; (chien) to wag its tail

fretin [frətɛ̃] nm: menu ~ small fry

friable [frijabl(ə)] adj crumbly

friand, e [frijɑ̃, -ɑ̃d] adj: ~ de fond of

friandise [frijɑ̃diz] nf sweet

fric [frik] (fam) nm cash, bread

friche [friʃ] : en ~ adj, adv (lying) fallow

friction [friksjɔ̃] nf (massage) rub, rub-down; (TECH, fig) friction; **frictionner** vt to rub (down); to massage

frigidaire [friʒidɛr] ® nm refrigerator

frigide [friʒid] adj frigid

frigo [frigo] nm fridge

frigorifier [frigɔrifje] vt to refrigerate; **frigorifique** adj refrigerating

frileux, euse [frilø, -øz] adj sensitive to (the) cold

frimer [frime] vi to put on an act

frimousse [frimus] nf (sweet) little face

fringale [frɛ̃gal] nf: avoir la ~ to be ravenous

fringant, e [frɛ̃gɑ̃, -ɑ̃t] adj dashing

fringues [frɛ̃g] (fam) nfpl clothes

fripé, e [fripe] adj crumpled

fripon, ne [fripɔ̃, -ɔn] adj roguish, mischievous ♦ nm/f rascal, rogue

fripouille [fripuj] nf scoundrel

frire [frir] vt, vi: faire ~ to fry

frisé, e [frize] adj curly; curly-haired

frisson [fʀisɔ̃] nm shudder, shiver; quiver; **frissonner** vi to shudder, shiver; to quiver

frit, e [fʀi, fʀit] pp de **frire**; **frite** nf: (pommes) **frites** chips (BRIT), French fries; **friteuse** nf chip pan; **friture** nf (huile) (deep) fat; (plat): **friture** (de poissons) fried fish; (RADIO) crackle

frivole [fʀivɔl] adj frivolous

froid, e [fʀwa, fʀwad] adj, nm cold; il fait ~ it's cold; avoir/prendre ~ to be/catch cold; être en ~ avec to be on bad terms with; **~ement** adv (accueillir) coldly; (décider) coolly

froisser [fʀwase] vt to crumple (up), crease; (fig) to hurt, offend; se ~ vi to crumple, crease; to take offence; se ~ un muscle to strain a muscle

frôler [fʀole] vt to brush against; (suj: projectile) to skim past; (fig) to come very close to

fromage [fʀɔmaʒ] nm cheese; ~ blanc soft white cheese; **fromager, ère** nm/f cheese merchant

froment [fʀɔmɑ̃] nm wheat

froncer [fʀɔ̃se] vt to gather; ~ les sourcils to frown

frondaisons [fʀɔ̃dɛzɔ̃] nfpl foliage sg

fronde [fʀɔ̃d] nf sling; (fig) rebellion, rebelliousness

front [fʀɔ̃] nm forehead, brow; (MIL) front; de ~ (se heurter) head-on; (rouler) together (i.e. 2 or 3 abreast); (simultanément) at once; faire ~ à to face up to; ~ de mer (sea) front

frontalier, ère [fʀɔ̃taljε, -εʀ] adj border cpd, frontier cpd ♦ nm/f: (travailleurs) ~s commuters from across the border

frontière [fʀɔ̃tjεʀ] nf frontier, border; (fig) frontier, boundary

fronton [fʀɔ̃tɔ̃] nm pediment

frotter [fʀɔte] vi to rub, scrape ♦ vt to rub; (pour nettoyer) to rub (up); to scrub; ~ une allumette to strike a match

fructifier [fʀyktifje] vi to yield a profit; **faire** ~ to turn to good account

fructueux, euse [fʀyktɥø, -øz] adj fruitful; profitable

fruit [fʀɥi] nm fruit gen no pl; ~s de mer seafood(s); ~s secs dried fruit sg; ~é, e adj fruity; ~ier, ère adj: arbre ~ier fruit tree ♦ nm/f **fruitier** (BRIT), fruit merchant (US)

fruste [fʀyst(ə)] adj unpolished, uncultivated

frustrer [fʀystʀe] vt to frustrate

fuel(-oil) [fjul(ɔjl)] nm fuel oil; heating oil

fugace [fygas] adj fleeting

fugitif, ive [fyʒitif, -iv] adj (lueur, amour) fleeting; (prisonnier etc) fugitive, runaway ♦ nm/f fugitive

fugue [fyg] nf: **faire une** ~ to run away, abscond

fuir [fɥiʀ] vt to flee from; (éviter) to shun ♦ vi to run away; (gaz, robinet) to leak

fuite [fɥit] nf flight; (écoulement, divulgation) leak; **être en** ~ to be on the run; **mettre en** ~ to put to flight

fulgurant, e [fylgyʀɑ̃, -ɑ̃t] adj lightning cpd, dazzling

fulminer [fylmine] vi to thunder forth

fumé, e [fyme] adj (CULIN) smoked; (verre) tinted

fume-cigarette [fymsigaʀɛt] nm inv cigarette holder

fumée [fyme] nf smoke

fumer [fyme] vi to smoke; (soupe) to steam ♦ vt to smoke; (terre, champ) to manure

fûmes etc vb voir **être**

fumet [fyme] nm aroma

fumeur, euse [fymœʀ, -øz] nm/f smoker

fumeux, euse [fymø, -øz] adj (péj) woolly, hazy

fumier [fymje] nm manure

fumiste [fymist(ə)] nm/f (péj: paresseux) shirker; (charlatan) phoney

fumisterie [fymistəʀi] (péj) nf fraud, con

funambule [fynɑ̃byl] nm tightrope walker

funèbre [fynɛbʀ(ə)] adj funeral

(fig) doleful; funereal

funérailles [fynerɑj] *nfpl* funeral *sg*

funeste [fynɛst(ə)] *adj* disastrous; deathly

fur [fyʀ] : **au ~ et à mesure** *adv* as one goes along; **au ~ et à mesure que as**

furet [fyʀɛ] *nm* ferret

fureter [fyʀte] *(péj) vi* to nose about

fureur [fyʀœʀ] *nf* fury; *(passion)*: **~ de passion for**; **faire ~** to be all the rage

furibond, e [fyʀibɔ̃, -ɔ̃d] *adj* furious

furie [fyʀi] *nf* fury; *(femme)* shrew, vixen; **en ~** *(mer)* raging; **furieux, euse** *adj* furious

furoncle [fyʀɔ̃kl(ə)] *nm* boil

furtif, ive [fyʀtif, -iv] *adj* furtive

fus [fy] *vb voir* **être**

fusain [fyzɛ̃] *nm (ART)* charcoal

fuseau, x [fyzo] *nm (pour filer)* spindle; *(pantalon)* (ski) pants; **~ horaire** time zone

fusée [fyze] *nf* rocket; **~ éclairante** flare

fuselé, e [fyzle] *adj* slender; tapering

fuser [fyze] *vi (rires etc)* to burst forth

fusible [fyzibl(ə)] *nm (ÉLEC: fil)* fuse wire; *(: fiche)* fuse

fusil [fyzi] *nm (de guerre, à canon rayé)* rifle, gun; *(de chasse, à canon lisse)* shotgun, gun; **fusillade** *nf* gunfire *no pl*, shooting *no pl*; shooting battle; **fusiller** *vt* to shoot; **fusil-mitrailleur** *nm* machine gun

fusionner [fyzjɔne] *vi* to merge

fustiger [fystiʒe] *vt* to denounce

fut *vb voir* **être**

fût [fy] *vb voir* **être** ♦ *nm (tonneau)* barrel, cask

futaie [fytɛ] *nf* forest, plantation

futé, e [fyte] *adj* crafty

futile [fytil] *adj* futile; frivolous

futur, e [fytyʀ] *adj, nm* future

fuyant, e [fɥijɑ̃, -ɑ̃t] *vb voir* **fuir** ♦ *adj (regard etc)* evasive; *(lignes etc)* receding; *(perspective)* vanishing

fuyard, e [fɥijaʀ, -aʀd(ə)] *nm/f* running

away

G

gabarit [gabaʀi] *nm (fig)* size; calibre

gâcher [gɑʃe] *vt (gâter)* to spoil, ruin; *(gaspiller)* to waste

gâchette [gɑʃɛt] *nf* trigger

gâchis [gɑʃi] *nm* waste *no pl*

gadoue [gadu] *nf* sludge

gaffe [gaf] *nf (instrument)* boat hook; *(erreur)* blunder; **faire ~** *(fam)* to be careful

gage [gaʒ] *nm (dans un jeu)* forfeit; *(fig: de fidélité)* token; **~s** *nmpl (salaire)* wages; *(garantie)* guarantee *sg*; **mettre en ~** to pawn

gager [gaʒe] *vt* to bet, wager

gageure [gaʒyʀ] *nf*: **c'est une ~** it's attempting the impossible

gagnant, e [gaɲɑ̃, -ɑ̃t] *nm/f* winner

gagne-pain [gaɲpɛ̃] *nm inv* job

gagner [gaɲe] *vt* to win; *(somme d'argent, revenu)* to earn; *(aller vers, atteindre)* to reach; *(envahir)* to overcome; to spread to ♦ *vi* to win; *(fig)* to gain; **~ du temps/de la place** to gain time/save space; **~ sa vie** to earn one's living

gai, e [ge] *adj* gay, cheerful; *(un peu ivre)* merry

gaieté [gete] *nf* cheerfulness; **de ~ de cœur** with a light heart

gaillard, e [gajaʀ, -aʀd(ə)] *adj (grivois)* bawdy, ribald ♦ *nm (strapping)* fellow

gain [gɛ̃] *nm (revenu)* earnings *pl*; *(bénéfice: gén pl)* profits *pl*; *(au jeu)* winnings *pl*; *(fig: de temps, place)* saving; **avoir ~ de cause** to win the case; *(fig)* to be proved right

gaine [gɛn] *nf (corset)* girdle; *(fourreau)* sheath

galant, e [galɑ̃, -ɑ̃t] *adj (courtois)* courteous, gentlemanly; *(entreprenant)* flirtatious, gallant; *(aventure, poésie)* amorous

galère [galɛʀ] *nf* galley

galérer [galeʀe] (fam) vi to slog away, work hard

galerie [galʀi] nf gallery; (THEATRE) circle; (de voiture) roof rack; (fig: spectateurs) audience; ~ **de peinture** (private) art gallery; ~ **marchande** shopping arcade

galet [galɛ] nm pebble; (TECH) wheel

galette [galɛt] nf flat cake

Galles [gal] nfpl: **le pays de** ~ Wales

gallois, e [galwa, -waz] adj Welsh ♦ nm (LING) Welsh ♦ nm/f: G~, e Welshman(woman)

galon [galɔ̃] nm (MIL) stripe; (décoratif) piece of braid

galop [galo] nm gallop

galoper [galɔpe] vi to gallop

galopin [galɔpɛ̃] nm urchin, ragamuffin

galvauder [galvode] vt to debase

gambader [gɑ̃bade] vi (animal, enfant) to leap about

gamelle [gamɛl] nf mess tin; billy can

gamin, e [gamɛ̃, -in] nm/f kid ♦ adj mischievous, playful

gamme [gam] nf (MUS) scale; (fig) range

gammé, e [game] adj: **croix ~e** swastika

gant [gɑ̃] nm glove; ~ **de toilette** face flannel (BRIT), face cloth

garage [gaʀaʒ] nm garage; **garagiste** nm/f garage owner; garage mechanic

garant, e [gaʀɑ̃, -ɑ̃t] nm/f guarantor ♦ nm guarantee; **se porter ~ de** to vouch for; to be answerable for

garantie [gaʀɑ̃ti] nf guarantee; (gage) security, surety; (bon de) ~ guarantee ou warranty slip

garantir [gaʀɑ̃tiʀ] vt to guarantee; (protéger): ~ **de** to protect from

garçon [gaʀsɔ̃] nm boy; (: célibataire) bachelor; (serveur): ~ (**de café**) waiter; ~ **de courses** messenger; **garçonnet** nm small boy; **garçonnière** nf bachelor flat

garde [gaʀd(ə)] nm (de prisonnier) guard; (de domaine etc) warden; (soldat, sentinelle) guardsman ♦ nf guarding; looking after; (soldats, BOXE, ESCRIME) guard; (faction) watch; (TYPO): (**page de**) ~ endpaper; flyleaf; **de** ~ on duty; **monter la** ~ to stand guard; **mettre en** ~ to warn; **prendre** ~ (**à**) to be careful (of); ~ **champêtre** nm rural policeman; ~ **du corps** nm bodyguard; ~ **des enfants** nf (après divorce) custody of the children; ~ **des Sceaux** nm ≈ Lord Chancellor (BRIT), ≈ Attorney General (US); **à vue** nf (JUR) ≈ police custody; ~**-à-vous** nm: **être/se mettre au** ~**-à-vous** to be at/stand to attention; ~**-barrière** nm/f level-crossing keeper; ~**-boue** nm inv mudguard; ~**-chasse** nm gamekeeper; ~**-fou** nm railing, parapet; ~**-malade** nf home nurse; ~**-manger** nm inv meat safe; pantry, larder

garder [gaʀde] vt (conserver) to keep; (surveiller: enfants) to look after; (: immeuble, lieu, prisonnier) to guard; **se** ~ vi (aliment: se conserver) to keep; **se** ~ **de faire** to be careful not to do; ~ **le lit/la chambre** to stay in bed/indoors; **pêche/chasse gardée** private fishing/hunting (ground)

garderie [gaʀdəʀi] nf day nursery, crèche

garde-robe [gaʀdərɔb] nf wardrobe

gardien, ne [gaʀdjɛ̃, -jɛn] nm/f (garde) guard; (de prison) warder; (de domaine, réserve) warden; (de musée etc) attendant; (de phare, cimetière) keeper; (d'immeuble) caretaker; (fig) guardian; ~ **de but** goalkeeper; ~ **de la paix** policeman; ~ **de nuit** night watchman

gare [gaʀ] nf (railway) station, train station (US) ♦ excl watch out!; ~ **routière** bus station

garer [gaʀe] vt to park; **se** ~ vi to park; (pour laisser passer) to draw into the side

gargariser [gaʁgaʁize] : se ~ vi to gargle; **gargarisme** nm gargling no pl; gargle

gargote [gaʁgɔt] nf cheap restaurant

gargouille [gaʁguj] nf gargoyle

gargouiller [gaʁguje] vi to gurgle

garnement [gaʁnəmã] nm rascal, scallywag

garni, e [gaʁni] adj (plat) served with vegetables (and chips or rice etc) ♦ nm furnished accommodation no pl

garnir [gaʁniʁ] vt (orner) to decorate; to trim; (approvisionner) to fill, stock; (protéger) to fit

garnison [gaʁnizõ] nf garrison

garniture [gaʁnityʁ] nf (CULIN) vegetables pl; filling; (décoration) trimming; (protection) fittings pl; ~ de frein brake lining

garrot [gaʁo] nm (MED) tourniquet

gars [gɑ] nm lad; guy

Gascogne [gaskɔɲ] nf Gascony; le golfe de ~ the Bay of Biscay

gas-oil [gazɔjl] nm diesel oil

gaspiller [gaspije] vt to waste

gastronomique [gastʁɔnɔmik] adj gastronomic

gâteau, x [gɑto] nm cake; ~ sec biscuit

gâter [gɑte] vt to spoil; se ~ vi (dent, fruit) to go bad; (temps, situation) to change for the worse

gâterie [gɑtʁi] nf little treat

gâteux, euse [gɑtø, øz] adj senile

gauche [goʃ] adj left, left-hand; (maladroit) awkward, clumsy ♦ nf (POL) left (wing); à ~ on the left; (direction) (to the) left; **gaucher, ère** adj left-handed; **gauchiste** nm/f leftist

gaufre [gofʁ(ə)] nf waffle

gaufrette [gofʁɛt] nf wafer

gaulois, e [golwa, -waz] adj Gallic; (grivois) bawdy ♦ nm/f: G~, e Gaul

gausser [gose] : se ~ de vi to deride

gaver [gave] vt to force-feed; (fig): ~ de to cram with, fill up with

gaz [gaz] nm inv gas

gaze [gaz] nf gauze

gazéifié, e [gazeifje] adj aerated

gazette [gazɛt] nf news sheet

gazeux, euse [gazø, -øz] adj gaseous; (boisson) fizzy; (eau) sparkling

gazoduc [gazɔdyk] nm gas pipeline

gazon [gazõ] nm (herbe) turf; grass; (pelouse) lawn

gazouiller [gazuje] vi to chirp; (enfant) to babble

geai [ʒɛ] nm jay

géant, e [ʒeã, -ãt] adj gigantic, giant; (COMM) giant-size ♦ nm/f giant

geindre [ʒɛ̃dʁ(ə)] vi to groan, moan

gel [ʒɛl] nm frost; freezing

gélatine [ʒelatin] nf gelatine

gelée [ʒəle] nf jelly; (gel) frost

geler [ʒəle] vt, vi to freeze; il gèle it's freezing

gélule [ʒelyl] nf (MED) capsule

gelures [ʒəlyʁ] nfpl frostbite sg

Gémeaux [ʒemo] nmpl: les ~ Gemini

gémir [ʒemiʁ] vi to groan, moan

gemme [ʒɛm] nf gem(stone)

gênant, e [ʒɛnã, -ãt] adj annoying; embarrassing

gencive [ʒãsiv] nf gum

gendarme [ʒãdaʁm(ə)] nm gendarme; ~**rie** nf military police force in countryside and small towns; their police station or barracks

gendre [ʒãdʁ(ə)] nm son-in-law

gêne [ʒɛn] nf (à respirer, bouger) discomfort, difficulty; (dérangement) bother, trouble; (manque d'argent) financial difficulties pl ou straits pl; (confusion) embarrassment

gêné, e [ʒene] adj embarrassed

gêner [ʒene] vt (incommoder) to bother; (encombrer) to hamper; to be in the way; (embarrasser): ~ qn to make sb feel ill-at-ease; se ~ vi to put o.s. out

général, e, aux [ʒeneʁal, -o] adj, nm general; en ~ usually, in general; ~**e** nf: (répétition) ~e final dress rehearsal; **~ement** adv generally

généraliser [ʒeneralize] vt, vi to generalize; **se ~** vi to become widespread

généraliste [ʒeneralist(ə)] nm/f general practitioner, G.P.

générateur, trice [ʒeneratœr, -tris] adj: **~ de** which causes

génération [ʒenerasjɔ̃] nf generation

généreux, euse [ʒenerø, -øz] adj generous

générique [ʒenerik] nm (CINÉMA) credits pl, credit titles pl

générosité [ʒenerozite] nf generosity

genêt [ʒənɛ] nm broom no pl (shrub)

génétique [ʒenetik] adj genetic

Genève [ʒənɛv] n Geneva

génial, e, aux [ʒenjal, -o] adj of genius; (fam: formidable) fantastic, brilliant

génie [ʒeni] nm genius; (MIL): **le ~** the Engineers pl; **~ civil** civil engineering

genièvre [ʒənjɛvr(ə)] nm juniper

génisse [ʒenis] nf heifer

genou, x [ʒnu] nm knee; **à ~x** on one's knees; **se mettre à ~x** to kneel down

genre [ʒɑ̃r] nm kind, type, sort; (allure) manner; (LING) gender

gens [ʒɑ̃] nmpl (f in some phrases) people pl

gentil, le [ʒɑ̃ti, -ij] adj kind; (enfant: sage) good; (endroit etc) nice; **gentillesse** nf kindness; **gentiment** adv kindly

géographie [ʒeɔgrafi] nf geography

geôlier [ʒolje] nm jailer

géologie [ʒeɔlɔʒi] nf (land) geology

géomètre [ʒeɔmɛtr(ə)] nm/f: (arpenteur-)**~** (land) surveyor

géométrie [ʒeɔmetri] nf geometry; **géométrique** adj geometric

gérance [ʒerɑ̃s] nf management; **mettre en ~** to appoint a manager for

géranium [ʒeranjɔm] nm geranium

gérant, e [ʒerɑ̃, -ɑ̃t] nm/f manager(eress)

gerbe [ʒɛrb(ə)] nf (de fleurs) spray; (de blé) sheaf; (fig) shower, burst

gercé, e [ʒɛrse] adj chapped

gerçure [ʒɛrsyr] nf crack

gérer [ʒere] vt to manage

germain, e [ʒɛrmɛ̃, -ɛn] adj: **cousin ~** first cousin

germe [ʒɛrm(ə)] nm germ; **~r** [ʒɛrme] vi to sprout; to germinate

geste [ʒɛst(ə)] nm gesture; move; motion

gestion [ʒɛstjɔ̃] nf management

gibecière [ʒibsjɛr] nf gamebag

gibet [ʒibɛ] nm gallows pl

gibier [ʒibje] nm (animaux) game; (fig) prey

giboulée [ʒibule] nf sudden shower

gicler [ʒikle] vi to spurt, squirt

gifle [ʒifl(ə)] nf slap (in the face); **gifler** vt to slap (in the face)

gigantesque [ʒigɑ̃tɛsk(ə)] adj gigantic

gigogne [ʒigɔɲ] adj: **~s** truckle lits (BRIT) ou trundle beds

gigot [ʒigo] nm leg of mutton ou lamb)

gigoter [ʒigɔte] vi to wriggle (about)

gilet [ʒilɛ] nm waistcoat; (pull) cardigan; (de corps) vest; **~ de sauvetage** life jacket

gingembre [ʒɛ̃ʒɑ̃br(ə)] nm ginger

girafe [ʒiraf] nf giraffe

giratoire [ʒiratwar] adj: **sens ~** roundabout

girofle [ʒirɔfl(ə)] nf: **clou de ~** clove

girouette [ʒirwɛt] nf weather vane ou cock

gisait etc vb voir **gésir**

gisement [ʒizmɑ̃] nm deposit

gît vb voir **gésir**

gitan, e [ʒitɑ̃, -an] nm/f gipsy

gîte [ʒit] nm home; shelter; **~ (rural)** holiday cottage ou apartment

givre [ʒivr(ə)] nm (hoar) frost

glabre [glɑbr(ə)] adj hairless; cleanshaven

glace [glas] nf ice; (crème glacée)

ice cream; (*verre*) sheet of glass; (*miroir*) mirror; (*de voiture*) window

glacé, e [glase] *adj* icy; (*boisson*) iced

glacer [glase] *vt* to freeze; (*boisson*) to chill, ice; (*gâteau*) to ice; (*papier, tissu*) to glaze; (*fig*): ~ **qn** to chill sb; to make sb's blood run cold

glacial, e [glasjal] *adj* icy

glacier [glasje] *nm* (GEO) glacier; (*marchand*) ice-cream maker

glacière [glasjɛʀ] *nf* icebox

glaçon [glasõ] *nm* icicle; (*pour boisson*) ice cube

glaise [glɛz] *nf* clay

gland [glɑ̃] *nm* acorn; (*décoration*) tassel

glande [glɑ̃d] *nf* gland

glaner [glane] *vt, vi* to glean

glapir [glapiʀ] *vi* to yelp

glas [glɑ] *nm* knell, toll

glauque [glok] *adj* dull blue-green

glissant, e [glisɑ̃, -ɑ̃t] *adj* slippery

glissement [glismɑ̃] *nm*: ~ **de terrain** landslide

glisser [glise] *vi* (*avancer*) to glide *ou* slide along; (*coulisser, tomber*) to slide; (*déraper*) to slip; (*être glissant*) to be slippery ♦ *vt* to slip; se ~ **dans** to slip into

global, e, aux [glɔbal, -o] *adj* overall

globe [glɔb] *nm* globe

globule [glɔbyl] *nm* (*du sang*) corpuscle

globuleux, euse [glɔbylø, -øz] *adj*: yeux ~ protruding eyes

gloire [glwaʀ] *nf* glory; (*mérite*) distinction, credit; (*personne*) celebrity; **glorieux, euse** *adj* glorious

glousser [gluse] *vi* to cluck; (*rire*) to chuckle

glouton, ne [glutõ, -ɔn] *adj* gluttonous

gluant, e [glyɑ̃, -ɑ̃t] *adj* sticky, gummy

glycine [glisin] *nf* wisteria

go [go] : **tout de** ~ *adv* straight out

G.O. *sigle* = **grandes ondes**

gobelet [gɔblɛ] *nm* tumbler; beaker;

(*à dés*) cup

gober [gɔbe] *vt* to swallow

godasse [gɔdas] (*fam*) *nf* shoe

godet [gɔdɛ] *nm* pot

goéland [gɔelɑ̃] *nm* (sea)gull

goélette [gɔelɛt] *nf* schooner

goémon [gɔemõ] *nm* wrack

gogo [gɔgo] : à ~ *adv* galore

goguenard, e [gɔgnaʀ, -aʀd(ə)] *adj* mocking

goinfre [gwɛ̃fʀ(ə)] *nm* glutton

golf [gɔlf] *nm* golf; golf course

golfe [gɔlf(ə)] *nm* gulf; bay

gomme [gɔm] *nf* (*à effacer*) rubber (BRIT), eraser; **gommer** *vt* to rub out (BRIT), erase

gond [gõ] *nm* hinge; sortir de ses ~s (*fig*) to fly off the handle

gondoler [gõdɔle] : se ~ *vi* to warp; to buckle

gonflé, e [gõfle] *adj* swollen; bloated

gonfler [gõfle] *vt* (*pneu, ballon*) to inflate, blow up; (*nombre, importance*) to inflate ♦ *vi* to swell (up); (CULIN: *pâte*) to rise

gonzesse [gõzɛs] (*fam*) *nf* chick, bird (BRIT)

goret [gɔʀɛ] *nm* piglet

gorge [gɔʀʒ(ə)] *nf* (ANAT) throat; (*poitrine*) breast

gorgé, e [gɔʀʒe] *adj*: ~ **de** filled with; (*eau*) saturated with; **gorgée** *nf* mouthful; sip; gulp

gorille [gɔʀij] *nm* gorilla; (*fam*) bodyguard

gosier [gozje] *nm* throat

gosse [gɔs] *nm/f* kid

goudron [gudʀõ] *nm* tar; **goudronner** *vt* to tar(mac) (BRIT), asphalt (US)

gouffre [gufʀ(ə)] *nm* abyss, gulf

goujat [guʒa] *nm* boor

goulot [gulo] *nm* neck; boire au ~ to drink from the bottle

goulu, e [guly] *adj* greedy

gourd, e [guʀ, guʀd(ə)] *adj* numb (with cold)

gourde [guʀd(ə)] *nf* (*récipient*) flask; (*fam*) (clumsy) clot *ou* oaf ♦ *adj* oafish

gourdin [guʀdɛ̃] nm club, bludgeon

gourmand, e [guʀmɑ̃, -ɑ̃d] adj greedy; **gourmandise** nf greed; (bonbon) sweet

gousse [gus] nf: ~ **d'ail** clove of garlic

goût [gu] nm taste; **de bon** ~ tasteful; **de mauvais** ~ tasteless; **prendre** ~ **à** to develop a taste ou a liking for

goûter [gute] vt (essayer) to taste; (apprécier) to enjoy ♦ vi to have (afternoon) tea ♦ nm (afternoon) tea

goutte [gut] nf drop; (MED) gout; (alcool) brandy

goutte-à-goutte [gutagut] nm (MED) drip; **tomber** ~ to drip

gouttière [gutjɛʀ] nf gutter

gouvernail [guvɛʀnaj] nm rudder; (barre) helm, tiller

gouvernante [guvɛʀnɑ̃t] nf governess

gouverne [guvɛʀn(ə)] nf: **pour sa** ~ for his guidance

gouvernement [guvɛʀnəmɑ̃] nm government; **gouvernemental, e, aux** adj government cpd; **pro-government**

gouverner [guvɛʀne] vt to govern

grâce [gʀɑs] nf grace; favour; (JUR) pardon; ~**s** nfpl (REL) grace sg; **faire** ~ **à qn de qch** to spare sb sth; **rendre** ~(**s**) **à** to give thanks to; **demander** ~ to beg for mercy; ~ **à** thanks to; **gracier** vt to pardon; **gracieux, euse** adj graceful

grade [gʀad] nm rank; **monter en** ~ to be promoted

gradé [gʀade] nm officer

gradin [gʀadɛ̃] nm tier; step; ~**s** nmpl (de stade) terracing sg

graduel, le [gʀaduɛl] adj gradual; progressive

graduer [gʀadue] vt (effort etc) to increase gradually; (règle, verre) to graduate

grain [gʀɛ̃] nm (gén) grain; (NAVIG) squall; ~ **de beauté** beauty spot; ~ **de café** coffee bean; ~ **de poivre** peppercorn; ~ **de poussière** speck

of dust; ~ **de raisin** grape

graine [gʀɛn] nf seed

graissage [gʀɛsaʒ] nm lubrication, greasing

graisse [gʀɛs] nf fat; (lubrifiant) grease; **graisser** vt to lubricate, grease; (tacher) to make greasy

grammaire [gʀamɛʀ] nf grammar; **grammatical, e, aux** adj grammatical

gramme [gʀam] nm gramme

grand, e [gʀɑ̃, gʀɑ̃d] adj (haut) tall; (gros, vaste, grave) big, large; (long) long; (sens abstraits) great ♦ adv: ~ **ouvert** wide open; **au** ~ **air** in the open (air); **les** ~**s blessés** the severely injured; ~ **ensemble** housing scheme; ~ **magasin** department store; ~**e personne** grown-up; ~ **surface** hypermarket; ~**es écoles** prestige schools of university level; ~**es lignes** (RAIL) main lines; ~**es vacances** summer holidays; **grand-chose** nm/f inv: **pas grand-chose** not much; **Grande-Bretagne** nf (Great) Britain; **grandeur** nf (dimension) size; magnitude; (fig) greatness; ~**eur nature** life-size; **grandir** vi to grow ♦ vt: **grandir qn** (suj: vêtement, chaussure) to make sb look taller; ~**mère** nf grandmother; ~**-messe** nf high mass: **à** ~**-peine** adv with difficulty; ~**-père** nm grandfather; ~**-route** nf main road; ~**s-parents** nmpl grandparents

grange [gʀɑ̃ʒ] nf barn

granit(e) [gʀanit] nm granite

graphique [gʀafik] adj graphic ♦ nm graph

grappe [gʀap] nf cluster; ~ **de raisin** bunch of grapes

grappiller [gʀapije] vt to glean

grappin [gʀapɛ̃] nm grapnel; **mettre le** ~ **sur** (fig) to get one's claws on

gras, se [gʀɑ, gʀɑs] adj (viande, soupe) fatty; (personne) fat; (surface, main) greasy; (plaisanterie) coarse; (TYPO) bold ♦ nm (CULIN) fat; **faire la** ~**se matinée** to have a lie-in (BRIT), sleep late (US); **gras-**

sement adv: **grassement payé** handsomely paid; **grassouillet, te** adj podgy, plump

gratifiant, e [gratifjɑ̃, -ɑ̃t] adj gratifying, rewarding

gratifier [gratifje] vt: ~ **qn de** to favour sb with; to reward sb with

gratiné, e [gratine] adj (CULIN) au gratin

gratis [gratis] adv free

gratitude [gratityd] nf gratitude

gratte-ciel [gratsjɛl] nm inv skyscraper

gratte-papier [gratpapje] (péj) nm inv penpusher

gratter [grate] vt (frotter) to scrape; (enlever) to scrape off; (bras, bouton) to scratch

gratuit, e [gratɥi, -ɥit] adj (entrée, billet) free; (fig) gratuitous

gravats [grava] nmpl rubble sg

grave [grav] adj (maladie, accident) serious, bad; (sujet, problème) serious, grave; (air) grave, solemn; (voix, son) deep, low-pitched; **gravement** adv seriously; gravely

graver [grave] vt to engrave

gravier [gravje] nm gravel no pl; **gravillons** [gravijɔ̃] nmpl loose gravel sg

gravir [gravir] vt to climb (up)

gravité [gravite] nf seriousness; gravity

graviter [gravite] vi to revolve

gravure [gravyr] nf engraving; (reproduction) print; plate

gré [gre] nm: **à son** ~ to his liking; as he pleases; **au** ~ **de** according to, following; **contre le** ~ **de qn** against sb's will; **de son (plein)** ~ of one's own free will; **bon** ~ **mal** ~ like it or not; **de** ~ **ou de force** whether one likes it or not; **savoir** ~ **à qn de qch** to be grateful to sb for sth

grec, grecque [grɛk] adj Greek; (classique: vase etc) Grecian ♦ nm/f Greek

Grèce [grɛs] nf: **la** ~ Greece

gréement [gremɑ̃] nm rigging

greffer [grefe] vt (BOT, MÉD: tissu) to graft; (MÉD: organe) to transplant

greffier [grefje] nm clerk of the court

grêle [grɛl] adj (very) thin ♦ nf hail

grêlé, e [grɛle] adj pockmarked

grêler [grɛle] vb impers: **il grêle** it's hailing; **grêlon** [grɛlɔ̃] nm hailstone

grelot [grəlo] nm little bell

grelotter [grəlɔte] vi to shiver

grenade [grənad] nf (explosive) grenade; (BOT) pomegranate

grenat [grəna] adj inv dark red

grenier [grənje] nm attic; (de ferme) loft

grenouille [grənuj] nf frog

grès [grɛ] nm sandstone; (poterie) stoneware

grésiller [grezije] vi to sizzle; (RADIO) to crackle

grève [grɛv] nf (d'ouvriers) strike; (plage) shore; **se mettre en/faire** ~ to go on/be on strike; ~ **de la faim** hunger strike; ~ **du zèle** work-to-rule (BRIT), slowdown (US)

grever [grəve] vt to put a strain on

gréviste [grevist(ə)] nm/f striker

gribouiller [gribuje] vt to scribble, scrawl

grief [grijɛf] nm grievance; **faire** ~ **à qn de** to reproach sb for

grièvement [grijɛvmɑ̃] adv seriously

griffe [grif] nf claw; (fig) signature

griffer [grife] vt to scratch

griffonner [grifɔne] vt to scribble

grignoter [griɲɔte] vt to nibble ou gnaw at

gril [gril] nm steak ou grill pan

grillade [grijad] nf grill

grillage [grijaʒ] nm (treillis) wire netting; wire fencing

grille [grij] nf (clôture) railings pl; (portail) (metal) gate; (d'égout) (metal) grate; (fig) grid

grille-pain [grijpɛ̃] nm inv toaster

griller [grije] vt (aussi: **faire** ~: pain) to toast; (: viande) to grill; (fig: ampoule etc) to burn out, blow

grillon [grijɔ̃] nm cricket

grimace [grimas] *nf* grimace; *(pour faire rire)*: **faire des ~s** to pull *ou* make faces

grimer [grime] *vt* to make up

grimper [grɛ̃pe] *vi*, *vt* to climb

grincer [grɛ̃se] *vi (porte, roue)* to grate; *(plancher)* to creak; **~ des dents** to grind one's teeth

grincheux, euse [grɛ̃ʃø, -øz] *adj* grumpy

grippe [grip] *nf* flu, influenza; **grippé, e** *adj*: **etre grippé** to have flu

gris, e [gri, griz] *adj* grey; *(ivre)* tipsy; **faire ~e mine** to pull a miserable *ou* wry face

grisaille [grizaj] *nf* greyness, dullness

griser [grize] *vt* to intoxicate

grisonner [grizɔne] *vi* to be going grey

grisou [grizu] *nm* firedamp

grive [griv] *nf* thrush

grivois, e [grivwa, -waz] *adj* saucy

Groenland [grɔɛnlɑ̃d] *nm* Greenland

grogner [grɔɲe] *vi* to growl; *(fig)* to grumble

groin [grwɛ̃] *nm* snout

grommeler [grɔmle] *vi* to mutter to o.s.

gronder [grɔ̃de] *vi* to rumble; *(fig: révolte)* to be brewing ♦ *vt* to scold

gros, se [gro, gros] *adj* big, large; *(obèse)* fat; *(travaux, dégâts)* extensive; *(large: trait, fil)* thick, heavy ♦ *adv*: **risquer/gagner ~** to risk/win a lot ♦ *nm (COMM)*: **le ~** the wholesale business; **prix de ~** wholesale price; **par ~ temps/grosse mer** in rough weather/heavy seas; **le ~ de** the main body of; **the bulk of; en ~** roughly; *(COMM)* wholesale; **~ lot** jackpot; **~ mot** coarse word; **~ œuvre** *nm (CONSTR)* shell of (building); **~ plan** *(PHOTO)* close-up; **~ sel** cooking salt; **~se caisse** big drum

groseille [grozej] *nf*: **~ (rouge)/ (blanche)** red/white currant; **~ à maquereau** gooseberry

gros: **~sesse** *nf* pregnancy; **~seur**

nf size; fatness; *(tumeur)* lump; **~sier, ière** *adj* coarse; *(travail)* rough; crude; *(évident: erreur)* gross

grosse [gros] *adj* voir **gros**

grossir [grosir] *vi (personne)* to put on weight; *(fig)* to grow, get bigger; *(rivière)* to swell ♦ *vt* to increase; to exaggerate; *(au microscope)* to magnify; *(suj: vêtement)*: **~ qn** to make sb look fatter

grossiste [grosist(ə)] *nm/f* wholesaler

grosso modo [grɔsomɔdo] *adv* roughly

grotte [grɔt] *nf* cave

grouiller [gruje] *vi* to mill about; to swarm about; **~ de** to be swarming with

groupe [grup] *nm* group; **le ~ des 7** Group of 7; **~ sanguin** *nm* blood group; **~ment** [grupmɑ̃] *nm* grouping; group

grouper [grupe] *vt* to group; **se ~** *vi* to get together

grue [gry] *nf* crane

grumeaux [grymo] *nmpl* lumps

gué [ge] *nm* ford; **passer à ~** to ford

guenilles [gənij] *nfpl* rags

guenon [gənɔ̃] *nf* female monkey

guépard [gepar] *nm* cheetah

guêpe [gɛp] *nf* wasp

guêpier [gepje] *nm (fig)* trap

guère [gɛr] *adv (avec adjectif, verbe)*: **ne ... ~** hardly; *(avec verbe)*: **ne ... ~** *tournure négative* + much; hardly ever; *tournure négative* + (very) long; **il n'y a ~ que/de** there's hardly anybody (*ou* anything) but/hardly any

guéridon [geridɔ̃] *nm* pedestal table

guérilla [gerija] *nf* guerrilla warfare

guérir [gerir] *vt (personne, maladie)* to cure; *(membre, plaie)* to heal ♦ *vi* to recover, be cured; to heal; **guérison** *nf* curing; healing; recovery

guérite [gerit] *nf* sentry box

guerre [gɛr] *nf* war; *(méthode)*: **~ atomique** atomic warfare *no pl*; **en ~** at war; **faire la ~ à** to wage war against; **de ~ lasse** finally;

d'usure war of attrition; **guerrier, ière** adj warlike ♦ nm/f warrior

guet [gɛ] nm: **faire le ~** to be on the watch ou look-out

guet-apens [gɛtapɑ̃] nm ambush

guetter [gete] vt (épier) to watch (intently); (attendre) to watch (out) for; to be lying in wait for

gueule [gœl] nf mouth; (fam) face; mouth; **ta ~!** (fam) shut up!; **~ de bois** (fam) hangover

gueuler [gœle] (fam) vi to bawl

gui [gi] nm mistletoe

guichet [giʃɛ] nm (de bureau, banque) counter, window; (d'une porte) wicket, hatch; **les ~s** (à la gare, au théâtre) the ticket office sg

guide [gid] nm guide

guider [gide] vt to guide

guidon [gidɔ̃] nm handlebars pl

guignol [giɲɔl] nm ≈ Punch and Judy show; (fig) clown

guillemets [gijmɛ] nmpl: **entre ~** in inverted commas

guillotiner [gijɔtine] vt to guillotine

guindé, e [gɛ̃de] adj stiff, starchy

guirlande [giʀlɑ̃d] nf garland; (de papier) paper chain

guise [giz] nf: **à votre ~** as you wish ou please; **en ~ de** by way of

guitare [gitaʀ] nf guitar

gymnase [ʒimnɑz] nm gym(nasium)

gymnastique [ʒimnastik] nf gymnastics sg; (au réveil etc) keep-fit exercises pl

gynécologie [ʒinekɔlɔʒi] nf gynaecology; **gynécologue** nm/f gynaecologist

H

habile [abil] adj skilful; (malin) clever; **habileté** nf skill, skilfulness; cleverness

habilité, e [abilite] adj: **~ à faire** entitled to do, empowered to do

habillé, e [abije] adj dressed; (chic) dressy; (TECH): **~ de** covered with; encased in

habillement [abijmɑ̃] nm clothes pl

habiller [abije] vt to dress; (fournir en vêtements) to clothe; **s'~** vi to dress (o.s.); (se déguiser, mettre des vêtements chic) to dress up

habit [abi] nm outfit; **~s** nmpl (vêtements) clothes; **~ (de soirée)** tails pl; evening dress

habitant, e [abitɑ̃, -ɑ̃t] nm/f inhabitant; (d'une maison) occupant

habitation [abitɑsjɔ̃] nf living; residence, home; house; **~s à loyer modéré** low-rent housing sg

habiter [abite] vt to live in; (suj: sentiment) to dwell in ♦ vi: **~ à/dans** to live in ou at/in

habitude [abityd] nf habit; **avoir l'~ de faire** to be in the habit of doing; (expérience) to be used to doing; **d'~** usually; **comme d'~** as usual

habitué, e [abitye] nm/f regular visitor; regular (customer)

habituel, le [abituɛl] adj usual

habituer [abitye] vt: **~ qn à** to get sb used to; **s'~ à** to get used to

'hache ['aʃ] nf axe

'hacher ['aʃe] vt (viande) to mince; (persil) to chop

'hachis ['aʃi] nm mince no pl

'hachoir ['aʃwaʀ] nm chopper; (meat) mincer; chopping board

'hagard, e ['agaʀ, -aʀd(ə)] adj wild, distraught

'haie ['ɛ] nf hedge; (SPORT) hurdle; (fig: rang) line, row

'haillons ['ajɔ̃] nmpl rags

'haine ['ɛn] nf hatred

'haïr ['aiʀ] vt to detest, hate

'hâlé, e ['ale] adj (sun)tanned, sun-burnt

haleine [alɛn] nf breath; **hors d'~** out of breath; **tenir en ~** to hold spellbound; to keep in suspense; **de longue ~** long-term

'haler ['ale] vt to haul in; to tow

'haleter ['alte] vt to pant

'hall ['ol] nm hall

'halle ['al] nf (covered) market; **~s** nfpl (d'une grande ville) central food market sg

hallucinant, e [alysinɑ̃, -ɑ̃t] adj staggering

hallucination [alysinɑsjɔ̃] nf hallucination

halte ['alt(ə)] nf stop, break; stopping place; (RAIL) halt ♦ excl stop!; **faire** ~ to stop

haltère [altɛʀ] nm dumbbell, barbell; ~s nmpl: (poids et) ~s (activité) weight lifting sg

'hamac ['amak] nm hammock

'hameau, x ['amo] nm hamlet

hameçon [amsɔ̃] nm (fish) hook

'hanche ['ɑ̃ʃ] nf hip

handicapé, e ['ɑ̃dikape] nm/f physically (ou mentally) handicapped person; ~ **moteur** spastic

hangar ['ɑ̃gaʀ] nm shed; (AVIAT) hangar

hanneton ['antɔ̃] nm cockchafer

'hanter ['ɑ̃te] vt to haunt

'hantise ['ɑ̃tiz] nf obsessive fear

'happer ['ape] vt to snatch; (suj: train etc) to hit

'haras ['aʀɑ] nm stud farm

'harassant, e ['aʀasɑ̃, -ɑ̃t] adj exhausting

'harceler ['aʀsəle] vt (MIL, CHASSE) to harass, harry; (importuner) to plague

'hardi, e ['aʀdi] adj bold, daring

'hareng ['aʀɑ̃] nm herring

'hargne ['aʀɲ(ə)] nf aggressiveness

'haricot ['aʀiko] nm bean; **haricot blanc** haricot bean; **haricot vert** green bean

harmonica [aʀmɔnika] nm mouth organ

harmonie [aʀmɔni] nf harmony

'harnacher ['aʀnaʃe] vt to harness

'harnais ['aʀnɛ] nm harness

'harpe ['aʀp(ə)] nf harp

'harponner ['aʀpɔne] vt to harpoon; (fam) to collar

hasard ['azaʀ] nm: **le** ~ chance, fate; **un** ~ a coincidence; a stroke of luck; **au** ~ aimlessly; at random; haphazardly; **par** ~ by chance; à **tout** ~ just in case; on the off chance (BRIT); **'hasarder** ['azaʀde] vt (mot) to venture; (fortune) to risk

'hâte ['ɑt] nf haste; à la ~ hurriedly hastily; **en** ~ posthaste, with all possible speed; **avoir** ~ **de** to be eager ou anxious to; ~ vt to hasten; **se** ~ vi to hurry

'hâtif, ive ['ɑtif, -iv] adj hurried hasty; (légume) early

'hausse ['os] nf rise, increase

'hausser ['ose] vt to raise; ~ **les épaules** to shrug (one's shoulders)

'haut, e ['o, 'ot] adj high; (grand tall; (son, voix) high(-pitched) ♦ adv high ♦ nm top (part); **de 3 m de** ~ 3 m high, 3 m in height; **des** ~**s e** **des bas** ups and downs; **en** ~ **lieu** in high places; à ~ **la voix, (tout)** ~ aloud, out loud; **du** ~ **de** from the top of; **de** ~ **en bas** from top to bot tom; downwards; **plus** ~ higher up further up; (dans un texte) above (parler) louder; **en** ~ up above; a (ou to) the top; (dans une maison upstairs; **en** ~ **de** at the top of

'hautain, e ['otɛ̃, -ɛn] adj haughty

'hautbois ['obwa] nm oboe

'haut-de-forme ['odfɔʀm(ə)] nm top hat

'hauteur ['otœʀ] nf height; (fig) loft iness; haughtiness; à la ~ **de** (sur la même ligne) level with; by; (fig equal to; à la ~ up to it

'haut-fond ['ofɔ̃] nm shallow, shoal

'haut-fourneau ['ofuʀno] nm blas ou smelting furnace

'haut-le-cœur ['olkœʀ] nm inv retch, heave

'haut-parleur ['opaʀlœʀ] nm (loud speaker

'havre ['ɑvʀ(ə)] nm haven

'Haye ['ɛ] n: **la Haye** the Hague

hebdo [ɛbdo] (fam) nm weekly

hebdomadaire [ɛbdɔmadɛʀ] adj nm weekly

héberger [ebɛʀʒe] vt to accommo date, lodge; (réfugiés) to take in

hébété, e [ebete] adj dazed

hébreu, x [ebʀø] adj m, nm Hebrew

hécatombe [ekatɔ̃b] nf slaughter

hectare [ɛktaʀ] nm hectare

'hein [ɛ̃] excl eh?

hélas ['elɑs] excl alas! ♦ adv unfortunately

héler [ele] vt to hail

hélice [elis] nf propeller

hélicoptère [elikɔptɛʀ] nm helicopter

helvétique [ɛlvetik] adj Swiss

hémicycle [emisikl(ə)] nm semicircle; (POL): l'~ ≈ the benches (of the Commons) (BRIT), ≈ the floor (of the House of Representatives) (US)

hémorragie [emɔʀaʒi] nf bleeding no pl, haemorrhage

hémorroïdes [emɔʀɔid] nfpl piles, haemorrhoids

'hennir [eniʀ] vi to neigh, whinny

herbe [ɛʀb(ə)] nf grass; (CULIN, MED) herb; en ~ unripe; (fig) budding; **herbicide** nm weed-killer; **herboriste** nm/f herbalist

'hère [ɛʀ] nm: pauvre hère poor wretch

héréditaire [eʀeditɛʀ] adj hereditary

'hérisser [eʀise] vt: ~ qn (fig) to ruffle sb; se ~ vi to bristle, bristle up

'hérisson [eʀisɔ̃] nm hedgehog

héritage [eʀitaʒ] nm inheritance; (fig) heritage; legacy

hériter [eʀite] vi: ~ de qch (de qn) to inherit sth (from sb); **héritier, ière** nm/f heir(ess)

hermétique [ɛʀmetik] adj airtight; watertight; (fig) abstruse; impenetrable

hermine [ɛʀmin] nf ermine

'hernie ['ɛʀni] nf hernia

héroïne [eʀɔin] nf heroine; (drogue) heroin

'héron ['eʀɔ̃] nm heron

'héros ['eʀo] nm hero

hésitation [ezitasjɔ̃] nf hesitation

hésiter [ezite] vi: ~ (à faire) to hesitate (to do)

hétéroclite [eteʀɔklit] adj heterogeneous; (objets) sundry

'hêtre ['ɛtʀ(ə)] nm beech

heure [œʀ] nf hour; (SCOL) period; (moment) time; c'est l'~ it's time; quelle ~ est-il? what time is it?; 2 ~s (du matin) 2 o'clock (in the morning); être à l'~ to be on time; (montre) to be right; mettre à l'~ to set right; à toute ~ at any time; 24 ~s sur 24 round the clock, 24 hours a day; à l'~ qu'il est at this time (of day); by now; sur l'~ at once; ~ de pointe rush hour; ~s supplémentaires overtime sg

heureusement [œʀøzmɑ̃] adv (par bonheur) fortunately, luckily

heureux, euse [œʀø, -øz] adj happy; (chanceux) lucky, fortunate; (judicieux) felicitous, fortunate

'heurt ['œʀ] nm (choc) collision; ~s nmpl (fig) clashes

'heurter ['œʀte] vt (mur) to strike, hit; (personne) to collide with; (fig) to go against, upset; se ~ à vt to come up against; **'heurtoir** nm door knocker

hexagone [ɛgzagɔn] nm hexagon; (la France) France (because of its shape)

hiberner [ibɛʀne] vi to hibernate

'hibou, x ['ibu] nm owl

'hideux, euse ['idø, -øz] adj hideous

hier [jɛʀ] adv yesterday; toute la journée d'~ all day yesterday; toute la matinée d'~ all yesterday morning

'hiérarchie ['jeʀaʀʃi] nf hierarchy

hilare [ilaʀ] adj mirthful

hippique [ipik] adj equestrian, horse cpd

hippodrome [ipɔdʀom] nm racecourse

hippopotame [ipɔpɔtam] nm hippopotamus

hirondelle [iʀɔ̃dɛl] nf swallow

hirsute [iʀsyt] adj hairy; shaggy; tousled

'hisser ['ise] vt to hoist, haul up

histoire [istwaʀ] nf (science, événements) history; (anecdote, récit, mensonge) story; (affaire) business

no pl; ~s nfpl (chichis) fuss no pl;
(ennuis) trouble sg; **historique** adj
historical; (important) historic

hiver [ivɛʀ] nm winter; **hivernal, e,
aux** adj winter cpd; wintry; **hiverner**
vi to winter

HLM sigle m/f = **habitation(s) à
loyer modéré**

'**hobby** [ɔbi] nm hobby

'**hocher** ['ɔʃe] vt: ~ **la tête** to nod;
(signe négatif ou dubitatif) to shake
one's head

'**hochet** ['ɔʃe] nm rattle

'**hockey** ['ɔke] nm: ~ **(sur glace/
gazon)** (ice/field) hockey

'**hold-up** ['ɔldœp] nm inv hold-up

'**hollandais, e** ['ɔlɑ̃dɛ, -ɛz] adj
Dutch ♦ nm (LING) Dutch ♦ nm/f:
Hollandais, e Dutchman(woman);
les Hollandais the Dutch

'**Hollande** ['ɔlɑ̃d] nf: la ~ Holland

'**homard** ['ɔmaʀ] nm lobster

homéopathique [ɔmeɔpatik] adj
homoeopathic

homicide [ɔmisid] nm murder; ~
involontaire manslaughter

hommage [ɔmaʒ] nm tribute; ~s
nmpl: **présenter ses** ~s to pay
one's respects; **rendre** ~ **à** to pay
tribute ou homage to

homme [ɔm] nm man; ~ **d'affaires**
businessman; ~ **d'État** statesman;
~ **de main** hired man; ~ **de paille**
stooge; ~**grenouille** nm frogman

homo: ~**gène** adj homogeneous;
~**logue** nm/f counterpart, opposite
number; ~**logué, e** adj (SPORT)
officially recognized, ratified; (tarif)
authorized; ~**nyme** nm (LING)
homonym; (d'une personne) name-
sake; ~**sexuel, le** adj homosexual

'**Hongrie** ['ɔ̃gʀi] nf: la ~ **Hongrie**
Hungary; '**hongrois, e** adj, nm/f
Hungarian

honnête [ɔnɛt] adj (intègre) honest;
(juste, satisfaisant) fair; ~**ment** adv
honestly; ~**té** nf honesty

honneur [ɔnœʀ] nm honour; (mérite) credit; **en l'**~ **de** in honour of;
(événement) on the occasion of; **fai-**

re ~ **à** (engagements) to honour;
(famille) to be a credit to; (fig: repas etc) to do justice to

honorable [ɔnɔʀabl(ə)] adj worthy,
honourable; (suffisant) decent

honoraire [ɔnɔʀɛʀ] adj honorary;
professeur ~ professor emeritus;
honoraires nmpl fees pl

honorer [ɔnɔʀe] vt to honour; (estimer) to hold in high regard; (faire
honneur à) to do credit to; **s'**~ **de** vt
to pride o.s. upon; **honorifique** adj
honorary

'**honte** ['ɔ̃t] nf shame; **avoir** ~ **de** to
be ashamed of; **faire** ~ **à qn** to
make sb (feel) ashamed; '**honteux,
euse** adj ashamed; (conduite, acte)
shameful, disgraceful

hôpital, aux [ɔpital, -o] nm hospital

'**hoquet** ['ɔke] nm: **avoir le hoquet**
to have (the) hiccoughs; '**hoqueter**
vi to hiccough

horaire [ɔʀɛʀ] adj hourly ♦ nm timetable, schedule; ~**s** nmpl (d'employé) hours; ~ **souple** flexitime

horizon [ɔʀizɔ̃] nm horizon; (paysage) landscape, view

horizontal, e, aux [ɔʀizɔ̃tal, -o]
adj horizontal

horloge [ɔʀlɔʒ] nf clock; **horloger,
ère** nm/f watchmaker; clockmaker;
horlogerie nf watch-making, watchmaker's (shop); clockmaker's (shop)

'**hormis** ['ɔʀmi] prép save

horoscope [ɔʀɔskɔp] nm horoscope

horreur [ɔʀœʀ] nf horror; **avoir** ~
de to loathe ou detest; **horrible** adj
horrible

horripiler [ɔʀipile] vt to exasperate

'**hors** ['ɔʀ] prép except (for); ~ **de**
out of; ~ **pair** outstanding; ~ **de
propos** inopportune; **être** ~ **de soi**
to be beside o.s.; ~ **d'usage** out of
service; ~**bord** nm inv speedboat
(with outboard motor); ~**concours**
adj ineligible to compete; (fig) out of
the running; ~**d'œuvre** nm inv hors
d'œuvre; ~**jeu** nm inv (SPORT)
offside; ~**la-loi** nm inv outlaw; ~
taxe (boutique, articles) duty-
free

hospice [ɔspis] *nm* (*de vieillards*) home

hospitalier, ière [ɔspitalje, -jɛʀ] *adj* (*accueillant*) hospitable; (MED: *service, centre*) hospital *cpd*

hospitalité [ɔspitalite] *nf* hospitality

hostie [ɔsti] *nf* host (REL)

hostile [ɔstil] *adj* hostile; **hostilité** *nf* hostility

hôte [ot] *nm* (*maître de maison*) host; (*invité*) guest

hôtel [otɛl] *nm* hotel; **aller à l'~** to stay in a hotel; **~ de ville** town hall; **~ (particulier)** (*private*) mansion; **hôtelier, ière** *adj* hotel *cpd* ♦ *nm/f* hotelier; **hôtellerie** *nf* hotel business; (*auberge*) inn

hôtesse [otɛs] *nf* hostess; **~ de l'air** air stewardess

hotte ['ɔt] *nf* (*panier*) basket (carried on the back); (*de cheminée*) hood; **hotte aspirante** cooker hood

houblon ['ublɔ̃] *nm* (BOT) hop; (*pour la bière*) hops *pl*

houille ['uj] *nf* coal; **houille blanche** hydroelectric power

houle ['ul] *nf* swell

houlette [ulɛt] *nf*: **sous la ~ de** under the guidance of

houleux, euse ['ulø, -øz] *adj* heavy, swelling; (*fig*) stormy, turbulent

houspiller ['uspije] *vt* to scold

housse ['us] *nf* cover; dust cover; loose *ou* stretch cover

houx ['u] *nm* holly

hublot ['yblo] *nm* porthole

huche ['yʃ] *nf*: **~ à pain** bread bin

huer ['ɥe] *vt* to boo

huile [ɥil] *nf* oil; **huiler** *vt* to oil; **huileux, euse** *adj* oily

huis [ɥi] *nm*: **à ~ clos** in camera

huissier [ɥisje] *nm* usher; (JUR): **~** bailiff

huit ['ɥit] *num* eight; **samedi en huit a week on Saturday; **'huitaine** *nf*: **une huitaine (de jours)** a week or so; **'huitième** *num* eighth

huître [ɥitʀ(ə)] *nf* oyster

humain, e [ymɛ̃, -ɛn] *adj* human;

(*compatissant*) humane ♦ *nm* human (being); **humanité** *nf* humanity

humble [œ̃bl(ə)] *adj* humble

humecter [ymɛkte] *vt* to dampen

humer ['yme] *vt* to smell; to inhale

humeur [ymœʀ] *nf* mood; (*tempérament*) temper; (*irritation*) bad temper; **de bonne/mauvaise ~** in a good/bad mood

humide [ymid] *adj* damp; (*main, yeux*) moist; (*climat, chaleur*) humid; (*saison, route*) wet

humilier [ymilje] *vt* to humiliate

humilité [ymilite] *nf* humility, humbleness

humoristique [ymɔʀistik] *adj* humorous; humoristic

humour [ymuʀ] *nm* humour; **avoir de l'~** to have a sense of humour; **~ noir** sick humour

hurlement ['yʀləmɑ̃] *nm* howling *no pl*, howl, yelling *no pl*, yell

hurler ['yʀle] *vi* to howl, yell

hurluberlu [yʀlybɛʀly] (*péj*) *nm* crank

hutte ['yt] *nf* hut

hydratant, e [idʀatɑ̃, -ɑ̃t] *adj* (*crème*) moisturizing

hydrate [idʀat] *nm*: **~s de carbone** carbohydrates

hydraulique [idʀolik] *adj* hydraulic

hydravion [idʀavjɔ̃] *nm* seaplane

hydrogène [idʀɔʒɛn] *nm* hydrogen

hydroglisseur [idʀoglisœʀ] *nm* hydroplane

hygiénique [iʒjenik] *adj* hygienic

hymne [imn(ə)] *nm* hymn; **~ national** national anthem

hypermarché [ipɛʀmaʀʃe] *nm* hypermarket

hypermétrope [ipɛʀmetʀɔp] *adj* long-sighted

hypnotiser [ipnotize] *vt* to hypnotize

hypocrite [ipɔkʀit] *adj* hypocritical

hypothèque [ipɔtɛk] *nf* mortgage

hypothèse [ipɔtɛz] *nf* hypothesis

hystérique [isteʀik] *adj* hysterical

I

iceberg [isbɛʀg] nm iceberg

ici [isi] adv here; **jusqu'~** as far as this; until now; **d'~ là** by then; in the meantime; **d'~ peu** before long

idéal, e, aux [ideal, -o] adj ideal ♦ nm ideal; ideals pl

idée [ide] nf idea; **avoir dans l'~ que** to have an idea that; **~s noires** black ou dark thoughts

identifier [idãtifje] vt to identify; **s'~ à** (héros etc) to identify with

identique [idãtik] adj: **~ (à)** identical (to)

identité [idãtite] nf identity

idiot, e [idjo, idjɔt] adj idiotic ♦ nm/f idiot

idole [idɔl] nf idol

if [if] nm yew

ignare [iɲaʀ] adj ignorant

ignoble [iɲɔbl(ə)] adj vile

ignorant, e [iɲɔʀã, -ãt] adj ignorant

ignorer [iɲɔʀe] vt (ne pas connaître) not to know, be unaware ou ignorant of; (être sans expérience de: plaisir, guerre etc) not to know about, have no experience of; (bouder: personne) to ignore

il [il] pron he; (animal, chose, en tournure impersonnelle) it; **~s** they; voir aussi **avoir**

île [il] nf island; **les ~s anglo-normandes** the Channel Islands; **les ~s Britanniques** the British Isles

illégal, e, aux [ilegal, -o] adj illegal

illégitime [ileʒitim] adj illegitimate

illettré, e [iletʀe] adj/nm/f illiterate

illimité, e [ilimite] adj unlimited

illisible [ilizibl(ə)] adj illegible; (roman) unreadable

illumination [ilyminasjɔ̃] nf illumination, floodlighting; (idée) flash of inspiration

illuminer [ilymine] vt to light up; (monument, rue: pour une fête) to illuminate, floodlight

illusion [ilyzjɔ̃] nf illusion; se faire

des **~s** to delude o.s.; **faire ~** to delude ou fool people; **illusionniste** nm/f conjuror

illustration [ilystʀasjɔ̃] nf illustration

illustre [ilystʀ(ə)] adj illustrious

illustré, e [ilystʀe] adj illustrated ♦ nm illustrated magazine; comic

illustrer [ilystʀe] vt to illustrate; **s'~** to become famous, win fame

îlot [ilo] nm small island, islet; (de maisons) block

ils [il] pron voir **il**

image [imaʒ] nf (gén) picture; (comparaison, ressemblance, OPTIQUE) image; **~ de marque** brand image; (fig) public image

imagination [imaʒinasjɔ̃] nf imagination; (chimère) fancy; **avoir de l'~** to be imaginative

imaginer [imaʒine] vt to imagine; (inventer: expédient) to devise, think up; **s'~** vt (se figurer: scène etc) to imagine, picture; **s'~ que** to imagine that

imbécile [ɛ̃besil] adj idiotic ♦ nm/f idiot

imberbe [ɛ̃bɛʀb(ə)] adj beardless

imbiber [ɛ̃bibe] vt to moisten, wet; **s'~** de to become saturated with

imbu, e [ɛ̃by] adj: **~ de** full of

imitateur, trice [imitatœʀ, -tʀis] nm/f (gén) imitator; (MUSIC-HALL) impersonator

imitation [imitasjɔ̃] nf imitation; (sketch) imitation, impression; impersonation

imiter [imite] vt to imitate; (contrefaire) to forge; (ressembler à) to look like

immaculé, e [imakyle] adj spotless; immaculate

immatriculation [imatʀikylasjɔ̃] nf registration

immatriculer [imatʀikyle] vt to register; **faire/se faire ~** to register

immédiat, e [imedja, -at] adj immediate ♦ nm: **dans l'~** for the time being; **~ement** adv immediately

immense [imãs] adj immense

immerger [imɛʀʒe] vt to immerse, submerge

immeuble [imœbl(ə)] nm building; ~ **locatif** block of rented flats (BRIT), rental building (US)

immigration [imigʀasjɔ̃] nf immigration

immigré, e [imigʀe] nm/f immigrant

imminent, e [iminɑ̃, -ɑ̃t] adj imminent

immiscer [imise]: s'~ vi to interfere in ou with

immobile [imɔbil] adj still, motionless; (fig) unchanging

immobilier, ière [imɔbilje, -jɛʀ] adj property cpd ♦ nm: l'~ the property business

immobiliser [imɔbilize] vt (gén) to immobilize; (circulation, véhicule, affaires) to bring to a standstill; s'~ (personne) to stand still; (machine, véhicule) to come to a halt

immonde [imɔ̃d] adj foul

immondices [imɔ̃dis] nmpl refuse sg; filth sg

immoral, e, aux [imɔʀal, -o] adj immoral

immuable [imɥabl(ə)] adj immutable; unchanging

immunisé, e [imynize] adj: ~ contre immune to

immunité [imynite] nf immunity

impact [ɛ̃pakt] nm impact

impair, e [ɛ̃pɛʀ] adj odd ♦ nm faux pas, blunder

impardonnable [ɛ̃paʀdɔnabl(ə)] adj unpardonable, unforgivable

imparfait, e [ɛ̃paʀfɛ, -ɛt] adj imperfect

impartial, e, aux [ɛ̃paʀsjal, -o] adj impartial, unbiased

impartir [ɛ̃paʀtiʀ] vt to assign; to bestow

impasse [ɛ̃pɑs] nf dead-end, cul-de-sac; (fig) deadlock

impassible [ɛ̃pasibl(ə)] adj impassive

impayable [ɛ̃pejabl(ə)] adj (drôle) priceless

impeccable [ɛ̃pekabl(ə)] adj faultless, impeccable; spotlessly clean; impeccably dressed; (fam) smashing

impensable [ɛ̃pɑ̃sabl(ə)] adj unthinkable; unbelievable

impératif, ive [ɛ̃peʀatif, -iv] adj imperative ♦ nm (LING) imperative; ~s nmpl (exigences) requirements; demands

impératrice [ɛ̃peʀatʀis] nf empress

impérial, e, aux [ɛ̃peʀjal, -o] adj imperial; **impériale** nf top deck

impérieux, euse [ɛ̃peʀjø, -øz] adj (caractère, ton) imperious; (obligation, besoin) pressing, urgent

impérissable [ɛ̃peʀisabl(ə)] adj undying; imperishable

imperméable [ɛ̃pɛʀmeabl(ə)] adj waterproof; (GEO) impermeable; (fig): ~ à impervious to ♦ nm raincoat

impertinent, e [ɛ̃pɛʀtinɑ̃, -ɑ̃t] adj impertinent

impétueux, euse [ɛ̃petɥø, -øz] adj fiery

impie [ɛ̃pi] adj impious, ungodly

impitoyable [ɛ̃pitwajabl(ə)] adj pitiless, merciless

implanter [ɛ̃plɑ̃te] vt (usine, industrie, usage) to establish; (colons etc) to settle; (idée, préjugé) to implant

impliquer [ɛ̃plike] vt to imply; ~ qn (dans) to implicate sb in

impoli, e [ɛ̃pɔli] adj impolite, rude

importance [ɛ̃pɔʀtɑ̃s] nf importance; sans ~ unimportant

important, e [ɛ̃pɔʀtɑ̃, -ɑ̃t] adj important; (en quantité) considerable, sizeable; extensive; (péj: airs, ton) self-important ♦ nm: l'~ the important thing

importateur, trice [ɛ̃pɔʀtatœʀ, -tʀis] nm/f importer

importation [ɛ̃pɔʀtasjɔ̃] nf importation; introduction; (produit) import

importer [ɛ̃pɔʀte] vt (COMM) to import; (maladies, plantes) to introduce ♦ vi (être important) to matter;

importe qu'il fasse it is important that he should do; **peu m'importe** I don't care; **peu importe (que)** it doesn't matter (if); *voir aussi* **n'importe**

importun, e [ɛ̃pɔrtœ̃, -yn] *adj* irksome, importunate; *(arrivée, visite)* inopportune, ill-timed ♦ *nm* intruder; **importuner** *vt* to bother

imposable [ɛ̃pozabl(ə)] *adj* taxable

imposant, e [ɛ̃pozɑ̃, -ɑ̃t] *adj* imposing

imposer [ɛ̃poze] *vt (taxer)* to tax; **s'~** *(être nécessaire)* to be imperative; *(montrer sa prominence)* to stand out, emerge; *(artiste: se faire connaître)* to win recognition; **~ qch à qn** to impose sth on sb; **en ~ à** to impress; **imposition** [ɛ̃pozisjɔ̃] *nf (ADMIN)* taxation

impossible [ɛ̃pɔsibl(ə)] *adj* impossible; **il m'est ~ de le faire** it is impossible for me to do it, I can't possibly do it; **faire l'~** to do one's utmost

impôt [ɛ̃po] *nm* tax; *(taxes)* taxation; **taxes** *pl*; **~s** *nmpl (contributions)* (income) tax *sg*; **payer 1000 F d'~s** to pay 1,000 F in tax; **~ foncier** land tax; **~ sur le chiffre d'affaires** corporation *(BRIT)* ou corporate *(US)* tax; **~ sur le revenu** income tax

impotent, e [ɛ̃pɔtɑ̃, -ɑ̃t] *adj* disabled

impraticable [ɛ̃pratikabl(ə)] *adj (projet)* impracticable, unworkable; *(piste)* impassable

imprécis, e [ɛ̃presi, -iz] *adj* imprecise

imprégner [ɛ̃preɲe] *vt (tissu, tampon)* to soak, impregnate; *(lieu, air)* to fill; **s'~ de** *(fig)* to absorb

imprenable [ɛ̃prənabl(ə)] *adj (forteresse)* impregnable; **vue ~** unimpeded outlook

impression [ɛ̃presjɔ̃] *nf* impression; *(d'un ouvrage, tissu)* printing; **faire bonne ~** to make a good impression

impressionnant, e [ɛ̃presjɔnɑ̃, -ɑ̃t]

adj impressive; upsetting

impressionner [ɛ̃presjɔne] *vt (frapper)* to impress; *(troubler)* to upset

imprévisible [ɛ̃previzibl(ə)] *adj* unforeseeable

imprévoyant, e [ɛ̃prevwajɑ̃, -ɑ̃t] *adj* lacking in foresight; *(en matière d'argent)* improvident

imprévu, e [ɛ̃prevy] *adj* unforeseen, unexpected ♦ *nm* unexpected incident; **en cas d'~** if anything unexpected happens

imprimante [ɛ̃primɑ̃t] *nf* printer; **~ matricielle** dot-matrix printer

imprimé [ɛ̃prime] *nm (formulaire)* printed form; *(POSTES)* printed matter *no pl*

imprimer [ɛ̃prime] *vt* to print; *(empreinte etc)* to imprint; *(publier)* to publish; *(communiquer: mouvement, impulsion)* to impart, transmit; **imprimerie** *nf* printing; *(établissement)* printing works *sg*; **imprimeur** *nm* printer

impromptu, e [ɛ̃prɔ̃pty] *adj* impromptu; sudden

impropre [ɛ̃prɔpr(ə)] *adj* inappropriate; **~ à** unsuitable for

improviser [ɛ̃provize] *vt, vi* to improvise

improviste [ɛ̃provist(ə)]: **à l'~** *adv* unexpectedly, without warning

imprudence [ɛ̃prydɑ̃s] *nf* carelessness *no pl*; imprudence *no pl*

imprudent, e [ɛ̃prydɑ̃, -ɑ̃t] *adj (conducteur, geste, action)* careless; *(remarque)* unwise, imprudent; *(projet)* foolhardy

impudent, e [ɛ̃pydɑ̃, -ɑ̃t] *adj* impudent; brazen

impudique [ɛ̃pydik] *adj* shameless

impuissant, e [ɛ̃pɥisɑ̃, -ɑ̃t] *adj* helpless; *(sans effet)* ineffectual; *(sexuellement)* impotent; **~ à faire** powerless to do

impulsif, ive [ɛ̃pylsif, -iv] *adj* impulsive

impulsion [ɛ̃pylsjɔ̃] *nf (ÉLEC, instinct)* impulse; *(élan, influence)* impetus

impunément [ɛ̃pynemɑ̃] adv with impunity

imputer [ɛ̃pyte] vt (attribuer) to ascribe, impute; (COMM): ~ à ou sur to charge to

inabordable [inabɔrdabl(ə)] adj (cher) prohibitive

inaccessible [inaksesibl(ə)] adj inaccessible; unattainable; (insensible): ~ à impervious to

inachevé, e [inaʃve] adj unfinished

inadapté, e [inadapte] adj (gén): ~ à not adapted to, unsuited to; (PSYCH) maladjusted

inadmissible [inadmisibl(ə)] adj inadmissible

inadvertance [inadvɛrtɑ̃s] : par ~ adv inadvertently

inaltérable [inalterabl(ə)] adj (matière) stable; (fig) unchanging; ~ à unaffected by

inamovible [inamɔvibl(ə)] adj fixed; (JUR) irremovable

inanimé, e [inanime] adj (matière) inanimate; (évanoui) unconscious; (sans vie) lifeless

inanition [inanisjɔ̃] nf: tomber d'~ to faint with hunger (and exhaustion)

inaperçu, e [inapɛrsy] adj: passer ~ to go unnoticed

inappréciable [inapresjabl(ə)] adj (service) invaluable

inapte [inapt(ə)] adj: ~ à incapable of; (MIL) unfit for

inattaquable [inatakabl(ə)] adj (texte, preuve) irrefutable

inattendu, e [inatɑ̃dy] adj unexpected

inattentif, ive [inatɑ̃tif, -iv] adj inattentive; ~ à (dangers, détails) heedless of; **inattention** nf: faute d'inattention careless mistake

inaugurer [inɔgyre] vt (monument) to unveil; (exposition, usine) to open; (fig) to inaugurate

inavouable [inavwabl(ə)] adj shameful; undisclosable

inavoué, e [inavwe] adj unavowed

incandescence [ɛ̃kɑ̃desɑ̃s] nf: porter à ~ to heat white-hot

incapable [ɛ̃kapabl(ə)] adj incapable; ~ de faire incapable of doing; (empêché) unable to do

incapacité [ɛ̃kapasite] nf incapability; (JUR) incapacity

incarcérer [ɛ̃karsere] vt to incarcerate, imprison

incarner [ɛ̃karne] vt to embody, personify; (THEATRE) to play

incartade [ɛ̃kartad] nf prank

incassable [ɛ̃kasabl(ə)] adj unbreakable

incendiaire [ɛ̃sɑ̃djɛr] adj incendiary; (fig: discours) inflammatory ♦ nm/f fire-raiser, arsonist

incendie [ɛ̃sɑ̃di] nm fire; ~ criminel arson no pl; ~ de forêt forest fire; ~r [ɛ̃sɑ̃dje] vt (mettre le feu à) to set fire to, set alight; (brûler complètement) to burn down

incertain, e [ɛ̃sɛrtɛ̃, -ɛn] adj uncertain; (temps) uncertain, unsettled; (imprécis: contours) indistinct, blurred; **incertitude** nf uncertainty

incessamment [ɛ̃sesamɑ̃] adv very shortly

incidemment [ɛ̃sidamɑ̃] adv in passing

incident [ɛ̃sidɑ̃] nm incident; ~ de parcours minor hitch ou setback; ~ technique technical difficulties pl

incinérer [ɛ̃sinere] vt (ordures) to incinerate; (mort) to cremate

incisive [ɛ̃siziv] nf incisor

inciter [ɛ̃site] vt: ~ qn à (faire) qch to encourage sb to do sth; (à la révolte etc) to incite sb to do sth

inclinable [ɛ̃klinabl(ə)] adj: siège à dossier ~ reclining seat

inclinaison [ɛ̃klinɛzɔ̃] nf (déclivité: d'une route etc) incline; (: d'un toit) slope; (état penché) tilt

inclination [ɛ̃klinɑsjɔ̃] nf: ~ de (la) tête nod (of the head); ~ (de buste) bow

incliner [ɛ̃kline] vt (tête, bouteille) to tilt ♦ vi: ~ à qch/à faire to incline towards sth/doing; s'~ (devant) to bow (before); (céder) to give in ou yield (to); ~ la tête ou le front to give a slight bow

inclure [ɛ̃klyʀ] *vt* to include; *(joindre à un envoi)* to enclose; **jusqu'au 10 mars inclus** until 10th March inclusive

incoercible [ɛ̃kɔɛʀsibl(ə)] *adj* uncontrollable

incohérent, e [ɛ̃kɔeʀã, -ãt] *adj* inconsistent; incoherent

incollable [ɛ̃kɔlabl(ə)] *adj*: **il est ~** he's got all the answers

incolore [ɛ̃kɔlɔʀ] *adj* colourless

incomber [ɛ̃kɔbe] : **~ à** *vt (suj: devoirs, responsabilité)* to rest upon; *(: frais, travail)* to be the responsibility of

incommensurable [ɛ̃kɔmãsyʀabl(ə)] *adj* immeasurable

incommode [ɛ̃kɔmɔd] *adj* inconvenient; *(posture, siège)* uncomfortable

incommoder [ɛ̃kɔmɔde] *vt*: **~ qn** to inconvenience sb; *(embarrasser)* to make sb feel uncomfortable

incompétent, e [ɛ̃kɔpetã, -ãt] *adj* incompetent

incompris, e [ɛ̃kɔpʀi, -iz] *adj* misunderstood

inconcevable [ɛ̃kɔsvabl(ə)] *adj* incredible

inconciliable [ɛ̃kɔsiljabl(ə)] *adj* irreconciliable

inconditionnel, le [ɛ̃kɔdisjɔnɛl] *adj* unconditional; *(partisan)* unquestioning

incongru, e [ɛ̃kɔgʀy] *adj* unseemly

inconnu, e [ɛ̃kɔny] *adj* unknown; new, strange ♦ *nm/f* stranger; unknown person *(ou artist etc)* ♦ *nm*: **l'~** the unknown ♦ *nf* unknown

inconsciemment [ɛ̃kɔsjamã] *adv* unconsciously

inconscient, e [ɛ̃kɔsjã, -ãt] *adj* unconscious; *(irréfléchi)* thoughtless, reckless ♦ *nm (PSYCH)*: **l'~** the unconscious; **~ de** unaware of

inconsidéré, e [ɛ̃kɔsideʀe] *adj* ill-considered

inconsistant, e [ɛ̃kɔsistã, -ãt] *adj* flimsy, weak; runny

incontestable [ɛ̃kɔtɛstabl(ə)] *adj* in-

disputable

incontournable [ɛ̃kɔtuʀnabl(ə)] *adj* unavoidable

inconvenant, e [ɛ̃kɔvnã, -ãt] *adj* unseemly, improper

inconvénient [ɛ̃kɔvenjã] *nm (d'une situation, d'un projet)* disadvantage, drawback; *(d'un remède, changement etc)* inconvenience; **si vous n'y voyez pas d'~** if you have no objections

incorporer [ɛ̃kɔʀpɔʀe] *vt*: **~ (à)** to mix in (with); *(paragraphe etc)*: **~ (dans)** to incorporate (in); *(MIL: appeler)* to recruit, call up

incorrect, e [ɛ̃kɔʀɛkt] *adj (impropre, inconvenant)* improper; *(défectueux)* faulty; *(inexact)* incorrect; *(impoli)* impolite; *(déloyal)* underhand

incrédule [ɛ̃kʀedyl] *adj* incredulous; *(REL)* unbelieving

increvable [ɛ̃kʀəvabl(ə)] *adj (fam)* tireless

incriminer [ɛ̃kʀimine] *vt (personne)* to incriminate; *(action, conduite)* to bring under attack; *(bonne foi, honnêteté)* to call into question

incroyable [ɛ̃kʀwajabl(ə)] *adj* incredible; unbelievable

incruster [ɛ̃kʀyste] *vt (ART)* to inlay; **s'~** *vi (invité)* to take root; *(radiateur etc)* to become coated with fur ou scale

inculpé, e [ɛ̃kylpe] *nm/f* accused

inculper [ɛ̃kylpe] *vt*: **~ (de)** to charge (with)

inculquer [ɛ̃kylke] *vt*: **~ qch à** to inculcate sth in qn instil sth into

inculte [ɛ̃kylt(ə)] *adj* uncultivated; *(esprit, peuple)* uncultured; *(barbe)* unkempt

Inde [ɛ̃d] *nf*: **l'~** India

indécis, e [ɛ̃desi, -iz] *adj* indecisive; *(perplexe)* undecided

indéfendable [ɛ̃defãdabl(ə)] *adj* indefensible

indéfini, e [ɛ̃defini] *adj (imprécis, incertain)* undefined; *(illimité, LING)* indefinite; **indéfiniment** *adv* indefinitely; **indéfini-**

nitely; **indéfinissable** adj indefinable
indélébile [ɛ̃delebil] adj indelible
indélicat, e [ɛ̃delika, -at] adj tactless; dishonest
indemne [ɛ̃demn(ə)] adj unharmed
indemniser [ɛ̃demnize] vt: ~ qn (de) to compensate sb (for)
indemnité [ɛ̃demnite] nf (dédommagement) compensation no pl; (allocation) allowance; ~ de **licenciement** redundancy payment
indépendamment [ɛ̃depɑ̃damɑ̃] adv independently; ~ de (abstraction faite de) irrespective of; (en plus de) over and above
indépendance [ɛ̃depɑ̃dɑ̃s] nf independence
indépendant, e [ɛ̃depɑ̃dɑ̃, -ɑ̃t] adj independent; ~ de independent of
indescriptible [ɛ̃deskriptibl(ə)] adj indescribable
indétermination [ɛ̃determinɑsjɔ̃] nf indecision; indecisiveness
indéterminé, e [ɛ̃detɛrmine] adj unspecified; indeterminate
index [ɛ̃dɛks] nm (doigt) index finger; (d'un livre etc) index; **mettre à l'**~ to blacklist
indexé, e [ɛ̃dɛkse] adj (ÉCON): ~ (**sur**) index-linked (to)
indicateur [ɛ̃dikatœr] nm (POLICE) informer; (livre) guide; directory; (TECH) gauge; indicator; ~ **des chemins de fer** railway timetable
indicatif, ive [ɛ̃dikatif, -iv] adj: à titre ~ for (your) information ♦ nm (LING) indicative; (RADIO) theme ou signature tune; (TEL) dialling code
indication [ɛ̃dikɑsjɔ̃] nf indication; (renseignement) information no pl; ~**s** nfpl (directives) instructions
indice [ɛ̃dis] nm (marque, signe) indication, sign; (POLICE: lors d'une enquête) clue; (JUR: présomption) piece of evidence; (SCIENCE, ÉCON, TECH) index
indicible [ɛ̃disibl(ə)] adj inexpressible
indien, ne [ɛ̃djɛ̃, -jɛn] adj, nm/f Indian
indifféremment [ɛ̃diferamɑ̃] adv (sans distinction) equally (well); indiscriminately
indifférence [ɛ̃diferɑ̃s] nf indifference; **indifférent, e** [ɛ̃diferɑ̃, -ɑ̃t] adj (peu intéressé) indifferent
indigence [ɛ̃diʒɑ̃s] nf poverty
indigène [ɛ̃diʒɛn] adj native, indigenous; local ♦ nm/f native
indigeste [ɛ̃diʒɛst(ə)] adj indigestible
indigestion [ɛ̃diʒɛstjɔ̃] nf indigestion no pl
indigne [ɛ̃diɲ] adj unworthy
indigner [ɛ̃diɲe] vt: s'~ (de ou contre) to be indignant (at)
indiqué, e [ɛ̃dike] adj (date, lieu) given; (adéquat, conseillé) suitable
indiquer [ɛ̃dike] vt (désigner): ~ qch/qn à qn to point sth/sb out to sb; (suj: pendule, aiguille) to show; (: étiquette, plan) to show, indicate; (faire connaître: médecin, restaurant): ~ qch/qn à qn to tell sb of sth/sb; (renseigner sur) to point out, tell; (déterminer: date, lieu) to give, state; (dénoter) to indicate, point to
indirect, e [ɛ̃dirɛkt] adj indirect
indiscipline [ɛ̃disiplin] nf lack of discipline; **indiscipliné, e** adj undisciplined; (fig) unmanageable
indiscret, ète [ɛ̃diskrɛ, -ɛt] adj indiscreet
indiscutable [ɛ̃diskytabl(ə)] adj indisputable
indispensable [ɛ̃dispɑ̃sabl(ə)] adj indispensable; essential
indisposé, e [ɛ̃dispoze] adj indisposed
indisposer [ɛ̃dispoze] vt (incommoder) to upset; (déplaire à) to antagonize
indistinct, e [ɛ̃distɛ̃, -ɛ̃kt(ə)] adj indistinct; **indistinctement** adv (voir, prononcer) indistinctly; (sans distinction) indiscriminately
individu [ɛ̃dividy] nm individual
individuel, le [ɛ̃dividɥɛl] adj (gén) individual; (opinion, livret, contrôle,

avantages) personal; **chambre ~le** single room; **maison ~le** detached house

indolore [ɛ̃dɔlɔr] *adj* painless

indomptable [ɛ̃dɔ̃tabl(ə)] *adj* untameable; (*fig*) invincible, indomitable

Indonésie [ɛ̃dɔnezi] *nf* Indonesia

indu, e [ɛ̃dy] *adj*: **à des heures ~es** at some ungodly hour

induire [ɛ̃dɥir] *vt*: **~ qn en erreur** to lead sb astray, mislead sb

indulgent, e [ɛ̃dylʒɑ̃, -ɑ̃t] *adj* (*parent, regard*) indulgent; (*juge, examinateur*) lenient

indûment [ɛ̃dymɔ̃] *adv* wrongfully; without due cause

industrie [ɛ̃dystri] *nf* industry; **industriel, le** *adj* industrial ♦ *nm* industrialist; manufacturer

inébranlable [inebrɑ̃labl(ə)] *adj* (*masse, colonne*) solid; (*personne, certitude, foi*) steadfast, unwavering

inédit, e [inedi, -it] *adj* (*correspondance etc*) hitherto unpublished; (*spectacle, moyen*) novel, original

ineffaçable [inefasabl(ə)] *adj* indelible

inefficace [inefikas] *adj* (*remède, moyen*) ineffective; (*machine, employé*) inefficient

inégal, e, aux [inegal, -o] *adj* unequal; uneven; **inégalable** [inegalabl(e)] *adj* matchless; **inégalé, e** [inegale] *adj* unmatched, unequalled

inerte [inɛrt(ə)] *adj* lifeless; inert

inestimable [inɛstimabl(ə)] *adj* priceless; (*fig: bienfait*) invaluable

inévitable [inevitabl(ə)] *adj* unavoidable; (*fatal, habituel*) inevitable

inexact, e [inɛgzakt] *adj* inaccurate, inexact; unpunctual

in extremis [inɛkstremis] *adv* at the last minute ♦ *adj* last-minute

infaillible [ɛ̃fajibl(ə)] *adj* infallible

infâme [ɛ̃fɑm] *adj* vile

infanticide [ɛ̃fɑ̃tisid] *nm/f* child-murderer(eress) ♦ *nm* (*meurtre*) infanticide

infarctus [ɛ̃farktys] *nm*: **~ (du**

myocarde) coronary (thrombosis)

infatigable [ɛ̃fatigabl(ə)] *adj* tireless

infect, e [ɛ̃fɛkt] *adj* vile; foul; (*repas, vin*) revolting

infecter [ɛ̃fɛkte] *vt* (*atmosphère, eau*) to contaminate; (*MED*) to infect; **s'~** to become infected *ou* septic; **infection** *nf* infection

inférieur, e [ɛ̃ferjœr] *adj* lower; (*en qualité, intelligence*) inferior; **à** (*somme, quantité*) less *ou* smaller than; (*moins bon que*) inferior to

infernal, e, aux [ɛ̃fɛrnal, -o] *adj* (*chaleur, rythme*) infernal; (*méchanceté, complot*) diabolical

infidèle [ɛ̃fidɛl] *adj* unfaithful

infiltrer [ɛ̃filtre]: **s'~** *vi* to penetrate into; (*liquide*) to seep into; (*fig: noyauter*) to infiltrate

infime [ɛ̃fim] *adj* minute, tiny; (*inférieur*) lowly

infini, e [ɛ̃fini] *adj* infinite ♦ *nm* infinity; **à l'~** (*MATH*) to infinity; (*agrandir, varier*) infinitely; (*interminablement*) endlessly; **infinité** *nf*: **une infinité de** an infinite number of

infinitif [ɛ̃finitif] *nm* infinitive

infirme [ɛ̃firm(ə)] *adj* disabled ♦ *nm/f* disabled person; **~ de guerre** war cripple

infirmerie [ɛ̃firmɔri] *nf* sick bay

infirmier, ière [ɛ̃firmje, -jɛr] *nm/f* nurse; **infirmière chef** sister; **infirmière visiteuse** = district nurse

infirmité [ɛ̃firmite] *nf* disability

inflammable [ɛ̃flamabl(ə)] *adj* (in)-flammable

inflation [ɛ̃flɑsjɔ̃] *nf* inflation

inflexion [ɛ̃flɛksjɔ̃] *nf* inflexion; **~ de la tête** slight nod (of the head)

infliger [ɛ̃fliʒe] *vt*: **~ qch (à qn)** to inflict sth (on sb); (*amende, sanction*) to impose sth (on sb)

influence [ɛ̃flyɑ̃s] *nf* influence; (*d'un médicament*) effect; **influencer** *vt* to influence; **influent, e** *adj* influential

influer [ɛ̃flye]: **~ sur** *vt* to have an influence upon

informaticien, ne [ɛ̃fɔrmatisjɛ̃, -jɛn] *nm/f* computer scientist

information [ɛ̃fɔʀmasjɔ̃] *nf* (*renseignement*) piece of information; (*PRESSE, TV: nouvelle*) item of news; (*diffusion de renseignements, INFORM*) information; (*JUR*) inquiry, investigation; ~s *nfpl* (*TV*) news *sg*; **voyage d'** ~ fact-finding trip

informatique [ɛ̃fɔʀmatik] *nf* (*technique*) data processing; (*science*) computer science ♦ *adj* computer *cpd*

informatiser *vt* to computerize

informe [ɛ̃fɔʀm(ə)] *adj* shapeless

informer [ɛ̃fɔʀme] *vt* (*de*) to inform sb (of); **s'~** (**de/si**) to inquire *ou* find out (about/whether *ou* if)

infortune [ɛ̃fɔʀtyn] *nf* misfortune

infraction [ɛ̃fʀaksjɔ̃] *nf* offence; ~ **à** violation *ou* breach of; **être en** ~ to be in breach of the law

infranchissable [ɛ̃fʀɑ̃ʃisabl(ə)] *adj* impassable; (*fig*) insuperable

infrastructure [ɛ̃fʀastʀyktyʀ] *nf* (*AVIAT, MIL*) ground installations *pl*; (*ÉCON: touristique etc*) infrastructure

infuser [ɛ̃fyze] *vt, vi* (*thé*) to brew; (*tisane*) to infuse; **infusion** *nf* (*tisane*) herb tea

ingénier [ɛ̃ʒenje]: **s'~** *vi* to strive to do

ingénierie [ɛ̃ʒenjʀi] *nf* engineering; ~ **génétique** genetic engineering

ingénieur [ɛ̃ʒenjœʀ] *nm* engineer; ~ **du son** sound engineer

ingénieux, euse [ɛ̃ʒenjø, -øz] *adj* ingenious, clever

ingénu, e [ɛ̃ʒeny] *adj* ingenuous, artless

ingérer [ɛ̃ʒeʀe]: **s'~** *vi* to interfere in

ingrat, e [ɛ̃gʀa, -at] *adj* (*personne*) ungrateful; (*sol*) poor; (*travail, sujet*) thankless; (*visage*) unprepossessing

ingrédient [ɛ̃gʀedjɑ̃] *nm* ingredient

ingurgiter [ɛ̃gyʀʒite] *vt* to swallow

inhabitable [inabitabl(ə)] *adj* uninhabitable

inhabituel, le [inabitɥɛl] *adj* unusual

inhérent, e [ineʀɑ̃, -ɑ̃t] *adj*: ~ **à** inherent in

inhibition [inibisjɔ̃] *nf* inhibition

inhumain, e [inymɛ̃, -ɛn] *adj* inhuman

inhumer [inyme] *vt* to inter, bury

inimitié [inimitje] *nf* enmity

initial, e, aux [inisjal, -o] *adj* initial; **initiale** *nf* initial

initiateur, trice [inisjatœʀ, -tʀis] *nm/f* initiator; (*d'une mode, technique*) innovator, pioneer

initiative [inisjativ] *nf* initiative

initier [inisje] *vt*: ~ **qn à** to initiate sb into; (*faire découvrir: art, jeu*) to introduce sb to

injecté, e [ɛ̃ʒɛkte] *adj*: **yeux** ~**s de sang** bloodshot eyes

injecter [ɛ̃ʒɛkte] *vt* to inject; **injection** *nf* injection; **à injection** (*AUTO*) fuel injection *cpd*

injure [ɛ̃ʒyʀ] *nf* insult, abuse *no pl*

injurier [ɛ̃ʒyʀje] *vt* to insult, abuse; **injurieux, euse** *adj* abusive, insulting

injuste [ɛ̃ʒyst(ə)] *adj* unjust, unfair; **injustice** *nf* injustice

inlassable [ɛ̃lasabl(ə)] *adj* tireless

inné, e [ine] *adj* innate, inborn

innocent, e [inɔsɑ̃, -ɑ̃t] *adj* innocent; **innocenter** *vt* to clear, prove innocent

innombrable [inɔ̃bʀabl(ə)] *adj* innumerable

innommable [inɔmabl(ə)] *adj* unspeakable

innover [inɔve] *vi* to break new ground

inoccupé, e [inɔkype] *adj* unoccupied

inoculer [inɔkyle] *vt* (*volontairement*) to inoculate; (*accidentellement*) to infect

inodore [inɔdɔʀ] *adj* (*gaz*) odourless; (*fleur*) scentless

inoffensif, ive [inɔfɑ̃sif, -iv] *adj* harmless, innocuous

inondation [inɔ̃dɑsjɔ̃] *nf* flooding *no pl*; flood; **inonder** [inɔ̃de] *vt* to flood;

(*fig*) to inundate, overrun

inopérant, e [inɔpeʀɑ̃, -ɑ̃t] *adj* inoperative, ineffective

inopiné, e [inɔpine] *adj* unexpected, sudden

inopportun, e [inɔpɔʀtœ̃, -yn] *adj* ill-timed, untimely; inappropriate

inoubliable [inublijabl(ə)] *adj* unforgettable

inouï, e [inwi] *adj* unheard-of, extraordinary

inox(ydable) [inɔks(idabl(ə))] *adj* stainless

inqualifiable [ɛ̃kalifjabl(ə)] *adj* unspeakable

inquiet, ète [ɛ̃kjɛ, -ɛt] *adj* anxious

inquiétant, e [ɛ̃kjetɑ̃, -ɑ̃t] *adj* worrying, disturbing

inquiéter [ɛ̃kjete] *vt* to worry; (*harceler*) to harass; s'~ to worry; s'~ de to worry about; (*s'enquérir de*) to inquire about

inquiétude [ɛ̃kjetyd] *nf* anxiety

insaisissable [ɛ̃sezisabl(ə)] *adj* elusive

insatisfait, e [ɛ̃satisfɛ, -ɛt] *adj* (*non comblé*) unsatisfied; unfulfilled; (*mécontent*) dissatisfied

inscription [ɛ̃skʀipsjɔ̃] *nf* inscription; (*voir s'inscrire*) enrolment; registration

inscrire [ɛ̃skʀiʀ] *vt* (*marquer: sur son calepin etc*) to note ou write down; (: *sur un mur, une affiche etc*) to write; (: *dans la pierre, le métal*) to inscribe; (*mettre: sur une liste, un budget etc*) to put down; s'~ (*pour une excursion etc*) to put one's name down; s'~ (à) (*club, parti*) to join; (*université*) to register ou enrol (at); (*examen, concours*) to register (for); s'~ en faux contre to challenge; ~ qn à (*club, parti*) to enrol sb at

insecte [ɛ̃sɛkt(ə)] *nm* insect; **insecticide** *nm* insecticide

insensé, e [ɛ̃sɑ̃se] *adj* mad

insensibiliser [ɛ̃sɑ̃sibilize] *vt* to anaesthetize

insensible [ɛ̃sɑ̃sibl(ə)] *adj* (*nerf, membre*) numb; (*dur, indifférent*) in-

sensitive; (*imperceptible*) imperceptible

insérer [ɛ̃seʀe] *vt* to insert; s'~ dans to fit into; to come within

insigne [ɛ̃siɲ] *nm* (*d'un parti, club*) badge ♦ *adj* distinguished

insignifiant, e [ɛ̃siɲifjɑ̃, -ɑ̃t] *adj* insignificant; trivial

insinuer [ɛ̃sinɥe] *vt* to insinuate, imply; s'~ dans (*fig*) to creep into

insister [ɛ̃siste] *vi* to insist; (*s'obstiner*) to keep on; ~ sur (*détail, note*) to stress

insolation [ɛ̃sɔlɑsjɔ̃] *nf* (MÉD) sunstroke *no pl*

insolent, e [ɛ̃sɔlɑ̃, -ɑ̃t] *adj* insolent

insolite [ɛ̃sɔlit] *adj* strange, unusual

insomnie [ɛ̃sɔmni] *nf* insomnia *no pl*, sleeplessness *no pl*

insondable [ɛ̃sɔ̃dabl(ə)] *adj* unfathomable

insonoriser [ɛ̃sɔnɔʀize] *vt* to soundproof

insouciant, e [ɛ̃susjɑ̃, -ɑ̃t] *adj* carefree; (*imprévoyant*) heedless

insoumis, e [ɛ̃sumi, -iz] *adj* (*caractère, enfant*) rebellious, refractory; (*contrée, tribu*) unsubdued

insoupçonnable [ɛ̃supsɔnabl(ə)] *adj* unsuspected; (*personne*) above suspicion

insoupçonné, e [ɛ̃supsɔne] *adj* unsuspected

insoutenable [ɛ̃sutnabl(ə)] *adj* (*argument*) untenable; (*chaleur*) unbearable

inspecter [ɛ̃spɛkte] *vt* to inspect

inspecteur, trice [ɛ̃spɛktœʀ, -tʀis] *nm/f* inspector; ~ d'Académie (regional) director of education; ~ des finances ≈ tax inspector (BRIT), ≈ Internal Revenue Service agent (US)

inspection [ɛ̃spɛksjɔ̃] *nf* inspection

inspirer [ɛ̃spiʀe] *vt* (*gén*) to inspire ♦ *vi* (*aspirer*) to breathe in; s'~ de (*suj: artiste*) to draw one's inspiration from

instable [ɛ̃stabl(ə)] *adj* (*meuble, équilibre*) unsteady; (*population, temps*) unsettled; (*régime, carac-*

tère) unstable

installation [ɛ̃stalɑsjɔ̃] *nf* putting in *ou* up; fitting out; settling in; (*appareils etc*) fittings *pl*, installations *pl*; ~s *nfpl* (*appareils*) equipment; (*équipements*) facilities

installer [ɛ̃stale] *vt* (*loger*): ~ qn to get sb settled; (*placer*) to put, place; (*meuble, gaz, électricité*) to put in; (*rideau, étagère, tente*) to put up; (*appartement*) to fit out; s'~ (*s'établir: artisan, dentiste etc*) to set o.s. up; (*se loger*) to settle (o.s.); (*emménager*) to settle in; (*sur un siège, à un emplacement*) to settle (down); (*fig: maladie, grève*) to take a firm hold

instamment [ɛ̃stamɑ̃] *adv* urgently

instance [ɛ̃stɑ̃s] *nf* (*ADMIN: autorité*) authority; ~s *nfpl* (*prières*) entreaties; **affaire en** ~ matter pending; **être en** ~ **de divorce** to be awaiting a divorce

instant [ɛ̃stɑ̃] *nm* moment, instant; **dans un** ~ in a moment; **à l'**~ this instant; **à tout** *ou* **chaque** ~ at any moment; constantly; **pour l'**~ for the moment, for the being; **par** ~s at times; **de tous les** ~s perpetual

instantané, e [ɛ̃stɑ̃tane] *adj* (*lait, café*) instant; (*explosion, mort*) instantaneous ♦ *nm* snapshot

instar [ɛ̃star] : **à l'**~ **de** *prép* following the example of, like

instaurer [ɛ̃stɔre] *vt* to institute

instinct [ɛ̃stɛ̃] *nm* instinct

instituer [ɛ̃stitɥe] *vt* to set up

institut [ɛ̃stity] *nm* institute; ~ **de beauté** beauty salon; **I**~ **Universitaire de Technologie** = polytechnic

instituteur, trice [ɛ̃stitytœr, -tris] *nm/f* (*primary school*) teacher

institution [ɛ̃stitysjɔ̃] *nf* institution; (*collège*) private school

instruction [ɛ̃stryksjɔ̃] *nf* (*enseignement, savoir*) education; (*JUR*: (preliminary) investigation and hearing; ~s *nfpl* (*ordres, mode d'emploi*) directions, instructions; ~ **civique** civ-

ics *sg*

instruire [ɛ̃strɥir] *vt* (*élèves*) to teach; (*recrues*) to train; (*JUR: affaire*) to conduct the investigation for; s'~ to educate o.s.; **instruit, e** *adj* educated

instrument [ɛ̃strymɑ̃] *nm* instrument; ~ **à cordes/vent** stringed/ wind instrument; ~ **de mesure** measuring instrument; ~ **de musique** musical instrument; ~ **de travail** (working) tool

insu [ɛ̃sy] *nm* : **à l'**~ **de qn** without sb knowing (it)

insubmersible [ɛ̃sybmɛrsibl(ə)] *adj* unsinkable

insubordination [ɛ̃sybɔrdinasjɔ̃] *nf* rebelliousness; (*MIL*) insubordination

insuccès [ɛ̃syksɛ] *nm* failure

insuffisant, e [ɛ̃syfizɑ̃, -ɑ̃t] *adj* insufficient; (*élève, travail*) inadequate

insuffler [ɛ̃syfle] *vt* to blow; to inspire

insulaire [ɛ̃sylɛr] *adj* island *cpd*; (*attitude*) insular

insuline [ɛ̃sylin] *nf* insulin

insulte [ɛ̃sylt(ə)] *nf* insult; **insulter** *vt* to insult

insupportable [ɛ̃sypɔrtabl(ə)] *adj* unbearable

insurger [ɛ̃syrʒe]: s'~ vi to rise up *ou* rebel (against)

insurmontable [ɛ̃syrmɔ̃tabl(ə)] *adj* (*difficulté*) insuperable; (*aversion*) unconquerable

intact, e [ɛ̃takt] *adj* intact

intangible [ɛ̃tɑ̃ʒibl(ə)] *adj* intangible; (*principe*) inviolable

intarissable [ɛ̃tarisabl(ə)] *adj* inexhaustible

intégral, e, aux [ɛ̃tegral, -o] *adj* complete

intégrant, e [ɛ̃tegrɑ̃, -ɑ̃t] *adj*: **faire partie** ~**e de** to be an integral part of

intègre [ɛ̃tɛgr(ə)] *adj* upright

intégrer [ɛ̃tegre] *vt* to integrate; s'~ **à** *ou* **dans** to become integrated into

intégrisme [ɛ̃tegrism(e)] *nm* fundamentalism

intellectuel, le [ɛtelɛktɥɛl] adj intellectual ♦ nm/f intellectual; (péj) highbrow

intelligence [ɛteliʒɑ̃s] nf intelligence; (compréhension): l'~ de the understanding of; (complicité): regard d'~ glance of complicity; (accord): vivre en bonne ~ avec qn to be on good terms with sb

intelligent, e [ɛteliʒɑ̃, -ɑ̃t] adj intelligent

intempéries [ɛtɑ̃peri] nfpl bad weather sg

intempestif, ive [ɛtɑ̃pɛstif, -iv] adj untimely

intenable [ɛtnabl(ə)] adj (chaleur) unbearable

intendant, e [ɛtɑ̃dɑ̃, -ɑ̃t] nm/f (MIL) quartermaster; (SCOL) bursar; (d'une propriété) steward

intense [ɛtɑ̃s] adj intense; **intensif, ive** adj intensive

intenter [ɛtɑ̃te] vt: ~ un procès contre ou à to start proceedings against

intention [ɛtɑ̃sjɔ̃] nf intention; (JUR) intent; avoir l'~ de faire to intend to do; à l'~ de for; (renseignement) for the benefit of; (film, ouvrage) aimed at; à cette ~ with this aim in view; **intentionné, e** adj: **bien intentionné** well-meaning ou -intentioned; **mal intentionné** ill-intentioned

interactif, ive [ɛteraktif, -iv] adj (COMPUT) interactive

intercaler [ɛterkale] vt to insert

intercepter [ɛtersɛpte] vt to intercept; (lumière, chaleur) to cut off

interchangeable [ɛterʃɑ̃ʒabl(ə)] adj interchangeable

interclasse [ɛterklɑs] nm (SCOL) break (between classes)

interdiction [ɛterdiksjɔ̃] nf ban

interdire [ɛterdir] vt to forbid; (ADMIN) to ban, prohibit; (: journal, livre) to ban; ~ à qn de faire to forbid sb to do, prohibit sb from doing; (suj: empêchement) to prevent sb from doing

interdit, e [ɛterdi, -it] adj (stupéfait) taken aback ♦ nm prohibition

intéressant, e [ɛteresɑ̃, -ɑ̃t] adj interesting

intéressé, e [ɛterese] adj (parties) involved, concerned; (amitié, motifs) self-interested

intéresser [ɛterese] vt (captiver) to interest; (toucher) to be of interest to; (ADMIN: concerner) to affect, concern; s'~ à to be interested in

intérêt [ɛterɛ] nm (aussi COMM) interest; (égoïsme) self-interest; avoir ~ à faire to do well to do

intérieur, e [ɛterjœr] adj (mur, escalier, poche) inside; (commerce, politique) domestic; (cour, calme, vie) inner; (navigation) inland ♦ nm (d'une maison, d'un récipient etc) inside; (d'un pays, aussi: décor, mobilier) interior; (POL): l'I~ the Interior; à l'~ (de) inside; (fig) within

intérim [ɛterim] nm interim period; assurer l'~ (de) to deputize (for); par ~ interim

intérimaire [ɛterimɛr] nm/f (secrétaire) temporary secretary, temp (BRIT); (suppléant) temporary replacement

intérioriser [ɛterjɔrize] vt to internalize

interlocuteur, trice [ɛterlɔkytœr, -tris] nm/f speaker; son ~ the person he was speaking to

interloquer [ɛterlɔke] vt to take aback

intermède [ɛtermɛd] nm interlude

intermédiaire [ɛtermedjɛr] adj intermediate; middle; half-way ♦ nm/f intermediary; (COMM) middleman; sans ~ directly; par l'~ de through

intermittence [ɛtermitɑ̃s] nf: par ~ sporadically, intermittently

internat [ɛterna] nm (SCOL) boarding school

international, e, aux [ɛternasjɔnal, -o] adj international

interne [ɛtern(ə)] adj internal ♦ nm/f (SCOL) boarder; (MED) houseman; **r** [ɛtɛʀnɛ] *vt* (*POL*) to intern; (*MED*) to confine to a mental institution

interpeller [ɛtɛʀpəle] *vt* (*appeler*) to call out to; (*apostropher*) to shout at; (*POLICE*) to take in for questioning; (*POL*) to question

interphone [ɛtɛʀfɔn] *nm* intercom

interposer [ɛtɛʀpoze] *vt* to interpose; **s'~** *vi* to intervene; **par personnes interposées** through a third party

interprète [ɛtɛʀpʀɛt] *nm/f* interpreter; (*porte-parole*) spokesperson

interpréter [ɛtɛʀpʀete] *vt* to interpret

interrogateur, trice [ɛtɛʀɔgatœʀ, -tʀis] *adj* questioning, inquiring

interrogatif, ive [ɛtɛʀɔgatif, -iv] *adj* (*LING*) interrogative

interrogation [ɛtɛʀɔgasjɔ̃] *nf* question; (*SCOL*) (written *ou* oral) test

interrogatoire [ɛtɛʀɔgatwaʀ] *nm* (*POLICE*) questioning *no pl*; (*JUR*) cross-examination

interroger [ɛtɛʀɔʒe] *vt* to question; (*INFORM*) to consult; (*SCOL*) to test

interrompre [ɛtɛʀɔ̃pʀ(ə)] *vt* (*gén*) to interrupt; (*travail, voyage*) to break off, interrupt; **s'~** to break off

interrupteur [ɛtɛʀyptœʀ] *nm* switch

interruption [ɛtɛʀypsjɔ̃] *nf* interruption; (*pause*) break

interstice [ɛtɛʀstis] *nm* crack; slit

interurbain [ɛtɛʀyʀbɛ̃] *nm* (*TEL*) long-distance call service ♦ *adj* long-distance

intervalle [ɛtɛʀval] *nm* (*espace*) space; (*de temps*) interval; **dans l'~** in the meantime

intervenir [ɛtɛʀvəniʀ] *vi* (*gén*) to intervene; (*survenir*) to take place; **~ auprès de qn** to intervene with sb

intervention [ɛtɛʀvɑ̃sjɔ̃] *nf* intervention; (*discours*) paper; **~ chirurgicale** (surgical) operation

intervertir [ɛtɛʀvɛʀtiʀ] *vt* to invert (the order of), reverse

interview [ɛtɛʀvju] *nf* interview

intestin, e [ɛtɛstɛ̃, -in] *adj* internal

♦ *nm* intestine

intime [ɛtim] *adj* intimate; (*vie, journal*) private; (*conviction*) inmost; (*dîner, cérémonie*) quiet ♦ *nm/f* close friend

intimer [ɛtime] *vt* (*JUR*) to notify; **~ à qn l'ordre de faire** to order sb to do

intimider [ɛtimide] *vt* to intimidate

intimité [ɛtimite] *nf*: **dans l'~** in private; (*sans formalités*) with only a few friends, quietly

intitulé, ée [ɛtityle] *adj* entitled

intolérable [ɛtɔleʀabl(ə)] *adj* intolerable

intoxication [ɛtɔksikasjɔ̃] *nf*: **~ alimentaire** food poisoning

intoxiquer [ɛtɔksike] *vt* to poison; (*fig*) to brainwash

intraduisible [ɛtʀadyizibl(ə)] *adj* untranslatable; (*fig*) inexpressible

intraitable [ɛtʀetabl(ə)] *adj* inflexible, uncompromising

intransigeant, e [ɛtʀɑ̃ziʒɑ̃, -ɑ̃t] *adj* intransigent; (*morale*) uncompromising

intransitif, ive [ɛtʀɑ̃zitif, -iv] *adj* (*LING*) intransitive

intrépide [ɛtʀepid] *adj* dauntless

intrigue [ɛtʀig] *nf* (*scénario*) plot

intriguer [ɛtʀige] *vi* to scheme ♦ *vt* to puzzle, intrigue

intrinsèque [ɛtʀɛ̃sɛk] *adj* intrinsic

introduction [ɛtʀɔdyksjɔ̃] *nf* introduction

introduire [ɛtʀɔdyiʀ] *vt* to introduce; (*visiteur*) to show in; (*aiguille, clef*): **~ qch dans** to insert *ou* introduce sth into; **s'~ dans** to gain entry into; to get *o.s.* accepted into; (*eau, fumée*) to get into

introuvable [ɛtʀuvabl(ə)] *adj* which cannot be found; (*COMM*) unobtainable

introverti, e [ɛtʀɔvɛʀti] *nm/f* introvert

intrus, e [ɛtʀy, -yz] *nm/f* intruder

intrusion [ɛtʀyzjɔ̃] *nf* intrusion; interference

intuition [ɛtyisjɔ̃] *nf* intuition

inusable [inyzabl(ə)] adj hard-wearing

inusité, e [inyzite] adj rarely used

inutile [inytil] adj useless; (superflu) unnecessary; **inutilisable** adj unusable

invalide [ēvalid] adj disabled ♦ nm: ~ **de guerre** disabled ex-serviceman

invasion [ēvazjɔ̃] nf invasion

invectiver [ēvɛktive] vt to hurl abuse at

invendable [ēvãdabl(ə)] adj unsaleable; unmarketable; **invendus** nmpl unsold goods

inventaire [ēvãtɛr] nm inventory; (COMM: liste) stocklist; (: opération) stocktaking no pl; (fig) survey

inventer [ēvãte] vt to invent; (subterfuge) to devise, invent; (histoire, excuse) to make up, invent; **inventeur** nm inventor; **inventif, ive** adj inventive; **invention** nf invention

inverse [ēvɛrs(ə)] adj reverse; opposite; inverse ♦ nm inverse, reverse; **dans l'ordre** ~ in the reverse order; **en sens** ~ in (ou from) the opposite direction; **inversement** adv conversely; **inverser** vt to invert, reverse; (ELEC) to reverse

investir [ēvestir] vt to invest; **investissement** nm investment; **investiture** nf investiture; (à une élection) nomination

invétéré, e [ēvetere] adj (habitude) ingrained; (bavard, buveur) inveterate

invisible [ēvizibl(ə)] adj invisible

invitation [ēvitasjɔ̃] nf invitation

invité, e [ēvite] nm/f guest

inviter [ēvite] vt to invite; ~ **qn à faire** (suj: chose) to induce ou tempt sb to do

involontaire [ēvolɔ̃tɛr] adj (mouvement) involuntary; (insulte) unintentional; (complice) unwitting

invoquer [ēvɔke] vt (Dieu, muse) to call upon, invoke; (prétexte) to put forward (as an excuse); (loi, texte) to refer to

invraisemblable [ēvrɛsãblabl(ə)]

adj unlikely, improbable; incredible

iode [jɔd] nm iodine

irai etc vb voir **aller**

Irak [irak] nm Iraq

Iran [irã] nm Iran

irions etc vb voir **aller**

irlandais, e [irlãdɛ, -ez] adj Irish ♦ nm/f: I~, e Irishman(woman); les I~ the Irish

Irlande [irlãd] nf Ireland; ~ **du Nord** Northern Ireland

ironie [irɔni] nf irony; **ironique** adj ironical; **ironiser** vi to be ironical

irons etc vb voir **aller**

irradier [iradje] vi to radiate ♦ vt (aliment) to irradiate

irraisonné, e [irɛzɔne] adj irrational, unreasoned

irrationnel, le [irasjɔnɛl] adj irrational

irréalisable [irealizabl(ə)] adj unrealizable; impracticable

irrécupérable [irekyperabl(ə)] adj unreclaimable, beyond repair; (personne) beyond redemption

irrécusable [irekyzabl(ə)] adj unimpeachable; incontestable

irréductible [iredyktibl(ə)] adj indomitable, implacable

irréel, le [ireɛl] adj unreal

irréfléchi, e [irefleʃi] adj thoughtless

irrégularité [iregylarite] nf irregularity; unevenness no pl

irrégulier, ière [iregylje, -jɛr] adj irregular, uneven; (élève, athlète) erratic

irrémédiable [iremedjabl(ə)] adj irreparable

irréprochable [irepRɔʃabl(ə)] adj irreproachable, beyond reproach; (tenue) impeccable

irrésistible [irezistibl(ə)] adj irresistible; (preuve, logique) compelling

irrespectueux, euse [irɛspɛktɥø, -øz] adj disrespectful

irriguer [irige] vt to irrigate

irritable [iritabl(ə)] adj irritable

irriter [irite] vt to irritate

irruption [irypsjɔ̃] nf irruption no pl; **faire** ~ **dans** to burst into

islamique [islamik] *adj* Islamic

Islande [islɑ̃d] *nf* Iceland

isolant, e [izɔlɑ̃, -ɑ̃t] *adj* insulating; *(insonorisant)* soundproofing

isolation [izɔlasjɔ̃] *nf* insulation

isolé, e [izɔle] *adj* isolated; insulated

isoler [izɔle] *vt* to isolate; *(prisonnier)* to put in solitary confinement; *(ville)* to cut off, isolate; *(ÉLEC)* to insulate; **isoloir** *nm* polling booth

Israël [israɛl] *nm* Israel; **israélien, ne** *adj, nmf* Israeli; **israélite** *adj* Jewish ♦ *nm* Jew(Jewess)

issu, e [isy] *adj:* ~ **de** descended from; *(fig)* stemming from; **~e** *nf (ouverture, sortie)* exit; *(solution)* way out, solution; *(dénouement)* outcome; **à l'~e de** at the conclusion *ou* close of; **rue sans ~e** dead end

Italie [itali] *nf* Italy; **italien, ne** *adj, nmf* Italian ♦ *nm (LING)* Italian

italique [italik] *nm:* **en** ~ in italics

itinéraire [itinerɛʀ] *nm* itinerary, route

IUT *sigle m* = Institut universitaire de technologie

IVG *sigle f* (= *interruption volontaire de grossesse)* abortion

ivoire [ivwaʀ] *nm* ivory

ivre [ivʀ(ə)] *adj* drunk; ~ **de** *(colère, bonheur)* wild with; **ivresse** *nf* drunkenness; **ivrogne** *nmf* drunkard

J

j' [ʒ] *pron* I

jachère [ʒaʃɛʀ] *nf:* (être) en ~ (to lie) fallow

jacinthe [ʒasɛ̃t] *nf* hyacinth

jack [ʒak] *nm* jack plug

jadis [ʒadis] *adv* in times past, formerly

jaillir [ʒajiʀ] *vi (liquide)* to spurt out; *(fig)* to burst out; to flood out

jais [ʒɛ] *nm* jet; **(d'un noir) de** ~ jet-black

jalon [ʒalɔ̃] *nm* range pole; *(fig)* milestone; **jalonner** *vt* to mark out; *(fig)* to mark, punctuate

jalousie [ʒaluzi] *nf* jealousy; *(store)* (Venetian) blind

jaloux, ouse [ʒalu, -uz] *adj* jealous

jamais [ʒamɛ] *adv* never; *(sans négation)* ever; **ne ...** ~ never; **à** ~ for ever

jambe [ʒɑ̃b] *nf* leg

jambon [ʒɑ̃bɔ̃] *nm* ham; **jambonneau, x** [ʒɑ̃bɔno] *nm* knuckle of ham

jante [ʒɑ̃t] *nf (wheel)* rim

janvier [ʒɑ̃vje] *nm* January

Japon [ʒapɔ̃] *nm* Japan; **japonais, e** *adj, nm (LING)* Japanese ♦ *nm* Japanese

japper [ʒape] *vi* to yap, yelp

jaquette [ʒakɛt] *nf (de cérémonie)* morning coat; *(de dame)* jacket

jardin [ʒaʀdɛ̃] *nm* garden; ~ **d'enfants** nursery school; **jardinage** *nm* gardening; **jardinier, ière** *nm/f* gardener; **jardinière** *nf (de fenêtre)* window box

jarre [ʒaʀ] *nf* (earthenware) jar

jarret [ʒaʀɛ] *nm* back of knee, ham; *(CULIN)* knuckle, shin

jarretelle [ʒaʀtɛl] *nf* suspender *(BRIT)*, garter *(US)*

jarretière [ʒaʀtjɛʀ] *nf* garter

jaser [ʒaze] *vi* to chatter, prattle; *(indiscrètement)* to gossip

jatte [ʒat] *nf* basin, bowl

jauge [ʒoʒ] *nf (instrument)* gauge; **jauger** *vt (fig)* to size up

jaune [ʒon] *adj, nm* yellow ♦ *adv (fam):* **rire** ~ to laugh on the other side of one's face; ~ **d'œuf** (egg) yolk; **jaunir** *vi, vt* to turn yellow

jaunisse [ʒonis] *nf* jaundice

Javel [ʒavɛl] *nf voir* eau

javelot [ʒavlo] *nm* javelin

J.-C. *sigle* = Jésus-Christ

je(j') [ʒ(ə)] *pron* I

jean [dʒin] *nm* jeans *pl*

Jésus-Christ [ʒezykri(st)] *n* Jesus Christ; **500 ans avant/après** ~ *ou* J.-C. 500 B.C./A.D.

jet¹ [ʒɛ] *nm (lancer)* throwing *no pl*, throw; *(jaillissement)* jet; spurt; *(de tuyau)* nozzle; **du premier jet** at the first attempt or shot; **jet d'eau** fountain; spray

jet² [dʒɛt] nm (avion) jet

jetable [ʒətabl(ə)] adj disposable

jetée [ʒəte] nf jetty; pier

jeter [ʒəte] vt (gén) to throw; (se défaire de) to throw away ou out; (son, lueur etc) to give out; **se ~ dans** to flow into; **~ qch à qn** to throw sth to sb; (de façon agressive) to throw sth at sb; **~ un coup d'œil (à)** to take a look (at); **~ un sort à qn** to cast a spell on sb

jeton [ʒɔtɔ] nm (au jeu) counter; (de téléphone) token

jette etc vb voir **jeter**

jeu, x [ʒø] nm (divertissement, TECH: d'une pièce) play; (TENNIS: partie, FOOTBALL etc: façon de jouer) game; (THÉÂTRE etc) acting; (au casino): **le ~** gambling; (fonctionnement) working, interplay; (série d'objets, jouet) set; (CARTES) hand; **en ~** at stake; at work; **remettre en ~** to throw in; **entrer/mettre en ~** to come/bring into play; **~ de cartes** pack of cards; **~ d'échecs** chess set; **~ de hasard** game of chance; **~ de mots** pun

jeudi [ʒødi] nm Thursday

jeun [ʒœ̃]: **à ~** adv on an empty stomach

jeune [ʒœn] adj young; **~ fille** girl; **~ homme** young man

jeûne [ʒøn] nm fast

jeunesse [ʒœnɛs] nf youth; (aspect) youthfulness; youngness

joaillerie [ʒɔajʀi] nf jewel trade; jewellery; **joaillier, ière** nm/f jeweller

joie [ʒwa] nf joy

joindre [ʒwɛ̃dʀ(ə)] vt to join; (à une lettre): **~ qch à** to enclose sth with; (contacter) to contact, get in touch with; **se ~ à** to join; **~ les mains** to put one's hands together

joint, e [ʒwɛ̃, ʒwɛ̃t] adj: **~ (à)** enclosure ♦ nm joint; (ligne) join; **~ de culasse** cylinder head gasket; **~ de robinet** washer

joli, e [ʒɔli] adj pretty, attractive;

c'est du **~!** (ironique) that's very nice!; **c'est bien ~, mais ...** that's all very well but ...

jonc [ʒɔ̃] nm (bul)rush

joncher [ʒɔ̃ʃe] vt (suj: choses) to be strewed on

jonction [ʒɔ̃ksjɔ̃] nf joining; (point de) **~** junction

jongleur, euse [ʒɔ̃glœʀ, -øz] nm/f juggler

jonquille [ʒɔ̃kij] nf daffodil

Jordanie [ʒɔʀdani] nf: **la ~** Jordan

joue [ʒu] nf cheek; **mettre en ~** to take aim at

jouer [ʒwe] vt to play; (somme d'argent, réputation) to stake, wager; (pièce, rôle) to perform; (film) to show; (simuler: sentiment) to affect, feign ♦ vi to play; (THÉÂTRE, CINEMA) to act, perform; (bois, porte: se voiler) to warp; (clef, pièce: avoir du jeu) to be loose; **se ~ de** (difficultés) to make light of; to deceive; **~ sur** (miser) to gamble on; **~ de** (MUS) to play; **~ des coudes** to play with one's elbows; **~ à** (jeu, sport, roulette) to play; **~ avec** (risquer) to gamble with; **~ un tour à qn** to play a trick on sb; **~ serré** to play a close game; **~ de malchance** to be dogged with ill-luck

jouet [ʒwe] nm toy; **être le ~ de** (illusion etc) to be the victim of

joueur, euse [ʒwœʀ, -øz] nm/f player; **être beau ~** to be a good loser

joufflu, e [ʒufly] adj chubby-cheeked

joug [ʒu] nm yoke

jouir [ʒwiʀ]: **~ de** vt to enjoy; **jouissance** nf pleasure; (JUR) use

joujou [ʒuʒu] (fam) nm toy

jour [ʒuʀ] nm day; (opposé à la nuit) day, daytime; (clarté) daylight; (fig: aspect) light; (ouverture) opening; **au ~ le ~** from day to day; **de nos ~s** these days; **il fait ~** it's daylight; **au grand ~** (fig) in the open; **mettre au ~** to disclose; **mettre à ~** to update; **donner le ~ à** to give birth to; **voir le ~** to be born; **~ férié** nm public holiday

journal, aux [ʒuʀnal, -o] nm (news)paper; (personnel) journal, diary; ~ **de bord** log; ~ **parlé/télévisé** radio/television news sg

journalier, ière [ʒuʀnalje, -jɛʀ] adj daily; (banal) everyday

journalisme [ʒuʀnalism(ə)] nm journalism; **journaliste** nmf journalist

journée [ʒuʀne] nf day; **la** ~ **continue** the 9 to 5 working day

journellement [ʒuʀnɛlmɑ̃] adv daily

joyau, x [ʒwajo] nm gem, jewel

joyeux, euse [ʒwajø, -øz] adj joyful, merry; ~ **Noël!** merry Christmas!; ~ **anniversaire!** happy birthday!

jubiler [ʒybile] vi to be jubilant, exult

jucher [ʒyʃe] vt, vi to perch

judas [ʒyda] nm (trou) spy-hole

judiciaire [ʒydisjɛʀ] adj judicial

judicieux, euse [ʒydisjø, -øz] adj judicious

judo [ʒydo] nm judo

juge [ʒyʒ] nm judge; ~ **d'instruction** examining (BRIT) ou committing (US) magistrate; ~ **de paix** justice of the peace

jugé [ʒyʒe] : **au** ~ adv by guesswork

jugement [ʒyʒmɑ̃] nm judgment; (JUR: au pénal) sentence; (: au civil) decision

juger [ʒyʒe] vt to judge; ~ **qn/qch satisfaisant** to consider sb/sth (to be) satisfactory; ~ **bon de faire** to see fit to do; ~ **de** to appreciate

juif, juive [ʒɥif, -iv] adj Jewish ♦ nm/f Jew(Jewess)

juillet [ʒɥijɛ] nm July

juin [ʒɥɛ̃] nm June

jumeau, elle, x [ʒymo, -ɛl] adj, nm/f twin; voir aussi **jumelle**

jumeler [ʒymle] vt to twin

jumelle [ʒymɛl] adj, nf voir **jumeau**; ~**s** nfpl (appareil) binoculars

jument [ʒymɑ̃] nf mare

jungle [ʒœ̃gl(ə)] nf jungle

jupe [ʒyp] nf skirt

jupon [ʒypɔ̃] nm waist slip

juré, e [ʒyʀe] nm/f juror

jurer [ʒyʀe] vt (obéissance etc) to swear, vow ♦ vi (dire des jurons) to swear, curse; (dissoner): ~ **(avec)** to clash (with); (s'engager): ~ **de faire/que** to swear ou vow to do/that; (affirmer): ~ **que** to swear ou vouch that; ~ **de qch** (s'en porter garant) to swear to sth

juridique [ʒyʀidik] adj legal

juron [ʒyʀɔ̃] nm curse, swearword

jury [ʒyʀi] nm jury; board

jus [ʒy] nm juice; (de viande) gravy; (meat) juice; ~ **de fruit** fruit juice

jusque [ʒysk(ə)] : **jusqu'à** prép (endroit) as far as, (up) to; (moment) until, till; (limite) up to; ~ **sur/dans** up to; (y compris) even on/in; **jusqu'à ce que** until; **jusqu'à présent** until now

juste [ʒyst(ə)] adj (équitable) just, fair; (légitime) just, justified; (exact, vrai) right; (étroit, insuffisant) tight ♦ adv right; (chanter) in tune; (seulement) just; ~ **assez/au-dessus** just enough/above; **au** ~ exactly; **le** ~ **milieu** the happy medium; **juste-ment** adv rightly, justly; (précisément) just, precisely; **justesse** nf (précision) accuracy; (d'une remarque) aptness; (d'une opinion) soundness; **de justesse** just

justice [ʒystis] nf (équité) fairness, justice; (ADMIN) justice; **rendre la** ~ to dispense justice; **rendre** ~ **à qn** to do sb justice; **justicier, ière** [ʒystisje, -jɛʀ] nm/f judge, righter of wrongs

justificatif, ive [ʒystifikatif, -iv] adj (document) supporting; **pièce jus-tificative** written proof

justifier [ʒystifje] vt to justify; ~ **de** to prove

juteux, euse [ʒytø, -øz] adj juicy

juvénile [ʒyvenil] adj young, youthful

K

K [ka] nm (INFORM) K
kaki [kaki] adj inv khaki
kangourou [kɑ̃guʀu] nm kangaroo
karaté [kaʀate] nm karate
karting [kaʀtiŋ] nm go-carting, karting
kermesse [kɛʀmɛs] nf bazaar, (charity) fête; village fair
kidnapper [kidnape] vt to kidnap
kilo [kilo] nm = **kilogramme**
kilo: ~**gramme** nm kilogramme; ~**métrage** nm number of kilometres travelled, ≈ mileage; ~**mètre** nm kilometre; ~**métrique** adj (distance) in kilometres
kinésithérapeute [kinezitéʀapøt] nm/f physiotherapist
kiosque [kjɔsk(ə)] nm kiosk, stall
klaxon [klaksɔn] nm horn; **klaxonner** vi, vt to hoot (BRIT), honk (US)
km. abr = **kilomètre**; **km/h** (= kilomètres/heure) ≈ m.p.h.
Ko [kao] abr (INFORM: kilooctet) K
K.-O. [kao] adj inv (knocked) out
kyste [kist(ə)] nm cyst

L

l' [l] dét voir le
la [la] dét le ♦ nm (MUS) A; (en chantant la gamme) la
là [la] adv there; (ici) here; (dans le temps) then; **elle n'est pas** ~ she isn't here; **c'est** ~ **que** this is where; ~ **où** where; **de** ~ (fig) hence; **par** ~ by that; **tout est** ~ that's what it's all about; voir aussi -**ci**; **celui**; **là-bas** adv there
label [label] nm stamp, seal
labeur [labœʀ] nm toil no pl, toiling no pl
labo [labo] abr m (= laboratoire) lab
laboratoire [labɔʀatwaʀ] nm laboratory; ~ **de langues** language laboratory

laborieux, euse [labɔʀjø, -øz] adj (tâche) laborious; **classes laborieuses** working classes
labour [labuʀ] nm ploughing no pl; ~**s** nmpl (champs) ploughed fields; **cheval de** ~ plough- ou cart-horse; **bœuf de** ~ ox
labourer [labuʀe] vt to plough; (fig) to make deep gashes ou furrows in
labyrinthe [labiʀɛ̃t] nm labyrinth, maze
lac [lak] nm lake
lacer [lase] vt to lace ou do up
lacérer [laseʀe] vt to tear to shreds
lacet [lase] nm (de chaussure) lace; (de route) sharp bend; (piège) snare
lâche [lɑʃ] adj (poltron) cowardly; (desserré) loose, slack ♦ nm/f coward
lâcher [lɑʃe] nm (de ballons, oiseaux) release ♦ vt to let go of; (ce qui tombe, abandonner) to drop; (oiseau, animal: libérer) to release, set free; (fig: mot, remarque) to let slip, come out with; (SPORT: distancer) to leave behind ♦ vi (fil, amarres) to break, give way; (freins) to fail; ~ **les amarres** (NAVIG) to cast off (the moorings); ~ **les chiens** to unleash the dogs; ~ **prise** to let go
lâcheté [lɑʃte] nf cowardice; lowness
lacrymogène [lakʀimɔʒɛn] adj: **gaz** ~ teargas
lacté, e [lakte] adj (produit, régime) milk cpd
lacune [lakyn] nf gap
là-dedans [ladədɑ̃] adv inside (there), in it; (fig) in that
là-dessous [ladsu] adv underneath, under there; (fig) behind that
là-dessus [ladsy] adv on there; (fig) at that point; about that
ladite [ladit] dét voir ledit
lagune [lagyn] nf lagoon
là-haut [la'o] adv up there
laïc [laik] adj, nm/f = **laïque**
laid, e [lɛ, lɛd] adj ugly; **laideur** nf ugliness no pl
lainage [lenaʒ] nm woollen garment; woollen material

laine [lɛn] *nf* wool

laïque [laik] *adj* lay, civil; (SCOL) state *cpd* ♦ *nm/f* layman(woman)

laisse [lɛs] *nf* (de chien) lead, leash; **tenir en ~** to keep on a lead *ou* leash

laisser [lese] *vt* to leave ♦ *vb aux:* **~ qn faire** to let sb do; **~ aller** to let o.s. go; **laisse-toi faire** let me (*ou* him) do it; **laisser-aller** *nm* carelessness, slovenliness; **laissez-passer** *nm inv* pass

lait [lɛ] *nm* milk; **frère/sœur de ~** foster brother/sister; **~ condensé/concentré** evaporated/condensed milk; **laiterie** *nf* dairy; **laitier, ière** *adj* dairy *cpd* ♦ *nm/f* milkman(dairywoman)

laiton [lɛtɔ̃] *nm* brass

laitue [lety] *nf* lettuce

laïus [lajys] (*péj*) *nm* spiel

lambeau, x [lɑ̃bo] *nm* scrap; **en ~x** in tatters, tattered

lambris [lɑ̃bʀi] *nm* panelling *no pl*

lame [lam] *nf* blade; (*vague*) wave; (*lamelle*) strip; **~ de fond** ground swell *no pl*; **~ de rasoir** razor blade

lamelle [lamɛl] *nf* thin strip *ou* blade

lamentable [lamɑ̃tabl(ə)] *adj* appalling; pitiful

lamenter [lamɑ̃te]: **se ~** *vi* to moan (over)

lampadaire [lɑ̃padɛʀ] *nm* (de salon) standard lamp; (dans la rue) street lamp

lampe [lɑ̃p(ə)] *nf* lamp; (TECH) valve; **~ à souder** blowlamp; **~ de poche** torch (BRIT), flashlight (US)

lampion [lɑ̃pjɔ̃] *nm* Chinese lantern

lance [lɑ̃s] *nf* spear; **~ d'incendie** fire hose

lancée [lɑ̃se] *nf:* **être/continuer sur sa ~** to be under way/keep going

lancement [lɑ̃smɑ̃] *nm* launching

lance-pierres [lɑ̃spjɛʀ] *nm inv* catapult

lancer [lɑ̃se] *nm* (SPORT) throwing *no pl*, throw ♦ *vt* to throw; (*émettre, projeter*) to throw out, send out; (*produit, fusée, bateau, artiste*) to launch; (*injure*) to hurl, fling; (*proclamation, mandat d'arrêt*) to issue; **se ~** *vi* (*prendre de l'élan*) to build up speed; (*se précipiter*): **se ~ sur** *ou* **contre** to rush at; **se ~ dans** (*discussion*) to launch into; (*aventure*) to embark on; **~ qch à qn** to throw sth to sb; (*de façon agressive*) to throw sth at sb; **~ du poids** *nm* putting the shot

lancinant, e [lɑ̃sinɑ̃, -ɑ̃t] *adj* (*regrets etc*) haunting; (*douleur*) shooting

landau [lɑ̃do] *nm* pram (BRIT), baby carriage (US)

lande [lɑ̃d] *nf* moor

langage [lɑ̃gaʒ] *nm* language

langer [lɑ̃ʒe] *vt* to change (the nappy (BRIT) *ou* diaper (US) of)

langouste [lɑ̃gust(ə)] *nf* crayfish *inv*; **langoustine** *nf* Dublin Bay prawn

langue [lɑ̃g] *nf* (ANAT, CULIN) tongue; (LING) language; **tirer la ~** (à) to stick out one's tongue (at); **de ~ française** French-speaking; **~ maternelle** native language, mother tongue; **~ verte** slang; **~ vivante** modern language

langueur [lɑ̃gœʀ] *nf* languidness

languir [lɑ̃giʀ] *vi* to languish; (*conversation*) to flag; **faire ~ qn** to keep sb waiting

lanière [lanjɛʀ] *nf* (de fouet) lash; (de valise, montre) strap

lanterne [lɑ̃tɛʀn(ə)] *nf* (portable) lantern; (électrique) light, lamp; (de voiture) (side)light

laper [lape] *vt* to lap up

lapidaire [lapidɛʀ] *adj* stone *cpd*; (*fig*) terse

lapin [lapɛ̃] *nm* rabbit; (peau) rabbitskin; (fourrure) cony

Laponie [laponi] *nf* Lapland

laps [laps] *nm:* **~ de temps** space of time, time *no pl*

laque [lak] *nf* lacquer; (brute) shellac; (pour cheveux) hair spray

laquelle [lakɛl] *pron voir* **lequel**

larcin [laʀsɛ̃] *nm* theft

lard [laʀ] nm (graisse) fat; (bacon) (streaky) bacon

lardon [laʀdɔ̃] nm: ~s chopped bacon

large [laʀʒ(ə)] adj wide; broad; (fig) generous ♦ adv: calculer/voir ~ to allow extra/think big ♦ nm (largeur): 5 m de ~ 5 m wide ou in width; (mer): le ~ the open sea; au ~ de off; (: ~) d'esprit broad-minded; **largement** adv widely; greatly; easily; generously; **largesse** nf generosity; ~sses nfpl (dons) liberalities; **largeur** nf (qu'on mesure) width; (impression visuelle) wideness, width; breadth; broadness

larguer [laʀɡe] vt to drop; ~ les amarres to cast off (the moorings)

larme [laʀm(ə)] nf tear; (fig) drop; en ~s in tears; **larmoyer** vi (yeux) to water; (se plaindre) to whimper

larvé, e [laʀve] adj (fig) latent

laryngite [laʀɛ̃ʒit] nf laryngitis

las, lasse [la, las] adj weary

laser [lazeʀ] nm: (rayon) ~ laser (beam); **chaîne** ~ compact disc (player); **disque** ~ compact disc

lasse [las] adj voir las

lasser [lase] vt to weary, tire; se ~ de vt to grow weary ou tired of

latéral, e, aux [lateʀal, -o] adj side cpd, lateral

latin, e [latɛ̃, -in] adj, nm/f Latin ♦ nm (LING) Latin

latitude [latityd] nf latitude

latte [lat] nf lath, slat; (de plancher) board

lauréat, e [loʀea, -at] nm/f winner

laurier [loʀje] nm (BOT) laurel; (CULIN) bay leaves pl; ~s nmpl (fig) laurels

lavable [lavabl(ə)] adj washable

lavabo [lavabo] nm washbasin; ~s nmpl (toilettes) toilet sg

lavage [lavaʒ] nm washing no pl, wash; ~ de cerveau brainwashing no pl

lavande [lavɑ̃d] nf lavender

lave [lav] nf lava no pl

lave-glace [lavɡlas] nm windscreen

(BRIT) ou windshield (US) washer

lave-linge [lavlɛ̃ʒ] nm inv washing machine

laver [lave] vt to wash; (tache) to wash off; se ~ vi to have a wash; se ~ les mains/dents to wash one's hands/clean one's teeth; ~ qn de (accusation) to clear sb of; **laverie** nf: laverie (automatique) launderette; **lavette** nf dish cloth; (fam) drip; **laveur, euse** nm/f cleaner; ~-vaisselle nm inv dishwasher; lavoir nm wash house

laxatif, ive [laksatif, -iv] adj, nm laxative

le(l'), la [l(ə)] (pl les) art déf **1** the; ~ livre/la pomme/l'arbre the book/the apple/the tree; les étudiants the students

2 (noms abstraits): ~ courage/l'amour/la jeunesse courage/love/youth

3 (indiquant la possession): se casser la jambe etc to break one's leg etc; levez la main put your hand up; avoir les yeux gris/~ nez rouge to have grey eyes/a red nose

4 (temps): le matin/soir in the morning/evening; mornings/evenings; ~ jeudi etc (d'habitude) on Thursdays etc; (ce jeudi-là etc) on (the) Thursday

5 (distribution, évaluation), a, an; 10F ~ mètre/kilo 10F a ou per metre/kilo; ~ tiers/quart a third/quarter of

♦ pron **1** (personne: mâle) him; (: femelle) her; (: pluriel) them; je ~/la/les vois I can see him/her/them

2 (animal, chose: singulier) it; (: pluriel) them; je le (ou la) vois I can see it; je les vois I can see them

3 (remplaçant une phrase): je ne ~ savais pas I didn't know (about it); il était riche et ne l'est plus he was once rich but no longer is

lécher [leʃe] *vt* to lick; (*laper: lait, eau*) to lick *ou* lap up; ~ **les vitrines** to go window-shopping

leçon [ləsɔ̃] *nf* lesson; **faire la** ~ **à** (*fig*) to give a lecture to; ~**s de conduite** driving lessons

lecteur, trice [lɛktœʀ, -tʀis] *nm/f* reader; (*d'université*) foreign language assistant ♦ *nm* (*TECH*): ~ **de cassettes** cassette player; ~ **de disque compact** compact disc player; ~ **de disquette** disk drive

lecture [lɛktyʀ] *nf* reading

ledit, ladite [ləd i] (*mpl* **lesdits**, *fpl* **lesdites**) *dét* the aforesaid

légal, e, aux [legal, -o] *adj* legal

légende [leʒɑ̃d] *nf* (*mythe*) legend; (*de carte, plan*) key; (*de dessin*) caption

léger, ère [leʒe, -ɛʀ] *adj* light; (*bruit, retard*) slight; (*superficiel*) thoughtless; (*volage*) free and easy, flighty; **à la légère** (*parler, agir*) rashly, thoughtlessly; **légèrement** *adv* lightly; thoughtlessly; slightly

législatif, ive [leʒislatif, -iv] *adj* legislative; **législatives** *nfpl* general election *sg*; **législature** [leʒislatyʀ] *nf* legislature; term (of office)

légitime [leʒitim] *adj* (*JUR*) lawful, legitimate; (*fig*) rightful, legitimate; **en état de** ~ **défense** in self-defence

legs [lɛg] *nm* legacy

léguer [lege] *vt*: ~ **qch à qn** (*JUR*) to bequeath sth to sb; (*fig*) to hand sth down *ou* pass sth on to sb

légume [legym] *nm* vegetable

lendemain [lɑ̃dmɛ̃] *nm*: **le** ~ **the next** *ou* following day; **le** ~ **matin/soir** the next *ou* following morning/evening; **le** ~ **de** the day after; **sans** ~ short-lived

lent, e [lɑ̃, lɑ̃t] *adj* slow; **lentement** *adv* slowly; **lenteur** *nf* slowness *no pl*

lentille [lɑ̃tij] *nf* (*OPTIQUE*) lens *sg*; (*CULIN*) lentil

léopard [leopaʀ] *nm* leopard

lèpre [lɛpʀ(ə)] *nf* leprosy

---

lequel, laquelle [ləkɛl, lakɛl] (*mpl* **lesquels**, *fpl* **lesquelles**; *à + lequel* **= auquel**, *de + lequel* **pron**) *pron* **1** (*interrogatif*) which, which one **2** (*relatif: personne: sujet*) who; (: *objet, après préposition*) whom; (: *chose*) ♦ *adj* ♦ *adj*: **auquel cas** in which case

les [le] *dét* voir **le**

lesbienne [lɛsbjɛn] *nf* lesbian

lesdites [ledit] *dét pl voir* **ledit**

lesdits [ledi] *dét pl voir* **ledit**

léser [leze] *vt* to wrong

lésiner [lezine] *vi*: ~ (**sur**) to skimp (on)

lésion [lezjɔ̃] *nf* lesion, damage *no pl*

lesquelles [lekɛl] *pron pl voir* **lequel**

lesquels [lekɛl] *pron pl voir* **lequel**

lessive [lesiv] *nf* (*poudre*) washing powder; (*linge*) washing *no pl*, wash

lessiver [lesive] *vt* to wash

lest [lɛst] *nm* ballast

leste [lɛst(ə)] *adj* sprightly, nimble

lettre [lɛtʀ(ə)] *nf* letter; ~**s** *nfpl* (*littérature*) literature *sg*; (*SCOL*) arts (subjects); **à la** ~ literally; **en toutes** ~**s** in full

lettré, e [letʀe] *adj* well-read

leucémie [løsemi] *nf* leukaemia

---

leur [lœʀ] *adj possessif* their; ~ **maison** their house; ~**s amis** their friends

♦ *pron* **1** (*objet indirect*) to them; (them); **je** ~ **ai dit la vérité** I told them the truth; **je le** ~ **ai donné** I gave it to them, I gave them it

2 (*possessif*): **le(la)** ~, ~**s** theirs

leurre [lœʀ] *nm* (*appât*) lure; (*fig*) delusion; snare

leurrer [lœʀe] *vt* to delude, deceive

leurs [lœʀ] *dét voir* **leur**

levain [ləvɛ̃] *nm* leaven

levé, e [ləve] *adj*: **être** ~ to be up

levée [l(ə)ve] *nf* (*POSTES*) collection; (*CARTES*) trick; ~ **de boucliers** general outcry

lever [l(ə)ve] *vt* (*vitre, bras etc*) to raise; (*soulever de terre, supprimer: interdiction, siège*) to lift; (*séance*) to close; (*impôts, armée*) to levy ♦ *vi* to rise ♦ *nm*: au ~ on getting up; se ~ *vi* to get up; (*soleil*) to rise; (*jour*) to break; (*brouillard*) to lift; ~ **de soleil** sunrise; ~ **du jour** daybreak

levier [ləvje] *nm* lever

lèvre [lɛvʀ(ə)] *nf* lip

lévrier [levʀije] *nm* greyhound

levure [l(ə)vyʀ] *nf* yeast; ~ **chimique** baking powder

lexique [lɛksik] *nm* vocabulary; lexicon

lézard [lezaʀ] *nm* lizard

lézarde [lezaʀd(ə)] *nf* crack

liaison [ljɛzɔ̃] *nf* (*lien*); (*amoureuse*) affair; (*PHONÉTIQUE*) liaison; entrer/être en ~ avec to get/be in contact with

liane [ljan] *nf* creeper

liant, e [ljɑ̃, -ɑ̃t] *adj* sociable

liasse [ljas] *nf* wad, bundle

Liban [libɑ̃] *nm*: le ~ (the) Lebanon; **libanais, e** *adj, nm/f* Lebanese

libeller [libele] *vt* (*chèque, mandat*): ~ (au nom de) to make out (to); (*lettre*) to word

libellule [libelyl] *nf* dragonfly

libéral, e, aux [libeʀal, -o] *adj, nm/f* liberal

libérer [libeʀe] *vt* (*délivrer*) to free, liberate; (: *moralement, PSYCH*) to liberate; (*relâcher, dégager: gaz*) to release; to discharge; se ~ *vi* (*de rendez-vous*) to get out of previous engagements

liberté [libɛʀte] *nf* freedom; (*loisir*) free time; ~s *nfpl* (*privautés*) liberties; **mettre/être en** ~ to set/be free; en ~ **provisoire/surveillée/conditionnelle** on bail/probation/parole; ~s **individuelles** personal freedom *sg*

libraire [libʀɛʀ] *nm/f* bookseller

librairie [libʀɛʀi] *nf* bookshop

libre [libʀ(ə)] *adj* free; (*route*) clear; (*place etc*) vacant; empty; not engaged; not taken; (*SCOL*) non-state; **de** ~ (*place*) free; ~ **de qch/de faire** free from sth/to do; ~ **arbitre** free will; ~-**échange** *nm* free trade; ~-**service** *nm* self-service store

Libye [libi] *nf*: la ~ Libya

licence [lisɑ̃s] *nf* (*permis*) permit; (*diplôme*) degree; (*liberté*) licence; licence (*BRIT*), license (*US*); licen- tiousness; **licencié, e** *nm/f* (*SCOL*): **licencié ès lettres/en droit** = Bachelor of Arts/Law; (*SPORT*) member of a sports federation

licencier [lisɑ̃sje] *vt* (*renvoyer*) to dismiss; (*débaucher*) to make redun- dant; to lay off

licite [lisit] *adj* lawful

lie [li] *nf* dregs *pl*, sediment

lié, e [lje] *adj*: très ~ avec very friendly with ou close to; ~ par (*ser- ment*) bound by

liège [ljɛʒ] *nm* cork

lien [ljɛ̃] *nm* (*corde, fig: affectif*) bond; (*rapport*) link, connection; ~ **de parenté** family tie

lier [lje] *vt* (*attacher*) to tie up; (*joindre*) to link up; (*fig: unir, enga- ger*) to bind; (*CULIN*) to thicken; se ~ avec to make friends with; ~ **qch à** to tie *ou* link sth to; ~ **conversa- tion avec** to strike up a conversation with

lierre [ljɛʀ] *nm* ivy

liesse [ljɛs] *nf*: être en ~ to be cele- brating *ou* jubilant

lieu, x [ljø] *nm* place; ~x *nmpl* (*ha- bitation*) premises; (*endroit: d'un ac- cident etc*) scene *sg*; en ~ **sûr** in a safe place; en **premier** ~ in the first place; en **dernier** ~ lastly; **avoir** ~ to take place; **avoir** ~ **de faire** to have grounds for doing; **tenir** ~ **de** to take the place of; to serve as; **donner** ~ **à** to give rise to; au ~ **de** instead of

lieu-dit [ljødi] (*pl* **lieux-dits**) *nm* lo- cality

lieutenant [ljøtnɑ̃] *nm* lieutenant

lièvre [ljɛvʀ(ə)] nm hare

ligament [ligamɑ̃] nm ligament

ligne [liɲ] nf (gén) line; (TRANSPORTS: liaison) service; (: trajet) route; (silhouette) figure; **entrer en ~ de compte** to come into it

lignée [liɲe] nf line; lineage; descendants pl

ligoter [ligɔte] vt to tie up

ligue [lig] nf league; **liguer** vt: **se liguer contre** (fig) to combine against

lilas [lila] nm lilac

limace [limas] nf slug

limaille [limɑj] nf: **~ de fer** iron filings pl

limande [limɑ̃d] nf dab

lime [lim] nf file; **~ à ongles** nail file; **limer** vt to file

limier [limje] nm bloodhound; (détective) sleuth

limitation [limitasjɔ̃] nf: **~ de vitesse** speed limit

limite [limit] nf (de terrain) boundary; (partie ou point extrême) limit; **vitesse/charge ~** maximum speed/load; **cas ~** borderline case; **date ~** deadline

limiter [limite] vt (restreindre) to limit, restrict; (délimiter) to border

limitrophe [limitʀɔf] adj border cpd

limoger [limɔʒe] vt to dismiss

limon [limɔ̃] nm silt

limonade [limɔnad] nf lemonade

linceul [lɛ̃sœl] nm shroud

linge [lɛ̃ʒ] nm (serviettes etc) linen; (pièce au corps) cloth; (aussi: ~ de corps) underwear; (: ~ de toilette) towels pl; (lessive) washing

lingerie [lɛ̃ʒʀi] nf lingerie, underwear

lingot [lɛ̃go] nm ingot

linguistique [lɛ̃gɥistik] adj linguistic ♦ nf linguistics sg

lion, ne [ljɔ̃, ljɔn] nm/f lion(lioness); (signe): **le L~** Leo; **lionceau, x** nm lion cub

liqueur [likœʀ] nf liqueur

liquide [likid] adj liquid ♦ nm liquid; (COMM): **en ~** in ready money ou cash; **liquider** [likide] vt (société, biens, témoin gênant) to liquidate; (compte, problème) to settle; (COMM: articles) to clear, sell off; **liquidités** [likidite] nfpl (COMM) liquid assets

lire [liʀ] nf (monnaie) lira ♦ vt, vi to read

lis [lis] nm = **lys**

lisible [lizibl(ə)] adj legible

lisière [lizjɛʀ] nf (de forêt) edge; (de tissu) selvage

lisons vb voir **lire**

lisse [lis] adj smooth

listing [listiŋ] nm (INFORM) printout

lit [li] nm (gén) bed; **faire son ~** to make one's bed; **aller/se mettre au ~** to go to/get into bed; **~ de camp** camp bed; **~ d'enfant** cot (BRIT), crib (US)

literie [litʀi] nf bedding, bedclothes pl

litière [litjɛʀ] nf litter

litige [litiʒ] nm dispute

litre [litʀ(ə)] nm litre; (récipient) litre measure

littéraire [literɛʀ] adj literary

littéral, e, aux [literal, -o] adj literal

littérature [literatyʀ] nf literature

littoral, aux [litoral, -o] nm coast

liturgie [lityʀʒi] nf liturgy

livraison [livʀɛzɔ̃] nf delivery

livre [livʀ(ə)] nm book ♦ nf (poids, monnaie) pound; **~ de bord** logbook; **~ de poche** paperback (pocket et size)

livré, e [livʀe] adj: **~ à soi-même** left to o.s. ou one's own devices; **livrée** nf livery

livrer [livʀe] vt (COMM) to deliver; (otage, coupable) to hand over; (secret, information) to give away; (se rendre, s'abandonner) to give o.s. up to; (faire: pratiques, actes) to indulge in; (: travail) to engage in; (: sport) to practise; (travail: enquête to carry out

livret [livʀɛ] *nm* booklet; (*d'opéra*) libretto; ~ **de caisse d'épargne** (savings) bank-book; ~ **de famille** (official) family record book; ~ **scolaire** (school) report book

livreur, euse [livʀœʀ, -øz] *nm/f* delivery boy *ou* man/girl *ou* woman

local, e, aux [lɔkal, -o] *adj* local ♦ *nm* (*salle*) premises *pl*; *voir aussi* locaux

localiser [lɔkalize] *vt* (*repérer*) to locate, place; (*limiter*) to confine

localité [lɔkalite] *nf* locality

locataire [lɔkatɛʀ] *nm/f* tenant; (*de chambre*) lodger

location [lɔkasjɔ̃] *nf* (*par le locataire, le loueur*) renting; (*par le propriétaire*) renting out, letting; (*THÉÂTRE*) booking office; "~ **de voitures**" "car rental"

location-vente [lɔkasjɔ̃vɑ̃t] (*pl* ~**s** ~**s**) *nf* hire purchase (*BRIT*), instalment plan (*US*)

locaux [lɔko] *nmpl* premises

locomotive [lɔkɔmɔtiv] *nf* locomotive, engine; (*fig*) pacesetter, pacemaker

locution [lɔkysjɔ̃] *nf* phrase

loge [lɔʒ] *nf* (*THÉÂTRE: d'artiste*) dressing room; (: *de spectateurs*) box; (*de concierge, franc-maçon*) lodge

logement [lɔʒmɑ̃] *nm* accommodation *no pl* (*BRIT*), accommodations *pl* (*US*); flat (*BRIT*), apartment (*US*); housing *no pl*

loger [lɔʒe] *vt* to accommodate ♦ *vi* to live; **se** ~ **dans** (*suj: balle, flèche*) to lodge itself in; **trouver à se** ~ to find accommodation; **logeur, euse** *nm/f* landlord(lady)

logiciel [lɔʒisjɛl] *nm* software

logique [lɔʒik] *adj* logical ♦ *nf* logic

logis [lɔʒi] *nm* home; abode, dwelling

loi [lwa] *nf* law; **faire la** ~ to lay down the law

loin [lwɛ̃] *adv* far; (*dans le temps*) a long way off; a long time ago; **plus** ~ further; ~ **de** far from; **au** ~ far

off; **de** ~ from a distance; (*fig: de beaucoup*) by far; **il vient de** ~ he's come a long way

lointain, e [lwɛ̃tɛ̃, -ɛn] *adj* faraway, distant; (*dans le futur, passé*) distant, far-off; (*cause, parent*) remote, distant ♦ *nm*: **dans le** ~ in the distance

loir [lwaʀ] *nm* dormouse

loisir [lwaziʀ] *nm*: **heures de** ~ spare time; ~**s** *nmpl* leisure *sg*; leisure activities; **avoir le** ~ **de faire** to have the time *ou* opportunity to do; **à** ~ at leisure; at one's pleasure

londonien, ne [lɔ̃dɔnjɛ̃, -jɛn] *adj* London *cpd*, of London ♦ *nm/f*: **L~, ne** Londoner

Londres [lɔ̃dʀ(ə)] *n* London

long, longue [lɔ̃, lɔ̃g] *adj* long ♦ *adv*: **en savoir** ~ to know a great deal ♦ *nm*: **de 3 m de** ~ 3 m long, 3 m in length; **ne pas faire** ~ **feu** not to last long; (*tout*) **le** ~ **de** (*all*) along; **tout au** ~ **de** (*année, vie*) throughout; **de** ~ **en large** (*marcher*) to and fro, up and down; *voir aussi* **longue**

longer [lɔ̃ʒe] *vt* to go (*ou* walk *ou* drive) along(side); (*suj: mur, route*) to border

longiligne [lɔ̃ʒiliɲ] *adj* long-limbed

longitude [lɔ̃ʒityd] *nf* longitude

longitudinal, e, aux [lɔ̃ʒitydinal, -o] *adj* (*running*) lengthways

longtemps [lɔ̃tɑ̃] *adv* (*for*) a long time, (*for*) long; **avant** ~ before long; **pour** *ou* **pendant** ~ for a long time; **mettre** ~ **à faire** to take a long time to do

longue [lɔ̃g] *adj voir* **long** ♦ *nf*: **à la** ~ in the end; **longuement** *adv* for a long time

longueur [lɔ̃gœʀ] *nf* length; ~**s** *nfpl* (*fig: d'un film etc*) tedious parts; **en** ~ lengthwise; **tirer en** ~ to drag on; **à** ~ **de journée** all day long; ~ **d'onde** wavelength

longue-vue [lɔ̃gvy] *nf* telescope

lopin [lɔpɛ̃] *nm*: ~ **de terre** patch of land

loque [lɔk] nf (personne) wreck; ~s
nfpl (habits) rags

loquet [lɔkɛ] nm latch

lorgner [lɔʀɲe] vt to eye; (fig) to
have one's eye on

lors [lɔʀ] : ~ de prép at the time of;
during; ~ même que even though

lorsque [lɔʀsk(ə)] conj when, as

losange [lɔzɑ̃ʒ] nm diamond;
(GEOM) lozenge

lot [lo] nm (part) share; (de loterie)
prize; (fig: destin) fate, lot; (COMM,
INFORM) batch

loterie [lɔtʀi] nf lottery; raffle

loti, e [lɔti] adj: bien/mal ~ well-/
badly off

lotion [losjɔ̃] nf lotion

lotir [lɔtiʀ] vt (terrain) to divide into
plots; to sell by lots; **lotissement** nm
housing development; plot, lot

loto [lɔto] nm lotto; numerical lottery

louable [lwabl(ə)] adj commendable

louanges [lwɑ̃ʒ] nfpl praise sg

loubard [lubaʀ] (fam) nm lout

louche [luʃ] adj shady, fishy, dubious
♦ nf ladle

loucher [luʃe] vi to squint

louer [lwe] vt (maison: suj: propriétaire) to let, rent (out); (: locataire)
to rent; (voiture etc: entreprise) to
hire out (BRIT), rent (out); (: locataire) to hire, rent; (réserver) to
book; (faire l'éloge de) to praise; "à
~" "to let" (BRIT), "for rent" (US)

loup [lu] nm wolf

loupe [lup] nf magnifying glass

louper [lupe] vt (manquer) to miss

lourd, e [luʀ, luʀd(ə)] adj, adv heav-
y; ~ de (conséquences, menaces)
charged with; **lourdaud, e** (péj) adj
clumsy

loutre [lutʀ(ə)] nf otter

louveteau, x [luvto] nm wolf-cub;
(scout) cub (scout)

louvoyer [luvwaje] vi (NAVIG) to
tack; (fig) to hedge, evade the issue

lover [lɔve] : se ~ vi to coil up

loyal, e, aux [lwajal, -o] adj (fidèle)
loyal, faithful; (fair-play) fair;
loyauté nf loyalty, faithfulness; fair-

ness

loyer [lwaje] nm rent

lu, e [ly] pp de lire

lubie [lybi] nf whim, craze

lubrifiant [lybʀifjɑ̃] nm lubricant

lubrifier [lybʀifje] vt to lubricate

lubrique [lybʀik] adj lecherous

lucarne [lykaʀn(ə)] nf skylight

lucratif, ive [lykʀatif, -iv] adj lucrative; profitable; **à but non ~** non
profit-making

lueur [lɥœʀ] nf (chatoyante) glimmer
no pl; (métallique, mouillée) gleam
no pl; (rougeoyante, chaude) glow no
pl; (pâle) (faint) light; (fig) glimmer; gleam

luge [lyʒ] nf sledge (BRIT), sled
(US)

lugubre [lygybʀ(ə)] adj gloomy; dismal

MOT-CLÉ

lui [lɥi] pron 1 (objet indirect: mâle)
(to) him; (: femelle) (to) her; (:
chose, animal) (to) it; **je ~ ai parlé**
I have spoken to him (ou to her); **il
~ a offert un cadeau** he gave him
(ou her) a present
2 (après préposition, comparatif:
personne) him; (: chose, animal) it;
elle est contente de ~ she is
pleased with him; **je le connais
mieux que ~** I know him better than
he does; I know her better than him
3 (sujet, forme emphatique) he; ~,
il est à Paris HE is in Paris
4: **~-même** himself; itself

---

luire [lɥiʀ] vi to shine; to glow

lumière [lymjɛʀ] nf light; ~s nfpl
(d'une personne) wisdom sg; **mettre
en ~** (fig) to highlight; **~ du jour**
daylight

luminaire [lyminɛʀ] nm lamp, light

lumineux, euse [lyminø, -øz] adj
(émettant de la lumière) luminous;
(éclairé) illuminated; (ciel, couleur)
bright; (relatif à la lumière: rayon
etc) of light, light cpd; (fig: regard)
radiant

lunaire [lynɛʀ] *adj* lunar, moon *cpd*
lunatique [lynatik] *adj* whimsical, temperamental
lundi [lœdi] *nm* Monday; ~ de Pâques Easter Monday
lune [lyn] *nf* moon; ~ de miel honeymoon
lunette [lynɛt] *nf*: ~s *nfpl* glasses, spectacles; (*protectrices*) goggles; ~ arrière (*AUTO*) rear window; ~s de soleil sunglasses; ~s noires dark glasses
lus *etc vb voir* lire
lustre [lystʀ(ə)] *nm* (*de plafond*) chandelier; (*fig: éclat*) lustre
lustrer [lystʀe] *vt* to shine
lut *vb voir* lire
luth [lyt] *nm* lute
lutin [lytɛ̃] *nm* imp, goblin
lutte [lyt] *nf* (*conflit*) struggle; (*sport*) wrestling; **lutter** *vi* to fight, struggle
luxe [lyks(ə)] *nm* luxury; de ~ luxury *cpd*
Luxembourg [lyksãbuʀ] *nm*: le ~ Luxembourg
luxer [lykse] *vt*: se ~ l'épaule to dislocate one's shoulder
luxueux, euse [lyksyø, -øz] *adj* luxurious
luxure [lyksyʀ] *nf* lust
lycée [lise] *nm* secondary school; **lycéen, ne** *nm/f* secondary school pupil
lyrique [liʀik] *adj* lyrical; (*OPERA*) lyric; artiste ~ opera singer
lys [lis] *nm* lily

M

M *abr* = Monsieur
m' [m] *pron voir* me
ma [ma] *dét* mon
macaron [makaʀɔ̃] *nm* (*gâteau*) macaroon; (*insigne*) (round) badge
macaronis [makaʀɔni] *nmpl* macaroni *sg*
macédoine [masedwan] *nf*: ~ de fruits fruit salad; ~ de légumes *nf* mixed vegetables

macérer [maseʀe] *vi*, *vt* to macerate; (*dans du vinaigre*) to pickle
mâcher [maʃe] *vt* to chew; ne pas ~ ses mots not to mince one's words
machin [maʃɛ̃] (*fam*) *nm* thing(umajig)
machinal, e, aux [maʃinal, -o] *adj* mechanical, automatic
machination [maʃinasjɔ̃] *nf* scheming, frame-up
machine [maʃin] *nf* machine; (*locomotive*) engine; (*fig: rouages*) machinery; ~ à écrire typewriter; ~ à laver/coudre washing/sewing machine; ~ à sous fruit machine; ~ à vapeur steam engine; **machinerie** *nf* machinery, plant; (*d'un navire*) engine room; **machiniste** *nm* (*de bus, métro*) driver
mâchoire [maʃwaʀ] *nf* jaw; ~ de frein brake shoe
mâchonner [maʃɔne] *vt* to chew (at)
maçon [masɔ̃] *nm* bricklayer; builder; ~**nerie** [masɔnʀi] *nf* (*murs*) brickwork; masonry, stonework; (*activité*) bricklaying; building
maculer [makyle] *vt* to stain
Madame [madam] (*pl* **Mesdames**) *nf*: ~ X Mrs X; occupez-vous de ~/Monsieur/Mademoiselle please serve this lady/gentleman/(young) lady; bonjour ~/Monsieur/Mademoiselle good morning; (*ton déférent*) good morning Madam/Sir/Madam; (*le nom est connu*) good morning Mrs/Mr/Miss X; ~/Monsieur/Mademoiselle! (*pour appeler*) Madam/Sir/Miss!; ~/Monsieur/Mademoiselle (*sur lettre*) Dear Madam/Sir/Madam; chère ~/cher Monsieur/chère Mademoiselle Dear Mrs/Mr/Miss X; Mesdames Ladies
Mademoiselle [madmwazɛl] (*pl* **Mesdemoiselles**) *nf* Miss; *voir* Madame
madère [madɛʀ] *nm* Madeira (wine)
magasin [magazɛ̃] *nm* (*boutique*)

shop; (*entrepôt*) warehouse; (*d'une arme*) magazine; **en ~** (COMM) in stock

magazine [magazin] *nm* magazine

magicien, ne [maʒisjɛ̃, -jɛn] *nm/f* magician

magie [maʒi] *nf* magic; **magique** *adj* magic; (*enchanteur*) magical

magistral, e, aux [maʒistral, -o] *adj* (*œuvre*, *addresse*) masterly; (*ton*) authoritative; (*ex cathedra*) enseignement ~ lecturing, lectures *pl*

magistrat [maʒistra] *nm* magistrate

magnétique [maɲetik] *adj* magnetic

magnétiser [maɲetize] *vt* to magnetize; (*fig*) to mesmerize, hypnotize

magnétophone [maɲetɔfɔn] *nm* tape recorder; **~ à cassettes** cassette recorder

magnétoscope [maɲetɔskɔp] *nm* video-tape recorder

magnifique [maɲifik] *adj* magnificent

magot [mago] *nm* (*argent*) pile (of money); nest egg

magouille [maguj] *nf* scheming

mai [me] *nm* May

maigre [mɛgR(ə)] *adj* (very) thin, skinny; (*viande*) lean; (*fromage*) low-fat; (*végétation*) thin, sparse; (*fig*) poor, meagre, skimpy ♦ *adv*: **faire ~** not to eat meat; **jours ~s** days of abstinence, fish days; **maigreur** *nf* thinness; **maigrir** *vi* to get thinner, lose weight

maille [maj] *nf* stitch; **avoir ~ à partir avec qn** to have a brush with sb; **~ à l'endroit/à l'envers** plain/purl stitch

maillet [majɛ] *nm* mallet

maillon [majɔ̃] *nm* link

maillot [majo] *nm* (*aussi: ~ de corps*) vest; (*de danseur*) leotard; (*de sportif*) jersey; **~ de bain** swimsuit; (*d'homme*) bathing trunks *pl*

main [mɛ̃] *nf* hand; **à la ~** in one's hand; **se donner la ~** to hold hands; **donner** *ou* **tendre la ~ à qn** to hold

out one's hand to sb; **se serrer la ~** to shake hands; **serrer la ~ à qn** to shake sb's hand; **sous la ~** to *ou* at hand; **attaque à ~ armée** armed attack; **à ~ droite/gauche** to the right/left; **à remettre en ~s propres** to be delivered personally; **de première ~** (COMM: *voiture etc*) second-hand with only one previous owner; **mettre la dernière ~ à** to put the finishing touches to; **se faire/perdre la ~** to get one's hand in/lose one's touch; **avoir qch bien en ~** to have (got) the hang of sth

main-d'œuvre [mɛ̃dœvʀ(ə)] *nf* manpower, labour

main-forte [mɛ̃fɔʀt(ə)] *nf*: **prêter ~ à qn** to come to sb's assistance

mainmise [mɛ̃miz] *nf* seizure; (*fig*): **~ sur** complete hold on

maint, e [mɛ̃, mɛ̃t] *adj* many a; **~s** many; **à ~es reprises** time and (time) again

maintenant [mɛ̃tnɑ̃] *adv* now; (*actuellement*) nowadays

maintenir [mɛ̃tniʀ] *vt* (*retenir, soutenir*) to support; (*conserver: foule etc*) to hold back; (*conserver, affirmer*) to maintain; **se ~** *vi* to hold; to keep steady; to persist

maintien [mɛ̃tjɛ̃] *nm* maintaining; (*attitude*) bearing

maire [mɛʀ] *nm* mayor

mairie [meʀi] *nf* (*bâtiment*) town hall; (*administration*) town council

mais [mɛ] *conj* but; **~ non!** of course not!; **~ enfin** but after all; (*indignation*) look here!; **~ encore?** is that all?

maïs [mais] *nm* maize (BRIT), corn (US)

maison [mɛzɔ̃] *nf* house; (*chez-soi*) home; (COMM) firm ♦ *adj inv* (CULIN) home-made; made by the chef; (*fig*) in-house, own; **à la ~** at home; (*direction*) home; **~ close** *ou* **de passe** brothel; **~ de correction** reformatory; **~ de repos** convalescent home; **~ de santé** mental home; **~ des jeunes** youth club; **~ mère**

parent company; **maisonnée** *nf* household, family; **maisonnette** *nf* small house, cottage

maître, esse [metʀ(ə), metʀεs] *nm/f* master(mistress); (SCOL) teacher, schoolmaster(mistress) ♦ *nm* (peintre etc) master; (titre): M∼ Maître, term of address gen for a barrister ♦ *adj* (principal, essentiel) main; **être** ∼ **de** (soi-même, situation) to be in control of; **une** ∼**sse femme** a managing woman; ∼ **chanteur** blackmailer; ∼**/maîtresse d'école** schoolmaster(mistress); ∼ **d'hôtel** (domestique) butler; (d'hôtel) head waiter; ∼ **nageur** lifeguard; **maîtresse** *nf* (amante) mistress; ∼**sse de maison** hostess; housewife

maîtrise [metʀiz] *nf* (aussi: ∼ de soi) self-control, self-possession; (habileté) skill, mastery; (suprématie) mastery, command; (diplôme) ≈ master's degree

maîtriser [metʀize] *vt* (cheval, incendie) to (bring under) control; (sujet) to master; (émotion) to control, master; **se** ∼ to control o.s.

majestueux, euse [maʒεstɥø, -øz] *adj* majestic

majeur, e [maʒœʀ] *adj* (important) major; (JUR) of age; (fig) adult ♦ *nm* (doigt) middle finger; **en** ∼ **partie** for the most part

majorer [maʒɔʀe] *vt* to increase

majoritaire [maʒɔʀitεʀ] *adj* majority *cpd*

majorité [maʒɔʀite] *nf* (gén) majority; (parti) party in power; **en** ∼ mainly

majuscule [maʒyskyl] *adj, nf*: (lettre) ∼ capital (letter)

mal [mal, mo] (*pl* **maux**) *nm* (opposé au bien) evil; (tort, dommage) harm; (douleur physique) pain, ache; (maladie) illness, sickness no pl ♦ *adv* badly ♦ *adj inv* bad, wrong; **être** ∼ to be uncomfortable; **être** ∼ **avec qn** to be on bad terms with sb; **être au plus** ∼ (malade) to be at death's door; (brouillé) to be at daggers drawn; **il a** ∼ **compris** he misunderstood; **dire/penser du** ∼ **de** to speak/think ill of; **ne voir aucun** ∼ **à** to see no harm in, see nothing wrong in; **craignant** ∼ **faire** fearing he was doing the wrong thing; **faire du** ∼ **à qn** to hurt sb; to harm sb; **se faire** ∼ to hurt o.s.; **se donner du** ∼ **pour faire qch** to go to a lot of trouble to do sth; **ça fait** ∼ it hurts; **j'ai** ∼ **au dos** my back hurts; **avoir** ∼ **à la tête/à la gorge/aux dents** to have a headache/a sore throat/toothache; **avoir le** ∼ **du pays** to be homesick; **prendre** ∼ to be taken ill, feel unwell; *voir aussi* **cœur; maux;** ∼ **de mer** seasickness; ∼ **en point** *adj inv* in a bad state

malade [malad] *adj* ill, sick; (poitrine, jambe) bad; (plante) diseased ♦ *nm/f* invalid, sick person; (à l'hôpital etc) patient; **tomber** ∼ to fall ill; **être** ∼ **du cœur** to have heart trouble *ou* a bad heart; ∼ **mental** mentally sick *ou* ill person

maladie [maladi] *nf* (spécifique) disease, illness; (mauvaise santé) illness, sickness; ∼ **d'Alzheimer** Alzheimer's (disease); **maladif, ive** *adj* sickly; (curiosité, besoin) pathological

maladresse [maladʀεs] *nf* clumsiness no pl; (gaffe) blunder

maladroit, e [maladʀwa, -wat] *adj* clumsy

malaise [malεz] *nm* (MÉD) feeling of faintness; feeling of discomfort; (fig) uneasiness, malaise

malaisé, e [maleze] *adj* difficult

malaria [malaʀja] *nf* malaria

malaxer [malakse] *vt* to knead; to mix

malchance [malʃɑ̃s] *nf* misfortune, ill luck no pl; **par** ∼ unfortunately

mâle [mɑl] *adj* (aussi ELEC, TECH) male; (viril: voix, traits) manly ♦ *nm* male

malédiction [malediksjɔ̃] *nf* curse

mal: ~**encontreux, euse** adj unfortunate, untoward; ~**-en-point** adj inv in a sorry state; ~**entendu** nm misunderstanding; ~**façon** nf fault; ~**faisant, e** adj evil, harmful; ~**faiteur** nm lawbreaker, criminal; burglar, thief; ~**famé, e** adj disreputable

malgache [malgaʃ] adj, nm/f Madagascan, Malagasy ♦ nm (LING) Malagasy

malgré [malgre] prép in spite of, despite; ~ **tout** all the same

malheur [malœr] nm (situation) adversity, misfortune; (événement) misfortune; disaster, tragedy; **faire un** ~ to be a smash hit; **malheureusement** adv unfortunately; **malheureux, euse** adj (triste) unhappy, miserable; (infortuné, regrettable) unfortunate; (malchanceux) unlucky; (insignifiant) wretched ♦ nm/f poor soul; unfortunate creature; **les** ~**eux** the destitute

malhonnête [malɔnɛt] adj dishonesty

malice [malis] nf mischievousness; (méchanceté): **par** ~ out of malice ou spite; **sans** ~ guileless; **malicieux, euse** adj mischievous

malin, igne [malɛ̃, -iɲ] adj (futé: f gén: maline) smart, shrewd; (MED) malignant

malingre [malɛ̃gʁ(ə)] adj puny

malle [mal] nf trunk

mallette [malɛt] nf (small) suitcase; overnight case; attaché case

malmener [malməne] vt to manhandle; (fig) to give a rough handling to

malodorant, e [malɔdɔʁɑ̃, -ɑ̃t] adj foul- ou ill-smelling

malotru [malɔtʁy] nm lout, boor

malpropre [malpʁɔpʁ(ə)] adj dirty

malsain, e [malsɛ̃, -ɛn] adj unhealthy

malt [malt] nm malt

Malte [malt] nf Malta

maltraiter [maltʁɛte] vt (brutaliser) to manhandle, ill-treat

malveillance [malvɛjɑ̃s] nf (animosité) ill will; (intention de nuire)

malevolence; (JUR) malicious intent no pl

malversation [malvɛʁsasjɔ̃] nf embezzlement

maman [mamɑ̃] nf mum(my), mother

mamelle [mamɛl] nf teat

mamelon [mamlɔ̃] nm (ANAT) nipple; (colline) knoll, hillock

mamie [mami] (fam) nf granny

mammifère [mamifɛʁ] nm mammal

manche [mɑ̃ʃ] nf (de vêtement) sleeve; (d'un jeu, tournoi) round; (GÉO): **la M~** the Channel ♦ nm (d'outil, casserole) handle; (de pelle, pioche etc) shaft; ~ **à balai** broomstick; (AVIAT, INFORM) joystick

manchette [mɑ̃ʃɛt] nf (de chemise) cuff; (coup) forearm blow; (titre) headline

manchon [mɑ̃ʃɔ̃] nm (de fourrure) muff

manchot [mɑ̃ʃo] nm one-armed man; armless man; (ZOOL) penguin

mandarine [mɑ̃daʁin] nf mandarin (orange), tangerine

mandat [mɑ̃da] nm (postal) postal ou money order; (d'un député etc) mandate; (procuration) power of attorney, proxy; (POLICE) warrant; ~ **d'amener** summons sg; ~ **d'arrêt** warrant for arrest; **mandataire** nm/f representative, proxy

manège [manɛʒ] nm riding school; (à la foire) roundabout, merry-go-round; (fig) game, ploy

manette [manɛt] nf lever, tap; ~ **de jeu** joystick

mangeable [mɑ̃ʒabl(ə)] adj edible, eatable

mangeoire [mɑ̃ʒwaʁ] nf trough, manger

manger [mɑ̃ʒe] vt to eat; (ronger: suj: rouille etc) to eat into ou away ♦ vi to eat

mangue [mɑ̃g] nf mango

maniable [manjabl(ə)] adj (outil) handy; (voiture, voilier) easy to handle

maniaque [manjak] adj finicky, fussy; suffering from a mania ♦ nm/f maniac

manie [mani] nf mania; (tic) odd habit

manier [manje] vt to handle

manière [manjɛʀ] nf (façon) way, manner; ~s nfpl (attitude) manners; (chichis) fuss sg; de ~ à so as to; de telle ~ que in such a way that; de cette ~ in this way ou manner; d'une certaine ~ in a way; d'une ~ générale generally speaking, as a general rule; de toute ~ in any case

maniéré, e [manjeʀe] adj affected

manifestant, e [manifɛstɑ̃, -ɑ̃t] nm/f demonstrator

manifestation [manifɛstasjɔ̃] nf (de joie, mécontentement) expression, demonstration; (symptôme) outward sign; (fête etc) event; (POL) demonstration

manifeste [manifɛst(ə)] adj obvious, evident ♦ nm manifesto

manifester [manifɛste] vt (volonté, intentions) to show, indicate; (joie, peur) to express, show ♦ vi to demonstrate; se ~ vi (émotion) to show ou express itself; (difficultés) to arise; (symptômes) to appear; (témoin etc) to come forward

manigance [manigɑ̃s] nf scheme

manigancer [manigɑ̃se] vt to plot

manipuler [manipyle] vt to handle; (fig) to manipulate

manivelle [manivɛl] nf crank

mannequin [mankɛ̃] nm (COUTURE) dummy; (MODE) model

manœuvre [manœvʀ(ə)] nf (gén) manœuvre (BRIT), maneuver (US) ♦ nm labourer; ~r [manœvʀe] vt to manœuvre (BRIT), maneuver (US); (levier, machine) to operate ♦ vi to manœuvre

manoir [manwaʀ] nm manor ou country house

manque [mɑ̃k] nm (insuffisance): ~ de lack of; (vide) emptiness, gap; (MED) withdrawal; ~s nmpl (lacunes) faults, defects

manqué, e [mɑ̃ke] adj failed; garçon ~ tomboy

manquer [mɑ̃ke] vi (faire défaut) to be lacking; (être absent) to be missing; (échouer) to fail ♦ vt to miss ♦ vb impers: il (nous) manque encore 100 F we are still 100 F short; il manque des pages (au livre) there are some pages missing (from the book); il/cela me manque I miss him/this; ~ à (règles etc) to be in breach of, fail to observe; ~ de to lack; il a manqué (de) se tuer he very nearly got killed

mansarde [mɑ̃saʀd(ə)] nf attic

mansuétude [mɑ̃sɥetyd] nf leniency

manteau, x [mɑ̃to] nm coat

manucure [manykyʀ] nf manicurist

manuel, le [manɥɛl] adj manual ♦ nm (ouvrage) manual, handbook

manufacture [manyfaktyʀ] nf factory; **manufacturé, e** [manyfaktyʀe] adj manufactured

manuscrit, e [manyskʀi, -it] adj handwritten ♦ nm manuscript

manutention [manytɑ̃sjɔ̃] nf (COMM) handling; (local) storehouse

mappemonde [mapmɔ̃d] nf (plane) map of the world; (sphère) globe

maquereau, x [makʀo] nm (ZOOL) mackerel inv; (fam) pimp

maquette [makɛt] nf (d'un décor, bâtiment, véhicule) (scale) model; (d'une page illustrée) paste-up

maquillage [makijaʒ] nm making up; faking; (crème etc) make-up

maquiller [makije] vt (personne, visage) to make up; (truquer: passeport, statistique) to fake; (: voiture volée) to do over (respray etc); se ~ vi to make up (one's face)

maquis [maki] nm (GEO) scrub; (MIL) maquis, underground fighting no pl

maraîcher, ère [maʀɛʃe, maʀɛʃɛʀ] adj: cultures maraîchères market gardening sg ♦ nm/f market gardener

marais [maʀɛ] nm marsh, swamp

marasme [maʀasm(ə)] nm stagnation

tion, slump

marathon [maʀatɔ̃] nm marathon

marâtre [maʀɑtʀ(ə)] nf cruel mother

maraudeur [maʀodœʀ] nm prowler

marbre [maʀbʀ(ə)] nm (pierre, statue) marble; (d'une table, commode) marble top; **marbrer** vt to mottle, blotch

marc [maʀ] nm (de raisin, pommes) marc; ~ **de café** coffee grounds pl ou dregs pl

marchand, e [maʀʃɑ̃, -ɑ̃d] nm/f shopkeeper, tradesman(woman); (au marché) stallholder ♦ adj: prix/valeur ~(e) market price/value; ~e de fruits fruiterer (BRIT), fruit seller (US); ~e de journaux newsagent; ~e de légumes greengrocer (BRIT), produce dealer (US); ~e de quatre saisons costermonger (BRIT), street vendor (selling fresh fruit and vegetables) (US)

marchander [maʀʃɑ̃de] vi to bargain, haggle

marchandise [maʀʃɑ̃diz] nf goods pl, merchandise no pl

marche [maʀʃ(ə)] nf (d'escalier) step; (activité) walking; (promenade, trajet, allure) walk; (démarche) walk, gait; (MIL etc, MUS) march; (fonctionnement) running; (progression) progress; course; ouvrir/fermer la ~ to lead the way/bring up the rear; dans le sens de la ~ (RAIL) facing the engine; en ~ (monter etc) while the vehicle is moving ou in motion; mettre en ~ to start; se mettre en ~ (personne) to get moving; (machine) to start; ~ à suivre (correct) procedure; (sur notice) (step by step) instructions pl; ~ arrière reverse (gear); faire ~ arrière to reverse; (fig) to backtrack, back-pedal

marché [maʀʃe] nm (lieu, COMM, ÉCON) market; (ville) trading centre; (transaction) bargain, deal; faire du ~ noir to buy and sell on the black market; ~ aux puces flea market; **M~ commun** Common

Market

marchepied [maʀʃəpje] nm (RAIL) step; (fig) stepping stone

marcher [maʀʃe] vi to walk; (MIL) to march; (aller: voiture, train, affaires) to go; (prospérer) to go well; (fonctionner) to work, run; (fam) to go along, agree; to be taken in; ~ sur to walk on; (mettre le pied sur) to step on ou in; (MIL) to march upon; ~ dans (herbe etc) to walk in ou on; (flaque) to step in; faire ~ qn to pull sb's leg; to lead sb up the garden path; **marcheur, euse** nm/f walker

mardi [maʀdi] nm Tuesday; **M~ gras** Shrove Tuesday

mare [maʀ] nf pond

marécage [maʀekaʒ] nm marsh, swamp

maréchal, aux [maʀeʃal, -o] nm marshal

marée [maʀe] nf tide; (poissons) fresh (sea) fish; ~ **haute/basse** high/low tide; ~ **montante/descendante** rising/ebb tide

marémotrice [maʀemɔtʀis] adj f tidal

margarine [maʀgaʀin] nf margarine

marge [maʀʒ(ə)] nf margin; **en** ~ **de** (fig) on the fringe of; cut off from; ~ **bénéficiaire** profit margin

marguerite [maʀgəʀit] nf marguerite, (oxeye) daisy; (d'imprimante) daisy-wheel

mari [maʀi] nm husband

mariage [maʀjaʒ] nm (union, état, fig) marriage; (noce) wedding; ~ **civil/religieux** registry office (BRIT) ou civil/church wedding

marié, e [maʀje] adj married ♦ nm (bride)groom; **les** ~**s** the bride and groom; **les (jeunes)** ~**s** the newly-weds; **mariée** nf bride

marier [maʀje] vt to marry; (fig) to blend; **se** ~ **(avec)** to marry

marin, e [maʀɛ̃, -in] adj sea cpd; **marine** ♦ nm sailor

marine [maʀin] adj voir marin ♦ adj inv navy (blue) ♦ nm (MIL) marine ♦ nf navy; ~ de guerre navy; ~ **marchande** merchant navy

marionnette [maʀjɔnɛt] nf puppet

maritime [maʀitim] adj sea cpd; maritime

mark [maʀk] nm mark

marmelade [maʀməlad] nf stewed fruit, compote; ~ **d'oranges** marmalade

marmite [maʀmit] nf (cooking-)pot

marmonner [maʀmɔne] vt, vi to mumble, mutter

marmotter [maʀmɔte] vt to mumble

Maroc [maʀɔk] nm: le ~ Morocco; **marocain, e** adj, nm/f Moroccan

maroquinerie [maʀɔkinʀi] nf leather craft; fine leather goods pl

marquant, e [maʀkɑ̃, -ɑ̃t] adj outstanding

marque [maʀk(ə)] nf mark; (SPORT, JEU: décompte des points) score; (COMM: de produits) brand; make; (de disques) label; de ~ (COMM) brand-name cpd; propriétary; (fig) high-class; distinguished; ~ **de fabrique** trademark; ~ **déposée** registered trademark

marquer [maʀke] vt to mark; (inscrire) to write down; (bétail) to brand; (SPORT: but etc) to score; (: joueur) to mark; (accentuer: taille etc) to emphasize; (manifester: refus, intérêt) to show ♦ vi (événement, personnalité) to stand out, be outstanding; (SPORT) to score; ~ **les points** (tenir la marque) to keep the score

marqueterie [maʀkətʀi] nf inlaid work, marquetry

marquis [maʀki] nm marquis ou marquess

marquise [maʀkiz] nf marchioness; (auvent) glass canopy ou awning

marraine [maʀɛn] nf godmother

marrant, e [maʀɑ̃, -ɑ̃t] (fam) adj funny

marre [maʀ] (fam) adv: en avoir ~ de to be fed up with

marrer [maʀe]: se ~ (fam) vi to have a (good) laugh

marron [maʀɔ̃] nm (fruit) chestnut ♦ adj inv brown; **marronnier** nm chestnut (tree)

mars [maʀs] nm March

marsouin [maʀswɛ̃] nm porpoise

marteau, x [maʀto] nm hammer; (de porte) knocker; **marteau-piqueur** nm pneumatic drill

marteler [maʀtəle] vt to hammer

martien, ne [maʀsjɛ̃, -jɛn] adj Martian, of ou from Mars

martinet [maʀtinɛ] nm (fouet) small whip; (ZOOL) swift

martyr, e [maʀtiʀ] nm/f martyr

martyre [maʀtiʀ] nm martyrdom; (fig: sens affaibli) agony, torture

martyriser [maʀtiʀize] vt (REL) to martyr; (fig) to bully; (enfant) to batter, beat

marxiste [maʀksist(ə)] adj, nm/f Marxist

masculin, e [maskylɛ̃, -in] adj masculine; (sexe, population) male; (équipe, vêtements) men's; (viril) manly ♦ nm masculine

masque [mask(ə)] nm mask; ~r [maske] vt (cacher: paysage, porte) to hide, conceal; (dissimuler: vérité, projet) to mask, obscure

massacre [masakʀ(ə)] nm massacre, slaughter; ~r [masakʀe] vt to massacre, slaughter; (fig: texte etc) to murder

massage [masaʒ] nm massage

masse [mas] nf mass; (péj): la ~ the masses pl; (ELEC) earth; (maillet) sledgehammer; une ~ de (fam) masses ou loads of; en ~ (adv: en bloc) in bulk; (: en foule) en masse ♦ adj (exécutions, production) mass cpd

masser [mase] vt (assembler) to gather; (pétrir) to massage; se ~ vi to gather; **masseur, euse** nm/f masseur(euse)

massif, ive [masif, -iv] adj (porte) solid, massive; (visage) heavy, large; (bois, or) solid; (dose) massive; (déportations etc) mass cpd ♦ nm (montagneux) massif; (de fleurs) clump, bank

massue [masy] *nf* club, bludgeon

mastic [mastik] *nm* (*pour vitres*) putty; (*pour fentes*) filler

mastiquer [mastike] *vt* (*aliment*) to chew, masticate; (*fente*) to fill; (*vitre*) to putty

mat, e [mat] *adj* (*couleur, métal*) mat(t); (*bruit, son*) dull ♦ *adj inv* (*ÉCHECS*): **être ~** to be checkmate

mât [mɑ] *nm* (*NAVIG*) mast; (*poteau*) pole, post

match [matʃ] *nm* match; **faire ~ nul** to draw; **~ aller** first leg; **~ retour** second leg, return match

matelas [matla] *nm* mattress; **~ pneumatique** air bed *ou* mattress

matelassé, e [matlase] *adj* padded; quilted

matelot [matlo] *nm* sailor, seaman

mater [mate] *vt* (*personne*) to bring to heel, subdue; (*révolte*) to put down

matérialiste [materjalist(ə)] *adj* materialistic

matériaux [materjo] *nmpl* material(s)

matériel, le [materjɛl] *adj* material ♦ *nm* equipment *no pl*; (*de camping etc*) gear *no pl*

maternel, le [matɛrnɛl] *adj* (*amour, geste*) motherly, maternal; (*grand-père, oncle*) maternal; **maternelle** *nf* (*aussi*: *école maternelle*) (state) nursery school

maternité [matɛrnite] *nf* (*établissement*) maternity hospital; (*état de mère*) motherhood, maternity; (*grossesse*) pregnancy

mathématique [matematik] *adj* mathematical; **mathématiques** *nfpl* (*science*) mathematics *sg*

matière [matjɛr] *nf* (*PHYSIQUE*) matter; (*COMM, TECH*) material, matter *no pl*; (*fig*: *d'un livre etc*) subject matter, material; (*SCOL*) subject; **en ~ de** as regards; **~s grasses** fat content *sg*; **~s premières** raw materials

matin [matɛ̃] *nm, adv* morning; **du ~ au soir** from morning till night;

de bon *ou* **grand ~** early in the morning; **matinal, e, aux** *adj* (*toilette, gymnastique*) morning *cpd*; (*de bonne heure*) early; **être matinal** (*personne*) to be up early; to be an early riser

matinée [matine] *nf* morning; (*spectacle*) matinée

matou [matu] *nm* tom(cat)

matraque [matrak] *nf* club; (*de policier*) truncheon (*BRIT*), billy (*US*)

matricule [matrikyl] *nf* roll, register ♦ *nm* (: *numéro ~*: *MIL*) regimental number; (: *ADMIN*) reference number

matrimonial, e, aux [matrimɔnjal, -o] *adj* marital, marriage *cpd*

maudire [modir] *vt* to curse

maudit, e [modi, -it] (*fam*) *adj* (*satané*) blasted, confounded

maugréer [mogree] *vi* to grumble

maussade [mosad] *adj* sullen

mauvais, e [mɔvɛ, -ɛz] *adj* bad; (*faux*): **le ~ numéro/moment** the wrong number/moment; (*méchant, malveillant*) malicious, spiteful; **il fait ~** the weather is bad; **la mer est ~e** the sea is rough; **~ plaisant** hoaxer; **~e herbe** weed; **~e langue** gossip, scandalmonger (*BRIT*); **~e passe** difficult situation; bad patch; **~e tête** rebellious *ou* headstrong customer

maux [mo] *nmpl de* **mal**; **~ de ventre** stomachache *sg*

maximum [maksimɔm] *adj, nm* maximum; **au ~** (*le plus possible*) to the full; as much as one can; (*tout au plus*) at the (very) most *ou* maximum

mayonnaise [majɔnɛz] *nf* mayonnaise

mazout [mazut] *nm* (fuel) oil

me(m') [m(ə)] *pron* me; (*réfléchi*) myself

Me *abr* = **Maître**

mec [mɛk] (*fam*) *nm* bloke, guy

mécanicien, ne [mekanisjɛ̃, -jɛn] *nm/f* mechanic; (*RAIL*) (train *ou* engine) driver

mécanique [mekanik] adj mechanical ♦ nf (science) mechanics sg; (technologie) mechanical engineering; (mécanisme) mechanism; engineering; works pl; ennui ~ engine trouble no pl

mécanisme [mekanism(ə)] nm mechanism

méchamment [meʃamɑ̃] adv nastily, maliciously, spitefully

méchanceté [meʃɑ̃ste] nf nastiness, maliciousness; nasty ou spiteful ou malicious remark (ou action)

méchant, e [meʃɑ̃, -ɑ̃t] adj nasty, malicious, spiteful; (enfant: pas sage) naughty; (animal) vicious; (avant le nom: valeur péjorative) nasty; miserable; (: intensive) terrific

mèche [meʃ] nf (de lampe, bougie) wick; (d'un explosif) fuse; (de vilebrequin, perceuse) bit; (de cheveux) lock; de ~ avec in league with

mécompte [mekɔ̃t] nm miscalculation; (déception) disappointment

méconnaissable [mekɔnɛsabl(ə)] adj unrecognizable

méconnaître [mekɔnɛtʀ(ə)] vt (ignorer) to be unaware of; (mésestimer) to misjudge

mécontent, e [mekɔ̃tɑ̃, -ɑ̃t] adj: ~ (de) discontented ou dissatisfied ou displeased (with); (contrarié) annoyed (at); **mécontentement** nm dissatisfaction, discontent, displeasure; annoyance

médaille [medaj] nf medal

médaillon [medajɔ̃] nm (portrait) medallion; (bijou) locket

médecin [mɛdsɛ̃] nm doctor; ~ légiste forensic surgeon

médecine [mɛdsin] nf medicine; ~ légale forensic medicine

média [medja] nmpl: les ~ the media

médiatique [medjatik] adj media cpd

médical, e, aux [medikal, -o] adj medical

médicament [medikamɑ̃] nm medi-

cine, drug

médiéval, e, aux [medjeval, -o] adj medieval

médiocre [medjɔkʀ(ə)] adj mediocre, poor

médire [mediʀ] vi: ~ de to speak ill of; **médisance** nf scandalmongering (BRIT); piece of scandal ou of malicious gossip

méditer [medite] vt (approfondir) to meditate on, ponder (over); (combiner) to meditate ♦ vi to meditate

Méditerranée [mediteʀane] nf: la (mer) ~ the Mediterranean (Sea); **méditerranéen, ne** adj, nm/f Mediterranean

méduse [medyz] nf jellyfish

meeting [mitiŋ] nm (POL, SPORT) rally

méfait [mefɛ] nm (faute) misdemeanour, wrongdoing; ~s nmpl (ravages) ravages, damage sg

méfiance [mefjɑ̃s] nf mistrust, distrust; **méfiant, e** [mefjɑ̃, -ɑ̃t] adj mistrustful, distrustful

méfier [mefje]: se ~ vi to be wary; to be careful; se ~ de to mistrust, distrust, be wary of; (faire attention) to be careful about

mégarde [megaʀd(ə)] nf: par ~ accidentally; by mistake

mégère [meʒɛʀ] nf shrew

mégot [mego] nm cigarette end

meilleur, e [mɛjœʀ] adj, adv better; (valeur superlative) best ♦ nm: le ~ (celui qui ...) the best (one); (ce qui ...) the best; le ~ des deux the better of the two; de ~e heure earlier; ~ marché cheaper; **meilleure** nf: la meilleure the best (one)

mélancolie [melɑ̃kɔli] nf melancholy, gloom; **mélancolique** adj melancholic, melancholy

mélange [melɑ̃ʒ] nm mixture

mélanger [melɑ̃ʒe] vt (substances) to mix; (vins, couleurs) to blend; (mettre en désordre) to mix up, muddle (up)

mélasse [melas] nf treacle, molasses sg

mêlée [mele] *nf* mêlée, scramble; (RUGBY) scrum(mage)

mêler [mele] *vt* (*substances, odeurs, races*) to mix; (*embrouiller*) to muddle (up), mix up; **se ~** *vi* to mix; to mingle; **se ~ à** (*suj: personne*) to join; to mix with; (*suj: odeurs etc*) to mingle with; **se ~ de** (: *personne*) to meddle with, interfere in; **~ qn à** (*affaire*) to get sb mixed up *ou* involved in

mélodie [melɔdi] *nf* melody

melon [m(ə)lɔ̃] *nm* (BOT) (honeydew) melon; (*aussi*: **chapeau ~**) bowler (hat)

membre [mɑ̃bʀ(ə)] *nm* (ANAT) limb; (*personne, pays, élément*) member ♦ *adj* member *cpd*

mémé [meme] *nf* (*fam*) granny

MOT-CLÉ

---

même [mɛm] *adj* **1** (*avant le nom*) same; **en ~ temps** at the same time **2** (*après le nom: renforcement*) il est la loyauté ~; he is loyalty itself; ce sont ses paroles/celles-là ~ they are his very words/the very ones

♦ *pron*: **le(la) ~** the same one

♦ *adv* **1** (*renforcement*): il n'a ~ pas pleuré he didn't even cry; ~ lui l'a dit even HE said it; ici ~ at this very place

2: **à ~**: **à ~ la bouteille** straight from the bottle; **à ~ la peau** next to the skin; **être à ~ de faire** to be in a position to do, be able to do

3: **de ~** to do likewise; **lui de ~** so does (*ou* did *ou* is) he; **~ que** just as; **il en va de ~ pour** the same goes for

---

mémento [memɛ̃to] *nm* (*agenda*) appointments diary; (*ouvrage*) summary

mémoire [memwaʀ] *nf* memory ♦ *nm* (ADMIN, JUR) memorandum; (SCOL) dissertation, paper; **~s** *nmpl* (*souvenirs*) memoirs; **à la ~ de** to the *ou* in memory of; **pour ~** for the

record; **de ~** from memory; **~ morte/vive** (INFORM) ROM/RAM

menace [mənas] *nf* threat

menacer [mənase] *vt* to threaten

ménage [menaʒ] *nm* (*travail*) housekeeping, housework; (*couple*) (married) couple; (*famille, ADMIN*) household; **faire le ~** to do the housework

ménagement [menaʒmɑ̃] *nm* care and attention; **~s** *nmpl* (*égards*) consideration *sg*, attention *sg*

ménager, ère [menaʒe, -ɛʀ] *vt* household *cpd*, domestic ♦ *vt* (*traiter*) to handle with tact; to treat considerately; (*utiliser*) to use sparingly; to use with care; (*prendre soin de*) to take (great) care of, look after; (*organiser*) to arrange; (*installer*) to put in; to make; **~ qch à qn** (*réserver*) to have sth in store for sb; **ménagère** *nf* housewife

mendiant, e [mɑ̃djɑ̃, ɑ̃t] *nm/f* beggar; **mendier** [mɑ̃dje] *vi* to beg ♦ *vt* to beg (for)

mener [məne] *vt* to lead; (*enquête*) to conduct; (*affaires*) to manage ♦ *vi*: (**à la marque**) to lead, be in the lead; **~ à/dans** (*emmener*) to take to/into; **~ qch à terme** *ou* **à bien** to see sth through (to a successful conclusion), complete sth successfully

meneur, euse [mənœʀ, -øz] *nm/f* leader; (*péj*) agitator; **~ de jeu** host, quizmaster

méningite [menɛ̃ʒit] *nf* meningitis *no pl*

ménopause [menɔpoz] *nf* menopause

menottes [mənɔt] *nfpl* handcuffs

mensonge [mɑ̃sɔ̃ʒ] *nm* lie; lying *no pl*; **mensonger, ère** *adj* false

mensualité [mɑ̃sɥalite] *nf* monthly payment; monthly salary

mensuel, le [mɑ̃sɥɛl] *adj* monthly

mensurations [mɑ̃syʀasjɔ̃] *nfpl* measurements

mentalité [mɑ̃talite] *nf* mentality

menteur, euse [mɑ̃tœʀ, -øz] *adj* lying

liar

menthe [mɑ̃t] nf mint

mention [mɑ̃sjɔ̃] nf (note) note, comment; (SCOL): ~ **bien** etc ≈ grade B etc (ou upper 2nd class etc) pass (BRIT), ≈ pass with (high) honors (US); **mentionner** vt to mention

mentir [mɑ̃tir] vi to lie; to be lying

menton [mɑ̃tɔ̃] nm chin

menu, e [məny] adj slim, slight; tiny; (frais, difficulté) minor ♦ adv (couper, hacher) very fine ♦ nm menu; par le ~ (raconter) in minute detail; ~e **monnaie** small change

menuiserie [mənɥizri] nf (travail) joinery, carpentry; woodwork; (local) joiner's workshop; (ouvrage) woodwork no pl; **menuisier** [mənɥizje] nm joiner, carpenter

méprendre [meprɑ̃dr(ə)]: se ~ vi to be mistaken (about)

mépris [mepri] nm (dédain) contempt, scorn; (indifférence): le ~ de contempt ou disregard for; au ~ de regardless of, in defiance of

méprisable [meprizabl(ə)] adj contemptible, despicable

méprise [mepriz] nf mistake, error; misunderstanding

mépriser [meprize] vt to scorn, despise; (gloire, danger) to scorn, spurn

mer [mɛr] nf sea; (marée) tide; en ~ at sea; prendre la ~ to put out to sea; en **haute** ou **pleine** ~ off shore, on the open sea; la ~ **du Nord/Rouge** the North/Red Sea

mercantile [mɛrkɑ̃til] adj (péj) mercenary

mercenaire [mɛrsənɛr] nm mercenary, hired soldier

mercerie [mɛrsəri] nf haberdashery (BRIT), notions (US); haberdasher's shop (BRIT), notions store (US)

merci [mɛrsi] excl thank you ♦ nf: à la ~ de qn/qch at sb's mercy/the mercy of sth; ~ **de** thank you for; **sans** ~ merciless(ly)

mercredi [mɛrkrədi] nm Wednesday

mercure [mɛrkyr] nm mercury

merde [mɛrd(ə)] (fam!) nf shit (!)

♦ excl (bloody) hell (!)

mère [mɛr] nf mother; ~ **célibataire** unmarried mother

méridional, e, aux [meridjɔnal, -o] adj southern ♦ nm/f Southerner

meringue [mərɛ̃g] nf meringue

mérite [merit] nm merit; le ~ **de** (ceci) lui **revient** the credit (for this) is his

mériter [merite] vt to deserve

merlan [mɛrlɑ̃] nm whiting

merle [mɛrl(ə)] nm blackbird

merveille [mɛrvɛj] nf marvel, wonder; **faire** ~ to work wonders; à ~ perfectly, wonderfully

merveilleux, euse [mɛrvɛjø, -øz] adj marvellous, wonderful

mes [me] dét voir **mon**

mésange [mezɑ̃ʒ] nf tit(mouse)

mésaventure [mezavɑ̃tyr] nf misadventure, misfortune

Mesdames [medam] nfpl de **Madame**

Mesdemoiselles [medmwazɛl] nfpl de **Mademoiselle**

mésentente [mezɑ̃tɑ̃t] nf dissension, disagreement

mesquin, e [mɛskɛ̃, -in] adj mean, petty

message [mesaʒ] nm message; **messager, ère** [mesaʒe, ɛr] nm/f messenger

messe [mɛs] nf mass; **aller à la** ~ to go to mass; ~ **de minuit** midnight mass

Messieurs [mesjø] nmpl de **Monsieur**

mesure [məzyr] nf (évaluation, dimension) measurement; (étalon, récipient, contenu) measure; (MUS: cadence) time, tempo; (: division) bar; (retenue) moderation; (disposition) measure, step; **sur** ~ (costume) made-to-measure; à la ~ **de** (fig) worthy of; on the same scale as; **dans la** ~ **où** insofar as, inasmuch as; à ~ **que** as; **être en** ~ **de** to be in a position to

mesurer [məzyre] vt to measure; (juger) to weigh up, assess; (limiter) to limit, ration; (modérer) to moderate; se ~ avec to have a confrontation with; to tackle; **il mesure 1 m 80** he's 1 m 80 tall

met vb voir **mettre**

métal, aux [metal, -o] nm metal; **métallique** adj metallic

météo [meteo] nf weather report; ≈ Met Office (BRIT), ≈ National Weather Service (US)

météorologie [meteɔrɔlɔʒi] nf meteorology

méthode [metɔd] nf method; (livre, ouvrage) manual, tutor

métier [metje] nm (profession: gén) job; (: manuel) trade; (: artisanal) craft; (technique, expérience) (acquired) skill ou technique; (aussi: ~ à tisser) (weaving) loom

métis, se [metis] adj, nm/f half-caste, half-breed

métisser [metise] vt to cross

métrage [metraʒ] nm (de tissu) length, ≈ yardage; (CINEMA) footage, length; **long/moyen/court ~** full-length/medium/short film

mètre [mɛtr(ə)] nm metre; (règle) (metre) rule; (ruban) tape measure; **métrique** adj metric

métro [metro] nm underground (BRIT), subway

métropole [metrɔpɔl] nf (capitale) metropolis; (pays) home country

mets [mɛ] nm dish

metteur [metœr] nm: ~ **en scène** (THEATRE) producer; (CINEMA) director; ~ **en ondes** producer

MOT-CLÉ

mettre [mɛtr(ə)] vt 1 (placer) to put; ~ **en bouteille/en sac** to bottle/put in bags ou sacks

2 (vêtements: revêtir) to put on; (: porter) to wear; **mets ton gilet** put your cardigan on; **je ne mets plus mon manteau** I no longer wear my coat

3 (faire fonctionner: chauffage, électricité) to put on; (: réveil, minuteur) to set; (installer: gaz, eau) to put in, to lay on; ~ **en marche** to

start up

4 (consacrer): ~ **du temps à faire qch** to take time to do sth ou over sth

5 (noter, écrire) to say, put (down); **qu'est-ce qu'il a mis sur la carte?** what did he say ou write on the card?; **mettez au pluriel** ... put ... into the plural

6 (supposer): **mettons que** ... let's say ou say that ...

7: **y ~ du sien** to pull one's weight

se ~ vi 1 (se placer): **vous pouvez vous ~ là** you can sit (ou stand) there; **où ça se met?** where does it go?; se ~ **au lit** to get into bed; se ~ **au piano** to sit down at the piano; se ~ **de l'encre sur les doigts** to get ink on one's fingers

2 (s'habiller): se ~ **en maillot de bain** to get into ou put on a swimsuit; **n'avoir rien à se ~** to have nothing to wear

3: se ~ **à** to begin, start; se ~ **à faire** to begin ou start doing ou to do; se ~ **au piano** to start learning the piano; se ~ **au travail/à l'étude** to get down to work/one's studies

meuble [mœbl(ə)] nm piece of furniture; furniture no pl ♦ adj (terre) loose, friable; **meublé** nm furnished flatlet (BRIT) ou room; **meubler** vt to furnish; (fig) meubler qch (de) to fill sth (with)

meugler [møgle] vi to low, moo

meule [møl] nf (à broyer) millstone; (à aiguiser) grindstone; (de foin, blé) stack; (de fromage) round

meunier [mønje] nm miller; **meunière** nf miller's wife

meure etc vb voir **mourir**

meurtre [mœrtr(ə)] nm murder; **meurtrier, ière** adj (arme etc) deadly; (fureur, instincts) murderous ♦ nm/f murderer(eress); **meurtrière** nf (ouverture) loophole

meurtrir [mœrtrir] vt to bruise; (fig) to wound; **meurtrissure** nf bruise; (fig) scar

meus *etc vb voir* **mouvoir**

meute [møt] *nf* pack

Mexico [mɛksiko] *n* Mexico City

Mexique [mɛksik] *nm*: le ~ Mexico

Mgr *abr* = **Monseigneur**

mi [mi] *nm* (MUS) E; (*en chantant la gamme*) mi ♦ *préfixe*: ~... half(-); mid-; à la ~-**janvier** in mid-January; à ~-**jambes/corps** (up *ou* down) to the knees/waist; à ~-**hauteur/pente** halfway up *ou* down/up *ou* down the hill

miauler [mjole] *vi* to miaow

miche [miʃ] *nf* round *ou* cob loaf

mi-chemin [miʃmɛ̃] : à ~ *adv* half-way, midway

mi-clos, e [miklo, -kloz] *adj* half-closed

micro [mikro] *nm* mike, microphone; (INFORM) micro

microbe [mikrob] *nm* germ, microbe

micro: ~-**onde** *nf*: four à ~s micro-wave oven; ~-**ordinateur** *nm* micro-computer; ~**scope** *nm* microscope

midi [midi] *nm* midday, noon; (*moment du déjeuner*) lunchtime; (*sud*) south; à ~ at 12 (o'clock) *ou* midday *ou* noon; en plein ~ (right) in the middle of the day; facing south; le M~ the South (of France), the Midi

mie [mi] *nf* crumb (of the loaf)

miel [mjɛl] *nm* honey

mien, ne [mjɛ̃, mjɛn] *pron*: le(la ~(ne), les ~(ne)s; les ~s my family

miette [mjɛt] *nf* (*de pain, gâteau*) crumb; (*fig: de la conversation etc*) scrap; en ~s in pieces *ou* bits

---

MOT-CLÉ

mieux [mjø] *adv* **1** (*d'une meilleure façon*): ~ (**que**) better (than); elle travaille/mange ~ she works/eats better; elle va ~ she is better

2 (*de la meilleure façon*) best; ce que je sais le ~ what I know best; les livres les ~ faits the best made books

3: de ~ en ~ better and better

♦ *adj* **1** (*plus à l'aise, en meilleure*

forme) better; se sentir ~ to feel better

2 (*plus satisfaisant*) better; c'est ~ ainsi it's better like this; c'est le ~ des deux it's the better of the two; le(la) ~, les ~ the best; demandez-lui, c'est le ~ ask him, it's the best thing

3 (*plus joli*) better-looking

4: au ~ at best; au ~ avec on the best of terms with; pour le ~ for the best

♦ *nm* **1** (*progrès*) improvement

2: de mon/ton ~ as best I/you can (*ou* could); faire de son ~ to do one's best

---

mièvre [mjɛvʀ(ə)] *adj* mawkish (BRIT), sickly sentimental

mignon, ne [miɲɔ̃, -ɔn] *adj* sweet, cute

migraine [migʀɛn] *nf* headache; migraine

mijoter [miʒɔte] *vt* to simmer; (*préparer avec soin*) to cook lovingly; (*affaire, projet*) to plot, cook up ♦ *vi* to simmer

mil [mil] *num* = **mille**

milieu, x [miljø] *nm* (*centre*) middle; (*fig*) middle course *ou* way; happy medium; (BIO, GEO) environment; (*entourage social*) milieu; background; circle; (*pègre*): le ~ the underworld; au ~ de in the middle of; au beau *ou* en plein ~ (de) right in the middle (of)

militaire [militɛʀ] *adj* military, army *cpd* ♦ *nm* serviceman

militant, e [militɑ̃, -ɑ̃t] *adj, nm/f* militant

militer [milite] *vi* to be a militant; ~ pour/contre (*suj: faits, raisons etc*) to militate in favour of/against

mille [mil] *num* a *ou* one thousand ♦ *nm* (*mesure*): ~ (**marin**) nautical mile; mettre dans le ~ to hit the bull's-eye; to be bang on target; **mil-lefeuille** *nm* cream *ou* vanilla slice; **millénaire** *nm* millennium ♦ *adj* thousand-year-old; (*fig*) ancient;

mille-pattes *nm inv* centipede
millésime [milezim] *nm* year; **millésimé, e** *adj* vintage *cpd*
millet [mijɛ] *nm* millet
milliard [miljaʀ] *nm* milliard, thousand million (BRIT), billion (US); **milliardaire** *nm/f* multimillionaire (BRIT), billionaire (US)
millier [milje] *nm* thousand; **un ~ (de)** a thousand or so, about a thousand; **par ~s** in (their) thousands, by the thousand
milligramme [miligram] *nm* milligramme
millimètre [milimɛtʀ(ə)] *nm* millimetre
million [miljɔ̃] *nm* million; **deux ~s de** two million; **millionnaire** *nm/f* millionaire
mime [mim] *nm/f* (*acteur*) mime(r) ♦ *nm* (*art*) mime, miming
mimer [mime] *vt* to mime; (*singer*) to mimic, take off
mimique [mimik] *nf* (*funny*) face; (*signes*) gesticulations *pl*, sign language *no pl*
minable [minabl(ə)] *adj* shabby-looking; pathetic
mince [mɛ̃s] *adj* thin; (*personne, taille*) slim, slender; (*fig: profit, connaissances*) slight, small, weak ♦ *excl:* **~ alors!** drat it!, darn it! (US); **minceur** *nf* thinness; slimness, slenderness
mine [min] *nf* (*physionomie*) expression, look; (*extérieur*) exterior, appearance; (*de crayon*) lead; (*gisement, exploitation, explosif, fig*) mine; **avoir bonne ~** (*personne*) to look well; (*ironique*) to look an utter idiot; **avoir mauvaise ~** to look unwell *ou* poorly; **faire ~ de faire** to make a pretence of doing; to make as if to do; **~ de rien** with a casual air; although you wouldn't think so
miner [mine] *vt* (*saper*) to undermine, erode; (*MIL*) to mine
minerai [minʀɛ] *nm* ore
minéral, e, aux [mineʀal, -o] *adj*, *nm* mineral

minéralogique [mineʀalɔʒik] *adj:* **numéro ~** registration number
minet, te [minɛ, -ɛt] *nm/f* (*chat*) pussy-cat; (*péj*) young trendy
mineur, e [minœʀ] *adj* minor ♦ *nm/ f* (JUR) minor, person under age ♦ *nm* (*travailleur*) miner
miniature [minjatyʀ] *adj*, *nf* miniature
minibus [minibys] *nm* minibus
mini-cassette [minikasɛt] *nf* cassette (recorder)
minier, ière [minje, -jɛʀ] *adj* mining
mini-jupe [miniʒyp] *nf* mini-skirt
minime [minim] *adj* minor, minimal
minimiser [minimize] *vt* to minimize; (*fig*) to play down
minimum [minimɔm] *adj*, *nm* minimum; **au ~** (*au moins*) at the very least
ministère [ministɛʀ] *nm* (*aussi REL*) ministry; (*cabinet*) government; **~ public** (JUR) Prosecution, public prosecutor
ministre [ministʀ(ə)] *nm* (*aussi REL*) minister; **~ d'Etat** senior minister
Minitel [minitɛl] (R) *nm* videotext terminal and service
minorité [minɔʀite] *nf* minority; **être en ~** to be in the *ou* a minority; **mettre en ~** (POL) to defeat
minoterie [minɔtʀi] *nf* flour-mill
minuit [minɥi] *nm* midnight
minuscule [minyskyl] *adj* minute, tiny ♦ *nf:* (*lettre*) ~ small letter
minute [minyt] *nf* minute; (JUR: *original*) minute, draft; **à la ~** (*just*) this instant; there and then; **minuter** *vt* to time; **minuterie** *nf* time switch
minutieux, euse [minysjø, -øz] *adj* meticulous; (*détail*) minutely detailed
mirabelle [miʀabɛl] *nf* (*cherry*) plum
miracle [miʀakl(ə)] *nm* miracle
mirage [miʀaʒ] *nm* mirage
mire [miʀ] *nf:* **point de ~** target; (*fig*) focal point; **ligne de ~** line of sight
miroir [miʀwaʀ] *nm* mirror

miroiter [miʀwate] *vi* to sparkle, shimmer; **faire ~ qch à qn** to paint sth in glowing colours for sb, dangle sth in front of sb's eyes

mis, e [mi, miz] *pp de* **mettre** ♦ *adj*: **bien ~** well-dressed

mise [miz] *nf (argent: au jeu)* stake; *(tenue)* clothing; attire; **être de ~** to be acceptable ou in season; **~ à feu** blast-off; **~ au point** *(fig)* clarification; **~ de fonds** capital outlay; **~ en plis** set; **~ en scène** production

miser [mize] *vt (enjeu)* to stake, bet; **~ sur** *(cheval, numéro)* to bet on; *(fig)* to bank ou count on

misérable [mizeʀabl(ə)] *adj (lamentable, malheureux)* pitiful, wretched; *(pauvre)* poverty-stricken; *(insignifiant, mesquin)* miserable ♦ *nm/f* wretch; *(miséreux)* poor wretch

misère [mizeʀ] *nf (extreme) poverty, destitution; **~s** *nfpl (malheurs)* woes, miseries; *(ennuis)* little troubles; **salaire de ~** starvation wage

miséricorde [mizeʀikɔʀd(ə)] *nf* mercy, forgiveness

missile [misil] *nm* missile

mission [misjɔ̃] *nf* mission; **partir en ~** *(ADMIN, POL)* to go on an assignment; **missionnaire** *nm/f* missionary

mit *vb voir* **mettre**

mité, e [mite] *adj* moth-eaten

mi-temps [mitɑ̃] *nf inv (SPORT: période)* half; *(: pause)* half-time; **à ~** part-time

mitigé, e [mitiʒe] *adj* lukewarm; mixed

mitonner [mitɔne] *vt* to cook with loving care; *(fig)* to cook up quietly

mitoyen, ne [mitwajɛ̃, -ɛn] *adj* common, party *cpd*

mitrailler [mitʀaje] *vt* to machinegun; *(fig)* to pelt, bombard; *(: photographier)* to take shot after shot of; **mitraillette** *nf* submachine gun; **mitrailleuse** *nf* machine gun

mi-voix [mivwa]: **à ~** *adv* in a low ou hushed voice

mixage [miksaʒ] *nm (CINÉMA)* (sound) mixing

mixer [miksœʀ] *nm* (food) mixer

mixte [mikst(ə)] *adj (gén)* mixed; *(SCOL)* mixed, coeducational; **à usage ~** dual-purpose

mixture [mikstyʀ] *nf* mixture; *(fig)* concoction

MLF *sigle m* = Mouvement de Libération de la femme

Mlle *(pl ~es) abr* = **Mademoiselle**

MM *abr* = **Messieurs**

Mme *(pl Mmes) abr* = **Madame**

Mo *abr* = **métro**

mobile [mɔbil] *adj* mobile; *(pièce de machine)* moving; *(élément de meuble etc)* movable ♦ *nm (motif)* motive; *(œuvre d'art)* mobile

mobilier, ière [mɔbilje, -jɛʀ] *adj (JUR)* personal ♦ *nm* furniture

mobiliser [mɔbilize] *vt (MIL, gén)* to mobilize

moche [mɔʃ] *(fam) adj* ugly; rotten

modalité [mɔdalite] *nf* form, mode; **~s** *nfpl (d'un accord etc)* clauses, terms

mode [mɔd] *nf* fashion ♦ *nm (manière)* form, mode; **à la ~** fashionable, in fashion; **~ d'emploi** directions *pl* (for use)

modèle [mɔdɛl] *adj, nm* model; *(qui pose: de peintre)* sitter; **~ déposé** registered design; **~ réduit** smallscale model; **modeler** [mɔdle] *vt (ART)* to model, mould; *(suj: vêtement, érosion)* to mould, shape

modem [mɔdɛm] *nm* modem

modéré, e [mɔdeʀe] *adj, nm/f* moderate

modérer [mɔdeʀe] *vt* to moderate; **se ~** *vi* to restrain o.s.

moderne [mɔdɛʀn(ə)] *adj* modern ♦ *nm* modern style; modern furniture; **moderniser** *vt* to modernize

modeste [mɔdɛst(ə)] *adj* modest; **modestie** *nf* modesty

modifier [mɔdifje] *vt* to modify, alter; **se ~** *vi* to alter

modique [mɔdik] *adj* modest

modiste [mɔdist(ə)] *nf* milliner

modulation [mɔdylɑsjɔ̃] *nf*: ~ de fréquence frequency modulation
module [mɔdyl] *nm* module
moelle [mwal] *nf* marrow
moelleux, euse [mwalø, -øz] *adj* soft; *(au goût, à l'ouïe)* mellow
moellon [mwalɔ̃] *nm* rubble stone
mœurs [mœr] *nfpl (conduite)* morals; *(manières)* manners; *(pratiques sociales, mode de vie)* habits
mohair [mɔɛr] *nm* mohair
moi [mwa] *pron m: (emphatique)*: ~, je ... for my part, I ..., I myself ...
moignon [mwaɲɔ̃] *nm* stump
moi-même [mwamɛm] *pron* myself; *(emphatique)* I myself
moindre [mwɛ̃dr(ə)] *adj* lesser; lower; le(la) ~, les ~s the least, the slightest
moine [mwan] *nm* monk, friar
moineau, x [mwano] *nm* sparrow

MOT-CLÉ
---

moins [mwɛ̃] *adv* **1** *(comparatif)*: ~ (que) less (than); ~ grand que less tall than, not as tall as; ~ je travaille, mieux je me porte the less I work, the better I feel
2 *(superlatif)*: le ~ (the) least; c'est ce que j'aime le ~ it's what I like (the) least; le(la) ~ doué*(e) the least gifted; au ~, du ~ at least; pour le ~ at the very least
3: ~ de *(quantité)* less (than); *(nombre)* fewer (than); ~ de sable/ d'eau less sand/water; ~ de livres/ gens fewer books/people; ~ de 2 ans less than 2 years; ~ de midi not yet midday
4: de ~, en ~ 100F/3 days less; 3 livres en ~ 3 books fewer; 3 books too few; l'argent en ~ less money; le soleil en ~ but for the sun, minus the sun; de ~ en ~ less and less
5: à ~ de, à ~ que unless; à ~ de faire unless we do (ou he does *etc*); à ~ que tu ne fasses unless you do; à ~ d'un accident barring any acci-

dent
♦ *prép*: 4 ~ 2 4 minus 2; il est ~ 5 it's 5 to; il fait ~ 5 it's 5 (degrees) below (freezing); il est ~ 5 it's minus 5

mois [mwa] *nm* month; ~ double *(COMM)* extra month's salary
moisi [mwazi] *nm* mould, mildew; odeur de ~ musty smell
moisir [mwazir] *vi* to go mouldy; *(fig)* to rot; to hang about
moisissure [mwazisyr] *nf* mould *no pl*
moisson [mwasɔ̃] *nf* harvest; **moissonner** *vt* to harvest, reap; **moissonneuse** *nf (machine)* harvester
moite [mwat] *adj* sweaty, sticky
moitié [mwatje] *nf* half; la ~ half; la ~ de half (of); la ~ du temps/ des gens half the time/the people; à la ~ de halfway through; à ~ *(avant le verbe)* half; à ~ *(avant l'adjectif)* half; de ~ by half; ~ half-and-half
mol [mɔl] *adj voir* mou
molaire [mɔlɛr] *nf* molar
molester [mɔlɛste] *vt* to manhandle, maul (about)
molle [mɔl] *adj voir* mou; **mollement** *adv* softly; *(péj)* sluggishly; *(protester)* feebly
mollet [mɔlɛ] *nm* calf ♦ *adj m*: œuf ~ soft-boiled egg
molletonné, e [mɔltɔne] *adj* fleece-lined
mollir [mɔlir] *vi* to give way; to relent; to go soft
môme [mom] *(fam) nm/f (enfant)* brat ♦ *nf (fille)* chick
moment [mɔmɑ̃] *nm* moment; ce n'est pas le ~ this is not the (right) time; à un certain ~ at some point; à un ~ donné at a certain point; pour un bon ~ for a good while; pour le ~ for the moment, for the time being; au ~ de at the time of; au ~ où as; at a time when; à tout ~ at any time *ou* moment; constantly, continually; en ce ~ at the moment; at present; sur le ~ at

time; par ~s now and then, at times; du ~ où *ou* que seeing that, since; **momentané, e** *adj* temporary, momentary

momie [mɔmi] *nf* mummy

mon, ma [mɔ̃, ma] (*pl* **mes**) *dét* my

Monaco [mɔnako] *nm*: le ~ Monaco

monarchie [mɔnaʀʃi] *nf* monarchy

monastère [mɔnastɛʀ] *nm* monastery

monceau, x [mɔ̃so] *nm* heap

mondain, e [mɔ̃dɛ̃, -ɛn] *adj* society *cpd*; social; fashionable; **~e** *nf*: la M~e, la police ~e ≈ the vice squad

monde [mɔ̃d] *nm* world; (*haute société*): le ~ (high) society; (*milieu*): être du même ~ to move in the same circles; (*gens*): il y a du ~ (*beaucoup de gens*) there are a lot of people; (*quelques personnes*) there are some people; **beaucoup/peu de ~** many/few people; **le meilleur** etc **du ~** the best etc in the world *ou* on earth; **mettre au** ~ to bring into the world; **pas le moins du** ~ not in the least; **se faire un** ~ **de qch** to make a great deal of fuss about sth; **mondial, e, aux** *adj* (*population*) world *cpd*; (*influence*) world-wide; **mondialement** *adv* throughout the world

monégasque [mɔnegask(ə)] *adj* Monegasque, of *ou* from Monaco

monétaire [mɔnetɛʀ] *adj* monetary

moniteur, trice [mɔnitœʀ, -tʀis] *nm/f* (*SPORT*) instructor(tress); (*de colonie de vacances*) supervisor ♦ *nm* (*écran*) monitor

monnaie [mɔnɛ] *nf* (*pièce*) coin; (*ECON, gén*: *moyen d'échange*) currency; (*petites pièces*): **avoir de la** ~ to have some change; **faire de la** ~ to get (some) change; **avoir/faire la** ~ **de 20 F** to have change of/get change for 20 F; **rendre à qn la** ~ (**sur 20 F**) to give sb the change (out of *ou* from 20 F); **monnayer** *vt* to convert into cash; (*talent*) to capitalize on

monologue [mɔnɔlɔg] *nm* monolo-

gue, soliloquy; **monologuer** *vi* to soliloquize

monopole [mɔnɔpɔl] *nm* monopoly

monotone [mɔnɔtɔn] *adj* monotonous

monseigneur [mɔ̃sɛɲœʀ] *nm* (*archevêque, évêque*) Your (*ou* His) Grace; (*cardinal*) Your (*ou* His) Eminence

Monsieur [məsjø] (*pl* **Messieurs**) *titre* Mr ♦ *nm* (*homme quelconque*): **un/le gentleman**; *voir aussi* **Madame**

monstre [mɔ̃stʀ(ə)] *nm* monster ♦ *adj*: **un travail** ~ a fantastic amount of work; an enormous job

mont [mɔ̃] *nm*: **par ~s et par vaux** up hill and down dale; **le M~ Blanc** Mont Blanc

montage [mɔ̃taʒ] *nm* putting up; mounting; setting; assembly; (*PHOTO*) photomontage; (*CINEMA*) editing

montagnard, e [mɔ̃taɲaʀ, -aʀd(ə)] *adj* mountain *cpd* ♦ *nm/f* mountain-dweller

montagne [mɔ̃taɲ] *nf* (*cime*) mountain; (*région*): **la** ~ the mountains *pl*; **~s russes** big dipper *sg*, switchback *sg*; **montagneux, euse** [mɔ̃taɲø, -øz] *adj* mountainous

montant, e [mɔ̃tɑ̃, -ɑ̃t] *adj* rising; (*robe, corsage*) high-necked ♦ *nm* (*somme, total*) (sum) total, (total) amount; (*de fenêtre*) upright; (*de lit*) post

monte-charge [mɔ̃tʃaʀʒ(ə)] *nm inv* goods lift, hoist

montée [mɔ̃te] *nf* rising, rise; ascent, climb; (*chemin*) way up; (*côte*) hill; **au milieu de la** ~ halfway up

monter [mɔ̃te] *vt* (*escalier, côte*) to go (*ou* come) up; (*valise, paquet*) to take (*ou* bring) up; (*cheval*) to mount; (*étagère*) to raise; (*tente, échafaudage*) to put up; (*machine*) to assemble; (*bijou*) to mount, set; (*COUTURE*) to set in; to sew on; (*CINEMA*) to edit; (*THÉÂTRE*) to put on, stage; (*société* etc) to plan

♦ *vi* to go (*ou* come) up; (*avion etc*) to climb, go up; (*chemin, niveau, température*) to go up, rise; (*passager*) to get on; (*à cheval*): ~ **bien/mal** to ride well/badly; **se ~ à** (*frais etc*) to add up to, come to; ~ **à pied** to walk up, go up on foot; ~ **à bicyclette/en voiture** to cycle/drive up, go up by bicycle/by car; ~ **dans le train/l'avion** to get into the train/plane, board the train/plane; ~ **sur** to climb up onto; ~ **à cheval** to get on *ou* mount a horse

monticule [mɔ̃tikyl] *nm* mound

montre [mɔ̃tʀ(ə)] *nf* watch; **faire ~ de** to show, display; **contre la ~** (*SPORT*) against the clock; **montre-bracelet** *nf* wristwatch

montrer [mɔ̃tʀe] *vt* to show; ~ **qch à qn** to show sb sth

monture [mɔ̃tyʀ] *nf* (*bête*) mount; (*d'une bague*) setting; (*de lunettes*) frame

monument [mɔnymɑ̃] *nm* monument; ~ **aux morts** war memorial

moquer [mɔke] : **se ~ de** *vt* to make fun of, laugh at; (*fam: se désintéresser de*) not to care about; (*tromper*): **se ~ de qn** to take sb for a ride

moquette [mɔket] *nf* fitted carpet

moqueur, euse [mɔkœʀ, -øz] *adj* mocking

moral, e, aux [mɔʀal, -o] *adj* moral ♦ *nm* morale; **avoir le ~ à zéro** to be really down; **morale** *nf* (*conduite*) morals *pl*; (*règles*) moral code, ethic; (*valeurs*) moral standards *pl*, morality; (*science*) ethics *sg*, moral philosophy; (*conclusion: d'une fable etc*) moral; **faire la morale à** to lecture, preach at; **moralité** *nf* morality; (*conduite*) morals *pl*; (*conclusion, enseignement*) moral

morceau, x [mɔʀso] *nm* piece, bit; (*d'une œuvre*) passage, extract; (*MUS*) piece; (*CULIN: de viande*) cut; **mettre en ~x** to pull to pieces *ou* bits

morceler [mɔʀsəle] *vt* to break up,

divide up

mordant, e [mɔʀdɑ̃, -ɑ̃t] *adj* scathing, cutting; biting

mordiller [mɔʀdije] *vt* to nibble at, chew at

mordre [mɔʀdʀ(ə)] *vt* to bite; (*suj: lime, vis*) to bite into ♦ *vi* (*poisson*) to bite; ~ **sur** (*fig*) to go over into, overlap into; ~ **à l'hameçon** to bite, rise to the bait

mordu, e [mɔʀdy] *nm/f*: **un ~ du jazz** a jazz fanatic

morfondre [mɔʀfɔ̃dʀ(ə)] : **se ~** *vi* to mope

morgue [mɔʀg(ə)] *nf* (*arrogance*) haughtiness; (*lieu: de la police*) morgue; (: *à l'hôpital*) mortuary

morne [mɔʀn(ə)] *adj* dismal, dreary

mors [mɔʀ] *nm* bit

morse [mɔʀs(ə)] *nm* (*ZOOL*) walrus; (*TEL*) Morse (code)

morsure [mɔʀsyʀ] *nf* bite

mort[1] [mɔʀ] *nf* death

mort[2]**, e** [mɔʀ, mɔʀt(ə)] *pp de* **mourir** ♦ *adj* dead ♦ *nm/f* (*défunt*) dead man(woman); (*victime*): **il y a eu plusieurs morts** several people were killed, there were several killed (*CARTES*) dummy; **mort ou vif** dead or alive; **mort de peur/fatigue** frightened to death/dead tired

mortalité [mɔʀtalite] *nf* mortality, death rate

mortel, le [mɔʀtɛl] *adj* (*poison etc*) deadly, lethal; (*accident, blessure*) fatal; (*REL*) mortal; (*fig*) deathly; deadly boring

mortier [mɔʀtje] *nm* (*gén*) mortar

mort-né, e [mɔʀne] *adj* (*enfant*) stillborn

mortuaire [mɔʀtɥeʀ] *adj* funeral *cpd*

morue [mɔʀy] *nf* (*ZOOL*) cod *inv*

mosaïque [mɔzaik] *nf* (*ART*) mosaic; (*fig*) patchwork

Moscou [mɔsku] *n* Moscow

mosquée [mɔske] *nf* mosque

mot [mo] *nm* word; (*message*) line, note; (*bon mot etc*) saying; sally; ~ **à ~** word for word; ~ **d'ordre** watchword; ~ **de passe** password;

~s croisés crossword (puzzle) sg

motard [mɔtaʀ] nm biker; (policier) motorcycle cop

motel [mɔtɛl] nm motel

moteur, trice [mɔtœʀ, -tʀis] adj (ANAT, PHYSIOL) motor; (TECH) driving; (AUTO): à 4 roues motrices 4-wheel drive ♦ nm engine, motor; à ~ power-driven, motor cpd

motif [mɔtif] nm (cause) motive; (décoratif) design, pattern, motif; (d'un tableau) subject, motif; ~s nmpl (JUR) grounds pl; sans ~ groundless

motiver [mɔtive] vt (justifier) to justify, account for; (ADMIN, JUR, PSYCH) to motivate

moto [mɔto] nf (motor)bike; **motocycliste** nm/f motorcyclist

motorisé, e [mɔtɔʀize] adj (troupe) motorized; (personne) having transport ou a car

motrice [mɔtʀis] adj voir moteur

motte [mɔt] nf: ~ de terre lump of earth, clod (of earth); ~ de beurre lump of butter; ~ de gazon turf, sod

mou (mol), molle [mu, mɔl] adj soft; (péj) flabby; sluggish ♦ nm (abats) lights pl, lungs pl; (de la corde): avoir du mou to be slack

mouche [muʃ] nf fly

moucher [muʃe] vt (enfant) to blow the nose of; (chandelle) to snuff (out); se ~ vi to blow one's nose

moucheron [muʃʀɔ̃] nm midge

moucheté, e [muʃte] adj dappled; flecked

mouchoir [muʃwaʀ] nm handkerchief, hanky; ~ en papier tissue, paper hanky

moudre [mudʀ(ə)] vt to grind

moue [mu] nf pout; faire la ~ to pout; (fig) to pull a face

mouette [mwɛt] nf (sea)gull

moufle [mufl(ə)] nf (gant) mitt(en)

mouillé, e [muje] adj wet

mouiller [muje] vt (humecter) to wet, moisten; (tremper): ~ qn/qch to make sb/sth wet; (couper, diluer) to water down; (mine etc) to lay

(NAVIG) to lie ou be at anchor; se ~ to get wet; (fam) to commit o.s.; to get o.s. involved

moule [mul] nf mussel ♦ nm (creux, CULIN) mould; (modèle plein) cast; ~ à gâteaux nm cake tin (BRIT) ou pan (US)

moulent vb voir moudre; mouler

mouler [mule] vt (suj: vêtement) to hug, fit closely round; ~ qch sur (fig) to model sth on

moulin [mulɛ̃] nm mill; ~ à café/à poivre coffee/pepper mill; ~ à légumes (vegetable) shredder; ~ à paroles (fig) chatterbox; ~ à vent windmill

moulinet [mulinɛ] nm (de treuil) winch; (de canne à pêche) reel; (mouvement): faire des ~s avec qch to whirl sth around

moulinette [mulinɛt] nf (vegetable) shredder

moulu, e [muly] pp de moudre

moulure [mulyʀ] nf (ornement) moulding

mourant, e [muʀɑ̃, -ɑ̃t] adj dying

mourir [muʀiʀ] vi to die; ~ d'envie de faire to be dying to do

mousse [mus] nf (BOT) moss; (écume: sur eau, bière) froth, foam; (: shampooing) lather; (CULIN) mousse ♦ nm (NAVIG) ship's boy; bas ~ stretch stockings; ~ à raser shaving foam; ~ carbonique (fire-fighting) foam

mousseline [muslin] nf muslin; chiffon

mousser [muse] vi to foam; to lather

mousseux, euse [musø, -øz] adj frothy ♦ nm: (vin) ~ sparkling wine

mousson [musɔ̃] nf monsoon

moustache [mustaʃ] nf moustache; ~s nfpl (du chat) whiskers pl

moustiquaire [mustikɛʀ] nf mosquito net (ou screen)

moustique [mustik] nm mosquito

moutarde [mutaʀd(ə)] nf mustard

mouton [mutɔ̃] nm (ZOOL, péj) sheep inv; (peau) sheepskin; (CULIN) mutton

mouvant, e [muvɑ̃, -ɑ̃t] adj unsettled; changing; shifting

mouvement [muvmɑ̃] nm (gén, aussi: mécanisme) movement; (fig) activity; impulse; gesture; (MUS: rythme) tempo; en ~ in motion, on the move; **mouvementé, e** adj (vie, poursuite) eventful; (réunion) turbulent

mouvoir [muvwaʀ] vt (levier, membre) to move; **se ~** vi to move

moyen, ne [mwajɛ̃, -ɛn] adj average; (tailles, prix) medium; (de grandeur moyenne) medium-sized ♦ nm (façon) means sg, way; **~s** nmpl (capacités) means; **au ~ de** by means of; **par tous les ~s** by every possible means, every possible way; **par ses propres ~s** all by oneself; ~ **âge** Middle Ages; ~ **de transport** means of transport

moyennant [mwajɛnɑ̃] prép (somme) for; (service, conditions) in return for; (travail, effort) with

moyenne [mwajɛn] nf average; (MATH) mean; (SCOL: à l'examen) pass mark; (AUTO) average speed; **en ~** on (an) average; ~ **d'âge** average age

Moyen-Orient [mwajɛnɔʀjɑ̃] nm: le ~ the Middle East

moyeu, x [mwajø] nm hub

MST sigle f (= maladie sexuellement transmissible) STD

mû, mue [my] pp de **mouvoir**

muer [mɥe] vi (oiseau, mammifère) to moult; (serpent) to slough; (jeune garçon): **il mue** his voice is breaking; **se ~ en** to transform into

muet, te [mɥɛ, -ɛt] adj dumb; (fig): ~ **d'admiration** etc speechless with admiration etc; (joie, douleur, CINEMA) silent; (carte) blank mute

mufle [myfl(ə)] nm (ZOOL: museau) (goujat) boor

mugir [myʒiʀ] vi (taureau) to bellow; (vache) to low; (fig) to howl

muguet [mygɛ] nm lily of the valley

mule [myl] nf (ZOOL) (she-)mule

mulet [mylɛ] nm (ZOOL) (he-)mule

multiple [myltipl(ə)] adj multiple, numerous; (varié) many, manifold ♦ nm (MATH) multiple

multiplication [myltiplikasjɔ̃] nf multiplication

multiplier [myltiplije] vt to multiply; **se ~** vi to multiply; to increase in number

municipal, e, aux [mynisipal, -o] adj municipal; town council; ~ borough cpd

municipalité [mynisipalite] nf (corps municipal) town council, corporation

munir [myniʀ] vt: ~ **qn/qch de** to equip sb/sth with

munitions [mynisjɔ̃] nfpl ammunition sg

mur [myʀ] nm wall; ~ **du son** sound barrier

mûr, e [myʀ] adj ripe; (personne) mature

muraille [myʀɑj] nf (high) wall

mural, e, aux [myʀal, -o] adj wall cpd; mural

mûre [myʀ] nf blackberry; mulberry

murer [myʀe] vt (enclos) to wall (in); (porte, issue) to wall up; (personne) to wall up ou in

muret [myʀɛ] nm low wall

mûrir [myʀiʀ] vi (fruit, blé) to ripen; (abcès, furoncle) to come to a head; (fig: idée, personne) to mature ♦ vt to ripen; to (make) mature

murmure [myʀmyʀ] nm murmur; ~s nmpl (plaintes) murmurings, mutterings; **murmurer** vi to murmur; (se plaindre) to mutter, grumble

muscade [myskad] nf (aussi: noix ~) nutmeg

muscat [myska] nm (raisin) muscat grape; (vin) muscatel (wine)

muscle [myskl(ə)] nm muscle; **musclé, e** adj muscular; (fig) strong-arm

museau, x [myzo] nm muzzle

musée [myze] *nm* museum; art gallery

museler [myzle] *vt* to muzzle; **muselière** *nf* muzzle

musette [myzɛt] *nf* (*sac*) lunchbag ♦ *adj inv* (*orchestre etc*) accordion *cpd*

musical, e, aux [myzikal, -o] *adj* musical

music-hall [myzikol] *nm* variety theatre; (*genre*) variety

musicien, ne [myzisjɛ̃, -jɛn] *adj* musical ♦ *nm/f* musician

musique [myzik] *nf* music; (*fanfare*) band; ~ **de chambre** chamber music

musulman, e [myzylmɑ̃, -an] *adj*, *nm/f* Moslem, Muslim

mutation [mytasjɔ̃] *nf* (*ADMIN*) transfer

mutilé, e [mytile] *nm/f* disabled person (*through loss of limbs*)

mutiler [mytile] *vt* to mutilate, maim

mutin, e [mytɛ̃, -in] *adj* (*air, ton*) mischievous, impish ♦ *nm/f* (*MIL, NAVIG*) mutineer

mutinerie [mytinʀi] *nf* mutiny

mutisme [mytism(ə)] *nm* silence

mutuel, le [mytɥɛl] *adj* mutual; **mutuelle** *nf* mutual benefit society

myope [mjɔp] *adj* short-sighted

myosotis [mjozotis] *nm* forget-me-not

myrtille [miʀtij] *nf* bilberry

mystère [mistɛʀ] *nm* mystery; **mystérieux, euse** *adj* mysterious

mystifier [mistifje] *vt* to fool; to mystify

mythe [mit] *nm* myth

mythologie [mitɔlɔʒi] *nf* mythology

N

n' [n] *adv voir* **ne**

nacre [nakʀ(ə)] *nf* mother of pearl

nage [naʒ] *nf* swimming; style of swimming, stroke; **traverser/s'éloigner à la ~** to swim across/away; **en ~** bathed in perspiration

nageoire [naʒwaʀ] *nf* fin

nager [naʒe] *vi* to swim; **nageur, euse** *nm/f* swimmer

naguère [nagɛʀ] *adv* formerly

naïf, ïve [naif, naiv] *adj* naïve

nain, e [nɛ̃, nɛn] *nm/f* dwarf

naissance [nɛsɑ̃s] *nf* birth; **donner ~ à** to give birth to; (*fig*) to give rise to

naître [nɛtʀ(ə)] *vi* to be born; (*fig*): **~ de** to arise from, be born out of; **il est né en 1960** he was born in 1960; **faire ~** (*fig*) to give rise to, arouse

naïve [naiv] *adj voir* **naïf**

nana [nana] (*fam*) *nf* (*fille*) chick, bird (*BRIT*)

nantir [nɑ̃tiʀ] *vt*: **~ qn de** to provide sb with; **les nantis** (*péj*) the well-to-do

nappe [nap] *nf* tablecloth; (*fig*) sheet; layer; **napperon** *nm* table-mat

naquit *etc vb voir* **naître**

narguer [naʀge] *vt* to taunt

narine [naʀin] *nf* nostril

narquois, e [naʀkwa, -waz] *adj* derisive, mocking

naseau, x [nazo] *nm* nostril

natal, e [natal] *adj* native

natalité [natalite] *nf* birth rate

natation [natasjɔ̃] *nf* swimming

natif, ive [natif, -iv] *adj* native

nation [nasjɔ̃] *nf* nation

national, e, aux [nasjɔnal, -o] *adj* national; **nationale** *nf*: (*route*) **nationale** ≈ A road (*BRIT*), ≈ state highway (*US*); **nationaliser** *vt* to nationalize; **nationalité** *nf* nationality

natte [nat] *nf* (*tapis*) mat; (*cheveux*) plait

naturaliser [natyralize] *vt* to naturalize

nature [natyʀ] *nf* nature ♦ *adj, adv* (*CULIN*) plain, without seasoning or sweetening; (*café, thé*) black, with-out sugar; **payer en ~** to pay in kind; ~ **morte** still-life; **naturel, le** *adj* (*gén, aussi: enfant*) natural ♦ *nm* naturalness; disposition, nature; (*autochtone*) native; **naturellement** *adv* naturally; (*bien sûr*) of course

naufrage [nofʀaʒ] nm (ship)wreck; (fig) wreck; **faire ~** to be shipwrecked

nauséabond, e [nozeabɔ̃, -ɔ̃d] adj foul, nauseous

nausée [noze] nf nausea; **je suis nausé** I'm so sorry

nautique [notik] adj nautical, water cpd

nautisme [notism(ə)] nm water sports

navet [navɛ] nm turnip

navette [navɛt] nf shuttle; **faire la ~ (entre)** to go to and fro ou shuttle (between)

navigateur [navigatœʀ] nm (NAVIG) seafarer, sailor; (AVIAT) navigator

navigation [navigasjɔ̃] nf navigation, sailing; shipping

naviguer [navige] vi to navigate, sail

navire [naviʀ] nm ship

navrer [navʀe] vt to upset, distress; **je suis navré** I'm so sorry

ne(n') [n(ə)] adv voir pas; plus; jamais etc; (explétif) non traduit

né, e [ne] pp (voir naître): en 1960 **né en** 1960 born in 1960; **~e Scott** née Scott

néanmoins [neɑ̃mwɛ̃] adv nevertheless

néant [neɑ̃] nm nothingness; **réduire à ~** to bring to nought; (espoir) to dash

nécessaire [neseseʀ] adj necessary ♦ nm necessary; (sac) kit; **~ de couture** sewing kit; **~ de toilette** toilet bag; **nécessité** nf necessity; **nécessiter** vt to require; **nécessiteux, euse** adj needy

nécrologique [nekʀɔlɔʒik] adj: **article ~** obituary; **rubrique ~** obituary column

nectar [nɛktaʀ] nm (sucré) nectar; (boisson) sweetened, diluted fruit juice

néerlandais, e [neɛʀlɑ̃dɛ, -ɛz] adj Dutch

nef [nɛf] nf (d'église) nave

néfaste [nefast(ə)] adj baneful; ill-fated

négatif, ive [negatif, -iv] adj negative ♦ nm (PHOTO) negative

négligé, e [negliʒe] adj (en désordre) slovenly ♦ nm (tenue) negligee

négligent, e [negliʒɑ̃, -ɑ̃t] adj careless; negligent

négliger [negliʒe] vt (épouse, jardin) to neglect; (tenue) to be careless about; (avis, précautions) to disregard; **~ de faire** to fail to do, not bother to do

négoce [negɔs] nm trade

négociant [negɔsjɑ̃] nm merchant

négociation [negɔsjasjɔ̃] nf negotiation

négocier [negɔsje] vi, vt to negotiate

nègre [nɛgʀ(ə)] nm Negro; ghost (writer)

négresse [negʀɛs] nf Negro woman

neige [nɛʒ] nf snow; **neiger** vi to snow

nénuphar [nenyfaʀ] nm water-lily

néon [neɔ̃] nm neon

néophyte [neofit] nm/f novice

néo-zélandais, e [neozelɑ̃dɛ, -ɛz] adj New Zealand cpd ♦ nm/f: **N~, e** New Zealander

nerf [nɛʀ] nm nerve; (fig) spirit; stamina; **nerveux, euse** adj nervous; (voiture) nippy, responsive; (tendineux) sinewy; **nervosité** nf excitability; state of agitation; nervousness

nervure [nɛʀvyʀ] nf vein

n'est-ce pas [nɛspa] adv isn't it?, won't you? etc, selon le verbe qui précède

net, nette [nɛt] adj (sans équivoque, distinct) clear; (évident) definite; (propre) neat, clean; (COMM: prix, salaire) net ♦ adv (refuser) flatly ♦ nm: **mettre au ~** to copy out; **s'arrêter ~** to stop dead; **nettement** adv clearly, distinctly; **netteté** nf clearness

nettoyage [nɛtwajaʒ] nm cleaning; **~ à sec** dry cleaning

nettoyer [nɛtwaje] vt to clean; (fig) to clean out

neuf[1] [nœf] num nine

neuf², **neuve** [nœf, nœv] adj new ♦ nm: remettre à ~ to redecorate; remettre à ~ to do up (as good as new); refurbish

neutre [nøtʀ(ə)] adj neutral; (LING) neuter ♦ nm neuter

neuve [nœv] adj voir neuf²

neuvième [nœvjɛm] num ninth

neveu, x [nəvø] nm nephew

névrosé, e [nevʀoze] adj, nm/f neurotic

nez [ne] nm nose; ~ à ~ avec face to face with; avoir du ~ to have flair

ni [ni] conj: l'un ~ l'autre ne sont neither one nor the other are; il n'a rien dit ~ fait he hasn't said or done anything

niais, e [njɛ, -ɛz] adj silly, thick

niche [niʃ] nf (du chien) kennel; (de mur) recess, niche

nicher [niʃe] vi to nest

nid [ni] nm nest; ~ de poule pothole

nièce [njɛs] nf niece

nier [nje] vt to deny

nigaud, e [nigo, -od] nm/f booby, fool

Nil [nil] nm: le ~ the Nile

n'importe [nɛ̃pɔʀt(ə)] adv: ~ qui/quoi/où anybody/anything/anywhere; ~ quand any time; ~ quel/quelle any; ~ lequel/laquelle any (one); ~ comment (sans soin) carelessly

niveau, x [nivo] nm level; (des élèves, études) standard; de ~ (avec) level (with); le ~ de la mer sea level; ~ de vie standard of living

niveler [nivle] vt to level

NN abr (= nouvelle norme) revised standard of hotel classification

noble [nɔbl(ə)] adj noble; **noblesse** nf nobility; (d'une action etc) nobleness

noce [nɔs] nf wedding; (gens) wedding party (ou guests pl); faire la ~ (fam) to be on a binge; ~s d'or/d'argent golden/silver wedding

nocif, ive [nɔsif, -iv] adj harmful, noxious

noctambule [nɔktɑ̃byl] nm night-bird

nocturne [nɔktyʀn(ə)] adj nocturnal ♦ nf late-night opening

Noël [nɔɛl] nm Christmas

nœud [nø] nm (de corde, du bois, NAVIG) knot; (ruban) bow; (fig: liens) bond, tie; ~ papillon bow tie

noir, e [nwaʀ] adj black; (obscur, sombre) dark ♦ nm/f black man(woman), Negro ♦ nm: dans le ~ in the dark; travail au ~ moonlighting; **noirceur** nf blackness; darkness; **noircir** vt, vi to blacken; **noire** nf (MUS) crotchet (BRIT), quarter note (US)

noisette [nwazɛt] nf hazelnut

noix [nwa] nf walnut; (CULIN): ~ de beurre a knob of butter; ~ de cajou cashew nut; ~ de coco coconut

nom [nɔ̃] nm name; (LING) noun; ~ d'emprunt assumed name; ~ de famille surname; ~ de jeune fille maiden name; ~ déposé nm trade name; ~ propre nm proper noun

nombre [nɔ̃bʀ(ə)] nm number; venir en ~ to come in large numbers; depuis ~ d'années for many years; ils sont au ~ de 3 there are 3 of them; au ~ de mes amis among my friends

nombreux, euse [nɔ̃bʀø, -øz] adj many, numerous; (avec nom sg: foule etc) large; peu ~ few; small

nombril [nɔ̃bʀi] nm navel

nommer [nɔme] vt (baptiser, mentionner) to name; (qualifier) to call; (élire) to appoint, nominate; se ~: il se nomme Pascal his name's Pascal, he's called Pascal

non [nɔ̃] adv (réponse) no; (avec loin, sans, seulement) not; ~ pas que = non que; ~ que not that; moi ~ plus neither do I, I don't either

non: ~**-alcoolisé, e** adj nonalcoholic; ~**-fumeur** nm non-smoker; ~**-lieu** nm: il y a eu ~ the case was dismissed; ~**-sens** nm absurdity

nord [nɔʀ] *nm* North ♦ *adj* northern; north; **au ~** (*situation*) in the north; (*direction*) to the north; **au ~ de** (*to the*) north of; **nord-est** *nm* North-East; **nord-ouest** *nm* North-West

normal, e, aux [nɔʀmal, -o] *adj* normal; **normale** *nf*: **la normale** the norm, the average; **normalement** *adv* (*en général*) normally; **normaliser** *vt* (*COMM, TECH*) to standardize

normand, e [nɔʀmɑ̃, -ɑ̃d] *adj* of Normandy

Normandie [nɔʀmɑ̃di] *nf* Normandy

norme [nɔʀm(ə)] *nf* norm; (*TECH*) standard

Norvège [nɔʀvɛʒ] *nf* Norway; **norvégien, ne** *adj, nm/f* Norwegian ♦ *nm* (*LING*) Norwegian

nos [no] *dét voir* **notre**

nostalgie [nɔstalʒi] *nf* nostalgia

notable [nɔtabl(ə)] *adj* notable, noteworthy; (*marqué*) noticeable, marked ♦ *nm* prominent citizen

notaire [nɔtɛʀ] *nm* notary; solicitor

notamment [nɔtamɑ̃] *adv* in particular, among others

note [nɔt] *nf* (*écrite, MUS*) note; (*SCOL*) mark (*BRIT*), grade; (*facture*) bill; **~ de service** memorandum

noté, e [nɔte] *adj*: **être bien/mal ~** (*employé etc*) to have a good/bad record

noter [nɔte] *vt* (*écrire*) to write down; (*remarquer*) to note, notice

notice [nɔtis] *nf* summary, short article; (*brochure*) leaflet, instruction book

notifier [nɔtifje] *vt*: **~ qch à qn** to notify sb of sth, notify sth to sb

notion [nɔsjɔ̃] *nf* notion, idea

notoire [nɔtwaʀ] *adj* widely known; (*en mal*) notorious

notre [nɔtʀ(ə), no] *pl* **nos**) *dét* our

nôtre [notʀ(ə)] *pron*: **le ~, la ~, les ~s ours** ♦ *pron*: **les ~s** ours; (*alliés etc*) our own people; **soyez des ~s** join us

nouer [nwe] *vt* to tie, knot; (*fig: alliance etc*) to strike up

noueux, euse [nwø, -øz] *adj* gnarled

nouilles [nuj] *nfpl* noodles; pasta *sg*

nourrice [nuʀis] *nf* wet-nurse

nourrir [nuʀiʀ] *vt* to feed; (*fig: espoir*) to harbour, nurse; **logé nourri** with board and lodging; **nourrissant, e** *adj* nourishing, nutritious

nourrisson [nuʀisɔ̃] *nm* (unweaned) infant

nourriture [nuʀityʀ] *nf* food

nous [nu] *pron* (*sujet*) we; (*objet*) us; **nous-mêmes** *pron* ourselves

nouveau(nouvel), elle, x [nuvo, -ɛl] *adj* new ♦ *nm/f* new pupil (*ou* employee); **de ~, à ~** again; **~ venu, nouvelle venue** newcomer; **~-né, e** *nm/f* newborn baby; **nouveau-té** *nf* novelty; (*COMM*) new film (*ou* book *ou* creation *etc*)

nouvel [nuvɛl] *adj voir* **nouveau**; **N~ An** New Year

nouvelle [nuvɛl] *adj voir* **nouveau** ♦ *nf* (piece of) news *sg*; (*LIT-TERATURE*) short story; **je suis sans ~s de lui** I haven't heard from him; **N~-Calédonie** *nf* New Caledonia; **N~-Zélande** *nf* New Zealand

novembre [nɔvɑ̃bʀ(ə)] *nm* November

novice [nɔvis] *adj* inexperienced

noyade [nwajad] *nf* drowning *no pl*

noyau, x [nwajo] *nm* (*de fruit*) stone; (*BIO, PHYSIQUE*) nucleus; (*ELEC, GEO, fig: centre*) core; **noyauter** *vt* (*POL*) to infiltrate

noyer [nwaje] *nm* walnut (tree); (*bois*) walnut ♦ *vt* to drown; (*fig*) to flood; to submerge; **se ~** *vi* to be drowned; drown; (*suicide*) to drown o.s.

nu, e [ny] *adj* naked (*membres*) naked, bare; (*chambre, fil, plaine*) bare ♦ *nm* (*ART*) nude; **se mettre ~** to strip; **mettre à ~** to bare

nuage [nɥaʒ] *nm* cloud; **nuageux, euse** *adj* cloudy

nuance [nɥɑ̃s] *nf* (*de couleur, sens*) shade; **il y a une ~ (entre)** there's a slight difference (between); **nuan-**

cer vt (opinion) to bring some reservations ou qualifications to

nucléaire [nyklɛɛʀ] adj nuclear

nudiste [nydist(ə)] nm/f nudist

nuée [nɥe] nf: **une ~ de** a cloud ou host ou swarm of

nues [ny] nfpl: **tomber des ~** to be taken aback; apporter; **porter qn aux ~** to praise sb to the skies

nuire [nɥiʀ] vi to be harmful; **~ à** to harm, to damage; to: **nuisible** adj harmful; **animal nuisible** pest

nuit [nɥi] nf night; **il fait ~** it's dark; **cette ~** last night; tonight; **~ blanche** sleepless night; **~ de noces** wedding night

nul, nulle [nyl] adj (aucun) no; (minime) nil, non-existent; (non valable) null; (péj) useless, hopeless ♦ pron none, no one; **match ~** draw; **résultat ~** match nul; **~ part** nowhere; **~ nullement** adv by no means

numérique [nymeʀik] adj numerical

numéro [nymeʀo] nm number; (spectacle) act, turn; **~ de téléphone** (tele)phone number; **~ vert** nm ≈ freefone (®) number (BRIT), ≈ toll-free number (US); **numéroter** vt to number

nu-pieds [nypje] adj inv barefoot

nuque [nyk] nf nape of the neck

nu-tête [nytɛt] adj inv bareheaded

nutritif, ive [nytʀitif, -iv] adj nutritional; (aliment) nutritious

nylon [nilɔ̃] nm nylon

O

oasis [ɔazis] nf oasis

obéir [ɔbeiʀ] vi to obey; **~ à** to obey; (suj: moteur, véhicule) to respond to; **obéissant, e** adj obedient

objecter [ɔbʒɛkte] vt (prétexter) to plead, put forward as an excuse; **~** (**à qn) que** to object (to sb)

objecteur [ɔbʒɛktœʀ] nm: **~ de conscience** conscientious objector

objectif, ive [ɔbʒɛktif, -iv] adj ob-

jective ♦ nm (OPTIQUE, PHOTO) lens sg, objective; (MIL, fig) objective; **~ à focale variable** zoom lens

objection [ɔbʒɛksjɔ̃] nf objection

objet [ɔbʒɛ] nm object; (d'une discussion, recherche) subject; **être ou faire l'~ de** (discussion) to be the subject of; (soins) to be given ou shown; **sans ~** purposeless; groundless; **~ d'art** object d'art; **~s personnels** personal items; **~s trouvés** lost property sg (BRIT), lost-and-found sg (US)

obligation [ɔbligasjɔ̃] nf obligation; (COMM) bond, debenture; **obligatoire** adj compulsory, obligatory

obligé, e [ɔbliʒe] adj (redevable): **être très ~ à qn** to be most obliged to sb

obligeance [ɔbliʒɑ̃s] nf: **avoir l'~ de ...** to be kind ou good enough to ...; **obligeant, e** adj obliging; kind

obliger [ɔbliʒe] vt (contraindre): **~ qn à faire** to force ou oblige sb to do; (JUR: engager) to bind; (rendre service à) to oblige; **je suis bien obligé** I have to

oblique [ɔblik] adj oblique; regard **~** sidelong glance; **en ~** diagonally; **obliquer** vi: **obliquer vers** to turn off towards

oblitérer [ɔbliteʀe] vt (timbre-poste) to cancel

obscène [ɔpsɛn] adj obscene

obscur, e [ɔpskyʀ] adj dark; obscure; lowly; **~cir** vt to darken; (fig) to obscure; **s'~cir** vi to grow dark; **~ité** nf darkness; **dans l'~ité** in the dark, in darkness

obséder [ɔpsede] vt to obsess, haunt

obsèques [ɔpsɛk] nfpl funeral sg

observateur, trice [ɔpsɛʀvatœʀ, -tʀis] adj observant, perceptive ♦ nm/f observer

observation [ɔpsɛʀvasjɔ̃] nf observation; (d'un règlement etc) observance; (reproche) reproof

observatoire [ɔpsɛʀvatwaʀ] nm observatory; (lieu élevé) observation post, vantage point

observer [ɔpsɛʁve] vt (regarder) to observe, watch; (examiner) to examine; (scientifiquement, aussi: règlement, jeûne etc) to observe; (surveiller) to watch; (remarquer) to observe, notice; **faire ~ qch à qn** (dire) to point out sth to sb

obstacle [ɔpstakl(ə)] nm obstacle; (ÉQUITATION) jump, hurdle; **faire ~ à** (lumière) to block out; (projet) to hinder, put obstacles in the path of

obstiné, e [ɔpstine] adj obstinate

obstiner [ɔpstine]: **s'~** vi to insist, dig one's heels in; **s'~ à faire** to persist (obstinately) in doing; **s'~ sur qch** to keep working at sth, labour away at sth

obstruer [ɔpstʁye] vt to block, obstruct

obtempérer [ɔptɑ̃peʁe] vi to obey

obtenir [ɔptəniʁ] vt to obtain, get; (total, résultat) to arrive at, reach; to achieve, obtain; **~ de pouvoir faire** to obtain permission to do; **~ de qn qu'il fasse** to get sb to agree to do; **obtention** nf obtaining

obturateur [ɔptyʁatœʁ] nm (PHOTO) shutter

obturer [ɔptyʁe] vt to close (up); (dent) to fill

obus [ɔby] nm shell

occasion [ɔkazjɔ̃] nf (aubaine, possibilité) opportunity; (circonstance) occasion; (COMM: article non neuf) secondhand buy; (: acquisition avantageuse) bargain; **à plusieurs ~s** on several occasions; **être l'~ de** to occasion, give rise to; **à l'~** sometimes, on occasions; some time; **d'~** secondhand; **occasionnel, le** adj (fortuit) chance cpd; (non régulier) occasional; casual

occasionner [ɔkazjɔne] vt to cause, bring about; **~ qch à qn** to cause sb sth

occident [ɔksidɑ̃] nm: **l'O~** the West; **occidental, e, aux** adj western; (POL) Western

occupation [ɔkypasjɔ̃] nf occupation

occupé, e [ɔkype] adj (MIL, POL)

occupied; (personne: affairé, pris) busy; (place, sièges) taken; (toilettes) engaged; (ligne) engaged (BRIT), busy (US)

occuper [ɔkype] vt to occupy; (main-d'œuvre) to employ; **s'~ de** (être responsable de) to be in charge of; (se charger de: affaire) to take charge of, deal with; (: clients etc) to attend to; (s'intéresser à, pratiquer) to be involved in; **s'~** to occupy o.s. ou keep o.s. busy (with sth); **ça occupe trop de place** it takes up too much room

occurrence [ɔkyʁɑ̃s] nf: **en l'~** in this case

océan [ɔseɑ̃] nm ocean; **l'~ Indien** the Indian Ocean

octet [ɔktɛt] nm byte

octobre [ɔktɔbʁ(ə)] nm October

octroyer [ɔktʁwaje] vt: **~ qch à qn** to grant sth to sb, grant sb sth

oculiste [ɔkylist(ə)] nm/f eye specialist

odeur [ɔdœʁ] nf smell

odieux, euse [ɔdjø, -øz] adj hateful

odorant, e [ɔdɔʁɑ̃, -ɑ̃t] adj sweet-smelling, fragrant

odorat [ɔdɔʁa] nm (sense of) smell

œil [œj] (pl **yeux**) nm eye; **à l'~** (fam) for free; **à l'~ nu** with the naked eye; **tenir qn à l'~** to keep an eye ou a watch on sb; **avoir l'~** to keep an eye on; **fermer les yeux** (sur) (fig) to turn a blind eye (to)

œillade [œjad] nf: **lancer une ~ à qn** to wink at sb, give sb a wink; **faire des ~s à** to make eyes at

œillères [œjɛʁ] nfpl blinkers (BRIT), blinders (US)

œillet [œjɛ] nm (BOT) carnation

œuf [œf, pl ø] nm egg; **~ à la coque** nm boiled egg; **~ au plat** fried egg; **~ de Pâques** Easter egg; **~ dur** hard-boiled egg; **~s brouillés** scrambled eggs

œuvre [œvʁ(ə)] nf (tâche) task, undertaking; (ouvrage achevé, livre, tableau etc) work; (ensemble de la production artistique) works pl; (or-

ganisation charitable) charity ♦ *nm*
(_d'un artiste_) works pl; (_CONSTR_):
le gros ~ the shell; être à l'~ to
be at work; mettre en ~ (_moyens_)
to make use of; ~ **d'art** work of art

offense [ɔfɑ̃s] *nf* insult

offenser [ɔfɑ̃se] *vt* to offend, hurt;
(_principes, Dieu_) to offend against;
s'~ **de** to take offence at

offert, e [ɔfɛʀ, -ɛʀt(ə)] *pp de* **offrir**

office [ɔfis] *nm* (_charge_) office;
(_agence_) bureau, agency; (_REL_)
service ♦ *nm ou nf* (_pièce_) pantry; **faire** ~ **de** to act as; to do duty as;
d'~ automatically; ~ **du tourisme**
tourist bureau

officiel, le [ɔfisjɛl] *adj, nm/f* official

officier [ɔfisje] *nm* officer ♦ *vi* to officiate; ~ **de l'état-civil** registrar

officieux, euse [ɔfisjø, -øz] *adj* unofficial

officinal, e, aux [ɔfisinal, -o] *adj*:
plantes ~es medicinal plants

officine [ɔfisin] *nf* (_de pharmacie_)
dispensary; (_bureau_) agency, office

offrande [ɔfʀɑ̃d] *nf* offering

offre [ɔfʀ(ə)] *nf* offer; (_aux enchères_)
bid; (_ADMIN: soumission_) tender;
(_ECON_): l'~ supply; "~s d'emploi
'situations vacant'"; ~ **d'emploi** job
advertised; ~ **publique d'achat**
takeover bid

offrir [ɔfʀiʀ] *vt*: ~ (**à qn**) (_donner_
to sb) to offer (to sb); (_faire cadeau de_) to give (to
sb); s'~ *vi* (_occasion, paysage_) to
present itself ♦ *vt* (_vacances, voi-
ture_) to treat o.s. to; ~ (**à qn**) **de
faire qch** to offer to do sth (for sb);
~ **à boire à qn** to offer sb a drink;
s'~ **comme guide/en otage** to offer
one's services as (a) guide/offer o.s.
as hostage

offusquer [ɔfyske] *vt* to offend

ogive [ɔʒiv] *nf*: ~ **nucléaire** nuclear
warhead

oie [wa] *nf* (_ZOOL_) goose

oignon [ɔɲɔ̃] *nm* (_BOT, CULIN_) onion; (_de tulipe etc: bulbe_) bulb;
(_MÉD_) bunion

oiseau, x [wazo] *nm* bird; ~ **de
proie** bird of prey

oiseux, euse [wazø, -øz] *adj* point-
less; trivial

oisif, ive [wazif, -iv] *adj* idle ♦ *nm/f*
(_péj_) man(woman) of leisure

oléoduc [ɔleɔdyk] *nm* (oil) pipeline

olive [ɔliv] *nf* (_BOT_) olive; **olivier**
nm olive (tree)

olympique [ɔlɛ̃pik] *adj* Olympic

ombrage [ɔ̃bʀaʒ] *nm* (_ombre_) (leaf-
y) shade; **ombragé, e** *adj* shaded,
shady; **ombrageux, euse** *adj* (_che-
val_) skittish, nervous; (_personne_)
touchy, easily offended

ombre [ɔ̃bʀ(ə)] *nf* (_espace non enso-
leillé_) shade; (~ _portée, tache_) shadow; à l'~ in the shade; **tu me fais
de l'~** you're in my light; **ça nous
donne de l'~** it gives us (some)
shade; **dans l'~** in obscurity;
in the dark; ~ **à paupières** eyeshad-
ow; **ombrelle** [ɔ̃bʀɛl] *nf* parasol, sunshade

omelette [ɔmlɛt] *nf* omelette

omettre [ɔmɛtʀ(ə)] *vt* to omit, leave
out

omnibus [ɔmnibys] *nm* slow _ou_ stopping train

omoplate [ɔmɔplat] *nf* shoulder
blade

MOT-CLÉ

---

on [ɔ̃] *pron* **1** (_indéterminé_) you, one;
~ **peut le faire ainsi** you _ou_ one
can do it like this, it can be done like
this

2 (_quelqu'un_): ~ **les a attaqués**
they were attacked; ~ **vous demande au téléphone** there's a phone call
for you, you're wanted on the phone

3 (_nous_) we; ~ **va y aller demain**
we're going tomorrow

4 (_les gens_) they; autrefois, ~
croyait ... they used to believe ...

5: ~ **ne peut plus** *adv*: ~ **ne peut
plus stupide** as stupid as can be

---

oncle [ɔ̃kl(ə)] *nm* uncle

onctueux, euse [ɔ̃ktɥø, -øz] *adj*
creamy, smooth; (_fig_) smooth, unc-

tuous

onde [ɔ̃d] nf (PHYSIQUE) wave; **sur les ~s** on the radio; **mettre en ~s** to produce for the radio; **sur ~s courtes** on short wave sg; **moyennes/longues ~s** medium/long wave sg

ondée [ɔ̃de] nf shower

on-dit [ɔ̃di] nm inv rumour

ondoyer [ɔ̃dwaje] vi to ripple, wave

onduler [ɔ̃dyle] vi to undulate; (cheveux) to wave

onéreux, euse [ɔnerø, -øz] adj costly; **à titre ~** in return for payment

ongle [ɔ̃gl(ə)] nm (ANAT) nail; **se faire les ~s** to do one's nails

onguent [ɔ̃gɑ̃] nm ointment

ont vb voir **avoir**

O.N.U. [ɔny] sigle f = **Organisation des Nations Unies**

onze [ɔ̃z] num eleven; **onzième** num eleventh

O.P.A. sigle f = **offre publique d'achat**

opaque [ɔpak] adj opaque

opéra [ɔpera] nm opera; (édifice) opera house

opérateur, trice [ɔperatœr, -tris] nm/f operator; **~ (de prise de vues)** cameraman

opération [ɔperasjɔ̃] nf operation; (COMM) dealing

opératoire [ɔperatwar] adj operating; (choc etc) post-operative

opérer [ɔpere] vt (MED) to operate on; (faire, exécuter) to carry out, make ♦ vi (remède: faire effet) to act, work; (procéder) to proceed; (MED) to operate; **s'~** vi (avoir lieu) to occur, take place; **se faire ~** to have an operation

opiner [ɔpine] vi: **~ de la tête** to nod assent

opinion [ɔpinjɔ̃] nf opinion; **l'~ (publique)** public opinion

opportun, e [ɔpɔrtœ̃, -yn] adj timely, opportune; **en temps ~** at the appropriate time; **~iste** [ɔpɔrtynist(ə)] nm/f opportunist

opposant, e [ɔpozɑ̃, -ɑ̃t] adj opposing; **opposants** nmpl opponents

opposé, e [ɔpoze] adj (direction, rive) opposite; (faction) opposing; (couleurs) contrasting; (opinions, intérêts) conflicting; (contre): **~ à** opposed to, against ♦ nm: **l'~** the other ou opposite side (ou direction); (contraire) the opposite; **à l'~** (fig) on the other hand; **à l'~ de** on the other ou opposite side from; (fig) contrary to, unlike

opposer [ɔpoze] vt (personnes, armées, équipes) to oppose; (couleurs, termes, tons) to contrast; **s'~** (sens réciproque) to conflict; to clash; to contrast; **s'~ à** (interdire, empêcher) to oppose; (tenir tête à) to rebel against; **~ qch à** (comme obstacle, défense) to set sth against; (comme objection) to put sth forward against

opposition [ɔpozisjɔ̃] nf opposition; **par ~ à** as opposed to, in contrast with; **entrer en ~ avec** to come into conflict with; **être en ~ avec** (idées, intérêts) to be at variance with; **faire ~ à un chèque** to stop a cheque

oppresser [ɔprese] vt to oppress; **oppression** nf oppression; (malaise) feeling of suffocation

opprimer [ɔprime] vt to oppress; (liberté, opinion) to suppress, stifle; (suj: chaleur etc) to suffocate, oppress

opter [ɔpte] vi: **~ pour** to opt for; **~ entre** to choose between

opticien, ne [ɔptisjɛ̃, -ɛn] nm/f optician

optimiste [ɔptimist(ə)] nm/f optimist ♦ adj optimistic

option [ɔpsjɔ̃] nf option; **matière à ~** (SCOL) optional subject

optique [ɔptik] adj (nerf) optic; (verres) optical ♦ nf (PHOTO: lentilles etc) optics pl; (science, industrie) optics sg; (fig: manière de voir) perspective

opulent, e [ɔpylɑ̃, -ɑ̃t] adj wealthy,

opulent; (formes, poitrine) ample, generous

or [ɔʀ] nm gold ♦ conj now, but; en ~ gold cpd; (fig) golden, marvellous

orage [ɔʀaʒ] nm (thunder)storm; **orageux, euse** adj stormy

oraison [ɔʀɛzɔ̃] nf orison, prayer; ~ **funèbre** funeral oration

oral, e, aux [ɔʀal, -o] adj, nm oral

orange [ɔʀɑ̃ʒ] nf orange ♦ adj inv orange; **oranger** nm orange tree

orateur [ɔʀatœʀ] nm speaker; orator

orbite [ɔʀbit] nf (ANAT) (eye-)socket; (PHYSIQUE) orbit

orchestre [ɔʀkɛstʀ(ə)] nm orchestra; (de jazz, danse) band; (places) stalls pl (BRIT), orchestra (US); **orchestrer** vt (MUS) to orchestrate; (fig) to mount, stage-manage

orchidée [ɔʀkide] nf orchid

ordinaire [ɔʀdinɛʀ] adj ordinary; everyday; standard ♦ nm ordinary; (menus) everyday fare ♦ nf (essence) ≈ two-star (petrol) (BRIT) (gas), ≈ regular gas (US); d'~ usually, normally; à l'~ usually, ordinarily

ordinateur [ɔʀdinatœʀ] nm computer; ~ **domestique** home computer; ~ **individuel** personal computer

ordonnance [ɔʀdɔnɑ̃s] nf organization; layout; (MED) prescription; (JUR) order; (MIL) orderly, batman (BRIT)

ordonné, e [ɔʀdɔne] adj tidy, orderly; (MATH) ordered

ordonner [ɔʀdɔne] vt (agencer) to organize, arrange; (donner un ordre): ~ **à qn de faire** to order sb to do; (REL) to ordain; (MED) to prescribe

ordre [ɔʀdʀ(ə)] nm (gén) order; (propreté et soin) orderliness, tidiness; (nature): **d'~ pratique** of a practical nature; ~s nmpl (REL) holy orders; **mettre en** ~ to tidy (up), put in order; **à l'~ de qn** payable to sb; **être aux ~s de qn/sous les ~s de qn** to be at sb's disposal/under sb's command; **jusqu'à nou-** vel ~ until further notice; **dans le même** ~ **d'idées** in this connection; **donnez-nous un** ~ **de grandeur** give us some idea as regards size (ou the amount); **de premier** ~ first-rate; ~ **du jour** (d'une réunion) agenda; (MIL) order of the day; **à l'ordre du jour** (fig) topical

ordure [ɔʀdyʀ] nf filth no pl; ~s nfpl (balayures, déchets) rubbish sg, (US) garbage sg; ~s **ménagères** household refuse

oreille [ɔʀɛj] nf (ANAT) ear; (de marmite, tasse) handle; **avoir de l'~** to have a good ear (for music)

oreiller [ɔʀeje] nm pillow

oreillons [ɔʀɛjɔ̃] nmpl mumps sg

ores [ɔʀ]: **d'~ et déjà** adv already

orfèvrerie [ɔʀfɛvʀəʀi] nf goldsmith's (ou silversmith's) trade; (ouvrage) gold (ou silver) plate

organe [ɔʀgan] nm organ; (porte-parole) representative, mouthpiece

organigramme [ɔʀganigʀam] nm organization chart; flow chart

organique [ɔʀganik] adj organic

organisateur, trice [ɔʀganizatœʀ, -tʀis] nm/f organizer

organisation [ɔʀganizasjɔ̃] nf organization; **O~ des Nations Unies** United Nations (Organization); **O~ du traité de l'Atlantique Nord** North Atlantic Treaty Organization

organiser [ɔʀganize] vt to organize; **mettre sur pied:** service etc) to set up; **s'~** to get organized

organisme [ɔʀganism(ə)] nm (BIO) organism; (corps, ADMIN) body

organiste [ɔʀganist(ə)] nm/f organist

orgasme [ɔʀgasm(ə)] nm orgasm, climax

orge [ɔʀʒ(ə)] nf barley

orgie [ɔʀʒi] nf orgy

orgue [ɔʀg(ə)] nm organ; ~s nfpl (MUS) organ sg

orgueil [ɔʀgœj] nm pride; **orgueilleux, euse** adj proud

Orient [ɔʀjɑ̃] nm: **l'~** the East, the Orient

oriental, e, aux [ɔʀjɑ̃tal, -o] adj

oriental, eastern; (*frontière*) eastern

orientation [ɔʀjɑ̃tasjɔ̃] *nf* positioning; orientation; (*d'une maison etc*) aspect; (*d'un journal*) leanings *pl*; **avoir le sens de l'~** to have a (good) sense of direction; **~ professionnelle** careers advising; careers advisory service

orienté, e [ɔʀjɑ̃te] *adj* (*fig: article, journal*) slanted; **bien/mal ~** (*appartement*) well/badly positioned; **~ au sud** facing south, with a southern aspect

orienter [ɔʀjɑ̃te] *vt* (*placer, disposer: pièce mobile*) to adjust, position; (*tourner*) to direct, turn; (*voyageur, touriste, recherches*) to direct; (*fig: élève*) to orientate; **s'~** (*se repérer*) to find one's bearings; **s'~ vers** (*fig*) to turn towards

origan [ɔʀigɑ̃] *nm* (BOT) oregano

originaire [ɔʀiʒinɛʀ] *adj:* **être ~ de** to be a native of

original, e, aux [ɔʀiʒinal, -o] *adj* original; (*bizarre*) eccentric ♦ *nm/f* eccentric ♦ *nm* (*document etc, ART*) original; (*dactylographie*) top copy

origine [ɔʀiʒin] *nf* origin; **dès l'~** at *ou* from the outset; **à l'~** originally; **originel, le** *adj* original

O.R.L. *sigle nm/f* = oto-rhino-laryngologue

orme [ɔʀm(ə)] *nm* elm

ornement [ɔʀnəmɑ̃] *nm* ornament; (*fig*) embellishment, adornment

orner [ɔʀne] *vt* to decorate, adorn

ornière [ɔʀnjɛʀ] *nf* rut

orphelin, e [ɔʀfəlɛ̃, -in] *adj* orphan(ed) ♦ *nm/f* orphan; **~ de père/mère** fatherless/motherless; **orphelinat** *nm* orphanage

orteil [ɔʀtɛj] *nm* toe; **gros ~** big toe

orthographe [ɔʀtɔgʀaf] *nf* spelling; **orthographier** *vt* to spell

orthopédiste [ɔʀtɔpedist(ə)] *nm/f* orthopaedic specialist

ortie [ɔʀti] *nf* (stinging) nettle

os [ɔs, *pl* o] *nm* bone

osciller [ɔsile] *vi* (*pendule*) to swing; (*au vent etc*) to rock; (TECH) to os-

cillate; (*fig*): **~ entre** to waver *ou* fluctuate between

osé, e [oze] *adj* daring, bold

oseille [ozɛj] *nf* sorrel

oser [oze] *vi, vt* to dare; **~ faire** to dare (to) do

osier [ozje] *nm* willow; **d'~** wicker(work); **en ~ = d'osier**

ossature [ɔsatyʀ] *nf* (ANAT) frame, skeletal structure; (*fig*) framework

osseux, euse [ɔsø, -øz] *adj* bony; (*tissu, maladie, greffe*) bone *cpd*

ostensible [ɔstɑ̃sibl(ə)] *adj* conspicuous

otage [ɔtaʒ] *nm* hostage; **prendre qn comme ~** to take sb hostage

O.T.A.N. [ɔtɑ̃] *sigle f* = Organisation du traité de l'Atlantique Nord

otarie [ɔtaʀi] *nf* sea-lion

ôter [ote] *vt* to remove; (*soustraire*) to take away; **~ qch à qn** to take sth (away) from sb; **~ qch de** to remove sth from

otite [ɔtit] *nf* ear infection

oto-rhino-(laryngologiste) [ɔtoʀino(laʀɛ̃gɔlɔʒist(ə))] *nm/f* ear nose and throat specialist

ou [u] *conj* or; **~ ... ~** either ... or; **~ bien** (or else)

MOT-CLÉ

où [u] *pron relatif* **1** (*position, situation*) where, that (*souvent omis*); **la chambre ~ il était** the room (that) he was in, the room where he was; **la ville ~ je l'ai rencontré** the town where I met him; **la pièce d'~ il est sorti** the room he came out of; **le village d'~ je viens** the village I come from; **les villes par ~ il est passé** the towns he went through

2 (*temps, état*) that (*souvent omis*); **le jour ~ il est parti** the day (that) he left; **au prix ~ c'est** at the price it is

♦ *adv* **1** (*interrogation*) where; **~ est-il/va-t-il?** where is he/is he going?; **par ~?** which way?; **d'~ vient que ...?** how come ...?

2 (*position*) where; **je sais ~ il est**

I know where he is; ~ que l'on aille wherever you go

ouate [wat] *nf* cotton wool (BRIT), cotton (US); (*bourre*) padding, wadding

oubli [ubli] *nm* (*acte*): **l'~ de** forgetting; (*étourderie*) forgetfulness *no pl*; (*négligence*) omission, oversight; (*absence de souvenirs*) oblivion

oublier [ublije] *vt* (*gén*) to forget; (*ne pas voir: erreurs etc*) to miss; (*ne pas mettre: virgule, nom*) to leave out; (*laisser quelque part: chapeau etc*) to leave behind; **s'~** to forget o.s.

oubliettes [ublijɛt] *nfpl* dungeon *sg*

ouest [wɛst] *nm* west ♦ *adj inv* west; (*région*) western; **à l'~** in the west; (*to the*) west, westwards; **à l'~ de** (*to the*) west of

ouf [uf] *excl* phew!

oui [wi] *adv* yes

ouï-dire [widiR]: **par ~** *adv* by hearsay

ouïe [wi] *nf* hearing; **~s** *nfpl* (*de poisson*) gills

ouïr [wiR] *vt* to hear; **avoir ouï dire que** to have heard it said that

ouragan [uRaɡɑ̃] *nm* hurricane

ourlet [uRlɛ] *nm* hem

ours [uRs] *nm* bear; **~ brun/blanc** brown/polar bear; **~ (en peluche)** teddy (bear)

oursin [uRsɛ̃] *nm* sea urchin

ourson [uRsɔ̃] *nm* (bear-)cub

ouste [ust(ə)] *excl* hop it!

outil [uti] *nm* tool

outiller [utije] *vt* (*ouvrier, usine*) to equip

outrage [utRaʒ] *nm* insult; **faire subir les derniers ~s à** (*femme*) to ravish; **~ à la pudeur** indecent conduct *no pl*; **~r** [utRaʒe] *vt* to offend gravely

outrance [utRɑ̃s]: **à ~** *adv* excessively, to excess

outre [utR(ə)] *nf* goatskin, water skin ♦ *prép* besides ♦ *adv*: **passer ~ à** to disregard, take no notice of; **en ~**

besides, moreover; **~ que** apart from the fact that; **~ mesure** immoderately; unduly; **~-Atlantique** *adv* across the Atlantic; **~-Manche** *adv* across the Channel; **~mer** *adj inv* ultramarine; **~-mer** *adv* overseas; **~passer** *vt* to go beyond, exceed

ouvert, e [uvɛR, -ɛRt(ə)] *pp de* ouvrir ♦ *adj* open; (*robinet, gaz etc*) on; **ouverture** *adv* openly

ouverture [uvɛRtyR] *nf* opening; (MUS) overture; (PHOTO): **~ (du diaphragme)** aperture; **~s** *fpl* (*propositions*) overtures; **~ d'esprit** open-mindedness

ouvrable [uvRabl(ə)] *adj*: **jour ~** working day, weekday

ouvrage [uvRaʒ] *nm* (*tâche, de tricot etc, MIL*) work *no pl*; (*texte, livre*) work

ouvragé, e [uvRaʒe] *adj* finely embroidered (*ou* worked *ou* carved)

ouvre-boîte(s) [uvRəbwat] *nm inv* tin (BRIT) *ou* can opener

ouvre-bouteille(s) [uvRəbutɛj] *nm inv* bottle-opener

ouvreuse [uvRøz] *nf* usherette

ouvrier, ière [uvRje, -jɛR] *nm/f* worker ♦ *adj* working-class; (*conflit*) industrial, labour *cpd*; **classe ouvrière** working class

ouvrir [uvRiR] *vt* (*gén*) to open; (*brèche, passage, MED: abcès*) to open up; (*commencer l'exploitation de, créer*) to open (up); (*eau, électricité, chauffage, robinet*) to turn on ♦ *vi* to open; to open up; **s'~** *vi* to open; **s'~ à qn** to open one's heart to sb; **~ l'appétit à qn** to whet sb's appetite

ovaire [ɔvɛR] *nm* ovary

ovale [ɔval] *adj* oval

ovni [ɔvni] *sigle m* (= objet volant non identifié) UFO

oxyder [ɔkside]: **s'~** *vi* to become oxidized

oxygène [ɔksiʒɛn] *nm* oxygen; (*fig*): **cure d'~** fresh air cure

oxygéné, e [ɔksiʒene] *adj*: **eau ~e** hydrogen peroxide

P

pacifique [pasifik] adj peaceful ♦ nm: le P~, l'océan P~ the Pacific (Ocean)

pacte [pakt(ə)] nm pact, treaty

pactiser [paktize] vi: ~ avec to come to terms with

pagaie [pagɛ] nf paddle

pagaille [pagaj] nf mess, shambles sg

page [paʒ] nf page ♦ nm page (boy); à la ~ (fig) up-to-date

paiement [pɛmã] nm payment

païen, ne [pajɛ̃, -jɛn] adj, nm/f pagan, heathen

paillard, e [pajaʀ, -aʀd(ə)] adj bawdy

paillasson [pajasɔ̃] nm doormat

paille [pɑj] nf straw; (défaut) flaw

paillettes [pajɛt] nfpl (décoratives) sequins, spangles; lessive en ~ soapflakes pl

pain [pɛ̃] nm (substance) bread; (unité) loaf (of bread); (morceau): ~ de cire etc bar of wax etc; ~ bis/complet brown/wholemeal (BRIT) ou wholewheat (US) bread; ~ d'épice gingerbread; ~ de mie sandwich loaf; ~ de sucre sugar loaf; ~ grillé toast

pair, e [pɛʀ] adj (nombre) even ♦ nm peer; aller de ~ to go hand in hand ou together; jeune fille au ~ au pair

paire [pɛʀ] nf pair

paisible [pezibl(ə)] adj peaceful, quiet

paître [pɛtʀ(ə)] vi to graze

paix [pɛ] nf peace; (fig) peacefulness, peace; faire/avoir la ~ to make/have peace

Pakistan [pakistã] nm: le ~ Pakistan

palace [palas] nm luxury hotel

palais [palɛ] nm palace; (ANAT) palate

pale [pal] nf (d'hélice, de rame) blade

pâle [pɑl] adj pale; bleu ~ pale blue

Palestine [palɛstin] nf: la ~ Palestine

palet [palɛ] nm disc; (HOCKEY) puck

palette [palɛt] nf (de peintre) palette; (produits) range

pâleur [pɑlœʀ] nf paleness

palier [palje] nm (d'escalier) landing; (fig) level, plateau; (TECH) bearing; par ~s in stages

pâlir [pɑliʀ] vi to turn ou go pale; (couleur) to fade

palissade [palisad] nf fence

palliatif [paljatif] nm palliative; (expédient) stopgap measure

pallier [palje] : ~ à vt to offset, make up for

palmarès [palmaʀɛs] nm record (of achievements); (SCOL) prize list; (SPORT) list of winners

palme [palm(ə)] nf (symbole) palm; (de plongeur) flipper; **palmé, e** adj (pattes) webbed

palmier [palmje] nm palm tree

palombe [palɔ̃b] nf woodpigeon

pâlot, te [palo, -ɔt] adj pale, peaky

palourde [paluʀd(ə)] nf clam

palper [palpe] vt to feel, finger

palpitant, e [palpitã, -ãt] adj thrilling

palpiter [palpite] vi (cœur, pouls) to beat; (: plus fort) to pound, throb

paludisme [palydism(ə)] nm malaria

pamphlet [pãflɛ] nm lampoon, satirical tract

pamplemousse [pãpləmus] nm grapefruit

pan [pã] nm section, piece ♦ excl bang!

panachage [panaʃaʒ] nm blend, mix

panache [panaʃ] nm plume; (fig) spirit, panache

panaché, e [panaʃe] adj: glace ~e mixed-flavour ice cream; bière ~e shandy

pancarte [pãkaʀt(ə)] nf sign, notice; (dans un défilé) placard

pancréas [pãkʀeas] nm pancreas

pané, e [pane] *adj* fried in bread-crumbs

panier [panje] *nm* basket; **mettre au ~** to chuck away; **~ à provisions** shopping basket

panique [panik] *nf, adj* panic; **paniquer** *vi* to panic

panne [pan] *nf* (*d'un mécanisme, moteur*) breakdown; **être en ~** to have broken down/break down; **être en ~ d'essence** *ou* **sèche** to have run out of petrol (BRIT) *ou* gas (US); **~ d'électricité** *ou* **de courant** power *ou* electrical failure

panneau, x [pano] *nm* (*écriteau*) sign, notice; **~** (*de boiserie, de tapisserie etc*) panel; **~ d'affichage** notice board; **~ de signalisation** roadsign

panonceau, x [panõso] *nm* sign

panoplie [panɔpli] *nf* (*jouet*) outfit; (*d'armes*) display; (*fig*) array

panorama [panɔrama] *nm* panorama

panse [pãs] *nf* paunch

pansement [pãsmã] *nm* dressing, bandage; **~ adhésif** sticking plaster

panser [pãse] *vt* (*plaie*) to dress, bandage; (*bras*) to put a dressing on, bandage; (*cheval*) to groom

pantalon [pãtalõ] *nm* (*aussi*: **~s, paire de ~s**) trousers *pl*, pair of trousers; **~ de ski** ski pants *pl*

pantelant, e [pãtlã, -ãt] *adj* gasping for breath, panting

panthère [pãtɛʀ] *nf* panther

pantin [pãtɛ̃] *nm* jumping jack; (*péj*) puppet

pantois [pãtwa] *adj m*: **rester ~** to be flabbergasted

pantomime [pãtɔmim] *nf* mime; (*pièce*) mime show

pantoufle [pãtufl(ə)] *nf* slipper

paon [pã] *nm* peacock

papa [papa] *nm* dad(dy)

pape [pap] *nm* pope

paperasse [papʀas] (*péj*) *nf* bumf *no pl*, papers *pl*; **paperasserie** (*péj*) *nf* red tape *no pl*; paperwork *no pl*

papeterie [papetʀi] *nf* (*usine*) paper mill; (*magasin*) stationer's (shop)

papier [papje] *nm* paper; (*article*) article; **~s** *nmpl* (*aussi*: **~s d'identité**) (identity) papers; **~ à lettres** writing paper, notepaper; **~ buvard** blotting paper; **~ carbone** carbon paper; **~ (d')aluminium** (BRIT) *ou* aluminum (US) foil, tinfoil; **~ de verre** sandpaper; **~ hygiénique** toilet paper; **~ journal** newsprint; (*pour emballer*) newspaper; **~ peint** wallpaper

papillon [papijõ] *nm* butterfly; (*fam: contravention*) (parking) ticket; (*TECH: écrou*) wing nut; **~ de nuit** moth

papilloter [papijɔte] *vi* to blink, flicker

paquebot [pakbo] *nm* liner

pâquerette [pɑkʀɛt] *nf* daisy

Pâques [pɑk] *nm, nfpl* Easter

paquet [pakɛ] *nm* packet; (*colis*) parcel; (*fig: tas*): **~ de** pile *ou* heap of; **paquet-cadeau** *nm* gift-wrapped parcel

par [paʀ] *prép* by; **finir** *etc* **~** to end *etc* with; **~ amour** out of love; **passer ~ Lyon/la côte** to go via *ou* through Lyons/along by the coast; **~ la fenêtre** (*jeter, regarder*) out of the window; **3 ~ jour/personne** 3 a *ou* per day/head; **2 ~ 2** two at a time; in twos; **~ ici** this way; (*dans le coin*) round here; **~-ci, ~-là** here and there

parabole [paʀabɔl] *nf* (REL) parable

parabole [paʀabɔl] *nf* (REL) para-

parachever [paʀaʃve] *vt* to perfect

parachute [paʀaʃyt] *nm* parachute

parachutiste [paʀaʃytist(ə)] *nm/f* parachutist; (MIL) paratrooper

parade [paʀad] *nf* (*spectacle, défilé*) parade; (ESCRIME, BOXE) parry

paradis [paʀadi] *nm* heaven, paradise

paradoxe [paʀadɔks(ə)] *nm* paradox

paraffine [paʀafin] *nf* paraffin

parages [paʀaʒ] *nmpl*: **dans les ~ (de)** in the area *ou* vicinity (of)

paragraphe [paʀagʀaf] *nm* paragraph

paraître [paʀɛtʀ(ə)] *vb* +*attrib* to seem, look, appear ♦ *vi* to appear; (*être visible*) to be seen; (*PRESSE, EDITION*) to be published, come out, appear; (*briller*) to show off ♦ *vb impers*: **il paraît que ...** it seems *ou* appears that ..., they say that ...; **il me paraît que ...** it seems to me that ...

parallèle [paʀalɛl] *adj* parallel; (*police, marché*) unofficial ♦ *nm* (*comparaison*): **faire un ~ entre** to draw a parallel between; (*GEO*) parallel ♦ *nf* parallel (line)

paralyser [paʀalize] *vt* to paralyse

paramédical, e, aux [paʀamedikal] *adj*: **personnel ~** paramedics *pl*, paramedical workers *pl*

parapet [paʀapɛ] *nm* parapet

parapher [paʀafe] *vt* to initial; to sign

paraphrase [paʀafʀaz] *nf* paraphrase

parapluie [paʀaplɥi] *nm* umbrella

parasite [paʀazit] *nm* parasite; **~s** *nmpl* (*TEL*) interference *sg*

parasol [paʀasɔl] *nm* parasol, sunshade

paratonnerre [paʀatɔnɛʀ] *nm* lightning conductor

paravent [paʀavɑ̃] *nm* folding screen

parc [paʀk] *nm* (*public*) park, gardens *pl*; (*de château etc*) grounds *pl*; (*pour le bétail*) pen, enclosure; (*d'enfant*) playpen; (*MIL: entrepôt*) depot; (*ensemble d'unités*) stock; (*de voitures etc*) fleet; **~ automobile** (*d'un pays*) number of cars on the roads; **~ (d'attractions)** à thème theme park; **~ de stationnement** car park

parcelle [paʀsɛl] *nf* fragment, scrap; (*de terrain*) plot, parcel

parce que [paʀs(ə)kə] *conj* because

parchemin [paʀʃəmɛ̃] *nm* parchment

parc(o)mètre [paʀk(ɔ)mɛtʀ(ə)] *nm* parking meter

parcourir [paʀkuʀiʀ] *vt* (*trajet, distance*) to cover; (*article, livre*) to skim *ou* glance through; (*lieu*) to go all over, travel up and down; (*suj: frisson, vibration*) to run through

parcours [paʀkuʀ] *nm* (*trajet*) journey; (*itinéraire*) route; (*SPORT: terrain*) course; (*: tour*) round; run; lap

par-dessous [paʀdəsu] *prép, adv* under(neath)

pardessus [paʀdəsy] *nm* overcoat

par-dessus [paʀdəsy] *prép* over (the top of) ♦ *adv* over (the top); **~ le marché** on top of all that

par-devant [paʀdəvɑ̃] *prép* in the presence of, before ♦ *adv* at the front; round the front

pardon [paʀdɔ̃] *nm* forgiveness *no pl* ♦ *excl* sorry!; (*pour interpeller etc*) excuse me!; **demander ~ à qn (de)** to apologize to sb (for); **je vous demande ~** I'm sorry; excuse me

pardonner [paʀdɔne] *vt* to forgive; **~ qch à qn** to forgive sb for sth

pare: ~-balles *adj inv* bulletproof; **~-boue** *nm inv* mudguard; **~-brise** *nm inv* windscreen (*BRIT*), windshield (*US*); **~-chocs** *nm inv* bumper

pareil, le [paʀɛj] *adj* (*identique*) the same, alike; (*similaire*) similar; (*tel*): **un courage/livre ~** such courage/a book, courage/a book like this; **de ~s livres** such books; **ses ~s** one's fellow men; one's peers; **ne pas avoir son(sa) ~(le)** to be second to none; **~ à** the same as; similar to; **sans ~** unparalleled, unequalled

parent, e [paʀɑ̃, -ɑ̃t] *nm/f*: **un/une ~/e** a relative *ou* relation ♦ *adj*: **être ~ de** to be related to; **~s** *nmpl* (*père et mère*) parents; **parenté** *nf* (*lien*) relationship

parenthèse [paʀɑ̃tɛz] *nf* (*ponctuation*) bracket, parenthesis; (*MATH*) bracket; (*digression*) parenthesis, digression; **ouvrir/fermer la ~** to open/close the brackets; **entre ~s** in brackets; (*fig*) incidentally

parer [paʀe] *vt* to adorn; (*CULIN*) to

dress, trim; (éviter) to ward off

paresse [parɛs] nf laziness; **paresseux, euse** adj lazy; (fig) slow, sluggish

parfaire [parfɛr] vt to perfect

parfait, e [parfɛ, -ɛt] adj perfect ♦ nm (LING) perfect (tense); **parfaitement** adv perfectly ♦ excl (most) certainly

parfois [parfwa] adv sometimes

parfum [parfœ̃] nm (produit) perfume, scent; (odeur: de fleur) scent, fragrance; (: de tabac, vin) aroma; (goût) flavour; **parfumé, e** adj (fleur, fruit) fragrant; (femme) perfumed; **parfumé au café** coffee-flavoured; **parfumer** vt (suj: odeur, bouquet) to perfume; (mouchoir) to put scent ou perfume on; (crème, gâteau) to flavour; **parfumerie** nf (commerce) perfumery; (produits) perfumes pl; (boutique) perfume shop

pari [pari] nm bet, wager; (SPORT) bet

paria [parja] nm outcast

parier [parje] vt to bet

Paris [pari] n Paris; **parisien, ne** adj Parisian; (GEO, ADMIN) Paris cpd ♦ nm/f: **Parisien, ne** Parisian

paritaire [paritɛr] adj joint

parjure [parʒyr] nm perjury

parking [parkiŋ] nm (lieu) car park

parlant, e [parlɑ̃, -ɑ̃t] adj (fig) graphic, vivid; eloquent; (CINEMA) talking

parlement [parləmɑ̃] nm parliament; **parlementaire** adj parliamentary ♦ nm/f member of parliament

parlementer [parləmɑ̃te] vi to negotiate, parley

parler [parle] vi to speak, talk; (avouer) to talk; ~ (à qn) de to talk ou speak (to sb) about; le/en français to speak French/in French; ~ affaires to talk business; ~ en dormant to talk in one's sleep; sans ~ de (fig) not to mention, to say nothing of; tu parles! you must be joking!

parloir [parlwar] nm (de prison,

d'hôpital) visiting room; (REL) parlour

parmi [parmi] prép among(st)

paroi [parwa] nf wall; (cloison) partition; ~ rocheuse rock face

paroisse [parwas] nf parish

parole [parɔl] nf (faculté): la ~ speech; (mot, promesse) word; ~s nfpl (MUS) words, lyrics; tenir ~ to keep one's word; prendre la ~ to speak; demander la ~ to ask for permission to speak; je le crois sur ~ I'll take his word for it

parquer [parke] vt (voiture, matériel) to park; (bestiaux) to pen (in ou up)

parquet [parkɛ] nm (parquet) floor; (JUR): le ~ the Public Prosecutor's department

parrain [parɛ̃] nm godfather; (d'un nouvel adhérent) sponsor, proposer

parrainer [parɛne] vt (suj: entreprise) to sponsor

pars vb voir partir

parsemer [parsəme] vt (suj: feuilles, papiers) to be scattered over; ~ qch de to scatter sth with

part [par] nf (qui revient à qn) share; (fraction, partie) part; (FINANCE) (non-voting) share; prendre ~ à (débat etc) to take part in; (soucis, douleur de qn) to share in; faire ~ de qch à qn to announce sth to sb, inform sb of sth; pour ma ~ as for me, as far as I'm concerned; à ~ entière full; de la ~ de (au nom de) on behalf of; (donné par) from; de toute(s) ~(s) from all sides ou quarters; de ~ et d'autre on both sides, on either side; de ~ en ~ right through; d'une ~ ... d'autre ~ on the one hand ... on the other hand; à ~ separately; (de côté) aside ♦ prép apart from, except for ♦ adj exceptional, special; faire ~ à des choses to make allowances

partage [partaʒ] nm dividing up; sharing (out) no pl, share-out; sharing; recevoir qch en ~ to receive sth as one's share (*ou* lot)

partager [partaʒe] vt to share; (*distribuer, répartir*) to share (out); (*morceler, diviser*) to divide (up); se ~ vt (*héritage etc*) to share between themselves (*ou* ourselves)

partance [partɑ̃s]: en ~ adv outbound, due to leave; en ~ pour (bound) for

partant [partɑ̃] vb voir **partir** ♦ nm (SPORT) starter; (HIPPISME) runner

partenaire [partənɛr] nm/f partner

parterre [partɛr] nm (*de fleurs*) (flower) bed; (THEATRE) stalls *pl*

parti [parti] nm (POL) party; (*décision*) course of action; (*personne à marier*) match; tirer ~ de to take advantage of, turn to good account; prendre le ~ de qn to stand up for sb, side with sb; prendre ~ (pour/contre) to take sides *ou* a stand (for/against); prendre son ~ de to come to terms with; ~ pris bias

partial, e, aux [parsjal, -o] adj biased, partial

participant, e [partisipɑ̃, -ɑ̃t] nm/f participant; (*à un concours*) entrant

participation [partisipasjɔ̃] nf participation; sharing; (COMM) interest; la ~ aux bénéfices profit-sharing

participe [partisip] nm participle

participer [partisipe]: ~ à vt (*course, réunion*) to take part in; (*profits etc*) to share in; (*frais etc*) to contribute to; (*chagrin, succès de qn*) to share in

particularité [partikylarite] nf particularity; (*distinctive*) characteristic

particule [partikyl] nf particle

particulier, ière [partikyljɛr, -jɛr] adj (*personnel, privé*) private; (*spécial*) special, particular; (*caractéristique*) characteristic, distinctive; (*spécifique*) particular ♦ nm (*individu*: ADMIN) private individual; ~ à peculiar to; en ~ (*surtout*) in particular, particularly; (*en privé*) in private; **particulièrement** adv particularly

partie [parti] nf (*gén*) part; (*profession, spécialité*) field, subject; (JUR etc: *protagonistes*) party; (*de cartes, tennis etc*) game; une ~ de campagne/de pêche an outing in the country/a fishing party *ou* trip; en ~ partly, in part; faire ~ de to belong to; (*suj: chose*) to be part of; prendre qn à ~ to take sb to task; (*malmener*) to set on sb; en grande ~ largely, in the main; ~ civile (JUR) party claiming damages in a criminal case

partiel, le [parsjɛl] adj partial ♦ nm (SCOL) class exam

partir [partir] vi (*gén*) to go; (*quitter*) to go, leave; (*s'éloigner*) to go (*ou* drive etc) away *ou* off; (*moteur*) to start; ~ de (*lieu: quitter*) to leave; (: *commencer à*) to start from; (*date*) to run *ou* start from; à ~ de from

partisan, e [partizɑ̃, -an] nm/f partisan ♦ adj: être ~ de qch/de faire to be in favour of sth/doing

partition [partisjɔ̃] nf (MUS) score

partout [partu] adv everywhere; ~ où il allait everywhere *ou* wherever he went; trente ~ (TENNIS) thirty all

paru pp *de* **paraître**

parure [paryr] nf (*bijoux etc*) finery *no pl*; jewellery *no pl*; (*assortiment*) set

parution [parysjɔ̃] nf publication, appearance

parvenir [parvənir]: ~ à vt (*atteindre*) to reach; (*réussir*): ~ à faire to manage to do, succeed in doing; faire ~ qch à qn to have sth sent to sb

parvis [parvi] nm (*in front of a church*) square

pas¹ [pɑ] nm (*allure, mesure*) pace; (*démarche*) tread; (*enjambée, DANSE*) step; (*bruit*) (foot)step; (*trace*) footprint; (TECH: *de vis, d'écrou*) thread; ~ à ~ step by step; au ~ at walking pace; à ~ de loup stealthily; faire les cent ~ to pace

up and down; **faire les premiers ~**
to make the first move; **sur le ~ de
la porte** on the doorstep

MOT-CLÉ

---

pas² [pɑ] *adv* **1** (*en corrélation avec
ne, non etc*) not; **il ne pleure ~** he
does not *ou* doesn't cry; he's not *ou*
isn't crying; **il n'a ~ pleuré/ne
pleura ~** he did not *ou* didn't/will not
ou won't cry; **ils n'ont ~ de
voiture/d'enfants** they haven't got a
car/any children, they have no car/
children; **il m'a dit de ne ~ le faire** he told me not to do it; **non ~
que ...** not that ...
2 (*employé sans ne etc*): **~ moi** not
me, not I, I don't (*ou* can't *etc*); **une
pomme ~ mûre** an apple which
isn't ripe; **~ plus tard qu'hier** only
yesterday; **~ du tout** not at all
3: **~ mal** not bad; not badly; **~
mal de** quite a lot of

passage [pɑsaʒ] *nm* (*fait de passer
voir passer*; (*lieu, prix de la traversée, extrait*) passage; (*chemin*) way;
de ~ (*touristes*) passing through;
(*amants etc*) casual; **~ à niveau**
level crossing; **~ clouté** pedestrian
crossing; **"~ interdit"** "no entry";
"~ protégé" right of way over secondary road(s) on your right; **~ souterrain** subway (*BRIT*), underpass
passager, ère [pɑsaʒe, -ɛʀ] *adj*
passing ♦ *nm/f* passenger; **~ clandestin** stowaway
passant, e [pɑsɑ̃, -ɑ̃t] *adj* (*rue, endroit*) busy ♦ *nm/f* passer-by; **en ~** in
passing
passe [pɑs] *nf* (*SPORT, magnétique,
NAVIG*) pass ♦ *nm* (*passe-partout*)
master *ou* skeleton key; **être en ~
de faire** to be on the way to doing

passé, e [pɑse] *adj* (*événement,
temps*) past; (*couleur, tapisserie*)
faded ♦ *prép* after ♦ *nm* past;
(*LING*) past (tense); **~ de mode** out
of fashion; **~ composé** perfect
(tense); **~ simple** past historic

passe: **~-droit** *nm* special privilege;
~-montagne *nm* balaclava;
partout *nm inv* master *ou* skeleton
key ♦ *adj inv* all-purpose; **~ nm:
tour de ~** trick, sleight of hand *no pl*
passeport [pɑspɔʀ] *nm* passport
passer [pɑse] *vi* (*se rendre, aller*) to
go; (*voiture, piétons: défiler*) to pass
(by), go by; (*faire une halte rapide:
facteur, laitier etc*) to come, call; (:
pour rendre visite) to call *ou* drop in;
(*air, lumière*) franchir un obstacle
to get through; (*accusé, projet
de loi*): **~ devant** to come before;
(*film, émission*) to be on; (*temps,
jours*) to pass, go by; (*couleur, papier*) to fade; (*mode*) to die out;
(*douleur*) to pass, go away;
(*CARTES*) to pass; (*SCOL*) to go up
(to the next class) ♦ *vt* (*frontière,
rivière etc*) to cross; (*obstacle*) to go
through; (*examen*) to sit, take; (*visite médicale etc*) to have; (*journée,
temps*) to spend; (*donner*): **~ qch à
qn** to pass sth to sb; to give sb sth;
(*transmettre*): **~ qch à qn** to pass
sth on to sb; (*enfiler: vêtement*) to
slip on; (*faire entrer, mettre*): **(faire) ~ qch dans/par** to get sth into/
through; (*café*) to pour the water on;
(*thé, soupe*) to strain; (*film, pièce*) to
show, put on; (*disque*) to play, put
on; (*marché, accord*) to agree on;
(*tolérer*): **~ qch à qn** to let sb get
away with sth; **se ~** *vi* (*avoir lieu:
scène, action*) to take place; (*se dérouler: entretien etc*) to go;
(*s'écouler: semaine etc*) to pass; (*arriver*): **que s'est-il passé?** what
happened?; **se ~** *vi* (*s'écouler: semaine etc*) to go by; **se ~ de** to go
without; **se ~ les mains sous
l'eau/de l'eau sur le visage** to put
one's hands under the tap/run water
over one's face; **~ par** to go
through; **~ sur** (*faute, détail inttime*)
to pass over; **~ avant qch/qn** (*fig*)
to come before sth/sb; **laisser ~**
(*air, lumière, personne*) to let
through; (*occasion*) to let slip, miss;

(erreur) to overlook; ~ **à la radio/ télévision** to be on the radio/on television; ~ **pour riche** to be taken for a rich man; ~ **en seconde**, ~ **la seconde** *(AUTO)* to change into second; ~ **le balai/l'aspirateur** to sweep up/hoover; **je vous passe M. X** *(je vous mets en communication avec lui)* I'm putting you through to Mr X; *(je lui passe l'appareil)* here I'll hand you over to Mr X

passerelle [pɑsʀɛl] *nf* footbridge; *(de navire, avion)* gangway

passe-temps [pɑstɑ̃] *nm inv* pastime

passeur, euse [pɑsœʀ, -øz] *nm/f* smuggler

passible [pɑsibl(ə)] *adj:* ~ **de** liable to

passif, ive [pɑsif, -iv] *adj* passive ♦ *nm* *(LING)* passive; *(COMM)* liabilities *pl*

passion [pɑsjɔ̃] *nf* passion; **passionnant, e** *adj* fascinating; **passionné, e** *adj* passionate; impassioned; **passionner** *vt (personne)* to fascinate, grip; **se ~ner pour** to take an avid interest in; to have a passion for

passoire [pɑswaʀ] *nf* sieve; *(à légumes)* colander; *(à thé)* strainer

pastèque [pɑstɛk] *nf* watermelon

pasteur [pɑstœʀ] *nm (protestant)* minister, pastor

pastille [pɑstij] *nf (à sucer)* lozenge, pastille; *(de papier etc)* (small) disc

patate [patat] *nf:* ~ **douce** sweet potato

patauger [patoʒe] *vi (pour s'amuser)* to splash about; *(avec effort)* to wade about

pâte [pɑt] *nf (à tarte)* pastry; *(à pain)* dough; *(à frire)* batter; *(substance molle)* paste; cream; ~**s** *(macaroni etc)* pasta *sg*; ~ **à modeler** modelling clay, Plasticine (®); ~ **brisée** shortcrust pastry; ~ **d'amandes** almond paste; ~ **de fruits** crystallized fruit *no pl*

pâté [pɑte] *nm (charcuterie)* pâté; *(tache)* ink blot; *(de sable)* sandpie;

~ **de maisons** block (of houses); ~ **en croûte** ≈ pork pie

pâtée [pɑte] *nf* mash, feed

patente [patɑ̃t] *nf (COMM)* trading licence

paternel, le [patɛʀnɛl] *adj (amour, soins)* fatherly; *(ligne, autorité)* paternal

pâteux, euse [pɑtø, -øz] *adj* thick; pasty

pathétique [patetik] *adj* moving

patience [pasjɑ̃s] *nf* patience

patient, e [pasjɑ̃, -ɑ̃t] *adj, nm/f* patient

patienter [pasjɑ̃te] *vi* to wait

patin [patɛ̃] *nm* skate; *(sport)* skating; ~**s** **(à glace)** (ice) skates; ~**s** **à roulettes** roller skates

patinage [patinaʒ] *nm* skating

patiner [patine] *vi* to skate; *(embrayage)* to slip; *(roue, voiture)* to spin; **se** ~ *vi (meuble, cuir)* to acquire a sheen; **patineur, euse** *nm/f* skater; **patinoire** *nf* skating rink, (ice) rink

pâtir [pɑtiʀ]: ~ **de** *vt* to suffer because of

pâtisserie [pɑtisʀi] *nf (boutique)* cake shop; *(métier)* confectionery; *(à la maison)* pastry- ou cake-making, baking; ~**s** *nfpl (gâteaux)* pastries, cakes; **pâtissier, ière** *nm/f* pastrycook; confectioner

patois [patwa] *nm* dialect, patois

patrie [patʀi] *nf* homeland

patrimoine [patʀimwan] *nm* inheritance, patrimony; *(culture)* heritage

patriote [patʀijɔt(ə)] *adj* patriotic

patron, ne [patʀɔ̃, -ɔn] *nm/f* boss; *(REL)* patron saint ♦ *nm (COUTURE)* pattern

patronat [patʀɔna] *nm* employers *pl*

patronner [patʀɔne] *vt* to sponsor, support

patrouille [patʀuj] *nf* patrol

patte [pat] *nf (jambe)* leg; *(pied: de chien, chat)* paw; *(: d'oiseau)* foot; *(languette)* strap

pâturage [pɑtyʀaʒ] *nm* pasture

pâture [pɑtyʀ] *nf* food

paume [pom] *nf* palm

paumé, e [pome] *(fam) nmf* drop-out

paumer [pome] *(fam) vt* to lose

paupière [popjɛʀ] *nf* eyelid

pause [poz] *nf (arrêt)* break; *(en parlant, MUS)* pause

pauvre [povʀ(ə)] *adj* poor; **pauvreté** *nf (état)* poverty

pavaner [pavane]: **se ~** *vi* to strut about

pavé, e [pave] *adj* paved; cobbled ♦ *nm (bloc)* paving stone; cobblestone; *(pavage)* paving

pavillon [pavijɔ̃] *nm (de banlieue)* small (detached) house; *(kiosque)* lodge; pavilion; *(drapeau)* flag

pavoiser [pavwaze] *vt* to put out flags; *(fig)* to rejoice, exult

pavot [pavo] *nm* poppy

payant, e [pejɑ̃, -ɑ̃t] *adj (spectateurs etc)* paying; *(fig: entreprise)* profitable; **c'est ~** you have to pay, there is a charge

paye [pɛj] *nf* pay, wages *pl*

payer [peje] *vt (créancier, employé, loyer)* to pay; *(achat, réparations, fig: faute)* to pay for ♦ *vi* to pay; *(métier)* to be well-paid; *(tactique etc)* to pay off; **il me l'a fait ~** 10 F he charged me 10 F for it; **~ qch à qn** to buy sth for sb, buy sb sth; **cela ne paie pas de mine** it doesn't look much

pays [pei] *nm* country; land; region; village; **du ~** local

paysage [peizaʒ] *nm* landscape

paysan, ne [peizɑ̃, -an] *nmf* countryman(woman); farmer; *(péj)* peasant ♦ *adj* country *cpd*; farming, farmers'

Pays-Bas [peiba] *nmpl*: **les ~** the Netherlands

PC *nm (INFORM)* PC

PDG *sigle m* = **président directeur général**

péage [peaʒ] *nm* toll; *(endroit)* tollgate; **pont à ~** toll bridge

peau, x [po] *nf* skin; **gants de ~** fine leather gloves; **~ de chamois**

(chiffon) chamois leather, shammy;
Peau-Rouge *nmf* Red Indian, redskin

péché [peʃe] *nm* sin

pêche [pɛʃ] *nf (sport, activité)* fishing; *(poissons pêchés)* catch; *(fruit)* peach; **~ à la ligne** *(en rivière)* angling

pécher [peʃe] *vi (REL)* to sin; *(fig: personne)* to err; *(: chose)* to be flawed

pêcher [peʃe] *nm* peach tree ♦ *vi* to go fishing ♦ *vt* to catch; to fish for

pécheur, eresse [peʃœʀ, peʃʀɛs] *nmf* sinner

pêcheur [peʃœʀ] *nm* fisherman; angler

pécule [pekyl] *nm* savings *pl*, nest egg

pécuniaire [pekynjɛʀ] *adj* financial

pédagogie [pedagoʒi] *nf* educational methods *pl*, pedagogy; **pédagogique** *adj* educational

pédale [pedal] *nf* pedal

pédalo [pedalo] *nm* pedal-boat

pédant, e [pedɑ̃, -ɑ̃t] *(péj) adj* pedantic

pédestre [pedɛstʀ(ə)] *adj*: **tourisme ~** hiking

pédiatre [pedjatʀ(ə)] *nmf* paediatrician, child specialist

pédicure [pedikyʀ] *nmf* chiropodist

pègre [pɛgʀ(ə)] *nf* underworld

peignais *etc* vb *voir* **peindre**; **peigner**

peigne [pɛɲ] *nm* comb

peigner [peɲe] *vt* to comb (the hair of); **se ~** to comb one's hair

peignoir [peɲwaʀ] *nm* dressing gown; **~ de bain** bathrobe

peindre [pɛ̃dʀ(ə)] *vt* to paint; *(fig)* to portray, depict

peine [pɛn] *nf (affliction)* sorrow, sadness *no pl*; *(mal, effort)* trouble *no pl*, effort; *(difficulté)* difficulty; *(punition, châtiment)* punishment; *(JUR)* sentence; **faire de la ~ à qn** to distress *ou* upset sb; **prendre la ~ de faire** to go to the trouble of doing; **se donner de la ~** to make an effort; ce n'est pas la ~ de faire there's no point in doing, it's not worth doing; à ~ scarcely, hardly, barely; à ~ ... que hardly .. than; défense d'afficher sous ~ d'amende billposters will be fined; ~ capital ou de mort capital punishment, death sentence; **peiner** vi to work hard; to struggle; (moteur, voiture) to labour ♦ vt to grieve, sadden

peintre [pɛ̃tʁ(ə)] nm painter; ~ en bâtiment house painter

peinture [pɛ̃tyʁ] nf painting; (couche de couleur, couleur) paint; (surfaces peintes: aussi: ~s) paintwork; "~ fraîche" "wet paint"; ~ mate/brillante matt/gloss paint

péjoratif, ive [peʒɔʁatif, -iv] adj pejorative, derogatory

pelage [pəlaʒ] nm coat, fur

pêle-mêle [pɛlmɛl] adv higgledy-piggledy

peler [pəle] vt, vi to peel

pèlerin [pɛlʁɛ̃] nm pilgrim

pelle [pɛl] nf shovel; (d'enfant, de terrassier) spade; ~ mécanique mechanical digger

pellicule [pelikyl] nf film; ~s nfpl (MED) dandruff sg

pelote [pəlɔt] nf (de fil, laine) ball; (d'épingles) pin cushion; ~ basque pelota

peloton [pəlɔtɔ̃] nm group, squad; (CYCLISME) pack; ~ d'exécution firing squad

pelotonner [pəlɔtɔne]: se ~ vi to curl (o.s.) up

pelouse [pəluz] nf lawn

peluche [pəlyʃ] nf: animal en ~ fluffy animal, soft toy

pelure [pəlyʁ] nf peeling, peel no pl

pénal, e [penal] adj penal

pénalité [penalite] nf penalty

penaud, e [pəno, -od] adj sheepish, contrite

penchant [pɑ̃ʃɑ̃] nm tendency, propensity; liking, fondness

pencher [pɑ̃ʃe] vi to tilt, lean over ♦ vt to tilt; se ~ vi to lean over; (se baisser) to bend down; se ~ sur

bend over; (fig: problème) to look into; se ~ au dehors to lean out; ~ pour to be inclined to favour

pendaison [pɑ̃dɛzɔ̃] nf hanging

pendant [pɑ̃dɑ̃] nm: faire ~ à to match; to be the counterpart of during; ~ que while

pendentif [pɑ̃dɑ̃tif] nm pendant

penderie [pɑ̃dʁi] nf wardrobe

pendre [pɑ̃dʁ(ə)] vt, vi to hang; se ~ (à) (se suicider) to hang o.s. (on); ~ à to hang (down) from; ~ qch à to hang sth (up) on

pendule [pɑ̃dyl] nf clock ♦ nm pendulum

pénétrer [penetʁe] vi, vt to penetrate; ~ dans to enter; (suj: projectile) to penetrate; (: air, eau) to come into, get into

pénible [penibl(ə)] adj (astreignant) hard; (affligeant) painful; (personne, caractère) tiresome; ~ment adv with difficulty

péniche [peniʃ] nf barge

pénicilline [penisilin] nf penicillin

péninsule [penɛ̃syl] nf peninsula

pénis [penis] nm penis

pénitence [penitɑ̃s] nf (repentir) penitence; (peine) penance

pénitencier [penitɑ̃sje] nm penitentiary

pénombre [penɔ̃bʁ(ə)] nf half-light; darkness

pensée [pɑ̃se] nf thought; (démarche, doctrine) thinking no pl; (BOT) pansy; en ~ in one's mind

penser [pɑ̃se] vi to think ♦ vt to think; (concevoir: problème, machine) to think out; ~ à to think of; (songer à: ami, vacances) to think of ou about; (réfléchir à: problème, offre) ~ à qch to think about sth ou think sth over; faire ~ à to remind one of; ~ faire qch to be thinking of doing sth, intend to do sth

pensif, ive [pɑ̃sif, -iv] adj pensive, thoughtful

pension [pɑ̃sjɔ̃] nf (allocation) pension; (prix du logement) board and lodgings, bed and board; (maison *particulière)* boarding house; *(hôtel)* guesthouse, hotel; *(école)* boarding school; **prendre qn en ~** to take sb (in) as a lodger; **mettre en ~** to send to boarding school; **~ alimentaire** *(d'étudiant)* living allowance; *(de divorcée)* maintenance allowance; alimony; **~ complète** full board; **~ de famille** boarding house, guesthouse; **pensionnaire** *nm/f* boarder; guest; **pensionnat** *nm* boarding school

pente [pɑ̃t] *nf* slope; **en ~** sloping

Pentecôte [pɑ̃tkot] *nf*: **la ~** Whitsun (BRIT), Pentecost

pénurie [penyri] *nf* shortage

pépé [pepe] *(fam) nm* grandad

pépin [pepɛ̃] *nm (BOT: graine)* pip; *(ennui)* snag, hitch

pépinière [pepinjɛʀ] *nf* nursery

perçant, e [pɛʀsɑ̃, -ɑ̃t] *adj* sharp, keen; piercing, shrill

percée [pɛʀse] *nf (trouée)* opening; *(MIL, technologique)* breakthrough; *(SPORT)* break

perce-neige [pɛʀsɔnɛʒ] *nf inv* snowdrop

percepteur [pɛʀsɛptœʀ] *nm* tax collector

perception [pɛʀsɛpsjɔ̃] *nf* perception; *(d'impôts etc)* collection; *(bureau)* tax office

percer [pɛʀse] *vt* to pierce; *(ouverture etc)* to make; *(mystère, énigme)* to penetrate ♦ *vi* to come through; to break through; **~ une dent** to cut a tooth; **perceuse** *nf* drill

percevoir [pɛʀsəvwaʀ] *vt (distinguer)* to perceive, detect; *(taxe, impôt)* to collect; *(revenu, indemnité)* to receive

perche [pɛʀʃ(ə)] *nf (bâton)* pole

percher [pɛʀʃe] *vt, vi* to perch; **se ~** *vi* to perch; **perchoir** *nm* perch

perçois etc *vb voir* **percevoir**

percolateur [pɛʀkɔlatœʀ] *nm* percolator

perçu, e *pp de* **percevoir**

percussion [pɛʀkysjɔ̃] *nf* percussion

percuter [pɛʀkyte] *vt* to strike; *(suj:*

véhicule) to crash into

perdant, e [pɛʀdɑ̃, -ɑ̃t] *nm/f* loser

perdition [pɛʀdisjɔ̃] *nf*: **en ~** *(NAVIG)* in distress; **lieu de ~** den of vice

perdre [pɛʀdʀ(ə)] *vt* to lose; *(gaspiller: temps, argent)* to waste; *(personne: moralement etc)* to ruin ♦ *vi* to lose; *(sur une vente etc)* to lose money; **se ~** *vi (s'égarer)* to get lost, lose one's way; *(fig)* to go to waste; to disappear, vanish

perdrix [pɛʀdri] *nf* partridge

perdu, e [pɛʀdy] *pp de* **perdre** ♦ *adj (isolé)* out-of-the-way; *(COMM: emballage)* non-returnable; *(malade)*: **il est ~** there's no hope left for him; **à vos moments ~s** in your spare time

père [pɛʀ] *nm* father; **~s** *nmpl (ancêtres)* forefathers; **~ de famille** family man; **le ~ Noël** Father Christmas

perfectionné, e [pɛʀfɛksjɔne] *adj* sophisticated

perfectionner [pɛʀfɛksjɔne] *vt* to improve, perfect

perforatrice [pɛʀfɔʀatʀis] *nf (pour cartes)* card-punch; *(de bureau)* punch

perforer [pɛʀfɔʀe] *vt* to perforate; to punch a hole (ou holes) in; *(ticket, bande, carte)* to punch

performant, e [pɛʀfɔʀmɑ̃, -ɑ̃t] *adj*: **très ~** high-performance *cpd*

perfusion [pɛʀfyzjɔ̃] *nf*: **faire une ~ à qn** to put sb on a drip

péril [peʀil] *nm* peril

périmé, e [peʀime] *adj* (out)dated; *(ADMIN)* out-of-date, expired

périmètre [peʀimɛtʀ(ə)] *nm* perimeter

période [peʀjɔd] *nf* period; **périodique** *adj (phases)* periodic; *(publication)* periodical ♦ *nm* periodical

péripéties [peʀipesi] *nfpl* events, episodes

périphérique [peʀifeʀik] *adj (quartiers)* outlying; *(ANAT, TECH)* peripheral; *(station de radio)* operating from outside France ♦ nm (AUTO) ring road; (INFORM) peripheral

périple [peripl(ə)] nm journey

périr [perir] vi to die, perish

périssable [perisabl(ə)] adj perishable

perle [perl(ə)] nf pearl; (de plastique, métal, sueur) bead

perlé, e [perle] adj: **grève ~e** go-slow

perler [perle] vi to form in droplets

permanence [permanɑ̃s] nf permanence; (local) (duty) office; emergency service; **assurer une ~** (service public, bureaux) to operate ou maintain a basic service; **être de ~** to be on call ou duty; **en ~** permanently; continuously

permanent, e [permanɑ̃, -ɑ̃t] adj permanent; (spectacle) continuous; **permanente** nf perm

perméable [permeabl(ə)] adj (terrain) permeable; **~ à** (fig) receptive ou open to

permettre [permetr(ə)] vt to allow, permit; **~ à qn de faire/qch** to allow sb to do/sth; **se ~ de faire** to take the liberty of doing; **permettez!** excuse me!

permis [permi] nm permit, licence; **~ de chasse** hunting permit; **~ (de conduire)** (driving) licence (BRIT), (driver's) license (US); **~ de construire** planning permission (BRIT), building permit (US); **~ de séjour** residence permit; **~ de travail** work permit

permission [permisjɔ̃] nf permission; (MIL) leave; **avoir la ~ de faire** to have permission to do; **en ~** on leave

permuter [permyte] vt to change around, permutate ♦ vi to change, swap

Pérou [peru] nm Peru

perpétuel, le [perpetɥɛl] adj perpetual; (ADMIN etc) permanent; for life

perpétuité [perpetɥite] nf: **à ~** adj, adv for life; **être condamné à ~** to

receive a life sentence

perplexe [perpleks(ə)] adj perplexed, puzzled

perquisitionner [perkizisjɔne] vi to carry out a search

perron [perɔ̃] nm steps pl (in front of mansion etc)

perroquet [perɔke] nm parrot

perruche [peryʃ] nf budgerigar (BRIT), budgie (BRIT), parakeet (US)

perruque [peryk] nf wig

persan, e [persɑ̃, -an] adj Persian

persécuter [persekyte] vt to persecute

persévérer [persevere] vi to persevere

persiennes [persjen] nfpl (metal) shutters

persiflage [persiflaʒ] nm mockery no pl

persil [persi] nm parsley

Persique [persik] adj: **le golfe ~** the (Persian) Gulf

persistant, e [persistɑ̃, -ɑ̃t] adj persistent; (feuilles) evergreen

persister [persiste] vi to persist; **~ à faire qch** to persist in doing sth

personnage [persɔnaʒ] nm (notable) personality; figure; (individu) character, individual; (THEATRE) character; (PEINTURE) figure

personnalité [persɔnalite] nf personality; (personnage) prominent figure

personne [persɔn] nf person ♦ pron nobody, no one; (quelqu'un) anybody, anyone; **~s** nfpl (gens) people pl; **il n'y a ~** there's nobody there, there isn't anybody there; **~ âgée** elderly person; **personnel, le** adj personal ♦ nm staff, personnel; **personnellement** adv personally

perspective [perspektiv] nf (ART) perspective; (vue, coup d'œil) view; (point de vue) viewpoint, angle; (chose escomptée, envisagée) prospect; **en ~** in prospect

perspicace [perspikas] adj clear-sighted, gifted with (ou showing) insight

persuader [pɛrsɥade] *vt*: ~ qn (de/de faire) to persuade sb (of/to do)

perte [pɛrt(ə)] *nf* loss; (*de temps*) waste; (*fig: morale*) ruin; **à ~** (COMM) at a loss; **à ~ de vue** as far as the eye can (ou could) see; **~ sèche** dead loss; **~s blanches** (vaginal) discharge *sg*

pertinemment [pɛrtinamɑ̃] *adv* to the point; full well

pertinent, e [pɛrtinɑ̃, -ɑ̃t] *adj* apt, relevant

perturbation [pɛrtyrbasjɔ̃] *nf* disruption; perturbation; **~ (atmosphérique)** atmospheric disturbance

perturber [pɛrtyrbe] *vt* to disrupt; (PSYCH) to perturb, disturb

pervers, e [pɛrvɛr, -ɛrs(ə)] *adj* perverted, depraved; perverse

pervertir [pɛrvɛrtir] *vt* to pervert

pesant, e [pəzɑ̃, -ɑ̃t] *adj* heavy; (*fig*) burdensome

pesanteur [pəzɑ̃tœr] *nf* gravity

pèse-personne [pɛzpɛrsɔn] *nm* (bathroom) scales *pl*

peser [pəze] *vt* to weigh ♦ *vi* to be heavy; (*fig*) to carry weight; **~ sur** to lie heavy on; to influence

pessimiste [pesimist(ə)] *adj* pessimistic ♦ *nm/f* pessimist

peste [pɛst(ə)] *nf* plague

pester [pɛste] *vi*: **~ contre** to curse

pétale [petal] *nm* petal

pétanque [petɑ̃k] *nf type of bowls*

pétarader [petarade] *vi* to backfire

pétard [petar] *nm* banger (BRIT), firecracker

péter [pete] *vi* (*fam: casser, sauter*) to burst; to bust; (*fam!*) to fart (!)

pétillant, e [petijɑ̃, -ɑ̃t] *adj* (*eau etc*) sparkling

pétiller [petije] *vi* (*flamme, bois*) to crackle; (*mousse, champagne*) to bubble; (*yeux*) to sparkle

petit, e [pəti, -it] *adj* (*gén*) small; (*main, objet, colline, en âge: enfant*) small, little; (*voyage*) short, little; (*bruit etc*) faint, slight; (*mesquin*)

mean; **~s** *nmpl* (*d'un animal*) young *pl*; **faire des ~s** to have kittens (ou puppies *etc*); **les tout-petits** the little ones, the tiny tots; **~ à ~** bit by bit, gradually; **~(e)** ami(e) boyfriend/girlfriend; **~ déjeuner** breakfast; **~ pain** (bread) roll; **les ~es annonces** the small ads; **~s pois** garden peas; **~-bourgeois** (*f ~-bourgeoise*: *péj*) *adj* middle-class; **~-fille** *nf* granddaughter; **~-fils** *nm* grandson

pétition [petisjɔ̃] *nf* petition

petits-enfants [pətizɑ̃fɑ̃] *nmpl* grandchildren

petit-suisse [pətisɥis] (*pl petits-suisses*) *nm small individual pot of cream cheese*

pétrin [petrɛ̃] *nm* kneading-trough; (*fig*): **dans le ~** in a jam ou fix

pétrir [petrir] *vt* to knead

pétrole [petrɔl] *nm* oil; (*pour lampe, réchaud etc*) paraffin (oil); **pétrolier, ière** *adj* oil *cpd* ♦ *nm* oil tanker

---

MOT-CLÉ

peu [pø] *adv* 1 (*modifiant verbe, adjectif, adverbe*): **il boit ~** he doesn't drink (very) much; **il est ~ bavard** he's not very talkative; **~ avant/après** shortly before/afterwards

2 (*modifiant nom*): **~ de: ~ de gens/d'arbres** few ou not (very) many people/trees; **il a ~ d'espoir** he hasn't got much hope, he has little hope; **pour ~ de temps** for (only) a short while

3: **~ à ~** little by little; **à ~ près** just about, more or less; **à ~ près 10 kg/10F** approximately 10 kg/10F
♦ *nm* 1: **le ~ de gens qui** the few people who; **le ~ de sable qui** what little sand, the little sand which
2: **un ~** a little; **un petit ~** a little bit; **un ~ d'espoir** a little hope
♦ *pron*: **le savent** few know (it); **avant** ou **sous ~** shortly, before long; **de ~** (only) just

---

peuple [pœpl(ə)] *nm* people

peupler [pœple] vt (pays, région) to populate; (étang) to stock; (suj: hommes, poissons) to inhabit; (suj: imagination, rêves) to fill

peuplier [pøplije] nm poplar (tree)

peur [pœr] nf fear; **avoir ~** (de/de faire/que) to be frightened ou afraid (of/of doing/that); **faire ~ à** to frighten; **de ~ de/que** for fear of/that; **peureux, euse** adj fearful, timorous

peut vb voir **pouvoir**

peut-être [pøtɛtr(ə)] adv perhaps, maybe; **~ que** perhaps, maybe; **~ bien qu'il fera/est** he may well do/be

peux etc vb voir **pouvoir**

phare [far] nm (en mer) lighthouse; (de véhicule) headlight; **mettre ses ~s** to put on one's headlights; **~s de recul** reversing lights

pharmacie [farmasi] nf (magasin) chemist's (BRIT), pharmacy; (officine) pharmacy; (de salle de bain) medicine cabinet; **pharmacien, ne** nm/f pharmacist, chemist (BRIT)

phénomène [fenɔmɛn] nm phenomenon; (monstre) freak

philanthrope [filɑ̃trɔp] nm/f philanthropist

philatélie [filateli] nf philately, stamp collecting

philosophe [filɔzɔf] nm/f philosopher ♦ adj philosophical

philosophie [filɔzɔfi] nf philosophy

phobie [fɔbi] nf phobia

phonétique [fɔnetik] nf phonetics sg

phoque [fɔk] nm seal; (fourrure) sealskin

phosphorescent, e [fɔsfɔresɑ̃, -ɑ̃t] adj luminous

photo [fɔto] nf photo(graph); **en ~** in ou on a photograph; **prendre en ~** to take a photo of; **aimer la/faire de la ~** to like taking/take photos; **~ d'identité** passport photograph; **~copie** nf photocopying; photocopy; **~copier** vt to photocopy; **~copieuse** [fɔtɔkɔpjøz] nf photocopier; **~graphe** nm/f photographer; **~graphie** nf

(procédé, technique) photography; (cliché) photograph; **~graphier** vt to photograph

phrase [fraz] nf (LING) sentence; (propos, MUS) phrase

physicien, ne [fizisjɛ̃, -ɛn] nm/f physicist

physionomie [fizjɔnɔmi] nf face

physique [fizik] adj physical ♦ nm physique ♦ nf physics sg; **au ~ ph** sically; **~ment** adv physically

piaffer [pjafe] vi to stamp

piailler [pjɑje] vi to squawk

pianiste [pjanist(ə)] nm/f pianist

piano [pjano] nm piano

pianoter [pjanɔte] vi to tinkle away (at the piano); (tapoter): **~ sur** to drum one's fingers on

pic [pik] nm (instrument) pick(axe); (montagne) peak; (ZOOL) woodpecker; **à ~** vertically; (fig) just at the right time

pichet [piʃɛ] nm jug

picorer [pikɔre] vi to peck

picoter [pikɔte] vt (suj: oiseau) to peck ♦ vi (irriter) to smart, prickle

pie [pi] nf magpie; (fig) chatterbox

pièce [pjɛs] nf (d'un logement) room; (THEATRE) play; (de mécanisme, machine) part; (de monnaie) coin; (COUTURE) patch; (document) document; (de drap, fragment, de collection) piece; **dix francs ~** ten francs each; **vendre à la ~** to sell separately; **travailler/payer à la ~** to do piecework/pay piece rate; **un maillot une ~** a one-piece swimsuit; **un deux-pièces cuisine** a two-room(ed) flat (BRIT) ou apartment (US) with kitchen; **~ à conviction** exhibit; **~ d'eau** ornamental lake ou pond; **~ d'identité:** avez-vous une (means of) identification?; **~ montée** tiered cake; **~s détachées** spares, (spare) parts; **~s justificatives** supporting documents

pied [pje] nm foot; (de verre) stem; (de table) leg; (de lampe) base; (plante) plant; **à ~** on foot; **à ~ sec**

without getting one's feet wet; **au ~
de la lettre** literally; **de ~ en cap**
from head to foot; **en ~** (*portrait*)
full-length; **avoir ~** to be able to
touch the bottom, not to be out of
one's depth; **avoir le ~ marin** to
be a good sailor; **sur ~** (*debout, réta-
bli*) up and about; **mettre sur ~**
(*entreprise*) to set up; **mettre à ~**
to dismiss; to lay off; **mettre à ~ de vigne**
vine

piédestal, aux [pjedɛstal, -o] nm
pedestal

pied-noir [pjɛnwaʀ] nm Algerian-
born Frenchman

piège [pjɛʒ] nm trap; **prendre au ~**
to trap; **piéger** vt (*avec une bombe*)
to booby-trap; **lettre/voiture piégée**
letter-/car-bomb

pierraille [pjɛʀɑj] nf loose stones pl

pierre [pjɛʀ] nf stone; **~ à briquet**
flint; **~ fine** semiprecious stone; **~
tombale** tombstone; **pierreries**
[pjɛʀʀi] nfpl gems, precious stones

piétiner [pjetine] vi (*trépigner*) to
stamp (one's foot); (*marquer le pas*)
to stand still; (*fig*) to be at a standstill ♦ vt to trample on

piéton, ne [pjetɔ̃, -ɔn] nm/f pedestrian; **piétonnier, ière** adj: **rue ou
zone piétonnière** pedestrian precinct

pieu, x [pjø] nm post; (*pointu*) stake

pieuvre [pjœvʀ(ə)] nf octopus

pieux, euse [pjø, -øz] adj pious

piffer [pife] (*fam*) vt: **je ne peux
pas le ~** I can't stand him

pigeon [piʒɔ̃] nm pigeon

piger [piʒe] (*fam*) vi, vt to understand

pigiste [piʒist(ə)] nm/f freelance(r)

pignon [piɲɔ̃] nm (*de mur*) gable;
(*d'engrenage*) cog(wheel), gearwheel

pile [pil] nf (*tas*) pile; (*ELEC*) battery ♦ adv (*s'arrêter etc*) dead; **à
deux heures ~** at two on the dot;
jouer à ~ ou face to toss up (for
it); **~ ou face?** heads or tails?

piler [pile] vt to crush, pound

pileux, euse [pilø, -øz] adj: sys-

tème ~ (*body*) hair

pilier [pilje] nm pillar

piller [pije] vt to pillage, plunder, loot

pilon [pilɔ̃] nm pestle

pilote [pilɔt] nm (*de char, voiture*) driver ♦ adj pilot cpd: **~ de
course** racing driver; **~ de ligne/
d'essai/de chasse** airline/test/fighter
pilot; **~r** [pilɔte] vt to pilot, fly; to
drive

pilule [pilyl] nf pill; **prendre la ~** to
be on the pill

piment [pimɑ̃] nm (*BOT*) pepper,
capsicum; (*fig*) spice, piquancy

pimpant, e [pɛ̃pɑ̃, -ɑ̃t] adj spruce

pin [pɛ̃] nm pine (tree); (*bois*)
pine(wood)

pinard [pinaʀ] (*fam*) nm (*cheap*)
wine, plonk (*BRIT*)

pince [pɛ̃s] nf (*outil*) pliers pl; (*de
homard, crabe*) pincer, claw; (*COU-
TURE*: pli) dart; **~ à épiler** tweezers pl; **~ à linge** clothes peg
(*BRIT*) ou pin (*US*); **~ à sucre** sugar tongs pl

pincé, e [pɛ̃se] adj (*air*) stiff

pinceau, x [pɛ̃so] nm (paint)brush

pincée [pɛ̃se] nf: **une ~ de** a pinch
of

pincer [pɛ̃se] vt to pinch; (*MUS*:
cordes) to pluck; (*fam*) to nab

pincettes [pɛ̃sɛt] nfpl (*pour le feu*)
(fire) tongs

pinède [pinɛd] nf pinewood, pine forest

pingouin [pɛ̃gwɛ̃] nm penguin

ping-pong [piŋpɔ̃g] ® nm table tennis

pingre [pɛ̃gʀ(ə)] adj niggardly

pinson [pɛ̃sɔ̃] nm chaffinch

pintade [pɛ̃tad] nf guinea-fowl

pioche [pjɔʃ] nf pickaxe; **piocher** vt
to dig up (with a pickaxe)

piolet [pjɔlɛ] nm ice axe

pion [pjɔ̃] nm (*ECHECS*) pawn;
(*DAMES*) piece

pionnier [pjɔnje] nm pioneer

pipe [pip] nf pipe

pipeau, x [pipo] nm (reed-)pipe

piquant, e [pikɑ̃, -ɑ̃t] adj (barbe,

rosier etc) prickly; (saveur, sauce) hot, pungent; (fig) racy; biting ♦ nm (épine) thorn, prickle; (fig) spiciness, spice

pique [pik] nf pike; (fig) cutting remark ♦ nm (CARTES: couleur) spades pl; (: carte) spade

pique-nique [piknik] nm picnic

piquer [pike] vt (percer) to prick; (planter): ~ qch dans to stick into; (MED) to give a jab to; (: animal blessé etc) to put to sleep; (: insecte, fumée, ortie) to sting; (: poivre) to burn; (: froid) to bite; (COUTURE) to machine (stitch); (intérêt etc) to arouse; (fam) to pick up; (: voler) to pinch; (: arrêter) to nab ♦ vi (avion) to go into a dive; se ~ de faire to pride o.s. on doing; ~ un galop/un cent mètres to break into a gallop/put on a sprint

piquet [pikɛ] nm (pieu) post, stake; (de tente) peg; ~ de grève (strike-) picket; ~ d'incendie fire-fighting squad

piqûre [pikyʀ] nf (d'épingle) prick; (d'ortie) sting; (de moustique) bite; (MED) injection, shot (US); (COUTURE) (straight) stitch; straight stitching; faire une ~ à qn to give sb an injection

pirate [piʀat] nm, adj pirate; ~ de l'air hijacker

pire [piʀ] adj worse; (superlatif): le(la) ~ ... the worst ♦ nm: le ~ (de) the worst (of)

pis [pi] nm (de vache) udder; (pire): le ~ the worst ♦ adj, adv worse; ~ aller nm inv stopgap

piscine [pisin] nf (swimming) pool; ~ couverte indoor (swimming) pool

pissenlit [pisɑ̃li] nm dandelion

pistache [pistaʃ] nf pistachio (nut)

piste [pist(ə)] nf (d'un animal, sentier) track, trail; (indice) lead; (de stade, de magnétophone) track; (de cirque) ring; (de danse) floor; (de patinage) rink; (de ski) run; (AVIAT) runway; ~ cyclable cycle track

pistolet [pistɔlɛ] nm (arme) pistol, gun; (à peinture) spray gun; ~ à air comprimé airgun; ~-mitrailleur nm submachine gun

piston [pistɔ̃] nm (TECH) piston; **pistonner** vt (candidat) to pull strings for

piteux, euse [pitø, -øz] adj pitiful (avant le nom), sorry (avant le nom)

pitié [pitje] nf pity; faire ~ to inspire pity; avoir ~ de (compassion) to pity, feel sorry for; (merci) to have pity ou mercy on

piton [pitɔ̃] nm (clou) peg; ~ rocheux rocky outcrop

pitoyable [pitwajabl(ə)] adj pitiful

pitre [pitʀ(ə)] nm clown; **pitrerie** nf tomfoolery no pl

pittoresque [pitɔʀɛsk(ə)] adj picturesque

pivot [pivo] nm pivot; **pivoter** vi to swivel; to revolve

P.J. sigle f (= police judiciaire) ≈ CID (BRIT); ≈ FBI (US)

placard [plakaʀ] nm (armoire) cupboard; (affiche) poster, notice; ~er vt (affiche) to put up

place [plas] nf (emplacement, situation, classement) place; (de ville, village) square; (espace libre) room, space; (de parking) space; (siège: de train, cinéma, voiture) seat; (emploi) job; en ~ (mettre) in its place; sur ~ on the spot; faire ~ à to give way to; faire de la ~ à to make room for; ça prend de la ~ it takes up a lot of room ou space; à la ~ de in place of, instead of; il y a 20 ~s assises/debout there are 20 seats/there is standing room for 20

placement [plasmɑ̃] nm placing; (FINANCE) investment; bureau de ~ employment agency

placer [plase] vt to place; (convive, spectateur) to seat; (capital, argent) to place, invest; (dans la conversation) to put ou get in; se ~ au premier rang to go and stand (ou sit) in the first row

plafond [plafɔ̃] nm ceiling

plafonner [plafɔne] vi to reach one's (ou à ceiling

plage [plaʒ] nf beach; (fig) band, bracket; (de disque) track, band; ~ **arrière** (AUTO) parcel ou back shelf

plagiat [plaʒja] nm plagiarism

plaider [plede] vi (avocat) to plead; (plaignant) to go to court, litigate ♦ vt to plead; ~ **pour** (fig) to speak for; **plaidoyer** nm (JUR) speech for the defence; (fig) plea

plaie [plɛ] nf wound

plaignant, e [plɛɲɑ̃, -ɑ̃t] nm/f plaintiff

plaindre [plɛ̃dr(ə)] vt to pity, feel sorry for; **se** ~ vi (gémir) to moan; (protester, souspéter): **se** ~ (**à qn**) (**de**) to complain (to sb) (about); **se** ~ vi; (souffrir): **se** ~ **de** to complain of

plaine [plɛn] nf plain

plain-pied [plɛ̃pje] adv: **de** ~ (**avec**) on the same level (as)

plainte [plɛ̃t] nf (gémissement) moan, groan; (doléance) complaint; **porter** ~ to lodge a complaint

plaire [plɛr] vi to please; ~ **à**: **cela me plaît** I like it; **se** ~ **quelque part** to like being somewhere ou like it somewhere; **s'il vous plaît** please

plaisance [plɛzɑ̃s] nf (aussi: navigation de ~) (pleasure) sailing, yachting

plaisant, e [plɛzɑ̃, -ɑ̃t] adj pleasant; (histoire, anecdote) amusing

plaisanter [plɛzɑ̃te] vi to joke; **plaisanterie** nf joke; joking no pl

plaise etc vb voir **plaire**

plaisir [plɛzir] nm pleasure; **faire** ~ **à qn** (délibérément) to be nice to sb, please sb; (suj: cadeau, nouvelle etc): **ceci me fait** ~ I'm delighted ou very pleased with this; **pour le** ou **par** ~ for pleasure

plaît vb voir **plaire**

plan, e [plɑ̃, -an] adj flat ♦ nm plan; (GEOM) plane; (fig) level, plane; (CINEMA) shot; **au premier/second** ~ in the foreground/middle distance;

à l'arrière ~ in the background; ~ **d'eau** lake; pond

planche [plɑ̃ʃ] nf (pièce de bois) plank, (wooden) board; (illustration) plate; **les** ~**s** nfpl (THEATRE) the stage sg, the boards; ~ **à repasser** ironing board; ~ **à roulettes** skateboard; ~ **de salut** (fig) sheet anchor

plancher [plɑ̃ʃe] nm floor; floorboards pl; (fig) minimum level ♦ vi to work hard

planer [plane] vi to glide; ~ **sur** (fig) to hang over; to hover above

planète [planɛt] nf planet

planeur [planœr] nm glider

planification [planifikasjɔ̃] nf (economic) planning

planifier [planifje] vt to plan

planning [planiŋ] nm programme, schedule; ~ **familial** family planning

planque [plɑ̃k] (fam) nf (emploi peu fatigant) cushy (BRIT) ou easy number; (cachette) hiding place

plant [plɑ̃] nm seedling, young plant

plante [plɑ̃t] nf plant; ~ **d'appartement** house ou pot plant; ~ **du pied** sole of the foot

planter [plɑ̃te] vt (plante) to plant; (enfoncer) to hammer ou drive in; (tente) to put up, pitch; (fam) to dump; to ditch; **se** ~ (fam: se tromper) to get it wrong

plantureux, euse [plɑ̃tyrø, -øz] adj copious, lavish; (femme) buxom

plaque [plak] nf plate; (de verglas, d'eczéma) patch; (avec inscription) plaque; ~ **chauffante** hotplate; ~ **de chocolat** bar of chocolate; ~ (**minéralogique** ou **d'immatriculation**) number (BRIT) ou license (US) plate; ~ **tournante** (fig) centre

plaqué, e [plake] adj: ~ **or/argent** gold-/silver-plated; ~ **acajou** veneered in mahogany

plaquer [plake] vt (aplatir): ~ **qch sur** ou **contre** to make sth stick ou cling to; (RUGBY) to bring down; (fam: laisser tomber) to drop

plaquette [plakɛt] nf (de chocolat)

bar; (*beurre*) pack(et)

plastic [plastik] *nm* plastic explosive

plastique [plastik] *adj, nm* plastic

plastiquer [plastike] *vt* to blow up (*with a plastic bomb*)

plat, e [pla, -at] *adj* flat; (*cheveux*) straight; (*personne, livre*) dull ♦ *nm* (*récipient, CULIN*) dish; (*d'un repas*): **le premier** ~ the first course; **à** ~ **ventre** face down; **à** ~ (*pneu, batterie*) flat; (*personne*) dead beat; ~ **cuisiné** pre-cooked meal; ~ **de résistance** main course; ~ **du jour** dish of the day

platane [platan] *nm* plane tree

plateau, x [plato] *nm* (*support*) tray; (*GEO*) plateau; (*de tourne-disques*) turntable; (*CINEMA*) set; ~ **à fromages** cheeseboard

plate-bande [platbãd] *nf* flower bed

plate-forme [platfɔʀm(ə)] *nf* platform; ~ **de forage/pétrolière** drilling/oil rig

platine [platin] *nm* platinum ♦ *nf* (*d'un tourne-disque*) turntable

plâtras [plɑtʀa] *nm* rubble *no pl*

plâtre [plɑtʀ(ə)] *nm* (*matériau*) plaster; (*statue*) plaster statue; (*MED*) (plaster) cast; **avoir un bras dans le** ~ to have an arm in plaster

plein, e [plɛ̃, -ɛn] *adj* full; (*porte, roue*) solid; (*chienne, jument*) big (*with young*) ♦ *nm*: **faire le** ~ (*d'essence*) to fill up (*with petrol*); **à** ~**es mains** (*ramasser*) in handfuls; (*empoigner*) firmly; **à** ~ **régime** at maximum revs; (*fig*) full steam; **à** ~ **temps** full-time; **en** ~ **air** in the open air; **en** ~ **soleil** in direct sunlight; **en** ~**e nuit/rue** in the middle of the night/street; **en** ~ **jour** in broad daylight; **en** ~ **sur** right on; **plein-emploi** *nm* full employment

plénitude [plenityd] *nf* fullness

pleurer [plœʀe] *vi* to cry; (*yeux*) to water ♦ *vt* to mourn (for); ~ **sur** to lament (over), to bemoan

pleurnicher [plœʀniʃe] *vi* to snivel, whine

pleurs [plœʀ] *nmpl*: **en** ~ in tears

pleut *vb voir* **pleuvoir**

pleuvoir [pløvwaʀ] *vb impers* to rain ♦ *vi* (*fig*): ~ (**sur**) to shower down (upon); to be showered upon; **il pleut** it's raining

pli [pli] *nm* fold; (*de jupe*) pleat; (*de pantalon*) crease; (*aussi: faux* ~) crease; (*enveloppe*) envelope; (*lettre*) letter; (*CARTES*) trick

pliant, e [plijã, -ãt] *adj* folding ♦ *nm* folding stool, campstool

plier [plije] *vt* to fold; (*pour ranger*) to fold up; (*table pliante*) to fold down; (*genou, bras*) to bend ♦ *vi* to bend; (*fig*) to yield; **se** ~ **à** to submit to

plinthe [plɛ̃t] *nf* skirting board

plisser [plise] *vt* (*rider, chiffonner*) to crease; (*jupe*) to put pleats in

plomb [plɔ̃] *nm* (*métal*) lead; (*d'une cartouche*) (lead) shot; (*PECHE*) sinker; (*sceau*) (lead) seal; (*ELEC*) fuse; **sans** ~ (*essence etc*) unleaded

plombage [plɔ̃baʒ] *nm* (*de dent*) filling

plomber [plɔ̃be] *vt* (*canne, ligne*) to weight (with lead); (*dent*) to fill

plomberie [plɔ̃bʀi] *nf* plumbing

plombier [plɔ̃bje] *nm* plumber

plongeant, e [plɔ̃ʒã, -ãt] *adj* plunging (*from above*; *tir, décolleté*) plunging

plongée [plɔ̃ʒe] *nf* (*SPORT*) diving *no pl*; (: *sans scaphandre*) skin diving

plongeoir [plɔ̃ʒwaʀ] *nm* diving board

plongeon [plɔ̃ʒɔ̃] *nm* dive

plonger [plɔ̃ʒe] *vi* to dive ♦ *vt*: ~ **qch dans** to plunge sth into

ployer [plwaje] *vt* to bend ♦ *vi* to sag; to bend

plu *pp de* **plaire; pleuvoir**

pluie [plɥi] *nf* rain; (*fig*): ~ **de** shower of

plume [plym] *nf* feather; (*pour écrire*) (pen) nib; (*fig*) pen; ~**r** (*plume*) *vt* to pluck; **plumier** [plymje] *nm* pencil box

plupart [plypaʀ]: **la** ~ *pron* the ma-

jority, most (of them); **la ~ des**
most, the majority of; **la ~ du
temps/d'entre nous** most of the
time/of us; **pour la ~** for the most
part, mostly

pluriel [plyʀjɛl] *nm* plural

plus¹ *vb voir* **plaire**

| MOT-CLÉ |

plus² [ply] *adv* 1 *(forme négative)*:
ne ... ~ no more, no longer; **je n'ai
~ d'argent** I've got no more money
ou no money left; **il ne travaille ~**
he's no longer working, he doesn't
work any more
2 [ply, plyz, + *voyelle*] *(comparatif)*
more, ...+er; *(superlatif)*: **le ~** the
most, the ...+est; **le ~ grand/
intelligent (que)** bigger/more intelligent (than); **le ~ grand/intelligent**
the biggest/most intelligent; **tout au
~ at** the very most
3 [plys] *(davantage)* more; **il travaille ~ (que)** he works more
(than); **~ il travaille, ~ il est heureux** the more he works, the happier
he is; **~ de pain** more bread; **~ de
10 personnes** more than 10 people,
over 10 people; **3 heures de ~ que** 3
hours more than; **de ~ what's** more,
moreover; **3 kilos en ~** 3 kilos
more; **en ~** in addition to; **de ~
en ~** more and more; **~ ou moins**
more or less; **ni ~ ni moins** no
more, no less

♦ *prép* [plys]: **4 ~ 2** 4 plus 2

plusieurs [plyzjœʀ] *dét, pron* several; **ils sont ~** there are several of
them

plus-que-parfait [plyskapaʀfɛ] *nm*
pluperfect, past perfect

plus-value [plyvaly] *nf* appreciation;
capital gain; surplus

plut *vb voir* **plaire**

plutôt [plyto] *adv* rather; **je ferais
~ ceci** I'd rather *ou* sooner do this;
fais ~ comme ça try this way instead, you'd better try this way; **~
que (de) faire** rather than *ou* in-

stead of doing

pluvieux, euse [plyvjø, -øz] *adj*
rainy, wet

PMU *sigle m* (= pari mutuel urbain)
system of betting on horses; *(café)*
betting agency

pneu [pnø] *nm* tyre (BRIT), tire
(US)

pneumatique [pnømatik] *nm* tyre
(BRIT), tire (US)

pneumonie [pnømɔni] *nf* pneumonia

poche [pɔʃ] *nf* pocket; *(déformation)*: **faire une** *ou* **des ~(s)** to
bag; *(sous les yeux)* bag, pouch; **de
~** pocket *cpd*

pocher [pɔʃe] *vt* (CULIN) to poach

pochette [pɔʃɛt] *nf (de timbres)*
wallet, envelope; *(d'aiguilles etc)*
case; *(mouchoir)* breast pocket handkerchief; **~ de disque** record sleeve

poêle [pwal] *nm* stove ♦ *nf*: **~ (à
frire)** frying pan

poêlon [pwalɔ̃] *nm* casserole

poème [pɔɛm] *nm* poem

poésie [pɔezi] *nf (poème)* poem;
(art): **la ~** poetry

poète [pɔɛt] *nm* poet

poids [pwa] *nm* weight; (SPORT)
shot; **vendre au ~** to sell by weight;
prendre du ~ to put on weight; **~
lourd** *(camion)* lorry (BRIT), truck
(US)

poignard [pwaɲaʀ] *nm* dagger; **~er**
vt to stab, knife

poigne [pwaɲ] *nf* grip; *(fig)*: **à ~**
firm-handed

poignée [pwaɲe] *nf (de sel etc, fig)*
handful; *(de couvercle, porte)* handle; **~ de main** handshake

poignet [pwaɲɛ] *nm* (ANAT) wrist;
(de chemise) cuff

poil [pwal] *nm* (ANAT) hair; *(de pinceau, brosse)* bristle; *(de tapis)*
strand; *(pelage)* coat; **à ~** *(fam)*
starkers; **au ~** hunky-dory; **poilu, e**
adj hairy

poinçon [pwɛ̃sɔ̃] *nm* awl; bodkin;
(marque) hallmark; **poinçonner** *vt*
to stamp; to hallmark; *(billet)* to
punch

poing [pwɛ̃] *nm* fist

point [pwɛ̃] *nm* (*marque, signe*) dot; (: *de ponctuation*) full stop, period (US); (*moment, de score etc, fig: question*) point; (*endroit*) spot; (*COUTURE, TRICOT*) stitch ♦ *adv* = **pas**; **faire le** ~ (*NAVIG*) to take a bearing; (*fig*) to take stock (of the situation); **en tout** ~ in every respect; **sur le** ~ **de faire** (just) about to do; **à tel** ~ **que** so much so that; **mettre au** ~ (*mécanisme, procédé*) to develop; (*appareil-photo*) to focus; (*affaire*) to settle; **à** ~ (*CULIN*) medium; just right; **à** ~ (*nommé*) just at the right time; ~ **de côté** stitch (*pain*); ~ **d'eau** spring; water point; ~ **d'exclamation** exclamation mark; ~ **d'interrogation** question mark; ~ **de repère** landmark; (*dans le temps*) point of reference; ~ **de vente** retail outlet; ~ **de vue** viewpoint; (*fig: opinion*) point of view; ~ **faible** weak point; ~ **final** full stop, period; ~ **mort** (*AUTO*): **au** ~ **mort** in neutral; ~**s de suspension** suspension points

pointe [pwɛ̃t] *nf* point; (*fig*): **une** ~ **de** a hint of; **être à la** ~ **de** to be in the forefront of; **sur la** ~ **des pieds** on tiptoe; **en** ~ (*tailler*) into a point ♦ *adj* pointed, tapered; **de** ~ (*technique etc*) leading; **heures/jours** ~ peak hours/days; ~ **de vitesse** burst of speed

pointer [pwɛ̃te] *vt* (*cocher*) to tick off; (*employés etc*) to check in; (*diriger: canon, doigt*): ~ **vers qch** to point at sth ♦ *vi* (*employé*) to clock in

pointillé [pwɛ̃tije] *nm* (*trait*) dotted line

pointilleux, euse [pwɛ̃tijø, -øz] *adj* particular, pernickety

pointu, e [pwɛ̃ty] *adj* pointed; (*clou*) sharp; (*voix*) shrill; (*analyse*) precise

pointure [pwɛ̃tyʀ] *nf* size

point-virgule [pwɛ̃viʀgyl] *nm* semicolon

poire [pwaʀ] *nf* pear; (*fam: péj*) mug

poireau, x [pwaʀo] *nm* leek

poirier [pwaʀje] *nm* pear tree

pois [pwa] *nm* (*BOT*) pea; (*sur une étoffe*) dot, spot; **à** ~ (*cravate etc*) spotted, polka-dot *cpd*

poison [pwazɔ̃] *nm* poison

poisse [pwas] *nf* rotten luck

poisseux, euse [pwasø, -øz] *adj* sticky

poisson [pwasɔ̃] *nm* fish *gén inv*; **les P~s** (*signe*) Pisces; ~ **d'avril!** April fool!; ~ **rouge** goldfish; **poissonnerie** *nf* fish-shop; **poissonnier, ière** *nm/f* fishmonger (*BRIT*), fish merchant (*US*)

poitrine [pwatʀin] *nf* chest; (*seins*) bust, bosom; (*CULIN*) breast; ~ **de bœuf** brisket

poivre [pwavʀ(ə)] *nm* pepper; **poivrier** *nm* (*ustensile*) pepperpot

poivron [pwavʀɔ̃] *nm* pepper, capsicum

pôle [pol] *nm* (*GÉO, ÉLEC*) pole

poli, e [pɔli] *adj* polite; (*lisse*) smooth; polished

police [pɔlis] *nf* police; **peine de simple** ~ *sentence given by magistrates' or police court*; ~ **d'assurance** insurance policy; ~ **des mœurs** vice squad; ~ **judiciaire** ≈ Criminal Investigation Department (*BRIT*), ≈ Federal Bureau of Investigation (*US*); ~ **secours** ≈ emergency services (*BRIT*), ≈ paramedics (*US*)

policier, ière [pɔlisje, -jɛʀ] *adj* police *cpd* ♦ *nm* policeman; (*aussi: roman* ~) detective novel

polio [pɔljo] *nf* polio

polir [pɔliʀ] *vt* to polish

polisson, ne [pɔlisɔ̃, -ɔn] *adj* naughty

politesse [pɔlitɛs] *nf* politeness

politicien, ne [pɔlitisjɛ̃, -ɛn] *nm/f* politician

politique [pɔlitik] *adj* political ♦ *nf* (*science, pratique, activité*) politics *sg*; (*mesures, méthode*) policies *pl*;

politiser vt to politicize

pollen [pɔlɛn] nm pollen

pollution [pɔlysjɔ̃] nf pollution

polo [pɔlo] nm polo shirt

Pologne [pɔlɔɲ] nf: **la ~** Poland;
polonais, e adj, nm (LING) Polish;
Polonais, e nm/f Pole

poltron, ne [pɔltrɔ̃, -ɔn] adj cowardly

polycopier [pɔlikɔpje] vt to duplicate

Polynésie [pɔlinezi] nf: **la ~** Polyne-
sia

polyvalent, e [pɔlivalɑ̃, -ɑ̃t] adj versatile; multi-purpose

pommade [pɔmad] nf ointment,
cream

pomme [pɔm] nf (BOT) apple; tomber dans les **~s** (fam) to pass out;
~ d'Adam Adam's apple; **~ d'arrosoir** (sprinkler) rose; **~ de pin** pine
ou fir cone; **~ de terre** potato

pommeau, x [pɔmo] nm (boule)
knob; (de selle) pommel

pommette [pɔmɛt] nf cheekbone

pommier [pɔmje] nm apple tree

pompe [pɔ̃p] nf pump; (faste) pomp
(and ceremony); **~ à essence** petrol
pump; **~s funèbres** funeral parlour
sg, undertaker's sg

pomper [pɔ̃pe] vt to pump; (évacuer) to pump out; (aspirer) to pump
up; (absorber) to soak up

pompeux, euse [pɔ̃pø, -øz] adj
pompous

pompier [pɔ̃pje] nm fireman

pompiste [pɔ̃pist(ə)] nm/f petrol
(BRIT) ou gas (US) pump attendant

poncer [pɔ̃se] vt to sand (down)

ponctuation [pɔ̃ktɥasjɔ̃] nf punctuation

ponctuel, le [pɔ̃ktɥɛl] adj (à
l'heure, aussi TECH) punctual; (fig:
opération etc) one-off, single; (scru-
puleux) punctilious, meticulous

ponctuer [pɔ̃ktɥe] vt to punctuate

pondéré, e [pɔ̃dere] adj level-
headed, composed

pondre [pɔ̃dʀ(ə)] vt to lay; (fig) to
produce

poney [pɔnɛ] nm pony

pont [pɔ̃] nm bridge; (AUTO) axle;
(NAVIG) deck; **faire le ~** to take
the extra day off; **~ de graissage**
ramp (in garage); **~ suspendu** suspension bridge; **P~s et Chaussées**
highways department

pont-levis [pɔ̃lvi] nm drawbridge

pop [pɔp] adj inv pop

populace [pɔpylas] (péj) nf rabble

populaire [pɔpylɛʀ] adj popular;
(manifestation) mass cpd; (milieux,
clientèle) working-class

population [pɔpylasjɔ̃] nf population; **~ active** nf working population

populeux, euse [pɔpylø, -øz] adj
densely populated

porc [pɔʀ] nm (ZOOL) pig; (CULIN)
pork; (peau) pigskin

porcelaine [pɔʀsəlɛn] nf porcelain,
china; piece of china (ware)

porc-épic [pɔʀkepik] nm porcupine

porche [pɔʀʃ(ə)] nm porch

porcherie [pɔʀʃəʀi] nf pigsty

pore [pɔʀ] nm pore

porno [pɔʀno] adj abr pornographic,
porno

port [pɔʀ] nm (NAVIG) harbour,
port; (ville) port; (de l'uniforme etc)
wearing; (pour lettre) postage; (pour
colis, aussi: posture) carriage; **~
d'arme** (JUR) carrying of a firearm

portable [pɔʀtabl(ə)] nm (COMPUT)
laptop (computer)

portail [pɔʀtaj] nm gate; (de cathédrale) portal

portant, e [pɔʀtɑ̃, -ɑ̃t] adj: **bien/
mal ~** in good/poor health

portatif, ive [pɔʀtatif, -iv] adj portable

porte [pɔʀt(ə)] nf door; (de ville, forteresse, SKI) gate; **mettre à la ~** to
throw out; **~ à ~** nm door-to-door
selling; **~ d'entrée** front door; **~ à
faux** nm: **en ~-à-faux** cantilevered;
(fig) in an awkward position; **~
avions** nm inv aircraft carrier; **~
bagages** nm inv luggage rack; **~
clefs** nm inv key ring; **~-documents**
nm inv attaché ou document case

portée [pɔrte] nf (d'une arme) range; (fig) impact, import; scope, capability; (de chatte etc) litter; (MUS) stave, staff; **à/hors de (de)** within/out of reach (of); **à ~ de (la) main** within (arm's) reach; **à ~ de voix** within earshot; **à la ~ de qn** (fig) at sb's level, within sb's capabilities

porte: **~-fenêtre** nf French window; **~feuille** nm wallet; (POL, BOURSE) portfolio; **~-jarretelles** nm inv suspender belt; **~-manteau, x** nm coat hanger; coat rack; **~-mine** nm propelling (BRIT) ou mechanical (US) pencil; **~-monnaie** nm inv purse; **~-parole** nm inv spokesman

porter [pɔrte] vt to carry; (sur soi: vêtement, barbe, bague) to wear; (fig: responsabilité etc) to bear, carry; (inscription, marque, titre, patronyme: suj: arbre, fruits, fleurs) to bear; (apporter): **~ qch quelque part/à qn** to take sth somewhere/to sb ♦ vi (voix, regard, canon) to carry; (coup, argument) to hit home; se **~** vi (se sentir): se **~ bien/mal** to be well/unwell; **~ sur** (peser) to rest on; (accent) to fall on; (conférence etc) to concern; (heurter) to strike; **être porté à faire** to be apt ou inclined to do; se **faire ~ malade** to report sick; **~ la main à son chapeau** to raise one's hand to one's hat; **~ son effort sur** to direct one's efforts towards; **~ à croire** to lead one to believe

porte-serviettes [pɔrtsɛrvjɛt] nm inv towel rail

porteur [pɔrtœr] nm (de bagages) porter; (de chèque) bearer

porte-voix [pɔrtəvwa] nm inv megaphone

portier [pɔrtje] nm doorman

portière [pɔrtjɛr] nf door

portillon [pɔrtijɔ̃] nm gate

portion [pɔrsjɔ̃] nf (part) portion, share; (partie) portion, section

portique [pɔrtik] nm (RAIL) gantry

porto [pɔrto] nm port (wine)

portrait [pɔrtrɛ] nm portrait; photograph; **portrait-robot** nm Identikit (®) ou photo-fit (®) picture

portuaire [pɔrtɥɛr] adj port cpd, harbour cpd

portugais, e [pɔrtygɛ, -ɛz] adj, nm/f Portuguese

Portugal [pɔrtygal] nm: **le ~** Portugal

pose [poz] nf laying; hanging; (attitude, d'un modèle) pose; (PHOTO) exposure

posé, e [poze] adj serious

poser [poze] vt (déposer): **~ qch (sur)/qn à** to put sth down (on)/ drop sb at; (placer): **~ qch sur/ quelque part** to put sth on somewhere; (installer: moquette, carrelage) to lay; (rideaux, papier peint) to hang; (question) to ask; (principe, conditions) to lay ou set down; (problème) to formulate; (difficulté) to pose ♦ vi (modèle) to pose; se **~** vi (oiseau, avion) to land; (question) to arise

positif, ive [pozitif, -iv] adj positive

position [pozisjɔ̃] nf position; **prendre ~** (fig) to take a stand

posologie [pozɔlɔʒi] nf directions for use, dosage

posséder [pɔsede] vt to own, possess; (qualité, talent) to have, possess; (bien connaître: métier, langue) to have mastered, have a thorough knowledge of; (sexuellement, aussi: suj: colère etc) to possess; **possession** nf ownership no pl; possession

possibilité [pɔsibilite] nf possibility; **~s** nfpl (moyens) means; (potentiel) potential sg

possible [pɔsibl(ə)] adj possible; (projet, entreprise) feasible ♦ nm: **faire son ~** to do all one can, do one's utmost; **le plus/moins de livres** ~ as many/few books as possible; **le plus/moins d'eau** ~ as much/little water as possible; **dès que** ~ as soon as possible

postal, e, aux [pɔstal, -o] adj postal

poste [pɔst(ə)] nf (service) post, postal service; (administration, bureau) post office ♦ nm (fonction, MIL) post (TEL) extension; (de radio etc) set; **mettre à la ~** to post; **P~s, Télécommunications et Télédiffusion** postal and telecommunications service; **~ d'essence** nm petrol ou filling station; **~ d'incendie** nm fire point; **~ de pilotage** nm cockpit; **~ (de police)** nm police station; **~ de secours** nm first-aid post; **~ de travail** nm work station; **poste restante** nf poste restante (BRIT), general delivery (US)

poster[1] [pɔste] vt to post

poster[2] [pɔstɛʀ] nm poster

postérieur, e [pɔsteʀjœʀ] adj (date) later; (partie) back ♦ nm (fam) behind

posthume [pɔstym] adj posthumous

postiche [pɔstiʃ] nm hairpiece

postuler [pɔstyle] vt (emploi) to apply for, put in for

posture [pɔstyʀ] nf posture; position

pot [po] nm jar, pot; (en plastique, carton) carton; (en métal) tin; **boire ou prendre un ~** (fam) to have a drink; **~ (de chambre)** (chamber)pot; **~ d'échappement** exhaust pipe; **~ de fleurs** plant pot, flowerpot; (plante) pot plant

potable [pɔtabl(ə)] adj: **eau (non) ~** (non-)drinking water

potage [pɔtaʒ] nm soup; soup course

potager, ère [pɔtaʒe, -ɛʀ] adj (plante) edible, vegetable cpd; (jardin) ~ kitchen ou vegetable garden

pot-au-feu [pɔtofø] nm inv (beef) stew

pot-de-vin [pɔdvɛ̃] nm bribe

pote [pɔt] (fam) nm pal

poteau, x [pɔto] nm post; **~ indicateur** signpost

potelé, e [pɔtle] adj plump, chubby

potence [pɔtɑ̃s] nf gallows sg

potentiel, le [pɔtɑ̃sjɛl] adj, nm potential

poterie [pɔtʀi] nf pottery; piece of pottery

potier [pɔtje] nm potter

potins [pɔtɛ̃] nmpl gossip sg

potiron [pɔtiʀɔ̃] nm pumpkin

pou, x [pu] nm louse

poubelle [pubɛl] nf (dust)bin

pouce [pus] nm thumb

poudre [pudʀ(ə)] nf powder; (fard) (face) powder; (explosif) gunpowder; **en ~: café en ~** instant coffee; **lait en ~** dried ou powdered milk; **poudrier** nm (powder) compact

pouffer [pufe] vi: **~ (de rire)** to snigger; to giggle

pouilleux, euse [pujø, -øz] adj flea-ridden; (fig) grubby; seedy

poulailler [pulaje] nm henhouse

poulain [pulɛ̃] nm foal; (fig) protégé

poule [pul] nf (ZOOL) hen; (CULIN) (boiling) fowl

poulet [pulɛ] nm chicken; (fam) cop

poulie [puli] nf pulley; block

pouls [pu] nm pulse; **prendre le ~ de** qn to feel sb's pulse

poumon [pumɔ̃] nm lung

poupe [pup] nf stern; **en ~** astern

poupée [pupe] nf doll

poupon [pupɔ̃] nm babe-in-arms; **pouponnière** nf crèche, day nursery

pour [puʀ] prép for ♦ nm: **le ~ et le contre** the pros and cons; **~ faire** (so as) to do, in order to do; **~ avoir fait** for having done; **~ que** so that, in order that; **~ 100 francs d'essence** 100 francs' worth of petrol; **~ cent per cent**; **~ ce qui est de** as for

pourboire [puʀbwaʀ] nm tip

pourcentage [puʀsɑ̃taʒ] nm percentage

pourchasser [puʀʃase] vt to pursue

pourparlers [puʀpaʀle] nmpl talks, negotiations

pourpre [puʀpʀ(ə)] adj crimson

pourquoi [puʀkwa] adv, conj why ♦ nm inv: **le ~ (de)** the reason (for)

pourrai etc vb voir **pouvoir**

pourri, e [puʀi] adj rotten

pourrir [puʀiʀ] vi to rot; (fruit) to go rotten ou bad ♦ vt to rot; (fig) to spoil thoroughly; **pourriture** nf rot

pourrons etc vb voir **pouvoir**

poursuite [puʀsɥit] nf pursuit, chase; ~s nfpl (JUR) legal proceedings

poursuivre [puʀsɥivʀ(ə)] vt to pursue, chase (after); (relancer) to hound, harry; (obséder) to haunt; (JUR) to bring proceedings against, prosecute; (: au civil) to sue; (but) to strive towards; (voyage, études) to carry on with, continue ♦ vi to carry on, go on; se ~ vi to go on, continue

pourtant [puʀtɑ̃] adv yet; c'est ~ facile (and) yet it's easy

pourtour [puʀtuʀ] nm perimeter

pourvoir [puʀvwaʀ] vt: ~ qch/qn de to equip sth/sb with ♦ vi: ~ à to provide for; (emploi) to fill; se ~ (JUR): se ~ en cassation to take one's case to the Court of Appeal

pourvoyeur [puʀvwajœʀ] nm supplier

pourvu, e [puʀvy] adj: ~ de equipped with; ~ que (si) provided that, so long as; (espérons que) let's hope (that)

pousse [pus] nf growth; (bourgeon) shoot

poussé, e [puse] adj exhaustive

poussée [puse] nf thrust; (coup) push; (MED) eruption; (fig) upsurge

pousser [puse] vt to push; (inciter): ~ qn à to urge ou press sb to +infin; (acculer): ~ qn à to drive sb to; (émettre: cri etc) to give; (stimuler) to urge on; to drive hard; (poursuivre) to carry on (further) ♦ vi to push; (croître) to grow; se ~ vi to move over; faire ~ (plante) to grow

poussette [puset] nf (voiture d'enfant) push chair (BRIT), stroller (US)

poussière [pusjɛʀ] nf dust; (grain) speck of dust; **poussiéreux, euse** adj dusty

poussin [pusɛ̃] nm chick

poutre [putʀ(ə)] nf beam; (en fer, ciment armé) girder

MOT-CLÉ

pouvoir [puvwaʀ] nm power; (POL: dirigeants): le ~ those in power; les ~s publics the authorities; ~ d'achat purchasing power

♦ vb semi-aux **1** (être en état de) can, be able to; je ne peux pas le réparer I can't ou I am not able to repair it; déçu de ne pas ~ le faire disappointed not to be able to do it **2** (avoir la permission) can, may, be allowed to; **vous pouvez aller au cinéma** you can ou may go to the pictures

3 (probabilité, hypothèse) may, might, could; **il a pu avoir un accident** he may ou might ou could have had an accident; **il aurait pu le dire!** he might ou could have said (so)!

♦ vb impers may, might, could; **il peut arriver que** it may ou might ou could happen that

♦ vt can, be able to; **j'ai fait tout ce que j'ai pu** I did all I could; **je n'en peux plus** (épuisé) I'm exhausted; (à bout) I can't take any more

se ~ vi: **il se peut que** it may ou might be that; **cela se pourrait** that's quite possible

---

prairie [pʀeʀi] nf meadow

praline [pʀalin] nf sugared almond

praticable [pʀatikabl(ə)] adj passable, practicable

praticien, ne [pʀatisjɛ̃, -jɛn] nm/f practitioner

pratique [pʀatik] nf practice ♦ adj practical

pratiquement [pʀatikmɑ̃] adv (pour ainsi dire) practically, virtually

pratiquer [pʀatike] vt to practise; (SPORT etc) to go in for; to play; (intervention, opération) to carry out; (ouverture, abri) to make

pré [pʀe] nm meadow

préalable [pʀealabl(ə)] adj preliminary; **condition ~ (de)** precondition (for), prerequisite (for); **au ~** beforehand

préambule [preɑ̃byl] *nm* preamble; (*fig*) prelude; **sans ~** straight away

préavis [preavi] *nm* notice; **communication avec ~** (*TEL*) personal *ou* person to person call

précaution [prekosjɔ̃] *nf* precaution; **avec ~** cautiously; **par ~** as a precaution

précédemment [presedamɑ̃] *adv* before, previously

précédent, e [presedɑ̃, -ɑ̃t] *adj* previous ♦ *nm* precedent; **le jour ~** the day before, the previous day; **sans ~** unprecedented

précéder [presede] *vt* to precede; (*marcher ou rouler devant*) to be in front of

précepteur, trice [preseptœr, -tris] *nm/f* (private) tutor

prêcher [preʃe] *vt* to preach

précieux, euse [presjø, -øz] *adj* precious; invaluable; (*style, écrivain*) précieux, precious

précipice [presipis] *nm* drop, chasm; (*fig*) abyss

précipitamment [presipitamɑ̃] *adv* hurriedly, hastily

précipitation [presipitasjɔ̃] *nf* (*hâte*) haste; **~s** *nfpl* (*pluie*) rain *sg*

précipité, e [presipite] *adj* hurried, hasty

précipiter [presipite] *vt* (*faire tomber*): **~ qn/qch du haut de** to throw *ou* hurl sb/sth off *ou* from; (*hâter: marche*) to quicken; (: *départ*) to hasten; **se ~** *vi* to speed up; **se ~ sur/vers** to rush at/towards

précis, e [presi, -iz] *adj* precise; (*tir, mesures*) accurate, precise ♦ *nm* handbook; **précisément** *adv* precisely; **préciser** *vt* (*expliquer*) to be more specific about, clarify; (*spécifier*) to state, specify; **se ~er** *vi* to become clear(er); **précision** *nf* precision; accuracy; point *ou* detail (*being or to be clarified*)

précoce [prekɔs] *adj* early; (*enfant*) precocious; (*calvitie*) premature

préconiser [prekɔnize] *vt* to advocate

prédécesseur [predesesœr] *nm* predecessor

prédilection [predilɛksjɔ̃] *nf*: **avoir une ~ pour** to be partial to; **de ~** favourite

prédire [predir] *vt* to predict

prédominer [predɔmine] *vi* to predominate; (*avis*) to prevail

préface [prefas] *nf* preface

préfecture [prefɛktyr] *nf* prefecture; **~ de police** police headquarters *pl*

préférable [preferabl(ə)] *adj* preferable

préféré, e [prefere] *adj, nm/f* favourite

préférence [preferɑ̃s] *nf* preference; **de ~** preferably

préférer [prefere] *vt*: **~ qn/qch (à)** to prefer sb/sth (to), like sb/sth better (than); **~ faire** to prefer to do; **j'~ais du thé** I would rather have tea, I'd prefer tea

préfet [prefɛ] *nm* prefect

préfixe [prefiks(ə)] *nm* prefix

préhistorique [preistɔrik] *adj* prehistoric

préjudice [preʒydis] *nm* (*matériel*) loss; (*moral*) harm *no pl*; **porter ~ à** to harm, be detrimental to; **au ou de** at the expense of

préjugé [preʒyʒe] *nm* prejudice; **avoir un ~ contre** to be prejudiced *ou* biased against

préjuger [preʒyʒe]: **~ de** *vt* to prejudge

prélasser [prelɑse]: **se ~** *vi* to lounge

prélèvement [prelɛvmɑ̃] *nm*: **faire un ~ de sang** to take a blood sample

prélever [prelve] *vt* (*échantillon*) to take; (*argent*): **~ (sur)** to deduct (from); (: *sur son compte*): **~ (sur)** to withdraw (from)

prématuré, e [prematyre] *adj* premature; (*retraite*) early ♦ *nm* premature baby

premier, ière [prəmje, -jɛr] adj first; (branche, marche) bottom; (fig) basic; prime; initial; le ~ venu the first person to come along; P~ Ministre Prime Minister; **première** nf (THÉÂTRE) first night; (AUTO) first (gear); (AVIAT, RAIL etc) first class; (CINEMA) première; (exploit) first; **premièrement** adv firstly

prémonition [premɔnisjɔ̃] nf premonition

prémunir [premynir]: se ~ vi to guard against

prenant, e [prənɑ̃, -ɑ̃t] adj absorbing, engrossing

prénatal, e [prenatal] adj (MÉD) antenatal

prendre [prɑ̃dr(ə)] vt to take; (ôter): ~ qch à to take sth from; (aller chercher) to get, fetch; (se procurer) to get; (malfaiteur, poisson) to catch; (passager) to pick up; (personnel, aussi: couleur, goût) to take on; (locataire) to take in; (élève etc: traiter) to handle; (voix, ton) to put on; (coincer): se ~ les doigts dans to get one's fingers caught in ♦ vi (liquide, ciment) to set; (greffe, vaccin) to take; (feu: foyer) to go; (: incendie) to start; (allumette) to light; (se diriger): ~ à gauche to turn (to the) left; à tout ~ on the whole, all in all; se ~ pour to think one is; s'en ~ à to attack; se ~ d'amitié/d'affection pour to befriend/become fond of; s'y ~ (procéder) to set about it

preneur [prənœr] nm: être/trouver ~ to be willing to buy/find a buyer

preniez vb voir prendre

prenne etc vb voir prendre

prénom [prenɔ̃] nm first ou Christian name

prénuptial, e, aux [prenypsjal, -o] adj premarital

préoccupation [preɔkypasjɔ̃] nf (souci) concern; (idée fixe) preoccupation

préoccuper [preɔkype] vt to concern; to preoccupy

préparatifs [preparatif] nmpl preparations

préparation [preparasjɔ̃] nf preparation; (SCOL) piece of homework

préparer [prepare] vt to prepare; (café) to make; (examen) to prepare for; (voyage, entreprise) to plan; se ~ vi (orage, tragédie) to brew, be in the air; se ~ (à qch/faire) to prepare (o.s.) ou get ready (for sth/to do); ~ qch à qn (surprise etc) to have sth in store for sb

prépondérant, e [prepɔ̃derɑ̃, -ɑ̃t] adj major, dominating

préposé, e [prepoze] adj: ~ à in charge of ♦ nm/f employee; official; attendant

préposition [prepozisjɔ̃] nf preposition

près [prɛ] adv near, close; ~ de near (to), close to; (environ) nearly, almost; de ~ closely; à 5 kg ~ to within about 5 kg; à cela ~ que apart from the fact that

présage [preza3] nm omen

présager [preza3e] vt to foresee

presbyte [presbit] adj long-sighted

presbytère [presbiter] nm presbytery

prescription [preskripsjɔ̃] nf (instruction) order, instruction; (MÉD, JUR) prescription

prescrire [preskrir] vt to prescribe

préséance [preseɑ̃s] nf precedence no pl

présence [prezɑ̃s] nf presence; (au bureau etc) attendance; ~ d'esprit presence of mind

présent, e [prezɑ̃, -ɑ̃t] adj, nm present; à ~ (que) now (that)

présentation [prezɑ̃tasjɔ̃] nf introduction; presentation; (allure) appearance

présenter [prezɑ̃te] vt to present; (sympathie, condoléances) to offer; (soumettre) to submit; (invité, conférencier): ~ qn (à) to introduce sb (to) ♦ vi: ~ mal/bien to have an unattractive/a pleasing appearance; se ~ vi (sur convocation) to report,

préservatif [prezervatif] *nm* sheath, condom

préserver [prezerve] *vt*: ~ **de** to protect from; to save from

président [prezidɑ̃] *nm* (POL) president; (*d'une assemblée, COMM*) chairman; ~ **directeur général** chairman and managing director

présider [prezide] *vt* to preside over; (*dîner*) to be the guest of honour at; ~ **à** to direct; to govern

présomptueux, euse [prezɔ̃ptɥø, -øz] *adj* presumptuous

presque [prɛsk(ə)] *adv* almost, nearly; ~ **rien** hardly anything; ~ **pas** hardly (at all); ~ **pas de** hardly any

presqu'île [prɛskil] *nf* peninsula

pressant, e [presɑ̃, -ɑ̃t] *adj* urgent; **se faire** ~ to become insistent

presse [prɛs] *nf* press; (*affluence*): **heures de** ~ busy times

pressé, e [prese] *adj* in a hurry; (*air*) hurried; (*besogne*) urgent; **orange** ~**e** fresh orange juice

pressentiment [presɑ̃timɑ̃] *nm* foreboding, premonition

pressentir [presɑ̃tir] *vt* to sense; (*prendre contact avec*) to approach

presse-papiers [prɛspapje] *nm inv* paperweight

presser [prese] *vt* (*fruit, éponge*) to squeeze; (*bouton*) to press; (*allure, affaire*) to speed up; (*inciter*): ~ **qn de faire** to urge ou press sb to do ♦ *vi* to be urgent; (*se hâter*) to hurry (up); **se** ~ *vi* (*se serrer*): **se** ~ **contre qn** to squeeze up against sb; **rien ne presse** there's no hurry

pressing [presiŋ] *nm* steam-pressing; (*magasin*) dry-cleaner's

pression [presjɔ̃] *nf* pressure; **faire** ~ **sur** to put pressure on; **artérielle** blood pressure

pressoir [preswar] *nm* (wine ou oil *etc*) press

prestance [prestɑ̃s] *nf* presence, imposing bearing

prestataire [prestatɛr] *nm/f* supplier

prestation [prestasjɔ̃] *nf* (*allocation*) benefit; (*d'une entreprise*) service provided; (*d'un artiste*) performance

prestidigitateur, trice [prestidiʒitatœr, -tris] *nm/f* conjurer

prestigieux, euse [prestiʒjø, -øz] *adj* prestigious

présumer [prezyme] *vt*: ~ **que** to presume ou assume that; ~ **de** to overrate

présupposer [presypoze] *vt* to presuppose

prêt, e [prɛ, prɛt] *adj* ready ♦ *nm* lending *no pl*; loan; **prêt-à-porter** ready-to-wear ou off-the-peg (BRIT) clothes *pl*

prétendant [pretɑ̃dɑ̃] *nm* pretender; (*d'une femme*) suitor

prétendre [pretɑ̃dr(ə)] *vt* (*affirmer*): ~ **que** to claim that; (*avoir l'intention de*): ~ **faire qch** to mean ou intend to do sth; ~ **à** (*droit, titre*) to lay claim to; **prétendu, e** (*supposé*) so-called

prête-nom [prɛtnɔ̃] *nm* (*péj*) figurehead

prétentieux, euse [pretɑ̃sjø, -øz] *adj* pretentious

prétention [pretɑ̃sjɔ̃] *nf* claim; pretentiousness

prêter [prete] *vt* (*livres, argent*): ~ **qch (à)** to lend sth (to); (*supposer*): ~ **à qn** (*caractère, propos*) to attribute to sb ♦ *vi* (*aussi*: **se** ~: *tissu, cuir*) to give; **se** ~ **à** to lend o.s. (ou itself) to; (*manigances etc*) to go along with; ~ **à** (*commentaires etc*) to be open to, give rise to; ~ **assistance à** to give help to; ~ **attention** à to pay attention to; ~ **serment** to take the oath; ~ **l'oreille** to listen

prétexte [pretɛkst(ə)] *nm* pretext, excuse; **sous aucun** ~ on no account; **prétexter** *vt* to give as a pretext ou an excuse

prêtre [prɛtr(ə)] *nm* priest

preuve [prœv] *nf* proof, proof;

proof, evidence *no pl*; **faire ~ de** to show; **faire ses ~s** to prove o.s. (*ou* itself)

prévaloir [prevalwar] *vi* to prevail; **se ~ de** *vt* to take advantage of; to pride o.s. on

prévenant, e [prɛvnɑ̃, -ɑ̃t] *adj* thoughtful, kind

prévenir [prɛvnir] *vt* (*avertir*): **~ qn de** to warn sb (about); (*informer*): **~ qn (de)** to tell *ou* inform sb (about); (*éviter*) to avoid, prevent; (*anticiper*) to forestall; to anticipate

prévention [prevɑ̃sjɔ̃] *nf* prevention; **~ routière** road safety

prévenu, e [prɛvny] *nm/f* (*JUR*) defendant, accused

prévision [previzjɔ̃] *nf*: **~s** predictions; forecast *sg*; **en ~ de** in anticipation of; **~s météorologiques** weather forecast *sg*

prévoir [prevwar] *vt* (*deviner*) to foresee; (*s'attendre à*) to expect, reckon on; (*prévenir*) to anticipate; (*organiser*) to plan; (*préparer, réserver*) to allow; **prévu pour 10h** scheduled for 10 o'clock

prévoyance [prevwajɑ̃s] *nf*: **caisse de ~** contingency fund

prévoyant, e [prevwajɑ̃, -ɑ̃t] *adj* gifted with (*ou* showing) foresight

prévu, e [prevy] *pp de* prévoir

prier [prije] *vi* to pray ♦ *vt* (*Dieu*) to pray to; (*implorer*) to beg; (*demander*): **~ qn de faire** to ask sb to do; **se faire ~** to need coaxing *ou* persuading; **je vous en prie** (*allez-y*) please do; (*de rien*) don't mention it

prière [prijer] *nf* prayer; **"~ de faire ..."** "please do ..."

primaire [primer] *adj* primary; (*péj*) simple-minded; simplistic ♦ *nm* (*SCOL*) primary education

prime [prim] *nf* (*bonification*) bonus; (*subside*) premium, allowance; (*COMM: cadeau*) free gift; (*ASSURANCES, BOURSE*) premium ♦ *adj*: **de ~ abord** at first glance

primer [prime] *vt* (*l'emporter sur*) to prevail over; (*récompenser*) to

award a prize to ♦ *vi* to dominate; to prevail

primeurs [primœr] *nfpl* early fruits and vegetables

primevère [primver] *nf* primrose

primitif, ive [primitif, -iv] *adj* primitive; (*originel*) original

prince [prɛ̃s] *nm* prince; **princesse** *nf* princess

principal, e, aux [prɛ̃sipal, -o] *adj* principal, main ♦ *nm* (*SCOL*) principal, head(master); (*essentiel*) main thing

principe [prɛ̃sip] *nm* principle; **pour le ~** on principle; **de ~** (*accord, hostilité*) automatic; **par ~** on principle; **en ~** (*habituellement*) as a rule; (*théoriquement*) in principle

printemps [prɛ̃tɑ̃] *nm* spring

priorité [prijorite] *nf* (*AUTO*): **avoir la ~ (sur)** to have right of way (over); **~ à droite** right of way to vehicles coming from the right

pris, e [pri, priz] *pp de* prendre ♦ *adj* (*place*) taken; (*journée, mains*) full; (*billets*) sold; (*personne*) busy; **avoir le nez/la gorge ~(e)** to have a stuffy nose/a hoarse throat; **être ~ de panique** to be panic-stricken

prise [priz] *nf* (*d'une ville*) capture; (*PÊCHE, CHASSE*) catch; (*point d'appui ou pour empoigner*) hold; (*ÉLEC: fiche*) plug; (*: femelle*) socket; **être aux ~s avec** to be grappling with; **~ de contact** (*rencontre*) initial meeting, first contact; **~ de courant** power point; **~ de sang** blood test; **~ de terre** earth; **~ de vue** (*photo*) shot; **~ multiple** adaptor

priser [prize] *vt* (*tabac, héroïne*) to take; (*estimer*) to prize, value ♦ *vt* to take snuff

prison [prizɔ̃] *nf* prison; **aller/être en ~** to go to/be in prison *ou* jail; **faire de la ~** to serve time; **prisonnier, ière** *nm/f* prisoner ♦ *adj* captive

prit [pri] *vb voir* prendre

privé, e [prive] *adj* private; **en ~** in private

priver [prive] vt: to ~ qn de to deprive
sb of; se ~ de to go ou do without

privilège [privilɛʒ] nm privilege

prix [pri] nm (valeur) price; (récompense, SCOL) prize; hors de ~ exor-
bitantly priced; à aucun ~ not at
any price; à tout ~ at all costs; ~
d'achat/de vente/de revient
purchasing/selling/cost price

probable [prɔbabl(ə)] adj likely,
probable; ~ment adv probably

probant, e [prɔbã, -ãt] adj convincing

problème [prɔblɛm] nm problem

procédé [prɔsede] nm (méthode)
process; (comportement) behaviour
no pl

procéder [prɔsede] vi to proceed; to
behave; ~ à to carry out

procès [prɔsɛ] nm trial; (poursuites)
proceedings pl; être en ~ avec to
be involved in a lawsuit with

processus [prɔsesys] nm process

procès-verbal, aux [prɔsɛvɛrbal,
-o] nm (constat) statement; (aussi:
P.V.): avoir un ~ to get a parking
ticket; to be booked; (de réunion)
minutes pl

prochain, e [prɔʃɛ̃, -ɛn] adj next;
(proche) impending; near ♦ nm fellow man; la ~e fois/semaine ~
next time/week; **prochainement** adv
soon, shortly

proche [prɔʃ] adj nearby; (dans le
temps) imminent; (parent, ami)
close; ~s nmpl (parents) close relatives; être ~ (de) to be near, be
close (to); de ~ en ~ gradually; le
P~ Orient the Middle East

proclamer [prɔklame] vt to proclaim

procuration [prɔkyrasjɔ̃] nf proxy;
power of attorney

procurer [prɔkyre] vt: ~ qch à qn
(fournir) to obtain sth for sb; (causer: plaisir etc) to bring sb sth; se ~
vt to obtain

procureur [prɔkyrœr] nm public
prosecutor

prodige [prɔdiʒ] nm marvel, won-

der; (personne) prodigy

prodigue [prɔdig] adj generous;
extravagant; fils ~ prodigal son

prodiguer [prɔdige] vt (argent,
biens) to be lavish with; (soins, attentions): ~ qch à qn to give sb sth

producteur, trice [prɔdyktœr,
-tris] nm/f producer

production [prɔdyksjɔ̃] nf (gén)
production; (rendement) output

produire [prɔdɥir] vt to produce; se
~ vi (acteur) to perform, appear;
(événement) to happen, occur

produit [prɔdɥi] nm (gén) product;
~ d'entretien cleaning product; ~
national brut gross national product; ~s agricoles farm produce
sg; ~s alimentaires nmpl foodstuffs

prof [prɔf] (fam) nm teacher

profane [prɔfan] adj (REL) secular
♦ nm/f layman(woman)

proférer [prɔfere] vt to utter

professeur [prɔfesœr] nm teacher;
(titulaire d'une chaire) professor; ~
(de faculté) (university) lecturer

profession [prɔfesjɔ̃] nf profession;
sans ~ unemployed; **professionnel,
le** adj, nm/f professional

profil [prɔfil] nm profile; (d'une voiture) line, contour; de ~ in profile;
profiler vt to streamline

profit [prɔfi] nm (avantage) benefit,
advantage; (COMM, FINANCE)
profit; au ~ de in aid of; tirer ~
to profit from

profitable [prɔfitabl(ə)] adj beneficial; profitable

profiter [prɔfite] vi: ~ de to take
advantage of; to make the most of;
~ à to benefit; to be profitable to

profond, e [prɔfɔ̃, -ɔ̃d] adj deep;
(méditation, mépris) profound; **profondeur** nf depth

progéniture [prɔʒenityr] nf offspring inv

programme [prɔgram] nm programme; (TV, RADIO) programmes
pl; (SCOL) syllabus, curriculum;
(INFORM) program; **programmer**
vt (TV, RADIO) to put on, show,

(INFORM) to program; **programmeur, euse** nm/f programmer

progrès [prɔgrɛ] nm progress no pl; **faire des ~** to make progress

progresser [prɔgrese] vi to progress; (troupes etc) to make headway ou progress; **progressif, ive** adj progressive

prohiber [prɔibe] vt to prohibit, ban

proie [prwa] nf prey no pl

projecteur [prɔʒɛktœr] nm projector; (de théâtre, cirque) spotlight

projectile [prɔʒɛktil] nm missile

projection [prɔʒɛksjɔ̃] nf projection; showing; **conférence avec ~s** lecture with slides (ou a film)

projet [prɔʒɛ] nm plan; (ébauche) draft; **~ de loi** bill

projeter [prɔʒte] vt (envisager) to plan; (film, photos) to project; (passer) to show; (ombre, lueur) to throw, cast; (jeter) to throw up (ou off ou out)

prolixe [prɔliks(ə)] adj verbose

prolongement [prɔlɔ̃ʒmɑ̃] nm extension; **~s** nmpl (fig) repercussions, effects; **dans le ~ de** the running on from

prolonger [prɔlɔ̃ʒe] vt (débat, séjour) to prolong; (délai, billet, rue) to extend; (suj: chose) to be a continuation ou an extension of; **se ~** vi to go on

promenade [prɔmnad] nf walk (ou drive ou ride); **faire une ~** to go for a walk; **une ~ en voiture/à vélo** a drive/(bicycle) ride

promener [prɔmne] vt (chien) to take out for a walk; (doigts, regard): **~ qch sur** to run sth over; **se ~** vi to go for (ou be out for) a walk

promesse [prɔmɛs] nf promise

promettre [prɔmɛtr(ə)] vt to promise ♦ vi to be ou look promising; **~ à qn de faire** to promise sb that one will do

promiscuité [prɔmiskɥite] nf crowding; lack of privacy

promontoire [prɔmɔ̃twar] nm headland

promoteur, trice [prɔmɔtœr, -tris] nm/f (instigateur) instigator, promoter; **~ (immobilier)** property developer (BRIT), real estate promoter (US)

promotion [prɔmɔsjɔ̃] nf promotion

promouvoir [prɔmuvwar] vt to promote

prompt, e [prɔ̃, prɔ̃t] adj swift, rapid

prôner [prone] vt to advocate

pronom [prɔnɔ̃] nm pronoun

prononcer [prɔnɔ̃se] vt (son, mot, jugement) to pronounce; (dire) to utter; (allocution) to deliver; **se ~** to reach a decision, give a verdict; **se ~ sur** to give an opinion on; **se ~ contre** to come down against; **prononciation** nf pronunciation

pronostic [prɔnɔstik] nm (MÉD) prognosis; (fig: aussi: **~s**) forecast

propagande [prɔpagɑ̃d] nf propaganda

propager [prɔpaʒe] vt to spread; **se ~** vi to spread

prophète [prɔfɛt] nm prophet

prophétie [prɔfesi] nf prophecy

propice [prɔpis] adj favourable

proportion [prɔpɔrsjɔ̃] nf proportion; **toute(s) ~(s) gardée(s)** making due allowance(s)

propos [prɔpo] nm (paroles) talk no pl, remark; (intention) intention, aim; (sujet): **à quel ~?** what about?; **à ~ de** about, regarding; **à tout ~** for no reason at all; **à ~** by the way; (opportunément) at the right moment

proposer [prɔpoze] vt (suggérer): **~ qch (à qn)** ou **de faire** to suggest sth (to sb)/doing, propose sth (to sb) ou to do; (offrir): **~ qch à qn/de faire** to offer sb sth/to do; (candidat) to put forward; (loi, motion) to propose; **~ de faire** to offer to do ou propose to do; **se ~** to offer one's services; **se ~ de faire** to intend ou propose to do; **proposition** nf suggestion; proposal; offer; (LING) clause

propre [prɔpr(ə)] adj clean; (net) neat, tidy; (possessif) own; (sens) literal; (*particulier*): ~ à peculiar to; (*approprié*): ~ à suitable for; (*de nature à*): ~ à faire likely to do ♦ nm: recopier au ~ to make a fair copy of; **proprement** [prɔprəmã] *adv* cleanly; neatly, tidily; le village proprement dit the village itself; à proprement parler strictly speaking; **propreté** nf cleanliness; neatness; tidiness

propriétaire [prɔprijetɛr] nm/f owner; (*pour le locataire*) landlord(lady)

propriété [prɔprijete] nf (*gén*) property; (*droit*) ownership; (*objet, immeuble, terres*) property gén no pl

propulser [prɔpylse] vt (*missile*) to propel; (*projeter*) to hurl, fling

proroger [prɔrɔʒe] vt to put back, defer; (*prolonger*) to extend

proscrire [prɔskrir] vt (*bannir*) to banish; (*interdire*) to ban, prohibit

prose [proz] nf (*style*) prose

prospecter [prɔspɛkte] vt to prospect; (*COMM*) to canvass

prospectus [prɔspɛktys] nm leaflet

prospère [prɔspɛr] adj prosperous

prosterner [prɔstɛrne]: se ~ vi to bow low, prostrate o.s.

prostituée [prɔstitɥe] nf prostitute

protecteur, trice [prɔtɛktœr, -tris] adj protective; (*air, ton*: *péj*) patronizing ♦ nm/f protector

protection [prɔtɛksjɔ̃] nf protection; (*d'un personnage influent*: *aide*) patronage

protéger [prɔteʒe] vt to protect; se ~ de ou contre to protect o.s. from

protéine [prɔtein] nf protein

protestant, e [prɔtɛstã, -ãt] adj, nm/f Protestant

protestation [prɔtɛstasjɔ̃] nf (*plainte*) protest

protester [prɔtɛste] vi: ~ (contre) to protest (against ou about); ~ de (*son innocence, sa loyauté*) to protest

prothèse [prɔtɛz] nf artificial limb, prosthesis; ~ dentaire denture

protocole [prɔtɔkɔl] nm (*fig*) etiquette

proue [pru] nf bow(s pl), prow

prouesse [prues] nf feat

prouver [pruve] vt to prove

provenance [prɔvnãs] nf origin; (*de mot, coutume*) source; **avion en ~ de** plane (arriving) from

provenir [prɔvnir]: ~ de vt to come from; (*résulter de*) to be the result of

proverbe [prɔvɛrb(ə)] nm proverb

province [prɔvɛ̃s] nf province

proviseur [prɔvizœr] nm ≈ head(teacher) (*BRIT*), ≈ principal (*US*)

provision [prɔvizjɔ̃] nf (*réserve*) stock, supply; (*avance*: à un avocat, avoué) retainer, retaining fee; (*COMM*) funds pl (in account); reserve; ~s nfpl (*vivres*) provisions, food no pl

provisoire [prɔvizwar] adj temporary; (*JUR*) provisional

provoquer [prɔvɔke] vt (*inciter*): ~ qn à to incite sb to; (*défier*) to provoke; (*causer*) to cause, bring about

proxénète [prɔksenɛt] nm procurer

proximité [prɔksimite] nf nearness, closeness; (*dans le temps*) imminence, closeness; à ~ near ou close by; à ~ de near (to), close to

prude [pryd] adj prudish

prudemment [prydamã] adv carefully, cautiously; wisely, sensibly

prudence [prydãs] nf carefulness; caution; avec ~ carefully; cautiously; par (mesure de) ~ as a precaution

prudent, e [prydã, -ãt] adj (*pas téméraire*) careful, cautious; (: *en général*) safety-conscious; (*sage*, *conseillé*) wise, sensible; (*réservé*) cautious

prune [pryn] nf plum

pruneau, x [pryno] nm prune

prunelle [prynɛl] nf plum; eye

prunier [prynje] nm plum tree

psaume [psom] nm psalm

pseudonyme [psødɔnim] nm (*gén*) fictitious name; (*d'écrivain*) pseudonym, pen name; (*de comédien*) pseudo name

psychiatre [psikjatʀ(ə)] nm/f psychiatrist

psychiatrique [psikjatʀik] adj psychiatric

psychique [psiʃik] adj psychological

psychologie [psikɔlɔʒi] nf psychology; **psychologique** adj psychological; **psychologue** nm/f psychologist

P.T.T. sigle fpl = Postes, Télécommunications et Télédiffusion

pu pp de pouvoir

puanteur [pɥɑ̃tœʀ] nf stink, stench

pub [pyb] (fam) abr f (= publicité): **la ~** advertising

public, ique [pyblik] adj public; (école, instruction) state cpd ♦ nm public; (assistance) audience; **en ~** in public

publicitaire [pyblisitɛʀ] adj advertising cpd; (film, voiture) publicity cpd

publicité [pyblisite] nf (méthode, profession) advertising; (annonce) advertisement; (révélations) publicity

publier [pyblije] vt to publish

publique [pyblik] adj voir public

puce [pys] nf flea; (INFORM) chip; **~s** nfpl (marché) flea market sg

pudeur [pydœʀ] nf modesty

pudique [pydik] adj (chaste) modest; (discret) discreet

puer [pɥe] (péj) vi to stink

puéricultrice [pɥeʀikyltʀis] nf p(a)ediatric nurse

puériculture [pɥeʀikyltyʀ] nf p(a)ediatric nursing; infant care

puéril, e [pɥeʀil] adj childish

puis [pɥi] vb voir pouvoir ♦ adv then

puiser [pɥize] vt: **~ (dans)** to draw (from)

puisque [pɥisk(ə)] conj since

puissance [pɥisɑ̃s] nf power; **en ~** potential

puissant, e [pɥisɑ̃, -ɑ̃t] adj powerful

puisse etc vb voir pouvoir

puits [pɥi] nm well; **~ de mine** mine shaft

pull(-over) [pul(ɔvœʀ)] nm sweater

pulluler [pylyle] vi to swarm

pulpe [pylp(ə)] nf pulp

pulvérisateur [pylveʀizatœʀ] nm spray

pulvériser [pylveʀize] vt to pulverize; (liquide) to spray

punaise [pynɛz] nf (ZOOL) bug; (clou) drawing pin (BRIT), thumbtack (US)

punch¹ [pɔ̃ʃ] nm (boisson) punch

punch² [pœnʃ] nm (BOXE, fig) punch

punir [pyniʀ] vt to punish; **punition** nf punishment

pupille [pypij] nf (ANAT) pupil ♦ nm/f (enfant) ward; **~ de l'Etat** child in care

pupitre [pypitʀ(ə)] nm (SCOL) desk; (REL) lectern; (de chef d'orchestre) rostrum

pur, e [pyʀ] adj pure; (vin) undiluted; (whisky) neat; **en ~e perte** to no avail

purée [pyʀe] nf: **~ (de pommes de terre)** mashed potatoes pl; **~ de marrons** chestnut purée

purger [pyʀʒe] vt (radiateur) to drain; (circuit hydraulique) to bleed; (MED, POL) to purge; (JUR: peine) to serve

purin [pyʀɛ̃] nm liquid manure

pur-sang [pyʀsɑ̃] nm inv thoroughbred

pusillanime [pyzilanim] adj fainthearted

putain [pytɛ̃] (fam!) nf whore (!)

puzzle [pœzl(ə)] nm jigsaw (puzzle)

P.V. sigle m = procès-verbal

pyjama [piʒama] nm pyjamas pl (BRIT), pajamas pl (US)

pyramide [piʀamid] nf pyramid

Pyrénées [piʀene] nfpl: **les ~** the Pyrenees

Q

QG [kyʒe] *sigle m* (= *quartier général*) HQ

QI [kyi] *sigle m* (= *quotient intellectuel*) IQ

quadragénaire [kadraʒenɛr] *nm/f* man/woman in his/her forties

quadriller [kadrije] *vt* (*papier*) to mark out in squares; (*POLICE*) to keep under tight control

quadruple [k(w)adrypl(ə)] *nm*: le ~ de four times as much as; **quadruplés, ées** *nm/fpl* quadruplets, quads

quai [ke] *nm* (*de port*) quay; (*de gare*) platform; **être à ~** (*navire*) to be alongside; (*train*) to be in the station

qualifier [kalifje] *vt* to qualify; se ~ *vi* to qualify; ~ **qch/qn de** to describe sth/sb as

qualité [kalite] *nf* quality; (*titre, fonction*) position

quand [kɑ̃] *conj, adv* when; ~ **je serai riche** when I'm rich; ~ **même** all the same; really; ~ **bien même** even though

quant [kɑ̃]: ~ **à** *prép* as for, as to; regarding

quant-à-soi [kɑ̃taswa] *nm*: **rester sur son** ~ to remain aloof

quantité [kɑ̃tite] *nf* quantity, amount; (*SCIENCE*) quantity; (*grand nombre*): **une** *ou* **des** ~(**s**) **de** a great deal of

quarantaine [karɑ̃tɛn] *nf* (*MÉD*) quarantine; **avoir la** ~ (*âge*) to be around forty; **une** ~ (**de**) forty or so, about forty

quarante [karɑ̃t] *num* forty

quart [kar] *nm* (*fraction, partie*) quarter; (*surveillance*) watch; **un** ~ **de beurre** a quarter kilo of butter; **un** ~ **de vin** a quarter litre of wine; **une livre un** ~ *ou* **et** ~ one and a quarter pounds; **le** ~ **de** a quarter of; ~ **d'heure** quarter of an hour

quartier [kartje] *nm* (*de ville*) dis-

trict, area; (*de bœuf*) quarter; (*de fruit, fromage*) piece; ~**s** *nmpl* (*MIL, BLASON*) quarters; **cinéma de** ~ local cinema; **avoir** ~ **libre** (*fig*) to be free; ~ **général** headquarters *pl*

quartz [kwarts] *nm* quartz

quasi [kazi] *adv* almost, nearly; **quasiment** *adv* almost, nearly

quatorze [katɔrz(ə)] *num* fourteen

quatre [katr(ə)] *num* four; **à ~ pattes** on all fours; **tiré à ~ épingles** dressed up to the nines; **faire les ~ cent coups** to get a bit wild; **se mettre en ~ pour qn** to go out of one's way for sb; ~ **à ~** (*monter, descendre*) four at a time; **quatre-vingt-dix** *num* ninety; **quatre-vingts** *num* eighty; **quatrième** *num* fourth

quatuor [kwatɥɔr] *nm* quartet(te)

MOT-CLÉ

que [kə] *conj* **1** (*introduisant complétive*) that; **il sait** ~ **tu es là** he knows (that) you're here; **je veux** ~ **tu acceptes** I want you to accept; **il a dit** ~ **oui** he said he would (*ou* it was *etc*)

2 (*reprise d'autres conjonctions*): **quand il rentrera et qu'il aura mangé** when he gets back and (when) he has eaten; **si vous y allez ou** ~ **vous** ... if you go there *ou* if you ...

3 (*en tête de phrase: hypothèse, souhait etc*): **qu'il le veuille ou non** whether he likes it or not let him do as he pleases!

4 (*après comparatif*) than; as; *voir aussi* **plus**; **aussi**; **autant** *etc*

5 (*seulement*): **ne** ... ~ only; **il ne boit** ~ **de l'eau** he only drinks water

♦ *adv* (*exclamation*): **qu'il** *ou* **qu'est-ce qu'il est bête/court vite!** he's so silly!/he runs so fast!; ~ **de livres!** what a lot of books!

♦ *pron* **1** (*relatif: personne*) whom; (*: chose*) that, which; **l'homme** ~ **je vois** the man (whom) I see; **le livre** ~ **tu vois** the book (that *ou*

which) you see; **un jour ~ j'étais
... a day when I was ...**
2 (*interrogatif*) what; **~ fais-tu?,
qu'est-ce ~ tu fais?** what are you
doing?; **qu'est-ce ~ c'est?** what is
it?, what's that?; **~ faire?** what can
one do?

MOT-CLÉ

quel, quelle [kɛl] *adj* **1** (*interrogatif: personne*) who; (: *chose*) what;
which; **~ est cet homme?** who is
this man?; **~ est ce livre?** what is
this book?; **~ livre/homme?** what
book/man?; (*parmi un certain choix*)
which book/man?; **~ acteurs
préférez-vous?** which actors do you
prefer?; **dans ~s pays êtes-vous
allé** which ou what countries did you
go to?
2 (*exclamatif*): **quelle surprise!**
what a surprise!
3: quel(le) que soit coupable whoever is guilty; **~ que soit votre
avis** whatever your opinion

quelconque [kɛlkɔ̃k] *adj* (*médiocre*)
indifferent, poor; (*sans attrait*) ordinary, plain; (*indéfini*): **un ami/
pretexte ~** some friend/pretext or
other

MOT-CLÉ

quelque [kɛlkə] *adj* **1** some; a few;
(*tournure interrogative*) any; **~ espoir** some hope; **il a ~s amis** he
has a few ou some friends; **a-t-il ~s
amis?** has he any friends?; **les ~s
livres qui** the few books which; **20
kg et ~(s)** a bit over 20 kg
2: ~ ... que whatever (ou whichever) book he chooses
3: ~ chose something; (*tournure interrogative*) anything; **~
chose d'autre** something else; anything
else; **~ part** somewhere; anywhere;
en ~ sorte as it were
♦ *adv* (*environ*): **~ 100 mètres**
some 100 metres

2: ~ peu rather, somewhat

quelquefois [kɛlkəfwa] *adv* sometimes

quelques-uns, -unes [kɛlkəzœ̃,
-yn] *pron* a few, some

quelqu'un [kɛlkœ̃] *pron* someone,
somebody, *tournure interrogative*
+anyone ou anybody; **~ d'autre**
someone ou somebody else; anybody
else

quémander [kemɑ̃de] *vt* to beg for

qu'en dira-t-on [kɑ̃diʀatɔ̃] *nm inv*:
le ~ gossip, what people say

querelle [kəʀɛl] *nf* quarrel

quereller [kəʀele]: **se ~** *vi* to quarrel

qu'est-ce que [kɛskə] *voir* que

qu'est-ce qui [kɛski] *voir* qui

question [kɛstjɔ̃] *nf* (*gén*) question;
(*fig*) matter; issue; **il a été ~ de**
(*ou* they) spoke about; **de quoi est-il
~?** what is it about?; **il n'en est
pas ~** there's no question of it; **hors
de ~** out of the question; **remettre
en ~** to question; **~naire** [kɛstjɔnɛʀ]
nm questionnaire; **~ner** [kɛstjɔne] *vt*
to question

quête [kɛt] *nf* collection; (*recherche*)
quest, search; **faire la ~** (*à l'église*)
to take the collection; (*artiste*) to
pass the hat round; **quêter** *vi* (*à
l'église*) to take the collection

quetsche [kwɛtʃ(ə)] *nf* damson

queue [kø] *nf* tail; (*fig: du classement*) bottom; (: *de poêle*) handle;
(: *de fruit, feuille*) stalk; (: *de train,
colonne, file*) rear; **faire la ~** to
queue (up) (BRIT), line up (US);
de cheval ponytail; **queue-de-pie** *nf*
(*habit*) tails *pl*, tail coat

qui [ki] *pron* (*personne*) who, *prép*
+whom; (*chose, animal*) which, that;
qu'est-ce ~ est sur la table? what
is on the table?; **~ est-ce ~** who?;
~ est-ce que? who?; (*objet*): **à ~
est ce sac?** whose bag is this?; **à ~
parlais-tu?** who were you talking
to?, to whom were you talking?;
amenez ~ vous voulez bring who

you like; ~ **que ce soit** whoever it may be

quiconque [kikɔ̃k] *pron* (*celui qui*) whoever, anyone who; (*personne*) anyone, anybody

quiétude [kjetyd] *nf* (*d'un lieu*) quiet, tranquillity; **en toute** ~ in complete peace

quille [kij] *nf*: (jeu de) ~s skittles *sg* (BRIT), bowling (US)

quincaillerie [kɛ̃kajʁi] *nf* (*ustensiles*) hardware; (*magasin*) hardware shop; **quincaillier, ière** *nm/f* hardware dealer

quinquagénaire [kɛ̃kaʒenɛʁ] *nm/f* man/woman in his/her fifties

quintal, aux [kɛ̃tal, -o] *nm* quintal (*100 kg*)

quinte [kɛ̃t] *nf*: ~ (de toux) coughing fit

quintuple [kɛ̃typl(ə)] *nm*: **le** ~ **de** five times as much as; **quintuplés, ées** *nm/fpl* quintuplets, quins

quinzaine [kɛ̃zɛn] *nf*: **une** ~ (de) about fifteen, fifteen or so; **une** ~ (de jours) a fortnight (BRIT), two weeks

quinze [kɛ̃z] *num* fifteen; **demain en** ~ a fortnight ou two weeks tomorrow; **dans** ~ **jours** in a fortnight's time), in two weeks (' time)

quiproquo [kipʁoko] *nm* misunderstanding

quittance [kitɑ̃s] *nf* (*reçu*) receipt; (*facture*) bill

quitte [kit] *adj*: **être** ~ **envers qn** to be no longer in sb's debt; (*fig*) to be quits with sb; **être** ~ **de** (*obligation*) to be clear of; **en être** ~ **à bon compte** to have got off lightly); ~ **à faire** even if it means doing

quitter [kite] *vt* to leave; (*espoir, illusion*) to give up; (*vêtement*) to take off; **se** ~ *vi* (*couples, interlocuteurs*) to part; **ne quittez pas** (*au téléphone*) hold the line

qui-vive [kiviv] *nm*: **être sur le** ~ to be on the alert

quoi [kwa] *pron* (*interrogatif*) what; ~ **de neuf?** what's the news?; **as-tu**

de ~ **écrire?** have you anything to write with?; **il n'a pas de** ~ **se l'acheter** he can't afford it; ~ **qu'il arrive** whatever happens; ~ **qu'il en soit** be that as it may; ~ **que ce soit** anything at all; **"il n'y a pas de** ~" "(please) don't mention it"; **à** ~ **bon?** what's the use?; **en** ~ **puis-je vous aider?** how can I help you?

quoique [kwak(ə)] *conj* (al)though

quolibet [kɔlibɛ] *nm* gibe, jeer

quote-part [kɔtpaʁ] *nf* share

quotidien, ne [kɔtidjɛ̃, -ɛn] *adj* daily; (*banal*) everyday ♦ *nm* (*journal*) daily (paper)

R

r. *abr* = **route; rue**

rab [ʁab] (*fam*) *abr* **nm** = **rabiot**

rabâcher [ʁabaʃe] *vt* to keep on repeating

rabais [ʁabɛ] *nm* reduction, discount

rabaisser [ʁabese] *vt* (*rabattre*) to reduce; (*dénigrer*) to belittle

rabattre [ʁabatʁ(ə)] *vt* (*couvercle, siège*) to pull down; (*gibier*) to drive; **se** ~ *vi* (*bords, couvercle*) to fall shut; (*véhicule, coureur*) to cut in; **se** ~ **sur** to fall back on

rabbin [ʁabɛ̃] *nm* rabbi

rabiot [ʁabjo] (*fam*) *nm* extra, more

râblé, e [ʁable] *adj* stocky

rabot [ʁabo] *nm* plane

rabougri, e [ʁabugʁi] *adj* stunted

rabrouer [ʁabʁue] *vt* to snub

racaille [ʁakaj] (*péj*) *nf* rabble, riffraff

raccommoder [ʁakɔmɔde] *vt* to mend, repair; (*chaussette etc*) to darn

raccompagner [ʁakɔ̃paɲe] *vt* to take *ou* see back

raccord [ʁakɔʁ] *nm* link

raccorder [ʁakɔʁde] *vt* to join (up), link up; (*suj: pont etc*) to connect, link

raccourci [ʁakuʁsi] *nm* short cut

raccourcir [ʁakuʁsiʁ] *vt* to shorten

raccrocher [rakrɔʃe] vt (tableau) to hang back up; (récepteur) to put down ♦ vi (TEL) to hang up, ring off; se ~ à vt to cling to, hang on to

race [ras] nf race; (d'animaux, fig) breed; (ascendance) stock, race; de ~ purebred, pedigree

rachat [raʃa] nm buying; buying back

racheter [raʃte] vt (article perdu) to buy another; (davantage): ~ du lait/3 œufs to buy more milk/another 3 eggs ou 3 more eggs; (après avoir vendu) to buy back; (d'occasion) to buy; (COMM: part, firme) to buy up; (: pension, rente) to redeem; se ~ vi (fig) to make amends

racial, e, aux [rasjal, -o] adj racial

racine [rasin] nf root; ~ carrée/cubique square/cube root

raciste [rasist(ə)] adj, nm/f raci(al)ist

racket [rakɛt] nm racketeering no pl

racler [rakle] vt (surface) to scrape; (tache, boue) to scrape off

racoler [rakɔle] vt (attirer: suj: prostituée) to solicit; (: parti, marchand) to tout for

racontars [rakɔ̃tar] nmpl gossip sg

raconter [rakɔ̃te] vt: ~ (à qn) (décrire) to relate (to sb), tell (sb) about; (dire) to tell (sb)

racorni, e [rakɔrni] adj hard(ened)

radar [radar] nm radar

rade [rad] nf (natural) harbour; rester en ~ (fig) to be left stranded

radeau, x [rado] nm raft

radiateur [radjatœr] nm radiator, heater; (AUTO) radiator; ~ électrique/à gaz electric/gas heater ou fire

radiation [radjosjɔ̃] nf (voir radier) striking off no pl; (PHYSIQUE) radiation

radical, e, aux [radikal, -o] adj radical

radier [radje] vt to strike off

radieux, euse [radjø, -øz] adj radiant; brilliant, glorious

radin, e [radɛ̃, -in] (fam) adj stingy

radio [radjo] nf radio; (MÉD) X-ray ♦ nm radio operator; à la ~ on the radio; **radioactif, ive** adj radioactive; **radiodiffuser** vt to broadcast; **radiographie** nf radiography; (photo) X-ray photograph; **radiophonique** adj radio cpd; **radio-réveil** (pl radios-réveils) nm radio alarm clock; **radiotélévisé, e** adj broadcast on radio and television

radis [radi] nm radish

radoter [radɔte] vi to ramble on

radoucir [radusir]: se ~ vi (se réchauffer) to become milder; (se calmer) to calm down; to soften

rafale [rafal] nf (vent) gust (of wind); (tir) burst of gunfire

raffermir [rafɛrmir] vt to firm up; (fig) to strengthen

raffiner [rafine] vt to refine; **raffinerie** nf refinery

raffoler [rafɔle]: ~ de vt to be very keen on

rafle [rafl(ə)] nf (de police) raid

rafler [rafle] (fam) vt to swipe, nick

rafraîchir [rafreʃir] vt (atmosphère, température) to cool (down); (aussi: mettre à ~) to chill; (fig: rénover) to brighten up; se ~ vi to grow cooler; to freshen up; to refresh o.s.; **rafraîchissant, e** adj refreshing; **rafraîchissement** nm cooling; (boisson) cool drink; **rafraîchissements** nmpl (boissons, fruits etc) refreshments

rage [raʒ] nf (MÉD): la ~ rabies; (fureur) rage, fury; faire ~ to rage; ~ de dents (raging) toothache

ragot [rago] (fam) nm malicious gossip no pl

ragoût [ragu] nm (plat) stew

raide [rɛd] adj (tendu) taut, tight; (escarpé) steep; (droit: cheveux) straight; (ankylosé, dur, guindé) stiff; (fam) steep, stiff; flat broke ♦ adv (en pente) steeply; ~ mort stone dead; **raidir** vt (muscles) to stiffen; (câble) to pull taut; se raidir vi to stiffen; to become taut; (personne) to tense up; to brace o.s.

raie [rɛ] nf (ZOOL) skate, ray;

(rayure) stripe; *(des cheveux)* parting

raifort [Rɛfɔʀ] nm horseradish

rail [ʀaj] nm rail; *(chemins de fer)* railways pl; par ~ by rail

railler [ʀɑje] vt to scoff at, jeer at

rainure [ʀɛnyʀ] nf groove; slot

raisin [ʀɛzɛ̃] nm *(aussi: ~s)* grapes pl; ~s secs raisins

raison [ʀɛzɔ̃] nf reason; avoir ~ to be right; donner ~ à qn to agree with sb; to prove sb right; se faire une ~ to learn to live with it; perdre la ~ to become insane; to take leave of one's senses; ~ de plus all the more reason; à plus forte ~ all the more so; en ~ de because of; according to; in proportion to; à ~ de at the rate of; ~ sociale corporate name; **raisonnable** adj reasonable, sensible

raisonnement [ʀɛzɔnmɑ̃] nm reasoning; arguing; argument

raisonner [ʀɛzɔne] vi *(penser)* to reason; *(argumenter, discuter)* to argue ♦ vt *(personne)* to reason with

rajeunir [ʀaʒœniʀ] vt *(suj: coiffure, robe)*: ~ qn to make sb look younger; *(: cure etc)* to rejuvenate; *(fig)* to give a new look to; to inject new blood into ♦ vi to become *(ou* look*)* younger

rajouter [ʀaʒute] vt: ~ du sel/un œuf to add some more salt/another egg

rajuster [ʀaʒyste] vt *(vêtement)* to straighten, tidy; *(salaires)* to adjust; *(machine)* to readjust

ralenti [ʀalɑ̃ti] nm: au ~ *(AUTO)* to tick over *(AUTO)*, idle; au ~ *(CINEMA)* in slow motion; *(fig)* at a slower pace

ralentir [ʀalɑ̃tiʀ] vt to slow down

râler [ʀɑle] vi to groan; *(fam)* to grouse, moan *(and groan)*

rallier [ʀalje] vt *(rassembler)* to rally; *(rejoindre)* to rejoin; *(gagner à sa cause)* to win over; se ~ à *(avis)* to come over *ou* round to

rallonge [ʀalɔ̃ʒ] nf *(de table)* (extra) leaf; *(argent etc)* extra no pl

rallonger [ʀalɔ̃ʒe] vt to lengthen

rallye [ʀali] nm rally; *(POL)* march

ramassage [ʀamasaʒ] nm: ~ scolaire school bus service

ramassé, e [ʀamase] adj *(trapu)* squat

ramasser [ʀamase] vt *(objet tombé ou par terre, fam)* to pick up; *(recueillir)* to collect; *(récolter)* to gather; se ~ *(sur soi-même)* to huddle up; to crouch; **ramassis** *(péj)* nm bunch; jumble

rambarde [ʀɑ̃baʀd(ə)] nf guardrail

rame [ʀam] nf *(aviron)* oar; *(de métro)* train; *(de papier)* ream

rameau, x [ʀamo] nm *(small)* branch; les R~x *(REL)* Palm Sunday sg

ramener [ʀamne] vt to bring back; *(reconduire)* to take back; *(rabattre: couverture, visière)*: ~ qch sur to pull sth back over; ~ qch à *(réduire à, aussi MATH)* to reduce sth to

ramer [ʀame] vi to row

ramollir [ʀamɔliʀ] vt to soften; se ~ vi to go soft

ramoner [ʀamɔne] vt to sweep

rampe [ʀɑ̃p] nf *(d'escalier)* banister(s pl); *(dans un garage, d'un terrain)* ramp; *(THEATRE)*: la ~ the footlights pl; ~ de lancement launching pad

ramper [ʀɑ̃pe] vi to crawl

rancard [ʀɑ̃kaʀ] *(fam)* nm date; tip

rancart [ʀɑ̃kaʀ] nm: mettre au ~ to scrap

rance [ʀɑ̃s] adj rancid

rancœur [ʀɑ̃kœʀ] nf rancour

rançon [ʀɑ̃sɔ̃] nf ransom; *(fig)* price

rancune [ʀɑ̃kyn] nf grudge, rancour; garder ~ à qn *(de qch)* to bear sb a grudge *(for sth)*; sans ~! no hard feelings!; **rancunier, ière** adj vindictive, spiteful

randonnée [ʀɑ̃dɔne] nf *(à pied)* walk, ramble; hike, hiking no pl

rang [ʀɑ̃] nm *(rangée)* row; *(grade, classement)* rank; ~s nmpl *(MIL)* ranks; se mettre en ~s/sur un ~ to get into ou form rows/a line; au premier ~ in the first row; (fig) ranking first

rangé, e [ʀɑ̃ʒe] adj (sérieux) orderly, steady

rangée [ʀɑ̃ʒe] nf row

ranger [ʀɑ̃ʒe] vt (classer, grouper) to order, arrange; (mettre à sa place) to put away; (voiture dans la rue) to park; (mettre de l'ordre dans) to tidy up; (arranger) to arrange; (fig: classer): ~ qn/qch parmi to rank sb/sth among; se ~ vi (véhicule, conducteur) to pull over ou in; (piéton) to step aside; (s'assagir) to settle down; se ~ à (avis) to come round to

ranimer [ʀanime] vt (personne) to bring round; (forces, courage) to restore; (troupes etc) to kindle new life in; (douleur, souvenir) to revive; (feu) to rekindle

rap [ʀap] nm rap (music)

rapace [ʀapas] nm bird of prey

râpe [ʀɑp] nf (CULIN) grater

râpé, e [ʀɑpe] adj (tissu) threadbare

râper [ʀɑpe] vt (CULIN) to grate

rapetisser [ʀaptise] vt to shorten

rapide [ʀapid] adj fast; (prompt) quick ♦ nm express (train); (de cours d'eau) rapid; **rapidement** adv fast; quickly

rapiécer [ʀapjese] vt to patch

rappel [ʀapɛl] nm (THÉÂTRE) curtain call; (MED: vaccination) booster; (ADMIN: de salaire) back pay no pl; (d'une aventure, d'un nom) reminder

rappeler [ʀaple] vt to call back; (ambassadeur, MIL) to recall; (faire se souvenir): ~ qch à qn to remind sb of sth; se ~ vt (se souvenir de) to remember, recall

rapport [ʀapɔʀ] nm (compte rendu) report; (profit) yield, return; revenue; (lien, analogie) relationship; (MATH, TECH) ratio; ~s nmpl (entre personnes, pays) relations; avoir ~ à to have something to do with;

être en ~ avec (idée de corrélation) to be related to; être/se mettre en ~ avec qn to be/get in touch with sb; par ~ à in relation to; ~ qualité-prix nm value (for money); ~s (sexuels) (sexual) intercourse sg

rapporter [ʀapɔʀte] vt (rendre, ramener) to bring back; (apporter davantage) to bring more; (suj: investissement) to yield; (: activité) to bring in; (relater) to report ♦ vi (investissement) to give a good return ou yield; (: activité) to be very profitable; se ~ à (correspondre à) to relate to; s'en ~ à to rely on; ~ qch à (rattacher) to relate sth to; **rapporteur, euse** nm/f (de procès, commission) reporter; (péj) telltale ♦ nm (GÉOM) protractor

rapprochement [ʀapʀɔʃmɑ̃] nm (de nations, familles) reconciliation; (analogie, rapport) parallel

rapprocher [ʀapʀɔʃe] vt (chaise d'une table): ~ qch (de) to bring sth closer to; (deux objets) to bring closer together; (réunir) to bring together; (comparer) to establish a parallel between; se ~ vi to draw closer ou nearer; se ~ de to come closer to; (présenter une analogie avec) to be close to

rapt [ʀapt] nm abduction

raquette [ʀakɛt] nf (de tennis) racket; (de ping-pong) bat; (à neige) snowshoe

rare [ʀaʀ] adj rare; (main-d'œuvre, denrées) scarce; (cheveux, herbe) sparse

rarement [ʀaʀmɑ̃] adv rarely, seldom

ras, e [ʀɑ, ʀɑz] adj (tête, cheveux) close-cropped; (poil, herbe) short ♦ adv short; en ~ campagne in open country; à ~ bords to the brim; au ~ de level with; en avoir ~ le bol (fam) to be fed up; ~ du cou adj (pull, robe) crew-neck

rasade [ʀazad] nf glassful

raser [ʀɑze] vt (barbe, cheveux) to shave off; (menton, personne) to shave; (*fam: ennuyer*) to bore; (*démolir*) to raze (to the ground); (*frôler*) to graze, skim; ~ *vi* to shave; (*fam*) to be bored (to tears); **rasoir** *nm* razor

rassasier [ʀasazje] *vt* to satisfy

rassemblement [ʀasɑ̃bləmɑ̃] *nm* (*groupe*) gathering; (*POL*) union

rassembler [ʀasɑ̃ble] *vt* (*réunir*) to assemble, gather; (*regrouper, amasser*) to gather together, collect; se ~ *vi* to gather

rassis, e [ʀasi, -iz] *adj* (*pain*) stale

rassurer [ʀasyʀe] *vt* to reassure; se ~ *vi* to be reassured; **rassure-toi** don't worry

rat [ʀa] *nm* rat

rate [ʀat] *nf* spleen

raté, e [ʀate] *adj* (*tentative*) unsuccessful, failed ♦ *nm/f* failure ♦ *nm* misfiring *no pl*

râteau, x [ʀato] *nm* rake

râtelier [ʀatəlje] *nm* rack; (*fam*) false teeth *pl*

rater [ʀate] *vi* (*affaire, projet etc*) to go wrong, fail ♦ *vt* (*cible, train, occasion*) to miss; (*démonstration, plat*) to spoil; (*examen*) to fail

ration [ʀasjɔ̃] *nf* ration; (*fig*) share

ratisser [ʀatise] *vt* (*allée*) to rake; (*feuilles*) to rake up; (*suj: armée, police*) to comb

R.A.T.P. *sigle f* (= *Régie autonome des transports parisiens*) *Paris transport authority*

rattacher [ʀataʃe] *vt* (*animal, cheveux*) to tie up again; (*incorporer: ADMIN etc*): ~ **qch à** to join sth to; (*fig: relier*): ~ **qch à** to link sth with; (: *lier*): ~ **qn à** to bind ou tie sb to

rattraper [ʀatʀape] *vt* (*fugitif*) to recapture; (*empêcher de tomber*) to catch (hold of); (*atteindre, rejoindre*) to catch up with; (*réparer: imprudence, erreur*) to make up for; se ~ *vi* to make good one's losses; to make up for it; se ~ (à) (*se raccrocher*) to stop ou.s. falling (by catching hold of)

rature [ʀatyʀ] *nf* deletion, erasure

rauque [ʀok] *adj* raucous; hoarse

ravages [ʀavaʒ] *nmpl*: **faire des ~** to wreak havoc

ravaler [ʀavale] *vt* (*mur, façade*) to restore; (*déprécier*) to lower

ravi, e [ʀavi] *adj*: **être ~ de/que** to be delighted with/that

ravin [ʀavɛ̃] *nm* gully, ravine

ravir [ʀaviʀ] *vt* (*enchanter*) to delight; (*enlever*): ~ **qch à qn** to rob sb of sth; **à ~** beautifully

raviser [ʀavize]: **se ~** *vi* to change one's mind

ravissant, e [ʀavisɑ̃, -ɑ̃t] *adj* delightful

ravisseur, euse [ʀavisœʀ, -øz] *nm/f* abductor, kidnapper

ravitailler [ʀavitaje] *vt* to resupply; (*véhicule*) to refuel; se ~ *vi* to get fresh supplies

raviver [ʀavive] *vt* (*feu, douleur*) to revive; (*couleurs*) to brighten up

rayé, e [ʀeje] *adj* (*à rayures*) striped

rayer [ʀeje] *vt* (*érafler*) to scratch; (*barrer*) to cross out; (*d'une liste*) to cross off

rayon [ʀɛjɔ̃] *nm* (*de soleil etc*) ray; (*GEOM*) radius; (*de roue*) spoke; (*étagère*) shelf; (*de grand magasin*) department; **dans un ~ de** within a radius of; ~ **d'action** range; ~ **de soleil** sunbeam; ~**s X** X-rays

rayonnement [ʀɛjɔnmɑ̃] *nm* radiation; (*fig*) radiance; influence

rayonner [ʀɛjɔne] *vi* (*chaleur, énergie*) to radiate; (*fig*) to shine forth; to be radiant; (*touriste*) to go touring (*from one base*)

rayure [ʀejyʀ] *nf* (*motif*) stripe; (*éraflure*) scratch; (*rainure, d'un fusil*) groove

raz-de-marée [ʀɑdmaʀe] *nm inv* tidal wave

ré [ʀe] *nm* (*MUS*) D; (*en chantant la gamme*) re

réacteur [ʀeaktœʀ] *nm* jet engine

réaction [ʀeaksjɔ̃] *nf* reaction; **moteur à** ~ jet engine

réadapter [ʀeadapte] *vt* to readjust;

(MÉD) to rehabilitate; **se ~ (à)** to readjust (to)

réagir [reaʒir] vi to react

réalisateur, trice [realizatœr, -tris] nm/f (TV, CINÉMA) director

réalisation [realizasjɔ̃] nf carrying out; realization, fulfilment; achievement; production; (œuvre) production; creation; work

réaliser [realize] vt (projet, opération) to carry out, realize; (rêve, souhait) to realize, fulfil; (exploit) to achieve; (achat, vente) to make; (film) to produce; (se rendre compte de, COMM: bien, capital) to realize; **se ~** vi to be realized

réaliste [realist(ə)] adj realistic

réalité [realite] nf reality; **en ~** in (actual) fact; **dans la ~** in reality; **~ virtuelle** [COMPUT] virtual reality

réanimation [reanimasjɔ̃] nf resuscitation; **service de ~** intensive care unit

réarmer [rearme] vt (arme) to reload ♦ vi (état) to rearm

rébarbatif, ive [rebarbatif, -iv] adj forbidding

rebattu, e [rəbaty] adj hackneyed

rebelle [rəbɛl] nm/f rebel ♦ adj (troupes) rebel; (enfant) rebellious; (mèche etc) unruly; **~ à** unamenable to

rebeller [rəbele]: **se ~** vi to rebel

rebondi, e [rəbɔ̃di] adj rounded, chubby

rebondir [rəbɔ̃dir] vi (ballon: au sol) to bounce; (: contre un mur) to rebound; (fig) to get moving again; **rebondissement** nm new development

rebord [rəbɔr] nm edge

rebours [rəbur]: **à ~** adv the wrong way

rebrousse-poil [rəbruspwaj]: **à ~** adv the wrong way

rebrousser [rəbruse] vt: **~ chemin** to turn back

rebut [rəby] nm: **mettre au ~** to scrap; **~er** [rəbyte] vt to put off

récalcitrant, e [rekalsitrɑ̃, -ɑ̃t] adj refractory

recaler [rəkale] vt (SCOL) to fail

récapituler [rekapityle] vt to recapitulate; to sum up

receler [rəsəle] vt (produit d'un vol) to receive; (malfaiteur) to harbour; (fig) to conceal; **receleur, euse** nm/f receiver

récemment [resamɑ̃] adv recently

recenser [rəsɑ̃se] vt (population) to take a census of; (inventorier) to list

récent, e [resɑ̃, -ɑ̃t] adj recent

récépissé [resepise] nm receipt

récepteur, trice [reseptœr, -tris] nm receiver; **~ (de radio)** radio set ou receiver

réception [resepsjɔ̃] nf receiving no pl; (accueil) reception, welcome; (bureau) reception desk; (réunion mondaine) reception, party; **réceptionniste** nm/f receptionist

recette [rəsɛt] nf (CULIN) recipe; (fig) formula, recipe; (COMM) takings pl; **~s** nfpl: (rentrées) receipts

receveur, euse [rəsvœr, -øz] nm/f (des contributions) tax collector; (des postes) postmaster(mistress); (d'autobus) conductor(tress)

recevoir [rəsvwar] vt to receive; (client, patient) to see ♦ vi to receive visitors; to give parties; to see patients etc; **se ~** vi (athlète) to land; **être reçu (à un examen)** to pass

rechange [rəʃɑ̃ʒ]: **de ~** adj (pièces, roue) spare; (fig: solution) alternative; **des vêtements de ~** a change of clothes

rechaper [rəʃape] vt to remould, retread

réchapper [reʃape]: **~ de** ou **à** vt (accident, maladie) to come through

recharge [rəʃarʒ(ə)] nf refill

recharger [rəʃarʒe] vt (camion, fusil, appareil-photo) to reload; (briquet, stylo) to refill; (batterie) to recharge

réchaud [reʃo] nm (portable) stove; plate-warmer

réchauffer [reʃofe] vt (plat) to reheat; (mains, personne) to warm; **se**

~ vi (température) to get warmer

rêche [ʀɛʃ] adj rough

recherche [ʀəʃɛʀʃ(ə)] nf (action): la ~ de the search for; (raffinement) affectedness, studied elegance; (scientifique etc): la ~ research; ~s nfpl (de la police) investigations; (scientifiques) research sg; se mettre à la ~ de to go in search of

recherché, e [ʀəʃɛʀʃe] adj (rare, demandé) much sought-after; (raffiné) studied, affected

rechercher [ʀəʃɛʀʃe] vt (objet égaré, personne) to look for; (causes, nouveau procédé) to try to find; (bonheur, amitié) to seek

rechute [ʀəʃyt] nf (MÉD) relapse

récidiver [ʀesidive] vi to commit a subsequent offence; (fig) to do it again

récif [ʀesif] nm reef

récipient [ʀesipjɑ̃] nm container

réciproque [ʀesipʀɔk] adj reciprocal

récit [ʀesi] nm story

récital [ʀesital] nm recital

réciter [ʀesite] vt to recite

réclamation [ʀeklamɑsjɔ̃] nf complaint; ~s nfpl (bureau) complaints department sg

réclame [ʀeklam] nf ad, advert(isement); **article en** ~ special offer

réclamer [ʀeklame] vt (aide, nourriture etc) to ask for; (revendiquer) to claim, demand; (nécessiter) to demand, require ♦ vi to complain

réclusion [ʀeklyzjɔ̃] nf imprisonment

recoin [ʀəkwɛ̃] nm nook, corner; (fig) hidden recess

reçois etc vb voir **recevoir**

récolte [ʀekɔlt(ə)] nf harvesting; gathering; (produits) harvest, crop; (fig) crop, collection

récolter [ʀekɔlte] vt to harvest, gather (in); (fig) to collect; to get

recommandé [ʀəkɔmɑ̃de] nm (POSTES): **en** ~ by registered mail

recommander [ʀəkɔmɑ̃de] vt to recommend; (suj: qualités etc) to commend; (POSTES) to register; **se** ~

de qn to give sb's name as a reference

recommencer [ʀəkɔmɑ̃se] vt (reprendre: lutte, séance) to resume, start again; (refaire: travail, explications) to start afresh, start (over) again; (récidiver: erreur) to make again ♦ vi to start again; (récidiver) to do it again

récompense [ʀekɔ̃pɑ̃s] nf reward; (prix) award; **récompenser** vt: **récompenser qn (de ou pour)** to reward sb (for)

réconcilier [ʀekɔ̃silje] vt to reconcile; **se** ~ **(avec)** to be reconciled (with)

reconduire [ʀəkɔ̃dɥiʀ] vt (raccompagner) to take ou see back; (JUR, POL: renouveler) to renew

réconfort [ʀekɔ̃fɔʀ] nm comfort; **réconforter** [ʀekɔ̃fɔʀte] vt (consoler) to comfort; (revigorer) to fortify

reconnaissance [ʀəkɔnesɑ̃s] nf recognition; acknowledgement; (gratitude) gratitude, gratefulness; (MIL) reconnaissance, recce; **reconnaissant, e** [ʀəkɔnesɑ̃, -ɑ̃t] adj grateful

reconnaître [ʀəkɔnɛtʀ(ə)] vt to recognize; (MIL: lieu) to reconnoitre; (JUR: enfant, dette, droit) to acknowledge; ~ **que** to admit ou acknowledge that; ~ **qn/qch à** to recognize sb/sth by

reconnu, e [ʀ(ə)kɔny] adj (indiscuté, connu) recognized

reconstituant, e [ʀəkɔ̃stitɥɑ̃, -ɑ̃t] adj (aliment, régime) strength-building

reconstituer [ʀəkɔ̃stitɥe] vt (monument ancien) to recreate; (fresque, vase brisé) to piece together, reconstitute; (événement, accident) to reconstruct; (fortune, patrimoine) to rebuild

reconstruire [ʀəkɔ̃stʀɥiʀ] vt to rebuild

reconvertir [ʀəkɔ̃vɛʀtiʀ]: **se** ~ vt (un métier, une branche) to go into

record [ʀəkɔʀ] nm, adj record

recoupement [ʀəkupmɑ̃] nm: **par**

~ by cross-checking

recouper [ʀəkupe] *vt*: **se** ~ *vi* (*témoignages*) to tie *ou* match up

recourbé, e [ʀəkuʀbe] *adj* curved; hooked; bent

recourir [ʀəkuʀiʀ] ~ à *vt* (*ami, agence*) to turn *ou* appeal to; (*force, ruse, emprunt*) to resort to

recours [ʀəkuʀ] *nm* (*JUR*) appeal; **avoir ~ à** — to resort to; **en dernier** ~ as a last resort; ~ **en grâce** plea for clemency

recouvrer [ʀəkuvʀe] *vt* (*vue, santé etc*) to recover, regain; (*impôts*) to collect; (*créance*) to recover

recouvrir [ʀəkuvʀiʀ] *vt* (*couvrir à nouveau*) to re-cover; (*couvrir entièrement, aussi fig*) to cover; (*cacher, masquer*) to conceal, hide; **se** ~ *vi* (*se superposer*) to overlap

récréation [ʀekʀeasjɔ̃] *nf* recreation, entertainment; (*SCOL*) break

récrier [ʀekʀije]: **se** ~ *vi* to exclaim

récriminations [ʀekʀiminasjɔ̃] *nfpl* remonstrations, complaints

recroqueviller [ʀəkʀɔkvije]: **se** ~ *vi* (*feuilles*) to curl *ou* shrivel up; (*personne*) to huddle up

recrudescence [ʀəkʀydesɑ̃s] *nf* fresh outbreak

recrue [ʀəkʀy] *nf* recruit

recruter [ʀəkʀyte] *vt* to recruit

rectangle [ʀɛktɑ̃gl(ə)] *nm* rectangle; **rectangulaire** *adj* rectangular

recteur [ʀɛktœʀ] *nm* ≈ (regional) director of education (*BRIT*), ≈ state superintendent of education (*US*)

rectificatif, -iv [ʀɛktifikatif, -iv] *nm* correction

rectifier [ʀɛktifje] *vt* (*tracé, virage*) to straighten; (*calcul, adresse*) to correct; (*erreur, faute*) to rectify

rectiligne [ʀɛktilin] *adj* straight; (*GEOM*) rectilinear

reçu, e [ʀəsy] *pp de* recevoir ♦ *adj* (*admis, consacré*) accepted ♦ *nm* (*COMM*) receipt

recueil [ʀəkœj] *nm* collection

recueillir [ʀəkœjiʀ] *vt* to collect; (*voix, suffrages*) to win; (*accueillir:* *réfugiés, chat*) to take in; **se** ~ *vi* to gather one's thoughts; to meditate

recul [ʀəkyl] *nm* retreat; recession; decline; (*d'arme à feu*) recoil, kick; **avoir un mouvement de** ~ to recoil; **prendre du** ~ to stand back

reculé, e [ʀəkyle] *adj* remote

reculer [ʀəkyle] *vi* to move back, back away; (*AUTO*) to reverse, back (up); (*fig*) to (be on the) decline; to be losing ground; (*: se dérober*) to shrink back ♦ *vt* to move back; to reverse, back (up); (*fig: possibilités, limites*) to extend; (*: date, décision*) to postpone

reculons [ʀəkylɔ̃]: à ~ *adv* backwards

récupérer [ʀekypeʀe] *vt* to recover, get back; (*heures de travail*) to make up; (*déchets*) to salvage; (*délinquant etc*) to rehabilitate ♦ *vi* to recover

récurer [ʀekyʀe] *vt* to scour

récuser [ʀekyze] *vt* to challenge; **se** ~ *vi* to decline to give an opinion

reçut *vb voir* recevoir

recycler [ʀəsikle] *vt* (*SCOL*) to re-orientate; (*employés*) to retrain; (*TECH*) to recycle

rédacteur, trice [ʀedaktœʀ, -tʀis] *nm/f* (*journaliste*) writer; subeditor; (*d'ouvrage de référence*) editor, compiler; ~ **en chef** chief editor; ~ **publicitaire** copywriter

rédaction [ʀedaksjɔ̃] *nf* writing; (*rédacteurs*) editorial staff; (*bureau*) editorial office(s); (*SCOL: devoir*) essay, composition

reddition [ʀedisjɔ̃] *nf* surrender

redemander [ʀədmɑ̃de] *vt* to ask again for; to ask for more of

redescendre [ʀədesɑ̃dʀ(ə)] *vi* to go back down ♦ *vt* (*pente etc*) to go down

redevable [ʀədvabl(ə)] *adj*: **être** ~ **de qch à qn** (*somme*) to owe sb sth; (*fig*) to be indebted to sb for sth

redevance [ʀədvɑ̃s] *nf* (*TEL*) rental charge; (*TV*) licence fee

rédiger [ʀediʒe] *vt* to write; (*con-*

trat) to draw up

redire [ʀədiʀ] *vt* to repeat; **trouver à ~ à** to find fault with

redoublé, e [ʀəduble] *adj*: **à coups ~s** even harder, twice as hard

redoubler [ʀəduble] *vi (tempête, violence)* to intensify; *(SCOL)* to repeat a year; **~ de** to be twice as +*adjectif*

redoutable [ʀədutabl(ə)] *adj* formidable, fearsome

redouter [ʀədute] *vt* to fear; *(appréhender)* to dread

redresser [ʀədʀese] *vt (arbre, mât)* to set upright; *(pièce tordue)* to straighten out; *(situation, économie)* to put right; **se ~** *vi (objet penché)* to right itself; *(personne)* to sit *(ou* stand) up *(straight)*

réduction [ʀedyksjɔ̃] *nf* reduction

réduire [ʀedɥiʀ] *vt* to reduce; *(prix, dépenses)* to cut, reduce; *(MED: fracture)* to set; **se ~ à** *(revenir à)* to boil down to; **se ~ en** *(se transformer en)* to be reduced to

réduit [ʀedɥi] *nm* tiny room; recess

rééducation [ʀeedykasjɔ̃] *nf (d'un membre)* re-education; *(de délinquants, d'un blessé)* rehabilitation

réel, le [ʀeɛl] *adj* real

réellement [ʀeɛlmɑ̃] *adv* really

réévaluer [ʀeevalɥe] *vt* to revalue

réexpédier [ʀeɛkspedje] *vt (à l'envoyeur)* to return, send back; *(au destinataire)* to send on, forward

refaire [ʀəfɛʀ] *vt (faire de nouveau, recommencer)* to do again; *(réparer, restaurer)* to do up

réfection [ʀefɛksjɔ̃] *nf* repair

réfectoire [ʀefɛktwaʀ] *nm* refectory

référence [ʀefeʀɑ̃s] *nf* reference; **~s** *nfpl (recommandations)* reference *sg*

référer [ʀefeʀe]: **se ~ à** *vt* to refer to; **en ~ à qn** to refer the matter to sb

réfléchi, e [ʀefleʃi] *adj (caractère)* thoughtful; *(action)* well-thought-out; *(LING)* reflexive

réfléchir [ʀefleʃiʀ] *vt* to reflect ♦ *vi* to think; **~ à** *ou* **sur** to think about

reflet [ʀəflɛ] *nm* reflection; *(sur l'eau etc)* sheen *no pl*, glint

refléter [ʀəflete] *vt* to reflect; **se ~** *vi* to be reflected

réflexe [ʀeflɛks(ə)] *nm, adj* reflex

réflexion [ʀeflɛksjɔ̃] *nf (de la lumière etc, pensée)* reflection; *(fait de penser)* thought; *(remarque)* remark; **~ faite, à la ~** on reflection

refluer [ʀəflɥe] *vi* to flow back; *(foule)* to surge back

reflux [ʀəfly] *nm (de la mer)* ebb

réforme [ʀefɔʀm(ə)] *nf* reform; *(REL)*: **la R~** the Reformation

réformer [ʀefɔʀme] *vt* to reform; *(MIL)* to declare unfit for service

refouler [ʀəfule] *vt (envahisseurs)* to drive back; *(liquide)* to force back; *(fig)* to suppress; *(PSYCH)* to repress

réfractaire [ʀefʀaktɛʀ] *adj*: **être ~ à** to resist

refrain [ʀəfʀɛ̃] *nm (MUS)* refrain, chorus; *(air, fig)* tune

refréner [ʀəfʀene] *vt* to curb, check

réfréner [ʀefʀene] *vt* = **refréner**

réfrigérateur [ʀefʀiʒeʀatœʀ] *nm* refrigerator, fridge

refroidir [ʀəfʀwadiʀ] *vt* to cool ♦ *vi* to cool (down); **se ~** *vi (prendre froid)* to catch a chill; *(temps)* to get cooler *ou* colder; *(fig)* to cool (off); **refroidissement** *nm (grippe etc)* chill

refuge [ʀəfyʒ] *nm* refuge; *(pour piétons)* (traffic) island

réfugié, e [ʀefyʒje] *adj, nm/f* refugee

réfugier [ʀefyʒje]: **se ~** *vi* to take refuge

refus [ʀəfy] *nm* refusal; **ce n'est pas de ~** I won't say no, it's welcome

refuser [ʀəfyze] *vt* to refuse; *(SCOL: candidat)* to fail; **~ qch à qn** to refuse sb sth; **~ du monde** to have to turn people away; **se ~ à faire** to refuse to do

réfuter [ʀefyte] *vt* to refute

regagner [ʀəgaɲe] *vt (argent, faveur)* to win back; *(lieu)* to get back to; **~ le temps perdu** to make up (for) lost time

regain [ʀəgɛ̃] nm (renouveau): un ~ de renewed +nom

régal [ʀegal] nm treat

régaler [ʀegale]: se ~ vi to have a delicious meal; (fig) to enjoy o.s.

regard [ʀəgaʀ] nm (coup d'œil) look, glance; (expression) look in (one's eye); au ~ de (loi, morale) from the point of view of; en ~ (vis à vis) opposite; en ~ de in comparison with

regardant, e [ʀəgaʀdɑ̃, -ɑ̃t] adj: très/peu ~ (sur) quite fussy/very free (about); (économe) very tight-fisted/quite generous (with)

regarder [ʀəgaʀde] vt (examiner, observer, lire) to look at; (film, télévision, match) to watch; (envisager: situation, avenir) to view; (considérer: son intérêt etc) to be concerned with; (être orienté vers): ~ (vers) to face; (concerner) to concern ♦ vi to look; ~ à (dépense) to be fussy with ou over; ~ qn/qch comme to regard sb/sth as

régie [ʀeʒi] nf (COMM, INDUSTRIE) state-owned company; (THEATRE, CINEMA) production; (RADIO, TV) control room

regimber [ʀəʒɛ̃be] vi to balk, jib

régime [ʀeʒim] nm (POL) régime; (ADMIN: carcéral, fiscal etc) system; (MED) diet; (TECH) (engine) speed; (fig) rate, pace; (de bananes, dattes) bunch; se mettre au/suivre un ~ to go on/be on a diet

régiment [ʀeʒimɑ̃] nm regiment; (fig: fam): un ~ de an army of

région [ʀeʒjɔ̃] nf region; **régional, e**, aux adj regional

régir [ʀeʒiʀ] vt to govern

régisseur [ʀeʒisœʀ] nm (d'un domaine) steward; (CINEMA, TV) assistant director; (THEATRE) stage manager

registre [ʀəʒistʀ(ə)] nm (livre) register; logbook; ledger; (MUS, LING) register

réglage [ʀeglaʒ] nm adjustment; tuning

règle [ʀɛgl(ə)] nf (instrument) ruler; (loi, prescription) rule; ~s nf/pl (PHYSIOL) period sg; en ~ (papiers d'identité) in order; en ~ générale as a (general) rule

réglé, e [ʀegle] adj well-ordered; steady; (papier) ruled; (arrangé) settled

règlement [ʀegləmɑ̃] nm (paiement) settlement; (arrêté) regulation; (règles, statuts) regulations pl, rules pl; ~ de compte(s) nm settling of old scores; **réglementaire** adj conforming to the regulations; (tenue) regulation cpd; **réglementer** [ʀegləmɑ̃te] vt to regulate

régler [ʀegle] vt (mécanisme, machine) to regulate, adjust; (moteur) to tune; (thermostat etc) to set, adjust; (conflit, facture) to settle; (fournisseur) to settle up with

réglisse [ʀeglis] nf liquorice

règne [ʀɛɲ] nm (d'un roi etc, fig) reign; (BIO): le ~ végétal/animal the vegetable/animal kingdom

régner [ʀeɲe] vi (roi) to rule, reign; (fig) to reign

regorger [ʀəgɔʀʒe] vi: ~ de to overflow with, be bursting with

regret [ʀəgʀɛ] nm regret; à ~ with regret; avec ~ regretfully; être au ~ de devoir faire to regret having to do

regrettable [ʀəgʀɛtabl(ə)] adj regrettable

regretter [ʀəgʀɛte] vt to regret; (personne) to miss; je regrette I'm sorry

regrouper [ʀəgʀupe] vt (grouper) to group together; (contenir) to include, comprise; se ~ vi to gather (together)

régulier, ière [ʀegylje, -jɛʀ] adj (gén) regular; (vitesse, qualité) steady; (répartition, pression, paysage) even; (TRANSPORTS: ligne, service) scheduled, regular; (légal, réglementaire) lawful, in order; (fam: correct) straight, on the level; **régulièrement** adv regularly; steadily; evenly; normally

rehausser [ʀəose] vt to heighten, raise

rein [ʀɛ̃] nm kidney; ~s nmpl (dos) back sg

reine [ʀɛn] nf queen

reine-claude [ʀɛnklod] nf greengage

réintégrer [ʀeɛ̃tegʀe] vt (lieu) to return to; (fonctionnaire) to reinstate

rejaillir [ʀəʒajiʀ] vi to splash up; ~ sur to splash up onto; (fig) to rebound on; to fall upon

rejet [ʀəʒɛ] nm (action, aussi MÉD) rejection

rejeter [ʀəʒte] vt (relancer) to throw back; (vomir) to bring ou throw up; (écarter) to reject; (déverser) to throw out, discharge; ~ **la responsabilité de qch sur qn** to lay the responsibility for sth on sb's door

rejoindre [ʀəʒwɛ̃dʀ(ə)] vt (famille, régiment) to rejoin, return to; (lieu) to get (back) to; (suj: route etc) to meet, join; (rattraper) to catch up (with); **se ~** vi to meet; **je te rejoins au café** ou I'll see ou meet you at the café

réjouir [ʀeʒwiʀ] vt to delight; **se ~** vi to be delighted; to rejoice; **réjouissances** nfpl (joie) rejoicing sg; (fête) festivities

relâche [ʀəlɑʃ]: **sans ~** without respite ou a break

relâché, e [ʀəlɑʃe] adj loose, lax

relâcher [ʀəlɑʃe] vt to release; (étreinte) to loosen; **se ~** vi to loosen; (discipline) to become slack ou lax; (élève etc) to slacken off

relais [ʀəlɛ] nm (SPORT): (**course de**) ~ relay (race); **équipe de** ~ shift team; (SPORT) relay team; **prendre le** ~ (**de**) to take over (from); ~ **routier** = transport café (BRIT), ~ truck stop (US)

relancer [ʀəlɑ̃se] vt (balle) to throw back; (moteur) to restart; (fig) to boost, revive; (personne): ~ **qn** to pester sb

relater [ʀəlate] vt to relate, recount

relatif, ive [ʀəlatif, -iv] adj relative

relation [ʀəlɑsjɔ̃] nf (récit) account, report; (rapport) relation(ship); ~s nfpl (rapports) relations; relationship sg; (connaissances) connections; **être/entrer en** ~(**s**) **avec** to be/get in contact with

relaxer [ʀəlakse] vt to relax; (JUR) to discharge; **se ~** vi to relax

relayer [ʀəleje] vt (collaborateur, coureur etc) to relieve; **se ~** vi (dans une activité) to take it in turns

reléguer [ʀəlege] vt to relegate

relent(s) [ʀəlɑ̃] nm(pl) (foul) smell

relevé, e [ʀəlve] adj (manches) rolled-up; (sauce) highly-seasoned ♦ nm (lecture) reading; (liste) statement; list; (facture) account; ~ **de compte** bank statement

relève [ʀəlɛv] nf relief; relief team (ou troops pl); **prendre la** ~ to take over

relever [ʀəlve] vt (statue, meuble) to stand up again; (personne tombée) to help up; (vitre, niveau de vie) to raise; (col) to turn up; (style, conversation) to elevate; (plat, sauce) to season; (sentinelle, équipe) to relieve; (fautes, points) to pick up; (constater: traces etc) to find, pick up; (répliquer à: remarque) to react to, reply to; (: défi) to accept, take up; (noter: adresse etc) to take down, note; (: plan) to sketch; (: cotes etc) to plot; (compteur) to read; (ramasser: cahiers) to collect, take in; **se ~** vi (se remettre debout) to get up; ~ **de** (maladie) to be recovering from; (être du ressort de) to be a matter for; (ADMIN: dépendre de) to come under; (fig) to pertain to; ~ **qn de** (fonctions) to relieve sb of; ~ **la tête** to look up; to hold up one's head

relief [ʀəljɛf] nm relief; ~s nmpl (restes) remains; **mettre en** ~ (fig) to bring out, highlight

relier [ʀəlje] vt to link up; (livre) to bind; ~ **qch à** to link with

religieuse [ʀəliʒjøz] nf nun; (gâteau) cream bun

religieux, euse [rəliʒjø, -øz] adj religious ♦ nm monk

religion [rəliʒjɔ̃] nf religion; (piété, dévotion) faith

relire [rəlir] vt (à nouveau) to re-read, read again; (vérifier) to read over

reliure [rəljyr] nf binding

reluire [rəlɥir] vi to gleam

remanier [rəmanje] vt to reshape, recast; (POL) to reshuffle

remarquable [rəmarkabl(ə)] adj remarkable

remarque [rəmark(ə)] nf remark; (écrite) note

remarquer [rəmarke] vt (voir) to notice; se ~ vi to be noticeable; faire ~ (à qn) que to point out (to sb) that; faire ~ qch (à qn) to point sth out (to sb); remarquez, ... mind you ...

remblai [rɑ̃ble] nm embankment

rembourrer [rɑ̃bure] vt to stuff; (dossier, vêtement, souliers) to pad

remboursement [rɑ̃bursəmɑ̃] nm repayment; envoi contre ~ cash on delivery; **rembourser** [rɑ̃burse] vt to pay back, repay

remède [rəmɛd] nm (médicament) medicine; (traitement, fig) remedy, cure

remémorer [rəmemɔre]: se ~ vt to recall, recollect

remerciements [rəmɛrsimɑ̃] nmpl thanks

remercier [rəmɛrsje] vt to thank; (congédier) to dismiss; ~ qn de/d'avoir fait to thank sb for/for having done

remettre [rəmɛtr(ə)] vt (vêtement): ~ qch to put sth back on; (replacer): ~ qch quelque part to put sth back somewhere; (ajouter): ~ du sel/un sucre to add more salt/another lump of sugar; (ajourner): ~ qch (à) to postpone sth (until); se ~ vi to get better, recover; se ~ de to recover from, get over; s'en ~ à to leave it up to; ~ qch à qn (rendre, restituer) to give sth back to sb;

(donner, confier: paquet, argent) to hand over sth to sb, deliver sth to sb; (: prix, décoration) to present sb with sth

remise [rəmiz] nf delivery; presentation; (rabais) discount; (local) shed; ~ de peine reduction of sentence; ~ en jeu (FOOTBALL) throw-in

remontant [rəmɔ̃tɑ̃] nm tonic, pick-me-up

remonte-pente [rəmɔ̃tpɑ̃t] nm ski-lift

remonter [rəmɔ̃te] vi to go back up; (jupe) to ride up ♦ vt (pente) to go up; (fleuve) to sail (ou swim etc) up; (manches, pantalon) to roll up; (col) to turn up; (niveau, limite) to raise; (fig: personne) to buck up; (moteur, meuble) to put back together, reassemble; (montre, mécanisme) to wind up; ~ le moral à qn to raise sb's spirits; ~ à (dater de) to date ou go back to

remontrance [rəmɔ̃trɑ̃s] nf reproof, reprimand

remontrer [rəmɔ̃tre] vt (fig): en ~ à to prove one's superiority over

remords [rəmɔr] nm remorse no pl; avoir des ~ to feel remorse

remorque [rəmɔrk(ə)] nf trailer; être en ~ to be on tow; **remorquer** vt to tow; **remorqueur** nm tug (boat)

remous [rəmu] nm (d'un navire) (back) wash no pl; (de rivière) swirl, eddy ♦ nmpl (fig) stir ég

remparts [rɑ̃par] nmpl walls, ramparts

remplaçant, e [rɑ̃plasɑ̃, -ɑ̃t] nm/f replacement, stand-in; (THEATRE) understudy; (SCOL) supply teacher

remplacement [rɑ̃plasmɑ̃] nm replacement; (job) replacement work no pl

remplacer [rɑ̃plase] vt to replace; (tenir lieu de) to take the place of; ~ qch/qn par to replace X with Y

rempli, e [rɑ̃pli] adj (emploi du temps) full, busy; ~ de full of, filled with

remplir [rɑ̃plir] vt to fill (up); (ques-

tionnaire) to fill out *ou* up; (*obligations, fonction, condition*) to fulfil; se ~ *vi* to fill up

remporter [ʀɑ̃pɔʀte] *vt* (*marchandise*) to take away; (*fig*) to win, achieve

remuant, e [ʀəmɥɑ̃, -ɑ̃t] *adj* restless

remue-ménage [ʀəmymenaʒ] *nm inv* commotion

remuer [ʀəmɥe] *vt* to move; (*café, sauce*) to stir ♦ *vi* to move; se ~ *vi* to move

rémunérer [ʀemyneʀe] *vt* to remunerate

renard [ʀənaʀ] *nm* fox

renchérir [ʀɑ̃ʃeʀiʀ] *vi* (*fig*): ~ (**sur**) to add something (to)

rencontre [ʀɑ̃kɔ̃tʀ(ə)] *nf* meeting; (*imprévue*) encounter; **aller à la** ~ **de qn** to go and meet sb

rencontrer [ʀɑ̃kɔ̃tʀe] *vt* to meet; (*mot, expression*) to come across; (*difficultés*) to meet with; se ~ *vi* to meet; (*véhicules*) to collide

rendement [ʀɑ̃dmɑ̃] *nm* (*d'un travailleur, d'une machine*) output; (*d'une culture*) return; **à plein** ~ at full capacity

rendez-vous [ʀɑ̃devu] *nm* (*rencontre*) appointment; (: *d'amoureux*) date; (*lieu*) meeting place; **donner** ~ **à qn** to arrange to meet sb; **avoir/prendre** ~ (**avec**) to have/make an appointment (with)

rendre [ʀɑ̃dʀ(ə)] *vt* (*livre, argent etc*) to give back, return; (*otages, visite etc*) to return; (*sang, aliments*) to bring up; (*exprimer, traduire*) to render; (*faire devenir*): ~ **qn célèbre/qch possible** to make sb famous/sth possible; se ~ *vi* (*capituler*) to surrender, give o.s. up; (*aller*): se ~ **quelque part** to go somewhere; se ~ **compte de qch** to realize sth

rênes [ʀɛn] *nfpl* reins

renfermé, e [ʀɑ̃fɛʀme] *adj* (*fig*) withdrawn ♦ *nm*: **sentir le** ~ to smell stuffy

renfermer [ʀɑ̃fɛʀme] *vt* to contain

renflement [ʀɑ̃fləmɑ̃] *nm* bulge

renflouer [ʀɑ̃flue] *vt* to refloat; (*fig*) to set back on its (*ou* his/her *etc*) feet

renfoncement [ʀɑ̃fɔ̃smɑ̃] *nm* recess

renforcer [ʀɑ̃fɔʀse] *vt* to reinforce

renfort [ʀɑ̃fɔʀ] : ~**s** *nmpl* reinforcements; **à grand** ~ **de** with a great deal of

renfrogné, e [ʀɑ̃fʀɔɲe] *adj* sullen

rengaine [ʀɑ̃gɛn] (*péj*) *nf* old tune

renier [ʀənje] *vt* (*parents*) to disown, repudiate; (*foi*) to renounce

renifler [ʀənifle] *vi, vt* to sniff

renne [ʀɛn] *nm* reindeer *inv*

renom [ʀənɔ̃] *nm* reputation; (*célébrité*) renown; **renommé, e** *adj* celebrated, renowned; **renommée** *nf* fame

renoncer [ʀənɔ̃se]: ~ **à** *vt* to give up; ~ **à faire** to give up the idea of doing

renouer [ʀənwe] *vt*: ~ **avec** (*tradition*) to revive; (*habitude*) to take up again; ~ **avec qn** to take up with sb again

renouvelable [ʀ(ə)nuvlabl(ə)] *adj* (*énergie etc*) renewable

renouveler [ʀənuvle] *vt* to renew; (*exploit, méfait*) to repeat; se ~ *vi* (*incident*) to recur, happen again; **renouvellement** *nm* renewal; recurrence

rénover [ʀenɔve] *vt* (*immeuble*) to renovate, do up; (*enseignement*) to reform; (*quartier*) to redevelop

renseignement [ʀɑ̃sɛɲmɑ̃] *nm* information *no pl*, piece of information; (**guichet des**) ~**s** information desk

renseigner [ʀɑ̃seɲe] *vt*: ~ **qn** (**sur**) to give information to sb (about); se ~ *vi* to ask for information, make inquiries

rentabilité [ʀɑ̃tabilite] *nf* profitability

rentable [ʀɑ̃tabl(ə)] *adj* profitable

rente [ʀɑ̃t] *nf* income; pension; (*gouvernment*) stock *ou* bond; **rentier, ière** *nm/f* person of private means

rentrée [ʀɑ̃tʀe] *nf*: ~ (**d'argent**) cash *no pl* coming in; **la** ~ (**des**

classes) the start of the new school year

rentrer [ʀɑ̃tʀe] vi (entrer de nouveau) to go (ou come) back in; (entrer) to go (ou come) in; (revenir chez soi) to go (ou come) (back) home; (air, clou: pénétrer) to go in; (revenu, argent) to come in ♦ vt (foins) to bring in; (véhicule) to put away; (chemise dans pantalon etc) to tuck in; (griffes) to draw in; (fig: larmes, colère etc) to hold back; ~ le ventre to pull in one's stomach; ~ dans (heurter) to crash into; ~ dans l'ordre to be back to normal; ~ dans ses frais to recover one's expenses

renversant, e [ʀɑ̃vɛʀsɑ̃, -ɑ̃t] adj astounding

renverse [ʀɑ̃vɛʀs(ə)]: à la ~ adv backwards

renverser [ʀɑ̃vɛʀse] vt (faire tomber: chaise, verre) to knock over, overturn; (piéton) to knock down; (liquide, contenu) to spill, upset; (retourner) to turn upside down; (: ordre des mots etc) to reverse; (fig: gouvernement etc) to overthrow; (stupéfier) to bowl over; se ~ vi to fall over; to overturn; to spill

renvoi [ʀɑ̃vwa] nm (référence) cross-reference; (éructation) belch

renvoyer [ʀɑ̃vwaje] vt to send back; (congédier) to dismiss; (lumière) to reflect; (son) to echo; (ajourner): ~ qch à to put sth off ou postpone sth (until); ~ qn à (fig) to refer sb to

repaire [ʀəpɛʀ] nm den

répandre [ʀepɑ̃dʀ(ə)] vt (renverser) to spill; (étaler, diffuser) to spread; (lumière) to shed; (chaleur, odeur) to give off; se ~ vi to spill; to spread; **répandu, e** adj (opinion, usage) widespread

réparation [ʀepaʀasjɔ̃] nf repair

réparer [ʀepaʀe] vt to repair; (fig: offense) to make up for, atone for; (: oubli, erreur) to put right

repartie [ʀəpaʀti] nf retort; avoir

de la ~ to be quick at repartee

repartir [ʀəpaʀtiʀ] vi to set off again; to leave again; (fig) to get going again; ~ à zéro to start from scratch (again)

répartir [ʀepaʀtiʀ] vt (pour attribuer) to share out; (pour disperser, disposer) to divide up; (poids, chaleur) to distribute; se ~ vt (travail, rôles) to share out between themselves; **répartition** nf sharing out; dividing up; distribution

repas [ʀəpa] nm meal

repasser [ʀəpase] vi to come (ou go) back ♦ vt (vêtement, tissu) to iron; (examen) to retake, resit; (film) to show again; (leçon, rôle: revoir) to go over (again)

repêcher [ʀəpeʃe] vt (noyé) to recover the body of; (candidat) to pass (by inflating marks)

repentir [ʀəpɑ̃tiʀ] nm repentance; se ~ vi to repent; se ~ de to repent of

répercussions [ʀepɛʀkysjɔ̃] nfpl repercussions

répercuter [ʀepɛʀkyte] vt (information, hausse des prix) to pass on; se ~ vi (bruit) to reverberate; (fig): se ~ sur to have repercussions on

repère [ʀəpɛʀ] nm mark; (monument etc) landmark

repérer [ʀəpeʀe] vt (erreur, connaissance) to spot; others (fam) to locate; se ~ to find one's way about

répertoire [ʀepɛʀtwaʀ] nm (liste) (alphabetical) list; (carnet) index notebook; (d'un artiste) repertoire

répéter [ʀepete] vt to repeat; (préparer: leçon: aussi vi) to learn, go over; (THÉÂTRE) to rehearse; se ~ vi (redire) to repeat o.s.; (se reproduire) to be repeated, recur

répétition [ʀepetisjɔ̃] nf repetition; (THÉÂTRE) rehearsal; ~ générale final dress rehearsal

répit [ʀepi] nm respite

replet, ète [ʀəplɛ, -ɛt] adj chubby

replier [ʀəplije] vt (rabattre) to fold down ou over; se ~ vi (troupes, armée) to withdraw, fall back

réplique 250 reproche

réplique [Replik] nf (repartie, fig) reply; (THEATRE) line; (copie) replica; ~r [Replike] vi to reply; (riposter) to retaliate

répondeur nm: ~ **automatique** (TEL) answering machine

répondre [RepɔdR(ə)] vi to answer, reply; (freins, mécanisme) to respond; ~ à to reply to, answer; (affection, salut) to return; (provocation, suj: mécanisme etc) to respond to; (correspondre à: besoin) to answer; (: conditions) to meet; (: description) to match; (avec impertinence): ~ à qn to answer sb back; ~ **de** to answer for

réponse [Repɔs] nf answer, reply; en ~ à in reply to

reportage [RəpɔRtaʒ] nm (bref) report; (écrit: documentaire) story; article; (en direct) commentary; (genre, activité): le ~ reporting

reporter1 [RəpɔRtɛR] nm reporter

reporter2 [RəpɔRte] vt (total): ~ qch sur to carry sth forward ou over to; (ajourner): ~ qch (à) to postpone sth (until); (transférer): ~ qch sur to transfer sth to; se ~ à (époque) to think back to; (document) to refer to

repos [Rəpo] nm rest; (fig) peace (and quiet); peace of mind; (MIL): ~! stand at ease!; en ~ at rest; de tout ~ safe

reposant, e [Rəpozɑ̃, -ɑ̃t] adj restful

reposer [Rəpoze] vt (verre, livre) to put down; (délasser) to rest; (problème) to reformulate ♦ vi (liquide, pâte) to settle, rest; se ~ vi to rest; se ~ sur qn to rely on sb; ~ sur to be built on; (fig) to rest on

repoussant, e [Rəpusɑ̃, -ɑ̃t] adj repulsive

repousser [Rəpuse] vi to grow again ♦ vt to repel, repulse; (offre) to turn down, reject; (tiroir, personne) to push back; (différer) to put back

reprendre [RəpRɑ̃dR(ə)] vt (prisonnier, ville) to recapture; (objet prêté, donné) to take back; (chercher): je

viendrai te ~ à 4h I'll come and fetch you at 4; (se resservir de): ~ **du pain/un œuf** to take (ou eat) more bread/another egg; (firme, entreprise) to take over; (travail, promenade) to resume; (emprunter: argument, idée) to take up, use; (refaire: article etc) to go over again; (jupe etc) to alter; (émission, pièce) to put on again; (réprimander) to tell off; (corriger) to correct ♦ vi (classes, pluie) to start (up) again; (activités, travaux, combats) to resume, start (up) again; (affaires, industrie) to pick up; (dire): **reprit-il** he went on; se ~ vi (se ressaisir) to recover; **s'y** ~ to make another attempt; ~ **des forces** to recover one's strength; ~ **courage** to take new heart; ~ **la route** to set off again; ~ **haleine** ou **son souffle** to get one's breath back

représailles [RəpRezaj] nfpl reprisals

représentant, e [RəpRezɑ̃tɑ̃, -ɑ̃t] nm/f representative

représentation [RəpRezɑ̃tasjɔ̃] nf (symbole, image) representation; (spectacle) performance

représenter [RəpRezɑ̃te] vt to represent; (donner: pièce, opéra) to perform; se ~ vt (se figurer) to imagine; to visualize

répression [RepResjɔ̃] nf (voir réprimer) suppression; repression

réprimer [RepRime] vt (émotions) to suppress; (peuple etc) to repress

repris [RəpRi] nm: ~ **de justice** ex-prisoner, ex-convict

reprise [RəpRiz] nf (recommencement) resumption; recovery; (TV) repeat; (CINEMA) rerun; (AUTO) acceleration no pl; (COMM) trade-in, part exchange; **à plusieurs** ~s on several occasions

repriser [RəpRize] vt to darn; to mend

reproche [RəpRɔʃ] nm (remontrance) reproach; **faire des** ~s à to reproach sb; **sans** ~(s) beyond reproach

reprocher [rəprɔʃe] *vt*: ~ qch à qn to reproach *ou* blame sb for sth; ~ qch à (machine, théorie) to have sth against

reproduction [rəprɔdyksjɔ̃] *nf* reproduction

reproduire [rəprɔdɥir] *vt* to reproduce; se ~ *vi* (BIO) to reproduce; (recommencer) to recur, re-occur

reptile [rɛptil] *nm* reptile

repu, e [rəpy] *adj* satisfied, sated

républicain, e [repyblikɛ̃, -ɛn] *adj, nm/f* republican

république [repyblik] *nf* republic

répugnant, e [repyɲɑ̃, -ɑ̃t] *adj* repulsive; loathsome

répugner [repyɲe]: ~ à *vt* to repel *ou* disgust sb; ~ à faire to be loath *ou* reluctant to do

réputation [repytasjɔ̃] *nf* reputation; **réputé, e** *adj* renowned

requérir [rəkerir] *vt* (nécessiter) to require, call for; (JUR: peine) to call for, demand

requête [rəkɛt] *nf* request; (JUR) petition

requin [rəkɛ̃] *nm* shark

requis, e [rəki, -iz] *adj* required

R.E.R. sigle m (= réseau express régional) Greater Paris high-speed train service

rescapé, e [rɛskape] *nm/f* survivor

rescousse [rɛskus] *nf*: aller à la ~ de qn to go to sb's aid *ou* rescue

réseau, x [rezo] *nm* network

réservation [rezɛrvasjɔ̃] *nf* booking, reservation

réserve [rezɛrv(ə)] *nf* (retenue) reserve; (entrepôt) storeroom; (restriction, d'Indiens) reservation; (de pêche, chasse) preserve; sous ~ de subject to; sans ~ unreservedly; de ~ (provisions etc) in reserve

réservé, e [rezɛrve] *adj* (discret) reserved; (chasse, pêche) private

réserver [rezɛrve] *vt* (gén) to reserve; (chambre, billet etc) to book, reserve; (garder): ~ qch pour/à to keep *ou* save sth for; ~ qch à qn to

reserve (*ou* book) sth for sb

réservoir [rezɛrvwar] *nm* tank

résidence [rezidɑ̃s] *nf* residence; (en) ~ surveillée (under) house arrest; ~ secondaire second home

résidentiel, le [rezidɑ̃sjɛl] *adj* residential

résider [rezide] *vi*: ~ à/dans/en to reside in; ~ dans (fig) to lie in

résidu [rezidy] *nm* residue no pl

résignor [reziɲe]: se ~ *vi* to resign o.s. (to sth/to doing)

résilier [rezilje] *vt* to terminate

résistance [rezistɑ̃s] *nf* resistance; (de réchaud, bouilloire: fil) element

résistant, e [rezistɑ̃, -ɑ̃t] *adj* (personne) robust, tough; (matériau) strong, hard-wearing

résister [reziste] *vi* to resist; ~ à (assaut, tentation) to resist; (effort, souffrance) to withstand; (désobéir à) to stand up to, oppose

résolu, e [rezɔly] *pp de* résoudre ♦ *adj*: être ~ à qch/faire to be set upon sth/doing

résolution [rezɔlysjɔ̃] *nf* solving; (fermeté, décision) resolution

résolve etc vb voir **résoudre**

résonner [rezɔne] *vi* (cloche, pas) to reverberate, resound; (salle) to be resonant; ~ de to resound with

résorber [rezɔrbe]: se ~ *vi* (fig) to be reduced; to be absorbed

résoudre [rezudr(ə)] *vt* to solve; se ~ à faire to bring o.s. to do

respect [rɛspɛ] *nm* respect; tenir en ~ to keep at bay

respecter [rɛspɛkte] *vt* to respect

respectueux, euse [rɛspɛktɥø, -øz] *adj* respectful; ~ de respectful of

respiration [rɛspirasjɔ̃] *nf* breathing no pl; ~ artificielle artificial respiration

respirer [rɛspire] *vi* to breathe; (fig) to get one's breath; to breathe again ♦ *vt* to breathe (in), inhale; (manifester: santé, calme etc) to exude

resplendir [rɛsplɑ̃dir] *vi* to shine; (fig): ~ (de) to be radiant (with)

responsabilité [rɛspɔ̃sabilite] *nf* responsibility; (*légale*) liability

responsable [ʀɛspɔ̃sabl(ə)] *adj* responsible ♦ *nm/f* (*du ravitaillement etc*) person in charge; (*firme*, *syndicat*) official; ~ **de** responsible for; (*chargé de*) in charge of, responsible for

ressaisir [ʀəsɛziʀ]: **se ~** *vi* to regain one's self-control

ressasser [ʀəsase] *vt* to keep going over

ressemblance [ʀəsɑ̃blɑ̃s] *nf* resemblance, similarity, likeness

ressemblant, e [ʀəsɑ̃blɑ̃, -ɑ̃t] *adj* (*portrait*) lifelike, true to life

ressembler [ʀəsɑ̃ble]: ~ **à** *vt* to be like; to resemble; (*visuellement*) to look like; **se ~** *vi* to be (*ou* look) alike

ressemeler [ʀəsəmle] *vt* to (re)sole

ressentiment [ʀəsɑ̃timɑ̃] *nm* resentment

ressentir [ʀəsɑ̃tiʀ] *vt* to feel; **se ~ de** to feel (*ou* show) the effects of

resserrer [ʀəseʀe] *vt* (*nœud, boulon*) to tighten (up); (*fig: liens*) to strengthen; **se ~** *vi* (*vallée*) to narrow

resservir [ʀəseʀviʀ] *vi* to do ou serve again ♦ *vt*: ~ **qn** (**d'un plat**) to give sb a second helping (of a dish)

ressort [ʀəsɔʀ] *nm* (*pièce*) spring; (*force morale*) spirit; (*recours*): **en dernier** ~ as a last resort; (*compétence*): **être du** ~ **de** to fall within the competence of

ressortir [ʀəsɔʀtiʀ] *vi* to go out (*ou* come) out (again); (*contraster*) to stand out; ~ **de** to emerge from; **faire** ~ (*fig: souligner*) to bring out

ressortissant, e [ʀəsɔʀtisɑ̃, -ɑ̃t] *nm/f* national

ressource [ʀəsuʀs(ə)] *nf*: **avoir la** ~ **de** to have the possibility of; ~**s** *nfpl* (*moyens*) resources; **leur seule** ~ **était de** the only course open to them was to

ressusciter [ʀesysite] *vt* (*fig*) to revive, bring back ♦ *vi* to rise (from the dead)

restant, e [ʀɛstɑ̃, -ɑ̃t] *adj* remaining ♦ *nm*: **le** ~ (**de**) the remainder (of); **un** ~ **de** (*de trop*) some leftover

restaurant [ʀɛstɔʀɑ̃] *nm* restaurant

restauration [ʀɛstɔʀasjɔ̃] *nf* restoration; (*hôtellerie*) catering; ~ **rapide** fast food

restaurer [ʀɛstɔʀe] *vt* to restore; **se** ~ *vi* to have something to eat

reste [ʀɛst(ə)] *nm* (*restant*): **le** ~ (**de**) the rest (of); (*de trop*): **un** ~ (**de**) some left-over; (*vestige*): **un** ~ **de** a remnant *ou* last trace of; (*MATH*) remainder; ~**s** *nmpl* (*nourriture*) left-overs; (*d'une cité etc*, *dépouille mortelle*) remains; **du** ~, **au** ~ besides, moreover

rester [ʀɛste] *vi* to stay, remain; (*subsister*) to remain, be left; (*durer*) to last, live on ♦ *vb impers*: **il reste du pain/2 œufs** there's some bread/there are 2 eggs left (over); **il me reste assez de temps** I have enough time left; **ce qui reste à faire** what remains to be done; **restons-en là** let's leave it at that

restituer [ʀɛstitɥe] *vt* (*objet, somme*): ~ **qch** (**à qn**) to return sth (to sb); (*TECH*) to release; (*: son*) to reproduce

restoroute [ʀɛstɔʀut] *nm* motorway (*BRIT*) *ou* highway (*US*) restaurant

restreindre [ʀɛstʀɛ̃dʀ(ə)] *vt* to restrict, limit

restriction [ʀɛstʀiksjɔ̃] *nf* restriction

résultat [ʀezylta] *nm* result; (*d'élection etc*) results *pl*

résulter [ʀezylte]: ~ **de** *vt* to result from, be the result of

résumé [ʀezyme] *nm* summary, résumé

résumer [ʀezyme] *vt* (*texte*) to summarize; (*récapituler*) to sum up; **se** ~ **à** to come down to

résurrection [ʀezyʀɛksjɔ̃] *nf* resurrection; (*fig*) revival

rétablir [ʀetabliʀ] *vt* to restore, re-establish; **se** ~ *vi* (*guérir*) to recover; (*silence, calme*) to return, be restored; **rétablissement** nm restoring; recovery; (SPORT) pull-up

retaper [ʀətape] vt (maison, voiture etc) to do up; (fam: revigorer) to buck up; (redactylographier) to retype

retard [ʀətaʀ] nm (d'une personne attendue) lateness no pl; (sur l'horaire, un programme) delay; (fig: scolaire, mental etc) backwardness; **en ~** (de 2 heures) (2 hours) late; **avoir du ~** to be late; (sur un programme) to be behind (schedule); **prendre du ~** (train, avion) to be delayed; (montre) to lose (time); **sans ~** without delay

retardement [ʀətaʀdəmã] : **à ~** adj delayed action cpd; **bombe à ~** time bomb

retarder [ʀətaʀde] vt (sur un horaire): **~ qn** (d'une heure) to delay sb (an hour); (départ, date): **~ qch** (de 2 jours) to put sth back (2 days), delay sth for ou (2 days); (horloge) to put back ♦ vi (montre) to be slow; to lose (time)

retenir [ʀətniʀ] vt (garder, retarder) to keep, detain; (maintenir: objet qui glisse, fig: colère, larmes) to hold back; (: objet suspendu) to hold; (fig: empêcher d'agir): **~ qn** (de faire) to hold sb back (from doing); (se rappeler) to retain; (réserver) to reserve; (accepter) to accept; (prélever): **~ qch** (sur) to deduct sth (from); **se ~** vi to restrain o.s. from doing; **se ~ de faire** to restrain o.s. from doing; **~ son souffle** to hold one's breath

retentir [ʀətãtiʀ] vi to ring out; (salle): **~ de** to ring ou resound with

retentissant, e [ʀətãtisã, -ãt] adj resounding; (fig) impact-making

retentissement [ʀətãtismã] nm repercussion; effect, impact; stir

retenu, e adj (place) reserved; (personne: emotion) restrained

retenue [ʀətny] nf (prélèvement) deduction; (SCOL) detention; (modéra-

tion) (self-)restraint; (réserve) reserve, reticence

réticence [ʀetisãs] nf hesitation, reluctance no pl

rétine [ʀetin] nf retina

retiré, e [ʀətiʀe] adj secluded; remote

retirer [ʀətiʀe] vt to withdraw; (vêtement, lunettes) to take off, remove; (extraire): **~ qch de** to take sth out of, remove sth from; (reprendre: bagages, billets) to collect, pick up

retombées [ʀətõbe] nfpl (radioactives) fallout sg; (fig) fallout; spinoffs

retomber [ʀətõbe] vi (à nouveau) to fall again; (atterrir: après un saut etc) to land; (tomber, redescendre) to fall back; (pendre) to fall, hang (down); (échoir): **~ sur qn** to fall on sb

rétorquer [ʀetɔʀke] vt: **~ (à qn) que** to retort (to sb) that

retors, e [ʀətɔʀ, -ɔʀs(ə)] adj wily

retouche [ʀətuʃ] nf (photographie) touch-up; (texte, vêtement) alteration

retoucher [ʀətuʃe] vt (photographie) to touch up; (texte, vêtement) to alter

retour [ʀətuʀ] nm return; **au ~** when we (ou they etc) get (ou got) back; (en route) on the way back; **être de ~** to be back (from); **par ~ du courrier** by return of post

retourner [ʀətuʀne] vt (dans l'autre sens: matelas, crêpe, foin, terre) to turn (over); (: caisse) to turn upside down; (: sac, vêtement) to turn inside out; (émouvoir: personne) to shake; (renvoyer, restituer): **~ qch à qn** to return sth to sb ♦ vi (aller, revenir): **~ quelque part/à** to go back ou return somewhere/to; **se ~** vi to turn over; (tourner la tête): **~ à** (état, activité) to return to, go back to; **se ~ contre** (fig) to turn against; **savoir de quoi il retourne** to know what it is all about

retracer [ʀətʀase] vt to relate, recount

retrait [ʀətʀɛ] nm (voir retirer) withdrawal; collection; en ~ set back; ~ **du permis (de conduire)** disqualification from driving (BRIT), revocation of driver's license (US)

retraite [ʀətʀɛt] nf (d'une armée, REL, refuge) retreat; (d'un employé) retirement; (revenu) pension; **prendre sa** ~ to retire; ~ **anticipée** early retirement; **retraité, e** adj retired ♦ nm/f pensioner

retrancher [ʀətʀɑ̃ʃe] vt (passage, détails) to take out, remove; (nombre, somme): ~ **qch de** to take ou deduct sth from; (couper) to cut off; se ~ **derrière/dans** to take refuge behind/in

retransmettre [ʀətʀɑ̃smɛtʀ(ə)] vt (RADIO) to broadcast; (TV) to show

rétrécir [ʀetʀesiʀ] vt (vêtement) to take in ♦ vi to shrink; se ~ vi to narrow

rétribution [ʀetʀibysjɔ̃] nf payment

rétro [ʀetʀo] adj inv: **la mode** ~ the nostalgia vogue

rétrograde [ʀetʀogʀad] adj reactionary, backward-looking

rétrograder [ʀetʀogʀade] vi (économie) to regress; (AUTO) to change down

rétroprojecteur [ʀetʀopʀɔʒɛktœʀ] nm overhead projector

rétrospective [ʀetʀospɛktiv] nf retrospective exhibition/season; **rétrospectivement** adv in retrospect

retrousser [ʀətʀuse] vt to roll up

retrouvailles [ʀətʀuvaj] nfpl reunion sg

retrouver [ʀətʀuve] vt (fugitif, objet perdu) to find; (occasion) to find again; (calme, santé) to regain; (revoir) to see again; (rejoindre) to meet (again), join; se ~ vi to meet; (s'orienter) to find one's way; se ~ **quelque part** to find o.s. somewhere; **s'y** ~ (rentrer dans ses frais) to break even

rétroviseur [ʀetʀovizœʀ] nm (rearview) mirror

réunion [ʀeynjɔ̃] nf bringing to-

gether; joining; (séance) meeting

réunir [ʀeyniʀ] vt (convoquer) to call together; (rassembler) to gather together; (cumuler) to combine; (rapprocher) to bring together (again), reunite; (rattacher) to join (together); se ~ vi (se rencontrer) to meet

réussi, e [ʀeysi] adj successful

réussir [ʀeysiʀ] vi to succeed, be successful; (à un examen) to pass; (plante, culture) to thrive, do well ♦ vt to make a success of; ~ **à faire** to succeed in doing; ~ **à qn** to go right for sb; (aliment) to agree with sb

réussite [ʀeysit] nf success; (CARTES) patience

revaloir [ʀəvalwaʀ] vt: **je vous le vaudrai cela** I'll repay you some day; (en mal) I'll pay you back for this

revaloriser [ʀəvaloʀize] vt (monnaie) to revalue; (salaires) to raise the level of

revanche [ʀəvɑ̃ʃ] nf revenge; **en** ~ on the other hand

rêve [ʀɛv] nm dream; (activité psychique): **le** ~ dreaming

revêche [ʀəvɛʃ] adj surly, sour-tempered

réveil [ʀevɛj] nm (d'un dormeur) waking up no pl; (fig) awakening; (pendule) alarm (clock); (MIL) reveille; **au** ~ on waking (up)

réveille-matin [ʀevɛjmatɛ̃] nm inv alarm clock

réveiller [ʀeveje] vt (personne) to wake up; (fig) to awaken, revive; se ~ vi to wake up; (fig) to reawaken

réveillon [ʀevɛjɔ̃] nm Christmas Eve; (de la Saint-Sylvestre) New Year's Eve; **réveillonner** vi to celebrate Christmas Eve (ou New Year's Eve)

révélateur, trice [ʀevelatœʀ, ʀis] adj: ~ **(de qch)** revealing (sth) ♦ nm (PHOTO) developer

révéler [ʀevele] vt (gén) to reveal; (faire connaître au public) to (qn/

qch to make sb/sth widely known, bring sb/sth to the public's notice; ~ vi to be revealed, reveal itself ♦ vb +attrib to prove (to be), to be revealed, reveal itself

revenant, e [rəvnɑ̃, -ɑ̃t] nm/f ghost

revendeur, euse [rəvɑ̃dœʀ, -øz] nm/f (détaillant) retailer; (d'occasions) secondhand dealer

revendication [rəvɑ̃dikasjɔ̃] nf claim, demand; **journée de ~** day of action

revendiquer [rəvɑ̃dike] vt to claim, demand; (responsabilité) to claim

revendre [rəvɑ̃dʀ(ə)] vt (d'occasion) to resell; (détailler) to sell; **à ~** (en abondance) to spare

revenir [rəvniʀ] vi to come back; (CULIN): **faire ~** to brown; (coûter): **~ cher/à 100 F (à qn)** to cost (sb) a lot/100 F; **~ à** (études, projet) to return to, go back to; (équivaloir à) to amount to; **~ à qn** (part, honneur) to go to sb, be sb's; (souvenir, nom) to come back to sb; **~ de** (fig: maladie, étonnement) to recover from; **~ sur** (question, sujet) to go back over; (engagement) to go back on; **~ à la charge** to return to the attack; **~ à soi** to come round; **n'en pas ~:** **je n'en reviens pas** I can't get over it; **faire revenir à dire que/au même** it amounts to saying that/the same thing

revenu [rəvny] nm income; (de l'Etat) revenue; (d'un capital) yield; **~s** nmpl income sg

rêver [ʀeve] vi, vt to dream; **~ de/à** to dream of

réverbère [ʀeveʀbɛʀ] nm street lamp ou light

réverbérer [ʀeveʀbeʀe] vt to reflect

révérence [ʀeveʀɑ̃s] nf (salut) bow; (: de femme) curtsey

rêverie [ʀevʀi] nf daydreaming no pl, daydream

revers [ʀəvɛʀ] nm (de feuille, main) back; (d'étoffe) wrong side; (de

pièce, médaille) back, reverse; (TENNIS, PING-PONG) backhand; (de veston) lapel; (de pantalon) turn-up; (fig: échec) setback

revêtement [ʀəvɛtmɑ̃] nm (de paroi) facing; (des sols) flooring; (de chaussée) surface; (de tuyau etc: enduit) coating

revêtir [ʀəvetiʀ] vt (habit) to don, put on; (fig) to take on; **~ qn de** to endow ou invest sb with; **~ qch de** to cover sth with; (fig) to cloak sth in

rêveur, euse [ʀevœʀ, -øz] adj dreamy ♦ nm/f dreamer

revient [rəvjɛ̃] vb voir revenir

revigorer [ʀəvigɔʀe] vt to invigorate, brace up; to revive, buck up

revirement [ʀəviʀmɑ̃] nm change of mind; (d'une situation) reversal

réviser [ʀevize] vt (texte, SCOL: matière) to revise; (machine, installation, moteur) to overhaul, service; (JUR: procès) to review

révision [ʀevizjɔ̃] nf revision; auditing no pl; overhaul; servicing no pl; review; **la ~ des 10000 km** (AUTO) the 10,000 km service

revivre [ʀəvivʀ(ə)] vi (reprendre des forces) to come alive again; (traditions) to be revived ♦ vt (épreuve, moment) to relive

revoir [ʀəvwaʀ] vt to see again; (réviser) to revise ♦ nm: **au ~** goodbye

révoltant, e [ʀevɔltɑ̃, -ɑ̃t] adj revolting; appalling

révolte [ʀevɔlt(ə)] nf rebellion, revolt

révolter [ʀevɔlte] vt to revolt; to outrage, appal; **se ~ (contre)** to rebel (against)

révolu, e [ʀevɔly] adj past; (ADMIN: âgé de 18 ans **~s** over 18 years of age; **après 3 ans ~s** when 3 full years have passed

révolution [ʀevɔlysjɔ̃] nf revolution; **révolutionnaire** adj, nm/f revolutionary

revolver [ʀevɔlvɛʀ] nm gun; (à barillet) revolver

révoquer [ʀevɔke] vt (fonctionnaire) to dismiss; (arrêt, contrat) to revoke

revue [rəvy] nf (inventaire, examen, MIL) review; (périodique) review, magazine; (de music-hall) variety show; **passer en ~ to** review; to go through

rez-de-chaussée [redʃose] nm inv ground floor

RF sigle = République Française

Rhin [rɛ̃] nm: le ~ the Rhine

rhinocéros [rinɔsɛrɔs] nm rhinoceros

Rhône [ron] nm: le ~ the Rhone

rhubarbe [rybarb(ə)] nf rhubarb

rhum [rɔm] nm rum

rhumatisme [rymatism(ə)] nm rheumatism no pl

rhume [rym] nm cold; ~ **de cerveau** head cold; **le ~ des foins** hay fever

ri [ri] pp de rire

riant, e [rjɑ̃, -ɑ̃t] adj smiling, cheerful

ricaner [rikane] vi (avec méchanceté) to snigger; (bêtement) to giggle

riche [riʃ] adj (gén) rich; (personne, pays) rich, wealthy; ~ **en** rich in; ~ **de** full of; rich in; **richesse** nf wealth; (fig) richness; **~sses** nfpl (ressources, argent) wealth sg; (fig: trésors) treasures

ricin [risɛ̃] nm: **huile de ~** castor oil

ricocher [rikɔʃe] vi: ~ **(sur)** to rebound (off); (sur l'eau) to bounce (on ou off)

ricochet [rikɔʃɛ] nm: **faire des ~s** to skip stones; **par ~** on the rebound; (fig) as an indirect result

rictus [riktys] nm grin; (snarling) grimace

ride [rid] nf wrinkle; (fig) ripple

rideau, x [rido] nm curtain; (POL): **le ~ de fer** the Iron Curtain

rider [ride] vt to wrinkle; (eau) to ripple; **se ~** vi to become wrinkled

ridicule [ridikyl] adj ridiculous ♦ nm: **le ~** : ridicule: **se ridiculiser** vi to make a fool of o.s.

rien [rjɛ̃] pron **1: (ne) ... ~** nothing;

tournure negative + anything; **qu'est-ce que vous avez?** - ~ **what have you got?** - nothing; **il n'a ~ dit/fait** he said/didn't say nothing; he hasn't said/done anything; **il n'a ~** (n'est pas blessé) he's all right; **de ~!** not at all!

2 (quelque chose): **a-t-il jamais ~ fait pour nous?** has he ever done anything for us?

3: ~ **de** nothing interesting; ~ **d'autre** nothing else; ~ **du tout** nothing at all

4: ~ **que** just, only; nothing but; ~ **que pour lui faire plaisir** only ou just to please him; ~ **que la vérité** nothing but the truth; ~ **que cela** that alone

♦ nm: **un petit** ~ (cadeau) a little something; **des ~s** trivia pl; **un ~ de** a hint of; **en un ~ de temps** in no time at all

rieur, euse [rjœr, -øz] adj cheerful

rigide [riʒid] adj stiff; (fig) rigid; strict

rigole [rigɔl] nf (conduit) channel; (filet d'eau) rivulet

rigoler [rigɔle] vi (rire) to laugh; (s'amuser) to have (some) fun; (plaisanter) to be joking ou kidding

rigolo, ote [rigɔlo, -ɔt] (fam) adj funny ♦ nm/f comic; (péj) fraud, phoney

rigoureux, euse [riguRø, -øz] adj (morale) rigorous, strict; (personne) stern, strict; (climat, châtiment) rigorous, harsh; (interdiction, neutralité) strict

rigueur [rigœr] nf rigour; strictness; harshness; **être de ~** to be the rule; **à la ~** at a pinch; possibly; **tenir ~ à qn de qch** to hold sth against sb

rime [rim] nf rhyme

rinçage [rɛ̃saʒ] nm rinsing (out); (opération) rinse

rincer [rɛ̃se] vt to rinse; (récipient) to rinse out

ring [riŋ] nm (boxing) ring

ringard, e [rɛ̃gar, -ard(ə)] adj old-fashioned

rions vb voir **rire**

riposter [ʀipɔste] vi to retaliate ◊ vt: ~ que to retort that; ~ à to counter; to reply to

rire [ʀiʀ] vi to laugh; (se divertir) to have fun ◊ nm laugh; le ~ laughter; ~ de to laugh at; pour ~ (pas sérieusement) for a joke ou a laugh

risée [ʀize] nf: être la ~ de to be the laughing stock of

risible [ʀizibl(ə)] adj laughable

risque [ʀisk(ə)] nm risk; le ~ danger; à ses ~s et périls at his own risk

risqué, e [ʀiske] adj risky; (plaisanterie) risqué, daring

risquer [ʀiske] vt to risk; (allusion, question) to venture, hazard; ça ne risque rien it's quite safe; ~ de: il risque de se tuer he could get himself killed; ce qui risque de se produire what might ou could well happen; il ne risque pas de recommencer there's no chance of him doing that again; se ~ à faire (tenter) to venture ou dare to

rissoler [ʀisɔle] vi, vt: (faire) ~ to brown

ristourne [ʀistuʀn(ə)] nf rebate

rite [ʀit] nm rite; (fig) ritual

rivage [ʀivaʒ] nm shore

rival, e, aux [ʀival, -o] adj, nm/f rival

rivaliser [ʀivalize] vi: ~ avec to rival, vie with; (être comparable) to hold its own against, compare with

rivalité [ʀivalite] nf rivalry

rive [ʀiv] nf shore; (de fleuve) bank

river [ʀive] vt (clou, pointe) to clinch; (plaques) to rivet together

riverain, e [ʀivʀɛ̃, -ɛn] nm/f riverside (ou lakeside) resident; local resident

rivet [ʀivɛ] nm rivet

rivière [ʀivjɛʀ] nf river

rixe [ʀiks(ə)] nf brawl, scuffle

riz [ʀi] nm rice

R.N. sigle f = route nationale

robe [ʀɔb] nf dress; (de juge, d'ecclésiastique) robe; (de professeur) gown; (de professeur) gown; (pelage) coat; ~ de chambre dressing gown; ~ de grossesse maternity dress; ~ de soirée/de mariée evening/wedding dress

robinet [ʀɔbinɛ] nm tap

robot [ʀɔbo] nm robot

robuste [ʀɔbyst(ə)] adj robust, sturdy

roc [ʀɔk] nm rock

rocaille [ʀɔkaj] nf loose stones pl; rocky ou stony ground; (jardin) rockery, rock garden

roche [ʀɔʃ] nf rock

rocher [ʀɔʃe] nm rock

rocheux, euse [ʀɔʃø, -øz] adj rocky

rodage [ʀɔdaʒ] nm: en ~ running in

roder [ʀɔde] vt (AUTO) to run in

rôder [ʀode] vi to roam about; (de façon suspecte) to lurk (about ou around); **rôdeur, euse** nm/f prowler

rogne [ʀɔɲ] nf: être en ~ to be in a temper

rogner [ʀɔɲe] vt to clip; ~ sur (fig) to cut down ou back on

rognons [ʀɔɲɔ̃] nmpl kidneys

roi [ʀwa] nm king; le jour ou la fête des R~s, les R~s Twelfth Night

roitelet [ʀwatlɛ] nm wren

rôle [ʀol] nm role; (contribution) part

romain, e [ʀɔmɛ̃, -ɛn] adj, nm/f Roman

roman, e [ʀɔmɑ̃, -an] adj (ARCHIT) Romanesque ◊ nm novel; ~ d'espionnage spy novel ou story; ~ photo romantic picture story

romance [ʀɔmɑ̃s] nf ballad

romancer [ʀɔmɑ̃se] vt to make into a novel; to romanticize

romancier, ière [ʀɔmɑ̃sje, -jɛʀ] nm/f novelist

romanesque [ʀɔmanɛsk(ə)] adj (fantastique) fantastic; storybook cpd; (sentimental) romantic

roman-feuilleton [ʀɔmɑ̃fœjtɔ̃] nm serialized novel

romanichel, le [ʀɔmaniʃɛl] nm/f gipsy

romantique [ʀɔmɑ̃tik] adj romantic

romarin [ʀɔmaʀɛ̃] nm rosemary

rompre [ʀɔ̃pʀ(ə)] vt to break; (entretien, fiançailles) to break off ♦ vi (fiancés) to break it off; **se ~** vi to break; (MED) to burst, rupture

rompu, e [ʀɔ̃py] adj: **~ à** with wide experience of; inured to

ronces [ʀɔ̃s] nfpl brambles

ronchonner [ʀɔ̃ʃɔne] (fam) vi to grouse, grouch

rond, e [ʀɔ̃, ʀɔ̃d] adj round; (joues, mollets) well-rounded; (fam: ivre) tight ♦ nm (cercle) ring; (fam: sou): **je n'ai plus un ~** I haven't a penny left; **en ~** (s'asseoir, danser) in a ring; **ronde** nf (gén: de surveillance) rounds pl, patrol; (danse) round (dance); (MUS) semibreve (BRIT), whole note (US); **à la ronde** (alentour): **à la ronde à 10 km** for 10 km round; **rondelet, te** adj plump

rondelle [ʀɔ̃dɛl] nf (TECH) washer; (tranche) slice, round

rondement [ʀɔ̃dmɑ̃] adv briskly; frankly

rondin [ʀɔ̃dɛ̃] nm log

rond-point [ʀɔ̃pwɛ̃] nm roundabout

ronflant, e [ʀɔ̃flɑ̃, -ɑ̃t] (péj) adj high-flown, grand

ronfler [ʀɔ̃fle] vi to snore; (moteur, poêle) to hum; to roar

ronger [ʀɔ̃ʒe] vt to gnaw (at); (suj: vers, rouille) to eat into; **se ~ les sangs** to worry o.s. sick; **se ~ les ongles** to bite one's nails; **rongeur** nm rodent

ronronner [ʀɔ̃ʀɔne] vi to purr

roquet [ʀɔkɛ] nm nasty little lap-dog

rosace [ʀozas] nf (vitrail) rose window

rosbif [ʀɔsbif] nm: **du ~** roasting beef; (cuit) roast beef; **un ~** a joint of beef

rose [ʀoz] nf rose ♦ adj pink

rosé, e [ʀoze] adj pinkish; (vin) ~ rosé

roseau, x [ʀozo] nm reed

rosée [ʀoze] nf dew

roseraie [ʀozʀɛ] nf rose garden

rosier [ʀozje] nm rosebush, rose tree

rosse [ʀɔs] nf (péj: cheval) nag ♦ adj nasty, vicious

rossignol [ʀɔsiɲɔl] nm (ZOOL) nightingale

rot [ʀo] nm belch; (de bébé) burp

rotatif, ive [ʀɔtatif, -iv] adj rotary

rotation [ʀɔtasjɔ̃] nf rotation; (fig) rotation, swap-around; turnover

roter [ʀɔte] (fam) vi to burp, belch

rôti [ʀoti] nm: **du ~** roasting meat; (cuit) roast meat; **~ de bœuf/porc** joint of beef/pork

rotin [ʀɔtɛ̃] nm rattan (cane); **fauteuil en ~** cane (arm)chair

rôtir [ʀotiʀ] vi, vt (aussi: **faire ~**) to roast; **rôtisserie** nf steakhouse; roast meat counter (ou shop); **rôtissoire** nf (roasting) spit

rotule [ʀɔtyl] nf kneecap, patella

roturier, ière [ʀɔtyʀje, -jɛʀ] nm/f commoner

rouage [ʀwaʒ] nm cog(wheel), gearwheel; (de montre) part; (fig) cog

roucouler [ʀukule] vi to coo

roue [ʀu] nf wheel; **~ dentée** cogwheel; **~ de secours** spare wheel

roué, e [ʀwe] adj wily

rouer [ʀwe] vt: **~ qn de coups** to give sb a thrashing

rouet [ʀwɛ] nm spinning wheel

rouge [ʀuʒ] adj, nm/f red ♦ nm red; (fard) rouge; (vin) ~ red wine; **sur la liste ~** ex-directory (BRIT), unlisted (US); **passer au ~** (signal) to go red; (automobiliste) to go through a red light; **~ (à lèvres)** lipstick; **rouge-gorge** nm robin (redbreast)

rougeole [ʀuʒɔl] nf measles sg

rougeoyer [ʀuʒwaje] vi to glow red

rouget [ʀuʒɛ] nm mullet

rougeur [ʀuʒœʀ] nf redness

rougir [ʀuʒiʀ] vi (de honte, timidité) to blush, flush; (de plaisir, colère) to flush; (fraise, tomate) to go ou turn red; (ciel) to redden

rouille [ʀuj] nf rust

rouillé, e [ʀuje] adj rusty

rouiller [ʀuje] vt to rust ♦ vi to rust, go rusty; **se ~** vi to rust

roulant, e [rulɑ̃, -ɑ̃t] *adj* (*meuble*) on wheels; (*surface, trottoir*) moving

rouleau, x [rulo] *nm* (*de papier, tissu, SPORT*) roll; (*de machine à écrire*) roller, platen; (*à mise en plis, à peinture, vague*) roller; ~ **compresseur** steamroller; ~ **à pâtisserie** rolling pin

roulement [rulmɑ̃] *nm* (*bruit*) rumbling *no pl*, rumble; (*rotation*) rotation; turnover; **par** ~ on a rota (*BRIT*) *ou* rotation (*US*) basis; ~ **(à billes)** ball bearings *pl*; ~ **de tambour** drum roll

rouler [rule] *vt* to roll; (*papier, tapis*) to roll up; (*CULIN: pâte*) to roll out; (*fam*) to do, con ♦ *vi* (*bille, boule*) to roll; (*voiture, train*) to go, run; (*automobiliste*) to drive; (*cycliste*) to ride; (*bateau*) to roll; (*tonnerre*) to rumble, roll; **se** ~ **dans** (*boue*) to roll in; (*couverture*) to roll o.s. (up) in

roulette [rulɛt] *nf* (*de table, fauteuil*) castor; (*de pâtissier*) pastry wheel; (*jeu*): **la** ~ **roulette**; **à** ~**s** on castors

roulis [ruli] *nm* roll(ing)

roulotte [rulɔt] *nf* caravan

Roumanie [rumani] *nf* Rumania

rouquin, e [rukɛ̃, -in] (*péj*) *nm/f* redhead

rouspéter [ruspete] (*fam*) *vi* to moan

rousse [rus] *adj voir* **roux**

roussi [rusi] *nm*: **ça sent le** ~ there's a smell of burning; (*fig*) I can smell trouble

roussir [rusir] *vt* to scorch ♦ *vi* (*feuilles*) to go *ou* turn brown; (*CULIN*): **faire** ~ to brown

route [rut] *nf* road; (*fig: chemin*) way; (*itinéraire, parcours*) route; (*fig: voie*) road, path; **par (la)** ~ by road; **il y a 3h de** ~ it's a 3-hour ride *ou* journey; **en** ~ on the way; **mettre en** ~ to start up; **se mettre en** ~ to set off; **faire** ~ **vers** to head towards; ~ **nationale** ≈ A road (*BRIT*), ≈ state highway (*US*); **rou-**

tier, ière *adj* road *cpd* ♦ *nm* (*camionneur*) (long-distance) lorry (*BRIT*) *ou* truck (*US*) driver; (*restaurant*) ≈ transport café (*BRIT*), ≈ truck stop (*US*); **routière** *nf* (*voiture*) touring car

routine [rutin] *nf* routine; **routinier, ière** (*péj*) *adj* humdrum; addicted to routine

rouvrir [ruvrir] *vt, vi* to reopen, open again; **se** ~ *vi* to reopen, open again

roux, rousse [ru, rus] *adj* red; (*personne*) red-haired ♦ *nm/f* redhead

royal, e, aux [rwajal, -o] *adj* royal; (*fig*) princely

royaume [rwajom] *nm* kingdom; (*fig*) realm; **le R~-Uni** the United Kingdom

royauté [rwajote] *nf* (*dignité*) kingship; (*régime*) monarchy

ruban [rybɑ̃] *nm* (*gén*) ribbon; (*d'acier*) strip; ~ **adhésif** adhesive tape

rubéole [rybeɔl] *nf* German measles *sg*, rubella

rubis [rybi] *nm* ruby

rubrique [rybrik] *nf* (*titre, catégorie*) heading; (*PRESSE: article*) column

ruche [ryʃ] *nf* hive

rude [ryd] *adj* (*barbe, toile*) rough; (*métier, tâche*) hard, tough; (*climat*) severe, harsh; (*bourru*) harsh, rough; (*fruste*) rugged, tough; (*fam*) jolly good

rudement [rydmɑ̃] (*fam*) *adv* (*très*) terribly; (*beaucoup*) terribly hard

rudimentaire [rydimɑ̃tɛr] *adj* rudimentary, basic

rudoyer [rydwaje] *vt* to treat harshly

rue [ry] *nf* street

ruée [rɥe] *nf* rush

ruelle [rɥɛl] *nf* alley(-way)

ruer [rɥe] *vi* (*cheval*) to kick out; **se** ~ *vi*: **se** ~ **sur** to pounce on; **se** ~ **vers/dans/hors de** to rush *ou* dash towards/into/out of

rugby [rygbi] *nm* rugby (football)

rugir [ʀyʒiʀ] vi to roar

rugueux, euse [ʀygø, -øz] adj rough

ruine [ʀɥin] nf ruin; ~s nfpl (de château etc) ruins

ruiner [ʀɥine] vt to ruin

ruineux, euse adj ruinous

ruisseau, x [ʀɥiso] nm stream, brook

ruisseler [ʀɥisle] vi to stream

rumeur [ʀymœʀ] nf (bruit confus) rumbling; hubbub no pl; murmur(ing); (nouvelle) rumour

ruminer [ʀymine] vt (herbe) to ruminate; (fig) to ruminate on ou over, chew over

rupture [ʀyptyʀ] nf (de câble, digue) breaking; (de tendon) rupture, tearing; (de négociations etc) breakdown; (de contrat) breach; (séparation, désunion) break-up, split

rural, e, aux [ʀyʀal, -o] adj rural, country cpd

ruse [ʀyz] nf: la ~ cunning, craftiness; trickery; une ~ a trick, a ruse; **rusé, e** adj cunning, crafty

russe [ʀys] adj, nm/f Russian ♦ nm (LING) Russian

Russie [ʀysi] nf: la ~ Russia

rustique [ʀystik] adj rustic

rustre [ʀystʀ(ə)] nm boor

rutilant, e [ʀytilɑ̃, -ɑ̃t] adj gleaming

rythme [ʀitm(ə)] nm rhythm; (vitesse) rate; (: de la vie) pace, tempo

S

s' [s] pron voir se

sa [sa] dét voir son[1]

S.A. sigle (= société anonyme) ≈ Ltd (BRIT), ≈ Inc. (US)

sable [sabl(ə)] nm sand; ~s mouvants quicksand(s)

sablé [sable] nm shortbread biscuit

sabler [sable] vt to sand; (contre le verglas) to grit; ~ le champagne to drink champagne

sablier [sablije] nm hourglass; (de cuisine) egg timer

sablonneux, euse [sablɔnø, -øz] adj sandy

saborder [sabɔʀde] vt (navire) to scuttle; (fig) to wind up, shut down

sabot [sabo] nm clog; (de cheval, bœuf) hoof; ~ de frein brake shoe

saboter [sabɔte] vt to sabotage

sac [sak] nm bag; (à charbon etc) sack; mettre à ~ to sack; ~ à dos rucksack; ~ à main handbag; ~ à provisions/de voyage shopping/travelling bag; ~ de couchage sleeping bag

saccade [sakad] nf jerk

saccager [sakaʒe] vt (piller) to sack; (dévaster) to create havoc in

saccharine [sakaʀin] nf saccharin

sacerdoce [saseʀdɔs] nm priesthood; (fig) calling, vocation

sache etc vb voir savoir

sachet [saʃe] nm (small) bag; (de lavande, poudre, shampooing) sachet; ~ de thé tea bag

sacoche [sakɔʃ] nf (gén) bag; (de bicyclette) saddlebag

sacre [sakʀ(ə)] nm coronation; consecration

sacré, e [sakʀe] adj sacred; (fam: satané) blasted; (: fameux): **un ~ ... a heck of a ...**

sacrement [sakʀəmɑ̃] nm sacrament

sacrifice [sakʀifis] nm sacrifice

sacrifier [sakʀifje] vt to sacrifice; ~ à to conform to

sacristie [sakʀisti] nf sacristy; (culte protestant) vestry

sadique [sadik] adj sadistic

sage [saʒ] adj wise; (enfant) good ♦ nm wise man; sage

sage-femme [saʒfam] nf midwife

sagesse [saʒes] nf wisdom

Sagittaire [saʒitɛʀ] nm: le ~ Sagittarius

Sahara [saaʀa] nm: le ~ the Sahara (desert)

saignant, e [sɛɲɑ̃, -ɑ̃t] adj (viande) rare

saignée [seɲe] nf (fig) heavy losses pl

saigner [seɲe] vi to bleed ♦ vt

bleed; (*animal*) to kill (by bleeding); ~ **du nez** to have a nosebleed

saillie [saji] *nf* (*sur un mur etc*) projection; (*trait d'esprit*) witticism

saillir [sajiʀ] *vi* to project, stick out; (*veine, muscle*) to bulge

sain, e [sɛ̃, sɛn] *adj* healthy; (*lectures*) wholesome; ~ **d'esprit** sound in mind, sane; ~ **et sauf** safe and sound, unharmed

saindoux [sɛ̃du] *nm* lard

saint, e [sɛ̃, sɛ̃t] *adj* holy; (*fig*) saintly ♦ *nm/f* saint; **le S~ Esprit** the Holy Spirit ou Ghost; **la S~e Vierge** the Blessed Virgin; **sainteté** *nf* holiness; **la S~Sylvestre** New Year's Eve

sais *etc vb voir* **savoir**

saisie [sezi] *nf* seizure; ~ **(de données)** (data) capture

saisir [seziʀ] *vt* to take hold of, grab; (*fig: occasion*) to seize; (*comprendre*) to grasp; (*entendre*) to get, catch; (*données*) to capture; (*suj: émotions*) to take hold of, come over; (*CULIN*) to fry quickly; (*JUR: biens, publication*) to seize; ~ **un tribunal d'une affaire** to submit ou refer a case to a court; **se ~ de** *vt* to seize; **saisissant, e** *adj* startling, striking

saison [sɛzɔ̃] *nf* season; **morte ~** slack season; **saisonnier, ière** *adj* seasonal

sait *vb voir* **savoir**

salade [salad] *nf* (*BOT*) lettuce *etc*; (*CULIN*) (green) salad; (*fam*) tangle, muddle; ~ **de fruits** fruit salad; **saladier** *nm* (salad) bowl

salaire [salɛʀ] *nm* (*annuel, mensuel*) salary; (*hebdomadaire, journalier*) pay, wages *pl*; (*fig*) reward; ~ **de base** basic salary (*ou* wage); ~ **minimum interprofessionnel de croissance** *index-linked guaranteed minimum wage*

salarié, e [salaʀje] *nm/f* salaried employee; wage-earner

salaud [salo] (*fam!*) *nm* sod (!), bastard (!)

sale [sal] *adj* dirty, filthy

salé, e [sale] *adj* (*liquide, saveur*) salty; (*CULIN*) salted; (*fig*) spicy; steep

saler [sale] *vt* to salt

saleté [salte] *nf* (*état*) dirtiness; (*crasse*) dirt, filth; (*tache etc*) dirt *no pl*; (*fig*) dirty trick; rubbish *no pl*; filth *no pl*

salière [saljɛʀ] *nf* saltcellar

salin, e [salɛ̃, -in] *adj* saline; **saline** *nf* saltworks *sg*; salt marsh

salir [saliʀ] *vt* to (make) dirty; (*fig*) to soil the reputation of; **se ~** to get dirty; **salissant, e** *adj* (*tissu*) which shows the dirt; (*métier*) dirty, messy

salle [sal] *nf* room; (*d'hôpital*) ward; (*de restaurant*) dining room; (*d'un cinéma*) auditorium; (: *public*) audience; **faire ~ comble** to have a full house; ~ **à manger** dining room; ~ **commune** (*d'hôpital*) ward; ~ **d'attente** waiting room; ~ **de bain(s)** bathroom; ~ **de classe** classroom; ~ **de concert** concert hall; ~ **de consultation** consulting room; ~ **d'eau** shower-room; ~ **d'embarquement** (*à l'aéroport*) departure lounge; ~ **de jeux** games room; playroom; ~ **d'opération** (*d'hôpital*) operating theatre; ~ **de séjour** living room; ~ **de spectacle** theatre; cinema; ~ **des ventes** saleroom

salon [salɔ̃] *nm* lounge, sitting room; (*mobilier*) lounge suite; (*exposition*) exhibition, show; ~ **de thé** tearoom

salopard [salɔpaʀ] (*fam!*) *nm* bastard (!)

salope [salɔp] (*fam!*) *nf* bitch (!)

saloperie [salɔpʀi] (*fam!*) *nf* filth *no pl*; dirty trick; rubbish *no pl*

salopette [salɔpɛt] *nf* dungarees *pl*; (*d'ouvrier*) overall(s)

salsifis [salsifi] *nm* salsify

salubre [salybʀ(ə)] *adj* healthy, salubrious

saluer [salɥe] *vt* (*pour dire bonjour, fig*) to greet; (*pour dire au revoir*) to take one's leave; (*MIL*) to salute

salut [saly] nm (sauvegarde) safety; (REL) salvation; (geste) greeting; (parole) greeting; (MIL) salute ♦ excl (fam) hi (there)

salutations [salytɔsjɔ̃] nfpl greetings; recevez mes ~ distinguées ou respectueuses yours faithfully

samedi [samdi] nm Saturday

SAMU [samy] sigle m (= service d'assistance médicale d'urgence) ≈ ambulance (service) (BRIT), ≈ paramedics pl (US)

sanction [sãksjɔ̃] nf sanction; (fig) penalty; **sanctionner** vt (loi, usage) to sanction; (punir) to punish

sandale [sãdal] nf sandal

sandwich [sãdwitʃ] nm sandwich

sang [sã] nm blood; en ~ covered in blood; se faire du mauvais ~ to fret, get in a state

sang-froid [sãfrwa] nm calm, sangfroid; de ~ in cold blood

sanglant, e [sãglã, -ãt] adj bloody, covered in blood; (combat) bloody

sangle [sãgl(ə)] nf strap

sanglier [sãglije] nm (wild) boar

sanglot [sãglo] nm sob

sangsue [sãsy] nf leech

sanguin, e [sãgɛ̃, -in] adj blood cpd; (fig) fiery; **sanguinaire** [sãginɛʀ] adj bloodthirsty; thirsty

sanisette [sanizɛt] nf (automatic) public toilet

sanitaire [sanitɛʀ] adj health cpd; ~s nmpl (lieu) bathroom sg

sans [sã] prép without; ~ qu'il s'en aperçoive without him ou his noticing; ~-abri nmpl homeless; ~-emploi [sãzãplwa] n inv unemployed person; les ~-emploi the unemployed; ~-façon adj inv fuss-free; free and easy; ~-gêne adj inv inconsiderate; ~-logis nmpl homeless

santé [sãte] nf health; en bonne ~ in good health; boire à la ~ de qn to drink (to) sb's health; "à la ~ de" "here's to"; à ta/votre ~! cheers!

saoudien, ne [saudjɛ̃, -jɛn] adj Saudi Arabian ♦ nm/f: S~(ne) Saudi

Arabian

saoul, e [su, sul] adj = soûl

saper [sape] vt to undermine, sap

sapeur-pompier [sapœʀpɔ̃pje] nm fireman

saphir [safiʀ] nm sapphire

sapin [sapɛ̃] nm fir (tree); (bois) fir; ~ de Noël Christmas tree

sarcastique [saʀkastik] adj sarcastic

sarcler [saʀkle] vt to weed

Sardaigne [saʀdɛɲ] nf: la ~ Sardinia

sardine [saʀdin] nf sardine

SARL sigle (= société à responsabilité limitée) ≈ plc (BRIT), ≈ Inc. (US)

sas [sas] nm (de sous-marin, d'engin spatial) airlock; (d'écluse) lock

satané, e [satane] adj confounded

satellite [satelit] nm satellite

satin [satɛ̃] nm satin

satire [satiʀ] nf satire; **satirique** adj satirical

satisfaction [satisfaksjɔ̃] nf satisfaction

satisfaire [satisfɛʀ] vt to satisfy; ~ à (engagement) to fulfil; (revendications, conditions) to satisfy, meet; to comply with; **satisfaisant, e** adj satisfactory; (qui fait plaisir) satisfying; **satisfait, e** adj satisfied; **satisfait de** happy ou satisfied with

saturer [satyʀe] vt to saturate

sauce [sos] nf sauce; (avec un rôti) gravy; **saucière** nf sauceboat

saucisse [sosis] nf sausage

saucisson [sosisɔ̃] nm (slicing) sausage

sauf, sauve [sof, sov] adj unharmed, unhurt; (fig: honneur) intact, saved ♦ prép except; laisser la vie sauve à qn to spare sb's life; ~ si (à moins que) unless; ~ erreur if I'm not mistaken; ~ avis contraire unless you hear to the contrary

sauge [soʒ] nf sage

saugrenu, e [sogʀəny] adj preposterous

saule [sol] nm willow (tree)

saumon [somɔ̃] nm salmon inv

saumure [somyʀ] nf brine

saupoudrer [sopudʀe] vt: ~ qch de to sprinkle sth with

saur [sɔʀ] adj m: **hareng** ~ smoked ou red herring, kipper

saurai etc vb voir **savoir**

saut [so] nm jump; (discipline sportive) jumping; **faire un** ~ **chez qn** to pop over to sb's (place); **au** ~ **du lit** on getting out of bed; ~ **à la corde** skipping; ~ **à la perche** pole vaulting; ~ **en hauteur/longueur** high/long jump; ~ **périlleux** somersault

saute [sot] nf sudden change

saute-mouton [sotmutɔ̃] nm: **jouer à** ~ to play leapfrog

sauter [sote] vi to jump, leap; (exploser) to blow up, explode; (: fusibles) to blow; (se rompre) to snap, burst; (se détacher) to pop out (ou off) ♦ vt to jump (over), leap (over); (fig: omettre) to skip, miss (out); **faire** ~ to blow up; to burst open; (CULIN) to sauté; ~ **au cou de qn** to fly into sb's arms

sauterelle [sotʀɛl] nf grasshopper

sautiller [sotije] vi to hop; to skip

sautoir [sotwaʀ] nm: ~ **(de perles)** string of pearls

sauvage [sovaʒ] adj (gén) wild; (peuplade) savage; (farouche) unsociable; (barbare) wild, savage; (non officiel) unauthorized, unofficial ♦ nm/f savage; (timide) unsociable type

sauve [sov] adj f voir **sauf**

sauvegarde [sovgaʀd(ə)] nf safeguard; **sauvegarder** vt to safeguard; (INFORM: enregistrer) to save; (: copier) to back up

sauve-qui-peut [sovkipø] excl run for your life!

sauver [sove] vt to save; (porter secours à) to rescue; (récupérer) to salvage, rescue; **se** ~ vi (s'enfuir) to run away; (fam: partir) to be off; **sauvetage** nm rescue; **sauveteur** nm rescuer; **sauvette: à la sauvette** adv (vendre) without authorization; (se marier etc) hastily, hurri-

edly; **sauveur** nm saviour (BRIT), savior (US)

savais etc vb voir **savoir**

savamment [savamɑ̃] adv (avec érudition) learnedly; (habilement) skilfully, cleverly

savant, e [savɑ̃, -ɑ̃t] adj scholarly, learned; (calé) clever ♦ nm scientist

saveur [savœʀ] nf flavour; (fig) savour

savoir [savwaʀ] vt to know; (être capable de): **il sait nager** he can swim ♦ nm knowledge; **se** ~ vi (être connu) to be known; **à** ~ that is, namely; **faire** ~ **qch à qn** to let sb know sth; **pas que je sache** not as far as I know

savon [savɔ̃] nm (produit) soap; (morceau) bar of soap; (fam): **passer un** ~ **à qn** to give sb a good dressing-down; **savonnette** nf bar of soap; **savonneux, euse** adj soapy

savons vb voir **savoir**

savourer [savuʀe] vt to savour

savoureux, euse [savuʀø, -øz] adj tasty; (fig) spicy, juicy

saxo(phone) [saksɔ(fɔn)] nm saxo(phone)

scabreux, euse [skabʀø, -øz] adj risky; (indécent) improper, shocking

scandale [skɑ̃dal] nm scandal; (tapage): **faire du** ~ to make a scene, create a disturbance; **faire** ~ to scandalize people; **scandaleux, euse** adj scandalous, outrageous

scandinave [skɑ̃dinav] adj, nm/f Scandinavian

Scandinavie [skɑ̃dinavi] nf Scandinavia

scaphandre [skafɑ̃dʀ(ə)] nm (de plongeur) diving suit; (de cosmonaute) space-suit

scarabée [skaʀabe] nm beetle

sceau, x [so] nm seal; (fig) stamp, mark

scélérat, e [seleʀa, -at] nm/f villain

sceller [sele] vt to seal

scénario [senaʀjo] nm (CINÉMA) scenario; script; (fig) scenario

scène [sɛn] nf (gén) scene; (estrade,

fig: théâtre) stage; **entrer en ~** to come on stage; **mettre en ~** *(THÉÂTRE)* to stage; *(CINÉMA)* to direct; *(fig)* to present, introduce; **~ de ménage** *nf* domestic scene

sceptique [sɛptik] *adj* sceptical

schéma [ʃema] *nm* *(diagramme)* diagram, sketch; *(fig)* outline; pattern; **~tique** *adj* diagrammatic(al), schematic; *(fig)* oversimplified

sciatique [sjatik] *nf* sciatica

scie [si] *nf* saw; **~ à découper** fretsaw; **~ à métaux** hacksaw

sciemment [sjamɑ̃] *adv* knowingly

science [sjɑ̃s] *nf* science; *(savoir)* knowledge; *(savoir-faire)* art, skill; **~s naturelles** *(SCOL)* natural science *sg*, biology *sg*; **~ po** *nfpl* political science *ou* studies *pl*; **scientifique** *adj* scientific ♦ *nm/f* scientist; science student

scier [sje] *vt* to saw; *(retrancher)* to saw off; **scierie** *nf* sawmill

scinder [sɛ̃de] *vt* to split up; **se ~** *vi* to split up

scintiller [sɛ̃tije] *vi* to sparkle

scission [sisjɔ̃] *nf* split

sciure [sjyr] *nf*: **~ (de bois)** sawdust

sclérose [skleroz] *nf*: **~ en plaques** multiple sclerosis

scolaire [skolɛr] *adj* school *cpd*; *(péj)* schoolish; **scolariser** *vt* to provide with schooling *(ou* schools); **scolarité** *nf* schooling

scooter [skutœr] *nm* (motor) scooter

score [skor] *nm* score

scorpion [skorpjɔ̃] *nm* *(signe)*: **le S~** Scorpio

Scotch [skotʃ] ® *nm* adhesive tape

scout, e [skut] *adj, nm* scout

script [skript] *nm* printing; *(CINÉMA)* (shooting) script

script-girl [skriptgœrl] *nf* continuity girl

scrupule [skrypyl] *nm* scruple

scruter [skryte] *vt* to scrutinize; *(l'obscurité)* to peer into

scrutin [skrytɛ̃] *nm* *(vote)* ballot; *(ensemble des opérations)* poll

sculpter [skylte] *vt* to sculpt; *(suj: érosion)* to carve; **sculpteur** *nm* sculptor

sculpture [skyltyr] *nf* sculpture; **~ sur bois** wood carving

---

MOT-CLÉ

---

se(s') [s(ə)] *pron* **1** *(emploi réfléchi)* oneself; *(: masc)* himself; *(: fém)* herself; *(: sujet non humain)* itself; *(: pl)* themselves; **se voir comme** l'on est to see o.s. as one is

2 *(réciproque)* one another, each other; **ils s'aiment** they love one another *ou* each other

3 *(passif)*: **cela se répare facilement** it is easily repaired

4 *(possessif)*: **se casser la jambe/laver les mains** to break one's leg/wash one's hands

---

séance [seɑ̃s] *nf* *(d'assemblée, récréative)* meeting, session; *(de tribunal)* sitting, session; *(musicale, CINÉMA, THÉÂTRE)* performance; **~ tenante** forthwith

seau, x [so] *nm* bucket, pail

sec, sèche [sɛk, sɛʃ] *adj* dry; *(raisins, figues)* dried; *(cœur, personne)* insensible) hard, cold ♦ *nm*: **tenir au ~** to keep in a dry place ♦ *adv* hard; **je le bois ~** I drink it straight *ou* neat; **à ~** *adj* dried up

sécateur [sekatœr] *nm* secateurs *pl* *(BRIT)*, shears *pl*

sèche [sɛʃ] *adj f voir* **sec**

sèche-cheveux [sɛʃʃəvø] *nm inv* hair-drier

sèche-linge [sɛʃlɛ̃ʒ] *nm inv* tumble dryer

sécher [seʃe] *vt* to dry; *(dessécher: peau, blé)* to dry (out); *(: étang)* to dry up ♦ *vi* to dry; to dry out; to dry up; *(fam: candidat)* to be stumped; **se ~** *(après le bain)* to dry o.s.

sécheresse [sɛʃrɛs] *nf* dryness; *(absence de pluie)* drought

séchoir [seʃwar] *nm* drier

second, e [səgɔ̃, -ɔ̃d] *adj* second ♦ *nm* *(assistant)* second in command;

(_NAVIG_) first mate; voyager en ~e to travel second-class; de ~e main second-hand; **secondaire** _adj_ secondary; **seconde** _nf_ second; **seconder** _vt_ to assist

secouer [səkwe] _vt_ to shake; (_passagers_) to rock; (_traumatiser_) to shake (up)

secourir [səkurir] _vt_ (_aller sauver_) to (go and) rescue; (_prodiguer des soins à_) to help, assist; (_venir en aide à_) to assist, aid; **secourisme** _nm_ first aid; life saving

secours [səkur] _nm_ help, aid, assistance ♦ _nmpl_ aid _sg_; au ~! help!; appeler au ~ to shout or call for help; **porter** ~ à qn to give sb assistance, help sb; les premiers ~ first aid _sg_

secousse [səkus] _nf_ jolt, bump; (_électrique_) shock; (_fig: psychologique_) jolt, shock; ~ **sismique** ou **tellurique** earth tremor

secret, ète [səkrɛ, -ɛt] _adj_ secret; (_fig: renfermé_) reticent, reserved ♦ _nm_ secret; (_discrétion absolue_): le ~ secrecy; au ~ in solitary confinement

secrétaire [səkretɛr] _nm/f_ secretary ♦ _nm_ (_meuble_) writing desk; ~ **de direction** private ou personal secretary; ~ **d'État** junior minister; ~ **général** _nm_ (_COMM_) company secretary; **secrétariat** _nm_ (_profession_) secretarial work; (_bureau_) office; (: _d'organisation internationale_) secretariat

secteur [sɛktœr] _nm_ sector; (_ADMIN_) district; (_ELEC_): **branché sur le** ~ plugged into the mains (supply)

section [sɛksjɔ̃] _nf_ section; (_de parcours d'autobus_) fare stage; (_MIL: unité_) platoon; **sectionner** _vt_ to sever

Sécu [seky] _abr f_ = **sécurité sociale**

séculaire [sekylɛr] _adj_ secular; (_très vieux_) age-old

sécuriser [sekyrize] _vt_ to give (a feeling of) security to

sécurité [sekyrite] _nf_ safety; security; **système de** ~ safety system; **être en** ~ to be safe; la ~ **routière** road safety; la ~ **sociale** ≈ (the) Social Security (_BRIT_), ≈ Welfare (_US_)

sédition [sedisjɔ̃] _nf_ insurrection; sedition

séduction [sedyksjɔ̃] _nf_ seduction; (_charme, attrait_) appeal, charm

séduire [seduir] _vt_ to charm; (_femme: abuser de_) to seduce; **séduisant, e** _adj_ (_femme_) seductive; (_homme, offre_) very attractive

ségrégation [segregasjɔ̃] _nf_ segregation

seigle [sɛgl(ə)] _nm_ rye

seigneur [sɛɲœr] _nm_ lord

sein [sɛ̃] _nm_ breast; (_entrailles_) womb; au ~ **de** (_équipe, institution_) within; (_flots, bonheur_) in the midst of

séisme [seism(ə)] _nm_ earthquake

seize [sɛz] _num_ sixteen; **seizième** _num_ sixteenth

séjour [seʒur] _nm_ stay; (_pièce_) living room; **séjourner** _vi_ to stay

sel [sɛl] _nm_ salt; (_fig_) wit; spice; ~ **de cuisine/de table** cooking/table salt

sélection [selɛksjɔ̃] _nf_ selection; **sélectionner** _vt_ to select

self-service [sɛlfsɛrvis] _adj, nm_ self-service

selle [sɛl] _nf_ saddle; ~s _nfpl_ (_MÉD_) stools; **seller** _vt_ to saddle

sellette [sɛlɛt] _nf_: **être sur la** ~ to be on the carpet

selon [səlɔ̃] _prép_ according to; (_en se conformant à_) in accordance with; ~ **que** according to whether; ~ **moi** as I see it

semaine [səmɛn] _nf_ week; en ~ during the week, on weekdays

semblable [sɑ̃blabl(ə)] _adj_ similar; (_de ce genre_): de ~s **mésaventures** such mishaps ♦ _nm_ fellow creature ou man; ~ **à** similar to, like

semblant [sɑ̃blɑ̃] _nm_: un ~ de vérité a semblance of truth; **faire** ~

(de faire), to pretend (to do)

sembler [sɑ̃ble] *vb* +*attrib* to seem
♦ *vb impers*: **il semble (bien) que/
inutile de** it (really) seems that/as appears that/useless to; **il me semble
que** it seems to me that; I think
(that); **comme bon lui semble** as
he sees fit

semelle [səmɛl] *nf* sole; (*intérieure*)
insole, inner sole

semence [səmɑ̃s] *nf* (*graine*) seed

semer [səme] *vt* to sow; (*fig: éparpiller*) to scatter; (: *confusion*) to
spread; (: *poursuivants*) to lose,
shake off; **semé de** (*difficultés*)
riddled with

semestre [səmɛstr(ə)] *nm* half-year;
(SCOL) semester

séminaire [semineʀ] *nm* seminar

semi-remorque [səmiʀəmɔʀk(ə)]
nm articulated lorry (BRIT),
semi(trailer) (US)

semonce [səmɔ̃s] *nf*: **un coup de ~**
a shot across the bows

semoule [səmul] *nf* semolina

sempiternel, le [sɛpitɛʀnɛl] *adj*
eternal, never-ending

sénat [sena] *nm* Senate; **sénateur**
nm Senator

sens [sɑ̃s] *nm* (PHYSIOL, *instinct*)
sense; (*signification*) meaning, sense;
(*direction*) direction; **à mon ~** to
my mind; **reprendre ses ~** to regain consciousness; **dans le ~ des
aiguilles d'une montre** clockwise;
~ commun common sense; **~ dessus dessous** upside down; **~ interdit** one-way street; **~ unique** one-
way street

sensass [sɑ̃sas] (*fam*) *adj* fantastic

sensation [sɑ̃sasjɔ̃] *nf* sensation sensation; **à ~** (*péj*) sensational

sensé, e [sɑ̃se] *adj* sensible

sensibiliser [sɑ̃sibilize] *vt*: **~ qn à**
to make sb sensitive to

sensibilité [sɑ̃sibilite] *nf* sensitivity

sensible [sɑ̃sibl(ə)] *adj* sensitive;
(*aux sens*) perceptible; (*appréciable:
différence, progrès*) appreciable, noticeable; **sensiblement** *adv* (*notable-*

ment) appreciably, noticeably; (*à
peu près*): **ils ont sensiblement le
même poids** they weigh approximately the same; **sensiblerie** *nf* sen-
timentality; squeamishness

sensuel, le [sɑ̃sɥɛl] *adj* sensual;
sensuous

sentence [sɑ̃tɑ̃s] *nf* (*jugement*) sentence; (*adage*) maxim

sentier [sɑ̃tje] *nm* path

sentiment [sɑ̃timɑ̃] *nm* feeling; re-
cevez mes ~s respectueux yours
faithfully; **sentimental, e, aux** *adj*
sentimental; (*vie, aventure*) love *cpd*

sentinelle [sɑ̃tinɛl] *nf* sentry

sentir [sɑ̃tiʀ] *vt* (*par l'odorat*) to
smell; (*par le goût*) to taste; (*par le
toucher, fig*) to feel; (*répandre une
odeur de*) to smell of; (: *ressemblance*) to smell like; (*avoir la saveur de*) to taste of; to taste like ♦ *vi*
to smell; **~ mauvais** to smell bad;
se ~ bien to feel good; **se ~ mal**
(*être indisposé*) to feel unwell *ou* ill;
se ~ le courage/la force de faire
to feel brave/strong enough to do; **il
ne peut pas le ~** (*fam*) he can't
stand him

séparation [separasjɔ̃] *nf* separation; (*cloison*) division, partition; **~
de corps** legal separation

séparé, e [separe] *adj* (*appartements, pouvoirs*) separate; (*époux*)
separated; **~ment** *adv* separately

séparer [separe] *vt* (*gén*) to separate; (*suj: divergences etc*) to divide;
(*suj*) to di-
vide; to drive apart; (*suj: diffé-
rences, obstacles*) to stand between;
(*détacher*): **~ qch de** to split sth
(off) from; (*diviser*): **~ qch par** to
divide sth (up) with; **se ~ vi** (*époux,
amis, adversaires*) to separate, part;
(*se diviser: route, tige etc*) to divide;
(*se détacher*): **se ~ (de)** to split off
(from); to come off; **se ~ de**
(*époux*) to separate *ou* part from;
(*employé, objet personnel*) to part
with; **~ une pièce en deux** to divide a room into two

sept [sɛt] *num* seven

septembre [sɛptɑ̃br(ə)] nm September

septennat [sɛptena] nm seven year term of office (of French President)

septentrional, e, aux [sɛptɑ̃trijɔnal, -o] adj northern

septicémie [sɛptisemi] nf blood poisoning, septicaemia

septième [sɛtjɛm] num seventh

septique [sɛptik] adj: fosse ~ septic tank

sépulture [sepyltyr] nf burial; burial place, grave

séquelles [sekɛl] nfpl after-effects; (fig) aftermath sg; consequences

séquestrer [sekɛstre] vt (personne) to confine illegally; (biens) to impound

serai etc vb voir être

serein, e [sarɛ̃, -ɛn] adj serene; (jugement) dispassionate

serez vb voir être

sergent [sɛrʒɑ̃] nm sergeant

série [seri] nf (de questions, d'accidents) series nv; (de clés, casseroles, outils) set; (catégorie: SPORT) rank; class; en ~ in quick succession; (COMM) mass cpd; de ~ standard; hors ~ (COMM) custom-built; (fig) outstanding

sérieusement [serjøzmɑ̃] adv seriously; reliably; responsibly

sérieux, euse [serjø, -øz] adj serious; (élève, employé) reliable, responsible; (client, maison) reliable, dependable ♦ nm seriousness; reliability; garder son ~ to keep a straight face; prendre qch/qn au ~ to take sth/sb seriously

serin [sarɛ̃] nm canary

seringue [sarɛ̃g] nf syringe

serions vb voir être

serment [sɛrmɑ̃] nm (juré) oath; (promesse) pledge, vow

sermon [sɛrmɔ̃] nm sermon

séro-positif, ive [sero-] adj (MED) HIV-positive

serpent [sɛrpɑ̃] nm snake

serpenter [sɛrpɑ̃te] vi to wind

serpentin [sɛrpɑ̃tɛ̃] nm (tube) coil;

(ruban) streamer

serpillière [sɛrpijɛr] nf floorcloth

serre [sɛr] nf (AGR) greenhouse; ~s nfpl (griffes) claws, talons

serré, e [sɛre] adj (réseau) dense; (écriture) close; (habits) tight; (fig: lutte, match) close, close-fought; (passagers etc) (tightly) packed

serrer [sɛre] vt (tenir) to grip ou hold tight; (comprimer, coincer) to squeeze; (poings, mâchoires) to clench; (suj: vêtement) to be too tight for; to fit tightly; (rapprocher) to close up, move closer together; (ceinture, nœud, frein, vis) to tighten ♦ vi: ~ à droite to keep ou get over to the right; se ~ vi (se rapprocher) to squeeze up; se ~ contre qn to huddle up to sb; ~ la main à qn to shake sb's hand; ~ qn dans ses bras to hug sb, clasp sb in one's arms

serrure [sɛryr] nf lock

serrurier [sɛryrje] nm locksmith

sert etc vb voir servir

sertir [sɛrtir] vt (pierre) to set

servante [sɛrvɑ̃t] nf (maid)servant

serveur, euse [sɛrvœr, -øz] nm/f waiter(waitress)

serviable [sɛrvjabl(ə)] adj obliging, willing to help

service [sɛrvis] nm (gén) service; (série de repas): premier ~ first sitting; (assortiment de vaisselle) set, service; (bureau: de la vente etc) department, section; (travail): pendant le ~ on duty; ~s nmpl (travail, ECON) services; faire le ~ to serve; rendre ~ à to help; rendre un ~ à qn to do sb a favour; mettre en ~ to put into service ou operation; hors ~ out of order; ~ après vente after-sales service; ~ d'ordre police (ou stewards) in charge of maintaining order; ~ militaire military service; ~s secrets secret service sg

serviette [sɛrvjɛt] nf (de table) napkin, serviette; (de toilette) towel; (porte-documents) briefcase;

~ **hygiénique** sanitary towel

servir [sɛʀviʀ] *vt* (*gén*) to serve; (*au restaurant*) to wait on; (*au magasin*) to serve, attend to; (*fig: aider*): ~ **qn** to aid sb; to serve sb's interests; (*COMM: rente*) to pay (*TENNIS*) to serve; (*CARTES*) to deal; **se** ~ *vi* (*prendre d'un plat*) to help o.s.; **se** ~ **de** (*plat*) to help o.s. to; (*voiture, outil, relations*) to use; **vous êtes servi?** are you being served?; **se** ~ **qn** (*diplôme, livre*) to make use of to sb; ~ **à qch/faire** (*outil etc*) to be used for sth/doing; **à quoi cela sert-il (de faire)?** what's the use (of doing)?; **cela ne sert à rien** it's no use; ~ (**à qn**) **de** to serve as (for sb); ~ **à dîner** (**à qn**) to serve dinner (to sb)

serviteur [sɛʀvitœʀ] *nm* servant

servitude [sɛʀvityd] *nf* servitude; (*fig*) constraint

ses [se] *dét voir* son[1]

seuil [sœj] *nm* doorstep; (*fig*) threshold

seul, e [sœl] *adj* (*sans compagnie*) alone; (*avec nuance affective: isolé*) lonely; (*unique*): **un** ~ **livre** only one book, a single book (*vivre*) alone, on one's own ♦ *nm, nf*: **il en reste un(e)** ~(**e**) there's only one left; **le** ~ **livre** the only book; ~ **ce livre, ce livre** ~ this book alone, only this book; **parler tout** ~ to talk to oneself; **faire qch (tout)** ~ to do sth (all) on one's own *ou* (all) by oneself; **à lui (tout)** ~ single-handed, on his own

seulement [sœlmɑ̃] *adv* only; **non** ~ ... **mais aussi** *ou* **encore** not only ... but also

sève [sɛv] *nf* sap

sévère [sevɛʀ] *adj* severe

sévices [sevis] *nmpl* (physical) cruelty *sg*, ill treatment *sg*

sévir [seviʀ] *vi* (*punir*) to use harsh measures, crack down; (*suj: fléau*) to rage, be rampant

sevrer [sɔvʀe] *vt* (*enfant etc*) to wean

sexe [sɛks(ə)] *nm* sex; (*organe mâle*) member

sexuel, le [sɛksɥɛl] *adj* sexual

seyant, e [sejɑ̃, ɑ̃t] *adj* becoming

shampooing [ʃɑ̃pwɛ̃] *nm* shampoo; **se faire un** ~ to shampoo one's hair

short [ʃɔʀt] *nm* (pair of) shorts *pl*

MOT-CLÉ

si [si] *nm* (*MUS*) B; (*en chantant la gamme*) ti

♦ *adv* **1** (*oui*) yes

2 (*tellement*) so; ~ **gentil/rapide** so kind/fast; (*tant et*) ~ **bien que** so much so that; ~ **rapide qu'il** soit however fast he may be

♦ *conj* if; ~ **tu veux** if you want; **je me demande** ~ I wonder if *ou* whether; ~ **seulement** if only

---

Sicile [sisil] *nf*: **la** ~ Sicily

SIDA [sida] *sigle m* (= *syndrome immuno-déficitaire acquis*) AIDS *sg*

sidéré, e [sideʀe] *adj* staggered

sidérurgie [sideʀyʀʒi] *nf* steel industry

siècle [sjɛkl(ə)] *nm* century; (*époque*) age

siège [sjɛʒ] *nm* seat; (*d'entreprise*) head office; (*d'organisation*) headquarters *pl*; (*MIL*) siege; ~ **social** registered office

siéger [sjeʒe] *vi* to sit

sien, ne [sjɛ̃, sjɛn] *pron*: **le(la)** ~(**ne**), **les** ~(**ne**)**s** his; hers; its; **les** ~**s** (*sa famille*) one's family; **faire des** ~**nes** (*fam*) to be up to one's (*usual*) tricks

sieste [sjɛst(ə)] *nf* (afternoon) snooze *ou* nap, siesta; **faire la** ~ to have a snooze *ou* nap

sifflement [sifləmɑ̃] *nm* whistle, whistling *no pl*; wheezing *no pl*; hissing *no pl*

siffler [sifle] *vi* (*gén*) to whistle; (*en respirant*) to wheeze; (*serpent, vapeur*) to hiss ♦ *vt* (*chanson*) to whistle; (*chien etc*) to whistle for; (*fille*) to whistle at; (*pièce, orateur*) to hiss, boo; (*faute*) to blow one's whistle at;

(fin du match, départ) to blow one's whistle for; *(fam: verre)* to guzzle

sifflet [siflɛ] nm whistle; **coup de ~** whistle

siffloter [siflɔte] vi, vt to whistle

sigle [sigl(ə)] nm acronym

signal, aux [siɲal, -o] nm *(signe convenu, appareil)* signal; *(indice, écriteau)* sign; **donner le ~ de** to give the signal for; **~ d'alarme** alarm signal; **signaux (lumineux)** *(AUTO)* traffic signals

signalement [siɲalmã] nm description, particulars pl

signaler [siɲale] vt to indicate; to announce; to report; *(faire remarquer)*: **~ qch à qn/(à qn) que** to point out sth to sb/(to sb) that; **se ~ (par)** to distinguish o.s. (by)

signature [siɲatyʀ] nf signature *(action)*, signing

signe [siɲ] nm sign; *(TYPO)* mark; **faire un ~ de la main** to give a sign with one's hand; **faire ~ à qn** *(fig)* to get in touch with sb; **faire ~ à qn d'entrer** to motion (to) sb to come in; **~s particuliers** nmpl distinguishing marks

signer [siɲe] vt to sign; **se ~** vi to cross o.s.

signet [siɲɛ] nm bookmark

significatif, ive [siɲifikatif, -iv] adj significant

signification [siɲifikasjɔ̃] nf meaning

signifier [siɲifje] vt *(vouloir dire)* to mean; *(faire connaître)*: **~ qch (à qn)** to make sth known to (sb); *(JUR)*: **~ qch à qn** to serve notice of sth on sb

silence [silɑ̃s] nm silence; *(MUS)* rest; **garder le ~** to keep silent, say nothing; **passer sous ~** to pass over (in silence); **silencieux, euse** adj quiet, silent ♦ nm silencer

silex [silɛks] nm flint

silhouette [silwɛt] nf outline, silhouette; *(lignes, contour)* outline; *(figure)* figure

silicium [silisjɔm] nm silicon; pla-

quette de ~ silicon chip

sillage [sijaʒ] nm wake; *(fig)* trail

sillon [sijɔ̃] nm furrow; *(de disque)* groove; **sillonner** vt to criss-cross

simagrées [simagʀe] nfpl fuss sg; airs and graces

similaire [similɛʀ] adj similar; **similicuir** nm imitation leather; **similitude** nf similarity

simple [sɛ̃pl(ə)] adj *(gén)* simple; *(non multiple)* single; **~s** nmpl *(MED)* medicinal plants; **~ d'esprit** nm/f simpleton; **~ messieurs** nm *(TENNIS)* men's singles sg; **un ~ particulier** an ordinary citizen; **~ soldat** private

simulacre [simylakʀ(ə)] nm *(péj)*: **~ de** a pretence of

simuler [simyle] vt to sham, simulate

simultané, e [simyltane] adj simultaneous

sincère [sɛ̃sɛʀ] adj sincere; genuine; **sincérité** nf sincerity

sine qua non [sinekwanɔn] adj: **condition ~** indispensable condition

singe [sɛ̃ʒ] nm monkey; *(de grande taille)* ape; **~r** [sɛ̃ʒe] vt to ape, mimic

singeries [sɛ̃ʒʀi] nfpl antics; *(simagrées)* airs and graces

singulariser [sɛ̃gylaʀize] vt to mark out; **se ~** vi to call attention to o.s.

singularité [sɛ̃gylaʀite] nf peculiarity

singulier, ière [sɛ̃gylje, -jɛʀ] adj remarkable, singular ♦ nm singular

sinistre [sinistʀ(ə)] adj sinister ♦ nm *(incendie)* blaze; *(catastrophe)* disaster; *(ASSURANCES)* damage *(giving rise to a claim)*; **sinistré, e** adj disaster-stricken ♦ nm/f disaster victim

sinon [sinɔ̃] conj *(autrement, sans quoi)* otherwise, or else; *(sauf)* except, other than; *(si ce n'est)* if not

sinueux, euse [sinɥø, -øz] adj winding; *(fig)* tortuous

sinus [sinys] nm *(ANAT)* sinus; *(GEOM)* sine; **sinusite** nf sinusitis

siphon [sifɔ̃] nm *(tube, d'eau ga-*

zeuse) siphon; (*d'évier etc*) U-bend

sirène [siʀɛn] *nf* siren; ~ **d'alarme** air-raid siren; fire alarm

sirop [siʀo] *nm* (*à diluer: de fruit etc*) syrup; (*boisson*) fruit drink; (*pharmaceutique*) syrup, mixture

siroter [siʀɔte] *vt* to sip

sismique [sismik] *adj* seismic

site [sit] *nm* (*paysage, environnement*) setting; (*d'une ville etc: emplacement*) site; ~ (*pittoresque*) beauty spot; ~s **touristiques** places of interest

sitôt [sito] *adv*: ~ **parti** as soon as he *etc* had left; ~ **après** straight after; **pas de** ~ not for a long time

situation [situɑsjɔ̃] *nf* (*gén*) situation; (*d'un édifice, d'une ville*) situation, position; location; ~ **de famille** *nf* marital status

situé, e [situe] *adj*: **bien** ~ well situated; ~ **à** situated at

situer [situe] *vt* to site, situate; (*en pensée*) to set, place; **se** ~ *vi*: (*en pensée*) to set, place; **se** ~ *vi*: **à/près de** to be situated at/near

six [sis] *num* six; **sixième** *num* sixth

ski [ski] *nm* (*objet*) ski; (*sport*) skiing; **faire du** ~ to ski; ~ **de fond** cross-country skiing; ~ **nautique** water-skiing; ~ **de piste** downhill skiing; ~ **de randonnée** crosscountry skiing; **skier** *vi* to ski; **skieur, euse** *nm/f* skier

slip [slip] *nm* (*sous-vêtement*) pants *pl*, briefs *pl*; (*de bain: d'homme*) trunks *pl*; (: *du bikini*) (bikini) briefs *pl*

slogan [slɔgã] *nm* slogan

S.M.I.C. [smik] *sigle m* = **salaire minimum interprofessionnel de croissance**

smicard, e [smikaʀ, -aʀd(ə)] (*fam*) *nm/f* minimum wage earner

smoking [smɔkiŋ] *nm* dinner ou evening suit

S.N.C.F. *sigle f* (= **société nationale des chemins de fer français**) French railways

snob [snɔb] *adj* snobbish ♦ *nm/f* snob

sobre [sɔbʀ(ə)] *adj* temperate, abste-

mious; (*élégance, style*) sober; ~ **de** (*gestes, compliments*) sparing of

sobriquet [sɔbʀikɛ] *nm* nickname

social, e, aux [sɔsjal, -o] *adj* social

socialisme [sɔsjalism(ə)] *nm* socialism; **socialiste** *nm/f* socialist

société [sɔsjete] *nf* society; (*sportive*) club; (*COMM*) company; **la** ~ **d'abondance/de consommation** the affluent/consumer society; ~ à **responsabilité limitée** *type of limited liability company*; ~ **anonyme** = limited (*BRIT*) ou incorporated (*US*) company

sociologie [sɔsjɔlɔʒi] *nf* sociology

socle [sɔkl(ə)] *nm* (*de colonne, statue*) plinth, pedestal; (*de lampe*) base

socquette [sɔkɛt] *nf* ankle sock

sœur [sœʀ] *nf* sister; (*religieuse*) nun, sister

soi [swa] *pron* oneself; **cela va de** ~ that *ou* it goes without saying; **soi-disant** *adj inv* so-called ♦ *adv* supposedly

soie [swa] *nf* silk; (*de porc, sanglier: poil*) bristle; **soierie** *nf* (*tissu*) silk

soif [swaf] *nf* thirst; **avoir** ~ to be thirsty; **donner** ~ **à qn** to make sb thirsty

soigné, e [swaɲe] *adj* (*tenue*) wellgroomed, neat; (*travail*) careful, meticulous; (*fam*) whopping; stiff

soigner [swaɲe] *vt* (*malade, maladie: suj: docteur*) to treat; (*suj: infirmière, mère*) to nurse, look after; (*blessé*) to tend; (*travail, détails*) to take care over; (*jardin, chevelure, invités*) to look after

soigneux, euse [swaɲø, -øz] *adj* (*propre*) tidy, neat; (*méticuleux*) painstaking, careful; ~ **de** careful with

soi-même [swamɛm] *pron* oneself

soin [swɛ̃] *nm* (*application*) care; (*propreté, ordre*) tidiness, neatness; ~**s** *nmpl* (*à un malade, blessé*) treatment *sg*, medical attention *sg*; (*attentions, prévenance*) care and attention *sg*; (*hygiène*) care *sg*; **prendre**

~ de to take care of, look after; **prendre** ~ **de faire** to take care to do; **les premiers** ~s first aid *sg*; **aux bons** ~s **de** c/o, care of

soir [swar] *nm* evening; **ce** ~ this evening, tonight; **demain** ~ tomorrow evening, tomorrow night

soirée [sware] *nf* evening; (*réception*) party

soit [swa] *vb voir* **être** ♦ *conj* (*a savoir*) namely; (*ou*): ~ ... ~ ... either ... or ♦ *adv* so be it, very well; ~ **que** ... ~ **que** *ou* **ou que** whether ... or whether

soixantaine [swasɑ̃tɛn] *nf*: **une** ~ (**de**) sixty or so, about sixty; **avoir la** ~ (*âge*) to be around sixty

soixante [swasɑ̃t] *num* sixty; **soixante-dix** *num* seventy

soja [sɔʒa] *nm* soya; (*graines*) soya beans *pl*

sol [sɔl] *nm* ground; (*de logement*) floor; (*revêtement*) flooring *no pl*; (*territoire, AGR, GÉO*) soil; (*MUS*) G; (: *en chantant la gamme*) so(h)

solaire [sɔlɛr] *adj* solar, sun *cpd*

soldat [sɔlda] *nm* soldier

solde [sɔld(ə)] *nf* pay ♦ *nm* (*COMM*) balance; ~s *nm ou f pl* sale goods; sales; **en** ~ at sale price

solder [sɔlde] *vt* (*compte*) to settle; (*marchandise*) to sell at sale price, sell off; **se** ~ **par** (*fig*) to end in; **article soldé (à)** 10 F item reduced to 10 F

sole [sɔl] *nf* sole *inv* (*fish*)

soleil [sɔlej] *nm* sun; (*lumière*) sun(light); (*temps ensoleillé*) sun(shine); (*BOT*) sunflower; **il fait du** ~ it's sunny, the sun's shining

solennel, le [sɔlanɛl] *adj* solemn; ceremonial; **solennité** *nf* (*d'une fête*) solemnity

solfège [sɔlfɛʒ] *nm* rudiments *pl* of music; (*exercices*) ear training *no pl*

solidaire [sɔlidɛr] *adj* (*personnes*) who stand together, who show solidarity; (*pièces mécaniques*) interdependent; **être** ~ **de** (*collègues*) to stand by; **solidarité** *nf* solidarity; in-

terdependence; **par solidarité (avec)** in sympathy (with)

solide [sɔlid] *adj* solid; (*mur, maison, meuble*) solid, sturdy; (*connaissances, argument*) sound; (*personne, estomac*) robust, sturdy ♦ *nm* solid

soliste [sɔlist(ə)] *nm/f* soloist

solitaire [sɔlitɛr] *adj* (*sans compagnie*) solitary, lonely; (*lieu*) lonely ♦ *nm/f* recluse; loner

solitude [sɔlityd] *nf* loneliness; (*paix*) solitude

solive [sɔliv] *nf* joist

sollicitations [sɔlisitɑsjɔ̃] *nfpl* entreaties, appeals; enticements; (*TECH*) stress *sg*

solliciter [sɔlisite] *vt* (*personne*) to appeal to; (*emploi, faveur*) to seek; (*suj: occupations, attractions etc*); ~ **qn** to appeal to sb's curiosity *etc*; to entice sb; to make demands on sb's time

sollicitude [sɔlisityd] *nf* concern

soluble [sɔlybl(ə)] *adj* soluble

solution [sɔlysjɔ̃] *nf* solution; ~ **de facilité** easy way out

solvable [sɔlvabl(ə)] *adj* solvent

sombre [sɔ̃br(ə)] *adj* dark; (*fig*) gloomy

sombrer [sɔ̃bre] *vi* (*bateau*) to sink; ~ **dans** (*misère, désespoir*) to sink into

sommaire [sɔmɛr] *adj* (*simple*) basic; (*expéditif*) summary ♦ *nm* summary

sommation [sɔmasjɔ̃] *nf* (*JUR*) summons *sg*; (*avant de faire feu*) warning

somme [sɔm] *nf* (*MATH*) sum; (*fig*) amount; (*argent*) sum, amount ♦ *nm*: **faire un** ~ to have a (short) nap; **en** ~ all in all; ~ **toute** all in all

sommeil [sɔmej] *nm* sleep; **avoir** ~ to be sleepy; **sommeiller** *vi* to doze; (*fig*) to lie dormant

sommelier [sɔməlje] *nm* wine waiter

sommer [sɔme] *vt*: ~ **qn de faire** to command *ou* order sb to do; (*JUR*) to summon sb to do

sommes vb voir **être**

sommet [sɔmɛ] nm top; (d'une montagne) summit, top; (fig: de la perfection, gloire) height

sommier [sɔmje] nm (bed) base

sommité [sɔmite] nf prominent person, leading light

somnambule [sɔmnɑ̃byl] nm/f sleepwalker

somnifère [sɔmnifɛr] nm sleeping drug no pl (ou pill)

somnoler [sɔmnɔle] vi to doze

somptueux, euse [sɔ̃ptɥø, -øz] adj sumptuous; lavish

son¹, sa [sɔ̃, sa] (pl **ses**) dét (antécédent humain: mâle) his; (: femelle) her; (: valeur indéfinie) one's, his/her; (antécédent non humain) its

son² [sɔ̃] nm sound; (de blé) bran

sondage [sɔ̃daʒ] nm: ~ **(d'opinion)** (opinion) poll

sonde [sɔ̃d] nf (NAVIG) lead ou sounding line; (MÉD) probe; catheter; feeding tube; (TECH) borer, driller; (pour fouiller etc) probe

sonder [sɔ̃de] vt (NAVIG) to sound; (atmosphère, plaie, bagages etc) to probe; (TECH) to bore, drill; (fig) to sound out; to probe

songe [sɔ̃ʒ] nm dream

songer [sɔ̃ʒe] vi: ~ à (penser à) to think of; ~ **que** to consider that; to think that; **songeur, euse** adj pensive

sonnant, e [sɔnɑ̃, -ɑ̃t] adj: à 8 heures ~es on the stroke of 8

sonné, e [sɔne] adj (fam) cracked; il est midi ~ it's gone twelve

sonner [sɔne] vi to ring ♦ vt (cloche) to ring; (glas, tocsin) to sound; (portier, infirmière) to ring for; (messe) to ring the bell for; **faux** (instrument) to sound out of tune; (rire) to ring false; ~ **les heures** to strike the hours

sonnerie [sɔnri] nf (son) ringing; (sonnette) bell; (mécanisme d'horloge) striking mechanism; ~ **d'alarme** alarm bell

sonnette [sɔnɛt] nf bell; ~ **d'alar-**

me alarm bell

sono [sɔno] abr f = **sonorisation**

sonore [sɔnɔr] adj (voix) sonorous, ringing; (salle, métal) resonant; (ondes, film, signal) sound cpd

sonorisation [sɔnɔrizasjɔ̃] nf (installations) public address system, P.A. system

sonorité [sɔnɔrite] nf (de piano, violon) tone; (de voix, mot) sonority; (d'une salle) resonance; acoustics pl

sont vb voir **être**

sophistiqué, e [sɔfistike] adj sophisticated

sorbet [sɔrbɛ] nm water ice, sorbet

sorcellerie [sɔrsɛlri] nf witchcraft no pl

sorcier [sɔrsje] nm sorcerer; **sorcière** nf witch ou sorceress

sordide [sɔrdid] adj sordid; squalid

sornettes [sɔrnɛt] nfpl twaddle sg

sort [sɔr] nm (fortune, destinée) fate; (condition, situation) lot; (magique) curse, spell; **tirer au** ~ to draw lots

sorte [sɔrt(ə)] nf sort, kind; **de la** ~ in that way; **de (telle)** ~ **que**, **en** ~ **que** so that; so much so that; **faire en** ~ **que** to see to it that

sortie [sɔrti] nf (issue) way out, exit; (MIL) sortie; (fig: verbale) outburst; sally; (promenade) outing; (le soir: au restaurant etc) night out; (COMM: somme): ~s items of expenditure; outgoings sans sg; ~ **de bain** (vêtement) bathrobe; ~ **de secours** emergency exit

sortilège [sɔrtilɛʒ] nm (magic) spell

sortir [sɔrtir] vi (gén) to come out; (partir, se promener, aller au spectacle) to go out; (numéro gagnant) to come up ♦ vt (gén) to take out; (produit, ouvrage, modèle) to bring out; (INFORM) to output; (: sur papier) to print out; (fam: expulser) to throw out; se ~ **de** (affaire, situation) to get out of; **s'en** ~ (malade) to pull through; (d'une difficulté etc) to get through; ~ **de** (gén) to leave; (endroit) to go (ou come) out of leave; (rainure etc) to come out of; (cadre, compétence) to be outside

sosie [sozi] nm double

sot, sotte [so, sɔt] adj silly, foolish ♦ nm/f fool; **sottise** nf silliness, foolishness; silly ou foolish thing

sou [su] nm: **près de ses ~s** tight-fisted; **sans le ~** penniless

soubresaut [subʀəso] nm start; jolt

souche [suʃ] nf (d'arbre) stump; (de carnet) counterfoil (BRIT); (de vieille ~) of old stock

souci [susi] nm (inquiétude) worry; (préoccupation) concern; (BOT) marigold; **se faire du ~** to worry; **soucier** [susje] : **se ~ de** vt to care about

soucieux, euse [susjø, -øz] adj concerned, worried

soucoupe [sukup] nf saucer; **~ volante** flying saucer

soudain, e [sudɛ̃, -ɛn] adj (douleur, mort) sudden ♦ adv suddenly, all of a sudden

soude [sud] nf soda

souder [sude] vt (avec fil à souder) to solder; (par chaleur autogène) to weld; (fig) to bind together

soudoyer [sudwaje] (péj) vt to bribe

soudure [sudyʀ] nf soldering; welding; (joint) soldered joint; weld

souffert, e [sufɛʀ, -ɛʀt(ə)] pp de souffrir

souffle [sufl(ə)] nm (en expirant) breath; (en soufflant) puff, blow; (respiration) breathing; (d'explosion, de ventilateur) blast; (du vent) blowing; **être à bout de ~** to be out of breath; **un ~ d'air** ou **de vent** a breath of air; **un ~ d'air** ou **de vent**, a puff of wind

soufflé, e [sufle] adj (fam: stupéfié) staggered ♦ nm (CULIN) soufflé

souffler [sufle] vi (gén) to blow; (haleter) to puff and blow ♦ vt (feu, bougie) to blow out; (chasser: poussière etc) to blow away; (TECH: verre) to blow; (suj: explosion) to destroy (with its blast); (dire): **~ qch à qn** to whisper sth to sb; (fam:

voler): **~ qch à qn** to pinch sth from sb

soufflet [sufle] nm (instrument) bellows pl; (gifle) slap (in the face)

souffleur [suflœʀ] nm (THEATRE) prompter

souffrance [sufʀɑ̃s] nf suffering; **en ~** (marchandise) awaiting delivery; (affaire) pending

souffrant, e [sufʀɑ̃, -ɑ̃t] adj unwell

souffre-douleur [sufʀədulœʀ] nm inv butt, underdog

souffrir [sufʀiʀ] vi to suffer; to be in pain ♦ vt to suffer, endure; (supporter) to bear, stand; (admettre: exception etc) to allow ou admit of; **~ de** (maladie, froid) to suffer from

soufre [sufʀ(ə)] nm sulphur

souhait [swɛ] nm wish; **tous nos ~s** de good wishes ou our best wishes for; **riche** etc **à ~** as rich etc as one could wish; **à vos ~s!** bless you!; **~able** [swɛtabl(ə)] adj desirable

souhaiter [swete] vt to wish for; **~ la bonne année à qn** to wish sb a happy New Year

souiller [suje] vt to dirty, soil; (fig) to sully, tarnish

soûl, e [su, sul] adj drunk ♦ nm: **tout son ~** to one's heart's content

soulagement [sulaʒmɑ̃] nm relief

soulager [sulaʒe] vt to relieve

soûler [sule] vt: **~ qn** to get sb drunk; (suj: boisson) to make sb drunk; (fig) to make sb's head spin ou reel; **se ~** to get drunk

soulever [sulve] vt to lift; (vagues, poussière) to send up; (peuple) to stir up (to revolt); (enthousiasme) to arouse; (question, débat) to raise; **se ~** vi (peuple) to rise up; (personne couchée) to lift o.s. up; **cela me soulève le cœur** it makes me feel sick

soulier [sulje] nm shoe

souligner [suliɲe] vt to underline; (fig) to emphasize; to stress

soumettre [sumɛtʀ(ə)] vt (pays) to subject, subjugate; (rebelle) to put down, subdue; **se ~ (à)** to submit (to); ~ qn/qch à to subject sb/sth to; ~ qch à qn (*projet etc*) to submit sth to sb

soumis, e [sumi, -iz] *adj* submissive; revenus ~ à l'impôt taxable income; **soumission** [sumisjɔ̃] *nf* submission; (*docilité*) submissiveness; (*COMM*) tender

soupape [supap] *nf* valve

soupçon [supsɔ̃] *nm* suspicion; (*petite quantité*): **un** ~ **de** a hint ou touch of; **soupçonner** *vt* to suspect; **soupçonneux, euse** *adj* suspicious

soupe [sup] *nf* soup; ~ **au lait** *adj inv* quick-tempered

souper [supe] *vi* to have supper ♦ *nm* supper

soupeser [supəze] *vt* to weigh in one's hand(s); (*fig*) to weigh up

soupière [supjɛʀ] *nf* (soup) tureen

soupir [supiʀ] *nm* sigh; (*MUS*) crotchet rest

soupirail, aux [supiʀaj, -o] *nm* (small) basement window

soupirer [supiʀe] *vi* to sigh; ~ **après qch** to yearn for sth

souple [supl(ə)] *adj* supple; (*fig: règlement, caractère*) flexible; (: *démarche, taille*) lithe, supple

source [suʀs(ə)] *nf* (*point d'eau*) spring; (*d'un cours d'eau, fig*) source; **de bonne** ~ on good authority

sourcil [suʀsij] *nm* (eye)brow

sourciller [suʀsije] *vi*: **sans** ~ without turning a hair ou batting an eyelid

sourcilleux, euse [suʀsijø, -øz] *adj* pernickety

sourd, e [suʀ, suʀd(ə)] *adj* deaf; (*bruit, voix*) muffled; (*douleur*) dull; (*lutte*) silent, hidden ♦ *nm/f* deaf person

sourdine [suʀdin] *nf* (*MUS*) mute; **en** ~ softly, quietly

sourd-muet, sourde-muette [suʀmɥɛ, suʀdmɥɛt] *adj* deaf-and-dumb ♦ *nm/f* deaf-mute

souriant, e [suʀjɑ̃, -ɑ̃t] *adj* cheerful

souricière [suʀisjɛʀ] *nf* mousetrap;

(*fig*) trap

sourire [suʀiʀ] *nm* smile ♦ *vi* to smile; ~ **à qn** to smile at sb; (*fig*) to appeal to sb; to smile on sb; **garder le** ~ to keep smiling

souris [suʀi] *nf* mouse

sournois, e [suʀnwa, -waz] *adj* deceitful, underhand

sous [su] *prép* (*gén*) under; ~ **la pluie/le soleil** in the rain/sunshine; ~ **terre** underground; ~ **peu** shortly, before long

sous-bois [subwa] *nm inv* undergrowth

souscrire [suskʀiʀ]: ~ **à** *vt* to subscribe to

sous-: ~directeur, trice *nm/f* assistant manager(manageress); **~entendre** *vt* to imply, infer; **~entendu, e** *adj* implied; (*LING*) understood ♦ *nm* innuendo, insinuation; **~estimer** *vt* to under-estimate; **~jacent, e** *adj* underlying; **~louer** *vt* to sublet; **~main** *nm inv* desk blotter; **en** ~ secretly; **~marin, e** *adj* (*flore, volcan*) submarine; (*navigation, pêche, explosif*) underwater ♦ *nm* submarine; **~officier** *nm* ≈ non-commissioned officer (N.C.O.); **~produit** *nm* by-product; (*fig: péj*) pale imitation; **~signé, e** *adj*: **je** ~ **I** the undersigned; **~sol** *nm* basement; **~titre** *nm* subtitle

soustraction [sustʀaksjɔ̃] *nf* subtraction

soustraire [sustʀɛʀ] *vt* to subtract, take away; (*dérober*) ~ **qch à qn** to remove sth from sb; **se** ~ **à** (*autorité etc*) to elude, escape from; (*danger*) à to shield sb from

sous-traitant [sutʀɛtɑ̃] *nm* subcontractor

sous-vêtements [suvɛtmɑ̃] *nmpl* underwear *sg*

soutane [sutan] *nf* cassock, soutane

soute [sut] *nf* hold

soutènement [sutɛnmɑ̃] *nm*: **mur de** ~ retaining wall

souteneur [sutnœʀ] *nm* procurer

soutenir [sutniʀ] *vt* to support; (*as-*

saut, choc) to stand up to, withstand; (*intérêt, effort*) to keep up; (*assurer*) ~ **que** to maintain that; ~ **la comparaison avec** to bear ou stand comparison with; **soutenu, e** *adj* (*efforts*) sustained, unflagging; (*style*) elevated

souterrain, e [suterɛ̃, -ɛn] *adj* underground ♦ *nm* underground passage

soutien [sutjɛ̃] *nm* support; ~ **de famille** breadwinner; ~~**gorge** [sutjɛ̃gɔrʒ(ə)] *nm* bra

soutirer [sutire] *vt*: ~ **qch à qn** to squeeze ou get sth out of sb

souvenir [suvnir] *nm* (*réminiscence*) memory; (*objet*) souvenir ♦ *vb*: **se** ~ **de** *vt* to remember; **se** ~ **que** to remember that; **en** ~ **de** in memory ou remembrance of

souvent [suvɑ̃] *adv* often; **peu** ~ seldom, infrequently

souverain, e [suvrɛ̃, -ɛn] *adj* sovereign; (*fig: mépris*) supreme ♦ *nm/f* sovereign, monarch

soviétique [sovjetik] *nm/f*: **Soviétique** Soviet citizen

soyeux, euse [swajø, øz] *adj* silky

soyons *etc vb voir* **être**

spacieux, euse [spasjø, -øz] *adj* spacious; roomy

spaghettis [spageti] *nmpl* spaghetti *sg*

sparadrap [sparadra] *nm* sticking plaster (*BRIT*), bandaid (®)

spatial, e, aux [spasjal, -o] *adj* (*AVIAT*) space *cpd*

speaker, ine [spikœr, -krin] *nm/f* announcer

spécial, e, aux [spesjal, -o] *adj* special; (*bizarre*) peculiar; **spécialement** *adv* especially, particularly; (*tout exprès*) specially

spécialiser [spesjalize] : **se** ~ *vi* to specialize

spécialiste [spesjalist(ə)] *nm/f* specialist

spécialité [spesjalite] *nf* speciality; (*SCOL*) special field

spécifier [spesifje] *vt* to specify, state

spécimen [spesimen] *nm* specimen; (*revue etc*) specimen ou sample copy

spectacle [spɛktakl(ə)] *nm* (*tableau, scène*) sight; (*représentation*) show; (*industrie*) show business; **spectaculaire** *adj* spectacular

spectateur, trice [spɛktatœr, -tris] *nm/f* (*CINEMA etc*) member of the audience; (*SPORT*) spectator; (*d'un événement*) onlooker, witness

spéculer [spekyle] *vi* to speculate; ~ **sur** (*COMM*) to speculate in; (*réfléchir*) to speculate on

spéléologie [speleɔlɔʒi] *nf* potholing

sperme [spɛrm(ə)] *nm* semen, sperm

sphère [sfɛr] *nf* sphere

spirale [spiral] *nf* spiral

spirituel, le [spirituɛl] *adj* spiritual; (*fin, piquant*) witty

spiritueux [spiritɥø] *nm* spirit

splendide [splɑ̃did] *adj* splendid; magnificent

spontané, e [spɔ̃tane] *adj* spontaneous

sport [spɔr] *nm* sport ♦ *adj inv* (*vêtement*) casual; **faire du** ~ to do sport; **sportif, ive** *adj* (*journal, association, épreuve*) sports *cpd*; (*allure, démarche*) athletic; (*attitude, esprit*) sporting; ~ **d'hiver** winter sports

spot [spɔt] *nm* (*lampe*) spot(light); (*annonce*): ~ (**publicitaire**) commercial (break)

square [skwar] *nm* public garden(s)

squelette [skəlɛt] *nm* skeleton; **squelettique** *adj* scrawny; (*fig*) skimpy

stabiliser [stabilize] *vt* to stabilize; (*terrain*) to consolidate

stable [stabl(ə)] *adj* stable, steady

stade [stad] *nm* (*SPORT*) stadium; (*phase, niveau*) stage

stage [staʒ] *nm* training period; training course; **stagiaire** *nm/f, adj* trainee

stalle [stal] *nf* stall, box

stand [stɑ̃d] *nm* (*d'exposition*) stand; (*de foire*) stall; ~ **de tir** (*à la foire, SPORT*) shooting range

standard [stɑ̃daʀ] adj inv standard ♦ nm switchboard; **standardiste** nm/f switchboard operator

standing [stɑ̃diŋ] nm standing; **immeuble de grand ~** block of luxury flats (BRIT), condo(minium) (US)

starter [staʀtɛʀ] nm (AUTO) choke

station [stasjɔ̃] nf station; (de bus) stop; (de villégiature) resort; (posture): **la ~ debout** standing, an upright posture; **~ de ski** ski resort; **~ de taxis** taxi rank (BRIT) ou stand (US)

stationnement [stasjɔnmɑ̃] nm parking; **stationner** [stasjɔne] vi to park

station-service [stasjɔ̃sɛʀvis] nf service station

statistique [statistik] nf (science) statistics sg; (rapport, étude) statistic ♦ adj statistical

statue [staty] nf statue

statuer [statɥe] vi: **~ sur** to rule on, give a ruling on

statut [staty] nm status; **~s** nmpl (JUR, ADMIN) statutes; **statutaire** adj statutory

Sté abr = **société**

steak [stɛk] nm steak

sténo(dactylo) [steno(daktilo)] nf shorthand typist (BRIT), stenographer (US)

sténo(graphie) [steno(grafi)] nf shorthand

stéréo(phonique) [stereo(fɔnik)] adj stereo(phonic)

stérile [steʀil] adj sterile; (terre) barren; (fig) fruitless, futile

stérilet [steʀilɛ] nm coil, loop

stériliser [steʀilize] vt to sterilize

stigmates [stigmat] nmpl scars, marks

stimulant [stimylɑ̃] nm (fig) stimulus, incentive

stimuler [stimyle] vt to stimulate

stipuler [stipyle] vt to stipulate

stock [stɔk] nm stock; **~ d'or** (FINANCE) gold reserves pl; **stocker** vt to stock

stop [stɔp] nm (AUTO: écriteau) stop

sign; (: signal) brake-light; **~per** [stɔpe] vt to stop, halt; (COUTURE) to mend ♦ vi to stop, halt

store [stɔʀ] nm blind; (de magasin) shade, awning

strabisme [stʀabism(ə)] nm squinting

strapontin [stʀapɔ̃tɛ̃] nm jump ou foldaway seat

stratégie [stʀateʒi] nf strategy; **stratégique** adj strategic

stressant, e [stʀɛsɑ̃, -ɑ̃t] adj stressful

strict, e [stʀikt(ə)] adj strict; (tenue, décor) severe, plain; **son droit le plus ~** his most basic right; **le ~ nécessaire/minimum** the bare essentials/minimum

strie [stʀi] nf streak

strophe [stʀɔf] nf verse, stanza

structure [stʀyktyʀ] nf structure; **~s d'accueil** reception facilities

studieux, euse [stydjø, -øz] adj studious; devoted to study

studio [stydjo] nm (logement) (one-roomed) flatlet (BRIT) ou apartment (US); (d'artiste, TV etc) studio

stupéfait, e [stypefɛ, -ɛt] adj astonished

stupéfiant [stypefjɑ̃] nm (MÉD) drug, narcotic

stupéfier [stypefje] vt to stupefy; (étonner) to stun, astonish

stupeur [stypœʀ] nf astonishment

stupide [stypid] adj stupid; **stupidité** nf stupidity; stupid thing (to do ou say)

style [stil] nm style; **meuble de ~** piece of period furniture

stylé, e [stile] adj well-trained

styliste [stilist(ə)] nm/f designer

stylo [stilo] nm: **~ (à encre)** (fountain) pen; **~ (à) bille** ball-point pen

su, e [sy] pp de **savoir** ♦ nm: **au ~ de** with the knowledge of

suave [sɥav] adj sweet; (goût) mellow

subalterne [sybaltɛʀn(ə)] adj (employé, officier) junior; (rôle) subordinate, subsidiary ♦ nm/f subordinate

subconscient [sybkɔ̃sjã] *nm* subconscious

subir [sybiʀ] *vt* (*affront, dégats*) to suffer; (*influence, charme*) to be under; (*opération, châtiment*) to undergo

subit, e [sybi, -it] *adj* sudden; **subitement** *adv* suddenly, all of a sudden

subjectif, ive [sybʒɛktif, -iv] *adj* subjective

subjonctif [sybʒɔ̃ktif] *nm* subjunctive

submerger [sybmɛʀʒe] *vt* to submerge; (*fig*) to overwhelm

subordonné, e [sybɔʀdɔne] *adj, nm/f* subordinate; ~ **à** subordinate to; subject to, depending on

subornation [sybɔʀnasjɔ̃] *nf* bribing

subrepticement [sybʀɛptismã] *adv* surreptitiously

subside [sypsid] *nm* grant

subsidiaire [sypsidjɛʀ] *adj*: **question** ~ deciding question

subsister [sybziste] *vi* (*rester*) to remain, subsist; (*vivre*) to live; (*survivre*) to live on

substance [sypstɑ̃s] *nf* substance

substituer [sypstitɥe] *vt*: ~ **qn/qch à** to substitute sb/sth for; **se** ~ **à qn** (*évincer*) to substitute o.s. for sb

substitut [sypstity] *nm* (*JUR*) deputy public prosecutor; (*succédané*) substitute

subterfuge [sybtɛʀfyʒ] *nm* subterfuge

subtil, e [sybtil] *adj* subtle

subtiliser [sybtilize] *vt*: ~ **qch** (à **qn**) to spirit sth away (from sb)

subvenir [sybvəniʀ]: ~ **à** *vt* to meet

subvention [sybvɑ̃sjɔ̃] *nf* subsidy, grant; **subventionner** *vt* to subsidize

suc [syk] *nm* (*BOT*) sap; (*de viande, fruit*) juice

succédané [syksedane] *nm* substitute

succéder [syksede]: ~ **à** *vt* (*directeur, roi etc*) to succeed; (*venir après dans une série*) to follow, succeed; **se** ~ *vi* (*accidents, années*) to follow one another

succès [syksɛ] *nm* success; **avoir du** ~ to be a success, be successful; **à** ~ successful; **de librairie** bestseller; ~ (**féminins**) conquests

succession [syksɛsjɔ̃] *nf* (*série, POL*) succession; (*JUR: patrimoine*) estate, inheritance

succomber [sykɔ̃be] *vi* to die, succumb; (*fig*): ~ **à** to give way to, succumb to

succursale [sykyʀsal] *nf* branch

sucer [syse] *vt* to suck

sucette [sysɛt] *nf* (*bonbon*) lollipop; (*de bébé*) dummy (*BRIT*), pacifier (*US*)

sucre [sykʀ(ə)] *nm* (*substance*) sugar; (*morceau*) lump of sugar, lump ou cube; ~ **d'orge** barley sugar; ~ **en morceaux/cristallisé/en poudre** lump/granulated/caster sugar; **sucré, e** *adj* (*produit alimentaire*) sweetened; (*au goût*) sweet; (*péj*) sugary, honeyed; **sucrer** *vt* (*thé, café*) to sweeten, put sugar in; **sucreries** *nfpl* (*bonbons*) sweets, sweet things; **sucrier** *nm* (*récipient*) sugar bowl

sud [syd] *nm*: **le** ~ **the** south ♦ *adj* *inv* south; (*côte*) south, southern; **au** ~ (*situation*) in the south; (*direction*) to the south; **au** ~ **de** (*to the*) south of; **sud-africain, e** *adj, nm/f* South African; **sud-américain, e** *adj, nm/f* South American; **sud-est** [sydɛst] *nm* south-east ♦ *adj inv* south-east; **sud-ouest** [sydwɛst] *nm* south-west ♦ *adj inv* south-west

Suède [sɥɛd] *nf*: **la** ~ Sweden; **suédois, e** *adj* Swedish ♦ *nm/f*: **Suédois, e** Swede ♦ *nm* (*LING*) Swedish

suer [sɥe] *vi* to sweat; (*suinter*) to ooze

sueur [sɥœʀ] *nf* sweat; **en** ~ sweating, in a sweat

suffire [syfiʀ] *vi* (*être assez*): ~ (à **qn/pour qch/pour faire**) to be enough ou sufficient (for sb/for sth/to do); **cela suffit pour les irriter/qu'ils se fâchent** it's enough to annoy them/for them to get angry; **f**

suffit d'une négligence ... it only takes one act of carelessness ...; **il suffit qu'on oublie pour que** ... one only needs to forget for ...

suffisamment [syfizamɑ̃] adv sufficiently, enough; **~ de** sufficient, enough

suffisant, e [syfizɑ̃, -ɑ̃t] adj (temps, ressources) sufficient; (résultats) satisfactory; (vaniteux) self-important, bumptious

suffixe [syfiks(ə)] nm suffix

suffoquer [syfɔke] vt to choke, suffocate; (stupéfier) to stagger, astound ♦ vi to choke, suffocate

suffrage [syfraʒ] nm (POL: voix) vote; (du public etc) approval no pl

suggérer [syɡʒere] vt to suggest; **suggestion** nf suggestion

suicide [sɥisid] nm suicide

suicider [sɥiside]: **se ~** vi to commit suicide

suie [sɥi] nf soot

suinter [sɥɛ̃te] vi to ooze

suis vb voir être; suivre

suisse [sɥis] adj Swiss ♦ nm: **S~** Swiss pl inv ♦ nf: **la S~** Switzerland; **la S~ romande/allemande** French-speaking/German-speaking Switzerland; **Suissesse** nf Swiss (woman ou girl)

suite [sɥit] nf (continuation d'énumération etc) rest, remainder; (: de feuilleton) continuation; (: film etc sur le même thème) sequel; (série: de maisons, succès) **une ~ de** a series ou succession of; (MATH) series sg; (conséquence) result; (ordre, liaison logique) coherence; (appartement, MUS) suite; (escorte) retinue, suite; **~s** nfpl (d'une maladie etc) effects; **prendre la ~ de** (directeur etc) to succeed, take over from; **donner ~ à** (requête, projet) to follow up; **faire ~ à** to follow; (faisant) **~** à **votre lettre du** further to your letter of the; **de ~** (d'affilée) in succession; (immédiatement) at once; **par la ~** afterwards, subsequently; **à la ~** one after the

other; **à la ~ de** (derrière) behind; (en conséquence de) following; **par ~** de owing to, as a result of

suivant, e [sɥivɑ̃, -ɑ̃t] adj next, following; (ci-après): **l'exercice ~** the following exercise ♦ prép (selon) according to; **au ~!** next!

suivi, e [sɥivi] adj (régulier) regular; (cohérent) consistent; (cours: très/peu ~) well-/poorly-attended

suivre [sɥivʀ(ə)] vt (gén) to follow; (SCOL: cours) to attend; (: programme) to keep up with; (: COMM: article) to continue to stock ♦ vi to follow; (élève) to attend; to keep up; **se ~** (accidents etc) to follow one after the other; (raisonnement) to be coherent; **faire ~** (lettre) to forward; **~ son cours** (suj: enquête etc) to run ou take its course; "à **~**" "to be continued"

sujet, te [syʒɛ, -ɛt] adj: **être ~ à** (vertige etc) to be liable ou subject to ♦ nm/f (d'un souverain) subject ♦ nm subject; **au ~ de** about; **~ à caution** questionable; **~ de conversation** topic ou subject of conversation; **~ d'examen** (SCOL) examination question; examination paper

summum [sɔmɔm] nm: **le ~ de** the height of

superbe [sypɛʀb(ə)] adj magnificent, superb

super(carburant) [sypɛʀ(kaʀbyʀɑ̃)] nm = 4-star petrol (BRIT), = high-octane gas (US)

supercherie [sypɛʀʃəʀi] nf trick

supérette [sypeʀɛt] nf (COMM) minimarket, superette (US)

superficie [sypɛʀfisi] nf (surface) area; (fig) surface

superficiel, le [sypɛʀfisjɛl] adj superficial

superflu, e [sypɛʀfly] adj superfluous

supérieur, e [sypeʀjœʀ] adj (lèvre, étages, classes) upper; (plus élevé: température, niveau): **~ (à)** higher (than); (meilleur: qualité, produit)

~ (à) superior (to); (*excellent, hautain*) superior ♦ *nm, nf* superior; à l'étage ~ on the next floor up; **supériorité** *nf* superiority

superlatif [syperlatif] *nm* superlative

supermarché [sypermarʃe] *nm* supermarket

superposer [syperpoze] *vt* (*faire chevaucher*) to superimpose; **lits superposés** bunk beds

superproduction [syperprɔdyksjɔ̃] *nf* (*film*) spectacular

superpuissance [syperpɥisɑ̃s] *nf* super-power

superstitieux, euse [syperstisjø, -øz] *adj* superstitious

superviser [sypervize] *vt* to supervise

suppléant, e [sypleɑ̃, -ɑ̃t] *adj* (*juge, fonctionnaire*) deputy *cpd*; (*professeur*) supply *cpd* ♦ *nm/f* deputy; supply teacher

suppléer [syplee] *vt* (*ajouter: mot manquant etc*) to supply, provide; (*compenser: lacune*) to fill in; (: *défaut*) to make up for; (*remplacer*) to stand in for; ~ à to make up for; to substitute for

supplément [syplemɑ̃] *nm* supplement; (*de frites etc*) extra portion; **un ~ de travail** extra *ou* additional work; **ceci est en ~** (*au menu etc*) this is extra, there is an extra charge for this; **~-aire** *cpd* additional, further; (*train, bus*) relief *cpd*, extra

supplications [syplikasjɔ̃] *nfpl* pleas, entreaties

supplice [syplis] *nm* (*peine corporelle*) torture *no pl*; form of torture; (*douleur physique, morale*) torture, agony

supplier [syplije] *vt* to implore, beseech

supplique [syplik] *nf* petition

support [sypɔr] *nm* support; (*pour livre, outils*) stand

supportable [sypɔrtabl(ə)] *adj* (*douleur*) bearable

supporter[1] [sypɔrter] *nm* supporter, fan

supporter[2] [sypɔrte] *vt* (*poids, poussée*) to support; (*conséquences, épreuve*) to bear, endure; (*défauts, personne*) to put up with; (*suj: chose: chaleur etc*) to withstand; (: *personne: chaleur, vin*) to be able to take

supposé, e [sypoze] *adj* (*nombre*) estimated; (*auteur*) supposed

supposer [sypoze] *vt* to suppose; (*impliquer*) to presuppose; **à ~ que** supposing (that)

suppositoire [sypozitwar] *nm* suppository

suppression [sypresjɔ̃] *nf* (*voir supprimer*) removal; deletion; cancellation; suppression

supprimer [syprime] *vt* (*cloison, cause, anxiété*) to remove; (*clause, mot*) to delete; (*congés, service d'autobus etc*) to cancel; (*emplois, privilèges, témoin gênant*) to do away with

supputer [sypyte] *vt* to calculate

suprême [syprem] *adj* supreme

MOT-CLÉ

sur *prép* **1** (*position*) on; (*pardessus*) over; (*au-dessus*) above; **pose-le ~ la table** put it on the table; **je n'ai pas d'argent ~ moi** I haven't any money on me

2 (*direction*) towards; **en allant ~ Paris** going towards Paris; ~ **votre droite** on *ou* to your right

3 (*à propos de*) on; about; **un livre/une conférence ~ Balzac** a book/lecture on *ou* about Balzac

4 (*proportion, mesures*) out of; by; **un ~ 10** one in 10; (*SCOL*) one out of 10; **4 m ~ 2** 4 m by 2

sur ce *adv* hereupon

---

sûr, e [syr] *adj* sure, certain; (*digne de confiance*) reliable; (*sans danger*) safe; **le plus ~** est de the safest thing is to; ~ **de soi** self-confident; ~ **et certain** absolutely certain

suranné, e [syrane] *adj* outdated, outmoded

surcharge [syʀʃaʀʒ(ə)] nf (de passagers, marchandises) excess load; (correction) alteration

surcharger [syʀʃaʀʒe] vt to overload

surchoix [syʀʃwa] adj inv top-quality

surclasser [syʀklɑse] vt to outclass

surcroît [syʀkʀwa] nm: un ~ de additional +nom; par ou de ~ moreover; en ~ in addition

surdité [syʀdite] nf deafness

surélever [syʀelve] vt to raise, heighten

sûrement [syʀmɑ̃] adv reliably; safely, securely; (certainement) certainly

surenchère [syʀɑ̃ʃɛʀ] nf (aux enchères) higher bid; (sur prix fixe) overbid; (fig) overstatement; outbidding tactics pl; **surenchérir** vi to bid higher; (fig) to try and outbid each other

surent vb voir **savoir**

surestimer [syʀɛstime] vt to overestimate

sûreté [syʀte] nf (voir sûr) reliability; safety; (JUR) guaranty; safety; **mettre en ~** to put in a safe place; **pour plus de ~** as an extra precaution; to be on the safe side

surf [syʀf] nm surfing

surface [syʀfas] nf surface; (superficie) surface area; **faire ~** to surface; **en ~** near the surface; (fig) superficially

surfait, e [syʀfɛ, -ɛt] adj overrated

surfin, e [syʀfɛ̃, -in] adj superfine

surgelé, e [syʀʒəle] adj (deep-)frozen

surgir [syʀʒiʀ] vi to appear suddenly; (jaillir) to shoot up; (fig: problème, conflit) to arise

sur: ~humain, e adj superhuman; **~impression** nf (PHOTO) double exposure; **en ~** superimposed; **~lechamp** adv immediately; **~lendemain** nm: **le ~** (soir) two days later (in the evening); **le ~** de two days after; **~mener** vt to overwork; **se ~** vi to overwork

surmonter [syʀmɔ̃te] vt (suj: coupole etc) to top; (vaincre) to overcome

surnager [syʀnaʒe] vi to float

surnaturel, le [syʀnatyʀɛl] adj, nm supernatural

surnom [syʀnɔ̃] nm nickname

surnombre [syʀnɔ̃bʀ(ə)] nm: **être en ~** to be too many (ou one too many)

surpeuplé, e [syʀpœple] adj overpopulated

sur-place [syʀplas] nm: **faire du ~** to mark time

surplomber [syʀplɔ̃be] vi to be overhanging ♦ vt to overhang; to tower above

surplus [syʀply] nm (COMM) surplus; (reste): **~ de bois** wood left over

surprenant, e [syʀpʀənɑ̃, -ɑ̃t] adj amazing

surprendre [syʀpʀɑ̃dʀ(ə)] vt (étonner, prendre à l'improviste) to surprise; (tomber sur: intrus etc) to catch; (fig) to detect; to chance upon; to overhear

surpris, e [syʀpʀi, -iz] adj: **~ (de/que)** surprised (at/that)

surprise [syʀpʀiz] nf surprise; **faire une ~ à qn** to give sb a surprise; **~-partie** [syʀpʀizpaʀti] nf party

sursaut [syʀso] nm start, jump; **~ de** (énergie, indignation) sudden fit ou burst of; **en ~** with a start; **sursauter** vi to (give a) start, jump

surseoir [syʀswaʀ] : **~ à** vt to overhear

sursis [syʀsi] nm (JUR: gén) suspended sentence; (à l'exécution capitale, aussi fig) reprieve; (MIL) deferment

surtaxe [syʀtaks(ə)] nf surcharge

surtout [syʀtu] adv (avant tout, d'abord) above all; (spécialement, particulièrement) especially; **~, ne dites rien!** whatever you do don't say anything!; **~ pas!** certainly ou definitely not!; **~ que ...** especially as ...

surveillance [syʀvejɑ̃s] nf watch; (POLICE, MIL) surveillance; **sous ~**

médicale under medical supervision

surveillant, e [syʀvɛjɑ̃, -ɑ̃t] nm/f (de prison) warder; (SCOL) monitor; (de travaux) supervisor, overseer

surveiller [syʀveje] vt (enfant, élèves, bagages) to watch, keep an eye on; (malade) to watch over; (prisonnier, suspect) to keep (a watch on; (territoire, bâtiment) to (keep) watch over; (travaux, cuisson) to supervise; (SCOL: examen) to invigilate; se ~ vi to keep a check ou watch on o.s.; ~ son langage/sa ligne to watch one's language/figure

survenir [syʀvəniʀ] vi (incident, retards) to occur, arise; (événement) to take place; (personne) to appear, arrive

survêt(ement) [syʀvɛt(mɑ̃)] nm tracksuit

survie [syʀvi] nf survival; (REL) afterlife

survivant, e [syʀvivɑ̃, -ɑ̃t] nm/f survivor

survivre [syʀvivʀ(ə)] vi to survive; ~ à (accident etc) to survive; (personne) to outlive

survoler [syʀvɔle] vt to fly over; (fig: livre) to skim through

survolté, e [syʀvɔlte] adj (fig) worked up

sus [sy(s)]: en ~ de prép in addition to, over and above; en ~ in addition; ~ à: au tyran! at the tyrant!

susceptible [syseptibl(ə)] adj touchy, sensitive; ~ d'amélioration that can be improved, open to improvement; ~ de faire able to do; liable to do

susciter [sysite] vt (admiration) to arouse; (obstacles, ennuis) ~ (à qn) to create (for sb)

suspect, e [syspɛ(kt), -ɛkt(ə)] adj suspicious; (témoignage, opinions) suspect ♦ nm/f suspect

suspecter [syspɛkte] vt to suspect; (honnêteté de qn) to question, have one's suspicions about

suspendre [syspɑ̃dʀ(ə)] vt (accrocher: vêtement) ~ qch (à) to hang sth up (on); (fixer: lustre etc): ~ qch à to hang sth from; (interrompre, démettre) to suspend; (remettre) to defer; se ~ à to hang from

suspendu, e [syspɑ̃dy] adj (accroché): ~ à hanging on (ou from); (perché): ~ au-dessus de suspended over

suspens [syspɑ̃]: en ~ adv (affaire) in abeyance; tenir en ~ to keep in suspense

suspense [syspɑ̃s] nm suspense

suspension [syspɑ̃sjɔ̃] nf suspension; ~ d'audience adjournment

sut vb voir **savoir**

suture [sytyʀ] nf (MÉD): point de ~ stitch

svelte [svɛlt(ə)] adj slender, svelte

S.V.P. sigle (= s'il vous plaît) please

syllabe [silab] nf syllable

sylviculture [silvikyltyʀ] nf forestry

symbole [sɛ̃bɔl] nm symbol; **symbolique** adj symbolic(al); (geste, offrande) token cpd; (salaire, dommage-intérêts) nominal; **symboliser** vt to symbolize

symétrique [simetʀik] adj symmetrical

sympa [sɛ̃pa] adj abr = **sympathique**

sympathie [sɛ̃pati] nf (inclination) liking; (affinité) fellow feeling; (condoléances) sympathy; accueillir avec ~ (projet) to receive favourably; croyez à toute ma ~ you have my deepest sympathy

sympathique [sɛ̃patik] adj nice, friendly; likeable; pleasant

sympathisant, e [sɛ̃patizɑ̃, -ɑ̃t] nm/f sympathizer

sympathiser [sɛ̃patize] vi (voisins etc: s'entendre) to get on (BRIT) ou along (US) (well)

symphonie [sɛ̃fɔni] nf symphony

symptôme [sɛ̃ptom] nm symptom

synagogue [sinagɔg] nf synagogue

syncope [sɛ̃kɔp] nf (MÉD) blackout; tomber en ~ to faint, pass out

syndic [sɛ̃dik] nm managing agent

syndical, e, aux [sɛ̃dikal, -o] *adj* (trade-)union *cpd*; **syndicaliste** *nm/f* trade unionist

syndicat [sɛ̃dika] *nm* (*d'ouvriers, employés*) (trade) union; (*autre association d'intérêts*) union, association; ~ **d'initiative** tourist office

syndiqué, e [sɛ̃dike] *adj* belonging to a (trade) union; **non** ~ non-union

syndiquer [sɛ̃dike]: **se** ~ *vi* to form a trade union; (*adhérer*) to join a trade union

synonyme [sinɔnim] *adj* synonymous ♦ *nm* synonym; ~ **de** synonymous with

syntaxe [sɛ̃taks(ə)] *nf* syntax

synthèse [sɛ̃tɛz] *nf* synthesis

synthétique [sɛ̃tetik] *adj* synthetic

Syrie [siʀi] *nf*: **la** ~ Syria

systématique [sistematik] *adj* systematic

système [sistɛm] *nm* system; ~ **D** resourcefulness

T

t' [t(ə)] *pron voir* te

ta [ta] *dét* ton[1]

tabac [taba] *nm* tobacco; tobacconist's (shop); ~ **blond/brun** light/dark tobacco

tabagie [tabaʒi] *nf*: ~ **passive** passive smoking

table [tabl(ə)] *nf* table; **à** ~! dinner *etc* is ready!; **se mettre à** ~ to sit down to eat; (*fig: fam*) to come clean; **mettre la** ~ to lay the table; **faire** ~ **rase de** to make a clean sweep of; ~ **de cuisson** (*à l'électricité*) hotplate; (*au gaz*) gas ring; ~ **de nuit** *ou* **de chevet** bedside table; ~ **des matières** (table of) contents *pl*

tableau, x [tablo] *nm* painting; (*reproduction, fig*) picture; (*panneau*) board; (*schéma*) table, chart; ~ **d'affichage** notice board; ~ **de bord** dashboard; (*AVIAT*) instrument panel; ~ **noir** blackboard

tabler [table] *vi*: ~ **sur** to bank on

tablette [tablɛt] *nf* (*planche*) shelf; ~ **de chocolat** bar of chocolate

tableur [tablœʀ] *nm* spreadsheet

tablier [tablije] *nm* apron

tabouret [tabuʀɛ] *nm* stool

tac [tak] *nm*: **du** ~ **au** ~ tit for tat

tache [taʃ] *nf* (*saleté*) stain, mark; (*ART, de couleur, lumière*) spot; splash, patch; ~ **de rousseur** *ou* **freckle**

tâche [taʃ] *nf* task; **travailler à la** ~ to do piecework

tacher [taʃe] *vt* to stain, mark; (*fig*) to sully, stain

tâcher [taʃe] *vi*: ~ **de faire** to try *ou* endeavour to do

tacot [tako] (*péj*) *nm* banger (*BRIT*), (old) heap

tact [takt] *nm* tact; **avoir du** ~ to be tactful

tactique [taktik] *adj* tactical ♦ *nf* (*technique*) tactics *sg*; (*plan*) tactic

taie [tɛ] *nf*: ~ **(d'oreiller)** pillowslip, pillowcase

taille [taj] *nf* cutting; pruning; (*milieu du corps*) waist; (*hauteur*) height; (*grandeur*) size; **de** ~ **à faire** capable of doing; **de** ~ **sizeable**

taille-crayon(s) [tajkʀɛjɔ̃] *nm* pencil sharpener

tailler [taje] *vt* (*pierre, diamant*) to cut; (*arbre, plante*) to prune; (*vêtement*) to cut out; (*crayon*) to sharpen

tailleur [tajœʀ] *nm* (*couturier*) tailor; (*vêtement*) suit; **en** ~ (*assis*) cross-legged

taillis [taji] *nm* copse

taire [tɛʀ] *vt* to keep to o.s., conceal ♦ *vi*: **faire** ~ **qn** to make sb be quiet; (*fig*) to silence sb; **se** ~ *vi* to be silent *ou* quiet

talc [talk] *nm* talc, talcum powder

talent [talɑ̃] *nm* talent

talon [talɔ̃] *nm* heel; (*de chèque, billet*) stub, counterfoil (*BRIT*); ~**s plats/aiguilles** flat/stiletto heels

talonner [talɔne] *vt* to follow hard behind; (*fig*) to hound

talus [taly] *nm* embankment

tambour [tābuʁ] *nm (MUS, aussi TECH)* drum; *(musicien)* drummer; *(porte)* revolving door(s *pl*)

tamis [tami] *nm* sieve

Tamise [tamiz] *nf*: **la ~** the Thames

tamisé, e [tamize] *adj (fig)* subdued, soft

tamiser [tamize] *vt* to sieve, sift

tampon [tāpɔ̃] *nm (de coton, d'ouate)* wad, pad; *(amortisseur)* buffer; *(bouchon)* plug, stopper; *(cachet, timbre)* stamp; *(mémoire)* ~ *(INFORM)* buffer; ~ *(hygiénique)* tampon; **tamponner** *vt (timbres)* to stamp; *(heurter)* to crash ou ram into; **tamponneuse** *adj*: **autos tamponneuses** dodgems

tandis [tādi]: ~ **que** *conj* while

tanguer [tɑ̃ge] *vi* to pitch (and toss)

tanière [tanjɛʁ] *nf* lair, den

tanné, e [tane] *adj* weather-beaten

tanner [tane] *vt* to tan

tant [tɑ̃] *adv* so much; ~ **de** *(sable, eau)* so much; *(gens, livres)* so many; ~ **que** as long as; *(comparatif)* as much as; ~ **mieux** that's great; so much the better; ~ **pis** never mind; too bad

tante [tɑ̃t] *nf* aunt

tantôt [tɑ̃to] *adv (parfois)*: ~ ... ~ now ... now; *(cet après-midi)* this afternoon

tapage [tapaʒ] *nm* uproar, din

tapageur, euse [tapaʒœʁ, -øz] *adj* loud, flashy; noisy

tape [tap] *nf* slap

tape-à-l'œil [tapalœj] *adj inv* flashy, showy

taper [tape] *vt (porte)* to bang, slam; *(dactylographier)* to type (out); *(fam: emprunter)*: ~ **qn de 10 F** to touch sb for 10 F ♦ *vi (soleil)* to beat down; ~ **sur qn** to thump sb; *(fig)* to run sb down; ~ **sur qch** to hit sth; to bang on sth; ~ **à** *(porte etc)* to knock on; ~ **dans** *(se servir)* to dig into; ~ **des mains/pieds** to clap one's hands/stamp one's feet; ~ **(à la machine)** to type; **se** ~ **un tra-**

vail to land o.s. with a job

tapi, e [tapi] *adj* crouching, cowering; hidden away

tapis [tapi] *nm* carpet; *(de table)* cloth; **mettre sur le** ~ *(fig)* to bring up for discussion; ~ **de sol** *(de tente)* groundsheet; ~ **roulant** conveyor belt

tapisser [tapise] *vt (avec du papier peint)* to paper; *(recouvrir)*: ~ **qch (de)** to cover sth (with)

tapisserie [tapisʁi] *nf (tenture, broderie)* tapestry; *(papier peint)* wallpaper

tapissier, ière [tapisje, -jɛʁ] *nm/f*: ~**(-décorateur)** upholsterer (and decorator)

tapoter [tapote] *vt* to pat, tap

taquiner [takine] *vt* to tease

tarabiscoté, e [taʁabiskote] *adj* over-ornate, fussy

tard [taʁ] *adv* late; **plus** ~ later (on); **au plus** ~ at the latest; **sur le** ~ late in life

tarder [taʁde] *vi (chose)* to be a long time coming; *(personne)*: ~ **à faire** to delay doing; **il me tarde d'être** I am longing to be; **sans (plus)** ~ without (further) delay

tardif, ive [taʁdif, -iv] *adj* late

targuer [taʁge]: **se** ~ **de** *vt* to boast about

tarif [taʁif] *nm (liste)* price list; tariff; *(barème)* rates *pl*; fares *pl*; tariff; *(prix)* rate; fare

tarir [taʁiʁ] *vt* to dry up, run dry

tarte [taʁt(ə)] *nf* tart

tartine [taʁtin] *nf* slice of bread; ~ **de miel** slice of bread and honey; **tartiner** *vt* to spread; **fromage à tartiner** cheese spread

tartre [taʁtʁ(ə)] *nm (des dents)* tartar; *(de chaudière)* fur, scale

tas [tɑ] *nm* heap, pile; *(fig)*: **un** ~ **de** heaps of, lots of; **en** ~ in a heap ou pile; **formé sur le** ~ trained on the job

tasse [tɑs] *nf* cup; ~ **à café** coffee cup

tassé, e [tɑse] *adj*: **bien** ~ *(café*

etc) strong

tasser [tɑse] *vt* (*terre, neige*) to pack down; (*entasser*): ~ **qch dans** to cram sth into; se ~ (*sol*) (*terrain*) to settle; (*fig*) to sort itself out, settle down

tâter [tɑte] *vt* to feel; (*fig*) to try out; se ~ (*hésiter*) to be in two minds; ~ **de** (*prison etc*) to have a taste of

tatillon, ne [tatijɔ̃, -ɔn] *adj* pernick-ety

tâtonnement [tɑtɔnmɑ̃] *nm*: par ~s (*fig*) by trial and error

tâtonner [tɑtɔne] *vi* to grope one's way along

tâtons [tɑtɔ̃]: à ~ *adv* to grope around for/grope one's way forward

tatouer [tatwe] *vt* to tattoo

taudis [todi] *nm* hovel, slum

taule [tol] (*fam*) nf nick (*fam*), pri-son

taupe [top] *nf* mole

taureau, x [tɔro] *nm* bull; (*signe*): le T~ Taurus

tauromachie [tɔromaʃi] *nf* bullfight-ing

taux [to] *nm* rate; (*d'alcool*) level; ~ **d'intérêt** interest rate

taxe [taks] *nf* tax; (*douanière*) duty; ~ **à la valeur ajoutée** value added tax; ~ **de séjour** tourist tax

taxer [takse] *vt* (*personne*) to tax; (*produit*) to put a tax on, tax; (*fig*): ~ **qn de** to call sb +*attrib*; to accuse sb of, tax sb with

taxi [taksi] *nm* taxi

Tchécoslovaquie [tʃekɔslɔvaki] *nf* Czechoslovakia; **tchèque** *adj*, *nm/f* Czech ♦ *nm* (*LING*) Czech

te(t') [t(ə)] *pron* you; (*réfléchi*) your-self

technicien, ne [tɛknisjɛ̃, -jɛn] *nm/f* technician

technique [tɛknik] *adj* technical ♦ *nf* technique; **techniquement** *adv* technically

technologie [tɛknɔlɔʒi] *nf* technolo-gy; **technologique** *adj* technologi-cal

teck [tɛk] *nm* teak

teignais *etc vb voir* **teindre**

teindre [tɛ̃dʀ(ə)] *vt* to dye

teint, e [tɛ̃, tɛ̃t] *adj* dyed ♦ *nm* (*du visage*) complexion; colour ♦ *nf* shade; **grand** ~ colourfast

teinté, e [tɛ̃te] *adj*: ~ **de** (*fig*) tinged with

teinter [tɛ̃te] *vt* to tint; (*bois*) to stain; **teinture** *nf* dyeing; (*sub-stance*) dye; (*MED*) tincture

teinturerie [tɛ̃tyʀʀi] *nf* dry cleaner's

teinturier [tɛ̃tyʀje] *nm* dry cleaner

tel, elle [tɛl] *adj* (*pareil*) such; (*comme*): ~ **un/des ...** like a/like ...; (*indéfini*) such-and-such a, a cer-tain; (*intensif*): **un** ~/de ~s ... such (a)/such ...; **rien de** ~ nothing like it, no such thing; ~ **que** like, such as; ~ **quel** as it is, (*as it stands* (*ou* was *etc*)

télé [tele] *abr f* (= *télévision*) TV, telly (*BRIT*); (*poste*) TV (set), telly; **à la** ~ on TV, on telly

télécabine [telekabin] *nf* (*benne*) cable car

télécarte [telekaʀt(ə)] *nf* phonecard

télé ~ commande *nf* remote control; **~copie** *nf* fax; **envoyer qch par** ~ to fax sth; **~distribution** *nf* cable TV; **~férique** *nm* = **téléphérique**; **~gramme** *nm* telegram; **~graphier** *vt* to telegraph, cable; **~guider** *vt* to operate by remote control, radio-control; **~journal** *nm* TV news mag-azine programme; **~matique** *nf* telematics *sg*; **~objectif** *nm* telepho-to lens *sg*

téléphérique [teleferik] *nm* cable car

téléphone [telefɔn] *nm* telephone; **avoir le** ~ to be on the (tele)phone; **au** ~ on the phone; ~ **de voiture** car phone; **téléphoner** *vi* to tele-phone, ring; to make a phone call; **téléphoner à** to phone, call up; **télé-phonique** *adj* telephone *cpd*

télescope [teleskɔp] *nm* telescope

télescoper [teleskɔpe] *vt* to smash up; se ~ (*véhicules*) to concertina

télé ~ scripteur *nm* teleprinter;

~**siège** nm chairlift; ~**ski** nm skitow; ~**spectateur, trice** nm/f (television) viewer; ~**viseur** nm television set; ~**vision** nf television; **à la** ~ on television

télex [teleks] nm telex

telle [tɛl] adj voir **tel**

tellement [tɛlmɑ̃] adv (tant) so much; (si) so; ~ **de** (sable, eau) so much; (gens, livres) so many; **il s'est endormi** ~ **il était fatigué** he was so tired (that) he fell asleep; **pas** ~ not (all) that much; not (all) that +adjectif

téméraire [temerɛr] adj reckless, rash; **témérité** nf recklessness, rashness

témoignage [temwaɲaʒ] nm (JUR: déclaration) testimony no pl, evidence no pl; (: faits) evidence no pl; (rapport, récit) account; (fig: d'affection etc) token, mark; expression

témoigner [temwaɲe] vt (intérêt, gratitude) to show ♦ vi (JUR) to testify, give evidence; ~ **de** to bear witness to, testify to

témoin [temwɛ̃] nm witness; (fig) testimony ♦ adj control cpd; **appartement** ~ show flat (BRIT); **être** ~ **de** to witness; ~ **oculaire** eyewitness

tempe [tɑ̃p] nf temple

tempérament [tɑ̃peramɑ̃] nm temperament, disposition; **à** ~ (vente) on deferred (payment) terms; (achat) by instalments, hire purchase cpd

température [tɑ̃peratyr] nf temperature; **avoir** ou **faire de la** ~ to be running ou have a temperature

tempéré, e [tɑ̃pere] adj temperate

tempête [tɑ̃pɛt] nf storm; ~ **de sable/neige** sand/snowstorm

temple [tɑ̃pl(ə)] nm temple; (protestant) church

temporaire [tɑ̃pɔrɛr] adj temporary

temps [tɑ̃] nm (atmosphérique) weather; (durée) time; (époque) time, times pl; (LING) tense; (MUS)

beat; (TECH) stroke; **il fait beau/mauvais** ~ the weather is fine/bad; **avoir le** ~**/tout le** ~ to have time/plenty of time; **en** ~ **de paix/guerre** in peacetime/wartime; **en** ~ **utile** ou **voulu** in due time ou course; **de** ~ **en** ~, **de** ~ **à autre** from time to time; **à** ~ (partir, arriver) in time; **à** ~ **partiel** part-time; **dans le** ~ at one time; **de tout** ~ always; ~ **d'arrêt** pause, halt; ~ **mort** (COMM) slack period

tenable [tənabl(ə)] adj bearable

tenace [tənas] adj tenacious, persistent

tenailler [tənaje] vt (fig) to torment

tenailles [tənaj] nfpl pincers

tenais etc vb voir **tenir**

tenancier, ière [tənɑ̃sje, -jɛr] nm/f manager/manageress

tenant, e [tənɑ̃, -ɑ̃t] nm/f (SPORT): ~ **du titre** title-holder

tendance [tɑ̃dɑ̃s] nf (opinions) leanings pl, sympathies pl; (inclination) tendency; (évolution) trend; **avoir** ~ **à** to have a tendency to, tend to

tendeur [tɑ̃dœr] nm (attache) elastic strap

tendre [tɑ̃dr(ə)] adj tender; (bois, roche, couleur) soft ♦ vt (élastique, peau) to stretch, draw tight; (muscle) to tense; (donner): ~ **qch à qn** to hold sth out to sb; to offer sb sth; (fig: piège) to set, lay; **se** ~ vi (corde) to tighten; (relations) to become strained; ~ **à qch/à faire** to tend towards sth/to do; ~ **l'oreille** to prick up one's ears; ~ **la main/le bras** to hold out one's hand/stretch out one's arm; **tendrement** adv tenderly; **tendresse** nf tenderness

tendu, e [tɑ̃dy] pp de **tendre** ♦ adj tight; tensed; strained

ténèbres [tenɛbr(ə)] nfpl darkness sg

teneur [tənœr] nf content; (d'une lettre) terms pl, content

tenir [tənir] vt to hold; (magasin, hôtel) to run; (promesse) to keep ♦ vi to hold; (neige, gel) to last; se ~

vi (avoir lieu) to be held, take place; *(être: personne)* to stand; se ~ **droit** to stand (*ou* sit) up straight; **bien se** ~ to behave well; se ~ à **qch** to hold on to sth; **s'en** ~ à **qch** to confine o.s. to sth; to stick to sth; ~ à to be attached to; to care about; to depend on; to stem from; ~ à **faire** to want to do; ~ **de** to partake of; to take after; **ça ne tient qu'à lui** it is entirely up to him; ~ **qn pour** to take sb for; ~ **qch de qn** (*histoire*) to have heard *ou* learnt sth from sb; *(qualité, défaut)* to have inherited *ou* got sth from sb; ~ **les comptes** to keep the books; ~ **le coup** to hold out; ~ **au chaud** to keep hot; **tiens/tenez, voilà le stylo** there's the pen!; **tiens, Alain!** look, here's Alain!; **tiens?** (*surprise*) really?

tennis [tenis] *nm* tennis; *(court)* **tennis court** ♦ *nm ou f pl (aussi:* **chaussures de** ~*)* tennis *ou* gym shoes; ~ **de table** table tennis; **tennisman** *nm* tennis player

tension [tɑ̃sjɔ̃] *nf* tension; *(fig)* tension; strain; *(MED)* blood pressure; **faire** *ou* **avoir de la** ~ to have high blood pressure

tentation [tɑ̃tasjɔ̃] *nf* temptation

tentative [tɑ̃tativ] *nf* attempt, bid

tente [tɑ̃t] *nf* tent

tenter [tɑ̃te] *vt (éprouver, attirer)* to tempt; *(essayer)* ~ **qch/de faire** to attempt *ou* try to do; ~ **sa chance** to try one's luck

tenture [tɑ̃tyr] *nf* hanging

tenu, e [təny] *pp de* **tenir** ♦ *adj (maison, comptes)* **bien** ~ well-kept; *(obligé)* ~ **de faire** under an obligation to do *(action de tenir)* running; keeping; holding; *(vêtements)* clothes *pl*, gear; *(allure)* dress *nm pl*, appearance; *(comportement)* manners *pl*, behaviour; **en petite tenue** scantily dressed *ou* clad; ~ **de route** *(AUTO)* road-holding; ~ **e de soi-rée** evening dress

ter [tɛr] *adj*: **16** ~ 16b *ou* B

térébenthine [terebɑ̃tin] *nf*: *(es-*

sence de) ~ (oil of) turpentine

terme [tɛrm(ə)] *nm* term; *(fin)* end; **à court/long** ~ short-/long-term; ~ **-range** ♦ *adv* in the short/long term; **avant** ~ *(MED)* prematurely; **mettre un** ~ à to put an end *ou* a stop to

terminaison [tɛrminɛzɔ̃] *nf (LING)* ending

terminal, e, aux [tɛrminal, -o] *adj* final ♦ *nm* terminal; **terminale** *nf (SCOL)* ≈ sixth form *ou* year *(BRIT)*, ≈ twelfth grade *(US)*

terminer [tɛrmine] *vt* to end; *(travail, repas)* to finish; **se** ~ *vi* to end

terne [tɛrn(ə)] *adj* dull

ternir [tɛrnir] *vt* to dull; *(fig)* to sully, tarnish; **se** ~ *vi* to become dull

terrain [tɛrɛ̃] *nm (sol, fig)* ground; *(COMM)* land *no pl*, plot (of land); site; **sur le** ~ *(fig)* on the field; ~ **d'aviation** airfield; ~ **de camping** campsite; ~ **de football/rugby** football/rugby pitch *(BRIT)* ou field *(US)*; ~ **de golf** golf course; ~ **de jeu** games field; playground; ~ **de sport** sports ground; ~ **vague** waste ground *no pl*

terrasse [tɛras] *nf* terrace; **à la** ~ *(café)* outside; ~ **ment** [tɛrasmɑ̃] *nm* earth-moving, earthworks *pl*; embankment; ~ **r** [tɛrase] *vt (adversaire)* to floor; *(suj: maladie etc)* to lay low

terre [tɛr] *nf (gén, aussi* ÉLEC*)* earth; *(substance)* soil, earth; *(opposé à mer)* land *no pl*; *(contrée)* land; ~ **s** *nfpl (terrains)* lands, land *sg*; **en** ~ *(pipe, poterie)* clay *cpd*; **à** ~ *ou* **par** ~ *(mettre, être)* on the ground *(ou* floor*)*; *(jeter, tomber)* to the ground, down; ~ **à** ~ *adj inv* down-to-earth; ~ **cuite** earthenware; terracotta; **la** ~ **ferme** dry land; ~ **glaise** clay

terreau [tɛro] *nm* compost

terre-plein [tɛrplɛ̃] *nm* platform

terrer [tɛre]: **se** ~ *vi* to hide away; to go to ground

terrestre [tɛrɛstr(ə)] *adj (surface)*

earth's, of the earth; *(BOT, ZOOL, MIL)* land *cpd*; *(REL)* earthly, worldly

terreur [tɛʀœʀ] *nf* terror no *pl*

terrible [tɛʀibl(ə)] *adj* terrible, dreadful; *(fam)* terrific

terrien, ne [tɛʀjɛ̃, -jɛn] *adj*: propriétaire ~ landowner ♦ *nm/f (non martien etc)* earthling

terrier [tɛʀje] *nm* burrow, hole; *(chien)* terrier

terril [tɛʀil] *nm* slag heap

terrine [tɛʀin] *nf (récipient)* terrine; *(CULIN)* pâté

territoire [tɛʀitwaʀ] *nm* territory

terroir [tɛʀwaʀ] *nm (AGR)* soil; region

terrorisme [tɛʀɔʀism(ə)] *nm* terrorism; **terroriste** *nm/f* terrorist

tertiaire [tɛʀsjɛʀ] *adj* tertiary ♦ *nm (ECON)* service industries *pl*

tertre [tɛʀtʀ(ə)] *nm* hillock, mound

tes [te] *dét voir* **ton**[1]

tesson [tesɔ̃] *nm*: ~ de bouteille piece of broken bottle

test [tɛst] *nm* test

testament [tɛstamɑ̃] *nm (JUR)* will; *(REL)* Testament; *(fig)* legacy

tester [tɛste] *vt* to test

testicule [tɛstikyl] *nm* testicle

tétanos [tetanos] *nm* tetanus

têtard [tɛtaʀ] *nm* tadpole

tête [tɛt] *nf* head; *(cheveux)* hair no *pl*; *(visage)* face; de ~ *(wagon etc)* front *cpd* ♦ *adv (calculer)* in one's head, mentally; **tenir** ~ à qn to stand up to sb; la ~ en bas with one's head down; la ~ la première *(tomber)* headfirst; **faire une** ~ *(FOOTBALL)* to head the ball; **faire la** ~ *(fig)* to sulk; **en** ~ *(SPORT)* in the lead; at the front; **de** ~ à ~ in private, alone together; **de la** ~ **aux pieds** from head to toe; ~ **de lecture** *(playback)* head; ~ **de liste** *(POL)* chief candidate; ~ **de série** *(TENNIS)* seeded player, seed

tête-à-queue [tɛtakø] *nm inv*: **faire un** ~ to spin round

téter [tete] *vt*: ~ **(sa mère)** to suck

at one's mother's breast, feed

tétine [tetin] *nf* teat; *(sucette)* dummy *(BRIT)*; pacifier *(US)*

têtu, e [tety] *adj* stubborn, pigheaded

texte [tɛkst(ə)] *nm* text

textile [tɛkstil] *adj* textile *cpd* ♦ *nm* textile; textile industry

texture [tɛkstyʀ] *nf* texture

TGV *sigle m (= train à grande vitesse)* high-speed train

thé [te] *nm* tea; **prendre le** ~ to have tea; **faire le** ~ to make the tea

théâtral, e, aux [teɑtʀal, -o] *adj* theatrical

théâtre [teɑtʀ(ə)] *nm* theatre; *(œuvres)* plays *pl*, dramatic works *pl*; *(fig:* lieu): **le** ~ **de** the scene of; *(péj)* histrionics *pl*, playacting; **faire du** ~ to be on the stage; to do some acting

théière [tejɛʀ] *nf* teapot

thème [tɛm] *nm* theme; *(SCOL: traduction)* prose (composition)

théologie [teɔlɔʒi] *nf* theology

théorie [teɔʀi] *nf* theory; **théorique** *adj* theoretical

thérapie [teʀapi] *nf* therapy

thermal, e, aux [tɛʀmal, -o] *adj*: **station** ~**e** spa; **cure** ~**e** water cure

thermes [tɛʀm(ə)] *nmpl* thermal baths

thermomètre [tɛʀmɔmɛtʀ(ə)] *nm* thermometer

thermos [tɛʀmos] ® *nm ou nf*: *(bouteille)* ~ vacuum *ou* Thermos ® flask

thermostat [tɛʀmɔsta] *nm* thermostat

thèse [tɛz] *nf* thesis

thon [tɔ̃] *nm* tuna (fish)

thym [tɛ̃] *nm* thyme

tibia [tibja] *nm* shinbone, tibia; shin

tic [tik] *nm* tic, *(nervous)* twitch; *(de langage etc)* mannerism

ticket [tikɛ] *nm* ticket; ~ **de caisse** *nm* receipt; ~ **de quai** platform ticket

tiède [tjɛd] *adj* lukewarm; tepid; *(vent, air)* mild, warm; **tiédir** *vi* to cool; to grow warmer

tien, ne [tjɛ̃, tjɛn] *pron*: le(la) ~(ne), les ~(ne)s yours; à la ~ne! cheers!

tiens [tjɛ̃] *vb, excl voir* tenir

tierce [tjɛʀs(ə)] *adj voir* tiers

tiercé [tjɛʀse] *nm system of forecast betting giving first 3 horses*

tiers, tierce [tjɛʀ, tjɛʀs(ə)] *adj* third ♦ *nm* (JUR) third party; (*fraction*) third; le ~ monde the Third World

tige [tiʒ] *nf* stem; (*baguette*) rod

tignasse [tiɲas] (*péj*) *nf* mop of hair

tigre [tigʀ(ə)] *nm* tiger

tigré, e [tigʀe] *adj* striped; spotted

tilleul [tijœl] *nm* lime tree(, linden (tree)); (*boisson*) lime-blossom tea

timbale [tɛ̃bal] *nf* (*metal*) tumbler; ~s *nfpl* (MUS) timpani, kettledrums

timbre [tɛ̃bʀ(ə)] *nm* (*tampon*) stamp; (*aussi*: ~poste) (postage) stamp; (MUS: de voix, instrument) timbre, tone

timbré, e [tɛ̃bʀe] (*fam*) *adj* daft

timide [timid] *adj* shy; timid; (*timoré*) timid, timorous; **timidement** *adv* shyly; timidly; **timidité** *nf* shyness; timidity

tins *etc vb voir* tenir

tintamarre [tɛ̃tamaʀ] *nm* din, uproar

tinter [tɛ̃te] *vi* to ring, chime; (*argent, clefs*) to jingle

tir [tiʀ] *nm* (*sport*) shooting; (*fait ou manière de tirer*) firing *no pl*; (*stand*) shooting gallery; ~ à l'arc archery; ~ au pigeon clay pigeon shooting

tirage [tiʀaʒ] *nm* (*action*) printing; (PHOTO) print; (*de journal*) circulation; (*de livre*) (print-)run; edition; (*de loterie*) draw; ~ au sort drawing lots

tirailler [tiʀaje] *vt* to pull at, tug at ♦ *vi* to fire at random

tirant [tiʀã] *nm*: ~ d'eau draught

tire [tiʀ] *nf*: vol à la ~ pickpocketing

tiré, e [tiʀe] *adj* (*traits*) drawn ♦ *nm* (COMM) drawee; ~ par les cheveux far-fetched

tire-au-flanc [tiʀoflã] (*péj*) *nm inv* skiver

tire-bouchon [tiʀbuʃɔ̃] *nm* corkscrew

tirelire [tiʀliʀ] *nf* moneybox

tirer [tiʀe] *vt* (*gén*) to pull; (*extraire*): ~ qch de to take *ou* pull sth out of; to get sth out of; to extract sth from; (*tracer*: ligne, trait) to draw, trace; (*fermer*: rideau) to draw, close; (*choisir*: carte, conclusion, aussi COMM: chèque*) to draw; (*en faisant feu*: balle, coup) to fire; (: *animal*) to shoot; (*journal, livre, photo*) to print; (FOOTBALL: corner etc) to take ♦ *vi* (*faire feu*) to fire; (*faire du tir*, FOOTBALL) to shoot; (*cheminée*) to draw; **se ~** *vi* (*fam*) to push off; **s'en ~** to pull through, get off; ~ **sur** to pull on *ou* at, to shoot *ou* fire at; (*pipe*) to draw on; (*fig: avoisiner*) to verge on *ou* border on; ~ **qn de** (*embarras etc*) to help *ou* get sb out of; ~ **à l'arc/la carabine** to shoot with a bow and arrow/ with a rifle

tiret [tiʀɛ] *nm* dash

tireur, euse [tiʀœʀ, -øz] *nm/f* (COMM) drawer ♦ *nm* gunman; ~ **d'élite** marksman

tiroir [tiʀwaʀ] *nm* drawer; **tiroir-caisse** *nm* till

tisane [tizan] *nf* herb tea

tisonnier [tizɔnje] *nm* poker

tisser [tise] *vt* to weave; **tisserand** *nm* weaver

tissu [tisy] *nm* fabric, material, cloth *no pl*; (ANAT, BIO) tissue

tissu-éponge [tisyepɔ̃ʒ] *nm* (terry) towelling *no pl*

titre [titʀ(ə)] *nm* (*gén*) title; (*de journal*) headline; (*diplôme*) qualification; (COMM) security; **en ~** (*champion*) official; à juste ~ with just cause, rightly; à quel ~? on what grounds?; à aucun ~ on no account; au même ~ (que) in the same way (as); à ~ **d'information** for your information; à ~ **gracieux** free of charge; à ~ **d'essai** on a trial basis; à ~ **privé** in a private capacity; ~ **de propriété** title deed; ~ **de trans-**

port ticket

tituber [titybe] *vi* to stagger (along)

titulaire [tityleʀ] *adj* (*ADMIN*) appointed, with tenure ♦ *nm/f* incumbent; **être ~ de** (*poste*) to hold; (*permis*) to be the holder of

toast [tost] *nm* slice *ou* piece of toast; (*de bienvenue*) (welcoming) toast; **porter un ~ à qn** to propose *ou* drink a toast to sb

toboggan [tɔbɔgɑ̃] *nm* toboggan; (*jeu*) slide

tocsin [tɔksɛ̃] *nm* alarm (bell)

toge [tɔʒ] *nf* toga; (*de juge*) gown

toi [twa] *pron you*

toile [twal] *nf* (*matériau*) cloth *no pl*; (*bâche*) piece of canvas; (*tableau*) canvas; **~ cirée** oilcloth; **~ d'araignée** cobweb; **~ de fond** (*fig*) backdrop

toilette [twalɛt] *nf* wash; (*habits*) outfit; dress *no pl*; **~s** *nfpl* (*w.-c.*) toilet *sg*; **faire sa ~** to have a wash, get washed; **articles de ~** toiletries

toi-même [twamɛm] *pron yourself*

toiser [twaze] *vt* to eye up and down

toison [twazɔ̃] *nf* (*de mouton*) fleece; (*cheveux*) mane

toit [twa] *nm* roof; **~ ouvrant** sunroof

toiture [twatyʀ] *nf* roof

tôle [tol] *nf* (*plaque*) steel *ou* iron sheet; **~ ondulée** corrugated iron

tolérable [tɔleʀabl(ə)] *adj* tolerable, bearable

tolérant, e [tɔleʀɑ̃, -ɑ̃t] *adj* tolerant

tolérer [tɔleʀe] *vt* to tolerate; (*ADMIN: hors taxe etc*) to allow

tollé [tɔle] *nm* outcry

tomate [tɔmat] *nf* tomato

tombe [tɔ̃b] *nf* (*sépulture*) grave; (*avec monument*) tomb

tombeau, x [tɔ̃bo] *nm* tomb

tombée [tɔ̃be] *nf*: **à la ~ de la nuit** at the close of day, at nightfall

tomber [tɔ̃be] *vi* to fall; **laisser ~** to drop; **~ sur** (*rencontrer*) to come across; (*attaquer*) to set about; **~ de fatigue/sommeil** to drop from exhaustion/be falling asleep on one's feet; **ça tombe bien** that's come at the right time; **il est bien tombé** he's been lucky

tome [tɔm] *nm* volume

ton¹, ta [tɔ̃, ta] (*pl tes*) *dét your*

ton² [tɔ̃] *nm* (*gén*) tone; (*MUS*) key; (*couleur*) shade, tone; **de bon ton** in good taste

tonalité [tɔnalite] *nf* (*au téléphone*) dialling tone; (*MUS*) key; (*fig*) tone

tondeuse [tɔ̃døz] *nf* (*à gazon*) (lawn)mower; (*du coiffeur*) clippers *pl*; (*pour la tonte*) shears *pl*

tondre [tɔ̃dʀ(ə)] *vt* (*pelouse, herbe*) to mow; (*haie*) to cut, clip; (*mouton, toison*) to shear; (*cheveux*) to crop

tonifier [tɔnifje] *vt* (*peau, organisme*) to tone up

tonique [tɔnik] *adj* fortifying ♦ *nm* tonic

tonne [tɔn] *nf* metric ton, tonne

tonneau, x [tɔno] *nm* (*à vin, cidre*) barrel; (*NAVIG*) ton; **faire des ~x** (*voiture, avion*) to roll over

tonnelle [tɔnɛl] *nf* bower, arbour

tonner [tɔne] *vi* to thunder; **il tonne** it is thundering, there's some thunder

tonnerre [tɔnɛʀ] *nm* thunder

tonus [tɔnys] *nm* dynamism

top [tɔp] *nm*: **au 3ème ~** at the 3rd stroke

topinambour [tɔpinɑ̃buʀ] *nm* Jerusalem artichoke

toque [tɔk] *nf* (*de fourrure*) fur hat; **~ de cuisinier** chef's hat; **~ de jockey/juge** jockey's/judge's cap

toqué, e [tɔke] *adj* (*fam*) cracked

torche [tɔʀʃ(ə)] *nf* torch

torchon [tɔʀʃɔ̃] *nm* cloth, duster; (*à vaisselle*) tea towel *ou* cloth

tordre [tɔʀdʀ(ə)] *vt* (*chiffon*) to wring; (*barre, fig: visage*) to twist; **se ~** *vi* (*barre*) to bend; (*roue*) to twist, buckle; (*ver, serpent*) to writhe; **se ~ le pied/bras** to twist one's foot/arm; **tordu, e** [tɔʀdy] *adj* (*fig*) warped, twisted

tornade [tɔʀnad] *nf* tornado

torpille [tɔʀpij] *nf* torpedo

torréfier [tɔʀefje] *vt* to roast

torrent [tɔʀɑ̃] nm torrent

torse [tɔʀs(ə)] nm (ANAT) torso; chest

torsion [tɔʀsjɔ̃] nf twisting; torsion

tort [tɔʀ] nm (défaut) fault; (préjudice) wrong no pl; ~s nmpl (JUR) fault sg; **avoir** ~ to be wrong; **être dans son** ~ to be in the wrong; **donner** ~ **à qn** to lay the blame on sb; (fig) to prove sb wrong; **causer du** ~ **à** to harm; to be harmful ou detrimental to; **à** ~ wrongly; **à** ~ **et à travers** wildly

torticolis [tɔʀtikɔli] nm stiff neck

tortiller [tɔʀtije] vt to twist; to twiddle; **se** ~ vi to wriggle, squirm

tortionnaire [tɔʀsjɔnɛʀ] nm torturer

tortue [tɔʀty] nf tortoise

tortueux, euse [tɔʀtɥø, -øz] adj (rue) twisting; (fig) tortuous

torture [tɔʀtyʀ] nf torture; **torturer** vt to torture; (fig) to torment

tôt [to] adv early; ~ **ou tard** sooner or later; **si** ~ so early; (déjà) so soon; **au plus** ~ at the earliest; **il eut** ~ **fait de faire** he soon did

total, e, aux [tɔtal, -o] adj total; **au** ~ in total ou all; **faire le** ~ to work out the total, add up; **totalement** adv totally, completely; **totaliser** vt to total (up)

totalité [tɔtalite] nf: **la** ~ **de** all of, the total amount (ou number) of; **the whole** +sg; **en** ~ entirely

toubib [tubib] (fam) nm doctor

touchant, e [tuʃɑ̃, -ɑ̃t] adj touching

touche [tuʃ] nf (de piano, de machine à écrire) key; (PEINTURE etc) stroke, touch; (fig: de nostalgie) touch, hint; (FOOTBALL: aussi: remise en ~) throw-in; (aussi: ligne de ~) touch-line

toucher [tuʃe] nm touch ♦ vt to touch; (palper) to feel; (atteindre: d'un coup de feu etc) to hit; (concerner) to concern, affect; (contacter) to reach, contact; (recevoir: récompense) to receive, get; (: salaire) to draw, get; (: chèque) to cash; **se** ~ (être en contact) to touch; **au** ~ to

the touch; ~ **à** to touch; (concerner) to have to do with, concern; **je vais lui en** ~ **un mot** I'll have a word with him about it; ~ **à sa fin** to be drawing to a close

touffe [tuf] nf tuft

touffu, e [tufy] adj thick, dense

toujours [tuʒuʀ] adv always; (encore) still; (constamment) forever; ~ **plus** more and more; **pour** ~ forever; ~ **est-il que** the fact remains that; **essaie** ~ (you can) try anyway

toupet [tupɛ] (fam) nm cheek

toupie [tupi] nf (spinning) top

tour [tuʀ] nf tower; (immeuble) high-rise block (BRIT) ou building (US); (ÉCHECS) castle, rook ♦ nm (excursion) stroll, walk; run, ride; trip; (SPORT: aussi: ~ **de piste**) lap; (: être servi ou de jouer etc) turn; (de roue etc) revolution; (circonférence): **de 3 m de** ~ 3 m round, with a circumference ou girth of 3 m; (POL: aussi: ~ **de scrutin**) ballot; (ruse, de prestidigitation) trick; (de potier) wheel; (à bois, métaux) lathe; **faire le** ~ **de** to go round; (à pied) to walk round; **c'est au** ~ **de Renée** it's Renée's turn; **à** ~ **de rôle**, **à** ~ **de rôle** in turn; **de chant** song recital; ~ **de contrôle** nf control tower; ~ **de garde** spell of duty; ~ **d'horizon** general survey; ~ **de taille/tête** waist/head measurement

tourbe [tuʀb(ə)] nf peat

tourbillon [tuʀbijɔ̃] nm whirlwind; (d'eau) whirlpool; (fig) whirl, swirl; **tourbillonner** vi to whirl (round)

tourelle [tuʀɛl] nf turret

tourisme [tuʀism(ə)] nm tourism; **agence de** ~ tourist agency; **faire du** ~ to go sightseeing; to go touring; **touriste** nm/f tourist; **touristique** adj tourist cpd; (région) touristic

tourment [tuʀmɑ̃] nm torment; **tourmenter** vt to torment; **se** ~ vi to fret, worry o.s.

tournant [tuʀnɑ̃] nm (de route)

bend; (*fig*) turning point

tournebroche [turnəbrɔʃ] *nm* roasting spit

tourne-disque [turnədisk(ə)] *nm* record player

tournée *nf* (*du facteur etc*) round; (*d'artiste, politicien*) tour; (*au café*) round of drinks

tournemain [turnəmɛ̃] : **en un ~** *adv* quick as a flash

tourner [turne] *vt* to turn; (*sauce, mélange*) to stir; (*contourner*) to get round; (*CINEMA*) to shoot; to make ♦ *vi* to turn; (*moteur*) to run; (*compteur*) to tick away; (*lait etc*) to turn (sour); **se ~** *vi* to turn round; **se ~ vers** to turn to; to turn towards; **bien ~** to turn out well; **~ autour de** to go round; (*péj*) to hang round; **~ à/en** to turn into; **~ le dos à** to turn one's back to; to have one's back to; **~ de l'œil** to pass out

tournesol [turnəsɔl] *nm* sunflower

tournevis [turnəvis] *nm* screwdriver

tourniquet [turnikɛ] *nm* (*pour arroser*) sprinkler; (*portillon*) turnstile; (*présentoir*) revolving stand, spinner

tournoi [turnwa] *nm* tournament

tournoyer [turnwaje] *vi* to whirl round; to swirl round

tournure [turnyr] *nf* (*LING*) turn of phrase; form; phrasing; (*évolution*): **la ~ de qch** the way sth is developing; (*aspect*): **la ~ de** the look of; **d'esprit** turn ou cast of mind; **la ~ des événements** the turn of events

tourte [turt(ə)] *nf* pie

tous [*adj* tu, *pron* tus] *adj, pron voir* **tout**

Toussaint [tusɛ̃] *nf*: **la ~** All Saints' Day

tousser [tuse] *vi* to cough

MOT-CLÉ

---

tout, e [tu, tut] (*mpl* tous, *fpl* toutes) *adj* 1 (*avec article singulier*) all; **~ le lait** all the milk; **~ la nuit** all night, the whole night; **~ le livre** the whole book; **~ un pain** a whole loaf; **~ le temps** all the time;

the whole time; **c'est ~ le contraire** it's quite the opposite

2 (*avec article pluriel*) every; all; **tous les livres** all the books; **~es les nuits** every night; **~es les fois** every time; **~es les trois/deux semaines** every third/two weeks; **~es les deux both** ou **each of us** (*ou* them *ou* you); **~es les trois** all three of us (*ou* them *ou* you)

3 (*sans article*): **à ~ âge** at any age; **pour ~e nourriture, il avait ...** his only food was ...

♦ *pron* everything, all; **il a ~ fait** he's done everything; **je les vois tous** I can see them all *ou* all of them; **nous y sommes tous allés** all of us went, we all went; **en ~** in all; **~ ce qu'il sait** all he knows

♦ *nm* whole; **le ~ de ...** all of it (*ou* them); **le ~ est de ...** the main thing is to ...; **pas du ~** not at all

♦ *adv* 1 (*très, complètement*) very; **~ près** very near; **le ~ premier** the very first; **~ seul** all alone; **le livre ~ entier** the whole book; **en ~ haut** right at the top; **~ droit** straight ahead

2: **~ en while**; **~ en travaillant** while working, as he *etc* works

3 **~ d'abord** first of all; **~ à coup** suddenly; **~ à fait** absolutely; **~ à l'heure** a short while ago; (*futur*) in a short while, shortly; **à ~ à l'heure!** see you later!; **~ de même** all the same; **~ le monde** everybody; **~ de suite** immediately, straight away; **~ terrain** ou **tous terrains** all-terrain

---

toutefois [tutfwa] *adv* however

toutes [tut] *adj, pron voir* **tout**

toux [tu] *nf* cough

toxicomane [tɔksikɔman] *nm/f* drug addict

trac [trak] *nm* nerves *pl*

tracasser [trakase] *vt* to worry, bother; to harass; **tracasseries** [trakasri] *nfpl* (*chicanes*) annoyances

trace [tʀas] *nf* (*empreintes*) tracks *pl*; (*marques*, *aussi fig*) mark; (*restes, vestige*) trace; (*indice*) sign; ~s de pas footprints

tracé [tʀase] *nm* line; layout

tracer [tʀase] *vt* to draw; (*mot*) to trace; (*piste*) to open up

tract [tʀakt] *nm* tract, pamphlet

tractations [tʀaktɑsjɔ̃] *nfpl* dealings, bargaining *sg*

tracteur [tʀaktœʀ] *nm* tractor

traction [tʀaksjɔ̃] *nf* ~ avant/arrière front-wheel/rear-wheel drive

tradition [tʀadisjɔ̃] *nf* tradition; **traditionnel, le** *adj* traditional

traducteur, trice [tʀadyktœʀ, -tʀis] *nm/f* translator

traduction [tʀadyksjɔ̃] *nf* translation

traduire [tʀadɥiʀ] *vt* to translate; (*exprimer*) to render, convey

trafic [tʀafik] *nm* traffic; ~ d'armes arms dealing; **trafiquant, e** *nm/f* trafficker; dealer; **trafiquer** (*péj*) *vt* to doctor, tamper with

tragédie [tʀaʒedi] *nf* tragedy

tragique [tʀaʒik] *adj* tragic

trahir [tʀaiʀ] *vt* to betray; (*fig*) to give away, reveal; **trahison** *nf* betrayal; (*JUR*) treason

train [tʀɛ̃] *nm* (*RAIL*) train; (*allure*) pace; (*fig: ensemble*) set; **mettre qch en ~** to get sth under way; **mettre qn en ~** to put sb in good spirits; **se mettre en ~** to get started; to warm up; **se sentir en ~** to feel in good form; ~ d'atterrissage undercarriage; ~ de vie style of living; ~ électrique (*jouet*) (electric) train set; ~autos-couchettes car-sleeper train

traîne [tʀɛn] *nf* (*de robe*) train; être à la ~ to be in tow; to lag behind

traîneau, x [tʀeno] *nm* sleigh, sledge

traînée [tʀene] *nf* streak, trail; (*péj*) slut

traîner [tʀene] *vt* (*remorque*) to pull; (*enfant, chien*) to drag *ou* trail along ♦ *vi* (*être en désordre*) to lie around; (*marcher*) to dawdle (along); (*vaga-*

bonder) to hang about; (*agir lentement*) to idle about; (*durer*) to drag on; **se** ~ *vi* to drag o.s. along; ~ **les pieds** to drag one's footprints

train-train [tʀɛ̃tʀɛ̃] *nm* humdrum routine

traire [tʀɛʀ] *vt* to milk

trait [tʀɛ] *nm* (*ligne*) line; (*de dessin*) stroke; (*caractéristique*) feature, trait; ~s *nmpl* (*du visage*) features; **d'un** ~ (*boire*) in one gulp; **de** ~ (*animal*) draught; **avoir** ~ **à** to concern; ~ **d'union** hyphen; (*fig*) link

traitant, e [tʀetɑ̃, -ɑ̃t] *adj*: **votre médecin** ~ your usual *ou* family doctor; **crème** ~**e** conditioning cream

traite [tʀɛt] *nf* (*COMM*) draft; (*AGR*) milking; **d'une** ~ without stopping; **la** ~ **des noirs** the slave trade

traité [tʀete] *nm* treaty

traitement [tʀetmɑ̃] *nm* treatment; processing; (*salaire*) salary; ~ **de données/texte** data/word processing

traiter [tʀete] *vt* (*gén*) to treat; (*TECH, INFORM*) to process; (*affaire*) to deal with, handle; (*qualifier*): ~ **qn d'idiot** to call sb a fool ♦ *vi* to deal; ~ **de** to deal with

traiteur [tʀetœʀ] *nm* caterer

traître, esse [tʀɛtʀ(ə), -tʀɛs] *adj* (*dangereux*) treacherous ♦ *nm* traitor

trajectoire [tʀaʒɛktwaʀ] *nf* path

trajet [tʀaʒɛ] *nm* journey; (*itinéraire*) route; (*fig*) path, course

trame [tʀam] *nf* (*de tissu*) weft; (*fig*) framework; texture

tramer [tʀame] *vt* to plot, hatch

tramway [tʀamwɛ] *nm* tram(way); tram(car) (*BRIT*); streetcar (*US*)

tranchant, e [tʀɑ̃ʃɑ̃, -ɑ̃t] *adj* sharp; (*fig*) peremptory ♦ *nm* (*d'un couteau*) cutting edge; (*de la main*) edge

tranche [tʀɑ̃ʃ] *nf* (*morceau*) slice; (*arête*) edge; (*partie*) section; (*série*) block; issue; bracket

tranché, e [tʀɑ̃ʃe] *adj* (*couleurs*) distinct, sharply contrasted; (*opi-*

nions) clear-cut, definite; **tranchée** *nf* trench

trancher [tʀɑ̃fe] *vt* to cut, sever; (*fig: résoudre*) to settle ♦ *vi* to take a decision; ~ **avec** to contrast sharply with

tranquille [tʀɑ̃kil] *adj* calm, quiet; (*enfant, élève*) quiet; (*rassuré*) easy in one's mind, with one's mind at rest; **se tenir** ~ (*enfant*) to be quiet; **laisse-moi/laisse-ça** ~ leave me/it alone; **tranquillité** *nf* quietness; peace (and quiet)

transat [tʀɑ̃zat] *nm* deckchair

transborder [tʀɑ̃sbɔʀde] *vt* to tran(s)ship

trans-: ~**férer** *vt* to transfer; ~**fert** *nm* transfer; ~**figurer** *vt* to transform; ~**formation** *nf* transformation; (*RUGBY*) conversion

transformer [tʀɑ̃sfɔʀme] *vt* to transform, alter; (*matière première, appartement, RUGBY*) to convert; ~ **en** to transform into; to turn into; to convert into

transfusion [tʀɑ̃sfyzjɔ̃] *nf*: ~ **sanguine** blood transfusion

transgresser [tʀɑ̃sgʀese] *vt* to contravene, disobey

transi, e [tʀɑ̃zi] *adj* numb (with cold), chilled to the bone

transiger [tʀɑ̃ziʒe] *vi* to compromise

transit [tʀɑ̃zit] *nm* transit; **transiter** *vi* to pass in transit

transitif, ive [tʀɑ̃zitif, -iv] *adj* transitive

transition [tʀɑ̃zisjɔ̃] *nf* transition; **transitoire** *adj* transitional; transient

translucide [tʀɑ̃slysid] *adj* translucent

transmetteur [tʀɑ̃smetœʀ] *nm* transmitter

transmettre [tʀɑ̃smetʀ(ə)] *vt* (*passer*): ~ **qch à qn** to pass sth on to sb; (*TECH, TEL, MED*) to transmit; (*TV, RADIO: re~*) to broadcast

trans-: ~**mission** *nf* transmission; ~**paraître** *vi* to show (through); ~**parence** *nf* transparence; **par** ~ (*regarder*) against the light; (*voir*)

showing through; ~**parent, e** *adj* transparent; ~**percer** *vt* to go through, pierce; ~**piration** *nf* perspiration; ~**pirer** *vi* to perspire; ~**planter** *vt* (*MED, BOT*) to transplant; (*personne*) to uproot; ~**port** *nm* transport; ~**s en commun** public transport *sg*

transporter [tʀɑ̃spɔʀte] *vt* to carry, move; (*COMM*) to transport, convey; **transporteur** *nm* haulage contractor (*BRIT*), trucker (*US*)

transversal, e, aux [tʀɑ̃svɛʀsal, -o] *adj* transverse, cross(-); cross-country; running at right angles

trapèze [tʀapɛz] *nm* (*au cirque*) trapeze

trappe [tʀap] *nf* trap door

trapu, e [tʀapy] *adj* squat, stocky

traquenard [tʀaknaʀ] *nm* trap

traquer [tʀake] *vt* to track down; (*harceler*) to hound

traumatiser [tʀomatize] *vt* to traumatize

travail, aux [tʀavaj, -o] *nm* (*gén*) work; (*tâche, métier*) work *no pl*, job; (*ECON, MED*) labour; **être sans** ~ (*employé*) to be out of work ou unemployed; *voir aussi* **travaux**; ~ (**au**) **noir** moonlighting

travailler [tʀavaje] *vi* to work; (*bois*) to warp ♦ *vt* (*bois, métal*) to work; (*objet d'art, discipline, fig: influencer*) to work on; **cela le travaille** it is on his mind; ~ **à** to work on; (*fig: contribuer à*) to work towards; **travailleur, euse** *adj* hard-working ♦ *nm/f* worker; **travailliste** *adj* ≈ Labour *cpd*

travaux [tʀavo] *nmpl* (*de réparation, agricoles etc*) work *sg*; (*sur route*) roadworks *pl*; (*de construction*) building (work); ~ **des champs** farmwork *sg*; ~ **dirigés** (*SCOL*) supervised practical work *sg*; ~ **forcés** hard labour *sg*; ~ **manuels** (*SCOL*) handicrafts; ~ **ménagers** housework *sg*

travée [tʀave] *nf* row; (*ARCHIT*) bay; span

travers [travɛʀ] nm fault, failing; en ~ (de) across; au ~ (de) through; de ~ askew ♦ adv sideways; (fig) the wrong way; à ~ through; regarder de ~ (fig) to look askance at

traverse [travɛʀs(ə)] nf (de voie ferrée) sleeper; chemin de ~ shortcut

traversée [travɛʀse] nf crossing

traverser [travɛʀse] vt (gén) to cross; (ville, tunnel, aussi: percer, fig) to go through; (suj: ligne, trait) to run across

traversin [travɛʀsɛ̃] nm bolster

travesti [travɛsti] nm transvestite

travestir [travɛstiʀ] vt (vérité) to misrepresent; se ~ vi to dress up; to dress as a woman

trébucher [trebyʃe] vi: ~ (sur) to stumble (over), trip (against)

trèfle [trɛfl(ə)] nm (BOT) clover; (CARTES: couleur) clubs pl; (: carte) club

treille [trɛj] nf vine arbour; climbing vine

treillis [trɛji] nm (métallique) wire-mesh

treize [trɛz] num thirteen; **treizième** num thirteenth

tréma [trema] nm diaeresis

tremblement [trɑ̃bləmɑ̃] nm: ~ de terre earthquake

trembler [trɑ̃ble] vi to tremble, shake; ~ de (froid, fièvre) to shiver ou tremble with; (peur) to shake ou tremble with; ~ pour qn to fear for sb

trémousser [tremuse]: se ~ vi to jig about, wriggle about

trempe [trɑ̃p] nf (fig): de cette/sa ~ of this/his calibre

trempé, e [trɑ̃pe] adj soaking (wet), drenched; (TECH) tempered

tremper [trɑ̃pe] vt to soak, drench; (aussi: faire ~, mettre à ~) to soak (plonger); ~ qch dans to dip sth into(n) ♦ vi to soak; (fig): ~ dans to be involved ou have a hand in; se ~ vi to have a quick dip; **trempette** nf: faire trempette to go paddling

tremplin [trɑ̃plɛ̃] nm springboard; (SKI) ski-jump

trentaine [trɑ̃tɛn] nf: une ~ (de) thirty or so, about thirty; avoir la ~ (âge) to be around thirty

trente [trɑ̃t] num thirty; **trentième** num thirtieth

trépidant, e [trepidɑ̃, -ɑ̃t] adj (fig: rythme) pulsating; (: vie) hectic

trépied [trepje] nm tripod

trépigner [trepiɲe] vi to stamp (one's feet)

très [trɛ] adv very; much +pp, highly +pp

trésor [trezɔʀ] nm treasure; (ADMIN) finances pl; funds pl; T~ (public) public revenue

trésorerie [trezɔʀʀi] nf (gestion) accounts pl; (bureaux) accounts department; **difficultés de** ~ cash problems, shortage of cash ou funds

trésorier, ière [trezɔʀje, -jɛʀ] nm/f treasurer

tressaillir [tresajiʀ] vi to shiver, shudder; to quiver

tressauter [tresote] vi to start, jump

tresse [trɛs] nf braid, plait

tresser [trese] vt (cheveux) to braid, plait; (fil, jonc) to plait; (corbeille) to weave; (corde) to twist

tréteau, x [treto] nm trestle

treuil [trœj] nm winch

trêve [trɛv] nf (MIL, POL) truce; (fig) respite; ~ de ... enough of this ...

tri [tri] nm sorting out no pl; selection; (POSTES) sorting; sorting office

triangle [trijɑ̃gl(ə)] nm triangle

tribord [tribɔʀ] nm: à ~ to starboard, on the starboard side

tribu [triby] nf tribe

tribunal, aux [tribynal, -o] nm (JUR) court; (MIL) tribunal

tribune [tribyn] nf (estrade) platform, rostrum; (débat) forum; (d'église, de tribunal) gallery; (de stade) stand

tribut [triby] nm tribute

tributaire [tribytɛʀ] adj: être ~ de to be dependent on

tricher [triʃe] vi to cheat

tricolore [trikɔlɔr] *adj* three-coloured; (*français*) red, white and blue

tricot [triko] *nm* (*technique, ouvrage*) knitting *no pl*; (*tissu*) knitted fabric; (*vêtement*) jersey, sweater

tricoter [trikɔte] *vt* to knit

trictrac [triktrak] *nm* backgammon

tricycle [trisikl(ə)] *nm* tricycle

triennal, e, aux [trijɛnal, -o] *adj* three-yearly; three-year

trier [trije] *vt* to sort out; (*POSTES, fruits*) to sort

trimestre [trimɛstr(ə)] *nm* (*SCOL*) term; (*COMM*) quarter; **trimestriel, le** *adj* quarterly; (*SCOL*) end-of-term

tringle [trɛ̃gl(ə)] *nf* rod

trinquer [trɛ̃ke] *vi* to clink glasses

triomphe [trijɔ̃f] *nm* triumph

triompher [trijɔ̃fe] *vi* to triumph, win; ~ **de** to triumph over, overcome

tripes [trip] *nfpl* (*CULIN*) tripe *sg*

triple [tripl(ə)] *adj* triple; treble ♦ *nm*: **le** ~ **(de)** (*comparaison*) three times as much (as); **en** ~ **exemplaire** in triplicate; **triplé** *vt, vi* to triple, treble

triplés, ées [triple] *nm/fpl* triplets

tripoter [tripɔte] *vt* to fiddle with

trique [trik] *nf* cudgel

triste [trist(ə)] *adj* sad; (*péj*): ~ **personnage/affaire** sorry individual/affair; **tristesse** *nf* sadness

trivial, e, aux [trivjal, -o] *adj* coarse, crude; (*commun*) mundane

troc [trɔk] *nm* barter

trognon [trɔɲɔ̃] *nm* (*de fruit*) core; (*de légume*) stalk

trois [trwa] *num* three; **troisième** *num* third; **trois-quarts** *nmpl*: **les trois-quarts de** three-quarters of

trombe [trɔ̃b] *nf*: **des ~s d'eau** a downpour; **en** ~ **like a whirlwind

trombone [trɔ̃bɔn] *nm* (*MUS*) trombone; (*de bureau*) paper clip

trompe [trɔ̃p] *nf* (*d'éléphant*) trunk; (*MUS*) trumpet, horn

tromper [trɔ̃pe] *vt* to deceive; (*vigilance, poursuivants*) to elude; **se** ~

vi to make a mistake, be mistaken; **se** ~ **de voiture/jour** to take the wrong car/get the day wrong; **se** ~ **de 3 cm/20 F** to be out by 3 cm/20 F; ~**ie** *nf* deception, trickery *no pl*

trompette [trɔ̃pɛt] *nf* trumpet; **en** ~ (*nez*) turned-up

tronc [trɔ̃] *nm* (*BOT, ANAT*) trunk; (*d'église*) collection box

tronçon [trɔ̃sɔ̃] *nm* section

tronçonner [trɔ̃sɔne] *vt* to saw up

trône [tron] *nm* throne

trop [tro] *adv* (+*vb*) too much; (+*adjectif, adverbe*) too; ~ (*nombreux*) too many; ~ **peu** (*nombreux*) too few; ~ (*souvent*) too often; ~ (*longtemps*) (for) too long; ~ **de** (*nombre*) too many; (*quantité*) too much; **de** ~, **en** ~: **des livres en** ~ a few books too many; **du lait en** ~ too much milk; **3 livres/3 F de** ~ = **3 books too many/3 F too much**

tropical, e, aux [trɔpikal, -o] *adj* tropical

tropique [trɔpik] *nm* tropic

trop-plein [trɔplɛ̃] *nm* (*tuyau*) overflow *ou* outlet (pipe); (*liquide*) overflow

troquer [trɔke] *vt*: ~ **qch contre** to barter *ou* trade sth for; (*fig*) to swap sth for

trot [tro] *nm* trot; ~**ter** [trɔte] *vi* to trot; (*fig*) to scamper along (*ou* about)

trottiner [trɔtine] *vi* (*fig*) to scamper along (*ou* about); **trottinette** [trɔtinɛt] *nf* (child's) scooter

trottoir [trɔtwar] *nm* pavement; **faire le** ~ (*péj*) to walk the streets; ~ **roulant** moving walkway, travellator

trou [tru] *nm* hole; (*fig*) gap; (*COMM*) deficit; ~ **d'air** air pocket; ~ **d'ozone** ozone hole; **le** ~ **de la serrure** the keyhole; ~ **de mémoire** blank, lapse of memory

trouble [trubl(ə)] *adj* (*liquide*) cloudy; (*image, mémoire*) indistinct, hazy; (*affaire*) shady, murky ♦ *nm* (*désarroi*) agitation; (*embarras*) confusion; (*zizanie*) unrest, discord; ~**s**

nmpl (POL) disturbances, troubles, unrest *sg*; (MED) trouble *sg*; disorders

troubler [tʀuble] *vt* (embarrasser) to confuse, disconcert; (émouvoir) to agitate; to disturb; (perturber: ordre etc) to disrupt; (liquide) to make cloudy; se ~ *vi* (personne) to become flustered *ou* confused

trouée [tʀue] *nf* gap; (MIL) breach

trouer [tʀue] *vt* to make a hole (*ou* holes) in; (*fig*) to pierce

trouille [tʀuj] (*fam*) *nf*: avoir la ~ to be scared to death

troupe [tʀup] *nf* troop; ~ (de théâtre) (theatrical) company

troupeau, x [tʀupo] *nm* (de moutons) flock; (de vaches) herd

trousse [tʀus] *nf* case, kit; (d'écolier) pencil case; (de médecin) instrument case; aux ~s de (*fig*) on the heels *ou* tail of; ~ à outils toolkit; ~ de toilette toilet bag

trousseau, x [tʀuso] *nm* (de mariée) trousseau; ~ de clefs bunch of keys

trouvaille [tʀuvaj] *nf* find

trouver [tʀuve] *vt* to find; (rendre visite): aller/venir ~ qn to go/come and see sb; je trouve que I find that; ~ à boire/critiquer to find something to drink/criticize ♦ *vi* (être) to be; (être soudain) to find o.s.; il se trouve que it happens that, it turns out that; se ~ bien to feel well; se ~ mal to pass out; je trouve que I find *ou* think that; ~ à boire/critiquer to find something to drink/criticize

truand [tʀyɑ̃] *nm* villain, crook

truander [tʀyɑ̃de] *vt* to cheat

truc [tʀyk] *nm* (astuce) way, device; (de cinéma, prestidigitateur) trick effect; (chose) thing, thingumajig; avoir le ~ to have the knack

truchement [tʀyʃmɑ̃] *nm*: par le ~ de qn through (the intervention of) sb

truelle [tʀyɛl] *nf* trowel

truffe [tʀyf] *nf* truffle; (nez) nose

truffé, e [tʀyfe] *adj*: ~ de (*fig*) peppered with; bristling with

truie [tʀyi] *nf* sow

truite [tʀyit] *nf* trout *inv*

truquer [tʀyke] *vt* (élections, serrure, dés) to fix; (CINEMA) to use special effects in

T.S.V.P. *sigle* = tournez s.v.p.

P.T.O.

T.T.C. *sigle* = toutes taxes comprises

tu¹ [ty] *pron* you

tu², e [ty] *pp de* taire

tuba [tyba] *nm* (MUS) tuba; (SPORT) snorkel

tube [tyb] *nm* tube; pipe; (chanson, disque) hit song *ou* record

tuer [tɥe] *vt* to kill; se ~ *vi* to be killed; (suicide) to kill o.s.; **tuerie** *nf* slaughter *no pl*

tue-tête [tytɛt] : à ~ *adv* at the top of one's voice

tueur [tɥœʀ] *nm* killer; ~ à gages hired killer

tuile [tɥil] *nf* tile; (*fam*) spot of bad luck, blow

tulipe [tylip] *nf* tulip

tuméfié, e [tymefje] *adj* puffy, swollen

tumeur [tymœʀ] *nf* growth, tumour

tumulte [tymylt(ə)] *nm* commotion

tumultueux, euse [tymyltɥø, -øz] *adj* stormy, turbulent

tunique [tynik] *nf* tunic

Tunisie [tynizi] *nf*: la ~ Tunisia; **tunisien, ne** *adj, nm/f* Tunisian

tunnel [tynɛl] *nm* tunnel

turbulences [tyʀbylɑ̃s] *nfpl* (AVIAT) turbulence *sg*

turbulent, e [tyʀbylɑ̃, -ɑ̃t] *adj* boisterous, unruly

turc, turque [tyʀk(ə)] *adj* Turkish ♦ *nm/f*: T~, Turque Turk/Turkish woman ♦ *nm* (LING) Turkish

turf [tyʀf] *nm* racing; **turfiste** *nm/f* racegoer

Turquie [tyʀki] *nf*: la ~ Turkey

turquoise [tyʀkwaz] *nf* turquoise ♦ *adj inv* turquoise

tus *etc vb voir* taire

tutelle [tytɛl] *nf* (JUR) guardianship; (POL) trusteeship; sous la ~ de *(fig)* under the supervision of

tuteur [tytœʀ] *nm (JUR)* guardian; *(de plante)* stake, support

tutoyer [tytwaje] *vt:* ~ **qn** to address sb as "tu"

tuyau, x [tɥijo] *nm* pipe; *(flexible)* tube; *(fam)* tip; *gen no pl;* ~ **d'arrosage** garden hose; ~ **d'échappement** exhaust pipe; **~terie** *nf* piping *no pl*

T.V.A. *sigle f (= taxe à la valeur ajoutée)* VAT

tympan [tɛ̃pɑ̃] *nm (ANAT)* eardrum

type [tip] *nm* type; *(fam)* chap, guy
♦ *adj* typical, standard

typé, e [tipe] *adj* ethnic

typhoïde [tifɔid] *nf* typhoid

typique [tipik] *adj* typical

tyran [tiʀɑ̃] *nm* tyrant

tzigane [dzigan] *adj* gipsy, tzigane

U

ulcère [ylsɛʀ] *nm* ulcer; **ulcérer** [ylseʀe] *vt (fig)* to sicken, appal

ultérieur, e [ylteʀjœʀ] *adj* later, subsequent; **remis à une date** ~e postponed to a later date

ultime [yltim] *adj* final

ultra... [yltʀa] *préfixe:* **ultramoderne/-rapide** ultra-modern/-fast

---

MOT-CLÉ

---

un, une [œ̃, yn] *art indéf* ♦ *art indéf:* (*devant voyelle*) an; ~ **garçon /vieillard** a boy/an old man; **une fille** a girl
♦ *pron* one; **l'**~ **des meilleurs** one of the best; **l'**~**, l'autre** (the) one ..., the other ...; **les** ~**s** ..., **les autres** some ..., others; **l'**~ **et l'autre** both (of them); **l'**~ **ou l'autre** either (of them); **l'**~ **l'autre, les** ~**s les autres** each other, one another; **pas** ~ **seul** not a single one; ~ **par** ~ one by one
♦ *num* one; **une pomme seulement** one apple only

---

unanime [ynanim] *adj* unanimous;

unanimité *nf:* **à l'unanimité** unanimously

uni, e [yni] *adj (ton, tissu)* plain; *(surface)* smooth, even; *(famille)* close(-knit); *(pays)* united

unifier [ynifje] *vt* to unite, unify

uniforme [ynifɔʀm(ə)] *adj (mouvement)* regular, uniform; *(surface, ton)* even; *(objets, maisons)* uniform
♦ *nm* uniform; **uniformiser** *vt* to make uniform; *(systèmes)* to standardize

union [ynjɔ̃] *nf* union; ~ **de consommateurs** consumers' association; **l'U~ soviétique** the Soviet Union

unique [ynik] *adj (seul)* only; *(le même)*: **un prix/système** ~ a single price/system; *(exceptionnel)* unique; **fils/fille** ~ only son/daughter, only child; **uniquement** *adv* only, solely; *(juste)* only, merely

unir [yniʀ] *vt (nations)* to unite; *(éléments, couleurs)* to combine; *(en mariage)* to unite, join together; **s'**~ to unite; *(en mariage)* to be joined together; ~ **qch à** to unite sth with; ~ **à** to combine sth with

unité [ynite] *nf (harmonie, cohésion)* unity; *(COMM, MIL, de mesure, MATH)* unit

univers [ynivɛʀ] *nm* universe

universel, le [ynivɛʀsɛl] *adj* universal; *(esprit)* all-embracing

universitaire [ynivɛʀsitɛʀ] *adj* university *cpd; (diplôme, études)* academic, university *cpd* ♦ *nm/f* academic

université [ynivɛʀsite] *nf* university

urbain, e [yʀbɛ̃, -ɛn] *adj* urban, city *cpd,* town *cpd; (poli)* urbane; **urbanisme** *nm* town planning

urgence [yʀʒɑ̃s] *nf* urgency; *(MÉD etc)* emergency; **d'**~ emergency *cpd*
♦ *adv* as a matter of urgency

urgent, e [yʀʒɑ̃, -ɑ̃t] *adj* urgent

urine [yʀin] *nf* urine; **urinoir** *nm* (public) urinal

urne [yʀn(ə)] *nf (électorale)* ballot box; *(vase)* urn

urticaire [yʀtikɛʀ] *nf* nettle rash

us [ys] *nmpl:* ~ **et coutumes** (habits

and) customs

USA *sigle mpl*: les ~ the USA

usage [yza3] *nm* (*emploi, utilisation*) use; (*coutume*) custom; (*LING*): l'~ usage; à l'~ de (*pour*) for (use of); en ~ in use; hors d'~ out of service; wrecked; à ~ interne to be taken; à ~ externe for external use only; **usagé, e** [yza3e] *adj* (*usé*) worn; (*d'occasion*) used; **usager, ère** [yza3e, -ɛʀ] *nm/f* user

usé, e [yze] *adj* worn; (*banal*) hackneyed

user [yze] *vt* (*outil*) to wear down; (*vêtement*) to wear out; (*matière*) to wear away; (*consommer: charbon etc*) to use; s'~ *vi* to wear; to wear out; (*fig*) to decline; ~ de (*moyen, procédé*) to use, employ; (*droit*) to exercise

usine [yzin] *nf* factory; ~ **marémotrice** tidal power station

usité, e [yzite] *adj* common

ustensile [ystɑ̃sil] *nm* implement; ~ **de cuisine** kitchen utensil

usuel, le [yzɥɛl] *adj* everyday, common

usure [yzyʀ] *nf* wear; worn state

ut [yt] *nm* (*MUS*) C

utérus [yteʀys] *nm* uterus, womb

utile [ytil] *adj* useful

utilisation [ytilizasjɔ̃] *nf* use

utiliser [ytilize] *vt* to use

utilitaire [ytilitɛʀ] *adj* utilitarian; (*objets*) practical

utilité [ytilite] *nf* usefulness *no pl*; use; **reconnu d'~ publique** state-approved

V

va *vb voir* **aller**

vacance [vakɑ̃s] *nf* (*ADMIN*) vacancy; ~**s** *nfpl* holiday(s *pl*), vacation *sg*; **prendre des/ses** ~**s** to take a holiday/one's holiday(s); **aller en** ~**s** to go on holiday; **vacancier, ière** [vakɑ̃sje, -jɛʀ] *nm/f* holiday-maker

vacant, e [vakɑ̃, -ɑ̃t] *adj* vacant

vacarme [vakaʀm(ə)] *nm* row, din

vaccin [vaksɛ̃] *nm* vaccine; (*opération*) vaccination; **vaccination** *nf* vaccination; **vacciner** *vt* to vaccinate; (*fig*) to make immune

vache [vaʃ] *nf* (*ZOOL*) cow; (*cuir*) cowhide ♦ *adj* (*fam*) rotten, mean; ~**ment** (*fam*) *adv* damned, hellish

vaciller [vasije] *vi* to sway, wobble; (*bougie, lumière*) to flicker; (*fig*) to be failing, falter

va-et-vient [vaevjɛ̃] *nm inv* (*de personnes, véhicules*) comings and goings *pl*, to-ings and fro-ings *pl*

vagabond [vagabɔ̃] *nm* (*rôdeur*) tramp, vagrant; (*voyageur*) wanderer; ~**er** [vagabɔ̃de] *vi* to roam, wander

vagin [vaʒɛ̃] *nm* vagina

vague [vag] *nf* wave ♦ *adj* vague; (*regard*) faraway; (*manteau, robe*) loose(-fitting); (*quelconque*): **un** ~ **bureau/cousin** some office/cousin or other; ~ **de fond** ground swell

vaillant, e [vajɑ̃, -ɑ̃t] *adj* (*courageux*) gallant; (*robuste*) hale and hearty

vaille *vb voir* **valoir**

vain, e [vɛ̃, vɛn] *adj* vain; **en** ~ in vain

vaincre [vɛ̃kʀ(ə)] *vt* to defeat; (*fig*) to conquer, overcome; **vaincu, e** *nm/f* defeated party; **vainqueur** *nm* victor; (*SPORT*) winner

vais *vb voir* **aller**

vaisseau, x [veso] *nm* (*ANAT*) vessel; (*NAVIG*) ship, vessel; ~ **spatial** spaceship

vaisselier [vesəlje] *nm* dresser

vaisselle [vesɛl] *nf* (*service*) crockery; (*plats etc à laver*) (dirty) dishes *pl*; (*lavage*) washing-up (*BRIT*), dishes *pl*

val [val] (*pl* **vaux** *ou* ~**s**) *nm* valley

valable [valabl(ə)] *adj* valid; (*acceptable*) decent, worthwhile

valent *etc vb voir* **valoir**

valet [valɛ] *nm* valet; (*CARTES*) jack

valeur [valœʀ] *nf* (*gén*) value; (*mé-*

rite) worth, merit; (COMM: *titre*) security; **mettre en ~** (*terrain*, *région*) to develop; (*fig*) to highlight; to show off to advantage; **avoir de la ~** to be valuable; **sans ~** worthless; **prendre de la ~** to go up *ou* gain in value

valide [valid] *adj* (*en bonne santé*) fit; (*valable*) valid; **valider** *vt* to validate

valions *vb voir* **valoir**

valise [valiz] *nf* (suit)case

vallée [vale] *nf* valley

vallon [val5] *nm* small valley

valoir [valwaʀ] *vi* (*être valable*) to hold, apply ♦ *vt* (*prix, valeur, effort*) to be worth; (*causer*): **~ qch à qn** to earn sb sth; **se ~** *vi* to be of equal merit; (*péj*) to be two-of-a-kind; **faire ~** (*droits, prérogatives*) to assert; **faire ~ que** to point out that; **à ~ sur** to be deducted from; **vaille que vaille** somehow or other; **cela ne me dit rien qui vaille** I don't like the look of it at all; **ce climat ne me vaut rien** this climate doesn't suit me; **la peine** to be worth the trouble *ou* worth it; **~ mieux**: **il vaut mieux se taire** it's better to say nothing; **ça ne vaut rien** it's worthless; **que vaut ce candidat?** how good is this applicant?

valoriser [valɔʀize] *vt* (ÉCON) to develop (the economy of); (PSYCH) to increase the standing of

valse [vals(ə)] *nf* waltz

valu, e [valy] *pp de* **valoir**

vandalisme [vɑ̃dalism(ə)] *nm* vandalism

vanille [vanij] *nf* vanilla

vanité [vanite] *nf* vanity; **vaniteux, euse** *adj* vain, conceited

vanne [van] *nf* gate; (*fig*) joke

vannerie [vanʀi] *nf* basketwork

vantard, e [vɑ̃taʀ, -aʀd(ə)] *adj* boastful

vanter [vɑ̃te] *vt* to speak highly of, vaunt; **se ~** *vi* to boast, brag; **se ~ de** to pride o.s. on; (*péj*) to boast of

vapeur [vapœʀ] *nf* steam; (*émana-*

tion) vapour, fumes *pl*; **~s** *nfpl* (*bouffées*) vapours; **à ~** steam-powered, steam *cpd*; **cuit à la ~** steamed

vaporeux, euse [vapɔʀø, -øz] *adj* (*flou*) hazy, misty; (*léger*) filmy

vaporisateur [vapɔʀizatœʀ] *nm* spray; **vaporiser** [vapɔʀize] *vt* (*parfum etc*) to spray

varappe [vaʀap] *nf* rock climbing

vareuse [vaʀøz] *nf* (*blouson*) pea jacket; (*d'uniforme*) tunic

variable [vaʀjabl(ə)] *adj* variable; (*temps, humeur*) changeable; (*divers: résultats*) varied, various

varice [vaʀis] *nf* varicose vein

varicelle [vaʀisɛl] *nf* chickenpox

varié, e [vaʀje] *adj* varied; (*divers*) various

varier [vaʀje] *vi* to vary; (*temps, humeur*) to change ♦ *vt* to vary

variété [vaʀjete] *nf* variety; **~s** *nfpl*: **spectacle/émission de ~s** variety show

variole [vaʀjɔl] *nf* smallpox

vas *vb voir* **aller**

vase [vaz] *nm* vase ♦ *nf* silt, mud

vaseux, euse [vazø, -øz] *adj* silty, muddy; (*fig: confus*) woolly, hazy; (*: fatigué*) peaky; woozy

vasistas [vazistɑs] *nm* fanlight

vaste [vast(ə)] *adj* vast, immense

vaudrai *etc vb voir* **valoir**

vaurien, ne [voʀjɛ̃, -ɛn] *nm/f* good-for-nothing, guttersnipe

vaut *vb voir* **valoir**

vautour [votuʀ] *nm* vulture

vautrer [votʀe]: **se ~** *vi* to wallow in/sprawl on

vaux [vo] *nmpl de* **val** ♦ *vb voir* **valoir**

va-vite [vavit]: **à la ~** *adv* in a rush *ou* hurry

veau, x [vo] *nm* (ZOOL) calf; (CU-LIN) veal; (*peau*) calfskin

vécu, e [veky] *pp de* **vivre**

vedette [vədɛt] *nf* (*artiste etc*) star; (*canot*) patrol boat; launch

végétal, e, aux [veʒetal, -o] *adj* vegetable ♦ *nm* vegetable, plant

végétarien, ne [veʒetaʀjɛ̃, -ɛn] adj, nm/f vegetarian

végétation [veʒetɑsjɔ̃] nf vegetation; ~s nfpl (MED) adenoids

véhicule [veikyl] nm vehicle; ~ utilitaire commercial vehicle

veille [vɛj] nf (garde) watch; (PSYCH) wakefulness; (jour): la ~ (de) the day before; la ~ au soir the previous evening; à la ~ de on the eve of

veillée [veje] nf (soirée) evening; (réunion) evening gathering; la ~ (mortuaire) watch

veiller [veje] vi to stay up; to be awake; to be on watch ♦ vt (malade, mort) to watch over, sit up with; ~ à to attend to, see to; ~ à ce que to make sure that; ~ sur to keep a watch on; **veilleur de nuit** nm night watchman

veilleuse [vɛjøz] nf (lampe) night light; (AUTO) sidelight; (flamme) pilot light; en ~ (lampe) dimmed

veine [vɛn] nf (ANAT, du bois etc) vein; (filon) vein, seam; (fam: chance): avoir de la ~ to be lucky

véliplanchiste [veliplɑ̃ʃist(ə)] nm/f windsurfer

velléités [veleite] nfpl vague impulses

vélo [velo] nm bike, cycle; faire du ~ to go cycling; ~ tout-terrain mountain bike

vélomoteur [velomotœʀ] nm moped

velours [vəluʀ] nm velvet; ~ côtelé corduroy

velouté, e [vəlute] adj (au toucher) velvety; (à la vue) soft, mellow; (au goût) smooth, mellow

velu, e [vəly] adj hairy

venais etc vb voir **venir**

venaison [vənɛzɔ̃] nf venison

vendange [vɑ̃dɑ̃ʒ] nf (opération, période: aussi: ~s) grape harvest; (raisins) grape crop, grapes pl; ~r [vɑ̃dɑ̃ʒe] vi to harvest the grapes

vendeur, euse [vɑ̃dœʀ, -øz] nm/f (de magasin) shop assistant; (COMM) salesman(woman) ♦ nm

(JUR) vendor, seller; ~ de journaux newspaper seller

vendre [vɑ̃dʀ(ə)] vt to sell; ~ qch à qn to sell sb sth; "à ~" "for sale"

vendredi [vɑ̃dʀədi] nm Friday; V~ saint Good Friday

vendu, e [vɑ̃dy] adj (péj: corrompu) corrupt

vénéneux, euse [venenø, -øz] adj poisonous

vénérien, ne [veneʀjɛ̃, -ɛn] adj venereal

vengeance [vɑ̃ʒɑ̃s] nf vengeance no pl, revenge no pl

venger [vɑ̃ʒe] vt to avenge; se ~ vi to avenge o.s.; se ~ de qch to avenge o.s. for sth; to take one's revenge for sth; se ~ de qn to take revenge on sb; se ~ sur to take revenge on; to take it out on

venimeux, euse [vənimø, -øz] adj poisonous, venomous; (fig: haineux) venomous, vicious

venin [vənɛ̃] nm venom, poison

venir [vəniʀ] vi to come; ~ de to come from; ~ de faire: je viens d'y aller/de le voir I've just been there/seen him; s'il vient à pleuvoir if it should rain; j'en viens à croire que I have come to believe that; faire ~ (docteur, plombier) to call (out)

vent [vɑ̃] nm wind; il y a du ~ it's windy; c'est du ~ it's all hot air; au ~ to windward; sous le ~ to leeward; avoir le ~ debout/arrière to head into the wind/have the wind astern; dans le ~ (fam) trendy

vente [vɑ̃t] nf sale; la ~ (activité) selling; (secteur) sales pl; mettre en ~ to put on sale; (objets personnels) to put up for sale; ~ aux enchères auction sale; ~ de charité jumble sale

venteux, euse [vɑ̃tø, -øz] adj windy

ventilateur [vɑ̃tilatœʀ] nm fan

ventiler [vɑ̃tile] vt to ventilate; (total, statistiques) to break down

ventouse [vɑ̃tuz] nf (de caoutchouc)

suction pad; (ZOOL) sucker

ventre [vɑ̃tr(ə)] nm (ANAT) stomach; (fig) belly; **avoir mal au ~** to have stomach ache (BRIT) ou a stomach ache (US)

ventriloque [vɑ̃trilɔk] nm/f ventriloquist

venu, e [vəny] pp de **venir** ♦ adj: **être mal ~ à** ou **de faire** to have no grounds for doing, be in no position to do coming

ver [vɛr] nm worm; (des fruits etc) maggot; (du bois) woodworm no pl; voir aussi **vers**; **~ à soie** silkworm; **~ de terre** earthworm; **~ luisant** glow-worm; **~ solitaire** tapeworm

verbaliser [vɛrbalize] vi (POLICE) to book ou report an offender

verbe [vɛrb(ə)] nm verb

verdeur [vɛrdœr] nf (vigueur) vigour, vitality; (crudité) forthrightness

verdict [vɛrdik(t)] nm verdict

verdir [vɛrdir] vi, vt to turn green

verdure [vɛrdyr] nf greenery

véreux, euse [verø, -øz] adj wormeaten; (malhonnête) shady, corrupt

verge [vɛrʒ(ə)] nf (ANAT) penis; (baguette) stick, cane

verger [vɛrʒe] nm orchard

verglacé, e [vɛrglase] adj icy, icedover

verglas [vɛrgla] nm (black) ice

vergogne [vɛrgɔɲ]: **sans ~** adv shamelessly

véridique [veridik] adj truthful

vérification [verifikasjɔ̃] nf checking no pl, check

vérifier [verifje] vt to check; (corroborer) to confirm, bear out

véritable [veritabl(ə)] adj real; (ami, amour) true

vérité [verite] nf truth; (d'un portrait romanesque) lifelikeness; (sincérité) truthfulness, sincerity

vermeil, le [vɛrmɛj] adj ruby red

vermine [vɛrmin] nf vermin pl

vermoulu, e [vɛrmuly] adj wormeaten, with woodworm

verni, e [vɛrni] adj (fam) lucky; **cuir ~** patent leather

vernir [vɛrnir] vt (bois, tableau, ongles) to varnish; (poterie) to glaze

vernis [vɛrni] nm (enduit) varnish; glaze; (fig) veneer; **~ à ongles** nail polish ou varnish; **vernissage** [vɛrnisaʒ] nm varnishing; glazing; (d'une exposition) preview

vérole [verɔl] nf (variole) smallpox

verrai etc vb voir **voir**

verre [vɛr] nm glass; (de lunettes) lens sg; **boire** ou **prendre un ~** to have a drink; **~s de contact** contact lenses; **verrerie** [vɛrri] nf (fabrique) glassworks sg; (activité) glassmaking; (objets) glassware; **verrière** [vɛrjɛr] nf (grand vitrage) window; (toit vitré) glass roof

verrons etc vb voir **voir**

verrou [vɛru] nm (targette) bolt; (fig) constriction; **mettre qn sous les ~s** to put sb behind bars; **verrouillage** nm locking; **verrouiller** vt to bolt; to lock

verrue [vɛry] nf wart

vers [vɛr] nm line ♦ nmpl (poésie) verse sg ♦ prép (en direction de) toward(s); (près de) around (about); (temporel) around, around

versant [vɛrsɑ̃] nm slopes pl, side

versatile [vɛrsatil] adj fickle, changeable

verse [vɛrs(ə)]: **à ~** adv it's pouring (with rain)

Verseau [vɛrso] nm: **le ~** Aquarius

versement [vɛrsəmɑ̃] nm payment; **en 3 ~s** in 3 instalments

verser [vɛrse] vt (liquide, grains) to pour; (larmes, sang) to shed; (argent) to pay ♦ vi (véhicule) to overturn; (fig): **~ dans** to lapse into

verset [vɛrse] nm verse

version [vɛrsjɔ̃] nf version; (SCOL) translation (into the mother tongue)

verso [vɛrso] nm back; **voir au ~** see over(leaf)

vert, e [vɛr, vɛrt(ə)] adj green; (vin) young; (vigoureux) sprightly; (cru) forthright ♦ nm green

vertèbre [vɛrtɛbr(ə)] nf vertebra

vertement [vɛrtəmɑ̃] adv (répri-

mander) sharply

vertical, e, aux [vɛʀtikal, -o] *adj* vertical; **~e** *nf* vertical; **à la ~e** vertically; **~ement** *adv* vertically

vertige [vɛʀtiʒ] *nm (peur du vide)* vertigo; *(étourdissement)* dizzy spell; *(fig)* fever; **vertigineux, euse** *adj* breathtaking

vertu [vɛʀty] *nf* virtue; **en ~ de** in accordance with; **vertueux, euse** *adj* virtuous

verve [vɛʀv(ə)] *nf* witty eloquence; **être en ~** to be in brilliant form

verveine [vɛʀvɛn] *nf (BOT)* verbena, vervain; *(infusion)* verbena tea

vésicule [vezikyl] *nf* vesicle; **~ bi-liaire** gall-bladder

vessie [vesi] *nf* bladder

veste [vɛst(ə)] *nf* jacket; **~ droite/croisée** single/double-breasted jacket

vestiaire [vɛstjɛʀ] *nm (au théâtre etc)* cloakroom; *(de stade etc)* changing-room *(BRIT)*, locker-room *(US)*

vestibule [vɛstibyl] *nm* hall

vestige [vɛstiʒ] *nm* relic; *(fig)* vestige; **~s** *nmpl* remains

vestimentaire [vɛstimɑ̃tɛʀ] *adj (détail)* of dress; *(élégance)* sartorial; **dépenses ~s** spending on clothes

veston [vɛstɔ̃] *nm* jacket

vêtement [vɛtmɑ̃] *nm* garment, item of clothing; **~s** *nmpl* clothes

vétérinaire [veteʀinɛʀ] *nm/f* vet, veterinary surgeon

vêtir [vetiʀ] *vt* to clothe, dress

veto [veto] *nm* veto; **opposer un ~ à** to veto

vêtu, e [vety] *pp de* **vêtir**

vétuste [vetyst(ə)] *adj* ancient, time-worn

veuf, veuve [vœf, vœv] *adj* widowed ♦ *nm* widower

veuille *vb voir* **vouloir**

veuillez *vb voir* **vouloir**

veule [vøl] *adj* spineless

veuve [vœv] *nf* widow

veux *vb voir* **vouloir**

vexations [vɛksasjɔ̃] *nfpl* humilia-

tions

vexer [vɛkse] *vt* to hurt, upset; **se ~** to be hurt, get upset

viabiliser [vjabilize] *vt* to provide with services *(water etc)*

viable [vjabl(ə)] *adj* viable; *(économie, industrie etc)* sustainable

viager, ère [vjaʒe, -ɛʀ] *adj*: **rente viagère** life annuity

viande [vjɑ̃d] *nf* meat

vibrer [vibʀe] *vi* to vibrate; *(son, voix)* to be vibrant; *(fig)* to be stirred; **faire ~** to (cause to) vibrate; to stir, thrill

vice [vis] *nm* vice; *(défaut)* fault ♦ *préfixe*: **~ ...** vice-; **~ de forme** legal flaw *ou* irregularity

vichy [viʃi] *nm (toile)* gingham

vicié, e [visje] *adj (air)* polluted, tainted; *(JUR)* invalidated

vicieux, euse [visjø, -øz] *adj (pervers)* dirty(-minded); nasty; *(fautif)* incorrect, wrong

vicinal, e, aux [visinal, -o] *adj*: **chemin ~** by-road, byway

victime [viktim] *nf* victim; *(d'accident)* casualty

victoire [viktwaʀ] *nf* victory

victuailles [viktɥɑj] *nfpl* provisions

vidange [vidɑ̃ʒ] *nf (d'un fossé, réservoir)* emptying; *(AUTO)* oil change; *(de lavabo: bonde)* waste outlet; **~s** *nfpl (matières)* sewage *sg*; **vidanger** *vt* to empty

vide [vid] *adj* empty ♦ *nm (PHYSIQUE)* vacuum; *(espace)* (empty) space, gap; *(futilité, néant)* void; **avoir peur du ~** to be afraid of heights; **emballé sous ~** vacuum packed; **à ~** *(sans occupants)* empty; *(sans charge)* unladen

vidéo [video] *nf* video ♦ *adj*: **cassette ~** video cassette

vide-ordures [vidɔʀdyʀ] *nm inv (rubbish)* chute

vide-poches [vidpɔʃ] *nm inv* tidy; *(AUTO)* glove compartment

vider [vide] *vt* to empty; *(CULIN: volaille, poisson)* to gut, clean out; **se ~** *vi* to empty; **~ les lieux** to quit

ou vacate the premises; **videur** *nm* (*de boîte de nuit*) bouncer

vie [vi] *nf* life; **être en ~** to be alive; **sans ~** lifeless; **à ~** for life

vieil [vjɛj] *adj voir* **vieux**

vieillard [vjɛjaʀ] *nm* old man; **les ~s** old people, the elderly

vieille [vjɛj] *adj*, *nf voir* **vieux**

vieilleries [vjɛjʀi] *nfpl* old things

vieillesse [vjɛjɛs] *nf* old age

vieillir [vjɛjiʀ] *vi* (*prendre de l'âge*) to grow old; (*population*, *vin*) to age; (*doctrine*, *auteur*) to become dated ♦ *vt* to age; **vieillissement** *nm* growing old; ageing

Vienne [vjɛn] *nf* Vienna

viens *vb voir* **venir**

vierge [vjɛʀʒ(ə)] *adj* virgin; (*page*) clean, blank ♦ *nf* virgin; (*signe*) la V~ Virgo; **~ de** (*sans*) free from, unsullied by

Vietnam [vjɛtnam] *nm* = **Viet-Nam**

Viet-Nam [vjɛtnam] *nm* Vietnam

vietnamien, ne [vjɛtnamjɛ̃, -jɛn] *adj*, *nm/f* Vietnamese

vieux(vieil), vieille [vjø, vjɛj] *adj* old ♦ *nm/f* old man(woman) ♦ *nmpl* old people; **mon vieux/ma vieille** (*fam*) old man/girl; **prendre un coup de vieux** to put years on; **vieux garçon** bachelor; **vieux jeu** *adj inv* old-fashioned

vif, vive [vif, viv] *adj* (*animé*) lively; (*alerte*, *brusque*, *aigu*) sharp; (*lumière*, *couleur*) brilliant; (*air*) crisp; (*vent*, *émotion*) keen; (*fort*: *regret*, *déception*) great, deep; (*vivant*): **brûlé ~** burnt alive; **de vive voix** personally; **piquer qn au ~** to cut sb to the quick; **à ~** (*plaie*) open; **avoir les nerfs à ~** to be on edge

vigie [viʒi] *nf* look-out; look-out post

vigne [viɲ] *nf* (*plante*) vine; (*plantation*) vineyard

vigneron [viɲʀɔ̃] *nm* wine grower

vignette [viɲɛt] *nf* (*motif*) vignette; (*de marque*) manufacturer's label ou seal; (*ADMIN*) ≈ (road) tax disc (*BRIT*), ≈ license plate sticker (*US*); price label (*used for reimbursement*)

vignoble [viɲɔbl(ə)] *nm* (*plantation*) vineyard; (*vignes d'une région*) vineyards *pl*

vigoureux, euse [viguʀø, -øz] *adj* vigorous, robust

vigueur [vigœʀ] *nf* vigour; **entrer en ~** to come into force; **en ~** current

vil, e [vil] *adj* vile, base; **à ~ prix** at a very low price

vilain, e [vilɛ̃, -ɛn] *adj* (*laid*) ugly; (*affaire*, *blessure*) nasty; (*pas sage*: *enfant*) naughty

villa [vila] *nf* (detached) house; **~ en multipropriété** time-share villa

village [vilaʒ] *nm* village; **villageois, e** *adj* village *cpd* ♦ *nm/f* villager

ville [vil] *nf* town; (*importante*) city; (*administration*): **la ~** ≈ the Corporation; ≈ the (town) council

villégiature [vileʒjatyʀ] *nf* holiday; (holiday) resort

vin [vɛ̃] *nm* wine; **avoir le ~ gai** to get happy after a few drinks; **~ d'honneur** reception (*with wine and snacks*); **~ de pays** local wine; **~ ordinaire** table wine

vinaigre [vinɛgʀ(ə)] *nm* vinegar; **vinaigrette** *nf* vinaigrette, French dressing

vindicatif, ive [vɛ̃dikatif, -iv] *adj* vindictive

vineux, euse [vinø, -øz] *adj* win(e)y

vingt [vɛ̃, vɛ̃t] *num* twenty; **~aine** *nf*: **une ~aine (de)** about twenty, twenty or so; **~tième** *num* twentieth

vinicole [vinikɔl] *adj* wine *cpd*, wine-growing

vins *etc vb voir* **venir**

vinyle [vinil] *nm* vinyl

viol [vjɔl] *nm* (*d'une femme*) rape; (*d'un lieu sacré*) violation

violacé, e [vjɔlase] *adj* purplish, mauvish

violemment [vjɔlamɑ̃] *adv* violently

violence [vjɔlɑ̃s] *nf* violence

violent, e [vjɔlɑ̃, -ɑ̃t] *adj* violent; (*remède*) drastic

violer [vjɔle] *vt* (*femme*) to rape;

(sépulture, loi, traité) to violate

violet, te [vjɔlɛ, -ɛt] *adj, nm* purple, mauve; **violette** *nf (fleur)* violet

violon [vjɔlɔ̃] *nm* violin; *(fam: prison)* lock-up

violoncelle [vjɔlɔ̃sɛl] *nm* cello

violoniste [vjɔlɔnist(ə)] *nmf* violinist

vipère [vipɛr] *nf* viper, adder

virage [viraʒ] *nm (d'un véhicule)* turn; *(d'une route, piste)* bend; *(fig: POL)* about-turn

virée [vire] *nf (courte)* run; (: *à pied)* walk; *(longue)* trip; hike, walking tour

virement [virmɑ̃] *nm (COMM)* transfer

virent *vb voir* **voir**

virer [vire] *vt (COMM):* ~ qch (sur) to transfer sth (into) ♦ *vi* to turn; *(CHIMIE)* to change colour; ~ **de bord** to tack

virevolter [virvɔlte] *vi* to twirl around

virgule [virgyl] *nf* comma; *(MATH)* point

viril, e [viril] *adj (propre à l'homme)* masculine; *(énergique, courageux)* manly, virile

virtuel, le [virtɥɛl] *adj* potential; *(théorique)* virtual

virtuose [virtɥoz] *nmf (MUS)* virtuoso; *(gén)* master

virus [virys] *nm (aussi: COMPUT)* virus

vis¹ [vi] *vb voir* **voir**; **vivre**

vis² [vis] *nf* screw

visa [viza] *nm (sceau)* stamp; *(validation de passeport)* visa

visage [vizaʒ] *nm* face

vis-à-vis [vizavi] *adv* face to face ♦ *nm* person opposite; house *etc* opposite; ~ **de** opposite; *(fig)* vis-à-vis; **en** ~ facing each other

viscéral, e, aux [viseral, -o] *adj (fig)* deep-seated, deep-rooted

visée [vize] : ~**s** *nfpl (intentions)* designs

viser [vize] *vi* to aim ♦ *vt* to aim at; *(concerner)* to be aimed *ou* directed at; *(apposer un visa sur)* to stamp,

visa; ~ **à qch/faire** to aim at sth/at doing *ou* to do; **viseur** [vizœr] *nm (d'arme)* sights *pl; (PHOTO)* viewfinder

visibilité [vizibilite] *nf* visibility

visible [vizibl(ə)] *adj (aussi: disponible)*: **est-il** ~ ? can he see me?, will he see visitors?

visière [vizjɛr] *nf (de casquette)* peak; *(qui s'attache)* eyeshade

vision [vizjɔ̃] *nf* vision; *(sens)* (eye)sight, vision; *(fait de voir)*: **la** ~ **de** the sight of

visionneuse [vizjɔnøz] *nf* viewer

visite [vizit] *nf (visiteur)* visitor; *(médicale, à domicile)* visit, call; **la** ~ *(MED)* medical examination; **faire une** ~ **à qn** to call on sb, pay sb a visit; **rendre** ~ **à qn** to visit sb, pay sb a visit; **être en** ~ **(chez qn)** to be visiting (sb); **heures de** ~ *(hôpital, prison)* visiting hours

visiter [vizite] *vt* to visit; *(musée, ville)* to visit, go round; **visiteur, euse** *nm/f* visitor

vison [vizɔ̃] *nm* mink

visser [vise] *vt:* ~ qch *(fixer, serrer)* to screw sth on

visuel, le [vizɥɛl] *adj* visual

vit *vb voir* **voir**; **vivre**

vital, e, aux [vital, -o] *adj* vital

vitamine [vitamin] *nf* vitamin

vite [vit] *adv (rapidement)* quickly, fast; *(sans délai)* quickly; soon; **faire** ~ to act quickly; to be quick

vitesse [vites] *nf* speed; *(AUTO: dispositif)* gear; **prendre qn de** ~ to outstrip sb; get ahead of sb; **prendre de la** ~ to pick up *ou* gather speed; **à toute** ~ at full *ou* top speed

viticole [vitikɔl] *adj* wine cpd, winegrowing

viticulteur [vitikyltœr] *nm* wine grower

vitrage [vitraʒ] *nm* glass *no pl; (rideau)* net curtain

vitrail, aux [vitraj, -o] *nm* stained-glass window

vitre [vitr(ə)] *nf* (window) pane [*

portière, voiture) window

vitré, e [vitre] adj glass cpd

vitrer [vitre] vt to glaze

vitreux, euse [vitRø, -øz] adj (terne) glassy

vitrine [vitRin] nf (devanture) (shop) window; (étalage) display; (petite armoire) display cabinet; ~ publicitaire display case, showcase

vitupérer [vitypeRe] vi to rant and rave

vivace [vivas] adj (arbre, plante) hardy; (fig) indestructible, inveterate

vivacité [vivasite] nf liveliness, vivacity; sharpness; brilliance

vivant, e [vivɑ̃, -ɑ̃t] adj (qui vit) living, alive; (animé) lively; (bruyant, exemple) living ♦ nm: du ~ de qn in sb's lifetime

vivats [viva] nmpl cheers

vive [viv] adj voir vif ♦ vb vivre ♦ excl: ~ le roi! long live the king!

vivement [vivmɑ̃] adv vivaciously; sharply ♦ excl: vivement les vacances! roll on the holidays!

viveur [vivœR] (péj) nm high liver, pleasure-seeker

vivier [vivje] nm fish tank; fishpond

vivifiant, e [vivifjɑ̃, -ɑ̃t] adj invigorating

vivions vb voir vivre

vivoter [vivɔte] vi (personne) to scrape a living, get by; (fig: affaire etc) to struggle along

vivre [vivR(ə)] vi, vt to live; il vit encore he is still alive; se laisser ~ to take life as it comes; ne plus ~ (être anxieux) to live on one's nerves; il a vécu (eu une vie aventureuse) he has seen life; être facile à ~ to be easy to get on with; faire ~ qn (pourvoir à sa subsistance) to provide (a living) for sb; vivres nmpl provisions, food supplies

vlan [vlɑ̃] excl wham!, bang!

vocable [vɔkabl(ə)] nm term

vocabulaire [vɔkabylɛR] nm vocabulary

vocation [vɔkasjɔ̃] nf vocation, calling

vociférer [vɔsifeRe] vi, vt to scream

vœu, x [vø] nm wish; (à Dieu) vow; faire ~ de to take a vow of; ~x de bonne année best wishes for the New Year

vogue [vɔg] nf fashion, vogue

voguer [vɔge] vi to sail

voici [vwasi] prép (pour introduire, désigner) here is +sg, here are +pl; et ~ que ... and now it (ou he) ...; voir aussi voilà

voie [vwa] nf way; (RAIL) track, line; (AUTO) lane; (fig) channel; ~ de garage (RAIL) siding; ~ ferrée track; railway line

voilà [vwala] prép (en désignant) there is +sg, there are +pl; les ~ ou voici here ou there they are; en ~ ou voici un here's one, there's one; ~ ou voici deux ans two years ago; ~ ou voici deux ans que c'est fini it is two years since; et ~! there we are!; ~ tout that's all; "~ ou voici" (en offrant etc) "there ou here you are"

voile [vwal] nm veil; (tissu léger) net ♦ nf sail; (sport) sailing

voiler [vwale] vt to veil; (fausser: roue) to buckle; (: bois) to warp; se ~ vi (lune, regard) to mist over; (voix) to become husky; (roue, disque) to buckle; (planche) to warp

voilier [vwalje] nm sailing ship; (de plaisance) sailing boat

voilure [vwalyR] nf (de voilier) sails pl

voir [vwaR] vi, vt to see; se ~ vt: se ~ critiquer/transformer to be criticized/transformed; cela se voit (cela arrive) it happens; (c'est visible) that's obvious, it shows; ~ venir (fig) to wait and see; faire ~ qch à qn to show sb sth; en faire ~ à qn (fig) to give sb a hard time; ne pas pouvoir voir qn not to be able to stand sb; voyons! let's see now; (indignation etc) come (along) now!; avoir quelque chose à voir avec to have something to do with

voire [vwaʀ] adv indeed; nay; or even

voisin, e [vwazɛ̃, -in] adj (proche) neighbouring; (contigu) next; (ressemblant) connected ♦ nm/f neighbour; **voisinage** nm (proximité) proximity; (environs) vicinity; (quartier, voisins) neighbourhood

voiture [vwatyʀ] nf car; (wagon) coach, carriage; ~ **d'enfant** pram (BRIT), baby carriage (US); ~ **de sport** sports car; ~**-lit** nf sleeper

voix [vwa] nf voice; (POL) vote; à **haute** ~ aloud; à ~ **basse** in a low voice; à 2/4 ~ (MUS) in 2/4 parts; **avoir** ~ **au chapitre** to have a say in the matter

vol [vɔl] nm (mode de locomotion) flying; (trajet, voyage, groupe d'oiseaux) flight; (larcin) theft; à ~ **d'oiseau** as the crow flies; **au** ~: **attraper qch au** ~ to catch sth as it flies past; **en** ~ in flight; ~ **à main armée** armed robbery; ~ **à voile** gliding; ~ **libre** hang-gliding

volage [vɔlaʒ] adj fickle

volaille [vɔlaj] nf (oiseaux) poultry pl; (viande) poultry no pl; (oiseau) fowl

volant, e [vɔlɑ̃, -ɑ̃t] adj voir **vole** etc ♦ nm (d'automobile) (steering) wheel; (de commande) wheel; (objet lancé) shuttlecock; (bande de tissu) flounce

volcan [vɔlkɑ̃] nm volcano

volée [vɔle] nf (TENNIS) volley; à **la** ~: **rattraper à la** ~ to catch in mid-air; à **toute** ~ (sonner les cloches) vigorously; (lancer un projectile) with full force; ~ **de coups/ de flèches** volley of blows/arrows

voler [vɔle] vi (avion, oiseau, fig) to fly; (voleur) to steal ♦ vt (objet) to steal; (personne) to rob; ~ **qch à qn** to steal sth from sb

volet [vɔle] nm (de fenêtre) shutter; (de feuillet, document) section

voleur, euse [vɔlœʀ, -øz] nm/f thief ♦ adj thieving

volontaire [vɔlɔ̃tɛʀ] adj voluntary; (caractère, personne: décidé) self-willed ♦ nm/f volunteer

volonté [vɔlɔ̃te] nf (faculté de vouloir) will; (énergie, fermeté) will(power); (souhait, désir) wish; à ~ as much as one likes; **bonne** ~ goodwill, willingness; **mauvaise** ~ lack of goodwill, unwillingness

volontiers [vɔlɔ̃tje] adv (de bonne grâce) willingly; (avec plaisir) willingly, gladly; (habituellement, souvent) readily, willingly

volt [vɔlt] nm volt

volte-face [vɔltəfas] nf inv about-turn

voltige [vɔltiʒ] nf (ÉQUITATION) trick riding; (au cirque) acrobatics sg; ~**r** [vɔltiʒe] vi to flutter (about)

volume [vɔlym] nm volume; (GÉOM: solide) solid; **volumineux, euse** adj voluminous, bulky

volupté [vɔlypte] nf sensual delight ou pleasure

vomir [vɔmiʀ] vi to vomit, be sick ♦ vt to vomit, bring up; (fig) to belch out, spew out; (exécrer) to loathe, abhor

vont [vɔ̃] vb voir **aller**

vos [vo] dét voir **votre**

vote [vɔt] nm vote; ~ **par correspondance/procuration** postal /proxy vote

voter [vɔte] vi to vote ♦ vt (loi, décision) to vote for

votre [vɔtʀ(ə)] (pl **vos**) dét your

vôtre [votʀ(ə)] pron: **le** ~, **la** ~, **les** ~**s** yours; **les** ~**s** (fig) your family ou folks; à **la** ~ (toast) your (good) health!

voudrai etc vb voir **vouloir**

voué, e [vwe] adj: ~ à doomed to

vouer [vwe] vt: ~ **qch à** (Dieu/un saint) to dedicate sth to; ~ **qch à** (étude, cause etc) to devote one's life to; ~ **une amitié éternelle à qn** to vow undying friendship to sb

---

MOT-CLÉ

---

vouloir [vulwar] *nm*: le bon ~ de qn sb's goodwill; sb's pleasure
♦ *vt* **1** (*exiger, désirer*) to want; ~ faire/que qn fasse to want to do/sb to do; voulez-vous du thé would you like *ou* do you want some tea?; que me veut-il? what does he want with me?; sans le ~ (*involontairement*) without meaning to, unintentionally; je voudrais ceci/faire I would *ou* I'd like this/to do
2 (*consentir*): je veux bien (*bonne volonté*) I'll be happy to; (*concession*) fair enough, that's fine; oui, si on veut (*en quelque sorte*) yes, if you like; veuillez attendre please wait; veuillez agréer ... (*formule épistolaire*) yours faithfully
3: en ~ à to bear sb a grudge; s'en ~ (de) to be annoyed with o.s. (for); il en veut à mon argent he's after my money
4: ~ de the firm doesn't want him any more; elle ne veut pas de son aide she doesn't want his help
5: ~ dire to mean

voulu, e [vuly] *adj* (*requis*) required, requisite; (*délibéré*) deliberate, intentional; *voir aussi* vouloir
vous [vu] *pron* you; (*objet indirect*) (to) you; (*réfléchi: sg*) yourself; (: *pl*) yourselves; (*réciproque*) each other; ~-même yourself; ~-mêmes yourselves
voûte [vut] *nf* vault
voûter [vute] *vt*: se ~ *vi* (*dos, personne*) to become stooped
vouvoyer [vuvwaje] *vt*: ~ qn to address sb as "vous"
voyage [vwajaʒ] *nm* journey, trip; (*fait de voyager*): le ~ travel(ling); partir/être en ~ to go off/be away on a journey *ou* trip; faire bon ~ to have a good journey; ~ d'agrément/d'affaires pleasure/business trip; ~ de noces honey-

moon; ~ organisé package tour
voyager [vwajaʒe] *vi* to travel; **voyageur, euse** *nm/f* traveller; (*passager*) passenger
voyant, e [vwajã, -ãt] *adj* (*couleur*) loud, gaudy ♦ *nm* (*signal*) (warning) light; **voyante** *nf* clairvoyant
voyelle [vwajel] *nf* vowel
voyons *etc vb voir* voir
voyou [vwaju] *nm* lout, hoodlum; (*enfant*) guttersnipe
vrac [vrak] : en ~ *adv* higgledy-piggledy; (*comm*) in bulk
vrai, e [vrɛ] *adj* (*véridique: récit, faits*) true; (*non factice, authentique*) real; à ~ dire to tell the truth
vraiment [vrɛmã] *adv* really
vraisemblable [vrɛsãblabl(ə)] *adj* likely, probable
vraisemblance [vrɛsãblãs] *nf* likelihood; (*romanesque*) verisimilitude
vrille [vrij] *nf* (*de plante*) tendril; (*outil*) gimlet; (*spirale*) spiral; (*AVIAT*) spin
vrombir [vrɔbir] *vi* to hum
vu, e [vy] *pp de* voir ♦ *adj*: bien/mal ~ (*fig*) well/poorly thought of; good/bad form (*en raison de*) in view of; ~ que in view of the fact that
vue [vy] *nf* (*fait de voir*): la ~ de the sight of; (*sens, faculté*) (eye)sight; (*panorama, image, photo*) view; ~s *nfpl* (*idées*) views; (*dessein*) designs; hors de ~ out of sight; tirer à ~ to shoot on sight; à ~ d'œil visibly; at a quick glance; en ~ (*visible*) in sight; (*comm*) in the public eye; en ~ de faire with a view to doing
vulgaire [vylgɛr] *adj* (*grossier*) vulgar, coarse; (*trivial*) commonplace, mundane; (*péj*): quelconque: de ~s touristes common tourists; (*BOT, ZOOL: non latin*) common; **vulgariser** *vt* to popularize
vulnérable [vylnerabl(ə)] *adj* vulnerable

W, X, Y, Z

wagon [vagɔ̃] *nm* (*de voyageurs*) carriage; (*de marchandises*) truck, wagon; **wagon-lit** *nm* sleeper, sleeping car; **wagon-restaurant** *nm* restaurant *ou* dining car

wallon, ne [walɔ̃, -ɔn] *adj* Walloon

waters [watɛʀ] *nmpl* toilet *sg*

watt [wat] *nm* watt

w.-c. [vese] *nmpl* toilet *sg*, lavatory *sg*

week-end [wikɛnd] *nm* weekend

western [wɛstɛʀn] *nm* western

whisky [wiski] (*pl* **whiskies**) *nm* whisky

xérès [gzeʀɛs] *nm* sherry

xylophone [ksilɔfɔn] *nm* xylophone

y [i] *adv* (*à cet endroit*) there; (*dessus*) on it (*ou* them); (*dedans*) in it (*ou* them) ♦ *pron* (*about ou* on *ou* of) it (*d'après le verbe employé*); **j'~** **pense** I'm thinking about it; *voir aussi* **aller**; **avoir**

yacht [jɔt] *nm* yacht

yaourt [jauʀt] *nm* yoghourt

yeux [jø] *nmpl* *de* **œil**

yoghourt [jɔguʀt] *nm* = **yaourt**

yougoslave [jugɔslav] *nm/f* Yugoslav(ian)

Yougoslavie [jugɔslavi] *nf* Yugoslavia

zèbre [zɛbʀ(ə)] *nm* (*ZOOL*) zebra

zébré, e [zebʀe] *adj* striped, streaked

zèle [zɛl] *nm* zeal; **faire du ~** (*péj*) to be over-zealous

zéro [zeʀo] *nm* zero, nought (*BRIT*); **au-dessous de ~** below zero (Centigrade) *ou* freezing; **partir de ~** to start from scratch; **trois (buts) à ~** 3 (goals) to nil

zeste [zɛst(ə)] *nm* peel, zest

zézayer [zezeje] *vi* to have a lisp

zigzag [zigzag] *nm* zigzag

zinc [zɛ̃g] *nm* (*CHIMIE*) zinc; (*comptoir*) bar, counter

zizanie [zizani] *nf*: **semer la ~** to stir up ill-feeling

zodiaque [zɔdjak] *nm* zodiac

zona [zona] *nm* shingles *sg*

zone [zon] *nf* zone, area; (*quartiers*): **la ~** the slum belt; **~ bleue** = restricted parking area; **~ industrielle** *nf* industrial estate

zoo [zoo] *nm* zoo

zoologie [zɔɔlɔʒi] *nf* zoology; **zoologique** *adj* zoological

zut [zyt] *excl* dash (it)! (*BRIT*), nuts! (*US*)

ENGLISH - FRENCH
ANGLAIS - FRANÇAIS

A

A [eɪ] n (MUS) la m

a [eɪ, ə] (before vowel or silent h: an) indef art **1** un(e); ~ book un livre; **an apple** une pomme; **she's ~ doctor** elle est médecin
2 (instead of the number 'one') un(e); ~ **year** ago il y a un an; ~ **hundred/thousand** etc pounds cent/mille etc livres
3 (in expressing ratios, prices etc): 3 ~ **day/week** 3 par jour/semaine; 10 **km ~n hour** 10 km à l'heure; **30p ~ kilo** 30p le kilo

A.A. n abbr = **Alcoholics Anonymous**; (BRIT: = Automobile Association) ≈ TCF m

A.A.A. (US) n abbr (= American Automobile Association) ≈ TCF m

aback [əˈbæk] adv: **to be taken ~** être stupéfait(e), être décontenancé(e)

abandon [əˈbændən] vt abandonner
♦ n: **with ~** avec désinvolture

abate [əˈbeɪt] vi s'apaiser, se calmer

abbey [ˈæbɪ] n abbaye f

abbot [ˈæbət] n père supérieur

abbreviation [əbriːvɪˈeɪʃən] n abréviation f

abdicate [ˈæbdɪkeɪt] vt, vi abdiquer

abdomen [ˈæbdəmən] n abdomen m

abduct [æbˈdʌkt] vt enlever

aberration [æbəˈreɪʃən] n anomalie f

abet [əˈbet] vt see **aid**

abeyance [əˈbeɪəns] n: **in ~** (law) tombé(e) en désuétude; (matter) en suspens

abide [əˈbaɪd] vt: **I can't ~ it/him** je ne peux pas le souffrir or supporter; ~ **by** vt fus observer, respecter

ability [əˈbɪlɪtɪ] n compétence f; capacité f; (skill) talent m

abject [ˈæbdʒekt] adj (poverty) sordide; (apology) plat(e)

ablaze [əˈbleɪz] adj en feu, en flammes

able [ˈeɪbl] adj capable, compétent(e); **to be ~ to do sth** être capable de faire qch, pouvoir faire qch; **~-bodied** adj robuste; **ably** [ˈeɪblɪ] adv avec compétence or talent, habilement

abnormal [æbˈnɔːməl] adj anormal(e)

aboard [əˈbɔːd] adv à bord ♦ prep à bord de

abode [əˈbəʊd] n (LAW): **of no fixed ~** sans domicile fixe

abolish [əˈbɒlɪʃ] vt abolir

aborigine [æbəˈrɪdʒɪniː] n aborigène m/f

abort [əˈbɔːt] vt faire avorter; **~ion** [əˈbɔːʃən] n avortement m; **to have an ~ion**; se faire avorter; **~ive** adj manqué(e)

abound [əˈbaʊnd] vi abonder; **to ~ in** or **with** abonder en, regorger de

about [əˈbaʊt] adv **1** (approximately) environ, à peu près; ~ **a hundred/thousand** etc environ cent/mille etc, une centaine/un millier etc; **it takes ~ 10 hours** ça prend environ or à peu près 10 heures; **at ~ 2 o'clock** vers 2 heures; **I've just ~ finished** j'ai presque fini
2 (referring to place) çà et là, de côté et d'autre; **to run ~** courir çà et là; **to walk ~** se promener, aller et venir
3: to be ~ to do sth être sur le point de faire qch
♦ prep **1** (relating to) au sujet de, à propos de; **a book ~ London** un livre sur Londres; **what is it ~?**

quoi s'agit-il?; **we talked ~ it** nous en avons parlé; **what** *or* **how ~ doing this?** et si nous faisions ceci? **2** (*referring to place*) dans; **to walk ~ the town** se promener dans la ville

about-face [ə'baʊt'feɪs] *n* demi-tour *m*

about-turn [ə'baʊt'tɜːn] *n* (*MIL*) demi-tour *m*; (*fig*) volte-face *f*

above [ə'bʌv] *adv* au-dessus ♦ *prep* au-dessus de; (*more*) plus de; **mentioned ~** mentionné ci-dessus; **~ all** par-dessus tout, surtout; **~board** *adj* franc(franche); honnête

abrasive [ə'breɪzɪv] *adj* abrasif(ive); (*fig*) caustique, agressif(ive)

abreast [ə'brɛst] *adv* de front; **to keep ~ of** se tenir au courant de

abridge [ə'brɪdʒ] *vt* abréger

abroad [ə'brɔːd] *adv* à l'étranger

abrupt [ə'brʌpt] *adj* (*steep, blunt*) abrupt(e); (*sudden, gruff*) brusque; **~ly** *adv* (*speak, end*) brusquement

abscess [æbsɪs] *n* abcès *m*

abscond [ab'skɒnd] *vi* disparaître, s'enfuir

absence ['æbsəns] *n* absence *f*

absent ['æbsənt] *adj* absent(e); **~ee** [æbsən'tiː] *n* absent(e); **~** (*habitual*) absentéiste *m/f*; **~-minded** *adj* distrait(e)

absolute ['æbsəluːt] *adj* absolu(e); **~ly** [æbsə'luːtlɪ] *adv* absolument

absolve [əb'zɒlv] *vt*: **to ~ sb (from)** (*blame, responsibility, sin*) absoudre qn (de)

absorb [əb'zɔːb] *vt* absorber; **to be ~ed in a book** être plongé(e) dans un livre; **~ent cotton** (*US*) *n* coton *m* hydrophile; **absorption** [əb'zɔːpʃən] *n* absorption *f*; (*fig*) concentration *f*

abstain [əb'steɪn] *vi*: **to ~ (from)** s'abstenir (de)

abstract ['æbstrækt] *adj* abstrait(e)

absurd [əb'sɜːd] *adj* absurde

abuse *n* ə'bjuːs, *vb* ə'bjuːz] *n* abus *m*; (*insults*) insultes *fpl*, injures *fpl* ♦ *vt* abuser de; (*insult*) insulter; **abusive** [ə'bjuːsɪv] *adj* grossier(ère), in-

jurieux(euse)

abysmal [ə'bɪzməl] *adj* exécrable; (*ignorance etc*) sans bornes

abyss [ə'bɪs] *n* abîme *m*, gouffre *m*

AC *abbr* (= *alternating current*) courant alternatif

academic [ækə'demɪk] *adj* universitaire; (*person: scholarly*) intellectuel(le); (*pej: issue*) oiseux(euse), purement théorique ♦ *n* universitaire *m/f*; **~ year** *n* année *f* universitaire

academy [ə'kædəmɪ] *n* (*learned body*) académie *f*; (*school*) collège *m*; **~ of music** conservatoire *m*

accelerate [æk'sɛləreɪt] *vt, vi* accélérer; **accelerator** [ək'sɛləreɪtə*] *n* accélérateur *m*

accent ['æksent] *n* accent *m*

accept [ək'sɛpt] *vt* accepter; **~able** *adj* acceptable; **~ance** *n* acceptation *f*

access ['æksɛs] *n* accès *m*; (*JUR: in divorce*) droit *m* de visite; **~ible** [æk'sɛsɪbl] *adj* accessible

accessory [æk'sɛsərɪ] *n* accessoire *m*; (*LAW*): **~ to** complice de

accident ['æksɪdənt] *n* accident *m*; (*chance*) hasard *m*; **by ~** accidentellement; par hasard; **~al** [æksɪ'dɛntl] *adj* accidentel(le); **~ally** [æksɪ'dɛntəlɪ] *adv* accidentellement; **~-prone** *adj* sujet(te) aux accidents

acclaim [ə'kleɪm] *n* acclamations *fpl* ♦ *vt* acclamer

accommodate [ə'kɒmədeɪt] *vt* loger, recevoir; (*oblige, help*) obliger; (*car etc*) contenir; **accommodating** [ə'kɒmədeɪtɪŋ] *adj* obligeant(e), arrangeant(e); **accommodation** [əkɒmə'deɪʃən] (*US* **~s**) *n* logement *m*

accompany [ə'kʌmpənɪ] *vt* accompagner

accomplice [ə'kʌmplɪs] *n* complice *m/f*

accomplish [ə'kʌmplɪʃ] *vt* accomplir; **~ment** *n* accomplissement *m*; réussite *f*; (*skill: gen pl*) talent *m*

accord [ə'kɔːd] *n* accord *m* ♦ *vt* accorder; **of his own ~** de son pro-

gré; ~**ance** *n*: in ~ance with
conformément à; ~**ing**: ~ing to
prep selon; ~**ingly** *adv* en conséquence

accordion [ə'kɔːdiən] *n* accordéon *m*

accost [ə'kɒst] *vt* aborder

account [ə'kaʊnt] *n* (COMM) compte
m; (report) compte rendu; récit *m*;
~**s** *npl* (COMM) comptabilité *f*,
comptes; of no ~ sans importance;
on ~ en acompte; on no ~ en aucun
cas; on ~ of à cause de; to take
into ~, take ~ of tenir compte de;
~ **for** *vt fus* expliquer, rendre compte de; ~**able** *adj*: ~able (to) responsable (devant); ~**ancy**
[ə'kaʊntənsi] *n* comptabilité *f*; ~**ant**
[ə'kaʊntənt] *n* comptable *m/f*; ~
number *n* (at bank etc) numéro *m*
de compte

accrued interest [ə'kjuːmjʊleit] *n* intérêt
m cumulé

accumulate [ə'kjuːmjʊleit] *vt* accumuler, amasser ♦ *vi* s'accumuler,
s'amasser

accuracy ['ækjʊrəsi] *n* exactitude *f*,
précision *f*

accurate ['ækjʊrit] *adj* exact(e), précis(e); ~**ly** *adv* avec précision

accusation [ækjuː'zeiʃən] *n* accusation *f*

accuse [ə'kjuːz] *vt*: to ~ **sb** (of sth)
accuser qn (de qch); ~**d** *n*: the ~d
l'accusé(e)

accustom [ə'kʌstəm] *vt* accoutumer,
habituer; ~**ed** *adj* (usual) habituel(le); (in the habit): ~ed to habitué(e) or accoutumé(e) à

ace [eis] *n* as *m*

ache [eik] *n* mal *m*, douleur *f* ♦ *vi*
(yearn): to ~ **to do sth** mourir d'envie de faire qch; my head ~s j'ai
mal à la tête

achieve [ə'tʃiːv] *vt* (aim) atteindre;
(victory, success) remporter, obtenir; ~**ment** *n* exploit *m*, réussite *f*

acid ['æsid] *adj* acide ♦ *n* acide *m*; ~
rain *n* pluies *fpl* acides

acknowledge [ək'nɒlidʒ] *vt* (letter:
also: ~ receipt of) accuser réception

de; (fact) reconnaître; ~**ment** *n* (of
letter) accusé *m* de réception

acne ['ækni] *n* acné *m*

acorn ['eikɔːn] *n* gland *m*

acoustic [ə'kuːstik] *adj* acoustique;
~**s** *n*, *npl* acoustique *f*

acquaint [ə'kweint] *vt*: to ~ **sb**
with sth mettre qn au courant de
qch; to be ~ed with connaître;
~**ance** *n* connaissance *f*

acquiesce [ækwi'es] *vi*: to ~ **to** accquiescer *or* consentir à

acquire [ə'kwaiə*] *vt* acquérir

acquit [ə'kwit] *vt* acquitter; to ~
o.s. well bien se comporter, s'en tirer très honorablement

acre ['eikə*] *n* acre *f* (= 4047 m²)

acrid ['ækrid] *adj* âcre

acrobat ['ækrəbæt] *n* acrobate *m/f*

across [ə'krɒs] *prep* (on the other
side) de l'autre côté de; (crosswise)
en travers de ♦ *adv* de l'autre côté;
en travers; to **run/swim** ~ traverser
en courant/à la nage; ~ **from** en
face de

acrylic [ə'krilik] *adj* acrylique

act [ækt] *n* acte *m*, action *f*; (of play)
acte; (in music-hall etc) numéro *m*;
(LAW) loi *f* ♦ *vi* agir; (THEATRE)
jouer; (pretend) jouer la comédie ♦
vt (part) jouer, tenir; in the ~ of en
train de; to ~ **as** servir de; ~**ing**
adj suppléant(e), par intérim ♦ *n*
(activity): to **do some** ~ing faire
du théâtre (or du cinéma)

action ['ækʃən] *n* action *f*; (MIL)
combat *m*(pl); (LAW) procès *m*,
action en justice; out of ~ hors de
combat; (machine) hors d'usage; to
take ~ agir, prendre des mesures;
~ **replay** *n* (TV) ralenti *m*

activate ['æktiveit] *vt* (mechanism)
actionner, faire fonctionner

active ['æktiv] *adj* actif(ive); (volcano) en activité; ~**ly** *adv* activement

activity [æk'tiviti] *n* activité *f*

actor ['æktə*] *n* acteur *m*

actress ['æktris] *n* actrice *f*

actual ['æktjʊəl] *adj* réel(le), véritable; ~**ly** *adv* (really) réellement, véritablement; *(in fact)* en fait

acumen ['ækjʊmen] *n* perspicacité *f*

acute [ə'kjuːt] *adj* aigu(ë); *(mind, observer)* pénétrant(e), perspicace

ad [æd] *n abbr* = **advertisement**

A.D. *adv abbr* (= *anno Domini*) ap. J.C.

adamant ['ædəmənt] *adj* inflexible

adapt [ə'dæpt] *vt* adapter ♦ *vi*: to ~ (to) s'adapter (à); ~**able** *adj* (*device*) adaptable; *(person)* qui s'adapte facilement; ~**er**, ~**or** *n (ELEC)* adapteur *m*, adaptateur *f*

add [æd] *vt* ajouter; *(figures: also: to ~ up)* additionner ♦ *vi*: to ~ to *(increase)* ajouter à, accroître

adder ['ædə⁰] *n* vipère *f*

addict ['ædɪkt] *n* intoxiqué(e); *(fig)* fanatique *m/f*; ~**ed** [ə'dɪktɪd] *adj*: to be ~**ed** to *(drugs, drink etc)* être adonné(e) à; *(fig: football etc)* être un(e) fanatique de; ~**ion** [ə'dɪkʃən] *n (MED)* dépendance *f*; ~**ive** *adj* qui crée une dépendance

addition [ə'dɪʃən] *n* addition *f*; *(thing added)* ajout *m*; **in** ~ de plus; de surcroît; **in** ~ **to** en plus de; ~**al** *adj* supplémentaire

additive ['ædɪtɪv] *n* additif *m*

address [ə'dres] *n* adresse *f*; *(talk)* discours *m*, allocution *f* ♦ *vt* adresser; *(speak to)* s'adresser à; **to** ~ (o.s. to) **a problem** s'attaquer à un problème

adept ['ædept] *adj*: ~ **at** expert(e) à or en

adequate ['ædɪkwɪt] *adj* adéquat(e); suffisant(e)

adhere [əd'hɪə⁰] *vi*: **to** ~ **to** adhérer à; *(fig: rule, decision)* se tenir à

adhesive [əd'hiːzɪv] *n* adhésif *m*; ~ **tape** *n (BRIT)* ruban adhésif; *(US: MED)* sparadrap *m*

ad hoc [æd'hɔk] *adj* improvisé(e), ad hoc

adjective ['ædʒektɪv] *n* adjectif *m*

adjoining [ə'dʒɔɪnɪŋ] *adj* voisin(e), adjacent(e), attenant(e)

adjourn [ə'dʒɜːn] *vt* ajourner ♦ *vi* suspendre la séance; lever la séance;

clore la session

adjust [ə'dʒʌst] *vt* ajuster, régler; rajuster ♦ *vi*: **to** ~ (**to**) s'adapter (à); ~**able** *adj* réglable; ~**ment** *n (PSYCH)* adaptation *f*; *(to machine)* ajustage *m*, réglage *m*; *(of prices, wages)* rajustement *m*

ad-lib [æd'lɪb] *vt, vi* improviser; **ad lib** *adv* à volonté, à loisir

administer [əd'mɪnɪstə⁰] *vt* administrer; *(justice)* rendre

administration [ədmɪnɪs'treɪʃən] *n* administration *f*

administrative [əd'mɪnɪstrətɪv] *adj* administratif(ive)

admiral ['ædmərəl] *n* amiral *m*; **A~ty** ['ædmərəltɪ] *(BRIT)* *n (also: A~ty Board)*: **the A~ty** ministère *m* de la Marine

admire [əd'maɪə⁰] *vt* admirer

admission [əd'mɪʃən] *n* admission *f*; *(to exhibition, night club etc)* entrée *f*; *(confession)* aveu *m*

admit [əd'mɪt] *vt* laisser entrer; admettre; *(agree)* reconnaître, admettre; ~ **to** *vt fus* reconnaître, avouer; ~**tance** *n* admission *f*, *(droit m d')*entrée *f*; ~**tedly** *adv* il faut admettre; il faut convenir

admonish [əd'mɒnɪʃ] *vt* donner un avertissement à; réprimander

ad nauseam [æd'nɔːsɪæm] *adv* (*repeat, talk*) à n'en plus finir

ado [ə'duː] *n*: **without (any) more** ~ sans plus de cérémonies

adolescence [ædə'lesns] *n* adolescence *f*; **adolescent** [ædə'lesnt] *adj, n* adolescent(e)

adopt [ə'dɒpt] *vt* adopter; ~**ed** *adj* adoptif(ive), adopté(e); ~**ion** [ə'dɒpʃən] *n* adoption *f*

adore [ə'dɔː⁰] *vt* adorer

adorn [ə'dɔːn] *vt* orner

Adriatic (Sea) [eɪdrɪ'ætɪk-] *n* Adriatique *f*

adrift [ə'drɪft] *adv* à la dérive

adult ['ædʌlt] *n* adulte *m/f* ♦ *adj* adulte; *(literature, education)* pour adultes

adultery [ə'dʌltərɪ] *n* adultère *m*

advance [əd'vɑ:ns] n avance f ♦
adj: ~ **booking** réservation f ♦ vt
avancer ♦ vi avancer, s'avancer; in
notice avertissement m; to make
~s (to sb) faire des propositions (à
qn); (amorously) faire des avances
(à qn); in ~ à l'avance, d'avance;
~d adj avancé(e); (SCOL: studies)
supérieur(e)

advantage [əd'vɑ:ntidʒ] n (also
TENNIS) avantage m; to take ~ of
(person) exploiter

advent ['ædvənt] n avènement m, venue f; A~ Avent m

adventure [əd'ventʃə*] n aventure f

adverb ['ædvə:b] n adverbe m

adverse ['ædvə:s] adj défavorable,
contraire

advert ['ædvə:t] (BRIT) n abbr =
advertisement

advertise ['ædvətaiz] vi(vt) faire de
la publicité (pour); mettre une annonce (pour vendre); to ~ for (staff,
accommodation) faire paraître une
annonce pour trouver; ~ment
[əd'və:tismənt] n (COMM) réclame f,
publicité f; (in classified ads) annonce f; ~r ['ædvətaizə*] n (in newspaper etc) annonceur m; **advertising**
['ædvətaiziŋ] n publicité f

advice [əd'vais] n conseils mpl; (notification) avis m; **piece of** ~
conseil; to take legal ~ consulter
un avocat

advisable [əd'vaizəbl] adj conseil-
lé(e), indiqué(e)

advise [əd'vaiz] vt conseiller; to ~
sb of sth aviser or informer qn de
qch; to ~ against sth/doing sth déconseiller qch/conseiller de ne pas
faire qch; ~dly [əd'vaizədli] adv (deliberately) délibérément; ~r n
conseiller(ère); **advisor** n = ~r;
advisory [əd'vaizəri] adj consulta-
tif(ive)

advocate [vb 'ædvəkeit] n 'ædvəkət]
n (upholder) défenseur m, avocat(e),
partisan(e) f; (LAW) avocat(e) ♦ vt
recommander, prôner

aerial ['ɛəriəl] n antenne f ♦ adj

aérien(ne)

aerobics [ɛə'rəubiks] n aérobic f

aeroplane ['ɛərəplein] (BRIT) n
avion m

aerosol ['ɛərəsɔl] n aérosol m

aesthetic [is'θetik] adj esthétique

afar [ə'fɑ:*] adv: from ~ de loin

affair [ə'fɛə*] n affaire f; (also: love
~) liaison f; aventure f

affect [ə'fɛkt] vt affecter; (disease)
atteindre; ~**ed** adj affecté(e)

affection [ə'fɛkʃən] n affection f;
~**ate** [ə'fɛkʃnit] adj affec-
tueux(euse)

affinity [ə'finiti] n: to have an ~
with/for avoir une affinité avec/pour;
(resemblance): to have an ~ with
avoir une ressemblance avec

afflict [ə'flikt] vt affliger

affluence ['æfluəns] n abondance f,
opulence f

affluent ['æfluənt] adj (person, family, surroundings) aisé(e), riche; the ~
society la société d'abondance

afford [ə'fɔ:d] vt se permettre; avoir
les moyens d'acheter or d'entretenir;
(provide) fournir, procurer

afield [ə'fi:ld] adv: (from) far ~
de loin

afloat [ə'fləut] adj, adv à flot; to
stay ~ surnager

afoot [ə'fut] adv: there is something ~ il se prépare quelque chose

afraid [ə'freid] adj effrayé(e); to be
~ of or to avoir peur de; I am ~
that ... je suis désolé(e), mais ...; I
am ~ so/not hélas oui/non

afresh [ə'frɛʃ] adv de nouveau

Africa ['æfrikə] n Afrique f; ~**n** adj
africain(e) ♦ n Africain(e)

aft [ɑ:ft] adv à l'arrière, vers l'arrière

after [ɑ:'ftə*] prep, adv après ♦ conj
après que, après avoir or être +pp;
what/who are you ~? que/qui
cherchez-vous?; to name sb ~ sb donner
à qn le nom de qn; twenty ~ eight

(US) huit heures vingt; ~ **all** après tout; ~ **you!** après vous, Monsieur *(or Madame etc)*; ~**effects** npl *(of disaster, radiation, drink etc)* répercussions fpl; *(of illness)* séquelles fpl, suites fpl; ~**math** n conséquences fpl, suites fpl; ~**noon** n après-midi m or f; ~**s** *(inf)* n *(dessert)* dessert m; ~**sales service** *(BRIT)* n *(for car, washing machine etc)* service m après-vente; ~**shave (lotion)** n after-shave m; ~**thought** n: **I had an** ~**thought** il m'est venu une idée après coup; ~**wards** *(US* ~**ward)** adv après

again [ə'gɛn] adv de nouveau; encore (une fois); **to do sth** ~ refaire qch; **not** ... ~ ne ... plus; ~ **and** ~ à plusieurs reprises

against [ə'gɛnst] prep contre; *(compared to)* par rapport à

age [eɪdʒ] n âge m ♦ vt, vi vieillir; **it's been** ~**s since** ça fait une éternité que ...; **he is 20 years of** ~ il a 20 ans; **to come of** ~ atteindre sa majorité; **to be** ~ majeur or mineur; ~**d¹** adj: ~**d 10** âgé(e) de 10 ans; ~**d²** ['eɪdʒɪd] npl: **the** ~**d** les personnes âgées; ~ **group** n tranche f d'âge; ~ **limit** n limite f d'âge

agency ['eɪdʒənsɪ] n agence f; *(government body)* organisme m, office m

agenda [ə'dʒɛndə] n ordre m du jour

agent ['eɪdʒənt] n agent m, représentant m; *(firm)* concessionnaire m

aggravate ['ægrəveɪt] vt aggraver; *(annoy)* exaspérer

aggregate ['ægrɪgɪt] n ensemble m, total m

aggressive [ə'grɛsɪv] adj agressif(ive)

aggrieved [ə'griːvd] adj chagriné(e), affligé(e)

aghast [ə'gɑːst] adj consterné(e), atterré(e)

agitate ['ædʒɪteɪt] vt *(person)* agiter, émouvoir, troubler ♦ vi: **to** ~ **for/ against** faire campagne pour/contre

AGM n abbr = *annual general meeting)* AG f, assemblée générale

ago [ə'gəu] adv: **2 days** ~ il y a deux jours; **not long** ~ il n'y a pas longtemps; **how long** ~? il y a combien de temps (de cela)?

agog [ə'gɒg] adj en émoi

agonizing ['ægənaɪzɪŋ] adj angoissant(e); déchirant(e)

agony ['ægənɪ] n *(pain)* douleur f atroce; **to be in** ~ souffrir le martyre

agree [ə'griː] vt *(price)* convenir de ♦ vi: **to** ~ **with** *(person)* être d'accord avec; *(statements etc)* concorder avec; *(LING)* s'accorder avec; **to** ~ **to do** accepter de or consentir à faire; **to** ~ **to sth** consentir à qch; **to** ~ **that** *(admit)* convenir or reconnaître que; **garlic doesn't** ~ **with me** je ne supporte pas l'ail; ~**able** adj agréable; *(willing)* consentant(e), d'accord; ~**d** adj *(time, place)* convenu(e); ~**ment** n accord m; **in** ~**ment** d'accord

agricultural [ægrɪ'kʌltʃərəl] adj agricole

agriculture ['ægrɪkʌltʃə*] n agriculture f

aground [ə'graund] adv: **to run** ~ échouer, s'échouer

ahead [ə'hɛd] adv *(in front: of position, place)* devant; *(: at the head)* en avant; *(look, plan, think)* en avant; ~ **of** devant; *(fig: schedule etc)* en avance sur; ~ **of time** en avance; **go right** or **straight** ~ allez tout droit; **go** ~! *(fig: permission)* allez-y!

aid [eɪd] n aide f; *(device)* appareil m ♦ vt aider; **in** ~ **of** en faveur de; **to** ~ **and abet** *(LAW)* se faire le complice de; *see also* **hearing**

aide [eɪd] n *(person)* aide m/f, assistant(e)

AIDS [eɪdz] n abbr = *acquired immune deficiency syndrome)* SIDA m

ailing ['eɪlɪŋ] adj malade

ailment ['eɪlmənt] n affection f

aim [eɪm] vt: **to** ~ **sth (at)** *(gun, camera)* braquer or pointer qch (sur); *(missile)* lancer qch (à or contre or en direction de); (*blow*) allonger qch (à); (*remark*) destiner or adresser qch (à) ♦ *vi* (*also: to take ~*) viser ♦ *n* but *m*; (*skill*): **his ~** is bad il vise mal; **to ~ at** viser; (*fig*) viser (à); **to ~ to do** avoir l'intention de faire; **~less** *adj* sans but

ain't [eɪnt] (*inf*) = **am not**; **aren't**; **isn't**

air [eə*] *n* air *m* ♦ *vt* (*room, bed, clothes*) aérer; (*grievances, views, ideas*) exposer, faire connaître ♦ *cpd* (*currents, attack etc*) aérien(ne); **to throw sth into the ~** jeter qch en l'air; **by ~** (*travel*) par avion; **to be on the ~** (*RADIO, TV: programme*) être diffusé(e); (*: station*) diffuser; **~bed** *n* matelas *m* pneumatique; **~borne** *adj* en vol; **~-conditioned** *adj* climatisé(e); **~ conditioning** *n* climatisation *f*; **~craft** *n* *inv* avion *m*; **~craft carrier** *n* porte-avions *m inv*; **~field** *n* terrain *m* d'aviation; **A~ Force** *n* armée *f* de l'air; **~ freshener** *n* désodorisant *m*; **~gun** *n* fusil *m* à air comprimé; **~ hostess** *n* (*BRIT*) hôtesse *f* de l'air; **~ letter** *n* (*BRIT*) aérogramme *m*; **~lift** *n* pont aérien; **~line** *n* ligne aérienne, compagnie *f* d'aviation; **~liner** *n* avion *m* de ligne; **~mail** *n*: **by ~mail** par avion; **~plane** *n* (*US*) avion *m*; **~port** *n* aéroport *m*; **~raid** *n* attaque *or* raid aérien(ne); **~sick** *adj*: **to be ~sick** avoir le mal de l'air; **~ terminal** *n* aérogare *f*; **~tight** *adj* hermétique; **~-traffic controller** *n* aiguilleur *m* du ciel; **~y** *adj* bien aéré(e); (*manners*) dégagé(e)

aisle [aɪl] *n* (*of church*) allée centrale; nef latérale; (*of theatre etc*) couloir *m*, passage *m*, allée

ajar [ə'dʒɑː*] *adj* entrouvert(e)

akin [ə'kɪn] *adj*: **~ to** (*similar*) qui tient de *or* ressemble à

alarm [ə'lɑːm] *n* alarme *f* ♦ *vt* alarmer; **~ call** *n* coup de fil *m* pour réveiller; **~ clock** *n* réveille-matin *m inv*, réveil *m*

alas [ə'læs] *excl* hélas!

albeit [ɔːl'biːɪt] *conj* (*although*) bien que +*sub*, encore que +*sub*

album ['ælbəm] *n* album *m*

alcohol ['ælkəhɔl] *n* alcool *m*; **~ic** [ælkə'hɔlɪk] *adj* alcoolique ♦ *n* alcoolique *m/f*; **A~ics Anonymous** Alcooliques anonymes

ale [eɪl] *n* bière *f*

alert [ə'lɜːt] *adj* alerte, vif(vive); vigilant(e) ♦ *n* alerte *f* ♦ *vt* alerter; **on the ~** sur le qui-vive; (*MIL*) en état d'alerte

algebra ['ældʒɪbrə] *n* algèbre *m*

Algeria [æl'dʒɪərɪə] *n* Algérie *f*

alias ['eɪlɪəs] *adv* alias ♦ *n* faux nom, nom d'emprunt; (*writer*) pseudonyme *m*

alibi ['ælɪbaɪ] *n* alibi *m*

alien ['eɪlɪən] *n* étranger(ère); (*from outer space*) extraterrestre *mf* ♦ *adj*: **~ (to)** étranger(ère) (à); **~ate** *vt* aliéner; s'aliéner

alight [ə'laɪt] *adj, adv* en feu ♦ *vi* mettre pied à terre; (*passenger*) descendre; (*bird*) se poser

alike [ə'laɪk] *adj* semblable, pareil(le) ♦ *adv* de même; **to look ~** se ressembler

alimony ['ælɪmənɪ] *n* (*payment*) pension *f* alimentaire

alive [ə'laɪv] *adj* vivant(e); (*lively*) plein(e) de vie

┌─────────────────────┐
│ **KEYWORD** │
└─────────────────────┘

all [ɔːl] *adj* (*singular*) tout(e); (*plural*) tous(toutes); **~ day** tout le jour; **~ night** toute la nuit; **~ men** tous les hommes; **~ five** tous les cinq; **~ the food** toute la nourriture; **~ the books** tous les livres; **~ the time** tous le temps; **~ his life** toute sa vie ♦ *pron* **1** tout; **I ate it ~**, **I ate ~ of it** j'ai tout mangé; **~ of us went** nous y sommes tous allés; **~ of the boys went** tous les garçons y sont allés

2 (*in phrases*): **above ~** surtout, par-dessus tout; **after ~** après tout; **at ~**: **not at ~** (*in answer to ques-*

tion) pas du tout; (*in answer to thanks*) je vous en prie!; **I'm not at ~ tired** je ne suis pas du tout fatigué(e); **anything at ~ will do** n'importe quoi fera l'affaire; **~ in ~** tout bien considéré, en fin de compte ♦ *adv*: **~ alone** tout (e) seul(e); **it's not as hard as ~ that** ce n'est pas si difficile que ça; **~ the more/the better** d'autant plus/mieux; **~ but** presque, pratiquement; **the score is 2 ~** le score est 2 partout

allay [əˈleɪ] *vt* (*fears*) apaiser, calmer

allege [əˈledʒ] *vt* alléguer, prétendre; **~dly** [əˈledʒɪdlɪ] *adv* à ce que l'on prétend, paraît-il

allegiance [əˈliːdʒəns] *n* allégeance *f*, fidélité *f*, obéissance *f*

allergic [əˈlɜːdʒɪk] *adj*: **~ to** allergique à; **allergy** [ˈælədʒɪ] *n* allergie *f*

alleviate [əˈliːvɪeɪt] *vt* soulager, adoucir

alley [ˈælɪ] *n* ruelle *f*

alliance [əˈlaɪəns] *n* alliance *f*

allied [ˈælaɪd] *adj* allié(e)

all-in [ˈɔːlɪn] (*BRIT*) *adj* (*also adv*: *charge*) tout compris; **~ wrestling** *n* lutte *f* libre

all-night [ˈɔːlnaɪt] *adj* ouvert(e) or qui dure toute la nuit

allocate [ˈæləkeɪt] *vt* (*share out*) répartir, distribuer; (*duties*): **to ~ sth to** assigner or attribuer qch à; (*sum*, *time*): **to ~ sth to** allouer qch à

allot [əˈlɒt] *vt*: **to ~ (to)** (*money*) répartir (entre), (*time*) allouer (à); **~ment** *n* (*share*) part *f*; (*garden*) lopin *m* de terre (*loué à la municipalité*)

all-out [ˈɔːlaʊt] *adj* (*effort etc*) total(e) ♦ *adv*: **all out** à fond

allow [əˈlaʊ] *vt* (*practice, behaviour*) permettre, autoriser; (*sum to spend etc*) accorder; allouer; (*sum, time estimated*) compter, prévoir; (*claim, goal*) admettre; (*concede*): **to ~ that** convenir que; **to ~ sb to do** permettre à qn de faire, autoriser qn

à faire; **he is ~ed to ...** on lui permet de ...; **~ for** *vt fus* tenir compte de; **~ance** *n* (*money received*) allocation *f*; subside *m*; indemnité *f*; (*TAX*) somme *f* déductible du revenu imposable, abattement *m*; **to make ~ances for** tenir compte de

alloy [ˈælɔɪ] *n* alliage *m*

all: **~ right** *adv* (*feel, check*) bien; (*as answer*) d'accord; **~rounder** *n*: **to be a good ~rounder** être doué(e) en tout; **~time** *adj* (*record*) sans précédent, absolu(e)

allude [əˈluːd] *vi*: **to ~ to** faire allusion à

alluring [əˈljʊərɪŋ] *adj* séduisant(e)

ally [ˈælaɪ, *vb* əˈlaɪ] *n* allié *m* ♦ *vt*: **to ~ o.s. with** s'allier avec

almighty [ɔːlˈmaɪtɪ] *adj* tout-puissant; (*tremendous*) énorme

almond [ˈɑːmənd] *n* amande *f*

almost [ˈɔːlməʊst] *adv* presque

alms [ɑːmz] *npl* aumône *f*

aloft [əˈlɒft] *adv* en l'air

alone [əˈləʊn] *adj, adv* seul(e); **to leave sb ~** laisser qn tranquille; **to leave sth ~** ne pas toucher à qch; **let ~ ...** sans parler de ...; encore moins ...

along [əˈlɒŋ] *prep* le long de ♦ *adv*: **is he coming ~ with us?** vient-il avec nous?; **he was hopping/limping ~** il avançait en sautillant/boitant; **~ with** (*together with*: *person*) en compagnie de; (: *thing*) avec, en plus de; **all ~** (*all the time*) depuis le début; **~side** *prep* le long de; à côté de ♦ *adv* bord à bord

aloof [əˈluːf] *adj* distant(e) ♦ *adv*: **to stand ~** se tenir à distance or à l'écart

aloud [əˈlaʊd] *adv* à haute voix

alphabet [ˈælfəbet] *n* alphabet *m*; **~ical** [ælfəˈbetɪkl] *adj* alphabétique

alpine [ˈælpaɪn] *adj* alpin(e), alpestre

Alps [ælps] *npl*: **the ~** les Alpes *fpl*

already [ɔːlˈredɪ] *adv* déjà

alright [ˈɔːlraɪt] (*BRIT*) *adv* = all right

Alsatian [ælˈseɪʃən] (*BRIT*) *n* (*dog*)

berger allemand

also ['ɔ:lsəu] adv aussi

altar ['ɔ:ltə*] n autel m

alter ['ɔ:ltə*] vt, vi changer

alternate [adj ɒl'tɜ:nɪt, vb 'ɔltɜ:neɪt] adj alterné(e), alternant(e), alternatif(ive) ♦ vi alterner; **on ~ days** un jour sur deux, tous les deux jours; **alternating current** n courant alternatif

alternative [ɒl'tɜ:nətɪv] adj (solutions) possible, au choix; (plan) autre, de rechange; (lifestyle, medicine) parallèle ♦ n (choice) alternative f; (other possibility) solution f de remplacement or de rechange, autre possibilité f; **an ~ comedian** un nouveau comique; **~ly** adv: **~ly one could** une autre or l'autre solution serait de, on pourrait aussi

alternator ['ɔltə:neɪtə*] n (AUT) alternateur m

although [ɔ:l'ðəu] conj bien que +sub

altitude ['æltɪtju:d] n altitude f

alto ['æltəu] n (female) contralto m; (male) haute-contre f

altogether [ɔːltə'geðə*] adv entièrement, tout à fait; (on the whole) tout compte fait; (in all) en tout

aluminium [æljʊ'mɪnɪəm] (BRIT), **aluminum** [ə'luːmɪnəm] (US) n aluminium m

always ['ɔːlweɪz] adv toujours

Alzheimer's (disease) [ælts'haɪməz] n maladie f d'Alzheimer

am [æm] vb see **be**

a.m. adv abbr (= ante meridiem) du matin

amalgamate [ə'mælgəmeɪt] vt, vi fusionner

amateur ['æmətə*] n amateur m; **~ish** (pej) adj d'amateur

amaze [ə'meɪz] vt stupéfier; **to be ~d (at)** être stupéfait(e) (de); **~ment** n stupéfaction f, stupeur f;

amazing [ə'meɪzɪŋ] adj étonnant(e); exceptionnel(le)

ambassador [æm'bæsədə*] n ambassadeur m

amber ['æmbə*] n ambre m; **at ~** (BRIT: AUT) à l'orange

ambiguous [æm'bɪgjʊəs] adj ambigu(ë)

ambition [æm'bɪʃən] n ambition f

ambitious [æm'bɪʃəs] adj ambitieux(euse)

amble ['æmbl] vi (also: **to ~ along**) aller d'un pas tranquille

ambulance ['æmbjʊləns] n ambulance f

ambush ['æmbʊʃ] n embuscade f ♦ vt tendre une embuscade à

amenable [ə'miːnəbl] adj: **~ to** (advice etc) disposé(e) à écouter

amend [ə'mend] vt (law) amender; (text) corriger; **to make ~s** réparer ses torts, faire amende honorable

amenities [ə'miːnɪtɪz] npl aménagements mpl, équipements mpl

America [ə'merɪkə] n Amérique f; **~n** adj américain(e) ♦ n Américain(e)

amiable ['eɪmɪəbl] adj aimable, affable

amicable ['æmɪkəbl] adj amical(e); (JUR) à l'amiable

amid(st) [ə'mɪd(st)] prep parmi, au milieu de

amiss [ə'mɪs] adj, adv: **there's something ~** il y a quelque chose qui ne va pas or qui cloche; **to take sth ~** prendre qch mal or de travers

ammonia [ə'məunɪə] n (gas) ammoniac m; (liquid) ammoniaque f

ammunition [æmjʊ'nɪʃən] n munitions fpl

amok [ə'mɒk] adv: **to run ~** être pris(e) d'un accès de folie furieuse

among(st) [ə'mʌŋ(st)] prep parmi, entre

amorous ['æmərəs] adj amoureux(euse)

amount [ə'maunt] n (sum) somme f, montant m; (quantity) quantité f, nombre m ♦ vi: **to ~ to** (total) s'élever à; (be same as) équivaloir à, revenir à

amp(ere) ['æmp(eə*)] n ampère m

ample ['æmpl] adj ample; spa-

cieux(euse); (*enough*): this is ~
c'est largement suffisant; **to have ~
time/room** avoir bien assez de
temps/place

amplifier ['æmplɪfaɪə*] n amplificateur m

amuse [ə'mjuːz] vt amuser, divertir;
~**ment** n amusement m; ~**ment arcade** n salle f de jeu

an [æn] indef art see a

anaemic [ə'niːmɪk] (US **anemic**) adj
anémique

anaesthetic [ænɪs'θetɪk] n anesthési-
que m

analog(ue) ['ænəlɔg] adj (*watch,
computer*) analogique

analyse ['ænəlaɪz] (US **analyze**) vt
analyser; **analysis** [ə'nælɪsɪs] (pl ana-
lyses) n analyse f; **analyst** ['ænəlɪst]
n (POL etc) spécialiste m/f; (US)
psychanalyste m/f

analyze ['ænəlaɪz] (US) vt = analyse

anarchist ['ænəkɪst] n anarchiste m/f

anarchy ['ænəkɪ] n anarchie f

anatomy [ə'nætəmɪ] n anatomie f

ancestor ['ænsɪstə*] n ancêtre m,
aïeul m

anchor ['æŋkə*] n ancre f ♦ vi (*also:
to drop* ~) jeter l'ancre, mouiller ♦
vt mettre à l'ancre; (*fig*): **to** ~ **sth
to** fixer qch à; **to weigh** ~ lever
l'ancre

anchovy ['æntʃəvɪ] n anchois m

ancient ['eɪnʃənt] adj ancien(ne),
antique; (*person*) d'un âge vénéra-
ble; (*car*) antédiluvien(ne)

ancillary [æn'sɪlərɪ] adj auxiliaire

and [ænd] conj et; ~ **so on** et ainsi
de suite; **try** ~ **come** tâchez de venir; **he talked** ~ **talked** il n'a pas
arrêté de parler; **better** ~ **better** de
mieux en mieux

anew [ə'njuː] adv à nouveau

angel ['eɪndʒəl] n ange m

anger ['æŋgə*] n colère f

angina [æn'dʒaɪnə] n angine f de poitrine

angle ['æŋgl] n angle m; **from their
~** de leur point de vue

angler ['æŋglə*] n pêcheur(euse) à la
ligne

Anglican ['æŋglɪkən] adj, n angli-
can(e)

angling ['æŋglɪŋ] n pêche f à la ligne

Anglo- ['æŋgləʊ] prefix anglo(-)

angrily ['æŋgrɪlɪ] adv avec colère

angry ['æŋgrɪ] adj en colère, fu-
rieux(euse); (*wound*) enflammé(e);
to be ~ with sb/at sth être furieux
contre qn/de qch; **to get ~** se fâcher,
se mettre en colère

anguish ['æŋgwɪʃ] n (*physical*) supplice m; (*mental*) angoisse f

angular ['æŋgjʊlə*] adj angu-
leux(euse)

animal ['ænɪməl] n animal m
adj animal(e) ♦

animate [vb 'ænɪmeɪt, adj 'ænɪmɪt]
adj animé(e), vivant(e); ~**d** adj ani-
mé(e)

aniseed ['ænɪsiːd] n anis m

ankle ['æŋkl] n cheville f; ~ **sock** n
socquette f

annex [n 'æneks, vb ə'neks] n (*also:
BRIT:* ~**e**) annexe f ♦ vt annexer

anniversary [ænɪ'vɜːsərɪ] n anniversaire m

announce [ə'naʊns] vt annoncer;
(*birth, death*) faire part de; ~**ment**
n annonce f; (*for births etc: in newspaper*) avis m de faire-part; (: *letter,
card*) faire-part m; ~**r** n (RADIO,
TV: *between programmes*) speak-
er(ine)

annoy [ə'nɔɪ] vt agacer, ennuyer,
contrarier; **don't get ~ed!** ne vous
fâchez pas!; ~**ance** n mécontentement m, contrariété f; ~**ing** adj aga-
çant(e), contrariant(e)

annual ['ænjʊəl] adj annuel(le) ♦ n
(BOT) plante annuelle; (*children's
book*) album m

annul [ə'nʌl] vt annuler

annum ['ænəm] n see **per**

anonymous [ə'nɒnɪməs] adj anonyme

anorak ['ænəræk] n anorak m

another [ə'nʌðə*] adj: ~ **book** (*one
more*) un autre livre, encore un livre,

un livre de plus; (*a different one*) un
autre livre ♦ *pron* un(e) autre, encore un(e), un(e) de plus; *see also* **one**
answer ['ɑːnsə*] *n* réponse *f*; (*to
problem*) solution *f* ♦ *vi* répondre ♦
vt (*reply to*) répondre à; (*problem*)
résoudre; (*prayer*) exaucer; **in ~ to
your letter** en réponse à votre lettre; **to ~ the phone** répondre (au téléphone); **to ~ the bell or the door**
aller or venir ouvrir (la porte); ~
back *vi* répondre, répliquer; ~ **for** *vt
fus* (*person*) répondre de, se porter
garant de; (*crime, one's actions*) être
responsable de; ~ **to** *vt fus* (*description*) répondre or correspondre à;
~**able** *adj*: ~**able** (**to sb/for sth**)
responsable (devant qn/de qch);
~**ing machine** *n* répondeur *m* automatique
ant [ænt] *n* fourmi *f*
antagonism [æn'tægənɪzəm] *n* anta-
gonisme *m*
antagonize [æn'tægənaɪz] *vt* éveiller
l'hostilité de, contrarier
Antarctic [ænt'ɑːktɪk] *n*: **the** ~ l'Antarctique *m*
antenatal [æntɪ'neɪtl] *adj* préna-
tal(e); ~ **clinic** *n* service *m* de
consultation prénatale
anthem ['ænθəm] *n*: **national** ~
hymne national
anti: ~**-aircraft** [æntɪ'ɛəkrɑːft] *adj*
(*missile*) anti-aérien(ne); ~**-biotic**
['æntɪbaɪ'ɒtɪk] *n* antibiotique *m*; ~**-
body** ['æntɪbɒdɪ] *n* anticorps *m*
anticipate [æn'tɪsɪpeɪt] *vt* s'attendre
à; prévoir; (*wishes, request*) aller au
devant de, devancer
anticipation [æntɪsɪ'peɪʃən] *n* attente *f*; **with** ~ impatiemment
anticlimax ['æntɪ'klaɪmæks] *n* déception *f*, douche froide (*col*)
anticlockwise ['æntɪ'klɒkwaɪz] *adj,
adv* dans le sens inverse des aiguilles
d'une montre
antics ['æntɪks] *npl* singeries *fpl*
antifreeze ['æntɪfriːz] *n* antigel *m*
antihistamine [æntɪ'hɪstəmɪn] *n*
antihistaminique *m*

antiquated ['æntɪkweɪtɪd] *adj*
vieilli(e), suranné(e), vieillot(te)
antique [æn'tiːk] *n* objet *m* d'art ancien, meuble ancien or d'époque,
antiquité *f* ♦ *adj* ancien(ne); ~ **dealer** *n* antiquaire *m*; ~ **shop** *n* magasin *m* d'antiquités
antiquity [æn'tɪkwɪtɪ] *n* antiquité *f*
anti: ~**-Semitism** [æntɪ'semɪtɪzəm] *n*
antisémitisme *m*; ~**-septic** [æntɪ'
septɪk] *n* antiseptique *m*; ~**-social**
[æntɪ'səʊʃl] *adj* peu liant(e), sauvage,
insociable; (*against society*) antiso-
cial(e)
antlers ['æntləz] *npl* bois *mpl*, ramu-
re *f*
anvil ['ænvɪl] *n* enclume *f*
anxiety [æŋ'zaɪətɪ] *n* anxiété *f*;
(*keenness*): ~ **to do** grand désir or
impatience *f* de faire
anxious ['æŋkʃəs] *adj* anxieux(euse),
angoissé(e); (*worrying: time, situation*) inquiétant(e); (*keen*): ~ **to do/
that** qui tient beaucoup à faire/à ce
que; impatient(e) de faire/que

KEYWORD

any ['enɪ] *adj* **1** (*in questions etc: singular*) du, de l', de la; (*in questions
etc: plural*) des; **have you ~
butter/children/ink?** avez-vous du
beurre/des enfants/de l'encre?
2 (*with negative*) de, d'; **I haven't ~
money/books** je n'ai pas
d'argent/de livres
3 (*no matter which*) n'importe
quel(le); **choose ~ book you like**
vous pouvez choisir n'importe quel livre
4 (*in phrases*): **in ~ case** de toute
façon; ~ **day now** d'un jour à l'autre; **at ~ moment** à tout moment,
d'un instant à l'autre; **at ~ rate** en
tout cas
♦ *pron* **1** (*in questions etc*): **have
you got ~?** est-ce que vous en
avez?; **can ~ of you sing?** est-ce
que parmi vous il y en a qui chan-
tent?
2 (*with negative*) en; **I haven't ~
(of them)** je n'en ai pas, je n'en ai

aucun

3 (*no matter which one(s)*) n'importe lequel (*or* laquelle); **take ~ of those books (you like)** vous pouvez prendre n'importe lequel de ces livres

♦ *adv* **1** (*in questions etc*): **do you want ~ more soup/sandwiches?** voulez-vous encore de la soupe/des sandwichs?; **are you feeling ~ better?** est-ce que vous vous sentez mieux?

2 (*with negative*): **I can't hear him ~ more** je ne l'entends plus; **don't wait ~ longer** n'attendez pas plus longtemps

any: ~body ['enɪbɔdɪ] *pron* n'importe qui; (*in interrogative sentences*) quelqu'un; (*in negative sentences*): **I don't see ~** je ne vois personne; **~how** *adv* (*at any rate*) de toute façon, quand même; (*haphazard*) n'importe comment; **~one** [-wʌn] *pron* = **anybody**; **~thing** *pron* n'importe quoi, quelque chose, ne ... rien; **~way** *adv* de toute façon; **~where** *adv* n'importe où, quelque part; **I don't see him ~** je ne le vois nulle part

apart [ə'pɑːt] *adv* (*to one side*) à part; de côté; (*separately*) séparément; **10 miles ~** à 10 miles l'un de l'autre; **to take ~** démonter; **~ from** à part, excepté

apartheid [ə'pɑːteɪt] *n* apartheid *m*

apartment [ə'pɑːtmənt] *n* (*US*) appartement *m*, logement *m*; (*room*) chambre *f*; **~ building** (*US*) *n* immeuble *m*; maison divisée en appartements

ape [eɪp] *n* (grand) singe ♦ *vt* singer

apéritif [ə'pɛrɪtɪf] *n* apéritif *m*

aperture ['æpətjʊə*] *n* orifice *m*, ouverture *f*; (*PHOT*) ouverture (du diaphragme)

apex ['eɪpɛks] *n* sommet *m*

apiece [ə'piːs] *adv* chacun(e)

apologetic [əpɔlə'dʒetɪk] *adj* (*tone, letter*) d'excuse; (*person*): **to be ~** s'excuser

apologize [ə'pɔlədʒaɪz] *vi*: **to ~ (for sth to sb)** s'excuser (de qch auprès de qn), présenter des excuses (à qn pour qch)

apology [ə'pɔlədʒɪ] *n* excuses *fpl*

apostrophe [ə'pɔstrəfɪ] *n* apostrophe *f*

appal [ə'pɔːl] *vt* consterner; **~ling** [ə'pɔːlɪŋ] *adj* épouvantable; (*stupidity*) consternant(e)

apparatus [æpə'reɪtəs] *n* appareil *m*, dispositif *m*; (*in gymnasium*) agrès *mpl*; (*of government*) dispositif *m*

apparel [ə'pærəl] (*US*) *n* habillement *m*

apparent [ə'pærənt] *adj* apparent(e); **~ly** *adv* apparemment

appeal [ə'piːl] *vi* (*LAW*) faire *or* interjeter appel ♦ *n* appel *m*; (*request*) prière *f*; appel *m*; (*charm*) attrait *m*, charme *m*; **to ~ for** lancer un appel pour; **to ~ to** (*beg*) faire appel à; (*be attractive*) plaire à; **it doesn't ~ to me** cela ne m'attire pas; **~ing** *adj* (*attractive*) attrayant(e)

appear [ə'pɪə*] *vi* apparaître, se montrer; (*LAW*) comparaître; (*publication*) paraître, sortir, être publié(e); (*seem*) paraître, sembler; **it would ~ that** il semble que; **to ~ in Hamlet** jouer dans Hamlet; **to ~ on TV** passer à la télé; **~ance** *n* apparition *f*; parution *f*; (*look, aspect*) apparence *f*, aspect *m*

appease [ə'piːz] *vt* apaiser, calmer

appendicitis [əpɛndɪ'saɪtɪs] *n* appendicite *f*; **appendix** [ə'pɛndɪks] (*pl* ap**pendices**) *n* appendice *m*

appetite ['æpɪtaɪt] *n* appétit *m*

appetizer ['æpɪtaɪzə*] *n* amuse-gueule *m*; (*drink*) apéritif *m*

applaud [ə'plɔːd] *vt, vi* applaudir

applause [ə'plɔːz] *n* applaudissements *mpl*

apple ['æpl] *n* pomme *f*; **~ tree** *n* pommier *m*

appliance [ə'plaɪəns] *n* appareil *m*

applicable [ə'plɪkəbl] *adj* (*revelant*): **to be ~ to** valoir pour

applicant ['æplɪkənt] *n*: **~ (for)**

candidat(e) (à)

application [æpli'keiʃən] n application f; (for a job, a grant etc) demande f; candidature f; ~ **form** n formulaire m de demande

applied [ə'plaid] adj appliqué(e)

apply [ə'plai] vt (paint, ointment) to ~ **(to)** appliquer (sur); (law etc): to ~ **(to)** appliquer (à) ♦ vi: to ~ (be suitable for, relevant to) s'appliquer à; (ask) s'adresser à; to ~ **(for)** (permit, grant) faire une demande (en vue d'obtenir); (job) poser sa candidature (pour), faire une demande d'emploi (concernant); to ~ **o.s. to** s'appliquer à

appoint [ə'point] vt nommer, engager; ~**ed** adj: at the ~**ed time** à l'heure dite; ~**ment** n nomination f; (meeting) rendez-vous m; to **make an** ~**ment (with)** prendre rendez-vous (avec)

appraisal [ə'preizl] n évaluation f

appreciate [ə'priːʃieit] vt (like) apprécier; (be grateful for) être reconnaissant(e) de; (understand) comprendre; se rendre compte de ♦ vi (FINANCE) prendre de la valeur

appreciation [əpriːʃi'eiʃən] n appréciation f; (gratitude) reconnaissance f; (COMM) hausse f, valorisation f

appreciative [ə'priːʃiətiv] adj (person) sensible; (comment) élogieux(euse)

apprehensive [æpri'hensiv] adj inquiet(ète), appréhensif(ive)

apprentice [ə'prentis] n apprenti m; ~**ship** n apprentissage m

approach [ə'prəutʃ] vi approcher ♦ vt (come near) approcher de; (ask, apply to) s'adresser à; (situation, problem) aborder ♦ n approche f; (access) accès m; ~**able** adj accessible

appropriate [adj ə'prəupriət, vb ə'prəuprieit] adj (moment, remark) opportun(e); (tool etc) approprié(e) ♦ vt (take) s'approprier

approval [ə'pruːvəl] n approbation f; **on** ~ (COMM) à l'examen

approve [ə'pruːv] vt approuver; ~ **of** vt fus approuver

approximate [adj ə'prɔksimit, vb ə'prɔksimeit] adj approximatif(ive) ♦ vt se rapprocher de, être proche de; ~**ly** adv approximativement

apricot ['eiprikɔt] n abricot m

April ['eiprəl] n avril m; ~ **Fool's Day** le premier avril

apron ['eiprən] n tablier m

apt [æpt] adj (suitable) approprié(e); (likely): ~ **to do** susceptible de faire; qui a tendance à faire

Aquarius [ə'kweəriəs] n le Verseau

Arab ['æræb] adj arabe ♦ n Arabe m/f; ~**ian** [ə'reibiən] adj arabe; ~**ic** ['æræbik] adj arabe ♦ n arabe m

arbitrary ['ɑːbitrəri] adj arbitraire

arbitration [ɑːbi'treiʃən] n arbitrage m

arcade [ɑː'keid] n arcade f; (passage with shops) passage m, galerie marchande

arch [ɑːtʃ] n arc m; (of foot) cambrure f, voûte f plantaire ♦ vt arquer, cambrer

archaeologist [ɑːki'ɔlədʒist] n archéologue m/f; **archaeology** [ɑːki'ɔlədʒi] n archéologie f

archbishop ['ɑːtʃ'biʃəp] n archevêque m

archenemy ['ɑːtʃ'enəmi] n ennemi m de toujours or juré

archaeology etc (US) = **archaeology** etc

archery ['ɑːtʃəri] n tir m à l'arc

architect ['ɑːkitekt] n architecte m; ~**ure** n architecture f

archives ['ɑːkaivz] npl archives fpl

Arctic ['ɑːktik] adj arctique ♦ n: the ~ l'Arctique m

ardent ['ɑːdənt] adj fervent(e)

are [ɑː*] vb see **be**

area ['ɛəriə] n (GEOM) superficie f; (zone) région f; (: smaller) secteur m, partie f; (in room) coin m; (knowledge, research) domaine m

aren't [ɑːnt] = **are not**

Argentina [ɑːdʒən'tiːnə] n Argentine f; **Argentinian** [ɑːdʒən'tiniən] adj argentin(e) ♦ *n* Argentin(e)

arguably [ɑ:gjʊəblɪ] *adv*: **it is ~ ...** on peut soutenir que c'est ...

argue [ˈɑ:gju:] *vi* (*quarrel*) se disputer; (*reason*) argumenter; **to ~ that** objecter *or* alléguer que

argument [ˈɑ:gjʊmənt] *n* (*reasons*) argument *m*; (*quarrel*) dispute *f*; **~ative** [ɑ:gjʊˈmentətɪv] *adj* ergoteur(euse), raisonneur(euse)

Aries [ˈɛərɪz] *n* le Bélier

arise [əˈraɪz] *vi* (*pt* **arose**, *pp* **arisen**) (*of* survenir, se présenter

aristocrat [ˈærɪstəkræt] *n* aristocrate *m/f*

arithmetic [əˈrɪθmətɪk] *n* arithmétique *f*

ark [ɑ:k] *n*: **Noah's A~** l'Arche *f* de Noé

arm [ɑ:m] *n* bras *m* ♦ *vt* armer; **~s** *npl* (*weapons, HERALDRY*) armes *fpl*; **~ in ~** bras dessus bras dessous

armaments [ˈɑ:məmənts] *npl* armement *m*

arm: **~chair** *n* fauteuil *m*; **~ed** *adj* armé(e); **~ed robbery** *n* vol *m* à main armée

armour [ˈɑ:mə*] (*US* **armor**) *n* armure *f*; (*MIL: tanks*) blindés *mpl*; **~ed car** *n* véhicule blindé

armpit [ˈɑ:mpɪt] *n* aisselle *f*

armrest [ˈɑ:mrest] *n* accoudoir *m*

army [ˈɑ:mɪ] *n* armée *f*

aroma [əˈrəʊmə] *n* arôme *m*

arose [əˈrəʊz] *pt of* **arise**

around [əˈraʊnd] *adv* autour; (*nearby*) dans les parages ♦ *prep* autour de; (*near*) près de; (*fig: about*) environ; (: *date, time*) vers

arouse [əˈraʊz] *vt* (*sleeper*) éveiller; (*curiosity, passions*) éveiller, susciter; (*anger*) exciter

arrange [əˈreɪndʒ] *vt* arranger; **to ~ to do sth** prévoir de faire qch; **~ment** *n* arrangement *m*; **~ments** *npl* (*plans etc*) arrangements *mpl*, dispositions *fpl*

array [əˈreɪ] *n*: **~ of** déploiement *m* or étalage *m* de

arrears [əˈrɪəz] *npl* arriéré *m*; **to be**

in ~ with one's rent devoir un arriéré de loyer

arrest [əˈrest] *vt* arrêter; (*sb's attention*) retenir, attirer ♦ *n* arrestation *f*; **under ~** en état d'arrestation

arrival [əˈraɪvl] *n* arrivée *f*; **new ~** nouveau venu, nouvelle venue; (*baby*) nouveau-né(e)

arrive [əˈraɪv] *vi* arriver

arrogant [ˈærəgənt] *adj* arrogant(e)

arrow [ˈærəʊ] *n* flèche *f*

arse [ɑ:s] (*BRIT: inf!*) *n* cul *m* (!)

arson [ˈɑ:sn] *n* incendie criminel

art [ɑ:t] *n* art *m*; **A~s** *npl* (*SCOL*) les lettres *fpl*

artery [ˈɑ:tərɪ] *n* artère *f*

artful [ˈɑ:tful] *adj* astucieux(euse), rusé(e)

art gallery *n* musée d'art; (*small and private*) galerie *f* de peinture

arthritis [ɑ:ˈθraɪtɪs] *n* arthrite *f*

artichoke [ˈɑ:tɪtʃəʊk] *n* (*also: globe ~*) artichaut *m*; (: *Jerusalem ~*) topinambour *m*

article [ˈɑ:tɪkl] *n* article *m*; **~s** *npl* (*BRIT: LAW: training*) ~ stage *m*; **~ of clothing** vêtement *m*

articulate *adj* [ɑ:ˈtɪkjʊlɪt], *vb* [ɑ:ˈtɪkjʊleɪt] *adj* (*person*) qui s'exprime bien; (*speech*) bien articulé(e), prononcé(e) clairement ♦ *vt* exprimer; **~d lorry** (*BRIT*) *n* (camion *m*) semi-remorque *m*

artificial [ɑ:tɪˈfɪʃəl] *adj* artificiel(le)

artist [ˈɑ:tɪst] *n* artiste *m/f*; **~ic** [ɑ:ˈtɪstɪk] *adj* artistique; **~ry** *n* art *m*, talent *m*

art school *n* ≈ école *f* des beaux-arts

KEYWORD

as [æz] *conj* **1** (*referring to time*) comme, alors que; à mesure que; **he came in ~ I was leaving** il est arrivé comme je partais; **~ the years went by** à mesure que les années passaient; **~ from tomorrow** à partir de demain

2 (*in comparisons*): **~ big** = aussi grand que; **twice ~ big** = deux fois plus grand que; ~ **much** or **many** ~ autant que; ~ **much money/many books** autant d'argent/de livres que; ~ **soon** ~ dès que

3 (since, because) comme, puisque; ~ **he had to be home by 10 ...** comme il or puisqu'il devait être de retour avant 10h ...

4 (referring to manner, way) comme; **do ~ you wish** faites comme vous voudrez

5 (concerning): ~ **for** or **to that** quant à cela, pour ce qui est de cela

6: ~ **for** or **though** comme si; **he looked** ~ **if he was ill** il avait l'air d'être malade; see also **long; such; well**

♦ prep: **he works** ~ **a driver** il travaille comme chauffeur; ~ **chairman of the company, he ...** en tant que président de la compagnie, il ...; **dressed up** ~ **a cowboy** déguisé en cowboy; **he gave me it** ~ **a present** il me l'a offert, il m'en a fait cadeau

a.s.a.p. abbr (= as soon as possible) dès que possible

asbestos [æz'bestɒs] n amiante f

ascend [ə'send] vt gravir; (throne) monter sur

ascent [ə'sent] n ascension f

ascertain [æsə'teɪn] vt vérifier

ascribe [ə'skraɪb] vt: to ~ **sth to** attribuer qch à

ash [æʃ] n (dust) cendre f; (also: ~ **tree**) frêne m

ashamed [ə'ʃeɪmd] adj honteux(euse), confus(e); **to be** ~ **of** avoir honte de

ashen ['æʃən] adj (pale) cendreux(euse), blême

ashore [ə'ʃɔː*] adv à terre

ashtray ['æʃtreɪ] n cendrier m

Ash Wednesday n mercredi m des cendres

Asia ['eɪʃə] n Asie f; ~**n** n Asiatique m/f ♦ adj asiatique

aside [ə'saɪd] adv de côté; à l'écart ♦ n aparté m

ask [ɑːsk] vt demander; (invite) inviter; **to** ~ **sb sth/to do sth** demander qch à qn de faire qch; **to** ~ **sb about sth** questionner qn sur qch; se renseigner auprès de qn sur qch; **to** ~ **(sb) a question** poser une question (à qn); **to** ~ **sb out to dinner** inviter qn au restaurant; ~ **after** vt fus demander des nouvelles de; ~ **for** vt fus demander; (trouble) chercher

askance [ə'kɑːns] adv: **to look** ~ **at sb** regarder qn de travers or d'un œil désapprobateur

asking price ['ɑːskɪŋ] n: **the** ~ le prix de départ

asleep [ə'sliːp] adj endormi(e); **to fall** ~ s'endormir

asparagus [əs'pærəgəs] n asperges fpl

aspect ['æspekt] n aspect m; (direction in which a building etc faces) orientation f, exposition f

aspersions [əs'pɜːʃənz] npl: **to cast** ~ **on** dénigrer

aspire [əs'paɪə*] vi: **to** ~ **to** aspirer à

aspirin ['æsprɪn] n aspirine f

ass [æs] n âne m; (inf) imbécile m/f; (US: inf!) cul m (!)

assailant [ə'seɪlənt] n agresseur m; assaillant m

assassinate [ə'sæsɪneɪt] vt assassiner; **assassination** [əsæsɪ'neɪʃən] n assassinat m

assault [ə'sɔːlt] n (MIL) assaut m; (gen: attack) agression f ♦ vt attaquer; (sexually) violenter

assemble [ə'sembl] vt assembler ♦ vi s'assembler, se rassembler

assembly [ə'semblɪ] n assemblée f, réunion f; (institution) assemblée; (construction) assemblage m; ~ **line** n chaîne f de montage

assent [ə'sent] n assentiment m, consentement m

assert [ə'sɜːt] vt affirmer, déclarer; (one's authority) faire valoir; (one's innocence) protester de

assess [ə'ses] vt évaluer; (tax, pay-

ment) établir *or* fixer le montant de; *(property etc: for tax)* calculer la valeur imposable de; *(person)* juger la valeur de; **~ment** *n* évaluation *f*, fixation *f*, calcul *m* de la valeur imposable de, jugement *m*; **~or** *n* expert *m* (*impôt et assurance*)

asset ['æset] *n* avantage *m*, atout *m*; **~s** *npl* (FINANCE) capital *m*; avoir(s) *m(pl)*; actif *m*

assign [ə'saɪn] *vt* (*date*) fixer; (*task*) assigner à; (*resources*) affecter à; **~ment** [ə'saɪnmənt] *n* tâche *f*, mission *f*

assist [ə'sɪst] *vt* aider, assister; **~ance** *n* aide *f*, assistance *f*; **~ant** *n* assistant(e), adjoint(e); (BRIT: *also:* **shop ~ant**) vendeur(euse)

associate [adj. *,* vb ə'səʊfɪɪt] *adj, n* associé(e) ♦ *vt* associer ♦ *vi*: to **~ with** sb fréquenter qn; **association** [əsəʊsɪ'eɪfən] *n* association *f*

assorted [ə'sɔːtɪd] *adj* assorti(e)

assortment [ə'sɔːtmənt] *n* assortiment *m*

assume [ə'sjuːm] *vt* supposer; (*responsibilities etc*) assumer; (*attitude, name*) prendre, adopter; **~d name** *n* nom m d'emprunt; **assumption** [ə'sʌmpfən] *n* supposition *f*, hypothèse *f*; (*of power*) assomption *f*, prise *f*

assurance [ə'fʊərəns] *n* assurance *f*

assure [ə'fʊə*] *vt* assurer

asthma ['æsmə] *n* asthme *m*

astonish [əs'tɒnɪʃ] *vt* étonner, stupéfier; **~ment** *n* étonnement *f*

astound [əs'taʊnd] *vt* stupéfier, sidérer

astray [əs'treɪ] *adv*: to **go ~** s'égarer; (*fig*) quitter le droit chemin; to **lead ~** détourner du droit chemin

astride [əs'traɪd] *prep* à cheval sur

astrology [əs'trɒlədʒɪ] *n* astrologie *f*

astronaut ['æstrənɔːt] *n* astronaute *m/f*

astronomy [əs'trɒnəmɪ] *n* astronomie *f*

astute [əs'tjuːt] *adj* astucieux(euse)

asylum [ə'saɪləm] *n* asile *m*

KEYWORD

at [æt] *prep* **1** (*referring to position, direction*) à; **~ the top** au sommet; **~ home/school** à la maison *or* chez soi/à l'école; **~ the baker's** à la boulangerie, chez le boulanger; to **look ~ sth** regarder qch

2 (*referring to time*): **~ 4 o'clock** à 4 heures; **~ Christmas** à Noël; **~ night** la nuit; **~ times** par moments, parfois

3 (*referring to rates, speed etc*) à; **~ £1 a kilo** une livre le kilo; **two ~ a time** deux à la fois; **~ 50 km/h** à 50 km/h

4 (*referring to manner*): **~ a stroke** d'un seul coup; **~ peace** en paix

5 (*referring to activity*): to **be ~ work** être à l'œuvre, travailler; to **play ~ cowboys** jouer aux cowboys; to **be good ~ sth** être bon en qch

6 (*referring to cause*): **shocked/surprised/annoyed ~ sth** choqué par/étonné de/agacé par qch; **I went ~ his suggestion** j'y suis allé sur son conseil

ate [et, eɪt] *pt of* eat

atheist ['eɪθɪɪst] *n* athée *m/f*

Athens ['æθɪnz] *n* Athènes *f*

athlete ['æθliːt] *n* athlète *m/f*

athletic [æθ'letɪk] *adj* athlétique; **~s** *n* athlétisme *m*

Atlantic [ət'læntɪk] *adj* atlantique ♦ *n*: **the ~ (Ocean)** l'Atlantique *m*, l'océan *m* Atlantique

atlas ['ætləs] *n* atlas *m*

atmosphere ['ætməsfɪə*] *n* atmosphère *f*

atom ['ætəm] *n* atome *m*; **~ic** [ə'tɒmɪk] *adj* atomique; **~(ic) bomb** *n* bombe *f* atomique; **~izer** ['ætəmaɪzə*] *n* atomiseur *m*

atone [ə'təʊn] *vi*: to **~ for** expier, racheter

atrocious [ə'trəʊfəs] *adj* (*very bad*) atroce, exécrable

attach [ə'tætʃ] *vt* attacher; (*document, letter*) joindre; to **be ~ed**

to sb/sth être attaché à qn/qch

attaché case [əˈtæʃeɪ-] n mallette f, attaché-case m

attachment [əˈtætʃmənt] n (tool) accessoire m; (love): ~ **(to)** affection f (pour), attachement m (à)

attack [əˈtæk] vt attaquer; (task etc) s'attaquer à ♦ n attaque f; (also: heart ~) crise f cardiaque

attain [əˈteɪn] vt (also: ~ **to**) parvenir à, atteindre; (: knowledge) acquérir; ~**ments** npl connaissances fpl, résultats mpl

attempt [əˈtempt] n tentative f ♦ vt essayer, tenter; **to make an** ~ **on sb's life** attenter à la vie de qn; ~**ed** adj: ~**ed murder/suicide** tentative f de meurtre/suicide

attend [əˈtend] vt (course) suivre; (meeting, talk) assister à; (school, church) aller à, fréquenter; (patient) soigner, s'occuper de; ~ **to** vt fus (needs, affairs etc) s'occuper de; (customer, patient) s'occuper de; ~**ance** n (being present) présence f; (people present) assistance f; ~**ant** n employé(e) ♦ adj (dangers) inhérent(e), concomitant(e)

attention [əˈtenʃən] n attention f; ~! (MIL) garde-à-vous!; **for the** ~ **of** (ADMIN) à l'attention de

attentive [əˈtentɪv] adj attentif(ive); (kind) prévenant(e)

attest [əˈtest] vi: **to** ~ (to demonstrate) démontrer; (confirm) témoigner

attic [ˈætɪk] n grenier m

attitude [ˈætɪtjuːd] n attitude f; pose f, maintien m

attorney [əˈtɜːnɪ] n (US: lawyer) avoué m; **A~ General** (BRIT) = procureur général; (US) = garde m des Sceaux, ministre m de la Justice

attract [əˈtrækt] vt attirer; ~**ion** [əˈtrækʃən] n (gen pl: pleasant things) attraction f, attrait m; (PHYSICS) attraction f; (fig: towards sb or sth) attirance f; ~**ive** adj attrayant(e); (person) séduisant(e)

attribute [n ˈætrɪbjuːt, vb əˈtrɪbjuːt] n attribut m ♦ vt: **to** ~ **sth to** attribuer qch à

attrition [əˈtrɪʃən] n: **war of** ~ guerre f d'usure

aubergine [ˈəʊbəʒiːn] n aubergine f

auction [ˈɔːkʃən] n (also: sale by ~) vente f aux enchères ♦ vt (: to sell by ~) vendre aux enchères; (: to put up for ~) mettre aux enchères; ~**eer** [ˌɔːkʃəˈnɪə*] n commissaire-priseur m

audience [ˈɔːdɪəns] n (people) assistance f; public m; spectateurs mpl; (interview) audience f

audiovisual [ˈɔːdɪəʊˈvɪzjuəl] adj audiovisuel(le); ~ **aids** npl supports or moyens audiovisuels

audit [ˈɔːdɪt] vt vérifier

audition [ɔːˈdɪʃən] n audition f

auditor [ˈɔːdɪtə*] n vérificateur m des comptes

augur [ˈɔːgə*] vi: **it** ~**s well** c'est bon signe or de bon augure

August [ˈɔːgəst] n août m

aunt [ɑːnt] n tante f; ~**ie** n dimin of aunt; ~**y** n dimin of aunt

au pair [ˈəʊˈpɛə*] n (also: ~ **girl**) jeune fille f au pair

auspicious [ɔːsˈpɪʃəs] adj de bon augure, propice

Australia [ɒsˈtreɪlɪə] n Australie f; ~**n** adj australien(ne) ♦ n Australien(ne)

Austria [ˈɒstrɪə] n Autriche f; ~**n** adj autrichien(ne) ♦ n Autrichien(ne)

authentic [ɔːˈθentɪk] adj authentique

author [ˈɔːθə*] n auteur m

authoritarian [ˌɔːθɒrɪˈtɛərɪən] adj autoritaire

authoritative [ɔːˈθɒrɪtətɪv] adj (account) digne de foi; (study, treatise) qui fait autorité; (person, manner) autoritaire

authority [ɔːˈθɒrɪtɪ] n autorité f; (permission) autorisation (formelle); **the authorities** npl (ruling body) les autorités fpl, l'administration f

authorize [ˈɔːθəraɪz] vt autoriser

auto [ˈɔːtəʊ] (US) n auto f, voiture f; ~**biography** [ɔːtəʊbaɪˈɒgrəfɪ] autobiographie f; **~graph** ['ɔːtəgrɑːf] n autographe m ♦ vt signer, dédicacer; **~mated** ['ɔːtəmeɪtɪd] adj automatisé(e), automatique; **~matic** [ɔːtə'mætɪk] adj automatique ♦ n (gun) automatique m; (washing machine) machine f à laver automatique; (BRIT: AUT) voiture f à transmission automatique; **~matically** adv automatiquement; **~mation** [ɔːtə'meɪʃən] n automatisation f (électronique); **~mobile** ['ɔːtəməbiːl] n (US) n automobile f; **~nomy** [ɔː'tɒnəmɪ] n autonomie f

autumn ['ɔːtəm] n automne m; **in ~** en automne

auxiliary [ɔːg'zɪlɪərɪ] adj auxiliaire ♦ n auxiliaire m/f

avail [ə'veɪl] vt: **to ~ o.s. of** profiter de ♦ n: **to no ~** sans résultat, en vain, en pure perte

availability [əveɪlə'bɪlɪtɪ] n disponibilité f

available [ə'veɪləbl] adj disponible

avalanche ['ævəlɑːnʃ] n avalanche f

Ave abbr = **avenue**

avenge [ə'vendʒ] vt venger

avenue [ə'vɛnjuː] n avenue f; (fig) moyen m

average ['ævərɪdʒ] n moyenne f; (fig) moyen m ♦ adj moyen(ne) ♦ vt (a certain figure) atteindre or faire etc en moyenne; **on ~** en moyenne; **~ out** vi: **to ~ out at** représenter en moyenne, donner une moyenne de

averse [ə'vɜːs] adj: **to be ~ to sth/doing sth** éprouver une forte répugnance envers qch/à faire qch

avert [ə'vɜːt] vt prévenir, écarter; (one's eyes) détourner

aviary ['eɪvɪərɪ] n volière f

avocado [ævə'kɑːdəʊ] n (also: BRIT: ~ **pear**) avocat m

avoid [ə'vɔɪd] vt éviter

await [ə'weɪt] vt attendre

awake [ə'weɪk] (pt **awoke**, pp **awoken**) adj éveillé(e) ♦ vt éveiller ♦ vi s'éveiller; **~ to** (dangers, possibilities) conscient(e) de; **to be ~** être réveillé(e); **he was still ~** il

ne dormait pas encore; **~ning** n réveil m

award [ə'wɔːd] n récompense f, prix m; (LAW: damages) dommages-intérêts mpl ♦ vt (prize) décerner; (LAW: damages) accorder

aware [ə'weə*] adj: **~ (of)** (conscious) conscient(e) (de); (informed) au courant (de); **to become ~ of/that** prendre conscience de/que; se rendre compte de/que; **~ness** n conscience f, connaissance f

awash [ə'wɒʃ] adj: **~ (with)** inondé(e) (de)

away [ə'weɪ] adj, adv au loin; absent(e); **two kilometres ~** à (une distance de) deux kilomètres, à deux kilomètres de distance; **two hours ~ by car** à deux heures de voiture or de route; **the holiday was two weeks ~** il restait deux semaines jusqu'aux vacances; **~ from** loin de; **he's ~ for a week** il est parti (pour) une semaine; **to pedal/work/laugh ~** être en train de pédaler/travailler/rire; **to fade ~** (sound) s'affaiblir; (colour) s'estomper; **to wither ~** (plant) se dessécher; **to take ~** emporter; (subtract) enlever; **~ game** n (SPORT) match m à l'extérieur

awe [ɔː] n respect mêlé de crainte; **~-inspiring** adj impressionnant(e); **~some** adj impressionnant(e)

awful ['ɔːfəl] adj affreux(euse); **an ~ lot (of)** un nombre incroyable (de); **~ly** adv (very) terriblement, vraiment

awhile [ə'waɪl] adv un moment, quelque temps

awkward ['ɔːkwəd] adj (clumsy) gauche, maladroit(e); (inconvenient) peu pratique; (embarrassing) gênant(e), délicat(e)

awning ['ɔːnɪŋ] n (of tent) auvent m; (of shop) store m; (of hotel etc) marquise f

awoke [ə'wəʊk] pt of **awake**; **~n** [ə'wəʊkən] pp of **awake**

awry [ə'raɪ] adv de travers; **to**

go ~ mal tourner

axe [æks] (US **ax**) n hache ♦ vt (project etc) abandonner; (jobs) supprimer; **axes** ['æksiz] npl of axe

axis ['æksis, pl -siz] (pl **axes**) n axe m

axle ['æksl] n (also: ~-tree: AUT) essieu m

ay(e) [aɪ] excl (yes) oui

B

B [biː] n (MUS) si m

B.A. abbr = **Bachelor of Arts**

babble ['bæbl] vi bredouiller; (baby, stream) gazouiller

baby ['beɪbɪ] n bébé m; (US: inf: darling): **come on, ~!** viens ma belle/mon gars!; ~ **carriage** (US) n voiture f d'enfant; ~-**sit** vi garder les enfants; ~-**sitter** n baby-sitter m/f

bachelor ['bætʃələ*] n célibataire m; **B~ of Arts/Science** = licencié(e) ès or en lettres/sciences

back [bæk] n (of person, horse, book) dos m; (of hand) dos, revers m; (of house) derrière m; (of car, train) arrière m; (of chair) dossier m; (of page) verso m; (of room, audience) fond m; (FOOTBALL) arrière m ♦ vt (candidate: also: ~ up) soutenir, appuyer; (horse: at races) parier or miser sur; (car) (faire) reculer ♦ vi (also: ~ up) reculer; (: car etc) faire marche arrière ♦ adj (in compounds) de derrière, à l'arrière ♦ adv (not forward) en arrière; (returned): **he's ~** il est rentré, il est de retour; (restitution): **throw the ball ~** renvoie la balle; (again): **he called ~** il a rappelé; ~ **seat/ wheels** (AUT) sièges mpl/roues fpl arrières; ~ **payments/rent** arriéré m de paiements/loyer; **he ran ~** il est revenu en courant; ~ **down** vi rabattre de ses prétentions; ~ **out** vi (of promise) se dédire; ~ **up** vt (candidate etc) soutenir, appuyer; (COMPUT) sauvegarder; ~-**bencher**

(BRIT) n membre du parlement sans portefeuille; ~-**bone** n colonne vertébrale, épine dorsale; ~-**cloth** (BRIT) n toile f de fond; ~-**date** vt (letter) antidater; ~-**dated** pay rise augmentation f avec effet rétroactif; ~-**drop** n = backcloth; ~-**fire** vi (AUT) pétarader; (plans) mal tourner; ~-**ground** n arrière-plan m; (of events) situation f, conjoncture f; (basic knowledge) éléments mpl de base; (experience) formation f; **family ~ground** milieu familial; ~-**hand** n (TENNIS: also: ~hand stroke) revers m; ~-**hander** (BRIT) n (bribe) pot-de-vin m; ~-**ing** n (fig) soutien m, appui m; ~-**lash** n contrecoup m, répercussion f; ~-**log** n: ~-**log of work** travail m en retard; ~ **number** n (of magazine etc) vieux numéro; ~-**pack** n sac m à dos; ~ **pay** n rappel m de salaire; ~-**side** (inf) n derrière m, postérieur m; ~-**stage** adv derrière la scène, dans la coulisse; ~-**stroke** n dos crawlé; ~-**up** adj (train, plane) supplémentaire, de réserve; (COMPUT) de sauvegarde ♦ n (support) appui m, soutien m; (also: ~**up disk/file**) sauvegarde f; ~-**ward** adj (movement) en arrière; (person, country) arriéré(e); attardé(e); ~-**wards** adv (move, go) en arrière; (read a list) à l'envers, à rebours; (fall) à la renverse; (walk) à reculons; ~-**water** n (fig) coin reculé; lieu perdu (péj); ~-**yard** n arrière-cour f

bacon ['beɪkən] n bacon m, lard m

bacteria [bæk'tɪərɪə] npl bactéries fpl

bad [bæd] adj mauvais(e); (child) vilain(e); (mistake, accident etc) grave; (meat, food) gâté(e), avarié(e); **his ~ leg** sa jambe malade; **to go ~** (meat, food) se gâter

bade [bæd] pt of **bid**

badge [bædʒ] n insigne m; (of policeman) plaque f

badger ['bædʒə*] n blaireau m

badly ['bædlɪ] adv (work, dress etc) mal; ~ **wounded** grièvement blessé;

he needs it ~ il en a absolument besoin; ~ **off** adj, adv dans la gêne

badminton ['bædmɪntən] n badminton m

bad-tempered ['bæd'tempəd] adj (person: by nature) ayant mauvais caractère; (: on one occasion) de mauvaise humeur

baffle ['bæfl] vt (puzzle) déconcerter

bag [bæg] n sac m ♦ vt (inf: take) empocher; s'approprier; ~s (inf: lots of) des masses de; ~**gage** n bagages mpl; ~**gy** adj avachi(e), qui fait des poches; ~**pipes** npl cornemuse f

bail [beɪl] n (payment) caution f; (release) mise f en liberté sous caution ♦ vt (prisoner: also: grant ~ to) mettre en liberté sous caution; (boat: also: ~ out) écoper; on ~ (prisoner) sous caution; see also **bale**; ~ **out** vt (prisoner) payer la caution de

bailiff ['beɪlɪf] n (BRIT) ≈ huissier m; (US) ≈ huissier-audiencier m

bait [beɪt] n appât m ♦ vt appâter; (fig: tease) tourmenter

bake [beɪk] vt (faire) cuire au four ♦ vi (bread etc) cuire (au four); (make cakes etc) faire de la pâtisserie; ~**d beans** npl haricots blancs à la sauce tomate; ~**r** n boulanger m; ~**ry** n boulangerie f, boulangerie industrielle; **baking** n cuisson f; **baking powder** n levure f (chimique)

balance ['bæləns] n équilibre m; (COMM: sum) solde m; (remainder) reste m; (scales) balance f ♦ vt mettre or faire tenir en équilibre; (pros and cons) peser; (budget) équilibrer; (account) balancer; ~ **of trade/payments** balance commerciale/des comptes or paiements; ~**d** adj (personality, diet) équilibré(e); (report) objectif(ive); ~ **sheet** n bilan m

balcony ['bælkənɪ] n balcon m; (in theatre) deuxième balcon

bald [bɔːld] adj chauve; (tyre) lisse

bale [beɪl] n balle f, ballot m; ~ **out** vi (of a plane) sauter en parachute

ball [bɔːl] n boule f; (football) ballon

m; (for tennis, golf) balle f; (of wool) pelote f; (of string) bobine f; (dance) bal m; **to play ~ (with sb)** (fig) coopérer (avec qn)

ballast ['bæləst] n lest m

ball bearings npl roulement m à billes

ballerina [bælə'riːnə] n ballerine f

ballet ['bæleɪ] n ballet m; (art) danse f (classique); ~ **dancer** n danceur(euse) m/f de ballet

balloon [bə'luːn] n ballon m; (in comic strip) bulle f

ballot ['bælət] n scrutin m; ~ **paper** n bulletin m de vote

ballpoint (pen) ['bɔːlpɔɪnt-] n stylo m à bille

ballroom ['bɔːlrum] n salle f de bal

balm [buːm] n baume m

ban [bæn] n interdiction f ♦ vt interdire

banana [bə'nɑːnə] n banane f

band [bænd] n bande f; (at a dance) orchestre m; (MIL) musique f, fanfare f; ~ **together** vi se liguer

bandage ['bændɪdʒ] n bandage m, pansement m ♦ vt bander

Bandaid ['bændeɪd] (US ®) n pansement adhésif

bandwagon ['bændwægən] n: **to jump on the ~** (fig) monter dans or prendre le train en marche

bandy ['bændɪ] vt (jokes, insults, ideas) échanger

bandy-legged ['bændɪ'legɪd] adj aux jambes arquées

bang [bæŋ] n détonation f; (of door) claquement m; (blow) coup (violent) ♦ vt frapper (violemment); (door) claquer ♦ vi détoner; claquer ♦ excl pan!

bangs [bæŋz] (US) npl (fringe) frange f

banish ['bænɪʃ] vt bannir

banister(s) ['bænɪstə(z)] n(pl) rampe f (d'escalier)

bank [bæŋk] n banque f; (of river, lake) bord m, rive f; (of earth) talus m, remblai m ♦ vi (AVIAT) virer sur l'aile; ~ **on** vt fus miser or tabler sur; ~ **account** n compte m en banque; ~ **card** n carte f d'identité bancaire; ~**er** n banquier m; ~**er's card** (BRIT) n = **bank card**; ~ **holiday** (BRIT) n jour férié (les banques sont fermées); ~**ing** n opérations fpl bancaires; profession f de banquier; ~**note** n billet m de banque; ~ **rate** n taux m de l'escompte

bankrupt ['bæŋkrʌpt] adj en faillite; to go ~ faire faillite; ~**cy** n faillite f

bank statement n relevé m de compte

banner ['bænə*] n bannière f

bannister(s) ['bænistə(z)] n(pl) = **banister(s)**

banns [bænz] npl bans mpl

baptism ['bæptizəm] n baptême m

bar [ba:*] n (pub) bar m; (counter: in pub) comptoir m, bar; (rod: of metal etc) barre f; (on window etc) barreau m; (of chocolate) tablette f, plaque f; (fig) obstacle m; (prohibition) mesure f d'exclusion; (MUS) mesure f ♦ vt (road) barrer; (window) munir de barreaux; (person) exclure; (activity) interdire; ~ of soap savonnette f; the B~ (LAW) le barreau; **behind** ~s (prisoner) sous les verrous; ~ **none** sans exception

barbaric [ba:'bærɪk] adj barbare

barbecue ['ba:bɪkju:] n barbecue m

barbed wire ['ba:bd-] n fil m de fer barbelé

barber ['ba:bə*] n coiffeur m (pour hommes)

bar code n (on goods) code m à barres

bare [bɛə*] adj nu(e) ♦ vt mettre à nu, dénuder; (teeth) montrer; the ~ **necessities** le strict nécessaire; ~**back** adv à cru, sans selle; ~**faced** adj impudent(e), effronté(e); ~**foot** adj, adv nu-pieds, (les) pieds nus; ~**ly** adv à peine

bargain ['ba:gɪn] n (transaction) marché m; (good buy) affaire f, occasion f ♦ vi (haggle) marchander; (negotiate): to ~ (with sb) négocier (avec qn), traiter (avec qn); **into**

the ~ par-dessus le marché; ~ **for** vt fus: he got more than he ~ed for il ne s'attendait pas à un coup pareil

barge [ba:dʒ] n péniche f; ~ **in** vi (walk in) faire irruption; (interrupt talk) intervenir mal à propos

bark [ba:k] n (of tree) écorce f; (of dog) aboiement m ♦ vi aboyer

barley ['ba:lɪ] n orge f; ~ **sugar** n sucre m d'orge

barmaid ['ba:meɪd] n serveuse f (de bar), barmaid f

barman ['ba:mən] (irreg) n barman m

barn [ba:n] n grange f

barometer [bə'rɔmɪtə*] n baromètre m

baron ['bærən] n baron m; ~**ess** n baronne f

barracks ['bærəks] npl caserne f

barrage ['bæra:ʒ] n (MIL) tir m de barrage; (dam) barrage m; (fig) pluie f

barrel ['bærəl] n tonneau m; (of oil) baril m; (of gun) canon m

barren ['bærən] adj stérile

barricade [bærɪ'keɪd] n barricade f

barrier ['bærɪə*] n barrière f; (fig: to progress etc) obstacle m

barring ['ba:rɪŋ] prep sauf

barrister ['bærɪstə*] (BRIT) n avocat (plaidant)

barrow ['bærəu] n (wheel~) charrette f à bras

bartender ['ba:tendə*] (US) n barman m

barter ['ba:tə*] vt: to ~ sth for échanger qch contre

base [beɪs] n base f; (of tree, post) pied m ♦ vt: to ~ sth on baser or fonder qch sur ♦ adj vil(e), bas(se)

baseball ['beɪsbɔ:l] n base-ball m

basement ['beɪsmənt] n sous-sol m

bases[1] ['beɪsɪz] npl of **base**

bases[2] ['beɪsi:z] npl of **basis**

bash [bæʃ] (inf) vt frapper, cogner

bashful ['bæʃful] adj timide; modeste

basic ['beɪsɪk] adj fondamental(e), de

base; (*minimal*) rudimentaire; ~**ally**
adv fondamentalement, à la base; (*in
fact*) en fait, au fond; ~**s** *npl*: **the
~s** l'essentiel *m*

basil ['bæzl] *n* basilic *m*

basin ['beɪsn] *n* (*vessel, also* GEO)
cuvette *f*, bassin *m*; (*also*: **wash~**)
lavabo *m*

basis ['beɪsɪs] (*pl* **bases**) *n* base *f*;
on a trial ~ à titre d'essai; **on a
part-time ~** à temps partiel

bask [bɑːsk] *vi*: **to ~ in the sun** se
chauffer au soleil

basket ['bɑːskɪt] *n* corbeille *f*; (*with
handle*) panier *m*; ~**ball** *n* basketball *m*

bass [beɪs] *n* (MUS) basse *f*

bassoon [bə'suːn] *n* (MUS) basson
m

bastard ['bɑːstəd] *n* enfant natu-
rel(le), bâtard(e); (*inf!*) salaud *m*
(!)

bat [bæt] *n* chauve-souris *f*; (*for baseball etc*) batte *f*; (BRIT: *for table
tennis*) raquette *f* ♦ *vt*: **he didn't ~
an eyelid** il n'a pas sourcillé *or* bron-
ché

batch [bætʃ] *n* (*of bread*) fournée *f*;
(*of papers*) liasse *f*

bated ['beɪtɪd] *adj*: **with ~ breath**
en retenant son souffle

bath [bɑːθ, *pl* bɑːðz] *n* bain *m*;
(~*tub*) baignoire *f* ♦ *vt* baigner, donner un bain à; **to have a ~** prendre
un bain; *see also* **baths**

bathe [beɪð] *vi* se baigner ♦ *vt*
(*wound*) laver

bathing ['beɪðɪŋ] *n* baignade *f*; ~
cap *n* bonnet *m* de bain; ~ **costume**
(US ~ **suit**) *n* maillot *m* (de bain)

bath: ~**robe** *n* peignoir *m* de bain;
~**room** *n* salle *f* de bains; ~**s** [bɑːðz]
npl (*also*: *swimming* ~) piscine *f*; ~
towel *n* serviette *f* de bain

baton ['bætən] *n* bâton *m*; (MUS) baguette *f*; (*club*) matraque *f*

batter ['bætə*] *vt* battre ♦ *n* pâte *f* à
frire; ~**ed** *adj* (*hat, pan*) cabossé(e)

battery ['bætərɪ] *n* batterie *f*; (*of
torch*) pile *f*

battle ['bætl] *n* bataille *f*, combat *m*
♦ *vi* se battre, lutter; ~**field** *n*
champ *m* de bataille; ~**ship** *n* cui-
rassé *m*

bawdy ['bɔːdɪ] *adj* paillard(e)

bawl [bɔːl] *vi* hurler; (*child*) brailler

bay [beɪ] *n* (*of sea*) baie *f*; **to hold
sb at ~** tenir qn à distance *or* en
échec; ~ **leaf** *n* laurier *m*; ~ **window** *n* baie vitrée

bazaar [bə'zɑː*] *n* bazar *m*; vente *f*
de charité

B & B *n abbr* = **bed and breakfast**

BBC *n abbr* (= *British Broadcasting
Corporation*) office de la radiodiffu-
sion et télévision britannique

B.C. *adv abbr* (= *before Christ*) av.
J.-C.

KEYWORD

---

be [biː] (*pt* **was**, **were**, *pp* **been**) *aux
vb* 1 (*with present participle: form-
ing continuous tenses*): **what are
you doing?** que faites-vous?;
they're coming tomorrow ils viennent demain; **I've been waiting for
you for 2 hours** je t'attends depuis 2
heures

2 (*with pp: forming passives*) être;
to ~ killed être tué(e); **he was nowhere to ~ seen** on ne le voyait
nulle part

3 (*in tag questions*): **it was fun,
wasn't it?** c'était drôle, n'est-ce-
pas?; **she's back, is she?** elle est
rentrée, n'est-ce pas *or* alors?

4 (+*to* +*infinitive*): **the house is to
~ sold** la maison doit être vendue;
he's not to open it il ne doit pas
l'ouvrir

♦ *vb* + *complement* 1 (*gen*) être;
I'm English je suis anglais(e); **I'm
tired** je suis fatigué(e); **I'm hot/
cold** j'ai chaud/froid; **he's a doctor**
il est médecin; **2 and 2 are 4** 2 et 2
font 4

2 (*of health*) aller; **how are you?**
comment allez-vous?; **he's fine now**
il va bien maintenant; **he's very ill**
il est très malade

3 (of age) avoir; **how old are you?** quel âge avez-vous?; **I'm sixteen (years old)** j'ai seize ans
4 (cost) coûter; **how much was the meal?** combien a coûté le repas?; **that'll ~ £5, please** ça fera 5 livres, s'il vous plaît
♦ vi **1** (exist, occur etc) être, exister; **the prettiest girl that ever was** la fille la plus jolie qui ait jamais existé; **~ that as it may** quoi qu'il en soit; **so ~ it** soit
2 (referring to place) être, se trouver; **I won't ~ here tomorrow** je ne serai pas là demain; **Edinburgh is in Scotland** Edimbourg est or se trouve en Ecosse
3 (referring to movement) aller; **where have you been?** où êtes-vous allé(s)?
♦ impers vb **1** (referring to time, distance) être; **it's 5 o'clock** il est 5 heures; **it's the 28th of April** c'est le 28 avril; **it's 10 km to the village** le village est à 10 km
2 (referring to the weather) faire; **it's too hot/cold** il fait trop chaud/froid; **it's windy** il y a du vent
3 (emphatic): **it's me/the postman** c'est moi/le facteur

beach [biːtʃ] n plage f ♦ vt échouer
beacon [ˈbiːkən] n (lighthouse) fanal m; (marker) balise f
bead [biːd] n perle f
beak [biːk] n bec m
beaker [ˈbiːkəʳ] n gobelet m
beam [biːm] n (of timber) poutre f; (of light) rayon m ♦ vi rayonner
bean [biːn] n haricot m; (of coffee) grain m; **runner ~** haricot m à rames); **broad ~** fève f; **~sprouts** npl germes mpl de soja
bear [bɛəʳ] (pt bore, pp borne) n ours m ♦ vt porter; (endure) supporter ♦ vi: **to ~ right/left** obliquer à droite/gauche; **se diriger vers la droite/gauche**; **~ out** vt corroborer, confirmer; **~ up** vi (person) tenir le coup

beard [biəd] n barbe f; **~ed** adj barbu(e)
bearer [ˈbɛərəʳ] n porteur m; (of passport) titulaire m/f
bearing [ˈbɛərɪŋ] n maintien m, allure f; (connection) rapport m; **~s** npl (also: ball **~s**) roulement m (à billes); **to take a ~** faire le point
beast [biːst] n bête f; (inf: person) brute f; **~ly** adj infect(e)
beat [biːt] (pt beat, pp beaten) n battement m; (MUS) temps m, mesure f; (of policeman) ronde f ♦ vt, vi battre; **off the ~en track** hors des chemins or sentiers battus; **~ it!** (inf) fiche(-moi) le camp!; **~ off** vt repousser; **~ up** vt (inf: person) tabasser; (eggs) battre; **~ing** n raclée f
beautiful [ˈbjuːtɪful] adj beau(belle); **~ly** adv admirablement
beauty [ˈbjuːti] n beauté f; **~ sal**on n institut m de beauté; **~ spo**t n (BRIT) (TOURISM) site naturel (d'une grande beauté)
beaver [ˈbiːvəʳ] n castor m
became [bɪˈkeɪm] pt of become
because [bɪˈkɒz] conj parce que; **~ of** prep à cause de
beck [bek] n: **to be at sb's ~ and call** être à l'entière disposition de qn
beckon [ˈbekən] vt (also: **~ to**) faire signe de (venir) à
become [bɪˈkʌm] (irreg: like come) vi devenir; **to ~ fat/thin** grossir/maigrir
becoming [bɪˈkʌmɪŋ] adj (behaviour) convenable, bienséant(e); (clothes) seyant(e)
bed [bed] n lit m; (of flowers) parterre m; (of coal, clay) couche f; (of sea) fond m; **to go to ~** aller se coucher; **~ and breakfast** n (terms) chambre et petit déjeuner; (place) ≈ chambre f d'hôte; **~clothes** npl couvertures fpl et draps mpl; **~ding** n literie f
bedraggled [bɪˈdrægld] adj (person, clothes) débraillé(e); (hair: wet) trempé(e)

bed: ~**ridden** *adj* cloué(e) au lit; ~**room** *n* chambre *f* (à coucher); ~**side** *n*: at sb's ~**side** au chevet de qn; ~**sit(ter)** (*BRIT*) *n* chambre meublée, studio *m*; ~**spread** *n* couvre-lit *m*, dessus-de-lit *m inv*; ~**time** *n* heure *f* du coucher

bee [biː] *n* abeille *f*

beech [biːtʃ] *n* hêtre *m*

beef [biːf] *n* boeuf *m*; **roast** ~ rosbif *m*; ~**burger** *n* hamburger *m*; ~**eater** *n* hallebardier *m* de la Tour de Londres

beehive ['biːhaɪv] *n* ruche *f*

beeline ['biːlaɪn] *n*: to make a ~ for se diriger tout droit vers

been [biːn] *pp* of **be**

beer [bɪə*] *n* bière *f*

beet [biːt] *n* (*vegetable*) betterave *f*; (*US: also: red* ~) betterave (potagère)

beetle ['biːtl] *n* scarabée *m*

beetroot ['biːtruːt] (*BRIT*) *n* betterave *f*

before [bɪ'fɔː*] *prep* (*in time*) avant; (*in space*) devant ♦ *conj* avant que +*sub*; avant de ♦ *adv* avant; devant; ~ **going** avant de partir; ~ **she goes** avant qu'elle ne parte; **the week** ~ la semaine précédente or d'avant; **I've seen it** ~ je l'ai déjà vu; ~**hand** *adv* au préalable, à l'avance

beg [bɛg] *vi* mendier ♦ *vt* mendier; (*forgiveness, mercy etc*) demander; (*entreat*) supplier; *see also* **pardon**

began [bɪ'gæn] *pt* of **begin**

beggar ['bɛgə*] *n* mendiant(e)

begin [bɪ'gɪn] (*pt* **began**, *pp* **begun**) *vt, vi* commencer; to ~ **doing** *or* to **do sth** commencer à or de faire qch; ~**ner** *n* débutant(e); ~**ning** *n* commencement *m*, début *m*

behalf [bɪ'hɑːf] *n*: **on** ~ **of**, (*US*) **in** ~ **of** (*representing*) de la part de; (*for benefit of*) pour le compte de; **on my/his** ~ pour moi/lui

behave [bɪ'heɪv] *vi* se conduire, se comporter; (*well: also:* ~ **o.s.**) se conduire bien or comme il faut

behaviour [bɪ'heɪvjə*] (*US behav-*

ior) *n* comportement *m*, conduite *f*

behead [bɪ'hɛd] *vt* décapiter

beheld [bɪ'hɛld] *pt, pp* of **behold**

behind [bɪ'haɪnd] *prep* derrière; (*time, progress*) en retard sur; (*work, studies*) en retard dans ♦ *adv* derrière ♦ *n* derrière *m*; to be ~ (**schedule**) avoir du retard; ~ **the scenes** dans les coulisses

behold [bɪ'həʊld] (*irreg: like* **hold**) *vt* apercevoir, voir

beige [beɪʒ] *adj* beige

Beijing ['beɪ'dʒɪŋ] *n* Bei-jing, Pékin

being ['biːɪŋ] *n* être *m*

Beirut [beɪ'ruːt] *n* Beyrouth

belated [bɪ'leɪtɪd] *adj* tardif(ive)

belch [bɛltʃ] *vi* avoir un renvoi, roter ♦ *vt* (*also:* ~ **out**: *smoke etc*) vomir, cracher

belfry ['bɛlfrɪ] *n* beffroi *m*

Belgian ['bɛldʒən] *adj* belge, de Belgique ♦ *n* Belge *m/f*

Belgium ['bɛldʒəm] *n* Belgique *f*

belie [bɪ'laɪ] *vt* démentir

belief [bɪ'liːf] *n* (*opinion*) conviction *f*; (*trust, faith*) foi *f*

believe [bɪ'liːv] *vt, vi* croire; to ~ **in** (*God*) croire en; (*method, ghosts*) croire à; ~**r** *n* (*in idea, activity*): ~**r in** partisan(e) de; (*REL*) croyant(e)

belittle [bɪ'lɪtl] *vt* déprécier, rabaisser

bell [bɛl] *n* cloche *f*; (*small*) clochette *f*, grelot *m*; (*on door*) sonnette *f*; (*electric*) sonnerie *f*

belligerent [bɪ'lɪdʒərənt] *adj* (*person, attitude*) agressif(ive)

bellow ['bɛləʊ] *vi* (*bull*) meugler; (*person*) brailler

belly ['bɛlɪ] *n* ventre *m*

belong [bɪ'lɒŋ] *vi*: to ~ **to** appartenir à; (*club etc*) faire partie de; **this book** ~**s here** ce livre va ici; ~**ings** *npl* affaires *fpl*, possessions *fpl*

beloved [bɪ'lʌvɪd] *adj* (bien-)aimé(e)

below [bɪ'ləʊ] *prep* sous, au-dessous de ♦ *adv* en dessous; **see** ~ voir plus bas *or* plus loin *or* ci-dessous

belt [bɛlt] *n* ceinture *f*; (*of land*) région *f*; (*TECH*) courroie *f* ♦ *vt*

(*thrash*) donner une raclée à; ~**way**
m ♦ *vi* (*in harbour*) venir à quai; (*at*
(US) *n* (AUT) route *f* de ceinture; (:
anchor) mouiller
motorway) périphérique *m*

beseech [bɪ'siːtʃ] (*pt, pp* **besought**)
bemused [bɪ'mjuːzd] *adj* stupéfié(e)
vt implorer, supplier

bench [bentʃ] *n* (*gen, also* BRIT:
beset [bɪ'set] (*pt, pp* **beset**) *vt* as-
POL) banc *m*; (*in workshop*) établi
saillir
m; **the B~** (LAW: *judge*) le juge; (:
beside [bɪ'saɪd] *prep* à côté de; **to be**
judges collectively) la magistrature,
~ **o.s.** (**with anger**) être hors de
la Cour
soi; **that's ~ the point** cela n'a rien

bend [bend] (*pt, pp* **bent**) *vt* cour-
à voir; ~**s** [-z] *adv* en outre, de plus;
ber; (*leg, arm*) plier ♦ *vi* se courber
(*in any case*) d'ailleurs ♦ *prep* (*as*
♦ *n* (BRIT: *in road*) virage *m*, tour-
well as) en plus de
nant *m*; (*in pipe, river*) coude *m*; ~
besiege [bɪ'siːdʒ] *vt* (*town*) assiéger;
down *vi* se baisser; ~ **over** *vi* se
(*fig*) assaillir
pencher
besought [bɪ'sɔːt] *pt, pp of* **beseech**

beneath [bɪ'niːθ] *prep* sous, au-
best [best] *adj* meilleur(e) ♦ *adv* le
dessous de; (*unworthy of*) indigne de
mieux; **the ~ part of** (*quantity*) le
♦ *adv* dessous, au-dessous, en bas
plus clair de, la plus grande partie

benefactor ['benɪfæktə*] *n* bienfai-
de; **at ~** au mieux; **to make the ~**
teur *m*
of sth s'accommoder de qch (du

beneficial [benɪ'fɪʃl] *adj* salutaire;
mieux que l'on peut); **to do one's ~**
avantageux(euse); ~ **to the health**
faire de son mieux; **to the ~ of my**
bon(ne) pour la santé
knowledge pour autant que je sa-

benefit ['benɪfɪt] *n* avantage *m*,
che; **to the ~ of my ability** du
profit *m*; (*allowance of money*) allo-
mieux que je pourrai; **~ man** *n* gar-
cation *f* ♦ *vt* faire du bien à, profiter
çon *m* d'honneur
à ♦ *vi*: **he'll ~ from it** cela lui fera
bestow [bɪ'stəu] *vt*: **to ~ sth on sb**
du bien, il y gagnera *or* s'en trouvera
accorder qch à qn; (*title*) conférer
bien
qch à qn

Benelux ['benɪlʌks] *n* Bénélux *m*
bet [bet] (*pt, pp* **bet** *or* **betted**) *n*

benevolent [bɪ'nevələnt] *adj* bien-
pari *m* ♦ *vt, vi* parier
veillant(e); (*organization*) bénévole
betray [bɪ'treɪ] *vt* trahir; ~**al** *n* trahi-

benign [bɪ'naɪn] *adj* (*person, smile*)
son *f*
bienveillant(e), affable; (MED) bé-
better ['betə*] *adj* meilleur(e) ♦ *adv*
nin(igne)
mieux ♦ *vt* améliorer ♦ *n*: **to get**

bent [bent] *pt, pp of* **bend** ♦ *n* incli-
the ~ of triompher de, l'emporter
nation *f*, penchant *m*; **to be ~ on**
sur; **you had ~ do it** vous feriez
être résolu(e) à
mieux de le faire; **he thought ~ of**

bequest [bɪ'kwest] *n* legs *m*
it il s'est ravisé; **to get ~** aller

bereaved [bɪ'riːvd] *n*: **the ~** la fa-
mieux; s'améliorer; ~ **off** *adj* plus à
mille du disparu
l'aise financièrement; (*fig*) **you'd be**

beret ['berɪ] *n* béret *m*
~ **off this way** vous vous en trouve-

Berlin [bɜːlɪn] *n* Berlin
riez mieux ainsi

berm [bɜːm] (US) *n* (AUT) accote-
betting ['betɪŋ] *n* paris *mpl*; ~ **shop**
ment *m*
(BRIT) *n* bureau *m* de paris

berry ['berɪ] *n* baie *f*
between [bɪ'twiːn] *prep* entre ♦

berserk [bə'sɜːk] *adj*: **to go ~** (*mad-*
adv: (**in**) ~ au milieu; dans l'inter-
man, crowd) se déchaîner
valle; (*in time*) dans l'intervalle

berth [bɜːθ] *n* (*bed*) couchette *f*; (*for*
beverage ['bevərɪdʒ] *n* boisson *f*
ship) poste *m* d'amarrage, mouillage
(*gén sans alcool*)

beware [bɪ'wɛə*] vi: to ~ (of) prendre garde (à); "~ of the dog" "(attention) chien méchant"

bewildered [bɪ'wɪldəd] adj dérouté(e), ahuri(e)

beyond [bɪ'jɒnd] prep (in space, time) au-delà de; (exceeding) au-dessus de ♦ adv au-delà; ~ doubt hors de doute; ~ **repair** irréparable

bias [ˈbaɪəs] n (prejudice) préjugé m, parti pris; ~**(s)ed** adj partial(e), montrant un parti pris

bib [bɪb] n bavoir m, bavette f

Bible [ˈbaɪbl] n Bible f

bicarbonate of soda [baɪˈkɑːbənɪt-] n bicarbonate m de soude

bicker [ˈbɪkə*] vi se chamailler

bicycle [ˈbaɪsɪkl] n bicyclette f

bid [bɪd] (pt **bid** or **bade**, pp **bid(den)**) n offre f; (at auction) enchère f; (attempt) tentative f ♦ vi faire une enchère or offre ♦ vt faire une enchère or offre de; to ~ sb good day souhaiter le bonjour à qn; ~**der** n: **the highest** ~**der** le plus offrant; ~**ding** n enchères fpl

bide [baɪd] vt: to ~ **one's time** attendre son heure

bifocals [baɪˈfəʊkəlz] npl verres mpl à double foyer, lunettes bifocales

big [bɪg] adj grand(e); gros(se)

bigheaded [ˈbɪgˈhedɪd] adj prétentieux(euse)

bigot [ˈbɪgət] n fanatique m/f, sectaire m/f; ~**ed** adj fanatique, sectaire; ~**ry** n fanatisme m, sectarisme m

big top n grand chapiteau

bike [baɪk] n vélo m, bécane f

bikini [bɪˈkiːnɪ] n bikini m

bilingual [baɪˈlɪŋgwəl] adj bilingue

bill [bɪl] n note f, facture f; (POL) projet m de loi; (US: banknote) billet m (de banque); (of bird) bec m; (THEATRE): **on the** ~ à l'affiche; **"post no ~s"** "défense d'afficher"; **to fit** or **fill the** ~ (fig) faire l'affaire; ~**board** n panneau m d'affichage

billet [ˈbɪlɪt] n cantonnement m (chez l'habitant)

billfold [ˈbɪlfəʊld] (US) n portefeuille m

billiards [ˈbɪljədz] n (jeu m de) billard m

billion [ˈbɪljən] n (BRIT) billion m (million de millions); (US) milliard m

bin [bɪn] n boîte f; (also: **dust~**) poubelle f; (for coal) coffre m

bind [baɪnd] (pt, pp **bound**) vt attacher; (book) relier; (oblige) obliger, contraindre ♦ n (inf: nuisance) scie f; ~**ing** adj (contract) constituant une obligation

binge [bɪndʒ] (inf) n: **to go on a/the** ~ (inf) aller faire la bringue

bingo [ˈbɪŋgəʊ] n jeu de loto pratiqué dans des établissements publics

binoculars [bɪˈnɒkjʊləz] npl jumelles fpl

bio... prefix: ~**chemistry** n biochimie f; ~**graphy** n biographie f; ~**logical** adj biologique; ~**logy** n biologie f

birch [bɜːtʃ] n bouleau m

bird [bɜːd] n oiseau m; (BRIT: inf: girl) nana f; ~**'s-eye view** n vue f à vol d'oiseau; (fig) vue d'ensemble or générale; ~**watcher** n ornithologue m/f amateur

Biro [ˈbaɪrəʊ] (®) n stylo m à bille

birth [bɜːθ] n naissance f; **to give** ~ **to** (subj: woman) donner naissance à; (: animal) mettre bas; ~ **certificate** n acte m de naissance; ~ **control** n (policy) limitation f des naissances; (method) méthode(s) contraceptive(s); ~**day** n anniversaire m ♦ cpd d'anniversaire; ~**place** n lieu m de naissance; (fig) berceau m; ~ **rate** n (taux m de) natalité f

biscuit [ˈbɪskɪt] n (BRIT) biscuit m; (US) petit pain au lait

bisect [baɪˈsekt] vt couper or diviser en deux

bishop [ˈbɪʃəp] n évêque m; (CHESS) fou m

bit [bɪt] pt of **bite** ♦ n morceau m; (of tool) mèche f; (of horse) mors m; (COMPUT) élément m binaire, bit m; **a** ~ **of** un peu de; **a** ~ **mad** un peu fou; ~ **by** ~ petit à petit

bitch [bɪtʃ] n (dog) chienne f; (inf!) salope f (!), garce f

bite [baɪt] (pt bit, pp bitten) vt, vi mordre; (insect) piquer ♦ n (insect ~) piqûre f; (mouthful) bouchée f; let's have a ~ (to eat) (inf) mangeons un morceau; to ~ one's nails se ronger les ongles

bitter ['bɪtə*] adj amer(ère); (weather, wind) glacial(e); (criticism) cinglant(e); (taste) acharné(e) ♦ n (BRIT: beer) bière f (forte); ~ness n amertume f; (taste) goût amer

blab [blæb] vi jaser, trop parler

black [blæk] adj noir(e) ♦ n (colour) noir m; (person): B~ noir(e) ♦ vt (BRIT: INDUSTRY) boycotter; to give sb a ~ eye pocher l'œil à qn, faire un œil au beurre noir à qn; ~ and blue couvert(e) de bleus; to be in the ~ (in credit) être créditeur(trice); ~berry n mûre f; ~bird n merle m; ~board n tableau noir; ~ coffee n café noir; ~currant n cassis m; ~en vt noircir; ~ ice n verglas m; ~leg (BRIT) n briseur m de grève, jaune m; ~list n liste noire; ~mail n chantage m ♦ vt faire chanter, soumettre au chantage; ~ market n marché noir; ~out n panne f d'électricité; (TV etc) interruption f d'émission; (fainting) syncope f; B~ Sea n: the B~ Sea la mer Noire; ~ sheep n brebis galeuse; ~smith n forgeron m; ~ spot n (AUT) point noir

bladder ['blædə*] n vessie f

blade [bleɪd] n lame f; (of propeller) pale f; ~ of grass brin m d'herbe

blame [bleɪm] n faute f, blâme m ♦ vt: to ~ sb/sth for sth attribuer à qn/qch la responsabilité de qch; reprocher qch à qn/qch; who's to ~? qui est le fautif or coupable or responsable?; ~less adj irréprochable

bland [blænd] adj (taste, food) doux(douce), fade

blank [blæŋk] adj blanc(blanche); (look) sans expression, dénué(e)

d'expression ♦ n espace m vide, blanc m; (cartridge) cartouche f à blanc; his mind was a ~ il avait la tête vide; ~ cheque n chèque m en blanc

blanket ['blæŋkɪt] n couverture f; (of snow, cloud) couche f

blare [blɛə*] vi beugler

blast [blɑːst] n souffle m; (of explosive) explosion f ♦ vt faire sauter or exploser; ~-off n (SPACE) lancement m

blatant ['bleɪtənt] adj flagrant(e), criant(e)

blaze [bleɪz] n (fire) incendie m; (fig) flamboiement m ♦ vi (fire) flamber; (fig: eyes) flamboyer; (: guns) crépiter ♦ vt: to ~ a trail (fig) montrer la voie

blazer ['bleɪzə*] n blazer m

bleach [bliːtʃ] n (also: household ~) eau f de Javel; (for linen etc) blanchir; ~ed adj (hair) oxygéné(e), décoloré(e); ~ers n ['bliːtʃəz] (US) npl (SPORT) gradins mpl (en plein soleil)

bleak [bliːk] adj morne; (countryside) désolé(e)

bleary-eyed ['blɪərɪ'aɪd] adj aux yeux pleins de sommeil

bleat [bliːt] vi bêler

bleed [bliːd] (pt, pp bled) vt, vi saigner; my nose is ~ing je saigne du nez

bleeper ['bliːpə*] n (device) bip m

blemish ['blemɪʃ] n défaut m; (on fruit, reputation) tache f

blend [blend] n mélange m ♦ vt mélanger ♦ vi (colours etc: also: ~ in) se mélanger, se fondre

bless [bles] (pt, pp blessed or blest) vt bénir; ~ you! (after sneeze) à vos souhaits!; ~ing n bénédiction f; (godsend) bienfait m

blew [bluː] pt of blow

blight [blaɪt] vt (hopes etc) anéantir; (life) briser

blimey ['blaɪmɪ] (BRIT: inf) excl mince alors!

blind [blaɪnd] adj aveugle ♦ n (for

blink 28 blunt

window) store *m* ♦ *vt* aveugler; ~
alley *n* impasse *f*; ~ **corner** (BRIT)
n virage *m* sans visibilité; ~**fold** *n*
bandeau *m* ♦ *adj, adv* les yeux ban-
dés ♦ *vt* bander les yeux à; ~**ly** *adv*
aveuglément; ~**ness** *n* cécité *f*; ~
spot *n* (AUT etc) angle mort; that
is her ~ **spot** (*fig*) elle refuse d'y
voir clair sur ce point

blink [blɪŋk] *vi* cligner des yeux;
(*light*) clignoter; ~**ers** *npl* œillères
fpl

bliss [blɪs] *n* félicité *f*, bonheur *m*
sans mélange

blister ['blɪstə*] *n* (on skin) ampoule
f, cloque *f*; (on paintwork, rubber)
boursouflure *f* ♦ *vi* (paint) se boursoufler, se cloquer

blithely ['blaɪðlɪ] *adv* (unconcerned-
ly) tranquillement

blizzard ['blɪzəd] *n* blizzard *m*, tempête *f* de neige

bloated ['bləʊtɪd] *adj* (face)
bouffi(e); (stomach, person) gon-
flé(e)

blob [blɒb] *n* (drop) goutte *f*; (stain,
spot) tache *f*

block [blɒk] *n* bloc *m*; (in pipes) obstruction *f*; (toy) cube *m*; (of buildings) pâté *m* (de maisons) ♦ *vt* bloquer; (fig) faire obstacle à; **mental**
~ trou *m* de mémoire; ~**ade** *n* blocus *m*; ~**age** *n* obstruction *f*;
~**buster** *n* (film, book) grand succès;
~ **letters** *npl* majuscules *fpl*; ~ **of
flats** (BRIT) *n* immeuble (locatif)

bloke [bləʊk] (BRIT: inf) *n* type *m*

blond(e) [blɒnd] *adj, n* blond(e)

blood [blʌd] *n* sang *m*; ~ **donor** *n*
donneur(euse) de sang; ~ **group** *n*
groupe sanguin; ~**hound** *n* limier *m*;
~ **poisoning** *n* empoisonnement *m*
du sang; ~ **pressure** *n* tension *f* (artérielle); ~**shed** *n* effusion *f* de sang,
carnage *m*; ~**shot** *adj:* ~**shot eyes**
yeux injectés de sang; ~**stream** *n*
sang *m*, système sanguin; ~ **test** *n*
prise *f* de sang; ~**thirsty** *adj* sanguinaire; ~ **vessel** *n* vaisseau sanguin;
~**y** *adj* sanglant(e); (nose) en sang;

(BRIT: inf!): this ~**y** ... ce foutu ...
(!), ce putain de ... (!); ~**y strong/
good** vachement or sacrément fort/
bon; ~**y-minded** (BRIT: inf) *adj*
contrariant(e), obstiné(e)

bloom [bluːm] *n* fleur *f* ♦ *vi* être en
fleur

blossom ['blɒsəm] *n* fleur(s) *f(pl)* ♦
vi être en fleurs; (fig) s'épanouir; to
~ **into** devenir

blot [blɒt] *n* tache *f* ♦ *vt* tacher; ~
out *vt* (memories) effacer; (view)
cacher, masquer

blotchy ['blɒtʃɪ] *adj* (complexion)
couvert(e) de marbrures

blotting paper ['blɒtɪŋ-] *n* buvard
m

blouse [blaʊz] *n* chemisier *m*, corsage *m*

blow [bləʊ] (*pt* blew, *pp* blown) *n*
coup *m* ♦ *vi* souffler ♦ *vt* souffler;
(*fuse*) faire sauter; (instrument)
jouer de; to ~ **one's nose** se moucher; to ~ **a whistle** siffler; ~
away *vt* chasser, faire s'envoler; ~
down *vt* faire tomber, renverser; ~
off *vt* emporter; ~ **out** *vi* (fire,
flame) s'éteindre; ~ **over** *vi* s'apaiser; ~ **up** *vi* faire sauter; (tyre)
gonfler; (PHOT) agrandir ♦ *vi* exploser, sauter; ~**dry** *n* brushing *m*;
~**lamp** (BRIT) *n* chalumeau *m*; ~
out *n* (of tyre) éclatement *m*; ~
torch *n* = blowlamp

blue [bluː] *adj* bleu(e); (fig) triste;
~**s** *n* (MUS): the ~**s** le blues; ~
film/joke film *m*/histoire *f* porno-
phique; to **come out of the** ~ (fig)
être complètement inattendu; ~**bell**
n jacinthe *f* des bois; ~**bottle** *n*
mouche *f* à viande; ~**print** *n* (fig)
projet *m*, plan directeur

bluff [blʌf] *vi* bluffer ♦ *n* bluff *m*; to
call sb's ~ mettre qn au défi d'exécuter ses menaces

blunder ['blʌndə*] *n* gaffe *f*, bévue *f*
♦ *vi* faire une gaffe or une bévue

blunt [blʌnt] *adj* (person) brusque,
ne mâchant pas ses mots; (knife)
émoussé(e), peu tranchant(e); (pen-

cil) mal taillé

blur [blə:*] *n* tache *or* masse floue *or* confuse ♦ *vt* brouiller

blurb [blə:b] *n* notice *f* publicitaire; (*for book*) texte *m* de présentation

blurt out [blə:t] *vt* (*reveal*) lâcher

blush [blʌʃ] *vi* rougir ♦ *n* rougeur *f*

blustery ['blʌstərɪ] *adj* (*weather*) à bourrasques

boar [bɔ:*] *n* sanglier *m*

board [bɔːd] *n* planche *f*; (*on wall*) panneau *m*; (*for chess*) échiquier *m*; (*cardboard*) carton *m*; (*committee*) conseil *m*, comité *m*; (*in firm*) conseil d'administration; (*NAUT, AVIAT*): **on ~** à bord ♦ *vt* (*ship*) monter à bord de; (*train*) monter dans; **full ~** (*BRIT*) pension complète; **half ~** demi-pension *f*; **~ and lodging** chambre *f* avec pension; **which goes by the ~** (*fig*) qu'on laisse tomber, qu'on abandonne; **~ up** *vt* (*door, window*) boucher; **~ing card** *n* = **boarding pass; ~ing house** *n* pension *f*; **~ing pass** *n* (*AVIAT, NAUT*) carte *f* d'embarquement; **~ing school** *n* internat *m*, pensionnat *m*; **~ room** *n* salle *f* du conseil d'administration

boast [bəʊst] *vi*: **to ~ (about** *or* **of)** se vanter (de)

boat [bəʊt] *n* bateau *m*; (*small*) canot *m*; barque *f*; **~er** *n* (*hat*) canotier *m*

bob [bɔb] *vi* (*boat, cork on water*: *also*: **~ up and down**) danser, se balancer

bobby ['bɔbɪ] (*BRIT*: *inf*) *n* ≈ agent *m* (de police)

bobsleigh ['bɔbsleɪ] *n* bob *m*

bode [bəʊd] *vi*: **to ~ well/ill** (**for**) être de bon/mauvais augure (pour)

bodily ['bɔdɪlɪ] *adj* corporel(le) ♦ *adv* dans ses bras

body ['bɔdɪ] *n* corps *m*; (*of car*) carrosserie *f*; (*of plane*) fuselage *m*; (*fig*: *society*) organe *m*, organisme *m*; (: *quantity*) ensemble *m*, masse *f*; (*of wine*) corps *m*; **~building** *n* cul-

turisme *m*; **~guard** *n* garde *m* du corps; **~work** *n* carrosserie *f*

bog [bɔg] *n* tourbière *f* ♦ *vi*: **to get ~ged down** (*fig*) s'enliser

boggle ['bɔgl] *vi*: **the mind ~s** c'est incroyable, on en reste sidéré

bogus ['bəʊgəs] *adj* bidon *inv*; fantôme

boil [bɔɪl] *vt* (faire) bouillir ♦ *vi* bouillir ♦ *n* (*MED*) furoncle *m*; **to come to the** (*BRIT*) *or* **a** (*US*) **~** bouillir; **~ down to** *vt fus* (*fig*) se réduire *or* ramener à; **~ over** *vi* déborder; **~ed egg** *n* œuf *m* à la coque; **~ed potatoes** *fpl* pommes *fpl* à l'anglaise *or* à l'eau; **~er** *n* chaudière *f*; **~ing point** *n* point *m* d'ébullition

boisterous ['bɔɪstərəs] *adj* bruyant(e), tapageur(euse)

bold [bəʊld] *adj* hardi(e), audacieux(euse); (*pej*) effronté(e); (*outline, colour*) franc(franche), tranché(e), marqué(e); (*pattern*) grand(e)

bollard ['bɔləd] (*BRIT*) (*AUT*) borne lumineuse *or* de signalisation

bolster ['bəʊlstə*]: **~ up** *vt* soutenir

bolt [bəʊlt] *n* (*lock*) verrou *m*; (*with nut*) boulon *m* ♦ *adv*: **~ upright** droit(e) comme un piquet ♦ *vt* verrouiller; (*TECH*: *also*: **~ on, ~ together**) boulonner; (*food*) engloutir ♦ *vi* (*horse*) s'emballer

bomb [bɔm] *n* bombe *f* ♦ *vt* bombarder

bombastic [bɔm'bæstɪk] *adj* pompeux(euse)

bomb: **~ disposal unit** *n* section *f* de déminage; **~er** *n* (*AVIAT*) bombardier *m*; **~shell** *n* (*fig*) bombe *f*

bona fide ['bəʊnə'faɪdɪ] *adj* (*traveller*) véritable

bond [bɔnd] *n* lien *m*; (*binding promise*) engagement *m*, obligation *f*; (*COMM*) obligation *f*; **in ~** (*of goods*) en douane

bondage ['bɔndɪdʒ] *n* esclavage *m*

bone [bəʊn] *n* os *m*; (*fish*) arête *f* ♦ *vt* désosser; ôter les arêtes de; **~idle** *adj* fainéant(e)

bonfire ['bɒnfaɪə*] n feu m (de joie); (for rubbish) feu

bonnet ['bɒnɪt] n bonnet m; (BRIT: of car) capot m

bonus ['bəʊnəs] n prime f, gratification f

bony ['bəʊnɪ] adj (arm, face, MED: tissue) osseux(euse); (meat) plein(e) d'os; (fish) plein d'arêtes

boo [bu:] excl hou!, peuh! ♦ vt huer

booby trap ['bu:bɪ-] n engin piégé

book [bʊk] n livre m; (of stamps, tickets) carnet m ♦ vt (ticket) prendre; (seat, room) réserver; (driver) dresser un procès-verbal à; (football player) prendre le nom de; ~s npl (accounts) comptes mpl, comptabilité f; ~case n bibliothèque f (meuble); ~ing office (BRIT) n bureau m de location; ~keeping n comptabilité f; ~let n brochure f; ~maker n bookmaker m; ~seller n libraire m/f; ~shop n librairie f; ~store n librairie f

boom [bu:m] n (noise) grondement m; (in prices, population) forte augmentation ♦ vi gronder; prospérer

boon [bu:n] n bénédiction f, grand avantage

boost [bu:st] n stimulant m, remontant m ♦ vt stimuler; ~er n (MED) rappel m

boot [bu:t] n botte f; (for hiking) chaussure f (de marche); (for football etc) soulier m; (BRIT: of car) coffre m ♦ vt (COMPUT) amorcer, initialiser; **to ~ in** (in addition) par-dessus le marché

booth [bu:ð] n (at fair) baraque (foraine); (telephone etc) cabine f; (also: voting ~) isoloir m

booty ['bu:tɪ] n butin m

booze [bu:z] (inf) n boissons fpl alcooliques, alcool m

border ['bɔːdə*] n bordure f; bord m; (of a country) frontière f ♦ vt border; (also: ~ on: country) être limitrophe de; **B~s** n (GEO): **the B~s** la région frontière entre l'Ecosse et l'Angleterre; ~ **on** vt fus être

voisin(e) de, toucher à; ~**line** n (fig) ligne f de démarcation; ~**line case** n cas m limite

bore [bɔː*] pt of **bear** ♦ vt (hole) percer; (oil well, tunnel) creuser; (person) ennuyer, raser ♦ n raseur(euse); (of gun) calibre m; **to be ~d** s'ennuyer; ~**dom** n ennui m; **boring** adj ennuyeux(euse)

born [bɔːn] adj: **to be ~** naître; **I was ~ in 1960** je suis né en 1960

borne [bɔːn] pp of **bear**

borough ['bʌrə] n municipalité f

borrow ['bɒrəʊ] vt: **to ~ sth (from sb)** emprunter qch (à qn)

Bosnia (and) Herzegovina ['bɒznɪə (ənd) ˌhɜːzəɡəʊviːnə] n Bosnie-Herzégovine f

bosom ['bʊzəm] n poitrine f; (fig) sein m; ~ **friend** n ami(e) intime

boss [bɒs] n patron(ne) ♦ vt (also: ~ around/about) commander; ~**y** adj autoritaire

bosun ['bəʊsn] n maître m d'équipage

botany ['bɒtənɪ] n botanique f

botch [bɒtʃ] vt (also: ~ up) saboter, bâcler

both [bəʊθ] adj les deux, l'un(e) et l'autre ♦ pron: ~ (of them) les deux, tous(toutes) les deux, l'un(e) et l'autre: **they sell ~ the fabric and the finished curtains** ils vendent (et) le tissu et les rideaux (finis), ils vendent à la fois le tissu et les rideaux (finis); ~ **of us went**, **we ~ went** nous en sommes allés (tous) les deux

bother ['bɒðə*] vt (worry) tracasser; (disturb) déranger ♦ vi (also: ~ o.s.) se tracasser, se faire du souci ♦ n: **it is a** ~ **to have to do** c'est vraiment ennuyeux d'avoir à faire; **it's no** ~ aucun problème; **to** ~ **doing** prendre la peine de faire

bottle ['bɒtl] n bouteille f; (baby's) biberon m ♦ vt mettre en bouteille(s); ~ **up** vt refouler, contenir; ~ **bank** n conteneur m à verre; ~**neck** n étranglement m; ~**opener**

n ouvre-bouteille *m*

bottom [ˈbɔtəm] *n* (*of container, sea etc*) fond *m*; (*buttocks*) derrière *m*; (*of page, list*) bas *m* ♦ *adj* du fond; du bas; the ~ **of the class** le dernier de la classe; **~less** *adj* (*funds*) inépuisable

bough [bau] *n* branche *f*, rameau *m*

bought [bɔːt] *pt, pp of* **buy**

boulder [ˈbəuldə*] *n* gros rocher

bounce [bauns] *vi* (*ball*) rebondir; (*cheque*) être refusé(e) (*étant sans provision*) ♦ *vt* faire rebondir ♦ *n* (*rebound*) rebond *m*; **~r** (*inf*) *n* (*at dance, club*) videur *m*

bound [baund] *pt, pp of* **bind** ♦ *n* (*gen pl*) limite *f*; (*leap*) bond *m* ♦ *vi* (*leap*) bondir ♦ *vt* (*limit*) borner ♦ *adj*: **to be ~ to do sth** (*obliged*) être obligé(e) ou avoir obligation de faire qch; **he's ~ to fail** (*likely*) il est sûr d'échouer, son échec est inévitable *ou* assuré; **~ for** à destination de; **out of ~s** dont l'accès est interdit

boundary [ˈbaundri] *n* frontière *f*

boundless [ˈbaundlɪs] *adj* sans bornes

bout [baut] *n* période *f*; (*of malaria etc*) accès *m*, crise *f*, attaque *f*; (*BOXING etc*) combat *m*, match *m*

bow[1] [bau] *n* nœud *m*; (*weapon*) arc *m*; (*MUS*) archet *m*

bow[2] [bau] *n* (*with body*) révérence *f*, inclination *f* (du buste *ou* corps); (*NAUT: also*: ~s) proue *f* ♦ *vi* faire une révérence, s'incliner; (*yield*): **to ~ to** *or* **before** s'incliner devant, se soumettre à

bowels [ˈbauəlz] *npl* intestins *mpl*; (*fig*) entrailles *fpl*

bowl [bəul] *n* (*for eating*) bol *m*; (*ball*) boule *f* ♦ *vi* (*CRICKET, BASEBALL*) lancer (la balle)

bow-legged [ˈbəuˈlegɪd] *adj* aux jambes arquées

bowler [ˈbəulə*] *n* (*CRICKET, BASEBALL*) lanceur *m* (de la balle); (*BRIT: also*: ~ **hat**) (chapeau *m* melon *m*

bowling [ˈbəulɪŋ] *n* (*game*) jeu *m* de boules; jeu *m* de quilles; ~ **alley** *n* bowling *m*; ~ **green** *n* terrain *m* de boules (*gazonné et carré*)

bowls [bəulz] *n* (*game*) (jeu *m* de) boules *fpl*

bow tie [ˈbəu-] *n* nœud *m* papillon

box [bɔks] *n* boîte *f*; (*also: cardboard* ~) carton *m*; (*THEATRE*) loge *f* ♦ *vt* mettre en boîte; (*SPORT*) boxer avec ♦ *vi* boxer, faire de la boxe; **~er** *n* (*person*) boxeur *m*; **~ing** *n* (*SPORT*) boxe *f*; **B~ing Day** (*BRIT*) *n* le lendemain de Noël; **~ing gloves** *npl* gants *mpl* de boxe; **~ing ring** *n* ring *m*; ~ **office** *n* bureau *m* de location; **~room** *n* débarras *m*; chambrette *f*

boy [bɔɪ] *n* garçon *m*

boycott [ˈbɔɪkɔt] *n* boycottage *m* ♦ *vt* boycotter

boyfriend [ˈbɔɪfrend] *n* (petit) ami

boyish [ˈbɔɪʃ] *adj* (*behaviour*) de garçon; (*girl*) garçonnier(ière)

BR *abbr* = **British Rail**

bra [brɑː] *n* soutien-gorge *m*

brace [breɪs] *n* (*on teeth*) appareil *m* (dentaire); (*tool*) vilbrequin *m* ♦ *vt* (*knees, shoulders*) appuyer; **~s** *npl* (*BRIT: for trousers*) bretelles *fpl*; **to ~ o.s.** (*lit*) s'arc-bouter; (*fig*) se préparer mentalement

bracelet [ˈbreɪslɪt] *n* bracelet *m*

bracing [ˈbreɪsɪŋ] *adj* tonifiant(e), tonique

bracket [ˈbrækɪt] *n* (*TECH*) tasseau *m*, support *m*; (*group*) classe *f*, tranche *f*; (*also: brace*) accolade *f*; (: *round* ~) parenthèse *f*; (: *square* ~) crochet *m* ♦ *vt* mettre entre parenthèse(s); (*fig: also*: ~ *together*) regrouper

brag [bræg] *vi* se vanter

braid [breɪd] *n* (*trimming*) galon *m*; (*of hair*) tresse *f*

brain [breɪn] *n* cerveau *m*; **~s** *npl* (*intellect, CULIN*) cervelle *f*; **he's got ~s** il est intelligent; **~child** *n* invention personnelle; **~wash** *vt* faire subir un lavage de cerveau à; ~**wave** n idée géniale; ~**y** adj intelligent(e), douée)

braise [breɪz] vt braiser

brake [breɪk] n (on vehicle, also fig) frein m ♦ vi freiner; ~ **fluid** n liquide m de freins; ~ **light** n feu m de stop

bran [bræn] n son m

branch [brɑːntʃ] n branche f; (COMM) succursale f ♦ vi bifurquer; ~ **out** vi (fig): to ~ **out** into étendre ses activités à

brand [brænd] n marque (commerciale) ♦ vt (cattle) marquer (au fer rouge); ~**new** adj tout(e) neuf(neuve), flambant neuf(neuve)

brandy [ˈbrændɪ] n cognac m, fine f

brash [bræʃ] adj effronté(e)

brass [brɑːs] n cuivre m (jaune), laiton m; the ~ (MUS) les cuivres; ~ **band** n fanfare f

brassière [ˈbræsɪə*] n soutien-gorge m

brat [bræt] (pej) n miocheme m/f, mômem/f

brave [breɪv] adj courageux(euse), brave ♦ n guerrier indien ♦ vt braver, affronter; ~**ry** n bravoure f, courage m

brawl [brɔːl] n rixe f, bagarre f

bray [breɪ] vi braire

brazen [ˈbreɪzn] adj impudent(e), effronté(e) ♦ vt: to ~ **it out** payer d'effronterie, crâner

brazier [ˈbreɪzɪə*] n brasero m

Brazil [brəˈzɪl] n Brésil m

breach [briːtʃ] vt ouvrir une brèche dans ♦ n (gap) brèche f (breaking): ~ **of contract** rupture f de contrat; ~ **of the peace** attentat m à l'ordre public

bread [bred] n pain m; ~ **and butter** n tartines (beurrées); (fig) subsistance f; ~**bin** (BRIT) n boîte f à pain; (bigger) huche f à pain; ~**box** (US) n = ~**bin**; ~**crumbs** npl miettes fpl de pain; (CULIN) chapelure f, panure f; ~**line** n: to be on the ~**line** être sans le sou or dans l'indigence

breadth [bretθ] n largeur f; (fig)

ampleur f

breadwinner [ˈbredwɪnə*] n soutien m de famille

break [breɪk] (pt broke, pp broken) vt casser; (promise) rompre; (law) violer ♦ vi (se) casser, se briser; (weather) tourner; (story, news) se répandre; (day) se lever ♦ n (gap) brèche f; (fracture) cassure f; (pause, interval) interruption f, arrêt m; (: short) pause f; (: at school) récréation f; (chance) chance f, occasion f favorable; to ~ **one's leg** etc se casser la jambe etc; to ~ **a record** battre un record; to ~ **the news to sb** annoncer la nouvelle à qn; to ~ **even** rentrer dans ses frais; ~ **free** or **loose** se dégager, s'échapper; ~ **open** (door etc) forcer, fracturer; ~ **down** vt (figures, data) décomposer, analyser ♦ vi s'effondrer; (MED) faire une dépression (nerveuse); (AUT) tomber en panne; ~ **in** vt (horse etc) dresser ♦ vi (burglar) entrer par effraction; (interrupt) interrompre; ~ **into** vt fus (house) s'introduire or pénétrer par effraction dans; ~ **off** vi (speaker) s'interrompre; (branch) se rompre; ~ **out** vi éclater, se déclarer; (prisoner) s'évader; to ~ **out in spots** or **a rash** avoir une éruption de boutons; ~ **up** vi (ship) se disloquer; (crowd, meeting) se disperser, se séparer; (marriage) se briser; (SCOL) entrer en vacances ♦ vt casser; (fight etc) interrompre, faire cesser; ~**age** n casse f; ~**down** n (AUT) panne f; (in communications, marriage) rupture f; (MED: also: nervous ~) dépression (nerveuse); (of statistics) ventilation f; ~**down van** (BRIT) n dépanneuse f; ~**er** n brisant m

breakfast [ˈbrekfəst] n petit déjeuner

break: ~**in** n cambriolage m; ~**ing and entering** n (LAW) effraction f; ~**through** n percée f; ~**water** n brise-lames m inv, digue f

breast [brest] n (of woman) sein m; (chest, of meat) poitrine f; ~**-feed**

(*irreg: like* feed) *vt, vi* allaiter; ~**stroke** *n* brasse *f*

breath [brεθ] *n* haleine *f*; **out of** ~ à bout de souffle, essoufflé(e)

Breathalyser ['brεθəlaɪzə*] (R) *n* Alcootest *m* (R)

breathe [bri:ð] *vt, vi* respirer; ~ **in** *vt, vi* aspirer, inspirer; ~ **out** *vt, vi* expirer; ~**r** *n* moment *m* de repos or de répit; **breathing** *n* respiration *f*; **breathing space** *n* (*fig*) (moment *m* de) répit *m*

breathless ['brεθlɪs] *adj* essoufflé(e), haletant(e); oppressé(e)

breathtaking ['brεθteɪkɪŋ] *adj* stupéfiant(e), à vous couper le souffle

breed [bri:d] (*pt, pp* bred) *vt* élever, faire l'élevage de ♦ *vi* se reproduire ♦ *n* race *f*, variété *f*; ~**ing** *n* (*upbringing*) éducation *f*

breeze [bri:z] *n* brise *f*; **breezy** ['bri:zɪ] *adj* frais(fraîche), aéré(e); (*manner etc*) désinvolte, jovial(e)

brevity ['brevɪtɪ] *n* brièveté *f*

brew [bru:] *vt* (*tea*) faire infuser; (*beer*) brasser ♦ *vi* (*fig*) se préparer, couver; ~**ery** *n* brasserie *f* (*fabrique*)

bribe [braɪb] *n* pot-de-vin *m* ♦ *vt* acheter; soudoyer; ~**ry** *n* corruption *f*

brick [brɪk] *n* brique *f*; ~**layer** *n* maçon *m*

bridal ['braɪdl] *adj* nuptial(e)

bride [braɪd] *n* mariée *f*, épouse *f*; ~**groom** *n* marié *m*, époux *m*; ~**smaid** *n* demoiselle *f* d'honneur

bridge [brɪdʒ] *n* pont *m*; (*NAUT*) passerelle *f* (de commandement); (*of nose*) arête *f*; (*CARDS, DENTISTRY*) bridge *m* ♦ *vt* (*fig: gap, gulf*) combler

bridle ['braɪdl] *n* bride *f*; ~ **path** *n* piste *or* allée cavalière

brief [bri:f] *adj* bref(brève) ♦ *n* (*LAW*) dossier *m*, cause *f*; (*gen*) tâche *f* ♦ *vt* mettre au courant; ~**s** *npl* (*undergarment*) slip *m*; ~**case** *n* serviette *f*; porte-documents *m inv*; ~**ly** *adv* brièvement

bright [braɪt] *adj* brillant(e); (*room, weather*) clair(e); (*clever: person, idea*) intelligent(e) (*cheerful: colour, person*) vif(vive)

brighten (*also* ~ **up**) *vt* (*room*) éclaircir, égayer; (*event*) égayer ♦ *vi* s'éclaircir; (*person*) retrouver un peu de sa gaieté; (*face*) s'éclairer; (*prospects*) s'améliorer

brilliance ['brɪljəns] *n* éclat *m*

brilliant ['brɪljənt] *adj* brillant(e); (*sunshine, light*) éclatant(e); (*in* holiday etc) super

brim [brɪm] *n* bord *m*

brine [braɪn] *n* (*CULIN*) sa▓

bring [brɪŋ] (*pt, pp* brou▓ porter; (*person*) amener; provoquer, entraîner; (*p porter; ramener; (*restore* réinstaurer; ~ **down** *vt* (*price* baisser; (*enemy plane*) descendre; (*government*) faire tomber; ~ **forward** *vt* avancer; ~ **off** *vt* (*task, plan*) réussir, mener à bien; ~ **out** *vt* (*meaning*) faire ressortir; (*book*) publier; (*object*) sortir; ~ **round** *vt* (*unconscious person*) ranimer; ~ **to** *vt* = ~ **round**; ~ **up** *vt* (*child*) élever; (*carry up*) monter; (*question*) soulever; (*food: vomit*) vomir, rendre

brink [brɪŋk] *n* bord *m*

brisk [brɪsk] *adj* vif(vive)

bristle ['brɪsl] *n* poil *m* ♦ *vi* se hérisser

Britain ['brɪtən] *n* (*also*: **Great** ~) Grande-Bretagne *f*

British ['brɪtɪʃ] *adj* britannique ♦ *npl*: **the** ~ les Britanniques *mpl*; ~ **Isles** *npl*: **the** ~ les Îles les Îles *fpl* Britanniques; ~ **Rail** *n* compagnie ferroviaire britannique

Briton ['brɪtən] *n* Britannique *m/f*

Brittany ['brɪtənɪ] *n* Bretagne *f*

brittle ['brɪtl] *adj* cassant(e), fragile

broach [brəʊtʃ] *vt* (*subject*) aborder

broad [brɔ:d] *adj* large; (*general: outlines*) grand(e); (: *distinction*) général(e); (*accent*) prononcé(e); **in** ~ **daylight** en plein jour; ~**cast** (*pt, pp*

~cast) n émission f ♦ vt radiodiffuser; téléviser ♦ vi émettre; **~en** vt élargir ♦ vi s'élargir; **to ~en one's mind** élargir ses horizons; **~ly** adv en gros, généralement; **~-minded** adj large d'esprit

broccoli ['brɒkəlɪ] n brocoli m

brochure ['brəʊʃʊə*] n prospectus m, dépliant m

broil [brɔɪl] vt griller

broke [brəʊk] pt of **break** ♦ adj (inf) fauché(e)

broke:1 ['brəʊkən] pp of **break** ♦ adj cassé(e); (machine: also: ~ down) fichu(e); **in ~ English/French** dans un anglais/français approximatif or hésitant; **~ leg** etc jambe etc cassée; **~-hearted** adj (ayant) le cœur brisé

~~~ker ['brəʊkə*] n courtier m

brolly ['brɒlɪ] (BRIT: inf) n pépin m, parapluie m

bronchitis [brɒŋ'kaɪtɪs] n bronchite f

bronze [brɒnz] n bronze m

brooch [brəʊtʃ] n broche f

brood [bruːd] n couvée f ♦ vi (person) méditer (sombrement), ruminer

broom [bruːm] n balai m; (BOT) genêt m; **~stick** n manche m à balai

Bros. abbr = **Brothers**

broth [brɒθ] n bouillon m de viande et de légumes

brothel ['brɒθl] n maison close, bordel m

brother ['brʌðə*] n frère m; **~-in-law** n beau-frère m

brought [brɔːt] pt, pp of **bring**

brow [braʊ] n front m; (eye~) sourcil m; (of hill) sommet m

brown [braʊn] adj brun(e), marron inv; (hair) châtain inv; brun; (eyes) marron inv; (tanned) bronzé(e) ♦ n (colour) brun m ♦ vt (CULIN) faire dorer; **~ bread** n pain m bis; **B~ie** ['braʊnɪ] n (also: ~ Guide) jeannette f, éclaireuse (cadette); **~ie** ['braʊnɪ] (US) n (cake) gâteau m au chocolat et aux noix; **~ paper** n papier m d'emballage; **~ sugar** n cassonade f

browse [braʊz] vi (among books)

bouquiner, feuilleter les livres; **to ~ through a book** feuilleter un livre

bruise [bruːz] n bleu m, contusion f ♦ vt contusionner, meurtrir

brunette [bruː'net] n (femme) brune

brunt [brʌnt] n: **the ~ of** (attack, criticism etc) le plus gros de

brush [brʌʃ] n brosse f; (painting) pinceau m; (shaving) blaireau m; (quarrel) accrochage m, prise f de bec ♦ vt brosser; (also: ~ against) effleurer, frôler; **~ aside** vt écarter, balayer; **~ up** vt (knowledge) rafraîchir, réviser; **~wood** n broussailles fpl, taillis m

Brussels ['brʌslz] n Bruxelles; **~ sprout** n chou m de Bruxelles

brutal ['bruːtl] adj brutal(e)

brute [bruːt] n brute f ♦ adj: **by ~ force** par la force

BSc abbr = **Bachelor of Science**

bubble ['bʌbl] n bulle f ♦ vi bouillonner, faire des bulles; (sparkle) pétiller; **~ bath** n bain moussant; **~ gum** n bubblegum m

buck [bʌk] n mâle m (d'un lapin, daim etc); (US: inf) dollar m ♦ vi ruer, lancer une ruade; **to pass the ~ (to sb)** se décharger de la responsabilité (sur qn); **~ up** vi (cheer up) reprendre du poil de la bête, se remonter

bucket ['bʌkɪt] n seau m

buckle ['bʌkl] n boucle f ♦ vt (belt etc) boucler, attacher ♦ vi (warp) tordre, gauchir; (: wheel) se voiler; se déformer

bud [bʌd] n bourgeon m; (of flower) bouton m ♦ vi bourgeonner; (flower) éclore

Buddhism ['bʊdɪzəm] n bouddhisme m

budding ['bʌdɪŋ] adj (poet etc) en herbe; (passion etc) naissant(e)

buddy ['bʌdɪ] (US) n copain m

budge [bʌdʒ] vt faire bouger; (fig: person) faire changer d'avis ♦ vi bouger; changer d'avis

budgerigar ['bʌdʒərɪgɑː*] (BRIT) n perruche f

budget ['bʌdʒɪt] n budget m ♦ vi: to ~ for sth inscrire qch au budget

budgie ['bʌdʒɪ] (BRIT) n = **budg-erigar**

buff [bʌf] adj (couleur f) chamois m ♦ n (inf: enthusiast) mordu(e)

buffalo ['bʌfələʊ] (pl ~ or ~es) n buffle m; (US) bison m

buffer ['bʌfə*] n tampon m; (COMPUT) mémoire f tampon

buffet¹ ['bʌfɪt] vt secouer, ébranler

buffet² ['bufeɪ] n (food, BRIT: bar) buffet m; ~ **car** (BRIT) n (RAIL) voiture-buffet f

bug [bʌg] n (insect) punaise f; (: gen) insecte m, bestiole f; (fig: germ) virus m, microbe m; (COM-PUT) erreur f; (fig: spy device) dispositif m d'écoute (électronique) ♦ vt garnir de dispositifs d'écoute; (inf: annoy) embêter

bugle ['bju:gl] n clairon m

build [bɪld] (pt, pp built) n (of per-son) carrure f, charpente f ♦ vt construire, bâtir; ~ **up** vt accumu-ler, amasser; accroître; ~**er** n entre-preneur m; ~**ing** n (trade) construc-tion f; (house, structure) bâtiment m, construction; (offices, flats) immeu-ble m; ~**ing society** (BRIT) n socié-té f de crédit immobilier

built [bɪlt] pt, pp of **build**; ~**-in** adj (cupboard, oven) encastré(e); (de-vice) incorporé(e); intégré(e); ~**-up area** n zone urbanisée

bulb [bʌlb] n (BOT) bulbe m, oignon m; (ELEC) ampoule f

bulge [bʌldʒ] n renflement m, gonfle-ment m ♦ vi (pocket, file etc) être plein(e) à craquer; (cheeks) être gonflé(e)

bulk [bʌlk] n masse f, volume m; (of person) corpulence f; **in** ~ (COMM) en vrac; **the** ~ **of** la plus grande or grosse partie de; ~**y** adj volumi-neux(euse), encombrant(e)

bull [bʊl] n taureau m; (male elephant/whale) mâle m; ~**dog** n bouledogue m

bulldozer ['bʊldəʊzə*] n bulldozer m

bullet ['bʊlɪt] n balle f (de fusil etc)

bulletin ['bʊlɪtɪn] n bulletin m, communiqué m; (news-) (bulletin d')informations fpl

bulletproof ['bʊlɪtpru:f] adj (car) blindé(e); (vest etc) pare-balles inv

bullfight ['bʊlfaɪt] n corrida f, course f de taureaux; ~**er** n torero m; ~**ing** n tauromachie f

bullion ['bʊlɪən] n or m or argent m en lingots

bull: ~**ock** ['bʊlək] n bœuf m; ~**ring** ['bʊlrɪŋ] n arènes fpl; ~'**s-eye** ['bʊlzaɪ] n centre m (de la cible)

bully ['bʊlɪ] n brute f, tyran m ♦ vt tyranniser, rudoyer

bum [bʌm] n (inf: backside) derrière m; (esp US: tramp) vagabond(e), traîne-savates m/f inv

bumblebee ['bʌmblbi:] n bourdon m

bump [bʌmp] n (in car: minor acci-dent) accrochage m; (jolt) cahot m; (on road etc, on head) bosse f ♦ vt heurter, cogner; ~ **into** vt fus ren-trer dans, tamponner; (meet) tomber sur; ~**er** n pare-chocs m inv ♦ adj: ~**er crop/harvest** récolte/moisson exceptionnelle; ~**er cars** npl autos tamponneuses

bumpy ['bʌmpɪ] adj cahoteux(euse)

bun [bʌn] n petit pain au lait; (of hair) chignon m

bunch [bʌntʃ] n (of flowers) bouquet m; (of keys) trousseau m; (of bana-nas) régime m; (of people) groupe m; ~**es** npl (in hair) couettes fpl; ~ **of grapes** grappe f de raisin

bundle ['bʌndl] n paquet m ♦ vt (also: ~ up) faire un paquet de; (put): to ~ sth/sb into fourrer or enfourner qch/qn dans

bungalow ['bʌŋgələʊ] n bungalow m

bungle ['bʌŋgl] vt bâcler, gâcher

bunion ['bʌnjən] n oignon m (au pied)

bunk [bʌŋk] n couchette f; ~ **beds** npl lits superposés

bunker ['bʌŋkə*] n (coal store) soute f à charbon; (MIL, GOLF) bunker m

bunny ['bʌnɪ] n (also: ~ rabbit)

Jeannot m lapin

bunting ['bʌntɪŋ] n pavoisement m, drapeaux mpl

buoy [bɔɪ] n bouée f; ~ **up** vt faire flotter; (fig) soutenir, épauler; ~**ant** adj capable de flotter; (carefree) gai(e), plein(e) d'entrain; (economy) ferme, actif

burden ['bɜːdn] n fardeau m ♦ vt (trouble) accabler, surcharger

bureau ['bjʊərəʊ] (pl ~x) n (BRIT: writing desk) bureau m, secrétaire m; (US: chest of drawers) commode f; (office) bureau, office m; ~**cracy** [bjʊˈrɔkrəsɪ] n bureaucratie f

burglar ['bɜːglə*] n cambrioleur m; ~ **alarm** n sonnerie f d'alarme; ~**y** n cambriolage m

Burgundy ['bɜːgəndɪ] n Bourgogne f

burial ['berɪəl] n enterrement m

burly ['bɜːlɪ] adj de forte carrure, costaud(e)

Burma ['bɜːmə] n Birmanie f

burn [bɜːn] (pt, pp burned or burnt) vt, vi brûler ♦ n brûlure f; ~ **down** vt incendier, détruire par le feu; ~**er** n brûleur m; ~**ing** adj brûlant(e); (house) en flammes; (ambition) dévorant(e)

burrow ['bʌrəʊ] n terrier m ♦ vt creuser

bursary ['bɜːsərɪ] (BRIT) n bourse f (d'études)

burst [bɜːst] (pt, pp burst) vt crever; faire éclater; (subj: river: banks etc) rompre ♦ vi éclater; (tyre) crever ♦ n (of gunfire) rafale f (de tir); (also: ~ pipe) rupture f, fuite f; a ~ of enthusiasm/energy un accès d'enthousiasme/d'énergie; to ~ into flames s'enflammer soudainement; to ~ out laughing éclater de rire; to ~ into tears fondre en larmes; to be ~ing with être plein (à craquer) de; (fig) être débordant(e) de; ~ **into** vt fus (room etc) faire irruption dans

bury ['berɪ] vt enterrer

bus [bʌs, pl -ɪz] (pl ~es) n autobus m

bush [bʊʃ] n buisson m; (scrubland)

brousse f; **to beat about the ~** tourner autour du pot; ~**y** ['bʊʃɪ] adj broussailleux(euse), touffu(e)

busily ['bɪzɪlɪ] adv activement

business ['bɪznɪs] n (matter, firm) affaire f; (trading) affaires fpl; (job, duty) travail m; **to be away on ~** être en déplacement d'affaires; **it's none of my ~** cela ne me regarde pas, ce ne sont pas mes affaires; **he means ~** il ne plaisante pas, il est sérieux; **like** adj sérieux(euse); efficace; ~**man** (irreg) n homme m d'affaires; ~ **trip** n voyage m d'affaires; ~**woman** (irreg) n femme f d'affaires

busker ['bʌskə*] (BRIT) n musicien ambulant

bus stop n arrêt m d'autobus

bust [bʌst] n buste m; (measurement) tour m de poitrine ♦ adj (inf: broken) fichu(e), fini(e); **to go ~** faire faillite

bustle ['bʌsl] n remue-ménage m, affairement m ♦ vi s'affairer, se démener; **bustling** adj (town) bruyant(e), affairé(e)

busy ['bɪzɪ] adj occupé(e); (shop, street) très fréquenté(e) ♦ vt: **to ~ o.s.** s'occuper; ~**body** n mouche f du coche, âme f charitable; ~ **signal** (US) n (TEL) tonalité f occupé inv

---

KEYWORD

but [bʌt] conj mais; **I'd love to come, ~ I'm busy** j'aimerais venir mais je suis occupé

♦ prep (apart from, except) sauf, excepté; **we've had nothing ~ trouble** nous n'avons eu que des ennuis; **no-one ~ him** can do it lui seul peut le faire; ~ **for you/your help** sans toi/ton aide; **anything ~ that** tout sauf ça, tout mais pas ça

♦ adv (just, only) ne ... que; **she's a child** elle n'est qu'une enfant; **had I ~ known** si seulement j'avais su; **all ~ finished** pratiquement terminé

butcher ['bʊtʃə*] n boucher m ♦ vt massacrer; (cattle etc for meat) tuer; ~'s (shop) n boucherie f

butler ['bʌtlə*] n maître m d'hôtel

butt [bʌt] n (large barrel) gros tonneau; (of gun) crosse f; (of cigarette) mégot m; (BRIT: fig: target) cible f ♦ vt donner un coup de tête à; ~ in vi (interrupt) s'immiscer dans la conversation

butter ['bʌtə*] n beurre m ♦ vt beurrer; ~cup n bouton m d'or; ~fly n papillon m; (SWIMMING: also: ~fly stroke) brasse f papillon

buttocks ['bʌtəks] npl fesses fpl

button ['bʌtn] n bouton m; (US: badge) insigne m ♦ vt (also: ~ up) boutonner ♦ vi se boutonner

buttress ['bʌtrɪs] n contrefort m

buxom ['bʌksəm] adj aux formes avantageuses or épanouies

buy [baɪ] (pt, pp bought) vt acheter ♦ n achat m; to ~ sb sth/sth from sb acheter qch à qn; to ~ sb a drink offrir un verre or à boire à qn; ~er n acheteur(euse)

buzz [bʌz] n bourdonnement m; (inf: phone call): to give sb a ~ passer un coup m de fil à qn ♦ vi bourdonner; ~er n timbre m électrique; ~ word (inf) n mot m à la mode

---

KEYWORD

by [baɪ] prep 1 (referring to cause, agent) par, de; killed ~ lightning tué par la foudre; surrounded ~ a fence entouré d'une barrière; a painting ~ Picasso un tableau de Picasso

2 (referring to method, manner, means): ~ bus/car en autobus/ voiture; ~ train par le or en train; to pay ~ cheque payer par chque; ~ saving hard, he ... à force d'économiser, il ...

3 (via, through) par; we came ~ Dover nous sommes venus de Douvres

4 (close to, past) à côté de; the

house ~ the school la maison à côté de l'école; a holiday ~ the sea des vacances au bord de la mer; she sat ~ his bed elle était assise à son chevet; she went ~ me elle est passée à côté de moi; I go ~ the post office every day je passe devant la poste tous les jours

5 (with time: not later than) avant; (: during): ~ daylight à la lumière du jour; ~ night la nuit, de nuit; ~ 4 o'clock avant 4 heures; ~ this time tomorrow d'ici demain à la même heure; ~ the time I got here it was too late lorsque je suis arrivé c'était déjà trop tard

6 (amount) à; ~ the kilo/metre au kilo/au mètre; paid ~ the hour payé à l'heure

7 (MATH, measure): to divide/ multiply ~ 3 diviser/multiplier par 3; a room 3 metres ~ 4 une pièce de 3 mètres sur 4; it's broader ~ a metre c'est plus large d'un mètre; one ~ one un à un; little ~ little petit à petit, peu à peu

8 (according to) d'après, selon; it's 3 o'clock ~ my watch il est 3 heures d'après ma montre; it's all right ~ me je n'ai rien contre

9: (all) ~ oneself etc tout(e) seul(e)

10: ~ the way au fait, à propos ♦ adv 1 see go; pass etc

2: ~ and ~ un peu plus tard, bientôt; ~ and large dans l'ensemble

bye(-bye) ['baɪ('baɪ)] excl au revoir!, salut!

bye(-)law ['baɪlɔː] n arrêté municipal

by: ~-election (BRIT) n élection (législative) partielle; ~gone adj passé(e) ♦ n: let ~s be ~s passons l'éponge, oublions le passé; ~pass n (route f de) contournement m; (MED) pontage m ♦ vt éviter; ~product n sous-produit m, dérivé m; (fig) conséquence f secondaire, retombée f; ~stander n ['baɪstændə*] spectateur(trice), badaud(e)

byte [baɪt] n (COMPUT) octet m

byword ['baɪwɜːd] n: to be a ~ for être synonyme de (fig)

by-your-leave ['baɪjɔː'liːv] n: without so much as a ~ sans même demander la permission

C

C [siː] n (MUS) do m

CA abbr = chartered accountant

cab [kæb] n taxi m; (of train, truck) cabine f

cabaret ['kæbəreɪ] n (show) spectacle m de cabaret

cabbage ['kæbɪdʒ] n chou m

cabin ['kæbɪn] n (house) cabane f, hutte f; (on ship) cabine f; (on plane) compartiment m; ~ **cruiser** n cruiser m

cabinet ['kæbɪnɪt] n (POL) cabinet m; (furniture) petit meuble à tiroirs et rayons; (also: display ~) vitrine f, petite armoire vitrée

cable ['keɪbl] n câble m ♦ vt câbler, télégraphier; ~-**car** n téléphérique m; ~ **television** n télévision f par câble

cache [kæʃ] n stock m

cackle ['kækl] vi caqueter

cactus ['kæktəs, pl -taɪ] (pl cacti) n cactus m

cadet [kə'dɛt] n (MIL) élève m officier

cadge [kædʒ] (inf) vt: to ~ (from or off) se faire donner (par)

café ['kæfeɪ] n ≈ café(-restaurant) m (sans alcool)

cage [keɪdʒ] n cage f

cagey ['keɪdʒɪ] (inf) adj réticent(e); méfiant(e)

cagoule [kə'guːl] n K-way m (®)

cajole [kə'dʒəul] vt couvrir de flatteries or de gentillesses

cake [keɪk] n gâteau m; ~ of soap savonnette f; ~**d** adj: ~**d with** raidi(e) par, couvert(e) d'une croûte de

calculate ['kælkjuleɪt] vt calculer;

(estimate: chances, effect) évaluer; **calculation** [kælkju'leɪʃən] n calcul m; **calculator** n machine f à calculer, calculatrice f; (pocket) calculette f

calendar ['kæləndə*] n calendrier m; ~ **year** n année civile

calf [kɑːf] (pl **calves**) n (of cow) veau m; (of other animals) petit m; (also: ~skin) veau m, vachette f; (ANAT) mollet m

calibre ['kælɪbə*] (US **caliber**) n calibre m

call [kɔːl] vt appeler; (meeting) convoquer ♦ vi appeler; (visit: also: ~ **in**, ~ **round**) passer ♦ n (shout) appel m, cri m; (also: telephone ~) coup m de téléphone; (visit) visite f; **she's** ~**ed Suzanne** elle s'appelle Suzanne; **to be on** ~ être de permanence; ~ **back** vi (return) repasser; (TEL) rappeler; ~ **for** vt fus (demand) demander; (fetch) passer prendre; ~ **off** vt annuler; ~ **on** vt fus (visit) rendre visite à, passer voir; (request): **to** ~ **on sb to do** inviter qn à faire; ~ **out** vi pousser un cri or des cris; ~ **up** vt (MIL) appeler, mobiliser; (TEL) appeler; ~**box** (BRIT) n (TEL) cabine f téléphonique; ~**er** n (TEL) personne f qui appelle; (visitor) visiteur m; ~ **girl** n call-girl f; ~-**in** (US) n (RADIO, TV: phone-in) programme m à ligne ouverte; ~**ing** n vocation f; (trade, occupation) état m; ~**ing card** (US) n carte f de visite

callous ['kæləs] adj dur(e), insensible

calm [kɑːm] adj calme ♦ n calme m ♦ vt calmer, apaiser; ~ **down** vi se calmer ♦ vt calmer, apaiser

Calor gas ['kælə*] (®) n butane m, butagaz m (®)

calorie ['kælərɪ] n calorie f

calves [kɑːvz] npl of **calf**

camber ['kæmbə*] n (of road) bombement m

Cambodia [kæm'bəudjə] n Cambodge m

camcorder ['kæmkɔːdə*] n camescope m

came [keɪm] pt of **come**

camel ['kæməl] n chameau m

camera ['kæmərə] n (PHOT) appareil-photo m; (also: cine-~, movie ~) caméra f; **in ~** à huis clos; **~man** (irreg) n caméraman m

camouflage ['kæməflɑːʒ] n camouflage m ♦ vt camoufler

camp [kæmp] n camp m ♦ vi camper ♦ adj (man) efféminé(e)

campaign [kæm'peɪn] n (MIL, POL etc) campagne f ♦ vi faire campagne

camp: **~bed** (BRIT) n lit m de camp; **~er** n campeur(euse); (vehicle) camping-car m; **~ing** n camping m; **to go ~ing** faire du camping; **~site** ['kæmpsaɪt] n campement m, (terrain m de) camping m

campus ['kæmpəs] n campus m

can¹ [kæn] n (of milk, oil, water) bidon m; (tin) boîte f de conserve ♦ vt mettre en conserve

KEYWORD

can² [kæn] (negative **cannot**, **can't**; conditional and pt **could**) aux vb 1 (be able to) pouvoir; **you ~ do it if you try** vous pouvez le faire si vous essayez; **I ~'t hear you** je ne t'entends pas

2 (know how to) savoir; **I ~ swim/play tennis/drive** je sais nager/jouer au tennis/conduire; **~ you speak French?** parlez-vous français?

3 (may) pouvoir; **~ I use your phone?** puis-je me servir de votre téléphone?

4 (expressing disbelief, puzzlement etc): **it ~'t be true!** ce n'est pas possible!; **what CAN he want?** qu'est-ce qu'il peut bien vouloir?

5 (expressing possibility, suggestion etc): **he could be in the library** il est peut-être dans la bibliothèque; **she could have been delayed** il se peut qu'elle ait été retardée

Canada ['kænədə] n Canada m; **Canadian** [kə'neɪdɪən] adj canadien(ne)

♦ n Canadien(ne)

canal [kə'næl] n canal m

canary [kə'nɛərɪ] n canari m, serin m

cancel ['kænsəl] vt annuler; (train) supprimer; (party, appointment) décommander; (cross out) barrer, rayer; **~lation** [kænsə'leɪʃən] n annulation f; suppression f

cancer ['kænsə*] n (MED) cancer m; **C~** (ASTROLOGY) le Cancer

candid ['kændɪd] adj (très) franc(franche), sincère

candidate ['kændɪdeɪt] n candidat(e)

candle ['kændl] n bougie f; (of tallow) chandelle f; (in church) cierge m; **~light:** **by ~light** à la lumière d'une bougie; (dinner) aux chandelles; **~stick** (also: ~ holder) bougeoir m; (bigger, ornate) chandelier m

candour ['kændə*] (US **candor**) n (grande) franchise f ou sincérité f

candy ['kændɪ] n sucre candi; (US) bonbon m; **~floss** (BRIT) n barbe f à papa

cane [keɪn] n canne f; (for furniture, baskets etc) rotin m ♦ vt (BRIT: SCOL) administrer des coups de bâton à

canister ['kænɪstə*] n boîte f; (of gas, pressurized substance) bombe f

cannabis ['kænəbɪs] n (drug) cannabis m

canned [kænd] adj (food) en boîte, en conserve

cannon ['kænən] (pl ~ or ~s) n (gun) canon m

cannot ['kænɒt] = **can not**

canoe [kə'nuː] n pirogue f; (SPORT) canoë m

canon ['kænən] n (clergyman) chanoine m; (standard) canon m

can-opener [-'əʊpnə*] n ouvre-boîte m

canopy ['kænəpɪ] n baldaquin m; dais m

can't [kɑːnt] = **can't**

cantankerous [kæn'tæŋkərəs] adj querelleur(euse), acariâtre

canteen [kæn'tiːn] n cantine f;
(BRIT: of cutlery) ménagère f

canter ['kæntə*] vi (horse) aller au
petit galop

canvas ['kænvəs] n toile f

canvass ['kænvəs] vi (POL): to ~
for faire campagne pour ♦ vt (investigate: opinions etc) sonder

canyon ['kænjən] n cañon m, gorge
(profonde)

cap [kæp] n casquette f; (of pen) capuchon m; (of bottle) capsule f;
(contraceptive: also: Dutch ~) diaphragme m; (for toy gun) amorce f ♦
vt (outdo) surpasser; (put limit on)
plafonner

capability [keɪpə'bɪlɪtɪ] n aptitude f,
capacité f

capable ['keɪpəbl] adj capable

capacity [kə'pæsɪtɪ] n capacité f;
(capability) aptitude f; (of factory)
rendement m

cape [keɪp] n (garment) cape f;
(GEO) cap m

caper ['keɪpə*] n (CULIN: gen: ~s)
câpre f; (prank) farce f

capital ['kæpɪtl] n (also: ~ city) capitale f; (money) capital m; (also: ~
letter) majuscule f; ~ **gains tax** n
(COMM) impôt m sur les plus-
values; ~**ism** n capitalisme m; ~**ist**
adj capitaliste ♦ n capitaliste m/f;
~**ize** vi: to ~**ize on** tirer parti de; ~
punishment n peine capitale

Capricorn ['kæprɪkɔːn] n (ASTROLOGY) le Capricorne

capsize [kæp'saɪz] vt faire chavirer
♦ vi chavirer

capsule ['kæpsjuːl] n capsule f

captain ['kæptɪn] n capitaine m

caption ['kæpʃən] n légende f

captive ['kæptɪv] adj, n captif(ive)

capture ['kæptʃə*] vt capturer, prendre; (attention) capter; (COMPUT)
saisir ♦ n capture f; (data) saisie
f de données

car [kɑː*] n voiture f, auto f; (RAIL)
wagon m, voiture

caramel ['kærəməl] n caramel m

caravan ['kærəvæn] n caravane f; ~

site (BRIT) n camping m pour caravanes

carbohydrate [kɑːbəʊ'haɪdreɪt] n
hydrate m de carbone; (food) féculent m

carbon ['kɑːbən] n carbone m; ~
dioxide n gaz m carbonique; ~
monoxide n oxyde m de carbone; ~
paper n papier m carbone

carburettor [kɑːbju'retə*] (US **carburetor**) n carburateur m

card [kɑːd] n carte f; (material) carton m; ~**board** n carton m; ~ **game**
n jeu m de cartes

cardiac ['kɑːdɪæk] adj cardiaque

cardigan ['kɑːdɪgən] n cardigan m

cardinal ['kɑːdɪnl] adj cardinal(e) ♦
n cardinal m

card index n fichier m

care [keə*] n soin m, attention f;
(worry) souci m; (charge) charge f,
garde f ♦ vi: to ~ **about** se soucier
de, s'intéresser à; (person) être attaché(e) à; ~ **of** chez, aux bons soins
de; **in sb's** ~ à la garde de qn,
confié(e) à qn; **to take** ~ (to do)
faire attention (à faire); **to take** ~
of s'occuper de; **I don't** ~ ça m'est
bien égal; **I couldn't** ~ **less** je m'en
fiche complètement (inf); ~ **for**
vt fus s'occuper de; (like) aimer

career [kə'rɪə*] n carrière f ♦ vi
(also: ~ **along**) aller à toute allure;
~ **woman** (irreg) n femme ambitieuse

care: ~**free** ['keəfriː] adj sans souci,
insouciant(e); ~**ful** ['keəfʊl] adj (thorough) soigneux(euse); (cautious)
prudent(e); **(be)** ~**ful!** (fais) attention!; ~**fully** adv avec soin, soigneusement; prudemment; ~**less** ['keəlɪs]
adj négligent(e); (heedless) insouciant(e); ~**r** [keərə*] n (MED) aide f

caress [kə'res] n caresse f ♦ vt caresser

caretaker ['keəteɪkə*] n gardien m,
concierge m/f

car-ferry ['kɑːferɪ] n (on sea) ferryboat m

cargo ['kɑːgəʊ] (pl ~**es**) n cargaison f

f, chargement *m*

car hire *n* location *f* de voitures

Caribbean [kærɪ'biːən] *adj*: the ~ (Sea) la mer des Antilles *or* Caraïbes

caring ['kɛərɪŋ] *adj* (person) bienveillant(e); (society, organization) humanitaire

carnal ['kɑːnl] *adj* charnel(le)

carnation [kɑː'neɪʃən] *n* œillet *m*

carnival ['kɑːnɪvəl] *n* (public celebration) carnaval *m*; (US: funfair) fête foraine

carol ['kærl] *n*: (Christmas) ~ chant *m* de Noël

carp [kɑːp] *n* (fish) carpe *f*; ~ at *vt fus* critiquer

car park (BRIT) *n* parking *m*, parc *m* de stationnement

carpenter ['kɑːpɪntə*] *n* charpentier *m*; **carpentry** ['kɑːpɪntrɪ] *n* menuiserie *f*

carpet ['kɑːpɪt] *n* tapis *m* ♦ *vt* recouvrir d'un tapis; ~ **slippers** *npl* pantoufles *fpl*; ~ **sweeper** *n* balai *m* mécanique

car phone *n* (TEL) téléphone *m* de voiture

carriage ['kærɪdʒ] *n* voiture *f*; (of goods) transport *m*; (: cost) port *m*; ~**way** (BRIT) *n* (part of road) chaussée *f*

carrier ['kærɪə*] *n* transporteur *m*, camionneur *m*; (company) entreprise *f* de transport; (MED) porteur(euse); ~ **bag** (BRIT) *n* sac *m* (en papier *or* en plastique)

carrot ['kærət] *n* carotte *f*

carry ['kærɪ] *vt* (subj: person) porter; (: vehicle) transporter; (involve: responsibilities etc) comporter, impliquer ♦ *vi* (sound) porter; to get **carried away** (fig) s'emballer, s'enthousiasmer; ~ **on** *vi*: to ~ on with sth/doing continuer qch/de faire ♦ *vt* poursuivre; ~ **out** *vt* (orders) exécuter; (investigation) mener; ~**cot** (BRIT) *n* porte-bébé *m*; ~**-on** (inf) *n* (fuss) histoires *fpl*

cart [kɑːt] *n* charrette *f* ♦ *vt* (inf)

transporter, trimballer (inf)

carton ['kɑːtən] *n* (box) carton *m*; (of yogurt) pot *m*; (of cigarettes) cartouche *f*

cartoon [kɑː'tuːn] *n* (PRESS) dessin *m* (humoristique), caricature *f*; (BRIT: comic strip) bande dessinée; (CINEMA) dessin animé

cartridge ['kɑːtrɪdʒ] *n* cartouche *f*

carve [kɑːv] *vt* (meat) découper; (wood, stone) tailler, sculpter; ~ **up** *vt* découper; (fig: country) morceler; **carving** ['kɑːvɪŋ] *n* sculpture *f*; **carving knife** *n* couteau *m* à découper

car wash *n* station *f* de lavage (de voitures)

case [keɪs] *n* cas *m*; (LAW) affaire *f*, procès *m*; (box) caisse *f*, boîte *f*, étui *m*; (BRIT: also: suit~) valise *f*; in ~ of en cas de; in ~ he ... au cas où il ...; just in ~ à tout hasard; in any ~ en tout cas, de toute façon

cash [kæʃ] *n* argent *m*; (COMM) argent liquide, espèces *fpl* ♦ *vt* encaisser; to pay (in) ~ payer comptant; ~ **on delivery** payable *or* paiement à la livraison; ~**book** *n* livre *m* de caisse; ~ **card** (BRIT) *n* carte *f* de retrait; ~ **desk** (BRIT) *n* caisse *f*; ~ **dispenser** (BRIT) *n* distributeur *m* automatique de billets, billetterie *f*

cashew [kæ'ʃuː] *n* (also: ~ nut) noix *f* de cajou

cashier [kæ'ʃɪə*] *n* caissier(ère)

cashmere ['kæʃmɪə*] *n* cachemire *m*

cash register *n* caisse (enregistreuse)

casing ['keɪsɪŋ] *n* revêtement (protecteur), enveloppe (protectrice)

casino [kə'siːnəʊ] *n* casino *m*

casket ['kɑːskɪt] *n* coffret *m*; (US: coffin) cercueil *m*

casserole ['kæsərəʊl] *n* (container) cocotte *f*; (food) ragoût *m* (en cocotte)

cassette [kæ'set] *n* cassette *f*, musicassette *f*; ~ **player** *n* lecteur *m* de cassettes; ~ **recorder** *n* magnétophone *m* à cassettes

cast [kɑːst] (pt, pp **cast**) *vt* (throw)

jeter; (shed) perdre; se dépouiller de; (statue) mouler; (THEATRE): to ~ sb as Hamlet attribuer à qn le rôle de Hamlet ♦ n (THEATRE) distribution f; (also: plaster ~) plâtre m; to ~ one's vote voter; ~ off vi (NAUT) larguer les amarres; (KNITTING) arrêter les mailles; ~ on vi (KNITTING) monter les mailles

castaway ['kɑːstəweɪ] n naufragé(e)

caster sugar ['kɑːstə-] (BRIT) n sucre m semoule

casting vote ['kɑːstɪŋ-] (BRIT) n voix prépondérante (pour départager)

cast iron n fonte f

castle ['kɑːsl] n château (fort); (CHESS) tour f

castor ['kɑːstə*] n (wheel) roulette f; ~ **oil** n huile f de ricin

castrate [kæs'treɪt] vt châtrer

casual ['kæʒjʊl] adj (by chance) de hasard, fait(e) au hasard, fortuit(e); (irregular: work etc) temporaire; (unconcerned) désinvolte; ~**ly** adv avec désinvolture, négligemment; (dress) décontracté

casualty ['kæʒjʊltɪ] n accidenté e, blessé(e); (dead) victime f, mort(e); (MED: department) urgences fpl

casual wear n vêtements mpl décontractés

cat [kæt] n chat m

catalogue ['kætəlɒg] (US catalog) n catalogue m ♦ vt cataloguer

catalyst ['kætəlɪst] n catalyseur m

catalytic convertor [kætə'lɪtɪk kən'vɜːtə*] n pot m catalytique

catapult ['kætəpʌlt] (BRIT) n (sling) lance-pierres m inv, fronde m

cataract ['kætərækt] n (MED) cataracte f

catarrh [kə'tɑː*] n rhume m chronique, catarrhe m

catastrophe [kə'tæstrəfɪ] n catastrophe f

catch [kætʃ] (pt, pp **caught**) vt attraper; (person: by surprise) prendre, surprendre; (understand, hear) saisir ♦ vi (fire) prendre; (become trapped) se prendre, s'accrocher ♦ n prise f; (trick) attrape f; (of lock) lo-

quet m; to ~ sb's attention or eye attirer l'attention de qn; to ~ one's breath retenir son souffle; to ~ fire prendre feu; to ~ sight of apercevoir; ~ on vi (grow popular) prendre; ~ up vi se rattraper, combler son retard ♦ vt (also: ~ up with) rattraper; ~ing adj (MED) contagieux(euse); ~ment area ['kætʃmənt-] (BRIT) n (SCOL) secteur m de recrutement; (of hospital) circonscription hospitalière; ~ phrase n slogan m; expression f (à la mode); ~y adj (tune) facile à retenir

category ['kætɪgərɪ] n catégorie f

cater ['keɪtə*] vi (provide food): to ~ (for) préparer des repas (pour), se charger de la restauration (pour); ~ **for** (BRIT) vt fus (needs) satisfaire, pourvoir à; (readers, consumers) s'adresser à; pourvoir aux besoins de; ~**er** n traiteur m; fournisseur m; ~**ing** n restauration f; approvisionnement m, ravitaillement m

caterpillar ['kætəpɪlə*] n chenille f; ~ **track** ® n chenille f

cathedral [kə'θiːdrəl] n cathédrale f

catholic ['kæθəlɪk] adj (tastes) éclectique, varié(e); **C~** adj catholique ♦ n catholique m/f

Catseye ® ['kæts'aɪ] n (BRIT: AUT) catadioptre m

cattle ['kætl] npl bétail m

catty ['kætɪ] adj méchant(e)

caucus ['kɔːkəs] n (POL: group) comité local d'un parti politique; (US: POL) comité électoral (pour désigner des candidats)

caught [kɔːt] pt, pp of **catch**

cauliflower ['kɒlɪflaʊə*] n chou-fleur m

cause [kɔːz] n cause f ♦ vt causer

caution ['kɔːʃən] n prudence f; (warning) avertissement m ♦ vt avertir, donner un avertissement à

cautious ['kɔːʃəs] adj prudent(e)

cavalry ['kævəlrɪ] n cavalerie f

cave [keɪv] n caverne f, grotte f; ~ **in** vi (roof etc) s'effondrer; ~**man**

(irreg) n homme *m* des cavernes

caviar(e) ['kævɪɑ:*] *n* caviar *m*

cavort [kə'vɔ:t] *vi* cabrioler, faire des cabrioles

CB *n abbr (= Citizens' Band (Radio))* CB *f*

CBI *n abbr (= Confederation of British Industries)* groupement du patronat

cc *abbr = carbon copy; cubic centimetres*

CD *n abbr (= compact disc (player))* CD *m*; **~-ROM** *n abbr (= compact disc read-only memory)* CD-ROM *m*

cease [si:s] *vt, vi* cesser; **~fire** *n* cessez-le-feu *m*; **~less** *adj* incessant(e), continuel(le)

cedar ['si:də*] *n* cèdre *m*

ceiling ['si:lɪŋ] *n* plafond *m*

celebrate ['sɛlɪbreɪt] *vt, vi* célébrer; **~d** *adj* célèbre; **celebration** [sɛlɪ'breɪʃən] *n* célébration *f*

celery ['sɛlərɪ] *n* céleri *m* (à côtes)

cell [sɛl] *n* cellule *f*; *(ELEC)* élément *m* (de pile)

cellar ['sɛlə*] *n* cave *f*

cello ['tʃɛləu] *n* violoncelle *m*

cellphone [sɛl'fəun] *n* téléphone *m* cellulaire; téléphone *m* sans fil

Celt [kɛlt, sɛlt] *n* Celte *m/f*; **~ic** ['kɛltɪk, 'sɛltɪk] *adj* celte

cement [sɪ'mɛnt] *n* ciment *m*; **~ mixer** *n* bétonneuse *f*

cemetery ['sɛmɪtrɪ] *n* cimetière *m*

censor ['sɛnsə*] *n* censeur *m* ♦ *vt* censurer; **~ship** *n* censure *f*

censure ['sɛnʃə*] *vt* blâmer, critiquer

census ['sɛnsəs] *n* recensement *m*

cent [sɛnt] *n (US etc: coin)* cent *m* (= un centième du dollar); *see also* **per**

centenary [sɛn'ti:nərɪ] *n* centenaire *m*

center ['sɛntə*] *(US) n* = **centre**

centigrade ['sɛntɪɡreɪd] *adj* centigrade

centimetre ['sɛntɪmi:tə*] *(US* **centimeter)** *n* centimètre *m*

centipede ['sɛntɪpi:d] *n* mille-pattes

m inv

central ['sɛntrəl] *adj* central(e); **C~ America** *n* Amérique centrale; **~ heating** *n* chauffage central; **~ reservation** *(BRIT) n (AUT)* terre-plein central

centre ['sɛntə*] *(US* **center)** *n* centre *m* ♦ *vt* centrer; **~-forward** *n (SPORT)* avant-centre *m*; **~-half** *n (SPORT)* demi-centre *m*

century ['sɛntjurɪ] *n* siècle *m*; **20th ~** XXe siècle

ceramic [sɪ'ræmɪk] *adj* céramique

cereal ['sɪərɪəl] *n* céréale *f*

ceremony ['sɛrɪmənɪ] *n* cérémonie *f*; **to stand on ~** faire des façons

certain ['sɜ:tən] *adj* certain(e); **for ~** certainement, sûrement; **~ly** *adv* certainement; **~ty** *n* certitude *f*

certificate [sə'tɪfɪkɪt] *n* certificat *m*

certified mail ['sɜ:tɪfaɪd-] *(US) n*: **by ~** en recommandé, avec avis de réception

certified public accountant *(US) n* expert-comptable *m*

certify ['sɜ:tɪfaɪ] *vt* certifier; *(award diploma to)* conférer un diplôme *etc* à; *(declare insane)* déclarer malade mental(e)

cervical ['sɜ:vɪkl] *adj*: **~ cancer** cancer *m* du col de l'utérus; **~ smear** frottis vaginal

cervix ['sɜ:vɪks] *n* col *m* de l'utérus

cf. *abbr (= compare)* cf., voir

CFC *n abbr = chlorofluorocarbon*; CFC *m (gen pl)*

ch. *abbr (= chapter)* chap.

chafe [tʃeɪf] *vt* irriter, frotter contre

chain [tʃeɪn] *n* chaîne *f* ♦ *vt (also: ~ up)* enchaîner, attacher (avec une chaîne); **~ reaction** *n* réaction *f* en chaîne; **~-smoke** *vi* fumer cigarette sur cigarette; **~ store** *n* magasin *m* à succursales multiples

chair [tʃeə*] *n* chaise *f*; *(arm~)* fauteuil *m*; *(of university)* chaire *f*; *(of meeting, committee)* présidence *f* ♦ *vt (meeting)* présider; **~lift** *n* télésiège *m*; **~man** *(irreg) n* président *m*

chalet ['ʃæleɪ] n chalet m

chalice ['tʃælɪs] n calice m

chalk ['tʃɔːk] n craie f

challenge ['tʃælɪndʒ] n défi m ♦ vt défier; (statement, right) mettre en question, contester; **to ~ sb to do** mettre qn au défi de faire; **challenging** ['tʃælɪndʒɪŋ] adj (tone, look) de défi, provocateur(trice); (task, career) qui représente un défi or une gageure

chamber ['tʃeɪmbə*] n chambre f; ~ **of commerce** chambre de commerce; **~maid** n femme f de chambre; **~ music** n musique f de chambre

champagne ['ʃæm'peɪn] n champagne m

champion ['tʃæmpɪən] n champion(ne); **~ship** n championnat m

chance [tʃɑːns] n (opportunity) occasion f, possibilité f; (hope, likelihood) chance f; (risk) risque m ♦ vt: **to ~ it** risquer (le coup), essayer ♦ adj fortuit(e), de hasard; **to take a ~** prendre un risque; **by ~** par hasard

chancellor ['tʃɑːnsələ*] n chancelier m; **C~ of the Exchequer** (BRIT) n chancelier m de l'Echiquier, ≈ ministre m des Finances

chandelier [ʃændɪ'lɪə*] n lustre m

change [tʃeɪndʒ] vt (alter, replace, COMM: money) changer; (hands, trains, clothes, one's name) changer de; (transform): **to ~ sb into** changer or transformer qn en ♦ vi (gen) changer; (one's clothes) se changer; (be transformed): **to ~ into** se changer or transformer en ♦ n changement m; (money) monnaie f; **to ~ gear** (AUT) changer de vitesse; **to ~ one's mind** changer d'avis; **a ~ of clothes** des vêtements de rechange; **for a ~** pour changer; **~able** adj (weather) variable; **~ machine** n distributeur m de monnaie; **~over** n (to new system) changement m, passage m

changing ['tʃeɪndʒɪŋ] adj changeant(e); **~ room** (BRIT) n (in shop) salon m d'essayage; (SPORT)

vestiaire m

channel ['tʃænl] n (TV) chaîne f; (navigable passage) chenal m; (irrigation) canal m ♦ vt canaliser; the (English) **C~** la Manche; the **C~ Islands** les îles de la Manche, les îles anglo-normandes

chant [tʃɑːnt] n chant m; (REL) psalmodie f ♦ vt chanter, scander

chaos ['keɪɒs] n chaos m

chap [tʃæp] n (BRIT: inf) (man) type m

chapel ['tʃæpəl] n chapelle f; (BRIT: nonconformist ~) église f

chaplain ['tʃæplɪn] n aumônier m

chapped ['tʃæpt] adj (skin, lips) gercé(e)

chapter ['tʃæptə*] n chapitre m

char [tʃɑː*] vt (burn) carboniser

character ['kærɪktə*] n caractère m; (in novel, film) personnage m; (eccentric) numéro m, phénomène m; **~istic** [kærɪktə'rɪstɪk] adj caractéristique ♦ n caractéristique f

charcoal ['tʃɑːkəʊl] n charbon m de bois; (for drawing) charbon m

charge [tʃɑːdʒ] n (cost) prix (demandé); (accusation) accusation f; (LAW) inculpation f ♦ vt: **to ~ sb** (with) inculper qn (de); (battery, enemy) charger; (customer, sum) faire payer ♦ vi foncer; **~s** npl (costs) frais mpl; **to reverse the ~s** (TEL) téléphoner en P.C.V.; **to take ~ of** se charger de; **to be in ~ of** être responsable de, s'occuper de; **how much do you ~?** combien prenez-vous?; **to ~ an expense (up) to sb** mettre une dépense sur le compte de qn; **~ card** n carte f de client

charity ['tʃærɪtɪ] n charité f; (organization) institution f charitable or de bienfaisance, œuvre f (de charité)

charm [tʃɑːm] n charme m; (on bracelet) breloque f ♦ vt charmer, enchanter; **~ing** adj charmant(e)

chart [tʃɑːt] n tableau m, diagramme m; graphique m; (map) carte marine ♦ vt dresser or établir la carte de; ~s *npl* (*hit parade*) hit-parade *m*

charter ['tʃɑːtə*] *vt* (*plane*) affréter ♦ *n* (*document*) charte *f*; **~ed accountant** (*BRIT*) *n* expert-comptable *m*; **~ flight** *n* charter *m*

chase [tʃeis] *vt* poursuivre, pourchasser; (*also: ~ away*) chasser ♦ *n* poursuite *f*, chasse *f*

chasm ['kæzəm] *n* gouffre *m*, abîme *m*

chat [tʃæt] *vi* (*also: have a ~*) bavarder, causer ♦ *n* conversation *f*; **~ show** (*BRIT*) *n* causerie télévisée

chatter ['tʃætə*] *vi* (*person*) bavarder; (*animal*) jacasser ♦ *n* bavardage *m*; jacassement *m*; **my teeth are ~ing** je claque des dents; **~box** (*inf*) *n* moulin *m* à paroles

chatty ['tʃæti] *adj* (*style*) familier(ère); (*person*) bavard(e)

chauffeur ['ʃəufə*] *n* chauffeur *m* (de maître)

chauvinist ['ʃəuvinist] *n* (*male ~*) phallocrate *m*; (*nationalist*) chauvin(e)

cheap [tʃiːp] *adj* bon marché *inv*, pas cher(chère); (*joke*) facile, d'un goût douteux; (*poor quality*) à bon marché, de qualité médiocre ♦ *adv* à bon marché, pour pas cher; **~er** *adj* moins cher(chère); **~ly** *adv* à bon marché, à bon compte

cheat [tʃiːt] *vi* tricher ♦ *vt* tromper, duper; (*rob*): **to ~ sb out of sth** escroquer qch à qn ♦ *n* tricheur(euse); escroc *m*

check [tʃek] *vt* vérifier; (*passport, ticket*) contrôler; (*halt*) arrêter; (*restrain*) maîtriser ♦ *n* vérification *f*, contrôle *m*; (*curb*) frein *m*; (*US: bill*) addition *f*; (*pattern: gen pl*) carreaux *mpl*; (*US*) = **cheque** ♦ *adj* (*pattern, cloth*) à carreaux; **~ in** *vi* (*in hotel*) remplir sa fiche (d'hôtel); (*at airport*) se présenter à l'enregistrement ♦ *vt* (*luggage*) (faire) enregistrer; **~ out** *vi* (*in hotel*) régler sa note; **~ up** *vi*: **to ~ up (on sth)** vérifier (qch); **to ~ up on sb** se renseigner sur le compte de qn; **~ered** (US) adj = **chequered**

(*US*) *adj* = **chequered**; **~ers** (*US*) *npl* jeu *m* de dames; **~-in** (**desk**) *n* enregistrement *m*; **~ing account** (*US*) *n* (*current account*) compte courant; **~mate** *n* échec et mat *m*; **~out** *n* (*in shop*) caisse *f*; **~point** *n* contrôle *m*; **~room** (*US*) *n* (*left-luggage office*) consigne *f*; **~up** *n* (*MED*) examen médical, check-up *m*

cheek [tʃiːk] *n* joue *f*; (*impudence*) toupet *m*, culot *m*; **~bone** *n* pommette *f*; **~y** *adj* effronté(e), culotté(e)

cheep [tʃiːp] *vi* piauler

cheer [tʃiə*] *vt* acclamer, applaudir; (*gladden*) réjouir, réconforter ♦ *vi* applaudir ♦ *n* (*gen pl*) acclamations *fpl*, applaudissements *mpl*; bravos *mpl*, hourras *mpl*; **~s!** à la vôtre!; **~ up** *vi* se dérider, reprendre courage ♦ *vt* remonter le moral à *or* de, dérider; **~ful** *adj* gai(e), joyeux(euse)

cheerio ['tʃiəri'əu] (*BRIT*) *excl* salut!, au revoir!

cheese [tʃiːz] *n* fromage *m*; **~board** *n* plateau *m* de fromages

cheetah ['tʃiːtə] *n* guépard *m*

chef [ʃef] *n* chef (cuisinier)

chemical ['kemikəl] *adj* chimique ♦ *n* produit *m* chimique

chemist ['kemist] *n* (*BRIT: pharmacist*) pharmacien(ne); (*scientist*) chimiste *m/f*; **~ry** *n* chimie *f*; **~'s (shop)** (*BRIT*) *n* pharmacie *f*

cheque [tʃek] (*BRIT*) *n* chèque *m*; **~book** *n* chéquier *m*, carnet *m* de chèques; **~ card** *n* carte *f* (d'identité) bancaire

chequered ['tʃekəd] (*US* **checkered**) *adj* (*fig*) varié(e)

cherish ['tʃeriʃ] *vt* chérir; **~ed** *adj* (*dream, memory*) cher(chère)

cherry ['tʃeri] *n* cerise *f*; (*also: ~ tree*) cerisier *m*

chess [tʃes] *n* échecs *mpl*; **~board** *n* échiquier *m*

chest [tʃest] *n* poitrine *f*; (*box*) coffre *m*, caisse *f*; **~ of drawers** *n* commode *f*

chestnut ['tʃesnʌt] n châtaigne f; (also: ~ tree) châtaignier m

chew [tʃu:] vt mâcher; **~ing gum** n chewing-gum m

chic [ʃi:k] adj chic inv, élégant(e)

chick [tʃɪk] n poussin m; (inf) nana f

chicken ['tʃɪkɪn] n poulet m; (inf: coward) poule mouillée; ~ **out** (inf) vi se dégonfler; **~pox** ['tʃɪkɪnpɔks] n varicelle f

chicory ['tʃɪkərɪ] n (for coffee) chicorée f; (salad) endive f

chief [tʃi:f] n chef ♦ adj principal(e); ~ **executive** (US **chief executive officer**) n directeur(trice) général(e); **~ly** adv principalement, surtout

chiffon ['ʃɪfɔn] n mousseline f de soie

chilblain ['tʃɪlbleɪn] n engelure f

child [tʃaɪld] (pl **~ren**) n enfant m/f; **~birth** n accouchement m; **~hood** n enfance f; **~ish** adj puéril(e), enfantin(e); **~like** adj d'enfant, innocent(e); ~ **minder** (BRIT) n garde f d'enfants

Chile ['tʃɪlɪ] n Chili m

chill [tʃɪl] n (of water) froid m; (of air) fraîcheur f; (MED) refroidissement m, coup m de froid ♦ vt (person) faire frissonner; (CULIN) mettre au frais, rafraîchir

chil(l)i ['tʃɪlɪ] n piment m (rouge)

chilly ['tʃɪlɪ] adj froid(e), glacé(e); (sensitive to cold) frileux(euse); to feel ~ avoir froid

chime [tʃaɪm] n carillon m ♦ vi carillonner, sonner

chimney ['tʃɪmnɪ] n cheminée f; ~ **sweep** n ramoneur m

chimpanzee [tʃɪmpæn'zi:] n chimpanzé m

chin [tʃɪn] n menton m

China ['tʃaɪnə] n Chine f

china ['tʃaɪnə] n porcelaine f; (crockery) vaisselle f en) porcelaine

Chinese [tʃaɪ'ni:z] adj chinois(e) ♦ n inv (person) Chinois(e); (LING) chinois m

chink [tʃɪŋk] n (opening) fente f, fissure f; (noise) tintement m

chip [tʃɪp] n (gen pl: CULIN: BRIT) frite f; (: US: potato ~) chip m; (of wood) copeau m; (of glass, stone) éclat m; (in game: also: micro~) puce f ♦ vt (cup, plate) ébrécher; ~ **in** vi mettre son grain de sel; (contribute) contribuer

chiropodist [kɪ'rɔpədɪst] (BRIT) n pédicure m/f

chirp [tʃə:p] vi pépier, gazouiller

chisel ['tʃɪzl] n ciseau m

chit [tʃɪt] n mot m, note f

chitchat ['tʃɪtʃæt] n bavardage m

chivalry ['ʃɪvəlrɪ] n esprit m chevaleresque, galanterie f

chives [tʃaɪvz] npl ciboulette f, civette f

chock-a-block ['tʃɔkə'blɔk], **chockful** ['tʃɔk'ful] adj plein(e) à craquer

chocolate ['tʃɔklɪt] n chocolat m

choice [tʃɔɪs] n choix m ♦ adj de choix

choir ['kwaɪə*] n chœur m, chorale f; **~boy** n jeune choriste m

choke [tʃəuk] vi étouffer ♦ vt étrangler; étouffer ♦ n (AUT) starter m; **street ~d with traffic** rue engorgée or emboutéillée

cholesterol [kə'lestərəl] n cholestérol m

choose [tʃu:z] (pt **chose**, pp **chosen**) vt choisir; to ~ to do décider de faire, juger bon de faire

choosy ['tʃu:zɪ] adj (to be) ~ (faire le/la) difficile

chop [tʃɔp] vt (wood) couper (à la hache); (CULIN: also: ~ **up**) couper (fin), émincer, hacher (en morceaux) ♦ n (CULIN) côtelette f; ~**s** npl (jaws) mâchoires fpl

chopper ['tʃɔpə*] n (helicopter) hélicoptère m, hélico m

choppy ['tʃɔpɪ] adj (sea) un peu agité(e)

chopsticks ['tʃɔpstɪks] npl baguettes fpl

chord [kɔ:d] n (MUS) accord m

chore [tʃɔ:*] n travail m de routine; **household ~s** travaux mpl de ménage

chortle ['tʃɔ:tl] vi glousser

chorus ['kɔ:rəs] n chœur m; (repeated part of song: also: fig) refrain m

chose [tʃəuz] pt of **choose**

chosen ['tʃəuzn] pp of **choose**

Christ [kraist] n Christ m

christen ['krisn] vt baptiser

Christian ['kristiən] adj, n chrétien(ne); **~ity** [kristi'æniti] n christianisme m; **~ name** n prénom m

Christmas ['krisməs] n Noël m or f; **Happy** or **Merry ~!** joyeux Noël!; **~ card** n carte f de Noël; **~ Day** n le jour de Noël; **~ Eve** n la veille de Noël, la nuit de Noël; **~ tree** n arbre m de Noël

chrome [krəum] n chrome m

chromium ['krəumiəm] n chrome m

chronic ['krɔnik] adj chronique

chronicle ['krɔnikl] n chronique f

chronological [krɔnə'lɔdʒikəl] adj chronologique

chrysanthemum [kri'sænθəməm] n chrysanthème m

chubby ['tʃʌbi] adj potelé(e), rondelet(te)

chuck [tʃʌk] (inf) vt (throw) lancer, jeter; (BRIT: also: **~ up**: job) lâcher; (: person) plaquer; **~ out** vt flanquer dehors or à la porte; (rubbish) jeter

chuckle ['tʃʌkl] vi glousser

chug [tʃʌg] vi faire teuf-teuf; (also: **~ along**) avancer en faisant teuf-teuf

chum [tʃʌm] n copain(copine)

chunk [tʃʌnk] n gros morceau

church [tʃə:tʃ] n église f; **~yard** n cimetière m

churn [tʃə:n] n (for butter) baratte f; (also: milk **~**) (grand) bidon à lait; **~ out** vt débiter

chute [ʃu:t] n glissoire f; (also: rubbish **~**) vide-ordures m inv

chutney ['tʃʌtni] n condiment m à base de fruits au vinaigre

CIA (US) n abbr (= Central Intelligence Agency) CIA f

CID (BRIT) n abbr = Criminal Investigation Department ≈ P.J. f

cider ['saidə*] n cidre m

cigar [si'gɑ:*] n cigare m

cigarette [sigə'ret] n cigarette f; **~ case** n étui m à cigarettes; **~ end** n mégot m

Cinderella [sində'relə] n Cendrillon

cine-camera ['sini'kæmərə] (BRIT) n caméra f

cinema ['sinəmə] n cinéma m

cinnamon ['sinəmən] n cannelle f

circle ['sə:kl] n cercle m; (in cinema, theatre) balcon m ♦ vi faire or décrire des cercles ♦ vt (move round) faire le tour de, tourner autour de; (surround) entourer, encercler

circuit ['sə:kit] n circuit m; **~ous** [sə:'kjuitəs] adj indirect(e), qui fait un détour

circular ['sə:kjulə*] adj circulaire ♦ n circulaire f

circulate ['sə:kjuleit] vi circuler ♦ vt faire circuler; **circulation** [sə:kju'leiʃən] n circulation f; (of newspaper) tirage m

circumflex ['sə:kəmfleks] n (also: **~ accent**) accent m circonflexe

circumstances ['sə:kəmstənsəz] npl circonstances fpl; (financial condition) moyens mpl, situation financière

circumvent [sə:kəm'vent] vt (rule, difficulty) tourner

circus ['sə:kəs] n cirque m

CIS n abbr (= Commonwealth of Independent States) CEI f

cistern ['sistən] n réservoir m (d'eau); (in toilet) réservoir de la chasse d'eau

citizen ['sitizn] n citoyen(ne); (resident): **the ~s of this town** les habitants de cette ville; **~ship** n citoyenneté f

citrus fruit ['sitrəs-] n agrume m

city ['siti] n ville f, cité f; **the C~** la Cité de Londres (centre des affaires)

civic ['sivik] adj civique; (authorities) municipal(e); **~ centre** (BRIT) n centre administratif (municipal)

civil ['sivil] adj civil(e); (polite) poli(e), courtois(e); (disobedience, defence) passif(ive); **~ engineer** n ingénieur *m* des travaux publics; **~ian** [sɪ'vɪlɪən] *adj, n* civil(e)

civilization [sɪvɪlaɪ'zeɪʃən] *n* civilisation *f*

civilized ['sɪvɪlaɪzd] *adj* civilisé(e); *(fig)* où règnent les bonnes manières

civil: **~ law** *n* code civil; *(study)* droit civil; **~ servant** *n* fonctionnaire *m/f*; **C~ Service** *n* fonction publique, administration *f*; **~ war** *n* guerre civile

clad [klæd] *adj*: **~ (in)** habillé(e) (de)

claim [kleɪm] *vt* revendiquer; *(rights, inheritance)* demander, prétendre à; *(assert)* déclarer, prétendre ♦ *vi (for insurance)* faire une déclaration de sinistre ♦ *n* revendication *f*; demande *f*; prétention *f*; déclaration *f*; *(right)* droit *m*, titre *m*; **~ant** *n (ADMIN, LAW)* requérant(e)

clairvoyant [klɛə'vɔɪənt] *n* voyant(e), extra-lucide *m/f*

clam [klæm] *n* palourde *f*

clamber ['klæmbə*] *vi* grimper, se hisser

clammy ['klæmɪ] *adj* humide (et froid(e)), moite

clamour ['klæmə*] *(US* **clamor**) *vi*: **to ~ for** réclamer à grands cris

clamp [klæmp] *n* agrafe *f*, crampon *m* ♦ *vt* serrer; *(sth to sth)* fixer; **~ down on** *vt fus* sévir ou prendre des mesures draconiennes contre

clan [klæn] *n* clan *m*

clang [klæŋ] *vi* émettre un bruit ou fracas métallique

clap [klæp] *vi* applaudir; **~ping** *n* applaudissements *mpl*

claret ['klærɪt] *n* (vin *m* de) bordeaux *m* (rouge)

clarinet [klærɪ'nɛt] *n* clarinette *f*

clarity ['klærɪtɪ] *n* clarté *f*

clash [klæʃ] *n* choc *m*; *(fig)* conflit *m* ♦ *vi* se heurter; être ou entrer en conflit; *(colours)* jurer; *(two events)* tomber en même temps

clasp [klɑːsp] *n (of necklace, bag)* fermoir *m*; *(hold, embrace)* étreinte *f* ♦ *vt* serrer, étreindre

class [klɑːs] *n* classe *f* ♦ *vt* classer, classifier

classic ['klæsɪk] *adj* classique ♦ *n (author, work)* classique *m*; **~al** *adj* classique

classified ['klæsɪfaɪd] *adj (information)* secret(ète); **~ advertisement** *n* petite annonce

classmate ['klɑːsmeɪt] *n* camarade *m/f* de classe

classroom ['klɑːsrʊm] *n* (salle *f* de) classe *f*

clatter ['klætə*] *n* cliquetis *m* ♦ *vi* cliqueter

clause [klɔːz] *n* clause *f*; *(LING)* proposition *f*

claw [klɔː] *n* griffe *f*; *(of bird of prey)* serre *f*; *(of lobster)* pince *f*; **~ at** *vt fus* essayer de s'agripper à ou griffer

clay [kleɪ] *n* argile *f*

clean [kliːn] *adj* propre; *(clear, smooth)* net(te); *(record, reputation)* sans tache; *(joke, story)* correct(e) ♦ *vt* nettoyer; **~ out** *vt* nettoyer (à fond); **~ up** *vt* nettoyer; *(fig)* remettre de l'ordre dans; **~-cut** *adj (person)* net(te), soigné(e); **~er** *n (person)* nettoyeur(euse), femme *f* de ménage; *(product)* détachant *m*; **~er's** *n (also:* dry **~er's)** teinturier *m*; **~ing** *n* nettoyage *m*; **~liness** ['klɛnlɪnɪs] *n* propreté *f*

cleanse [klɛnz] *vt* nettoyer; *(purify)* purifier; **~r** *n (for face)* démaquillant *m*

clean-shaven ['kliːn'ʃeɪvn] *adj* rasé(e) de près

cleansing department ['klɛnzɪŋ-] *(BRIT)* *n* service *m* de voirie

clear [klɪə*] *adj* clair(e); *(glass, plastic)* transparent(e); *(road, way)* libre, dégagé(e); *(conscience)* net(te) ♦ *vt (room)* débarrasser; *(of people)* faire évacuer; *(cheque)* compenser; *(LAW: suspect)* innocenter; *(obstacle)* franchir ou sauter sans heurter ♦ *vi (weather)* s'éclaircir; *(fog)* se dissiper ♦ *adv*: **~ of** à distance de, à l'écart de; **to ~ the table** débarrasser la table, desservir; ~ **up** *vt* ranger, mettre en ordre; *(mystery)* éclaircir, résoudre; **~ance** ['klɪərns] *n (removal)* déblaiement *m*; *(permission)* autorisation *f*; **~cut** *adj* clair(e), nettement défini(e); **~ing** *n (in forest)* clairière *f*; **~ing bank** *(BRIT) n* banque qui appartient à une chambre de compensation; **~ly** *adv* clairement; *(evidently)* de toute évidence; **~way** *(BRIT) n* route *f* à stationnement interdit

clef [klɛf] *n (MUS)* clé *f*

cleft [klɛft] *n (in rock)* crevasse *f*, fissure *f*

clench [klɛntʃ] *vt* serrer

clergy ['klɜːdʒɪ] *n* clergé *m*; **~man** *(irreg) n* ecclésiastique *m*

clerical ['klɛrɪkəl] *adj* de bureau, d'employé de bureau; *(REL)* clérical(e), du clergé

clerk [klɑːk, *(US)* klɜːk] *n* employé(e) de bureau; *(US: salesperson)* vendeur(euse)

clever ['klɛvə*] *adj (mentally)* intelligent(e); *(deft, crafty)* habile, adroit(e); *(device, arrangement)* ingénieux(euse), astucieux(euse)

clew [kluː] *(US) n* = **clue**

click [klɪk] *vi* faire un bruit sec *ou* un déclic ♦ *vt*: to ~ **one's tongue** faire claquer sa langue; to ~ **one's heels** claquer des talons

client ['klaɪənt] *n* client(e)

cliff [klɪf] *n* falaise *f*

climate ['klaɪmɪt] *n* climat *m*

climax ['klaɪmæks] *n* apogée *m*, point culminant; *(sexual)* orgasme *m*

climb [klaɪm] *vi* grimper, monter ♦ *vt* gravir, escalader, monter sur ♦ *n* montée *f*, escalade *f*; **~-down** *n* reculade *f*, dérobade *f*; **~er** *n (mountaineer)* grimpeur(euse), varappeur(euse); *(plant)* plante grimpante; **~ing** *n (mountaineering)* escalade *f*, varappe *f*

clinch [klɪntʃ] *vt (deal)* conclure, sceller

cling [klɪŋ] *(pt, pp* clung) *vi*: to ~

(to) se cramponner (à), s'accrocher (à); *(of clothes)* coller (à)

clinic ['klɪnɪk] *n* centre médical; **~al** *adj* clinique; *(attitude)* froid(e), détaché(e)

clink [klɪŋk] *vi* tinter, cliqueter

clip [klɪp] *n (for hair)* barrette *f*; *(also: paper ~)* trombone *m* ♦ *vt (fasten)* attacher; *(hair, nails)* couper; *(hedge)* tailler; **~pers** *npl (for hedge)* sécateur *m*; *(also: nail ~pers)* coupe-ongles *m inv*; **~ping** *n (from newspaper)* coupure *f* de journal

cloak [kləʊk] *n* grande cape ♦ *vt (fig)* masquer, cacher; **~room** *n (for coats etc)* vestiaire *m*; *(BRIT: WC)* toilettes *fpl*

clock [klɒk] *n (large)* horloge *f*; *(small)* pendule *f*; ~ **in** *(BRIT) vi* pointer (en arrivant); ~ **off** *(BRIT) vi* pointer (en partant); ~ **on** *(BRIT) vi* = **clock in**; ~ **out** *(BRIT) vi* = **clock off**; **~wise** *adv* dans le sens des aiguilles d'une montre; **~work** *n* rouages *mpl*, mécanisme *m*; *(of clock)* mouvement *m* (d'horlogerie) ♦ *adj* mécanique

clog [klɒg] *n* sabot *m* ♦ *vt* boucher ♦ *vi (also: ~ up)* se boucher

cloister ['klɔɪstə*] *n* cloître *m*

close[1] [kləʊs] *adj (near)*: ~ **(to)** près (de), proche (de); *(contact, link)* étroit(e); *(contest)* très serré(e); *(watch)* étroit(e), strict(e); *(examination)* attentif(ive), minutieux(euse); *(weather)* lourd(e), étouffant(e) ♦ *adv* près, à proximité; ~ **to** *prep*: ~ **by** *adj* proche ♦ *adv* tout(e) près; ~ **at hand** = ~ **by**; **a** ~ **friend** un ami intime; **to have a** ~ **shave** *(fig)* l'échapper belle

close[2] [kləʊz] *vt* fermer ♦ *vi (shop etc)* fermer; *(lid, door etc)* se fermer; *(end)* se terminer, se conclure ♦ *n (end)* conclusion *f*, fin *f*; ~ **down** *vt, vi* fermer *(définitivement)*

closed [kləʊzd] *adj* fermé(e); ~ **shop** *n* organisation *f* qui n'admet que des travailleurs syndiqués

close-knit [kləʊs'nɪt] *adj* (*family, community*) très uni(e)

closely [ˈkləʊslɪ] *adv* (*examine, watch*) de près

closet [ˈklɒzɪt] *n* (*cupboard*) placard *m*, réduit *m*

close-up [ˈkləʊsʌp] *n* gros plan

closure [ˈkləʊʒə*] *n* fermeture *f*

clot [klɒt] *n* (*gen: blood* ~) caillot *m*; (*inf: person*) ballot *m* ♦ *vi* (*blood*) se coaguler

cloth [klɒθ] *n* (*material*) tissu *m*, étoffe *f*; (*also: tea~*) torchon *m*; lavette *f*

clothe [kləʊð] *vt* habiller, vêtir; ~s *npl* vêtements *mpl*, habits *mpl*; ~s **brush** *n* brosse *f* à habits; ~s **line** *n* corde *f* (à linge); ~s **peg** (*US* ~s **pin**) *n* pince *f* à linge

clothing [ˈkləʊðɪŋ] *n* = **clothes**

cloud [klaʊd] *n* nuage *m*; ~**burst** *n* grosse averse; ~**y** *adj* nuageux(euse), couvert(e); (*liquid*) trouble

clout [klaʊt] *vt* flanquer une taloche à

clove [kləʊv] *n* (*CULIN: spice*) clou *m* de girofle; ~ **of garlic** gousse *f* d'ail

clover [ˈkləʊvə*] *n* trèfle *m*

clown [klaʊn] *n* clown *m* ♦ *vi* (*also:* ~ *about*, ~ *around*) faire le clown

cloying [ˈklɔɪɪŋ] *adj* (*taste, smell*) écœurant(e)

club [klʌb] *n* (*society, place: also: golf* ~) club *m*; (*weapon*) massue *f*, matraque *f* ♦ *vt* matraquer ♦ *vi*: to ~ **together** s'associer; ~s (*CARDS*) trèfle *m*; ~ **car** (*US*) *n* (*RAIL*) wagon-restaurant *m*; ~**house** *n* club *m*

cluck [klʌk] *vi* glousser

clue [kluː] *n* indice *m*; (*in crosswords*) définition *f*; **I haven't a** ~ je n'en ai pas la moindre idée

clump [klʌmp] *n*: ~ **of trees** bouquet *m* d'arbres; **a** ~ **of buildings** un ensemble de bâtiments

clumsy [ˈklʌmzɪ] *adj* gauche, maladroit(e)

clung [klʌŋ] *pt, pp* of **cling**

cluster [ˈklʌstə*] *n* (*of people*) (petit) groupe; (*of flowers*) grappe *f*; (*of stars*) amas *m* ♦ *vi* se rassembler

clutch [klʌtʃ] *n* (*grip, grasp*) étreinte *f*, prise *f*; (*AUT*) embrayage *m* ♦ *vt* (*grasp*) agripper; (*hold tightly*) serrer fort; (*hold on to*) se cramponner à

clutter [ˈklʌtə*] *vt* (*also:* ~ *up*) encombrer

CND *n abbr* (= *Campaign for Nuclear Disarmament*) mouvement pour le désarmement nucléaire

Co. *abbr* = **county**; **company**

c/o *abbr* (= *care of*) c/o, aux bons soins de

coach [kəʊtʃ] *n* (*bus*) autocar *m*; (*horse-drawn*) diligence *f*; (*of train*) voiture *f*, wagon *m*; (*SPORT: trainer*) entraîneur(euse); (*SCOL: tutor*) répétiteur(trice) ♦ *vt* entraîner; (*student*) faire travailler; ~ **trip** *n* excursion *f* en car

coal [kəʊl] *n* charbon *m*; ~ **face** *n* front *m* de taille; ~**field** *n* bassin houiller

coalition [kəʊəˈlɪʃən] *n* coalition *f*

coal: ~**man** [ˈkəʊlmən] (*irreg*) *n* charbonnier *m*, marchand *m* de charbon; ~ **merchant** *n* = ~**man**; ~**mine** [ˈkəʊlmaɪn] *n* mine *f* de charbon

coarse [kɔːs] *adj* grossier(ère), rude

coast [kəʊst] *n* côte *f* ♦ *vi* (*car, cycle etc*) descendre en roue libre; ~**al** *adj* côtier(ère); ~**guard** *n* garde-côte *m*; (*service*) gendarmerie *f* maritime; ~**line** *n* côte *f*, littoral *m*

coat [kəʊt] *n* manteau *m*; (*of animal*) pelage *m*, poil *m*; (*of paint*) couche *f* ♦ *vt* couvrir; ~ **hanger** *n* cintre *m*; ~**ing** *n* couche *f*, revêtement *m*; ~ **of arms** *n* blason *m*, armoiries *fpl*

coax [kəʊks] *vt* persuader par des cajoleries

cob [kɒb] *n* see **corn**

cobbler [ˈkɒblə*] *n* cordonnier *m*

cobbles [ˈkɒblz] (*also:* **cobblestones**) *npl* pavés (ronds)

cobweb ['kɒbweb] *n* toile *f* d'araignée

cocaine [kə'keɪn] *n* cocaïne *f*

cock [kɒk] *n* (*rooster*) coq *m*; (*male bird*) mâle *m* ♦ *vt* (*gun*) armer; **~erel** *n* jeune coq *m*; **~-eyed** *adj* (*idea, method*) absurde, qui ne tient pas debout

cockle ['kɒkl] *n* coque *f*

cockney ['kɒknɪ] *n* cockney *m*, habitant des quartiers populaires de l'East End de Londres, = faubourien(ne)

cockpit ['kɒkpɪt] *n* (*in aircraft*) poste *m* de pilotage, cockpit *m*

cockroach ['kɒkrəʊtʃ] *n* cafard *m*

cocktail ['kɒkteɪl] *n* cocktail *m* (*fruit* ~ *etc*) salade *f*; ~ **cabinet** *n* (meuble-)bar *m*; ~ **party** *n* cocktail *m*

cocoa ['kəʊkəʊ] *n* cacao *m*

coconut ['kəʊkənʌt] *n* noix *f* de coco

COD *abbr* = **cash on delivery**

cod [kɒd] *n* morue fraîche, cabillaud *m*

code [kəʊd] *n* code *m*

cod-liver oil ['kɒdlɪvər-] *n* huile *f* de foie de morue

coercion [kəʊ'ɜːʃən] *n* contrainte *f*

coffee ['kɒfɪ] *n* café *m*; ~ **bar** (*BRIT*) *n* café *m*; ~ **bean** *n* grain de café; ~ **break** *n* pause-café *f*; **~pot** *n* cafetière *f*; ~ **table** *n* (petite) table basse

coffin ['kɒfɪn] *n* cercueil *m*

cog [kɒg] *n* dent *f* (d'engrenage); (*wheel*) roue dentée

cogent ['kəʊdʒənt] *adj* puissant(e), convaincant(e)

coil [kɔɪl] *n* rouleau *m*, bobine *f*; (*contraceptive*) stérilet *m* ♦ *vt* enrouler

coin [kɔɪn] *n* pièce *f* de monnaie ♦ *vt* (*word*) inventer; **~age** *n* monnaie *f*, système *m* monétaire; ~ **box** (*BRIT*) *n* cabine *f* téléphonique

coincide [kəʊɪn'saɪd] *vi* coïncider; **~nce** [kəʊ'ɪnsɪdəns] *n* coïncidence *f*

Coke [kəʊk] ® *n* coca *m*

coke [kəʊk] *n* coke *m*

colander ['kʌləndə*] *n* passoire *f*

cold [kəʊld] *adj* froid(e) ♦ *n* froid *m*; (*MED*) rhume *m*; **it's** ~ il fait froid; **to be** or **feel** ~ (*person*) avoir froid; **to catch** ~ prendre or attraper froid; **to catch a** ~ attraper un rhume; **in** ~ **blood** de sang-froid; **~-shoulder** *vt* se montrer froid(e) envers, snober; ~ **sore** *n* bouton de fièvre

coleslaw ['kəʊlslɔː] *n* sorte de salade de chou cru

colic ['kɒlɪk] *n* colique(s) *f(pl)*

collapse [kə'læps] *vi* s'effondrer, s'écrouler ♦ *n* effondrement *m*, écroulement *m*; **collapsible** [kə'læpsəbl] *adj* pliant(e); télescopique

collar ['kɒlə*] *n* (*of coat, shirt*) col *m*; (*for animal*) collier *m*; **~bone** *n* clavicule *f*

collateral [kɒ'lætərəl] *n* nantissement *m*

colleague ['kɒliːg] *n* collègue *m/f*

collect [kə'lɛkt] *vt* rassembler; ramasser; (*as a hobby*) collectionner; (*BRIT*: *call and pick up*) (passer) prendre; (*mail*) faire la levée de, ramasser; (*money owed*) encaisser; (*donations, subscriptions*) recueillir ♦ *vi* (*people*) se rassembler; (*things*) s'amasser; **to call** ~ (*US*: *TEL*) téléphoner en P.C.V.; **~ion** [kə'lɛkʃən] *n* collection *f*; (*of mail*) levée *f*; (*for money*) collecte *f*, quête *f*; **~or** [kə'lɛktə*] *n* collectionneur *m*

college ['kɒlɪdʒ] *n* collège *m*

collide [kə'laɪd] *vi* entrer en collision

collie ['kɒlɪ] *n* (*dog*) colley *m*

colliery ['kɒlɪərɪ] (*BRIT*) *n* mine *f* de charbon, houillère *f*

collision [kə'lɪʒən] *n* collision *f*

colloquial [kə'ləʊkwɪəl] *adj* familier(ère)

colon ['kəʊlən] *n* (*sign*) deux-points *m inv*; (*MED*) côlon *m*

colonel ['kɜːnl] *n* colonel *m*

colony ['kɒlənɪ] *n* colonie *f*

colour ['kʌlə*] (*US* **color**) *n* couleur *f* ♦ *vt* (*paint*) peindre; (*dye*) teindre;

(news) fausser, exagérer ♦ vi *(blush)* rougir; ~s npl *(of party, club)* couleurs fpl; ~ **in** vt colorier; ~ **bar** n discrimination raciale *(dans un établissement)*; ~**blind** adj daltonien(ne); ~**ed** adj *(person)* de couleur; *(illustration)* en couleur; ~**film** n *(for camera)* pellicule f *(en)* couleur; ~**ful** adj colorée(e), vif(vive); *(personality)* pittoresque, haut(e) en couleurs; ~**ing** n colorant m; *(complexion)* teint m; ~ **scheme** n combinaison f de(s) couleurs; ~ **television** n télévision f (en) couleur

colt [kəʊlt] n poulain m

column ['kɒləm] n colonne f; ~**ist** ['kɒləmnɪst] n chroniqueur(euse) m

coma ['kəʊmə] n coma m

comb [kəʊm] n peigne m ♦ vt *(hair)* peigner; *(area)* ratisser, passer au peigne fin

combat ['kɒmbæt] n combat m ♦ vt combattre, lutter contre

combination [kɒmbɪ'neɪʃən] n combinaison f

combine [vb kəm'baɪn, n 'kɒmbaɪn] vt: to ~ **sth with sth** combiner qch avec qch; *(one quality with another)* joindre ou allier qch à qch ♦ vi s'associer; *(CHEM)* se combiner ♦ n *(ECON)* trust m; ~ **(harvester)** n moissonneuse-batteuse-lieuse f

come [kʌm] *(pt came, pp come)* vi venir, arriver; **to ~ to** *(decision etc)* parvenir ou arriver à; **to ~ undone/loose** se défaire/desserrer; ~ **about** vi se produire, arriver; ~ **across** vt fus rencontrer par hasard, tomber sur; ~ **along** vi = to come on; ~ **away** vi partir, s'en aller, se détacher; ~ **back** vi revenir; ~ **by** vt fus *(acquire)* obtenir, se procurer; ~ **down** vi descendre; *(prices)* baisser; *(buildings)* s'écrouler, être démoli(e); ~ **forward** vi s'avancer, se présenter, s'annoncer; ~ **from** vt fus être originaire de, venir de; ~ **in** vi entrer; ~ **in for** vt fus *(criticism etc)* être l'objet de; ~ **into** vt fus *(money etc)* hériter de; ~ **out** vi *(button)* se

détacher; *(stain)* s'enlever; *(attempt)* réussir; ~ **on** vi *(pupil, work, project)* faire des progrès, s'avancer; *(lights, electricity)* s'allumer; *(central heating)* se mettre en marche; ~ on! viens!, allons!, allez!; ~ **out** vi sortir; *(book)* paraître; *(strike)* cesser le travail, se mettre en grève; ~ **round** vi *(after faint, operation)* revenir à soi, reprendre connaissance; ~ **to** vi revenir à soi; ~ **up** vi monter; ~ **up against** vt fus *(resistance, difficulties)* rencontrer; ~ **up with** vt fus: **he came up with an idea** il a eu une idée, il a proposé quelque chose; ~ **upon** vt fus tomber sur; ~**back** ['kʌmbæk] n *(THEATRE etc)* rentrée f

comedian [kə'miːdɪən] n *(in music hall etc)* comique m; *(THEATRE)* comédien m

comedy ['kɒmədɪ] n comédie f

comeuppance [kʌm'ʌpəns] n: **to get one's ~** recevoir ce qu'on mérite

comfort ['kʌmfət] n confort m, bien-être m; *(relief)* soulagement m, réconfort m ♦ vt consoler, réconforter; **the ~s of home** les commodités fpl de la maison; ~**able** adj confortable; *(person)* à l'aise; *(patient)* dont l'état est stationnaire; *(walk etc)* facile; ~**ably** *(sit)* confortablement; *(live)* à l'aise; ~ **station** n *(US)* toilettes fpl

comic ['kɒmɪk] adj *(also: ~al)* comique ♦ n comique m; *(BRIT: magazine)* illustré m; ~ **strip** n bande dessinée

coming ['kʌmɪŋ] n arrivée f ♦ adj prochain(e), à venir; ~**(s) and going(s)** n(pl) va-et-vient m inv

comma ['kɒmə] n virgule f

command [kə'mɑːnd] n ordre m, commandement m; *(MIL: authority)* commandement; *(mastery)* maîtrise f ♦ vt *(troops)* commander; **to ~ sb to do** ordonner à qn de faire; ~**er** [kə'mɑːndɪə°] n *(MIL)* commandant m

commando [kə'mɑːndəʊ] n commando m; membre m d'un commando

commemorate [kə'meməreit] vt commémorer

commence [kə'mens] vt, vi commencer

commend [kə'mend] vt louer; (recommend) recommander

commensurate [kə'menʃurit] adj: ~ with or to en proportion de, proportionné(e) à

comment ['kɔment] n commentaire m ♦ vi: to ~ (on) faire des remarques (sur); "no" ~ "je n'ai rien à dire"; ~ary ['kɔmɛntri] n commentaire m; (SPORT) reportage m (en direct); ~ator ['kɔmɛnteitə*] n commentateur m; reporter m

commerce ['kɔmə:s] n commerce m

commercial [kə'mə:ʃəl] adj commercial(e) ♦ n (TV, RADIO) annonce f publicitaire, spot m (publicitaire); ~ **radio** n radio privée; ~ **television** n télévision privée

commiserate [kə'mizəreit] vi: to ~ with sb témoigner de la sympathie pour qn

commission [kə'miʃən] n (order for work) commande f; (committee, fee) commission f ♦ vt (work of art) commander, charger un artiste de l'exécution de; **out of** ~ (not working) hors service; ~**aire** [kəmiʃə'nɛə*] (BRIT) n (at shop, cinema etc) portier m (en uniforme); ~**er** n (POLICE) préfet m de police

commit [kə'mit] vt (act) commettre; (resources) consacrer; (to sb's care) confier (à); **to** ~ **o.s.** (to do) s'engager à (faire); **to** ~ **suicide** se suicider; ~**ment** n engagement m, (obligation) responsabilité(s) f(pl)

committee [kə'miti] n comité m

commodity [kə'mɔditi] n produit m, marchandise f, article m

common ['kɔmən] adj commun(e); (usual) courant(e) ♦ n terrain communal; **the C~s** npl la chambre des Communes; **in** ~ en commun; ~**er** n roturier(ière); ~ **law** n droit

coutumier; ~**ly** adv communément, généralement; couramment; **C~ Market** n: **the C~ Market** le Marché commun; ~**place** adj banal(e), ordinaire; ~ **room** n salle commune; ~ **sense** n bon sens; **C~wealth** (BRIT) n: **the C~wealth** le Commonwealth

commotion [kə'məuʃən] n désordre m, tumulte m

communal ['kɔmju:nl] adj (life) communautaire; (for common use) commun(e)

commune [n 'kɔmju:n, vb kə'mju:n] n (group) communauté f ♦ vi: **to** ~ **with** communier avec

communicate [kə'mju:nikeit] vt, vi communiquer

communication [kəmju:ni'keiʃən] n communication f; ~ **cord** (BRIT) n sonnette f d'alarme

communion [kə'mju:niən] n (also: **Holy C~**) communion f

communism ['kɔmjunizəm] n communisme m; **communist** ['kɔmjunist] adj communiste ♦ n communiste m/f

community [kə'mju:niti] n communauté f; ~ **centre** n centre m de loisirs; ~ **chest** (US) n fonds commun; ~ **home** n (school) centre m d'éducation surveillée

commutation ticket [kɔmju'teiʃən-] (US) n carte f d'abonnement

commute [kə'mju:t] vi faire un trajet journalier (de son domicile à son bureau) ♦ vt (LAW) commuer; ~**r** n banlieusard(e) (qui ... see vi)

compact [adj kəm'pækt, n 'kɔmpækt] adj compact(e) ♦ n (also: powder ~) poudrier m; ~ **disc** n disque compact; ~ **disk player** n lecteur m de disque compact

companion [kəm'pæniən] n compagnon(compagne); ~**ship** n camaraderie f

company ['kʌmpəni] n compagnie f; **to keep sb** ~ tenir compagnie à qn; ~ **secretary** (BRIT) n (COMM) secrétaire général (d'une société)

comparative [kəm'pærətɪv] adj (study) comparatif(ive); (relative) relatif(ive); **~ly** adv (relatively) relativement

compare [kəm'pɛə*] vt: to ~ sth/sb with/to comparer qch/qn avec or et/à ♦ vi: to ~ (with) se comparer (à), être comparable (à); **comparison** [kəm'pærɪsn] n comparaison f

compartment [kəm'pɑːtmənt] n compartiment m

compass ['kʌmpəs] n boussole f; ~es npl (GEOM: also: pair of ~es) compas m

compassion [kəm'pæʃən] n compassion f; **~ate** adj compatissant(e)

compatible [kəm'pætɪbl] adj compatible

compel [kəm'pel] vt contraindre, obliger; **~ling** adj (fig: argument) irrésistible

compensate ['kɒmpənseɪt] vt indemniser, dédommager ♦ vi: to ~ for compenser; **compensation** [kɒmpən'seɪʃn] n compensation f; (money) dédommagement m, indemnité f

compère ['kɒmpɛə*] n (TV) animateur(trice)

compete [kəm'piːt] vi: to ~ (with) rivaliser (avec), faire concurrence (à)

competent ['kɒmpɪtənt] adj compétent(e), capable

competition [kɒmpɪ'tɪʃn] n (contest) compétition f, concours m; (ECON) concurrence f

competitive [kəm'petɪtɪv] adj (ECON) concurrentiel(le); (sport) de compétition; (person) qui a l'esprit de compétition

competitor [kəm'petɪtə*] n concurrent(e)

complacency [kəm'pleɪsnsɪ] n suffisance f, vaine complaisance

complain [kəm'pleɪn] vi: to ~ (about) se plaindre (de); (in shop etc) réclamer (au sujet de); to ~ of (pain) se plaindre de; **~t** n plainte f; réclamation f; (MED) affection f

complement [n 'kɒmplɪmənt, vb 'kɒmplɪment] n complément m; (especially of ship's crew etc) effectif complet ♦ vt (enhance) compléter; **~ary** [kɒmplɪ'mentərɪ] adj complémentaire

complete [kəm'pliːt] adj complet(ète) ♦ vt achever, parachever; (set, group) compléter; (a form) remplir; **~ly** adv complètement; **completion** [kəm'pliːʃən] n achèvement m; (of contract) exécution f

complex ['kɒmpleks] adj complexe ♦ n complexe m

complexion [kəm'plekʃən] n (of face) teint m

compliance [kəm'plaɪəns] n (submission) docilité f; (agreement): ~ with le fait de se conformer à; **in** ~ **with** en accord avec

complicate ['kɒmplɪkeɪt] vt compliquer; **~d** adj compliqué(e); **complication** [kɒmplɪ'keɪʃn] n complication f

compliment [n 'kɒmplɪmənt, vb 'kɒmplɪment] n compliment m ♦ vt complimenter; **~s** npl (respects) compliments mpl, hommages mpl; **to pay sb a** ~ faire or adresser un compliment à qn; **~ary** [kɒmplɪ'mentərɪ] adj flatteur(euse); (free) (offert(e)) à titre gracieux; **free ticket** n billet m de faveur

comply [kəm'plaɪ] vi: to ~ with se soumettre à, se conformer à

component [kəm'pəʊnənt] n composant m, élément m

compose [kəm'pəʊz] vt composer; (form): **to be ~d of** se composer de; **to ~ o.s.** se calmer, se maîtriser; prendre une contenance; **~d** adj calme, posé(e); **~r** n (MUS) compositeur m; **composition** [kɒmpə'zɪʃən] n composition f; **composure** [kəm'pəʊʒə*] n calme m, maîtrise f de soi

compound ['kɒmpaʊnd] n composé m; (enclosure) enclos m, enceinte f; (LING) composé m ♦ adj composé(e); **~ fracture** n fracture compliquée; **~ interest** n intérêt composé

comprehend [kɒmprɪ'hend] vt

comprendre; **comprehension** [kɔmprɪ'henʃən] n compréhension f

comprehensive [kɔmprɪ'hensɪv] adj (très) complet(ète); ~ **policy** n (INSURANCE) assurance f tous risques; ~ **(school)** (BRIT) n école secondaire polyvalente, ≈ C.E.S. m

compress [vb kəm'pres, n 'kɔmpres] vt comprimer; (text, information) condenser ♦ n (MED) compresse f

comprise [kəm'praɪz] vt (also: be ~d of) comprendre; (constitute) constituer, représenter

compromise ['kɔmprəmaɪz] n compromis m ♦ vt compromettre ♦ vi transiger, accepter un compromis

compulsion [kəm'pʌlʃən] n contrainte f, force f

compulsive [kəm'pʌlsɪv] adj (PSYCH) compulsif(ive); (book, film etc) captivant(e)

compulsory [kəm'pʌlsərɪ] adj obligatoire

computer [kəm'pjuːtə*] n ordinateur m; ~ **game** n jeu m vidéo; ~**ize** vt informatiser; ~ **programmer** n programmeur(euse); ~ **programming** n programmation f; ~ **science** n = ~ **science**

comrade ['kɔmrɪd] n camarade m/f

con [kɔn] vt duper; (cheat) escroquer ♦ n escroquerie f

conceal [kən'siːl] vt cacher, dissimuler

conceit [kən'siːt] n vanité f, suffisance f, prétention f; ~**ed** adj vaniteux(euse), suffisant(e)

conceive [kən'siːv] vt, vi concevoir

concentrate ['kɔnsəntreɪt] vi se concentrer ♦ vt concentrer

concentration [kɔnsən'treɪʃən] n concentration f; ~ **camp** n camp m de concentration

concept ['kɔnsept] n concept m

concern [kən'sɜːn] n affaire f; (COMM) entreprise f, firme f; (anxiety) inquiétude f, souci m ♦ vt concerner; to be ~ed (about) s'inquiéter (de), être inquiet(e) au sujet

de); ~**ing** prep en ce qui concerne, à propos de

concert ['kɔnsət] n concert m; ~**ed** adj concerté(e); ~ **hall** n salle f de concert

concerto [kən'tʃɜːtəʊ] n concerto m

concession [kən'seʃən] n concession f; tax ~ dégrèvement fiscal

conclude [kən'kluːd] vt conclure; **conclusion** [kən'kluːʒən] n conclusion f; **conclusive** [kən'kluːsɪv] adj concluant(e), définitif(ive)

concoct [kən'kɔkt] vt confectionner, composer; (fig) inventer; ~**ion** [kən'kɔkʃən] n mélange m

concourse ['kɔŋkɔːs] n (hall) hall m, salle f des pas perdus

concrete ['kɔŋkriːt] n béton m ♦ adj concret(ète); (floor etc) en béton

concur [kən'kɜː*] vi (agree) être d'accord

concurrently [kən'kʌrəntlɪ] adv simultanément

concussion [kən'kʌʃən] n (MED) commotion (cérébrale)

condemn [kən'dem] vt condamner

condensation [kɔnden'seɪʃən] n condensation f

condense [kən'dens] vi se condenser ♦ vt condenser; ~**d milk** n lait concentré (sucré)

condition [kən'dɪʃən] n condition f; (MED) état m ♦ vt déterminer, conditionner; **on ~ that** à condition que +sub, à condition de; ~**al** adj conditionnel(le); ~**er** n (for hair) baume après-shampooing m; (for fabrics) assouplissant m

condolences [kən'dəʊlənsɪz] npl condoléances fpl

condom ['kɔndəm] n préservatif m

condominium [kɔndə'mɪnɪəm] (US) n (building) immeuble m (en copropriété)

condone [kən'dəʊn] vt fermer les yeux sur, approuver (tacitement)

conducive [kən'djuːsɪv] adj: ~ **to** favorable à, qui contribue à

conduct [n 'kɔndʌkt, vb kən'dʌkt] n conduite f ♦ vt conduire; (MUS) diriger; to ~ o.s. se conduire, se comporter; **~ed tour** *n* voyage organisé; *(of building)* visite guidée; **~or** [kən'dʌktə*] *n* (of orchestra) chef *m* d'orchestre; *(on bus)* receveur *m*; *(US: on train)* chef *m* de train; (ELEC) conducteur *m*; **~ress** [kən'dʌktrɪs] *n* (on bus) receveuse *f*

cone [kəun] *n* cône *m*; (for ice-cream) cornet *m*; (BOT) pomme *f* de pin, cône

confectioner [kən'fekʃənə*] *n* confiseur(euse); **~'s (shop)** *n* confiserie *f*; **~y** *n* confiserie *f*

confer [kən'fɜː*] *vt*: to ~ sth on conférer qch à ♦ *vi* conférer, s'entretenir

conference ['kɒnfərəns] *n* conférence *f*

confess [kən'fes] *vt* confesser, avouer ♦ *vi* se confesser; **~ion** [kən'feʃən] *n* confession *f*

confetti [kən'feti] *n* confettis *mpl*

confide [kən'faid] *vi*: to ~ in se confier à

confidence ['kɒnfidəns] *n* confiance *f*; *(also: self-~)* assurance *f*, confiance en soi; *(secret)* confidence *f*; **in ~** *(speak, write)* en confidence, confidentiellement; **~ trick** *n* escroquerie *f*; **confident** ['kɒnfidənt] *adj* sûr(e), assuré(e); **confidential** [kɒnfi'denʃəl] *adj* confidentiel(le)

confine [kən'fain] *vt* limiter, borner; *(shut up)* confiner, enfermer; **~d** *adj* *(space)* restreint(e), réduit(e); **~ment** *n* emprisonnement *m*, détention *f*; **~s** ['kɒnfainz] *npl* confins *mpl*, bornes *fpl*

confirm [kən'fɜːm] *vt* confirmer; *(appointment)* ratifier; **~ation** [kɒnfə'meiʃən] *n* confirmation *f*; **~ed** *adj* invétéré(e), incorrigible

confiscate ['kɒnfiskeit] *vt* confisquer

conflict [n 'kɒnflikt, vb kən'flikt] *n* conflit *m*, lutte *f* ♦ *vi* être or entrer en conflit; *(opinions)* s'opposer, se heurter; **~ing** [kən'fliktiŋ] *adj* contradictoire

conform [kən'fɔːm] *vi*: to ~ (to) se

conformer (à)

confound [kən'faund] *vt* confondre

confront [kən'frʌnt] *vt* confronter, mettre en présence; *(enemy, danger)* affronter, faire face à; **~ation** [kɒnfrən'teiʃən] *n* confrontation *f*

confuse [kən'fjuːz] *vt* (person) troubler; (situation) embrouiller; (one thing with another) confondre; **~d** *adj* (person) dérouté(e), désorienté(e); **confusing** *adj* peu clair(e), déroutant(e); **confusion** [kən'fjuːʒən] *n* confusion *f*

congeal [kən'dʒiːl] *vi* (blood) se coaguler; (oil etc) se figer

congenial [kən'dʒiːniəl] *adj* sympathique, agréable

congested [kən'dʒestid] *adj* (MED) congestionné(e); (area) surpeuplé(e); (road) bloqué(e)

congestion [kən'dʒestʃən] *n* congestion *f*; (fig) encombrement *m*

congratulate [kən'grætjuleit] *vt*: to ~ sb (on) féliciter qn (de); **congratulations** [kəngrætju'leiʃənz] *npl* félicitations *fpl*

congregate ['kɒngrigeit] *vi* se rassembler, se réunir

congregation [kɒngri'geiʃən] *n* assemblée *f* (des fidèles)

congress ['kɒngres] *n* congrès *m*; **~man** (*irreg: US*) *n* membre *m* du Congrès

conjunction [kən'dʒʌŋkʃən] *n* (LING) conjonction *f*

conjunctivitis [kəndʒʌŋkti'vaitis] *n* conjonctivite *f*

conjure ['kʌndʒə*] *vi* faire des tours de passe-passe; **~ up** *vt* (ghost, spirit) faire apparaître; (memories) évoquer; **~r** *n* prestidigitateur *m*, illusionniste *m/f*

conk out [kɒŋk-] (inf) *vi* tomber or rester en panne

con man (*irreg*) *n* escroc *m*

connect [kə'nekt] *vt* joindre, relier; (ELEC) connecter; (TEL: caller) mettre en connection (with avec); (fig) établir un rapport entre, faire un rapprochement entre ♦ *vi* (*train*): **to ~ with** assurer la correspondance avec; **to be ~ed with** (*fig*) avoir un rapport avec; avoir des rapports avec, être en relation avec; **~ion** [kə'nekʃə] *n* relation *f*, lien *m*; (*ELEC*) connexion *f*; (*train, bus etc*) correspondance *f*; (*TEL*) branchement *m*, communication *f*

connive [kə'naɪv] *vi*: **to ~ at** se faire le complice de

conquer ['kɔŋkə*] *vt* conquérir; (*feelings*) vaincre, surmonter

conquest ['kɔŋkwest] *n* conquête *f*

cons [kɔnz] *npl see* **convenience**; **pro**

conscience ['kɔnʃəns] *n* conscience *f*; **conscientious** [kɔnʃɪ'enʃəs] *adj* consciencieux(euse)

conscious ['kɔnʃəs] *adj* conscient(e); **~ness** *n* conscience *f*; (*MED*) connaissance *f*

conscript ['kɔnskrɪpt] *n* conscrit *m*

consent [kən'sent] *n* consentement *m* ♦ *vi*: **to ~ (to)** consentir (à)

consequence ['kɔnsɪkwəns] *n* conséquence *f*, suites *fpl*; (*significance*) importance *f*

consequently ['kɔnsɪkwəntlɪ] *adv* par conséquent, donc

conservation [kɔnsə'veɪʃən] *n* préservation *f*, protection *f*

conservative [kən'sɜ:vətɪv] *adj* conservateur(trice); at a ~ estimate au bas mot; **C~** (*BRIT*) *adj, n* (*POL*) conservateur(trice)

conservatory [kən'sɜ:vətrɪ] *n* (*greenhouse*) serre *f*

conserve [kən'sɜ:v] *vt* conserver, préserver; (*supplies, energy*) économiser ♦ *n* confiture *f*

consider [kən'sɪdə*] *vt* (*study*) considérer, réfléchir à; (*take into account*) penser à, prendre en considération; (*regard, judge*) considérer, estimer; **to ~ doing sth** envisager de faire qch; **~able** [kən'sɪdərəbl] *adj* considérable; **~ably** *adv* nettement; **~ate** [kən'sɪdərɪt] *adj* prévenant(e), plein(e) d'égards; **~ation** [kɔns-

idə'reɪʃən] *n* considération *f*; **~ing** [kən'sɪdərɪŋ] *prep* étant donné

consign [kən'saɪn] *vt* expédier; (*to sb's care*) confier; (*fig*) livrer; **~ment** *n* arrivage *m*, envoi *m*

consist [kən'sɪst] *vi*: **to ~ of** consister en, se composer de

consistency [kən'sɪstənsɪ] *n* consistance *f*; (*fig*) cohérence *f*

consistent [kən'sɪstənt] *adj* logique, cohérent(e)

consolation [kɔnsə'leɪʃən] *n* consolation *f*

console ['kɔnsəul] *n* (*COMPUT*) console *f*

consonant ['kɔnsənənt] *n* consonne *f*

conspicuous [kən'spɪkjuəs] *adj* voyant(e), qui attire l'attention

conspiracy [kən'spɪrəsɪ] *n* conspiration *f*, complot *m*

constable ['kʌnstəbl] (*BRIT*) *n* ≈ agent *m* de police, gendarme *m*; **chief ~** ≈ préfet *m* de police

constabulary [kən'stæbjulərɪ] (*BRIT*) *n* ≈ police *f*, gendarmerie *f*

constant ['kɔnstənt] *adj* constant(e); incessant(e); **~ly** *adv* constamment, sans cesse

constipated ['kɔnstɪpeɪtəd] *adj* constipé(e); **constipation** [kɔnstɪ'peɪʃən] *n* constipation *f*

constituency [kən'stɪtjuənsɪ] *n* circonscription électorale

constituent [kən'stɪtjuənt] *n* (*POL*) électeur(trice); (*part*) élément constitutif, composant *m*

constitution [kɔnstɪ'tju:ʃən] *n* constitution *f*; **~al** *adj* constitutionnel(le)

constraint [kən'streɪnt] *n* contrainte *f*

construct [kən'strʌkt] *vt* construire; **~ion** [kən'strʌkʃən] *n* construction *f*; **~ive** *adj* constructif(ive)

construe [kən'stru:] *vt* interpréter, expliquer

consul ['kɔnsl] *n* consul *m*; **~ate** ['kɔnsjulət] *n* consulat *m*

consult [kən'sʌlt] *vt* consulter; **~ant** *n* (*MED*) médecin consultant; (*other* *specialist*) consultant *m*, (*expert-*) conseil *m*; ~**ing room** (*BRIT*) *n* cabinet *m* de consultation

consume [kən'sjuːm] *vt* consommer; ~**r** *n* consommateur(trice); ~**r goods** *npl* biens *mpl* de consommation; ~**r society** *n* société *f* de consommation

consummate ['kɔnsʌmeɪt] *vt* consommer

consumption [kən'sʌmpʃən] *n* consommation *f*

cont. *abbr* (= continued) suite

contact ['kɔntækt] *n* contact *m*; (*person*) connaissance *f*, relation *f* ♦ *vt* contacter, se mettre en contact ou en rapport avec; ~ **lenses** *npl* verres *mpl* de contact, lentilles *fpl*

contagious [kən'teɪdʒəs] *adj* contagieux(euse)

contain [kən'teɪn] *vt* contenir; to ~ o.s. se contenir, se maîtriser; ~**er** *n* récipient *m*; (*for shipping etc*) container *m*

contaminate [kən'tæmɪneɪt] *vt* contaminer

cont'd *abbr* (= continued) suite

contemplate ['kɔntəmpleɪt] *vt* contempler; (*consider*) envisager

contemporary [kən'tempərərɪ] *adj* contemporain(e); (*design, wallpaper*) moderne ♦ *n* contemporain(e)

contempt [kən'tempt] *n* mépris *m*, dédain *m*; ~ **of court** (*LAW*) outrage *m* à l'autorité de la justice; ~**uous** *adj* dédaigneux(euse), méprisant(e)

contend [kən'tend] *vt*: to ~ **that** soutenir ou prétendre que ♦ *vi*: to ~ **with** (*compete*) rivaliser avec; (*struggle*) lutter avec; ~**er** *n* concurrent(e); (*POL*) candidat(e)

content [*adj, vb* kən'tent, *n* 'kɔntent] *adj* content(e), satisfait(e) ♦ *vt* contenter, satisfaire ♦ *n* contenu *m*; (*of fat, moisture*) teneur *f*; ~**s** *npl* (*of container etc*) contenu *m*; (*table of*) ~**s** table *f* des matières; ~**ed** *adj* content(e), satisfait(e)

contention [kən'tenʃən] *n* dispute *f*,

contestation *f*; (*argument*) assertion *f*, affirmation *f*

contest [*n* 'kɔntest, *vb* kən'test] *n* combat *m*, lutte *f*; (*competition*) concours *m* ♦ *vt* (*decision, statement*) contester, discuter; (*compete for*) disputer; ~**ant** *n* concurrent(e); (*in fight*) adversaire *m/f*

context ['kɔntekst] *n* contexte *m*

continent ['kɔntɪnənt] *n* continent *m*; the C~ (*BRIT*) l'Europe continentale; ~**al** [kɔntɪ'nentl] *adj* continental(e); ~**al quilt** (*BRIT*) *n* couette *f*

contingency [kən'tɪndʒənsɪ] *n* éventualité *f*, événement imprévu

continual [kən'tɪnjuəl] *adj* continuel(le)

continuation [kəntɪnju'eɪʃən] *n* continuation *f*; (*after interruption*) reprise *f*; (*of story*) suite *f*

continue [kən'tɪnjuː] *vi, vt* continuer; (*after interruption*) reprendre, poursuivre

continuity [kɔntɪ'njuːɪtɪ] *n* continuité *f*; (*TV etc*) enchaînement *m*

continuous [kən'tɪnjuəs] *adj* continu(e); (*LING*) progressif(ive); ~ **stationery** *n* papier *m* en continu

contort [kən'tɔːt] *vt* tordre, crisper

contour ['kɔntuə*] *n* contour *m*, profil *m*; (*on map: also*: ~ **line**) courbe *f* de niveau

contraband ['kɔntrəbænd] *n* contrebande *f*

contraceptive [kɔntrə'septɪv] *adj* contraceptif(ive), anticonceptionnel(le) ♦ *n* contraceptif *m*

contract [*n* 'kɔntrækt, *vb* kən'trækt] *n* contrat *m* ♦ *vi* (*become smaller*) se contracter, se rétrécir; (*COMM*): to ~ **to do sth** s'engager (par contrat) à faire qch; ~**ion** [kən'trækʃən] *n* contraction *f*; ~**or** [kən'træktə*] *n* entrepreneur *m*

contradict [kɔntrə'dɪkt] *vt* contredire

contraption [kən'træpʃən] (*pej*) *n* machin *m*, truc *m*

contrary¹ ['kɒntrərɪ] *adj* contraire, opposé(e) ♦ *n* contraire *m*; **on the ~** au contraire; **unless you hear to the ~** sauf avis contraire

contrary² [kən'trɛərɪ] *adj* (*perverse*) contrariant(e), entêté(e)

contrast [*n* 'kɒntrɑːst, *vb* kən'trɑːst] *n* contraste *m* ♦ *vt* mettre en contraste, contraster; **in ~ to** *or* **with** contrairement à

contravene [kɒntrə'viːn] *vt* enfreindre, violer, contrevenir à

contribute [kən'trɪbjuːt] *vi* contribuer ♦ *vt*: **to ~ £10/an article to** donner 10 livres/un article à; **to ~ to** contribuer à; (*newspaper*) collaborer à; **contribution** [kɒntrɪ'bjuːʃən] *n* contribution *f*; **contributor** [kən'trɪbjutə*] *n* (*to newspaper*) collaborateur(trice)

contrive [kən'traɪv] *vi*: **to ~ to do** s'arranger pour faire, trouver le moyen de faire

control [kən'trəul] *vt* maîtriser, commander; (*check*) contrôler ♦ *n* contrôle *m*, autorité *f*; maîtrise *f*; ~s *npl* (*of machine etc*) commandes *fpl*; (*on radio, TV*) boutons *mpl* de réglage; **everything is under ~** tout va bien, j'ai (*or* il a *etc*) la situation en main; **to be in ~ of** être maître de, maîtriser; **the car went out of ~** j'ai (*or* il a *etc*) perdu le contrôle du véhicule; ~ **panel** *n* tableau *m* de commande; ~ **room** *n* salle *f* des commandes; ~ **tower** *n* (*AVIAT*) tour *f* de contrôle

controversial [kɒntrə'vəːʃəl] *adj* (*topic*) discutable, contestable; (*person*) qui fait beaucoup parler de lui; **controversy** ['kɒntrəvəːsɪ] *n* controverse *f*, polémique *f*

convalesce [kɒnvə'lɛs] *vi* relever de maladie, se remettre (d'une maladie)

convector [kən'vɛktə*] *n* (*heater*) radiateur *m* (à convexion)

convene [kən'viːn] *vt* convoquer, assembler ♦ *vi* se réunir, s'assembler

convenience [kən'viːnɪəns] *n* commodité *f*; **at your ~** quand *or* comme cela vous convient; **all modern ~s**, (*BRIT*) **all mod cons** avec tout le confort moderne, tout confort

convenient [kən'viːnɪənt] *adj* commode

convent ['kɒnvənt] *n* couvent *m*

convention [kən'vɛnʃən] *n* convention *f*; ~**al** *adj* conventionnel(le)

conversant [kən'vəːsənt] *adj*: **to be ~ with** s'y connaître en; être au courant de

conversation [kɒnvə'seɪʃən] *n* conversation *f*

converse [*n* 'kɒnvəːs, *vb* kən'vəːs] *n* contraire *m*, inverse *m* ♦ *vi* s'entretenir; ~**ly** [kɒn'vəːslɪ] *adv* inversement, réciproquement

convert [*vb* kən'vəːt, *n* 'kɒnvəːt] *vt* (*REL, COMM*) convertir; (*alter*) transformer; (*house*) aménager ♦ *n* converti(e); ~**ible** *n* (*voiture f*) décapotable *f*

convey [kən'veɪ] *vt* transporter; (*thanks*) transmettre; (*idea*) communiquer; ~**or belt** *n* convoyeur *m*, tapis roulant

convict [*vb* kən'vɪkt, *n* 'kɒnvɪkt] *vt* déclarer (*or* reconnaître) coupable ♦ *n* forçat *m*, détenu *m*; ~**ion** [kən'vɪkʃən] *n* (*LAW*) condamnation *f*; (*belief*) conviction *f*

convince [kən'vɪns] *vt* convaincre, persuader; **convincing** *adj* persuasif(ive), convaincant(e)

convoluted [kɒnvə'luːtɪd] *adj* (*argument*) compliqué(e)

convulse [kən'vʌls] *vt*: **to be ~d with laughter/pain** se tordre de rire/douleur

coo [kuː] *vi* roucouler

cook [kʊk] *vt* faire cuire ♦ *vi* cuire; (*person*) faire la cuisine ♦ *n* cuisinier(ière); ~**book** *n* livre *m* de cuisine; ~**er** *n* cuisinière *f*; ~**ery** *n* cuisine *f*; ~**ery book** (*BRIT*) *n* = cookbook; ~**ie** (*US*) *n* biscuit *m*, petit gâteau sec; ~**ing** *n* cuisine *f*

cool [kuːl] *adj* frais(fraîche); (*calm, unemotional*) calme; (*unfriendly*) froid(e) ♦ *vt, vi* rafraîchir, refroidir

coop [ku:p] *n* poulailler *m*; (*for rabbits*) clapier *m* ♦ *vt*: to ~ **up** (*fig*) cloîtrer, enfermer

cooperate [kəu'ɔpəreɪt] *vi* coopérer, collaborer; **cooperation** [kəuɔpə'reɪʃən] *n* coopération *f*, collaboration *f*; **cooperative** [kəu'ɔpərətɪv] *adj* coopératif(ive) ♦ *n* coopérative *f*

coordinate [*vb* kəu'ɔ:dɪneɪt, *n* kəu'ɔ:dɪnət] *vt* coordonner ♦ *n* (*MATH*) coordonnée *f*; ~**s** *npl* (*clothes*) ensemble *m*, coordonnés *mpl*

co-ownership ['kəu'əunəʃɪp] *n* copropriété *f*

cop [kɔp] (*inf*) *n* flic *m*

cope [kəup] *vi*: to ~ **with** faire face à; (*solve*) venir à bout de

copper ['kɔpə*] *n* cuivre *m*; (*BRIT*: *inf*: *policeman*) flic *m*; ~**s** *npl* (*coins*) petite monnaie; ~ **sulphate** *n* sulfate *m* de cuivre

copy ['kɔpɪ] *n* copie *f*; (*of book etc*) exemplaire *m* ♦ *vt* copier; ~**right** *n* droit *m* d'auteur, copyright *m*

coral ['kɔrəl] *n* corail *m*; ~ **reef** *n* récif *m* de corail

cord [kɔ:d] *n* corde *f*; (*fabric*) velours côtelé; (*ELEC*) cordon *m*, fil *m*

cordial ['kɔ:dɪəl] *adj* cordial(e), chaleureux(euse) ♦ *n* cordial *m*

cordon ['kɔ:dn] *n* cordon *m*; ~ **off** *vt* boucler (*par cordon de police*)

corduroy ['kɔ:dərɔɪ] *n* velours côtelé

core [kɔ:*] *n* noyau *m*; (*of fruit*) trognon *m*, cœur *m*; (*of building*, *problem*) cœur ♦ *vt* enlever le trognon *or* le cœur de

cork [kɔ:k] *n* liège *m*; (*of bottle*) bouchon *m*; ~**screw** *n* tire-bouchon *m*

corn [kɔ:n] *n* (*BRIT*: *wheat*) blé *m*; (*US*: *maize*) maïs *m*; (*on foot*) cor *m*; ~ **on the cob** (*CULIN*) épi *m* de maïs; ~**ed beef** ['kɔ:nd-] *n* corned-beef *m*

corner ['kɔ:nə*] *n* coin *m*; (*AUT*) tournant *m*, virage *m*; (*FOOTBALL*: *also*: ~ *kick*) corner *m* ♦ *vt* acculer, mettre au pied du mur; coincer; (*COMM*: *market*) accaparer ♦ *vi* prendre un virage; ~**stone** *n* pierre *f* angulaire

cornet ['kɔ:nɪt] *n* (*MUS*) cornet *m* à pistons; (*BRIT*: *of ice-cream*) cornet (de glace)

cornflakes ['kɔ:nfleɪks] *npl* cornflakes *mpl*

cornflour (*BRIT*), **cornstarch** (*US*) ['kɔ:nflauə*] *n* farine *f* de maïs, maïzena *f* (®)

Cornwall ['kɔ:nwəl] *n* Cornouailles *f*

corny ['kɔ:nɪ] (*inf*) *adj* rebattu(e)

coronary ['kɔrənərɪ] *n* (*also*: ~ *thrombosis*) infarctus *m* (du myocarde), thrombose *f* coronarienne

coronation [kɔrə'neɪʃən] *n* couronnement *m*

coroner ['kɔrənə*] *n* officiel chargé de déterminer les causes d'un décès

corporal ['kɔ:pərəl] *n* caporal *m*, brigadier *m* ♦ *adj*: ~ **punishment** châtiment corporel

corporate ['kɔ:pərɪt] *adj* en commun, collectif(ive); (*COMM*) de l'entreprise

corporation [kɔ:pə'reɪʃən] *n* (*of town*) municipalité *f*, conseil municipal; (*COMM*) société *f*

corps [kɔ:*, *pl* kɔ:z] (*pl* **corps**) *n* corps *m*

corpse [kɔ:ps] *n* cadavre *m*

correct [kə'rekt] *adj* (*accurate*) correct(e), exact(e); (*proper*) correct, convenable ♦ *vt* corriger; ~**ion** [kə'rekʃən] *n* correction *f*

correspond [kɔrɪs'pɔnd] *vi* correspondre; ~**ence** *n* correspondance *f*; ~**ence course** *n* cours *m* par correspondance; ~**ent** *n* correspondant(e)

corridor ['kɔrɪdɔ:*] *n* couloir *m*, corridor *m*

corrode [kə'rəud] *vt* corroder, ronger ♦ *vi* se corroder

corrugated ['kɔrəgeɪtɪd] *adj* plissé(e); ondulé(e); ~ **iron** *n* tôle ondulée

corrupt [kə'rʌpt] *adj* corrompu(e) ♦ *vt* corrompre; ~**ion** [kə'rʌpʃən] *n* corruption *f*

Corsica ['kɔ:sɪkə] *n* Corse *f*

cosmetic [kɔz'metɪk] *n* produit *m* de

beauté, cosmétique m

cosset ['kɔsɪt] vt choyer, dorloter

cost [kɔst] (pt, pp cost) n coût m ♦ vi coûter ♦ vt établir ou calculer le prix de revient de; ~s npl (COMM) frais mpl; (LAW) dépens mpl; it ~s £5/too much cela coûte cinq livres/ c'est trop cher; **at all** ~s coûte que coûte, à tout prix

co-star ['kəʊstɑ:*] n partenaire m/f

cost-effective ['kɔst'fɛktɪv] adj rentable

costly ['kɔstlɪ] adj coûteux(euse)

cost-of-living ['kɔstəv'lɪvɪŋ] adj: ~ **allowance** indemnité f de vie chère; ~ **index** index m du coût de la vie

cost price (BRIT) n prix coûtant ou de revient

costume ['kɔstjuːm] n costume m; (lady's suit) tailleur m; (BRIT: also: swimming ~) maillot m (de bain); ~ **jewellery** n bijoux mpl fantaisie

cosy ['kəʊzɪ] (US cozy) adj douillet(te); (person) à l'aise, au chaud

cot [kɔt] n (BRIT: child's) lit m d'enfant, petit lit; (US: campbed) lit de camp

cottage ['kɔtɪdʒ] n petite maison (à la campagne), cottage m; ~ **cheese** n fromage blanc (maigre)

cotton ['kɔtn] n coton m; ~ **on** (inf) vi: **to** ~ **on to** piger; ~ **candy** (US) n barbe f à papa; ~ **wool** (BRIT) n ouate f, coton m hydrophile

couch [kaʊtʃ] n canapé m; divan m

couchette [kuː'ʃɛt] n couchette f

cough [kɔf] vi tousser ♦ n toux f; ~ **drop** n pastille f pour ou contre la toux

could [kʊd] pt of **can**[2]; ~**n't** = could not

council ['kaʊnsl] n conseil m; **city** ou **town** ~ conseil municipal; ~ **estate** (BRIT) n (zone f de) logements loués à/par la municipalité; ~ **house** (BRIT) n maison m (à loyer modéré) louée par la municipalité; ~**lor** ['kaʊnslə*] n conseiller(ère)

counsel ['kaʊnsl] n (lawyer) avocat(e); (advice) conseil m, consulta-

tion f; ~**lor** n conseiller(ère); (US: lawyer) avocat(e)

count [kaʊnt] vt, vi compter ♦ n compte m; (nobleman) comte m; ~ **on** vt fus compter sur; ~**down** n compte m à rebours

countenance ['kaʊntɪnəns] n expression f ♦ vt approuver

counter ['kaʊntə*] n comptoir m; (in post office, bank) guichet m; (in game) jeton m ♦ vt aller à l'encontre de, opposer ♦ adv: ~ **to** contrairement à; ~**act** [kaʊntə'rækt] vt neutraliser, contrebalancer; ~**feit** ['kaʊntəfɪt] n faux m, contrefaçon f ♦ vt contrefaire ♦ adj faux(fausse); ~**foil** ['kaʊntəfɔɪl] n talon m, souche f; ~**mand** ['kaʊntəmɑːnd] vt annuler; ~**part** ['kaʊntəpɑːt] n (of person etc) homologue m/f

countess ['kaʊntɪs] n comtesse f

countless ['kaʊntlɪs] adj innombrable

country ['kʌntrɪ] n pays m; (native land) patrie f; (as opposed to town) campagne f; (region) région f, pays; ~ **dancing** (BRIT) n danse f folklorique; ~ **house** n manoir m, (petit) château; ~**man** (irreg) n (compatriot) compatriote m; (country dweller) habitant m de la campagne, campagnard m; ~**side** n campagne f

county ['kaʊntɪ] n comté m

coup [kuː] (pl ~s) n beau coup; (also: ~ **d'état**) coup d'Etat

couple ['kʌpl] n couple m; **a** ~ **of** deux; (a few) quelques

coupon ['kuːpɔn] n coupon m, bon-prime m, bon-réclame m; (COMM) coupon

courage ['kʌrɪdʒ] n courage m

courier ['kʊrɪə*] n messager m, courrier m; (for tourists) accompagnateur/trice, guide m/f

course [kɔːs] n cours m; (of ship) route f; (for golf) terrain m; (part of meal) plat m; **first** ~ entrée f; **of** ~ bien sûr; ~ **of action** parti m, ligne f de conduite; ~ **of treatment** (MED) traitement m

court [kɔːt] n cour f; (LAW) cour,
tribunal m; (TENNIS) court m ♦ vt
(woman) courtiser, faire la cour à;
to take to ~ actionner ou poursuivre
en justice

courteous ['kɜːtɪəs] adj courtois(e),
poli(e)

courtesy ['kɜːtəsɪ] n courtoisie f, politesse f; **(by) ~ of** avec l'aimable
autorisation de

court: **~-house** ['kɔːthaus] n (US) n
palais m de justice; **~ier** ['kɔːtɪə*] n
courtisan m, dame f de la cour; **~
martial** (pl **~s martial**) n cour martiale, conseil m de guerre; **~room**
['kɔːtrum] n salle f de tribunal; **~
yard** ['kɔːtjɑːd] n cour f

cousin ['kʌzn] n cousin(e) f; **first ~**
cousin(e) germain(e)

cove [kəuv] n petite baie, anse f

covenant ['kʌvənənt] n engagement
m

cover ['kʌvə*] vt couvrir ♦ n couverture f; (of pan) couvercle m; (over
furniture) housse f; (shelter) abri m;
to take ~ se mettre à l'abri; **under
~** à l'abri; **under ~ of darkness** à
la faveur de la nuit; **under separate
~** (COMM) sous pli séparé; **to ~ up
for sb** couvrir qn; **~age** n (TV,
PRESS) reportage m; **~ charge** n
couvert m (supplément à payer);
~ing n couche f, **~ing letter** (US **~
letter**) n lettre explicative; **~ note** n
(INSURANCE) police f provisoire

covert ['kʌvət] adj (threat) voilé(e),
caché(e); (glance) furtif(ive)

cover-up ['kʌvərʌp] n tentative f
pour étouffer une affaire

covet ['kʌvɪt] vt convoiter

cow [kau] n vache f ♦ vt effrayer, intimider

coward ['kauəd] n lâche m/f; **~ice**
['kauədɪs] n lâcheté f; **~ly** adj lâche

cowboy ['kaubɔɪ] n cow-boy m

cower ['kauə*] vi se recroqueviller

coy [kɔɪ] adj faussement effarouché(e) ou timide

cozy ['kauzɪ] (US) adj = cosy

CPA (US) n abbr = certified public

accountant

crab [kræb] n crabe m; **~ apple** n
pomme f sauvage

crack [kræk] n fente f, fissure f;
fêlure f; (: in bone) fissure, (noise) craquement m, coup (sec); (drug) crack m
♦ vt fendre, fissurer; fêler; lézarder;
(whip) faire claquer; (nut) casser;
(code) déchiffrer; (problem) résoudre ♦ adj (athlete) de première classe, d'élite; **~ down on** vt fus mettre
un frein à; **~ up** vi être au bout du
rouleau, s'effondrer; **~er** n (Christmas ~er) pétard m; (biscuit) biscuit
(salé)

crackle ['krækl] vi crépiter, grésiller

cradle ['kreidl] n berceau m

craft [krɑːft] n métier (artisanal); (pl
inv: boat) embarcation f, barque f;
(: plane) appareil m; **~sman** (irreg)
n artisan m, ouvrier (qualifié);
~smanship n travail m; **~y** adj rusé(e), malin(igne)

crag [kræg] n rocher escarpé

cram [kræm] vt (fill): **to ~ sth with**
bourrer qch de; (put): **to ~ sth into**
fourrer qch dans ♦ vi (for exams)
bachoter

cramp [kræmp] n crampe f ♦ vt
gêner, entraver; **~ed** adj à l'étroit,
très serré(e)

cranberry ['krænbərɪ] n canneberge f

crane [krein] n grue f

crank [kræŋk] n manivelle f; (person) excentrique m/f; **~shaft** n vilebrequin m

cranny ['krænɪ] n see nook

crash [kræʃ] n fracas m; (of car) collision f; (of plane) accident m ♦ vt
(plane) avoir un accident avec ♦ vi
s'écraser; (two cars) se percuter,
s'emboutir; (COMM) s'effondrer; **to
~ into** se jeter ou se fracasser
contre; **~ course** n cours intensif;
~ helmet n casque (protecteur); **~
landing** n atterrissage forcé or en catastrophe

crate [kreit] n cageot m; (for bottles)
caisse f

cravat(e) [krə'væt] n foulard (noué

autour du cou)

crave [kreɪv] *vt, vi*: **to ~ (for)** avoir une envie irrésistible de

crawl [krɔːl] *vi* ramper; *(vehicle)* avancer au pas ♦ *n* (SWIMMING) crawl *m*

crayfish ['kreɪfɪʃ] *n inv* *(freshwater)* écrevisse *f*; *(saltwater)* langoustine *f*

crayon ['kreɪən] *n* crayon *m* (de couleur)

craze [kreɪz] *n* engouement *m*

crazy ['kreɪzɪ] *adj* fou(folle)

creak [kriːk] *vi* grincer; craquer

cream [kriːm] *n* crème *f* ♦ *adj* (colour) crème *inv*; **~ cake** *n* (petit) gâteau à la crème; **~ cheese** *n* fromage *m* à la crème, fromage blanc; **~y** *adj* crémeux(euse)

crease [kriːs] *n* pli *m* ♦ *vt* froisser, chiffonner ♦ *vi* se froisser, se chiffonner

create [kriːˈeɪt] *vt* créer; **creation** [kriːˈeɪʃən] *n* création *f*; **creative** [kriːˈeɪtɪv] *adj* (artistic) créatif(ive); (ingenious) ingénieux(euse)

creature ['kriːtʃə*] *n* créature *f*

crèche [kreʃ] *n* garderie *f*, crèche *f*

credence ['kriːdəns] *n*: **to lend** *or* **give ~ to** ajouter foi à

credentials [krɪˈdenʃəlz] *npl* (references) références *fpl*; (papers of identity) pièce *f* d'identité

credit ['kredɪt] *n* crédit *m*; (recognition) honneur *m* ♦ *vt* (COMM) créditer; (believe: also: **give ~ to**) ajouter foi à, croire; **~s** *npl* (CINEMA, TV) générique *m*; **to be in ~** (person, bank account) être créditeur(trice); **to ~ sb with** (*fig*) prêter or attribuer à qn; **~ card** *n* carte *f* de crédit; **~or** *n* créancier(ière)

creed [kriːd] *n* croyance *f*; credo *m*

creek [kriːk] *n* crique *f*, anse *f*; (US: stream) ruisseau *m*, petit cours d'eau

creep [kriːp] (*pt, pp* crept) *vi* ramper; **~er** *n* plante grimpante; **~y** *adj* (frightening) qui fait frissonner, qui donne la chair de poule

cremate [krɪˈmeɪt] *vt* incinérer

crematorium [kremə'tɔːrɪəm] *n* (*pl*

~ia) *n* four *m* crématoire

crêpe [kreɪp] *n* crêpe *m*; **~ bandage** (BRIT) *n* bande *f* Velpeau ®

crept [krept] *pt, pp of* creep

crescent ['kresnt] *n* croissant *m*; (street) rue *f* (en arc de cercle)

cress [kres] *n* cresson *m*

crest [krest] *n* crête *f*; **~fallen** *adj* déconfit(e), découragé(e)

crevice ['krevɪs] *n* fissure *f*, lézarde *f*, fente *f*

crew [kruː] *n* équipage *m*; (CINEMA etc) équipe *f*; **~-cut** *n*: **to have a ~-cut** avoir les cheveux en brosse; **~-neck** *n* col ras du cou

crib [krɪb] *n* lit *m* d'enfant; (for baby) berceau *m* ♦ *vt* (*inf*) copier

crick [krɪk] *n*: **~ in the neck** torticolis *m*; **~ in the back** tour *m* de reins

cricket ['krɪkɪt] *n* (insect) grillon *m*, cri-cri *m inv*; (game) cricket *m*

crime [kraɪm] *n* crime *m*; **criminal** ['krɪmɪnl] *adj*, *n* criminel(le)

crimson ['krɪmzn] *adj* cramoisi(e)

cringe [krɪndʒ] *vi* avoir un mouvement de recul

crinkle ['krɪŋkl] *vt* froisser, chiffonner

cripple ['krɪpl] *n* boiteux(euse), infirme *m/f* ♦ *vt* estropier

crisis ['kraɪsɪs] (*pl* crises) *n* crise *f*

crisp [krɪsp] *adj* croquant(e); (weather) vif(vive); (manner etc) brusque; **~s** (BRIT) *npl* (pommes) chips *fpl*

crisscross ['krɪskrɒs] *adj* entrecroisé(e)

criterion [kraɪˈtɪərɪən] (*pl* **~ia**) *n* critère *m*

critic ['krɪtɪk] *n* critique *m*; **~al** *adj* critique; **~ally** *adv* (examine) d'un œil critique; (speak also) sévèrement; **~ally ill** gravement malade; **~ism** ['krɪtɪsɪzəm] *n* critique *f*; **~ize** ['krɪtɪsaɪz] *vt* critiquer

croak [krəʊk] *vi* (frog) coasser; (raven) croasser; (person) parler d'une voix rauque

Croatia [krəʊˈeɪʃə] *n* Croatie *f*

crochet ['krəʊʃeɪ] n travail m au crochet

crockery ['krɒkərɪ] n vaisselle f

crocodile ['krɒkədaɪl] n crocodile m

crocus ['krəʊkəs] n crocus m

croft [krɒft] (BRIT) n petite ferme

crony ['krəʊnɪ] (inf: pej) n copain(copine)

crook [krʊk] n escroc m; (of shepherd) houlette f; ~ed ['krʊkɪd] adj courbé(e), tordu(e); (action) malhonnête

crop [krɒp] n (produce) culture f; (amount produced) récolte f; (riding ~) cravache f ♦ vt (hair) tondre; ~ up vi surgir, se présenter, survenir

cross [krɒs] n croix f; (BIO etc) croisement m ♦ vt (street etc) traverser; (arms, legs, BIO) croiser; (cheque) barrer ♦ adj en colère, fâché(e); ~ out vt barrer, biffer; ~ over vi traverser; ~bar n barre (transversale); ~-country (race) n cross(-country) m; ~-examine vt (LAW) faire subir un examen contradictoire à; ~-eyed adj qui louche; ~fire n feux croisés; ~ing n (sea passage) traversée f; (also: pedestrian ~ing) passage clouté; ~ing guard (US) n contractuel(le) qui fait traverser la rue aux enfants; ~ purposes: to be at ~ purposes with sb comprendre qn de travers; ~-reference n renvoi m, référence f; ~roads n carrefour m; ~ section n (of object) coupe transversale; (in population) échantillon m; ~walk (US) n passage clouté; ~wind n vent m de travers; ~word n mots croisés mpl

crotch [krɒtʃ] n (ANAT, of garment) entre-jambes m

crouch [kraʊtʃ] vi s'accroupir; se tapir

crow [krəʊ] n (bird) corneille f; (of cock) chant m du coq, cocorico m ♦ vi (cock) chanter

crowbar ['krəʊbɑ:*] n levier m

crowd [kraʊd] n foule f ♦ vt remplir ♦ vi affluer, s'attrouper, s'entasser;

to ~ in entrer en foule; ~ed adj bondé(e), plein(e)

crown [kraʊn] n couronne f; (of head) sommet m de la tête; (of hill) sommet ♦ vt couronner; ~ jewels npl joyaux mpl de la Couronne; ~ prince n prince héritier

crow's-feet ['krəʊzfi:t] npl pattes fpl d'oie

crucial ['kru:ʃəl] adj crucial(e), décisif(ive)

crucifix ['kru:sɪfɪks] n (REL) crucifix m; ~ion [kru:sɪ'fɪkʃən] n (REL) crucifixion f

crude [kru:d] adj (materials) brut(e); non raffiné(e); (fig: basic) rudimentaire, sommaire; (: vulgar) cru(e), grossier(ère); ~ (oil) n (pétrole) brut m

cruel ['krʊəl] adj cruel(le); ~ty n cruauté f

cruise [kru:z] n croisière f ♦ vi (ship) croiser; (car) rouler; ~r n croiseur m; (motorboat) yacht m de croisière

crumb [krʌm] n miette f

crumble ['krʌmbl] vt émietter ♦ vi (plaster etc) s'effriter; (land, earth) s'ébouler; (building) s'écrouler, crouler; (fig) s'effondrer; **crumbly** ['krʌmblɪ] adj friable

crumpet ['krʌmpɪt] n petite crêpe (épaisse)

crumple ['krʌmpl] vt froisser, friper

crunch [krʌntʃ] vt croquer; (underfoot) faire craquer or crisser, écraser ♦ n (fig) instant m or moment m critique, moment de vérité; ~y adj croquant(e), croustillant(e)

crusade [kru:'seɪd] n croisade f

crush [krʌʃ] n foule f, cohue f; (love): to **have a ~ on sb** avoir le béguin pour qn (inf); (drink): **lemon ~** citron pressé ♦ vt écraser; (crumple) froisser; (fig: hopes) anéantir

crust [krʌst] n croûte f

crutch [krʌtʃ] n béquille f

crux [krʌks] n point crucial

cry [kraɪ] vi pleurer; (shout: also: ~ out) crier ♦ n cri m; ~ off (inf) vi se dédire; se décommander

cryptic ['krɪptɪk] adj énigmatique

crystal ['krɪstl] n cristal m; **~-clear** adj clair(e) comme de l'eau de roche

cub [kʌb] n petit m (d'un animal); (also: C~ scout) louveteau m

Cuba ['kjuːbə] n Cuba m

cubbyhole ['kʌbɪhəʊl] n cagibi m

cube [kjuːb] n cube m ♦ vt (MATH) élever au cube; **cubic** ['kjuːbɪk] adj cubique; cubic metre etc mètre m etc cube; **cubic capacity** n cylindrée f

cubicle ['kjuːbɪkl] n (in hospital) box m; (at pool) cabine f

cuckoo ['kʊkuː] n coucou m; **~ clock** n (pendule f à) coucou m

cucumber ['kjuːkʌmbə*] n concombre m

cuddle ['kʌdl] vt câliner, caresser ♦ vi se blottir l'un contre l'autre

cue [kjuː] n (snooker ~) queue f de billard; (THEATRE etc) signal m

cuff [kʌf] n (BRIT: of shirt, coat etc) poignet m, manchette f; (US: of trousers) revers m; (blow) tape f; **off the** ~ à l'improviste; **~ links** npl boutons mpl de manchette

cul-de-sac ['kʌldəsæk] n cul-de-sac m, impasse f

cull [kʌl] vt sélectionner ♦ n (of animals) massacre m

culminate ['kʌlmɪneɪt] vi: **to** ~ **in** finir or se terminer par; (end in) mener à; **culmination** [kʌlmɪ'neɪʃən] n point culminant

culottes [kjuː'lɒts] npl jupe-culotte f

culprit ['kʌlprɪt] n coupable m/f

cult [kʌlt] n culte m

cultivate ['kʌltɪveɪt] vt cultiver; **cultivation** [kʌltɪ'veɪʃən] n culture f

cultural ['kʌltʃərəl] adj culturel(le)

culture ['kʌltʃə*] n culture f; **~d** adj (person) cultivé(e)

cumbersome ['kʌmbəsəm] adj encombrant(e), embarrassant

cunning ['kʌnɪŋ] n ruse f, astuce f ♦ adj rusé(e), malin(igne); (device, idea) astucieux(euse)

cup [kʌp] n tasse f; (as prize) coupe

f; (of bra) bonnet m

cupboard ['kʌbəd] n armoire f; (built-in) placard m

cup tie (BRIT) n match m de coupe

curate ['kjuərɪt] n vicaire m

curator [kjʊ'reɪtə*] n conservateur m (d'un musée etc)

curb [kɜːb] vt refréner, mettre un frein à ♦ n (fig) frein m, restriction f; (US: kerb) bord m du trottoir

curdle ['kɜːdl] vi se cailler

cure [kjʊə*] vt guérir; (CULIN: salt) saler; (: smoke) fumer; (: dry) sécher ♦ n remède m

curfew ['kɜːfjuː] n couvre-feu m

curio ['kjʊərɪəʊ] n bibelot m, curiosité f

curiosity [kjʊərɪ'ɒsɪtɪ] n curiosité f

curious ['kjʊərɪəs] adj curieux(euse)

curl [kɜːl] n boucle f (de cheveux) ♦ vt, vi boucler; (tightly) friser; **~ up** vi s'enrouler; se pelotonner; **~er** n bigoudi m, rouleau m; (fig) bouclé(e); frisé(e)

currant ['kʌrənt] n (dried) raisin m de Corinthe, raisin sec; (bush) groseiller m; (fruit) groseille f

currency ['kʌrənsɪ] n monnaie f; **to gain** ~ (fig) s'accréditer

current ['kʌrənt] n courant m ♦ adj courant(e); ~ **account** (BRIT) n compte courant; ~ **affairs** npl (questions fpl d')actualité f; **~ly** adv actuellement

curriculum [kə'rɪkjʊləm] (pl **~s** or **curricula**) n programme m d'études; ~ **vitae** n curriculum vitae m

curry ['kʌrɪ] n curry m ♦ vt: **to** ~ **favour with** chercher à s'attirer les bonnes grâces de

curse [kɜːs] vi jurer, blasphémer ♦ vt maudire ♦ n (spell) malédiction f; (problem, scourge) fléau m; (swearword) juron m

cursor ['kɜːsə*] n (COMPUT) curseur m

cursory ['kɜːsərɪ] adj superficiel(le), hâtif(ive)

curt [kɜːt] adj brusque, sec(sèche)

curtail [kɜː'teɪl] vt (visit etc) écourter; (*expenses, freedom etc*) réduire

curtain ['kɜ:tn] n rideau m

curts(e)y ['kɜ:tsɪ] vi faire une révérence

curve [kɜ:v] n courbe f; (*in the road*) tournant m, virage m ♦ vi se courber; (*road*) faire une courbe

cushion ['kʊʃən] n coussin m ♦ vt (*fall, shock*) amortir

custard ['kʌstəd] n (*for pouring*) crème anglaise

custody ['kʌstədɪ] n (*of child*) garde f; **to take sb into ~** (*suspect*) placer qn en détention préventive

custom ['kʌstəm] n coutume f, usage m; (COMM) clientèle f; **~ary** adj habituel(le)

customer ['kʌstəmə*] n client(e)

customized ['kʌstəmaɪzd] adj (*car etc*) construit(e) sur commande

custom-made ['kʌstəm'meɪd] adj (*clothes*) fait(e) sur mesure; (*other goods*) hors série, fait(e) sur commande

customs ['kʌstəmz] npl douane f; **~ officer** n douanier(ière)

cut [kʌt] (pt, pp **cut**) vt couper; (*meat*) découper; (*reduce*) réduire ♦ vi couper ♦ n coupure f; (*of clothes*) coupe f; (*in salary etc*) réduction f; (*of meat*) morceau m; **to ~ one's hand** se couper la main; **to ~ a tooth** percer une dent; **~ down** vt fus (*tree etc*) couper, abattre; (*consumption*) réduire; **~ off** vt couper; (*fig*) isoler; **~ out** vt découper; (*stop*) arrêter; (*remove*) ôter; **~ up** vt (*paper, meat*) découper; **~back** n réduction f

cute [kju:t] adj mignon(ne), adorable

cuticle remover ['kju:tɪkl-] n (*on nail*) repousse-peaux m inv

cutlery ['kʌtlərɪ] n couverts mpl

cutlet ['kʌtlɪt] n côtelette f

cut: ~out n (*switch*) coupe-circuit m inv; (*cardboard ~out*) découpage m; **~-price** (US **~-rate**) adj au rabais, à prix réduit; **~throat** n assassin m ♦ adj acharné(e)

cutting ['kʌtɪŋ] adj tranchant(e),

coupant(e); (*fig*) cinglant(e), mordant(e) ♦ n (BRIT: *from newspaper*) coupure f (de journal); (*from plant*) bouture f

CV n abbr = **curriculum vitae**

cwt abbr = **hundredweight(s)**

cyanide ['saɪənaɪd] n cyanure m

cycle ['saɪkl] n cycle m; (*bicycle*) bicyclette f, vélo m ♦ vi faire de la bicyclette; **cycling** ['saɪklɪŋ] n cyclisme m; **cyclist** ['saɪklɪst] n cycliste m/f

cygnet ['sɪgnɪt] n jeune cygne m

cylinder ['sɪlɪndə*] n cylindre m; **~- head gasket** n joint m de culasse

cymbals ['sɪmblz] npl cymbales fpl

cynic ['sɪnɪk] n cynique m/f; **~al** adj cynique; **~ism** ['sɪnɪsɪzəm] n cynisme m

Cypriot ['sɪprɪət] adj cypriote, chypriote ♦ n Cypriote m/f, Chypriote m/f

Cyprus ['saɪprəs] n Chypre f

cyst [sɪst] n kyste m

cystitis [sɪs'taɪtɪs] n cystite f

czar [zɑ:*] n tsar m

Czech [tʃek] adj tchèque ♦ n Tchèque m/f; (LING) tchèque m

Czechoslovak [tʃekə'sləʊvæk] adj, n = **Czechoslovakian**

Czechoslovakia [tʃekəslə'vækɪə] n Tchécoslovaquie f; **~n** adj tchécoslovaque ♦ n Tchécoslovaque m/f

D

D [di:] n (MUS) ré m

dab [dæb] vt (*eyes, wound*) tamponner; (*paint, cream*) appliquer (par petites touches ou rapidement)

dabble ['dæbl] vi: **to ~ in** faire ou se mêler ou s'occuper un peu de

dad [dæd] n papa m

daddy ['dædɪ] n papa m

daffodil ['dæfədɪl] n jonquille f

daft [dɑ:ft] adj idiot(e), stupide

dagger ['dægə*] n poignard m

daily ['deɪlɪ] adj quotidien(ne), journalier(ère) ♦ n quotidien m ♦ adv

dainty ['deɪntɪ] *adj* délicat(e), mignon(ne)

dairy ['dɛərɪ] *n* (BRIT: shop) crémerie *f*, laiterie *f*; (on farm) laiterie; ~ **products** *npl* produits laitiers; ~ **store** (US) *n* crémerie *f*, laiterie *f*

dais ['deɪɪs] *n* estrade *f*

daisy ['deɪzɪ] *n* pâquerette *f*; ~ **wheel** *n* (on printer) marguerite *f*

dale [deɪl] *n* vallon *m*

dam [dæm] *n* barrage *m* ♦ *vt* endiguer

damage ['dæmɪdʒ] *n* dégâts *mpl*, dommages *mpl*; (fig) tort *m* ♦ *vt* endommager, abîmer; (fig) faire du tort à; ~**s** *npl* (LAW) dommages-intérêts *mpl*

damn [dæm] *vt* condamner; (curse) maudire ♦ *n* (inf): **I don't give a** ~ je m'en fous ♦ *adj* (inf: also: ~ed): **this** ~ ... ce sacré ou foutu ...; ~ (**it**)! zut!; ~**ing** *adj* accablant(e)

damp [dæmp] *adj* humide ♦ *n* humidité *f* ♦ *vt* (also: ~en: cloth, rag) humecter; (: enthusiasm) refroidir

damson ['dæmzən] *n* prune *f* de Damas

dance [dɑːns] *n* danse *f*; (social event) bal *m* ♦ *vi* danser; ~ **hall** *n* salle *f* de bal, dancing *m*; ~**r** *n* danseur(euse); **dancing** ['dɑːnsɪŋ] *n* danse *f*

dandelion ['dændɪlaɪən] *n* pissenlit *m*

dandruff ['dændrəf] *n* pellicules *fpl*

Dane [deɪn] *n* Danois(e)

danger ['deɪndʒə*] *n* danger *m*; **there is a** ~ **of fire** il y a (un) risque d'incendie; **in** ~ en danger; **he was in** ~ **of falling** il risquait de tomber; ~**ous** *adj* dangereux(euse)

dangle ['dæŋgl] *vt* balancer ♦ *vi* pendre

Danish ['deɪnɪʃ] *adj* danois(e) ♦ *n* (LING) danois *m*

dapper ['dæpə*] *adj* pimpant(e)

dare [dɛə*] *vt*: **to** ~ **sb to do** défier qn de faire ♦ *vi*: **to** ~ (**to**) **do** sth oser faire qch; **I** ~ **say** (I suppose)

il est probable (que); ~**devil** *n* casse-cou *m inv*; **daring** ['dɛərɪŋ] *adj* hardi(e), audacieux(euse); (dress) osé(e) ♦ *n* audace *f*, hardiesse *f*

dark [dɑːk] *adj* (night, room) obscur(e), sombre; (colour, complexion) foncé(e), sombre ♦ *n*: **in the** ~ dans le noir; **in the** ~ **about** (fig) ignorant tout de; **after** ~ après la tombée de la nuit; ~**en** *vt* obscurcir, assombrir ♦ *vi* s'obscurcir, s'assombrir; ~ **glasses** *npl* lunettes noires; ~**ness** *n* obscurité *f*; ~**room** *n* chambre noire

darling ['dɑːlɪŋ] *adj* chéri(e) ♦ *n* chéri(e); (favourite): **to be the** ~ **of** être la coqueluche de

darn [dɑːn] *vt* repriser, raccommoder

dart [dɑːt] *n* fléchette *f*; (sewing) pince *f* ♦ *vi*: **to** ~ **towards** (also: make a ~ towards) se précipiter ou s'élancer vers; **to** ~ **away/along** partir/passer comme une flèche; ~**board** *n* cible *f* (de jeu de fléchettes)

dash [dæʃ] *n* (sign) tiret *m*; (small quantity) goutte *f*, larme *f* ♦ *vt* (missile) jeter ou lancer violemment; (hopes) anéantir ♦ *vi*: **to** ~ **towards** (also: make a ~ towards) se précipiter ou se ruer vers; ~ **away** ou partir à toute allure, filer; ~ **off** *vi* = ~ away

dashboard ['dæʃbɔːd] *n* (AUT) tableau *m* de bord

dashing ['dæʃɪŋ] *adj* fringant(e)

data ['deɪtə] *npl* données *fpl*; ~**base** *n* (COMPUT) base *f* de données; ~ **processing** *n* traitement *m* de données

date [deɪt] *n* date *f*; (with sb) rendez-vous *m*; (fruit) datte *f* ♦ *vt* dater; (person) sortir avec; ~ **of birth** date de naissance; **to** ~ (until now) à ce jour; **out of** ~ (passport) périmé; (theory etc) dépassé(e); (clothes etc) démodé(e); **up to** ~ moderne; (news) très récent; ~**d** *adj* démodé(e)

daub [dɔːb] *vt* barbouiller

daughter ['dɔːtə*] n fille f; ~-in-law
n belle-fille f, bru f

daunting ['dɔːntɪŋ] adj découra-
geant(e)

dawdle ['dɔːdl] vi traîner, lambiner

dawn [dɔːn] n aube f, aurore f ♦ vi
(day) se lever, poindre; (fig): it ~ed
on him that ...: il lui vint à l'esprit
que ...

day [deɪ] n jour m; (as duration)
journée f; (period of time, age) époque f, temps m; the ~ before the
veille, le jour précédent; the ~
after, the following ~ le lendemain, le jour suivant; the ~ after
tomorrow après-demain; the ~ before yesterday avant-hier; by ~ de
jour; ~break n point m du jour;
~dream vi rêver (tout éveillé);
~light n (lumière f du) jour m; ~
return (BRIT) n billet m d'aller-
retour (valable pour la journée);
~time n jour m, journée f; ~-to-day
adj quotidien(ne); (event) journa-
lier(ère)

daze [deɪz] vt (stun) étourdir ♦ n: in
a ~ étourdi(e), hébété(e)

dazzle ['dæzl] vt éblouir, aveugler

DC abbr (= direct current) courant
continu

D-day ['diːdeɪ] n le jour J

dead [ded] adj mort(e); (numb) en-
gourdi(e), insensible; (battery) à
plat; (telephone): the line is ~ la ligne est coupée ♦ adv absolument,
complètement ♦ npl: the ~ les
morts; he was shot ~ il a été tué
d'un coup de revolver; ~ on time à
l'heure pile; ~ tired éreinté(e),
complètement fourbu(e); to stop ~
s'arrêter pile or net; ~en vt (blow,
sound) amortir; (pain) calmer; ~
end n impasse f; ~ heat n
(SPORT): to finish in a ~ heat terminer exæquo; ~line n date f or heure f limite; ~lock n (fig) impasse f;
~ loss n: to be a ~ loss (inf: person) n'être bon(ne) à rien; ~ly adj
mortel(le); (weapon) meurtrier(ère);
(accuracy) extrême; ~pan adj im-

passible; D~ Sea n: the D~ Sea la
mer Morte

deaf [def] adj sourd(e); ~en vt rendre sourd; ~-mute n sourd(e)-
muet(te); ~ness n surdité f.

deal [diːl] (pt, pp dealt) n affaire f,
marché m ♦ vt (blow) porter;
(cards) donner, distribuer; a great
~ (of) beaucoup (de); ~ in vt fus
faire le commerce de; ~ with vt fus
(person, problem) s'occuper or se
charger de; (be about: book etc)
traiter de; ~er n marchand m;
~ings npl (COMM) transactions fpl;
(relations) relations fpl, rapports mpl

dean [diːn] n (REL, BRIT: SCOL)
doyen m; (US) conseiller(ère) (prin-
cipal(e)) d'éducation

dear [dɪə*] adj cher(chère); (expensive) cher, coûteux(euse) ♦ n: my ~
mon cher/ma chère; ~ me! mon
Dieu!; D~ Sir/Madam (in letter)
Monsieur/Madame; D~ Mr/Mrs X
Cher Monsieur/Chère Madame; ~ly
adv (love) tendrement; (pay) cher

death [deθ] n mort f; (fatality) mort
m; (ADMIN) décès m; ~ certificate
n acte m de décès; ~ly adj de mort;
~ penalty n peine f de mort; ~ rate
n (taux m de) mortalité f; ~ toll n
nombre m de morts

debar [dɪˈbɑː*] vt: to ~ sb from
doing interdire à qn de faire

debase [dɪˈbeɪs] vt (value) déprécier, dévaloriser

debatable [dɪˈbeɪtəbl] adj discutable

debate [dɪˈbeɪt] n discussion f, débat
m ♦ vt discuter, débattre

debit [ˈdebɪt] n débit m ♦ vt: to ~ a
sum to sb or to sb's account porter une somme au débit de qn, débiter qn d'une somme; see also direct

debt [det] n dette f; to be in ~ avoir
des dettes, être endetté(e); ~or n dé-
biteur(trice)

debunk [diːˈbʌŋk] vt (theory, claim)
montrer le ridicule de

decade [ˈdekeɪd] n décennie f, déca-
de f

decadence [ˈdekədəns] n décadence

f

decaffeinated [di:'kæfineitid] *adj* décaféiné(e)

decanter [dɪ'kæntə*] *n* carafe *f*

decay [dɪ'keɪ] *n* (*of building*) délabrement *m*; (*also: tooth* ~) carie *f* (dentaire) ♦ *vi* (*rot*) se décomposer, pourrir; (*teeth*) se carier

deceased [dɪ'si:st] *n* défunt(e) *f*

deceit [dɪ'si:t] *n* tromperie *f*, supercherie *f*; ~**ful** *adj* trompeur(euse); **deceive** [dɪ'si:v] *vt* tromper

December [dɪ'sembə*] *n* décembre *m*

decent ['di:sənt] *adj* décent(e), convenable; **they were very** ~ **about it** ils se sont montrés très *f* chic

deception [dɪ'sepʃən] *n* tromperie *f*

deceptive [dɪ'septiv] *adj* trompeur(euse)

decide [dɪ'said] *vt* (*person*) décider; (*question, argument*) trancher, régler ♦ *vi* se décider, décider; **to** ~ **to do/that** décider de faire/que; **to** ~ **on** décider, se décider pour; ~**d** *adj* (*clear, definite*) net(te), marqué(e); ~**dly** [dɪ'saididli] *adv* résolument; (*distinctly*) incontestablement, nettement

deciduous [dɪ'sidjuəs] *adj* à feuilles caduques

decimal ['desɪml] *adj* décimal(e) ♦ *n* décimale *f*; ~ **point** *n* ≈ virgule *f*

decipher [dɪ'saifə*] *vt* déchiffrer

decision [dɪ'sɪʒən] *n* décision *f*

decisive [dɪ'saɪsɪv] *adj* décisif(ive); (*person*) décidé(e)

deck [dek] *n* (*NAUT*) pont *m*; (*of bus*) **top** ~ impériale *f*; (*of cards*) jeu *m*; (*record* ~) platine *f*; ~**chair** *n* chaise longue

declare [dɪ'kleə*] *vt* déclarer

decline [dɪ'klaɪn] *n* (*decay*) déclin *m*; (*lessening*) baisse *f* ♦ *vt* refuser, décliner ♦ *vi* décliner; (*business*) baisser

decoder [di:'kəʊdə*] *n* (*TV*) décodeur *m*

decorate ['dekəreɪt] *vt* (*adorn, give*

a medal to) décorer; (paint and paper) peindre et tapisser; **decoration** [dekə'reɪʃən] *n* (medal etc, adornment) décoration *f*; **decorator** ['dekəreɪtə*] *n* peintre-décorateur *m*

decoy ['di:kɔɪ] *n* piège *m*; (*person*) compère *m*

decrease [*n* 'di:kri:s, *vb* di:'kri:s] *n*: ~ **(in)** diminution *f* (de) ♦ *vt, vi* diminuer

decree [dɪ'kri:] *n* (POL, REL) décret *m*; (LAW) arrêt *m*, jugement *m*; ~ **nisi** [-'naɪsaɪ] *n* jugement *m* provisoire de divorce

dedicate [dɪ'dedɪkeɪt] *vt* consacrer; (book etc) dédier; **dedication** [dedɪ'keɪʃən] *n* (devotion) dévouement *m*; (in book) dédicace *f*

deduce [dɪ'dju:s] *vt* déduire, conclure

deduct [dɪ'dʌkt] *vt*: **to** ~ **sth (from)** déduire qch (de), retrancher qch (de); ~**ion** [dɪ'dʌkʃən] *n* (deducting, deducing) déduction *f*; (from wage etc) prélèvement *m*, retenue *f*

deed [di:d] *n* action *f*, acte *m*; (LAW) acte notarié, contrat *m*

deem [di:m] *vt* (formal) juger

deep [di:p] *adj* profond(e); (*voice*) grave ♦ *adv*: **spectators stood 20** ~ il y avait 20 rangs de spectateurs; **4 metres** ~ de 4 mètres de profondeur; ~**en** *vt* approfondir ♦ *vi* (fig) s'épaissir; ~**freeze** *n* congélateur *m*; ~**fry** *vt* faire frire (en friteuse); ~**ly** *adv* profondément; (interested) vivement; ~**sea diver** *n* sous-marin(e); ~**sea diving** *n* plongée sous-marine; ~**sea fishing** *n* grande pêche; ~**seated** *adj* profond(e), profondément enraciné(e)

deer [dɪə*] *n inv*: **(red)** ~ cerf *m*, biche *f*; **(fallow)** ~ daim *m*; **(roe)** ~ chevreuil *m*; ~**skin** *n* daim *m*

deface [dɪ'feɪs] *vt* dégrader; (notice, poster) barbouiller

default [dɪ'fɔ:lt] *n* (COMPUT: also: ~ value) valeur *f* par défaut; **by** ~ (LAW) par défaut, par contumace; (SPORT) par forfait

defeat [dɪˈfiːt] n défaite f ♦ vt (team, opponents) battre

defect [n ˈdiːfɛkt, vb dɪˈfɛkt] n défaut m ♦ vi: to ~ to the enemy/the West passer à l'ennemi/à l'Ouest; ~ive [dɪˈfɛktɪv] adj défectueux(euse)

defence [dɪˈfɛns] (US **defense**) n défense f; ~less adj sans défense

defend [dɪˈfɛnd] vt défendre; ~ant n défendeur(deresse); (in criminal case) accusé(e), prévenu(e); ~er n défenseur m

defer [dɪˈfəː*] vt (postpone) différer, ajourner

defiance [dɪˈfaɪəns] n défi m; **in** ~ **of** au mépris de; **defiant** [dɪˈfaɪənt] adj provocant(e), de défi; (person) rebelle, intraitable

deficiency [dɪˈfɪʃənsɪ] n insuffisance f, déficience f; **deficient** adj (inadequate) insuffisant(e); **to be deficient in** manquer de

deficit [ˈdɛfɪsɪt] n déficit m

defile [vb dɪˈfaɪl, n ˈdiːfaɪl] vt souiller, profaner

define [dɪˈfaɪn] vt définir

definite [ˈdɛfɪnɪt] adj (fixed) défini(e), (bien) déterminé(e); (clear, obvious) net(te), manifeste; (certain) sûr(e); **he was** ~ **about it** il a été catégorique; ~ly adv sans aucun doute

definition [dɛfɪˈnɪʃən] n définition f; (clearness) netteté f

deflate [diːˈfleɪt] vt dégonfler

deflect [dɪˈflɛkt] vt détourner, faire dévier

deformed [dɪˈfɔːmd] adj difforme

defraud [dɪˈfrɔːd] vt frauder; **to** ~ **sb of sth** escroquer qch à qn

defrost [diːˈfrɔst] vt dégivrer; (food) décongeler; ~er (US) n (demister) dispositif m anti-buée inv

deft [dɛft] adj adroit(e), preste

defunct [dɪˈfʌŋkt] adj défunt(e)

defuse [diːˈfjuːz] vt désamorcer

defy [dɪˈfaɪ] vt défier; (efforts etc) résister à

degenerate [vb dɪˈdʒɛnəreɪt, adj dɪˈdʒɛnərɪt] vi dégénérer ♦ adj dégé-

néré(e)

degree [dɪˈgriː] n degré m; (SCOL) diplôme m (universitaire); **a (first)** ~ **in maths** une licence en maths; **by** ~s (gradually) par degrés; **to some** ~ jusqu'à un certain point, dans une certaine mesure

dehydrated [diːhaɪˈdreɪtɪd] adj déshydraté(e); (milk, eggs) en poudre

de-ice [diːˈaɪs] vt (windscreen) dégivrer

deign [deɪn] vi: **to** ~ **to do** daigner faire

dejected [dɪˈdʒɛktɪd] adj abattu(e), déprimé(e)

delay [dɪˈleɪ] vt retarder ♦ vi s'attarder ♦ n délai m, retard m; **to be** ~ed être en retard

delectable [dɪˈlɛktəbl] adj délicieux(euse)

delegate [n ˈdɛlɪgɪt, vb ˈdɛlɪgeɪt] n délégué(e) ♦ vt déléguer

delete [dɪˈliːt] vt rayer, supprimer

deliberate [adj dɪˈlɪbərɪt, vb dɪˈlɪbəreɪt] adj (intentional) délibéré(e); (slow) mesuré(e) ♦ vi délibérer, réfléchir; ~ly adv (on purpose) exprès, délibérément

delicacy [ˈdɛlɪkəsɪ] n délicatesse f; (food) mets fin or délicat, friandise f

delicate [ˈdɛlɪkɪt] adj délicat(e)

delicatessen [dɛlɪkəˈtɛsn] n épicerie fine

delicious [dɪˈlɪʃəs] adj délicieux (euse)

delight [dɪˈlaɪt] n (grande) joie, grand plaisir ♦ vt enchanter; **to take (a)** ~ **in** prendre grand plaisir à; ~ed adj: ~ed (at or with/to do) ravi(e) (de/de faire); ~ful adj (person) adorable; (meal, evening) merveilleux(euse)

delinquent [dɪˈlɪŋkwənt] adj, n délinquant(e)

delirious [dɪˈlɪrɪəs] adj: **to be** ~ délirer

deliver [dɪˈlɪvə*] vt (mail) distribuer; (goods) livrer; (message) remettre; (speech) prononcer; (MED:

baby) mettre au monde; **~y** n distribution f; livraison f; (of speaker) élocution f; (MED) accouchement m; **to take ~y** of prendre livraison de

delude [dɪ'lu:d] vt tromper, leurrer

delusion [dɪ'lu:ʒən] n illusion f

delve [delv] vi: **~ into** fouiller dans; (subject) approfondir

demand [dɪ'mɑ:nd] vt réclamer, exiger ♦ n exigence f; (claim) revendication f; (ECON) demande f; **in ~** demandé(e), recherché(e); **on ~** sur demande; **~ing** adj (person) exigeant(e); (work) astreignant(e)

demean [dɪ'mi:n] vt: **to ~ o.s.** s'abaisser

demeanour [dɪ'mi:nə*] (US demeanor) n comportement m; maintien m

demented [dɪ'mentɪd] adj dément(e), fou(folle)

demise [dɪ'maɪz] n mort f

demister [di:'mɪstə*] (BRIT) n (AUT) dispositif m anti-buée inv

demo ['deməu] (inf) n abbr (= demonstration) f

democracy [dɪ'mɒkrəsɪ] n démocratie f; **democrat** ['deməkræt] n démocrate m/f; **democratic** [demə'krætɪk] adj démocratique

demolish [dɪ'mɒlɪʃ] vt démolir

demonstrate ['demənstreɪt] vt démontrer, prouver; (show) faire une démonstration de ♦ vi: **to ~** (for/against) manifester (en faveur de/contre); **demonstration** [demən'streɪʃən] n démonstration f, manifestation f; **demonstrator** ['demənstreɪtə*] n (POL) manifestant(e)

demote [dɪ'məut] vt rétrograder

demure [dɪ'mjuə*] adj sage, réservé(e)

den [den] n tanière f, antre m

denatured alcohol [di:'neɪtʃəd-] (US) n alcool m à brûler

denial [dɪ'naɪəl] n démenti m; (refusal) dénégation f

denim ['denɪm] n jean m; **~s** npl (jeans) (blue-)jean(s) m(pl)

Denmark ['denmɑ:k] n Danemark m

denomination [dɪnɒmɪ'neɪʃən] n (of

money) valeur f; (REL) confession f

denounce [dɪ'nauns] vt dénoncer

dense [dens] adj dense; (stupid) obtus(e), bouché(e); **~ly** adv: **~ly populated** à forte densité de population

density ['densɪtɪ] n densité f; **double/high-~ diskette** disquette f double densité/haute densité

dent [dent] n bosse f ♦ vt (also: **make a ~ in**) cabosser

dental ['dentl] adj dentaire; **~ surgeon** n (chirurgien(ne)) dentiste

dentist ['dentɪst] n dentiste m/f

dentures ['dentʃəz] npl dentier m sg

deny [dɪ'naɪ] vt nier; (refuse) refuser

deodorant [di:'əudərənt] n déodorant m, désodorisant m

depart [dɪ'pɑ:t] vi partir; **to ~ from** (fig: differ from) s'écarter de

department [dɪ'pɑ:tmənt] n (COMM) rayon m; (SCOL) section f; (POL) ministère m, département m; **~ store** n grand magasin

departure [dɪ'pɑ:tʃə*] n départ m; **a new ~** une nouvelle voie; **~ lounge** n (at airport) salle f d'embarquement

depend [dɪ'pend] vi: **to ~ on** dépendre de; (rely on) compter sur; **it ~s** cela dépend; **~ing on the result** selon le résultat; **~able** adj (person) sérieux(euse), sûr(e); (car, watch) solide, fiable; **~ant** n personne f à charge; **~ent** adj: **to be ~ent (on)** dépendre (de) ♦ n = **dependant**

depict [dɪ'pɪkt] vt (in picture) représenter; (in words) dépeindre, décrire

depleted [dɪ'pli:tɪd] adj (considérablement) réduit(e) or diminué(e)

deport [dɪ'pɔ:t] vt expulser

deposit [dɪ'pɒzɪt] n (CHEM, COMM, GEO) dépôt m; (of ore, oil) gisement m; (part payment) arrhes fpl, acompte m; (on bottle etc) consigne f; (for hired goods etc) cautionnement m, garantie f ♦ vt déposer; **~ account** n compte m sur livret

depot ['depəu] n dépôt m; (US:

RAIL) gare *f*

depress [dɪ'pres] *vt* déprimer; (*press down*) appuyer sur, abaisser; (*prices, wages*) faire baisser; **~ed** *adj* (*person*) déprimé(e); (*area*) en déclin, touché(e) par le sous-emploi; **~ing** *adj* déprimant(e); **~ion** [dɪ'preʃən] *n* dépression *f*; (*hollow*) creux *m*

deprivation [deprɪ'veɪʃən] *n* privation *f*; (*loss*) perte *f*

deprive [dɪ'praɪv] *vt*: **to ~ sb of** priver qn de; **~d** *adj* déshérité(e)

depth [depθ] *n* profondeur *f*; **in the ~s of despair** au plus profond du désespoir; **to be out of one's ~** avoir perdu pied, nager

deputize [ˈdepjʊtaɪz] *vi*: **to ~ for** assurer l'intérim de

deputy [ˈdepjʊtɪ] *adj* adjoint(e) ♦ *n* (*second in command*) adjoint(e); (*US: also ~ sheriff*) shérif adjoint; **~ head** directeur adjoint, sous-directeur *m*

derail [dɪ'reɪl] *vt*: **to be ~ed** dérailler

deranged [dɪ'reɪndʒd] *adj*: **to be (mentally) ~** avoir le cerveau dérangé

derby [ˈdɑːbɪ] (*US*) *n* (*bowler hat*) (chapeau *m*) melon *m*

derelict [ˈderɪlɪkt] *adj* abandonné(e), à l'abandon

derisory [dɪ'raɪsərɪ] *adj* (*sum*) dérisoire; (*smile, person*) moqueur(euse)

derive [dɪ'raɪv] *vt*: **to ~ sth from** tirer qch de; trouver qch dans: **to ~ from** provenir de, dériver de

derogatory [dɪ'rɒgətərɪ] *adj* désobligeant(e); péjoratif(ive)

descend [dɪ'send] *vt, vi* descendre; **to ~ from** descendre de, être issu(e) de; **to ~ to** (*doing*) **sth** s'abaisser à (faire) qch; **descent** [dɪ'sent] *n* descente *f*; (*origin*) origine *f*

describe [dɪs'kraɪb] *vt* décrire; **description** [dɪs'krɪpʃən] *n* description *f*; (*sort*) sorte *f*, espèce *f*

desecrate [ˈdesɪkreɪt] *vt* profaner

desert [*n* ˈdezət, *vb* dɪ'zɜːt] *n* désert *m* ♦ *vt* déserter, abandonner ♦ *vi* (*MIL*) déserter; **~s** *npl*: **to get one's just ~s** n'avoir que ce qu'on mérite; **to ~ n** déserter or mc; **~ion** [dɪ'zɜːʃən] *n* (*MIL*) désertion *f*; (*LAW: of spouse*) abandon *m* du domicile conjugal; **~ island** *n* île déserte

deserve [dɪ'zɜːv] *vt* mériter; **deserving** [dɪ'zɜːvɪŋ] *adj* (*person*) méritant(e); (*action, cause*) méritoire

design [dɪ'zaɪn] *n* (*sketch*) plan *m*, dessin *m*; (*layout, shape*) conception *f*, ligne *f*; (*pattern*) dessin *m*, motif(s) *m(pl)*; (*COMM, art*) design *m*, stylisme *m*; (*intention*) dessein *m* ♦ *vt* dessiner; élaborer; **~er** [dɪ'zaɪnə*] *n* (*TECH*) concepteur-projeteur *m*; (*ART*) dessinateur(trice), designer *m*; (*fashion*) styliste *m/f*

desire [dɪ'zaɪə*] *n* désir *m* ♦ *vt* désirer

desk [desk] *n* (*in office*) bureau *m*; (*for pupil*) pupitre *m*; (*BRIT: in shop, restaurant*) caisse *f*; (*in hotel, at airport*) réception *f*

desolate [ˈdesəlɪt] *adj* désolé(e); (*person*) affligé(e)

despair [dɪs'pɛə*] *n* désespoir *m* ♦ *vi*: **to ~ of** désespérer de

despatch [dɪs'pætʃ] *n, vt* = **dispatch**

desperate [ˈdespərɪt] *adj* désespéré(e); (*criminal*) prêt(e) a tout; **to be ~ for sth/to do sth** avoir désespérément besoin de qch/de faire qch; **~ly** [ˈdespərɪtlɪ] *adv* désespérément; (*very*) terriblement, extrêmement

desperation [despə'reɪʃən] *n* désespoir *m*; **in (sheer) ~** en désespoir de cause

despicable [dɪs'pɪkəbl] *adj* méprisable

despise [dɪs'paɪz] *vt* mépriser

despite [dɪs'paɪt] *prep* malgré, en dépit de

despondent [dɪs'pɒndənt] *adj* découragé(e), abattu(e)

dessert [dɪ'zɜːt] *n* dessert *m*; **~spoon** *n* cuiller *f* à dessert

destination [destɪ'neɪʃən] *n* destination f

destined ['destɪnd] adj: to be ~ to do/for sth être destiné(e) à faire/à qch

destiny ['destɪnɪ] n destinée f, destin m

destitute ['destɪtjuːt] adj indigent(e)

destroy [dɪs'trɔɪ] vt détruire; (injured horse) abattre; (dog) faire piquer; ~**er** n (NAUT) contre-torpilleur m

destruction [dɪs'trʌkʃən] n destruction f

detach [dɪ'tætʃ] vt détacher; ~**ed** adj (attitude, person) détaché(e); ~**ed house** n pavillon m, maison(nette) (individuelle); ~**ment** n (MIL) détachement m; (fig) détachement, indifférence f

detail ['diːteɪl] n détail m ♦ vt raconter en détail, énumérer; **in** ~ en détail; ~**ed** adj détaillé(e)

detain [dɪ'teɪn] vt retenir; (in captivity) détenir; (in hospital) hospitaliser

detect [dɪ'tɛkt] vt déceler, percevoir; (MED, POLICE) dépister; (MIL, RADAR, TECH) détecter; ~**ion** [dɪ'tɛkʃən] n découverte f; ~**ive** n agent m de la sûreté, policier m; private ~**ive** détective privé; ~**ive story** n roman policier

detention [dɪ'tɛnʃən] n détention f; (SCOL) retenue f, consigne f

deter [dɪ'təː*] vt dissuader

detergent [dɪ'təːdʒənt] n détergent m, détersif m

deteriorate [dɪ'tɪərɪəreɪt] vi se détériorer, se dégrader

determine [dɪ'təːmɪn] vt déterminer; to ~ to do résoudre de faire, se déterminer à faire; ~**d** adj (person) déterminé(e), décidé(e)

deterrent [dɪ'tɛrənt] n effet m de dissuasion; force f de dissuasion

detonate ['dɛtəneɪt] vt faire détoner or exploser

detour ['diːtuə*] n détour m; (US: AUT: diversion) déviation f

detract [dɪ'trækt] vt: to ~ from

(quality, pleasure) diminuer; (reputation) porter atteinte à

detriment ['dɛtrɪmənt] n: to the ~ of au détriment de, au préjudice de; ~**al** [dɛtrɪ'mɛntl] adj: ~**al to** préjudiciable or nuisible à

devaluation [dɪvæljʊ'eɪʃən] n dévaluation f

devastate ['dɛvəsteɪt] vt (also fig) dévaster; **devastating** adj dévastateur(trice); (news) accablant(e)

develop [dɪ'vɛləp] vt (gen) développer; (disease) commencer à souffrir de; (resources) mettre en valeur, exploiter ♦ vi se développer; (situation, disease: evolve) évoluer; (facts, symptoms: appear) se manifester, se produire; ~**ing country** pays m en voie de développement; **the machine has** ~**ed a fault** un problème s'est manifesté dans cette machine; ~**er** n (also: property ~**er**) promoteur m; ~**ment** n développement m; (of affair, case) rebondissement m, fait(s) nouveau(x)

device [dɪ'vaɪs] n (apparatus) engin m, dispositif m

devil ['dɛvl] n diable m; démon m

devious ['diːvɪəs] adj (person) sournois(e), dissimulé(e)

devise [dɪ'vaɪz] vt imaginer, concevoir

devoid [dɪ'vɔɪd] adj: ~ **of** dépourvu(e) de, dénué(e) de

devolution [diːvə'luːʃən] n (POL) décentralisation f

devote [dɪ'vəʊt] vt: to ~ **sth to** consacrer qch à; ~**d** adj dévoué(e); to be ~**d to** (book etc) être consacré(e) à; (person) être très attaché(e) à; ~**e** [dɛvəʊ'tiː] n (REL) adepte m/f; (MUS, SPORT) fervent(e)

devotion [dɪ'vəʊʃən] n dévouement m, attachement m; (REL) dévotion f, piété f

devour [dɪ'vauə*] vt dévorer

devout [dɪ'vaut] adj pieux(euse), dévot(e)

dew [djuː] n rosée f

diabetes 74 diligent

diabetes [daɪə'biːtiːz] *n* diabète *m*;
diabetic [daɪə'bɛtɪk] *adj* diabétique ♦
n diabétique *m/f*

diabolical [daɪə'bɔlɪkl] *(inf)* *adj*
(weather) atroce; *(behaviour)* infer-
nal(e)

diagnosis [daɪəg'nəʊsɪs, *pl* daɪg'-
nəʊsiːz] *(pl* **diagnoses)** *n* diagnostic
m

diagonal [daɪ'ægənl] *adj* diagonal(e)
♦ *n* diagonale *f*

diagram ['daɪəgræm] *n* diagramme
m, schéma *m*

dial ['daɪəl] *n* cadran *m* ♦ *vt* (number) faire, composer; ~ **code** (US) *n*
= **dialling code**

dialect ['daɪəlɛkt] *n* dialecte *m*

dialling code ['daɪəlɪŋ-] (BRIT) *n*
indicatif *m* (téléphonique)

dialling tone ['daɪəlɪŋ-] (BRIT) *n*
tonalité *f*

dialogue ['daɪəlɔg] *n* dialogue *m*

dial tone (US) *n* = **dialling tone**

diameter [daɪ'æmɪtə*] *n* diamètre *m*

diamond ['daɪəmənd] *n* diamant *m*;
(shape) losange *m*; ~s *npl* (CARDS)
carreau *m*

diaper ['daɪəpə*] (US) *n* couche *f*

diaphragm ['daɪəfræm] *n* diaphragme *m*

diarrhoea [daɪə'riːə] (US **diarrhea)**
n diarrhée *f*

diary ['daɪərɪ] *n* (daily account) journal *m*; (book) agenda *m*

dice [daɪs] *n inv* dé *m* ♦ *vt* (CULIN)
couper en dés or en cubes

dictate [vb dɪk'teɪt, *n* 'dɪkteɪt] *vt* dicter

dictation [dɪk'teɪʃən] *n* dictée *f*

dictator [dɪk'teɪtə*] *n* dictateur *m*;
~**ship** *n* dictature *f*

dictionary ['dɪkʃənrɪ] *n* dictionnaire
m

did [dɪd] *pt* of **do**; ~**n't** = **did not**

die [daɪ] *vi* mourir; **to be dying for**
sth avoir une envie folle de qch; **to**
be dying to do sth mourir d'envie
de faire qch; ~ **away** *vi* s'éteindre;
~ **down** *vi* se calmer, s'apaiser; ~
out *vi* disparaître

die-hard ['daɪhɑːd] *n* réactionnaire
m/f, jusqu'au-boutiste *m/f*

diesel ['diːzəl] *n* (vehicle) diesel *m*;
(also: ~ **oil**) carburant *m* diesel,
gas-oil *m*; ~ **engine** *n* moteur *m* diesel

diet ['daɪət] *n* alimentation *f*;
(restricted food) régime *m* ♦ *vi*
(also: **be on a ~)** suivre un régime

differ ['dɪfə*] *vi* (be different): **to ~**
(from) être différent (de); différer
(de); (disagree): **to ~ (from sb**
over sth) ne pas être d'accord (avec
qn au sujet de qch); ~**ence** *n* différence *f*; (quarrel) différend *m*,
désaccord *m*; ~**ent** *adj* différent(e);
~**entiate** [dɪfə'rɛnʃɪeɪt] *vi*: **to ~enti-**
ate (between) faire une différence
(entre)

difficult ['dɪfɪkəlt] *adj* difficile; ~**y** *n*
difficulté *f*

diffident ['dɪfɪdənt] *adj* qui manque
de confiance or d'assurance

dig [dɪg] (pt, pp **dug)** *vt* (hole) creuser; (garden) bêcher ♦ *n* (prod)
coup *m* de coude; (fig) coup de griffe
or de patte; (archeological) fouilles
fpl; ~ **in** *vi* (MIL: also: ~ o.s. **in)** se
retrancher; ~ **into** *vt fus* (savings)
puiser dans; **to ~ one's nails into**
sth enfoncer ses ongles dans qch; ~
up *vt* déterrer

digest [vb daɪ'dʒɛst, *n* 'daɪdʒɛst] *vt*
digérer ♦ *n* sommaire *m*, résumé *m*;
~**ion** *n* digestion *f*

digit ['dɪdʒɪt] *n* (number) chiffre *m*;
(finger) doigt *m*; ~**al** *adj* digital(e),
à affichage numérique or digital; ~**al**
computer calculateur *m* numérique

dignified ['dɪgnɪfaɪd] *adj* digne

dignity ['dɪgnɪtɪ] *n* dignité *f*

digress [daɪ'grɛs] *vi*: **to ~ from**
s'écarter de, s'éloigner de

digs [dɪgz] (BRIT: inf) *npl* piaule *f*,
chambre meublée

dilapidated [dɪ'læpɪdeɪtɪd] *adj* déla-
bré(e)

dilemma [daɪ'lɛmə] *n* dilemme *m*

diligent ['dɪlɪdʒənt] *adj* appliqué(e),
assidu(e)

dilute [daɪ'luːt] vt diluer

dim [dɪm] adj (light) faible; (memory, outline) vague, indécis(e); (figure) vague, indistinct(e); (room) sombre; (stupid) borné(e), obtus(e) ♦ vt (light) réduire, baisser; (US: AUT) mettre en code

dime [daɪm] (US) n = 10 cents

dimension [dɪ'menʃən] n dimension f

diminish [dɪ'mɪnɪʃ] vt, vi diminuer

diminutive [dɪ'mɪnjʊtɪv] adj minuscule, tout(e) petit(e)

dimmers ['dɪməz] (US) npl (AUT) phares mpl de code inv; feux mpl de position

dimple ['dɪmpl] n fossette f

din [dɪn] n vacarme m

dine [daɪn] vi dîner; ~r n (person) dîneur(euse) m/f; (US: restaurant) petit restaurant

dinghy ['dɪŋgɪ] n youyou m; (also: rubber ~) canot m pneumatique; (: sailing ~) voilier m, dériveur m

dingy ['dɪndʒɪ] adj miteux(euse), minable

dining car ['daɪnɪŋ-] (BRIT) n wagon-restaurant m

dining room ['daɪnɪŋ-] n salle f à manger

dinner ['dɪnə*] n dîner m; (lunch) déjeuner m; (public) banquet m; ~ jacket n smoking m; ~ party n dîner m; ~ time n heure f du dîner; (midday) heure du déjeuner

dint [dɪnt] n: by ~ of (doing) à force de (faire)

dip [dɪp] n déclivité f; (in sea) baignade f, bain m; (CULIN) ≈ sauce f ♦ vt tremper, plonger; (BRIT: AUT: lights) mettre en code, baisser ♦ vi plonger

diploma [dɪ'pləʊmə] n diplôme m

diplomacy [dɪ'pləʊməsɪ] n diplomatie f

diplomat ['dɪpləmæt] n diplomate m; ~ic [dɪplə'mætɪk] adj diplomatique

dipstick ['dɪpstɪk] n (AUT) jauge f de niveau d'huile

dipswitch ['dɪpswɪtʃ] (BRIT) n (AUT) interrupteur m de lumière réduite

dire [daɪə*] adj terrible, extrême, affreux(euse)

direct [daɪ'rekt] adj direct(e) ♦ vt diriger, orienter (letter, remark) adresser; (film, programme) réaliser; (play) mettre en scène; (order): to ~ sb to do sth ordonner à qn de faire qch ♦ adv directement; can you ~ me to ...? pouvez-vous m'indiquer le chemin de ...?; ~ debit (BRIT) n prélèvement m automatique

direction [dɪ'rekʃən] n direction f; ~s npl (advice) indications fpl; sense of ~ sens m de l'orientation; ~s for use mode m d'emploi

directly [dɪ'rektlɪ] adv (in a straight line) directement, tout droit; (at once) tout de suite, immédiatement

director [dɪ'rektə*] n directeur m; (THEATRE) metteur m en scène; (CINEMA, TV) réalisateur(trice)

directory [dɪ'rektərɪ] n annuaire m; (COMPUT) répertoire m

dirt [dɜːt] n saleté f; crasse f; (earth) terre f, boue f; ~cheap adj très bon marché inv; ~y adj sale ♦ vt salir; ~y trick coup tordu

disability [dɪsə'bɪlɪtɪ] n invalidité f, infirmité f

disabled [dɪs'eɪbld] adj infirme, invalide ♦ npl: the ~ les handicapés

disadvantage [dɪsəd'vɑːntɪdʒ] n désavantage m, inconvénient m

disagree [dɪsə'griː] vi (be different) ne pas concorder; (be against, think otherwise): to ~ (with) ne pas être d'accord (avec); ~able adj désagréable; ~ment n désaccord m, différend m

disallow ['dɪsə'laʊ] vt rejeter

disappear [dɪsə'pɪə*] vi disparaître; ~ance n disparition f

disappoint [dɪsə'pɔɪnt] vt décevoir; ~ed adj déçu(e); ~ing adj décevant(e); ~ment n déception f

disapproval [dɪsə'pruːvəl] n désapprobation f

disapprove [dɪsə'pruːv] vi: to ~ (of) désapprouver

disarmament [dɪs'ɑːməmənt] n désarmement m

disarray [dɪsə'reɪ] n: **in** ~ (army) en déroute; (organization) en désarroi; (hair, clothes) en désordre

disaster [dɪ'zɑːstə*] n catastrophe f, désastre m

disband [dɪs'bænd] vt démobiliser; disperser ♦ vi se séparer; se disperser

disbelief ['dɪsbə'liːf] n incrédulité f

disc [dɪsk] n disque m; (COMPUT) = disk

discard ['dɪskɑːd] vt (old things) se débarrasser de; (fig) écarter, renoncer à

discern [dɪ'sɜːn] vt discerner, distinguer; **~ing** adj perspicace

discharge [vb dɪs'tʃɑːdʒ, n 'dɪstʃɑːdʒ] vt décharger; (duties) s'acquitter de; (patient) renvoyer (chez lui); (employee) congédier, licencier; (soldier) rendre à la vie civile, réformer; (defendant) relaxer, élargir ♦ n décharge f; (dismissal) renvoi m; licenciement m; élargissement m; (MED) écoulement m

discipline ['dɪsɪplɪn] n discipline f

disc jockey n disc-jockey m

disclaim [dɪs'kleɪm] vt nier

disclose [dɪs'kləʊz] vt révéler, divulguer; **disclosure** [dɪs'kləʊʒə*] n révélation f

disco ['dɪskəʊ] n abbr = discotheque

discomfort [dɪs'kʌmfət] n malaise m, gêne f; (lack of comfort) manque m de confort

disconcert [dɪskən'sɜːt] vt déconcerter

disconnect ['dɪskə'nekt] vt (ELEC, RADIO, pipe) débrancher; (TEL, water) couper

discontent [dɪskən'tent] n mécontentement m; **~ed** adj mécontent(e)

discontinue ['dɪskən'tɪnjuː] vt cesser, interrompre; "~d" (COMM) "fin de série"

discord ['dɪskɔːd] n discorde f, dissension f; (MUS) dissonance f

discotheque ['dɪskəʊtek] n discothèque f

discount [n 'dɪskaʊnt, vb dɪs'kaʊnt] n remise f, rabais m ♦ vt (sum) faire une remise de; (fig) ne pas tenir compte de

discourage [dɪs'kʌrɪdʒ] vt décourager

discover [dɪs'kʌvə*] vt découvrir; **~y** n découverte f

discredit [dɪs'kredɪt] vt (idea) mettre en doute; (person) discréditer

discreet [dɪs'kriːt] adj discret(ète)

discrepancy [dɪs'krepənsɪ] n divergence f, contradiction f

discretion [dɪs'kreʃən] n discrétion f; use your own ~ à vous de juger

discriminate [dɪs'krɪmɪneɪt] vi: to ~ **between** établir une distinction entre, faire la différence entre; to ~ **against** pratiquer une discrimination contre; **discriminating** adj qui a du discernement; **discrimination** [dɪskrɪmɪ'neɪʃən] n discrimination f; (judgment) discernement m

discuss [dɪs'kʌs] vt discuter de; (debate) discuter; **~ion** [dɪs'kʌʃən] n discussion f

disdain [dɪs'deɪn] n dédain m

disease [dɪ'ziːz] n maladie f

disembark [dɪsɪm'bɑːk] vt, vi débarquer

disengage [dɪsɪn'geɪdʒ] vt: to ~ the clutch (AUT) débrayer

disentangle [dɪsɪn'tæŋgl] vt (wool, wire) démêler, débrouiller; (from wreckage) dégager

disfigure [dɪs'fɪgə*] vt défigurer

disgrace [dɪs'greɪs] n honte f; (disfavour) disgrâce f ♦ vt déshonorer, couvrir de honte; **~ful** adj scandaleux(euse), honteux(euse)

disgruntled [dɪs'grʌntld] adj mécontent(e)

disguise [dɪs'gaɪz] n déguisement m ♦ vt déguiser; **in** ~ déguisé(e)

disgust [dɪs'gʌst] n dégoût m, aversion f ♦ vt dégoûter, écœurer; **~ing**

adj dégoûtant(e); révoltant(e)

dish [dɪʃ] *n* plat *m*; **to do** *or* **wash the ~es** faire la vaisselle; **~ out** *vt* servir, distribuer; **~ up** *vt* servir; **~cloth** *n* (*for washing*) lavette *f*

dishearten [dɪs'hɑːtn] *vt* décourager

dishevelled [dɪ'ʃevəld] (*US* **disheveled**) *adj* ébouriffé(e); décoiffé(e); débraillé(e)

dishonest [dɪs'ɒnɪst] *adj* malhonnête

dishonour [dɪs'ɒnə*] (*US* **dishonor**) *n* déshonneur *m*; **~able** *adj* (*behaviour*) déshonorant(e); (*person*) peu honorable

dishtowel [dɪʃtaʊəl] (*US*) *n* torchon *m*

dishwasher [dɪʃwɒʃə*] *n* lave-vaisselle *m*

disillusion [dɪsɪ'luːʒən] *vt* désabuser, désillusionner

disincentive [dɪsɪn'sentɪv] *n*: **to be a ~** être démotivant(e)

disinfect [dɪsɪn'fekt] *vt* désinfecter; **~ant** *n* désinfectant *m*

disintegrate [dɪs'ɪntɪgreɪt] *vi* se désintégrer

disinterested [dɪs'ɪntrɪstɪd] *adj* désintéressé(e)

disjointed [dɪs'dʒɔɪntɪd] *adj* décousu(e), incohérent(e)

disk [dɪsk] *n* (*COMPUT*) disque *m*; (: *floppy ~*) disquette *f*; **single-/double-sided ~** disquette simple/double face; **~ drive** *n* lecteur *m* de disquettes; **~ette** [dɪs'ket] *n* disquette *f*, disque *m* souple

dislike [dɪs'laɪk] *n* aversion *f*, antipathie *f* ♦ *vt* ne pas aimer

dislocate [dɪsləʊkeɪt] *vt* disloquer; déboîter

dislodge [dɪs'lɒdʒ] *vt* déplacer, faire bouger

disloyal [dɪs'lɔɪəl] *adj* déloyal(e)

dismal [dɪzməl] *adj* lugubre, maussade

dismantle [dɪs'mæntl] *vt* démonter

dismay [dɪs'meɪ] *n* consternation *f*

dismiss [dɪs'mɪs] *vt* congédier, renvoyer; (*soldiers*) faire rompre les rangs à; (*idea*) écarter; (*LAW*): **to**

~ a case rendre une fin de non-recevoir; **~al** *n* renvoi *m*

dismount [dɪs'maʊnt] *vi* mettre pied à terre, descendre

disobedient [dɪsə'biːdɪənt] *adj* désobéissant(e)

disobey [dɪsə'beɪ] *vt* désobéir à

disorder [dɪs'ɔːdə*] *n* désordre *m*; (*rioting*) désordres *mpl*; (*MED*) troubles *mpl*; **~ly** *adj* (*dɪs'ɔːdəlɪ*) en désordre; désordonné(e)

disorientated [dɪs'ɔːrɪenteɪtɪd] *adj* désorienté(e)

disown [dɪs'əʊn] *vt* renier

disparaging [dɪs'pærɪdʒɪŋ] *adj* désobligeant(e)

dispassionate [dɪs'pæʃnɪt] *adj* calme, froid(e); impartial(e), objectif(ive)

dispatch [dɪs'pætʃ] *vt* expédier, envoyer ♦ *n* envoi *m*, expédition *f*; (*MIL, PRESS*) dépêche *f*

dispel [dɪs'pel] *vt* dissiper, chasser

dispense [dɪs'pens] *vt* distribuer, administrer; **~ with** *vt fus* se passer de; **~r** *n* (*machine*) distributeur *m*; **dispensing chemist** (*BRIT*) *n* pharmacie *f*

disperse [dɪs'pɜːs] *vt* disperser ♦ *vi* se disperser

dispirited [dɪs'pɪrɪtɪd] *adj* découragé(e), déprimé(e)

displace [dɪs'pleɪs] *vt* déplacer

display [dɪs'pleɪ] *n* étalage *m*; déploiement *m*; affichage *m*; (*screen*) écran *m*, visuel *m*; (*of feeling*) manifestation *f* ♦ *vt* montrer; (*goods*) mettre à l'étalage, exposer; (*results, departure times*) afficher; (*pej*) faire étalage de

displease [dɪs'pliːz] *vt* mécontenter, contrarier; **~d** *adj*: **~d with** mécontent(e) de; **displeasure** [dɪs'pleʒə*] *n* mécontentement *m*

disposable [dɪs'pəʊzəbl] *adj* (*pack etc*) jetable, à jeter; (*income*) disponible; **~ nappy** (*BRIT*) *n* couche *f* à jeter, couche-culotte *f*

disposal [dɪs'pəʊzəl] *n* (*of goods for sale*) vente *f*; (*of property*) disposition f, cession f; (of rubbish) enlèvement m; destruction f; **at one's ~** à sa disposition

dispose [dɪs'pəʊz] vt disposer; **~ of** vt fus (unwanted goods etc) se débarrasser de, se défaire de; (problem) expédier; **~d** [dɪs'pəʊzd] adj: **to be ~d to do sth** être disposé(e) à faire qch; **disposition** [dɪspə'zɪʃən] n disposition f; (temperament) naturel m

disprove [dɪs'pruːv] vt réfuter

dispute [dɪs'pjuːt] n discussion f; (also: **industrial ~**) conflit m ♦ vt contester; (matter) discuter; (victory) disputer

disqualify [dɪs'kwɒlɪfaɪ] vt (SPORT) disqualifier; **to ~ sb for sth/from doing** rendre qn inapte à qch/à faire qch

disquiet [dɪs'kwaɪət] n inquiétude f, trouble m

disregard [dɪsrɪ'gɑːd] vt ne pas tenir compte de

disrepair [dɪsrɪ'pɛə*] n: **to fall into ~** (building) tomber en ruine

disreputable [dɪs'rɛpjʊtəbl] adj (person) de mauvaise réputation; (behaviour) déshonorant(e)

disrespectful [dɪsrɪ'spɛktfʊl] adj irrespectueux(euse)

disrupt [dɪs'rʌpt] vt (plans) déranger; (conversation) interrompre

dissatisfied [dɪs'sætɪsfaɪd] adj: **~ (with)** insatisfait(e)

dissect [dɪ'sɛkt] vt disséquer

dissent [dɪ'sɛnt] n dissentiment m, différence f d'opinion

dissertation [dɪsə'teɪʃən] n mémoire m

disservice [dɪs'sɜːvɪs] n: **to do sb a ~** rendre un mauvais service à qn

dissimilar ['dɪ'sɪmɪlə*] adj: **~ (to)** dissemblable (à), différent(e) (de)

dissipate ['dɪsɪpeɪt] vt dissiper; (money, efforts) disperser

dissolute ['dɪsəluːt] adj débauché(e), dissolu(e)

dissolve [dɪ'zɒlv] vt dissoudre ♦ vi se dissoudre, fondre; **to ~ in(to) tears** fondre en larmes

distance ['dɪstəns] n distance f; **in**

the ~ au loin

distant ['dɪstənt] adj lointain(e), éloigné(e); (manner) distant(e), froid(e)

distaste [dɪs'teɪst] n dégoût m; **~ful** adj déplaisant(e), désagréable

distended [dɪs'tɛndɪd] adj (stomach) dilaté(e)

distil [dɪs'tɪl] vt distiller; **~lery** n distillerie f

distinct [dɪs'tɪŋkt] adj distinct(e); (clear) marqué(e); **as ~ from** par opposition à; **~ion** [dɪs'tɪŋkʃən] n distinction f; (in exam) mention f très bien; **~ive** adj distinctif(ive)

distinguish [dɪs'tɪŋgwɪʃ] vt distinguer; **~ed** adj (eminent) distingué(e); **~ing** adj (feature) distinctif(ive), caractéristique

distort [dɪs'tɔːt] vt déformer

distract [dɪs'trækt] vt distraire, déranger; **~ed** adj distrait(e); (anxious) éperdu(e), égaré(e); **~ion** [dɪs'trækʃən] n distraction f; égarement m

distraught [dɪs'trɔːt] adj éperdu(e)

distress [dɪs'trɛs] n détresse f ♦ vt affliger; **~ing** adj douloureux(euse), pénible

distribute [dɪs'trɪbjuːt] vt distribuer; **distribution** [dɪstrɪ'bjuːʃn] n distribution f; **distributor** [dɪs'trɪbjʊtə*] n distributeur m

district ['dɪstrɪkt] n (of country) région f; (of town) quartier m; (ADMIN) district m; **~ attorney** (US) n ≈ procureur m de la République; **~ nurse** (BRIT) n infirmière visiteuse

distrust [dɪs'trʌst] n méfiance f ♦ vt se méfier de

disturb [dɪs'tɜːb] vt troubler; (inconvenience) déranger; **~ance** n dérangement m; (violent event, political etc) troubles mpl; **~ed** adj (worried, upset) agité(e), troublé(e); **to be emotionally ~ed** avoir des problèmes affectifs; **~ing** adj troublant(e), inquiétant(e)

disuse [dɪs'juːs] n: **to fall into ~** tomber en désuétude

disused ['dɪs'juːzd] adj désaffecté(e)

ditch [dɪtʃ] n fossé m; (irrigation) rigole *f* ♦ *vt* (*inf*) abandonner; (*person*) plaquer

dither ['dɪðə*] *vi* hésiter

ditto ['dɪtəu] *adv* idem

dive [daɪv] *n* plongeon *m*; (*of submarine*) plongée *f* ♦ *vi* plonger; **to ~ into** (*bag, drawer etc*) plonger la main dans; (*shop, car etc*) se précipiter dans; **~r** *n* plongeur *m*

diversion [daɪ'vɜːʃən] *n* (*BRIT: AUT*) déviation *f*; (*distraction, MIL*) diversion *f*

divert [daɪ'vɜːt] *vt* (*funds, BRIT: traffic*) dévier; (*river, attention*) détourner

divide [dɪ'vaɪd] *vt* diviser; (*separate*) séparer ♦ *vi* se diviser; **~d highway** (*US*) *n* route *f* à quatre voies

dividend ['dɪvɪdend] *n* dividende *m*

divine [dɪ'vaɪn] *adj* divin(e)

diving ['daɪvɪŋ] *n* plongée (sous-marine); **~ board** *n* plongeoir *m*

divinity [dɪ'vɪnɪtɪ] *n* divinité *f*; (*SCOL*) théologie *f*

division [dɪ'vɪʒən] *n* division *f*

divorce [dɪ'vɔːs] *n* divorce *m* ♦ *vt* divorcer d'avec; (*dissociate*) séparer; **~d** *adj* divorcé(e); **~e** [dɪvɔː'siː] *n* divorcé(e)

D.I.Y. (*BRIT*) *n abbr* = **do-it-yourself**

dizzy ['dɪzɪ] *adj*: **to make sb ~** donner le vertige à qn; **to feel ~** avoir la tête qui tourne

DJ *n abbr* = **disc jockey**

KEYWORD

do [duː] (*pt* **did**, *pp* **done**) *n* (*inf: party etc*) soirée *f*, fête *f*
♦ *vb* **1** (*in negative constructions*) *non traduit*; **I ~n't understand** je ne comprends pas

2 (*to form questions*) *non traduit*; **didn't you know?** vous ne le saviez pas?; **why didn't you come?** pourquoi n'êtes-vous pas venu?

3 (*for emphasis, in polite expressions*): **she does seem rather late** je trouve qu'elle est bien en retard; **~ sit down/help yourself** asseyez-

vous/servez-vous je vous en prie

4 (*used to avoid repeating vb*): **she swims better than I ~** elle nage mieux que moi; **~ you agree?** - **yes, I ~/no, I ~n't** vous êtes d'accord? - oui/non; **she lives in Glasgow** - **so ~ I** elle habite Glasgow - moi aussi; **who broke it?** - **I did** qui l'a cassé? - c'est moi

5 (*in question tags*): **he laughed, didn't he?** il a ri, n'est-ce pas?; **I ~n't know him, ~ I?** je ne le connais pas, je crois

♦ *vt* (*gen: carry out, perform etc*) faire; **what are you ~ing tonight?** qu'est-ce que vous faites ce soir?; **to ~ the cooking/washing-up** faire la cuisine/la vaisselle; **to ~ one's teeth/hair/nails** se brosser les dents/se coiffer/se faire les ongles; **the car was ~ing 100** la voiture faisait du 100 (à l'heure)

♦ *vi* **1** (*act, behave*) faire; **~ as I ~** faites comme moi

2 (*get on, fare*) marcher; **the firm is ~ing well** l'entreprise marche bien; **how ~ you ~?** comment allez-vous?; (*on being introduced*) enchanté(e)!

3 (*suit*) aller; **will it ~?** est-ce que ça ira?

4 (*be sufficient*) suffire, aller; **will £10 ~?** est-ce que 10 livres suffiront?; **that'll ~** ça suffit, ça ira; **that'll ~!** (*in annoyance*) ça va ou suffit comme ça!; **to make ~ (with)** se contenter (de)

do away with *vt fus* supprimer

do up *vt* (*laces, dress*) attacher; (*buttons*) boutonner; (*zip*) fermer; (*renovate: room*) refaire; (*: house*) remettre à neuf

do with *vt fus* (*need*): **I could do with a drink/some help** quelque chose à boire/un peu d'aide ne serait pas de refus; (*be connected*): **that has nothing to ~ with you** cela ne vous concerne pas; **I won't have anything to ~ with it** je ne veux pas m'en mêler

do without *vi* s'en passer ♦ *vt fus* se passer de

dock [dɔk] *n* dock *m*; (*LAW*) banc *m* des accusés ♦ *vi* se mettre à quai; (*SPACE*) s'arrimer; ~**er** *n* docker *m*; ~**yard** *n* chantier *m* de construction navale

doctor ['dɔktə*] *n* médecin *m*, docteur *m*; (*PhD etc*) docteur *m* ♦ *vt* (*drink*) frelater; **D~ of Philosophy** *n* (*degree*) doctorat *m*; (*person*) Docteur *m* en Droit or Lettres *etc*, titulaire *m/f* d'un doctorat

document ['dɔkjəmənt] *n* document *m*; ~**ary** [dɔkju'mentəri] *adj* documentaire ♦ *n* documentaire *m*

dodge [dɔdʒ] *n* truc *m*; combine *f* ♦ *vt* esquiver, éviter

dodgems ['dɔdʒəmz] *npl* (*BRIT*) autos tamponneuses

doe [dəu] *n* (*deer*) biche *f*; (*rabbit*) lapine *f*

does [dʌz] *vb see* **do**; ~**n't** = **does not**

dog [dɔg] *n* chien(ne) ♦ *vt* suivre de près; poursuivre, harceler; ~ **collar** *n* collier *m* de chien; (*fig*) faux-col *m* d'ecclésiastique; ~**eared** *adj* corné(e)

dogged ['dɔgid] *adj* obstiné(e), opiniâtre

dogsbody ['dɔgzbɔdi] *n* bonne *f* à tout faire, tâcheron *m*

doings ['du:iŋz] *npl* activités *fpl*

do-it-yourself ['du:itjɔ'self] *n* bricolage *m*

doldrums ['dɔldrəmz] *npl*: **to be in the** ~ avoir le cafard; (*business*) être dans le marasme

dole [dəul] *n* (*BRIT: payment*) allocation *f* de chômage; **on the** ~ au chômage; ~ **out** *vt* donner au compte-goutte

doleful ['dəulful] *adj* plaintif(ive), lugubre

doll [dɔl] *n* poupée *f*

dollar ['dɔlə*] *n* dollar *m*

dolled up ['dɔld-] (*inf*) *adj*: (**all**) ~ sur son trente et un

dolphin ['dɔlfin] *n* dauphin *m*

dome [dəum] *n* dôme *m*

domestic [də'mestik] *adj* (*task, appliances*) ménager(ère); (*of country: trade, situation etc*) intérieur(e); (*animal*) domestique; ~**ated** *adj* (*animal*) domestiqué(e); (*husband*) pantouflard(e)

dominate ['dɔmineit] *vt* dominer

domineering [dɔmi'niəriŋ] *adj* dominateur(trice), autoritaire

dominion [də'miniən] *n* (*territory*) territoire *m*; **to have** ~ **over** contrôler

domino ['dɔminəu] (*pl* ~**es**) *n* domino *m*; ~**es** *n* (*game*) dominos *mpl*

don [dɔn] (*BRIT*) *n* professeur *m* d'université

donate [dəu'neit] *vt* faire don de, donner

done [dʌn] *pp of* **do**

donkey ['dɔŋki] *n* âne *m*

donor ['dəunə*] *n* (*of blood etc*) donneur(euse); (*to charity*) donateur(trice)

don't [dəunt] *vb* = **do not**

donut (*US*) *n* = **doughnut**

doodle ['du:dl] *vi* griffonner, gribouiller

doom [du:m] *n* destin *m* ♦ *vt*: **to be** ~**ed** (**to failure**) être voué(e) à l'échec; ~**sday** *n* le Jugement dernier

door [dɔ:*] *n* porte *f*; (*RAIL, car*) portière *f*; ~**bell** *n* sonnette *f*; ~**handle** *n* poignée *f* de la porte; (*car*) poignée de portière; ~**man** (*irreg*) *n* (*in hotel*) portier *m*; ~**mat** *n* paillasson *m*; ~**step** *n* pas *m* de la porte, seuil *m*; ~**way** *n* (*embrasure f de la*) porte *f*

dope [dəup] *n* (*inf: drug*) drogue *f*; (*: person*) andouille *f* ♦ *vt* (*horse etc*) doper

dopey ['dəupi] (*inf*) *adj* à moitié endormi(e)

dormant ['dɔ:mənt] *adj* assoupi(e), en veilleuse

dormitory ['dɔ:mitri] *n* dortoir *m*; (*US: building*) résidence *f* universitaire

dormouse ['dɔ:maus, *pl* 'dɔ:maɪs] (*pl* **dormice**) *n* loir *m*

dose [dəus] *n* dose *f*

doss house ['dɔs-] (*BRIT*) *n* asile *m de nuit*

dot [dɔt] *n* point *m*; (*on material*) pois *m* ♦ *vt*: ~**ted with** parsemé(e) de; **on the** ~ à l'heure tapante ou pile

dote [dəut]: **to** ~ **on** *vt fus* être fou(folle) de

dot-matrix printer [dɔt'meɪtrɪks-] *n* imprimante matricielle

dotted line *n* pointillé(s) *m(pl)*

double ['dʌbl] *adj* double ♦ *adv* (*twice*): **to cost** ~ (**sth**) coûter le double (de qch) ou deux fois plus (que qch) ♦ *n* double *m* ♦ *vt* doubler; (*fold*) plier en deux ♦ *vi* doubler; ~**s** *n* (*TENNIS*) double *m*; **on** *or* (*BRIT*) **at the** ~ au pas de course; ~ **bass** (*BRIT*) *n* contrebasse *f*; ~ **bed** *n* grand lit; ~ **bend** (*BRIT*) *n* virage *m* en S; ~**-breasted** *adj* croisé(e); ~**cross** *vt* doubler, trahir; ~**decker** *n* autobus *m* à impériale; ~ **glazing** (*BRIT*) *n* double vitrage *m*; ~ **room** *n* chambre *f* pour deux personnes; **doubly** ['dʌblɪ] *adv* doublement, deux fois plus

doubt [daut] *n* doute *m* ♦ *vt* douter de; **to** ~ **that** douter que; ~**ful** *adj* douteux(euse); (*person*) incertain(e); ~**less** *adv* sans doute, sûrement

dough [dəu] *n* pâte *f*; ~**nut** (*US* **donut**) *n* beignet *m*

douse [dauz] *vt* (*drench*) tremper, inonder; (*extinguish*) éteindre

dove [dʌv] *n* colombe *f*

Dover ['dəuvə*] *n* Douvres

dovetail ['dʌvteɪl] *vi* (*fig*) concorder

dowdy ['daudɪ] *adj* démodé(e); mal fagoté(e) (*inf*)

down [daun] *n* (*soft feathers*) duvet *m* ♦ *adv* en bas, vers le bas; (*on the ground*) par terre ♦ *prep* en bas de; (*along*) le long de ♦ *vt* (*inf*: *drink, food*) s'envoyer; ~ **with X!** à bas X!; ~**-and-out** *n* clochard(e); ~**at-**

heel *adj* éculé(e); (*fig*) miteux(euse); ~**cast** *adj* démoralisé(e); ~**fall** *n* chute *f*; ruine *f*; ~**hearted** *adj* découragé(e); ~**hill** *adv*: **to go** ~**hill** descendre; (*fig*) péricliter; ~ **payment** *n* acompte *m*; ~**pour** *n* pluie torrentielle, déluge *m*; ~**right** *adj* (*lie etc*) effronté(e); (*refusal*) catégorique

Down's syndrome [daunz-] *n* (*MED*) trisomie *f*

down: ~**stairs** *adv* en-dessous-de-chaussée; à l'étage inférieur; ~**stream** *adv* en aval; ~**-to-earth** *adj* terre à terre *inv*; ~**town** *adv* en ville; ~ **under** *adv* en Australie (*or* Nouvelle-Zélande); ~**ward** *adj, adv* vers le bas; ~**wards** *adv* vers le bas

dowry ['dauri] *n* dot *f*

doz. *abbr* = **dozen**

doze [dəuz] *vi* sommeiller; ~ **off** *vi* s'assoupir

dozen ['dʌzn] *n* douzaine *f*; **a** ~ **books** une douzaine de livres; ~**s of** des centaines de

Dr. *abbr* = **doctor**; **drive**.

drab [dræb] *adj* terne, morne

draft [drɑ:ft] *n* ébauche *f*; (*of letter, essay etc*) brouillon *m*; (*COMM*) traite *f*; (*US*: *call-up*) conscription *f* ♦ *vt* faire le brouillon *or* un projet de; (*MIL*: *send*) détacher; *see also* **draught**

draftsman ['drɑ:ftsmən] (*irreg*: *US*) *n* = **draughtsman**

drag [dræg] *vt* traîner ♦ *vi* (*river*) draguer ♦ *vi* traîner ♦ *n* (*inf*) casse-pieds *m/f*; (*women's clothing*): **in** ~ (en) travesti; ~ **on** *vi* s'éterniser

dragon ['drægn] *n* dragon *m*

dragonfly ['drægnflaɪ] *n* libellule *f*

drain [dreɪn] *n* égout *m*, canalisation *f*; (*on resources*) saignée *f* ♦ *vt* (*land, marshes etc*) drainer, assécher; (*vegetables*) égoutter; (*glass*) vider ♦ *vi* (*water*) s'écouler; ~**age** *n* drainage *m*; système *m* d'égouts *or* de canalisations; ~**ing board** (*US* ~**board**) *n* égouttoir *m*; ~**pipe** *n* tuyau *m* d'écoulement

drama ['drɑːmə] n (art) théâtre m, art m dramatique; (play) pièce f (de théâtre); (event) drame m; ~**tic** [drə'mætɪk] adj dramatique; spectaculaire; ~**tist** ['dræmətɪst] n auteur m dramatique; ~**tize** vt (events) dramatiser; (adapt: for TV/cinema) adapter pour la télévision/pour l'écran

drank [dræŋk] pt of **drink**

drape [dreɪp] vt draper; ~**s** (US) npl rideaux mpl

drastic ['dræstɪk] adj sévère; énergique; (change) radical(e)

draught [drɑːft] (US **draft**) n courant m d'air; (NAUT) tirant m d'eau; on ~ (beer) à la pression; ~**board** (BRIT) n damier m; ~**s** (BRIT) n (jeu m de) dames fpl

draughtsman ['drɑːftsmən] (irreg) n dessinateur(trice) (industriel(le))

draw [drɔː] (pt **drew**, pp **drawn**) vt tirer; (tooth) arracher, extraire; (attract) attirer; (picture) dessiner; (line, circle) tracer; (money) retirer; (wages) toucher ♦ vi (SPORT) faire match nul ♦ n match nul; (lottery) tirage m au sort; loterie f; to ~ near s'approcher; approcher; ~ **out** vi (lengthen) s'allonger ♦ vt (money) retirer; ~ **up** vi (stop) s'arrêter ♦ vt (chair) approcher; (document) établir, dresser; ~**back** n inconvénient m, désavantage m; ~**bridge** n pont-levis m; ~**er** [drɔː*] n tiroir m

drawing ['drɔːɪŋ] n dessin m; ~ **board** n planche f à dessin; ~ **pin** (BRIT) n punaise f; ~ **room** n salon m

drawl [drɔːl] n accent traînant

drawn [drɔːn] pp of **draw**

dread [dred] n terreur f, effroi m ♦ vt redouter, appréhender; ~**ful** adj affreux(euse)

dream [driːm] (pt, pp **dreamed** or **dreamt**) n rêve m ♦ vt, vi rêver; ~**y** adj rêveur(euse); (music) langoureux(euse)

dreary ['drɪərɪ] adj morne; monotone

dredge [dredʒ] vt draguer

dregs [dregz] npl lie f

drench [drentʃ] vt tremper

dress [dres] n robe f; (no pl: clothing) habillement m, tenue f ♦ vi s'habiller ♦ vt habiller; (wound) panser; to get ~**ed** s'habiller; ~ **up** vi s'habiller; (in fancy ~) se déguiser; ~ **circle** n (BRIT) (THEATRE) premier balcon; ~**er** n (furniture) vaisselier m; (: US) coiffeuse f, commode f; ~**ing** n (MED) pansement m; (CULIN) sauce f, assaisonnement m; ~**ing gown** (BRIT) n robe f de chambre; ~**ing room** n (THEATRE) loge f; (SPORT) vestiaire m; ~**ing table** n coiffeuse f; ~**maker** n couturière f; ~ **rehearsal** n (répétition) générale

drew [druː] pt of **draw**

dribble ['drɪbl] vi (baby) baver ♦ vt (ball) dribbler

dried [draɪd] adj (fruit, beans) sec(sèche); (eggs, milk) en poudre

drier ['draɪə*] n = **dryer**

drift [drɪft] n (of current etc) force f; direction f, mouvement m; (of snow) rafale f; (: on ground) congère f; (general meaning) sens (général) m; (of sand, snow) s'amonceler, s'entasser; ♦ vi (boat) aller à la dérive, dériver; ~**wood** n bois flotté

drill [drɪl] n perceuse f; (~ bit) foret m, mèche f; (of dentist) roulette f, fraise f; (MIL) exercice m ♦ vt percer; (troops) entraîner ♦ vi (for oil) faire un or des forage(s)

drink [drɪŋk] (pt **drank**, pp **drunk**) n boisson f; (alcoholic) verre m, vi boire; to have a ~ boire quelque chose, boire un verre; prendre l'apéritif; a ~ **of water** un verre d'eau; ~**er** n buveur(euse); ~**ing water** n eau f potable

drip [drɪp] n goutte f; (MED) goutte-à-goutte m inv; perfusion f ♦ vi tomber goutte à goutte; (tap) goutter; ~**-dry** adj (shirt) sans repassage; ~**ping** n graisse f (de rôti)

drive [draɪv] (pt **drove**, pp **driven**) n promenade f or trajet m en voiture;

(also: ~**way**) allée f; (energy) dynamisme m, énergie f; (push) effort (concerté), campagne f (also: disk ~) lecteur m de disquettes ♦ vt conduire; (push) chasser, pousser; (TECH: motor, wheel) faire fonctionner; entraîner; (nail, stake etc): to ~ **sth into sth** enfoncer qch dans qch ♦ vi (AUT: at controls) conduire; (: travel) aller en voiture; **left-/right-hand** ~ conduite f à gauche/droite; **to** ~ **sb mad** rendre qn fou(folle); **to** ~ **sb home/to the airport** reconduire qn chez lui/conduire qn à l'aéroport

drivel ['drɪvl] n idioties fpl

driver ['draɪvə*] n conducteur(trice); (of taxi, bus) chauffeur m; ~'**s license** (US) n permis m de conduire

driveway ['draɪvweɪ] n allée f

driving ['draɪvɪŋ] n conduite f; ~ **instructor** n moniteur m d'auto-école; ~ **lesson** n leçon f de conduite; ~ **licence** (BRIT) n permis m de conduire; ~ **school** n auto-école f; ~ **test** n examen m du permis de conduire

drizzle ['drɪzl] n bruine f, crachin m

drone [drəʊn] n bourdonnement m; (male bee) faux bourdon

drool [druːl] vi baver

droop [druːp] vi (shoulders) tomber; (head) pencher; (flower) pencher la tête

drop [drɒp] n goutte f; (fall) baisse f; (also: parachute ~) saut m ♦ vt laisser tomber; (voice, eyes, price) baisser; (set down from car) déposer ♦ vi tomber; ~**s** npl (MED) gouttes; ~ **off** vi (sleep) s'assoupir ♦ vt (passenger) déposer; ~ **out** vi (withdraw) se retirer; (student etc) abandonner, décrocher; ~**out** n marginal(e); ~**per** n compte-gouttes m inv; ~**pings** npl crottes fpl

drought [draʊt] n sécheresse f

drove [drəʊv] pt of **drive**

drown [draʊn] vt noyer ♦ vi se noyer

drowsy ['draʊzɪ] adj somnolent(e)

drudgery ['drʌdʒərɪ] n corvée f

drug [drʌg] n médicament m; (narcotic) drogue f ♦ vt droguer; **to be on** ~**s** se droguer; ~ **addict** n toxicomane m/f; ~**gist** (US) n pharmacien(ne)-droguiste; ~**store** (US) n pharmacie-droguerie f, drugstore m

drum [drʌm] n tambour m; (for oil, petrol) bidon m; ~**s** npl (kit) batterie f; ~**mer** n (joueur m de) tambour m

drunk [drʌŋk] pp of **drink** ♦ adj ivre, soûl(e) ♦ n (also: ~**ard**) ivrogne m/f; ~**en** adj (person) ivre, soûl(e); (rage, stupor) ivrogne, d'ivrogne

dry [draɪ] adj sec(sèche); (day) sans pluie; (humour) pince-sans-rire inv; (lake, riverbed, well) à sec ♦ vt sécher; (clothes) faire sécher ♦ vi sécher; ~ **up** vi tarir; ~**cleaner's** n teinturerie f; ~**er** n séchoir m; (US: spin-~er) essoreuse f; ~**ness** n sécheresse f; ~ **rot** n pourriture sèche (du bois)

dual [djuəl] adj double; ~ **carriageway** (BRIT) n route f à quatre voies or à chaussées séparées; ~ **purpose** adj à double usage

dubbed [dʌbd] adj (CINEMA) doublé(e)

dubious ['djuːbɪəs] adj hésitant(e), incertain(e); (reputation, company) douteux(euse)

duchess ['dʌtʃɪs] n duchesse f

duck [dʌk] n canard m ♦ vi se baisser vivement, baisser subitement la tête; ~**ling** n caneton m

duct [dʌkt] n conduite f, canalisation f; (ANAT) conduit m

dud [dʌd] n (object, tool): **it's a** ~ c'est de la camelote, ça ne marche pas ♦ adj: ~ **cheque** (BRIT) chèque sans provision

due [djuː] adj dû(due); (expected) attendu(e); (fitting) qui convient ♦ n: **to give sb his (or her)** ~ être juste envers qn ♦ adv: ~ **north** droit vers le nord; ~**s** npl (for club, union) cotisation f; (in harbour) droits mpl de port); **in** ~ **course** en temps utile or voulu; finalement; ~ to dû(due) à; causé(e) par; **he's** ~ **to finish to-morrow** normalement il doit finir de-main

duet [dju:'et] n duo m

duffel bag [dʌfl] n sac m marin

duffel coat n duffel-coat m

dug [dʌg] pt, pp of **dig**

duke [dju:k] n duc m

dull [dʌl] adj terne, morne; (boring) ennuyeux(euse), (sound, pain) sourd(e); (weather, day) gris(e), maussade ♦ vt (pain, grief) atté-nuer; (mind, senses) engourdir

duly ['dju:lɪ] adv (on time) en temps voulu; (as expected) comme il se doit

dumb [dʌm] adj muet(te); (stupid) bête; ~**founded** [dʌm'faundɪd] adj si-déré(e)

dummy ['dʌmɪ] n (tailor's model) mannequin m; (mock-up) factice m, maquette f; (BRIT: for baby) tétine f ♦ adj faux(fausse), factice

dump [dʌmp] n (also: rubbish dump) décharge (publique); (pej) trou m ♦ vt (put down) déposer; déverser; (get rid of) se débarrasser de; (COMPUT: data) vider, transférer

dumpling ['dʌmplɪŋ] n boulette f (de pâte)

dumpy ['dʌmpɪ] adj boulot(te)

dunce [dʌns] n âne m, cancre m

dune [dju:n] n dune f

dung [dʌŋ] n fumier m

dungarees [dʌŋgə'ri:z] npl salopette f; bleu(s) m(pl)

dungeon ['dʌndʒən] n cachot m

duplex ['dju:pleks] (US) n maison ju-melée; (apartment) duplex m

duplicate [n 'dju:plɪkɪt, vb 'dju:plɪkeɪt] n double m ♦ vt faire un double de; (on machine) polycopier; photocopier; **in** ~ en deux exemplai-res

durable ['djuərəbl] adj durable; (clothes, metal) résistant(e), solide

duration [djuə'reɪʃən] n durée f

duress [djuə'res] n: **under** ~ sous la contrainte

during ['djuərɪŋ] prep pendant, au cours de

dusk [dʌsk] n crépuscule m

dust [dʌst] n poussière f ♦ vt (furni-ture) épousseter, essuyer; (cake etc): **to** ~ **with** saupoudrer de; ~**bin** (BRIT) n poubelle f; ~**er** n chiffon m; ~**man** (BRIT irreg) n boueux m, éboueur m; ~**y** adj poussié-reux(euse)

Dutch [dʌtʃ] adj hollandais(e), néer-landais(e) ♦ n (LING) hollandais m ♦ adv (inf): **to go** ~ partager les frais; **the** ~ npl (people) les Hollan-dais; ~**man** (irreg) n Hollandais; ~**woman** (irreg) n Hollandaise f

dutiful ['dju:tɪful] adj (child) respec-tueux(euse)

duty ['dju:tɪ] n devoir m; (tax) droit m, taxe f; **on** ~ de service; (at night etc) de garde; **off** ~ libre, pas de service or de garde; ~**free** adj exempté(e) de douane, hors taxe inv

duvet ['du:veɪ] (BRIT) n couette f

dwarf [dwɔ:f] (pl **dwarves**) n nain(e) ♦ vt écraser

dwell [dwel] (pt, pp **dwelt**) vi de-meurer; ~ **on** vt fus s'appesantir sur; ~**ing** n habitation f, demeure f

dwindle ['dwɪndl] vi diminuer, dé-croître

dye [daɪ] n teinture f ♦ vt teindre

dying ['daɪɪŋ] adj mourant(e), agoni-sant(e)

dyke [daɪk] (BRIT) n digue f

dynamic [daɪ'næmɪk] adj dynamique

dynamite ['daɪnəmaɪt] n dynamite f

dynamo ['daɪnəməu] n dynamo f

dyslexia [dɪs'leksɪə] n dyslexie f

E

E [i:] n (MUS) mi m

each [i:tʃ] adj chaque ♦ pron chac-un(e); ~ **other** l'un(e) l'autre; **they hate** ~ **other** ils se détestent (mutuellement); **you are jealous of** ~ **other** vous êtes jaloux l'un de l'au-tre; **they have 2 books** ~ ils ont 2 livres chacun

eager ['i:gə*] adj (keen) avide; **to be ~ to do sth** avoir très envie de faire qch; **to be ~ for** désirer vivement, être avide de

eagle ['i:gl] n aigle m

ear [ɪə*] n oreille f; (of corn) épi m; **~ache** n mal m aux oreilles; **~drum** n tympan m

earl [ɜːl] (BRIT) n comte m

earlier ['ɜːlɪə*] adj (date etc) plus rapproché(e); (edition, fashion etc) plus ancien(ne), antérieur(e) ♦ adv plus tôt

early ['ɜːlɪ] adv tôt, de bonne heure; (ahead of time) en avance; (near the beginning) au début ♦ adj qui se manifeste (ou se fait) tôt ou de bonne heure; (work) de jeunesse; (settler, Christian) premier(ère); (reply) rapide; (death) prématuré(e); **to have an ~ night** se coucher tôt ou de bonne heure; **in the ~ or ~ in the spring/19th century** au début du printemps/19ème siècle; **~ retirement** n: **to take ~ retirement** prendre sa retraite anticipée

earmark ['ɪəmɑːk] vt: **to ~ sth for** réserver ou destiner qch à

earn [ɜːn] vt gagner; (COMM: yield) rapporter

earnest ['ɜːnɪst] adj sérieux(euse); **in ~** adv sérieusement

earnings ['ɜːnɪŋz] npl salaire m; (of company) bénéfices mpl

earphones ['ɪəfəʊnz] npl écouteurs mpl

earring ['ɪərɪŋ] n boucle f d'oreille

earshot ['ɪəʃɔt] n: **within ~** à portée de voix

earth [ɜːθ] n (gen, also BRIT: ELEC) terre f ♦ vt relier à la terre; **~enware** n poterie f; faïence f; **~quake** n tremblement m de terre, séisme m; **~y** [ɜːθɪ] adj (vulgar: humour) truculent(e)

ease [i:z] n facilité f, aisance f; (comfort) bien-être m ♦ vt (soothe) calmer; (loosen) relâcher, détendre; **to ~ sth in/out** faire pénétrer/sortir

qch délicatement or avec douceur; faciliter la pénétration/la sortie de qch; **at ~!** (MIL) repos!; **~ off** vi diminuer; (slow down) ralentir; **~ up** vi = ease off

easel ['i:zl] n chevalet m

easily ['i:zɪlɪ] adv facilement

east [i:st] n est m; (wind) d'est; (side) est inv ♦ adv à l'est, vers l'est; **the E~** l'Orient m; (POL) les pays mpl de l'Est

Easter ['i:stə*] n Pâques fpl; **~ egg** n œuf m de Pâques

east: ~erly ['i:stəlɪ] adj (wind) d'est; (direction) est inv; (point) à l'est; **~ern** ['i:stən] adj de l'est, oriental(e); **~ward(s)** ['i:stwəd(z)] adv vers l'est, à l'est

easy ['i:zɪ] adj facile; (manner) aisé(e) ♦ adv: **to take it or things ~** ne pas se fatiguer; (not worry) ne pas (trop) s'en faire; **~ chair** n fauteuil m; **~going** adj accommodant(e), facile à vivre

eat [i:t] (pt ate, pp eaten) vt, vi manger; **~ away at** vt fus ronger, attaquer; (savings) entamer; **~ into** vt fus = eat away at

eaves [i:vz] npl avant-toit m

eavesdrop ['i:vzdrɔp] vi: **to ~ (on a conversation)** écouter (une conversation) de façon indiscrète

ebb [eb] n reflux m ♦ vi refluer; (fig: also: **~ away**) décliner

ebony ['ebənɪ] n ébène f

EC n abbr (= European Community) C.E.E.

eccentric [ɪk'sentrɪk] adj excentrique ♦ n excentrique m/f

echo ['ekəʊ] (pl ~es) n écho m ♦ vt répéter ♦ vi résonner, faire écho

eclipse [ɪ'klɪps] n éclipse f

ecology [ɪ'kɔlədʒɪ] n écologie f

economic [i:kə'nɔmɪk] adj économique; (business etc) rentable; **~al** adj économique; (person) économe; **~s** n économie f politique ♦ npl (of project, situation) aspect m financier

economize [ɪ'kɔnəmaɪz] vi économiser, faire des économies

economy [ɪˈkɒnəmɪ] n économie f; ~ **class** n classe f touriste; ~ **size** n format m économique

ecstasy [ˈekstəsɪ] n extase f; **ecstatic** adj extatique

ECU [ˈeɪkjuː] n abbr (= European Currency Unit) ECU m

eczema [ˈeksɪmə] n eczéma m

edge [edʒ] n bord m; (of knife etc) tranchant m, fil m ♦ vt border; **on** ~ (fig) crispé(e), tendu(e); **to ~ away from** s'éloigner furtivement de; **~ways** adv: **he couldn't get a word in** ~**ways** il ne pouvait pas placer un mot

edgy [ˈedʒɪ] adj crispé(e), tendu(e)

edible [ˈedɪbl] adj comestible

edict [ˈiːdɪkt] n décret m

Edinburgh [ˈedɪnbərə] n Édimbourg

edit [ˈedɪt] vt (text, book) éditer; (report) préparer; (film) monter; (broadcast) réaliser; **~ion** [ɪˈdɪʃən] n édition f; **~or** n (of column) rédacteur(trice); (of newspaper) rédacteur(trice) en chef; (of sb's work) éditeur(trice); **~orial** [edɪˈtɔːrɪəl] adj de la rédaction, éditorial(e) ♦ n éditorial m

educate [ˈedjʊkeɪt] vt (teach) instruire; (instruct) éduquer

education [edjʊˈkeɪʃən] n éducation f; (studies) études fpl; (teaching) enseignement m, instruction f; **~al** adj (experience, toy) pédagogique; (institution) scolaire; (policy) d'éducation

eel [iːl] n anguille f

eerie [ˈɪərɪ] adj inquiétant(e)

effect [ɪˈfekt] n effet m ♦ vt effectuer; **to take** ~ (law) entrer en vigueur, prendre effet; (drug) agir, faire son effet; **in** ~ en fait; **~ive** adj efficace; (actual) véritable; **~ively** adv efficacement; (in reality) effectivement; **~iveness** n efficacité f

effeminate [ɪˈfemɪnɪt] adj efféminé(e)

effervescent [efəˈvesnt] adj (drink) gazeux(euse)

efficiency [ɪˈfɪʃənsɪ] n efficacité f;

(of machine) rendement m

efficient [ɪˈfɪʃənt] adj efficace; (machine) qui a un bon rendement

effort [ˈefət] n effort m; **~less** adj (style) aisé(e); (achievement) facile

effusive [ɪˈfjuːsɪv] adj chaleureux(euse)

e.g. adv abbr (= exempli gratia) par exemple, p.e.

egg [eg] n œuf m; **hard-boiled/soft-boiled** ~ œuf dur/à la coque; ~ **on** vt pousser; **~cup** n coquetier m; **~plant** n (esp US) aubergine f; **~shell** n coquille f d'œuf

ego [ˈiːgəʊ] n (self-esteem) amour-propre m

egotism [ˈegəʊtɪzəm] n égotisme m

egotist [ˈegəʊtɪst] n égocentrique m/f

Egypt [ˈiːdʒɪpt] n Égypte f; **~ian** [ɪˈdʒɪpʃən] adj égyptien(ne) ♦ n Égyptien(ne)

eiderdown [ˈaɪdədaʊn] n édredon m

eight [eɪt] num huit; **~een** num dix-huit; **~h** [eɪtθ] num huitième; **~y** num quatre-vingts

Eire [ˈɛərə] n République f d'Irlande

either [ˈaɪðə*] adj l'un ou l'autre; (both, each) chaque ♦ pron: ~ (of them) l'un ou l'autre ♦ adv non plus ♦ conj: ~ **good or bad** ou bon ou mauvais, soit bon soit mauvais; **on** ~ **side** de chaque côté; **I don't like** ~ je n'aime ni l'un ni l'autre; **no, I don't** ~ moi non plus

eject [ɪˈdʒekt] vt (tenant etc) expulser; (object) éjecter

eke [iːk] : **to** ~ **out** vt faire durer

elaborate [adj ɪˈlæbərɪt, vb ɪˈlæbəreɪt] adj compliqué(e), recherché(e) ♦ vt élaborer ♦ vi: **to** ~ **(on)** entrer dans les détails (de)

elapse [ɪˈlæps] vi s'écouler, passer

elastic [ɪˈlæstɪk] adj élastique ♦ n élastique m; **to** ~ **band** n élastique m

elated [ɪˈleɪtɪd] adj transporté(e) de joie

elation [ɪˈleɪʃən] n allégresse f

elbow [ˈelbəʊ] n coude m

elder [ˈeldə*] adj aîné(e) ♦ n (tree) sureau m; **one's** ~**s** ses aînés; **~ly**

adj âgé(e) ♦ *npl*: **the ~ly** les personnes âgées

eldest ['ɛldɪst] *adj, n*: **the ~ (child)** l'aîné(e) (des enfants)

elect [ɪ'lɛkt] *vt* élire ♦ *adj*: **the president ~** le président désigné; **to ~ to do** choisir de faire; **~ion** [ɪ'lɛkʃən] *n* élection *f*; **~ioneering** [ɪlɛkʃə'nɪərɪŋ] *n* propagande électorale, manœuvres électorales; **~or** *n* électeur(trice); **~orate** *n* électorat *m*

electric [ɪ'lɛktrɪk] *adj* électrique; **~al** *adj* électrique; **~ blanket** *n* couverture chauffante; **~ fire** (*BRIT*) *n* radiateur *m* électrique; **~ian** [ɪlɛk'trɪʃən] *n* électricien *m*

electricity [ɪlɛk'trɪsɪtɪ] *n* électricité *f*

electrify [ɪ'lɛktrɪfaɪ] *vt* (*RAIL, fence*) électrifier; (*audience*) électriser

electronic [ɪlɛk'trɒnɪk] *adj* électronique; **~s** *n* électronique *f*

elegant ['ɛlɪɡənt] *adj* élégant(e)

element ['ɛlɪmənt] *n* (*gen*) élément *m*; (*of heater, kettle etc*) résistance *f*; **~ary** [ɛlɪ'mɛntərɪ] *adj* élémentaire; (*school, education*) primaire

elephant ['ɛlɪfənt] *n* éléphant *m*

elevation [ɛlɪ'veɪʃən] *n* (*raising, promotion*) avancement *m*, promotion *f*; (*height*) hauteur *f*

elevator ['ɛlɪveɪtə*] *n* (*in warehouse etc*) élévateur *m*, monte-charge *m inv*; (*US: lift*) ascenseur *m*

eleven [ɪ'lɛvn] *num* onze; **~ses** *npl* ~ pause-café *f*; **~th** *num* onzième

elicit [ɪ'lɪsɪt] *vt*: **to ~ (from)** obtenir (de), arracher (à)

eligible ['ɛlɪdʒəbl] *adj*: **to be ~ for** remplir les conditions requises pour; **an ~ young man/woman** un beau parti

elm [ɛlm] *n* orme *m*

elongated ['iːlɒŋɡeɪtɪd] *adj* allongé(e)

elope [ɪ'ləʊp] *vi* (*lovers*) s'enfuir (ensemble); **~ment** [ɪləʊpmənt] *n* fugue amoureuse

eloquent ['ɛləkwənt] *adj* éloquent(e)

else [ɛls] *adv* d'autre; **something ~** quelque chose d'autre, autre chose;

somewhere ~ ailleurs, autre part; **everywhere ~** partout ailleurs; **nobody ~** personne d'autre; **where ~?** à quel endroit?; **little ~** pas grand-chose d'autre; **~where** *adv* ailleurs, autre part

elude [ɪ'luːd] *vt* échapper à

elusive [ɪ'luːsɪv] *adj* insaisissable

emaciated [ɪ'meɪsɪeɪtɪd] *adj* émacié(e), décharné(e)

emancipate [ɪ'mænsɪpeɪt] *vt* émanciper

embankment [ɪm'bæŋkmənt] *n* (*of road, railway*) remblai *m*, talus *m*; (*of river*) berge *f*, quai *m*

embark [ɪm'bɑːk] *vi* embarquer; **to ~ on** (*journey*) entreprendre; (*fig*) se lancer ou s'embarquer dans; **~ation** [ɛmbɑː'keɪʃən] *n* embarquement *m*

embarrass [ɪm'bærəs] *vt* embarrasser, gêner; **~ed** *adj* gêné(e); **~ing** *adj* gênant(e), embarrassant(e); **~ment** *n* embarras *m*, gêne *f*

embassy ['ɛmbəsɪ] *n* ambassade *f*

embedded [ɪm'bɛdɪd] *adj* enfoncé(e)

embellish [ɪm'bɛlɪʃ] *vt* orner, décorer; (*fig: account*) enjoliver

embers ['ɛmbəz] *npl* braise *f*

embezzle [ɪm'bɛzl] *vt* détourner

embezzlement [ɪm'bɛzlmənt] *n* détournement *m* de fonds

embitter [ɪm'bɪtə*] *vt* (*person*) aigrir; (*relations*) envenimer

embody [ɪm'bɒdɪ] *vt* (*features*) réunir, comprendre; (*ideas*) formuler, exprimer

embossed [ɪm'bɒst] *adj* (*metal*) estampé(e); (*leather*) frappé(e); **~ wallpaper** papier gaufré

embrace [ɪm'breɪs] *vt* embrasser, étreindre; (*include*) embrasser ♦ *vi* s'étreindre, s'embrasser ♦ *n* étreinte *f*

embroider [ɪm'brɔɪdə*] *vt* broder; **~y** *n* broderie *f*

emerald ['ɛmərəld] *n* émeraude *f*

emerge [ɪ'mɜːdʒ] *vi* apparaître; (*from room, car*) surgir; (*from* _sleep, imprisonment_) sortir

emergency [ɪˈmɜːdʒənsɪ] _n_ urgence _f_; **in an ~** en cas d'urgence; **~ cord** _n_ sonnette _f_ d'alarme; **~ exit** _n_ sortie _f_ de secours; **~ landing** _n_ atterrissage forcé; **~ services** _npl_: **the ~ services** (_fire, police, ambulance_) les services _mpl_ d'urgence

emergent [ɪˈmɜːdʒənt] _adj_ (_nation_) en voie de développement; (_group_) en développement

emery board [ˈemərɪ-] _n_ lime _f_ à ongles (_en carton émerisé_)

emigrate [ˈemɪɡreɪt] _vi_ émigrer

eminent [ˈemɪnənt] _adj_ éminent(e)

emissions [ɪˈmɪʃənz] _npl_ émissions _fpl_

emit [ɪˈmɪt] _vt_ émettre

emotion [ɪˈməuʃən] _n_ émotion _f_; **~al** _adj_ (_person_) émotif(ive), très sensible; (_needs, exhaustion_) affectif(ive); (_scene_) émouvant(e); (_tone, speech_) qui fait appel aux sentiments

emotive [ɪˈməutɪv] _adj_ chargé(e) d'émotion; (_subject_) sensible

emperor [ˈempərə*] _n_ empereur _m_

emphasis [ˈemfəsɪs] (_pl_ -**ases**) _n_ (_stress_) accent _m_; (_importance_) insistance _f_

emphasize [ˈemfəsaɪz] _vt_ (_syllable, word, point_) appuyer or insister sur; (_feature_) souligner, accentuer

emphatic [ɪmˈfætɪk] _adj_ (_strong_) énergique, vigoureux(euse); (_unambiguous, clear_) catégorique; **~ally** [ɪmˈfætɪkəlɪ] _adv_ avec vigueur or énergie; catégoriquement

empire [ˈempaɪə*] _n_ empire _m_

employ [ɪmˈplɔɪ] _vt_ employer; **~ee** _n_ employé(e); **~er** _n_ employeur(euse); **~ment** _n_ emploi _m_; **~ment agency** _n_ agence _f_ or bureau _m_ de placement

empower [ɪmˈpauə*] _vt_: **to ~ sb to do** autoriser or habiliter qn à faire

empress [ˈemprɪs] _n_ impératrice _f_

emptiness [ˈemptɪnəs] _n_ (_of area, region_) aspect _m_ désertique _m_; (_of life_) vide _m_, vacuité _f_

empty [ˈemptɪ] _adj_ vide; (_threat,_

promise) en l'air, vain(e) ♦ _vt_ vider ♦ _vi_ se vider; (_liquid_) s'écouler; **~-handed** _adj_ les mains vides

emulate [ˈemjuleɪt] _vt_ rivaliser avec, imiter

emulsion [ɪˈmʌlʃən] _n_ émulsion _f_; **~ (paint)** _n_ peinture mate

enable [ɪˈneɪbl] _vt_: **to ~ sb to do** permettre à qn de faire

enact [ɪnˈækt] _vt_ (_law_) promulguer; (_play_) jouer

enamel [ɪˈnæməl] _n_ émail _m_; (_also: ~ paint_) peinture laquée

enamoured [ɪnˈæməd] _adj_: **to be ~ of** être entiché(e) de

encased [ɪnˈkeɪst] _adj_: **~ in** enfermé(e) or enchassé(e) dans

enchant [ɪnˈtʃɑːnt] _vt_ enchanter; **~ing** _adj_ ravissant(e), enchanteur(teresse)

encl. _abbr_ = **enclosed**

enclose [ɪnˈkləuz] _vt_ (_land_) clôturer; (_space, object_) entourer; (_letter etc_): **to ~ (with)** joindre (à); **please find ~d** veuillez trouver ci-joint

enclosure [ɪnˈkləuʒə*] _n_ enceinte _f_

encompass [ɪnˈkʌmpəs] _vt_ (_include_) contenir, inclure

encore [ˈɒŋkɔː*] _excl_ bis ♦ _n_ bis _m_

encounter [ɪnˈkauntə*] _n_ rencontre _f_ ♦ _vt_ rencontrer

encourage [ɪnˈkʌrɪdʒ] _vt_ encourager; **~ment** _n_ encouragement _m_

encroach [ɪnˈkrəutʃ] _vi_: **to ~ (up)on** empiéter sur

encyclop(a)edia [ensaɪkləuˈpiːdɪə] _n_ encyclopédie _f_

end [end] _n_ (_gen, also: aim_) fin _f_; (_of table, street, rope etc_) bout _m_, extrémité _f_ ♦ _vt_ terminer; (_also: bring to an ~, put an ~ to_) mettre fin à ♦ _vi_ se terminer, finir; **in the ~** finalement; **on** (_object_) debout, dressé(e); **to stand on ~** (_hair_) se dresser sur la tête; **for hours on ~** pendant des heures et des heures; **~ up** _vi_: **to ~ up in** (_condition_) finir or se terminer par; (_place_) finir or aboutir à

endanger [ɪnˈdeɪndʒə*] _vt_ mettre en

endearing

endearing 89 **enrol**

danger

endearing [ɪn'dɪərɪŋ] adj attachant(e)

endeavour [ɪn'devə*] (US **endeavor**) n tentative f, effort m ♦ vi: **to ~** to do tenter or s'efforcer de faire

ending ['endɪŋ] n dénouement m, fin f; (LING) terminaison f

endive ['endaɪv] n chicorée f; (smooth) endive f

endless ['endlɪs] adj sans fin, interminable

endorse [ɪn'dɔːs] vt (cheque) endosser; (approve) appuyer, approuver, sanctionner; **~ment** n (approval) appui m, aval m; (BRIT: on driving licence) contravention portée au permis de conduire

endow [ɪn'dau] vt: **to ~ with** (fig) doter (de)

endure [ɪn'djuə*] vt supporter, endurer ♦ vi durer

enemy ['enɪmɪ] adj, n ennemi(e)

energetic [enə'dʒetɪk] adj énergique; (activity) qui fait se dépenser (physiquement)

energy ['enədʒɪ] n énergie f

enforce [ɪn'fɔːs] vt (LAW) appliquer, faire respecter

engage [ɪn'geɪdʒ] vt engager; (attention etc) retenir ♦ vi (TECH) s'enclencher, s'engrener; **to ~ in** se lancer dans; **~d** adj (BRIT: busy, in use) occupé(e); (betrothed) fiancé(e); **to get ~d** se fiancer; **~d tone** n (TEL) tonalité f occupé inv or pas libre; **~ment** n obligation f, engagement m; rendez-vous m inv; (to marry) fiançailles fpl; **~ment ring** n bague f de fiançailles

engaging [ɪn'geɪdʒɪŋ] adj engageant(e), attirant(e)

engender [ɪn'dʒendə*] vt produire, causer

engine ['endʒɪn] n (AUT) moteur m; (RAIL) locomotive f; **~ driver** n mécanicien m

engineer [endʒɪ'nɪə*] n ingénieur m; (BRIT: repairer) dépanneur m; (NAVY, US RAIL) mécanicien m;

~ing [-'nɪərɪŋ] n engineering m, ingénierie f; (of bridges, ships) génie m; (of machine) mécanique f

England ['ɪŋglənd] n Angleterre f

English ['ɪŋglɪʃ] adj anglais(e) ♦ n (LING) anglais m; the **~** npl (people) les Anglais; the **~ Channel** la Manche; **~man** (irreg) n Anglais; **~woman** (irreg) n Anglaise f

engraving [ɪn'greɪvɪŋ] n gravure f

engrossed [ɪn'grəust] adj: **~ in** absorbé(e) par, plongé(e) dans

engulf [ɪn'gʌlf] vt engloutir

enhance [ɪn'hɑːns] vt rehausser, mettre en valeur

enjoy [ɪn'dʒɔɪ] vt aimer, prendre plaisir à; (have: health, fortune) jouir de; (: success) connaître; **to ~ o.s.** s'amuser; **~able** adj agréable; **~ment** n plaisir m

enlarge [ɪn'lɑːdʒ] vt accroître; (PHOT) agrandir ♦ vi: **to ~ on** (subject) s'étendre sur; **~ment** n (PHOT) agrandissement m

enlighten [ɪn'laɪtn] vt éclairer; **~ed** adj éclairé(e); **~ment** n: the **E~ment** (HISTORY) ≈ le Siècle des lumières

enlist [ɪn'lɪst] vt recruter; (support) s'assurer ♦ vi s'engager

enmity ['enmɪtɪ] n inimitié f

enormous [ɪ'nɔːməs] adj énorme

enough [ɪ'nʌf] adj, pron: **~ time/ books** assez or suffisamment de temps/livres ♦ adv: **big ~** assez or suffisamment grand; **have you got ~?** en avez-vous assez?; **he has not worked ~** il n'a pas assez or suffisamment travaillé; **~ to eat** assez à manger; **~!** assez!, ça suffit!; **that's ~, thanks** cela suffit or c'est assez, merci; **I've had ~ of him** j'en ai assez de lui; ... **which, funnily or oddly ~** ... qui, chose curieuse

enquire [ɪn'kwaɪə*] vt, vi = **inquire**

enrage [ɪn'reɪdʒ] vt mettre en fureur or en rage, rendre furieux(euse)

enrol [ɪn'rəul] (US **~l**) vt inscrire ♦ vi s'inscrire; **~ment** (US **~lment**) n inscription f

ensue [ɪn'sjuː] vi s'ensuivre, résulter

ensure [ɪn'ʃʊə*] vt assurer; garantir; to ~ that s'assurer que

entail [ɪn'teɪl] vt entraîner, occasionner

entangled [ɪn'tæŋgld] adj: to become ~ (in) s'empêtrer (dans)

enter ['entə*] vt (room) entrer dans, pénétrer dans; (club, army) entrer à; (competition) s'inscrire à or pour; (sb for a competition) (faire) inscrire; (write down) inscrire, noter; (COMPUT) entrer, introduire ♦ vi entrer; ~ **for** vt fus s'inscrire à, se présenter pour or à; ~ **into** vt fus (explanation) se lancer dans; (discussion, negotiations) entamer; (agreement) conclure

enterprise ['entəpraɪz] n entreprise f; (initiative) (esprit m d')initiative f; **free** ~ libre entreprise; **private** ~ entreprise privée

enterprising ['entəpraɪzɪŋ] adj entreprenant(e), dynamique; (scheme) audacieux(euse)

entertain [entə'teɪn] vt amuser, distraire; (invite) recevoir (à dîner); (idea, plan) envisager; ~**er** n artiste m/f de variétés; ~**ing** adj amusant(e), distrayant(e); ~**ment** n (amusement) divertissement m, amusement m; (show) spectacle m

enthralled [ɪn'θrɔːld] adj captivé(e)

enthusiasm [ɪn'θuːzɪæzəm] n enthousiasme m

enthusiast [ɪn'θuːzɪæst] n enthousiaste m/f; ~**ic** [ɪnθuːzɪ'æstɪk] adj enthousiaste; to be ~**ic about** être enthousiasmé(e) par

entice [ɪn'taɪs] vt attirer, séduire

entire [ɪn'taɪə*] adj (tout) entier(ère); ~**ly** adv entièrement, complètement; ~**ty** [ɪn'taɪərətɪ] n: in its ~**ty** dans sa totalité

entitle [ɪn'taɪtl] vt: to ~ **sb to sth** donner droit à qch à qn; ~**d** adj (book) intitulé(e); to be ~**d to do** avoir le droit de or être habilité à faire

entrance [n 'entrəns, vb ɪn'trɑːns] n entrée f ♦ vt enchanter, ravir; to **gain** ~ **to** (university etc) être admis à; ~ **examination** n examen m d'entrée; ~ **fee** n (to museum etc) prix m d'entrée; (to join club etc) droit m d'inscription; ~ **ramp** (US) n (AUT) bretelle f d'accès

entrant ['entrənt] n participant(e); concurrent(e); (BRIT: in exam) candidat(e)

entrenched [ɪn'trentʃt] adj retranché(e); (ideas) arrêté(e)

entrepreneur [ɒntrəprə'nɜː*] n entrepreneur m

entrust [ɪn'trʌst] vt: to ~ **sth to** confier qch à

entry ['entrɪ] n entrée f; (in register) inscription f; **no** ~ défense d'entrer, entrée interdite; (AUT) sens interdit; ~ **form** n feuille f d'inscription; ~ **phone** (BRIT) n interphone m

enunciate [ɪ'nʌnsɪeɪt] vt énoncer; (word) articuler, prononcer

envelop [ɪn'veləp] vt envelopper

envelope ['envələʊp] n enveloppe f

envious ['envɪəs] adj envieux(euse)

environment [ɪn'vaɪərənmənt] n environnement m; (social, moral) milieu m; ~**al** [ɪnvaɪərən'mentl] adj écologique; du milieu; ~**friendly** adj écologique

envisage [ɪn'vɪzɪdʒ] vt (foresee) prévoir

envoy ['envɔɪ] n (diplomat) ministre m plénipotentiaire

envy ['envɪ] n envie f ♦ vt envier; to ~ **sb sth** envier qch à qn

epic ['epɪk] n épopée f ♦ adj épique

epidemic [epɪ'demɪk] n épidémie f

epilepsy ['epɪlepsɪ] n épilepsie f

episode ['epɪsəʊd] n épisode m

epitome [ɪ'pɪtəmɪ] n modèle m;

epitomize [ɪ'pɪtəmaɪz] vt incarner

equable ['ekwəbl] adj égal(e); de tempérament égal

equal ['iːkwl] adj égal(e) ♦ n égal(e) ♦ vt égaler; to ~ (to) (task) à la hauteur de; ~**ity** [iː'kwɒlɪtɪ] n égalité f; ~**ize** vi (SPORT) égaliser; ~**ly** adv également; *(just as)* tout aussi

equanimity [ɛkwə'nɪmɪtɪ] n égalité f d'humeur

equate [ɪ'kweɪt] vt: to ~ sth with comparer qch à; assimiler qch à; **equation** [ɪ'kweɪʒən] n *(MATH)* équation f

equator [ɪ'kweɪtə*] n équateur m

equilibrium [iːkwɪ'lɪbrɪəm] n équilibre m

equip [ɪ'kwɪp] vt: to ~ (with) équiper (de); **to be well** ~**ped** *(office etc)* être bien équipé(e); **he is well** ~**ped for the job** il a les compétences requises pour ce travail; ~**ment** n équipement m; *(electrical etc)* appareillage m, installation f

equities ['ɛkwɪtɪz] *(BRIT)* npl *(COMM)* actions cotées en Bourse

equivalent [ɪ'kwɪvələnt] adj: ~ (to) équivalent(e) (à) ♦ n équivalent m

equivocal [ɪ'kwɪvəkəl] adj équivoque; *(open to suspicion)* douteux (euse)

era ['ɪərə] n ère f, époque f

eradicate [ɪ'rædɪkeɪt] vt éliminer

erase [ɪ'reɪz] vt effacer; ~**r** n gomme f

erect [ɪ'rɛkt] adj droit(e) ♦ vt construire; *(monument)* ériger; élever; *(tent etc)* dresser; ~**ion** [ɪ'rɛkʃən] n érection f

ERM n abbr (= *Exchange Rate Mechanism*) SME m

erode [ɪ'rəud] vt éroder; *(metal)* ronger

erotic [ɪ'rɒtɪk] adj érotique

err [ɜː*] vi *(formal: make a mistake)* se tromper

errand ['ɛrənd] n course f, commission f

erratic [ɪ'rætɪk] adj irrégulier(ère), inconstant(e)

error ['ɛrə*] n erreur f

erupt [ɪ'rʌpt] vi entrer en éruption; *(fig)* éclater; ~**ion** [ɪ'rʌpʃən] n éruption f

escalate ['ɛskəleɪt] vi s'intensifier

escalator ['ɛskəleɪtə*] n escalier roulant

escapade [ɛskə'peɪd] n fredaine f; équipée f

escape [ɪs'keɪp] n fuite f; *(from prison)* évasion f ♦ vi s'échapper, fuir; *(from jail)* s'évader; *(fig)* s'en tirer; *(leak)* échapper ♦ vt échapper à; **to** ~ **from** *(person)* échapper à; *(place)* s'échapper de; *(fig)* fuir; **es-capism** [-ɪzəm] n *(fig)* évasion f

escort [n 'ɛskɔːt, vb ɪs'kɔːt] n escorte f ♦ vt escorter

Eskimo ['ɛskɪməu] n Esquimau(de)

esophagus [iː'sɒfəgəs] *(US)* n = **oesophagus**

especially [ɪs'pɛʃəlɪ] adv *(particularly)* particulièrement; *(above all)* surtout

espionage ['ɛspɪənɑːʒ] n espionnage m

Esquire [ɪs'kwaɪə*] n: **J Brown,** ~ Monsieur J. Brown

essay ['ɛseɪ] n *(SCOL)* dissertation f; *(LITERATURE)* essai m

essence ['ɛsəns] n essence f

essential [ɪ'sɛnʃəl] adj essentiel(le); *(basic)* fondamental(e) ♦ n: ~**s** éléments essentiels; ~**ly** adv essentiellement

establish [ɪs'tæblɪʃ] vt établir; *(business)* fonder, créer; *(one's power etc)* asseoir, affirmer; ~**ed** adj bien établi(e); ~**ment** n établissement m; *(founding)* création f; **the E~ment** les pouvoirs établis; l'ordre établi; les milieux dirigeants

estate [ɪs'teɪt] n *(land)* domaine m, propriété f; *(LAW)* biens mpl, succession f; *(BRIT: also: housing ~)* lotissement m, cité f; ~ **agent** n agent immobilier; ~ **car** *(BRIT)* n break m

esteem [ɪs'tiːm] n estime f

esthetic [ɪs'θɛtɪk] *(US)* adj = **aesthetic**

estimate [n 'ɛstɪmət, vb 'ɛstɪmeɪt] n estimation f; *(COMM)* devis m ♦ vt estimer; **estimation** [ɛstɪ'meɪʃən] n opinion f; *(calculation)* estimation f

estranged [ɪs'streɪndʒd] adj séparé(e); dont on s'est séparé(e)

etc. *abbr* (= *et cetera*) etc

etching ['etʃɪŋ] *n* eau-forte *f*

eternal [ɪ'tɜːnl] *adj* éternel(le)

eternity [ɪ'tɜːnɪtɪ] *n* éternité *f*

ethical ['eθɪkəl] *adj* moral(e); **ethics** ['eθɪks] *n* éthique *f* ♦ *npl* moralité *f*

Ethiopia [iːθɪ'əupɪə] *n* Éthiopie *f*

ethnic ['eθnɪk] *adj* ethnique; (*music etc*) folklorique

ethos ['iːθɔs] *n* génie *m*

etiquette ['etɪket] *n* convenances *fpl*, étiquette *f*

Eurocheque ['juərəutʃek] *n* eurochèque *m*

Europe ['juərəp] *n* Europe *f*; **~an** [juərə'piːən] *adj* européen(ne) ♦ *n* Européen(ne)

evacuate [ɪ'vækjueɪt] *vt* évacuer

evade [ɪ'veɪd] *vt* échapper à; (*question etc*) éluder; (*duties*) se dérober à; **to ~ tax** frauder le fisc

evaporate [ɪ'væpəreɪt] *vi* s'évaporer; **~d milk** *n* lait condensé non sucré

evasion [ɪ'veɪʒən] *n* dérobade *f*; **tax ~** fraude fiscale

eve [iːv] *n*: **on the ~ of** à la veille de

even ['iːvən] *adj* (*level, smooth*) régulier(ère); (*equal*) égal(e); (*number*) pair(e) ♦ *adv* même; **~ if** même si +*indic*; **~ though** alors même que +*cond*; **~ more** encore plus; **~ so** quand même; **not ~** pas même; **to get ~ with sb** prendre sa revanche sur qn; **~ out** *vi* s'égaliser

evening ['iːvnɪŋ] *n* soir *m*; (*as duration, event*) soirée *f*; **in the ~** le soir; **~ class** *n* cours *m* du soir; **~ dress** *n* tenue *f* de soirée

event [ɪ'vent] *n* événement *m*; (*SPORT*) épreuve *f*; **in the ~ of** en cas de; **~ful** *adj* mouvementé(e)

eventual [ɪ'ventʃuəl] *adj* final(e); **~ity** [ɪventʃu'ælɪtɪ] *n* possibilité *f*, éventualité *f*; **~ly** *adv* finalement

ever ['evə'] *adv* jamais; (*at all times*) toujours; **the best ~** le meilleur qu'on ait jamais vu; **have you ~ seen it?** l'as-tu déjà vu?, as-tu eu l'occasion ou t'est-il arrivé de le

voir?; **why ~ not?** mais enfin, pourquoi pas?; **~ since** *adv* depuis ♦ *conj* depuis que; **~green** *n* arbre *m* à feuilles persistantes; **~lasting** *adj* éternel(le)

every ['evrɪ] *adj* chaque; **~ day** tous les jours, chaque jour; **~ other/third day** tous les deux/trois jours; **~ other car** une voiture sur deux; **~ now and then** de temps en temps; **~body** *pron* tout le monde, tous *pl*; **~day** *adj* quotidien(ne); de tous les jours; **~one** *pron* = **everybody**; **~thing** *pron* tout; **~where** *adv* partout

evict [ɪ'vɪkt] *vt* expulser; **~ion** [ɪ'vɪkʃən] *n* expulsion *f*

evidence ['evɪdəns] *n* (*proof*) preuve(s) *f(pl)*; (*of witness*) témoignage *m*; (*sign*): **to show ~** présenter des signes de; **to give ~** témoigner, déposer

evident ['evɪdənt] *adj* évident(e); **~ly** *adv* de toute évidence; (*apparently*) apparemment

evil ['iːvl] *adj* mauvais(e) ♦ *n* mal *m*

evoke [ɪ'vəuk] *vt* évoquer

evolution [iːvə'luːʃən] *n* évolution *f*

evolve [ɪ'vɔlv] *vt* élaborer ♦ *vi* évoluer

ewe [juː] *n* brebis *f*

ex- [eks] *prefix* ex-

exact [ɪg'zækt] *adj* exact(e) ♦ *vt*: **to ~ sth (from)** extorquer qch (à); exiger qch (de); **~ing** *adj* exigeant(e); (*work*) astreignant(e); **~ly** *adv* exactement

exaggerate [ɪg'zædʒəreɪt] *vt, vi* exagérer; **exaggeration** [ɪgzædʒə'reɪʃən] *n* exagération *f*

exalted [ɪg'zɔːltɪd] *adj* (*prominent*) élevé(e); (*: person*) haut placé(e)

exam [ɪg'zæm] *n abbr* (*SCOL*) = **examination**

examination [ɪgzæmɪ'neɪʃən] *n* (*SCOL, MED*) examen *m*

examine [ɪg'zæmɪn] *vt* (*gen*) examiner; (*SCOL: person*) interroger; **~r** *n* examinateur(trice)

example [ɪg'zɑːmpl] *n* exemple *m*;

for ~ par exemple

exasperate [ɪg'zɑːspəreɪt] vt exaspérer; **exasperation** [ɪgzɑːspə'reɪʃən] n exaspération f, irritation f

excavate ['ekskəveɪt] vt excaver; **excavation** [ekskə'veɪʃən] n fouilles fpl

exceed [ɪk'siːd] vt dépasser; (one's powers) outrepasser; **~ingly** adv extrêmement

excellent ['eksələnt] adj excellent(e)

except [ɪk'sept] prep (also: ~ for, ~ing) sauf, excepté ♦ vt excepter; ~ if/when sauf si/quand; ~ that sauf que, si ce n'est que; **~ion** [ɪk'sepʃən] n exception f; to take ~ion to s'offusquer de; **~ional** [ɪk'sepʃənl] adj exceptionnel(le)

excerpt ['eksɜːpt] n extrait m

excess [ɪk'ses] n excès m; ~ **baggage** n excédent m de bagages; ~ **fare** (BRIT) n supplément m; **~ive** adj excessif(ive)

exchange [ɪks'tʃeɪndʒ] n échange m; (also: telephone ~) central m ♦ vt: to ~ (for) échanger (contre); ~ **rate** n taux m de change

Exchequer [ɪks'tʃekə*] (BRIT) n: the ~ l'Echiquier m, ≈ le ministère des Finances

excise [n 'eksaɪz, vb ek'saɪz] n taxe f ♦ vt exciser

excite [ɪk'saɪt] vt exciter; to get ~d s'exciter; **~ment** n excitation f; **exciting** adj passionnant(e)

exclaim [ɪks'kleɪm] vi s'exclamer; **exclamation** [ekskla'meɪʃən] n exclamation f; **exclamation mark** n point m d'exclamation

exclude [ɪks'kluːd] vt exclure

exclusive [ɪks'kluːsɪv] adj exclusif(ive); (club, district) sélect(e); (item of news) en exclusivité; ~ of VAT TVA non comprise; **mutually** ~ qui s'excluent l'un(e) l'autre

excruciating [ɪks'kruːʃɪeɪtɪŋ] adj atroce

excursion [ɪks'kɜːʃən] n excursion f

excuse [n ɪks'kjuːs, vb ɪks'kjuːz] n excuse f ♦ vt excuser; to ~ sb from

(activity) dispenser qn de; ~ **me!** excusez-moi!, pardon!; now if you will ~ me, ... maintenant, si vous (le) permettez ...

ex-directory ['eksdɪ'rektərɪ] (BRIT) adj sur la liste rouge

execute ['eksɪkjuːt] vt exécuter; **execution** [eksɪ'kjuːʃən] n exécution f; **~er** n bourreau m

executive [ɪg'zekjʊtɪv] n (COMM) cadre m; (of organization, political party) bureau m ♦ adj exécutif(ive)

exemplify [ɪg'zemplɪfaɪ] vt illustrer; (typify) incarner

exempt [ɪg'zempt] adj: ~ **from** exempté(e) or dispensé(e) de ♦ vt: to ~ **sb from** exempter or dispenser qn de

exercise ['eksəsaɪz] n exercice m ♦ vt exercer; (patience etc) faire preuve de; (dog) promener ♦ vi prendre de l'exercice; ~ **bike** n vélo m d'appartement; ~ **book** n cahier m

exert [ɪg'zɜːt] vt exercer, employer; to ~ o.s. se dépenser; **~ion** [ɪg'zɜːʃən] n effort m

exhale [eks'heɪl] vt exhaler ♦ vi expirer

exhaust [ɪg'zɔːst] n (also: ~ fumes) gaz mpl d'échappement; (: ~ pipe) tuyau m d'échappement ♦ vt épuiser; **~ed** adj épuisé(e); **~ion** [ɪg'zɔːstʃən] n épuisement m; **nervous ~ion** fatigue nerveuse; surmenage mental; **~ive** adj très complet(ète)

exhibit [ɪg'zɪbɪt] n (ART) pièce exposée, objet exposé; (LAW) pièce à conviction ♦ vt exposer; (courage, skill) faire preuve de; **~ion** [eksɪ'bɪʃən] n exposition f; (of ill-temper, talent etc) démonstration f

exhilarating [ɪg'zɪləreɪtɪŋ] adj grisant(e); stimulant(e)

exile ['eksaɪl] n exil m; (person) exilé(e) ♦ vt exiler

exist [ɪg'zɪst] vi exister; **~ence** n existence f; **~ing** adj actuel(le)

exit ['eksɪt] n sortie f ♦ vi (COMPUT, THEATRE) sortir; ~ **ramp** n (AUT) bretelle f d'accès

exodus ['eksədəs] n exode m

exonerate [ɪg'zɒnəreɪt] vt: to ~ **from** disculper de

exotic [ɪg'zɒtɪk] adj exotique

expand [ɪks'pænd] vt agrandir; accroître ♦ vi (trade etc) se développer, s'accroître; (gas, metal) se dilater

expanse [ɪks'pæns] n étendue f

expansion [ɪks'pænʃən] n développement m, accroissement m

expect [ɪks'pɛkt] vt (anticipate) s'attendre à, s'attendre à ce que +sub; (count on) compter sur, escompter; (require) demander, exiger; (suppose) supposer; (await, also baby) attendre ♦ vi: to be ~ing être enceinte; ~ancy n (anticipation) attente f; life ~ancy espérance f de vie; ~ant mother n future maman; ~ation [ekspek'teɪʃən] n attente f, espérance(s) f(pl)

expedient [ɪks'pi:dɪənt] adj indiqué(e), opportun(e) ♦ n expédient m

expedition [ekspɪ'dɪʃən] n expédition f

expel [ɪks'pɛl] vt chasser, expulser; (SCOL) renvoyer

expend [ɪks'pɛnd] vt consacrer; (money) dépenser; ~iture [ɪk'spɛndɪtʃə*] n dépense f; dépenses fpl

expense [ɪks'pɛns] n dépense f, frais mpl; (high cost) coût m; ~s npl (COMM) frais mpl; at the ~ of aux dépens de; ~ account n (note f de) frais mpl

expensive [ɪks'pɛnsɪv] adj cher(chère), coûteux(euse); to be ~ coûter cher

experience [ɪks'pɪərɪəns] n expérience f ♦ vt connaître, faire l'expérience de; (feeling) éprouver; ~d adj expérimenté(e)

experiment [n ɪks'pɛrɪmənt, vb ɪks'pɛrɪment] n expérience f ♦ vi faire une expérience; to ~ with expérimenter

expert ['ekspɜ:t] adj expert(e) ♦ n

expert m; ~**ise** [ekspə'ti:z] n (grande) compétence f

expire [ɪks'paɪə*] vi expirer; **expiry** n expiration f

explain [ɪks'pleɪn] vt expliquer; **explanation** [eksplə'neɪʃən] n explication f; **explanatory** [ɪks'plænətərɪ] adj explicatif(ive)

explicit [ɪks'plɪsɪt] adj explicite; (definite) formel(le)

explode [ɪks'pləʊd] vi exploser

exploit [n 'eksplɔɪt, vb ɪks'plɔɪt] n exploit m ♦ vt exploiter; ~**ation** [eksplɔɪ'teɪʃən] n exploitation f

exploratory [eks'plɔrətərɪ] adj (expedition) d'exploration; (fig: talks) préliminaire; ~ **operation** n (MED) sondage m

explore [ɪks'plɔ:*] vt explorer; (possibilities) étudier, examiner; ~**r** n explorateur(trice)

explosion [ɪks'pləʊʒən] n explosion f; **explosive** [ɪks'pləʊzɪv] adj explosif(ive) ♦ n explosif m

exponent [eks'pəʊnənt] n (of school of thought etc) interprète m, représentant m

export [vb eks'pɔ:t, n 'ekspɔ:t] vt exporter ♦ n exportation f ♦ cpd d'exportation; ~**er** n exportateur m

expose [ɪks'pəʊz] vt exposer; (unmask) démasquer, dévoiler; ~**d** [ɪks'pəʊzd] adj (position, house) exposé(e)

exposure [ɪks'pəʊʒə*] n exposition f; (publicity) couverture f; (PHOT) (temps m de) pose f; (: shot) pose; to die ~ **from** ~ (MED) mourir de froid; ~ **meter** n posemètre m

express [ɪks'prɛs] adj (definite) formel(le), exprès(esse); (BRIT: letter etc) exprès inv ♦ n (train) rapide m; (bus) car m express ♦ vt exprimer; ~**ion** [ɪks'prɛʃən] n expression f; ~**ly** adv expressément, formellement; ~**way** (US) n (urban motorway) voie f express (à plusieurs files)

exquisite [ɛks'kwɪzɪt] adj exquis(e)

extend [ɪks'tɛnd] vt (visit, street) prolonger; (building) agrandir; (of-

fer) présenter, offrir; (*hand, arm*) tendre ♦ *vi* s'étendre

extension [ɪksˈtɛnʃən] *n* prolongation *f*; agrandissement *m*; (*building*) annexe *f*; (*to wire, table*) rallonge *f*; (*telephone: in offices*) poste *m*; (: *in private house*) téléphone *m* supplémentaire

extensive [ɪksˈtɛnsɪv] *adj* étendu(e), vaste; (*damage, alterations*) considérable; (*inquiries*) approfondi(e); **~ly** *adv*: **he's travelled ~ly** il a beaucoup voyagé

extent [ɪksˈtɛnt] *n* étendue *f*; **to some ~** dans une certaine mesure; **to what ~?** dans quelle mesure?, jusqu'à quel point?; **to the ~ of ...** au point de ...; **to such an ~ that ...** à tel point que ...

extenuating [ɛksˈtɛnjʊeɪtɪŋ] *adj*: **~ circumstances** circonstances atténuantes

exterior [ɛksˈtɪərɪə*] *adj* extérieur(e) ♦ *n* extérieur *m*; dehors *m*

external [ɛksˈtə:nl] *adj* externe

extinct [ɪksˈtɪŋkt] *adj* éteint(e)

extinguish [ɪksˈtɪŋgwɪʃ] *vt* éteindre; **~er** *n* (*also*: **fire ~er**) extincteur *m*

extort [ɪksˈtɔ:t] *vt*: **to ~ sth (from)** extorquer qch (à); **~ionate** [ɪksˈtɔ:ʃənɪt] *adj* exorbitant(e)

extra [ˈɛkstrə] *adj* supplémentaire, de plus ♦ *adv* (*in addition*) en plus ♦ *n* supplément *m*; (*perk*) à-côté *m*; (*THEATRE*) figurant(e) ♦ *prefix* extra-

extract [*vb* ɪksˈtrækt, *n* ˈɛkstrækt] *vt* extraire; (*tooth*) arracher; (*money, promise*) soutirer ♦ *n* extrait *m*

extracurricular [ˈɛkstrəkəˈrɪkjulə*] *adj* parascolaire

extradite [ˈɛkstrədaɪt] *vt* extrader

extra: **~marital** [ɛkstrəˈmærɪtl] *adj* extra-conjugal(e); **~mural** [ɛkstrəˈmjuərl] *adj* hors faculté *inv*; (*lecture*) public(que); **~ordinary** [ɪksˈtrɔ:dnrɪ] *adj* extraordinaire

extravagance [ɪksˈtrævəgəns] *n* prodigalités *fpl*; (*thing bought*) folie *f*, dépense excessive; **extravagant** [ɪksˈtrævəgənt] *adj* extravagant(e);

(*in spending: person*) prodigue, dépensier(ère); (: *tastes*) dispendieux(euse)

extreme [ɪksˈtri:m] *adj* extrême ♦ *n* extrême *m*; **~ly** *adv* extrêmement

extricate [ˈɛkstrɪkeɪt] *vt*: **to ~ sth (from)** dégager qch (de)

extrovert [ˈɛkstrəuvə:t] *n* extraverti(e)

eye [aɪ] *n* œil *m* (*pl* **yeux**); (*of needle*) trou *m*, chas *m* ♦ *vt* examiner; **to keep an ~ on** surveiller; **~ball** *n* globe *m* oculaire; **~bath** (*BRIT*) *n* œillère *f* (*pour bains d'œil*); **~brow** *n* sourcil *m*; **~brow pencil** *n* crayon *m* à sourcils; **~drops** *npl* gouttes *fpl* pour les yeux; **~lash** *n* cil *m*; **~lid** *n* paupière *f*; **~liner** *n* eye-liner *m*; **~opener** *n* révélation *f*; **~shadow** *n* ombre *f* à paupières; **~sight** *n* vue *f*; **~sore** *n* horreur *f*; **~ witness** *n* témoin *m* oculaire

F

F [ɛf] *n* (*MUS*) fa *m* ♦ *abbr* = **Fahrenheit**

fable [ˈfeɪbl] *n* fable *f*

fabric [ˈfæbrɪk] *n* tissu *m*

fabrication [fæbrɪˈkeɪʃən] *n* (*lies*) invention(s) *f(pl)*, fabulation *f*; (*making*) fabrication *f*

fabulous [ˈfæbjuləs] *adj* fabuleux(euse); (*inf: super*) formidable

face [feɪs] *n* visage *m*, figure *f*; (*expression*) expression *f*; (*of clock*) cadran *m*; (*of cliff*) paroi *f*; (*of mountain*) face *f*; (*of building*) façade *f* ♦ *vt* faire face à; **~ down** (*person*) à plat ventre; (*card*) face en dessous; **to lose/save ~** perdre/sauver la face; **to make** *or* **pull a ~** faire une grimace; **in the ~ of** (*difficulties etc*) face à, devant; **on the ~ of it** à première vue; **~ to ~** face à face; **up to** *vt fus* faire face à, affronter; **~ cloth** (*BRIT*) *n* gant *m* de toilette; **~ cream** *n* crème *f* pour le visage; **~ lift** *n* lifting *m*; (*of building etc*) ravalement *m*, retapage *m*; ~ **powder** *n* poudre *f* de riz; ~ **value** *n* (*of coin*) valeur nominale; **to take sth at** ~ **value** (*fig*) prendre qch pour argent comptant

facilities [fə'sɪlɪtɪz] *npl* installations *fpl*, équipement *m*; **credit** ~ facilités *fpl* de paiement

facing ['feɪsɪŋ] *prep* face à, en face de

facsimile [fæk'sɪmɪlɪ] *n* (*exact replica*) fac-similé *m*; (*fax*) télécopie *f*

fact [fækt] *n* fait *m*; **in** ~ en fait

factor ['fæktə*] *n* facteur *m*

factory ['fæktərɪ] *n* usine *f*, fabrique *f*

factual ['fæktjuəl] *adj* basé(e) sur les faits

faculty ['fæklətɪ] *n* faculté *f*; (*US: teaching staff*) corps enseignant

fad [fæd] *n* (*craze*) engouement *m*

fade [feɪd] *vi* se décolorer, passer; (*light, sound*) s'affaiblir; (*flower*) se faner

fag [fæg] *n* (*BRIT: inf*) (*cigarette*) sèche *f*

fail [feɪl] *vt* (*exam*) échouer à; (*candidate*) recaler; (*subj: courage, memory*) faire défaut à ♦ *vi* échouer; (*brakes*) lâcher; (*eyesight, health, light*) baisser, s'affaiblir; **to** ~ **to do sth** (*neglect*) négliger de faire qch; (*be unable*) ne pas arriver or parvenir à faire qch; **without** ~ à coup sûr; sans faute; ~**ing** *n* défaut *m* ♦ *prep* faute de; ~**ure** *n* échec *m*; (*person*) raté(e); (*mechanical etc*) défaillance *f*

faint [feɪnt] *adj* faible; (*recollection*) vague; (*mark*) à peine visible ♦ *n* évanouissement *m* ♦ *vi* s'évanouir; **to feel** ~ défaillir

fair [fɛə*] *adj* équitable, juste, impartial(e); (*hair*) blond(e); (*skin, complexion*) clair, blanc(blanche); (*weather*) beau(belle); (*good enough*) assez bon(ne); (*sizeable*) considérable ♦ *adv*: **to play** ~ jouer franc-jeu ♦ *n* foire *f*; (*BRIT: fun~*) fête (foraine); ~**ly** *adv* équitablement; (*quite*) assez; ~**ness** *n* justice

f, équité *f*, impartialité *f*

fairy ['fɛərɪ] *n* fée *f*; ~ **tale** *n* conte *m* de fées

faith [feɪθ] *n* foi *f*; (*trust*) confiance *f*; (*specific religion*) religion *f*; ~**ful** *adj* fidèle; ~**fully** *adv* see **yours**

fake [feɪk] *n* (*painting etc*) faux *m*; (*person*) imposteur *m* ♦ *adj* faux(fausse) ♦ *vt* simuler; (*painting*) faire un faux de

falcon ['fɔːlkən] *n* faucon *m*

fall [fɔːl] (*pt* fell, *pp* fallen) *n* chute *f*; (*US: autumn*) automne *m* ♦ *vi* tomber; (*price, temperature, dollar*) baisser; ~ **s** *npl* (*waterfall*) chute *f* d'eau, cascade *f*; **to** ~ **flat** (*on one's face*) tomber de tout son long, s'étaler; (*joke*) tomber à plat; (*plan*) échouer; ~ **back** *vi* reculer, se retirer; ~ **back on** *vt fus* se rabattre sur; ~ **behind** *vi* prendre du retard; ~ **down** *vi* (*person*) tomber; (*building*) s'effondrer, s'écrouler; ~ **for** *vt fus* (*trick, story etc*) se laisser prendre à; (*person*) tomber amoureux de; ~ **in** *vi* s'effondrer; (*MIL*) se mettre en rangs; ~ **off** *vi* tomber; (*diminish*) baisser, diminuer; ~ **out** *vi* (*hair, teeth*) tomber; (*MIL*) rompre les rangs; (*friends etc*) se brouiller; ~ **through** *vi* (*plan, project*) tomber à l'eau

fallacy ['fæləsɪ] *n* erreur *f*, illusion *f*

fallout ['fɔːlaut] *n* retombées (radioactives); ~ **shelter** *n* abri *m* anti-atomique

fallow ['fæləu] *adj* en jachère; en friche

false [fɔːls] *adj* faux(fausse); ~ **alarm** *n* fausse alerte; ~ **pretences** *npl*: **under** ~ **pretences** sous un faux prétexte; ~ **teeth** (*BRIT*) *npl* fausses dents

falter ['fɔːltə*] *vi* chanceler, vaciller

fame [feɪm] *n* renommée *f*, renom *m*

familiar [fə'mɪlɪə*] *adj* familier(ère); **to be** ~ **with** (*subject*) connaître

family ['fæmɪlɪ] *n* famille *f* ♦ *cpd* (*business, doctor etc*) de famille; **has he any** ~? (*children*) a-t-il des enfants?

famine ['fæmɪn] n famine f

famished ['fæmɪʃt] (inf) adj affamé(e)

famous ['feɪməs] adj célèbre; ~ly adv (get on) fameusement, à merveille

fan [fæn] n (folding) éventail m; (ELEC) ventilateur m; (of person) fan m, admirateur(trice); (of team, sport etc) supporter m/f ♦ vt éventer; (fire, quarrel) attiser; ~ out vi se déployer (en éventail)

fanatic [fə'nætɪk] n fanatique m/f

fan belt n courroie f de ventilateur

fanciful ['fænsɪful] adj fantaisiste

fancy ['fænsɪ] n fantaisie f, envie f; imagination f ♦ adj (de) fantaisie inv ♦ vt (feel like, want) avoir envie de; (imagine, think) imaginer; **to take a ~ to** se prendre d'affection pour; s'enticher de; **he fancies her** (inf) elle lui plaît; **~ dress** n déguisement m, travesti m; **~-dress ball** n bal masqué or costumé

fang [fæŋ] n croc m; (of snake) crochet m

fantastic [fæn'tæstɪk] adj fantastique

fantasy ['fæntəzɪ] n imagination f, fantaisie f; (dream) chimère f

far [fɑː] adj lointain(e), éloigné(e) ♦ adv loin; **~ away** or **off** au loin, dans le lointain; **at the ~ side/end** à l'autre côté/bout; **~ better** beaucoup mieux; **~ from** loin de; **by ~** de loin, de beaucoup; **go as ~ as the ~m** allez jusqu'à la ferme; **as ~ as I know** pour autant que je sache; **how ~ is it to ...?** combien y a-t-il jusqu'à ...?; **how ~ have you got?** où en êtes-vous?; **~away** adj lointain(e); (look) distrait(e)

farce [fɑːs] n farce f

farcical ['fɑːsɪkl] adj grotesque

fare [feər] n (on trains, buses) prix m du billet; (in taxi) prix de la course; (food) table f, chère f; **half ~** demi-tarif; **full ~** plein tarif

Far East n: **the ~** l'Extrême-Orient m

farewell [feə'wel] excl adieu ♦ n adieu

farm [fɑːm] n ferme f ♦ vt cultiver; **~er** n fermier(ère); cultivateur(trice); **~hand** n ouvrier(ère) agricole; **~house** n (maison f de) ferme f; **~ing** n agriculture f; (of animals) élevage m; **~land** n terres cultivées; **~ worker** n = farmhand; **~yard** n cour f de ferme

far-reaching ['fɑː'riːtʃɪŋ] adj d'une grande portée

fart [fɑːt] (inf!) vi péter

farther ['fɑːðər] adv plus loin ♦ adj plus éloigné(e), plus lointain(e)

farthest ['fɑːðɪst] superl of far

fascinate ['fæsɪneɪt] vt fasciner; **fascinating** adj fascinant(e)

fascism ['fæʃɪzəm] n fascisme m

fashion ['fæʃən] n mode f; (manner) façon f, manière f ♦ vt façonner; **in ~** à la mode; **out of ~** démodé(e); **~able** adj à la mode; **~ show** n défilé m de mannequins or de mode

fast [fɑːst] adj rapide; (clock): **to be ~** avancer; (dye, colour) grand or bon teint inv ♦ adv vite, rapidement; (stuck, held) solidement ♦ n jeûne m ♦ vi jeûner; **~ asleep** profondément endormi

fasten ['fɑːsn] vt attacher, fixer; (coat) attacher, fermer ♦ vi se fermer, s'attacher; **~er** n attache f; **~ing** n = fastener

fast food n fast food m, restauration f rapide

fastidious [fæs'tɪdɪəs] adj exigeant(e), difficile

fat [fæt] adj gros(se) ♦ n graisse f; (on meat) gras m; (for cooking) matière grasse

fatal ['feɪtl] adj (injury etc) mortel(le); (mistake) fatal(e); **~ity** [fə'tælɪtɪ] n (road death etc) victime f, décès m

fate [feɪt] n destin m; (of person) sort m; **~ful** adj fatidique

father ['fɑːðər] n père m; **~-in-law** n beau-père m; **~ly** adj paternel(le)

fathom ['fæðəm] n brasse f (= 1828

mm) ♦ vt (mystery) sonder, pénétrer

fatigue [fə'ti:g] n fatigue f

fatten ['fætn] vt engraisser

fatty ['fætɪ] adj (food) gras(se) ♦ n (inf) gros(se)

fatuous ['fætjʊəs] adj stupide

faucet ['fɔ:sɪt] (US) n robinet m

fault [fɔ:lt] n faute f; (defect) défaut m; (GEO) faille f ♦ vt trouver des défauts à; it's my ~ c'est de ma faute; to find ~ with trouver à redire or à critiquer à; at ~ fautif(ive), coupable; ~y adj défectueux(euse)

fauna ['fɔ:nə] n faune f

faux pas ['fəʊ'pɑ:] n inv impair m, bévue f, gaffe f

favour ['feɪvə*] (US **favor**) n faveur f; (help) service m ♦ vt (proposition) être en faveur de; (pupil etc) favoriser; (team, horse) donner gagnant; to do sb a ~ rendre un service à qn; to find ~ with trouver grâce aux yeux de; in ~ of en faveur de; ~able adj favorable; ~ite ['feɪvərɪt] adj, n favori(te)

fawn [fɔ:n] n faon m ♦ adj (also: ~-coloured) fauve ♦ vi: to ~ (up)on flatter servilement

fax [fæks] n (document) télécopie f; (machine) télécopieur m ♦ vt envoyer par télécopie

FBI ['efbi:'aɪ] n abbr (US: = Federal Bureau of Investigation) F.B.I. m

fear [fɪə*] n crainte f, peur f ♦ vt craindre; for ~ of de peur que +sub, de peur de +infin; ~ful adj craintif(ive); (sight, noise) affreux(euse), épouvantable; ~less adj intrépide

feasible ['fi:zəbl] adj faisable, réalisable

feast [fi:st] n festin m, banquet m; (REL: also: ~ day) fête f ♦ vi festoyer

feat [fi:t] n exploit m, prouesse f

feather ['feðə*] n plume f

feature ['fi:tʃə*] n caractéristique f; (article) chronique f, rubrique f ♦ vt

(subj: film) avoir pour vedette(s) ♦ vi: to ~ in figurer (en bonne place) dans; (in film) jouer dans; ~s npl (of face) traits mpl; ~ film n long métrage

February ['februərɪ] n février m

fed [fed] pt, pp of **feed**

federal ['fedərəl] adj fédéral(e)

fed up adj: to be ~ en avoir marre, en avoir plein le dos

fee [fi:] n rémunération f; (of doctor, lawyer) honoraires mpl; (for examination) droits mpl; **school** ~s frais mpl de scolarité

feeble ['fi:bl] adj faible; (pathetic: attempt, excuse) pauvre; (:joke) piteux(euse)

feed [fi:d] (pt, pp **fed**) n (of baby) tétée f; (of animal) fourrage m, pâture f; (on printer) mécanisme m d'alimentation ♦ vt (person) nourrir; (BRIT: baby) allaiter; (: with bottle) donner le biberon à; (horse etc) donner à manger à; (machine) alimenter; (data, information): to ~ sth into fournir qch à; ~ on vt fus se nourrir de; ~back n feed-back m inv; ~ing bottle (BRIT) n biberon m

feel [fi:l] (pt, pp **felt**) n sensation f; (impression) impression f ♦ vt toucher; (explore) tâter, palper; (cold, pain) sentir; (grief, anger) ressentir; to ~ hungry/cold avoir faim/froid; to ~ lonely/better se sentir seul/mieux; I don't ~ well je ne me sens pas bien; it ~s soft c'est doux(douce) au toucher; to ~ like (want) avoir envie de; ~ about vi fouiller, tâtonner; ~er n (of insect) antenne f; to put out ~ers or a ~ler tâter le terrain; ~ing n (physical) sensation f; (emotional) sentiment m

feet [fi:t] npl of **foot**

feign [feɪn] vt feindre, simuler

fell [fel] pt of **fall** ♦ vt (tree, person) abattre

fellow ['feləʊ] n type m; (comrade) compagnon m; (of learned society) membre *m* ♦ *cpd:* **their ~ prisoners/students** leurs camarades prisonniers/d'étude; **~ citizen** *n* concitoyen(ne) *m/f*; **~ countryman** (*irreg*) *n* compatriote *m*; **~ men** *npl* semblables *mpl*; **~ship** *n* (*in society*) association *f*; (*comradeship*) amitié *f*, camaraderie *f*; (*grant*) sorte de bourse universitaire

felony ['fɛlənɪ] *n* crime *m*, forfait *m*

felt [fɛlt] *pt*, *pp of* **feel** ♦ *n* feutre *m*; **~-tip pen** *n* stylo-feutre *m*

female ['fiːmeɪl] *n* (*ZOOL*) femelle *f*; (*pej: woman*) bonne femme *f* ♦ *adj* (*BIO*) femelle; (*sex, character*) féminin(e); (*vote etc*) des femmes

feminine ['fɛmɪnɪn] *adj* féminin(e)

feminist ['fɛmɪnɪst] *n* féministe *m/f*

fence [fɛns] *n* barrière *f* ♦ *vt* (*also:* **~ in**) clôturer ♦ *vi* faire de l'escrime; **fencing** ['fɛnsɪŋ] *n* escrime *m*

fend [fɛnd] *vi:* **to ~ for o.s.** se débrouiller (tout seul); **~ off** *vt* (*attack etc*) parer

fender ['fɛndə*] *n* garde-feu *m inv*; (*on boat*) défense *f*; (*US: of car*) aile *f*

ferment [*vb* fə'mɛnt, *n* 'fɜːmɛnt] *vi* fermenter ♦ *n* agitation *f*, effervescence *f*

fern [fɜːn] *n* fougère *f*

ferocious [fə'rəʊʃəs] *adj* féroce

ferret ['fɛrɪt] *n* furet *m*

ferry ['fɛrɪ] *n* (*small*) bac *m*; (*large: also:* **~boat**) ferry(-boat) *m* ♦ *vt* transporter

fertile ['fɜːtaɪl] *adj* fertile; (*BIO*) fécond(e); **fertilizer** ['fɜːtɪlaɪzə*] *n* engrais *m*

fester ['fɛstə*] *vi* suppurer

festival ['fɛstɪvəl] *n* (*REL*) fête *f*; (*ART, MUS*) festival *m*

festive ['fɛstɪv] *adj* de fête; **the ~ season** (*BRIT: Christmas*) la période des fêtes; **festivities** [fɛs'trvɪtɪz] *npl* réjouissances *fpl*

festoon [fɛs'tuːn] *vt:* **to ~ with** orner de

fetch [fɛtʃ] *vt* aller chercher; (*sell for*) se vendre

fetching ['fɛtʃɪŋ] *adj* charmant(e)

fête [feɪt] *n* fête *f*, kermesse *f*

fetish ['fɛtɪʃ] *n:* **to make a ~ of** être obsédé(e) par

feud [fjuːd] *n* dispute *f*, dissension *f*

fever ['fiːvə*] *n* fièvre *f*; **~ish** *adj* fiévreux(euse), fébrile

few [fjuː] *adj* (*not many*) peu de; **a ~** *adj* quelques ♦ *pron* quelques-uns(unes); **~er** *adj* moins de; moins (*nombreux*); **~est** *adj* le moins (de)

fiancé, e [fɪ'ɑ̃nseɪ] *n* fiancé(e) *m/f*

fib [fɪb] *n* bobard *m*

fibre ['faɪbə*] (*US* **fiber**) *n* fibre *f*; **~-glass** (®) *n* fibre de verre

fickle ['fɪkl] *adj* inconstant(e), volage, capricieux(euse)

fiction ['fɪkʃən] *n* romans *mpl*, littérature *f* romanesque; (*invention*) fiction *f*; **~al** *adj* fictif(ive)

fictitious [fɪk'tɪʃəs] *adj* fictif(ive), imaginaire

fiddle ['fɪdl] *n* (*MUS*) violon *m*; (*cheating*) combine *f*; escroquerie *f* ♦ *vt* (*BRIT: accounts*) falsifier, maquiller; **~ with** *vt fus* tripoter

fidget ['fɪdʒɪt] *vi* se trémousser, remuer

field [fiːld] *n* champ *m*; (*fig*) domaine *m*, champ; (*SPORT: ground*) terrain *m*; **~ marshal** *n* maréchal *m*; **~work** *n* travaux *mpl* pratiques (sur le terrain)

fiend [fiːnd] *n* démon *m*; **~ish** *adj* diabolique, abominable

fierce [fɪəs] *adj* (*look, animal*) féroce, sauvage; (*wind, attack, person*) (très) violent(e); (*fighting, enemy*) acharné(e)

fiery ['faɪərɪ] *adj* ardent(e), brûlant(e); (*temperament*) fougueux(euse)

fifteen [fɪf'tiːn] *num* quinze

fifth [fɪfθ] *num* cinquième

fifty ['fɪftɪ] *num* cinquante; **~-fifty** *adj:* **a ~-fifty chance** *etc* une chance *etc* sur deux ♦ *adv* moitié-moitié

fig [fɪg] *n* figue *f*

fight [faɪt] (*pt, pp* **fought**) *n* (*MIL*)

combat m; (between persons) bagarre f; (against cancer etc) lutte f ♦ vt se battre contre; (cancer, alcoholism, emotion) combattre, lutter contre; (election) se présenter à ♦ vi se battre; ~**er** n (fig) lutteur m; (plane) chasseur m; ~**ing** n combats mpl (brawl) bagarres fpl

figment ['fɪgmənt] n: **a ~ of the imagination** une invention

figurative ['fɪgjʊrətɪv] adj figuré(e)

figure ['fɪgə*] n figure f; (number, cipher) chiffre m; (body, outline) silhouette f; (shape) ligne f, formes fpl ♦ vt (think: esp US) supposer ♦ vi (appear) figurer; ~ **out** vt (work out) calculer; ~**head** n (NAUT) figure f de proue; (pej) prête-nom m; ~ **of speech** n figure f de rhétorique

file [faɪl] n (dossier) dossier m; (folder) dossier, chemise f; (: with hinges) classeur m; (COMPUT) fichier m; (row) file f; (tool) lime f ♦ vt (nails, wood) limer; (papers) classer; (LAW: claim) faire enregistrer; déposer ♦ vi: **to ~ in/out** entrer/sortir l'un derrière l'autre; **to ~ for divorce** faire une demande en divorce; **filing cabinet** n classeur m (meuble)

fill [fɪl] vt remplir; (need) répondre à ♦ n: **to eat one's ~** manger à sa faim; **to ~ with** remplir de; ~ **in** vt (hole) boucher; (form) remplir; ~ **up** vt remplir; ~ **it up, please** (AUT) le plein, s'il vous plaît

fillet ['fɪlɪt] n filet m; ~ **steak** n filet m de bœuf, tournedos m

filling ['fɪlɪŋ] n (CULIN) garniture f, farce f; (for tooth) plombage m; ~ **station** n station-service f

film [fɪlm] n film m; (PHOT) pellicule f, film m; (of powder, liquid) couche f, pellicule f ♦ vt (scene) filmer ♦ vi tourner; ~ **star** n vedette f de cinéma

filter ['fɪltə*] n filtre m ♦ vt filtrer; ~ **lane** n (AUT) voie f de sortie; ~ **tipped** adj à bout filtre

filth [fɪlθ] n saleté f; ~**y** adj sale, dé-

goûtant(e); (language) ordurier(ère)

fin [fɪn] n (of fish) nageoire f

final ['faɪnl] adj final(e); (definitive) définitif(ive) ♦ n (SPORT) finale f; ~**s** npl (SCOL) examens mpl de dernière année; ~**e** [fɪˈnɑːlɪ] n finale m; ~**ize** vt mettre au point; ~**ly** adv (eventually) enfin, finalement; (lastly) en dernier lieu

finance [faɪˈnæns] n finance f ♦ vt financer; ~**s** npl (financial position) finances fpl; **financial** [faɪˈnænʃəl] adj financier(ère)

find [faɪnd] (pt, pp **found**) vt trouver; (lost object) retrouver ♦ n trouvaille f, découverte f; **to ~ sb guilty** (LAW) déclarer qn coupable; ~ **out** vt (truth, secret) découvrir; (person) démasquer ♦ vi: **to ~ out about** (make enquiries) se renseigner; (by chance) apprendre; ~**ings** npl (LAW) conclusions fpl, verdict m; (of report) conclusions

fine [faɪn] adj (excellent) excellent(e); (thin, not coarse, subtle) fin(e); (weather) beau(belle) ♦ adv (well) très bien ♦ n (LAW) amende f, contravention f ♦ vt (LAW) condamner à une amende; donner une contravention à; **to be ~** (person) aller bien; (weather) être beau; ~ **arts** npl beaux-arts mpl

finery ['faɪnərɪ] n parure f

finger ['fɪŋgə*] n doigt m ♦ vt palper, toucher; **little ~** n auriculaire m, petit doigt; **index ~** n index m; ~**nail** n ongle m (de la main); ~**print** n empreinte digitale; ~**tip** n bout m du doigt

finicky ['fɪnɪkɪ] adj tatillon(ne), méticuleux(euse); minutieux(euse)

finish ['fɪnɪʃ] n fin f; (SPORT) arrivée f; (polish etc) finition f ♦ vt finir, terminer ♦ vi finir, se terminer; ~ **doing sth** finir de faire qch; **to ~ third** arriver or terminer troisième; ~ **off** vt finir, terminer; (kill) achever; ~ **up** vi, vt finir; **finishing line** n ligne f d'arrivée; ~**ing school** n institution privée (pour jeunes filles)

finite ['faɪnaɪt] adj fini(e); (verb) conjugué(e)

Finland ['fɪnlənd] n Finlande f

Finn [fɪn] n Finnois(e); Finlandais(e); **~ish** adj finnois(e); finlandais(e) ♦ n (LING) finnois m

fir [fɜ:*] n sapin m

fire [faɪə*] n feu m; (accidental) incendie m; (heater) radiateur m ♦ vt (discharge): **to ~ a gun** tirer un coup de feu; (fig) enflammer, animer; (inf: dismiss) mettre à la porte, renvoyer ♦ vi (shoot) tirer, faire feu; **on ~** en feu; **~ alarm** n avertisseur m d'incendie; **~arm** n arme f à feu; **~ brigade** n (sapeurs-)pompiers mpl; **~ department** (US) n = **fire brigade**; **~ engine** n (vehicle) voiture f de pompiers; **~ escape** n escalier m de secours; **~ extinguisher** n extincteur m; **~man** n pompier m; **~place** n cheminée f; **~side** n foyer m, coin m du feu; **~ station** n caserne f de pompiers; **~wood** n bois m de chauffage; **~works** npl feux mpl d'artifice; (display) feu(x) d'artifice

firing squad ['faɪərɪŋ-] n peloton m d'exécution

firm [fɜ:m] adj ferme ♦ n compagnie f, firme f

first [fɜ:st] adj premier(ère) ♦ adv (before all others) le premier, la première; (before all other things) en premier, d'abord; (when listing reasons etc) en premier lieu, premièrement ♦ n (person: in race) premier(ère); (BRIT: SCOL) mention f très bien; (AUT) première f; **at ~** au commencement, au début; **~ of all** tout d'abord, pour commencer; **~ aid** n premiers secours or soins; **~ aid kit** n trousse f à pharmacie; **~ class** adj de première classe; (excellent) excellent(e), exceptionnel(le); **~-hand** adj de première main; **~ lady** (US) n femme f du président; **~ly** adv premièrement, en premier lieu; **~ name** n prénom m; **~-rate** adj excellent(e)

fish [fɪʃ] n inv poisson m ♦ vt, vi pêcher; **to go ~ing** aller à la pêche; **~erman** n pêcheur m; **~ farm** n établissement m piscicole; **~ fingers** (BRIT) npl bâtonnets de poisson (congelés); **~ing boat** n barque f or bateau m de pêche; **~ing line** n ligne f (de pêche); **~ing rod** n canne f à pêche; **~monger's (shop)** n poissonnerie f; **~ sticks** (US) npl = **fish fingers**; **~y** (inf) adj suspect(e), louche

fist [fɪst] n poing m

fit [fɪt] adj (healthy) en (bonne) forme; (proper) convenable; approprié(e) ♦ vt (subj: clothes) aller à; (put, attach) installer, poser; adapter; (equip) équiper, garnir, munir; (suit) convenir à ♦ vi (clothes) aller; (parts) s'adapter; (in space, gap) entrer, s'adapter ♦ n (MED) accès m, crise f; (of anger) accès; (of hysterics, jealousy) crise; **~ to** en état de; **~ for** digne de; apte à; **~ of coughing** quinte f de toux; **a ~ of giggles** le fou rire; **this dress is a good ~** cette robe (me) va très bien; **by ~s and starts** par à-coups; **~ in** vi s'accorder; s'adapter; **~ful** adj (sleep) agité(e); **~ment** n meuble encastré, élément m; **~ness** n (MED) forme f physique; **~ted carpet** n moquette f; **~ted kitchen** (BRIT) n cuisine équipée; **~ter** n monteur m; **~ting** adj approprié(e) ♦ n (of dress) essayage m; (of piece of equipment) pose f, installation f; **~tings** npl (in building) installations fpl; **~ting room** n cabine f d'essayage

five [faɪv] num cinq; **~r** (BRIT) n billet m de cinq livres; (US) billet de cinq dollars

fix [fɪks] vt (date, amount etc) fixer; (organize) arranger; (mend) réparer; (meal, drink) préparer ♦ n: **to be in a ~** être dans le pétrin; **~ up** vt (meeting) arranger; **to ~ sb up with sth** faire avoir qch à qn; **~ation** [fɪk'seɪʃən] n (PSYCH) fixa-

tion f; (fig) obsession f; **~ed** [frkst]
adj (prices etc) fixe; (smile) figée(e);
~ture ['frkstʃə*] n installation f
(fixe); (SPORT) rencontre f (au programme)

fizzle ['frzl] vi: **~ out** vi (interest)
s'estomper; (strike, film) se terminer
en queue de poisson

fizzy ['frzɪ] adj pétillant(e); ga-
zeux(euse)

flabbergasted ['flæbəgɑːstɪd] adj si-
déré(e), ahuri(e)

flabby ['flæbɪ] adj mou(molle)

flag [flæg] n drapeau m; (also:
~stone) dalle f ♦ vi faiblir; fléchir;
~ down vt héler, faire signe de
s'arrêter à; **~pole** ['flægpəʊl] n mât
m; **~ship** n vaisseau m amiral; (fig)
produit m vedette

flair [flɛə*] n flair m

flak [flæk] n (MIL) tir antiaérien;
(inf: criticism) critiques fpl

flake [flerk] n (of rust, paint) écaille
f; (of snow, soap powder) flocon m ♦
vi (also: ~ off) s'écailler

flamboyant [flæm'bɔɪənt] adj flam-
boyant(e), éclatant(e); (person) haut
(e) en couleur

flame [flerm] n flamme f

flamingo [flə'mɪŋgəʊ] n flamant m
(rose)

flammable ['flæməbl] n inflammable

flan [flæn] (BRIT) n tarte f

flank [flæŋk] n flanc m ♦ vt flanquer

flannel ['flænl] n (fabric) flanelle f;
(BRIT: also: face~) gant m de toilette; **~s** npl (trousers) pantalon m
de flanelle

flap [flæp] n (of pocket, envelope) ra-
bat m ♦ vt (wings) battre (de) ♦ vi
(sail, flag) claquer; (inf: also: be in
a ~) paniquer

flare [flɛə*] n (signal) signal lumineux; (in skirt etc) évasement m; **~
up** vi s'embraser; (fig) se
mettre en colère, s'emporter; (: revolt etc) éclater

flash [flæʃ] n éclair m; (also: news
~) flash m (d'information); (PHOT)

flash ♦ vt (light) projeter; (send:
message) câbler; (look) jeter;
(smile) lancer ♦ vi (light) clignoter;
a ~ of lightning un éclair; in a ~
en un clin d'œil; to ~ one's headlights faire un appel de phares; to ~
by or past (person) passer comme
un éclair (devant); **~bulb** n ampoule
f de flash; **~cube** n cube-flash m;
~light n lampe f de poche

flashy ['flæʃɪ] (pej) adj tape-à-l'œil
inv, tapageur(euse)

flask [flɑːsk] n flacon m, bouteille f;
(vacuum) ~ thermos m or f ®

flat [flæt] adj plat(e); (tyre) dégon-
flé(e), à plat; (beer) éventé(e); (denial) catégorique; (MUS) bémol inv;
(: voice) faux(fausse); (fee, rate)
fixe ♦ n (BRIT: apartment) appartement m; (AUT) crevaison f; (MUS)
bémol m; to work ~ out travailler
d'arrache-pied; **~ly** adv catégoriquement; **~ten** vt (also: ~ten out) aplatir
(: crop) coucher; (building(s)) raser

flatter ['flætə*] vt flatter; **~ing** adj
flatteur(euse); **~y** n flatterie f

flaunt [flɔːnt] vt faire étalage de

flavour ['fleɪvə*] (US flavor) n goût
m, saveur f; (of ice cream etc) parfum m ♦ vt parfumer; **vanilla-
flavoured** à l'arôme de vanille, à la
vanille; **~ing** n arôme m

flaw [flɔː] n défaut m; **~less** adj sans
défaut

flax [flæks] n lin m; **~en** adj blond(e)

flea [fliː] n puce f

fleck [flek] n tacheture f; moucheture
f

flee [fliː] (pt, pp fled) vt fuir ♦ vi
fuir, s'enfuir

fleece [fliːs] n toison f ♦ vt (inf) voler, filouter

fleet [fliːt] n flotte f; (of lorries etc)
parc m, convoi m

fleeting ['fliːtɪŋ] adj fugace, fugi-
tif(ive); (visit) très bref(brève)

Flemish ['flemɪʃ] adj flamand(e)

flesh [fleʃ] n chair f; **~ wound** n
blessure superficielle

flew [flu:] pt of **fly**

flex [fleks] n fil m or câble m électrique ♦ vt (knee) fléchir; (muscles) tendre

flexible adj flexible

flick [flik] n petite tape; chiquenaude f; (of duster) petit coup ♦ vt donner un petit coup à; (switch) appuyer sur; ~ **through** vt fus feuilleter

flicker ['flikə*] vi (light) vaciller; **his eyelids** ~**ed** il a cligné

flier ['flaiə*] n aviateur m

flight [flait] n vol m; (escape) fuite f; (also: ~ **of steps**) escalier m; ~ **attendant** (US) n steward m, hôtesse f de l'air; ~ **deck** n (AVIAT) poste m de pilotage; (NAUT) pont m d'envol

flimsy ['flimzi] adj peu solide; (clothes) trop léger(ère); (excuse) pauvre, mince

flinch [flintʃ] vi tressaillir; **to** ~ **from** se dérober à, reculer devant

fling [fliŋ] (pt, pp **flung**) vt jeter, lancer

flint [flint] n silex m; (in lighter) pierre f (à briquet)

flip [flip] vt (throw) lancer (d'une chiquenaude); **to** ~ **a coin** jouer à pile ou face; **to** ~ **sth over** retourner qch

flippant ['flipənt] adj désinvolte, irrévérencieux(euse)

flipper ['flipə*] n (of seal etc) nageoire f; (for swimming) palme f

flirt [flə:t] vi flirter ♦ n flirteur(euse) m/f

flit [flit] vi voleter

float [fləut] n flotteur m; (in procession) char m; (money) réserve f ♦ vi flotter

flock [flɔk] n troupeau m; (of birds) vol m; (REL) ouailles fpl ♦ vi: **to** ~ **to** se rendre en masse à

flog [flɔg] vt fouetter

flood [flʌd] n inondation f; (of letters, refugees etc) flot m ♦ vi inonder ♦ vi (people): **to** ~ **into** envahir; ~**ing** n inondation f; ~**light** n projecteur m

floor [flɔ:*] n sol m; (storey) étage m; (of sea, valley) fond m ♦ vt (subj: question) décontenancer; (: blow) terrasser; **on the** ~ par terre; **ground** ~, (US) **first** ~ rez-de-chaussée m inv; **first** ~, (US) **second** ~ premier étage; ~**board** n planche f (du plancher); ~ **show** n spectacle m de variétés

flop [flɔp] n fiasco m ♦ vi être un fiasco; (fall: into chair) s'affaler, s'effondrer

floppy ['flɔpi] adj lâche, flottant(e); ~ (**disk**) n (COMPUT) disquette f

flora ['flɔ:rə] n flore f

floral ['flɔ:rəl] adj (dress) à fleurs

florid ['flɔrid] adj (complexion) coloré(e); (style) plein(e) de fioritures

florist ['flɔrist] n fleuriste m/f

flounce [flauns] n: **to** ~ **out** sortir dans un mouvement d'humeur

flounder ['flaundə*] vi patauger ♦ n (ZOOL) flet m

flour ['flauə*] n farine f

flourish ['flʌriʃ] vi prospérer ♦ n (gesture) moulinet m

flout [flaut] vt se moquer de, faire fi de

flow [fləu] n (ELEC, of river) courant m; (of blood in veins) circulation f; (of tide) flux m; (of orders, data) flot m ♦ vi couler; (traffic) s'écouler; (robes, hair) flotter; **the** ~ **of traffic** l'écoulement m de la circulation; ~ **chart** n organigramme m

flower ['flauə*] n fleur f ♦ vi fleurir; ~ **bed** n plate-bande f; ~**pot** n pot m (de fleurs); ~**y** adj fleuri(e)

flown [fləun] pp of **fly**

flu [flu:] n grippe f

fluctuate ['flʌktjueit] vi varier, fluctuer

fluent ['flu:ənt] adj (speech) coulant(e), aisé(e); **he speaks** ~ **French, he's** ~ **in French** il parle couramment le français

fluff [flʌf] n duvet m; (on jacket, carpet) peluche f; ~**y** adj duveteux(euse); (toy) en peluche

fluid ['flu:id] adj fluide ♦ n fluide m

fluke [flu:k] (inf) n (luck) coup m de

veine

flung [flʌŋ] *pt, pp* of **fling**

fluoride ['fluoraid] *n* fluorure *f*; ~ **toothpaste** *n* dentifrice *m* au fluor

flurry ['flʌrɪ] *n* (*of snow*) rafale *f*, bourrasque *f*; ~ **of activity/ excitement** affairement *m*/excitation *f* soudain(e)

flush [flʌʃ] *n* (*on face*) rougeur *f*; (*fig: of youth, beauty etc*) éclat *m* ♦ *vt* nettoyer à grande eau ♦ *vi* rougir ♦ *adj*: ~ **with** au ras de, de niveau avec; **to** ~ **the toilet** tirer la chasse (d'eau); ~ **out** *vt* (*game, birds*) débusquer; ~**ed** *adj* (tout(e)) rouge

flustered ['flʌstəd] *adj* énervé(e)

flute [flu:t] *n* flûte *f*

flutter ['flʌtə*] *n* (*of panic, excitement*) agitation *f*; (*of wings*) battement *m* ♦ *vi* (*bird*) battre des ailes, voleter

flux [flʌks] *n*: **in a state of** ~ fluctuant sans cesse

fly [flaɪ] (*pt* **flew**, *pp* **flown**) *n* (*insect*) mouche *f*; (*on trousers: also:* **flies**) braguette *f* ♦ *vt* (*aircraft*) piloter; (*passengers, cargo*) transporter ♦ *vi* voler; (*passengers*) aller en avion; (*escape*) s'enfuir, fuir; (*flag*) se déployer; ~ **away** *vi* (*bird, insect*) s'envoler; ~ **off** *vi* = **fly away**; ~**ing** *n* (*activity*) aviation *f*; (*action*) vol *m* ♦ *adj*: a ~**ing visit** une visite éclair; **with** ~**ing colours** haut la main; ~**ing saucer** *n* soucoupe volante; ~**ing start** *n*: **to get off to a** ~**ing start** prendre un excellent départ; ~**over** *n* (*BRIT*) (*bridge*) saut-de-mouton *m*; ~**sheet** *n* (*for tent*) double toit *m*

foal [fəul] *n* poulain *m*

foam [fəum] *n* écume *f*; (*on beer*) mousse *f*; (*also:* ~ **rubber**) caoutchouc *m* mousse ♦ *vi* (*liquid*) écumer; (*soapy water*) mousser

fob [fɔb] *vt*: **to** ~ **sb off** se débarrasser de qn

focal point ['fəukəl-] *n* (*fig*) point central

focus ['fəukəs] (*pl* ~**es**) *n* foyer *m*;

(*of interest*) centre *m* ♦ *vt* (*field glasses etc*) mettre au point ♦ *vi*: **to** ~ (**on**) (*with camera*) régler la mise au point (sur); (*person*) fixer son regard (sur); **out of/in** ~ (*picture*) flou(e)/net(te); (*camera*) pas au point/au point

fodder ['fɔdə*] *n* fourrage *m*

foe [fəu] *n* ennemi *m*

fog [fɔg] *n* brouillard *m*; ~**gy** *adj*: **it's** ~**gy** il y a du brouillard; ~ **lamp** *n* (*AUT*) phare *m* antibrouillard; ~ **light** (*US*) *n* = **fog lamp**

foil [fɔɪl] *vt* déjouer, contrecarrer ♦ *n* feuille *f* de métal; (*kitchen* ~) papier *m* d'alu(minium); (*complement*) repoussoir *m*; (*FENCING*) fleuret *m*

fold [fəuld] *n* (*bend, crease*) pli *m*; (*AGR*) parc *m* à moutons; (*fig*) bercail *m* ♦ *vt* plier; (*arms*) croiser; ~ **up** *vi* (*map, table etc*) se plier; (*business*) fermer boutique ♦ *vt* (*map, clothes*) plier; ~**er** *n* (*for papers*) chemise *f*; (*: with hinges*) classeur *m*; ~**ing** *adj* (*chair, bed*) pliant(e)

foliage ['fəulɪɪdʒ] *n* feuillage *m*

folk [fəuk] *npl* gens *mpl* ♦ *cpd* folklorique; ~**s** *npl* (*parents*) parents *mpl*; ~**lore** ['fəuklɔ:*] *n* folklore *m*; ~ **song** *n* chanson *f* folklorique

follow ['fɔləu] *vt* suivre ♦ *vi* suivre; (*result*) s'ensuivre; **to** ~ **suit** (*fig*) faire de même; ~ **up** *vt* (*letter, offer*) donner suite à; (*case*) suivre; ~**er** *n* disciple *m/f*, partisan(e); ~**ing** *adj* suivant(e) ♦ *n* partisans *mpl*, disciples *mpl*

folly ['fɔlɪ] *n* inconscience *f*; folie *f*

fond [fɔnd] *adj* (*memory, look*) tendre; (*hopes, dreams*) un peu fou(folle); **to be** ~ **of** aimer beaucoup

fondle ['fɔndl] *vt* caresser

font [fɔnt] *n* (*in church: for baptism*) fonts baptismaux; (*TYP*) fonte *f*

food [fu:d] *n* nourriture *f*; ~ **mixer** *n* mixer *m*; ~ **poisoning** *n* intoxication *f* alimentaire; ~ **processor** *n* robot *m* de cuisine; ~**stuffs** *npl* denrées *fpl* alimentaires

fool [fu:l] *n* idiot(e); (*CULIN*) mousse *f* de fruits ♦ *vi* faire l'idiot *or* l'imbécile; **~hardy** *adj* téméraire, imprudent(e); **~ish** *adj* idiot(e), stupide; (*rash*) imprudent(e); insensé; **~proof** *adj* (*plan etc*) infaillible

foot [fut] (*pl* **feet**) *n* pied *m*; (*of animal*) patte *f*; (*measure*) pied (= 30,48 cm; 12 inches) ♦ *vt* (*bill*) payer; **on ~** à pied; **~age** *n* (*CINEMA: length*) ≃ métrage *m*; (: *material*) séquences *fpl*; **~ball** *n* ballon *m* (de football); (*sport: BRIT*) football *m*; (: *US*) football américain; **~ball player** (*BRIT*) *n* (*also: footballer*) joueur *m* de football; **~brake** *n* frein *m* à pédale; **~bridge** *n* passerelle *f*; **~hills** *npl* contreforts *mpl*; **~hold** *n* prise *f* (de pied); **~ing** *n* (*fig*) position *f*; **to lose one's ~ing** perdre pied; **~lights** *npl* rampe *f*; **~man** (*irreg*) *n* valet *m* de pied; **~note** *n* note *f* (en bas de page); **~path** *n* sentier *m*; (*in street*) trottoir *m*; **~print** *n* trace *f* (de pas); **~step** *n* pas *m*; **~wear** *n* chaussure(s) *f(pl)*

KEYWORD

for [fɔ:*] *prep* **1** (*indicating destination, intention, purpose*) pour; **the train ~ London** le train pour *or* (à destination) de Londres; **he went ~ the paper** il est allé chercher le journal; **it's time ~ lunch** c'est l'heure du déjeuner; **what's it ~?** ça sert à quoi?; **what ~?** (*why*) pourquoi?

2 (*on behalf of, representing*) pour; **the MP ~ Hove** le député de Hove; **to work ~ sb/sth** travailler pour qn/qch; **G ~ George** G comme George

3 (*because of*) pour; **~ this reason** pour cette raison; **~ fear of being criticized** de peur d'être critiqué

4 (*with regard to*) pour; **it's cold ~ July** il fait froid pour juillet; **a gift ~ languages** un don pour les langues

5 (*in exchange for*): **I sold it ~ £5** je l'ai vendu 5 livres; **to pay 50 pence ~ a ticket** payer 50 pence un billet

6 (*in favour of*) pour; **are you ~ or against us?** êtes-vous pour ou contre nous?

7 (*referring to distance*) pendant (*referring to distance*), sur; **there are roadworks ~ 5 km** il y a des travaux sur *or* pendant 5 km; **we walked ~ miles** nous avons marché pendant des kilomètres

8 (*referring to time*) pendant; depuis; pour; **he was away ~ 2 years** il a été absent pendant 2 ans; **she will be away ~ a month** elle sera absente (pendant) un mois; **I have known her ~ years** je la connais depuis des années; **can you do it ~ tomorrow?** est-ce que tu peux le faire pour demain?

9 (*with infinitive clauses*): **it is not ~ me to decide** ce n'est pas à moi de décider; **it would be best ~ you to leave** le mieux serait que vous partiez; **there is still time ~ you to do it** vous avez encore le temps de le faire; **~ this to be possible ...** pour que cela soit possible ...

10 (*in spite of*): **~ all his work/efforts** malgré tout son travail/tous ses efforts; **~ all his complaints, he's very fond of her** il a beau se plaindre, il l'aime beaucoup

♦ *conj* (*since, as: rather formal*) car

---

forage ['fɔrɪdʒ] *vi* fourrager

foray ['fɔreɪ] *n* incursion *f*

forbid [fə'bɪd] (*pt* **forbad(e)**, *pp* **forbidden**) *vt* défendre, interdire; **to ~ sb to do** défendre *or* interdire à qn de faire; **~ding** *adj* sévère, sombre

force [fɔːs] *n* force *f* ♦ *vt* forcer; (*push*) pousser (de force); **the F~s** *npl* (*MIL*) l'armée *f*; **in ~** en vigueur; **~feed** *vt* nourrir de force; **~ful** *adj* énergique, volontaire

forcibly ['fɔːsəblɪ] *adv* par la force,

de force; (express) énergiquement

ford [fɔːd] n gué m

fore [fɔː*] n: to come to the ~ se faire remarquer

fore: ~arm ['fɔːrɑːm] n avant-bras m inv; **~boding** [fɔː'bəudɪŋ] n pressentiment m (néfaste); **~cast** ['fɔːkɑːst] (irreg: like cast) n prévision f ♦ vt prévoir; **~court** ['fɔːkɔːt] n (of garage) devant m; **~fathers** ['fɔːfɑːðəz] npl ancêtres mpl; **~finger** ['fɔːfɪŋgə*] n index m

forefront ['fɔːfrʌnt] n: in the ~ of au premier rang or plan de

forego [fɔː'gəu] (irreg: like go) vt renoncer à; **~ne** ['fɔːgɔn] adj: it's a **~ne conclusion** c'est couru d'avance

foreground ['fɔːgraund] n premier plan

forehead ['fɔrɪd] n front m

foreign ['fɔrɪn] adj étranger(ère); (trade) extérieur(e); **~er** n étranger(ère); **~ exchange** n change m; **F~ Office** (BRIT) n ministère m des affaires étrangères; **F~ Secretary** (BRIT) n ministre m des affaires étrangères

foreleg ['fɔːleg] n (cat, dog) patte f de devant; (horse) jambe antérieure

foreman ['fɔːmən] (irreg) n (factory, building site) contremaître m, chef m d'équipe

foremost ['fɔːməust] adj le(la) plus en vue; premier(ère) ♦ adv: **first and ~** avant tout, tout d'abord

forensic [fə'rensɪk] adj: **~ medicine** médecine légale; **~ scientist** n médecin m légiste

forerunner ['fɔːrʌnə*] n précurseur m

foresee [fɔː'siː] (irreg: like see) vt prévoir; **~able** adj prévisible

foreshadow [fɔː'ʃædəu] vt présager, annoncer, laisser prévoir

foresight ['fɔːsaɪt] n prévoyance f

forest ['fɔrɪst] n forêt f

forestall [fɔː'stɔːl] vt devancer

forestry ['fɔrɪstrɪ] n sylviculture f

foretaste ['fɔːteɪst] n avant-goût m

foretell [fɔː'tel] (irreg: like tell) vt prédire

foretold [fɔː'təuld] pt, pp of foretell

forever [fə'revə*] adv pour toujours; (fig) continuellement

forewent [fɔː'went] pt of forego

foreword ['fɔːwɜːd] n avant-propos m inv

forfeit ['fɔːfɪt] vt (lose) perdre

forgave [fə'geɪv] pt of forgive

forge [fɔːdʒ] n forge f ♦ vt (signature) contrefaire; (wrought iron) forger; **to ~ money** (BRIT) fabriquer de la fausse monnaie; **~ ahead** vi pousser de l'avant, prendre de l'avance; **~r** n faussaire m; **~ry** n faux m, contrefaçon f

forget [fə'get] (pt forgot, pp forgotten) vt, vi oublier; **~ful** adj distrait(e), étourdi(e); **~-me-not** n myosotis m

forgive [fə'gɪv] (pt forgave, pp forgiven) vt pardonner; **to ~ sb for sth/for doing sth** pardonner qch à qn/à qn de faire qch; **~ness** n pardon m

forgo [fɔː'gəu] (pt forwent, pp forgone) vt = forego

fork [fɔːk] n (for eating) fourchette f; (for gardening) fourche f; (of roads) bifurcation f; (of railways) embranchement m ♦ vi (road) bifurquer; **~ out** vt (inf) allonger; **~-lift truck** n chariot élévateur

forlorn [fə'lɔːn] adj (deserted) abandonné(e); (attempt, hope) désespéré(e)

form [fɔːm] n forme f; (SCOL) classe f; (questionnaire) formulaire m ♦ vt former; (habit) contracter; **in top ~** en pleine forme

formal ['fɔːməl] adj (offer, receipt) en bonne et due forme; (person) cérémonieux(euse); (dinner) officiel(le); (clothes) de soirée; (garden) à la française; (education) à proprement parler; **~ly** adv officiellement; cérémonieusement

format ['fɔːmæt] n format m ♦ vt (COMPUT) formater

formative ['fɔːmətɪv] adj: ~ **years** années fpl d'apprentissage or de formation

former ['fɔːmə*] adj ancien(ne) (before n), précédent(e); **the ~ ... the** latter le premier ... le second, celui-là ... celui-ci; ~**ly** adv autrefois

formidable ['fɔːmɪdəbl] adj redoutable

formula ['fɔːmjʊlə] (pl ~s or formulae) n formule f

forsake [fə'seɪk] (pt forsook, pp forsaken) vt abandonner

fort [fɔːt] n fort m

forte ['fɔːtɪ] n (point) fort m

forth [fɔːθ] adv en avant; **to go back and ~** aller et venir; **and so ~** et ainsi de suite; ~**coming** adj (event) qui va avoir lieu prochainement; (character) ouvert(e), communicatif(ive); (available) disponible; ~**right** adj franc(franche), direct(e); ~**with** adv sur-le-champ

fortify ['fɔːtɪfaɪ] vt fortifier

fortitude ['fɔːtɪtjuːd] n courage m

fortnight ['fɔːtnaɪt] (BRIT) n quinzaine f, quinze jours mpl; ~**ly** (BRIT) adj bimensuel(le) ♦ adv tous les quinze jours

fortunate ['fɔːtʃənɪt] adj heureux(euse); (person) chanceux(euse); **it is ~ that** c'est une chance que; ~**ly** adv heureusement

fortune ['fɔːtʃən] n chance f; (wealth) fortune f; ~**-teller** n diseuse f de bonne aventure

forty ['fɔːtɪ] num quarante

forward ['fɔːwəd] adj (ahead of schedule) en avance; (movement, position) en avant, vers l'avant; (not shy) direct(e); effronté(e) ♦ n (SPORT) avant m ♦ vt (letter) faire suivre; (parcel, goods) expédier; (fig) promouvoir, favoriser; ~(**s**) adv en avant; **to move ~** avancer

fossil ['fɔsl] n fossile m

foster ['fɔstə*] vt encourager, favoriser; (child) élever (sans obligation d'adopter); ~ **child** n enfant adoptif(ive)

fought [fɔːt] pt, pp of **fight**

foul [faʊl] adj (weather, smell, food) infect(e); (language) ordurier(ère) ♦ n (SPORT) faute f ♦ vt (dirty) salir, encrasser; **he's got a ~ temper** il a un caractère de chien; ~ **play** n (LAW) acte criminel

found [faʊnd] pt, pp of **find** ♦ vt (establish) fonder; ~**ation** [faʊn'deɪʃən] n (act) fondation f; (base) fondement m; (also: ~**ation cream**) fond m de teint; ~**ations** npl (of building) fondations fpl

founder ['faʊndə*] n fondateur m ♦ vi couler, sombrer

foundry ['faʊndrɪ] n fonderie f

fountain ['faʊntɪn] n fontaine f; ~ **pen** n stylo m (à encre)

four [fɔː*] num quatre; **on all ~s** à quatre pattes; ~**-poster** n (also: ~-poster bed) lit m à baldaquin; ~**some** n (game) partie f à quatre; (outing) sortie f à quatre

fourteen [fɔː'tiːn] num quatorze

fourth [fɔːθ] num quatrième

fowl [faʊl] n volaille f

fox [fɒks] n renard m ♦ vt mystifier

foyer ['fɔɪeɪ] n (hotel) hall m; (THEATRE) foyer m

fraction ['frækʃən] n fraction f

fracture ['fræktʃə*] n fracture f

fragile ['frædʒaɪl] adj fragile

fragment ['frægmənt] n fragment m

fragrant ['freɪgrənt] adj parfumé(e), odorant(e)

frail [freɪl] adj fragile, délicat(e)

frame [freɪm] n charpente f; (of picture, bicycle) cadre m; (of door, window) encadrement m, chambranle m; (of spectacles: also: ~s) monture f ♦ vt encadrer; ~ **of mind** disposition f d'esprit; ~**work** n structure f

France [frɑːns] n France f

franchise ['fræntʃaɪz] n (POL) droit m de vote; (COMM) franchise f

frank [fræŋk] adj franc(franche) ♦ vt (letter) affranchir; ~**ly** adv franchement

frantic ['fræntɪk] adj (hectic) frénétique; (distraught) hors de soi

fraternity [frə'tɜːnɪtɪ] n (spirit) fraternité f; (club) communauté f, confrérie f

fraud [frɔːd] n supercherie f, fraude f, tromperie f; (person) imposteur m

fraught [frɔːt] adj: ~ with chargé(e) de, plein(e) de

fray [freɪ] n bagarre f ♦ vi s'effilocher; tempers were ~ed les gens commençaient à s'énerver

freak [friːk] n (also cpd) phénomène m, créature ou événement exceptionnel(le) par sa rareté

freckle ['frɛkl] n tache f de rousseur

free [friː] adj libre; (gratis) gratuit(e) ♦ vt (prisoner etc) libérer; (jammed object or person) dégager; ~ (of charge), for ~ gratuitement; ~dom ['friːdəm] n liberté f; ~-for-all n mêlée générale; ~ gift n prime f; ~hold n propriété foncière libre; ~ kick n coup franc; ~lance adj indépendant(e); ~ly adv librement; (liberally) libéralement; F~mason n franc-maçon m; F~post ⓡ n port payé; ~-range adj (hen, eggs) de ferme; ~ trade n libre-échange m; ~way (US) n autoroute f; ~ will n libre arbitre m; of one's own ~ will de son plein gré

freeze [friːz] (pt froze, pp frozen) vi geler ♦ vt geler; (food) congeler; (prices, salaries) bloquer, geler ♦ n gel m; (fig) blocage m; ~-dried adj lyophilisé(e); ~r n congélateur m

freezing ['friːzɪŋ] adj: ~ (cold) (weather, water) glacial(e) ♦ n 3 degrees below ~ 3 degrés au-dessous de zéro; ~ point n point m de congélation

freight [freɪt] n (goods) fret m, cargaison f; (money charged) fret, prix m du transport; ~ train n train m de marchandises

French [frɛntʃ] adj français(e) ♦ n (LING) français m; the ~ npl (people) les Français; ~ bean n haricot vert; ~ fried (potatoes), ~ fries (US) npl (pommes de terre fpl) frites fpl; ~man (irreg) n Français m; ~

window n porte-fenêtre f; ~woman (irreg) n Française f

frenzy ['frɛnzɪ] n frénésie f

frequency ['friːkwənsɪ] n fréquence f

frequent [adj 'friːkwənt, vb friː'kwɛnt] adj fréquent(e) ♦ vt fréquenter; ~ly adv fréquemment

fresh [frɛʃ] adj frais (fraîche); (new) nouveau(nouvelle); (cheeky) familier(ère), culotté(e); ~en vi (wind, air) fraîchir; ~en up vi faire un brin de toilette; ~er n (SCOL: inf: in 1st year) étudiant(e) de 1ère année; ~ly adv nouvellement, récemment; ~man (US: irreg) n = fresher; ~ness n fraîcheur f; ~water adj (fish) d'eau douce

fret [frɛt] vi s'agiter, se tracasser

friar ['fraɪə*] n moine m, frère m

friction ['frɪkʃən] n friction f

Friday ['fraɪdeɪ] n vendredi m

fridge [frɪdʒ] (BRIT) n frigo m, frigidaire m (ⓡ)

fried [fraɪd] adj frit(e); ~ egg œuf m sur le plat

friend [frɛnd] n ami(e); ~ly adj amical(e); gentil(le); (place) accueillant(e); ~ship n amitié f

frieze [friːz] n frise f

fright [fraɪt] n peur f, effroi m; to take ~ prendre peur, s'effrayer; ~en vt effrayer, faire peur à; ~ened adj: to be ~ened (of) avoir peur (de); ~ening adj effrayant(e); ~ful adj affreux(euse)

frigid ['frɪdʒɪd] adj (woman) frigide

frill [frɪl] n (of dress) volant m; (of shirt) jabot m

fringe [frɪndʒ] n (BRIT: of hair) frange f; (edge: of forest etc) bordure f; ~ benefits npl avantages sociaux or en nature

frisk [frɪsk] vt fouiller

fritter ['frɪtə*] n beignet m; ~ away vt gaspiller

frivolous ['frɪvələs] adj frivole

frizzy ['frɪzɪ] adj crépu(e)

fro [frəu] adv: to go to and ~ aller et venir

frock [frɔk] n robe f

frog [frog] *n* grenouille *f*; **~man** *n* homme-grenouille *m*

frolic [ˈfrɒlɪk] *vi* folâtrer, batifoler

KEYWORD

from [frɒm] *prep* **1** (*indicating starting place, origin etc*) de; **where do you come from ~?**, **where are you ~?** d'où venez-vous?; **~ London to Paris** de Londres à Paris; **a letter ~ my sister** une lettre de ma sœur; **to drink ~ the bottle** boire à (même) la bouteille
2 (*indicating time*) (à partir) de; **~ one o'clock to** *or* **until** *or* **till two** d'une heure à deux heures; **~ January (on)** à partir de janvier
3 (*indicating distance*) de; **the hotel is one kilometre ~ the beach** l'hôtel est à un kilomtre de la plage
4 (*indicating price, number etc*) de; **the interest rate was increased ~ 9% to 10%** le taux d'intérêt a augmenté de 9 à 10%
5 (*indicating difference*) de; **he can't tell red ~ green** il ne peut pas distinguer le rouge du vert
6 (*because of, on the basis of*): **~ what he says** d'après ce qu'il dit; **weak ~ hunger** affaibli par la faim

front [frʌnt] *n* (*of house, dress*) devant *m*; (*of coach, train*) avant *m*; (*promenade: also: sea ~*) bord *m* de mer; (*MIL, METEOROLOGY*) front *m*; (*fig: appearances*) contenance *f*, façade ♦ *adj* de devant; (*seat*) avant *inv*; **in ~ (of)** devant; (*fig*) ['frʌntɪdʒ] *n* (*of building*) façade *f*; **~ door** *n* porte *f* d'entrée; (*of car*) portière *f* avant; **~ier** ['frʌntɪə*] *n* frontière *f*; **~ page** *n* première page; **~ room** *n* (*BRIT*) *n* pièce *f* de devant, salon *m*; **~-wheel drive** *n* traction *f* avant

frost [frɒst] *n* gel *m*, gelée *f*; (*also: hoar-~*) givre *m*; **~bite** *n* gelures *fpl*; **~ed** *adj* (*glass*) dépoli(e); **~y** *adj* (*weather, welcome*) glacial(e)

froth [frɒθ] *n* mousse *f*; écume *f*

frown [fraʊn] *vi* froncer les sourcils

froze [frəʊz] *pt of* **freeze**

frozen [ˈfrəʊzn] *pp of* **freeze**

fruit [fruːt] *n inv* fruit *m*; ~ **~erer** *n* fruitier *m*, marchand(e) de fruits; **~ful** *adj* (*fig*) fructueux(euse); **~ion** [fruːˈɪʃən] *n*: **to come to ~ion** se réaliser; **~ juice** *n* jus *m* de fruit; **~ machine** *n* (*BRIT*) machine *f* à sous; **~ salad** *n* salade *f* de fruits

frustrate [frʌsˈtreɪt] *vt* frustrer

fry [fraɪ] (*pt, pp* **fried**) *vt* (faire) frire; *see also* **small**; **~ing pan** *n* poêle *f* (à frire)

fuddy-duddy [ˈfʌdɪdʌdɪ] (*pej*) *n* vieux schnock

ft. *abbr* = **foot**; **feet**

fudge [fʌdʒ] *n* (*CULIN*) caramel *m*

fuel [fjʊəl] *n* (*for heating*) combustible *m*; (*for propelling*) carburant *m*; ~ **~oil** *n* mazout *m*; **~ tank** *n* (*in vehicle*) réservoir *m*

fugitive [ˈfjuːdʒɪtɪv] *n* fugitif(ive)

fulfil [fʊlˈfɪl] (*US* **~l**) *vt* (*function, condition*) remplir; (*order*) exécuter; (*wish, desire*) satisfaire, réaliser; **~ment** *n* (*of wishes etc*) réalisation *f*; (*feeling*) contentement *m*

full [fʊl] *adj* plein(e); (*details, skirt*) complet(ète), (*skirt*) ample, large ♦ *adv*: **to know ~ well that** savoir fort bien que; **I'm ~ (up)** j'ai bien mangé; **a ~ two hours** deux bonnes heures; **at ~ speed** à toute vitesse; **in ~** (*reproduce, quote*) intégralement; (*write*) en toutes lettres; **~ employment** plein emploi; **to pay in ~** tout payer; **~-length** *adj* (*film*) long métrage; (*portrait, mirror*) en pied; (*coat*) long(ue); **~ moon** *n* pleine lune; **~-scale** *adj* (*attack, war*) complet(ète), total(e); (*model*) grandeur nature *inv*; **~ stop** *n* point *m*; **~-time** *adj, adv* (*work*) à plein temps; **~y** *adv* entièrement, complètement; (*at least*) au moins; **~y-fledged** *adj* (*teacher, barrister*) diplômé(e); (*citizen, member*) à part entière

fumble [ˈfʌmbl] *vi*: **~ with** tripoter

fume [fjuːm] vi rager; ~s npl vapeurs fpl, émanations fpl, gaz mpl

fun [fʌn] n amusement m, divertissement m; **to have** ~ s'amuser; **for** ~ pour rire; **to make** ~ **of** se moquer de

function ['fʌŋkʃən] n fonction f; (social occasion) cérémonie f, soirée officielle ♦ vi fonctionner; **~al** adj fonctionnel(le)

fund [fʌnd] n caisse f, fonds m; (source, store) source f, mine f; ~s npl (money) fonds mpl

fundamental [fʌndə'mentl] adj fondamental(e)

funeral ['fjuːnərəl] n enterrement m, obsèques fpl; ~ **parlour** n entreprise f de pompes funèbres; ~ **service** n service m funèbre

funfair ['fʌnfɛə*] (BRIT) n fête f (foraine)

fungus ['fʌŋgəs] (pl **fungi**) n champignon m; (mould) moisissure f

funnel ['fʌnl] n entonnoir m; (of ship) cheminée f

funny ['fʌnɪ] adj amusant(e), drôle; (strange) curieux(euse), bizarre

fur [fɜː*] n fourrure f; (BRIT: in kettle etc) (dépôt m de) tartre m; ~ **coat** n manteau m de fourrure

furious ['fjuərɪəs] adj furieux(euse); (effort) acharné(e)

furlong ['fɜːlɔŋ] n = 201,17 m

furlough ['fɜːləu] n permission f, congé m

furnace ['fɜːnɪs] n fourneau m

furnish ['fɜːnɪʃ] vt meubler; (supply): **to** ~ **sb with sth** fournir qch à qn; ~**ings** npl mobilier m, ameublement m

furniture ['fɜːnɪtʃə*] n meubles mpl, mobilier m; **piece of** ~ meuble m

furrow ['fʌrəu] n sillon m

furry ['fɜːrɪ] adj (animal) à fourrure; (toy) en peluche

further ['fɜːðə*] adj (additional) supplémentaire, autre; nouveau (nouvelle) ♦ adv plus loin; (more) davantage; (moreover) de plus ♦ vt faire avancer or progresser, promou-

voir; ~ **education** n enseignement m postscolaire; ~**more** adv de plus, en outre

furthest ['fɜːðɪst] superl of **far**

fury ['fjuərɪ] n fureur f

fuse [fjuːz] (US **fuze**) n fusible m; (for bomb etc) amorce f, détonateur m ♦ vt, vi (metal) fondre; **to** ~ **the lights** (BRIT) faire sauter les plombs; ~ **box** n boîte f à fusibles

fuss [fʌs] n (excitement) agitation f; (complaining) histoire(s) f(pl); **to make a** ~ faire des histoires; **to make a** ~ **of sb** être aux petits soins pour qn; ~**y** adj (person) tatillon(ne), difficile; (dress, style) tarabiscoté(e)

future ['fjuːtʃə*] adj futur(e) ♦ n avenir m; (LING) futur m; **in** ~ à l'avenir

fuze [fjuːz] (US) n, vt, vi = **fuse**

fuzzy ['fʌzɪ] adj (PHOT) flou(e); (hair) crépu(e)

G

G [dʒiː] n (MUS) sol m

G7 n abbr (= Group of 7) le groupe des 7

gabble ['gæbl] vi bredouiller

gable ['geɪbl] n pignon m

gadget ['gædʒɪt] n gadget m

Gaelic ['geɪlɪk] adj gaélique ♦ n (LING) gaélique m

gag [gæg] n (on mouth) bâillon m; (joke) gag m ♦ vt bâillonner

gaiety ['geɪətɪ] n gaieté f

gain [geɪn] n (improvement) gain m; (profit) gain, profit m; (increase): ~ (in) augmentation f (de) ♦ vt gagner ♦ vi (watch) avancer; **to** ~ **3 lbs** (in weight) prendre 3 livres; **to** ~ **on sb** (catch up) rattraper qn; **to** ~ **from/by** gagner de/à

gait [geɪt] n démarche f

gal. abbr = **gallon**

gale [geɪl] n rafale f de vent; coup m de vent

gallant ['gælənt] adj vaillant(e),

brave; (towards ladies) galant
gall bladder ['gɔːl-] n vésicule f biliaire
gallery ['gælərɪ] n galerie f; (also: art ~) musée m; (: private) galerie
galley ['gælɪ] n (ship's kitchen) cambuse f
gallon ['gælən] n gallon m (BRIT = 4,5 l; US = 3,8 l)
gallop ['gæləp] n galop m ♦ vi galoper
gallows ['gæləʊz] n potence f
gallstone ['gɔːlstəʊn] n calcul m biliaire
galore [gə'lɔː*] adv en abondance, à gogo
Gambia n: (The) ~ la Gambie
gambit ['gæmbɪt] n (fig: (opening) ~ manœuvre f stratégique
gamble ['gæmbl] n pari m, risque calculé ♦ vt, vi jouer; to ~ on (fig) miser sur; ~r n joueur m; **gambling** ['gæmblɪŋ] n jeu m
game [geɪm] n jeu m; (match) match m; (strategy, scheme) plan m; projet m; (HUNTING) gibier m ♦ adj (willing): to be ~ (for) être prêt(e) (à or pour); **big** ~ gros gibier; **~keeper** n garde-chasse m
gammon ['gæmən] n (bacon) quartier m de lard fumé; (ham) jambon fumé
gamut ['gæmət] n gamme f
gang [gæŋ] n bande f; (of workmen) équipe f; ~ **up** vi: to ~ up on sb se liguer contre qn; **~ster** ['gæŋstə*] n gangster m; **~way** n passerelle f; (BRIT: of bus, plane) couloir central; (: in cinema) allée centrale
gaol [dʒeɪl] (BRIT) n = **jail**
gap [gæp] n trou m; (in time) intervalle m; (difference): ~ **between** écart m entre
gape [geɪp] vi (person) être or rester bouche bée; (hole, shirt) être ouvert(e); **gaping** ['geɪpɪŋ] adj (hole) béant(e)
garage ['gærɑːʒ] n garage m
garbage ['gɑːbɪdʒ] n (US: rubbish) ordures fpl, détritus mpl; (inf: nonsense) foutaises fpl; ~ **can** (US) n poubelle f, boîte f à ordures
garbled ['gɑːbld] adj (account, message) embrouillé(e)
garden ['gɑːdn] n jardin m; **~s** npl jardin public; **~er** n jardinier m; **~ing** n jardinage m
gargle ['gɑːgl] vi se gargariser
garish ['gɛərɪʃ] adj criard(e), voyant(e); (light) cru(e)
garland ['gɑːlənd] n guirlande f; couronne f
garlic ['gɑːlɪk] n ail m
garment ['gɑːmənt] n vêtement m
garrison ['gærɪsən] n garnison f
garrulous ['gærʊləs] adj volubile, loquace
garter ['gɑːtə*] n jarretière f; (US) jarretelle f
gas [gæs] n gaz m; (US: ~oline) essence f ♦ vt asphyxier; ~ **cooker** (BRIT) n cuisinière f à gaz; ~ **cylinder** n bouteille f de gaz; ~ **fire** (BRIT) n radiateur m à gaz
gash [gæʃ] n entaille f; (on face) balafre f
gasket ['gæskɪt] n (AUT) joint m de culasse
gas mask n masque m à gaz
gas meter n compteur m à gaz
gasoline ['gæsəliːn] (US) n essence f
gasp [gɑːsp] vi haleter; ~ **out** (say) dire dans un souffle or d'une voix entrecoupée
gas station (US) n station-service f
gas tap n bouton m (de cuisinière à gaz); (on pipe) robinet m à gaz
gastric adj gastrique; ~ **flu** grippe f intestinale
gate [geɪt] n (of garden) portail m; (of field) barrière f; (of building, at airport) porte f; **~crash** vt s'introduire sans invitation dans; **~way** n porte f
gather ['gæðə*] vt (flowers, fruit) cueillir; (pick up) ramasser; (assemble) rassembler, réunir; recueillir; (understand) comprendre; (SEWING) froncer ♦ vi (assemble) se rassembler; to ~ **speed** prendre de la

vitesse; **~ing** *n* rassemblement *m*

gaudy ['gɔːdɪ] *adj* voyant(e)

gauge [geɪdʒ] *n* (*instrument*) jauge *f* ♦ *vt* jauger

gaunt [gɔːnt] *adj* (*thin*) décharné(e); (*grim, desolate*) désolé(e)

gauntlet ['gɔːntlɪt] *n* (*glove*) gant *m*; (*fig*): **to run the ~ through** an angry crowd se frayer un passage à travers une foule hostile; **to throw down the ~** jeter le gant

gauze [gɔːz] *n* gaze *f*

gave [geɪv] *pt of* **give**

gay [geɪ] *adj* (*homosexual*) homosexuel(le); (*cheerful*) gai(e), réjoui(e); (*colour etc*) gai, vif(vive)

gaze [geɪz] *n* regard *m* fixe ♦ *vi*: **to ~ at** fixer du regard

gazump (*BRIT*) *vi* revenir sur une promesse de vente (*pour accepter une offre plus intéressante*)

GB *abbr* = **Great Britain**

GCE *n abbr* (*BRIT*) = **General Certificate of Education**

GCSE *n abbr* (*BRIT*) = **General Certificate of Secondary Education**

gear [gɪə*] *n* matériel *m*, équipement *m*; attirail *m*; (*TECH*) engrenage *m*; (*AUT*) vitesse *f* ♦ *vt* (*fig: adapt*): **to ~ sth to** adapter qch à; **top** (*or US* **high**) **~** quatrième (*or* cinquième) vitesse; **low ~** première vitesse; **in ~** en prise; **~ box** *n* boîte *f* de vitesses; **~ lever** (*US* **~ shift**) *n* levier *m* de vitesse

geese [giːs] *npl of* **goose**

gel [dʒel] *n* gel *m*

gelignite ['dʒelɪgnaɪt] *n* plastic *m*

gem [dʒem] *n* pierre précieuse

Gemini ['dʒemɪnaɪ] *n* les Gémeaux *mpl*

gender ['dʒendə*] *n* genre *m*

general ['dʒenərəl] *n* général *m* ♦ *adj* général(e); **in ~** en général; **~ delivery** *n* poste restante; **~ election** *n* élection(s) législative(s); **~ly** *adv* généralement; **~ practitioner** *n* généraliste *m/f*

generate ['dʒenəreɪt] *vt* engendrer;

(*electricity etc*) produire

generation [dʒenə'reɪʃən] *n* génération *f*; (*of electricity etc*) production *f*

generator ['dʒenəreɪtə*] *n* générateur *m*

generosity [dʒenə'rɒsɪtɪ] *n* générosité *f*; **generous** ['dʒenərəs] *adj* généreux(euse); (*copious*) copieux(euse)

genetic engineering [dʒɪ'netɪk-] *n* ingénierie *f* génétique

genetics [dʒɪ'netɪks] *n* génétique *f*

Geneva [dʒɪ'niːvə] *n* Genève

genial ['dʒiːnɪəl] *adj* cordial(e), chaleureux(euse)

genitals ['dʒenɪtlz] *npl* organes génitaux

genius ['dʒiːnɪəs] *n* génie *m*

genteel [dʒen'tiːl] *adj* de bon ton, distingué(e)

gentle ['dʒentl] *adj* doux(douce)

gentleman ['dʒentlmən] *n* monsieur *m*; (*well-bred man*) gentleman *m*

gently ['dʒentlɪ] *adv* doucement

gentry ['dʒentrɪ] *n inv*: **the ~** la petite noblesse

gents [dʒents] *n* W.C. *mpl* (*pour hommes*)

genuine ['dʒenjuɪn] *adj* véritable, authentique; (*person*) sincère

geography [dʒɪ'ɒgrəfɪ] *n* géographie *f*

geology [dʒɪ'ɒlədʒɪ] *n* géologie *f*

geometric(al) [dʒɪə'metrɪk(l)] *adj* géométrique

geometry [dʒɪ'ɒmɪtrɪ] *n* géométrie *f*

geranium [dʒɪ'reɪnɪəm] *n* géranium *m*

geriatric [dʒerɪ'ætrɪk] *adj* gériatrique

germ [dʒɜːm] *n* (*MED*) microbe *m*

German ['dʒɜːmən] *adj* allemand(e) ♦ *n* Allemand(e); (*LING*) allemand *m*; **~ measles** (*BRIT*) *n* rubéole *f*

Germany ['dʒɜːmənɪ] *n* Allemagne *f*

gesture ['dʒestʃə*] *n* geste *m*

KEYWORD

get [get] (*pt, pp* **got**, *pp* **gotten** (*US*)) *vi* **1** (*become, be*) devenir; **to ~ old/tired** devenir vieux/fatigué, vieillir/se fatiguer; to ~ **drunk** s'enivrer; to ~ **killed** se faire tuer; **when do I ~ paid?** quand est-ce que je serai payé?; **it's ~ting late** il se fait tard

2 (go): **to ~ to/from** aller à/de; **to ~ home** rentrer chez soi; **how did you ~ here?** comment es-tu arrivé ici?

3 (begin) commencer ou se mettre à; **I'm ~ting to like him** je commence à l'apprécier; **let's ~ going** or **started** allons-y

4 (modal aux vb): **you've got to do it** il faut que vous le fassiez; **I've got to tell the police** je dois le dire à la police

♦ vt **1**: **to ~ sth done** (do) faire qch; (have done) faire faire qch; **to ~ one's hair cut** se faire couper les cheveux; **to ~ sb to do sth** faire faire qch à qn; **to ~ sb drunk** enivrer qn

2 (obtain: money, permission, results) obtenir, avoir; (find: job, flat) trouver; (fetch: person, doctor, object) aller chercher; **to ~ sth for sb** procurer qch à qn; **~ me Mr Jones, please** (on phone) passez-moi Mr Jones, s'il vous plaît; **can I ~ you a drink?** est-ce que je peux vous servir à boire?

3 (receive: present, letter) recevoir, avoir; (acquire: reputation) avoir; (: prize) obtenir; **what did you ~ for your birthday?** qu'est-ce que tu as eu pour ton anniversaire?

4 (catch) prendre, saisir, attraper; (hit: target) atteindre; **to ~ sb by the arm/throat** prendre ou saisir ou attraper qn par le bras/à la gorge; **~ him!** arrête-le!

5 (take, move) faire parvenir; **do you think we'll ~ it through the door?** on arrivera à le faire passer par la porte?; **I'll ~ you there somehow** je me débrouillerai pour t'y emmener

6 (catch, take: plane, bus etc) prendre

7 (understand) comprendre, saisir; (hear) entendre; **I've got it!** j'ai compris!; **I didn't ~ your name** je n'ai pas entendu votre nom

8 (have, possess): **to have got** avoir; **how many have you got?** vous en avez combien?

get about vi se déplacer; (news) se répandre

get along vi (agree) s'entendre; (depart) s'en aller; (manage) = **get by**

get at vt fus (attack) s'en prendre à; (reach) attraper, atteindre

get away vi partir, s'en aller, s'en aller; (escape) s'échapper

get away with vt fus en être quitte pour; se faire passer or pardonner

get back vi (return) rentrer ♦ vt récupérer, recouvrer

get by vi (pass) passer; (manage) se débrouiller

get down vi, vt fus descendre ♦ vt (depress) déprimer

get down to vt fus (work) se mettre à

get in vi rentrer; (train) arriver; **get into** vt fus entrer dans; (car, train etc) monter dans; (clothes) mettre, enfiler, endosser; **to get into bed/a rage** se mettre au lit/en colère

get off vi (from train etc) descendre; (depart: person, car) s'en aller; (escape) s'en tirer ♦ vt fus (remove: clothes, stain) enlever ♦ vt fus (train, bus) descendre de

get on vi (at exam etc) se débrouiller; (agree): **to get on (with)** s'entendre (avec) ♦ vt fus monter dans; (horse) monter sur

get out vi sortir; (of vehicle) descendre ♦ vt sortir

get out of vt fus sortir de; (duty etc) échapper à, se soustraire à

get over vt fus (illness) se remettre de

get round vt fus contourner; (fig: person) entortiller

get through vi (TEL) avoir la communication; **to get through to sb** atteindre qn

get together vi se réunir ♦ vt assembler

get up vi (rise) se lever ♦ vt fus monter

get up to vt fus (reach) arriver à; (prank etc) faire

getaway ['getəweɪ] n: **to make one's ~** filer

geyser ['giːzə*] n (GEO) geyser m; (BRIT: water heater) chauffe-eau m inv

Ghana ['gɑːnə] n Ghana m

ghastly ['gɑːstlɪ] adj atroce, horrible; (pale) livide, blême

gherkin ['gɜːkɪn] n cornichon m

ghetto blaster ['getəʊ-] n stéréo f portable

ghost [gəʊst] n fantôme m, revenant m

giant ['dʒaɪənt] n géant(e) ♦ adj géant(e), énorme

gibberish ['dʒɪbərɪʃ] n charabia m

giblets ['dʒɪblɪts] npl abats mpl

Gibraltar [dʒɪ'brɔːltə*] n Gibraltar m

giddy ['gɪdɪ] adj (dizzy): **to be** or **feel ~** avoir le vertige

gift [gɪft] n cadeau m; (donation, ability) don m; **~ed** adj doué(e); **~ token** n chèque-cadeau m

gigantic [dʒaɪ'gæntɪk] adj gigantesque

giggle ['gɪgl] vi pouffer (de rire), rire sottement

gill [dʒɪl] n (measure) = 0.25 pints (BRIT = 0.15 l, US = 0.12 l)

gills [gɪlz] npl (of fish) ouïes fpl, branchies fpl

gilt [gɪlt] adj doré(e) ♦ n dorure f; **~-edged** adj (COMM) de premier ordre

gimmick ['gɪmɪk] n truc m

gin [dʒɪn] n (liquor) gin m

ginger ['dʒɪndʒə*] n gingembre m; **~ ale**, **~ beer** n boisson gazeuse au gingembre; **~bread** n pain m d'épices

gingerly ['dʒɪndʒəlɪ] adv avec précaution

gipsy ['dʒɪpsɪ] n = gypsy

giraffe [dʒɪ'rɑːf] n girafe f

girder ['gɜːdə*] n poutrelle f

girdle ['gɜːdl] n (corset) gaine f

girl [gɜːl] n fille f, fillette f; (young unmarried woman) jeune fille; (daughter) fille f; **an English ~** une jeune Anglaise; **~friend** n (of girl) amie f; (of boy) petite amie; **~ish** adj de petite or de jeune fille; (for a boy) efféminé(e)

giro ['dʒaɪərəʊ] n (bank ~) virement m bancaire; (post office ~) mandat m; (BRIT: welfare cheque) mandat d'allocation chômage

girth [gɜːθ] n circonférence f; (of horse) sangle f

gist [dʒɪst] n essentiel m

give [gɪv] (pt **gave**, pp **given**) vt donner ♦ vi (break) céder; (stretch: fabric) se prêter; **to ~ sb sth**, **~ sth to sb** donner qch à qn; **to ~ a cry/sigh** pousser un cri/un soupir; **~ away** vt donner; (~ free) faire cadeau de; (betray) donner, trahir; (disclose) révéler; (bride) conduire à l'autel; **~ back** vt rendre; **~ in** vi céder ♦ vt donner; **~ off** vt dégager; **~ out** vt distribuer; annoncer; **~ up** vi renoncer ♦ vt renoncer à; **to ~ up smoking** arrêter de fumer; **to ~ o.s. up** se rendre; **~ way** (BRIT) vi céder; (AUT) céder la priorité

glacier ['glæsɪə*] n glacier m

glad [glæd] adj content(e); **~ly** adv volontiers

glamorous ['glæmərəs] adj (person) séduisant(e); (job) prestigieux (euse)

glamour ['glæmə*] n éclat m, prestige m

glance [glɑːns] n coup m d'œil ♦ vi: **to ~ at** jeter un coup d'œil à; **~ off** vt fus (bullet) ricocher sur; **glancing** ['glɑːnsɪŋ] adj (blow) oblique

gland [glænd] n glande f

glare [gleə*] n (of anger) regard furieux; (of light) lumière éblouissante; (of publicity) feux mpl ♦ vi briller d'un éclat aveuglant; **to ~ at** lancer un regard furieux à; **glaring** ['gleərɪŋ] adj (mistake) criant(e), qui saute aux yeux

glass [glɑːs] n verre m; ~es npl (spectacles) lunettes fpl; ~**house** (BRIT) n (for plants) serre f; ~**ware** n verrerie f

glaze [gleɪz] vt (door, window) vitrer; (pottery) vernir ♦ n (on pottery) vernis m; (: AVIAT) verni(e); (eyes) vitreux(euse); **glazier** ['gleɪzɪə*] n vitrier m

gleam [gliːm] vi luire, briller

glean [gliːn] vt (information) glaner

glee [gliː] n joie f

glib [glɪb] adj (person) qui a du bagou; (response) désinvolte, facile

glide [glaɪd] vi glisser; (AVIAT, birds) planer; **glider** n (AVIAT) planeur m; **gliding** ['glaɪdɪŋ] n (SPORT) vol m à voile

glimmer ['glɪmə*] n lueur f

glimpse [glɪmps] n vision passagère, aperçu m ♦ vt entrevoir, apercevoir

glint [glɪnt] vi étinceler

glisten ['glɪsn] vi briller, luire

glitter ['glɪtə*] vi scintiller, briller

gloat [gləʊt] vi: to ~ (over) jubiler (à propos de)

global ['gləʊbl] adj mondial(e)

globe [gləʊb] n globe m

gloom [gluːm] n obscurité f; (sadness) tristesse f, mélancolie f; ~**y** adj sombre, triste, lugubre

glorious ['glɔːrɪəs] adj glorieux(euse); splendide

glory ['glɔːrɪ] n gloire f; (splendour) splendeur f

gloss [glɒs] n (shine) brillant m, vernis m; (also: ~ paint) peinture brillante or laquée; ~ **over** vt fus glisser sur

glossary ['glɒsərɪ] n glossaire m

glossy ['glɒsɪ] adj brillant(e); ~ magazine magazine m de luxe

glove [glʌv] n gant m; ~ **compartment** n (AUT) boîte f à gants, vide-poches m inv

glow [gləʊ] vi rougeoyer; (face) rayonner; (eyes) briller

glower ['glaʊə*] vi: to ~ (at) lancer des regards mauvais (à

glucose ['gluːkəʊz] n glucose m

glue [gluː] n colle f ♦ vt coller

glum [glʌm] adj sombre, morne

glut [glʌt] n surabondance f

glutton ['glʌtn] n glouton(ne); a ~ for work un bourreau de travail; a ~ for punishment un masochiste (fig)

gnarled [nɑːld] adj noueux(euse)

gnat [næt] n moucheron m

gnaw [nɔː] vt ronger

go [gəʊ] (pt went, pp gone; pl ~es) vi aller; (depart) partir; (work) marcher; (be sold): to ~ for £10 se vendre 10 livres; (fit, suit): to ~ with aller avec; (become): to ~ pale/mouldy pâlir/moisir; (break etc) céder ♦ n: to have a ~ (at) essayer (de faire); to be on the ~ être en mouvement; whose ~ is it? à qui est-ce de jouer?; he's ~ing to do it va le faire, il est sur le point de faire; to ~ for a walk aller se promener; to ~ dancing aller danser; how did it ~? comment s'est-ce passé?; to ~ round the back/by the shop passer par derrière/devant le magasin; ~ **about** vi (rumour) se répandre ♦ vt fus: how do I ~ about this? comment dois-je m'y prendre (pour faire ceci?); ~ **ahead** vi (make progress) avancer; (get going) y aller; ~ **along** vi aller, avancer ♦ vt fus longer, parcourir; ~ **away** vi partir, s'en aller; ~ **back** vi rentrer, revenir; (go again) retourner; ~ **back on** vt fus (promise) revenir sur; ~ **by** vi (years, time) passer, s'écouler ♦ vt fus (believe) se fier à; en croire; ~ **down** vi descendre; (ship) couler; (sun) se coucher ♦ vt fus descendre; ~ **for** vt fus (fetch) aller chercher; (like) aimer; (attack) s'en prendre à, attaquer; ~ **in** vi entrer; ~ **in for** vt fus (competition) se présenter à; (like) aimer; ~ **into** vt fus entrer dans; (investigate) étudier, examiner; (embark on) se lancer dans; ~ **off** vi partir, s'en aller; (food) se gâter; (explode) sauter; (event) se dérouler ♦ vt fus ne plus aimer; **the gun went off** le coup est parti; ~ **on** vi continuer; (happen) se passer; **to** ~ **on doing** continuer à faire; ~ **out** vi sortir; (fire, light) s'éteindre; ~ **over** vt fus (check) revoir, vérifier; ~ **through** vt fus (town etc) traverser; ~ **up** vi monter; (price) augmenter ♦ vt fus gravir; ~ **without** vt fus se passer de

goad [gəʊd] vt aiguillonner

go-ahead ['gəʊəhed] adj dynamique, entreprenant(e) ♦ n feu vert

goal [gəʊl] n but m; ~**keeper** n gardien m de but; ~**post** n poteau m de but

goat [gəʊt] n chèvre f

gobble ['gɔbl] vt (also: ~ **down**, ~ **up**) engloutir

go-between ['gəʊbɪtwiːn] n intermédiaire m/f

god [gɔd] n dieu m; **G**~ n Dieu m; ~**child** n filleul(e); ~**daughter** n filleule f; ~**dess** n déesse f; ~**father** n parrain m; ~**forsaken** adj maudit(e); ~**mother** n marraine f; ~**send** n aubaine f; ~**son** n filleul m

goggles ['gɔglz] npl (for skiing etc) lunettes protectrices

going ['gəʊɪŋ] n (conditions) état m du terrain ♦ adj: **the** ~ **rate** le tarif (en vigueur)

gold [gəʊld] n or m ♦ adj en or; (reserves) d'or; ~**en** adj (made of gold) en or; (gold in colour) doré(e); ~**fish** n poisson m rouge; ~**plated** adj plaqué(e or inv); ~**smith** n orfèvre m

golf [gɔlf] n golf m; ~ **ball** n balle f de golf; (on typewriter) boule f; ~ **club** n club m de golf; (stick) club m, crosse f de golf; ~ **course** n (terrain m de) golf m; ~**er** n joueur(euse) de golf

gone [gɔn] pp of **go**

gong [gɔŋ] n gong m

good [gʊd] adj bon(ne); (kind) gentil(le); (child) sage ♦ n bien m; ~**s** npl (COMM) marchandises fpl, articles mpl; ~! bon!, très bien!; **to**

be ~ **at** être bon to; **to be** ~ **for** être bon pour; **would you be** ~ **enough to ...?** auriez-vous la bonté or l'amabilité de ...?; **a** ~ **deal (of)** beaucoup (de); **a** ~ **many** beaucoup (de); **to make** ~ vi (succeed) faire son chemin, réussir ♦ vt (deficit) combler; (losses) compenser; **it's no** ~ **complaining** cela ne sert à rien de se plaindre; **for** ~ pour de bon, une fois pour toutes; ~ **morning/afternoon!** bonjour!; ~ **evening!** bonsoir!; ~ **night!** bonsoir!; (on going to bed) bonne nuit!; ~**bye** excl au revoir!; **G**~ **Friday** n Vendredi saint; ~**looking** adj beau(belle), bien inv; ~**natured** adj (person) qui a un bon naturel; ~**ness** n (of person) bonté f; **for** ~**ness sake!** je vous en prie!; ~**ness gracious!** mon Dieu!; ~**s train** (BRIT) n train m de marchandises; ~**will** n bonne volonté

goose [guːs] (pl **geese**) n oie f

gooseberry ['gʊzbərɪ] n groseille f à maquereau; **to play** ~ (BRIT) tenir la chandelle

gooseflesh ['guːsfleʃ] n, **goose pimples** npl chair f de poule

gore [gɔːɹ] vt encorner ♦ n sang m

gorge [gɔːdʒ] n gorge f ♦ vt: **to** ~ **o.s. (on)** se gorger (de)

gorgeous ['gɔːdʒəs] adj splendide, superbe

gorilla [gə'rɪlə] n gorille m

gorse [gɔːs] n ajoncs mpl

gory ['gɔːrɪ] adj sanglant(e); (details) horrible

go-slow ['gəʊ'sləʊ] (BRIT) n grève perlée

gospel ['gɔspəl] n évangile m

gossip ['gɔsɪp] n (chat) bavardages mpl; commérage m, cancans mpl; (person) commère f ♦ vi bavarder; (maliciously) cancaner, faire des commérages

got [gɔt] pt, pp of **get**

gotten ['gɔtn] (US) pp of **get**

gout [gaʊt] n goutte f

govern ['gʌvən] vt gouverner; ~**ess** ['gʌvənɪs] n gouvernante f; ~**ment**

['gaʊnmənt] n gouvernement m; (BRIT: ministers) ministère m; ~or ['gʌvənə*] n (of state, bank) gouverneur m; (of school, hospital) ≈ membre m/f du conseil d'établissement; (BRIT: of prison) directeur(trice)

gown [gaʊn] n robe f; (of teacher, BRIT: of judge) toge f

GP n abbr = general practitioner

grab [græb] vt saisir, empoigner ♦ vi: to ~ at essayer de saisir

grace [greɪs] n grâce f ♦ vt honorer; (adorn) orner; 5 days' ~ cinq jours de répit; ~ful adj gracieux(euse), élégant(e); **gracious** ['greɪʃəs] adj bienveillant(e)

grade [greɪd] n (COMM) qualité f; (in hierarchy) catégorie f, grade m, échelon m; (SCOL) note f; (US: school class) classe f ♦ vt classer; ~ crossing (US) n passage m à niveau; ~ school (US) n école f primaire

gradient ['greɪdɪənt] n inclinaison f, pente f

gradual ['grædjʊəl] adj graduel(le), progressif(ive); ~ly adv peu à peu, graduellement

graduate [n 'grædjʊɪt, vb 'grædjʊeɪt] n diplômé(e), licencié(e); (US: of high school) bachelier(ère) ♦ vi obtenir son diplôme; (US) obtenir son baccalauréat; **graduation** [grædʊ'eɪʃən] n (cérémonie f de) remise f des diplômes

graffiti [grə'fiːtɪ] npl graffiti mpl

graft [grɑːft] n (AGR, MED) greffe f; (bribery) corruption f ♦ vt greffer; hard ~ (BRIT: inf) boulot acharné

grain [greɪn] n grain m

gram [græm] n gramme m

grammar ['græmə*] n grammaire f; ~ school (BRIT) n ≈ lycée m; **grammatical** [grə'mætɪkl] adj grammatical(e)

gramme [græm] n = gram

grand [grænd] adj magnifique, splendide; (gesture etc) noble; ~children npl petits-enfants mpl; ~dad (inf) n grand-papa m; ~daughter n petite-fille f; ~father n grand-père m;

~ma (inf) n grand-maman f; ~mother n grand-mère f; ~pa (inf) n = ~dad; ~parents npl grands-parents mpl; ~ piano n piano m à queue; ~son n petit-fils m; ~stand n (SPORT) tribune f

granite ['grænɪt] n granit m

granny ['grænɪ] (inf) n grand-maman f

grant [grɑːnt] vt accorder; (a request) accéder à; (admit) concéder ♦ n (SCOL) bourse f; (ADMIN) subside m, subvention f; to take it for ~ed that trouver tout naturel que +sub; to take sb for ~ed considérer qn comme faisant partie du décor

granulated sugar ['grænjʊleɪtɪd-] n sucre m en poudre

grape [greɪp] n raisin m; ~fruit ['greɪpfruːt] n pamplemousse m

graph [grɑːf] n graphique m; ~ic ['græfɪk] adj graphique; (account, description) vivant(e); ~ics n arts mpl graphiques; graphisme m ♦ npl représentations fpl graphiques

grapple ['græpl] vi: to ~ with être aux prises avec

grasp [grɑːsp] vt saisir ♦ n (grip) prise f; (understanding) compréhension f, connaissance f; ~ing adj cupide

grass [grɑːs] n herbe f; (lawn) gazon m; ~hopper n sauterelle f; ~roots adj de la base, du peuple

grate [greɪt] n grille f de cheminée ♦ vi grincer ♦ vt (CULIN) râper

grateful ['greɪtfʊl] adj reconnaissant(e)

grater ['greɪtə*] n râpe f

gratifying ['grætɪfaɪɪŋ] adj agréable

grating ['greɪtɪŋ] n (iron bars) grille f ♦ adj (noise) grinçant(e)

gratitude ['grætɪtjuːd] n gratitude f

gratuity [grə'tjuːɪtɪ] n pourboire m

grave [greɪv] n tombe f ♦ adj grave, sérieux(euse)

gravel ['grævəl] n gravier m

gravestone ['greɪvstəʊn] n pierre f tombale

graveyard ['greɪvjɑːd] n cimetière m

gravity ['grævɪtɪ] n (PHYSICS) gravité f; pesanteur f; (seriousness) gravité

gravy ['greɪvɪ] n jus m (de viande); sauce f

gray [greɪ] (US) adj = **grey**

graze [greɪz] vi paître, brouter ♦ vt (touch lightly) frôler, effleurer; (scrape) écorcher ♦ n écorchure f

grease [griːs] n (fat) graisse f; (lubricant) lubrifiant m ♦ vt graisser; lubrifier; **~proof paper** (BRIT) n papier sulfurisé; **greasy** ['griːsɪ] adj gras(se), graisseux(euse)

great [greɪt] adj grand(e); (inf: formidable; **G~ Britain** n Grande-Bretagne f; **~-grandfather** n arrière-grand-père m; **~-grandmother** n arrière-grand-mère f; **~ly** adv très, grandement; (with verbs) beaucoup; **~ness** n grandeur f

Greece [griːs] n Grèce f

greed [griːd] n (also: **~iness**) avidité f; (for food) gourmandise f, gloutonnerie f; **~y** adj avide; gourmand(e), glouton(ne)

Greek [griːk] adj grec(grecque) ♦ n Grec(Grecque); (LING) grec m

green [griːn] adj vert(e); (inexperienced) (bien) jeune, naïf(naïve); (POL) vert(e), écologiste; (ecological) écologique ♦ n vert m; (stretch of grass) pelouse f; **~s** npl (vegetables) légumes verts; (POL): the **G~s** les Verts mpl; **The G~ Party** (BRIT: POL) le parti écologiste; **~ belt** n (round town) ceinture verte; **~ card** n (AUT) carte verte; (US) permis m de travail; **~ery** n verdure f; **~grocer** (BRIT) n marchand m de fruits et légumes; **~house** n serre f; **~house effect** n effet m de serre; **~house gas** n gaz m à effet de serre; **~ish** adj verdâtre

Greenland ['griːnlənd] n Groenland m

greet [griːt] vt accueillir; **~ing** n salutation f; **~ing(s) card** n carte f de vœux

gregarious [grɪ'gɛərɪəs] adj (person)

sociable

grenade [grɪ'neɪd] n grenade f

grew [gruː] pt of **grow**

grey [greɪ] (US **gray**) adj gris(e); (dismal) sombre; **~-haired** adj grisonnant(e); **~hound** n lévrier m

grid [grɪd] n grille f; (ELEC) réseau m

grief [griːf] n chagrin m, douleur f

grievance ['griːvəns] n doléance f, grief m

grieve [griːv] vi avoir du chagrin; se désoler ♦ vt faire de la peine à, affliger; **to ~ for sb** (dead person) pleurer qn

grievous ['griːvəs] adj (LAW): **~ bodily harm** coups mpl et blessures fpl

grill [grɪl] n (on cooker) gril m; (food: also mixed ~) grillade(s) f(pl) ♦ vt (BRIT) griller; (inf: question) cuisiner

grille [grɪl] n grille f, grillage m; (AUT) calandre f

grim [grɪm] adj sinistre, lugubre; (serious, stern) sévère

grimace [grɪ'meɪs] n grimace f ♦ vi grimacer, faire une grimace

grime [graɪm] n crasse f, saleté f

grin [grɪn] n large sourire m ♦ vi sourire

grind [graɪnd] (pt, pp **ground**) vt écraser; (coffee, pepper etc) moudre; (US: meat) hacher; (make sharp) aiguiser ♦ n (work) corvée f

grip [grɪp] n (hold) prise f, étreinte f; (control) emprise f; (grasp) connaissance f; (handle) poignée f; (holdall) sac m de voyage ♦ vt saisir, empoigner; to come to ~s with en venir aux prises avec; **~ping** adj prenant(e), palpitant(e)

grisly ['grɪzlɪ] adj sinistre, macabre

gristle ['grɪsl] n cartilage m

grit [grɪt] n gravillon m; (courage) cran m ♦ vt (road) sabler; **to ~ one's teeth** serrer les dents

groan [grəʊn] n (of pain) gémissement m ♦ vi gémir

grocer ['grəʊsə*] n épicier m; **~ies**

npl provisions *fpl*; **~'s (shop)** *n* épicerie *f*

groin [grɔɪn] *n* aine *f*

groom [gruːm] *n* palefrenier *m*; *(also: bride~)* marié *m* ♦ *vt (horse)* panser; *(fig)*: **to ~ sb for** former qn pour; **well-groomed** très soigné(e)

groove [gruːv] *n* rainure *f*

grope [grəʊp] *vi*: **to ~ for** chercher à tâtons

gross [grəʊs] *adj* grossier(ère); *(COMM)* brut(e); **~ly** *adv (greatly)* très, grandement

grotto [grɒtəʊ] *n* grotte *f*

grotty [grɒtɪ] *(inf) adj* minable, affreux(euse)

ground [graʊnd] *pt, pp of* **grind** ♦ *n* sol *m*, terre *f*; *(land)* terrain *m*, terres *fpl*; *(SPORT)* terrain *m*; *(US: also: ~ wire)* terre; *(reason: gen pl)* raison *f* ♦ *vt (plane)* empêcher de décoller, retenir au sol; *(US: ELEC)* équiper d'une prise de terre; **~s** *npl (of coffee etc)* marc *m*; *(gardens etc)* parc *m*, domaine *m*; **on the ~, to the ~** par terre; **to gain/lose ~** gagner/perdre du terrain; **~ cloth** *(US)* *n* = **groundsheet**; **~ing** *n (in education)* connaissances *fpl* de base; **~less** *adj* sans fondement; **~sheet** *(BRIT)* *n* tapis *m* de sol; **~ staff** *n* personnel *m* au sol; **~swell** *n* lame *f* ou vague *f* de fond; **~work** *n* préparation *f*

group [gruːp] *n* groupe *m* ♦ *vt (also: ~ together)* grouper ♦ *vi* se grouper

grouse [graʊs] *n inv (bird)* grouse *f* ♦ *vi (complain)* rouspéter, râler

grove [grəʊv] *n* bosquet *m*

grovel [grɒvl] *vi (fig)* ramper

grow [grəʊ] *(pt* grew, *pp* grown) *vi* pousser, croître; *(person)* grandir; *(increase)* augmenter, se développer; *(become)*: **to ~ rich/weak** s'enrichir/s'affaiblir; *(develop)*: **he's ~n out of his jacket** sa veste est (devenue) trop petite pour lui; **he'll ~ out of it!** ça lui passera! ♦ *vt* cultiver, faire pousser; *(beard)* laisser pousser; **~ up** *vi* grandir; **~er** *n* produc-

teur *m*; **~ing** *adj (fear, amount)* croissant(e), grandissant(e)

growl [graʊl] *vi* grogner

grown [grəʊn] *pp of* **grow**; **~-up** *n* adulte *m/f*, grande personne

growth [grəʊθ] *n* croissance *f*, développement *m*; *(what has grown)* pousse *f*, poussée *f*; *(MED)* grosseur *f*, tumeur *f*

grub [grʌb] *n* larve *f*; *(inf: food)* bouffe *f*

grubby [grʌbɪ] *adj* crasseux(euse)

grudge [grʌdʒ] *n* rancune *f* ♦ *vt*: **to ~ sb sth** *(in giving)* donner qch à qn à contre-cœur; *(resent)* reprocher qch à qn; **to bear sb a ~ (for)** garder rancune *or* en vouloir à qn

gruelling [grʊəlɪŋ] *(US* **grueling***)* *adj* exténuant(e)

gruesome [gruːsəm] *adj* horrible

gruff [grʌf] *adj* bourru(e)

grumble [grʌmbl] *vi* rouspéter, ronchonner

grumpy [grʌmpɪ] *adj* grincheux(euse)

grunt [grʌnt] *vi* grogner

G-string [dʒiː-] *n (garment)* cache-sexe *m inv*

guarantee [gærən'tiː] *n* garantie *f* ♦ *vt* garantir

guard [gɑːd] *n* garde *f*; *(one man)* garde *m*; *(BRIT: RAIL)* chef *m* de train; *(on machine)* dispositif *m* de sûreté; *(also: fire~)* garde-feu *m* ♦ *vt* garder, surveiller; *(protect)*: **to ~ (against** *or* **from)** protéger (contre); **~ against** *vt (prevent)* empêcher, se protéger de; **~ed** *adj (fig)* prudent(e); **~ian** *n* gardien(ne); *(of minor)* tuteur(trice); **~'s van** *(BRIT)* *n (RAIL)* fourgon *m*

guerrilla [ɡə'rɪlə] *n* guérillero *m*

guess [ɡes] *vt* deviner; *(estimate)* évaluer; *(US)* croire, penser ♦ *vi* deviner ♦ *n* supposition *f*, hypothèse *f*; **to take** *or* **have a ~** essayer de deviner; **~work** *n* hypothèse *f*

guest [ɡest] *n* invité(e); *(in hotel)* client(e); **~-house** *n* pension *f*; **~-room** *n* chambre *f* d'amis

guffaw [gʌ'fɔ:] vi pouffer de rire
guidance ['gaɪdəns] n conseils mpl
guide [gaɪd] n (person, book etc)
guide m; (BRIT: also: girl ~) guide
f ♦ vt guider; ~**book** n guide m; ~
dog n chien m d'aveugle; ~**lines** npl
(fig) instructions (générales),
conseils mpl
guild [gɪld] n corporation f; cercle m,
association f
guile [gaɪl] n astuce f
guillotine [gɪlə'ti:n] n guillotine f
guilt [gɪlt] n culpabilité f; ~**y** adj
coupable
guinea pig ['gɪnɪ-] n cobaye m
guise [gaɪz] n aspect m, apparence f
guitar [gɪ'tɑ:*] n guitare f
gulf [gʌlf] n golfe m; (abyss) gouffre
m
gull [gʌl] n mouette f; (larger) goéland m
gullet ['gʌlɪt] n gosier m
gullible ['gʌlɪbl] adj crédule
gully ['gʌlɪ] n ravin m; ravine f; couloir m
gulp [gʌlp] vi avaler sa salive ♦ vt
(also: ~ down) avaler
gum [gʌm] n (ANAT) gencive f;
(glue) colle f; (sweet: also ~drop)
boule f de gomme; (also: chewing ~)
chewing-gum m ♦ vt coller; ~**boots**
(BRIT) npl bottes fpl en caoutchouc
gun [gʌn] n (small) revolver m, pistolet m; (rifle) fusil m, carabine f;
(cannon) canon m; ~**boat** n canon-
nière f; ~**fire** n fusillade f; ~**man** n
bandit armé; ~**point** n: at ~**point**
sous la menace du pistolet (or fusil);
~**powder** n poudre f à canon; ~**shot**
n coup m de feu
gurgle ['gɜ:gl] vi gargouiller; (baby)
gazouiller
gush [gʌʃ] vi jaillir; (fig) se répandre en effusions
gust [gʌst] n (of wind) rafale f; (of
smoke) bouffée f
gusto ['gʌstəu] n enthousiasme m
gut [gʌt] n intestin m, boyau m; ~**s**
npl (inf: courage) cran m
gutter ['gʌtə*] n (in street) caniveau

m; (of roof) gouttière f
guy [gaɪ] n (inf: man) type m; (also:
~**rope**) corde f; (BRIT: figure) effi-
gie de Guy Fawkes (brûlée en plein
air le 5 novembre)
guzzle ['gʌzl] vt avaler gloutonne-
ment
gym [dʒɪm] n (also: ~nasium) gymnase m; (also: ~nastics) gym f;
~**nast** ['dʒɪmnæst] n gymnaste m/f;
~**nastics** [dʒɪm'næstɪks] n, npl gymnastique f; ~ **shoes** npl chaussures
fpl de gym; ~**slip** (BRIT) n tunique f
(d'écolière)
gynaecologist [gaɪnɪ'kɔlədʒɪst] (US
gynecologist) n gynécologue m/f
gypsy ['dʒɪpsɪ] n gitan(e), bohé-
mien(ne)

H

haberdashery [hæbə'dæʃərɪ] (BRIT)
n mercerie f
habit ['hæbɪt] n habitude f; (REL:
costume) habit m
habitual [hə'bɪtjuəl] adj habituel(le);
(drinker, liar) invétéré(e)
hack [hæk] vt hacher, tailler ♦ n
(pej: writer) nègre m; ~**er** n
(COMPUT) pirate m (informatique);
(: enthusiast) passionné(e) m/f des
ordinateurs
hackneyed ['hæknɪd] adj usé(e), re-
battu(e)
had [hæd] pt, pp of **have**
haddock ['hædək] (pl ~ or ~s) n
églefin m; **smoked** ~ haddock m
hadn't ['hædnt] = **had not**
haemorrhage ['hemərɪdʒ] (US
hemorrhage) n hémorragie f
haemorrhoids ['hemərɔɪdz] (US
hemorroids) npl hémorroïdes fpl
haggle ['hægl] vi marchander
Hague [heɪg] n: The ~ La Haye
hail [heɪl] n grêle f ♦ vt (call) héler;
(acclaim) acclamer ♦ vi grêler;
~**stone** n grêlon m
hair [hɛə*] n cheveux mpl; (of animal) pelage m; (single hair: on

head) cheveu m; (: on body; of animal) poil m; **to do one's** ~ se coiffer; ~**brush** n brosse f à cheveux; ~**cut** n coupe f (de cheveux); ~**do** n coiffure f; ~**dresser** n coiffeur(euse); ~**dresser's** n salon m de coiffure, coiffeur m; ~**dryer** n sèche-cheveux m; ~**grip** n pince f à cheveux; ~**net** n filet m à cheveux; ~**piece** n perruque f; ~**pin** n épingle f à cheveux; ~**pin bend** (US ~**pin curve**) n virage m en épingle à cheveux; ~**raising** adj à (vous) faire dresser les cheveux sur la tête; ~ **removing cream** n crème f dépilatoire; ~ **spray** n laque f (pour les cheveux); ~**style** n coiffure f; ~**y** adj poilu(e); (inf: fig) effrayant(e)

hake [heɪk] (pl ~ or ~s) n colin m, merlu m

half [hɑːf] (pl **halves**) n moitié f; (of beer: also: ~ **pint**) ≈ demi-litre m ♦ adj demi(e) ♦ adv à moitié, à demi; ~ **a dozen** une demi-douzaine; ~ **a pound** une demi-livre, ≈ 250 g; **two and a** ~ deux et demi; **to cut sth in** ~ couper qch en deux; ~**baked** adj (plan) qui ne tient pas debout; ~**caste** n métis(se); ~**hearted** adj tiède, sans enthousiasme; ~**hour** n demi-heure f; ~**mast**: **at** ~**mast** adv (flag) en berne; ~**penny** ['heɪpnɪ] (BRIT) n demi-penny m; ~**price** adj, adv: **(at)** ~**price** à moitié prix; ~ **term** (BRIT) n (SCOL) congé m de demi-trimestre; ~**time** n mi-temps f; ~**way** adv à mi-chemin

hall [hɔːl] n salle f; (entrance way) hall m, entrée f

hallmark ['hɔːlmɑːk] n poinçon m; (fig) marque f

hallo [hʌ'ləʊ] excl = hello

hall of residence (BRIT: pl **halls of residence**) n résidence f universitaire

Hallowe'en ['hæləʊ'iːn] n veille f de la Toussaint

hallucination [həluːsɪ'neɪʃən] n hal-

lucination f

hallway ['hɔːlweɪ] n vestibule m

halo ['heɪləʊ] n (of saint etc) auréole f

halt [hɔːlt] n halte f, arrêt m ♦ vt (progress etc) interrompre ♦ vi faire halte, s'arrêter

halve [hɑːv] vt (apple etc) partager or diviser en deux; (expense) réduire de moitié; ~**s** [hɑːvz] npl of **half**

ham [hæm] n jambon m

hamburger ['hæmbɜːgə*] n hamburger m

hamlet ['hæmlɪt] n hameau m

hammer ['hæmə*] n marteau m ♦ vt (nail) enfoncer; (fig) démolir ♦ vi (on door) frapper à coups redoublés; **to** ~ **an idea into sb** faire entrer de force une idée dans la tête de qn

hammock ['hæmək] n hamac m

hamper ['hæmpə*] vt gêner ♦ n panier m (d'osier)

hamster ['hæmstə*] n hamster m

hand [hænd] n main f; (of clock) aiguille f; (handwriting) écriture f; (worker) ouvrier(ère); (at cards) jeu m ♦ vt passer, donner; **to give** or **lend sb a** ~ donner un coup de main à qn; **at** ~ à portée de la main; **in** ~ (time) à disposition; (job, situation) en main; **to be on** ~ (person) être disponible; (emergency services) se tenir prêt(e) (à intervenir); **to** ~ (information etc) sous la main, à portée de la main; **on the one** ~ ..., **on the other** ~ ..., d'une part ..., d'autre part ...; ~ **in** vt remettre; ~ **out** vt distribuer; ~ **over** vt transmettre; céder; ~**bag** n sac m à main; ~**book** n manuel m; ~**brake** n frein m à main; ~**cuffs** npl menottes fpl; ~**ful** n poignée f

handicap ['hændɪkæp] n handicap m ♦ vt handicaper; **mentally/physically** ~**ped** handicapé(e) mentalement/physiquement

handicraft ['hændɪkrɑːft] n (travail m d')artisanat m, technique artisanale; (object) objet artisanal

handiwork ['hændɪwɜːk] n ouvrage

m

handkerchief [ˈhæŋkətʃɪf] *n* mouchoir *m*

handle [ˈhændl] *n* (of door etc) poignée *f*; (of cup etc) anse *f*; (of knife etc) manche *m*; (of saucepan) queue *f*; (for winding) manivelle *f* ♦ *vt* toucher, manier; (deal with) s'occuper de; (treat: people) prendre; "~ **with care**" "fragile"; **to fly off the ~** s'énerver; **~bar(s)** *n(pl)* guidon *m*

hand: ~**luggage** *n* bagages *mpl* à main; ~**made** *adj* fait(e) à la main; ~**out** *n* (from government, parents) aide *f*; (leaflet) documentation *f*, prospectus *m*; (summary of lecture) polycopié *m*; ~**rail** *n* rampe *f*, main courante; ~**shake** *n* poignée *f* de main

handsome [ˈhænsəm] *adj* beau (belle); (profit, return) considérable

handwriting [ˈhændraɪtɪŋ] *n* écriture *f*

handy [ˈhændɪ] *adj* (person) adroit(e); (close at hand) sous la main; (convenient) pratique; ~**man** [ˈhændɪmən] (irreg) *n* bricoleur *m*; (servant) homme *m* à tout faire

hang [hæŋ] (pt, pp **hung**) *vt* accrocher; (criminal: pt, pp: **hanged**) pendre ♦ *vi* pendre; (hair, drapery) tomber; **to get the ~ of (doing) sth** (inf) attraper le coup pour faire qch; ~ **about** *vi* traîner; ~ **around** *vi* = **hang about**; ~ **on** *vi* (wait) attendre; ~ **up** *vi* (TEL): **to ~ up on sb** raccrocher (au nez de qn) ♦ *vt* (coat, painting etc) accrocher, suspendre

hangar [ˈhæŋə*] *n* hangar *m*

hanger [ˈhæŋə*] *n* cintre *m*, portemanteau *m*; ~**on** [ˈhæŋər'ɒn] *n* parasite *m*; ~**gliding** [ˈhæŋɡlaɪdɪŋ] *n* deltaplane *m*, vol *m* libre; ~**over** [ˈhæŋəʊvə*] *n* (after drinking) gueule *f* de bois; ~**up** [ˈhæŋʌp] *n* complexe *m*

hanker [ˈhæŋkə*] *vi*: **to ~ after** avoir envie de

hankie, hanky [ˈhæŋkɪ] *n abbr* =

haphazard [ˈhæpˈhæzəd] *adj* fait(e) au hasard, fait(e) au petit bonheur

happen [ˈhæpən] *vi* arriver; se passer, se produire; **it so ~s that** il se trouve que; **as it ~s** justement; ~**ing** *n* événement *m*

happily [ˈhæpɪlɪ] *adv* heureusement; (cheerfully) joyeusement

happiness [ˈhæpɪnɪs] *n* bonheur *m*

happy [ˈhæpɪ] *adj* heureux(euse); ~ **with** (arrangements etc) satisfait(e) de; **to be ~ to do** faire volontiers; ~ **birthday!** bon anniversaire!; ~**go-lucky** *adj* insouciant(e)

harass [ˈhærəs] *vt* accabler, tourmenter; ~**ment** *n* tracasseries *fpl*

harbour [ˈhɑːbə*] (US **harbor**) *n* port *m* ♦ *vt* héberger, abriter; (hope, fear etc) entretenir

hard [hɑːd] *adj* (question, problem) difficile, dur(e); (facts, evidence) concret(ète) ♦ *adv* (work) dur; (think, try) sérieusement; **to look ~ at** regarder fixement; (thing) regarder de près; **no ~ feelings!** sans rancune!; **to be ~ of hearing** être dur(e) d'oreille; **to be ~ done by** être traité(e) injustement; ~**back** *n* livre relié; ~ **cash** *n* espèces *fpl*; ~ **disk** *n* (COMPUT) disque dur; ~**en** *vt* durcir; (fig) endurcir ♦ *vi* durcir; ~**headed** *adj* réaliste, décidé(e); ~ **labour** *n* travaux forcés

hardly [ˈhɑːdlɪ] *adv* (scarcely, no sooner) à peine; ~ **anywhere/ever** presque nulle part/jamais

hard: ~**ship** *n* épreuves *fpl*; ~ **up** (inf) *adj* fauché(e); ~**ware** *n* quincaillerie *f*; (COMPUT, MIL) matériel *m*; ~**ware shop** *n* quincaillerie *f*; ~**wearing** *adj* solide; ~**working** *adj* travailleur(euse)

hardy [ˈhɑːdɪ] *adj* robuste, (plant) résistant(e) au gel

hare [hɛə*] *n* lièvre *m*; ~**brained** *adj* farfelu(e)

harm [hɑːm] *n* mal *m*; (wrong) tort *m* ♦ *vt* (person) faire du mal ou du tort à; (thing) endommager; **out of**

~'s way à l'abri du danger, en lieu sûr; ~ful *adj* nuisible; ~less *adj* inoffensif(ive); sans méchanceté

harmony ['hɑ:mənɪ] *n* harmonie *f*

harness ['hɑ:nɪs] *n* harnais *m*; (safety ~) harnais de sécurité ♦ *vt* (horse) harnacher; (resources) exploiter

harp [hɑ:p] *n* harpe *f* ♦ *vi*: to ~ on about rabâcher

harrowing ['hærəʊɪŋ] *adj* déchirant(e), très pénible

harsh [hɑ:ʃ] *adj* (hard) dur(e); (severe) sévère; (unpleasant: sound) discordant(e); (: light) cru(e)

harvest ['hɑ:vɪst] *n* (of corn) moisson *f*; (of fruit) récolte *f*; (of grapes) vendange *f* ♦ *vt* moissonner; récolter; vendanger

has [hæz] *vb* see **have**

hash [hæʃ] *n* (CULIN) hachis *m*; (fig: mess) gâchis *m*

hasn't ['hæznt] = **has not**

hassle ['hæsl] *n* (inf: bother) histoires *fpl*, tracas *mpl*

haste [heɪst] *n* hâte *f*; précipitation *f*; ~n ['heɪsn] *vt* hâter, accélérer ♦ *vi* se hâter, s'empresser; **hastily** *adv* à la hâte; précipitamment; **hasty** ['heɪstɪ] *adj* hâtif(ive); précipité(e)

hat [hæt] *n* chapeau *m*

hatch [hætʃ] *n* (NAUT: also: ~way) écoutille *f*; (also: service ~) passeplats *m inv* ♦ *vi* éclore

hatchback ['hætʃbæk] *n* (AUT) modèle *m* avec hayon arrière

hatchet ['hætʃɪt] *n* hachette *f*

hate [heɪt] *vt* haïr, détester ♦ *n* haine *f*; ~ful *adj* odieux(euse), détestable; **hatred** ['heɪtrɪd] *n* haine *f*

haughty ['hɔ:tɪ] *adj* hautain(e), arrogant(e)

haul [hɔ:l] *vt* traîner, tirer ♦ *n* (of fish) prise *f*; (of stolen goods etc) butin *m*; ~age *n* transport routier; (costs) frais *mpl* de transport; ~ier (US hauler) *n* (company) transporteur (routier); (driver) camionneur *m*

haunch [hɔ:ntʃ] *n* hanche *f*; (of

meat) cuissot *m*

haunt [hɔ:nt] *vt* hanter ♦ *n* repaire *m*

KEYWORD

have [hæv] (pt, pp had) aux vb 1 (gen) avoir; être; to ~ arrived/gone être arrivé(e)/allé(e); to ~ eaten/slept avoir mangé/dormi; he has been promoted il a été promu
2 (in tag questions): you've done it, ~n't you? vous l'avez fait, n'est-ce pas?
3 (in short answers and questions): no I ~n't/yes we have! mais non!/mais si!; so I ~! ah oui!, oui c'est vrai!; I've been there before, ~ you? j'y suis déjà allé, et vous?
♦ modal aux vb (be obliged): to ~ (got) to do sth devoir faire qch; être obligé de faire qch; she has (got) to do it elle doit le faire, il faut qu'elle le fasse; you ~n't to tell her vous ne devez pas le lui dire
♦ vt 1 (possess, obtain) avoir; he has (got) blue eyes/dark hair il a les yeux bleus/les cheveux bruns; may I ~ your address? puis-je avoir votre adresse?
2 (+noun: take, hold etc): to ~ breakfast/a bath/a shower prendre le petit déjeuner/un bain/une douche; to ~ dinner/lunch déjeuner/dîner; to ~ a swim nager; to ~ a meeting se réunir; to ~ a party organiser une fête
3 to ~ sth done faire faire qch; to ~ one's hair cut se faire couper les cheveux; to ~ sb do sth faire faire qch à qn
4 (experience, suffer) avoir; to ~ a cold/flu avoir un rhume/la grippe; to ~ an operation se faire opérer
5 (inf: dupe) avoir; he's been had il s'est fait avoir ou roulé

have out *vt*: to ~ it out with sb (settle a problem etc) s'expliquer (franchement) avec qn

haven ['heɪvn] *n* port *m*; (fig) havre

m

haven't ['hævnt] = have not

havoc ['hævək] *n* ravages *mpl*

hawk [hɔːk] *n* faucon *m*

hay [heɪ] *n* foin *m*; ~ **fever** *n* rhume *m* des foins; ~**stack** *n* meule *f* de foin

haywire ['heɪwaɪə*] (*inf*) *adj*: to go ~ (*machine*) se détraquer; (*plans*) mal tourner

hazard ['hæzəd] *n* (*danger*) danger *m*, risque *m* ♦ *vt* risquer, hasarder; ~ (**warning**) **lights** *npl* (AUT) feux *mpl* de détresse

haze [heɪz] *n* brume *f*

hazelnut ['heɪzlnʌt] *n* noisette *f*

hazy ['heɪzɪ] *adj* brumeux(euse); (*idea*) vague

he [hiː] *pron* il; it is ~ who ... c'est lui qui ...

head [hed] *n* tête *f*; (*leader*) chef *m*; (*of school*) directeur(trice) ♦ *vt* (*list*) être en tête de; (*group*) être à la tête de; ~**s** (*or* **tails**) pile (ou face); ~ **first** la tête la première; ~ **over heels in love** follement et éperdument amoureux(euse); to ~ a ball faire une tête; ~ **for** *vt fus* se diriger vers; ~**ache** *n* mal *m* de tête; ~**dress** (BRIT) *n* (*of Red Indian etc*) coiffure *f*; ~**ing** *n* titre *m*; ~**lamp** (BRIT) *n* = **headlight**; ~**land** *n* promontoire *m*, cap *m*; ~**light** *n* phare *m*; ~**line** *n* titre *m*; ~**long** *adv* (*fall*) la tête la première; (*rush*) tête baissée; ~**master** *n* directeur *m*; ~**mistress** *n* directrice *f*; ~ **office** *n* bureau central, siège *m*; ~**on** *adj* (*collision*) de plein fouet; (*confrontation*) en face à face; ~**phones** *npl* casque *m* (à écouteurs); ~**quarters** *npl* bureau *m* ou siège central; (MIL) quartier général; ~**rest** *n* appui-tête *m*; ~**room** *n* (*in car*) hauteur *f* de plafond; (*under bridge*) hauteur limite; ~**scarf** *n* foulard *m*; ~**strong** *adj* têtu(e), entêté(e); ~**waiter** *n* maître *m* d'hôtel; ~**way** *n*: to make ~**way** avancer, faire des progrès; ~**wind**

vent *m* contraire; (NAUT) vent debout; ~**y** *adj* capiteux(euse); enivrant(e); (*experience*) grisant(e)

heal [hiːl] *vt, vi* guérir

health [helθ] *n* santé *f*; ~ **food** *n* aliment(s) naturel(s); ~ **food shop** *n* magasin *m* diététique; **H~ Service** (BRIT) *n*: the **H~ Service** = la Sécurité sociale; ~**y** *adj* (*person*) en bonne santé; (*climate, food, attitude etc*) sain(e); bon(ne) pour la santé

heap [hiːp] *n* tas *m*; ~ *vt* (+ **up**) (*up*) entasser, amonceler; she ~**ed her plate with cakes** elle a chargé son assiette de gâteaux

hear [hɪə*] (*pt, pp* **heard**) *vt* entendre; (*news*) apprendre ♦ *vi* entendre; to ~ **about** entendre parler de; avoir des nouvelles de; to ~ **from sb** recevoir or avoir des nouvelles de qn; ~**ing** ['hɪərɪŋ] *n* (*sense*) ouïe *f*; (*of witnesses*) audition *f*; (*of a case*) audience *f*; ~ **aid** *n* appareil *m* acoustique; ~**say** ['hɪəseɪ] *n*: by ~ *adv* par ouï-dire *m*

hearse [hɜːs] *n* corbillard *m*

heart [hɑːt] *n* cœur *m*; ~**s** *npl* (CARDS) cœur *m*; to lose/take ~ perdre/prendre courage; at ~ au fond; by ~ (*learn, know*) par cœur; ~ **attack** *n* crise *f* cardiaque; ~**beat** *n* battement *m* du cœur; ~**breaking** *adj* déchirant(e), qui fend le cœur; ~**broken** *adj*: to be ~**broken** avoir beaucoup de chagrin or le cœur brisé; ~**burn** *n* brûlures *fpl* d'estomac; ~ **failure** *n* arrêt du cœur; ~**felt** *adj* sincère

hearth [hɑːθ] *n* foyer *m*, cheminée *f*

heartily ['hɑːtɪlɪ] *adv* chaleureusement; (*laugh*) de bon cœur; (*eat*) de bon appétit; to agree ~ être entièrement d'accord

heartland ['hɑːtlænd] *n* (*of country, region*) centre *m*

hearty ['hɑːtɪ] *adj* chaleureux(euse); (*appetite*) robuste; (*dislike*) cordial(e)

heat [hiːt] *n* chaleur *f*; (*fig*) feu *m*, agitation *f*; (SPORT: *also*: qualifying

~ éliminatoire f ♦ vt chauffer; ~ **up** vi (water) chauffer; (room) se réchauffer ♦ vt réchauffer; ~**ed** adj chauffé(e); (fig) passionné(e), échauffé(e); ~**er** n appareil m de chauffage; radiateur m; (in car) chauffage m; (water ~) chauffe-eau m

heath [hi:θ] (BRIT) n lande f

heather ['hɛðə*] n bruyère f

heating ['hi:tɪŋ] n chauffage m

heatstroke ['hi:tstrəuk] n (MED) coup m de chaleur

heatwave n vague f de chaleur

heave [hi:v] vt soulever (avec effort); (drag) traîner ♦ vi se soulever; (retch) avoir un haut-le-cœur; to ~ **a sigh** pousser un soupir

heaven ['hɛvn] n ciel m, paradis m; (fig) paradis; ~**ly** adj céleste, divin(e)

heavily ['hɛvɪlɪ] adv lourdement; (drink, smoke) beaucoup; (sleep, sigh) profondément

heavy ['hɛvɪ] adj lourd(e); (work, sea, rain, eater) gros(se); (snow) beaucoup; (drinker, smoker) grand(e); (breathing) bruyant(e); (schedule, week) chargé(e); ~ **goods vehicle** n poids lourd; ~**weight** n (SPORT) poids lourd

Hebrew ['hi:bru:] adj hébraïque ♦ n (LING) hébreu m

Hebrides ['hɛbrɪdi:z] npl: **the** ~ les Hébrides fpl

heckle ['hɛkl] vt interpeller (un orateur)

hectic ['hɛktɪk] adj agité(e), trépidant(e)

he'd [hi:d] = he would; he had

hedge [hɛdʒ] n haie f ♦ vi se dérober; to ~ **one's bets** (fig) se couvrir

hedgehog ['hɛdʒhɔg] n hérisson m

heed [hi:d] vt (also: take ~ of) tenir compte de; ~**less** adj insouciant(e)

heel [hi:l] n talon m ♦ vt (shoe) retalonner

hefty ['hɛftɪ] adj (person) costaud(e); (parcel) lourd(e); (profit) gros(se)

heifer ['hɛfə*] n génisse f

height [haɪt] n (of person) taille f, grandeur f; (of object) hauteur f; (of plane, mountain) altitude f; (high ground) hauteur, éminence f; (fig: of glory) sommet m; (: of luxury, stupidity) comble m; ~**en** vt (fig) augmenter

heir [ɛə*] n héritier m; ~**ess** ['ɛərɪs] n héritière f; ~**loom** n héritage m, meuble m (or bijou m or tableau m) de famille

held [hɛld] pt, pp of **hold**

helicopter ['hɛlɪkɔptə*] n hélicoptère m

hell [hɛl] n enfer m; ~! (infl) merde!

he'll [hi:l] = he will; he shall

hellish ['hɛlɪʃ] (inf) adj infernal(e)

hello [hə'ləu] excl bonjour!; (to attract attention) hé!; (surprise) tiens!

helm [hɛlm] n (NAUT) barre f

helmet ['hɛlmɪt] n casque m

help [hɛlp] n aide f; (charwoman) femme f de ménage ♦ vt aider; ~! au secours!; ~ **yourself** servez-vous; **he can't** ~ **it** il n'y peut rien; ~**er** n aide m/f, assistant(e); ~**ful** adj serviable, obligeant(e); (useful) utile; ~**ing** n portion f; ~**less** adj impuissant(e); (defenceless) faible

hem [hɛm] n ourlet m ♦ vt ourler; ~ **in** vt cerner

hemorrhage ['hɛmərɪdʒ] (US) n = **haemorrhage**

hemorroids ['hɛmərɔɪdz] (US) npl = **haemorroids**

hen [hɛn] n poule f

hence [hɛns] adv (therefore) d'où, de là; **2 years** ~ d'ici 2 ans, dans 2 ans; ~**forth** adv dorénavant

henchman ['hɛntʃmən] (pej: irreg) n acolyte m

her [hɜ:*] pron (direct) la, l'; (indirect) lui; (stressed, after prep) elle ♦ adj son(sa), ses pl; see also me; my

herald ['hɛrəld] n héraut m ♦ vt annoncer; ~**ry** n (herald's) n héraldique f; (coat of arms) blason m

herb [hɜ:b] n herbe f

herd [hɜːd] n troupeau m

here [hɪə*] adv ici; (time) alors ♦ excl tiens!, tenez!; ~! présent!; ~ is, ~ are voici; ~ he/she is! le/la voici!; ~ **after** adv après, plus tard; ~**by** adv (formal: in letter) par la présente

hereditary [hɪˈredɪtərɪ] adj héréditaire

heresy ['herəsɪ] n hérésie f

heritage ['herɪtɪdʒ] n (of country) patrimoine m

hermit ['hɜːmɪt] n ermite m

hernia ['hɜːnɪə] n hernie f

hero ['hɪərəu] (pl ~es) n héros m

heroin ['herəuɪn] n héroïne f

heroine ['herəuɪn] n héroïne f

heron ['herən] n héron m

herring ['herɪŋ] n hareng m

hers [hɜːz] pron le(la) sien(ne), les siens(siennes); see also mine

herself [hɜːˈself] pron (reflexive) se; (emphatic) elle-même; (after prep) elle; see also oneself

he's [hiːz] = he is; he has

hesitant ['hezɪtənt] adj hésitant(e), indécis(e)

hesitate ['hezɪteɪt] vi hésiter; **hesitation** [hezɪˈteɪʃən] n hésitation f

hew [hjuː] (pp hewed or hewn) vt (stone) tailler; (wood) couper

heyday ['heɪdeɪ] n: the ~ of l'âge m d'or de, les beaux jours de

HGV n abbr = heavy goods vehicle

hi [haɪ] excl salut!; (to attract attention) hé!

hiatus [haɪˈeɪtəs] n (gap) lacune f; (interruption) pause f

hibernate ['haɪbəneɪt] vi hiberner

hiccough, hiccup ['hɪkʌp] vi hoqueter; ~**s** npl hoquet m

hide [haɪd] (pt hid, pp hidden) n (skin) peau f ♦ vt cacher ♦ vi: to ~ (from sb) se cacher (de qn); ~-**and-seek** n cache-cache m; ~**away** n cachette f

hideous ['hɪdɪəs] adj hideux(euse)

hiding ['haɪdɪŋ] n (beating) correction f, volée f de coups; to be in ~ (concealed) se tenir caché(e)

hierarchy ['haɪərɑːkɪ] n hiérarchie f

hi-fi ['haɪfaɪ] n hi-fi f inv ♦ adj hi-fi inv

high [haɪ] adj (speed, respect, number) grand(e); (price) élevé(e); (wind) fort(e), violent(e); (voice) aigu(aiguë) ♦ adv haut; 20 m ~ haut de 20 m; ~**brow** adj, n intellectuel(le); ~**chair** n (child's) chaise haute; ~**er education** n études supérieures; ~**-handed** adj très autoritaire; très cavalier(ère); ~ **jump** n (SPORT) saut m en hauteur; ~**lands** npl: the H~**lands** the Highlands mpl; ~**light** n (fig: of event) point culminant ♦ vt faire ressortir, souligner; ~**lights** npl (in hair) reflets mpl; ~**ly** adv très, fort, hautement; to speak/think ~**ly** of sb dire/penser beaucoup de bien de qn; ~**ly paid** adj très bien payé(e); ~**ly strung** adj nerveux(euse), toujours tendu(e); ~**ness** n: Her (or His) H~**ness** Son Altesse f; ~-**pitched** adj aigu(aiguë); ~-**rise block**, ~-**rise flats** tour f (d'habitation); ~ **school** n lycée m; (US) établissement m d'enseignement supérieur; ~ **season** (BRIT) n haute saison; ~ **street** (BRIT) n grand-rue f; ~**way** ['haɪweɪ] n route nationale; H~**way Code** (BRIT) n code m de la route

hijack ['haɪdʒæk] vt (plane) détourner; ~**er** n pirate m de l'air

hike [haɪk] vi aller or faire des excursions à pied ♦ n excursion f à pied, randonnée f; ~**r** n promeneur(euse), excursionniste m/f

hilarious [hɪˈlɛərɪəs] adj (account, event) désopilant(e)

hill [hɪl] n colline f; (fairly high) montagne f; (on road) côte f; ~**side** n (flanc m de) coteau m; ~**y** adj vallonné(e); montagneux(euse)

hilt [hɪlt] n (of sword) garde f; to the ~ (fig: support) à fond

him [hɪm] pron (direct) le; (stressed, indirect, after prep) lui; see also me; ~**self** [hɪmˈself] pron *(reflexive)* se; *(emphatic)* lui-même; *(after prep)* lui; *see also* oneself

hind [haɪnd] *adj* de derrière

hinder ['hɪndə*] *vt* gêner; *(delay)* retarder; **hindrance** ['hɪndrəns] *n* gêne *f*, obstacle *m*

hindsight ['haɪndsaɪt] *n*: **with ~** avec du recul, rétrospectivement

Hindu ['hɪnduː] *adj* hindou(e)

hinge [hɪndʒ] *n* charnière *f* ♦ *vi (fig)*: **to ~ on** dépendre de

hint [hɪnt] *n* allusion *f*; *(advice)* conseil *m* ♦ *vt*: **to ~ that** insinuer que ♦ *vi*: **to ~ at** faire une allusion à

hip [hɪp] *n* hanche *f*

hippopotamus [hɪpə'pɔtəməs] *(pl* **~es** *or* **~mi)** *n* hippopotame *m*

hire ['haɪə*] *vt (BRIT: car, equipment)* louer; *(worker)* embaucher, engager ♦ *n* location *f*; **for ~** à louer; *(taxi)* libre; **~ purchase** *(BRIT) n* achat *m (or* vente *f)* à tempérament *or* crédit

his [hɪz] *pron* le(la) sien(ne), les siens(siennes) ♦ *adj* son(sa), ses *pl*; *see also* my; mine

hiss [hɪs] *vi* siffler

historic [hɪ'stɔrɪk] *adj* historique

historical [hɪ'stɔrɪkl] *adj* historique

history ['hɪstərɪ] *n* histoire *f*

hit [hɪt] *(pt, pp* **hit)** *vt* frapper; *(reach: target)* atteindre, toucher; *(collide with: car)* entrer en collision avec, heurter; *(fig: affect)* toucher ♦ *n* coup *m*; *(success)* succès *m*; *(: song)* tube *m*; **to ~ it off** bien s'entendre avec qn; **~-and-run driver** *n* chauffard *m* (coupable du délit de fuite)

hitch [hɪtʃ] *vt (fasten)* accrocher, attacher; *(also: ~ up)* remonter d'une saccade ♦ *n (difficulty)* anicroche *f*, contretemps *m*; **to ~ a lift** faire du stop

hitchhike ['hɪtʃhaɪk] *vi* faire de l'auto-stop; **~r** *n* auto-stoppeur(euse)

hi-tech ['haɪ'tek] *adj* de pointe

hitherto ['hɪðə'tuː] *adv* jusqu'ici

HIV: **~-negative/-positive** séro-

négatif(ive)/-positif(ive)

hive [haɪv] *n* ruche *f*; **~ off** *(inf) vt* mettre à part, séparer

HMS *abbr* = Her (His) Majesty's Ship

hoard [hɔːd] *n (of food)* provisions *fpl*, réserves *fpl*; *(of money)* trésor *m* ♦ *vt* amasser; **~ing** ['hɔːdɪŋ] *(BRIT) n (for posters)* panneau *m* d'affichage *or* publicitaire

hoarse [hɔːs] *adj* enroué(e)

hoax [həʊks] *n* canular *m*

hob [hɔb] *n* plaque (chauffante)

hobble ['hɔbl] *vi* boitiller

hobby ['hɔbɪ] *n* passe-temps favori; **~-horse** *n (fig)* dada *m*

hobo ['həʊbəʊ] *(US) n* vagabond *m*

hockey ['hɔkɪ] *n* hockey *m*

hog [hɔg] *n* porc (châtré) ♦ *vt (fig)* accaparer; **to go the whole ~** aller jusqu'au bout

hoist [hɔɪst] *n (apparatus)* palan *m* ♦ *vt* hisser

hold [həʊld] *(pt, pp* **held)** *vt* tenir; *(contain)* contenir; *(believe)* considérer; *(possess)* avoir; *(detain)* détenir ♦ *vt (withstand pressure)* tenir (bon); *(be valid)* valoir ♦ *n (also fig)* prise *f*; *(NAUT)* cale *f*; **~ the line!** *(TEL)* ne quittez pas!; **to ~ one's own** *(fig)* bien se défendre; **to catch or get (a) ~ of** saisir; **to get ~ of** *(fig)* trouver; **~ back** *vt* retenir; *(secret)* taire; **~ down** *vt (person)* maintenir à terre; *(job)* occuper; **~ off** *vt* tenir à distance; **~ on** *vi* tenir bon; *(wait)* attendre; **~ on!** *(TEL)* ne quittez pas!; **~ on to** *vt* fus se cramponner à; *(keep)* conserver, garder; **~ out** *vt* offrir ♦ *vi (resist)* tenir bon; **~ up** *vt (raise)* lever; *(support)* soutenir; *(delay)* retarder; *(rob)* braquer; **~all** *(BRIT) n* fourre-tout *m inv*; **~er** *n (of ticket, record)* détenteur(trice); *(of office, title etc)* titulaire *m/f*; *(container)* support *m*; **~ing** *n (share)* intérêts *mpl*; *(farm)* ferme *f*; **~up** *n (robbery)* hold-up *m*; *(delay)* retard *m*; *(BRIT: in traffic)* bouchon *m*

hole [həʊl] n trou m

holiday ['hɒlədɪ] n vacances fpl; (day off) jour m de congé; (public) jour férié; **on ~** en congé; **~ camp** n (also: ~ centre) camp m de vacances; **~-maker** (BRIT) n vacancier(ère); **~ resort** n centre m de villégiature or de vacances

Holland ['hɒlənd] n Hollande f

hollow ['hɒləʊ] adj creux(euse) ♦ n creux m ♦ vt: **to ~ out** creuser, évider

holly ['hɒlɪ] n houx m

holocaust ['hɒləkɔːst] n holocauste m

holster ['həʊlstə*] n étui m de revolver

holy ['həʊlɪ] adj saint(e); (bread, water) bénit(e); (ground) sacré(e); **H~ Ghost** n Saint-Esprit m

homage ['hɒmɪdʒ] n hommage m; **to pay ~ to** rendre hommage à

home [həʊm] n foyer m, maison f; (country) pays natal, patrie f; (institution) maison ♦ adj de famille; (ECON, POL) national(e), intérieur(e); (SPORT: game) sur leur (or notre) terrain; (team) qui reçoit ♦ adv chez soi, à la maison; au pays natal; (right in: nail etc) à fond; **at ~** chez soi, à la maison; **make yourself at ~** faites comme chez vous; **~ address** n domicile permanent; **~land** n patrie f; **~less** adj sans foyer; sans abri; **~ly** adj (plain) simple, sans prétention; (: US) fait(e) à la maison; **~-made** adj fait(e) à la maison; **H~ Office** (BRIT) n ministère m de l'Intérieur; **~ rule** n autonomie f; **H~ Secretary** (BRIT) n ministre m de l'Intérieur; **~sick** adj: **to be ~sick** avoir le mal du pays; s'ennuyer de sa famille; **~ town** n ville natale; **~ward** adj (journey) du retour; **~work** n devoirs mpl

homogeneous [hɒmə'dʒiːnɪəs] adj homogène

homosexual [hɒməʊ'sɛksjuəl] adj, n homosexuel(le)

honest ['ɒnɪst] adj honnête; (sincere) franc(franche); **~ly** adv hon-

nêtement; franchement; **~y** n honnêteté f

honey ['hʌnɪ] n miel m; **~comb** n rayon m de miel; **~moon** n lune f de miel, voyage m de noces; **~suckle** ['hʌnɪsʌkl] (BOT) n chèvrefeuille m

honk [hɒŋk] vi (AUT) klaxonner

honorary ['ɒnərərɪ] adj honoraire; (duty, title) honorifique

honour ['ɒnə*] (US **honor**) vt honorer ♦ n honneur m; **hono(u)rable** adj honorable; **hono(u)rs degree** n (SCOL) licence avec mention

hood [hʊd] n capuchon m; (of cooker) hotte f; (AUT: BRIT) capote f; (: US) capot m

hoof [huːf] (pl **hooves**) n sabot m

hook [hʊk] n crochet m; (on dress) agrafe f; (for fishing) hameçon m ♦ vt accrocher; (fish) prendre

hooligan ['huːlɪgən] n voyou m

hoop [huːp] n cerceau m

hooray [huː'reɪ] excl hourra

hoot [huːt] vi (AUT) klaxonner; (siren) mugir; (owl) hululer; **~er** n (BRIT: AUT) klaxon m; (NAUT, factory) sirène f

Hoover [®:BRIT] n aspirateur m ♦ vt: **h~** passer l'aspirateur dans or sur

hooves [huːvz] npl of **hoof**

hop [hɒp] vi (on one foot) sauter à cloche-pied; (bird) sautiller

hope [həʊp] vt, vi espérer ♦ n espoir m; **I ~ so** je l'espère; **I ~ not** j'espère que non; **~ful** adj (person) plein(e) d'espoir; (situation) prometteur(euse), encourageant(e); **~fully** adv (expectantly) avec espoir, avec optimisme; (one hopes) avec un peu de chance; **~less** adj désespéré(e); (useless) nul(le)

hops [hɒps] npl houblon m

horizon [hə'raɪzn] n horizon m; **~tal** [hɒrɪ'zɒntl] adj horizontal(e)

horn [hɔːn] n corne f; (MUS: also: French ~) cor m; (AUT) klaxon m

hornet ['hɔːnɪt] n frelon m

horny ['hɔːnɪ] adj (inf) (aroused) en rut, excité(e)

horoscope ['hɒrəskəʊp] n horoscope m

horrendous [hə'rendəs] adj horrible, affreux(euse)

horrible ['hɒrɪbl] adj horrible, affreux(euse)

horrid ['hɒrɪd] adj épouvantable

horrify ['hɒrɪfaɪ] vt horrifier

horror ['hɒrə*] n horreur f; ~ **film** n film m d'épouvante

hors d'oeuvre [ɔː'dəːvrə] n (CULIN) hors-d'œuvre m inv

horse [hɔːs] n cheval m; ~**back** n: on ~**back** à cheval; ~ **chestnut** n marron m (d'Inde); ~**man** (irreg) n cavalier m; ~**power** n puissance f (en chevaux); ~**racing** n courses fpl de chevaux; ~**radish** n raifort m; ~**shoe** n fer m à cheval

hose [həʊz] n (also: ~pipe) tuyau m; (: garden~) tuyau d'arrosage

hospitable [hɒs'pɪtəbl] adj hospitalier(ère)

hospital ['hɒspɪtl] n hôpital m; **in** ~ à l'hôpital

hospitality [hɒspɪ'tælɪtɪ] n hospitalité f

host [həʊst] n hôte m; (TV, RADIO) animateur(trice); (REL) hostie f; (large number): **a** ~ **of** une foule de

hostage ['hɒstɪdʒ] n otage m

hostel ['hɒstəl] n foyer m; (also: youth~) auberge f de jeunesse

hostess ['həʊstes] n hôtesse f; (TV, RADIO) animatrice f

hostile ['hɒstaɪl] adj hostile; **hostility** [hɒs'tɪlɪtɪ] n hostilité f

hot [hɒt] adj chaud(e); (as opposed to only warm) très chaud; (spicy) fort(e); (contest etc) acharné(e); (temper) passionné(e); **to be** ~ (person) avoir chaud; (object) être (très) chaud; **it is** ~ (weather) il fait chaud; ~**bed** n (fig) foyer m, pépinière f; ~ **dog** n hot-dog m

hotel [həʊ'tel] n hôtel m

hot: ~**headed** adj impétueux(euse); ~**house** n serre (chaude); ~**line** n (POL) téléphone m rouge, ligne directe; ~**ly** adv passionnément, violemment; ~**plate** n (on cooker) plaque chauffante; ~**water bottle** n bouillotte f

hound [haʊnd] vt poursuivre avec acharnement ♦ n chien courant

hour ['aʊə*] n heure f; ~**ly** adj, adv toutes les heures; (rate) horaire

house [n haʊs, pl 'haʊzɪz, vb haʊz] n maison f; (POL) chambre f; (THEATRE) salle f; auditoire m ♦ vt (person) loger, héberger; (objects) abriter; **on the** ~ (fig) aux frais de la maison; ~ **arrest** n assignation f à résidence; ~**boat** n bateau m (aménagé en habitation); ~**bound** adj confiné(e) chez soi; ~**breaking** n cambriolage m (avec effraction); ~**coat** n peignoir m; ~**hold** n (persons) famille f, maisonnée f; (ADMIN etc) ménage m; ~**keeper** n gouvernante f; ~**keeping** n (work) ménage m; ~**keeping (money)** n argent m du ménage; ~**warming (party)** n pendaison f de crémaillère; ~**wife** (irreg) n ménagère f; femme f au foyer; ~**work** n (travaux mpl du) ménage m

housing ['haʊzɪŋ] n logement m; ~ **development**, ~ **estate** n lotissement m

hovel ['hɒvəl] n taudis m

hover ['hɒvə*] vi planer; ~**craft** n aéroglisseur m

how [haʊ] adv comment; ~ **are you?** comment allez-vous?; ~ **do you do?** bonjour; enchanté(e); ~ **far is it?** combine y a-t-il jusqu'à ...?; ~ **long have you been here?** depuis combine de temps êtes-vous là?; ~ **lovely!** que or comme c'est joli!; ~ **many/much?** combien?; ~ **many people/much milk?** combien de gens/lait?; ~ **old are you?** quel âge avez-vous?

however [haʊ'evə*] adv de quelque façon or manière que +subj; (+adj) quelque or si ... que +subj; (in questions) comment ♦ conj pourtant, cependant

howl [haʊl] vi hurler

H.P. abbr = hire purchase

h.p. abbr = horsepower

HQ abbr = headquarters

hub [hʌb] n (of wheel) moyeu m; (fig) centre m, foyer m

hubbub [ˈhʌbʌb] n brouhaha m

hubcap [ˈhʌbkæp] n enjoliveur m

huddle [ˈhʌdl] vi: to ~ together se blottir les uns contre les autres

hue [hju:] n teinte f, nuance f; ~ and cry n tollé (général), clameur f

huff [hʌf] n: in a ~ fâché(e)

hug [hʌg] vt serrer dans ses bras; (shore, kerb) serrer

huge [hju:dʒ] adj énorme, immense

hulk [hʌlk] n (ship) épave f; (car, building) carcasse f; (person) masto-donte m

hull [hʌl] n coque f

hullo [hʌˈləʊ] excl = hello

hum [hʌm] vt (tune) fredonner ♦ vi fredonner; (insect) bourdonner; (plane, tool) vrombir

human [ˈhju:mən] adj humain(e) ♦ n ~ (being) être humain; **~e** [hju:ˈmeɪn] adj humain(e), humanitai-re; **~itarian** [hju:mænɪˈteərɪən] adj humanitaire; **~ity** [hju:ˈmænɪtɪ] n hu-manité f

humble [ˈhʌmbl] adj humble, mo-deste ♦ vt humilier

humbug [ˈhʌmbʌg] n fumisterie f; (BRIT) bonbon m à la menthe

humdrum [ˈhʌmdrʌm] adj mono-tone, banal(e)

humid [ˈhju:mɪd] adj humide

humiliate [hju:ˈmɪlɪeɪt] vt humilier; **humiliation** n humiliation f

humorous [ˈhju:mərəs] adj humoris-tique; (person) doué(e) d'humour

humour [ˈhju:mə*] (US **humor**) n humeur m; (mood) humeur f ♦ vt (person) faire plaisir à; se prêter aux caprices de

hump [hʌmp] n bosse f

humpbacked [ˈhʌmpbækt] adj: ~ bridge pont m en dos d'âne

hunch [hʌntʃ] n (premonition) intui-tion f; **~back** n bossu(e); **~ed** adj voûté(e)

hundred [ˈhʌndrɪd] num cent; ~s of des centaines de; **~weight** n (BRIT) = 50.8 kg; (US) = 45.3 kg

hung [hʌŋ] pt, pp of **hang**

Hungary [ˈhʌŋgərɪ] n Hongrie f

hunger [ˈhʌŋgə*] n faim f ♦ vi: to ~ for avoir faim de, désirer ardem-ment

hungry [ˈhʌŋgrɪ] adj affamé(e); (keen): ~ for avide de; to be ~ avoir faim

hunk [hʌŋk] n (of bread etc) gros morceau

hunt [hʌnt] vt chasser; (criminal) pourchasser ♦ vi chasser; (search): to ~ for chercher (partout) ♦ n chasse f; **~er** n chasseur m; **~ing** n chasse f

hurdle [ˈhɜ:dl] n (SPORT) haie f; (fig) obstacle m

hurl [hɜ:l] vt lancer (avec violence); (abuse, insults) lancer

hurrah [hʊˈrɑ:] excl = hooray

hurray [hʊˈreɪ] excl = hooray

hurricane [ˈhʌrɪkən] n ouragan m

hurried [ˈhʌrɪd] adj pressé(e), préci-pité(e); (work) fait(e) à la hâte; **~ly** adv précipitamment, à la hâte

hurry [ˈhʌrɪ] (vb: also: ~ up) n hâte f, précipitation f ♦ vi se presser, se dépêcher ♦ vt (person) faire presser, faire se dépêcher; (work) presser; to be in a ~ être pressé(e); to do sth in a ~ faire qch en vitesse; to ~ in/out entrer/sortir précipitamment

hurt [hɜ:t] (pt, pp **hurt**) vt (cause pain to) faire mal à; (injure, fig) blesser ♦ vi faire mal ♦ adj bles-sé(e); **~ful** adj (remark) blessant(e)

hurtle [ˈhɜ:tl] vi: to ~ past passer en trombe; to ~ down dégringoler

husband [ˈhʌzbənd] n mari m

hush [hʌʃ] n calme m, silence m ♦ vt faire taire; ~! chut!; ~ up vt (scandal) étouffer

husk [hʌsk] n (of wheat) balle f; (of rice, maize) enveloppe f

husky [ˈhʌskɪ] adj rauque ♦ n chien m esquimau or de traîneau

hustle [ˈhʌsl] vt pousser, bousculer ♦

n: ~ **and bustle** tourbillon m (d'activité)

hut [hʌt] n hutte f; (shed) cabane f

hutch [hʌtʃ] n clapier m

hyacinth ['haɪəsɪnθ] n jacinthe f

hydrant ['haɪdrənt] n (also: fire ~) bouche f d'incendie

hydraulic [haɪ'drɔlɪk] adj hydraulique

hydroelectric [haɪdrəʊ'lektrɪk] adj hydro-électrique

hydrofoil ['haɪdrəʊfɔɪl] n hydrofoil m

hydrogen ['haɪdrədʒən] n hydrogène m

hyena [haɪ'i:nə] n hyène f

hygiene ['haɪdʒi:n] n hygiène f

hymn [hɪm] n hymne m; cantique m

hype [haɪp] (inf) n battage m publicitaire

hypermarket ['haɪpəmɑ:kɪt] (BRIT) n hypermarché m

hyphen ['haɪfən] n trait m d'union

hypnotize ['hɪpnətaɪz] vt hypnotiser

hypocrisy [hɪ'pɔkrɪsɪ] n hypocrisie f

hypocrite ['hɪpəkrɪt] n hypocrite m/f; **hypocritical** adj hypocrite

hypothesis [haɪ'pɒθɪsɪs] (pl ~es) n hypothèse f

hysterical [hɪs'terɪkəl] adj hystérique; (funny) hilarant(e); ~ **laughter** fou rire m

hysterics [hɪs'terɪks] npl: to be in/ have ~ (anger, panic) avoir une crise de nerfs; (laughter) attraper un fou rire

I

I [aɪ] pron je; (before vowel) j'; (stressed) moi

ice [aɪs] n glace f; (on road) verglas m ♦ vt (cake) glacer ♦ vi (also: ~ over, ~ up) geler; (: window) se givrer; **~berg** n iceberg m; **~box** n (US) réfrigérateur m; (BRIT) compartiment m à glace; (insulated box) glacière f; ~ **cream** n glace f; ~ **cube** n glaçon m; **~d** adj glacé(e); ~ **hockey** n hockey m sur glace; **I~land** ['aɪslənd] n Islande f; **~ lolly** n (BRIT) esquimau m (glace); ~ **rink** n patinoire f; **~skating** n patinage m (sur glace)

icicle ['aɪsɪkl] n glaçon m (naturel)

icing ['aɪsɪŋ] n (CULIN) glace f; ~ **sugar** (BRIT) n sucre m glace

icy ['aɪsɪ] adj glacé(e); (road) verglacé(e); (weather, temperature) glacial(e)

I'd [aɪd] = I would; I had

idea [aɪ'dɪə] n idée f

ideal [aɪ'dɪəl] n idéal m ♦ adj idéal(e)

identical [aɪ'dentɪkəl] adj identique

identification [aɪdentɪfɪ'keɪʃən] n identification f; **means of** ~ pièce f d'identité

identify [aɪ'dentɪfaɪ] vt identifier

Identikit picture (®) n portrait-robot m

identity [aɪ'dentɪtɪ] n identité f; ~ **card** n carte f d'identité

ideology [aɪdɪ'ɒlədʒɪ] n idéologie f

idiom ['ɪdɪəm] n expression f idiomatique; (style) style m

idiosyncrasy [ɪdɪə'sɪŋkrəsɪ] n (of person) particularité f, petite manie

idiot ['ɪdɪət] n idiot(e), imbécile m/f; **~ic** [ɪdɪ'ɒtɪk] adj idiot(e), bête, stupide

idle ['aɪdl] adj sans occupation, désœuvré(e); (lazy) oisif(ive), paresseux(euse); (unemployed) au chômage; (question, pleasures) vain(e), futile ♦ vi (engine) tourner au ralenti; to lie ~ être arrêté(e), ne pas fonctionner; ~ **away** vt: to ~ **away** the time passer son temps à ne rien faire

idol ['aɪdl] n idole f; **~ize** vt idolâtrer, adorer

i.e. adv abbr (= id est) c'est-à-dire

if [ɪf] conj si; ~ **necessary** si c'est nécessaire; ~ **so** si c'est le cas; ~ **not** sinon; ~ **only** si seulement

ignite [ɪg'naɪt] vt mettre le feu à, enflammer ♦ vi s'enflammer

ignition [ɪg'nɪʃən] n (AUT) allumage m; **to switch on/off the** ~ mettre/couper le contact; ~ **key** n clé f de contact

ignorant ['ɪgnərənt] adj ignorant(e); **to be ~ of** (subject) ne rien connaître à; (events) ne pas être au courant de

ignore [ɪg'nɔː*] vt ne tenir aucun compte de; (person) faire semblant de ne pas reconnaître, ignorer; (fact) méconnaître

ill [ɪl] adj (sick) malade; (bad) mauvais(e) ♦ n mal m ♦ adv: **to speak/think ~ of** dire/penser du mal de; **~s** npl (misfortunes) maux mpl, malheurs mpl; **to be taken ~** tomber malade; **~-advised** adj (decision) peu judicieux(euse); (person) malavisé(e); **~-at-ease** adj mal à l'aise

I'll [aɪl] = **I will**; **I shall**

illegal [ɪ'liːgl] adj illégal(e)

illegible [ɪ'ledʒəbl] adj illisible

illegitimate [ɪlɪ'dʒɪtɪmət] adj illégitime

ill: **~-fated** [ɪl'feɪtɪd] adj malheureux(euse); (day) néfaste; **~ feeling** n ressentiment m, rancune f

illiterate [ɪ'lɪtərət] adj illettré(e); (letter) plein(e) de fautes

ill: **~-mannered** [ɪl'mænəd] adj (child) mal élevé(e); **~ness** [ɪlnəs] n maladie f; **~-treat** [ɪl'triːt] vt maltraiter

illuminate [ɪ'luːmɪneɪt] vt (room, street) éclairer; (for special effect) illuminer; **illumination** [ɪluːmɪ'neɪʃən] n éclairage m; illumination f

illusion [ɪ'luːʒən] n illusion f

illustrate ['ɪləstreɪt] vt illustrer; **illustration** [ɪlə'streɪʃən] n illustration f

ill will n malveillance f

I'm [aɪm] = **I am**

image ['ɪmɪdʒ] n image f; (public face) image de marque; **~ry** n images fpl

imaginary [ɪ'mædʒɪnərɪ] adj imaginaire

imagination [ɪmædʒɪ'neɪʃən] n imagination f

imaginative [ɪ'mædʒɪnətɪv] adj imaginatif(ive); (person) plein(e) d'ima-

gination

imagine [ɪ'mædʒɪn] vt imaginer, s'imaginer; (suppose) imaginer, supposer

imbalance [ɪm'bæləns] n déséquilibre m

imbue [ɪm'bjuː] vt: **to ~ sb/sth with** imprégner qn/qch de

imitate ['ɪmɪteɪt] vt imiter; **imitation** [ɪmɪ'teɪʃən] n imitation f

immaculate [ɪ'mækjʊlɪt] adj impeccable; (REL) immaculé(e)

immaterial [ɪmə'tɪərɪəl] adj sans importance, insignifiant(e)

immature [ɪmə'tjʊə*] adj (fruit) (qui n'est pas mûr(e); (person) qui manque de maturité

immediate [ɪ'miːdɪət] adj immédiat(e); **~ly** adv (at once) immédiatement; **~ly next to** juste à côté de

immense [ɪ'mɛns] adj immense, énorme

immerse [ɪ'mɜːs] vt immerger, plonger; **immersion heater** [ɪ'mɜːʃən-] (BRIT) n chauffe-eau m électrique

immigrant ['ɪmɪgrənt] n immigrant(e); immigré(e); **immigration** [ɪmɪ'greɪʃən] n immigration f

imminent ['ɪmɪnənt] adj imminent(e)

immoral [ɪ'mɒrəl] adj immoral(e)

immortal [ɪ'mɔːtl] adj, n immortel(le)

immune [ɪ'mjuːn] adj: **~ (to)** immunisé(e) (contre); (fig) à l'abri de; **immunity** [ɪ'mjuːnɪtɪ] n immunité f

imp [ɪmp] n lutin m; (child) petit diable

impact ['ɪmpækt] n choc m, impact m; (fig) impact m

impair [ɪm'pɛə*] vt détériorer, diminuer

impart [ɪm'pɑːt] vt communiquer, transmettre; (flavour) donner

impartial [ɪm'pɑːʃəl] adj impartial(e)

impassable [ɪm'pɑːsəbl] adj infranchissable; (road) impraticable

impassive [ɪm'pæsɪv] adj impassible

impatience [ɪm'peɪʃəns] n impa-

tience f
impatient [ɪm'peɪʃənt] *adj* impatient(e); **to get** *or* **grow ~** s'impatienter
impeccable [ɪm'pekəbl] *adj* impeccable, parfait(e)
impede [ɪm'piːd] *vt* gêner
impediment [ɪm'pedɪmənt] *n* obstacle *m*; (*also*: **speech ~**) défaut *m* d'élocution
impending [ɪm'pendɪŋ] *adj* imminent(e)
imperative [ɪm'perətɪv] *adj* (*need*) urgent(e), pressant(e); (*tone*) impérieux(euse) ♦ *n* (*LING*) impératif *m*
imperfect [ɪm'pɜːfɪkt] *adj* imparfait(e); (*goods etc*) défectueux(euse)
imperial [ɪm'pɪərɪəl] *adj* impérial(e); (*BRIT*: *measure*) légal(e)
impersonal [ɪm'pɜːsnl] *adj* impersonnel(le)
impersonate [ɪm'pɜːsəneɪt] *vt* se faire passer pour; (*THEATRE*) imiter
impertinent [ɪm'pɜːtɪnənt] *adj* impertinent(e), insolent(e)
impervious [ɪm'pɜːvɪəs] *adj* (*fig*): **~ to** insensible à
impetuous [ɪm'petjʊəs] *adj* impétueux(euse), fougueux(euse)
impetus ['ɪmpɪtəs] *n* impulsion *f*; (*of runner*) élan *m*
impinge [ɪm'pɪndʒ]: **to ~ on** *vt fus* (*person*) affecter, toucher; (*rights*) empiéter sur
implement [*n* 'ɪmplɪmənt, *vb* 'ɪmplɪment] *n* outil *m*, instrument *m*; (*for cooking*) ustensile *m* ♦ *vt* exécuter
implicit [ɪm'plɪsɪt] *adj* implicite; (*complete*) absolu(e), sans réserve
imply [ɪm'plaɪ] *vt* suggérer, laisser entendre; indiquer, supposer
impolite [ɪmpə'laɪt] *adj* impoli(e)
import [*vb* ɪm'pɔːt, *n* 'ɪmpɔːt] *vt* importer ♦ *n* (*COMM*) importation *f*
importance [ɪm'pɔːtns] *n* importance *f*
important [ɪm'pɔːtənt] *adj* important(e)

importer [ɪm'pɔːtə*] *n* importateur(trice)
impose [ɪm'pəʊz] *vt* imposer ♦ *vi*: **to ~ on sb** abuser de la gentillesse de qn; **imposing** [ɪm'pəʊzɪŋ] *adj* imposant(e), impressionnant(e); **imposition** [ɪmpə'zɪʃən] *n* (*of tax etc*) imposition *f*; **to be an imposition on** (*person*) abuser de la gentillesse *or* la bonté de
impossible [ɪm'pɒsəbl] *adj* impossible
impotent ['ɪmpətənt] *adj* impuissant(e)
impound [ɪm'paʊnd] *vt* confisquer, saisir
impoverished [ɪm'pɒvərɪʃt] *adj* appauvri(e), pauvre
impractical [ɪm'præktɪkəl] *adj* pas pratique; (*person*) qui manque d'esprit pratique
impregnable [ɪm'pregnəbl] *adj* (*fortress*) imprenable
impress [ɪm'pres] *vt* impressionner, faire impression sur; (*mark*) imprimer, marquer; **to ~ sth on sb** faire bien comprendre qch à qn
impression [ɪm'preʃən] *n* impression *f*; (*of stamp, seal*) empreinte *f*; (*imitation*) imitation *f*; **to be under the ~ that** avoir l'impression que; **~ist** *n* (*ART*) impressionniste *m/f*; (*entertainer*) imitateur(trice) *m/f*
impressive [ɪm'presɪv] *adj* impressionnant(e)
imprint ['ɪmprɪnt] *n* (*outline*) marque *f*, empreinte *f*
imprison [ɪm'prɪzn] *vt* emprisonner, mettre en prison
improbable [ɪm'prɒbəbl] *adj* improbable; (*excuse*) peu plausible
improper [ɪm'prɒpə*] *adj* (*unsuitable*) déplacé(e), de mauvais goût; indécent(e); (*dishonest*) malhonnête
improve [ɪm'pruːv] *vt* améliorer ♦ *vi* s'améliorer; (*pupil etc*) faire des progrès; **~ment** *n* amélioration *f* (*in* de); progrès *m*
improvise ['ɪmprəvaɪz] *vt, vi* improviser

impudent ['ɪmpjʊdənt] *adj* impudent(e)

impulse ['ɪmpʌls] *n* impulsion *f*; on ~ impulsivement, sur un coup de tête; **impulsive** [ɪm'pʌlsɪv] *adj* impulsif(ive)

KEYWORD

---

in [ɪn] *prep* **1** (*indicating place, position*) dans; ~ **the house/the fridge** dans la maison/le frigo; ~ **the garden** dans le or au jardin; ~ **town** en ville; ~ **the country** à la campagne; ~ **school** à l'école; ~ **here/there** ici/là

2 (*with place names: of town, region, country*): ~ **London** à Londres; ~ **England** en Angleterre; ~ **Japan** au Japon; ~ **the United States** aux Etats-Unis

3 (*indicating time: during*): ~ **spring** au printemps; ~ **summer** en été; ~ **May/1992** en mai/1992; ~ **the afternoon** (dans) l'après-midi; **at 4 o'clock** ~ **the afternoon** à 4 heures de l'après-midi

4 (*indicating time: in the space of*) en; (: *future*) dans; **I did it** ~ **3 hours/days** je l'ai fait en 3 heures/jours; **I'll see you** ~ **2 weeks** *or* ~ **2 weeks' time** je te verrai dans 2 semaines

5 (*indicating manner etc*) à; ~ **a loud/soft voice** à voix haute/basse; ~ **pencil** au crayon; ~ **French** en français; **the boy** ~ **the blue shirt** le garçon à or avec la chemise bleue

6 (*indicating circumstances*): ~ **the sun** au soleil; ~ **the shade** à l'ombre; ~ **the rain** sous la pluie

7 (*indicating mood, state*): ~ **tears** en larmes; ~ **anger** sous le coup de la colère; ~ **despair** au désespoir; ~ **good condition** en bon état; **to live** ~ **luxury** vivre dans le luxe

8 (*with ratios, numbers*): **1** ~ **10 (households)**, **1 (household)** ~ **10** **1** ménage sur 10; **20 pence** ~ **the pound** 20 pence par livre sterling; **they lined up** ~ **twos** ils se mirent

en rangs (deux) par deux; ~ **hundreds** par centaines

9 (*referring to people, works*) chez; **the disease is common** ~ **children** c'est une maladie courante chez les enfants; ~ **(the works of) Dickens** chez Dickens, dans (l'œuvre de) Dickens

10 (*indicating profession etc*) dans; **to be** ~ **teaching** être dans l'enseignement

11 (*after superlative*) de; **the best pupil** ~ **the class** le meilleur élève de la classe

12 (*with present participle*): ~ **saying this** en disant ceci

♦ *adv*: **to be** ~ (*person: at home, work*) être là; (*train, ship, plane*) être arrivé(e); (*in fashion*) être à la mode; **to ask sb** ~ inviter qn à entrer; **to run/limp** *etc* ~ entrer en courant/boitant *etc*

♦ *n*: **the** ~**s and outs** (*of proposal, situation etc*) les tenants et aboutissants (de)

---

in. *abbr* = **inch**

inability [ɪnə'bɪlɪtɪ] *n* incapacité *f*

inaccurate [ɪn'ækjʊrɪt] *adj* inexact(e); (*person*) qui manque de précision

inadequate [ɪn'ædɪkwət] *adj* insuffisant(e), inadéquat(e)

inadvertently [ɪnəd'vɜːtəntlɪ] *adv* par mégarde

inadvisable [ɪnəd'vaɪzəbl] *adj* (*action*) à déconseiller

inane [ɪ'neɪn] *adj* inepte, stupide

inanimate [ɪn'ænɪmət] *adj* inanimé(e)

inappropriate [ɪnə'prəʊprɪət] *adj* inopportun(e), mal à propos; (*word, expression*) impropre

inarticulate [ɪnɑː'tɪkjʊlət] *adj* (*person*) qui s'exprime mal; (*speech*) indistinct(e)

inasmuch as [ɪnəz'mʌtʃəz] *adv* (*insofar as*) dans la mesure où; (*seeing that*) attendu que

inauguration [ɪnɔːgjʊ'reɪʃən] *n* inauguration f; (of president) investiture f

inborn ['ɪn'bɔːn] adj (quality) in-né(e)

inbred ['ɪn'bred] adj inné(e), natu-rel(le); (family) consanguin(e)

Inc. abbr = **incorporated**

incapable [ɪn'keɪpəbl] adj incapable

incapacitate [ɪnkə'pæsɪteɪt] vt: to ~ sb from doing rendre qn incapable de faire

incense [n 'ɪnsens, vb ɪn'sens] n en-cens m ♦ vt (anger) mettre en colère

incentive [ɪn'sentɪv] n encourage-ment m, raison f de se donner de la peine

incessant [ɪn'sesnt] adj inces-sant(e); **~ly** adv sans cesse, constamment

inch [ɪntʃ] n pouce m (= 25 mm; 12 in a foot); **within an** ~ **of** à deux doigts de; **he didn't give an** ~ (fig) il n'a pas voulu céder d'un pouce; ~ **forward** vi avancer petit à petit

incident ['ɪnsɪdənt] n incident m

incidental [ɪnsɪ'dentl] adj (additio-nal) accessoire; ~ **to** qui accompa-gne; **~ly** adv (by the way) à propos

inclination [ɪnklɪ'neɪʃən] n (fig) in-clination f

incline [n 'ɪnklaɪn, vb ɪn'klaɪn] n pente f ♦ vt incliner ♦ vi (surface) s'incliner; **to be ~d to do** avoir ten-dance à faire

include [ɪn'kluːd] vt inclure, comprendre; **including** [ɪn'kluːdɪŋ] prep y compris

inclusive [ɪn'kluːsɪv] adj inclus(e), compris(e); ~ **of tax** etc taxes etc comprises

income ['ɪnkʌm] n revenu m; ~ **tax** n impôt m sur le revenu

incoming ['ɪnkʌmɪŋ] adj qui arrive; (president) entrant(e); ~ **mail** cour-rier m du jour; ~ **tide** marée mon-tante

incompetent [ɪn'kɒmpɪtənt] adj in-compétent(e), incapable

incomplete [ɪnkəm'pliːt] adj in-complet(ète)

incongruous [ɪn'kɒŋgruəs] adj in-congru(e)

inconsiderate [ɪnkən'sɪdərɪt] adj (person) qui manque d'égards; (ac-tion) inconsidéré(e)

inconsistency [ɪnkən'sɪstənsɪ] n (of actions etc) inconséquence f; (of work) irrégularité f; (of statement etc) incohérence f

inconsistent [ɪnkən'sɪstənt] adj in-conséquent(e); irrégulier(ère); peu cohérent(e); ~ **with** incompatible avec

inconspicuous [ɪnkən'spɪkjuəs] adj qui passe inaperçu(e); (colour, dress) discret(ète)

inconvenience [ɪnkən'viːnɪəns] n in-convénient m; (trouble) dérangement m ♦ vt déranger

inconvenient [ɪnkən'viːnɪənt] adj (house) malcommode; (time, place) mal choisi(e), qui ne convient pas; (visitor) importun(e)

incorporate [ɪn'kɔːpəreɪt] vt incor-porer; (contain) contenir; ~**d com-pany** (US) n société f anonyme

incorrect [ɪnkə'rekt] adj incorrect(e)

increase [n 'ɪnkriːs, vb ɪn'kriːs] n augmentation f ♦ vi, vt augmenter; **increasing** [ɪn'kriːsɪŋ] adj (number) croissant(e); **increasingly** [ɪn'kriːsɪŋ-lɪ] adv de plus en plus

incredible [ɪn'kredəbl] adj in-croyable

incredulous [ɪn'kredjuləs] adj incré-dule

incubator ['ɪnkjubeɪtə*] n (for babies) couveuse f

incumbent [ɪn'kʌmbənt] n (presi-dent) président m en exercice; (REL) titulaire m/f ♦ adj: **it is** ~ **on him to ...** il lui incombe or appar-tient de ...

incur [ɪn'kɜː*] vt (expenses) encou-rir; (anger, risk) s'exposer à; (debt) contracter; (loss) subir

indebted [ɪn'detɪd] adj: **to be** ~ **to sb** (for) être redevable à qn (de)

indecent [ɪn'diːsnt] adj indécent(e), inconvenant(e); ~ **assault** (BRIT) n attentat m à la pudeur; ~ **exposure** n outrage m (public) à la pudeur

indecisive [ɪndɪ'saɪsɪv] adj (person) indécis(e)

indeed [ɪn'diːd] adv vraiment; en effet; (furthermore) d'ailleurs; yes ~! certainement!

indefinitely [ɪn'dɛfɪnɪtlɪ] adv (wait) indéfiniment

indemnity [ɪn'dɛmnɪtɪ] n (safeguard) assurance f, garantie f; (compensation) indemnité f

independence [ɪndɪ'pɛndəns] n indépendance f; **independent** [ɪndɪ'pɛndənt] adj indépendant(e); (school) privée(e); (radio) libre

index ['ɪndɛks] n (pl: ~es: in book) index m; (: in library etc) catalogue m; (pl: indices: ratio, sign) indice m; ~ **card** n fiche f; ~ **finger** n index m; ~**linked** adj indexée(e) (sur le coût de la vie etc)

India ['ɪndɪə] n Inde f; ~**n** adj indien(ne) ♦ n Indien(ne); (American) ~n Indien(ne) (d'Amérique)

indicate ['ɪndɪkeɪt] vt indiquer; **indication** [ɪndɪ'keɪʃən] n indication f, signe m; **indicative** [ɪn'dɪkətɪv] adj; **indicative** of symptomatique de ♦ n (LING) indicatif m; **indicator** ['ɪndɪkeɪtə*] n (sign) indicateur m; (AUT) clignotant m

indices ['ɪndɪsiːz] npl of **index**

indictment [ɪn'daɪtmənt] n accusation f

indifferent [ɪn'dɪfrənt] adj indifférent(e); (poor) médiocre, quelconque

indigenous [ɪn'dɪdʒɪnəs] adj indigène

indigestion [ɪndɪ'dʒɛstʃən] n indigestion f, mauvaise digestion

indignant [ɪn'dɪgnənt] adj: ~ (at sth/with sb) indigné(e) (de qch/contre qn)

indignity [ɪn'dɪgnɪtɪ] n indignité f, affront m

indirect [ɪndɪ'rɛkt] adj indirect(e)

indiscreet [ɪndɪs'kriːt] adj indiscret(ète); (rash) imprudent(e)

indiscriminate [ɪndɪs'krɪmɪnət] adj

(person) qui manque de discernement; (killings) commis(e) au hasard

indisputable [ɪndɪs'pjuːtəbl] adj incontestable, indéniable

individual [ɪndɪ'vɪdjuəl] n individu m ♦ adj individuel(le); (characteristic) particulier(ère), original(e)

indoctrination [ɪndɒktrɪ'neɪʃən] n endoctrinement m

Indonesia [ɪndəʊ'niːzɪə] n Indonésie f

indoor ['ɪndɔː*] adj (plant) d'appartement; (swimming pool) couvert(e); (sport, games) pratiqué(e) en salle; ~**s** [ɪn'dɔːz] adv à l'intérieur

induce [ɪn'djuːs] vt (persuade) persuader; (bring about) provoquer; ~**ment** n (incentive) récompense f, (pej: bribe) pot-de-vin m

indulge [ɪn'dʌldʒ] vt (whim) céder à, satisfaire; (child) gâter ♦ vi: to ~ in sth (luxury) se permettre qch; (fantasies etc) se livrer à qch; ~**nce** n fantaisie f (que l'on s'offre); (leniency) indulgence f; ~**nt** adj indulgent(e)

industrial [ɪn'dʌstrɪəl] adj industriel(le); (injury) du travail; ~ **action** n action revendicative; ~ **estate** (BRIT) n zone industrielle; ~**ist** n industriel m; ~ **park** (US) n = industrial estate

industrious [ɪn'dʌstrɪəs] adj travailleur(euse)

industry ['ɪndəstrɪ] n industrie f; (diligence) zèle m, application f

inebriated [ɪ'niːbrɪeɪtɪd] adj ivre

inedible [ɪn'ɛdɪbl] adj immangeable; (plant etc) non comestible

ineffective [ɪnɪ'fɛktɪv], **ineffectual** [ɪnɪ'fɛktjuəl] adj inefficace

inefficient [ɪnɪ'fɪʃənt] adj inefficace

inequality [ɪnɪ'kwɒlɪtɪ] n inégalité f

inescapable [ɪnɪs'keɪpəbl] adj inéluctable, inévitable

inevitable [ɪn'ɛvɪtəbl] adj inévitable; **inevitably** adv inévitablement

inexhaustible [ɪnɪg'zɔːstəbl] adj inépuisable

inexpensive [ɪnɪks'pensɪv] adj bon marché inv

inexperienced [ɪnɪks'pɪərɪənst] adj inexpérimenté(e)

infallible [ɪn'fæləbl] adj infaillible

infamous ['ɪnfəməs] adj infâme, abominable

infancy ['ɪnfənsɪ] n petite enfance, bas âge

infant ['ɪnfənt] n (baby) nourrisson m; (young child) petit(e) enfant; ~ **school** (BRIT) n classes fpl préparatoires (entre 5 et 7 ans)

infatuated [ɪn'fætjʊeɪtɪd] adj: ~ **with** entiché(e); **infatuation** [ɪnfætjʊ'eɪʃən] n engouement m

infect [ɪn'fekt] vt infecter, contaminer; **~ion** [ɪn'fekʃən] n infection f; (contagion) contagion f; **~ious** [ɪn'fekʃəs] adj infectieux(euse); (also fig) contagieux(euse)

infer [ɪn'fɜː*] vt conclure, déduire; (imply) suggérer

inferior [ɪn'fɪərɪə*] adj inférieur(e); (goods) de qualité inférieure ♦ n inférieur(e); (in rank) subalterne m/f; **~ity** [ɪnfɪərɪ'ɔrɪtɪ] n infériorité f; **~ity complex** n complexe m d'infériorité

inferno [ɪn'fɜːnəʊ] n (blaze) brasier m

infertile [ɪn'fɜːtaɪl] adj stérile

infighting ['ɪnfaɪtɪŋ] n querelles fpl internes

infinite ['ɪnfɪnɪt] adj infini(e)

infinitive [ɪn'fɪnɪtɪv] n infinitif m

infinity [ɪn'fɪnɪtɪ] n infinité f; (also MATH) infini m

infirmary [ɪn'fɜːmərɪ] n (hospital) hôpital m

inflamed [ɪn'fleɪmd] adj enflammé(e)

inflammable [ɪn'flæməbl] (BRIT) adj inflammable

inflammation [ɪnflə'meɪʃən] n inflammation f

inflatable [ɪn'fleɪtəbl] adj gonflable

inflate [ɪn'fleɪt] vt (tyre, balloon) gonfler; (price) faire monter; **inflation** [ɪn'fleɪʃən] n (ECON) inflation f;

inflationary [ɪn'fleɪʃnərɪ] adj inflationniste

inflict [ɪn'flɪkt] vt: to ~ **on** infliger à

influence ['ɪnfluəns] n influence f ♦ vt influencer; **under the ~ of** alcohol en état d'ébriété; **influential** [ɪnfluˈenʃl] adj influent(e)

influenza [ɪnfluˈenzə] n grippe f

influx ['ɪnflʌks] n afflux m

inform [ɪn'fɔːm] vt: to ~ **sb (of)** informer or avertir qn (de) ♦ vi: to ~ **on sb** dénoncer qn

informal [ɪn'fɔːml] adj (person, manner, party) simple; (visit, discussion) dénué(e) de formalités; (announcement, invitation) non officiel(le); (colloquial) familier (ère); **~ity** [ɪnfɔːˈmælɪtɪ] n simplicité f, absence f de cérémonie; caractère non officiel

informant [ɪn'fɔːmənt] n informateur(trice)

information [ɪnfəˈmeɪʃən] n information f; renseignements mpl; (knowledge) connaissances fpl; **a piece of ~** un renseignement; **~ office** n bureau m de renseignements

informative [ɪn'fɔːmətɪv] adj instructif(ive)

informer [ɪn'fɔːmə*] n (also: police ~) indicateur(trice)

infringe [ɪn'frɪndʒ] vt enfreindre ♦ vi: to ~ **on** empiéter sur; **~ment** n: **~ment (of)** infraction f (à)

infuriating [ɪn'fjʊərɪeɪtɪŋ] adj exaspérant(e)

ingenious [ɪn'dʒiːnɪəs] adj ingénieux(euse); **ingenuity** [ɪndʒɪˈnjuːɪtɪ] n ingéniosité f

ingenuous [ɪn'dʒenjuəs] adj naïf(naïve), ingénu(e)

ingot ['ɪŋɡət] n lingot m

ingrained [ɪn'ɡreɪnd] adj enraciné(e)

ingratiate [ɪn'ɡreɪʃɪeɪt] vt: to ~ **o.s. with** s'insinuer dans les bonnes grâces de, se faire bien voir de

ingredient [ɪn'ɡriːdɪənt] n ingrédient m; (fig) élément m

inhabit [ɪn'hæbɪt] vt habiter; **~ant** [ɪn'hæbɪtnt] n habitant(e)

inhale [ɪn'heɪl] vt respirer; (smoke) avaler ♦ vi aspirer; (in smoking) avaler la fumée

inherent [ɪn'hɪərənt] adj: ~ (in or to) inhérent(e) (à)

inherit [ɪn'herɪt] vt hériter de; ~ance n héritage m

inhibit [ɪn'hɪbɪt] vt (PSYCH) inhiber; (growth) freiner; ~ion [ɪnhɪ'bɪʃən] n inhibition f

inhuman [ɪn'hju:mən] adj inhumain(e)

initial [ɪ'nɪʃl] adj initial(e) ♦ n initiale f ♦ vt parafer; ~s npl (letters) initiales fpl; (as signature) parafe m; ~ly adv initialement, au début

initiate [ɪ'nɪʃɪeɪt] vt (start) entreprendre; amorcer; lancer; (person) initier; to ~ proceedings against sb intenter une action à qn

initiative [ɪ'nɪʃətɪv] n initiative f

inject [ɪn'dʒekt] vt injecter; (person): to ~ sb with sth faire une piqûre de qch à qn; ~ion [ɪn'dʒekʃən] n injection f, piqûre f

injure ['ɪndʒə*] vt blesser; (reputation etc) compromettre; ~d adj blessé(e); **injury** ['ɪndʒərɪ] n blessure f; **injury time** n (SPORT) arrêts mpl de jeu

injustice [ɪn'dʒʌstɪs] n injustice f

ink [ɪŋk] n encre f

inkling ['ɪŋklɪŋ] n: to have an/no ~ of avoir une (vague) idée de/n'avoir aucune idée de

inlaid ['ɪn'leɪd] adj incrusté(e); (table etc) marqueté(e)

inland [adj 'ɪnlənd, adv 'ɪnlænd] adj intérieur(e) ♦ adv à l'intérieur, dans les terres; **I~ Revenue** (BRIT) n fisc m

in-laws ['ɪnlɔ:z] npl beaux-parents mpl; belle famille

inlet ['ɪnlet] n (GEO) crique f

inmate ['ɪnmeɪt] n (in prison) détenu(e); (in asylum) interné(e)

inn [ɪn] n auberge f

innate [ɪ'neɪt] adj inné(e)

inner ['ɪnə*] adj intérieur(e); ~ **city** n centre m de zone urbaine; ~ **tube**

n (of tyre) chambre f à air

innings ['ɪnɪŋz] n (CRICKET) tour m de batte

innocent ['ɪnəsnt] adj innocent(e)

innocuous [ɪ'nɒkjuəs] adj inoffensif(ive)

innuendo [ɪnju'endəu] (pl ~es) n insinuation f, allusion (malveillante)

innumerable [ɪ'nju:mərəbl] adj innombrable

inordinately [ɪ'nɔ:dɪnɪtlɪ] adv démesurément

inpatient ['ɪnpeɪʃənt] n malade hospitalisé(e)

input ['ɪnput] n (resources) ressources fpl; (COMPUT) entrée f (de données); (: data) données fpl

inquest ['ɪnkwest] n enquête f; (coroner's) enquête judiciaire

inquire [ɪn'kwaɪə*] vi demander ♦ vt demander; to ~ about se renseigner sur; ~ **into** vt fus faire une enquête sur; **inquiry** [ɪn'kwaɪərɪ] n demande f de renseignements; (investigation) enquête f, investigation f; **inquiry office** (BRIT) n bureau m de renseignements

inquisitive [ɪn'kwɪzɪtɪv] adj curieux(euse)

inroads ['ɪnrəudz] npl: to make ~ into (savings etc) entamer

ins abbr = inches

insane [ɪn'seɪn] adj fou(folle); (MED) aliéné(e); **insanity** [ɪn'sænɪtɪ] n folie f; (MED) aliénation (mentale)

inscription [ɪn'skrɪpʃən] n inscription f; (in book) dédicace f

inscrutable [ɪn'skru:təbl] adj impénétrable; (comment) obscur(e)

insect ['ɪnsekt] n insecte m; ~**icide** [ɪn'sektɪsaɪd] n insecticide m

insecure [ɪnsɪ'kjuə*] adj peu solide; peu sûr(e); (person) anxieux(euse)

insensitive [ɪn'sensɪtɪv] adj insensible

insert [ɪn'sɜ:t] vt insérer; ~**ion** n insertion f

in-service [ɪn'sɜ:vɪs] adj (training) continu(e), en cours d'emploi; (course) de perfectionnement; de recyclage

inshore ['ɪn'ʃɔː*] adj côtier(ère) ♦ adv près de la côte; (move) vers la côte

inside ['ɪn'saɪd] n intérieur m ♦ adj intérieur(e) ♦ adv à l'intérieur, dedans ♦ prep à l'intérieur de; (of time): ~ **10 minutes** en moins de 10 minutes; ~s npl (inf) intestins mpl; ~ **information** n renseignements obtenus à la source; ~ **lane** n (AUT: BRIT) voie f de gauche; (: US, Europe etc) voie de droite; ~ **out** adv à l'envers; (know) à fond

insider dealing, insider trading n (St Ex) délit m d'initié

insight ['ɪnsaɪt] n perspicacité f; (glimpse, idea) aperçu m

insignificant [ɪnsɪg'nɪfɪkənt] adj insignifiant(e)

insincere [ɪnsɪn'sɪə*] adj hypocrite

insinuate [ɪn'sɪnjʊeɪt] vt insinuer

insist [ɪn'sɪst] vi insister; to ~ on doing insister pour faire; to ~ on sth exiger qch; to ~ that insister pour que; (claim) maintenir or soutenir que; ~**ent** adj insistant(e), pressant(e); (noise, action) interrompu(e)

insole ['ɪnsəʊl] n (removable) semelle intérieure

insolent ['ɪnsələnt] adj insolent(e)

insolvent [ɪn'sɒlvənt] adj insolvable

insomnia [ɪn'sɒmnɪə] n insomnie f

inspect [ɪn'spekt] vt inspecter; (ticket) contrôler; ~**ion** [ɪn'spekʃən] n inspection f; contrôle m; ~**or** n inspecteur(trice); (BRIT: on buses, trains) contrôleur(euse)

inspire [ɪn'spaɪə*] vt inspirer

install [ɪn'stɔːl] vt installer; ~**ation** [ɪnstə'leɪʃən] n installation f

instalment [ɪn'stɔːlmənt] (US **installment**) n acompte m, versement partiel; (of TV serial etc) épisode m; **in** ~**s** (pay) à tempérament; (receive) en plusieurs fois

instance ['ɪnstəns] n exemple m; for ~ par exemple; **in the first** ~ tout d'abord, en premier lieu

instant ['ɪnstənt] n instant m ♦ adj immédiat(e); (coffee, food) instantané(e), en poudre; ~**ly** adv immédiatement, tout de suite

instead [ɪn'sted] adv au lieu de cela; ~ **of** au lieu de; ~ **of sb** à la place de qn

instep ['ɪnstep] n cou-de-pied m; (of shoe) cambrure f

instigate ['ɪnstɪgeɪt] vt (rebellion) fomenter, provoquer; (talks etc) promouvoir

instil [ɪn'stɪl] vt: to ~ (into) inculquer (à); (courage) insuffler (à)

instinct ['ɪnstɪŋkt] n instinct m

institute ['ɪnstɪtjuːt] n institut m ♦ vt instituer, établir; (inquiry) ouvrir; (proceedings) entamer

institution [ɪnstɪ'tjuːʃən] n institution f; (educational) établissement m (scolaire); (mental home) établissement (psychiatrique)

instruct [ɪn'strʌkt] vt: to ~ **sb** in sth enseigner qch à qn; to ~ **sb** to do charger qn or ordonner à qn de faire; ~**ion** [ɪn'strʌkʃən] n instruction f; ~**ions** npl (orders) directives fpl; ~**ions** (for use) mode m d'emploi; ~**or** n professeur m; (for skiing, driving) moniteur m

instrument ['ɪnstrʊmənt] n instrument m; ~**al** [ɪnstrʊ'mentl] adj: to be ~**al** in contribuer à; ~ **panel** n tableau m de bord

insufficient [ɪnsə'fɪʃənt] adj insuffisant(e)

insular ['ɪnsjʊlə*] adj (outlook) borné(e); (person) aux vues étroites

insulate ['ɪnsjʊleɪt] vt isoler; (against sound) insonoriser; **insulating tape** n ruban isolant; **insulation** [ɪnsjʊ'leɪʃən] n isolation f; insonorisation f

insulin ['ɪnsjʊlɪn] n insuline f

insult n ['ɪnsʌlt, vb ɪn'sʌlt] n insulte f, affront m ♦ vt insulter, faire affront à

insurance [ɪn'ʃʊərəns] n assurance f; **fire/life** ~ assurance-incendie/-vie; ~ **policy** n police f d'assurance

insure [ɪn'ʃuə*] vt assurer; **to ~ (o.s.) against** (fig) parer à

intact [ɪn'tækt] adj intact(e)

intake ['ɪnteɪk] n (of food, oxygen) consommation f; (BRIT: SCOL): an ~ **of 200 a year** 200 admissions fpl par an

integral ['ɪntɪgrəl] adj (part) intégrant(e)

integrate ['ɪntɪgreɪt] vt intégrer ♦ vi s'intégrer

intellect ['ɪntɪlekt] n intelligence f; **~ual** [ɪntɪ'lektjuəl] adj, n intellectuel(le)

intelligence [ɪn'telɪdʒəns] n intelligence f; (MIL etc) informations fpl, renseignements mpl; **~ service** n services secrets; **intelligent** [ɪn'telɪdʒənt] adj intelligent(e)

intend [ɪn'tend] vt (gift etc): **to ~ sth for** destiner qch à; **to ~ to do** avoir l'intention de faire; **~ed** adj (journey) projeté(e); (effect) voulu(e); (insult) intentionnel(le)

intense [ɪn'tens] adj intense; (person) véhément(e); **~ly** adv intensément; profondément

intensive [ɪn'tensɪv] adj intensif(ive); **~ care unit** n service m de réanimation

intent [ɪn'tent] n intention f ♦ adj attentif(ive); (absorbed): **~ (on)** absorbé(e) (par); **to all ~s and purposes** en fait, pratiquement; **to be ~ on doing sth** être (bien) décidé à faire qch

intention [ɪn'tenʃən] n intention f; **~al** adj intentionnel(le), délibéré(e)

intently [ɪn'tentlɪ] adv attentivement

interact [ɪntər'ækt] vi avoir une action réciproque; (people) communiquer; **~ive** adj (COMPUT) interactif(ive)

interchange [n 'ɪntətʃeɪndʒ, vb ɪntə'tʃeɪndʒ] n (exchange) échange m; (on motorway) échangeur m; **~able** [ɪntə'tʃeɪndʒəbl] adj interchangeable

intercom ['ɪntəkɒm] n interphone m

intercourse ['ɪntəkɔːs] n (sexual)

rapports mpl

interest ['ɪntrest] n intérêt m; (pastime): **my main ~** ce qui m'intéresse le plus; (COMM) intérêts mpl ♦ vt intéresser; **to be ~ed in** sth s'intéresser à qch; **I am ~ed in going** ça m'intéresse d'y aller; **~ing** adj intéressant(e); **~ rate** n taux m d'intérêt

interface ['ɪntəfeɪs] n (COMPUT) interface f

interfere [ɪntə'fɪə*] vi: **to ~ in** (quarrel) s'immiscer dans; (other people's business) se mêler de; **to ~ with** (object) toucher à; (plans) contrecarrer; (duty) être en conflit avec; **~nce** [ɪntə'fɪərəns] n (in affairs) ingérance f; (RADIO, TV) parasites mpl

interim ['ɪntərɪm] adj provisoire ♦ n: **in the ~** dans l'intérim, entre-temps

interior [ɪn'tɪərɪə*] n intérieur m ♦ adj intérieur(e); (minister, department) de l'Intérieur; **~ designer** n styliste m/f, designer m/f

interjection [ɪntə'dʒekʃən] n (interruption) interruption f; (LING) interjection f

interlock [ɪntə'lɒk] vi s'enclencher

interlude ['ɪntəluːd] n intervalle m; (THEATRE) intermède m

intermediate [ɪntə'miːdɪət] adj intermédiaire; (SCOL: course, level) moyen(ne)

intermission [ɪntə'mɪʃən] n pause f; (THEATRE, CINEMA) entracte m

intern [vb ɪn'tɜːn, n 'ɪntɜːn] vt interner ♦ n (US) interne m/f

internal [ɪn'tɜːnl] adj interne; (politics) intérieur(e); **~ly** adv: **"not to be taken ~ly"** "pour usage externe"; **I~ Revenue Service** (US) n fisc m

international [ɪntə'næʃnəl] adj international(e)

interplay ['ɪntəpleɪ] n effet m réciproque, interaction f

interpret [ɪn'tɜːprɪt] vt interpréter ♦ vi servir d'interprète; **~er** n interprète m/f

interrelated [ɪntərɪ'leɪtɪd] adj en

correlation, en rapport étroit

interrogate [ɪn'terəgeɪt] vt interroger; (suspect etc) soumettre à un interrogatoire; **interrogation** [ɪnterə'geɪʃən] n interrogation f; interrogatoire m

interrupt [ɪntə'rʌpt] vt, vi interrompre; **~ion** n interruption f

intersect [ɪntə'sekt] vi (roads) se croiser, se couper; **~ion** [ɪntə'sekʃən] n (of roads) croisement m

intersperse [ɪntə'spɜ:s] vt: to ~ with parsemer de

intertwine [ɪntə'twaɪn] vi s'entrelacer

interval ['ɪntəvəl] n intervalle m; (BRIT: THEATRE) entracte m; (: SPORT) mi-temps f; at ~s par intervalles

intervene [ɪntə'vi:n] vi (person) intervenir; (event) survenir; (time) s'écouler (entre-temps); **intervention** [ɪntə'venʃən] n intervention f

interview ['ɪntəvju:] n (RADIO, TV etc) interview f; (for job) entrevue f ♦ vt interviewer; avoir une entrevue avec; **~er** n (RADIO, TV) interviewer m

intestine [ɪn'testɪn] n intestin m

intimacy ['ɪntɪməsɪ] n intimité f

intimate [adj 'ɪntɪmət, vb 'ɪntɪmeɪt] adj intime; (friendship) profond(e); (knowledge) approfondi(e) ♦ vt (hint) suggérer, laisser entendre

into ['ɪntu] prep dans; ~ pieces/ French en morceaux/français

intolerant [ɪn'tɔlərənt] adj: ~ (of) intolérant(e) (de)

intoxicated [ɪn'tɔksɪkeɪtd] adj (drunk) ivre; **intoxication** [ɪntɔksɪ'keɪʃən] n ivresse f

intractable [ɪn'træktəbl] adj (child) indocile, insoumis(e); (problem) insoluble

intransitive [ɪn'trænsɪtɪv] adj intransitif(ive)

intravenous [ɪntrə'vi:nəs] adj intraveineux(euse)

in-tray ['ɪntreɪ] n courrier m "arrivée"

intricate ['ɪntrɪkət] adj complexe, compliqué(e)

intrigue [ɪn'tri:g] n intrigue f ♦ vt intriguer; **intriguing** [ɪn'tri:gɪŋ] adj fascinant(e)

intrinsic [ɪn'trɪnsɪk] adj intrinsèque

introduce [ɪntrə'dju:s] vt introduire; (TV show, people to each other) présenter; ~ sb to (pastime, technique) initier qn à; **introduction** [ɪntrə'dʌkʃən] f; (of person) initiation f; (to new experience) initiation f; **introductory** [ɪntrə'dʌktərɪ] adj préliminaire, d'introduction; **introductory offer** n (COMM) offre f de lancement

intrude [ɪn'tru:d] vi (person) être importun(e); to ~ on (conversation etc) s'immiscer dans; ~r n intrus(e)

intuition [ɪntju:'ɪʃən] n intuition f

inundate ['ɪnʌndeɪt] vt: to ~ with inonder de

invade [ɪn'veɪd] vt envahir

invalid [n 'ɪnvəlɪd, adj ɪn'vælɪd] n malade m/f; (with disability) invalide m/f ♦ adj (not valid) non valide or valable

invaluable [ɪn'væljuəbl] adj inestimable, inappréciable

invariably [ɪn'veərɪəblɪ] adv invariablement; toujours

invent [ɪn'vent] vt inventer; ~ion [ɪn'venʃən] n invention f; ~ive adj inventif(ive); ~or n inventeur(trice)

inventory ['ɪnvəntrɪ] n inventaire m

invert [ɪn'vɜ:t] vt intervertir; (cup, object) retourner; **~ed commas** (BRIT) npl guillemets mpl

invest [ɪn'vest] vt investir ♦ vi: to ~ in sth placer son argent dans (fig) s'offrir qch

investigate [ɪn'vestɪgeɪt] vt (crime etc) faire une enquête sur; **investigation** [ɪnvestɪ'geɪʃən] n (of crime) enquête f

investment [ɪn'vestmənt] n investissement m, placement m

investor [ɪn'vestə*] n investisseur m; actionnaire m/f

invigilator [ɪn'vɪdʒɪleɪtə*] n surveillant(e)

invigorating [ɪn'vɪɡəreɪtɪŋ] adj vivifiant(e); (fig) stimulant(e)

invisible [ɪn'vɪzəbl] adj invisible

invitation [ɪnvɪ'teɪʃən] n invitation f

invite [ɪn'vaɪt] vt inviter; (opinions etc) demander; **inviting** [ɪn'vaɪtɪŋ] adj engageant(e); attrayant(e)

invoice ['ɪnvɔɪs] n facture f

involuntary [ɪn'vɒləntərɪ] adj involontaire

involve [ɪn'vɒlv] vt (entail) entraîner, nécessiter; (concern) concerner; (associate): **to ~ sb (in)** impliquer qn (dans), mêler qn (à); faire participer qn (à); **to be ~d in** particiver à; (engrossed) être absorbé(e) par; **~ment** n: **~ment (in)** participation f (à); rôle m (dans); (enthusiasm) enthousiasme m (pour)

inward ['ɪnwəd] adj (thought, feeling) profond(e), intime; (movement) vers l'intérieur; **~(s)** adv vers l'intérieur

I/O abbr (COMPUT: = input/output) E/S

iodine ['aɪədiːn] n iode m

iota [aɪ'əʊtə] n (fig) brin m, grain m

IOU n abbr (= I owe you) reconnaissance f de dette

IQ n abbr (= intelligence quotient) Q.I. m

IRA n abbr (US = Irish Republican Army) IRA f

Iran [ɪ'rɑːn] n Iran m

Iraq [ɪ'rɑːk] n Irak m

irate [aɪ'reɪt] adj courroucé(e)

Ireland ['aɪələnd] n Irlande f

iris ['aɪrɪs] (pl ~es) n iris m

Irish ['aɪrɪʃ] adj irlandais(e) ♦ npl: **the ~** les Irlandais; **~man** (irreg) n Irlandais m; **~ Sea** n mer f d'Irlande; **~woman** (irreg) n Irlandaise f

iron ['aɪən] n fer m; (for clothes) fer m à repasser ♦ cpd de fer; en fer; (fig) de fer ♦ vt (clothes) repasser; **~ out** vt (fig) aplanir; faire disparaître; **the I~ Curtain** n le rideau de fer

ironic(al) [aɪ'rɒnɪk(əl)] adj ironique

ironing ['aɪənɪŋ] n repassage m; **~ board** n planche f à repasser

ironmonger's (shop) ['aɪənmʌŋgəz-] n quincaillerie f

irony ['aɪərənɪ] n ironie f

irrational [ɪ'ræʃənl] adj irrationnel(le)

irregular [ɪ'reɡjʊlə*] adj irrégulier(ère); (surface) inégal(e)

irrelevant [ɪ'reləvənt] adj sans rapport, hors de propos

irresistible [ɪrɪ'zɪstəbl] adj irrésistible

irrespective [ɪrɪ'spektɪv]: **~ of** prep sans tenir compte de

irresponsible [ɪrɪ'spɒnsəbl] adj (act) irréfléchi(e); (person) irresponsable, inconscient(e)

irrigate ['ɪrɪɡeɪt] vt irriguer; **irrigation** [ɪrɪ'ɡeɪʃən] n irrigation f

irritate ['ɪrɪteɪt] vt irriter; **irritating** adj irritant(e); **irritation** [ɪrɪ'teɪʃən] n irritation f

IRS n abbr = **Internal Revenue Service**

is [ɪz] vb see **be**

Islam ['ɪzlɑːm] n Islam m

island ['aɪlənd] n île f; **~er** n habitant(e) d'une île, insulaire m/f

isle [aɪl] n île f

isn't ['ɪznt] = **is not**

isolate ['aɪsəleɪt] vt isoler; **~d** adj isolé(e); **isolation** [aɪsə'leɪʃən] n isolation f

Israel ['ɪzreɪl] n Israël m; **~i** [ɪz'reɪlɪ] adj israélien(ne) ♦ n Israélien(ne)

issue ['ɪʃuː] n question f, problème m; (of book) publication f, parution f; (of banknotes etc) émission f; (of newspaper etc) numéro m ♦ vt (rations, equipment) distribuer; (statement) publier, faire; (banknotes etc) émettre, mettre en circulation; **at ~** en jeu, en cause; **to take ~ with sb (over)** exprimer son désaccord avec qn (sur); **to make an ~ of sth** faire une montagne de qch

J

it [ɪt] *pron* **1** (*specific: subject*) il(elle); (: *direct object*) la, l'); (: *indirect object*) lui; ~'s on the table c'est or il (elle) est sur la table; about/from/of ~ en; I spoke to him about ~ je lui en ai parlé; what did you learn from ~? qu'est-ce que vous en avez retiré?; I'm proud of ~ j'en suis fier; in/to ~ y; put the book in ~ mettez-y le livre; he agreed to ~ il y a consenti; did you go to ~? (*party, concert etc*) est-ce que vous y êtes allé(s)?
2 (*impersonal*) il; ce; ~'s raining il pleut; ~'s Friday tomorrow demain c'est vendredi or nous sommes vendredi; ~'s 6 o'clock il est 6 heures; who is ~? — ~'s me qui est-ce? — c'est moi

Italian [ɪ'tæljən] *adj* italien(ne) ♦ *n* Italien(ne); (*LING*) italien *m*
italics [ɪ'tælɪks] *npl* italiques *fpl*
Italy ['ɪtəlɪ] *n* Italie *f*
itch [ɪtʃ] *n* démangeaison *f* ♦ *vi* (*person*) éprouver des démangeaisons; (*part of body*) démanger; I'm ~ing to do l'envie me démange de faire; ~y *adj* qui démange; to be ~y avoir des démangeaisons
it'd ['ɪtd] = it would; it had
item ['aɪtəm] *n* article *m*; (*on agenda*) question *f*, point *m*; (*also: news* ~) nouvelle *f*; ~ize *vt* détailler, faire une liste de
itinerary [aɪ'tɪnərərɪ] *n* itinéraire *m*
it: ~'ll [ɪtl] = it will; it shall; ~s [ɪts] *adj son(sa), ses [ɪts]* = it is; it has; ~self [ɪt'sɛlf] *pron* (*reflexive*) se; (*emphatic*) lui-même(elle-même)
ITV *n abbr* (*BRIT: = Independent Television*) chaîne privée
IUD *n abbr* (= *intra-uterine device*) DIU *m*, stérilet *m*
I've [aɪv] = I have
ivory ['aɪvərɪ] *n* ivoire *m*
ivy ['aɪvɪ] *n* lierre *m*

jab [dʒæb] *vt*: to ~ sth into enfoncer or planter qch dans ♦ *n* (*inf: injection*) piqûre *f*
jack [dʒæk] *n* (*AUT*) cric *m*; (*CARDS*) valet *m*; ~ up *vt* soulever (au cric)
jackal ['dʒækəl] *n* chacal *m*
jackdaw ['dʒækdɔː] *n* choucas *m*
jacket ['dʒækɪt] *n* veste *f*, veston *m*; (*of book*) jaquette *f*, couverture *f*
jackknife ['dʒæknaɪf] *vi*: the lorry ~d la remorque (du camion) s'est mise en travers
jack plug *n* (*ELEC*) prise jack mâle *f*
jackpot ['dʒækpɔt] *n* gros lot
jaded ['dʒeɪdɪd] *adj* éreinté(e), fatigué(e)
jagged ['dʒægɪd] *adj* dentelé(e)
jail [dʒeɪl] *n* prison *f* ♦ *vt* emprisonner, mettre en prison
jam [dʒæm] *n* confiture *f*; (*also: traffic* ~) embouteillage *m* ♦ *vt* (*passage etc*) encombrer, obstruer; (*mechanism, drawer etc*) bloquer, coincer; (*RADIO*) brouiller ♦ *vi* se coincer, se bloquer; (*gun*) s'enrayer; to be in a ~ (*inf*) être dans le pétrin; to ~ sth into entasser qch dans; enfoncer qch dans
jangle ['dʒæŋɡl] *vi* cliqueter
janitor ['dʒænɪtə*] *n* concierge *m*
January ['dʒænjuərɪ] *n* janvier *m*
Japan [dʒə'pæn] *n* Japon *m*; ~ese [dʒæpə'niːz] *adj* japonais(e) ♦ *n inv* Japonais(e); (*LING*) japonais *m*
jar [dʒɑː*] *n* (*stone, earthenware*) pot *m*; (*glass*) bocal *m* ♦ *vi* (*sound discordant*) produire un son grinçant or discordant; (*colours etc*) jurer
jargon ['dʒɑːɡən] *n* jargon *m*
jaundice ['dʒɔːndɪs] *n* jaunisse *f*; ~d *adj* (*fig*) envieux(euse), désapprobateur(trice)
javelin ['dʒævlɪn] *n* javelot *m*
jaw [dʒɔː] *n* mâchoire *f*

jay [dʒeɪ] n geai m; **~walker** ['dʒeɪwɔːkə*] n piéton indiscipliné

jazz [dʒæz] n jazz m; **~ up** vt animer, égayer

jealous ['dʒeləs] adj jaloux(ouse); **~y** n jalousie f

jeans [dʒiːnz] npl jean m

jeer [dʒɪə*] vi: to **~ (at)** se moquer cruellement (de), railler

jelly ['dʒelɪ] n gelée f; **~fish** n méduse f

jeopardy ['dʒepədɪ] n: to be in **~** être en danger or péril

jerk [dʒɜːk] n secousse f; saccade f; sursaut m, spasme m; (inf: idiot) pauvre type m ♦ vt (pull) tirer brusquement ♦ vi (vehicles) cahoter

jersey ['dʒɜːzɪ] n (pullover) tricot m; (fabric) jersey m

Jesus ['dʒiːzəs] n Jésus

jet [dʒet] n (gas, liquid) jet m; (AVIAT) avion m à réaction, jet m; **~-black** adj (d'un noir) de jais; **~ engine** n moteur m à réaction; **~ lag** n (fatigue due au) décalage m horaire

jettison ['dʒetɪsn] vt jeter par-dessus bord

jetty ['dʒetɪ] n jetée f, digue f

Jew [dʒuː] n Juif m

jewel ['dʒuːəl] n bijou m, joyau m; (in watch) rubis m; **~ler** (US **~er**) n bijoutier(ère), joaillier m; **~ler's (shop)** n bijouterie f, joaillerie f; **~lery** (US **~ry**) n bijoux mpl

Jewess ['dʒuːɪs] n Juive f

Jewish ['dʒuːɪʃ] adj juif(juive)

jibe [dʒaɪb] n sarcasme m

jiffy ['dʒɪfɪ] (inf) n: in a **~** en un clin d'œil

jigsaw ['dʒɪgsɔː] n (also: **~ puzzle**) puzzle m

jilt [dʒɪlt] vt laisser tomber, plaquer

jingle ['dʒɪŋgl] n (for advert) couplet m publicitaire ♦ vi cliqueter, tinter

jinx [dʒɪŋks] (inf) n (mauvais) sort

jitters ['dʒɪtəz] (inf) npl: to get the **~** (inf) avoir la trouille or la frousse

job [dʒɒb] n (chore, task) travail m, tâche f; (employment) emploi m,

poste m, place f; it's a good **~** that ... c'est heureux or c'est une chance que ...; just the **~**! (c'est) juste or exactement ce qu'il faut!; **~ centre** (BRIT) n agence f pour l'emploi; **~less** adj sans travail, au chômage

jockey ['dʒɒkɪ] n jockey m ♦ vi: to **~ for position** manœuvrer pour être bien placé

jocular ['dʒɒkjulə*] adj jovial(e), enjoué(e); facétieux(euse)

jog [dʒɒg] vt secouer ♦ vi (SPORT) faire du jogging; to **~ sb's memory** rafraîchir la mémoire de qn; **~ along** vi cheminer; trotter; **~ging** n jogging m

join [dʒɔɪn] vt (put together) unir, assembler; (become member of) s'inscrire à; (meet) rejoindre, retrouver; (queue) se joindre à ♦ vi (roads, rivers) se rejoindre, se rencontrer ♦ n raccord m; **~ in** vi se mettre de la partie, participer ♦ vt fus participer à, se mêler à; **~ up** vi (meet) se rejoindre; (MIL) s'engager; **~er** ['dʒɔɪnə*] (BRIT) n menuisier m

joint [dʒɔɪnt] n (TECH) jointure f; joint m; (ANAT) articulation f, jointure; (BRIT: CULIN) rôti m; (inf: place) boîte f; (: of cannabis) joint m ♦ adj commun(e); **~ account** n (with bank etc) compte joint

joke [dʒəʊk] n plaisanterie f; (also: practical **~**) farce f ♦ vi plaisanter; to play a **~ on** jouer un tour à, faire une farce à; **~r** n (CARDS) joker m

jolly ['dʒɒlɪ] adj gai(e), enjoué(e); (enjoyable) amusant(e), plaisant(e) ♦ adv (BRIT: inf) rudement, drôlement

jolt [dʒəʊlt] n cahot m, secousse f; (shock) choc m ♦ vt cahoter, secouer

Jordan ['dʒɔːdən] n (country) Jordanie f

jostle ['dʒɒsl] vt bousculer, pousser

jot [dʒɒt] n: not one **~** pas un brin; **~ down** vt noter; **~ter** (BRIT) n cahier m (de brouillon); (pad) bloc-notes m

journal ['dʒɜːnl] n journal m; **~ism**

n journalisme *m*; **~ist** *n* journaliste *m/f*

journey ['dʒɜːnɪ] *n* voyage *m*; *(distance covered)* trajet *m*

joy [dʒɔɪ] *n* joie *f*; **~ful** *adj* joyeux(euse); **~rider** *n* personne qui fait une virée dans une voiture volée; **~stick** *n* (AVIAT, COMPUT) manche *m* à balai

JP *n abbr* = Justice of the Peace

Jr *abbr* = junior

jubilant ['dʒuːbɪlənt] *adj* triomphant(e); réjoui(e)

judge [dʒʌdʒ] *n* juge *m* ♦ *vt* juger; **judg(e)ment** *n* jugement *m*

judicial [dʒuːˈdɪʃəl] *adj* judiciaire

judiciary [dʒuːˈdɪʃɪərɪ] *n* (pouvoir *m*) judiciaire *m*

judo ['dʒuːdəʊ] *n* judo *m*

jug [dʒʌg] *n* pot *m*, cruche *f*

juggernaut ['dʒʌgənɔːt] (BRIT) *n* (huge truck) énorme poids lourd

juggle ['dʒʌgl] *vi* jongler; **~r** *n* jongleur *m*

Jugoslav *etc* = Yugoslav *etc*

juice [dʒuːs] *n* jus *m*; **juicy** ['dʒuːsɪ] *adj* juteux(euse)

jukebox ['dʒuːkbɒks] *n* juke-box *m*

July [dʒuːˈlaɪ] *n* juillet *m*

jumble ['dʒʌmbl] *n* fouillis *m* ♦ *vt* (also: **~ up**) mélanger, brouiller; **~ sale** (BRIT) *n* vente *f* de charité

jumbo (jet) ['dʒʌmbəʊ-] *n* jumbo-jet *m*, gros porteur

jump [dʒʌmp] *vi* sauter, bondir; *(start)* sursauter; *(increase)* monter en flèche ♦ *vt* sauter, franchir ♦ *n* saut *m*, bond *m*; sursaut *m*; **to ~ the queue** (BRIT) passer avant son tour

jumper ['dʒʌmpə*] *n* (BRIT: pullover) pull-over *m*; *(US: dress)* robe-chasuble *f*

jumper cables (US), **jump leads** (BRIT) *npl* câbles *mpl* de démarrage

jumpy ['dʒʌmpɪ] *adj* nerveux(euse), agité(e)

Jun. *abbr* = junior

junction ['dʒʌŋkʃən] (BRIT) *n* (of roads) carrefour *m*; *(of rails)* em-

branchement *m*

juncture ['dʒʌŋktʃə*] *n*: **at this ~** à ce moment-là, sur ces entrefaites

June [dʒuːn] *n* juin *m*

jungle ['dʒʌŋgl] *n* jungle *f*

junior ['dʒuːnɪə*] *adj, n*: **he's ~ to me** (by 2 years), **he's my ~** (by 2 years) il est mon cadet (de 2 ans), il est plus jeune que moi (de 2 ans); **he's ~ to me** (seniority) il est en dessous de moi (dans la hiérarchie), j'ai plus d'ancienneté que lui; **~ school** (BRIT) *n* école *f* primaire

junk [dʒʌŋk] *n* (rubbish) camelote *f*; (cheap goods) bric-à-brac *m inv*; **~ food** *n* aliments *mpl* sans grande valeur nutritive; **~ mail** *n* prospectus *mpl* (non sollicités); **~ shop** *n* (boutique *f* du) brocanteur *m*

Junr *abbr* = junior

juror ['dʒuərə*] *n* juré *m*

jury ['dʒuərɪ] *n* jury *m*

just [dʒʌst] *adj* juste ♦ *adv*: **he's done it/left** il vient de le faire/partir; **~ right/two o'clock** exactement *ou* juste ce qu'il faut/deux heures; **she's ~ as clever as you** elle est tout aussi intelligente que vous; **it's ~ as well that ...** heureusement que ...; **~ as he was leaving** au moment *ou* à l'instant précis où il partait; **~ before/enough/here** juste avant/ assez/ici; **it's ~ a mistake** ce n'est que moi/(rien) qu'une erreur; **~ missed/caught** manqué/attrapé de justesse; **~ listen to this!** écoutez un peu ça!

justice ['dʒʌstɪs] *n* justice *f*; (US: judge) juge *m* de la Cour suprême; **J~ of the Peace** *n* juge *m* de paix

justify ['dʒʌstɪfaɪ] *vt* justifier

jut [dʒʌt] *vi* (also: **~ out**) dépasser, faire saillie

juvenile ['dʒuːvənaɪl] *adj* juvénile; (court, books) pour enfants ♦ *n* adolescent(e)

K

K *abbr* (= *one thousand*) K; (= *kilobyte*) Ko

kangaroo [kæŋgə'ruː] *n* kangourou *m*

karate [kə'rɑːtɪ] *n* karaté *m*

kebab [kə'bæb] *n* kébab *m*

keel [kiːl] *n* quille *f*

keen [kiːn] *adj* (*eager*) plein(e) d'enthousiasme; (*interest, desire, competition*) vif(vive); (*eye, intelligence*) pénétrant(e); (*edge*) effilé(e); to be ~ to do or on doing sth désirer vivement faire qch, tenir beaucoup à faire qch; to be ~ on sth/sb aimer beaucoup qch/qn

keep [kiːp] (*pt, pp* **kept**) *vt* (*retain, preserve*) garder; (*detain*) retenir; (*shop, accounts, diary, promise*) tenir; (*house*) avoir; (*support*) entretenir; (*chickens, bees etc*) élever ♦ *vi* (*remain*) rester; (*food*) se conserver ♦ *n* (*of castle*) donjon *m*; (*food etc*): **enough for his ~** assez pour (assurer) sa subsistance; (*inf*): **for ~s** pour de bon, pour toujours; **to ~ doing sth** ne pas arrêter de faire qch; **to ~ sb from doing/sth from happening** empêcher qn de faire or que qch ne se fasse; **to ~ sb happy/a place tidy** faire en sorte que qn soit content/qu'un endroit reste propre; **to ~ sth to o.s.** garder qch pour soi, tenir qch secret; **to ~ sth (back) from sb** cacher qch à qn; **to ~ time** (*clock*) être à l'heure, ne pas retarder; **well kept** bien entretenu(e); **~ on** *vi*: **to ~ on doing** continuer à faire; **don't ~ on about it!** arrête (d'en parler)!; **~ out** *vt* empêcher d'entrer; **"~ out"** "défense d'entrer"; **~ up** *vt* continuer, maintenir ♦ *vi*: **to ~ up with sb** (*in race etc*) aller aussi vite que qn; (*in work etc*) se maintenir au niveau de qn; **~er** *n* gardien(ne); **~-fit** *n* gymnastique *f* d'entretien; **~ing** *n* (*care*) garde *f*; **in ~ing with** en accord

avec; **~sake** *n* souvenir *m*

kennel ['kɛnl] *n* niche *f*; **~s** *npl* (*boarding* ~s) chenil *m*

kerb [kɜːb] (*BRIT*) *n* bordure *f* du trottoir

kernel ['kɜːnl] *n* (*of nut*) amande *f*; (*fig*) noyau *m*

kettle ['kɛtl] *n* bouilloire *f*; **~drum** *n* timbale *f*

key [kiː] *n* (*gen, MUS*) clé *f*; (*of piano, typewriter*) touche *f* ♦ *vt* (*also:* ~ **in**) introduire (au clavier), saisir; **~board** *n* clavier *m*; **~ed up** *adj* (*person*) surexcité(e); **~hole** *n* trou *m* de la serrure; **~note** *n* (*of speech*) note dominante; (*MUS*) tonique *f*; **~ ring** *n* porte-clés *m*

khaki ['kɑːki] *n* kaki *m*

kick [kɪk] *vt* donner un coup de pied à ♦ *vi* (*horse*) ruer ♦ *n* coup *m* de pied; (*thrill*): **he does it for ~s** il le fait parce que ça l'excite, il le fait pour le plaisir; **to ~ the habit** (*inf*) arrêter; **~ off** *vi* (*SPORT*) donner le coup d'envoi

kid [kɪd] *n* (*inf: child*) gamin(e), gosse *m/f*; (*animal, leather*) chevreau *m* ♦ *vi* (*inf*) plaisanter, blaguer

kidnap ['kɪdnæp] *vt* enlever, kidnapper; **~per** *n* ravisseur(euse); **~ping** *n* enlèvement *m*

kidney ['kɪdnɪ] *n* (*ANAT*) rein *m*; (*CULIN*) rognon *m*

kill [kɪl] *vt* tuer ♦ *n* mise *f* à mort; **~er** *n* tueur(euse); meurtrier(ère); **~ing** *n* meurtre *m*; (*of group of people*) tuerie *f*, massacre *m*; **to make a ~ing** (*inf*) réussir un beau coup (de filet); **~joy** *n* rabat-joie *m/f*

kiln [kɪln] *n* four *m*

kilo ['kiːləu] *n* kilo *m*; **~byte** *n* (*COMPUT*) kilo-octet *m*; **~gram(me)** ['kɪləugræm] *n* kilogramme *m*; **~metre** ['kɪləmiːtə*] (*US* **~meter**) *n* kilomètre *m*; **~watt** *n* kilowatt *m*

kilt [kɪlt] *n* kilt *m*

kin [kɪn] *n* see **next; kith**

kind [kaɪnd] *adj* gentil(le), aimable ♦ *n* sorte *f*, espèce *f*, genre *m*; **to be**

two of a ~ se ressembler; **in ~** (COMM) en nature

kindergarten ['kɪndəɡɑːtn] n jardin m d'enfants

kind-hearted ['kaɪnd'hɑːtɪd] adj bon(bonne)

kindle ['kɪndl] vt allumer, enflammer

kindly ['kaɪndlɪ] adj bienveillant(e), plein(e) de gentillesse ♦ adv avec bonté; **will you ~ ...!** auriez-vous la bonté or l'obligeance de ...?

kindness ['kaɪndnɪs] n bonté f, gentillesse f

kindred ['kɪndrɪd] adj: **~ spirit** âme f sœur

kinetic [kɪ'netɪk] adj cinétique

king [kɪŋ] n roi m; **~dom** n royaume m; **~fisher** n martin-pêcheur m; **~-size bed** n grand lit (de 1,95 m de large); **~-size(d)** adj format géant inv; (cigarettes) long(longue)

kinky ['kɪŋkɪ] (pej) adj (person) excentrique; (sexually) aux goûts spéciaux

kiosk ['kiːɒsk] n kiosque m; (BRIT: TEL) cabine f (téléphonique)

kipper ['kɪpə*] n hareng fumé et salé

kiss [kɪs] n baiser m ♦ vt embrasser; **to ~ (each other)** s'embrasser; **~ of life** (BRIT) n bouche à bouche m

kit [kɪt] n équipement m, matériel m; (set of tools etc) trousse f; (for assembly) kit m

kitchen ['kɪtʃɪn] n cuisine f; **~ sink** n évier m

kite [kaɪt] n (toy) cerf-volant m

kith [kɪθ] n: **~ and kin** parents et amis mpl

kitten ['kɪtn] n chaton m, petit chat

kitty ['kɪtɪ] n (money) cagnotte f

knack [næk] n: **to have the ~ of doing** avoir le coup pour faire

knapsack ['næpsæk] n musette f

knead [niːd] vt pétrir

knee [niː] n genou m; **~cap** n rotule f

kneel [niːl] (pt, pp **knelt**) vi (also: **~ down**) s'agenouiller

knew [njuː] pt of **know**

knickers ['nɪkəz] (BRIT) npl culotte f (de femme)

knife [naɪf] (pl **knives**) n couteau m ♦ vt poignarder, frapper d'un coup de couteau

knight [naɪt] n chevalier m; (CHESS) cavalier m; **~hood** n (title): **to get a ~hood** être fait chevalier

knit [nɪt] vt tricoter ♦ vi tricoter; (broken bones) se ressouder; **to ~ one's brows** froncer les sourcils; **~ting** n tricot m; **~ting needle** n aiguille f à tricoter; **~wear** n tricots mpl, lainages mpl

knives [naɪvz] npl of **knife**

knob [nɒb] n bouton m

knock [nɒk] vt frapper; (bump into) heurter; (inf) dénigrer ♦ vi (at door etc): **to ~ at or on** frapper à ♦ n coup m; **~ down** vt renverser; **~ off** vi (inf: finish) s'arrêter (de travailler) ♦ vt (from price) faire un rabais de; (inf: steal) piquer; **~ out** vt assommer; (BOXING) mettre k.-o.; (defeat) éliminer; **~ over** vt renverser, faire tomber; **~er** n (on door) heurtoir m; **~out** n (BOXING) knock-out m, K.-O. m; **~out competition** n compétition f avec épreuves éliminatoires

knot [nɒt] n (gen) nœud m ♦ vt nouer; **~ty** adj (fig) épineux(euse)

know [nəʊ] (pt knew, pp known) vt savoir; (person, place) connaître; **to ~ how to do** savoir (comment) faire; **to ~ how to swim** savoir nager; **to ~ about or of sth** être au courant de qch; **to ~ about or of sb** avoir entendu parler de qn; **~-all** (pej) n je-sais-tout m/f; **~-how** n savoir-faire m; **~ing** adj (look etc) entendu(e); **~ingly** adv sciemment; (smile, look) d'un air entendu

knowledge ['nɒlɪdʒ] n connaissance f; (learning) connaissances, savoir m; **~able** adj bien informé(e)

knuckle ['nʌkl] n articulation f (des doigts), jointure f

Koran [kɔ'rɑːn] n Coran m

Korea [kə'rɪə] n Corée f

kosher ['kəʊʃə*] adj kascher inv

L

L abbr (= lake, large) L; (= left) g; (= BRIT: AUT: = learner) signale un conducteur débutant

lab [læb] n abbr (= laboratory) labo m

label ['leibl] n étiquette f ♦ vt étiqueter

labor etc (US) = **labour** etc

laboratory [lə'bɒrətəri] n laboratoire m

labour ['leibə*] (US labor) n (work) travail m; (workforce) main-d'œuvre f ♦ vi: to ~ (at) travailler dur (à), peiner (sur) ♦ vt: to ~ a point insister sur un point; **in** ~ (MED) en travail, en train d'accoucher; **L~, the L~ party** (BRIT) le parti travailliste, les travaillistes; **~ed** adj (breathing) pénible, difficile; ~ er n manœuvre m; **farm** ~ er ouvrier m agricole

lace [leis] n dentelle f; (of shoe) lacet m ♦ vt (shoe: also: ~ up) lacer

lack [læk] n manque m ♦ vt manquer de; **through** or **for** ~ of faute de, par manque de; **to be** ~ing manquer, faire défaut; **to be** ~ing **in** manquer de

lacquer ['lækə*] n laque f

lad [læd] n garçon m, gars m

ladder ['lædə*] n échelle f; (BRIT: in tights) maille filée

laden ['leidn] adj: ~ (**with**) chargé(e) (de)

ladle ['leidl] n louche f

lady ['leidi] n dame f; (in address): **ladies and gentlemen** Mesdames (et) Messieurs; **young** ~ jeune fille f; (married) jeune femme f; **the ladies' (room)** les toilettes fpl (pour dames); ~**bird** n coccinelle f; ~**bug** (US) n = **ladybird**; ~**like** adj distingué(e); ~**ship** n: **your** ~**ship** Madame la comtesse (or la baronne etc)

lag [læg] n retard m ♦ vi (also: be-

hind) rester en arrière, traîner; (fig) rester en traîne ♦ vt (pipes) calorifuger

lager ['lɑːgə*] n bière blonde

lagoon [lə'guːn] n lagune f

laid [leid] pt, pp of **lay**; ~-**back** (inf) adj relaxe, décontracté(e); ~ **up** adj alité(e)

lain [lein] pp of **lie**

lake [leik] n lac m

lamb [læm] n agneau m; ~ **chop** n côtelette f d'agneau

lame [leim] adj boiteux(euse)

lament [lə'ment] n lamentation f ♦ vt pleurer, se lamenter sur

laminated ['læmineitid] adj laminé(e); (windscreen) (en verre) feuilleté

lamp [læmp] n lampe f; ~**post** (BRIT) n réverbère m; ~**shade** n abat-jour m inv

lance [lɑːns] vt (MED) inciser

land [lænd] n (as opposed to sea) terre f (ferme); (soil) terre; terrain m; (estate) terre(s), domaine(s) m(pl); (country) pays m ♦ vi (AVIAT) atterrir; (fig) (re)tomber ♦ vt (passengers, goods) débarquer; **to** ~ **sb with sth** (inf) coller qch à qn; ~ **up** vi atterrir, (finir par) se retrouver; ~**fill site** n décharge f; ~**ing** n (AVIAT) atterrissage m; (of staircase) palier m; (of troops) débarquement m; ~**ing stage** n train m d'atterrissage; ~**ing strip** n piste f d'atterrissage; ~**lady** n propriétaire f, logeuse f; (of pub) patronne f; ~**locked** adj sans littoral; ~**lord** n propriétaire m, logeur m; (of pub etc) patron m; ~**mark** n (point m de) repère m; **to be a** ~**mark** (fig) faire date or époque; ~**owner** n propriétaire foncier or terrien; ~**scape** n paysage m; ~**scape gardener** n jardinier(ère) paysagiste; ~**slide** ['lændslaid] n (GEO) glissement m (de terrain); (fig: POL) raz-de-marée (électoral)

lane [lein] n (in country) chemin m; (AUT) voie f, file f; (in race) couloir

m

language ['læŋgwɪdʒ] *n* langue *f*; (way one speaks) langage *m*; **bad ~** grossièretés *fpl*, langage grossier; **~ laboratory** *n* laboratoire *m* de langues

lank [læŋk] *adj* (hair) raide et terne

lanky ['læŋkɪ] *adj* grand(e) et maigre, efflanqué(e)

lantern ['læntən] *n* lanterne *f*

lap [læp] *n* (of track) tour *m* (de piste); (of body): **in** or **on one's ~** sur les genoux ♦ *vt* (also: **~ up**) laper ♦ *vi* (waves) clapoter; **~ up** *vt* (fig) accepter béatement, gober

lapel [lə'pɛl] *n* revers *m*

Lapland ['læplænd] *n* Laponie *f*

lapse [læps] *n* défaillance *f*; (in behaviour) écart *m* de conduite ♦ *vi* (LAW) cesser d'être en vigueur; (contract) expirer; **to ~ into bad habits** prendre de mauvaises habitudes; **~ of time** laps *m* de temps, intervalle *m*

laptop (computer) ['læptɒp-] *n* portable *m*

larceny ['lɑːsənɪ] *n* vol *m*

larch [lɑːtʃ] *n* mélèze *m*

lard [lɑːd] *n* saindoux *m*

larder ['lɑːdə*] *n* garde-manger *m* *inv*

large [lɑːdʒ] *adj* grand(e); (person, animal) gros(se); **at ~** (free) en liberté; (generally) en général; *see also* **by**; **~ly** *adv* en grande partie; (principally) surtout; **~-scale** *adj* (action) d'envergure; (map) à grande échelle

lark [lɑːk] *n* (bird) alouette *f*; (joke) blague *f*, farce *f*; **~ about** *vi* faire l'idiot, rigoler

laryngitis [lærɪn'dʒaɪtɪs] *n* laryngite *f*

laser ['leɪzə*] *n* laser *m*; **~ printer** *n* imprimante *f* laser

lash [læʃ] *n* coup *m* de fouet; (also: **eye~**) cil *m* ♦ *vt* fouetter; (tie) attacher; **~ out** *vi*: **to ~ out at** or **against** attaquer violemment

lass [læs] *n* (BRIT) (jeune) fille *f*

lasso [læ'suː] *n* lasso *m*

last [lɑːst] *adj* dernier(ère) ♦ *adv* en dernier; (finally) finalement ♦ *vi* durer; **~ week** la semaine dernière; **~ night** (evening) hier soir; (night) la nuit dernière; **at ~** enfin; **~ but one** avant-dernier(ère); **~-ditch** *adj* (attempt) ultime, désespéré(e); **~ing** *adj* durable; **~ly** *adv* en dernier lieu, pour finir; **~-minute** *adj* de dernière minute

latch [lætʃ] *n* loquet *m*

late [leɪt] *adj* (not on time) en retard; (far on in day etc) tardif(ive); (edition, delivery) dernier(ère); (former) ancien(ne) ♦ *adv* tard; (behind time, schedule) en retard; **of ~** dernièrement; **in ~ May** vers la fin (du mois) de mai, fin mai; **the ~ Mr X** feu M. X; **~comer** *n* retardataire *m/f*; **~ly** *adv* récemment; **~r** ['leɪtə*] *adj* (date etc) ultérieur(e); (version etc) plus récent(e) ♦ *adv* plus tard; **~r on** plus tard; **~st** ['leɪtɪst] *adj* tout(e) dernier(ère); **at the ~st** au plus tard

lathe [leɪð] *n* tour *m*

lather ['lɑːðə*] *n* mousse *f* (de savon) ♦ *vt* savonner

Latin ['lætɪn] *n* latin *m* ♦ *adj* latin(e); **~ America** *n* Amérique latine; **~ American** *adj* latino-américain(e)

latitude ['lætɪtjuːd] *n* latitude *f*

latter ['lætə*] *adj* deuxième, dernier(ère) ♦ *n*: **the ~** ce dernier, celui-ci; **~ly** *adv* dernièrement, récemment

laudable ['lɔːdəbl] *adj* louable

laugh [lɑːf] *n* rire *m* ♦ *vi* rire; **~ at** *vt fus* se moquer de; rire de; **~ off** *vt* écarter par une plaisanterie or par une boutade; **~able** *adj* risible, ridicule; **~ing stock** *n*: **the ~ing stock** of la risée de; **~ter** *n* rire *m*; rires *mpl*

launch [lɔːntʃ] *n* lancement *m*; (motorboat) vedette *f* ♦ *vt* lancer; **~ into** *vt fus* se lancer dans

launderette [lɔːn'drɛt] (BRIT), **Laundromat** ['lɔːndrəmæt] (US: ®) *n* laverie f (automatique)

laundry ['lɔ:ndrɪ] n (clothes) linge m; (business) blanchisserie f; (room) buanderie f

laureate ['lɔ:rɪət] adj see poet

laurel ['lɔrəl] n laurier m

lava ['lɑ:və] n lave f

lavatory ['lævətrɪ] n toilettes fpl

lavender ['lævɪndə*] n lavande f

lavish ['lævɪʃ] adj (amount) co-pieux(euse); (person): ~ with prodigue à ♦ vt: to ~ sth on sb prodiguer qch à qn; (money) dépenser qch sans compter pour qn/qch

law [lɔ:] n loi f; (science) droit m; ~-abiding adj respectueux(euse) des lois; ~ and order n l'ordre public; ~ court n tribunal m, cour f de justice; ~ful adj légal(e); ~less adj (action) illégal(e)

lawn [lɔ:n] n pelouse f; ~mower n tondeuse f à gazon; ~ tennis n tennis m

law school (US) n faculté f de droit

lawsuit ['lɔ:su:t] n procès m

lawyer ['lɔ:jə*] n (consultant, with company) juriste m; (for sales, wills etc) notaire m; (partner, in court) avocat m

lax [læks] adj relâché(e)

laxative ['læksətɪv] n laxatif m

lay [leɪ] (pt, pp laid) pt of lie ♦ adj laïque; (not expert) profane ♦ vt poser, mettre; (eggs) pondre; to ~ the table mettre la table; ~ aside vt mettre de côté; ~ by vt = lay aside; ~ down vt poser; to ~ down the law faire la loi; to ~ down one's life sacrifier sa vie; ~ off vt (workers) licencier; ~ on vt (provide) fournir; ~ out vt (display) disposer, étaler; (about) (inf) n fainéant(e); ~by (BRIT) n aire f de stationnement (sur le bas-côté)

layer ['leɪə*] n couche f

layman ['leɪmən] (irreg) n profane m

layout ['leɪaʊt] n disposition f, plan m, agencement f; (PRESS) mise f en page

laze [leɪz] vi (also: ~ about) paresser

lazy ['leɪzɪ] adj paresseux(euse)

lb abbr = pound (weight)

lead¹ [li:d] (pt, pp led) n (distance, time ahead) avance f; (clue) piste f; (THEATRE) rôle principal; (ELEC) fil m; (for dog) laisse f ♦ vt mener, conduire; (be leader of) être à la tête de; (SPORT) mener, être en tête; in the ~ en tête; to ~ the way montrer le chemin; ~ away vt emmener; ~ back vt: to ~ back to ramener à; ~ on vt (tease) faire marcher; ~ to vt fus mener à; conduire à; ~ up to vt fus conduire à

lead² [led] n (metal) plomb m; (in pencil) mine f; ~en ['ledn] adj (sky, sea) de plomb

leader ['li:də*] n chef m; dirigeant(e), leader m; (SPORT: in league) leader; (: in race) coureur m de tête; ~ship n direction f; (quality) qualités fpl de chef

lead-free ['led'fri:] adj (petrol) sans plomb

leading ['li:dɪŋ] adj principal(e); de premier plan; (in race) de tête; ~ lady n (THEATRE) vedette (féminine); ~ light n (person) vedette f, sommité f; ~ man (irreg) n vedette (masculine)

lead singer [li:d-] n (in pop group) (chanteur m) vedette f

leaf [li:f] (pl leaves) n feuille f ♦ vi: to ~ through feuilleter; to turn over a new ~ changer de conduite or d'existence

leaflet ['li:flɪt] n prospectus m, brochure f; (POL, REL) tract m

league [li:g] n ligue f; (FOOTBALL) championnat m; to be in ~ with avoir partie liée avec, être de mèche avec

leak [li:k] n fuite f ♦ vi (pipe, liquid etc) fuir; (shoes) prendre l'eau; (ship) faire eau ♦ vt (information) divulguer

lean [li:n] (pt, pp leaned or leant) adj maigre ♦ vt: to ~ sth on sth appuyer qch sur qch ♦ vi (slope) pencher; (rest): to ~ against s'appuyer contre; être appuyé(e) contre; to ~ on s'appuyer sur; to ~ back/ forward se pencher en arrière/ avant; ~ out vi se pencher au dehors; ~ over se pencher; ~ing n: ~ing (towards) tendance f (à), penchant m (à)

leap [li:p] (pt, pp leaped or leapt) n bond m, saut m ♦ vi bondir, sauter; ~frog n saute-mouton m; ~ year n année f bissextile

learn [lɜːn] (pt, pp ~ed or learnt) vt, vi apprendre; to ~ to do sth apprendre à faire qch; to ~ about or of sth (hear, read) apprendre qch; ~ed ['lɜːnɪd] adj érudit(e), savant(e); ~er (BRIT) n (also: ~ driver) conducteur(trice) débutant(e); ~ing n (knowledge) savoir m

lease [li:s] n bail m ♦ vt louer à bail

leash [li:ʃ] n laisse f

least [li:st] adj: the ~ (+noun) le(la) plus petit(e), le(la) moindre; (: smallest amount of) le moins de ♦ adv (+verb) le moins; (+adj): the ~ le(la) moins; at ~ au moins; (or rather) du moins; not in the ~ pas le moins du monde

leather ['lɛðə*] n cuir m

leave [li:v] (pt, pp left) vt laisser; (go away from) quitter; (forget) oublier ♦ vi partir, s'en aller ♦ n (time off) congé m; (MIL: also: consent) permission f; to be left rester; there's some milk left over il reste du lait; on ~ en permission; ~ behind vt (person, object) laisser; (forget) oublier; ~ out vt oublier, omettre; ~ of absence n congé exceptionnel; (MIL) permission spéciale

leaves [li:vz] npl of leaf

Lebanon ['lɛbənən] n Liban m

lecherous ['lɛtʃərəs] (pej) adj lubrique

lecture ['lɛktʃə*] n conférence f; (SCOL) cours m ♦ vi donner des cours; enseigner ♦ vt (scold) ser-

monner, réprimander; to give a ~ on faire une conférence sur; donner un cours sur; ~r ['lɛktʃərə*] (BRIT) n (at university) professeur m (d'université)

led [lɛd] pt, pp of lead

ledge [lɛdʒ] n (of window, on wall) rebord m; (of mountain) saillie f, corniche f

ledger ['lɛdʒə*] n (COMM) registre m, grand livre

leech [li:tʃ] n (also fig) sangsue f

leek [li:k] n poireau m

leer [lɪə*] vi: to ~ at sb regarder qn d'un air mauvais or concupiscent

leeway ['li:weɪ] n (fig): to have some ~ avoir une certaine liberté d'action

left [lɛft] pt, pp of leave ♦ adj (not right) gauche ♦ n gauche f ♦ adv à gauche; on the ~, to the ~ à gauche; the L~ (POL) la gauche; ~-handed adj gaucher(ère); ~-hand side n gauche f, côté m gauche; ~- luggage (office) (BRIT) n consigne f; ~overs npl restes mpl; ~-wing adj (POL) de gauche

leg [lɛg] n jambe f; (of animal) patte f; (of furniture) pied m; (CULIN: of chicken, pork) cuisse f; (: of lamb) gigot m; (of journey) étape f; 1st/ 2nd ~ (SPORT) match m aller/ retour

legacy ['lɛgəsɪ] n héritage m, legs m

legal ['li:gəl] adj légal(e); ~ holiday (US) n jour férié; ~ tender n monnaie légale

legend ['lɛdʒənd] n légende f

legible ['lɛdʒəbl] adj lisible

legislation [lɛdʒɪs'leɪʃən] n législation f; **legislature** ['lɛdʒɪslətʃə*] n (corps) m législature

legitimate [lɪ'dʒɪtɪmət] adj légitime

leg-room [lɛgrum] n place f pour les jambes

leisure ['lɛʒə*] n loisir m, temps m libre; loisirs mpl; at ~ (tout) à loisir; à tête reposée; ~ centre n centre m de loisirs; ~ly adj tranquille; fait(e) sans se presser

lemon ['lemən] n citron m; **~ade** n limonade f; **~ tea** n thé m au citron

lend [lend] (pt, pp **lent**) vt: **to ~ sth (to sb)** prêter qch (à qn)

length [leŋθ] n longueur f; (section: of road, pipe etc) morceau m, bout m; (of time) durée f; **at ~** (at last) enfin, à la fin; (lengthily) longuement; **~en** vt allonger, prolonger ♦ vi s'allonger; **~ways** adv dans le sens de la longueur, en long; **~y** adj (très) long(longue)

lenient ['li:nɪənt] adj indulgent(e), clément(e)

lens [lenz] n lentille f; (of spectacles) verre m; (of camera) objectif m

Lent [lent] n Carême m

lent [lent] pt, pp of **lend**

lentil ['lentl] n lentille f

Leo ['li:əu] n le Lion

leotard ['li:əta:d] n maillot m (de danseur etc), collant m

leprosy ['leprəsi] n lèpre f

lesbian ['lezbɪən] n lesbienne f

less [les] adj moins de ♦ pron, adv moins ♦ prep moins; **~ than that/ you** moins que cela/vous; **~ than half** moins de la moitié; **~ than ever** moins que jamais; **~ and ~** de moins en moins; **the ~ he works ...** moins il travaille ...

lessen ['lesn] vi diminuer, s'atténuer ♦ vt diminuer, réduire, atténuer

lesser ['lesə*] adj moindre; **to a ~ extent** à un degré moindre

lesson ['lesn] n leçon f; **to teach sb a ~** (fig) donner une bonne leçon à qn

lest [lest] conj de peur que +sub

let [let] (pt, pp **let**) vt laisser; (BRIT: lease) louer; **to ~ sb do sth** laisser qn faire qch; **to ~ sb know sth** faire savoir qch à qn, prévenir qn de qch; **~'s go** allons-y; **~ him come** qu'il vienne; **"to ~"** "à louer"; **~ down** vt (tyre) dégonfler; (person) décevoir, faire faux bond à; **~ go** vi lâcher prise ♦ vt lâcher; **~ in** vt laisser entrer; (visitor etc) faire entrer; **~ off** vt (culprit) ne

pas punir; (firework etc) faire partir; **~ on** (inf) vi dire; **~ out** vt laisser sortir; (scream) laisser échapper; **~ up** vi diminuer, (cease) s'arrêter

lethal ['li:θəl] adj mortel(le), fatal(e)

letter ['letə*] n lettre f; **~ bomb** n lettre piégée; **~box** (BRIT) n boîte f aux or à lettres; **~ing** n lettres fpl, caractères mpl

lettuce ['letɪs] n laitue f, salade f

let-up ['letʌp] n répit m, arrêt m

leukaemia [lu:'ki:mɪə] (US **leukemia**) n leucémie f

level ['levl] adj plat(e), plan(e), uni(e); horizontal(e) ♦ n niveau m ♦ vt niveler, aplanir; **to be ~ with** être au même niveau que; **to draw ~ with** (person, vehicle) arriver à la hauteur de; **"A" ~s** (BRIT) = baccalauréat m; **"O" ~s** (BRIT) = B.E.P.C.; **on the ~** (fig: honest) régulier(ère); **~ off** vi (prices etc) se stabiliser; **~ out** vi = level off; **~ crossing** (BRIT) n passage m à niveau; **~-headed** adj équilibré(e)

lever ['li:və*] n levier m; **~age** n: **~age** (on or with) prise f (sur)

levity ['levɪtɪ] n légèreté f

levy ['levɪ] n taxe f, impôt m ♦ vt prélever, imposer, percevoir

lewd [lu:d] adj obscène, lubrique

liability [laɪə'bɪlɪtɪ] n responsabilité f; (handicap) handicap m; **liabilities** npl (on balance sheet) passif m

liable ['laɪəbl] adj (subject): **~ to** sujet(te) à; passible de; (responsible): **~ (for)** responsable (de); (likely): **~ to do** susceptible de faire

liaise [lɪ'eɪz] vi: **to ~ with** assurer la liaison avec; **liaison** [lɪ'eɪzɒn] n liaison f

liar ['laɪə*] n menteur(euse)

libel ['laɪbl] n diffamation f; (document) écrit m diffamatoire ♦ vt diffamer

liberal ['lɪbərəl] adj libéral(e); (generous): **~ with** prodigue de, généreux(euse) avec; **the L~ Democrats** (BRIT) le parti libéral-démocrate

liberation [lɪbəˈreɪʃən] n libération f
liberty [ˈlɪbətɪ] n liberté f; **to be at ~** to do être libre de faire
Libra [ˈliːbrə] n la Balance
librarian [laɪˈbrɛərɪən] n bibliothécaire m/f
library [ˈlaɪbrərɪ] n bibliothèque f
libretto [lɪˈbrɛtəʊ] n livret m
Libya [ˈlɪbɪə] n Libye f
lice [laɪs] npl of **louse**
licence [ˈlaɪsəns] (US **license**) n autorisation f, permis m; (RADIO, TV) redevance f; **driving ~**, (US) **driver's license** permis m (de conduire); **~ number** n numéro m d'immatriculation; **~ plate** n plaque f minéralogique
license [ˈlaɪsəns] n (US) = **licence** ♦ vt donner une licence à; **~d** adj (car) muni(e) de la vignette; (to sell alcohol) patenté(e) pour la vente des spiritueux, qui a une licence de débit de boissons
lick [lɪk] vt lécher; (inf: defeat) écraser; **to ~ one's lips** (fig) se frotter les mains
licorice [ˈlɪkərɪs] (US) n = **liquorice**
lid [lɪd] n couvercle m; (eye~) paupière f
lie [laɪ] (pt **lay**, pp **lain**) vi (rest) être étendu(e) or allongé(e) or couché(e); (in grave) être enterré(e), reposer; (be situated) se trouver, être; (be untruthful: pt, pp **lied**) mentir ♦ n mensonge m; **to ~ low** (fig) se cacher; **~ about** vi traîner; **~ around** vi = **lie about**; **~down** (BRIT) n: **to have a ~down** se reposer; **~in** (BRIT) n: **to have a ~in** faire la grasse matinée
lieutenant [lɛfˈtɛnənt, (US) luːˈtɛnənt] n lieutenant m

life [laɪf] (pl **lives**) n vie f; **to come to ~** (fig) s'animer; **~ assurance** (BRIT) n = **life insurance**; **~belt** (BRIT) n bouée f de sauvetage; **~boat** n canot m or chaloupe f de sauvetage; **~buoy** n bouée f de sauvetage; **~guard** n surveillant m de

baignade; **~ insurance** n assurance-vie f; **~ jacket** n gilet m or ceinture f de sauvetage; **~less** adj sans vie, inanimé(e); (dull) manquant de vie or de vigueur; **~like** adj qui semble vrai(e) or vivant(e); (painting) réaliste; **~line** n: **it was his ~line** ça l'a sauvé; **~long** adj de toute une vie, de toujours; **~ preserver** (US) n = **lifebelt** or **life jacket**; **~ sentence** n condamnation f à perpétuité; **~size(d)** adj grandeur nature inv; **~ span** n (durée f de) vie f; **~ style** n style m or mode m de vie; **~ support system** n (MED) respirateur artificiel; **~time** n vie f; **in his ~time** de son vivant
lift [lɪft] vt soulever, lever; (end) supprimer, lever ♦ vi (fog) se lever ♦ n (BRIT: elevator) ascenseur m; **to give sb a ~** (: AUT) emmener or prendre qn en voiture; **~off** n décollage m
light [laɪt] (pt, pp **lit**) n lumière f; (lamp) lampe f; (AUT: rear ~) feu m; (: head~) phare m; (for cigarette etc) have you got a **~?** avez-vous du feu? ♦ vt (candle, cigarette, fire) allumer; (room) éclairer ♦ adj (room, colour) clair(e); (not heavy) léger(ère); (not strenuous) peu fatigant(e) ♦ npl (AUT: traffic ~s) feux mpl; **to come to ~** être dévoilé(e) or découvert(e); **~ up vi** (face) s'éclairer ♦ vt (illuminate) éclairer, illuminer; **~ bulb** n ampoule f; **~en** vt (make less heavy) alléger; **~er** n (also: cigarette ~er) briquet m; **~headed** adj (excited) grisé(e); (fire) allumer; **~hearted** adj gai(e), joyeux(euse), enjoué(e); **~house** n phare m; **~ing** n (on road) éclairage m; (in theatre) éclairages; **~ly** adv légèrement; **to get off ~ly** s'en tirer à bon compte; **~ness** n (in weight) légèreté f
lightning [ˈlaɪtnɪŋ] n éclair m, foudre f; **~ conductor** n paratonnerre m; **~ rod** (US) n = **lightning conductor**

light pen n crayon m optique
lightweight ['laɪtweɪt] adj (suit) léger(ère) ♦ n (BOXING) poids léger
like [laɪk] vt aimer (bien) ♦ prep comme ♦ adj semblable, pareil(le) ♦ n: and the ~ et d'autres du même genre; **his ~s** and **dislikes** ses goûts mpl or préférences fpl; **I would ~, I'd ~** je voudrais, j'aimerais; **would you ~ a coffee?** voulez-vous du café?; **to be/look ~ sb/sth** ressembler à qn/qch; **what does it look ~?** de quoi est-ce que ça a l'air?; **what does it taste ~?** quel goût est-ce que ça a?; **that's just ~ him** c'est bien de lui, ça lui ressemble; **do it ~ this** fais-le comme ceci; **it's nothing ~ ...** ce n'est pas du tout comme ...; ~**able** adj sympathique, agréable
likelihood ['laɪklɪhʊd] n probabilité f
likely ['laɪklɪ] adj probable; plausible; **he's ~** to leave il va sûrement partir, il risque fort de partir; **not ~!** (inf) pas de danger!
likeness ['laɪknɪs] n ressemblance f; **that's a good ~** c'est très ressemblant
likewise ['laɪkwaɪz] adv de même, pareillement
liking ['laɪkɪŋ] n (for person) affection f; (for thing) penchant m, goût m
lilac ['laɪlək] n lilas m
lily ['lɪlɪ] n lis m; ~ **of the valley** n muguet m
limb [lɪm] n membre m
limber up ['lɪmbə*-] vi se dégourdir, faire des exercices d'assouplissement
limbo ['lɪmbəʊ] n: **to be in ~** (fig) être tombé(e) dans l'oubli
lime [laɪm] n (tree) tilleul m; (fruit) lime f, citron vert; (GEO) chaux f
limelight ['laɪmlaɪt] n: **in the ~** (fig) en vedette, au premier plan
limerick ['lɪmərɪk] n poème m humoristique (de 5 vers)
limestone ['laɪmstəʊn] n pierre f à chaux; (GEO) calcaire m
limit ['lɪmɪt] n limite f ♦ vt limiter;

~**ed** adj limité(e), restreint(e); **to be ~ed to** se limiter à, ne concerner que; ~**ed (liability) company** (BRIT) n ≈ société f anonyme
limp [lɪmp] n: **to have a ~** boiter ♦ vi boiter ♦ adj mou(molle)
limpet ['lɪmpɪt] n patelle f
line [laɪn] n ligne f; (stroke) trait m; (wrinkle) ride f; (rope) corde f; (wire) fil m; (of poem) vers m; (row, series) rangée f; (of people) file f, queue f; (railway track) voie f; (COMM: series of goods) article(s) m(pl); (work) métier m, type m d'activité; (attitude, policy) position f ♦ vt: **to ~ (with)** (clothes) doubler (de); (box) garnir or tapisser (de); (subj: trees, crowd) border; **in a ~** aligné(e); **in ~ with** dans sa partie, dans son rayon; **in ~ with** en accord avec; ~ **up** vi s'aligner, se mettre en rang(s) ♦ vt aligner; (event) prévoir, préparer
lined [laɪnd] adj (face) ridé(e), marqué(e); (paper) réglé(e)
linen ['lɪnɪn] n linge m (de maison); (cloth) lin m
liner ['laɪnə*] n paquebot m (de ligne); (for bin) sac m à poubelle
linesman ['laɪnzmən] (irreg) n juge m de touche; (TENNIS) juge m de ligne
line-up ['laɪnʌp] n (US: queue) file f; (SPORT) composition f de l'équipe
linger ['lɪŋgə*] vi s'attarder; traîner; (smell, tradition) persister
lingo ['lɪŋgəʊ] (inf: pl ~**es**) n pej jargon m
linguist ['lɪŋgwɪst] n: **to be a good ~** être doué(e) par les langues
linguistics [lɪŋ'gwɪstɪks] n linguistique f
lining ['laɪnɪŋ] n doublure f
link [lɪŋk] n lien m, rapport m; (of a chain) maillon m ♦ vt relier, lier, unir; ~**s** npl (GOLF) (terrain m de) golf m; ~ **up** vt relier ♦ vi se rejoindre; s'associer
lino ['laɪnəʊ] n = linoleum

linoleum [lɪˈnəʊliəm] n linoléum m

lion [ˈlaɪən] n lion m; **~ess** n lionne f

lip [lɪp] n lèvre f; **~-read** vi lire sur les lèvres; **~ salve** n pommade f rosat or pour les lèvres; **~ service**: to pay **~ service to sth** ne reconnaître le mérite de qch que pour la forme; **~stick** n rouge m à lèvres

liqueur [lɪˈkjʊə*] n liqueur f

liquid [ˈlɪkwɪd] adj liquide ♦ n liquide m; **~ize** [ˈlɪkwɪdaɪz] vt (CULIN) passer au mixer; **~izer** n mixer m

liquor [ˈlɪkə*] n spiritueux mpl, alcool m

liquorice [ˈlɪkərɪs] (BRIT) n réglisse f

liquor store (US) n magasin m de vins et spiritueux

lisp [lɪsp] vi zézayer

list [lɪst] n liste f ♦ vt (write down) faire une or la liste de; (mention) énumérer; **~ed building** (BRIT) n monument classé

listen [ˈlɪsn] vi écouter; to **~ to** écouter; **~er** n auditeur(trice)

listless [ˈlɪstlɪs] adj indolent(e), apathique

lit [lɪt] pt, pp of **light**

liter [ˈliːtə*] (US) n = **litre**

literacy [ˈlɪtərəsɪ] n degré m d'alphabétisation, fait m de savoir lire et écrire

literal [ˈlɪtərl] adj littéral(e); **~ly** adv littéralement; (really) réellement

literary [ˈlɪtərərɪ] adj littéraire

literate [ˈlɪtərət] adj qui sait lire et écrire, instruit(e)

literature [ˈlɪtrɪtʃə*] n littérature f; (brochures etc) documentation f

lithe [laɪð] adj agile, souple

litigation [lɪtɪˈgeɪʃən] n litige m; contentieux m

litre [ˈliːtə*] (US **liter**) n litre m

litter [ˈlɪtə*] n (rubbish) détritus mpl, ordures fpl; (young animals) portée f; **~ bin** (BRIT) n boîte f à ordures, poubelle f; **~ed** adj: **~ed with** jonché(e) de, couvert(e) de

little [ˈlɪtl] adj (small) petit(e) ♦ adv peu; **~ milk/time** peu de lait/temps; **a ~** un peu (de); **a ~ bit** un peu; **~ by ~** petit à petit, peu à peu

live¹ [laɪv] adj (animal) vivant(e), en vie; (wire) sous tension; (bullet, bomb) non explosé(e); (broadcast) en direct; (performance) en public

live² [lɪv] vi vivre; (reside) vivre, habiter; **~ down** vt faire oublier (avec le temps); **~ on** vt fus (food, salary) vivre de; **~ together** vi vivre ensemble, cohabiter; **~ up to** vt fus se montrer à la hauteur de

livelihood [ˈlaɪvlɪhʊd] n moyens mpl d'existence

lively [ˈlaɪvlɪ] adj vif/vive, plein(e) d'entrain; (place, book) vivant(e)

liven up [ˈlaɪvn-] vt animer ♦ vi s'animer

liver [ˈlɪvə*] n foie m

lives [laɪvz] npl of **life**

livestock [ˈlaɪvstɒk] n bétail m, cheptel m

livid [ˈlɪvɪd] adj livide, blafard(e); (inf: furious) furieux(euse), furibond(e)

living [ˈlɪvɪŋ] adj vivant(e), en vie ♦ n: **to earn** or **make a ~** gagner sa vie; **~ conditions** npl conditions fpl de vie; **~ room** n salle f de séjour; **~ standards** npl niveau m de vie; **~ wage** n salaire m permettant de vivre (décemment)

lizard [ˈlɪzəd] n lézard m

load [ləʊd] n (weight) poids m; (thing carried) chargement m, charge f ♦ vt (also: **~ up**): to **~ (with)** charger (de); (gun, camera) charger (avec); (COMPUT) charger; **a ~ of, ~s of** (fig) un or des tas de, des masses de; **to talk a ~ of rubbish** dire des bêtises; **~ed** adj (question) insidieux(euse); (inf: rich) bourré(e) de fric

loaf [ləʊf] (pl **loaves**) n pain m, miche f

loan [ləʊn] n prêt m ♦ vt prêter; **on ~** prêt(e), en prêt

loath [ləʊθ] adj: **to be ~ to do** répugner à faire

loathe [ləʊð] vt détester, avoir en horreur

loaves [ləʊvz] npl of loaf

lobby ['lɒbɪ] n hall m, entrée f; (POL) groupe m de pression, lobby m ♦ vt faire pression sur

lobster ['lɒbstə*] n homard m

local ['ləʊkəl] adj local(e) ♦ n (pub) pub m ou café m du coin; **the ~s** npl (inhabitants) les gens mpl du pays ou du coin; **~ anaesthetic** n anesthésie locale; **~ call** n communication urbaine; **~ government** n administration locale ou municipale; **~ity** [ləʊ'kælɪtɪ] n région f, environs mpl; (position) lieu m

locate [ləʊ'keɪt] vt (find) trouver, repérer; (situate) to be ~d in être situé(e) à or en

location [ləʊ'keɪʃən] n emplacement m; **on ~** (CINEMA) en extérieur

loch [lɒx] n lac m, loch m

lock [lɒk] n (of door, box) serrure f; (of canal) écluse f; (of hair) mèche f, boucle f ♦ vt (with key) fermer à clé ♦ vi (door etc) fermer à clé; (wheels) se bloquer; **~ in** vt enfermer; **~ out** vt enfermer dehors; (deliberately) mettre à la porte; **~ up** vt (person) enfermer; (house) fermer à clé ♦ vt tout fermer (à clé)

locker ['lɒkə*] n casier m; (in station) consigne f automatique

locket ['lɒkɪt] n médaillon m

locksmith ['lɒksmɪθ] n serrurier m

lockup ['lɒkʌp] n (prison) prison f

locum ['ləʊkəm] n (MED) suppléant(e) (de médecin)

lodge [lɒdʒ] n (house) pavillon m (de gardien); (hunting ~) pavillon de chasse ♦ vi (person): **to ~** (with) être logé(e) (chez), être en pension (chez); (bullet) se loger ♦ vt: **to ~ a complaint** porter plainte; **~r** n locataire m/f; (with meals) pensionnaire m/f; **lodgings** ['lɒdʒɪŋz] npl chambre f, meublé m

loft [lɒft] n grenier m

lofty ['lɒftɪ] adj (noble) noble, élevé(e); (haughty) hautain(e)

log [lɒg] n (of wood) bûche f; (book) = **logbook** ♦ vt (record) noter

logbook ['lɒgbʊk] n (NAUT) livre m or journal m de bord; (AVIAT) carnet m de vol; (of car) ≈ carte grise

loggerheads ['lɒgəhedz] npl: **at ~** (with) à couteaux tirés (avec)

logic ['lɒdʒɪk] n logique f; **~al** adj logique

loin [lɔɪn] n (CULIN) filet m, longe f

loiter ['lɔɪtə*] vi traîner

loll [lɒl] vi (also: **~ about**) se prélasser, fainéanter

lollipop ['lɒlɪpɒp] n sucette f; **~ man/lady** (BRIT: irreg) n contractuel(le) qui fait traverser la rue aux enfants

London ['lʌndən] n Londres m; **~er** n Londonien(ne)

lone [ləʊn] adj solitaire

loneliness ['ləʊnlɪnəs] n solitude f, isolement m; **lonely** ['ləʊnlɪ] adj seul(e); solitaire, isolé(e)

long [lɒŋ] adj long(longue) ♦ adv longtemps ♦ vi: **to ~ for sth** avoir très envie de qch; attendre qch avec impatience; **so or as ~ as** pourvu que; **don't be ~!** dépêchez-vous!; **how ~ is this river/course?** quelle est la longueur de ce fleuve/la durée de ce cours?; **6 metres ~** (long) de 6 mètres; **6 months ~** qui dure 6 mois, de 6 mois; **all night ~** toute la nuit; **he no ~er comes** il ne vient plus; **~ before/after** longtemps avant/après; **before ~** (+future) avant peu, dans peu de temps; (+past) peu de temps après; **at ~ last** enfin; **~-distance** adj (call) interurbain(e); **~hand** n écriture normale or courante; **~ing** n désir m, envie f, nostalgie f

longitude ['lɒŋgɪtjuːd] n longitude f

long: ~ jump n saut m en longueur; **~-life** adj (batteries etc) longue durée inv; (milk) upérisé(e); **~-lost** adj (person) perdu(e) de vue depuis longtemps; **~-playing record** n (disque m) 33 tours inv; **~-range** adj à longue portée; **~-sighted** adj (MED) presbyte; **~-standing** adj de longue date; **~-suffering** adj empreint(e) d'une patience résignée; extrêmement patient(e); **~-term** adj à long terme; **~-wave** n grandes ondes; **~-winded** adj intarissable, interminable

loo [luː] (BRIT: inf) n W.-C. mpl, petit coin

look [luk] vi regarder; (seem) sembler, paraître, avoir l'air; (building etc): to ~ south/(out) onto the sea donner au sud/sur la mer ♦ n (gen) regard m; (appearance) air m, allure f, aspect m; **~s** npl (good ~s) physique m, beauté f; to have a ~ regarder; ~! regardez!; ~ (here)! (annoyance) écoutez!; ~ after vt fus s'occuper de; ~ at vt fus regarder; (problem etc) examiner; ~ back vi: to ~ back on (event etc) évoquer, repenser à; ~ down on vt fus (fig) regarder de haut, dédaigner; ~ for vt fus chercher; ~ forward to vt fus attendre avec impatience; we ~ forward to hearing from you (in letter) dans l'attente de vous lire; ~ into vt fus examiner, étudier; ~ on vi regarder (en spectateur); ~ out vi (beware): to ~ out (for) prendre garde (à), faire attention (à); ~ out for vt fus être à la recherche de; guetter; ~ round vi regarder derrière soi, se retourner; ~ to vt fus (rely on) compter sur; ~ up vi lever les yeux; (improve) s'améliorer ♦ vt (word, name) chercher; ~ up to vt fus avoir du respect pour; **~out** n poste m de guet; (person) guetteur m; to be on the ~out (for) guetter

loom [luːm] vi (also: ~ up) surgir; (approach: event etc) être imminent(e); (threaten) menacer ♦ n (for weaving) métier m à tisser

loony ['luːnɪ] (inf) adj n timbré(e), cinglé(e)

loop [luːp] n boucle f; **~hole** n (fig) porte f de sortie; échappatoire f

loose [luːs] adj (knot, screw) desserré(e); (clothes) ample, lâche; (hair) dénoué(e), épars(e); (not firmly fixed) pas solide; (morals, discipline) relâché(e) ♦ n: on the ~ en liberté; ~ change n petite monnaie; ~ chippings npl (on road) gravillons mpl; ~ end n: to be at a ~ end or (US) at ~ ends ne pas trop savoir quoi faire; **~ly** adv sans serrer; (imprecisely) approximativement; **~n** vt desserrer

loot [luːt] n (inf: money) pognon m, fric m ♦ vt piller

lopsided ['lɔp'saɪdɪd] adj de travers, asymétrique

lord [lɔːd] n seigneur m; L~ Smith lord Smith; the L~ le Seigneur; good L~! mon Dieu!; the (House of) L~s (BRIT) la Chambre des lords; my L~ ~ your lordship Monsieur le comte (or le baron or le juge); (to bishop) Monseigneur; **L~ship** n: your L~ship Monsieur le comte (or le baron or le juge); (to bishop) Monseigneur

lore [lɔː¹] n tradition(s) f(pl)

lorry ['lɔrɪ] (BRIT) n camion m; ~ driver (BRIT) n camionneur m, routier m

lose [luːz] (pt, pp lost) vt, vi perdre; to ~ (time) (clock) retarder; to get lost vi se perdre; ~ vi perdant(e)

loss [lɔs] n perte f; to be at a ~ être perplexe ou embarrassé(e)

lost [lɔst] pt, pp of lose ♦ adj perdu(e); ~ and found (US), ~ property n objets trouvés

lot [lɔt] n (set) lot m; the ~ le tout; a ~ (of) beaucoup (de); **~s of** des tas de; to draw ~s (for sth) tirer (qch) au sort

lotion ['ləʊʃən] n lotion f

lottery ['lɔtərɪ] n loterie f

loud [laʊd] adj bruyant(e), sonore; (voice) fort(e); (support, condemnation) vigoureux(euse); (gaudy) voyant(e), tapageur(euse) ♦ adv fort; (speak etc) fort; out ~ tout haut; **~-hailer** (BRIT) n porte-voix m inv; **~ly** adv fort, bruyamment; **~speaker** n haut-parleur m

lounge [laʊndʒ] n salon m; (at airport) salle f; (BRIT: also: ~

(salle) de café m or bar m ♦ vi (also: ~ about or around) se prélasser, paresser; ~ suit (BRIT) n complet m; (on invitation) "tenue de ville"

louse [laus] (pl lice) n poux m

lousy ['lauzɪ] (inf) adj infect(e), moche; I feel ~ je suis mal fichu(e)

lout [laut] n rustre m, butor m

lovable ['lʌvəbl] adj adorable; très sympathique

love [lʌv] n amour m ♦ vt aimer; (caringly, kindly) aimer beaucoup; "~ (from) Anne" "affectueusement, Anne"; I ~ chocolate j'adore le chocolat; to be/fall in ~ with être/tomber amoureux(euse) de; to make ~ faire l'amour; "15 ~" (TENNIS) "15 à rien ou zéro"; ~ affair n liaison (amoureuse); ~ life n vie sentimentale

lovely ['lʌvlɪ] adj (très) joli(e), ravissant(e); (delightful: person) charmant(e); (: holiday etc) (très) agréable

lover ['lʌvə*] n amant m; (person in love) amoureux(euse); (amateur): a ~ of un amateur de; un(e) amoureux(euse) de

loving ['lʌvɪŋ] adj affectueux(euse), tendre

low [ləu] adj bas(basse); (quality mauvais(e), inférieur(e); (person: depressed) déprimé(e); (: ill) bas(basse), affaibli(e) ♦ adv bas ♦ n (METEOROLOGY) dépression f; to be ~ on être à court de; to feel ~ se sentir déprimé(e); to reach an all-time ~ être au plus bas; ~-alcohol adj peu alcoolisé(e); ~-cut adj (dress) décolleté(e)

lower ['ləuə*] adj inférieur m ♦ vt abaisser, baisser

low: ~-fat adj maigre; ~-lands npl (GEO) plaines fpl; ~ly adj humble, modeste

loyalty ['lɔɪəltɪ] n loyauté f, fidélité f

lozenge ['lɔzɪndʒ] n (MED) pastille f

LP n abbr = long-playing record

L-plates ['elpleits] (BRIT) npl

plaques fpl d'apprenti conducteur

Ltd abbr (= limited) = S.A.

lubricant ['lu:brɪkənt] n lubrifiant m

lubricate ['lu:brɪkeɪt] vt lubrifier, graisser

luck [lʌk] n chance f; bad ~ malchance f, malheur m; bad or hard or tough ~! pas de chance!; good ~! bonne chance!; ~ily adv heureusement, par bonheur; ~y adj (person) qui a de la chance; (coincidence, event) heureux(euse); (object) porte-bonheur inv

ludicrous ['lu:dɪkrəs] adj ridicule, absurde

lug [lʌg] (inf) vt traîner, tirer

luggage ['lʌgɪdʒ] n bagages mpl; ~ rack n (on car) galerie f

lukewarm ['lu:kwɔ:m] adj tiède

lull [lʌl] n accalmie f; (in conversation) pause f ♦ vt: to ~ sb to sleep bercer qn pour qu'il s'endorme; to be ~ed into a false sense of security s'endormir dans une fausse sécurité

lullaby ['lʌləbaɪ] n berceuse f

lumbago [lʌm'beɪgəu] n lumbago m

lumber ['lʌmbə*] n (wood) bois m de charpente; (junk) bric-à-brac m inv ♦ vt: to ~ed with (inf) se farcir; ~jack n bûcheron m

luminous ['lu:mɪnəs] adj lumineux(euse)

lump [lʌmp] n morceau m; (swelling) grosseur f ♦ vt: to ~ together réunir, mettre en tas; ~ sum n somme globale or forfaitaire; ~y adj (sauce) avec des grumeaux; (bed) défoncé(e), peu confortable

lunar ['lu:nə*] adj lunaire

lunatic ['lu:nətɪk] adj fou(folle), cinglé(e) (inf)

lunch [lʌntʃ] n déjeuner m

luncheon ['lʌntʃən] n déjeuner m (chic); ~ meat n sorte de mortadelle; ~ voucher (BRIT) n chèque-repas m

lung [lʌŋ] n poumon m

lunge [lʌndʒ] vi (also: ~ forward) faire un mouvement brusque en avant; **to ~ at** envoyer or assener un coup à

lurch [lə:tʃ] vi vaciller, tituber ♦ n écart m brusque; **to leave sb in the ~** laisser qn se débrouiller or se dépêtrer tout(e) seul(e)

lure [ljuə*] n (attraction) attrait m, charme m ♦ vt attirer or persuader par la ruse

lurid ['ljuərid] adj affreux(euse), atroce; (pej: colour, dress) criard(e)

lurk [lə:k] vi se tapir, se cacher

luscious ['lʌʃəs] adj succulent(e); appétissant(e)

lush [lʌʃ] adj luxuriant(e)

lust [lʌst] n (sexual) luxure f; lubricité f; désir m; (fig): ~ **for** soif f de; ~ **after**, ~ **for** vt fus (sexually) convoiter, désirer; ~**y** ['lʌsti] adj vigoureux(euse), robuste

Luxembourg ['lʌksəmbə:g] n Luxembourg m

luxurious [lʌg'zjuəriəs] adj luxueux(euse); **luxury** ['lʌkʃəri] n luxe m ♦ cpd de luxe

lying ['laiiŋ] n mensonge(s) m(pl) ♦ vb see **lie**

lyrical adj lyrique

lyrics ['liriks] npl (of song) paroles fpl

M

m. abbr = **metre**; **mile**; **million**

M.A. abbr = **Master of Arts**

mac [mæk] n (BRIT) imper(méable) m

macaroni [mækə'rəuni] n macaroni mpl

machine [mə'ʃi:n] n machine f ♦ vt (TECH) façonner à la machine; (dress etc) coudre à la machine; ~ **gun** n mitrailleuse f; ~ **language** n (COMPUT) langage-machine m; ~**ry** n machinerie f, machines fpl; (fig) mécanisme(s) m(pl)

mackerel ['mækrəl] n inv maquereau m

mackintosh ['mækintɔʃ] n (BRIT) imperméable m

mad [mæd] adj fou(folle); (foolish) insensé(e); (angry) furieux(euse); (keen): **to be ~ about** être fou(folle) de

madam ['mædəm] n madame f

madden ['mædn] vt exaspérer

made [meid] pt, pp of **make**

Madeira [mə'diərə] n (GEO) Madère f; (wine) madère m

made-to-measure ['meidtə'meʒə*] (BRIT) adj fait(e) sur mesure

madly ['mædli] adv follement; ~ **in love** éperdument amoureux(euse)

madman ['mædmən] (irreg) n fou m

madness ['mædnəs] n folie f

magazine [mægə'zi:n] n (PRESS) magazine m, revue f; (RADIO, TV; also: ~ **programme**) magazine

maggot ['mægət] n ver m, asticot m

magic ['mædʒik] n magie f ♦ adj magique; ~**al** adj magique; (experience, evening) merveilleux (euse); ~**ian** [mə'dʒiʃən] n magicien (ne); (conjurer) prestidigitateur m

magistrate ['mædʒistreit] n magistrat m; juge m

magnet ['mægnit] n aimant m; ~**ic** [mæg'netik] adj magnétique

magnificent [mæg'nifisənt] adj superbe, magnifique; (splendid: robe, building) somptueux(euse), magnifique

magnify ['mægnifai] vt grossir; (sound) amplifier; ~**ing glass** n loupe f; **magnitude** ['mægnitju:d] n ampleur f

magpie ['mægpai] n pie f

mahogany [mə'hɔgəni] n acajou m

maid [meid] n bonne f; **old ~** (pej) vieille fille

maiden ['meidn] n jeune fille f ♦ adj (aunt etc) non mariée; (speech, voyage) inaugural(e); ~ **name** n nom m de jeune fille

mail [meil] n poste f; (letters) courrier m ♦ vt envoyer (par la poste); ~**box** (US) n boîte f aux lettres; ~**ing list** n liste f d'adresses; ~**order** n vente f or achat m par correspondance

maim [meɪm] vt mutiler

main [meɪn] adj principal(e) ♦ n: the ~(s) n (pl) (gas, water) conduite principale, canalisation f; the ~s n (ELEC) le secteur; **in the** ~ dans l'ensemble; ~**frame** n (COMPUT) (gros) ordinateur, unité centrale; ~**land** n continent m; ~**ly** adv principalement, surtout; ~**road** n grand-route f; ~**stay** n (fig) pilier m; ~**stream** n courant principal

maintain [meɪnˈteɪn] vt entretenir; (continue) maintenir; (affirm) soutenir; **maintenance** [ˈmeɪntənəns] n entretien m; (alimony) pension f alimentaire

maize [meɪz] n maïs m

majestic [məˈdʒestɪk] adj majestueux(euse)

majesty [ˈmædʒɪstɪ] n majesté f

major [ˈmeɪdʒə*] n (MIL) commandant m ♦ adj (important) important(e); (most important) principal(e); (MUS) majeur(e)

Majorca [məˈjɔːkə] n Majorque f

majority [məˈdʒɒrɪtɪ] n majorité f

make [meɪk] (pt, pp made) vt faire; (manufacture) faire, fabriquer; (earn) gagner; (cause to be): **to** ~ **sb sad etc** rendre qn triste etc; (force): **to** ~ **sb do sth** obliger qn à faire qch, faire faire qch à qn; (equal): **2 and 2** ~ **4** 2 et 2 font 4 ♦ n fabrication f; (brand) marque f; **to** ~ **a fool of sb** (ridicule) ridiculiser qn; (trick) avoir ou duper qn; **to** ~ **a profit** faire un ou des bénéfice(s); **to** ~ **a loss** essuyer une perte; **to** ~ **it** (arrive) arriver; (achieve sth) parvenir à qch, réussir; **what time do you** ~ **it?** quelle heure est-vous?; **to** ~ **do with** se contenter de; ~ **for** vt fus (place) se diriger vers; ~ **out** vt (write out: cheque) faire; (decipher) déchiffrer; (understand) comprendre; (see) distinguer; ~ **up** vt (constitute) constituer; (invent) inventer, imaginer; (parcel, bed) faire ♦ vi se réconcilier; (with cosmetics) se maquiller;

~ **up for** vt fus compenser; ~**believe** n: **it's just** ~**believe** (game) c'est pour faire semblant; (invention) c'est de l'invention pure; ~**r** n fabricant m; ~**shift** adj provisoire, improvisé(e); ~**up** n maquillage m; ~**up remover** n démaquillant m

making [ˈmeɪkɪŋ] n (fig): **in the** ~ en formation ou gestation; **to have the** ~**s of** (actor, athlete etc) avoir l'étoffe de

malaria [məˈleərɪə] n malaria f

Malaysia [məˈleɪzɪə] n Malaisie f

male [meɪl] n (BIO) mâle m ♦ adj mâle; (sex, attitude) masculin(e); (child etc) du sexe masculin

malevolent [məˈlevələnt] adj malveillant(e)

malfunction [mælˈfʌŋkʃən] n fonctionnement défectueux

malice [ˈmælɪs] n méchanceté f, malveillance f; **malicious** [məˈlɪʃəs] adj méchant(e), malveillant(e)

malign [məˈlaɪn] vt diffamer, calomnier

malignant [məˈlɪɡnənt] adj (MED) malin(igne)

mall [mɔːl] n (also: shopping ~) centre commercial

mallet [ˈmælɪt] n maillet m

malpractice [mælˈpræktɪs] n faute professionnelle; négligence f

malt [mɔːlt] n malt m ♦ cpd (also: ~ whisky) pur malt

Malta [ˈmɔːltə] n Malte f

mammal [ˈmæməl] n mammifère m

mammoth [ˈmæməθ] n mammouth m ♦ adj géant(e), monstre

man [mæn] (pl **men**) n homme m ♦ vt (NAUT: ship) garnir d'hommes; (MIL: gun) servir; (: post) être de service à; (machine) assurer le fonctionnement de; **an old** ~ un vieillard; ~ **and wife** mari et femme

manage [ˈmænɪdʒ] vi se débrouiller ♦ vt (be in charge of) s'occuper de; (: business etc) gérer; (control: ship) manier, manœuvrer; (: person) savoir s'y prendre avec; **to** ~ **to do**

réussir à faire; **~able** adj (task) faisable; (number) raisonnable; **~ment** n gestion f, administration f, direction f; **~r** n directeur m; administrateur m; (SPORT) manager m; (of artist) impresario m; **~ress** [mænɪ'dʒɛˈrəs] n directrice f; gérante f; **~rial** [mænə'dʒɪərɪəl] adj directorial(e); (skills) de cadre, de gestion; **managing director** [mænɪdʒɪŋ] n directeur général

mandarin ['mændərɪn] n (also: ~ orange) mandarine f; (person) mandarin m

mandatory ['mændətərɪ] adj obligatoire

mane [meɪn] n crinière f

maneuver (US) vt, vi, n = manoeuvre

manfully ['mænfʊlɪ] adv vaillamment

mangle ['mæŋgl] vt déchiqueter; mutiler

mango ['mæŋgəʊ] (pl **~es**) n mangue f

mangy ['meɪndʒɪ] adj galeux(euse)

manhandle ['mænhændl] vt malmener

man: **~hole** ['mænhəʊl] n trou m d'homme; **~hood** ['mænhʊd] n âge m d'homme; virilité f; **~hour** ['mæn'aʊə*] n heure f de main-d'œuvre; **~hunt** ['mænhʌnt] n (POLICE) chasse f à l'homme

mania ['meɪnɪə] n manie f; **~c** ['meɪnɪæk] n maniaque m/f; (fig) fou(folle) m/f; **manic** ['mænɪk] adj maniaque

manicure ['mænɪkjʊə*] n manucure f; **~ set** n trousse f à ongles

manifest ['mænɪfɛst] vt manifester ♦ adj manifeste, évident(e); **~o** [mænɪ'fɛstəʊ] n manifeste m

manipulate [mə'nɪpjʊleɪt] vt manipuler; (system, situation) exploiter

man: **~kind** [mæn'kaɪnd] n humanité f, genre humain; **~ly** ['mænlɪ] adj viril(e); **~made** ['mæn'meɪd] adj artificiel(le); (fibre) synthétique

manner ['mænə*] n manière f, façon

f; (behaviour) attitude f, comportement m; (sort): **all** ~ **of** toutes sortes de; **~s** npl (behaviour) manières; **~ism** n particularité f de langage (or de comportement), tic m

manoeuvre [mə'nuːvə*] (US **maneuver**) vt (move) manœuvrer; (manipulate: person) manipuler; (: situation) exploiter ♦ vi manœuvrer ♦ n manœuvre f

manor ['mænə*] n (also: ~ house) manoir m

manpower ['mænpaʊə*] n main-d'œuvre f

mansion ['mænʃən] n château m, manoir m

manslaughter ['mænslɔːtə*] n homicide m involontaire

mantelpiece ['mæntlpiːs] n cheminée f

manual ['mænjʊəl] adj manuel(le) ♦ n manuel m

manufacture [mænjʊ'fæktʃə*] vt fabriquer ♦ n fabrication f; **~r** n fabricant m

manure [mə'njʊə*] n fumier m

manuscript ['mænjʊskrɪpt] n manuscrit m

many ['mɛnɪ] adj beaucoup de, de nombreux(euses) ♦ pron beaucoup, un grand nombre; **a great** ~ un grand nombre (de); ~ **a** ... bien des ..., plus d'un(e) ...

map [mæp] n carte f; (of town) plan m; ~ **out** vt tracer; (task) planifier

maple ['meɪpl] n érable m

mar [mɑː*] vt gâcher, gâter

marathon ['mærəθən] n marathon m

marble ['mɑːbl] n marbre m; (toy) bille f

March [mɑːtʃ] n mars m

march [mɑːtʃ] vi marcher au pas; (fig: protesters) défiler ♦ n marche f; (demonstration) manifestation f

mare [mɛə*] n jument f

margarine [mɑːdʒə'riːn] n margarine f

margin ['mɑːdʒɪn] n marge f; **~al** (seat) n (POL) siège disputé

marigold ['mærɪɡəʊld] *n* souci *m*

marijuana [mærɪ'wɑːnə] *n* marijuana *f*

marina [mə'riːnə] *n* (*harbour*) marina *f*

marine [mə'riːn] *adj* marin(e) ♦ *n* fusilier marin; (*US*) marine *m*; ~ **engineer** *n* ingénieur *m* en génie maritime

marital ['mærɪtl] *adj* matrimonial(e); ~ **status** situation *f* de famille

marjoram ['mɑːdʒərəm] *n* marjolaine *f*

mark [mɑːk] *n* marque *f*; (*of skid etc*) trace *f*; (*BRIT: SCOL*) note *f*; (*currency*) mark *m* ♦ *vt* marquer; (*stain*) tacher; (*BRIT: SCOL*) noter, corriger; **to ~ time** marquer le pas; **~er** *n* (*sign*) jalon *m*; (*bookmark*) signet *m*

market ['mɑːkɪt] *n* marché *m* ♦ *vt* (*COMM*) commercialiser; ~ **garden** (*BRIT*) *n* jardin maraîcher; **~ing** *n* marketing *m*; **~place** *n* place *f* du marché; (*COMM*) marché *m*; **~ research** *n* étude *f* de marché

marksman ['mɑːksmən] (*irreg*) *n* tireur *m* d'élite

marmalade ['mɑːməleɪd] *n* confiture *f* d'oranges

maroon [mə'ruːn] *vt*: **to be ~ed** être abandonné(e); (*fig*) être bloqué(e) ♦ *adj* bordeaux *inv*

marquee [mɑː'kiː] *n* chapiteau *m*

marriage ['mærɪdʒ] *n* mariage *m*; ~ **bureau** *n* agence matrimoniale; ~ **certificate** *n* extrait *m* d'acte de mariage

married ['mærɪd] *adj* marié(e); (*life, love*) conjugal(e)

marrow ['mærəʊ] *n* moelle *f*; (*vegetable*) courge *f*

marry ['mærɪ] *vt* épouser, se marier avec; (*subj: father, priest etc*) marier ♦ *vi* (*also: get married*) se marier

Mars [mɑːz] *n* (*planet*) Mars *f*

marsh [mɑːʃ] *n* marais *m*, marécage *m*

marshal ['mɑːʃəl] *n* maréchal *m*;

(*US: fire, police*) ≈ capitaine *m*; (*SPORT*) membre *m* du service d'ordre ♦ *vt* rassembler

marshy ['mɑːʃɪ] *adj* marécageux(euse)

martyr ['mɑːtə*] *n* martyr(e); **~dom** *n* martyre *m*

marvel ['mɑːvəl] *n* merveille *f* ♦ *vi*: **to ~ (at)** s'émerveiller (de); **~lous** (*US* **~ous**) *adj* merveilleux(euse)

Marxist ['mɑːksɪst] *adj* marxiste ♦ *n* marxiste *m/f*

marzipan ['mɑːzɪpæn] *n* pâte *f* d'amandes

mascara [mæs'kɑːrə] *n* mascara *m*

masculine ['mæskjʊlɪn] *adj* masculin(e)

mash [mæʃ] *vt* écraser, réduire en purée; **~ed potatoes** *npl* purée *f* de pommes de terre

mask [mɑːsk] *n* masque *m* ♦ *vt* masquer

mason ['meɪsn] *n* (*also: stone~*) maçon *m*; (*: free~*) franc-maçon *m*; **~ry** *n* maçonnerie *f*

masquerade [mæskə'reɪd] *vi*: **to ~** as se faire passer pour

mass [mæs] *n* multitude *f*, masse *f*; (*PHYSICS*) masse; (*REL*) messe *f* ♦ *cpd* (*communication*) de masse; (*unemployment*) massif(ive) ♦ *vi* se masser; **the ~ es** les masses; **~es of** des tas de

massacre ['mæsəkə*] *n* massacre *m*

massage ['mæsɑːʒ] *n* massage *m* ♦ *vt* masser

massive ['mæsɪv] *adj* énorme, massif(ive)

mass media *n inv* mass-media *mpl*

mass production *n* fabrication *f* en série

mast [mɑːst] *n* mât *m*; (*RADIO*) pylône *m*

master ['mɑːstə*] *n* maître *m*; (*in secondary school*) professeur *m*; (*title for boys*): **M~ X** Monsieur X ♦ *vt* maîtriser; (*learn*) apprendre à fond; **~ly** *adj* magistral(e); **~mind** *n* esprit supérieur ♦ *vt* diriger, être le cerveau de; **M~ of Arts/Science**

n = maîtrise *f* (en lettres/sciences);
~piece *n* chef-d'œuvre *m*; **~plan** *n*
stratégie *f* d'ensemble; **~y** *n*
maîtrise *f*; connaissance parfaite

mat [mæt] *n* petit tapis; (*also:*
door~) paillasson *m*; (: *table*~) napperon *m* ♦ *adj* = **matt**

match [mætʃ] *n* allumette *f*; (*game*)
match *m*, partie *f*; (*fig*) égal(e) ♦ *vt*
(*also: ~ up*) assortir; (*go well with*)
aller bien avec, s'assortir à; (*equal*)
égaler, valoir ♦ *vi* être assorti(e); **to**
be a good ~ être bien assorti(e);
~box *n* boîte *f* d'allumettes; **~ing**
adj assorti(e)

mate [meɪt] *n* (*inf*) copain(copine);
(*animal*) partenaire *m/f*, mâle/
femelle; (*in merchant navy*) second
m ♦ *vi* s'accoupler

material [mə'tɪərɪəl] *n* (*substance*)
matière *f*, matériau *m*; (*cloth*) tissu
m, étoffe *f*; (*information, data*) données *fpl* ♦ *adj* matériel(le); (*relevant: evidence*) pertinent(e); **~s** *npl*
(*equipment*) matériaux *mpl*

maternal [mə'tɜ:nl] *adj* maternel(le)

maternity [mə'tɜ:nɪtɪ] *n* maternité *f*;
~ dress *n* robe *f* de grossesse; **~**
hospital *n* maternité *f*

mathematical [mæθə'mætɪkl] *adj*
mathématique; **mathematics**
[mæθə'mætɪks] *n* mathématiques *fpl*

maths [mæθs] (*US* **math**) *n* math(s)
fpl

matinée ['mætɪneɪ] *n* matinée *f*

mating call ['meɪtɪŋ-] *n* appel *m* du
mâle

matrices ['meɪtrɪsi:z] *npl* of **matrix**

matriculation [mətrɪkju'leɪʃən] *n*
inscription *f*

matrimonial [mætrɪ'məʊnɪəl] *adj*
matrimonial(e), conjugal(e)

matrimony ['mætrɪmənɪ] *n* mariage
m

matrix ['meɪtrɪks] (*pl* **matrices**) *n*
matrice *f*

matron ['meɪtrən] *n* (*in hospital*)
infirmière-chef *f*; (*in school*) infirmière

mat(t) [mæt] *adj* mat(e)

matted ['mætɪd] *adj* emmêlé(e)

matter ['mætə*] *n* question *f*; (*PHYSICS*) matière *f*; (*content*) contenu
m, fond *m*; (*MED: pus*) pus *m* ♦ *vi*
importer; **~s** *npl* (*affairs, situation*)
la situation; **it doesn't ~** cela n'a
pas d'importance; (*I don't mind*)
cela ne fait rien; **what's the ~?**
qu'est-ce qu'il y a?, qu'est-ce qui ne
va pas?; **no ~ what** quoiqu'il arrive; **as a ~ of course** tout naturellement; **as a ~ of fact** en fait; **~-**
of-fact *adj* terre à terre; (*voice*) neutre

mattress ['mætrəs] *n* matelas *m*

mature [mə'tjʊə*] *adj* mûr(e);
(*cheese*) fait(e); (*wine*) arrivé(e) à
maturité ♦ *vi* (*person*) mûrir; (*wine,
cheese*) se faire

maul [mɔːl] *vt* lacérer

mausoleum [mɔːsə'lɪəm] *n* mausolée *m*

mauve [məʊv] *adj* mauve

maverick ['mævərɪk] *n* (*fig*) nonconformiste *m/f*

maximum ['mæksɪməm] (*pl* **maxima**) *adj* maximum ♦ *n* maximum *m*

May [meɪ] *n* mai *m*; **~ Day** *n* le Premier Mai; *see also* **mayday**

may [meɪ] (*conditional* **might**) *vi* (*indicating possibility*): **he ~ come** il
se peut qu'il vienne; (*be allowed to*):
~ I smoke? puis-je fumer?;
(*wishes*): **~ God bless you!** (que)
Dieu vous bénisse!; **you ~ as well**
go à votre place, je partirais

maybe ['meɪbi:] *adv* peut-être; **~**
he'll ... peut-être qu'il ...

mayday ['meɪdeɪ] *n* SOS *m*

mayhem ['meɪhem] *n* grabuge *m*

mayonnaise [meɪə'neɪz] *n* mayonnaise *f*

mayor [mɛə*] *n* maire *m*; **~ess** *n*
épouse *f* du maire

maze [meɪz] *n* labyrinthe *m*, dédale
m

MD *n abbr* (= *Doctor of Medicine*)
titre universitaire; = **managing director**

me [mi:] *pron* me, m' +*vowel*;

(stressed, after prep) moi; **he heard ~ il m'a entendu**; **give ~ a book** donnez-moi un livre; **after ~** après moi

meadow ['medəu] n prairie f, pré m
meagre ['mi:gə*] (US meager) adj maigre
meal [mi:l] n repas m; (flour) farine f; **~time** n l'heure f du repas
mean [mi:n] (pt, pp meant) adj (with money) avare, radin(e); (unkind) méchant(e); (shabby) misérable; (average) moyen(ne) ♦ vt signifier, vouloir dire; (refer to) faire allusion à, parler de; (intend): **to ~ to do sth** avoir l'intention de faire ♦ n moyenne f; **~s** npl (way, money) moyens mpl; **by ~s of** par l'intermédiaire de; au moyen de; **by all ~s!** je vous en prie!; **to be ~t for sb/sth** être destiné à qn/qch; **do you ~ it?** vous êtes sérieux?; **what do you ~?** que voulez-vous dire?
meander [mı'ændə*] vi faire des méandres
meaning ['mi:nıŋ] n signification f, sens m; **~ful** adj significatif(ive); (relationship, occasion) important(e); **~less** adj dénué(e) de sens
meanness ['mi:nnıs] n (with money) avarice f; (unkindness) méchanceté f; (shabbiness) médiocrité f
meant [ment] pt, pp of **mean**
meantime ['mi:ntaım] adv (also: in the ~) pendant ce temps
meanwhile ['mi:nwaıl] adv = meantime
measles ['mi:zlz] n rougeole f
measly ['mi:zlı] (inf) adj minable
measure ['meʒə*] vt, vi mesurer ♦ n mesure f; (ruler) règle f (graduée); **~ments** npl mesures fpl; **chest/hip ~ment** tour m de poitrine/hanches
meat [mi:t] n viande f; **~ball** n boulette f de viande
Mecca ['mekə] n la Mecque
mechanic [mı'kænık] n mécanicien m; **~al** adj mécanique; **~s** n (PHYSICS) mécanique f ♦ npl (of reading, government etc) mécanisme m

mechanism ['mekənızəm] n mécanisme m
medal ['medl] n médaille f; **~lion** n médaillon m; **~list** (US **~ist**) n (SPORT) médaillé(e)
meddle ['medl] vi: **to ~ in** se mêler de, s'occuper de; **to ~ with** toucher à
media ['mi:dıə] npl media mpl
mediaeval [medı'i:vəl] adj = medieval
median ['mi:dıən] (US) n (also: ~ strip) bande médiane
mediate ['mi:dıeıt] vi servir d'intermédiaire
Medicaid ['medıkeıd] (®:US) n assistance médicale aux indigents
medical ['medıkəl] adj médical(e) ♦ n visite médicale
Medicare ['medıkeə*] (®:US) n assistance médicale aux personnes âgées
medication [medı'keıʃən] n (drugs) médicaments mpl
medicine ['medsın] n médecine f; (drug) médicament m
medieval [medı'i:vəl] adj médiéval(e)
mediocre [mi:dı'əukə*] adj médiocre
meditate ['medıteıt] vi méditer
Mediterranean [medıtə'reınıən] adj méditerranéen(ne); **the ~ (Sea)** la (mer) Méditerranée
medium ['mi:dıəm] (pl media) adj moyen(ne) ♦ n (means) moyen m; (pl mediums: person) médium m; **the happy ~** le juste milieu; **~ wave** n ondes moyennes
medley ['medlı] n mélange m; (MUS) pot-pourri m
meek [mi:k] adj doux(douce), humble
meet [mi:t] (pt, pp met) vt rencontrer; (by arrangement) retrouver, rejoindre; (for the first time) faire la connaissance de; (go and fetch): **I'll ~ you at the station** j'irai te chercher à la gare; (opponent, danger) faire face à; (obligations) satisfaire à

♦ vi (friends) se rencontrer, se retrouver; (in session) se réunir; (join: lines, roads) se rejoindre; ~ **with** vi fus rencontrer; ~**ing** n rencontre f; (session: of club etc) réunion f; (POL) meeting m; **she's at a ~ing** (COMM) elle est en conférence

megabyte ['megəbaɪt] n (COMPUT) méga-octet m

megaphone ['megəfəʊn] n porte-voix m inv

melancholy ['melənkəlɪ] n mélancolie f ♦ adj mélancolique

mellow ['meləʊ] adj velouté(e), doux(douce); (sound) mélodieux(euse) ♦ vi (person) s'adoucir

melody ['melədɪ] n mélodie f

melon ['melən] n melon m

melt [melt] vi fondre ♦ vt faire fondre; (metal) fondre; ~ **away** vi fondre complètement; ~ **down** vt fondre; ~**down** n fusion f (du cœur d'un réacteur nucléaire); ~**ing pot** n (fig) creuset m

member ['membə*] n membre m; M~ **of Parliament** (BRIT) député m; M~ **of the European Parliament** Eurodéputé m; ~**ship** n adhésion f; statut m de membre; (members) membres mpl, adhérents mpl; ~**ship card** n carte f de membre

memento [mə'mentəʊ] n souvenir m

memo ['meməʊ] n note f (de service)

memoirs ['memwɑːz] npl mémoires mpl

memorandum [memə'rændəm] (pl **memoranda**) n note f (de service)

memorial [mɪ'mɔːrɪəl] n mémorial m ♦ adj commémoratif(ive)

memorize ['meməraɪz] vt apprendre par cœur; retenir

memory ['memərɪ] n mémoire f; (recollection) souvenir m

men [men] npl of **man**

menace ['menɪs] n menace f; (nuisance) plaie f ♦ vt menacer; **menacing** adj menaçant(e)

mend [mend] vt réparer; (darn) raccommoder, repriser ♦ n: **on the ~**

en voie de guérison; **to ~ one's ways** s'amender; ~**ing** n réparation f; (clothes) raccommodage m

menial ['miːnɪəl] adj subalterne

meningitis [menɪn'dʒaɪtɪs] n méningite f

menopause ['menəʊpɔːz] n ménopause f

menstruation [menstru'eɪʃən] n menstruation f

mental ['mentl] adj mental(e); ~**ity** [men'tælɪtɪ] n mentalité f

mention ['menʃən] n mention f ♦ vt mentionner, faire mention de; **don't ~ it!** je vous en prie, il n'y a pas de quoi!

menu ['menjuː] n (set ~, COMPUT) menu m; (list of dishes) carte f

MEP n abbr = **Member of the European Parliament**

mercenary ['mɜːsɪnərɪ] adj intéressé(e), mercenaire ♦ n mercenaire m

merchandise ['mɜːtʃəndaɪz] n marchandises fpl

merchant ['mɜːtʃənt] n négociant m, marchand m; ~ **bank** (BRIT) n banque f d'affaires; ~ **navy** (US **marine**) n marine marchande

merciful ['mɜːsɪfʊl] adj miséricordieux(euse), clément(e); **a ~ release** une délivrance

merciless ['mɜːsɪləs] adj impitoyable, sans pitié

mercury ['mɜːkjʊrɪ] n mercure m

mercy ['mɜːsɪ] n pitié f, indulgence f; (REL) miséricorde f; **at the ~ of** à la merci de

mere [mɪə*] adj simple; (chance) pur(e); **a ~ two hours** seulement deux heures; ~**ly** adv simplement, purement

merge [mɜːdʒ] vt unir ♦ vi (colours, shapes, sounds) se mêler; (roads) se joindre; (COMM) fusionner; ~**r** n (COMM) fusion f

meringue [mə'ræŋ] n meringue f

merit ['merɪt] n mérite m, valeur f

mermaid ['mɜːmeɪd] n sirène f

merry ['merɪ] adj gai(e); M~ **Christmas!** Joyeux Noël!; ~**go-**

round n manège m
mesh [meʃ] n maille f
mesmerize ['mezməraɪz] vt hypnotiser; fasciner
mess [mes] n désordre m, fouillis m, pagaille f; (muddle: of situation) gâchis m; (dirt) saleté f; (MIL) mess m, cantine f; ~ **about** (inf) vi perdre son temps; ~ **about with** (inf) vt fus tripoter; ~ **around** (inf) vi = mess about; ~ **around with** vt fus = mess about with; ~ **up** vt (dirty) salir; (spoil) gâcher
message ['mesɪdʒ] n message m
messenger ['mesɪndʒə*] n messager m
Messrs ['mesəz] abbr (on letters) MM
messy ['mesɪ] adj sale; en désordre
met [met] pt, pp of **meet**
metal ['metl] n métal m; ~**lic** adj métallique
meteorology [miːtɪə'rɔlədʒɪ] n météorologie f
mete out [miːt-] vt infliger; (justice) rendre
meter ['miːtə*] n (instrument) compteur m; (also: parking ~) parcmètre m; (US: unit) = **metre**
method ['meθəd] n méthode f; ~**ical** adj méthodique; M~**ist** ['meθədɪst] n méthodiste m/f
meths [meθs] (BRIT), **methylated spirit** ['meθɪleɪtɪd-] (BRIT) n alcool m à brûler
metre ['miːtə*] (US **meter**) n mètre m
metric ['metrɪk] adj métrique
metropolitan [metrə'pɔlɪtən] adj métropolitain(e); the M~ **Police** (BRIT) la police londonienne
mettle ['metl] n: to be on one's ~ être d'attaque
mew [mjuː] vi (cat) miauler
mews [mjuːz] (BRIT) n: ~ **cottage** cottage aménagé dans une ancienne écurie
Mexico ['meksɪkəʊ] n Mexique m
miaow [miːˈaʊ] vi miauler
mice [maɪs] npl of **mouse**

micro ['maɪkrəʊ] n (also: ~**computer**) micro-ordinateur m
microchip ['maɪkrəʊtʃɪp] n puce f
microphone ['maɪkrəfəʊn] n microphone m
microscope ['maɪkrəskəʊp] n microscope m
microwave ['maɪkrəʊweɪv] n (also: ~ **oven**) four m à micro-ondes
mid [mɪd] adj: in ~ **May** à la mi-mai; in ~ **afternoon** au milieu de l'après-midi; in ~ **air** en plein ciel; ~**day** n midi m
middle ['mɪdl] n milieu m; (waist) taille f; ♦ adj du milieu; (average) moyen(ne); in the ~ of the night au milieu de la nuit; ~**-aged** adj d'un certain âge; M~ **Ages** npl: the M~ Ages le moyen âge; ~**-class(es)** adj ~ bourgeois(e); ~**-class(es)** n(pl): the ~ **class(es)** ~ les classes moyennes; M~ **East** n Proche-Orient m, Moyen-Orient m; ~**man** (irreg) n intermédiaire m; ~ **name** n deuxième nom m; ~**-of-the-road** adj (politician) modéré(e); (music) neutre; ~**weight** n (BOXING) poids moyen; **middling** ['mɪdlɪŋ] adj moyen(ne)
midge [mɪdʒ] n moucheron m
midget ['mɪdʒɪt] n nain(e)
Midlands ['mɪdləndz] npl comtés du centre de l'Angleterre
midnight ['mɪdnaɪt] n minuit m
midriff ['mɪdrɪf] n estomac m, taille f
midst [mɪdst] n: in the ~ of au milieu de
midsummer ['mɪd'sʌmə*] n milieu m de l'été
midway ['mɪd'weɪ] adj, adv: ~ (between) à mi-chemin (entre); ~ **through** ... au milieu de ..., en plein(e) ...
midweek ['mɪd'wiːk] n milieu m de la semaine
midwife ['mɪdwaɪf] (pl **midwives**) n sage-femme f
midwinter ['mɪd'wɪntə*] n: in ~ en plein hiver
might [maɪt] vb see **may** ♦ n puis-

sance f, force f; **~y** adj puissant(e)

migraine ['mi:grein] n migraine f

migrant ['maigrnt] adj (bird) migrateur(trice); (worker) saisonnier(ère)

migrate [mai'greit] vi émigrer

mike [maik] n abbr (= microphone) micro m

mild [maild] adj doux(douce); (reproach, infection) léger(ère); (illness) bénin(igne); (interest) modéré(e); (taste) peu relevé(e)

mildly ['maildli] adv doucement; légèrement; **to put it ~** c'est le moins qu'on puisse dire

mile [mail] n mil(l)e m (= 1609 m); **~age** n distance f en milles, ≈ kilométrage m; **~ometer** [mai'lɔmitə*] n compteur m (kilométrique); **~stone** n borne f; (fig) jalon m

militant ['militnt] adj militant(e)

military ['militəri] adj militaire

militate ['militeit] vi: **to ~ against** (prevent) empêcher

militia [mi'liʃə] n milice(s) f(pl)

milk [milk] n lait m ♦ vt (cow) traire; (fig: person) dépouiller, plumer; (: situation) exploiter à fond; **~ chocolate** n chocolat m au lait; **~man** (irreg) n laitier m; **~ shake** n milk-shake m; **~y** adj (drink) au lait; (colour) laiteux(euse); **M~y Way** n voie lactée

mill [mil] n moulin m; (steel ~) aciérie f; (spinning ~) filature f; (flour ~) minoterie f ♦ vt moudre, broyer ♦ vi (also: ~ about) grouiller; **~er** n meunier m

milligram(me) ['miligræm] n milligramme m

millimetre ['milimi:tə*] (US millimeter) n millimètre m

millinery ['milinəri] n chapellerie f

million ['miljən] n million m; **~aire** [miljə'neə*] n millionnaire m

milometer [mai'lɔmitə*] n ≈ compteur m kilométrique

mime [maim] n mime m ♦ vt, vi mimer

mimic ['mimik] n imitateur(trice) ♦

vt imiter, contrefaire

min. abbr = minute(s); minimum

mince [mins] vt hacher ♦ vi (in walking) marcher à petits pas maniérés ♦ n (BRIT: CULIN) viande hachée, hachis m; **~meat** n (fruit) hachis de fruits secs utilisé en pâtisserie; (US: meat) viande hachée, hachis; **~ pie** n (sweet) sorte de tarte aux fruits secs; **~r** n hachoir m

mind [maind] n esprit m ♦ vt (attend to, look after) s'occuper de; (be careful) faire attention à; (object to): **I don't ~ the noise** le bruit ne me dérange pas; **I don't ~ cela ne me dérange pas; it is on my ~** cela me préoccupe; **to my ~** à mon avis or sens; **to be out of one's ~** ne plus avoir toute sa raison; **to keep or bear sth in ~** tenir compte de qch; **to make up one's ~** se décider; **never ~** ça ne fait rien; (don't worry) ne vous en faites pas; **"~ the step"** "attention à la marche"; **~er** n (child~er) gardienne f; (inf: bodyguard) ange gardien (fig); **~ful** adj: **~ful of** attentif(ive) à, soucieux(euse) de; **~less** adj irréfléchi(e); (boring: job) idiot(e)

mine¹ [main] pron le(la) mien(ne), les miens(miennes) ♦ adj: **this book is mine** ce livre est à moi

mine² [main] n mine f ♦ vt (coal) extraire; (ship, beach) miner; **~field** n champ m de mines; (fig) situation (très délicate); **~r** n mineur m

mineral ['minərəl] adj minéral(e) ♦ n minéral m; **~s** npl (BRIT: soft drinks) boissons gazeuses; **~ water** n eau minérale

mingle ['mingl] vi: **to ~ with** se mêler à

miniature ['minitʃə*] adj (en) miniature ♦ n miniature f

minibus ['minibʌs] n minibus m

minim ['minim] n (MUS) blanche f

minimal ['miniməl] adj minime

minimize ['mɪnɪmaɪz] *vt (reduce)* réduire au minimum; *(play down)* minimiser

minimum ['mɪnɪməm] *(pl* **minima**) *adj, n* minimum *m*

mining ['maɪnɪŋ] *n* exploitation minière

miniskirt ['mɪnɪskɜ:t] *n* mini-jupe *f*

minister ['mɪnɪstə*] *n (BRIT: POL)* ministre *m*; *(REL)* pasteur *m* ♦ *vi:* **to ~ to sb's needs)** pourvoir aux besoins de qn; **~ial** [mɪnɪs'tɪərɪəl] *(BRIT) adj (POL)* ministériel(le)

ministry ['mɪnɪstrɪ] *n (BRIT: POL)* ministère *m*; *(REL)*: **to go into the ~** devenir pasteur

mink [mɪŋk] *n* vison *m*

minor ['maɪnə*] *adj* petit(e), de peu d'importance; *(MUS, poet, problem)* mineur(e) ♦ *n (LAW)* mineur(e)

minority [maɪ'nɒrɪtɪ] *n* minorité *f*

mint [mɪnt] *n (plant)* menthe *f*; *(sweet)* bonbon *m* à la menthe ♦ *vt (coins)* battre; **the (Royal) M~,** *(US)* **the (US) M~** = l'Hôtel m de la Monnaie; **in ~ condition** à l'état de neuf

minus ['maɪnəs] *n (also: ~ sign)* signe *m* moins ♦ *prep* moins

minute¹ [maɪ'nju:t] *adj* minuscule; *(detail, search)* minutieux(euse)

minute² ['mɪnɪt] *n* minute *f*; **~s** *npl (official record)* procès-verbal, compte rendu

miracle ['mɪrəkl] *n* miracle *m*

mirage ['mɪrɑ:ʒ] *n* mirage *m*

mirror ['mɪrə*] *n* miroir *m*, glace *f*; *(in car)* rétroviseur *m*

mirth [mɜːθ] *n* gaieté *f*

misadventure [mɪsəd'ventʃə*] *n* mésaventure *f*

misapprehension ['mɪsæprɪ'henʃən] *n* malentendu *m*, méprise *f*

misappropriate [mɪsə'prəʊprɪeɪt] *vt* détourner

misbehave ['mɪsbɪ'heɪv] *vi* se conduire mal

miscalculate [mɪs'kælkjʊleɪt] *vt* mal calculer

miscarriage ['mɪskærɪdʒ] *n (MED)*

fausse couche; **~ of justice** erreur *f* judiciaire

miscellaneous [mɪsɪ'leɪnɪəs] *adj (items)* divers(es); *(selection)* varié(e)

mischief ['mɪstʃɪf] *n (naughtiness)* sottises *fpl*; *(fun)* farce *f*; *(playfulness)* espièglerie *f*; *(maliciousness)* méchanceté *f*; **mischievous** ['mɪstʃɪvəs] *adj (playful, naughty)* coquin(e), espiègle

misconception ['mɪskən'sepʃən] *n* idée fausse

misconduct [mɪs'kɒndʌkt] *n* inconduite *f*; **professional ~** faute professionnelle

misdemeanour [mɪsdɪ'mi:nə*] *(US)* **misdemeanor** *n* écart *m* de conduite; infraction *f*

miser ['maɪzə*] *n* avare *m/f*

miserable ['mɪzərəbl] *adj (person, expression)* malheureux(euse); *(conditions)* misérable; *(weather)* maussade; *(offer, donation)* minable; *(failure)* pitoyable

miserly ['maɪzəlɪ] *adj* avare

misery ['mɪzərɪ] *n (unhappiness)* tristesse *f*; *(pain)* souffrances *fpl*; *(wretchedness)* misère *f*

misfire ['mɪs'faɪə*] *vi* rater

misfit ['mɪsfɪt] *n (person)* inadapté(e)

misfortune [mɪs'fɔ:tʃən] *n* malchance *f*, malheur *m*

misgiving [mɪs'gɪvɪŋ] *n (apprehension)* craintes *fpl*; **to have ~s about** avoir des doutes quant à

misguided ['mɪs'gaɪdɪd] *adj* malavisé(e)

mishandle ['mɪs'hændl] *vt (mismanage)* mal s'y prendre pour faire *or* résoudre *etc*

mishap ['mɪshæp] *n* mésaventure *f*

misinform [mɪsɪn'fɔ:m] *vt* mal renseigner

misinterpret ['mɪsɪn'tɜ:prɪt] *vt* mal interpréter

misjudge ['mɪs'dʒʌdʒ] *vt* méjuger

mislay [mɪs'leɪ] *vt (irreg: like lay) vt* égarer

mislead [mɪs'liːd] (*irreg: like lead*) vt induire en erreur; **~ing** adj trompeur(euse)

mismanage [mɪs'mænɪdʒ] vt mal gérer

misnomer [mɪs'nəʊmə*] n terme or qualificatif trompeur or peu approprié

misplace [mɪs'pleɪs] vt égarer

misprint [mɪs'prɪnt] n faute f d'impression

Miss [mɪs] n Mademoiselle

miss [mɪs] vt (*fail to get, attend or see*) manquer, rater; (*regret the absence of*): **I ~ him/it** il/cela me manque ♦ vi manquer ♦ n (*shot*) coup manqué; **to ~ out** (*BRIT*) vt oublier

misshapen [mɪs'ʃeɪpən] adj difforme

missile [ˈmɪsaɪl] n (*MIL*) missile m; (*object thrown*) projectile m

missing [ˈmɪsɪŋ] adj manquant(e); (*after escape, disaster: person*) disparu(e); **to go ~** disparaître; **to be ~** avoir disparu

mission [ˈmɪʃən] n mission f; **~ary** n missionnaire m/f

misspent [ˈmɪsˈspent] adj: **his ~ youth** sa folle jeunesse

mist [mɪst] n (*light*) brume f; (*heavy*) brouillard m ♦ vi (*also: ~ over: eyes*) s'embuer; **~ over** vi (*windows etc*) s'embuer; **~ up** vi = mist over

mistake [mɪs'teɪk] (*irreg: like take*) n erreur f, faute f ♦ vt (*meaning, remark*) mal comprendre; **se méprendre sur**; **to make a ~** se tromper, faire une erreur; **by ~** par erreur, par inadvertance; **to ~ for** prendre pour; **~n** (*pp of mistake*) ♦ adj (*idea etc*) erroné(e); **to be ~n** faire erreur, se tromper

mister [ˈmɪstə*] n (*inf*) Monsieur m; *see also* **Mr**

mistletoe [ˈmɪsltəʊ] n gui m

mistook [mɪs'tʊk] pt of mistake

mistress [ˈmɪstrɪs] n maîtresse f; (*BRIT: in primary school*) institu-

trice f; (: *in secondary school*) professeur m

mistrust [ˈmɪsˈtrʌst] vt se méfier de

misty [ˈmɪstɪ] adj brumeux(euse); (*glasses, window*) embué(e)

misunderstand [ˈmɪsʌndə'stænd] (*irreg*) vt, vi mal comprendre; **~ing** n méprise f, malentendu m

misuse [n ˈmɪs'juːs, vb ˈmɪs'juːz] n mauvais emploi; (*of power*) abus m ♦ vt mal employer; abuser de; **~ of funds** détournement m de fonds

mitigate [ˈmɪtɪgeɪt] vt atténuer

mitt(en) [ˈmɪt(n)] n mitaine f; moufle f

mix [mɪks] vt mélanger; (*sauce, drink etc*) préparer ♦ vi se mélanger; (*socialize*): **he doesn't ~ well** il est peu sociable ♦ n mélange m; **to ~ with** (*people*) fréquenter; **~ up** vt mélanger; (*confuse*) confondre; **~ed** adj (*feelings, reactions*) contradictoire; (*salad*) mélangé(e); (*school, marriage*) mixte; **~ed grill** n assortiment de grillades; **~ed-up** adj (*confused*) désorienté(e), embrouillé(e); **~er** n (*for food*) batteur m, mixer m; (*person*): **he is a good ~er** il est très liant; **~ture** n assortiment m, mélange m; (*MED*) préparation f; **~-up** n confusion f

mm abbr (= millimeter) mm

moan [məʊn] n gémissement m ♦ vi gémir; (*inf: complain*): **to ~ (about)** se plaindre (de)

moat [məʊt] n fossé m, douves fpl

mob [mɒb] n foule f; (*disorderly*) cohue f ♦ vt assaillir

mobile [ˈməʊbaɪl] adj mobile ♦ n mobile m; **~ home** n (grande) caravane; **~ phone** n téléphone portatif

mock [mɒk] vt ridiculiser; (*laugh at*) se moquer de ♦ adj faux(fausse); **~ exam** examen blanc; **~ery** n moquerie f, raillerie f; **to make a ~ery of** tourner en dérision; **~-up** n maquette f

mod [mɒd] adj *see* convenience

mode [məʊd] n mode m

model [ˈmɒdl] n modèle m; (*person:*

for fashion) mannequin *m*; (: *for artist)* modèle ♦ *vi* travailler comme mannequin ♦ *adj (railway: toy)* modèle réduit *inv*; *(child, factory)* modèle; to ~ clothes présenter des vêtements; to ~ o.s. on imiter

modem ['məʊdem] (COMPUT) *n* modem *m*

moderate *[adj, n* 'mɒdərət, *vb* 'mɒdəreɪt] *adj* modéré(e); *(amount, change)* peu important(e) ♦ *vi* se calmer ♦ *vt* modérer

modern ['mɒdən] *adj* moderne; **~ize** *vt* moderniser

modest ['mɒdɪst] *adj* modeste; **~y** *n* modestie *f*

modicum ['mɒdɪkəm] *n*: a ~ of un minimum de

modify ['mɒdɪfaɪ] *vt* modifier

mogul ['məʊgəl] *n (fig)* nabab *m*

mohair ['məʊhɛə*] *n* mohair *m*

moist [mɔɪst] *adj* humide, moite; **~en** ['mɔɪsn] *vt* humecter, mouiller légèrement; **~ure** ['mɔɪstʃə*] *n* humidité *f*; **~urizer** ['mɔɪstʃəraɪzə*] *n* produit hydratant

molar ['məʊlə*] *n* molaire *f*

molasses [mə'læsɪz] *n* mélasse *f*

mold [məʊld] (US) *n*, *vt* = **mould**

mole [məʊl] *n (animal, fig: spy)* taupe *f*; *(spot)* grain *m* de beauté

molest [mə'lest] *vt (harass)* molester; (JUR: *sexually)* attenter à la pudeur de

mollycoddle ['mɒlɪkɒdl] *vt* chouchouter, couver

molt [məʊlt] (US) *vi* = **moult**

molten ['məʊltən] *adj* fondu(e); *(rock)* en fusion

mom [mɒm] (US) *n* = **mum**

moment ['məʊmənt] *n* moment *m*, instant *m*; at the ~ en ce moment; at that ~ à ce moment-là; **~ary** *adj* momentané(e), passager(ère); **~ous** [mə'mentəs] *adj* important(e), capital(e)

momentum [məʊ'mentəm] *n* élan *m*, vitesse acquise; *(fig)* dynamique *f*; to gather ~ prendre de la vitesse

mommy ['mɒmɪ] (US) *n* = **mummy**

Monaco ['mɒnəkəʊ] *n* Monaco *m*

monarch ['mɒnək] *n* monarque *m*; **~y** *n* monarchie *f*

monastery ['mɒnəstrɪ] *n* monastère *m*

Monday ['mʌndeɪ] *n* lundi *m*

monetary ['mʌnɪtərɪ] *adj* monétaire

money ['mʌnɪ] *n* argent *m*; to make ~ gagner de l'argent; **~ order** *n* mandat *m*; **~-spinner** (*inf*) *n* mine *f* d'or (*fig*)

mongrel ['mʌngrəl] *n (dog)* bâtard *m*

monitor ['mɒnɪtə*] *n* (TV, COMPUT) moniteur *m* ♦ *vt* contrôler; *(broadcast)* être à l'écoute de; *(progress)* suivre (de près)

monk [mʌŋk] *n* moine *m*

monkey ['mʌŋkɪ] *n* singe *m*; ~ **nut** (BRIT) *n* cacahuète *f*; ~ **wrench** *n* clé *f* à molette

monopoly [mə'nɒpəlɪ] *n* monopole *m*

monotone ['mɒnətəʊn] *n* ton *m* (*or* voix *f*) monocorde

monotonous [mə'nɒtənəs] *adj* monotone

monsoon [mɒn'suːn] *n* mousson *f*

monster ['mɒnstə*] *n* monstre *m*

monstrous ['mɒnstrəs] *adj* monstrueux(euse); *(huge)* gigantesque

month [mʌnθ] *n* mois *m*; **~ly** *adj* mensuel(le) ♦ *adv* mensuellement

monument ['mɒnjʊmənt] *n* monument *m*

moo [muː] *vi* meugler, beugler

mood [muːd] *n* humeur *f*, disposition *f*; to be in a good/bad ~ être de bonne/mauvaise humeur; **~y** *adj* (*variable)* d'humeur changeante, lunatique; *(sullen)* morose, maussade

moon [muːn] *n* lune *f*; **~light** *n* clair *m* de lune; **~lighting** *n* travail *m* au noir; **~lit** *adj*: a **~lit night** une nuit de lune

moor [mʊə*] *n* lande *f* ♦ *vt (ship)* amarrer ♦ *vi* mouiller; **~land** ['mʊələnd] *n* lande *f*

moose [muːs] *n inv* élan *m*

mop [mɔp] n balai m à laver; (for dishes) lavette f (à vaisselle) ♦ vt essuyer; ~ **of hair** tignasse f; ~ **up** vt éponger

mope [məup] vi avoir le cafard, se morfondre

moped ['məuped] n cyclomoteur m

moral ['mɔrəl] adj moral(e) ♦ n morale f; ~s npl (attitude, behaviour) moralité f

morale [mɔ'rɑːl] n moral m

morality [mə'rælɪtɪ] n moralité f

morass [mə'ræs] n marais m, marécage m

KEYWORD

more [mɔː*] adj 1 (greater in number etc) plus (de), davantage; ~ **people/work (than)** plus de gens/de travail (que)
2 (additional) encore un; **do you want (some)** ~ **tea?** voulez-vous encore du thé?; **I have no or I don't have any** ~ **money** je n'ai plus d'argent; **it'll take a few** ~ **weeks** ça prendra encore quelques semaines ♦ pron plus, davantage; ~ **than 10** plus de 10; **it cost** ~ **than we expected** cela a coûté plus que prévu; **I want** ~ j'en veux plus or davantage; **is there any** ~? est-ce qu'il en reste?; **there's no** ~ il n'y en a plus; **a little** ~ un peu plus; **many/much** ~ beaucoup plus, bien davantage
♦ adv: ~ **dangerous/easily (than)** plus dangereux/facilement (que); ~ **and** ~ **expensive** de plus en plus cher; ~ **or less** plus ou moins; ~ **than ever** plus que jamais

moreover [mɔː'rəuvə*] adv de plus

morning ['mɔːnɪŋ] n matin m; matinée f ♦ cpd matinal(e); (paper) du matin; **in the** ~ le matin; **7 o'clock in the** ~ 7 heures du matin; ~ **sickness** n nausées matinales

Morocco [mə'rɔkəu] n Maroc m

moron ['mɔːrɔn] (inf) n idiot(e)

Morse [mɔːs] n: ~ **(code)** morse m

morsel ['mɔːsl] n bouchée f

mortar ['mɔːtə*] n mortier m

mortgage ['mɔːgɪdʒ] n hypothèque f; (loan) prêt m (or crédit m) hypothécaire ♦ vt hypothéquer; ~ **company** (US) n société f de crédit immobilier

mortuary ['mɔːtjuərɪ] n morgue f

mosaic [məu'zeɪk] n mosaïque f

Moscow ['mɔskəu] n Moscou

Moslem ['mɔzləm] adj, n = Muslim

mosque [mɔsk] n mosquée f

mosquito [mɔs'kiːtəu] (pl ~es) n moustique m

moss [mɔs] n mousse f

most [məust] adj la plupart de; le plus de ♦ pron la plupart ♦ adv le plus; (very) très, extrêmement; **the** ~ (also: + adjective) le plus; ~ **of** la plus grande partie de; ~ **of them** la plupart d'entre eux; **I saw (the)** ~ j'en ai vu la plupart; c'est moi qui en ai vu le plus; **at the (very)** ~ au plus; **to make the** ~ **of** profiter au maximum de; **~ly** adv (chiefly) surtout; (usually) généralement

MOT n abbr (BRIT: = Ministry of Transport): **the** ~ **(test)** la visite technique (annuelle) obligatoire des véhicules à moteur

motel [məu'tel] n motel m

moth [mɔθ] n papillon m de nuit; (in clothes) mite f; **~ball** n boule f de naphtaline

mother ['mʌðə*] n mère f ♦ vt (act as mother to) servir de mère à; (pamper, protect) materner; ~ **country** mère patrie; **~hood** n maternité f; **~-in-law** n belle-mère f; **~ly** adj maternel(le); **~-of-pearl** n nacre f; **~-to-be** n future maman; ~ **tongue** langue maternelle

motion ['məuʃən] n mouvement m; (gesture) geste m; (at meeting) motion f ♦ vt, vi: **to** ~ **(to) sb to do** sth faire signe à qn de or de faire; **~less** adj immobile, sans mouvement; ~ **picture** n film m

motivated ['məutɪveɪtɪd] adj motivé(e); **motive** ['məutɪv] n motif m, mobile *m*

motley ['mɒtlɪ] *adj* hétéroclite

motor ['məʊtə*] *n* moteur *m*; (BRIT: inf: vehicle) auto ♦ cpd (industry, vehicle) automobile; ~**bike** *n* moto *f*; ~**boat** *n* bateau *m* à moteur; ~**car** (BRIT) *n* automobile *f*; ~**cycle** *n* vélomoteur *m*; ~**cycle racing** *n* course *f* de motos; ~**cyclist** *n* motocycliste *m/f*; ~**ing** (BRIT) *n* tourisme *m* automobile; ~**ist** ['məʊtərɪst] *n* automobiliste *m/f*; ~ **mechanic** *n* mécanicien *m* garagiste; ~ **racing** (BRIT) *n* course *f* automobile; ~ **trade** (BRIT) *n* secteur *m* de l'automobile; ~**way** (BRIT) *n* autoroute *f*

mottled ['mɒtld] *adj* tacheté(e), marbré(e)

motto ['mɒtəʊ] (*pl* ~**es**) *n* devise *f*

mould [məʊld] (US **mold**) *n* moule *m*; (mildew) moisissure *f* ♦ *vt* mouler, modeler; (fig) façonner; **mo(u)ldy** *adj* moisi(e); (smell) de moisi

moult [məʊlt] (US **molt**) *vi* muer

mound [maʊnd] *n* monticule *m*, tertre *m*; (heap) monceau *m*, tas *m*

mount [maʊnt] *n* mont *m*, montagne *f* ♦ *vt* monter ♦ *vi* (inflation, tension) augmenter; (also: ~ **up**: problems etc) s'accumuler; ~ **up** *vi* (bills, costs, savings) s'accumuler

mountain ['maʊntɪn] *n* montagne *f* ♦ *cpd* de montagne; ~ **bike** *n* VTT *m*, vélo tout-terrain; ~**eer** [maʊntɪ-ˈnɪə*] *n* alpiniste *m/f*; ~**eering** *n* alpinisme *m*; ~**ous** *adj* montagneux(-euse); ~ **rescue team** *n* équipe *f* de secours en montagne; ~**side** *n* flanc *m* or versant *m* de la montagne

mourn [mɔːn] *vt* pleurer ♦ *vi*: **to** ~ (**for**) (person) pleurer la mort de; ~**er** *n* parent(e) *or* ami(e) du défunt; personne *f* en deuil; ~**ful** *adj* triste, lugubre; ~**ing** *n* deuil *m*; **in** ~**ing** en deuil

mouse [maʊs] (*pl* **mice**) *n* (also COMPUT) souris *f*; ~**trap** *n* souricière *f*

mousse [muːs] *n* mousse *f*

moustache [məsˈtɑːʃ] (US **mustache**) *n* moustache(s) *f(pl)*

mousy ['maʊsɪ] *adj* (hair) d'un châtain terne

mouth [maʊθ, *pl* maʊðz] (*pl* ~**s**) *n* bouche *f*; (of dog, cat) gueule *f*; (of river) embouchure *f*; (of hole, cave) ouverture *f*; ~**ful** *n* bouchée *f*; ~**organ** *n* harmonica *m*; ~**piece** *n* (of musical instrument) embouchure *f*; (spokesman) porte-parole *m inv*; ~**wash** *n* eau *f* dentifrice; ~**watering** *adj* qui met l'eau à la bouche

movable ['muːvəbl] *adj* mobile

move [muːv] *n* (movement) mouvement *m*; (in game) coup *m*; (: turn to play) tour *m*; (change: of house) déménagement *m*; (: of job) changement *m* d'emploi ♦ *vt* déplacer, bouger; (emotionally) émouvoir; (POL: resolution etc) proposer; (in game) jouer ♦ *vi* (gen) bouger, remuer; (traffic) circuler; (also: ~ **house**) déménager; (situation) évoluer; **that was a good** ~ bien joué!; **to** ~ **sb to do sth** pousser *or* inciter qn à faire qch; **to get a** ~ **on** se dépêcher, se remuer; ~ **about** *vi* (fidget) remuer; (travel) voyager, se déplacer; (change residence, job) ne pas rester au même endroit; ~ **along** *vi* se pousser; ~ **around** *vi* = **move about**; ~ **away** *vi* s'en aller; ~ **back** *vi* revenir, retourner; ~ **forward** *vi* avancer; ~ **in** *vi* (to a house) emménager; (police, soldiers) intervenir; ~ **on** *vi* se remettre en route; ~ **out** *vi* (of house) déménager; ~ **over** *vi* se pousser, se déplacer; ~ **up** *vi* (pupil) passer dans la classe supérieure; (employee) avoir de l'avancement; ~**able** *adj* = **movable**

movement ['muːvmənt] *n* mouvement *m*

movie ['muːvɪ] *n* film *m*; **the** ~**s** le cinéma; ~ **camera** *n* caméra *f*

moving ['muːvɪŋ] *adj* en mouvement; (emotional) émouvant(e)

mow [məʊ] (*pt* mowed or mown) *vt* faucher; (*lawn*) tondre; ~ **down** *vt* faucher; ~**er** *n* (*also*: lawnmower) tondeuse *f* à gazon

MP *n abbr* = Member of Parliament

mph *abbr* = miles per hour

Mr ['mɪstə*] *n*: ~ Smith Monsieur Smith, M. Smith

Mrs ['mɪsɪz] (*US* Mrs.) *n*: ~ Smith Madame Smith, Mme Smith

Ms [mɪz] (*US* Ms.) *n* (= Miss or Mrs): ~ Smith = Madame Smith, Mme Smith

MSc *n abbr* = Master of Science

much [mʌtʃ] *adj* beaucoup de ♦ *adv, n, pron* beaucoup; how ~ is it? combien est-ce que ça coûte?; too ~ trop (de); as ~ as autant de

muck [mʌk] *n* (*dirt*) saleté *f*; ~ **about** (*or*) **around** (*inf*) *vi* faire l'imbécile; ~ **up** (*inf*) *vt* (*exam, interview*) se planter à (*fam*); ~**y** *adj* (*très sale*) (*book, film*) cochon(ne)

mud [mʌd] *n* boue *f*

muddle ['mʌdl] *n* (*mess*) pagaille *f*, désordre *m*; (*mix-up*) confusion *f* ♦ *vt* (*also*: ~ up) embrouiller; ~ **through** *vi* se débrouiller

muddy ['mʌdɪ] *adj* boueux(euse); **mudguard** ['mʌdɡɑːd] *n* garde-boue *m inv*

muffin ['mʌfɪn] *n* muffin *m*

muffle ['mʌfl] *vt* (*sound*) assourdir, étouffer; (*against cold*) emmitoufler; ~**d** *adj* (*sound*) étouffé(e); (*person*) emmitouflé(e); ~**r** (*US*) *n* (*AUT*) silencieux *m*

mug [mʌɡ] *n* (*cup*) grande tasse (*sans soucoupe*); (*for beer*) chope *f*; (*inf*: *face*) bouille *f*; (: *fool*) poire *f* ♦ *vt* (*assault*) agresser; ~**ging** *n* agression *f*

muggy ['mʌɡɪ] *adj* lourd(e), moite

mule [mjuːl] *n* mule *f*

mull over [mʌl-] *vt* réfléchir à

multi-level ['mʌltɪlevl] (*US*) *adj* = multistorey

multiple ['mʌltɪpl] *adj* multiple ♦ *n* multiple *m*; ~ **sclerosis** *n* sclérose *f* en plaques

multiplication [mʌltɪplɪ'keɪʃən] *n* multiplication *f*; **multiply** ['mʌltɪplaɪ] *vt* multiplier ♦ *vi* se multiplier

multistorey ['mʌltɪ'stɔːrɪ] (*BRIT*) *adj* (*building*) à étages; (*car park*) à étages *or* niveaux multiples

mum [mʌm] (*BRIT*: *inf*) *n* maman *f* ♦ *adj*: to keep ~ ne pas souffler mot

mumble ['mʌmbl] *vt, vi* marmotter, marmonner

mummy ['mʌmɪ] *n* (*BRIT*: *mother*) maman *f*; (*embalmed*) momie *f*

mumps [mʌmps] *n* oreillons *mpl*

munch [mʌntʃ] *vt, vi* mâcher

mundane [mʌn'deɪn] *adj* banal(e), terre à terre *inv*

municipal [mjuː'nɪsɪpəl] *adj* municipal(e)

murder ['mɜːdə*] *n* meurtre *m*, assassinat *m* ♦ *vt* assassiner; ~**er** *n* meurtrier *m*, assassin *m*; ~**ous** *adj* meurtrier(ère)

murky ['mɜːkɪ] *adj* sombre, ténébreux(euse); (*water*) trouble

murmur ['mɜːmə*] *n* murmure *m* ♦ *vt, vi* murmurer

muscle ['mʌsl] *n* muscle *m*; (*fig*) force *f*; ~ **in** *vi* (*on territory*) envahir; (*on success*) exploiter

muscular ['mʌskjʊlə*] *adj* musculaire; (*person, arm*) musclé(e)

muse [mjuːz] *vi* méditer, songer

museum [mjuː'zɪəm] *n* musée *m*

mushroom ['mʌʃrʊm] *n* champignon *m* ♦ *vi* pousser comme un champignon

music ['mjuːzɪk] *n* musique *f*; ~**al** *adj* musical(e); (*person*) musicien(ne) ♦ *n* (*show*) comédie musicale; ~**al instrument** *n* instrument *m* de musique; ~**ian** [mjuː'zɪʃən] *n* musicien(ne)

Muslim ['mʌzlɪm] *adj, n* musulman(e)

muslin ['mʌzlɪn] *n* mousseline *f*

mussel ['mʌsl] *n* moule *f*

must [mʌst] *aux vb* (*obligation*): **I** ~ do it je dois le faire, il faut que je le fasse; (*probability*): he ~ be there by now il doit y être maintenant, il y est probablement maintenant; (*suggestion, invitation*): you ~ come and see me il faut que vous veniez me voir; (*indicating sth unwelcome*): why ~ he behave so badly? qu'est-ce qu'il le pousse à se conduire si mal? ♦ *n* nécessité *f*, impératif *m*; it's a ~ c'est indispensable

mustache (*US*) *n* = moustache

mustard ['mʌstəd] *n* moutarde *f*

muster ['mʌstə*] *vt* rassembler

mustn't ['mʌsnt] = must not

mute [mjuːt] *adj* muet(te)

muted ['mjuːtɪd] *adj* (*colour*) sourd(e); (*reaction*) voilé(e)

mutiny ['mjuːtɪnɪ] *n* mutinerie *f* ♦ *vi* se mutiner

mutter ['mʌtə*] *vt, vi* marmonner, marmotter

mutton ['mʌtn] *n* mouton *m*

mutual ['mjuːtjuəl] *adj* mutuel(le), réciproque; (*benefit, interest*) commun(e); **~ly** *adv* mutuellement

muzzle ['mʌzl] *n* museau *m*; (*protective device*) muselière *f*; (*of gun*) gueule *f* ♦ *vt* museler

my [maɪ] *adj* mon(ma), mes *pl*; ~ house/car/gloves ma maison/mon auto/mes gants; I've washed ~ hair/cut ~ finger je me suis lavé les cheveux/coupé le doigt; **~self** [maɪˈself] *pron* (*reflexive*) me; (*emphatic*) moi-même; (*after prep*) moi; *see also* oneself

mysterious [mɪsˈtɪərɪəs] *adj* mystérieux(euse); **mystery** ['mɪstərɪ] *n* mystère *m*

mystify ['mɪstɪfaɪ] *vt* mystifier; (*puzzle*) ébahir

myth [mɪθ] *n* mythe *m*; **~ology** [mɪˈθɒlədʒɪ] *n* mythologie *f*

N

n/a *abbr* = not applicable

nag [næg] *vt* (*scold*) être toujours après, reprendre sans arrêt; **~ging** *adj* (*doubt, pain*) persistant(e)

nail [neɪl] *n* (*human*) ongle *m*; (*metal*) clou *m* ♦ *vt* clouer; to ~ sb down to a date/price contraindre qn à accepter *or* donner une date/un prix; **~brush** *n* brosse *f* à ongles; **~file** *n* lime *f* à ongles; **~ polish** *n* vernis *m* à ongles; **~ polish remover** *n* dissolvant *m*; **~ scissors** *npl* ciseaux *mpl* à ongles; **~ varnish** (*BRIT*) *n* = nail polish

naïve [naɪˈiːv] *adj* naïf(ïve)

naked ['neɪkɪd] *adj* nu(e)

name [neɪm] *n* nom *m*; (*reputation*) réputation *f* ♦ *vt* nommer; (*identify: accomplice etc*) citer; (*price, date*) fixer, donner; **by ~** par son nom; **in the ~ of** au nom de; **what's your ~?** comment vous appelez-vous?; **~less** *adj* sans nom; (*witness, contributor*) anonyme; **~ly** *adv* à savoir; **~sake** *n* homonyme *m*

nanny ['nænɪ] *n* bonne *f* d'enfants

nap [næp] *n* (*sleep*) (petit) somme *m* ♦ *vi*: to be caught **~ping** être pris à l'improviste *or* en défaut

nape [neɪp] *n*: ~ of the neck nuque *f*

napkin ['næpkɪn] *n* serviette *f* (de table)

nappy ['næpɪ] (*BRIT*) *n* couche *f* (*gen pl*); ~ **rash** *n*: to have ~ rash avoir les fesses rouges

narcissus [naːˈsɪsəs, *pl* naːˈsɪsɪ] (*pl* narcissi) *n* narcisse *m*

narcotic [naːˈkɒtɪk] *n* (*drug*) stupéfiant *m*; (*MED*) narcotique *m*

narrative ['nærətɪv] *n* récit *m*

narrow ['nærəu] *adj* étroit(e); (*fig*) restreint(e), limité(e) ♦ *vi* (*road*) devenir plus étroit, se rétrécir; (*gap, difference*) se réduire; to have a ~ escape l'échapper belle; to ~ sth down to réduire qch à; **~ly** adv: he **~ly missed injury/the tree** il a failli se blesser/rentrer dans l'arbre; **~minded** adj à l'esprit étroit, borné(e); (attitude) borné

nasty ['nɑːstɪ] adj (person: malicious) méchant(e); (: rude) très désagréable; (smell) dégoûtant(e); (wound, situation, disease) mauvais(e)

nation ['neɪʃən] n nation f

national ['næʃənl] adj national(e) ♦ n (abroad) ressortissant(e); (when home) national(e); **~ dress** n costume national; **N~ Health Service** (BRIT) n service national de santé, ≈ Sécurité Sociale; **N~ Insurance** (BRIT) n ≈ Sécurité Sociale; **~ism** ['næʃnəlɪzəm] n nationalisme m; **~ist** ['næʃnəlɪst] adj nationaliste ♦ n nationaliste m/f; **~ity** [næʃə'nælɪtɪ] n nationalité f; **~ize** vt nationaliser; **~ly** adv (as a nation) du point de vue national; (nationwide) dans le pays entier

nationwide ['neɪʃənwaɪd] adj s'étendant à l'ensemble du pays; (problem) à l'échelle du pays entier ♦ adv à travers ou dans tout le pays

native ['neɪtɪv] n autochtone m/f, habitant(e) du pays ♦ adj du pays, indigène; (country) natal(e); (ability) inné(e); **a ~ of Russia** une personne originaire de Russie; **a ~ speaker of French** une personne de langue maternelle française; **~ language** n langue maternelle

NATO ['neɪtəʊ] n abbr (= North Atlantic Treaty Organization) OTAN f

natural ['nætʃrəl] adj naturel(le); **gas** n gaz naturel; **~ize** vt naturaliser; (plant) acclimater; **to become ~ized** (person) se faire naturaliser; **~ly** adv naturellement

nature ['neɪtʃə*] n nature f; **by ~** par tempérament, de nature

naught [nɔːt] n = nought

naughty ['nɔːtɪ] adj (child) vilain(e), pas sage

nausea ['nɔːsɪə] n nausée f; **~te**

['nɔːsɪeɪt] vt écœurer, donner la nausée à

naval ['neɪvl] adj naval(e); **~ officer** n officier m de marine

nave [neɪv] n nef f

navel ['neɪvl] n nombril m

navigate ['nævɪgeɪt] vt (steer) diriger; (plot course) naviguer ♦ vi naviguer; **navigation** [nævɪ'geɪʃən] n navigation f

navvy ['nævɪ] (BRIT) n terrassier m

navy ['neɪvɪ] n marine f; **~(-blue)** adj bleu marine inv

Nazi ['nɑːtsɪ] n Nazi(e)

NB abbr (= nota bene) NB

near [nɪə*] adj proche ♦ adv près ♦ prep (also: **~ to**) près de ♦ vt approcher de; **~by** adj proche ♦ adv tout près, à proximité; **~ly** adv presque, près; **I ~ly fell** j'ai failli tomber; **~ miss** n (AVIAT) quasi-collision f; **that was a ~ miss** (gen) il s'en est fallu de peu; (of shot) c'est passé très près; **~side** n (AUT: BRIT) côté m gauche; (in US, Europe) côté droit; **~-sighted** adj myope

neat [niːt] adj (person, work) soigné(e); (room etc) bien tenu(e) or rangé(e); (skilful) habile; (spirits) pur(e); **~ly** adv avec soin or ordre; habilement

necessarily ['nesɪsrɪlɪ] adv nécessairement

necessary ['nesɪsərɪ] adj nécessaire

necessity [nɪ'sesɪtɪ] n nécessité f; (thing needed) chose nécessaire or essentielle; **necessities** npl nécessaire m

neck [nek] n cou m; (of animal, garment) encolure f; (of bottle) goulot m ♦ vi (inf) se peloter; **~ and ~** à égalité; **~lace** ['neklɪs] n collier m; **~line** n encolure f; **~tie** n cravate f

need [niːd] n besoin m ♦ vt avoir besoin de; **to ~ to do** devoir faire; avoir besoin de faire; **you don't ~ to go** vous n'avez pas besoin ou n'êtes pas obligé de partir

needle ['niːdl] n aiguille f ♦ vt asticoter, tourmenter

needless ['niːdlɪs] adj inutile

needlework ['niːdlwɜːk] n (activity) travaux mpl d'aiguille; (object(s)) ouvrage m

needn't ['niːdnt] = need not

needy ['niːdɪ] adj nécessiteux(euse)

negative ['negətɪv] n (PHOT, ELEC) négatif m; (LING) terme m de négation ♦ adj négatif(ive)

neglect [nɪ'glekt] vt négliger ♦ n (of person, duty, garden) le fait de négliger; (state of ~) abandon m

negligee ['neglɪʒeɪ] n déshabillé m

negotiate [nɪ'gəuʃɪeɪt] vi, vt négocier; **negotiation** [nɪgəuʃɪ'eɪʃən] n négociation f, pourparlers mpl

Negro ['niːgrəu] (!; pl ~es) n Noir(e)

neigh [neɪ] vi hennir

neighbour ['neɪbə*] (US neighbor) n voisin(e); **~hood** n (place) quartier m; (people) voisinage m; **~ing** adj voisin(e), avoisinant(e); **~ly** adj obligeant(e); (action etc) amical(e)

neither ['naɪðə*] adj, pron aucun(e) (des deux), ni l'un(e) ni l'autre ♦ conj: **I didn't move and ~ did Claude** je n'ai pas bougé, (et) Claude non plus; ..., ~ **did I refuse** ..., (et or mais) je n'ai pas non plus refusé ... ♦ adv: ~ **good nor bad** ni bon ni mauvais

neon [niːɔn] n néon m; ~ **light** n lampe f au néon

nephew ['nefjuː] n neveu m

nerve [nɜːv] n nerf m; (fig: courage) sang-froid m, courage m; (: impudence) aplomb m, toupet m; **to have a fit of ~s** avoir le trac; **~-racking** adj angoissant(e)

nervous ['nɜːvəs] adj nerveux(euse); (anxious) inquiet(ète), plein(e) d'appréhension; (timid) intimidé(e); **~ breakdown** n dépression nerveuse

nest [nest] n nid m ♦ vi (se) nicher, faire son nid; ~ **egg** n (fig) bas m de laine, magot m

nestle ['nesl] vi se blottir

net [net] n filet m ♦ adj net(te) ♦ vt (fish etc) prendre au filet; (profit)

rapporter; **~ball** n netball m; ~ **curtains** npl voilages mpl

Netherlands ['neðələndz] npl: **the ~** les Pays-Bas mpl

nett [net] adj = net

netting ['netɪŋ] n (for fence etc) treillis m, grillage m

nettle ['netl] n ortie f

network ['netwɜːk] n réseau m

neurotic [njuə'rɔtɪk] adj, n névrosé(e)

neuter ['njuːtə*] adj neutre ♦ vt (cat etc) châtrer, couper

neutral ['njuːtrəl] adj neutre ♦ n (AUT) point mort; **~ize** vt neutraliser

never ['nevə*] adv (ne ...) jamais; ~ **again** plus jamais; ~ **in my life** jamais de ma vie; see also **mind**; **~-ending** adj interminable; **~theless** [nevəðə'les] adv néanmoins, malgré tout

new [njuː] adj nouveau(nouvelle); (brand new) neuf(neuve); **~born** adj nouveau-né(e); **~comer** ['njuːkʌmə*] n nouveau venu/nouvelle venue; **~fangled** (pej) adj ultramoderne (et farfelu(e)); **~found** adj (enthusiasm) de fraîche date; (friend) nouveau(nouvelle); **~ly** adv nouvellement, récemment; **~ly-weds** npl jeunes mariés mpl

news [njuːz] n nouvelle(s) f(pl); (RADIO, TV) informations fpl, actualités fpl; **a piece of ~** une nouvelle; **~ agency** n agence f de presse; **~agent** (BRIT) n marchand m de journaux; **~caster** n présentateur(trice); **~dealer** (US) n = newsagent; **~ flash** n flash m d'information; **~letter** n bulletin m; **~paper** n journal m; **~print** n papier m (de journal; **~reader** n = newscaster; **~reel** n actualités (filmées); **~ stand** n kiosque m à journaux

newt [njuːt] n triton m

New Year n Nouvel An; **~'s Day** n le jour de l'An; **~'s Eve** n la Saint-Sylvestre

New Zealand [-'ziːlənd] n la

Nouvelle-Zélande; ~**er** n Néo-zélandais(e)

next [nekst] adj (seat, room) voisin(e), d'à côté; (meeting, bus stop) suivant(e); (in time) prochain(e) ♦ adv (place) à côté; (time) la fois suivante, la prochaine fois; (afterwards) ensuite; the ~ day le lendemain, le jour suivant or d'après; ~ year l'année prochaine; ~ time adv la prochaine fois; ~ to à côté de; ~ to nothing presque rien; ~, please! (at doctor's) au suivant!; ~ **door** adv à côté ♦ adj d'à côté; ~**-of-kin** n parent m le plus proche

NHS n abbr = **National Health Service**

nib [nɪb] n (bec m de) plume f

nibble ['nɪbl] vt grignoter

nice [naɪs] adj (pleasant, likeable) agréable; (pretty) joli(e); (kind) gentil(le); ~**ly** adv agréablement; joliment; gentiment

niceties ['naɪsɪtɪz] npl subtilités fpl

nick [nɪk] n (indentation) encoche f; (wound) entaille f ♦ vt (BRIT: inf) faucher, piquer; **in the ~ of time** juste à temps

nickel ['nɪkl] n nickel m; (US) pièce f de 5 cents

nickname ['nɪkneɪm] n surnom m ♦ vt surnommer

niece [niːs] n nièce f

Nigeria [naɪ'dʒɪərɪə] n Nigéria m or f

niggling ['nɪglɪŋ] adj (person) tatillon(ne); (detail) insignifiant(e); (doubts, injury) persistant(e)

night [naɪt] n nuit f; (evening) soir m; **at** ~ la nuit; **by** ~ de nuit; **the** ~ **before last** avant-hier soir; ~**cap** n boisson prise avant le coucher; ~**club** n boîte f de nuit; ~**dress** n chemise f de nuit; ~**fall** n tombée f de la nuit; ~**gown** n chemise f de nuit; ~**ie** ['naɪtɪ] n chemise f de nuit; ~**ingale** ['naɪtɪŋgeɪl] n rossignol m; ~**life** n vie f nocturne; ~**ly** ['naɪtlɪ] adj de chaque nuit or soir; (by night) nocturne ♦ adv chaque nuit or soir; ~**mare**

['naɪtmeə*] n cauchemar m; ~ **porter** n gardien m de nuit, concierge m de service la nuit; ~ **school** n cours mpl du soir; ~ **shift** n équipe f de nuit; ~**time** n nuit f; ~ **watchman** n veilleur m de nuit, gardien m de nuit

nil [nɪl] n rien m; (BRIT: SPORT) zéro m

Nile [naɪl] n: **the** ~ le Nil

nimble ['nɪmbl] adj agile

nine [naɪn] num neuf; ~**teen** num dix-neuf; ~**ty** num quatre-vingt-dix

ninth [naɪnθ] num neuvième

nip [nɪp] vt pincer

nipple ['nɪpl] n (ANAT) mamelon m, bout m du sein

nitrogen ['naɪtrədʒən] n azote m

KEYWORD

no [nəʊ] (pl ~**es**) adv (opposite of "yes") non; **are you coming?** - ~ (**I'm not**) est-ce que vous venez? - non; **would you like some more?** - ~ **thank you** non je vous en voulez encore?, - non merci

♦ adj (not any) pas de, aucun(e) (used with "ne"); **I have no money/books** je n'ai pas d'argent/de livres; ~ **student would have done it** aucun étudiant ne l'aurait fait; "~ **smoking**" "défense de fumer"; "~ **dogs**" "les chiens ne sont pas admis"

♦ n non m

---

nobility [nəʊ'bɪlɪtɪ] n noblesse f

noble ['nəʊbl] adj noble

nobody ['nəʊbədɪ] pron personne

nod [nɒd] vi faire un signe de tête (affirmatif ou amical); (sleep) somnoler ♦ vt: **to ~ one's head** faire un signe de (la) tête; (in agreement) faire signe que oui ♦ n signe m de (la) tête; ~ **off** vi s'assoupir

noise [nɔɪz] n bruit m; **noisy** ['nɔɪzɪ] adj bruyant(e)

nominal ['nɒmɪnl] adj (rent, leader) symbolique

nominate ['nɒmɪneɪt] vt (propose) proposer; (appoint) nommer; **nomi-**

nee [nɔmiˈniː] n candidat agréé; personne nommée

non... prefix non-; **~-alcoholic** adj non-alcoolisé(e); **~-committal** adj évasif(ive)

nondescript [ˈnɔndɪskrɪpt] adj quelconque, indéfinissable

none [nʌn] pron aucun(e); **~ of** you aucun d'entre vous, personne parmi vous; **I've ~** left je n'en ai plus; **he's ~** the worse for it il ne s'en porte pas plus mal

nonentity [nɔˈnentɪtɪ] n personne insignifiante

nonetheless [ˈnʌnðəˈles] adv néanmoins

non-existent [nɔnɪgˈzɪstənt] adj inexistant(e)

non-fiction [nɔnˈfɪkʃən] n littérature f non-romanesque

nonplussed [ˈnɔnˈplʌst] adj perplexe

nonsense [ˈnɔnsəns] n absurdités fpl, idioties fpl; **~!** ne dites pas d'idioties!

non: **~-smoker** n non-fumeur m; **~-stick** adj qui n'attache pas; **~-stop** adj direct(e), sans arrêt (or escale) ♦ adv sans arrêt

noodles [ˈnuːdlz] npl nouilles fpl

nook [nuk] n: **~s and crannies** recoins mpl

noon [nuːn] n midi m

no one [ˈnəuwʌn] pron = **nobody**

noose [nuːs] n nœud coulant; (hangman's) corde f

nor [nɔː*] conj = **neither** ♦ adv = **neither**

norm [nɔːm] n norme f

normal [ˈnɔːməl] adj normal(e); **~ly** adv normalement

Normandy [ˈnɔːməndɪ] n Normandie f

north [nɔːθ] n nord m ♦ adj du nord, nord inv ♦ adv au or vers le nord; **N~ America** n Amérique f du Nord; **~-east** n nord-est m; **~erly** [ˈnɔːðəlɪ] adj du nord; **~ern** [ˈnɔːðən] adj du nord, septentrional(e); **N~ern Ireland** n Irlande f du Nord; **N~ Pole** n

pôle m Nord; **N~ Sea** n mer f du Nord; **~ward(s)** [ˈnɔːθwəd(z)] adv vers le nord; **~-west** n nord-ouest m

Norway [ˈnɔːweɪ] n Norvège f

Norwegian [nɔːˈwiːdʒən] adj norvégien(ne) ♦ n Norvégien(ne); (LING) norvégien m

nose [nəuz] n nez m; **~ about, around** vi fouiner or fureter (partout); **~bleed** n saignement m du nez; **~-dive** n (descente f en) piqué m; **~y** (inf) adj = **nosy**

nostalgia [nɔsˈtældʒɪə] n nostalgie f

nostril [ˈnɔstrɪl] n narine f; (of horse) naseau m

nosy [ˈnəuzɪ] (inf) adj curieux(euse)

not [nɔt] adv (ne ...) pas; **he is ~** isn't here il n'est pas ici; **you must ~ or** you mustn't do that tu ne dois pas faire ça; **it's too late, isn't it or is it ~?** c'est trop tard, n'est-ce pas?; **~ yet/now** pas encore/maintenant; **~ at all** pas du tout; see also **all; only**

notably [ˈnəutəblɪ] adv (particularly) en particulier; (markedly) spécialement

notary [ˈnəutərɪ] n notaire m

notch [nɔtʃ] n encoche f

note [nəut] n note f; (letter) mot m; (banknote) billet m ♦ vt (also: **~ down**) noter; (observe) constater; **~book** n carnet m; **~d** [ˈnəutɪd] adj réputé(e); **~pad** n bloc-notes m; **~paper** n papier m à lettres

nothing [ˈnʌθɪŋ] n rien m; **he does ~** il ne fait rien; **~ new** rien de nouveau; **for ~** pour rien

notice [ˈnəutɪs] n (announcement, warning) avis m; (period of time) délai m; (resignation) démission f; (dismissal) congé m ♦ vt remarquer, s'apercevoir de; **to take ~ of** prêter attention à; **to bring sth to sb's ~** porter qch à la connaissance de qn; **at short ~** dans un délai très court; **until further ~** jusqu'à nouvel ordre; **to hand in one's ~** donner sa démission, démissionner; **~able** adj visible; **~ board** (BRIT) n panneau *m* d'affichage

notify ['nəʊtɪfaɪ] *vt*: to ~ sth to sb notifier qch à qn; to ~ sb (of sth) avertir qn (de qch)

notion ['nəʊʃən] *n* idée *f*; (*concept*) notion *f*

notorious [nəʊ'tɔːrɪəs] *adj* notoire (*souvent en mal*)

notwithstanding [nɒtwɪθ'stændɪŋ] *adv* néanmoins ♦ *prep* en dépit de

nought [nɔːt] *n* zéro *m*

noun [naʊn] *n* nom *m*

nourish ['nʌrɪʃ] *vt* nourrir; ~**ing** *adj* nourrissant(e); ~**ment** *n* nourriture *f*

novel ['nɒvl] *n* roman *m* ♦ *adj* nouveau(nouvelle), original(e); ~**ist** *n* romancier *m*; ~**ty** *n* nouveauté *f*

November [nəʊ'vembə*] *n* novembre *m*

now [naʊ] *adv* maintenant ♦ *conj*: ~ (that) maintenant que; right ~ tout de suite; by ~ à l'heure qu'il est; just ~: that's the fashion just ~ c'est la mode en ce moment; ~ and then, ~ and again de temps en temps; from ~ on dorénavant; ~**adays** ['naʊədeɪz] *adv* de nos jours

nowhere ['nəʊwεə*] *adv* nulle part

nozzle ['nɒzl] *n* (*of hose etc*) ajutage *m*; (*of vacuum cleaner*) suceur *m*

nuclear ['njuːklɪə*] *adj* nucléaire

nucleus ['njuːklɪəs, *pl* 'njuːklɪaɪ] (*pl* nuclei) *n* noyau *m*

nude [njuːd] *adj* nu(e) ♦ *n* nu *m*; in the ~ (tout(e)) nu(e)

nudge [nʌdʒ] *vt* donner un (petit) coup de coude à

nudist ['njuːdɪst] *n* nudiste *m/f*

nuisance ['njuːsns] *n*: it's a ~ c'est (très) embêtant; he's a ~ il est assommant *or* casse-pieds; what a ~! quelle barbe!

null [nʌl] *adj*: ~ and void nul(le) et non avenu(e)

numb [nʌm] *adj* engourdi(e); (*with fear*) paralysé(e)

number ['nʌmbə*] *n* nombre *m*; (*numeral*) chiffre *m*; (*of house, bank account etc*) numéro *m* ♦ *vt* numéroter; (*amount to*) compter; a ~ of un

certain nombre de; to be ~ed among compter parmi; they were seven in ~ ils étaient (au nombre de) sept; ~ **plate** *n* (AUT) plaque *f* minéralogique *or* d'immatriculation

numeral ['njuːmərəl] *n* chiffre *m*

numerate ['njuːmərɪt] (BRIT) *adj*: to be ~ avoir les notions d'arithmétique

numerical [njuː'merɪkəl] *adj* numérique

numerous ['njuːmərəs] *adj* nombreux(euse)

nun [nʌn] *n* religieuse *f*, sœur *f*

nurse [nɜːs] *n* infirmière *f* ♦ *vt* (*patient, cold*) soigner

nursery ['nɜːsəri] *n* (*room*) nursery *f*; (*institution*) crèche *f*; (*for plants*) pépinière *f*; ~ **rhyme** *n* comptine *f*, chansonnette *f* pour enfants; ~ **school** *n* école maternelle; ~ **slope** *n* (SKI) piste *f* pour débutants

nursing ['nɜːsɪŋ] *n* (*profession*) profession *f* d'infirmière; (*care*) soins *mpl*; ~ **home** *n* clinique *f*; maison *f* de convalescence; ~ **mother** *n* mère *f* qui allaite

nut [nʌt] *n* (*of metal*) écrou *m*; (*fruit*) noix *f*, noisette *f*; cacahuète *f*; ~**crackers** ['nʌtkrækəz] *npl* casse-noix *m inv*, casse-noisette(s) *m*

nutmeg ['nʌtmeg] *n* (noix *f*) muscade *f*

nutritious [njuː'trɪʃəs] *adj* nutritif(ive), nourrissant(e)

nuts (*inf*) *adj* dingue

nutshell ['nʌtʃel] *n*: in a ~ en un mot

nylon ['naɪlɒn] *n* nylon *m* ♦ *adj* de *or* en nylon

O

oak [əʊk] *n* chêne *m* ♦ *adj* de *or* en chêne

OAP (BRIT) *n abbr* = **old-age pensioner**

oar [ɔː*] *n* aviron *m*, rame *f*

oasis [əʊ'eɪsɪs, *pl* əʊ'eɪsiːz] (*pl* oa-

ses) n oasis f

oath [əʊθ] n serment m; (swear word) juron m; **under ~,** (BRIT) on ~ sous serment

oatmeal ['əʊtmiːl] n flocons mpl d'avoine

oats [əʊts] n avoine f

obedience [ə'biːdɪəns] n obéissance f; **obedient** [ə'biːdɪənt] adj obéissant(e)

obey [ə'beɪ] vt obéir à; (instructions) se conformer à

obituary [ə'bɪtjʊərɪ] n nécrologie f

object [n 'ɒbdʒɪkt, vb əb'dʒekt] n objet m; (purpose) but m, objet; (LING) complément m d'objet ♦ vi: **to ~ to** (attitude) désapprouver; (proposal) protester contre; **expense is no ~** l'argent n'est pas un problème; **he ~ed that ...** il a fait valoir or a objecté que ...; **I ~!** je proteste!; **~ion** [əb'dʒekʃən] n objection f; **~ionable** [əb'dʒekʃnəbl] adj très désagréable; (language) choquant(e); **~ive** [əb'dʒektɪv] n objectif m ♦ adj objectif(ive)

obligation [ɒblɪ'geɪʃən] n obligation f, devoir m; **without ~** sans engagement

oblige [ə'blaɪdʒ] vt (force): **to ~ sb to do** obliger or forcer qn à faire; (do a favour) rendre service à, obliger; **to be ~d to sb for sth** être obligé(e) à qn de qch; **obliging** [ə'blaɪdʒɪŋ] adj obligeant(e), serviable

oblique [ə'bliːk] adj oblique; (allusion) indirect(e)

obliterate [ə'blɪtəreɪt] vt effacer

oblivion [ə'blɪvɪən] n oubli m; **oblivious** [ə'blɪvɪəs] adj: **oblivious of** oublieux(euse) de

oblong ['ɒblɒŋ] adj oblong(ue) ♦ n rectangle m

obnoxious [əb'nɒkʃəs] adj odieux (euse); (smell) nauséabond(e)

oboe ['əʊbəʊ] n hautbois m

obscene [əb'siːn] adj obscène

obscure [əb'skjʊə*] adj obscur(e) ♦ vt obscurcir; (hide: sun) cacher

observant [əb'zɜːvənt] adj observateur(trice)

observation [ɒbzə'veɪʃən] n (remark) observation f; (watching) surveillance f; **observatory** [əb'zɜːvətrɪ] n observatoire m

observe [əb'zɜːv] vt observer; (remark) faire observer or remarquer; **~r** n observateur(trice)

obsess [əb'ses] vt obséder; **~ive** adj obsédant(e)

obsolescence [ɒbsə'lesns] n vieillissement m

obsolete ['ɒbsəliːt] adj dépassé(e); démodé(e)

obstacle ['ɒbstəkl] n obstacle m; **~ race** n course f d'obstacles

obstinate ['ɒbstɪnət] adj obstiné(e)

obstruct [əb'strʌkt] vt (block) boucher, obstruer; (hinder) entraver

obtain [əb'teɪn] vt obtenir; **~able** adj qu'on peut obtenir

obvious ['ɒbvɪəs] adj évident(e), manifeste; **~ly** adv manifestement; **~ly not!** bien sûr que non!

occasion [ə'keɪʒən] n occasion f; (event) événement m; **~al** adj pris(e) or fait(e) etc de temps en temps; occasionnel(le); **~ally** adv de temps en temps, quelquefois

occupation [ɒkjʊ'peɪʃən] n occupation f; (job) métier m, profession f; **~al hazard** n risque m du métier

occupier ['ɒkjʊpaɪə*] n occupant(e)

occupy ['ɒkjʊpaɪ] vt occuper; **to ~ o.s. with** or **by doing** s'occuper à faire

occur [ə'kɜː*] vi (event) se produire; (phenomenon, error) se rencontrer; **to ~ to sb** venir à l'esprit de qn; **~rence** n (existence) présence f, existence f; (event) cas m, fait m

ocean ['əʊʃən] n océan m; **~-going** adj de haute mer

o'clock [ə'klɒk] adv: **it is 5 ~** il est 5 heures

OCR n abbr = optical character reader; optical character recognition

October [ɒk'təʊbə*] n octobre m

octopus ['ɔktəpəs] n pieuvre f

odd [ɔd] adj (strange) bizarre, curieux(euse); (number) impair(e); (not of a set) dépareillé(e); **60-odd** 60 et quelques; **at ~ times** de temps en temps; **the ~ one out** l'exception f; **~ity** n (person) excentrique m/f; (thing) curiosité f; **~-job man** n homme à tout faire; **~ jobs** npl petits travaux divers; **~ly** adv bizarrement, curieusement; **~ments** npl (COMM) fins fpl de série; **~s** npl (in betting) cote f; **it makes no ~s** cela n'a pas d'importance; **at ~s** en désaccord; **~s and ends** npl petites choses

odour ['əʊdə*] (US **odor**) n odeur f

of [ɔv, əv] prep 1 (gen) de; **a friend ~ ours** un de nos amis; **a boy ~ 10** un garçon de 10 ans; **that was kind ~ you** c'était gentil de votre part
2 (expressing quantity, amount, dates etc) de; **a kilo ~ flour** un kilo de farine; **how much ~ this do you need?** combien vous en faut-il?; **there were 3 ~ them** (people) ils étaient 3; (objects) il y en avait 3; **3 ~ us went** 3 d'entre nous sont allé(e)s; **the 5th ~ July** le 5 juillet
3 (from, out of) en, de; **a statue ~ marble** une statue de or en marbre; **made ~ wood** (fait) en bois

off [ɔf] adj, adv (engine) coupé(e); (tap) fermé(e); (BRIT: food: bad) mauvais(e); (: milk) tourné(e); (absent) absent(e); (cancelled) annulé(e) ♦ prep de; sur; **to be ~** (to leave) partir, s'en aller; **to be ~ sick** être absent pour cause de maladie; **a day ~** un jour de congé; **to have an ~ day** n'être pas dans son assiette; **he had his coat ~** il avait enlevé son manteau; **10% ~** (COMM) 10% de rabais; **~ the coast** au large de la côte; **I'm ~ meat** je ne mange plus de viande, je n'aime plus la viande; **on the ~ chance** à tout ha-

sard

offal ['ɔfəl] n (CULIN) abats mpl

off-colour ['ɔf'kʌlə*] (BRIT) adj (ill) malade, mal fichu(e)

offence [ə'fɛns] (US **offense**) n (crime) délit m, infraction f; **to take ~ at** se vexer de, s'offenser de

offend [ə'fɛnd] vt (person) offenser, blesser; **~er** n délinquant e

offense [ə'fɛns] (US) n = **offence**

offensive [ə'fɛnsɪv] adj offensant(e), choquant(e); (smell etc) très déplaisant(e); (weapon) offensif(ive) ♦ n (MIL) offensive f

offer ['ɔfə*] n offre f, proposition f ♦ vt offrir, proposer; **"on ~"** (COMM) "en promotion"; **~ing** n offrande f

offhand ['ɔf'hænd] adj désinvolte ♦ adv spontanément

office ['ɔfɪs] n (place, room) bureau m; (position) charge f, fonction f; **doctor's ~** (US) cabinet (médical); **to take ~** entrer en fonctions; **~ automation** n bureautique f; **~ block** (US ~ **building**) n immeuble m de bureaux; **~ hours** npl heures fpl de bureau; (US: MED) heures de consultation

officer ['ɔfɪsə*] n (MIL etc) officier m; (also: **police ~**) agent m (de police); (of organization) membre m du bureau directeur

office worker n employé(e) de bureau

official [ə'fɪʃəl] adj officiel(le) ♦ n officiel m; (civil servant) fonctionnaire m/f; employé(e); **~dom** n administration f, bureaucratie f

officiate [ə'fɪʃɪeɪt] vi (REL) officier; **to ~ at a marriage** célébrer un mariage

officious [ə'fɪʃəs] adj trop empressé(e)

offing ['ɔfɪŋ] n: **in the ~** (fig) en perspective

off: **~-licence** n (BRIT) (shop) débit m de vins et de spiritueux; **~-line** adj, adv (COMPUT) en autonome; (: switched off) non connecté(e); **~-peak** adj aux heures creuses; (electricity, heating, ticket) au tarif heures creuses; ~**-putting** (BRIT) adj (remark) rébarbatif(ive); (person) rebutant(e), peu engageant(e); ~**-season** n adv hors-saison inv

offset ['ɔfset] (irreg) vt (counteract) contrebalancer, compenser

offshoot ['ɔfʃuːt] n (fig) ramification f, antenne f

offshore [ɔf'ʃɔː*] adj (breeze) de terre; (fishing) côtier(ère)

offside [ɔf'saɪd] adj (SPORT) hors jeu; (AUT: with right-hand drive) de droite; (: with left-hand drive) de gauche

offspring ['ɔfsprɪŋ] n inv progéniture f

off: ~**stage** adv dans les coulisses; ~**-the-peg** (US ~**-the-rack**) adv en prêt-à-porter; ~**-white** adj blanc cassé inv

often ['ɔfən] adv souvent; how ~ do you go? vous y allez tous les combien?; how ~ have you gone there? vous y êtes allé combien de fois?

ogle ['əʊgl] vt lorgner

oh [əʊ] excl ô!, oh!, ah!

oil [ɔɪl] n huile f; (petroleum) pétrole m; (for central heating) mazout m ♦ vt (machine) graisser; ~**can** n burette f de graissage; (for storing) bidon m à huile; ~**field** n gisement m de pétrole; ~**filter** n (AUT) filtre m à huile; ~**painting** n peinture f à l'huile; ~**refinery** n raffinerie f; ~**rig** n derrick m; (at sea) plate-forme pétrolière; ~**skins** npl ciré m; ~**tanker** n (ship) pétrolier m; (truck) camion-citerne m; ~**well** n puits m de pétrole; ~**y** adj huileux(euse); (food) gras(se)

ointment ['ɔɪntmənt] n onguent m

O.K., okay ['əʊ'keɪ] excl d'accord! ♦ adj (average) pas mal ♦ vt approuver, donner son accord à; is it ~?, are you ~? ça va?

old [əʊld] adj vieux(vieille); (person) vieux, âgé(e); (former) ancien(ne), vieux; how ~ are you? quel âge avez-

vous?; he's 10 years ~ il a 10 ans, il est âgé de 10 ans; ~**er brother/sister** frère/sœur aîné(e); ~**age** n vieillesse f; ~**age pensioner** (BRIT) n retraité(e); ~**-fashioned** adj démodé(e); (person) vieux jeu inv

olive ['ɔlɪv] n (fruit) olive f; (tree) olivier m ♦ adj (also: ~**-green**) (vert) olive inv; ~ **oil** n huile f d'olive

Olympic [əʊ'lɪmpɪk] adj olympique; the ~ **Games, the** ~**s** les Jeux mpl olympiques

omelet(te) ['ɔmlɪt] n omelette f

omen ['əʊmən] n présage m.

ominous ['ɔmɪnəs] adj menaçant(e), inquiétant(e); (event) de mauvais augure

omit [əʊ'mɪt] vt omettre; **to** ~ **to do** omettre de faire

---

KEYWORD

on [ɔn] prep 1 (indicating position) sur; ~ **the table** sur la table; ~ **the wall** sur le or au mur; ~ **the left** à gauche

2 (indicating means, method, condition etc): ~ **foot** à pied; ~ **the train/plane** (be) dans le train/ l'avion; (go) en train/avion; ~ **the telephone/radio/television** au téléphone/à la radio/à la television; **to be** ~ **drugs** se droguer; ~ **holiday** en vacances

3 (referring to time): ~ **Friday** vendredi; ~ **Fridays** le vendredi; ~ **June 20th** le 20 juin; **a week** ~ **Friday** vendredi en huit; ~ **arrival** à l'arrivée; ~ **seeing this** en voyant cela

4 (about, concerning) sur, de; **a book** ~ **Balzac/physics** un livre sur Balzac/de physique

♦ adv 1 (referring to dress, covering): **to have one's coat** ~ avoir (mis) son manteau; **to put one's coat** ~ mettre son manteau; **what's she got** ~? qu'est-ce qu'elle porte?; **screw the lid** ~ **tightly** vissez bien le couvercle

2 (further, continuously): to walk etc ~ continuer à marcher etc; ~ and off de temps à autre

♦ adj **1** (in operation: machine) en marche; (: radio, TV, light) allumé(e); (: tap, gas) ouvert(e); (: brakes) mise(e); **is the meeting still ~?** (not cancelled) est-ce que la réunion a bien lieu?; (in progress) la réunion dure-t-elle encore?; **when is this film ~?** quand passe ce film?

2 (inf): that's not ~! (not acceptable) cela ne se fait pas!; (not possible) pas question!

once [wʌns] adv une fois; (formerly) autrefois ♦ conj une fois que; ~ **he had left/it was done** une fois qu'il fut parti/que ce fut terminé; **at ~** tout de suite, immédiatement; (simultaneously) à la fois; ~ **a week** une fois par semaine; ~ **more** encore une fois; ~ **and for all** une fois pour toutes; ~ **upon a time** il y avait une fois, il était une fois

oncoming ['ɒnkʌmɪŋ] adj (traffic) venant en sens inverse

KEYWORD

one [wʌn] num un(e); ~ **hundred and fifty** cent cinquante; ~ **day** un jour

♦ adj **1** (sole) seul(e), unique; **the ~ book which** l'unique or le seul livre qui; **the ~ man who** le seul (homme) qui

2 (same) même; **they came in the ~ car** ils sont venus dans la même voiture

♦ pron **1**: **this ~** celui-ci(celle-ci); **that ~** celui-là(celle-là); **I've already got ~/a red ~** j'en ai déjà un(e)/un(e) rouge; ~ **by ~** un(e) à or par un(e)

2: ~ **another** l'un(e) l'autre; **to look at ~ another** se regarder

3 (impersonal) on; ~ **never knows** on ne sait jamais; **to cut ~'s finger** se couper le doigt

one: ~**-day excursion** (US) n billet m d'aller-retour (valable pour la journée); ~**-man** (business) dirigé(e) etc par un seul homme; ~**-man band** n homme-orchestre m; ~**-off** (BRIT: inf) n exemplaire m unique

oneself [wʌn'self] pron (reflexive) se; (after prep) soi(-même); (emphatic) soi-même; **to hurt ~** se faire mal; **to keep sth for ~** garder qch pour soi; **to talk to ~** se parler à soi-même

one: ~**-sided** adj (argument) unilatéral; ~**-to-~** adj (relationship) univoque; ~**-upmanship** n: **the art of ~** l'art de faire mieux que les autres; ~**-way** adj (street, traffic) à sens unique

ongoing ['ɒngəʊɪŋ] adj en cours; (relationship) suivi(e)

onion ['ʌnjən] n oignon m

on-line ['ɒn'laɪn] adj, adv (COMPUT) en ligne; (: switched on) connecté(e)

onlooker ['ɒnlʊkə*] n spectateur (trice)

only ['əʊnlɪ] adv seulement ♦ adj seul(e), unique ♦ conj seulement, mais; **an ~ child** un enfant unique; **not ~ ... but also** non seulement ... mais aussi

onset ['ɒnset] n début m; (of winter, old age) approche f

onshore ['ɒnʃɔː*] adj (wind) du large

onslaught ['ɒnslɔːt] n attaque f, assaut m

onto ['ɒntʊ] prep = **on to**

onus ['əʊnəs] n responsabilité f

onward(s) ['ɒnwəd(z)] adv (move) en avant; **from that time ~** à partir de ce moment

ooze [uːz] vi suinter

opaque [əʊ'peɪk] adj opaque

OPEC ['əʊpek] n abbr (= Organization of Petroleum Exporting Countries) O.P.E.P. f

open ['əʊpən] adj ouvert(e); (car) découvert(e); (road, view) déga-

opera géé(e); (*meeting*) public(ique); (*admiration*) manifeste ♦ *vt* ouvrir ♦ *vi* (*flower, eyes, door, debate*) s'ouvrir; (*shop, bank, museum*) ouvrir; (*book etc: commence*) commencer, débuter; **in the ~** (*air*) en plein air; **~ on to** *vt fus* (*subj: room, door*) donner sur; **~ up** *vt* ouvrir; (*blocked road*) dégager ♦ *vi* s'ouvrir; **~ing** *n* ouverture *f*; (*opportunity*) occasion *f* ♦ *adj* (*remarks*) préliminaire; **~ly** *adv* ouvertement; **~-minded** *adj* à l'esprit ouvert; **~-necked** *adj* à col ouvert; **~-plan** *adj* sans cloisons

opera ['ɒpərə] *n* opéra *m*; **~ singer** *n* chanteur(euse) d'opéra

operate ['ɒpəreɪt] *vt* (*machine*) faire marcher, faire fonctionner ♦ *vi* fonctionner; (*MED*): **to ~ (on sb)** opérer (qn)

operatic [ɒpə'rætɪk] *adj* d'opéra

operating ['ɒpəreɪtɪŋ]: **~-table** *n* table *f* d'opération; **~-theatre** *n* salle *f* d'opération

operation [ɒpə'reɪʃən] *n* opération *f*; (*of machine*) fonctionnement *m*; **to be in ~** (*system, law*) être en vigueur; **to have an ~** (*MED*) se faire opérer

operative ['ɒpərətɪv] *adj* (*measure*) en vigueur

operator ['ɒpəreɪtə*] *n* (*of machine*) opérateur(trice); (*TEL*) téléphoniste *m/f*

opinion [ə'pɪnjən] *n* opinion *f*, avis *m*; **in my ~** à mon avis; **~ated** *adj* aux idées bien arrêtées; **~ poll** *n* sondage *m* (d'opinion)

opponent [ə'pəunənt] *n* adversaire *m/f*

opportunity [ɒpə'tju:nɪtɪ] *n* occasion *f*; **to take the ~ of doing** profiter de l'occasion pour faire; en profiter pour faire

oppose [ə'pəuz] *vt* s'opposer à; **to ~d to** opposé(e) à; **as ~d to** par opposition à; **opposing** [ə'pəuzɪŋ] *adj* (*side*) opposé(e)

opposite ['ɒpəzɪt] *adj* (*house etc*) d'en face ♦ *adv* en face ♦ *prep* en face de ♦ *n* opposé *m*, contraire *m*; **the ~ sex** l'autre sexe, le sexe opposé

opposition [ɒpə'zɪʃən] *n* opposition *f*

oppress [ə'pres] *vt* opprimer

oppressive *adj* (*political regime*) oppressif(ive); (*weather*) lourd(e); (*heat*) accablant(e)

opt [ɒpt] *vi*: **to ~ for** opter pour; **to ~ to do** choisir de faire; **~ out** *vi*: **to ~ out of** choisir de ne pas participer à *or* de ne pas faire

optical ['ɒptɪkəl] *adj* optique; (*instrument*) d'optique; **~ character recognition/reader** *n* lecture *f*/lecteur *m* optique

optician [ɒp'tɪʃən] *n* opticien(ne)

optimist ['ɒptɪmɪst] *n* optimiste *m/f*; **~ic** *adj* optimiste

option ['ɒpʃən] *n* choix *m*, option *f*; (*SCOL*) matière *f* à option; (*COMM*) option; **~al** *adj* facultatif(ive); (*COMM*) en option

or [ɔː*] *conj* ou; (*with negative*): **he hasn't seen ~ heard anything** il n'a rien vu ni entendu; **~ else** sinon; ou bien

oral ['ɔːrəl] *adj* oral(e) ♦ *n* oral *m*

orange ['ɒrɪndʒ] *n* (*fruit*) orange *f* ♦ *adj* orange *inv*

orator ['ɒrətə*] *n* orateur/trice

orbit ['ɔːbɪt] *n* orbite *f* ♦ *vt* graviter autour de

orchard ['ɔːtʃəd] *n* verger *m*

orchestra ['ɔːkɪstrə] *n* orchestre *m*; (*US: seating*) (fauteuils *mpl* d')orchestre

orchid ['ɔːkɪd] *n* orchidée *f*

ordain [ɔː'deɪn] *vt* (*REL*) ordonner

ordeal [ɔː'diːl] *n* épreuve *f*

order ['ɔːdə*] *n* ordre *m*; (*COMM*) commande *f* ♦ *vt* ordonner; (*COMM*) commander; **in ~** en ordre; (*document*) en règle; **in (working) ~** en état de marche; **out of ~** (*not in correct order*) en désordre; (*not working*) en dérangement; **in ~ to do/that** pour faire/que **+sub**; **on ~** (*COMM*) en commande; **to ~ sb to do** ordonner à qn de faire; **~ form** *n* bon *m* de commande; **~ly** *n* (*MIL*)

ordonnance f; (MED) garçon m de salle ♦ adj (room) en ordre; (person) qui a de l'ordre

ordinary ['ɔːdnrɪ] adj ordinaire, normal(e); (pej) quelconque; out of the ~ exceptionnel(le)

Ordnance Survey map n = carte f d'État-Major

ore [ɔːʳ] n mineral m

organ ['ɔːgən] n organe m; (MUS) orgue m, orgues fpl; ~**ic** [ɔː'gænɪk] adj organique

organization [ɔːgənaɪ'zeɪʃən] n organisation f

organize ['ɔːgənaɪz] vt organiser; ~**r** n organisateur(trice)

orgasm ['ɔːgæzəm] n orgasme m

Orient ['ɔːrɪənt] n: the ~ l'Orient m; o~**al** [ɔːrɪ'entl] adj oriental(e)

origin ['ɒrɪdʒɪn] n origine f

original [ə'rɪdʒɪnl] adj original(e); (earliest) originel(le) ♦ n original m; ~**ly** adv (at first) à l'origine

originate [ə'rɪdʒɪneɪt] vi: to ~ from (person) être originaire de; (suggestion) provenir de; to ~ in prendre naissance dans; avoir son origine dans

Orkneys ['ɔːknɪz] npl: the ~ (also: the Orkney Islands) les Orcades fpl

ornament ['ɔːnəmənt] n ornement m; (trinket) bibelot m; ~**al** [ɔːnə'mentl] adj décoratif(ive); (garden) d'agrément

ornate [ɔː'neɪt] adj très orné(e)

orphan ['ɔːfən] n orphelin(e); ~**age** n orphelinat m

orthopaedic [ɔːθəʊ'piːdɪk] (US orthopedic) adj orthopédique

ostensibly [ɒs'tensəblɪ] adv en apparence

ostentatious [ɒsten'teɪʃəs] adj prétentieux(euse)

ostracize ['ɒstrəsaɪz] vt frapper d'ostracisme

ostrich ['ɒstrɪtʃ] n autruche f

other ['ʌðəʳ] adj autre ♦ pron: the ~ (one) l'autre m/f; ~**s** (~ people) d'autres; ~ **than** autrement que; à part; ~**wise** adv, conj autrement

otter ['ɒtəʳ] n loutre f

ouch [autʃ] excl aïe!

ought [ɔːt] (pt ought) aux vb: I ~ to do it je devrais le faire, il faudrait que je le fasse; this ~ to have been corrected cela aurait dû être corrigé; he ~ to win il devrait gagner

ounce [auns] n once f (= 28.35g; 16 in a pound)

our [auəʳ] adj notre, nos pl; see also my; ~**s** pron le(la) nôtre, les nôtres; see also mine; ~**selves** pron pl (reflexive, after preposition) nous; (emphatic) nous-mêmes; see also oneself

oust [aust] vt évincer

out [aut] adv dehors; (published, not at home etc) sorti(e); (light, fire) éteint(e); ~ **here** ici; ~ **there** là-bas; he's ~ (absent) il est sorti; (unconscious) il est sans connaissance; to be ~ **in one's calculations** s'être trompé dans ses calculs; to **run/back** etc ~ sortir en courant/en reculant etc; ~ **loud** à haute voix; ~ **of** (outside) en dehors de; (because of: anger etc) par; (from among): ~ **of** 10 sur 10; (without): ~ **of petrol** sans essence, à court d'essence; ~ **of order** (machine) en panne; (TEL: line) en dérangement; ~**and-out** adj (liar, thief etc) véritable

outback ['autbæk] n (in Australia): the ~ l'intérieur m

outboard ['autbɔːd] n (also: ~ motor) (moteur m) hors-bord m

outbreak ['autbreɪk] n (of war, disease) début m; (of violence) éruption f; ~**burst** ['autbɜːst] n explosion f, accès m; ~**cast** ['autkɑːst] n exilé(e); (socially) paria m; ~**come** ['autkʌm] n issue f, résultat m; ~**crop** ['autkrɒp] n (of rock) affleurement m; ~**cry** ['autkraɪ] n tollé (général); ~**dated** [aut'deɪtɪd] adj démodé(e); ~**do** [aut'duː] (irreg) vt surpasser

outdoor ['autdɔːʳ] adj de or en plein air; ~**s** adv dehors; au grand air

outer ['aʊtə*] adj extérieur(e); ~
space n espace m cosmique

outfit ['aʊtfɪt] n (clothes) tenue f

outgoing ['aʊtgəʊɪŋ] adj (character)
ouvert(e), extraverti(e); (retiring)
sortant(e); ~**s** (BRIT) npl (expenses) dépenses fpl

outgrow [aʊt'grəʊ] (irreg) vt
(clothes) devenir trop grand(e) pour

outhouse ['aʊthaʊs] n appentis m,
remise f

outing ['aʊtɪŋ] n sortie f; excursion f

outlandish [aʊt'lændɪʃ] adj étrange

outlaw ['aʊtlɔː] n hors-la-loi m inv ♦
vt mettre hors-la-loi

outlay ['aʊtleɪ] n dépenses fpl; (investment) mise f de fonds

outlet ['aʊtlet] n (for liquid etc) issue
f, sortie f; (US: ELEC) prise f de
courant; (also: retail ~) point m de
vente

outline ['aʊtlaɪn] n (shape) contour
m; (summary) esquisse f, grandes lignes f ♦ vt (fig: theory, plan) exposer
à grands traits

out: ~**live** [aʊt'lɪv] vt survivre à;
~**look** ['aʊtlʊk] n perspective f;
~**lying** ['aʊtlaɪŋ] adj écarté(e);
~**moded** [aʊt'məʊdɪd] adj démodé(e); dépassé(e); ~**number**
[aʊt'nʌmbə*] vt surpasser en nombre

out-of-date [aʊtəv'deɪt] adj (passport) périmé(e); (theory etc) dépassé(e); (clothes etc) démodé(e)

out-of-the-way [aʊtəvðə'weɪ] adj
(place) loin de tout

outpatient ['aʊtpeɪʃənt] n malade
m/f en consultation externe

outpost ['aʊtpəʊst] n avant-poste m

output ['aʊtpʊt] n rendement m, production f; (COMPUT) sortie f

outrage ['aʊtreɪdʒ] n (anger) indignation f; (violent act) atrocité f;
(scandal) scandale m ♦ vt outrager;
~**ous** [aʊt'reɪdʒəs] adj atroce; scandaleux(euse)

outright [adv aʊt'raɪt, adj 'aʊtraɪt]
adv complètement; (deny, refuse) catégoriquement; (ask) carrément;
(kill) sur le coup ♦ adj complet(ète);

catégorique

outset ['aʊtset] n début m

outside [aʊt'saɪd] n extérieur m ♦
adj extérieur(e) ♦ adv (au) dehors, à
l'extérieur ♦ prep hors de, à l'extérieur de; **at the ~** (fig) au plus or
maximum; ~ **lane** n (AUT: in Britain) voie f de droite; (: in US, Europe) voie de gauche; ~ **line** n (TEL)
ligne extérieure; ~**r** n (stranger)
étranger(ère)

out: ~**size** ['aʊtsaɪz] adj énorme;
(clothes) grande taille inv; ~**skirts**
['aʊtskɜːts] npl faubourgs mpl; ~**spoken** [aʊt'spəʊkən] adj très
franc(franche)

outstanding [aʊt'stændɪŋ] adj remarquable, exceptionnel(le); (unfinished) en suspens; (debt) impayé(e);
(problem) non réglé(e)

outstay [aʊt'steɪ] vt: **to ~ one's
welcome** abuser de l'hospitalité de
son hôte

out: ~**stretched** ['aʊtstretʃt] adj
(hand) tendu(e); ~**strip** [aʊt'strɪp] vt
(competitors, demand) dépasser; ~**tray** n courrier m "départ"

outward ['aʊtwəd] adj (sign, appearances) extérieur(e); (journey)
(d')aller; ~**ly** adv extérieurement;
en apparence

outweigh [aʊt'weɪ] vt l'emporter sur

outwit [aʊt'wɪt] vt se montrer plus
malin que

oval ['əʊvəl] adj ovale ♦ n ovale m

ovary ['əʊvərɪ] n ovaire m

oven ['ʌvn] n four m; ~**proof** adj allant au four

over ['əʊvə*] adv (par-)dessus ♦ adj
(finished) fini(e), terminé(e); (too
much) en plus ♦ prep sur; par-
dessus; (above) au-dessus de; (on
the other side of) de l'autre côté de;
(more than) plus de; (during) pendant; ~ **here** ici; ~ **there** là-bas;
all ~ (everywhere) partout; (finished) fini(e); ~ **and** ~ (again) à
plusieurs reprises; ~ **and above** en
plus de; **to ask sb ~** inviter qn (à
passer)

overall [adj, n 'əʊvərɔːl, adv əʊvər'ɔːl] adj (length, cost etc) total(e); (study) d'ensemble ♦ n (BRIT) blouse f ♦ adj dans l'ensemble, en général; ~s npl bleus mpl (de travail)

overawe [əʊvər'ɔː] vt impressionner

over: ~**balance** [əʊvə'bæləns] vi basculer; ~**bearing** [əʊvə'bɛərɪŋ] adj impérieux(euse), autoritaire; ~**board** ['əʊvəbɔːd] adv (NAUT) par-dessus bord; ~**book** [əʊvə'bʊk] vt faire du surbooking; ~**cast** ['əʊvəkɑːst] adj couvert(e)

overcharge [əʊvə'tʃɑːdʒ] vt: to ~ sb for sth faire payer qch trop cher à qn

overcoat ['əʊvəkəʊt] n pardessus m

overcome [əʊvə'kʌm] (irreg) vt (defeat) triompher de; (difficulty) surmonter

overcrowded [əʊvə'kraʊdɪd] adj bondé(e)

overdo [əʊvə'duː] (irreg) vt exagérer; (overcook) trop cuire; to ~ it (work etc) se surmener

overdose ['əʊvədəʊs] n dose excessive

overdraft ['əʊvədrɑːft] n découvert m; **overdrawn** ['əʊvə'drɔːn] adj (account) à découvert; (person) dont le compte est à découvert

overdue [əʊvə'djuː] adj en retard; (change, reform) qui tarde

overestimate [əʊvər'ɛstɪmeɪt] vt surestimer

overexcited [əʊvərɪk'saɪtɪd] adj surexcité(e)

overflow [vb əʊvə'fləʊ, n 'əʊvəfləʊ] vi déborder ♦ n (also: ~ pipe) tuyau m d'écoulement, trop-plein m

overgrown [əʊvə'grəʊn] adj (garden) envahi(e) par la végétation

overhaul [vb əʊvə'hɔːl, n 'əʊvəhɔːl] vt réviser ♦ n révision f

overhead [adv əʊvə'hɛd, adj, n 'əʊvəhɛd] adv au-dessus ♦ adj aérien(ne); (lighting) vertical(e) ♦ n (US) = **overheads;** ~**s** npl (expenses) frais généraux

overhear [əʊvə'hɪə*] (irreg) vt entendre (par hasard)

overheat [əʊvə'hiːt] vi (engine) chauffer

overjoyed [əʊvə'dʒɔɪd] adj: ~ (at) ravi(e) (de), enchanté(e) (de)

overkill ['əʊvəkɪl] n: that would be ~ ce serait trop

overland adj, adv par voie de terre

overlap [vb əʊvə'læp, n 'əʊvəlæp] vi se chevaucher

overleaf [əʊvə'liːf] adv au verso

overload ['əʊvələʊd] vt surcharger

overlook [əʊvə'lʊk] vt (have view of) donner sur; (miss: by mistake) oublier; (forgive) fermer les yeux sur

overnight [adv 'əʊvə'naɪt, adj 'əʊvənaɪt] adv (happen) durant la nuit; (fig) soudain ♦ adj d'une (or de) nuit; **he stayed there** ~ il y a passé la nuit

overpass n pont autoroutier

overpower [əʊvə'paʊə*] vt vaincre; (fig) accabler; ~**ing** adj (heat, stench) suffocant(e)

overrate ['əʊvə'reɪt] vt surestimer

override [əʊvə'raɪd] (irreg: like ride) vt (order, objection) passer outre à; **overriding** [əʊvə'raɪdɪŋ] adj prépondérant(e)

overrule [əʊvə'ruːl] vt (decision) annuler; (claim) rejeter; (person) rejeter l'avis de

overrun [əʊvə'rʌn] (irreg: like run) vt (country) occuper; (time limit) dépasser

overseas ['əʊvə'siːz] adv outre-mer; (abroad) à l'étranger ♦ adj (trade) extérieur(e); (visitor) étranger(ère)

overshadow [əʊvə'ʃædəʊ] vt (fig) éclipser

oversight ['əʊvəsaɪt] n omission f, oubli m

oversleep [əʊvə'sliːp] (irreg) vi se réveiller (trop) tard

overstate vt exagérer

overstep [əʊvə'stɛp] vt: to ~ the mark dépasser la mesure

overt [əʊ'vɜːt] adj non dissimulé(e)

overtake [əuvə'teɪk] (irreg) vt (AUT) dépasser, doubler

overthrow [əuvə'θrəu] (irreg) vt (government) renverser

overtime ['əuvətaɪm] n heures fpl supplémentaires

overtone ['əuvətəun] n (also: ~s) note f, sous-entendus mpl

overture ['əuvətʃuə*] n (MUS, fig) ouverture f

overturn [əuvə'tə:n] vt renverser ♦ vi se retourner

overweight [əuvə'weɪt] adj (person) trop gros(se)

overwhelm [əuvə'wɛlm] vt (subj: emotion) accabler; (enemy, opponent) écraser; ~**ing** adj (victory, defeat) écrasant(e); (desire) irrésistible

overwork [əuvə'wə:k] n surmenage m

overwrought ['əuvə'rɔ:t] adj excédé(e)

owe [əu] vt: to ~ sb sth, to ~ sth to sb devoir qch à qn; owing to ['əuɪŋ-] prep à cause de, en raison de

owl [aul] n hibou m

own [əun] vt posséder ♦ adj propre; a room of my ~ une chambre à moi, ma propre chambre; to get one's ~ back prendre sa revanche; on one's ~ tout(e) seul(e); ~ **up** vi avouer; ~**er** n propriétaire m/f; ~**ership** n possession f

ox [ɔks] (pl oxen) n bœuf m

oxtail ['ɔksteɪl] n: ~ soup soupe f à la queue de bœuf

oxygen ['ɔksɪdʒən] n oxygène m; ~ **mask** n masque m à oxygène

oyster ['ɔɪstə*] n huître f

oz. abbr = ounce(s)

ozone hole n trou m d'ozone

ozone layer n couche f d'ozone

P

p [pi:] abbr = penny; pence

PA n abbr = personal assistant; public address system

pa [pɑ:] (inf) n papa m

p.a. abbr = per annum

pace [peɪs] n pas m; (speed) allure f; vitesse f ♦ vi: to ~ up and down faire les cent pas; to keep ~ with aller à la même vitesse que; ~**maker** n (MED) stimulateur m cardiaque; (SPORT: also: pacesetter) meneur(euse) de train

Pacific n: the ~ (Ocean) le Pacifique, l'océan m Pacifique

pack [pæk] n (packet; US: of cigarettes) paquet m; (of hounds) meute f; (of thieves etc) bande f; (back pack) sac m à dos; (of cards) jeu m ♦ vt (goods) empaqueter, emballer; (box) remplir; (cram) entasser; to ~ one's suitcase faire sa valise; to ~ (one's bags) faire ses bagages; to ~ sb off to expédier qn à.; ~ **it in!** laisse tomber!; écrase!

package ['pækɪdʒ] n paquet m; (also: ~ **deal**) forfait m; ~ **tour** (BRIT) n voyage organisé

packed lunch [pækt-] (BRIT) n repas froid

packet ['pækɪt] n paquet m

packing ['pækɪŋ] n emballage m; ~ **case** n caisse f (d'emballage)

pact [pækt] n pacte m; traité m

pad [pæd] n bloc(-notes) m; (to prevent friction) tampon m; (inf: home) piaule f ♦ vt rembourrer; ~**ding** n rembourrage m

paddle ['pædl] n (oar) pagaie f; (US: for table tennis) raquette f de ping-pong ♦ vt: to ~ a canoe etc pagayer ♦ vi barboter, faire trempette; ~ **steamer** n bateau m à aubes; **paddling pool** (BRIT) n petit bassin

paddock ['pædək] n enclos m; (RACING) paddock m

paddy field ['pædɪ-] n rizière f

padlock ['pædlɔk] n cadenas m

paediatrics [piːdɪ'ætrɪks] (US **pediatrics**) n pédiatrie f

pagan ['peɪɡən] adj, n païen(ne)

page [peɪdʒ] n (of book) page f; (also: ~ boy) groom m, chasseur m; (at wedding) garçon m d'honneur ♦ vt (in hotel etc) (faire) appeler

pageant ['pædʒənt] n spectacle m historique; **~ry** n apparat m, pompe f

pager, paging device n (TEL) récepteur m d'appels

paid [peɪd] pt, pp of **pay** ♦ adj (work, official) rémunéré(e); (holiday) payé(e); **to put ~ to** (BRIT) mettre fin à, régler; **~ gunman** n tueur m à gages

pail [peɪl] n seau m

pain [peɪn] n douleur f; **to be in ~** souffrir, avoir mal; **to take ~s to do sth** se donner du mal pour faire; **~ed** adj peiné(e), chagrin(e); **~ful** adj douloureux(euse); (fig) difficile, pénible; **~fully** adv (fig: very) terriblement; **~killer** n analgésique m; **~less** adj indolore; **~staking** ['peɪnzteɪkɪŋ] adj (person) soigneux(euse); (work) soigné(e)

paint [peɪnt] n peinture f ♦ vt peindre; **to ~ the door blue** peindre la porte en bleu; **~brush** n pinceau m; **~er** n peintre m; **~ing** n peinture f; (picture) tableau m; **~work** n peinture f

pair [peə*] n (of shoes, gloves etc) paire f; (of people) couple m; **~ of scissors** (paire de) ciseaux mpl; **~ of trousers** pantalon m

pajamas [pə'dʒɑːməz] (US) npl pyjama(s) m(pl)

Pakistan [pɑːkɪ'stɑːn] n Pakistan m; **~i** adj pakistanais(e) ♦ n Pakistanais(e)

pal [pæl] (inf) n copain(copine)

palace ['pæləs] n palais m

palatable ['pælətəbl] adj bon(bonne), agréable au goût

palate ['pælɪt] n palais m (ANAT)

pale [peɪl] adj pâle ♦ n: **beyond the**

~ (behaviour) inacceptable; **to grow ~** pâlir

Palestine ['pælɪstaɪn] n Palestine f; **Palestinian** adj palestinien(ne) ♦ n Palestinien(ne)

palette ['pælɪt] n palette f

pall [pɔːl] n (of smoke) voile m ♦ vi devenir lassant(e)

pallet ['pælɪt] n (for goods) palette f

pallid ['pælɪd] adj blême

palm [pɑːm] n (of hand) paume f; (also: ~ tree) palmier m ♦ vt: **to ~ sth off on sb** (inf) refiler qch à qn; **P~ Sunday** n le dimanche des Rameaux

palpable ['pælpəbl] adj évident(e), manifeste

paltry ['pɔːltrɪ] adj dérisoire

pamper ['pæmpə*] vt gâter, dorloter

pamphlet ['pæmflət] n brochure f

pan [pæn] n (also: sauce~) casserole f; (: frying ~) poêle f

pancake ['pænkeɪk] n crêpe f

panda ['pændə] n panda m; **~ car** (BRIT) n ≈ voiture f pie inv (de police)

pandemonium [pændɪ'məʊnɪəm] n tohu-bohu m

pander ['pændə*] vi: **to ~ to** flatter bassement; obéir servilement à

pane [peɪn] n carreau m, vitre f

panel ['pænl] n (of wood, cloth etc) panneau m; (RADIO, TV) experts mpl; (for interview, exams) jury m; **~ling** (US **~ing**) n boiseries fpl

pang [pæŋ] n: **~s of remorse/jealousy** affres mpl du remords/de la jalousie; **~s of hunger/conscience** tiraillements mpl d'estomac/de la conscience

panic ['pænɪk] n panique f, affolement m ♦ vi s'affoler, paniquer; **~ky** adj (person) qui panique or s'affole facilement; **~-stricken** adj affolé(e)

pansy ['pænzɪ] n (BOT) pensée f; (inf: pej) tapette f, pédé m

pant [pænt] vi haleter

panther ['pænθə*] n panthère f

panties ['pæntɪz] npl slip m

pantihose ['pæntɪhəʊz] (US) npl collant m

pantomime ['pæntəmaɪm] (BRIT) n spectacle m de Noël

pantry ['pæntrɪ] n garde-manger m inv

pants [pænts] npl (BRIT: woman's) slip m; (: man's) slip, caleçon m; (US: trousers) pantalon m

paper ['peɪpə*] n papier m; (also: wall~) papier peint; (: news~) journal m; (academic essay) article m; (exam) épreuve écrite ♦ adj en or de papier ♦ vt tapisser (de papier peint); ~s npl (also: identity ~s) papiers (d'identité); ~back n livre m de poche; livre broché or non relié; ~ bag n sac m en papier; ~ clip n trombone m; ~ hankie n mouchoir m en papier; ~weight n presse-papiers m inv; ~work n papiers mpl; (pej) paperasserie f

par [pɑ:*] n pair m; (GOLF) normale f du parcours; on a ~ with à égalité avec, au même niveau que

parable ['pærəbl] n parabole f (REL)

parachute ['pærəʃu:t] n parachute m

parade [pə'reɪd] n défilé m ♦ vt (fig) faire étalage de ♦ vi défiler

paradise ['pærədaɪs] n paradis m

paradox ['pærədɔks] n paradoxe m; ~ically [pærə'dɔksɪkəlɪ] adv paradoxalement

paraffin ['pærəfɪn] (BRIT) n (also: ~ oil) pétrole m (lampant)

paragon ['pærəgən] n modèle m

paragraph ['pærəgrɑːf] n paragraphe m

parallel ['pærəlɛl] adj parallèle; (fig) semblable ♦ n (line) parallèle f; (fig, GEO) parallèle m

paralyse ['pærəlaɪz] (BRIT) vt paralyser

paralysis [pə'ræləsɪs] n paralysie f

paralyze ['pærəlaɪz] (US) vt = paralyse

paramount ['pærəmaunt] adj: of ~ importance de la plus haute or grande importance

paranoid ['pærənɔɪd] adj (PSYCH) paranoïaque

paraphernalia ['pærəfə'neɪlɪə] n attirail m

parasol ['pærəsɔl] n ombrelle f; (over table) parasol m

paratrooper ['pærətru:pə*] n parachutiste (soldat)

parcel ['pɑːsl] n paquet m, colis m ♦ vt (also: ~ up) empaqueter

parch [pɑːtʃ] vt dessécher; ~ed adj (person) assoiffé(e)

parchment ['pɑːtʃmənt] n parchemin m

pardon ['pɑːdn] n pardon m; grâce f ♦ vt pardonner à; ~ me!, I beg your ~! pardon!, je suis désolé!; I beg your(~)?, (US) ~ me? pardon?

parent ['pɛərənt] n père m or mère f; ~s npl parents mpl

Paris ['pærɪs] n Paris

parish ['pærɪʃ] n paroisse f; (BRIT: civil) ≈ commune f

Parisian [pə'rɪzɪən] adj parisien(ne) ♦ n Parisien(ne)

park [pɑːk] n parc m, jardin public ♦ vt garer ♦ vi se garer

parking ['pɑːkɪŋ] n stationnement m; "no ~" "stationnement interdit"; ~ lot (US) n parking m, parc m de stationnement; ~ meter n parcomètre m; ~ ticket n P.V. m

parlance ['pɑːləns] n langage m

parliament ['pɑːləmənt] n parlement m; ~ary [pɑːlə'mɛntərɪ] adj parlementaire

parlour ['pɑːlə*] (US **parlor**) n salon m

parochial [pə'rəukɪəl] (pej) adj à l'esprit de clocher

parody ['pærədɪ] n parodie f

parole [pə'rəul] n: on ~ en liberté conditionnelle

parrot ['pærət] n perroquet m

parry ['pærɪ] vt (blow) esquiver

parsley ['pɑːslɪ] n persil m

parsnip ['pɑːsnɪp] n panais m

parson ['pɑːsn] n ecclésiastique m; (Church of England) pasteur m

part [pɑːt] n partie f; (of machine) pièce f; (THEATRE etc) rôle m; (of serial) épisode m; (US: in hair) raie f ♦ adv = **partly** ♦ vt séparer ♦ vi (people) se séparer; (crowd) s'ouvrir; **to take ~** in participer à, prendre part à; **to take sth in good ~** prendre qch du bon côté; **to take sb's ~** prendre le parti de qn, prendre parti pour qn; **for my ~** en ce qui me concerne; **for the most ~** dans la plupart des cas; **~** vt fus se séparer de; **~ exchange** (BRIT) n: **in ~ exchange** en reprise

partial ['pɑːʃəl] adj (not complete) partiel(le); **to be ~ to** avoir un faible pour

participate [pɑː'tɪsɪpeɪt] vi: **to ~ (in)** participer à, prendre part à

participation [pɑːtɪsɪ'peɪʃən] n participation f

participle ['pɑːtɪsɪpl] n participe m

particle ['pɑːtɪkl] n particule f

particular [pə'tɪkjʊlə*] adj particulier(ère); (special) spécial(e); (fussy) difficile, méticuleux(euse); **~s** npl (details) détails mpl; (personal) nom, adresse etc; **in ~** en particulier; **~ly** adv particulièrement

parting ['pɑːtɪŋ] n séparation f; (BRIT: in hair) raie f ♦ adj d'adieu

partisan [pɑːtɪ'zæn] n partisan(e) ♦ adj partisan(e), de parti

partition [pɑː'tɪʃən] n (wall) cloison f; (POL) partition f, division f

partly ['pɑːtlɪ] adv en partie, partiellement

partner ['pɑːtnə*] n partenaire m/f; (in marriage) conjoint(e); (boyfriend, girlfriend) ami(e); (COMM) associé(e); (at dance) cavalier(ère); **~ship** n association f

partridge ['pɑːtrɪdʒ] n perdrix f

part-time ['pɑːt'taɪm] adj, adv à mi-temps, à temps partiel

party ['pɑːtɪ] n (POL) parti m; (group) groupe m; (LAW) partie f; (celebration) réception f, soirée f; fête f ♦ cpd (POL) de or du parti; **~ dress** n robe habillée; **~ line** n (TEL) ligne partagée

pass [pɑːs] vt passer; (place) passer

devant; (friend) croiser; (overtake) dépasser; (exam) être reçu(e) à, réussir; (approve) approuver, accepter ♦ vi passer; (SCOL) être reçu(e) ou admis(e); réussir ♦ n (permit) laissez-passer m inv; carte f d'accès ou d'abonnement; (in mountains) col m; (SPORT) passe f; (SCOL: also: ~ mark): **to get a ~** être reçu(e) (sans mention); **to make a ~ at sb** (inf) faire des avances à qn; **~ away** vi mourir; **~ by** vi passer ♦ vt négliger; **~ on** vt (news, object) transmettre; (illness) passer; **~ out** vi s'évanouir; **~ up** vt (opportunity) laisser passer; **~able** adj (road) praticable; (work) acceptable

passage ['pæsɪdʒ] n (also: ~way) couloir m; (gen, in book) passage m; (by boat) traversée f

passbook ['pɑːsbʊk] n livret m

passenger ['pæsɪndʒə*] n passager(ère)

passer-by ['pɑːsə'baɪ] (pl ~s-by) n passant(e)

passing ['pɑːsɪŋ] adj (fig) passager(ère); **in ~** en passant

passing place n (AUT) aire f de croisement

passion ['pæʃən] n passion f; **~ate** adj passionné(e)

passive ['pæsɪv] adj (also LING) passif(ive); **~ smoking** n tabagie m passive

Passover ['pɑːsəʊvə*] n Pâque (juive)

passport ['pɑːspɔːt] n passeport m; **~ control** n contrôle m des passeports

password ['pɑːswɜːd] n mot m de passe

past [pɑːst] prep (in front of) devant; (further than) au delà de, plus loin que; (later than) après ♦ adj passé(e); (president etc) ancien(ne) ♦ n passé m; **he's ~ forty** il a de passé la quarantaine, il a plus de or passé quarante ans; **for the ~ few days** depuis quelques/3 jours; ces derniers/3 derniers jours; **ten/**

quarter ~ **eight** huit heures dix/un
or et quart

pasta ['pæstə] n pâtes fpl

paste [peist] n pâte f; (meat ~) pâté
m (à tartiner); (tomato ~) purée f,
concentré m; (glue) colle f (de pâte)
♦ vt coller

pasteurized ['pæstəraizd] adj pas-
teurisé e

pastille ['pæstl] n pastille f

pastime ['pɑ:staim] n passe-temps m
inv

pastry ['peistri] n pâte f; (cake)
pâtisserie f

pasture ['pɑ:stʃə*] n pâturage m

pasty [n 'pæsti, adj 'peisti] n petit
pâté (en croûte) ♦ adj (complexion)
terreux(euse)

pat [pæt] vt tapoter; (dog) caresser

patch [pætʃ] n (of material) pièce f;
(eye ~) cache m; (spot) tache f; (on
tyre) rustine f ♦ vt (clothes) rapiécer; (to go through) a bad ~ (passer par) une période difficile; ~ **up**
vt réparer (grossièrement); to ~ **up**
a quarrel se raccommoder; ~**y** adj
inégal(e); (incomplete) fragmentaire

pâté ['pætei] n pâté m, terrine f

patent ['peitnt] n brevet m (d'invention) ♦ vt faire breveter ♦ adj
patent(e), manifeste; ~ **leather** n
cuir verni

paternal [pə'tə:nl] adj paternel(le)

path [pɑ:θ] n chemin m, sentier m;
(in garden) allée f; (trajectory) trajectoire f

pathetic [pə'θetik] adj (pitiful) pitoyable; (very bad) lamentable, minable

pathological [pæθə'lɒdʒikl] adj pa-
thologique

pathos ['peiθɒs] n pathétique m

pathway ['pɑ:θwei] n sentier m, passage m

patience ['peiʃəns] n patience f;
(BRIT: CARDS) réussite f

patient ['peiʃnt] n patient(e); malade m/f ♦ adj patient(e)

patriotic [pætri'ɒtik] adj patriotique;
(person) patriote

patrol [pə'trəul] n patrouille f ♦ vt
patrouiller dans; ~ **car** n voiture f de
police; ~**man** (irreg: US) n agent m
de police

patron ['peitrən] n (in shop)
client(e); (of charity) patron(ne); ~
of the arts mécène m; ~**ize** vt
traiter avec condescendance; (shop,
club) être un client or un habitué
de

patter ['pætə*] n crépitement m, ta-
potement m; (sales talk) boniment m

pattern ['pætən] n (design) motif m;
(SEWING) patron m

paunch [pɔ:ntʃ] n gros ventre, bedaine f

pauper ['pɔ:pə*] n indigent(e)

pause [pɔ:z] n pause f, arrêt m ♦ vi
faire une pause, s'arrêter

pave [peiv] vt paver, daller; to ~
the way for ouvrir la voie à;
~**ment** ['peivmənt] (BRIT) n trottoir m

pavilion [pə'viliən] n pavillon m;
tente f

paving ['peiviŋ] n (material) pavé
m, dalle f; ~ **stone** n pavé m

paw [pɔ:] n patte f

pawn [pɔ:n] n (CHESS, also fig) pion
m ♦ vt mettre en gage; ~**broker** n
prêteur m sur gages; ~**shop** n
mont-de-piété m

pay [pei] (pt, pp **paid**) n salaire m;
paie f ♦ vt payer ♦ vi payer; (be
profitable) être rentable; to ~ **attention** (to) prêter attention (à); to ~
sb a visit rendre visite à qn; to ~
one's respects to qn se présenter à
qn; ~ **back** vt rembour-
ser; ~ **for** vt fus payer; ~ **in** vt verser; ~ **off** vt régler, acquitter; (person) rembourser ♦ vi (scheme, decision) se révéler payant(e); ~ **up** vt
(money) payer; ~**able** adj: **~able
to sb** (cheque) à l'ordre de qn; ~**ee**
[pei'i:] n bénéficiaire m/f; ~ **envelope** (US) n = pay packet; ~**ment**
n paiement m; règlement m; monthly
~**ment** mensualité f; ~ **packet**
(BRIT) n paie f; ~ **phone** n cabine f

téléphonique, téléphone public; ~**roll** n registre m du personnel; ~ **slip** (BRIT) n bulletin m de paie; ~ **television** n chaînes fpl payantes

PC n abbr = **personal computer**.

p.c. abbr = **per cent**

pea [pi:] n (petit) pois

peace [pi:s] n paix f; (calm) calme m, tranquillité f; ~**ful** adj paisible, calme

peach [pi:tʃ] n pêche f

peacock ['pi:kɔk] n paon m

peak [pi:k] n (mountain) pic m, cime f; (of cap) visière f; (fig: highest level) maximum m; (: of career, fame) apogée m; ~ **hours** npl heures fpl de pointe

peal [pi:l] n (of bells) carillon m; ~ **of laughter** éclat m de rire

peanut ['pi:nʌt] n arachide f, cacahuète f

pear [pɛə*] n poire f

pearl [pɜ:l] n perle f

peasant ['pɛznt] n paysan(ne)

peat [pi:t] n tourbe f

pebble ['pɛbl] n caillou m, galet m

peck [pɛk] vt (also: ~ at) donner un coup de bec à ♦ n coup m de bec; (kiss) bécot m; ~**ing order** n ordre m des préséances; ~**ish** (BRIT: inf) adj: **I feel** ~**ish** je mangerais bien quelque chose

peculiar [pɪ'kju:lɪə*] adj étrange, bizarre, curieux(euse); ~ **to** particulier(ère) à

pedal ['pɛdl] n pédale f ♦ vi pédaler

pedantic [pɪ'dæntɪk] adj pédant(e)

peddler ['pɛdlə*] n (of drugs) revendeur(euse)

pedestal ['pɛdɪstl] n piédestal m

pedestrian [pɪ'dɛstrɪən] n piéton m; ~ **crossing** (BRIT) n passage clouté

pediatrics [pi:dɪ'ætrɪks] (US) n = **paediatrics**

pedigree ['pɛdɪgri:] n ascendance f; (of animal) pedigree m ♦ cpd (animal) de race

pee [pi:] (inf) vi faire pipi, pisser

peek [pi:k] n jeter un coup d'œil (furtif)

peel [pi:l] n pelure f, épluchure f; (of orange, lemon) écorce f ♦ vt peler, éplucher ♦ vi (paint etc) s'écailler; (wallpaper) se décoller; ~ **off** vi (label etc) se décoller

peep [pi:p] n (BRIT: look) coup d'œil furtif; (sound) pépiement m ♦ vi (BRIT) jeter un coup d'œil (furtif); ~ **out** (BRIT) vi se montrer (furtivement); ~**hole** n judas m

peer [pɪə*] n: ~ **at** regarder attentivement, scruter ♦ n (noble) pair m; (equal) pair m, égal(e); ~**age** n pairie f

peeved [pi:vd] adj irrité(e), fâché(e)

peg [pɛg] n (for coat etc) patère f; (BRIT: also: clothes ~) pince f à linge

Peking [pi:'kɪŋ] n Pékin m; **Peking(g)ese** [pi:kɪ'ni:z] n (dog) pékinois m

pelican ['pɛlɪkən] n pélican m; ~ **crossing** (BRIT) n (AUT) feu à commande manuelle

pellet ['pɛlɪt] n boulette f; (of lead) plomb m

pelt [pɛlt] vt: **to** ~ **sb (with)** bombarder qn (de) ♦ vi (rain) tomber à seaux; (inf: run) courir à toutes jambes ♦ n peau f

pelvis ['pɛlvɪs] n bassin m

pen [pɛn] n (for writing) stylo m; (for sheep) parc m

penal ['pi:nl] adj pénal(e); (system, colony) pénitentiaire; ~**ize** vt pénaliser

penalty ['pɛnltɪ] n pénalité f; sanction f; (fine) amende f; (SPORT) pénalisation f; (FOOTBALL) penalty m; (RUGBY) pénalité f

penance ['pɛnəns] n pénitence f

pence [pɛns] (BRIT) npl of **penny**

pencil ['pɛnsl] n crayon m; ~ **case** n trousse f (d'écolier); ~ **sharpener** n taille-crayon(s) m inv

pendant ['pɛndənt] n pendentif m

pending ['pɛndɪŋ] prep en attendant ♦ adj en suspens

pendulum ['pɛndjuləm] n (of clock) balancier m

penetrate ['pɛnɪtreɪt] vt pénétrer

dans; pénétrer

penfriend ['penfrend] (BRIT) n correspondant(e)

penguin ['peŋgwɪn] n pingouin m

penicillin [penɪ'sɪlɪn] n pénicilline f

peninsula [pɪ'nɪnsjʊlə] n péninsule f

penis ['piːnɪs] n pénis m, verge f

penitentiary [penɪ'tenʃərɪ] n prison f

penknife ['pennaɪf] n canif m

pen name n nom m de plume, pseudonyme m

penniless ['penɪləs] adj sans le sou

penny ['penɪ] (pl pennies or (BRIT) pence) n penny m; (US) = cent

penpal ['penpæl] n correspondant(e)

pension ['penʃən] n pension f; (from company) retraite f; **~er** (BRIT) n retraité(e); **~ fund** n caisse f de pension

Pentecost ['pentɪkɒst] n Pentecôte f

penthouse ['penthaʊs] n appartement m (de luxe) (en attique)

pent-up ['pentʌp] adj (feelings) refoulé(e)

penultimate [pɪ'nʌltɪmɪt] adj avant-dernier(ère)

people ['piːpl] npl gens mpl; personnes fpl; (inhabitants) population f; (POL) peuple m ♦ n (nation, race) peuple m; **several ~ came** plusieurs personnes sont venues; **~ say that ...** on dit que ...

pep [pep] (inf) n entrain m, dynamisme m; **~ up** vt remonter

pepper ['pepə*] n poivre m; (vegetable) poivron m ♦ vt (fig): **to ~ with** bombarder de; **~mint** n (sweet) pastille f de menthe

peptalk ['peptɔːk] (inf) n (petit) discours d'encouragement

per [pəːr] (inf) prep par; **~ hour** (miles etc) à l'heure; (fee) de l'heure; **~ kilo** etc le kilo etc; **~ annum** par an; **~ capita** adj, adv par personne, par habitant

perceive [pə'siːv] vt percevoir; (notice) remarquer, s'apercevoir de

per cent [pə'sent] adv pour cent

percentage [pə'sentɪdʒ] n pourcen-

tage m

perception [pə'sepʃən] n perception f; (insight) perspicacité f

perceptive [pə'septɪv] adj pénétrant(e); (person) perspicace

perch [pɜːtʃ] n (fish) perche f; (for bird) perchoir m ♦ vi: **to ~ on** se percher sur

percolator ['pɜːkəleɪtə*] n cafetière f (électrique)

perennial [pə'renɪəl] adj perpétuel(le); (BOT) vivace

perfect [adj, n 'pɜːfɪkt, vb pə'fekt] adj parfait(e) ♦ n (also: **~ tense**) parfait m ♦ vt parfaire; mettre au point; **~ly** adv parfaitement

perforate ['pɜːfəreɪt] vt perforer, percer; **perforation** [pɜːfə'reɪʃən] n perforation f

perform [pə'fɔːm] vt (carry out) exécuter; (concert etc) jouer, donner ♦ vi jouer; **~ance** n représentation f, spectacle m; (of an artist) interprétation f; (SPORT) performance f; (of car, engine) fonctionnement m; (of company, economy) résultats mpl; **~er** n artiste m/f, interprète m/f

perfume ['pɜːfjuːm] n parfum m

perfunctory [pə'fʌŋktərɪ] adj négligent(e), pour la forme

perhaps [pə'hæps] adv peut-être

peril ['perɪl] n péril m

perimeter [pə'rɪmɪtə*] n périmètre m

period ['pɪərɪəd] n période f; (HISTORY) époque f; (SCOL) cours m; (full stop) point m; (MED) règles fpl ♦ adj (costume, furniture) d'époque; **~ic(al)** [pɪərɪ'ɒdɪk(əl)] adj périodique; **~ical** n périodique m

peripheral [pə'rɪfərəl] adj périphérique ♦ n (COMPUT) périphérique m

perish ['perɪʃ] vi périr; (decay) se détériorer; **~able** adj périssable

perjury ['pɜːdʒərɪ] n parjure m, faux serment

perk [pɜːk] n avantage m; accessoire, à-côté m; **~ up** vi (cheer up) se ragaillardir; **~y** adj (cheerful) guilleret(te)

perm [pɜːm] n (for hair) permanente f

permanent ['pɜːmənənt] adj permanent(e)

permeate ['pɜːmieit] vi s'infiltrer ♦ vt s'infiltrer dans; pénétrer

permissible [pə'misəbl] adj permis(e), acceptable

permission [pə'mɪʃən] n permission f, autorisation f

permissive [pə'mɪsɪv] adj tolérant(e), permissif(ive)

permit [n 'pɜːmɪt, vb pə'mɪt] n permis m ♦ vt permettre

perpendicular [pɜːpən'dɪkjulə*] adj perpendiculaire

persecute ['pɜːsɪkjuːt] vt persécuter

persevere [pɜːsɪ'vɪə*] vi persévérer

Persian ['pɜːʃən] adj persan(e) ♦ n (LING) persan m; the (~) Gulf le golfe Persique

persist [pə'sɪst] vi: to ~ (in doing) persister ou s'obstiner (à faire); **~ent** adj persistant(e), tenace

person ['pɜːsn] n personne f; in ~ en personne; **~al** adj personnel(le); **~al assistant** n secrétaire privé(e); **~al call** n communication privée; **~al column** n annonces personnelles; **~al computer** n ordinateur personnel; **~ality** [-'nælɪtɪ] n personnalité f; **~ally** adv personnellement; to take sth **~ally** se sentir visé(e) (par qch); **~al organizer** n filofax m (®); **~al stereo** n balladeur m

personnel [pɜːsə'nel] n personnel m

perspective [pə'spektɪv] n perspective f; to get things into ~ faire la part des choses

Perspex ['pɜːspeks] (®) n plexiglas m (®)

perspiration [pɜːspə'reɪʃən] n transpiration f

persuade [pə'sweid] vt: to ~ sb to do sth persuader qn de faire qch

persuasion [pə'sweɪʒən] n persuasion f; (creed) religion f

pertaining [pɜː'teɪnɪŋ] : ~ to prep

relatif(ive) à

peruse [pə'ruːz] vt lire (attentivement)

pervade [pə'veid] vt se répandre dans, envahir

perverse [pə'vɜːs] adj pervers(e); (contrary) contrariant(e); **pervert** [n 'pɜːvɜːt, vb pə'vɜːt] n perverti(e) ♦ vt pervertir; (words) déformer

pessimist ['pesɪmɪst] n pessimiste m/f; **~ic** [pesɪ'mɪstɪk] adj pessimiste

pest [pest] n animal m (ou insecte m) nuisible; (fig) fléau m

pester ['pestə*] vt importuner, harceler

pet [pet] n animal familier ♦ cpd (favourite) favori(te) ♦ vt (stroke) caresser, câliner ♦ vi (inf) se peloter; teacher's ~ chouchou m du professeur; ~ hate bête noire

petal ['petl] n pétale m

peter out ['piːtə-] vi (stream, conversation) tarir; (meeting) tourner court; (road) se perdre

petite [pə'tiːt] adj menu(e)

petition [pə'tɪʃən] n pétition f

petrified ['petrɪfaid] adj (fig) mort(e) de peur

petrol ['petrəl] (BRIT) n essence f; **two-star** ~ essence f ordinaire; **four-star** ~ super m; ~ **can** n bidon m à essence

petroleum [pɪ'trəulɪəm] n pétrole m

petrol: ~ **pump** (BRIT) n pompe f à essence; ~ **station** (BRIT) n station-service f; ~ **tank** (BRIT) n réservoir m (d'essence)

petticoat ['petɪkəut] n combinaison f

petty ['petɪ] adj (mean) mesquin(e); (unimportant) insignifiant(e), sans importance; ~ **cash** n caisse f des dépenses courantes; ~ **officer** n second-maître m

petulant ['petjulənt] adj boudeur(euse), irritable

pew [pjuː] n banc m (d'église)

pewter ['pjuːtə*] n étain m

phantom ['fæntəm] n fantôme m

pharmacy ['fɑːməsɪ] n pharmacie f

phase [feiz] n phase f ♦ vt: to ~ sth

in/out introduire/supprimer qch progressivement

PhD abbr = Doctor of Philosophy n (title) ≈ docteur m (en droit ou lettres etc) ≈ doctorat m; titulaire m/f d'un doctorat

pheasant ['fɛznt] n faisan m

phenomenon [fɪ'nɔmɪnən] (pl phenomena) n phénomène m

philosophical [fɪlə'sɔfɪkl] adj philosophique

philosophy [fɪ'lɔsəfɪ] n philosophie f

phobia ['fəʊbjə] n phobie f

phone [fəʊn] n téléphone m ♦ vt téléphoner; to be on the ~ avoir le téléphone; (be calling) être au téléphone; ~ **back** vt, vi rappeler; ~ **up** vt téléphoner à ♦ vi téléphoner; ~**book** n annuaire m; ~ **booth** n = phone box; ~ **box** (BRIT) n cabine f téléphonique; ~ **call** n coup m de fil or de téléphone; ~**card** n carte f de téléphone; ~-**in** n (BRIT, RADIO, TV) programme m à ligne ouverte

phonetics [fə'nɛtɪks] n phonétique f

phoney ['fəʊnɪ] adj faux(fausse), factice; (person) pas franc(he), poseur(euse)

photo ['fəʊtəʊ] n photo f

photo...: ~**copier** ['-kɔpɪə*] n photocopieuse f; ~**copy** [-kɔpɪ] n photocopie f ♦ vt photocopier; ~**graph** [-grɑːf] n photographie f ♦ vt photographier; ~**grapher** [-grəfə*] n photographe m/f; ~**graphy** [-grəfɪ] n photographie f

phrase [freɪz] n expression f; (LING) locution f ♦ vt exprimer; ~ **book** n recueil m d'expressions (pour touristes)

physical ['fɪzɪkl] adj physique; ~ **education** n éducation f physique; ~**ly** adv physiquement

physician [fɪ'zɪʃən] n médecin m

physicist ['fɪzɪsɪst] n physicien(ne)

physics ['fɪzɪks] n physique f

physiotherapy [fɪzɪə'θɛrəpɪ] n kinésithérapie f

physique [fɪ'ziːk] n physique m; constitution f

pianist ['pɪənɪst] n pianiste m/f

piano [pɪ'ænəʊ] n piano m

pick [pɪk] n (tool: also: ~axe) pic m, pioche f ♦ vt choisir; (fruit etc) cueillir; (remove) prendre; (lock) forcer; **take your** ~ faites votre choix; **the** ~ **of** le(la) meilleur(e) de; to ~ **one's nose** se mettre les doigts dans le nez; to ~ **one's teeth** se curer les dents; to ~ **a quarrel with sb** chercher noise à qn; ~ **at** vt fus: to ~ **at one's food** manger du bout des dents, chipoter; ~ **on** vt fus (person) harceler; ~ **out** vt choisir; (distinguish) distinguer; ~ **up** vi (improve) s'améliorer ♦ vt ramasser; (collect) passer prendre; (AUT: give lift to) prendre, emmener; (learn) apprendre; (RADIO) capter; to ~ **up speed** prendre de la vitesse; to ~ **o.s. up** se relever

picket ['pɪkɪt] n (in strike) piquet m de grève ♦ vt mettre un piquet de grève devant

pickle ['pɪkl] n (also: ~s: as condiment) pickles mpl, petits légumes macérés dans du vinaigre ♦ vt conserver dans du vinaigre or dans de la saumure; **to be in a** ~ (mess) être dans le pétrin

pickpocket ['pɪkpɔkɪt] n pickpocket m

pick-up ['pɪkʌp] n (small truck) pick-up m inv

picnic ['pɪknɪk] n pique-nique m

picture ['pɪktʃə*] n image f; (painting) peinture f, tableau m; (etching) gravure f; (photograph) photo(graphie) f; (drawing) dessin m; (film) film m; (fig) description f; tableau m ♦ vt se représenter; **the** ~**s** (BRIT: inf) le cinéma; ~ **book** n livre m d'images

picturesque [pɪktʃə'rɛsk] adj pittoresque

pie [paɪ] n tourte f; (of fruit) tarte f; (of meat) pâté m en croûte

piece [piːs] n morceau m; (item): a ~ **of furniture/advice** un meuble/ conseil ♦ vt: to ~ **together** rassembler; **to take to ~s** démonter; **~meal** *adv* (*irregularly*) au coup par coup; (*bit by bit*) par bouts; **~work** *n* travail *m* aux pièces

pie chart *n* graphique *m* circulaire, camembert *m*

pier [pɪə*] *n* jetée *f*

pierce [pɪəs] *vt* percer, transpercer

pigeon ['pɪdʒən] *n* pigeon *m*; **~hole** *n* casier *m*

piggy bank ['pɪgɪ-] *n* tirelire *f*

pig: **~headed** ['hɛdɪd] *adj* entêté(e), têtu(e); **~let** *n* porcelet *m*, petit cochon; **~skin** [-skɪn] *n* peau *m* de porc; **~sty** [-staɪ] *n* porcherie *f*; **~tail** [-teɪl] *n* natte *f*, tresse *f*

pike [paɪk] *n* (*fish*) brochet *m*

pilchard ['pɪltʃəd] *n* pilchard *m* (*sorte de sardine*)

pile [paɪl] *n* (*pillar, of books*) pile *f*; (*heap*) tas *m*; (*of carpet*) poils *mp* ♦ *vt* (*also: ~ up*) empiler, entasser ♦ *vi* (*also: ~up*) s'entasser, s'accumuler; **to ~ into** (*car*) s'engouffrer dans

piles [paɪlz] *npl* hémorroïdes *fpl*

pile-up ['paɪlʌp] *n* (*AUT*) télescopage *m*, collision *f* en série

pilfering ['pɪlfərɪŋ] *n* chapardage *m*

pilgrim ['pɪlgrɪm] *n* pèlerin *m*

pill [pɪl] *n* pilule *f*

pillage ['pɪlɪdʒ] *vt* piller

pillar ['pɪlə*] *n* pilier *m*; **~ box** (*BRIT*) *n* boîte *f* aux lettres

pillion ['pɪljən] *n*: **to ride ~** (*on motorcycle*) monter derrière

pillow ['pɪləʊ] *n* oreiller *m*; **~case** *n* taie *f* d'oreiller

pilot ['paɪlət] *n* pilote *m* ♦ *cpd* (*scheme etc*) pilote, expérimental(e) ♦ *vt* piloter; **~ light** *n* veilleuse *f*

pimp [pɪmp] *n* souteneur *m*, maquereau *m*

pimple ['pɪmpl] *n* bouton *m*

pin [pɪn] *n* épingle *f*; (*TECH*) cheville *f* ♦ *vt* épingler; **~s and needles** fourmis *fpl*; **to ~ sb down** (*fig*) obliger qn à répondre; **to ~ sth on sb** (*fig*) mettre qch sur le dos de qn

pinafore ['pɪnəfɔ:*] *n* tablier *m*

pinball ['pɪnbɔ:l] *n* flipper *m*

pincers ['pɪnsəz] *npl* tenailles *fpl*; (*of crab etc*) pinces *fpl*

pinch [pɪntʃ] *n* (*of salt etc*) pincée *f* ♦ *vt* pincer; (*inf: steal*) piquer, chiper; **at a ~** à la rigueur

pincushion ['pɪnkʊʃən] *n* pelote *f* à épingles

pine [paɪn] *n* (*also: ~ tree*) pin *m* ♦ *vi*: **to ~ for** s'ennuyer de, désirer ardemment; **~ away** *vi* dépérir

pineapple ['paɪnæpl] *n* ananas *m*

ping [pɪŋ] *n* (*noise*) tintement *m*; **~pong** (®) *n* ping-pong *m* (®)

pink [pɪŋk] *adj* rose ♦ *n* (*colour*) rose *m*; (*BOT*) œillet *m*, mignardise *f*

PIN (number) *n* code *m* confidentiel

pinpoint ['pɪnpɔɪnt] *vt* indiquer or localiser (*avec précision*); (*problem*) mettre le doigt sur

pint [paɪnt] *n* pinte *f* (*BRIT = 0.57l; US = 0.47l*) (*BRIT: inf*) ≈ demi *m*

pioneer [paɪə'nɪə*] *n* pionnier *m*

pious ['paɪəs] *adj* pieux(euse)

pip [pɪp] *n* (*seed*) pépin *m*; **the ~s** *npl* (*BRIT: time signal on radio*) le(s) top(s) sonore(s)

pipe [paɪp] *n* tuyau *m*, conduite *f*; (*for smoking*) pipe *f* ♦ *vt* amener par tuyau; **~s** *npl* (*also: bag~s*) cornemuse *f*; **~ down** (*inf*) *vi* se taire; **~ cleaner** *n* cure-pipe *m*; **~ dream** *n* chimère *f*, château *m* en Espagne; **~line** *n* pipe-line *m*; **~r** *n* joueur(euse) de cornemuse

piping ['paɪpɪŋ] *adv*: **~ hot** très chaud(e)

pique [pi:k] *n* dépit *m*

pirate ['paɪərɪt] *n* pirate *m*

Pisces ['paɪsi:z] *n* les Poissons *mpl*

piss [pɪs] (*inf!*) *vi* pisser; **~ed** (*inf!*) *adj* (*drunk*) bourré(e)

pistol ['pɪstl] *n* pistolet *m*

piston ['pɪstən] *n* piston *m*

pit [pɪt] *n* trou *m*, fosse *f*; (*also: coal ~*) puits *m* de mine; (*quarry*) carrière *f* ♦ *vt*: **to ~ one's wits against sb** se mesurer à qn; **~s** *npl* (*AUT*) aire *f* de service

pitch [pɪtʃ] n (MUS) ton m; (BRIT: SPORT) terrain m; (tar) poix f; (fig) degré m; point m ♦ vt (throw) lancer ♦ vi (fall) tomber; to ~ a tent dresser une tente; ~**black** adj noir(e) (comme du cirage); ~**ed battle** n bataille rangée

piteous ['pɪtɪəs] adj pitoyable

pitfall ['pɪtfɔ:l] n piège m

pith [pɪθ] n (of orange etc) intérieur m de l'écorce

pithy ['pɪθɪ] adj piquant(e)

pitiful ['pɪtɪful] adj (touching) pitoyable

pitiless ['pɪtɪləs] adj impitoyable

pittance ['pɪtəns] n salaire m de misère

pity ['pɪtɪ] n pitié f ♦ vt plaindre; what a ~! quel dommage!

pizza ['pi:tsə] n pizza f

placard ['plæka:d] n affiche f; (in march) pancarte f

placate [plə'keɪt] vt apaiser, calmer

place [pleɪs] n endroit m, lieu m; (proper position, job, rank, seat) place f; (home): **at/to his** ~ chez lui ♦ vt (object) placer, mettre; (identify) situer; reconnaître; **to take** ~ avoir lieu; out of ~ (not suitable) déplacé(e), inopportun(e); **to change** ~s with sb changer de place avec qn; **in the first** ~ d'abord, en premier

plague [pleɪg] n fléau m; (MED) peste f ♦ vt tourmenter

plaice [pleɪs] n inv carrelet m

plaid [plæd] n tissu écossais

plain [pleɪn] adj (in one colour) uni(e); (simple) simple; (clear) clair(e), évident(e); (not handsome) quelconque, ordinaire ♦ adv franchement, carrément ♦ n plaine f; ~ **chocolate** n chocolat m à croquer; ~ **clothes** adj (police officer) en civil; ~**ly** adv clairement; (frankly) carrément, sans détours

plaintiff ['pleɪntɪf] n plaignant(e)

plait [plæt] n tresse f, natte f

plan [plæn] n plan m; (scheme) projet m ♦ vt (think in advance) projeter; (prepare) organiser; (house)

dresser les plans de, concevoir ♦ vi faire des projets; **to** ~ **to do** prévoir de faire

plane [pleɪn] n (AVIAT) avion m; (ART, MATH etc) plan m; (fig) niveau m, plan; (tool) rabot m; (also: ~ **tree**) platane m ♦ vt raboter

planet ['plænɪt] n planète f

plank [plæŋk] n planche f

planner ['plænə*] n planificateur(trice); (town ~) urbaniste m/f

planning ['plænɪŋ] n planification f; **family** ~ planning familial; ~ **permission** n permis de construire

plant [plɑ:nt] n plante f; (machinery) matériel m; (factory) usine f ♦ vt planter; (bomb) mettre; (microphone, incriminating evidence) cacher

plaster ['plɑ:stə*] n plâtre m; (also: ~ **of Paris**) plâtre à mouler; (BRIT: also: sticking ~) pansement adhésif ♦ vt plâtrer; (cover): **to** ~ **with** couvrir de; ~**ed** (inf) adj soûl(e)

plastic ['plæstɪk] n plastique m ♦ adj (made of ~) en plastique; ~ **bag** n sac m en plastique

Plasticine ['plæstɪsi:n] (®) n pâte f à modeler

plastic surgery n chirurgie f esthétique

plate [pleɪt] n (dish) assiette f; (in book) gravure f, planche f; (dental ~) dentier m

plateau ['plætəʊ] (pl ~s or ~x) n plateau m

plate glass n verre m (de vitrine)

platform ['plætfɔ:m] n plate-forme f; (at meeting) tribune f; (stage) estrade f; (RAIL) quai m

platinum ['plætɪnəm] n platine m

platter ['plætə*] n plat m

plausible ['plɔ:zɪbl] adj plausible; (person) convaincant(e)

play [pleɪ] n (THEATRE) pièce f de théâtre ♦ vt (game) jouer à; (team, opponent) jouer contre; (instrument) jouer de; (play, part, piece of music, note) jouer; (record etc) passer ♦ vi jouer; **to** ~ **safe** ne prendre aucun risque; ~ **down** vt minimiser; ~ **up**

vi (cause trouble) faire des siennes; ~boy n playboy m; ~er n joueur(euse); (THEATRE) acteur(trice); (MUS) musicien(ne); ~ful adj enjoué(e); ~ground n cour f de récréation; (in park) aire f de jeux; ~group n garderie f; ~ing card n carte f à jouer; ~ing field n terrain m de sport; ~mate n camarade m/f, copain(copine); ~off n (SPORT) belle f; ~pen n parc m (pour bébé); ~thing n jouet m; ~time n récréation f; ~wright n dramaturge m

plc abbr (= public limited company) ≈ SARL f

plea [pli:] n (request) appel m; (LAW) défense f

plead [pli:d] vi plaider; (give as excuse) invoquer ♦ vi (LAW) plaider; (beg): to ~ with sb implorer qn

pleasant ['plɛznt] adj agréable; ~ries npl (polite remarks) civilités fpl

please [pli:z] excl s'il te (or vous) plaît ♦ vt plaire à ♦ vi plaire; (think fit): do as you ~ faites comme il vous plaira; ~ yourself! à ta (or votre) guise!; ~d adj: ~d (with) content(e) (de); ~d to meet you enchanté (de faire votre connaissance); pleasing ['pli:zɪŋ] adj plaisant(e), qui fait plaisir

pleasure ['plɛʒə*] n plaisir m; "it's a ~" "je vous en prie"; ~ boat n bateau m de plaisance

pleat [pli:t] n pli m

pledge [plɛdʒ] n (promise) promesse f ♦ vt engager; promettre

plentiful ['plɛntɪful] adj abondant(e), copieux(euse)

plenty ['plɛntɪ] n: ~ of beaucoup de; (bien) assez de

pliable ['plaɪəbl] adj flexible; (person) malléable

pliers ['plaɪəz] npl pinces fpl

plight [plaɪt] n situation f critique

plimsolls ['plɪmsəlz] (BRIT) npl chaussures fpl de tennis, tennis mpl

plinth [plɪnθ] n (of statue) socle m

plod [plɒd] vi avancer péniblement; (fig) peiner

plonk [plɒŋk] (inf) n (BRIT: wine) pinard m, piquette f ♦ vt: to ~ sth down poser brusquement qch

plot [plɒt] n complot m, conspiration f; (of story, play) intrigue f; (of land) lot m de terre, lopin m ♦ vt (sb's downfall) comploter; (mark out) pointer; relever, déterminer ♦ vi comploter

plough [plau] (US plow) n charrue f ♦ vt (earth) labourer; ~ money into investir dans; ~ through vt fus (snow etc) avancer péniblement dans; ~man's lunch (BRIT) n assiette froide avec du pain, du fromage et des pickles

ploy [plɔɪ] n stratagème m

pluck [plʌk] vt (fruit) cueillir; (musical instrument) pincer; (bird) plumer; (eyebrow) épiler ♦ n courage m, cran m; to ~ up courage prendre son courage à deux mains

plug [plʌg] n (ELEC) prise f de courant; (stopper) bouchon m, bonde f; (AUT: also: spark(ing) ~) bougie f ♦ vt (hole) boucher; (inf: advertise) faire de la battage pour; ~ in vt (ELEC) brancher

plum [plʌm] n (fruit) prune f ♦ cpd: ~ job (inf) travail m en or

plumb [plʌm] vt: to ~ the depths (fig) toucher le fond (du désespoir)

plumber ['plʌmə*] n plombier m

plumbing ['plʌmɪŋ] n (trade) plomberie f; (piping) tuyauterie f

plummet ['plʌmɪt] vi: to ~ (down) plonger, dégringoler

plump [plʌmp] adj rondelet(te), dodu(e), bien en chair ♦ vi: to ~ for (col: choose) se décider pour

plunder ['plʌndə*] n pillage m (loot) butin m ♦ vt piller

plunge [plʌndʒ] n plongeon m; (fig) chute f ♦ vt plonger ♦ vi (dive) plonger (fall) tomber, dégringoler; to take the ~ se jeter à l'eau; ~r n (for drain) (déboucher m à) ventouse f; plunging adj: plunging neckline décolleté plongeant

pluperfect [pluːˈpɜːfɪkt] n plus-que-parfait m

plural [ˈplʊərəl] adj pluriel(le) ♦ n pluriel m

plus [plʌs] n (also: ~ sign) signe m plus ♦ prep plus; **ten/twenty** ~ plus de dix/vingt

plush [plʌʃ] adj somptueux(euse)

ply [plaɪ] vt (a trade) exercer ♦ vi (ship) faire la navette ♦ n (of wool, rope) fil m, brin m; **to** ~ **sb with drink** donner continuellement à boire à qn; **to** ~ **sb with questions** presser qn de questions; ~**wood** n contre-plaqué m

PM abbr = **Prime Minister**

p.m. adv abbr (= post meridiem) de l'après-midi

pneumatic drill [njuːˈmætɪk-] n marteau-piqueur m

pneumonia [njuːˈməʊnɪə] n pneumonie f

poach [pəʊtʃ] vt (cook) pocher; (steal) pêcher (or chasser) sans permis ♦ vi braconner; ~**ed egg** n œuf poché; ~**er** n braconnier m

P.O. Box n abbr = **Post Office Box**

pocket [ˈpɒkɪt] n poche f ♦ vt empocher; **to be out of** ~ (BRIT) en être de sa poche; ~**book** n (US) (wallet) portefeuille m; ~ **knife** n canif m; ~ **money** n argent m de poche

pod [pɒd] n cosse f

podgy [ˈpɒdʒɪ] adj rondelet(te)

podiatrist [pɒˈdiːətrɪst] (US) n pédicure m/f, podologue m/f

poem [ˈpəʊɪm] n poème m

poet [ˈpəʊɪt] n poète m; ~**ic** adj poétique; ~ **laureate** n poète lauréat (nommé par la Cour royal); ~**ry** n poésie f

poignant [ˈpɔɪnjənt] adj poignant(e); (sharp) vif(vive)

point [pɔɪnt] n (tip) pointe f; (in time) moment m; (in space) endroit m; (subject, idea) point, sujet m; (purpose) sens m; (ELEC) prise f; (also: decimal ~): **2** ~ **3** (2.3) 2 virgule 3 (2,3) ♦ vt (show) indiquer;

(gun etc): **to** ~ **sth at** braquer or diriger qch sur ♦ vi: **to** ~ **at** montrer du doigt; ~**s** npl (AUT) vis platinées; (RAIL) aiguillage m; **to be on the** ~ **of doing sth** être sur le point de faire qch; **to make a** ~ **of doing** ne pas manquer de faire; **to get the** ~ comprendre, saisir; **to miss the** ~ ne pas comprendre; **to come to the** ~ en venir au fait; **there's no** ~ (in doing) cela ne sert à rien (de faire); ~ **out** vt faire remarquer, souligner; ~ **to** vt fus (fig) indiquer; ~**-blank** adv (fig) catégoriquement; (also: at ~-blank range) à bout portant; ~**ed** adj (shape) pointu(e); (remark) plein(e) de sous-entendus; ~**er** n (needle) aiguille f; (piece of advice) conseil m; (clue) indice m; ~**less** adj inutile, vain(e); ~ **of view** n point m de vue

poise [pɔɪz] n (composure) calme m

poison [ˈpɔɪzn] n poison m ♦ vt empoisonner; ~**ous** adj (snake) venimeux(euse); (plant) vénéneux(euse); (fumes etc) toxique

poke [pəʊk] vt (fire) tisonner; (jab with finger, stick etc) piquer; pousser du doigt; (put): **to** ~ **sth in(to)** fourrer or enfoncer qch dans; ~ **about** vi fureter

poker [ˈpəʊkə*] n tisonnier m; (CARDS) poker m

poky [ˈpəʊkɪ] adj exigu(ë)

Poland [ˈpəʊlənd] n Pologne f

polar [ˈpəʊlə*] adj polaire; ~ **bear** n ours blanc

Pole [pəʊl] n Polonais(e)

pole [pəʊl] n poteau m; (of wood) mât m, perche f; (GEO) pôle m; ~ **bean** (US) n haricot m (à rames); ~ **vault** n saut m à la perche

police [pəˈliːs] npl police f ♦ vt maintenir l'ordre dans; ~ **car** n voiture f de police; ~**man** (irreg) n agent m de police, policier m; ~ **station** n commissariat m de police; ~**woman** (irreg) n femme-agent f

policy [ˈpɒlɪsɪ] n politique f; (also: insurance ~) police f (d'assurance)

polio ['pəʊlɪəʊ] n polio f

Polish ['pəʊlɪʃ] adj polonais(e) ♦ n (LING) polonais m

polish ['pɒlɪʃ] n (for shoes) cirage m; (for floor) cire f, encaustique f; (shine) éclat m, poli m; (fig: refinement) raffinement m ♦ vt (put polish on shoes, wood) cirer; (make shiny) astiquer, faire briller; ~ **off** vt (work) expédier; (food) liquider; ~**ed** adj (fig) raffiné(e)

polite [pə'laɪt] adj poli(e); **in ~ society** dans la bonne société; ~**ness** n politesse f

political [pə'lɪtɪkəl] adj politique

politician [pɒlɪ'tɪʃən] n homme m politique, politicien m

politics ['pɒlɪtɪks] npl politique f

poll [pəʊl] n scrutin m, vote m; (also: opinion ~) sondage m (d'opinion) ♦ vt obtenir

pollen ['pɒlən] n pollen m

polling day ['pəʊlɪŋ-] (BRIT) n jour m des élections

polling station (BRIT) n bureau m de vote

pollute [pə'luːt] vt polluer; **pollution** n pollution f

polo ['pəʊləʊ] n polo m; ~-**necked** adj à col roulé; ~ **shirt** n polo m

poltergeist ['pɒltəgaɪst] n esprit frappeur

polyester [pɒlɪ'estə*] n polyester m

polytechnic [pɒlɪ'teknɪk] (BRIT) n (college) I.U.T. m, Institut m Universitaire de Technologie

polythene ['pɒlɪθiːn] n polyéthylène m; ~ **bag** n sac m en plastique

pomegranate ['pɒmɪgrænɪt] n grenade f

pomp [pɒmp] n pompe f, faste m, apparat m; ~**ous** adj pompeux(euse)

pond [pɒnd] n étang m; mare f

ponder ['pɒndə*] vt considérer, peser; ~**ous** adj pesant(e), lourd(e)

pong [pɒŋ] (BRIT: inf) n puanteur f

pony ['pəʊnɪ] n poney m; ~**tail** n queue f de cheval; ~ **trekking** (BRIT) n randonnée f à cheval

poodle ['puːdl] n caniche m

pool [puːl] n (of rain) flaque f; (pond) mare f; (also: swimming ~) piscine f; (billiards) billard m ♦ vt mettre en commun; ~**s** npl (football pools) ≈ loto sportif

poor [pʊə*] adj pauvre; (mediocre) médiocre, faible, mauvais(e) ♦ npl: **the** ~ les pauvres mpl; ~**ly** adj souffrant(e), malade ♦ adv mal; médiocrement

pop [pɒp] n (MUS) musique f pop; (drink) boisson gazeuse; (US: inf: father) papa m; (noise) bruit sec ♦ vt (put) mettre (rapidement) ♦ vi éclater; (cork) sauter; ~ **in** vi entrer en passant; ~ **out** vi sortir (brièvement); ~ **up** vi apparaître, surgir

pope [pəʊp] n pape m

poplar ['pɒplə*] n peuplier m

popper ['pɒpə*] (BRIT: inf) n bouton-pression m

poppy ['pɒpɪ] n coquelicot m; pavot m

Popsicle ['pɒpsɪkl] (® US) n esquimau m (glace)

popular ['pɒpjʊlə*] adj populaire; (fashionable) à la mode

population [pɒpjʊ'leɪʃən] n population f

porcelain ['pɔːslɪn] n porcelaine f

porch [pɔːtʃ] n porche m; (US) véranda f

porcupine ['pɔːkjʊpaɪn] n porc-épic m

pore [pɔː*] n pore m ♦ vi: **to** ~ **over** s'absorber dans, être plongé(e) dans

pork [pɔːk] n porc m

pornography [pɔː'nɒgrəfɪ] n pornographie f

porpoise ['pɔːpəs] n marsouin m

porridge ['pɒrɪdʒ] n porridge m

port [pɔːt] n (harbour) port m; (NAUT: left side) bâbord m; (wine) porto m; ~ **of call** escale f

portable ['pɔːtəbl] adj portatif(ive)

porter ['pɔːtə*] n (for luggage) porteur m; (doorkeeper) gardien m; portier m

portfolio [pɔːtˈfəʊliəʊ] n portefeuille m; (of artist) portfolio m

porthole [ˈpɔːthəʊl] n hublot m

portion [ˈpɔːʃən] n portion f, part f

portly [ˈpɔːtli] adj corpulent(e)

portrait [ˈpɔːtrɪt] n portrait m

portray [pɔːˈtreɪ] vt faire le portrait de; (in writing) dépeindre, représenter; (subj: actor) jouer; ~al n portrait m, représentation f

Portugal [ˈpɔːtjʊɡəl] n Portugal m

Portuguese [pɔːtjʊˈɡiːz] adj portugais(e) ♦ n inv Portugais(e); (LING) portugais m

pose [pəʊz] n pose f ♦ vi (pretend): to ~ as se poser en ♦ vt poser; (problem) créer

posh [pɒʃ] (inf) adj chic inv

position [pəˈzɪʃən] n position f; (job) situation f ♦ vt placer

positive [ˈpɒzɪtɪv] adj positif(ive); (certain) sûr(e), certain(e); (definite) formel(le), catégorique

posse [ˈpɒsɪ] (US) n détachement m

possess [pəˈzɛs] vt posséder; ~ion n possession f

possibility [pɒsəˈbɪlɪtɪ] n possibilité f; éventualité f

possible [ˈpɒsəbl] adj possible; as big as ~ aussi gros que possible

possibly [ˈpɒsəblɪ] adv (perhaps) peut-être; **if you** ~ **can** si cela vous est possible; **I cannot** ~ **come** il m'est impossible de venir

post [pəʊst] n poste f; (BRIT: letters, delivery) courrier m; (job, situation, MIL) poste m; (pole) poteau m ♦ vt (BRIT: send by ~) poster; (: appoint): **to** ~ **to** affecter à; ~**age** n tarifs mpl d'affranchissement; ~**al order** n mandat-(poste) m; ~**box** (BRIT) n boîte f aux lettres; ~**card** n carte postale; ~**code** (BRIT) n code postal

poster [ˈpəʊstə*] n affiche f

poste restante [ˈpəʊstˈrɛstɑ̃ːt] (BRIT) n poste restante

postgraduate [ˈpəʊstˈɡrædjʊət] n (= étudiant(e)) de troisième cycle

posthumous [ˈpɒstjʊməs] adj posthume

postman [ˈpəʊstmən] (irreg) n facteur m

postmark [ˈpəʊstmɑːk] n cachet m (de la poste)

postmortem [ˈpəʊstˈmɔːtəm] n autopsie f

post office n (building) poste f; (organization): **the Post Office** les Postes; **Post Office Box** n boîte postale

postpone [pəˈspəʊn] vt remettre (à plus tard)

posture [ˈpɒstʃə*] n posture f; (fig) attitude f

postwar [ˈpəʊstˈwɔː*] adj d'après-guerre

posy [ˈpəʊzɪ] n petit bouquet

pot [pɒt] n pot m; (for cooking) marmite f; casserole f; (tea~) théière f; (coffee~) cafetière f; (inf: marijuana) herbe f ♦ vt (plant) mettre en pot; **to go to** ~ (inf: work, performance) aller à vau-l'eau

potato [pəˈteɪtəʊ] (pl ~es) n pomme f de terre; ~ **peeler** n épluchelégumes m inv

potent [ˈpəʊtənt] adj puissant(e); (drink) fort(e), très alcoolisé(e); (man) viril

potential [pəˈtɛnʃəl] adj potentiel(le) ♦ n potentiel m

pothole [ˈpɒthəʊl] n (in road) nid m de poule; (BRIT: underground) gouffre m, caverne f; **potholing** [ˈpɒthəʊlɪŋ] (BRIT) n: **to go potholing** faire de la spéléologie

potluck [ˈpɒtˈlʌk] n: **to take** ~ tenter sa chance

potted [ˈpɒtɪd] adj (food) en conserve; (plant) en pot; (abbreviated) abrégé(e)

potter [ˈpɒtə*] n potier m ♦ vi: **to** ~ **around**, ~ **about** (BRIT) bricoler; ~**y** n poterie f

potty [ˈpɒtɪ] adj (inf: mad) dingue ♦ n (child's) pot m

pouch [paʊtʃ] n (ZOOL) poche f; (for tobacco) blague f; (for money) bourse f

poultry [ˈpəʊltrɪ] n volaille f

pounce [paʊns] vi: to ~ (on) bondir (sur), sauter (sur)

pound [paʊnd] n (unit of money) livre f; (unit of weight) livre f ♦ vt (beat) bourrer de coups, marteler; (crush) piler, pulvériser ♦ vi (heart) battre violemment, taper

pour [pɔ:*] vt verser ♦ vi couler à flots; to ~ (with rain) pleuvoir à verse; to ~ sb a drink verser ou servir à boire à qn; ~ **away** vt vider; ~ **in** vi (people) affluer, se précipiter; (news, letters etc) arriver en masse; ~ **off** vt = **pour away**; ~ **out** vi (people) sortir en masse ♦ vt vider; (fig) déverser; (serve: a drink) verser; ~**ing** adj: ~**ing rain** pluie torrentielle

pout [paʊt] vi faire la moue

poverty [ˈpɒvətɪ] n pauvreté f, misère f; ~-**stricken** adj pauvre, déshérité(e)

powder [ˈpaʊdə*] n poudre f ♦ vt: to ~ one's face se poudrer; ~ **compact** n poudrier m; ~**ed milk** n lait m en poudre; ~ **puff** n houppette f; ~ **room** n toilettes fpl (pour dames)

power [ˈpaʊə*] n (strength) puissance f, force f; (ability, authority) pouvoir m; (of speech, thought) faculté f; (ELEC) courant m; to be in ~ (POL etc) être au pouvoir; ~ **cut** (BRIT) n coupure f de courant; ~**ed** adj: ~**ed by** actionné(e) par, fonctionnant à; ~**ful** adj puissant(e); ~**less** adj impuissant(e); ~ **point** (BRIT) n prise f de courant; ~ **station** n centrale f électrique

p.p. abbr (= per procurationem): ~ J. Smith pour M. J. Smith

PR n abbr = **public relations**

practical [ˈpræktɪkl] adj pratique; ~**ities** npl (of situation) aspect m pratique; ~**ity** (no pl) n (of person) sens m pratique; ~ **joke** n farce f; ~**ly** adv (almost) pratiquement

practice [ˈpræktɪs] n pratique f; (of profession) exercice m; (at football etc) entraînement m; (business) ca-

binet m ♦ vt, vi (US) = **practise**; in ~ (in reality) en pratique; out of ~ rouillé(e)

practise [ˈpræktɪs] (US **practice**) vt (musical instrument) travailler; (train for: sport) s'entraîner à; (a sport, religion) pratiquer; (profession) exercer ♦ vi s'exercer, travailler; (train) s'entraîner; (lawyer, doctor) exercer; **practising** [ˈpræktɪsɪŋ] adj (Christian etc) pratiquant(e); (lawyer) en exercice

practitioner [prækˈtɪʃənə*] n praticien(ne)

prairie [ˈprɛərɪ] n steppe f, prairie f

praise [preɪz] n éloge(s) m(pl), louange(s) f(pl) ♦ vt louer, faire l'éloge de; ~**worthy** adj digne d'éloges

pram [præm] (BRIT) n landau m, voiture f d'enfant

prance [prɑːns] vi (also: to ~ about: person) se pavaner

prank [præŋk] n farce f

prawn [prɔːn] n crevette f (rose)

pray [preɪ] vi prier; ~**er** [prɛə*] n prière f

preach [priːtʃ] vt, vi prêcher

precaution [prɪˈkɔːʃən] n précaution f

precede [prɪˈsiːd] vt précéder

precedent [ˈprɛsɪdənt] n précédent m

precinct [ˈpriːsɪŋkt] n (US) circonscription f, arrondissement m; ~**s** npl (neighbourhood) alentours mpl, environs mpl; **pedestrian** ~ (BRIT) zone piétonnière; **shopping** ~ (BRIT) centre commercial

precious [ˈprɛʃəs] adj précieux(euse)

precipitate [adj prɪˈsɪpɪtɪt, vb prɪˈsɪpɪteɪt] vt précipiter

precise [prɪˈsaɪs] adj précis(e); ~**ly** adv précisément

preclude [prɪˈkluːd] vt exclure

precocious [prɪˈkəʊʃəs] adj précoce

precondition [ˈpriːkənˈdɪʃən] n condition f nécessaire

predecessor [ˈpriːdɪsesə*] n prédécesseur m

predicament [prɪ'dɪkəmənt] n situation f difficile

predict [prɪ'dɪkt] vt prédire; **~able** adj prévisible

predominantly [prɪ'dɒmɪnntlɪ] adv en majeure partie; surtout

preempt vt anticiper, devancer

preen [pri:n] vt: to ~ itself (bird) se lisser les plumes; to ~ o.s. s'admirer

prefab ['pri:fæb] n bâtiment préfabriqué

preface ['prefɪs] n préface f

prefect ['pri:fekt] (BRIT) n (in school) élève chargé(e) de certaines fonctions de discipline

prefer [prɪ'fɜ:*] vt préférer; **~ably** adv de préférence; **~ence** n préférence f; **~ential** adj: **~ential treatment** traitement m de faveur ou préférentiel

prefix ['pri:fɪks] n préfixe m

pregnancy ['pregnənsɪ] n grossesse f

pregnant ['pregnənt] adj enceinte; (animal) pleine

prehistoric ['pri:hɪs'tɔrɪk] adj préhistorique

prejudice ['predʒʊdɪs] n préjugé m; **~d** adj (person) plein(e) de préjugés; (in a matter) partial(e)

premarital ['pri:'mærɪtl] adj avant le mariage

premature ['premətʃʊə*] adj prématuré(e)

premier ['premɪə*] adj premier(ère), principal(e) ♦ n (POL) Premier ministre

première [premɪ'ɛə*] n première f

premise ['premɪs] n prémisse f; **~s** npl (building) locaux mpl; **on the ~s** sur les lieux, sur place

premium ['pri:mɪəm] n prime f; to be at a ~ faire prime; ~ **bond** (BRIT) n bon m à lot, obligation f à prime

premonition [premə'nɪʃən] n prémonition f

preoccupied [prɪ'ɒkjʊpaɪd] adj préoccupé(e)

prep [prep] n (SCOL: study) étude f

prepaid ['pri:'peɪd] adj payée(e) d'avance

preparation [prepə'reɪʃən] n préparation f; **~s** npl (for trip, war) préparatifs mpl

preparatory [prɪ'pærətərɪ] adj préliminaire; ~ **school** n école primaire privée

prepare [prɪ'pɛə*] vt préparer ♦ vi: to ~ for se préparer à; **~d to** prêt(e) à

preposition [prepə'zɪʃən] n préposition f

preposterous [prɪ'pɒstərəs] adj absurde

prep school n = preparatory school

prerequisite ['pri:'rekwɪzɪt] n condition f préalable

prescribe [prɪs'kraɪb] vt prescrire

prescription [prɪs'krɪpʃən] n (MED) ordonnance f; (: medicine) médicament (obtenu sur ordonnance)

presence ['prezns] n présence f; ~ **of mind** présence d'esprit

present [adj, n 'preznt, vb prɪ'zent] adj présent(e) ♦ n (gift) cadeau m; (actuality) présent m ♦ vt présenter; (prize, medal) remettre; (give): to ~ **sb with sth** ou **sth to sb** offrir qch à qn; to give sb a ~ offrir un cadeau à qn; at ~ en ce moment; **~ation** n présentation f; (ceremony) remise f du cadeau (or de la médaille etc); **~-day** adj contemporain(e), actuel(le); **~er** n (RADIO, TV) présentateur(trice); **~ly** adv (with verb in past) peu après; (soon) tout à l'heure, bientôt; (at present) en ce moment

preservative [prɪ'zɜ:vətɪv] n agent m de conservation

preserve [prɪ'zɜ:v] vt (keep safe) préserver, protéger; (maintain) conserver, garder; (food) mettre en conserve ♦ n (often pl: jam) confiture f

president ['prezɪdənt] n président; **~ial** adj présidentiel(le)

press [pres] n presse f; (for wine)

pressoir *m* ♦ *vt* (*squeeze*) presser, serrer; (*push*) appuyer sur; (*clothes: iron*) repasser; (*put pressure on*) faire pression sur; (*insist*): to ~ sth on sb presser qn d'accepter qch ♦ *vi* appuyer, peser; to ~ for sth faire pression pour obtenir qch; we are ~ed for time/money le temps/l'argent nous manque; ~ on *vi* continuer; ~ **conference** *n* conférence *f* de presse; ~ing *adj* urgent(e), pressant(e); ~ **stud** (*BRIT*) *n* bouton-pression *m*; ~-up (*BRIT*) *n* traction *f*

pressure ['prɛʃə*] *n* pression *f*; (*stress*) tension *f*; to put ~ on sb (to do) faire pression sur qn (pour qu'il/elle fasse); ~ **cooker** *n* cocotte-minute *f*; ~ **gauge** *n* manomètre *m*; ~ **group** *n* groupe *m* de pression

prestige [prɛs'ti:ʒ] *n* prestige *m*

presumably [prɪ'zju:məblɪ] *adv* vraisemblablement

presume [prɪ'zju:m] *vt* présumer, supposer

pretence [prɪ'tɛns] (*US* pretense) *n* (*claim*) prétention *f*; under false ~s sous des prétextes fallacieux

pretend [prɪ'tɛnd] *vt* (*feign*) feindre, simuler ♦ *vi* faire semblant

pretext ['pri:tɛkst] *n* prétexte *m*

pretty ['prɪtɪ] *adj* joli(e) ♦ *adv* assez

prevail [prɪ'veɪl] *vi* (*be usual*) avoir cours; (*win*) l'emporter, prévaloir; ~ing *adj* dominant(e)

prevalent ['prɛvələnt] *adj* répandu(e), courant(e)

prevent [prɪ'vɛnt] *vt*: to ~ (from doing) empêcher (de faire); ~ative *adj* = preventive; ~ive *adj* préventif(ive)

preview ['pri:vju:] *n* (*of film etc*) avant-première *f*

previous ['pri:vɪəs] *adj* précédent(e); antérieur(e); ~ly *adv* précédemment, auparavant

prewar [pri:'wɔ:*] *adj* d'avant-guerre

prey [preɪ] *n* proie *f* ♦ *vi*: to ~ on s'attaquer à; it was ~ing on his mind cela le travaillait

price [praɪs] *n* prix *m* ♦ *vt* (*goods*) fixer le prix de; ~less *adj* sans prix, inestimable; ~ **list** *n* liste *f* des prix, tarif *m*

prick [prɪk] *n* piqûre *f* ♦ *vt* piquer; to ~ up one's ears dresser *or* tendre l'oreille

prickle ['prɪkl] *n* (*of plant*) épine *f*; (*sensation*) picotement *m*; **prickly** ['prɪklɪ] *adj* piquant(e), épineux(euse); **prickly heat** *n* fièvre *f* miliaire

pride [praɪd] *n* orgueil *m*; fierté *f* ♦ *vt*: to ~ o.s. on se flatter de; s'enorgueillir de

priest [pri:st] *n* prêtre *m*; ~hood *n* prêtrise *f*, sacerdoce *m*

prim [prɪm] *adj* collet monté *inv*, guindé(e)

primarily ['praɪmərɪlɪ] *adv* principalement, essentiellement

primary ['praɪmərɪ] *adj* (*first in importance*) premier(ère), primordial(e), principal(e) ♦ *n* (*US: election*) (élection *f*) primaire *f*; ~ **school** (*BRIT*) *n* école primaire *f*

prime [praɪm] *adj* primordial(e), fondamental(e); (*excellent*) excellent(e) ♦ *n*: in the ~ of life dans la fleur de l'âge ♦ *vt* (*wood*) apprêter; (*fig*) mettre au courant; P~ **Minister** *n* Premier ministre *m*

primeval [praɪ'mi:vəl] *adj* primitif(ive); ~ **forest** forêt *f* vierge

primitive ['prɪmɪtɪv] *adj* primitif(ive)

primrose ['prɪmrəʊz] *n* primevère *f*

primus (**stove**) ['praɪməs] (®:*BRIT*) *n* réchaud *m* de camping

prince [prɪns] *n* prince *m*

princess [prɪn'sɛs] *n* princesse *f*

principal ['prɪnsəpl] *adj* principal(e) ♦ *n* (*headmaster*) directeur(trice), principal *n*

principle ['prɪnsəpl] *n* principe *m*; in/on ~ en/par principe

print [prɪnt] *n* (*mark*) empreinte *f*; (*letters*) caractères *mpl*; (*ART*) gravure *f*, estampe *f*; (: *photograph*) photo *f* ♦ *vt* imprimer; (*publish*) publier; (*write in block letters*) écrire en caractères d'imprimerie; **out of ~** épuisé(e); **~ed matter** *n* imprimés *m*(*pl*); **~er** *n* imprimeur *m*; (*machine*) imprimante *f*; **~ing** *n* impression *f*; **~out** *n* copie *f* papier

prior ['praɪə*] *adj* antérieur(e), précédent(e); (*more important*) prioritaire ♦ *adv*: **~ to doing** avant de faire

priority [praɪ'ɔrɪtɪ] *n* priorité *f*

prise [praɪz] *vt*: **to ~ open** forcer

prison ['prɪzn] *n* prison *f* ♦ *cpd* pénitentiaire; **~er** *n* prisonnier(ère)

pristine ['prɪstiːn] *adj* parfait(e)

privacy ['prɪvəsɪ] *n* intimité *f*, solitude *f*

private ['praɪvɪt] *adj* privé(e), (*personal*) personnel(le); (*house, lesson*) particulier(ère); (*quiet: place*) tranquille; (*reserved: person*) secret(ète) ♦ *n* soldat de deuxième classe; **"~"** (*on envelope*) "personnelle"; **in ~** en privé; **~ enterprise** *n* l'entreprise privée; **~ eye** *n* détective privé; **~ property** *n* propriété privée; **privatize** *vt* privatiser

privet ['prɪvɪt] *n* troène *m*

privilege ['prɪvɪlɪdʒ] *n* privilège *m*

privy ['prɪvɪ] *adj*: **to be ~ to** être au courant de

prize [praɪz] *n* prix *m* ♦ *adj* (*example, idiot*) parfait(e); (*bull, novel*) primé(e) ♦ *vt* priser, faire grand cas de; **~giving** *n* distribution *f* des prix; **~winner** *n* gagnant(e)

pro [prəu] *n* (*SPORT*) professionnel(le), *m*; **the ~s and cons** le pour et le contre

probability [prɔbə'bɪlɪtɪ] *n* probabilité *f*; **probable** ['prɔbəbl] *adj* probable; **probably** *adv* probablement

probation [prə'beɪʃən] *n*: **on ~** (*LAW*) en liberté surveillée, en sursis; (*employee*) à l'essai

probe [prəub] *n* (*MED, SPACE*) sonde *f*; (*enquiry*) enquête *f*, investigation *f* ♦ *vt* sonder, explorer

problem ['prɔbləm] *n* problème *m*

procedure [prə'siːdʒə*] *n* (*ADMIN, LAW*) procédure *f*; (*method*) marche *f* à suivre, façon *f* de procéder

proceed [prə'siːd] *vi* continuer; (*go forward*) avancer; **to ~** (*with*) continuer, poursuivre; **to ~ to** se mettre à faire; **~ings** *npl* (*LAW*) poursuites *fpl*; (*meeting*) réunion *f*, séance *f*; **~s** ['prəusiːdz] *npl* produit *m*, recette *f*

process ['prəuses] *n* processus *m*; (*method*) procédé *m* ♦ *vt* traiter; **~ing** *n* (*PHOT*) développement *m*; **~ion** [prə'seʃən] *n* défilé *m*, cortège *m*; (*REL*) procession *f*; **funeral ~ion** (*on foot*) cortège *m* funèbre; (*in cars*) convoi *m* mortuaire

proclaim [prə'kleɪm] *vt* déclarer, proclamer

procrastinate [prəu'kræstɪneɪt] *vi* faire traîner les choses, vouloir tout remettre au lendemain

procure [prə'kjuə*] *vt* obtenir

prod [prɔd] *vt* pousser

prodigal ['prɔdɪgəl] *adj* prodigue

prodigy ['prɔdɪdʒɪ] *n* prodige *m*

produce [*n* 'prɔdjuːs, *vb* prə'djuːs] *n* (*AGR*) produits *mpl* ♦ *vt* produire; (*to show*) présenter; (*cause*) provoquer, causer; (*THEATRE*) monter, mettre en scène; **~r** *n* producteur *m*; (*THEATRE*) metteur en scène

product ['prɔdʌkt] *n* produit *m*

production [prə'dʌkʃən] *n* production *f*; (*THEATRE*) mise *f* en scène; **~ line** *n* chaîne *f* (de fabrication)

productivity [prɔdʌk'tɪvɪtɪ] *n* productivité *f*

profession [prə'feʃən] *n* profession *f*; **~al** *n* professionnel(le) ♦ *adj* professionnel(le); (*work*) de professionnel

professor [prə'fesə*] *n* professeur *m* (titulaire d'une chaire)

proficiency [prə'fɪʃənsɪ] *n* compétence *f*, aptitude *f*

profile ['prəufaɪl] *n* profil *m*

profit ['prɔfɪt] *n* bénéfice *m*; profit *m* ♦ *vi*: **to ~ (by** or **from)** profiter (de); **~able** *adj* lucratif(ive), rentable

profound [prə'faʊnd] *adj* profond(e)

profusely [prə'fju:slɪ] *adv* abondamment; avec effusion

prognosis [prɒg'nəʊsɪs] (*pl* **prognoses**) *n* pronostic *m*

programme [prəʊgræm] (*US* **program**) *n* programme *m*; (*RADIO, TV*) émission *f* ♦ *vt* programmer; ~**r** (*US* **programer**) *n* programmeur(euse)

progress [*n* 'prəʊgres, *vb* prə'gres] *n* progrès *m*(*pl*) ♦ *vi* progresser, avancer; **in** ~ en cours; ~**ive** *adj* progressif(ive); (*person*) progressiste

prohibit [prə'hɪbɪt] *vt* interdire, défendre

project [*n* 'prɒdʒekt, *vb* prə'dʒekt] *n* (*plan*) projet *m*, plan *m*; (*venture*) opération *f*, entreprise *f*; (*research*) étude *f*, dossier *m* ♦ *vt* projeter ♦ *vi* (*stick out*) faire saillie, s'avancer; ~**ion** [prə'dʒekʃən] *n* projection *f*; (*overhang*) saillie *f*; ~**or** [prə'dʒektə*] *n* projecteur *m*

prolong [prə'lɒŋ] *vt* prolonger

prom [prɒm] *n abbr* = **promenade**; (*US: ball*) bal *m* d'étudiants

promenade [prɒmɪ'nɑ:d] *n* (*by sea*) esplanade *f*, promenade *f*; ~ **concert** (*BRIT*) *n* concert *m* populaire (de musique classique)

prominent ['prɒmɪnənt] *adj* (*standing out*) proéminent(e); (*important*) important(e)

promiscuous [prə'mɪskjʊəs] *adj* (*sexually*) de mœurs légères

promise ['prɒmɪs] *n* promesse *f* ♦ *vt, vi* promettre; **promising** ['prɒmɪsɪŋ] *adj* prometteur(euse)

promote [prə'məʊt] *vt* promouvoir; (*new product*) faire la promotion de; ~**r** *n* (*of event*) organisateur(trice); (*of cause, idea*) promoteur(trice); **promotion** [prə'məʊʃən] *n* promotion *f*

prompt [prɒmpt] *adj* rapide ♦ *adv* (*punctually*) à l'heure ♦ *n* (*COMPUT*) message *m* (de guidage) ♦ *vt* provoquer; (*person*) inciter,

pousser; (*THEATRE*) souffler (son rôle or ses répliques) à; ~**ly** *adv* rapidement, sans délai; ponctuellement

prone [prəʊn] *adj* (*lying*) couché(e) (face contre terre); ~ **to** enclin(e) à

prong [prɒŋ] *n* (of fork) dent *f*

pronoun ['prəʊnaʊn] *n* pronom *m*

pronounce [prə'naʊns] *vt* prononcer

pronunciation [prənʌnsɪ'eɪʃən] *n* prononciation *f*

proof [pru:f] *n* preuve *f*; (*TYP*) épreuve *f* ♦ *adj*: ~ **against** à l'épreuve de

prop [prɒp] *n* support *m*, étai *m*; (*fig*) soutien *m* ♦ *vt* (*also*: ~ **up**) étayer, soutenir; (*lean*): **to** ~ **sth against** appuyer qch contre or à

propaganda [prɒpə'gændə] *n* propagande *f*

propel [prə'pel] *vt* propulser, faire avancer; ~**ler** *n* hélice *f*

propensity [prə'pensɪtɪ] *n*: **a** ~ **for** or **to/to do** une propension à/à faire

proper ['prɒpə*] *adj* (*suited, right*) approprié(e), bon(bonne); (*seemly*) correct(e), convenable; (*authentic*) vrai(e), véritable; (*referring to place*): **the village** ~ le village proprement dit; ~**ly** *adv* correctement, convenablement; ~ **noun** *n* nom *m* propre

property ['prɒpətɪ] *n* propriété *f*; (*things owned*) biens *mpl*; (*land*) terres *fpl*

prophecy ['prɒfɪsɪ] *n* prophétie *f*

prophesy ['prɒfɪsaɪ] *vt* prédire

prophet ['prɒfɪt] *n* prophète *m*

proportion [prə'pɔ:ʃən] *n* proportion *f*; (*share*) part *f*, partie *f*; ~**al, ~ate** *adj* proportionnel(le)

proposal [prə'pəʊzl] *n* proposition *f*, offre *f*; (*plan*) projet *m*; (*of marriage*) demande *f* en mariage

propose [prə'pəʊz] *vt* proposer, suggérer ♦ *vi* faire sa demande en mariage; **to** ~ **to do** avoir l'intention de faire; **proposition** [prɒpə'zɪʃən] *n* proposition *f*

propriety [prə'praɪətɪ] *n* (*seemliness*) bienséance *f*, convenance *f*

prose [prəuz] n (not poetry) prose f

prosecute ['prɒsɪkjuːt] vt poursuivre; **prosecution** [prɒsɪ'kjuːʃən] n poursuites fpl judiciaires; (accusing side) partie plaignante; **prosecutor** ['prɒsɪkjuːtə*] n (US: plaintiff) plaignant(e); (also: public ~) procureur m, ministère public

prospect [n 'prɒspekt, vb prə'spekt] n perspective f ♦ vt, vi prospecter; ~s npl (for work etc) possibilités fpl d'avenir, débouchés mpl; ~ing n (for gold, oil etc) prospection f; ~ive adj (possible) éventuel(le); (future) futur(e)

prospectus [prə'spektəs] n prospectus m

prosperity [prɒ'spɛrɪtɪ] n prospérité f

prostitute ['prɒstɪtjuːt] n prostitué(e)

protect [prə'tɛkt] vt protéger; ~ion n protection f; ~ive adj protecteur(trice); (clothing) de protection

protein ['prəutiːn] n protéine f

protest [n 'prəutɛst, vb prə'tɛst] n protestation f ♦ vi, vt: to ~ (that) protester (que)

Protestant ['prɒtɪstənt] adj, n protestant(e)

protester [prə'tɛstə*] n manifestant(e)

protracted [prə'træktɪd] adj prolongé(e)

protrude [prə'truːd] vi avancer, dépasser

proud [praud] adj fier(ère); (pej) orgueilleux(euse)

prove [pruːv] vt prouver, démontrer ♦ vi: to ~ (to be) correct etc s'avérer juste etc; to ~ o.s. montrer ce dont on est capable

proverb ['prɒvɜːb] n proverbe m

provide [prə'vaɪd] vt fournir; to ~ sb with sth fournir qch à qn; ~ for vt fus (person) subvenir aux besoins de; (future event) prévoir; ~d (that) conj à condition que +sub; **providing** [prə'vaɪdɪŋ] conj: providing (that) à condition que +sub

province ['prɒvɪns] n province f; (fig) domaine m; **provincial** [prə'vɪnʃəl] adj provincial(e)

provision [prə'vɪʒən] n (supplying) fourniture f; (stipulation) disposition f; ~s npl (food) provisions fpl; ~al adj provisoire

proviso [prə'vaɪzəu] n condition f

provocative [prə'vɒkətɪv] adj provocateur(trice), provocant(e)

provoke [prə'vəuk] vt provoquer

prow [prau] n proue f

prowess ['praues] n prouesse f

prowl [praul] vi (also: ~ about, ~ around) rôder ♦ n: on the ~ à l'affût; ~er n rôdeur(euse)

proxy ['prɒksɪ] n procuration f

prudent ['pruːdənt] adj prudent(e)

prune [pruːn] n pruneau m ♦ vt élaguer

pry [praɪ] vi: to ~ into fourrer son nez dans

PS n abbr (= postscript) p.s.

psalm [sɑːm] n psaume m

pseudo- ['sjuːdəu] prefix pseudo-; ~**nym** ['sjuːdənɪm] n pseudonyme m

psyche [praul] vi (also: ~al) psyché f

psychiatrist [saɪ'kaɪətrɪst] n psychiatre m/f

psychic ['saɪkɪk] adj (also: ~al) (méta)psychique; (person) doué(e) d'un sixième sens

psychoanalyst [saɪkəu'ænəlɪst] n psychanalyste m/f

psychological [saɪkə'lɒdʒɪkəl] adj psychologique; **psychologist** [saɪ'kɒlədʒɪst] n psychologue m/f; **psychology** [saɪ'kɒlədʒɪ] n psychologie f

PTO abbr (= please turn over) T.S.V.P.

pub [pʌb] n (= public house) pub m

public ['pʌblɪk] n public m ♦ adj public(ique); **in** ~ en public; **to make** ~ rendre public; ~ **address system** n (système m de) sonorisation f; hauts-parleurs mpl

publican ['pʌblɪkən] n patron m de pub

public: ~ **company** n société f anonyme (cotée en bourse); ~ **convenience** n (BRIT) toilettes fpl; ~ **holiday** n jour férié; ~ **house** (BRIT) n pub m

publicity [pʌb'lɪsɪtɪ] n publicité f

publicize ['pʌblɪsaɪz] vt faire connaître, rendre public(ique)

public: ~ **opinion** n opinion publique; ~ **relations** n relations publiques; ~ **school** n (BRIT) école (secondaire) privée; (US) école publique; ~-**spirited** adj qui fait preuve de civisme; ~ **transport** n transports mpl en commun

publish ['pʌblɪʃ] vt publier; ~**er** n éditeur m; ~**ing** n édition f

pucker ['pʌkə*] vt plisser

pudding ['pudɪŋ] n pudding m; (BRIT: sweet) dessert m, entremets m; **black** ~, (US) **blood** ~ boudin (noir)

puddle ['pʌdl] n flaque f (d'eau)

puff [pʌf] n bouffée f ♦ vt: **to** ~ **one's pipe** tirer sur sa pipe ♦ vi (pant) haleter; ~ **out** vt (fill with air) gonfler; ~**ed** (out) adj (inf: out of breath) tout(e) essoufflé(e); ~ **pastry** (US ~ **paste**) n pâte feuilletée; ~**y** adj bouffi(e), boursouflé(e)

pull [pul] n (tug): **to give sth a** ~ tirer sur qch ♦ vt tirer; (trigger) presser ♦ vi tirer; ~ **to pieces** mettre en morceaux; **to** ~ **one's punches** ménager son adversaire; **to** ~ **one's weight** faire sa part (du travail); **to** ~ **o.s. together** se ressaisir; **to** ~ **sb's leg** (fig) faire marcher qn; ~ **apart** vt (break) mettre en pièces, démantibuler; ~ **down** vt (house) démolir; ~ **in** vi (AUT) entrer; (RAIL) entrer en gare; ~ **off** vt enlever, ôter; (deal etc) mener à bien, conclure; ~ **out** vi démarrer, partir ♦ vt sortir; arracher; ~ **over** vi (AUT) se ranger; ~ **through** vi s'en sortir; ~ **up** vi (stop) s'arrêter ♦ vt remonter; (uproot) déraciner, arracher

pulley ['pulɪ] n poulie f

pullover ['puləuvə*] n pull(-over) m, tricot m

pulp [pʌlp] n (of fruit) pulpe f

pulpit ['pulpɪt] n chaire f

pulsate [pʌl'seɪt] vi battre, palpiter; (music) vibrer

pulse [pʌls] n (of blood) pouls m; (of heart) battement m; (of music, engine) vibrations fpl; (BOT, CULIN) légume sec

pump [pʌmp] n pompe f; (shoe) escarpin m ♦ vt pomper; ~ **up** vt gonfler

pumpkin ['pʌmpkɪn] n potiron m, citrouille f

pun [pʌn] n jeu de mots, calembour m

punch [pʌntʃ] n (blow) coup m de poing; (tool) poinçon m; (drink) punch m ♦ vt (hit): **to** ~ **sb/sth** donner un coup de poing à qn/sur qch; ~-**line** n (of joke) conclusion f; ~-**up** (BRIT: inf) n bagarre f

punctual ['pʌŋktjuəl] adj ponctuel(le)

punctuation [pʌŋktjʊ'eɪʃən] n ponctuation f

puncture ['pʌŋktʃə*] n crevaison f

pundit ['pʌndɪt] n individu m qui pontifie, pontife m

pungent ['pʌndʒənt] adj piquant(e), âcre

punish ['pʌnɪʃ] vt punir; ~**ment** n punition f, châtiment m

punk [pʌŋk] n (also: ~-**rocker**) punk m/f; (: ~ **rock**) le punk rock; (US: inf: hoodlum) voyou m

punt [pʌnt] n (boat) bachot m

punter ['pʌntə*] n (BRIT) (gambler) parieur(euse); (inf): **the** ~**s** le public

puny ['pju:nɪ] adj chétif(ive); (effort) piteux(euse)

pup [pʌp] n chiot m

pupil ['pju:pl] n (SCOL) élève m/f; (of eye) pupille f

puppet ['pʌpɪt] n marionnette f, pantin m

puppy ['pʌpɪ] n chiot m, jeune chien(ne)

purchase ['pɜːtʃɪs] n achat m ♦ vt acheter; ~r n acheteur(euse)
pure [pjuə] adj pur(e); ~ly ['pjuəlɪ] adv purement
purge [pɜːdʒ] n purge f
purple ['pɜːpl] adj violet(te); (face) cramoisi(e)
purport [pɜː'pɔːt] vi: to ~ be/do prétendre être/faire
purpose ['pɜːpəs] n intention f, but m; on ~ exprès; ~ful adj déterminé(e), résolu(e)
purr [pɜː] vi ronronner
purse [pɜːs] n (BRIT: for money) porte-monnaie m inv; (US: handbag) sac m à main ♦ vt serrer, pincer
purser ['pɜːsə*] n (NAUT) commissaire m du bord
pursue [pə'sjuː] vt poursuivre
pursuit [pə'sjuːt] n poursuite f; (occupation) occupation f, activité f

push [puʃ] n poussée f ♦ vt pousser; (button) appuyer sur; (thrust): to ~ sth (into) enfoncer qch (dans); (product) faire de la publicité pour ♦ vi pousser; (demand): to ~ for exiger, demander avec insistance; ~ aside vt écarter; ~ off (inf) vi filer, ficher le camp; ~ on vi (continue) continuer; ~ through vi se frayer un chemin ♦ vt (measure) faire accepter; ~ up vt (total, prices) faire monter; ~chair (BRIT) n poussette f; ~er n (drug ~er) revendeur(euse) (de drogue); ~over (inf) n: it's a ~over c'est un jeu d'enfant; ~up (US) n traction f; ~y (pej) adj arriviste
puss [pus] (inf) n minet m
pussy (cat) ['pusɪ (kæt)] (inf) n minet m
put [put] (pt, pp put) vt mettre, poser, placer; (say) dire, exprimer; (a question) poser; (case, view) exposer, présenter; (estimate) estimer; ~ about (rumour) faire courir; ~ across (ideas etc) communiquer; ~ away vt (store) ranger; ~ back vt (replace) remettre, replacer;

(postpone) remettre; (delay) retarder; ~ by vt (money) mettre de côté, économiser; ~ down vt (parcel etc) poser, déposer; (in writing) mettre par écrit, inscrire; (suppress: revolt etc) réprimer, faire cesser; (animal) abattre; (dog, cat) faire piquer; (attribute) attribuer; ~ forward vt (ideas) avancer; ~ in vt (gas, electricity) installer; (application, complaint) soumettre; (time, effort) consacrer; ~ off vt (light etc) éteindre; (postpone) remettre à plus tard, ajourner; (discourage) dissuader; ~ on vt (clothes, lipstick, record) mettre; (light etc) allumer; (play etc) monter; (food: cook) mettre à cuire or à chauffer; (gain): to ~ on weight prendre du poids, grossir; to ~ the brakes on freiner; to ~ the kettle on mettre l'eau à chauffer; ~ out vt (take out) mettre dehors; (one's hand) tendre; (light etc) éteindre; (person: inconvenience) déranger, gêner; ~ through vt (TEL: call) passer; (: person) mettre en communication; (plan) faire accepter; ~ up vt (raise) lever, relever, remonter; (pin up) afficher; (hang) accrocher; (build) construire, ériger; (tent) monter; (umbrella) ouvrir; (increase) augmenter; (accommodate) loger; ~ up with vt fus supporter
putt [pʌt] n coup roulé; ~ing green n green m
putty ['pʌtɪ] n mastic m
put-up ['putʌp] (BRIT) adj: ~ job coup monté
puzzle ['pʌzl] n énigme f, mystère m; (jigsaw) puzzle m ♦ vt intriguer, rendre perplexe ♦ vi se creuser la tête; **puzzling** adj déconcertant(e)
pyjamas [pɪ'dʒɑːməz] (BRIT) npl pyjama(s) m(pl)
pyramid ['pɪrəmɪd] n pyramide f
Pyrenees [pɪrɪ'niːz] npl: the ~ les Pyrénées fpl

Q

quack [kwæk] n (of duck) coin-coin m inv; (pej: doctor) charlatan m

quad [kwod] n abbr = **quadrangle** ♦ abbr = **quadruplet**

quadrangle [ˈkwɔdræŋgl] n (courtyard) cour f

quadruple [kwoˈdruːpl] vt, vi quadrupler; ~s npl [kwoˈdruːplɔts] npl quadruplés

quagmire [ˈkwæɡmaɪə*] n bourbier m

quail [kweɪl] n (ZOOL) caille f ♦ vi: to ~ at or before reculer devant

quaint [kweɪnt] adj bizarre; (house, village) au charme vieillot, pittoresque

quake [kweɪk] vi trembler

qualification [kwɔlɪfɪˈkeɪʃən] n (often pl: degree etc) diplôme m; (: training) qualification(s) f(pl), expérience f; (ability) compétence(s) f(pl); (limitation) réserve f, restriction f

qualified [ˈkwɔlɪfaɪd] adj (trained) qualifié(e); (professionally) diplômé(e); (fit, competent) compétent(e), qualifié(e); (limited) conditionnel(le)

qualify [ˈkwɔlɪfaɪ] vt qualifier; (modify) atténuer, nuancer ♦ vi: to ~ (as) obtenir son diplôme (de); to ~ (for) remplir les conditions requises (pour); (SPORT) se qualifier (pour)

quality [ˈkwɔlɪtɪ] n qualité f

qualm [kwɑːm] n doute m; scrupule m

quandary [ˈkwɔndərɪ] n: **in a ~** devant un dilemme, dans l'embarras

quantity [ˈkwɔntɪtɪ] n quantité f; ~ **surveyor** n métreur m vérificateur

quarantine [ˈkwɔrəntiːn] n quarantaine f

quarrel [ˈkwɔrəl] n querelle f, dispute f ♦ vi se disputer, se quereller; **~some** adj querelleur(euse)

quarry [ˈkwɔrɪ] n (for stone) carrière

f; (animal) proie f, gibier m

quart [kwɔːt] n ≈ litre m

quarter [ˈkwɔːtə*] n quart m; (US: coin: 25 cents) quart de dollar; (of year) trimestre m; (district) quartier m ♦ vt (divide) partager en quartiers or en quatre; ~**s** npl (living ~) logement m; (MIL) quartiers mpl, cantonnement m; **a ~ of an hour** un quart d'heure; **~ final** n quart m de finale; **~ly** adj trimestriel(le) ♦ adv tous les trois mois

quartet(te) [kwɔːˈtet] n quatuor m; (jazz players) quartette m

quartz [kwɔːts] n quartz m

quash [kwɔʃ] vt (verdict) annuler

quaver [ˈkweɪvə*] n (BRIT: MUS) croche f ♦ vi trembler

quay [kiː] n (also: ~side) quai m

queasy [ˈkwiːzɪ] adj: **to feel ~** avoir mal au cœur

queen [kwiːn] n reine f; (CARDS etc) dame f; **~ mother** n reine mère f

queer [kwɪə*] adj étrange, curieux(euse); (suspicious) louche ♦ n (inf!) homosexuel m

quell [kwel] vt réprimer, étouffer

quench [kwentʃ] vt: **to ~ one's thirst** se désaltérer

querulous [ˈkwerʊləs] adj (person) récriminateur(trice); (voice) plaintif(ive)

query [ˈkwɪərɪ] n question f ♦ vt remettre en question, mettre en doute

quest [kwest] n recherche f, quête f

question [ˈkwestʃən] n question f ♦ vt (person) interroger; (plan, idea) remettre en question, mettre en doute; **beyond ~** sans aucun doute; **out of the ~** hors de question; **~able** adj discutable; **~ mark** n point m d'interrogation; **~naire** [kwestʃəˈnɛə*] n questionnaire m

queue [kjuː] n (BRIT) n queue f, file f ♦ vi (also: ~ up) faire la queue

quibble [ˈkwɪbl] vi: **to ~ (about)** or (over) or (with sth) ergoter (sur qch)

quick [kwɪk] adj rapide; (agile) agi-

le, vif(vive) ♦ n: **cut to the ~** (fig)
touché(e) au vif; **be ~!** dépêche-
toi!; **~en** vt accélérer, presser ♦ vi
s'accélérer, devenir plus rapide; **~ly**
adv vite, rapidement; **~sand** n
sables mouvants; **~-witted** adj à
l'esprit vif

quid [kwɪd] (BRIT: inf) n, pl inv
livre f

quiet ['kwaɪət] adj tranquille; (silence:
(voice) bas(se); (ceremony, colour)
discret(ète) ♦ n tranquillité f, calme
m; (silence) silence m ♦ vt, vi (US)
= **quieten;** **keep ~!** tais-toi!; **~en**
vi (also: ~ down) se calmer, s'apaiser ♦ vt calmer, apaiser; **~ly** adv
tranquillement, calmement; (silently)
silencieusement; **~ness** n tranquillité
f, calme m; (silence) silence m

quilt [kwɪlt] n édredon m; (continen-
tal ~) couette f

quin [kwɪn] n abbr = **quintuplet**

quintuplets [kwɪn'tjuːplɪts] npl quin-
tuplé(e)s

quip [kwɪp] n remarque piquante or
spirituelle, pointe f

quirk [kwɜːk] n bizarrerie f

quit [kwɪt] (pt, pp ~ or ~**ted**) vt
quitter; (smoking, grumbling) arrêter de ♦ vi (give up) abandonner,
renoncer; (resign) démissionner

quite [kwaɪt] adv (rather) assez, plutôt; (entirely) complètement, tout à
fait; (following a negative = almost):
that's not ~ big enough ce n'est
pas tout à fait assez grand; I ~ understand je comprends très bien; ~
a few of them un assez grand nombre d'entre eux; ~ (so)! exactement!

quits [kwɪts] adj: ~ (**with**) quitte
(envers); **let's call it ~** restons-en
là

quiver ['kwɪvə*] vi trembler, frémir

quiz [kwɪz] n (game) jeu-concours m
♦ vt interroger; **~zical** adj nar-
quois(e)

quota ['kwəʊtə] n quota m

quotation [kwəʊ'teɪʃən] n citation f;
(estimate) devis m; **~ marks** npl

guillemets mpl

quote [kwəʊt] n citation f; (estimate) devis m ♦ vt citer; (price) ind
quer; ~s npl guillemets mpl

R

rabbi ['ræbaɪ] n rabbin m

rabbit ['ræbɪt] n lapin m; ~ **hutch**
n clapier m

rabble ['ræbl] (pej) n populace f

rabies ['reɪbiːz] n rage f

RAC n abbr (BRIT) = Royal Automo
bile Club

rac(c)oon [rə'kuːn] n raton laveur

race [reɪs] n (species) race f
(competition, rush) course f ♦ vt
(horse) faire courir ♦ vi (compete)
faire la course, courir; (hurry) aller
à toute vitesse, courir; (engine)
s'emballer; (pulse) augmenter; ~
car (US) n = **racing car**; ~ **car driver** (US) = **racing driver**; **~course**
n champ m de course; **~horse** n
cheval m de course; **~track** n piste f

racial ['reɪʃəl] adj racial(e)

racing ['reɪsɪŋ] n courses fpl; ~ **car**
(BRIT) n voiture f de course; ~ **driver** (BRIT) n pilote m de course

racism ['reɪsɪzəm] n racisme m; **ra-
cist** adj raciste ♦ n raciste m/f

rack [ræk] n (for guns, tools) râtelier
m; (also: luggage ~) porte-bagages
m inv, filet m à bagages; (: roof ~)
galerie f; (dish ~) égouttoir m ♦ vt
tourmenter; **to ~ one's brains** se
creuser la cervelle

racket ['rækɪt] n (for tennis) raquette
f; (noise) tapage m; vacarme m;
(swindle) escroquerie f

racquet ['rækɪt] n raquette f

racy ['reɪsɪ] adj plein(e) de verve;
(slightly indecent) osé(e)

radar ['reɪdɑː*] n radar m

radial ['reɪdɪəl] adj (also: ~-ply) à
carcasse radiale

radiant ['reɪdɪənt] adj rayonnant(e)

radiate ['reɪdɪeɪt] vt (heat) émettre,
dégager; (emotion) rayonner de ♦ vi

(lines) rayonner

radiation [reɪdɪ'eɪʃən] n rayonnement m; *(radioactive)* radiation f

radiator ['reɪdɪeɪtə*] n radiateur m

radical ['rædɪkəl] adj radical(e)

radii ['reɪdɪaɪ] npl of **radius**

radio ['reɪdɪəʊ] n radio f ♦ vt appeler par radio; **on the** ~ à la radio; **~active** [reɪdɪəʊ'æktɪv] adj radioactif(ive); **~station** n station f de radio

radish ['rædɪʃ] n radis m

radius ['reɪdɪəs] *(pl* **radii)** n rayon m

RAF n abbr = **Royal Air Force**

raffle ['ræfl] n tombola f

raft [rɑːft] n *(craft; also: life ~)* radeau m

rafter ['rɑːftə*] n chevron m

rag [ræg] n chiffon m; *(pej: newspaper)* feuille f de chou, torchon m; *(student ~)* attractions organisées au profit d'œuvres de charité; **~s** npl *(torn clothes etc)* haillons mpl; **~ doll** n poupée f de chiffon

rage [reɪdʒ] n *(fury)* rage f, fureur f ♦ vi *(person)* être fou(folle) de rage; *(storm)* faire rage, être déchaîné(e); **it's all the** ~ cela fait fureur

ragged ['rægɪd] adj *(edge)* inégal(e); *(clothes)* en loques; *(appearance)* déguenillé(e)

raid [reɪd] n *(attack; also: MIL)* raid m; *(criminal)* hold-up m inv; *(by police)* descente f, rafle f ♦ vt faire un raid sur *ou* un hold-up *ou* une descente dans

rail [reɪl] n *(on stairs)* rampe f; *(on bridge, balcony)* balustrade f; *(of ship)* bastingage m; **~s** npl *(track)* rails mpl, voie ferrée; **by** ~ par chemin de fer, en train; **~ing(s)** n(pl) grille f; **~road** *(US)*, **~way** *(BRIT)* n *(track)* voie ferrée; *(company)* chemin m de fer; **~way line** *(BRIT)* n ligne f de chemin de fer; **~wayman** *(BRIT: irreg)* n cheminot m; **~way station** *(BRIT)* n gare f

rain [reɪn] n pluie f ♦ vi pleuvoir; **in the** ~ sous la pluie; **it's ~ing** il pleut; **~bow** n arc-en-ciel m; **~coat**

n imperméable m; **~drop** n goutte f de pluie; **~fall** n chute f de pluie; *(measurement)* hauteur f des précipitations; **~forest** n forêt f tropicale humide; **~y** adj pluvieux(euse)

raise [reɪz] n augmentation f ♦ vt *(lift)* lever; hausser; *(increase)* augmenter; *(morale)* remonter; *(standards)* améliorer; *(question, doubt)* provoquer, soulever; *(cattle, family)* élever; *(crop)* faire pousser; *(funds)* rassembler; *(loan)* obtenir; *(army)* lever; **to** ~ **one's voice** élever la voix

raisin ['reɪzən] n raisin sec

rake [reɪk] n *(tool)* râteau m ♦ vt *(garden, leaves)* ratisser; *(with machine gun)* balayer

rally ['rælɪ] n *(POL etc)* meeting m, rassemblement m; *(AUT)* rallye m; *(TENNIS)* échange m ♦ vt *(support)* gagner ♦ vi *(sick person)* aller mieux; *(Stock Exchange)* reprendre; **~ round** vt fus venir en aide à

RAM [ræm] n abbr = **random access memory)** mémoire vive

ram [ræm] n bélier m ♦ vt enfoncer; *(crash into)* emboutir; percuter

ramble ['ræmbl] n randonnée f ♦ vi *(walk)* se promener, faire une randonnée; *(talk: also:* ~ **on)** discourir, pérorer; **~r** n promeneur(euse), randonneur(euse); *(BOT)* rosier grimpant; **~ing** ['ræmblɪŋ] adj *(speech)* décousu(e); *(house)* plein(e) de coins et de recoins; *(BOT)* grimpant(e)

ramp [ræmp] n *(incline)* rampe f; dénivellation f; **on** ~, **off** ~ *(US: AUT)* bretelle f d'accès

rampage [ræm'peɪdʒ] n: **to be on the** ~ se déchaîner

rampant ['ræmpənt] adj *(disease etc)* qui sévit

ramshackle ['ræmʃækl] adj *(house)* délabré(e); *(car etc)* déglingué(e)

ran [ræn] pt of **run**

ranch [rɑːntʃ] n ranch m; **~er** n propriétaire m de ranch

rancid ['rænsɪd] adj rance

rancour ['ræŋkə*] (*US* **rancor**) *n* rancune *f*

random ['rændəm] *adj* fait(e) or établi(e) au hasard; (*MATH*) aléatoire ♦ *n*: **at ~** au hasard; **~ access** *n* (*COMPUT*) accès sélectif

randy ['rændi] (*BRIT: inf*) *adj* excité(e); lubrique

rang [ræŋ] *pt of* **ring**

range [reɪndʒ] *n* (*of mountains*) chaîne *f*; (*of missile, voice*) portée *f*; (*of products*) choix *m*, gamme *f*; (*MIL: also: shooting ~*) champ *m* de tir; (*indoor*) stand *m* de tir; (*also: kitchen ~*) fourneau *m* (de cuisine) ♦ *vt* (*place in a line*) mettre en rang, ranger ♦ *vi*: **to ~ over** (*extend*) couvrir; **to ~ from ... to** aller de ... à; **a ~ of** (*series: of proposals etc*) divers(e)

ranger ['reɪndʒə*] *n* garde forestier

rank [ræŋk] *n* rang *m*; (*MIL*) grade *m*; (*BRIT: also: taxi ~*) station *f* de taxis ♦ *vi*: **to ~ among** compter or se classer parmi ♦ *adj* (*stinking*) fétide, puant(e); **the ~ and file** (*fig*) la masse, la base

rankle ['ræŋkl] *vi* (*insult*) rester sur le cœur

ransack ['rænsæk] *vt* fouiller (à fond); (*plunder*) piller

ransom ['rænsəm] *n* rançon *f*; **to hold to ~** (*fig*) exercer un chantage sur

rant [rænt] *vi* fulminer

rap [ræp] *vt* frapper sur or à; taper sur; *n*: **~** (*music*) rap *m*

rape [reɪp] *n* viol *m*; (*BOT*) colza *m* ♦ *vt* violer; **~(seed) oil** *n* huile *f* de colza

rapid ['ræpɪd] *adj* rapide; **~s** *npl* (*GEO*) rapides *mpl*

rapist ['reɪpɪst] *n* violeur *m*

rapport [ræ'pɔː*] *n* entente *f*

rapture ['ræptʃə*] *n* extase *f*, ravissement *m*; **rapturous** ['ræptʃərəs] *adj* enthousiaste, frénétique

rare [rɛə*] *adj* rare; (*CULIN: steak*) saignant(e)

raring ['rɛərɪŋ] *adj*: **~ to go** (*inf*)

très impatient(e) de commencer

rascal ['rɑːskl] *n* vaurien *m*

rash [ræʃ] *adj* imprudent(e), irréfléchi(e) ♦ *n* (*MED*) rougeur *f*, éruption *f*; (*spate: of events*) série (noire)

rasher ['ræʃə*] *n* fine tranche (de lard)

raspberry ['rɑːzbərɪ] *n* framboise *f*; **~ bush** *n* framboisier *m*

rasping ['rɑːspɪŋ] *adj*: **~ noise** grincement *m*

rat [ræt] *n* rat *m*

rate [reɪt] *n* taux *m*; (*speed*) vitesse *f*, rythme *m*; (*price*) tarif *m* ♦ *vt* classer; évaluer; **~s** *npl* (*BRIT: tax*) impôts locaux; (*fees*) tarifs *mpl*; **to ~ sb/sth as** considérer qn/qch comme; **~able value** (*BRIT*) *n* valeur locative imposable; **~payer** (*BRIT*) *n* contribuable *m/f* (*payant les impôts locaux*)

rather ['rɑːðə*] *adv* plutôt; **it's ~ expensive** c'est assez cher; (*too much*) c'est un peu cher; **there's ~ a lot** il y en a beaucoup; **I would** or **I'd ~ go** j'aimerais mieux or je préférerais partir

rating ['reɪtɪŋ] *n* (*assessment*) évaluation *f*; (*score*) classement *m*; (*NAUT: BRIT: sailor*) matelot *m*; **~s** *npl* (*RADIO, TV*) indice *m* d'écoute

ratio ['reɪʃɪəʊ] *n* proportion *f*

ration ['ræʃən] *n* (*gen pl*) ration(s) *f(pl)*

rational ['ræʃənl] *adj* raisonnable, sensé(e); (*solution, reasoning*) logique; **~e** [ræʃə'nɑːl] *n* raisonnement *m*; **~ize** [ræʃnəlaɪz] *vt* rationaliser; (*conduct*) essayer d'expliquer or de motiver

rat race *n* foire *f* d'empoigne

rattle ['rætl] *n* (*of door, window*) battement *m*; (*of coins, chain*) cliquetis *m*; (*of train, engine*) bruit *m* de ferraille; (*object: for baby*) hochet *m* ♦ *vi* cliqueter; (*car, bus*): **to ~ along** rouler dans un bruit de ferraille ♦ *vt* agiter (bruyamment); (*unnerve*) décontenancer; ~**snake** n serpent m à sonnettes

raucous ['rɔːkəs] adj rauque; (noisy) bruyant(e), tapageur(euse)

rave [reɪv] vi (in anger) s'emporter; (with enthusiasm) s'extasier; (MED) délirer

raven ['reɪvn] n corbeau m

ravenous ['rævənəs] adj affamé(e)

ravine [rə'viːn] n ravin m

raving ['reɪvɪŋ] adj: ~ **lunatic** n fou(folle) furieux(euse)

ravishing ['rævɪʃɪŋ] adj enchanteur(eresse)

raw [rɔː] adj (uncooked) cru(e); (not processed) brut(e); (sore) à vif, irrité(e); (inexperienced) inexpérimenté(e); (weather, day) froid(e) et humide; ~ **deal** (inf) n sale coup m; ~ **material** n matière première

ray [reɪ] n rayon m; ~ **of hope** lueur f d'espoir

raze [reɪz] vt (also: ~ **to the ground**) raser, détruire

razor ['reɪzə*] n rasoir m; ~ **blade** n lame f de rasoir

Rd abbr = **road**

re [riː] prep concernant

reach [riːtʃ] n portée f, atteinte f; (of river etc) étendue f ♦ vt atteindre; (conclusion, decision) parvenir à ♦ vi s'étendre, étendre le bras; **out of/within** ~ hors de/à portée; **within** ~ **of the shops** pas trop loin des or à proximité des magasins; ~ **out** vt tendre ♦ vi: **to** ~ **out (for)** allonger le bras (pour prendre)

react [riː'ækt] vi réagir; ~**ion** [riː'ækʃən] n réaction f

reactor [riː'æktə*] n réacteur m

read¹ [riːd] (pt, pp **read**) vi lire ♦ vt (understand) comprendre, interpréter; (study) étudier; (meter) relever; ~ **out** vt lire à haute voix; ~**able** adj facile or agréable à lire; (writing) lisible; ~**er** n lecteur(trice); (book) livre m de lecture; (BRIT: at university) chargé(e) d'enseignement; ~**ership** n (of paper etc) (nombre m de) lecteurs mpl

read² [red] pt, pp of **read¹**

readily ['redɪlɪ] adv volontiers, avec empressement; (easily) facilement

readiness ['redɪnəs] n empressement m; **in** ~ (prepared) prêt(e)

reading ['riːdɪŋ] n lecture f; (understanding) interprétation f; (on instrument) indications fpl

ready ['redɪ] adj prêt(e); (willing) prêt, disposé(e); (available) disponible ♦ n: **at the** ~ (MIL) prêt à faire feu; **to get** ~ se préparer ♦ vt préparer; ~**-made** adj tout(e) fait(e); ~ **money** (argent m) liquide m; ~**-to-wear** adj prêt(e) à porter

real [rɪəl] adj véritable; réel(le); **in** ~ **terms** dans la réalité; ~ **estate** n biens fonciers or immobiliers; ~**istic** adj réaliste; ~**ty** [rɪ'ælɪtɪ] n réalité f

realization [rɪəlaɪ'zeɪʃən] n (awareness) prise f de conscience; (fulfilment; also: of asset) réalisation f

realize ['rɪəlaɪz] vt (understand) se rendre compte de; (a project, COMM: asset) réaliser

really ['rɪəlɪ] adv vraiment; ~? vraiment?, c'est vrai?

realm [relm] n royaume m; (fig) domaine m

realtor ['rɪəltɔː*] n (®: US) n agent immobilier

reap [riːp] vt moissonner; (fig) récolter

reappear ['riːə'pɪə*] vi réapparaître, reparaître

rear [rɪə*] adj de derrière, arrière inv; (AUT: wheel etc) arrière ♦ n arrière m ♦ vt (cattle, family) élever ♦ vi (also: ~ **up**: animal) se cabrer; ~**guard** n (MIL) arrière-garde f

rear-view mirror ['rɪəvjuː-] n (AUT) rétroviseur m

reason ['riːzn] n raison f ♦ vi: **to** ~ **with sb** raisonner qn, faire entendre raison à qn; **to have** ~ **to think** avoir lieu de penser; **it stands to** ~ **that** il va sans dire que; ~**able** adj raisonnable; (not bad) acceptable; ~**ably** adv raisonnablement; ~**ing** n raisonnement m

reassurance [ˌriːəˈʃʊərəns] *n* réconfort *m*; (*factual*) assurance *f*, garantie *f*; **reassure** [ˌriːəˈʃʊə*] *vt* rassurer

rebate [ˈriːbeɪt] *n* (*on tax etc*) dégrèvement *m*

rebel [*n* ˈrɛbl, *vb* rɪˈbɛl] *n* rebelle *m/f* ♦ *vi* se rebeller, se révolter; **~lious** *adj* rebelle

rebound [*vb* rɪˈbaʊnd, *n* ˈriːbaʊnd] *vi* (*ball*) rebondir ♦ *n* rebond *m*; **to marry on the ~** se marier immédiatement après une déception amoureuse

rebuff [rɪˈbʌf] *n* rebuffade *f*

rebuke [rɪˈbjuːk] *vt* réprimander

rebut [rɪˈbʌt] *vt* réfuter

recall [rɪˈkɔːl] *vt* rappeler; (*remember*) se rappeler, se souvenir de ♦ *n* rappel *m*; (*ability to remember*) mémoire *f*

recant [rɪˈkænt] *vi* se rétracter; (*REL*) abjurer

recap [ˈriːkæp], **recapitulate** [ˌriːkəˈpɪtjʊleɪt] *vt, vi* récapituler

rec'd *abbr* = received

recede [rɪˈsiːd] *vi* (*tide*) descendre; (*disappear*) disparaître peu à peu; (*memory, hope*) s'estomper; **receding** [rɪˈsiːdɪŋ] *adj* (*chin*) fuyant(e); **receding hairline** front dégarni

receipt [rɪˈsiːt] *n* (*document*) reçu *m*; (*for parcel etc*) accusé *m* de réception; (*act of receiving*) réception *f*; **~s** *npl* (*COMM*) recettes *fpl*

receive [rɪˈsiːv] *vt* recevoir

receiver [rɪˈsiːvə*] *n* (*TEL*) récepteur *m*, combiné *m*; (*RADIO*) récepteur *m*; (*of stolen goods*) receleur *m*; (*LAW*) administrateur *m* judiciaire

recent [ˈriːsnt] *adj* récent(e); **~ly** *adv* récemment

receptacle [rɪˈsɛptəkl] *n* récipient *m*

reception [rɪˈsɛpʃən] *n* réception *f*; (*welcome*) accueil *m*, réception; **~ desk** *n* réception *f*; **~ist** *n* réceptionniste *m/f*

recess [rɪˈsɛs] *n* (*in room*) renfoncement *m*, alcôve *f*; (*secret place*) recoin *m*; (*POL etc*: *holiday*) vacances

fpl

recession [rɪˈsɛʃən] *n* récession *f*

recipe [ˈrɛsɪpɪ] *n* recette *f*

recipient [rɪˈsɪpɪənt] *n* (*of payment*) bénéficiaire *m/f*; (*of letter*) destinataire *m/f*

recital [rɪˈsaɪtl] *n* récital *m*

recite [rɪˈsaɪt] *vt* (*poem*) réciter

reckless [ˈrɛklɪs] *adj* (*driver etc*) imprudent(e)

reckon [ˈrɛkən] *vt* (*count*) calculer, compter; (*think*): **I ~ that ...** je pense que ...; **~ on** *vt fus* compter sur, s'attendre à; **~ing** *n* compte *m*, calcul *m*; estimation *f*

reclaim [rɪˈkleɪm] *vt* (*demand back*) réclamer (le remboursement *or* la restitution de); (*land*: *from sea*) assécher; (*waste materials*) récupérer

recline [rɪˈklaɪn] *vi* être allongé(e) *or* étendu(e); **reclining** [rɪˈklaɪnɪŋ] *adj* (*seat*) à dossier réglable

recluse [rɪˈkluːs] *n* reclus(e), ermite *m*

recognition [ˌrɛkəgˈnɪʃən] *n* reconnaissance *f*; **to gain ~** être reconnu(e); **transformed beyond ~** méconnaissable

recognize [ˈrɛkəgnaɪz] *vt*: **to ~ (by/as)** reconnaître (à/comme étant)

recoil [rɪˈkɔɪl] *vi* (*person*): **to ~ (from sth/doing sth)** reculer (devant qch/l'idée de faire qch) ♦ *n* (*of gun*) recul *m*

recollect [ˌrɛkəˈlɛkt] *vt* se rappeler, se souvenir de; **~ion** [ˌrɛkəˈlɛkʃən] *n* souvenir *m*

recommend [ˌrɛkəˈmɛnd] *vt* recommander

reconcile [ˈrɛkənsaɪl] *vt* (*two people*) réconcilier; (*two facts*) concilier, accorder; **to ~ o.s. to** se résigner à

recondition [ˌriːkənˈdɪʃən] *vt* remettre à neuf; réviser entièrement

reconnoitre [ˌrɛkəˈnɔɪtə*] (*US* **reconnoiter**) *vt* (*MIL*) reconnaître

reconstruct [ˌriːkənˈstrʌkt] *vt* (*building*) reconstruire; (*crime, policy, system*) reconstituer

record [*n* ˈrɛkɔːd, *vb* rɪˈkɔːd] *n* rapport *m*, récit *m*; (*of meeting etc*) procès-verbal *m*; (*register*) registre *m*; (*file*) dossier *m*; (*also: criminal* ~) casier *m* judiciaire; (*MUS: disc*) disque *m*; (*SPORT*) record *m*; (*COMPUT*) article *m* ♦ *vt* (*set down*) noter; (*MUS: song etc*) enregistrer; **in ~ time** en un temps record *inv*; **~ off the** ~ *adj* officieux(euse) ♦ *adv* officieusement; **~-card** *n* (*in file*) fiche *f*; **~ed delivery** *n* (*BRIT: POST*): **~ed delivery letter** *n* lettre *f* recommandée; **~er** [rɪˈkɔːdə*] *n* (*MUS*) flûte *f* à bec; **~ holder** *n* (*SPORT*) détenteur(trice) du record; **~ing** [rɪˈkɔːdɪŋ] *n* (*MUS*) enregistrement *m*; **~ player** *n* tourne-disque *m*

recount [rɪˈkaʊnt] *vt* raconter

re-count [ˈriːkaʊnt] *n* (*POL: of votes*) deuxième compte *m* ♦ *vt* recompter

recoup [rɪˈkuːp] *vt*: **to ~ one's losses** récupérer ce qu'on a perdu, se refaire

recourse [rɪˈkɔːs] *n*: **to have ~ to** avoir recours à

recover [rɪˈkʌvə*] *vt* récupérer ♦ *vi*: **to ~ (from)** (*illness*) se rétablir (de); (*from shock*) se remettre (de); **~y** [rɪˈkʌvərɪ] *n* récupération *f*; rétablissement *m*; (*ECON*) redressement *m*

recreation [rɛkrɪˈeɪʃən] *n* récréation *f*, détente *f*; **~al** *adj* pour la détente, récréatif(ive)

recruit [rɪˈkruːt] *n* recrue *f* ♦ *vt* recruter

rectangle [ˈrɛktæŋgl] *n* rectangle *m*; **rectangular** [rɛkˈtæŋgjulə*] *adj* rectangulaire

rectify [ˈrɛktɪfaɪ] *vt* (*error*) rectifier, corriger

rector [ˈrɛktə*] *n* (*REL*) pasteur *m*

recuperate [rɪˈkuːpəreɪt] *vi* récupérer; (*from illness*) se rétablir

recur [rɪˈkɜː*] *vi* se reproduire; (*symptoms*) réapparaître; **~rence** *n* répétition *f*; réapparition *f*; **~rent** *adj* périodique, fréquent(e)

recycle *vt* recycler

red [rɛd] *n* rouge *m*; (*POL: pej*) rouge *m/f* ♦ *adj* rouge; (*hair*) roux(rousse); (*in the* ~ (*account*) à découvert; (*business*) en déficit; **~ carpet treatment** *n* réception *f* en grande pompe; **R~ Cross** *n* Croix-Rouge *f*; **~currant** *n* groseille *f* (rouge); **~den** *vt*, *vi* rougir; **~dish** *adj* rougeâtre; (*hair*) qui tirent sur le roux

redeem [rɪˈdiːm] *vt* (*debt*) rembourser; (*sth in pawn*) dégager; (*fig, also REL*) racheter; **~ing** *adj* (*feature*) qui sauve, qui rachète (le reste)

redeploy [ˈriːdɪˈplɔɪ] *vt* (*resources*) réorganiser

red: **~-haired** [ˈhɛəd] *adj* roux(rousse); **~-handed** [ˈhændɪd] *adj*: **to be caught ~-handed** être pris(e) en flagrant délit *or* la main dans le sac; **~head** [-hɛd] *n* roux(rousse); **~ herring** *n* (*fig*) diversion *f*, fausse piste; **~-hot** [-hɔt] *adj* chauffé(e) au rouge, brûlant(e)

redirect [ˈriːdaɪˈrɛkt] *vt* (*mail*) faire suivre

red light *n*: **to go through a ~** (*AUT*) brûler un feu rouge; **red-light district** *n* quartier *m* des prostituées

redo [riːˈduː] *vt* (*irreg*) *vt* refaire

redolent [ˈrɛdəulənt] *adj*: **~ of** qui sent; (*fig*) qui évoque

redress [rɪˈdrɛs] *n* réparation *f* ♦ *vt* redresser

Red Sea *n*: **the ~** la mer Rouge

redskin [ˈrɛdskɪn] *n* Peau-Rouge *m/f*

red tape *n* (*fig*) paperasserie (administrative)

reduce [rɪˈdjuːs] *vt* réduire; (*lower*) abaisser; **"~ speed now"** (*AUT*) "ralentir"; **reduction** [rɪˈdʌkʃən] *n* réduction *f*; (*discount*) rabais *m*

redundancy [rɪˈdʌndənsɪ] (*BRIT*) *n* licenciement *m*, mise *f* au chômage

redundant [rɪˈdʌndənt] *adj* (*BRIT: worker*) mis(e) au chômage, licencié(e); (*detail, object*) superflu(e); **to be made ~** être licencié(e), être mis(e) au chômage

reed [ri:d] n (BOT) roseau m; (MUS: of clarinet etc) hanche f

reef [ri:f] n (at sea) récif m, écueil m

reek [ri:k] vi: to ~ (of) puer, empester

reel [ri:l] n bobine f; (FISHING) moulinet m; (CINEMA) bande f; (dance) quadrille écossais ♦ vi (sway) chanceler; ~ in vt (fish, line) ramener

ref [ref] (inf) n abbr (= referee) arbitre m

refectory [rɪ'fektərɪ] n réfectoire m

refer [rɪ'fɜ:*] vt: to ~ sb to (inquirer: for information, patient: to specialist) adresser qn à; (reader: to text) renvoyer qn à; (dispute, decision): to ~ sth to soumettre qch à ♦ vi: to ~ to (allude to) parler de, faire allusion à; (consult) se reporter à

referee [refə'ri:] n arbitre m; (BRIT: for job application) répondant/e

reference ['refrəns] n référence f, renvoi m; (mention) allusion f, mention f; (for job application: letter) références, lettre f de recommandation; with ~ to (COMM: in letter) me référant à, suite à; ~ book n ouvrage m de référence

refill [vb ri:'fɪl, n 'ri:fɪl] vt remplir à nouveau; (pen, lighter etc) recharger ♦ n (for pen etc) recharge f

refine [rɪ'faɪn] vt (sugar, oil) raffiner; (taste) affiner; (theory, idea) fignoler (inf); ~d adj (person, taste) raffiné(e)

reflect [rɪ'flekt] vt (light, image) réfléchir, refléter; (fig) refléter ♦ vi (think) réfléchir, méditer; it ~s badly on him cela le discrédite; it ~s well on him c'est tout à son honneur; ~ion [rɪ'flekʃən] n réflexion f; (image) reflet m; (criticism): ~ion on critique f; atteinte f à; on ~ion réflexion faite

reflex ['ri:fleks] adj réflexe ♦ n réflexe m; ~ive [rɪ'fleksɪv] adj (LING) réfléchi(e)

reform [rɪ'fɔ:m] n réforme f ♦ vt reformer; R~ation [refə'meɪʃən] n: the R~ation la Réforme; ~atory (US) n

≈ centre m d'éducation surveillée

refrain [rɪ'freɪn] vi: to ~ from doing s'abstenir de faire ♦ n refrain m

refresh [rɪ'freʃ] vt rafraîchir; (subj: sleep) reposer; ~er course (BRIT) n cours m de recyclage; ~ing adj (drink) rafraîchissant(e); (sleep) réparateur(trice); ~ments npl rafraîchissements mpl

refrigerator [rɪ'frɪdʒəreɪtə*] n réfrigérateur m, frigidaire m (®)

refuel [ri:'fjʊəl] vi se ravitailler en carburant

refuge ['refju:dʒ] n refuge m; to take ~ in se réfugier dans

refugee [refjʊ'dʒi:] n réfugié(e)

refund [n 'ri:fʌnd, vb rɪ'fʌnd] n remboursement m ♦ vt rembourser

refurbish [ri:'fɜ:bɪʃ] vt remettre à neuf

refusal [rɪ'fju:zəl] n refus m; to have first ~ on avoir droit de préemption sur

refuse¹ [rɪ'fju:z] vt, vi refuser

refuse² ['refju:s] n ordures fpl, détritus mpl; ~ collection n ramassage m d'ordures

regain [rɪ'geɪn] vt regagner; retrouver

regal ['ri:gəl] adj royal(e)

regard [rɪ'gɑ:d] n respect m, estime f, considération f ♦ vt considérer; to give one's ~s to faire ses amitiés à; "with kindest ~s" "bien amicalement"; as ~s, with ~ to = regarding; ~ing prep en ce qui concerne; ~less adv quand même; ~less of sans se soucier de

régime [reɪ'ʒi:m] n régime m

regiment [n 'redʒɪmənt, vb 'redʒɪment] n régiment m; ~al [redʒɪ'mentl] adj d'un ou du régiment

region ['ri:dʒən] n région f; in the ~ of (fig) aux alentours de; ~al adj régional(e)

register ['redʒɪstə*] n registre m; (also: electoral ~) liste électorale ♦ vt enregistrer; (birth, death) déclarer; (vehicle) immatriculer; (POST:

letter) envoyer en recommandé; *(subj: instrument)* marquer ♦ vi s'inscrire; *(at hotel)* signer le registre; *(make impression)* être (bien) compris(e); **~ed** *adj (letter, parcel)* recommandé(e); **~ed trademark** *n* marque déposée; **registrar** [redʒɪs'trɑ:*] *n* officier *m* de l'état civil; **registration** [redʒɪs'treɪʃən] *n* enregistrement *m*; *(AUT: also: ~ number)* numéro *m* d'immatriculation

registry ['redʒɪstrɪ] *n* bureau *m* de l'enregistrement; **~ office** *(BRIT)* *n* bureau *m* de l'état civil; **to get married in a ~ office** ≈ se marier à la mairie

regret [rɪ'gret] *n* regret *m* ♦ *vt* regretter; **~fully** *adv* à ou avec regret

regular ['regjulə*] *adj* régulier(ère); *(usual)* habituel(le); *(soldier)* de métier ♦ *n (client etc)* habitué(e); **~ly** *adv* régulièrement

regulate ['regjuleɪt] *vt* régler; **regulation** [regju'leɪʃən] *n (rule)* règlement *m*; *(adjustment)* réglage *m*

rehabilitation ['ri:həbɪlɪ'teɪʃən] *n* *(of offender)* réinsertion *f*; *(of addict)* réadaptation *f*

rehearsal [rɪ'hɜ:səl] *n* répétition *f*

rehearse [rɪ'hɜ:s] *vt* répéter

reign [reɪn] *n* règne *m* ♦ *vi* régner

reimburse [ri:ɪm'bɜ:s] *vt* rembourser

rein [reɪn] *n (for horse)* rêne *f*

reindeer ['reɪndɪə*] *n, pl inv* renne *m*

reinforce [ri:ɪn'fɔ:s] *vt* renforcer; **~d concrete** *n* béton armé; **~ments** *npl* *(MIL)* renfort(s) *m(pl)*

reinstate ['ri:ɪn'steɪt] *vt* rétablir, réintégrer

reject [*n* 'ri:dʒekt, *vb* rɪ'dʒekt] *n (COMM)* article *m* de rebut ♦ *vt* refuser; *(idea)* rejeter; **~ion** [rɪ'dʒek-ʃən] *n* rejet *m*, refus *m*

rejoice [rɪ'dʒɔɪs] *vi*: **to ~ (at** ou **over)** se réjouir (de)

rejuvenate [rɪ'dʒu:vɪneɪt] *vt* rajeunir

relapse [rɪ'læps] *n (MED)* rechute *f*

relate [rɪ'leɪt] *vt (tell)* raconter; *(connect)* établir un rapport entre ♦

vi: **this ~s to** cela se rapporte à; **to ~ to sb** s'entretenir des rapports avec qn; **~d** *adj* apparenté(e); **~d to** prep concernant

relation [rɪ'leɪʃən] *n (person)* parent(e); *(link)* rapport *m*, lien *m*; **~ship** *n* rapport *m*, lien *m*; *(personal ties)* relations *fpl*, rapports; *(also: family ~ship)* lien de parenté

relative ['relətɪv] *n* parent(e) ♦ *adj* relatif(ive); **all her ~s** toute sa famille; **~ly** *adv* relativement

relax [rɪ'læks] *vi (muscle)* se relâcher; *(person: unwind)* se détendre ♦ *vt* relâcher; *(mind, person)* détendre; **~ation** [ri:læk'seɪʃən] *n* relâchement *m*; *(of mind)* détente *f*, relaxation *f*; *(recreation)* détente *f*, délassement *m*; **~ed** *adj* détendu(e); **~ing** *adj* délassant(e)

release [rɪ'li:s] *n (from prison, obligation)* libération *f*; *(of gas etc)* émission *f*; *(of film etc)* sortie *f*; *(new recording)* disque *m* ♦ *vt (prisoner)* libérer; *(gas etc)* émettre, dégager; *(free: from wreckage etc)* dégager; *(TECH: catch, spring etc)* faire jouer; *(book, film)* sortir; *(news)* rendre public, publier

relegate ['relɪgeɪt] *vt* reléguer; *(BRIT: SPORT)*: **to be ~d** descendre dans une division inférieure

relent [rɪ'lent] *vi* se laisser fléchir; **~less** *adj* implacable; *(unceasing)* continuel(le)

relevant ['reləvənt] *adj (question)* pertinent(e); *(fact)* significatif(ive); *(information)* utile; **~ to** ayant rapport à, approprié à

reliable [rɪ'laɪəbl] *adj (person, firm)* sérieux(euse), fiable; *(method, machine)* fiable; *(news, information)* sûr(e); **reliably** *adv*: **to be reliably informed** savoir de source sûre

reliance [rɪ'laɪəns] *n*: **~ (on)** *(person)* confiance *f* (en); *(drugs, promises)* besoin *m* (de), dépendance *f*

(de)

relic ['rɛlɪk] n (REL) relique f; (of the past) vestige m

relief [rɪ'liːf] n (from pain, anxiety etc) soulagement m; (help, supplies) secours m(pl); (ART, GEO) relief m

relieve [rɪ'liːv] vt (pain, patient) soulager; (fear, worry) dissiper; (bring help) secourir; (take over from: gen) relayer; (: guard) relever; to ~ sb of sth débarrasser qn de qch; to ~ o.s. se soulager

religion [rɪ'lɪdʒən] n religion f; **religious** [rɪ'lɪdʒəs] adj religieux(euse); (book) de piété

relinquish [rɪ'lɪŋkwɪʃ] vt abandonner; (plan, habit) renoncer à

relish ['rɛlɪʃ] n (CULIN) condiment m; (enjoyment) délectation f ♦ vt (food etc) savourer; to ~ doing se délecter à faire

relocate ['riːləʊ'keɪt] vt installer ailleurs ♦ vi déménager, s'installer ailleurs

reluctance [rɪ'lʌktəns] n répugnance f

reluctant [rɪ'lʌktənt] adj peu disposé(e), qui hésite; ~**ly** adv à contrecœur

rely on [rɪlaɪ] vt fus (be dependent) dépendre de; (trust) compter sur

remain [rɪ'meɪn] vi rester; ~**der** n reste m; ~**ing** adj qui reste; ~**s** npl restes mpl

remand [rɪ'mɑːnd] n: on ~ en détention préventive ♦ vt: to be ~ed in custody être placé(e) en détention préventive; ~ **home** (BRIT) n maison f d'arrêt

remark [rɪ'mɑːk] n remarque f, observation f ♦ vt (faire) remarquer, dire; ~**able** adj remarquable

remedial [rɪ'miːdɪəl] adj (tuition, classes) de rattrapage; ~ **exercises** gymnastique corrective

remedy ['rɛmədɪ] n: ~ (for) remède m (contre or à) ♦ vt remédier à

remember [rɪ'mɛmbə*] vt se rappeler, se souvenir de; (send greetings): ~ me to him saluez-le de ma part;

remembrance [rɪ'mɛmbrəns] n souvenir m; mémoire f

remind [rɪ'maɪnd] vt: to ~ sb of sb rappeler à qn; to ~ sb to do faire penser à qn à faire, rappeler à qn qu'il doit faire; ~**er** n (souvenir) souvenir m; (letter) rappel m

reminisce [rɛmɪ'nɪs] vi: to ~ (about) évoquer ses souvenirs (de)

reminiscent [rɛmɪ'nɪsnt] adj: to be ~ of rappeler, faire penser à

remiss [rɪ'mɪs] adj négligent(e)

remission [rɪ'mɪʃən] n (of illness, sins) rémission f; (of debt, prison sentence) remise f

remit [rɪ'mɪt] vt (send: money) envoyer; ~**tance** n paiement m

remnant ['rɛmnənt] n reste m, restant m; (of cloth) coupon m; ~**s** npl (COMM) fins fpl de série

remorse [rɪ'mɔːs] n remords m; ~**ful** adj plein(e) de remords; ~**less** adj (fig) impitoyable

remote [rɪ'məʊt] adj éloigné(e), lointain(e); (person) distant(e); (possibility) vague; ~ **control** n télécommande f; ~**ly** adv au loin; (slightly) très vaguement

remould ['riːməʊld] (BRIT) n (tyre) pneu rechapé

removable [rɪ'muːvəbl] adj (detachable) amovible

removal [rɪ'muːvəl] n (taking away) enlèvement m; suppression f; (BRIT: from house) déménagement m; (from office: dismissal) renvoi m; (of stain) nettoyage m; (MED) ablation f; ~ **van** (BRIT) n camion m de déménagement

remove [rɪ'muːv] vt enlever, retirer; (employee) renvoyer; (stain) faire partir; (abuse) supprimer; (doubt) chasser

render ['rɛndə*] vt rendre; ~**ing** n (MUS etc) interprétation f

rendezvous n rendez-vous m inv

renew [rɪ'njuː] vt renouveler; (negotiations) reprendre; (acquaintance) renouer; ~**able** adj (energy) renouvelable; ~**al** n renouvellement m; reprise f

renounce [rɪ'naʊns] vt renoncer à

renovate ['renəveɪt] vt rénover; (art work) restaurer

renown [rɪ'naʊn] n renommée f; **~ed** adj renommé(e)

rent [rent] n loyer m ♦ vt louer; **~al** n (for television, car) (prix m de) location f

rep [rep] n abbr = **representative**; = **repertory**

repair [rɪ'peə*] n réparation f ♦ vt réparer; **in good/bad ~** en bon/mauvais état; **~ kit** n trousse f de réparation

repatriate [riː'pætrɪeɪt] vt rapatrier

repay [riː'peɪ] (irreg) vt (money, creditor) rembourser; (sb's efforts) récompenser; **~ment** n remboursement m

repeal [rɪ'piːl] n (of law) abrogation f ♦ vt (law) abroger

repeat [rɪ'piːt] n (RADIO, TV) reprise f ♦ vt répéter; (COMM: order) renouveler; (SCOL: a class) redoubler ♦ vi répéter; **~edly** adv souvent, à plusieurs reprises

repel [rɪ'pel] vt repousser ♦ **~lent** n: **insect ~lent** insectifuge m

repent [rɪ'pent] vi: **to ~ (of)** se repentir (de); **~ance** n repentir m

repertory ['repətərɪ] n (also: **~ theatre**) théâtre m de répertoire

repetition [repɪ'tɪʃən] n répétition f

repetitive [rɪ'petɪtɪv] adj (movement, work) répétitif(ive); (speech) plein(e) de redites

replace [rɪ'pleɪs] vt (put back) remettre, replacer; (take the place of) remplacer; **~ment** n (substitution) remplacement m; (person) remplaçant(e)

replay ['riːpleɪ] n (of match) match rejoué(e) m; (of tape, film) répétition f

replenish [rɪ'plenɪʃ] vt (glass) remplir (de nouveau); (stock etc) réapprovisionner

replica ['replɪkə] n réplique f, copie exacte

reply [rɪ'plaɪ] n réponse f ♦ vi répon-

dre; **~ coupon** n coupon-réponse m

report [rɪ'pɔːt] n rapport m; (PRESS etc) reportage m; (BRIT: also: **school ~**) bulletin m (scolaire); (of gun) détonation f ♦ vt rapporter, faire un compte rendu de; (PRESS etc) faire un reportage sur; (bring to notice: occurrence) signaler ♦ vi (make a ~) faire un rapport (or un reportage); (present o.s.): **to ~ (to sb)** se présenter (chez qn); (be responsible to): **to ~ to sb** être sous les ordres de qn; **~ card** n (US, SCOTTISH) bulletin m scolaire; **~edly** adv: **she is ~edly living in ...** elle habiterait ...; **he ~edly told them to ...** il leur aurait ordonné de ...; **~er** n reporter m

repose [rɪ'pəʊz] n: **in ~** en or au repos

represent [reprɪ'zent] vt représenter; (view, belief) présenter, expliquer; (describe): **to ~ sth as** présenter or décrire qch comme; **~ation** [reprɪzen'teɪʃən] n représentation f; **~ations** npl (protest) démarche f; **~ative** n représentant(e); (US: POL) député m ♦ adj représentatif(ive), caractéristique

repress [rɪ'pres] vt réprimer; **~ion** [rɪ'preʃən] n répression f

reprieve [rɪ'priːv] n (LAW) grâce f; (fig) sursis m, délai m

reprisal [rɪ'praɪzəl] n: **~s** npl représailles fpl

reproach [rɪ'prəʊtʃ] vt: **to ~ sb with sth** reprocher qch à qn; **~ful** adj de reproche

reproduce [riːprə'djuːs] vt reproduire ♦ vi se reproduire; **reproduction** [riːprə'dʌkʃən] n reproduction f

reproof [rɪ'pruːf] n reproche m

reptile ['reptaɪl] n reptile m

republic [rɪ'pʌblɪk] n république f; **~an** adj républicain(e)

repudiate [rɪ'pjuːdɪeɪt] vt répudier, rejeter

repulsive [rɪ'pʌlsɪv] adj repoussant(e), répulsif(ive)

reputable ['repjʊtəbl] adj de bonne

réputation; (*occupation*) honorable

reputation [rɪpjʊˈteɪʃən] *n* réputation *f*

reputed [rɪˈpjuːtɪd] *adj* (*supposed*) supposé(e); **~ly** *adv* d'après ce qu'on dit

request [rɪˈkwɛst] *n* demande *f*; (*formal*) requête *f* ♦ *vt*: to ~ (of or from sb) demander (à qn); ~ **stop** (BRIT) *n* (*for bus*) arrêt facultatif

require [rɪˈkwaɪə*] *vt* (*need: subj: person*) avoir besoin de; (*: thing, situation*) demander; (*want*) exiger; (*order*): to ~ **sb** to do **sth**/**sth** of **sb** exiger que qn fasse qch/qch de qn; **~ment** *n* exigence *f*; besoin *m*; condition requise

requisite [ˈrɛkwɪzɪt] *n* chose *f* nécessaire ♦ *adj* (*appropriate*) nécessaire, requis(e); **toilet ~s** accessoires *mpl* de toilette

requisition [rɛkwɪˈzɪʃən] *n*: ~ (for) demande *f* (de) ♦ *vt* (MIL) réquisitionner

rescue [ˈrɛskjuː] *n* (*from accident*) sauvetage *m*; (*help*) secours *mpl* ♦ *vt* sauver; ~ **party** *n* équipe *f* de sauvetage; **~r** *n* sauveteur *m*

research [rɪˈsɜːtʃ] *n* recherche(s) *f(pl)* ♦ *vt* faire des recherches sur

resemblance [rɪˈzɛmbləns] *n* ressemblance *f*

resemble [rɪˈzɛmbl] *vt* ressembler à

resent [rɪˈzɛnt] *vt* être contrarié(e) par; **~ful** *adj* irrité(e), plein(e) de ressentiment; **~ment** *n* ressentiment *m*

reservation [rɛzəˈveɪʃən] *n* (*booking*) réservation *f*; (*doubt*) réserve *f*; (*for tribe*) réserve; **to make a ~** (*in a hotel/a restaurant/on a plane*) réserver or retenir une chambre/une table/une place

reserve [rɪˈzɜːv] *n* réserve *f*; (SPORT) remplaçant *m* ♦ *vt* (*seats etc*) réserver, retenir; ~**s** *npl* (MIL) réservistes *mpl*; **in ~** en réserve; **~d** *adj* réservé(e)

reshuffle [ˈriːʃʌfl] *n*: Cabinet ~ (POL) remaniement ministériel

residence [ˈrɛzɪdəns] *n* résidence *f*;

~ **permit** (BRIT) *n* permis *m* de séjour

resident [ˈrɛzɪdənt] *n* résident(e) ♦ *adj* résidant(e); **~ial** [rɛzɪˈdɛnʃəl] *adj* (*area*) résidentiel(le); (*course*) avec hébergement sur place; **~ial school** *n* internat *m*

residue [ˈrɛzɪdjuː] *n* reste *m*; (CHEM, PHYSICS) résidu *m*

resign [rɪˈzaɪn] *vt* (*one's post*) démissionner de ♦ *vi* démissionner; to ~ **o.s.** to se résigner à; **~ation** [rɛzɪɡˈneɪʃən] *n* (*of post*) démission *f*; (*state of mind*) résignation *f*; **~ed** *adj* résigné(e)

resilient [rɪˈzɪlɪənt] *adj* (*material*) élastique; (*person*) qui réagit, qui a du ressort

resist [rɪˈzɪst] *vt* résister à; **~ance** *n* résistance *f*

resolution [rɛzəˈluːʃən] *n* résolution *f*

resolve [rɪˈzɒlv] *n* résolution *f* ♦ *vt* (*problem*) résoudre ♦ *vi*: to ~ to do résoudre or décider de faire

resort [rɪˈzɔːt] *n* (*town*) station *f*; (*recourse*) recours *m* ♦ *vi*: to ~ to avoir recours à; **in the last** ~ en dernier ressort

resound [rɪˈzaʊnd] *vi*: to ~ (with) retentir or résonner (de); **~ing** [rɪˈzaʊndɪŋ] *adj* retentissant(e)

resource [rɪˈsɔːs] *n* ressource *f*; ~**s** *npl* (*supplies, wealth etc*) ressources; **~ful** *adj* ingénieux(euse), débrouillard(e)

respect [rɪsˈpɛkt] *n* respect *m* ♦ *vt* respecter; ~**s** *npl* (*compliments*) respects, hommages *mpl*; **with ~ to** en ce qui concerne; **in this ~** à cet égard; **~able** *adj* respectable; **~ful** *adj* respectueux(euse)

respite [ˈrɛspaɪt] *n* répit *m*

resplendent [rɪsˈplɛndənt] *adj* resplendissant(e)

respond [rɪsˈpɒnd] *vi* répondre; (*react*) réagir; **response** [rɪsˈpɒns] *n* réponse *f*; réaction *f*

responsibility [rɪspɒnsəˈbɪlɪtɪ] *n* responsabilité *f*

responsible [rɪs'pɒnsəbl] adj (liable): ~ (for) responsable (de); (person) digne de confiance; (job) qui comporte des responsabilités

responsive [rɪs'pɒnsɪv] adj qui réagit; (person) qui n'est pas réservé(e) or indifférent(e)

rest [rest] n repos m (stop) arrêt m, pause f; (MUS) silence m; (support) support m, appui m; (remainder) reste m, restant m ♦ vi se reposer; (be supported): to ~ on appuyer or reposer sur; (remain) rester ♦ vt (lean): to ~ sth on/against appuyer qch sur/contre; the ~ of them les autres; it ~s with him to ... c'est à lui de ...

restaurant ['restərɒŋ] n restaurant m; ~ car (BRIT) n wagon-restaurant m

restful ['restful] adj reposant(e)

restive ['restɪv] adj agité(e), impatient(e); (horse) rétif(ive)

restless ['restləs] adj agité(e)

restoration [restə'reɪʃən] n restauration f; restitution f; rétablissement m

restore [rɪ'stɔ:*] vt (building) restaurer; (sth stolen) restituer; (peace, health) rétablir; to ~ to (former state) ramener à

restrain [rɪs'treɪn] vt contenir; (person): to ~ (from doing) retenir (de faire); ~ed adj (style) sobre; (manner) mesuré(e); ~t n (restriction) contrainte f; (moderation) retenue f

restrict [rɪs'trɪkt] vt restreindre, limiter; ~ion [rɪs'trɪkʃən] n restriction f, limitation f

rest room (US) n toilettes fpl

result [rɪ'zʌlt] n résultat m ♦ vi: to ~ in aboutir à, se terminer par; as a ~ of à la suite de

resume [rɪ'zju:m] vt, vi (work, journey) reprendre

résumé ['reɪzju:meɪ] n résumé m; (US) curriculum vitae m

resumption [rɪ'zʌmpʃən] n reprise f

resurgence [rɪ'sɜ:dʒəns] n (of energy, activity) regain m

resurrection [rezə'rekʃən] n resurrection f

resuscitate [rɪ'sʌsɪteɪt] vt (MED) réanimer

retail [n, adj 'ri:teɪl, vb 'ri:teɪl] adj de or au détail ♦ adv au détail; ~er ['ri:teɪlə*] n détaillant(e); ~ price n prix m de détail

retain [rɪ'teɪn] vt (keep) garder, conserver; ~er n (fee) acompte m, provision f

retaliate [rɪ'tælɪeɪt] vi: to ~ (against) se venger (de); **retaliation** [rɪtælɪ'eɪʃən] n représailles fpl, vengeance f

retarded [rɪ'tɑ:dɪd] adj retardé(e)

retch [retʃ] vi avoir des haut-le-cœur

retentive [rɪ'tentɪv] adj: ~ memory excellente mémoire

retina ['retɪnə] n rétine f

retinue ['retɪnju:] n suite f, cortège m

retire [rɪ'taɪə*] vi (give up work) prendre sa retraite; (withdraw) se retirer, partir; (go to bed) (aller) se coucher; ~d adj (person) retraité(e); ~ment n retraite f; retiring [rɪ'taɪərɪŋ] adj (shy) réservé(e); (leaving) sortant(e)

retort [rɪ'tɔ:t] vi riposter

retrace [rɪ'treɪs] vt: to ~ one's steps revenir sur ses pas

retract [rɪ'trækt] vt (statement, claws) rétracter; (undercarriage, aerial) rentrer, escamoter

retrain [rɪ'treɪn] vt (worker) recycler

retread ['ri:tred] n (tyre) pneu rechapé

retreat [rɪ'tri:t] n retraite f ♦ vi battre en retraite

retribution [retrɪ'bju:ʃən] n châtiment m

retrieval [rɪ'tri:vəl] n (see vb) récupération f; réparation f

retrieve [rɪ'tri:v] vt (sth lost) récupérer; (situation, honour) sauver; (error, loss) réparer; ~r n chien m d'arrêt

retrospect ['retrəʊspekt] n: in ~ rétrospectivement, après coup; ~ive [retrəʊ'spektɪv] adj rétrospectif(ive); (law) rétroactif(ive)

return [rɪ'tɜːn] n (going or coming back) retour m; (of sth stolen etc) restitution f; (FINANCE: from land, shares) rendement m, rapport m ♦ cpd (journey) de retour; (BRIT: ticket) aller et retour; (match) retour ♦ vi (come back) revenir; (go back) retourner ♦ vt rendre; (bring back) rapporter; (send back: also: ball) renvoyer; (put back) remettre; (POL: candidate) élire; ~s npl (COMM) recettes fpl; (FINANCE) bénéfices mpl; in ~ (for) en échange (de); by ~ (of post) par retour (du courrier); many happy ~s (of the day)! bon anniversaire!

reunion [riː'juːnjən] n réunion f

reunite [riːju'naɪt] vt réunir

rev [rev] n abbr (AUT: = revolution) tour m ♦ vt (also: ~ up) emballer

revamp ['riː'væmp] vt (firm, system etc) réorganiser

reveal [rɪ'viːl] vt (make known) révéler; (display) laisser voir; ~ing adj révélateur(trice); (dress) au décolleté généreux ou suggestif

revel ['revl] vi: to ~ in sth/in doing se délecter de qch/à faire

revelry ['revlrɪ] n festivités fpl

revenge [rɪ'vendʒ] n vengeance f; to take ~ on (enemy) se venger sur

revenue ['revənjuː] n revenu m

reverberate [rɪ'vɜːbəreɪt] vi (sound) retentir, se répercuter; (fig: shock etc) se propager

reverence ['revərəns] n vénération f, révérence f

Reverend ['revərənd] adj (in titles): the ~ John Smith (Anglican) le révérend John Smith; (Catholic) l'abbé (John) Smith; (Protestant) le pasteur (John) Smith

reversal [rɪ'vɜːsl] n (of opinion) revirement m; (of order) renversement m; (of direction) changement m

reverse [rɪ'vɜːs] n contraire m, opposé m; (back) dos m, envers m; (of paper) verso m; (of coin: also: back) revers m; (AUT: also: ~ gear) marche f arrière ♦ adj (order,

direction) opposé(e), inverse ♦ vt (order, position) changer, inverser; (direction, policy) changer complètement de; (decision) annuler; (roles) renverser; (car) faire marche arrière avec ♦ vi (BRIT: AUT) faire marche arrière; he ~d (the car) into a wall m'a embouti un mur en marche arrière; ~d charge call (BRIT) (TEL) communication f en PCV; reversing lights (BRIT) npl (AUT) feux mpl de marche arrière ou de recul

revert [rɪ'vɜːt] vi: to ~ to revenir à, retourner à

review [rɪ'vjuː] n revue f; (of book, film) critique f, compte rendu; (of situation, policy) examen m, bilan m ♦ vt passer en revue; faire la critique de; examiner; ~er n critique m

revile [rɪ'vaɪl] vt injurier

revise [rɪ'vaɪz] vt (manuscript) réviser, modifier; (manuscript) revoir, corriger ♦ vi (study) réviser; **revision** [rɪ'vɪʒən] n révision f

revival [rɪ'vaɪvl] n reprise f; (recovery) rétablissement m; (of faith) renouveau m

revive [rɪ'vaɪv] vt (person) ranimer; (custom) rétablir; (economy) relancer; (hope, courage) raviver, faire renaître; (play) reprendre ♦ vi (person) reprendre connaissance; (: from ill health) se rétablir; (hope etc) renaître; (activity) reprendre

revoke [rɪ'vəʊk] vt révoquer; (law) abroger

revolt [rɪ'vəʊlt] n révolte f ♦ vi se révolter, se rebeller ♦ vt révolter, dégoûter; ~ing adj dégoûtant(e)

revolution [revə'luːʃən] n révolution f; (of wheel etc) tour m, révolution; ~ary adj révolutionnaire ♦ n révolutionnaire m/f

revolve [rɪ'vɒlv] vi tourner

revolver [rɪ'vɒlvə*] n revolver m

revolving [rɪ'vɒlvɪŋ] adj tournant(e); (chair) pivotant(e); ~ door n (porte f à) tambour m

revulsion [rɪ'vʌlʃən] n dégoût m, répugnance f

reward [rɪ'wɔːd] n récompense f ♦
vt: **to ~ (for)** récompenser (de);
~ing adj (fig) qui (en) vaut la peine,
gratifiant(e)

rewind [riː'waɪnd] (irreg) vt (tape)
rembobiner

rewire [riː'waɪə*] vt (house) refaire
l'installation électrique de

rheumatism ['ruːmətɪzm] n rhumatisme m

Rhine [raɪn] n: **the ~** le Rhin

rhinoceros [raɪ'nɔsərəs] n rhinocéros
m

Rhone [rəʊn] n: **the ~** le Rhône

rhubarb ['ruːbɑːb] n rhubarbe f

rhyme [raɪm] n rime f; (verse) vers
mpl

rhythm ['rɪðəm] n rythme m

rib [rɪb] n (ANAT) côte f

ribbon ['rɪbən] n ruban m; **in ~s**
(torn) en lambeaux

rice [raɪs] n riz m; **~ pudding** n riz
au lait

rich [rɪtʃ] adj riche; (gift, clothes)
somptueux(euse) ♦ npl: **the ~** les riches mpl; **~es** npl richesses fpl; **~ly**
adv richement; (deserved, earned)
largement

rickets ['rɪkɪts] n rachitisme m

rickety ['rɪkɪtɪ] adj branlant(e)

rickshaw ['rɪkʃɔː] n pousse-pousse m
inv

rid [rɪd] (pt, pp rid) vt: **to ~ sb of**
débarrasser qn de; **to get ~ of** se
débarrasser de

riddle ['rɪdl] n (puzzle) énigme f ♦
vt: **to be ~d with** être criblé(e) de;
(fig: guilt, corruption, doubts) être en
proie à

ride [raɪd] (pt rode, pp ridden) n
promenade f, tour m; (distance covered) trajet m ♦ vi (as sport) monter
(à cheval), faire du cheval; (go
somewhere: on horse, bicycle) aller
(à cheval or bicyclette etc); (journey: on bicycle, motorcycle, bus)
rouler ♦ vt (a certain horse) monter;
(distance) parcourir, faire; **to take
sb for a ~** (fig) faire marcher qn;

to ~ a horse/bicycle monter à
cheval/à bicyclette; **~r** n cava-
lier(ère); (in race) jockey m; (on bicycle) cycliste m/f; (on motorcycle)
motocycliste m/f

ridge [rɪdʒ] n (of roof, mountain)
arête f; (of hill) faîte m; (on object)
strie f

ridicule ['rɪdɪkjuːl] n ridicule m; dérision f

ridiculous [rɪ'dɪkjʊləs] adj ridicule

riding ['raɪdɪŋ] n équitation f; **~
school** n manège m, école f d'équitation

rife [raɪf] adj répandu(e); **~ with**
abondant(e) en, plein(e) de

riffraff ['rɪfræf] n racaille f

rifle ['raɪfl] n fusil m (à canon rayé)
♦ vt vider, dévaliser; **~ through** vt
(belongings) fouiller; (papers) feuilleter; **~ range** n champ m de tir;
(at fair) stand m de tir

rift [rɪft] n fente f, fissure f; (fig: disagreement) désaccord m

rig [rɪg] n (also: oil ~: at sea) plate-
forme pétrolière ♦ vt (election etc)
truquer; **~ out** (BRIT) vt: **to ~ out
as/in** habiller en/de; **~ up** vt arranger, faire avec des moyens de fortune; **~ging** n (NAUT) gréement m

right [raɪt] adj (correctly chosen:
answer, road etc) bon(bonne); (true)
juste, exact(e); (suitable) appro-
prié(e), convenable; (just) juste,
équitable; (morally good) bien; (not
left) droit(e) ♦ n (what is morally right) bien m; (title, claim)
droit m; (not left) droite f ♦ adv
(answer) correctement, juste; (treat)
bien, comme il faut; (not on the left)
à droite ♦ vt redresser ♦ excl bon!;
to be ~ (person) avoir raison; (answer) être juste or correct(e); (clock)
à l'heure (juste); **by ~s** en toute justice; **on the ~** à droite; **to be in the
~** avoir raison; **~ now** en ce moment même; tout de suite; **~ in the
middle** en plein milieu; **~ away** immédiatement; **~ angle** n (MATH)
angle droit; **~eous** ['raɪtʃəs] adj

droit(e), vertueux(euse); (*anger*) justifié(e); ~**ful** *adj* légitime; ~**handed** *adj* (*person*) droitier(ère); ~**hand man** *n* bras droit (*fig*); ~**hand side** *n* côté droit; ~**ly** *adv* (*with reason*) à juste titre; ~ **of way** *n* droit *m* de passage; (*AUT*) priorité *f*; ~**wing** *adj* (*POL*) de droite

rigid ['rɪdʒɪd] *adj* rigide; (*principle, control*) strict(e)

rigmarole ['rɪgmərəul] *n* comédie *f*

rigorous ['rɪgərəs] *adj* rigoureux(euse)

rile [raɪl] *vt* agacer

rim [rɪm] *n* bord *m*; (*of spectacles*) monture *f*; (*of wheel*) jante *f*

rind [raɪnd] *n* (*of bacon*) couenne *f*; (*of lemon etc*) écorce *f*, zeste *m*; (*of cheese*) croûte *f*

ring [rɪŋ] (*pt* rang, *pp* rung) *n* anneau *m*; (*on finger*) bague *f*; (*also: wedding* ~) alliance *f*; (*of people, objects*) cercle *m*; (*of spies*) réseau *m*; (*of smoke etc*) rond *m*; (*arena*) piste *f*, arène *f*; (*for boxing*) ring *m*; (*sound of bell*) sonnerie *f* ♦ *vi* (*telephone, bell*) sonner; (*person: by telephone*) téléphoner; (*also: ~ out: voice, words*) retentir; (*ears*) bourdonner ♦ *vt* (*BRIT: TEL: also: ~ up*) téléphoner à, appeler; (*bell*) faire sonner; **to ~ the bell** sonner; **to give sb a ~** (*BRIT: TEL*) appeler qn; **~ back** *vt, vi* (*TEL*) rappeler; **~ off** *vi* (*BRIT*) (*TEL*) raccrocher; **~ up** *vt* (*BRIT*) (*TEL*) appeler; **~ing** *n* (*of telephone*) sonnerie *f*; (*of bell*) tintement *m*; (*in ears*) bourdonnement *m*; **~ing tone** *n* (*BRIT*) (*TEL*) sonnerie *f*; **~leader** *n* (*of gang*) chef *m*, meneur *m*

ringlets ['rɪŋlɪts] *npl* anglaises *fpl*

ring road *n* (*BRIT*) route *f* de ceinture; (*motorway*) périphérique *m*

rink [rɪŋk] *n* (*also: ice* ~) patinoire *f*

rinse [rɪns] *vt* rincer

riot ['raɪət] *n* émeute *f*; (*of flowers, colour*) profusion *f* ♦ *vi* faire une émeute, manifester avec violence; **to run ~** se déchaîner; **~ous** *adj* (*mob,*

assembly) séditieux(euse), déchaîné(e); (*living, behaviour*) débauché(e); (*party*) très animé(e); (*welcome*) délirant(e)

rip [rɪp] *n* déchirure *f* ♦ *vt* déchirer ♦ *vi* se déchirer; ~**cord** ['rɪpkɔ:d] *n* poignée *f* d'ouverture

ripe [raɪp] *adj* (*fruit*) mûr(e); (*cheese*) fait(e); ~**n** *vt* mûrir ♦ *vi* mûrir

ripple ['rɪpl] *n* ondulation *f*; (*of applause, laughter*) cascade *f* ♦ *vi* onduler

rise [raɪz] (*pt* rose, *pp* risen) *n* (*slope*) côte *f*, pente *f*; (*hill*) hauteur *f*; (*increase: in wages: BRIT*) augmentation *f*; (: *in prices, temperature*) hausse *f*, augmentation; (*fig: to power etc*) ascension *f* ♦ *vi* s'élever, monter; (*prices, numbers*) monter; (*waters*) monter; (*sun: person: from chair, bed*) se lever; (*also: ~ up: tower, building*) s'élever; (: *rebel*) se révolter; se rebeller; (*in rank*) s'élever; **to give ~ to** donner lieu à; **to ~ to the occasion** se montrer à la hauteur; **rising** *adj* (*increasing: number, prices*) en hausse; (*tide*) montant(e); (*sun, moon*) levant(e)

risk [rɪsk] *n* risque *m* ♦ *vt* risquer; **at ~** en danger; **at one's own ~** à ses risques et périls; ~**y** *adj* risqué(e)

rissole ['rɪsəul] *n* croquette *f*

rite [raɪt] *n* rite *m*; **last ~s** derniers sacrements; **ritual** ['rɪtjuəl] *adj* rituel(le) ♦ *n* rituel *m*

rival ['raɪvl] *adj, n* rival(e); (*in business*) concurrent(e) ♦ *vt* (*match*) égaler; ~**ry** *n* rivalité *f*, concurrence *f*

river ['rɪvə*] *n* rivière *f*; (*major, also fig*) fleuve *m* ♦ *cpd* (*port, traffic*) fluvial(e); **up/down** ~ en amont/aval; ~**bank** *n* rive *f*, berge *f*

rivet ['rɪvɪt] *n* rivet *m* ♦ *vt* (*fig*) river, fixer

Riviera [rɪvɪ'eərə] *n*: **the (French)** ~ la Côte d'Azur; **the Italian** ~ la Riviera (italienne)

road [rəud] *n* route *f*; (*in town*) rue

f; (*fig*) chemin, voie *f*; **major/minor ~** route principale *or* à priorité/voie secondaire; **~ accident** *n* accident *m* de la circulation; **~block** *n* barrage routier; **~hog** *n* chauffard *m*; **~ map** *n* carte routière; **~ safety** *n* sécurité routière; **~side** *n* bord de la route, bas-côté *m*; **~sign** *n* panneau *m* de signalisation; **~way** *n* chaussée *f*; **~ works** *npl* travaux *mpl* de réfection des routes); **~worthy** *adj* en bon état de marche

roam [rəum] *vi* errer, vagabonder

roar [rɔ:*] *n* rugissement *m*; (*of crowd*) hurlements *mpl*; (*of vehicle, thunder, storm*) grondement *m* ♦ *vi* rugir; hurler; gronder; **to ~ with laughter** éclater de rire; **to do a ~ing trade** faire des affaires d'or

roast [rəust] *n* rôti *m* ♦ *vt* (faire) rôtir; (*coffee*) griller, torréfier; **~ beef** *n* rôti *m* de bœuf, rosbif *m*

rob [rɔb] *vt* (*person*) voler; (*bank*) dévaliser; **to ~ sb of sth** voler *or* dérober qch à qn; (*fig*: *deprive*) priver qn de qch; **~ber** *n* bandit *m*, voleur *m*; **~bery** *n* vol *m*

robe [rəub] *n* (*for ceremony etc*) robe *f*; (*also*: *bath~*) peignoir *m*; (*US*) couverture *f*

robin [ˈrɔbɪn] *n* rouge-gorge *m*

robust [rəuˈbʌst] *adj* robuste; (*material, appetite*) solide

rock [rɔk] *n* (*substance*) roche *f*, roc *m*; (*boulder*) rocher *m*; (*US*: *small stone*) caillou *m*; (*BRIT*: *sweet*) ≈ sucre *m* d'orge ♦ *vt* (*swing gently*: *cradle*) balancer; (: *child*) bercer; (*shake*) ébranler, secouer ♦ *vi* se balancer; être ébranlé(e) *or* secoué(e); **on the ~s** (*drink*) avec des glaçons; (*marriage etc*) en train de craquer; **~ and roll** *n* rock (and roll) *m*, rock'n'roll *m*; **~-bottom** *adj* (*fig*: *prices*) sacrifié(e); **~ery** *n* (*jardin m* de) rocaille *f*

rocket [ˈrɔkɪt] *n* fusée *f*; (*MIL*) fusée, roquette *f*

rocking chair [ˈrɔkɪŋ-] *n* fauteuil *m* à bascule

rocking horse *n* cheval *m* à bascule

rocky [ˈrɔkɪ] *adj* (*hill*) rocheux(euse); (*path*) rocailleux(euse)

rod [rɔd] *n* (*wooden*) baguette *f*; (*metallic*) tringle *f*; (*TECH*) tige *f*; (*also*: *fishing ~*) canne *f* à pêche

rode [rəud] *pt of* **ride**

rodent [ˈrəudənt] *n* rongeur *m*

rodeo [ˈrəudɪəu] *n* (*US*) rodéo *m*

roe [rəu] *n* (*species*: *also*: **~ deer**) chevreuil *m*; (*of fish, also*: **hard ~**) œufs *mpl* de poisson; **soft ~** laitance *f*

rogue [rəug] *n* coquin(e)

role [rəul] *n* rôle *m*

roll [rəul] *n* rouleau *m*; (*of banknotes*) liasse *f*; (*also*: **bread ~**) petit pain; (*register*) liste *f*; (*sound: of drums etc*) roulement *m* ♦ *vt* rouler; (*also*: **~ up**: *string*) enrouler; (*sleeves*) retrousser; (: **~ out**: *pastry*) étendre au rouleau, abaisser ♦ *vi* rouler; **~ about** *vi* rouler çà et là; (*person*) se rouler par terre; **~ around** *vi* = **roll about**; **~ by** *vi* (*time*) s'écouler, passer; **~ in** *vi* (*mail, cash*) affluer; **~ over** *vi* se retourner; **~ up** *vi* (*inf*: *arrive*) s'amener ♦ *vt* rouler; **~ call** *n* appel *m*; **~er** *n* rouleau *m*; (*wheel*) roulette *f*; (*for road*) rouleau compresseur; **~er coaster** *n* montagnes *fpl* russes; **~er skates** *npl* patins *mpl* à roulettes; **~ing** [ˈrəulɪŋ] *adj* (*landscape*) onduleux(euse); **~ing pin** *n* rouleau *m* à pâtisserie; **~ing stock** *n* (*RAIL*) matériel roulant

ROM [rɔm] *n abbr* (= *read only memory*) mémoire morte

Roman [ˈrəumən] *adj* romain(e); **~ Catholic** *adj*, *n* catholique (*m/f*)

romance [rəˈmæns] *n* (*love affair*) idylle *f*; (*charm*) poésie *f*; (*novel*) roman *m* d'amour

Romania [rəuˈmeɪnɪə] *n* Roumanie *f*; **~n** *adj* roumain(e) ♦ *n* Roumain(e); (*LING*) roumain *m*

Roman numeral *n* chiffre romain

romantic [rəʊˈmæntɪk] adj romantique; sentimental(e)

Rome [rəʊm] n Rome

romp [rɒmp] n jeux bruyants ♦ vi (also: ~ about) s'ébattre, jouer bruyamment; **~ers** [ˈrɒmpəz] npl barboteuse f

roof [ruːf] (pl ~s) n toit m ♦ vt couvrir (d'un toit); **~ of the mouth** la voûte du palais; **~ing** n toiture f; **~ rack** n (AUT) galerie f

rook [rʊk] n (bird) freux m; (CHESS) tour f

room [rʊm] n (in house) pièce f; (also: bed~) chambre f (à coucher); (in school etc) salle f; (space) place f; **~s** npl (lodging) meublé m; **"~s to let"** (BRIT) or **"for rent"** (US) "chambres à louer"; **single/double ~** chambre pour une personne/deux personnes; **there is ~ for improvement** cela laisse à désirer; **~ing house** (US) n maison f or immeuble m de rapport; **~mate** n camarade m/f de chambre; **~ service** n service m des chambres (dans un hôtel); **~y** adj spacieux(euse); (garment) ample

roost [ruːst] vi se jucher

rooster [ˈruːstəʳ] n (esp US) coq m

root [ruːt] n (BOT, MATH) racine f; (fig: of problem) origine f, fond m ♦ vi (plant) s'enraciner; **~ about** vi (fig) fouiller; **~ for** vt fus encourager, applaudir; **~ out** vt (find) dénicher

rope [rəʊp] n corde f; (NAUT) cordage m ♦ vt (tie up or together) attacher; (climbers: also: ~ together) encorder; (area: ~ off) interdire l'accès de; (divide off) séparer; **to know the ~s** (fig) être au courant, connaître les ficelles; **~ in** vt (fig: person) embringuer

rosary [ˈrəʊzərɪ] n chapelet m

rose [rəʊz] pt of rise ♦ n rose f; (also: ~bush) rosier m; (on watering can) pomme f

rosé [ˈrəʊzeɪ] n rosé m

rosebud [ˈrəʊzbʌd] n bouton m de rose

rosemary [ˈrəʊzmərɪ] n romarin m

roster [ˈrɒstəʳ] n: **duty ~** tableau m de service

rostrum [ˈrɒstrəm] n tribune f (pour un orateur etc)

rosy [ˈrəʊzɪ] adj rose; **a ~ future** un bel avenir

rot [rɒt] n (decay) pourriture f; (fig: pej) idioties fpl ♦ vt, vi pourrir

rota [ˈrəʊtə] n liste f, tableau m de service; **on a ~ basis** par roulement

rotary [ˈrəʊtərɪ] adj rotatif(ive)

rotate [rəʊˈteɪt] vt (revolve) faire tourner; (change round: jobs) faire à tour de rôle ♦ vi (revolve) tourner; **rotating** adj (movement) tournant(e)

rote [rəʊt] n: **by ~** machinalement, par cœur

rotten [ˈrɒtn] adj (decayed) pourri(e); (dishonest) corrompu(e); (inf: bad) mauvais(e), moche; **to feel ~** (ill) être mal fichu(e)

rotund [rəʊˈtʌnd] adj (person) rondelet(te)

rough [rʌf] adj (cloth, skin) rêche, rugueux(euse); (terrain) accidenté(e); (path) rocailleux(euse); (voice) rauque, rude; (person, manner: coarse) rude, fruste; (: violent) brutal(e); (district, weather) mauvais(e); (sea) houleux(euse); (plan etc) ébauché(e); (guess) approximatif(ive) ♦ n (GOLF) rough m; **to ~ it** vivre à la dure; **to sleep ~** (BRIT) coucher à la dure; **~age** n fibres fpl alimentaires; **~-and-ready** adj rudimentaire; **~ copy, ~draft** n brouillon m; **~ly** adv (handle) rudement, brutalement; (speak) avec brusquerie; (make) grossièrement; (approximately) à peu près, en gros

roulette [ruːˈlet] n roulette f

Roumania [ruːˈmeɪnɪə] n = Romania

round [raʊnd] adj rond(e) ♦ n (BRIT: of toast) tranche f; (duty: of policeman, milkman etc) tournée f; (: of doctor) visites fpl; (game: of cards, in competition) partie f; (BOXING) round m; (of talks) série *f* ♦ *vt* (*corner*) tourner ♦ *prep* autour de ♦ *adv*: **all** ~ tout autour; **the long way** ~ (par) le chemin le plus long; **all the year** ~ toute l'année; **it's just** ~ **the corner** (*fig*) c'est tout près; **the clock 24 hours** ~ les 24 heures sur 24; **to go** ~ **to sb's (house)** aller chez qn; **to go** ~ **the back** passer par derrière; **to go** ~ **a house** visiter une maison, faire le tour d'une maison; **enough to go** ~ assez pour tout le monde; ~ **of ammunition** cartouche *f*; ~ **of applause** ban *m*, applaudissements *mpl*; ~ **of drinks** tournée *f*; ~ **of sandwiches** sandwich *m*; ~ **off** *vt* (*speech etc*) terminer; ~ **up** *vt* rassembler; (*criminals*) effectuer une rafle de; (*price, figure*) arrondir (au chiffre supérieur); **~about** *n* (*BRIT: AUT*) rond-point *m* (à sens giratoire); (*at fair*) manège *m* (de chevaux de bois) ♦ *adj* (*route, means*) détourné(e); **~ers** *n* (*game*) sorte de baseball; **~ly** *adv* (*fig*) tout net, carrément; **~-shouldered** *adj* au dos rond; **~trip** *n* (*voyage* m) aller et retour m; **~up** *n* rassemblement m; (*of criminals*) rafle *f*

rouse [rauz] *vt* (*wake up*) réveiller; (*stir up*) susciter; provoquer; éveiller; **rousing** ['rauzɪŋ] *adj* (*welcome*) enthousiaste

rout [raut] *n* (*MIL*) déroute *f*

route [ruːt] *n* itinéraire *m*; (*of bus*) parcours *m*; (*of trade, shipping*) route *f*; ~ **map** (*BRIT*) *n* (*for journey*) croquis *m* d'itinéraire

routine [ruː'tiːn] *adj* (*work*) ordinaire, courant(e); (*procedure*) d'usage ♦ *n* (*habits*) habitudes *fpl*; (*THEATRE*) numéro *m*

rove [rəuv] *vt* (*area, streets*) errer dans

row¹ [rəu] *n* (*line*) rangée *f*; (*of people, seats, KNITTING*) rang *m*; (*behind one another: of cars, people*) file *f* ♦ *vi* (*in boat*) ramer; (*as sport*) faire de l'aviron ♦ *vt* (*boat*) faire al-

ler à la rame *or* à l'aviron; **in a row** (*fig*) affilée

row² [rau] *n* (*noise*) vacarme *m*; (*dispute*) dispute *f*, querelle *f*; (*scolding*) réprimande *f*, savon *m* ♦ *vi* se disputer, se quereller

rowboat ['rəubəut] (*US*) *n* canot *m* (à rames)

rowdy ['raudɪ] *adj* chahuteur(euse); (*occasion*) tapageur(euse)

rowing ['rəuɪŋ] *n* canotage *m*; (*as sport*) aviron *m*; ~ **boat** (*BRIT*) *n* canot *m* (à rames)

royal ['rɔɪəl] *adj* royal(e); **R~ Air Force** (*BRIT*) *n* armée de l'air britannique

royalty ['rɔɪəltɪ] *n* (*royal persons*) (membres *mpl* de la) famille royale; (*payment: to author*) droits *mpl* d'auteur; (*: to inventor*) royalties *fpl*

rpm *abbr* (*AUT*: = *revs per minute*) tr/mn

RSVP *abbr* (= *répondez s'il vous plaît*) R.S.V.P.

Rt Hon. *abbr* (*BRIT*: = *Right Honourable*) *titre donné aux députés de la Chambre des communes*

rub [rʌb] *vt* frotter; frictionner; (*hands*) se frotter ♦ *n* (*with cloth*) coup *m* chiffon *or* de torchon; **to give sth a** ~ donner un coup de chiffon *or* de torchon à; **to** ~ **sb up** (*BRIT*) *or* **to** ~ **sb** (*US*) **the wrong way** prendre qn à rebrousse-poil; ~ **off** *vi* partir; ~ **off on** *vt fus* déteindre sur; ~ **out** *vt* effacer

rubber ['rʌbə*] *n* caoutchouc *m*; (*BRIT: eraser*) gomme *f* (à effacer); ~ **band** *n* élastique *m*; ~ **plant** *n* caoutchouc *m* (*plante verte*)

rubbish ['rʌbɪʃ] *n* (*from household*) ordures *fpl*; (*fig: pej*) camelote *f*; (*: nonsense*) bêtises *fpl*, idioties *fpl*; ~ **bin** (*BRIT*) *n* poubelle *f*; ~ **dump** *n* décharge publique, dépotoir *m*

rubble ['rʌbl] *n* décombres *mpl*; (*smaller*) gravats *mpl*; (*CONSTR*) blocage *m*

ruby ['ruːbɪ] *n* rubis *m*

rucksack ['rʌksæk] *n* sac *m* à dos

rudder ['rʌdə*] n gouvernail m
ruddy ['rʌdɪ] adj (face) coloré(e);
(inf: damned) sacré(e), fichu(e)
rude [ruːd] adj (impolite) impoli(e);
(coarse) grossier(ère); (shocking) in-
décent(e), inconvenant(e)
ruffian ['rʌfɪən] n brute f, voyou m
ruffle ['rʌfl] vt (hair) ébouriffer; (clothes) chiffonner; (fig: person): to
get ~d s'énerver
rug [rʌg] n petit tapis; (BRIT: blanket) couverture f
rugby ['rʌgbɪ] n (also: ~ football)
rugby m
rugged ['rʌgɪd] adj (landscape) acci-
denté(e); (features, character) rude
rugger ['rʌgə*] n (BRIT: inf) rugby
m
ruin ['ruːɪn] n ruine f ♦ vt ruiner;
(spoil, clothes) abimer; (event)
gâcher; ~s npl (of building) ruine(s)
rule [ruːl] n règle f; (regulation)
règlement m; (government) autorité
f, gouvernement m ♦ vt (country)
gouverner; (person) dominer ♦ vi
commander; (LAW) statuer; as a ~
normalement, en règle générale; to
rule out vt exclure; ~d adj (paper) ré-
glé(e); ~r n (sovereign) souve-
rain(e); (for measuring) règle f; ~l-
ing adj (party) au pouvoir; (class)
dirigeant(e) ♦ n (LAW) décision f
rum [rʌm] n rhum m
Rumania [ruːˈmeɪnɪə] n = Romania
rumble ['rʌmbl] vi gronder; (stomach, pipe) gargouiller
rummage ['rʌmɪdʒ] vi fouiller
rumour ['ruːmə*] (US rumor) n rumeur f, bruit m (qui court) ♦ vt: it
is ~ed that le bruit court que
rump [rʌmp] n (of animal) croupe f;
(inf: of person) postérieur m; ~
steak n rumsteck m
rumpus ['rʌmpəs] (inf) n tapage m,
chahut m
run [rʌn] (pt ran, pp run) n (fast
pace) (pas m de) course f; (outing)
tour m or promenade f (en voiture);
(distance travelled) parcours m, trajet m; (series) suite f, série f;

(THEATRE) série de représentations; (SKI) piste f; (CRICKET, BA-
SEBALL) point m; (in tights, stockings) maille filée, échelle f ♦ vt
(operate: business) diriger; (:
competition, course) organiser; (: hotel, house) tenir; (race) participer à;
(COMPUT) exécuter; (to pass: hand,
finger) passer; (water, bath) faire
couler; (PRESS: feature) publier ♦
vi courir; (flee) s'enfuir; (work: machine, factory) marcher; (bus, train)
circuler; (continue: play) se jouer;
(: contract) être valide; (flow: river,
bath; nose) couler; (colours, washing) déteindre; (in election) être
candidat, se présenter; to go for a
~ faire un peu de course à pied;
there was a ~ on ... (meat, tickets)
les gens se sont rués sur ...; in the
long ~ à longue échéance; à la longue; en fin de compte; on the ~ en
fuite; I'll ~ you to the station je
vais vous emmener or conduire à la
gare; to ~ a risk courir un risque;
~ about vi (children) courir çà et
là; ~ across vt fus (find) trouver
par hasard; ~ around vi = run
about; ~ down vt (production) réduire progressivement; (factory) réduire progressivement la production
de; (AUT) renverser; (criticize) critiquer, dénigrer; to be ~ down (person: tired) être fatigué(e) or à plat;
~ in (BRIT) vt (car) roder; ~ into
vt fus (meet: person) rencontrer par
hasard; (: trouble) se heurter à;
(collide with) heurter; ~ off vi s'enfuir ♦ vt (water) laisser s'écouler;
(copies) tirer; ~ out vi (person) sortir en courant; (liquid) couler; (lease) expirer; (money) être épuisé(e);
~ out of vt fus se trouver à court
de; ~ over vt (AUT) écraser ♦ vt
fus (revise) revoir, reprendre; ~
through vt fus (recapitulate) reprendre; (play) répéter; ~ up vt: to ~
up against (difficulties) se heurter
à; to ~ up a debt s'endetter;
~away adj (horse) emballé(e)

(truck) fou(folle); (person) fugitif(ive); (teenager) fugueur(euse)

rung [rʌŋ] pp of **ring ♦** n (of ladder) barreau m

runner ['rʌnə*] n (in race: person) coureur(euse); (: horse) partant m; (on sledge) patin m; (for drawer etc) coulisseau m; ~ **bean** (BRIT) n haricot m (à rames); **~-up** n second(e)

running ['rʌnɪŋ] n course f; (of business, organization) gestion f, direction f ♦ adj (water) courant(e); to be in/out of the ~ pour qch être/ne pas être sur les rangs pour qch; 6 days ~ 6 jours de suite; ~ **commentary** n commentaire détaillé; ~ **costs** npl frais mpl d'exploitation

runny ['rʌnɪ] adj qui coule

run-of-the-mill ['rʌnəvðə'mɪl] adj ordinaire, banal(e)

runt [rʌnt] n (also pej) avorton m

run-up ['rʌnʌp] n: ~ **to sth** (election etc) période f précédant qch

runway ['rʌnweɪ] n (AVIAT) piste f

rupee [ru:'pi:] n roupie f

rupture ['rʌptʃə*] n (MED) hernie f

rural ['ruərəl] adj rural(e)

rush [rʌʃ] n (hurry) hâte f, précipitation f; (of crowd, COMM: sudden demand) ruée f; (current) flot m; (of emotion) vague f; (BOT) jonc m ♦ vt (hurry) transporter ou envoyer d'urgence ♦ vi se précipiter; ~ **hour** n heures fpl de pointe

rusk [rʌsk] n biscotte f

Russia ['rʌʃə] n Russie f; ~**n** adj russe ♦ n Russe m/f; (LING) russe m

rust [rʌst] n rouille f ♦ vi rouiller

rustic ['rʌstɪk] adj rustique

rustle ['rʌsl] vi bruire, produire un bruissement ♦ vt (paper) froisser; (US: cattle) voler

rustproof ['rʌstpru:f] adj inoxydable

rusty ['rʌstɪ] adj rouillé(e)

rut [rʌt] n ornière f; (ZOOL) rut m; to be in a ~ suivre l'ornière, s'encroûter

ruthless ['ru:θlɪs] adj sans pitié, impitoyable

rye [raɪ] n seigle m; ~ **bread** n pain de seigle

S

Sabbath ['sæbəθ] n (Jewish) sabbat m; (Christian) dimanche m

sabotage ['sæbətɑ:ʒ] n sabotage m ♦ vt saboter

saccharin(e) ['sækərɪn] n saccharine f

sachet ['sæʃeɪ] n sachet m

sack [sæk] n (bag) sac m ♦ vt (dismiss) renvoyer, mettre à la porte; (plunder) piller, mettre à sac; to get the ~ être renvoyé(e), être mis(e) à la porte; (dismissal) renvoi m; ~**ing** n (material) toile f à sac; (dismissal) renvoi m

sacrament ['sækrəmənt] n sacrement m

sacred ['seɪkrɪd] adj sacré(e)

sacrifice ['sækrɪfaɪs] n sacrifice m ♦ vt sacrifier

sad [sæd] adj triste; (deplorable) triste, fâcheux(euse)

saddle ['sædl] n selle f ♦ vt (horse) seller; to be ~**d with sth** (inf) avoir qch sur les bras; ~**bag** n sacoche f

sadistic [sə'dɪstɪk] adj sadique

sadly ['sædlɪ] adv tristement; (unfortunately) malheureusement; (seriously) fort

sadness ['sædnɪs] n tristesse f

s.a.e. n abbr = **stamped addressed envelope**

safe [seɪf] adj (out of danger) hors de danger, en sécurité; (not dangerous) sans danger; (unharmed): ~ **journey!** bon voyage!; (cautious) prudent(e); (sure: bet etc) assuré(e) ♦ n coffre-fort m; ~ **from** à l'abri de; ~ **and sound** sain(e) et sauf(sauve); (just) to be on the ~ **side** pour plus de sûreté, par précaution; ~-**conduct** n sauf-conduit m; ~-**deposit** n (vault) dépôt m de coffres-forts; (box) coffre-fort m; ~**guard** n sauvegarde f, protection f ♦ vt sauvegarder, protéger; ~**keeping** n bonne garde; ~**ly** adv (assume, say) risque d'erreur; (*drive, arrive*) sans accident; ~ **sex** *n* rapports *mpl* sexuels sans risque, sexe *m* sans risques

safety ['seiftɪ] *n* sécurité *f*; ~ **belt** *n* ceinture *f* de sécurité; ~ **pin** *n* épingle *f* de sûreté or de nourrice; ~ **valve** *n* soupape *f* de sûreté

sag [sæg] *vi* s'affaisser; (*hem, breasts*) pendre

sage [seɪdʒ] *n* (*herb*) sauge *f*; (*person*) sage *m*

Sagittarius [sædʒɪ'tɛərɪəs] *n* le Sagittaire

Sahara [sə'hɑːrə] *n*: the ~ (Desert) le (désert du) Sahara

said [sɛd] *pt, pp* of **say**

sail [seɪl] *n* (*on boat*) voile *f*; (*trip*): to go for a ~ faire un tour en bateau ♦ *vt* (*boat*) manœuvrer, piloter ♦ *vi* (*travel: ship*) avancer, naviguer; (*set off*) partir, prendre la mer; (*SPORT*) faire de la voile; they ~ed into Le Havre ils sont entrés dans le port du Havre; ~ **through** *vi, vt fus* (*fig*) réussir haut la main; ~**boat** *n* (*US*) *n* bateau *m* à voiles, voilier *m*; ~**ing** *n* (*SPORT*) voile *f*; to go ~**ing** faire de la voile; ~**ing boat** *n* bateau *m* à voiles, voilier *m*; ~**ing ship** *n* grand voilier; ~**or** *n* marin *m*, matelot *m*

saint [seɪnt] *n* saint(e)

sake [seɪk] *n*: for the ~ of pour (l'amour de), dans l'intérêt de; par égard pour

salad ['sæləd] *n* salade *f*; ~ **bowl** *n* saladier *m*; ~ **cream** *n* (*BRIT*) (sorte *f* de) mayonnaise *f*; ~ **dressing** *n* vinaigrette *f*

salary ['sælərɪ] *n* salaire *m*

sale [seɪl] *n* vente *f*; (*at reduced prices*) soldes *mpl*; "**for** ~" "à vendre"; **on** ~ en vente; **on** ~ **or return** vendu(e) avec faculté de retour; ~**room** *n* salle *f* des ventes; ~**s assistant** *n* vendeur(euse); ~**s clerk** (*US*) *n* vendeur(euse); ~**sman** (*irreg*) *n* vendeur *m*; (*representative*) représentant *m* de commerce;

~**swoman** (*irreg*) *n* vendeuse *f*; (*representative*) représentante *f* de commerce

sallow ['sæləʊ] *adj* cireux(euse)

salmon ['sæmən] *n inv* saumon *m*

saloon [sə'luːn] *n* (*US*) bar *m*; (*BRIT: AUT*) berline *f*; (*ship's lounge*) salon *m*

salt [sɔːlt] *n* sel *m* ♦ *vt* saler; ~ **cellar** *n* salière *f*; ~**water** *adj* de mer; ~**y** *adj* salé(e)

salute [sə'luːt] *n* salut *m* ♦ *vt* saluer

salvage ['sælvɪdʒ] *n* (*saving*) sauvetage *m*; (*things saved*) biens sauvés or récupérés ♦ *vt* sauver, récupérer

salvation [sæl'veɪʃən] *n* salut *m*; **S~ Army** *n* armée *f* du Salut

same [seɪm] *adj* même ♦ *pron*: the ~ le(la) même, les mêmes; the ~ **book as** le même livre que; **at the** ~ **time** en même temps; **all** or **just the** ~ tout de même, quand même; **to do the** ~ faire de même, en faire autant; **to do the** ~ **as sb** faire comme qn; **the** ~ **to you!** à vous de même!; (*after insult*) toi-même!

sample ['sɑːmpl] *n* échantillon *m*; (*blood*) prélèvement *m* ♦ *vt* (*food, wine*) goûter

sanctimonious [sæŋktɪ'məʊnɪəs] *adj* moralisateur(trice)

sanction ['sæŋkʃən] *n* approbation *f*, sanction *f*

sanctity ['sæŋktɪtɪ] *n* sainteté *f*, caractère sacré

sanctuary ['sæŋktjʊərɪ] *n* (*holy place*) sanctuaire *m*; (*refuge*) asile *m*; (*for wild life*) réserve *f*

sand [sænd] *n* sable *m* ♦ *vt* (*furniture: also:* ~ **down**) poncer

sandal ['sændl] *n* sandale *f*

sand: ~**box** (*US*) *n* tas *m* de sable; ~**castle** *n* château *m* de sable; ~**paper** *n* papier *m* de verre; ~**pit** (*BRIT*) *n* (*for children*) tas *m* de sable; ~**stone** *n* grès *m*

sandwich ['sænwɪdʒ] *n* sandwich *m*; cheese/ham ~ sandwich au fromage/jambon; ~ **course** (*BRIT*) *n* cours *m* de formation professionnelle

sandy ['sændɪ] adj sablonneux(euse); (colour) sable inv, blond roux inv

sane [seɪn] adj sain(e), sain(e) d'esprit; (outlook) sensé(e), sain(e)

sang [sæŋ] pt of sing

sanitary ['sænɪtərɪ] adj (system, arrangements) sanitaire; (clean) hygiénique; ~ **towel** (US **napkin**) n serviette f hygiénique

sanitation [sænɪ'teɪʃən] n (in house) installations fpl sanitaires; (in town) système m sanitaire; ~ **department** (US) n service m de voirie

sanity ['sænɪtɪ] n santé mentale; (common sense) bon sens

sank [sæŋk] pt of sink

Santa Claus [sæntə'klɔːz] n le père Noël

sap [sæp] n (of plants) sève f ♦ vt (strength) saper, miner

sapling ['sæplɪŋ] n jeune arbre m

sapphire ['sæfaɪə*] n saphir m

sarcasm ['sɑːkæzəm] n sarcasme m, raillerie f

sardine [sɑː'diːn] n sardine f

Sardinia [sɑː'dɪnɪə] n Sardaigne f

sash [sæʃ] n écharpe f

sat [sæt] pt, pp of sit

satchel ['sætʃəl] n cartable m

satellite ['sætəlaɪt] n satellite m; ~ **dish** n antenne f parabolique; ~ **television** n télévision f par câble

satin ['sætɪn] n satin m ♦ adj en or de satin, satiné(e)

satire ['sætaɪə*] n satire f

satisfaction [sætɪs'fækʃən] n satisfaction f; **satisfactory** [sætɪs'fæktərɪ] adj satisfaisant(e)

satisfy ['sætɪsfaɪ] vt satisfaire, contenter; (convince) convaincre, persuader; ~**ing** adj satisfaisant(e)

Saturday ['sætədeɪ] n samedi m

sauce [sɔːs] n sauce f; ~**pan** n casserole f; ~**er** ['sɔːsə*] n soucoupe f; **saucy** ['sɔːsɪ] adj impertinent(e)

Saudi ['saʊdɪ]: ~ **Arabia** n Arabie Saoudite; ~ (**Arabian**) adj saoudien(ne)

sauna ['sɔːnə] n sauna m

saunter ['sɔːntə*] vi: to ~ **along/in/**

out etc marcher/entrer/sortir etc d'un pas nonchalant

sausage ['sɒsɪdʒ] n saucisse f; ~ **roll** n (cold meat) saucisson m; ~ friand m

savage ['sævɪdʒ] adj (cruel, fierce) brutal(e), féroce; (primitive) primitif(ive), sauvage ♦ n sauvage m/f

save [seɪv] vt (person, belongings) sauver; (money) mettre de côté, économiser; (time) (faire) gagner; (keep) garder; (COMPUT) sauvegarder; (SPORT: stop) arrêter; (avoid: trouble) éviter ♦ vi (also: ~ up) mettre de l'argent de côté ♦ n (SPORT) arrêt m (du ballon) ♦ prep sauf, à l'exception de

saving ['seɪvɪŋ] n économie f ♦ adj: the ~ **grace** of sth ce qui rachète qch; ~**s** npl (money saved) économies fpl; ~**s account** n compte m d'épargne; ~**s bank** n caisse f d'épargne

saviour ['seɪvjə*] (US **savior**) n sauveur m

savour ['seɪvə*] (US **savor**) vt savourer; ~**y** (US **savory**) adj (dish: not sweet) salé(e)

saw [sɔː] (pt ~ed, pp ~ed or **sawn**) vt scier ♦ n (tool) scie f ♦ pt of see; ~**dust** n sciure f; ~**mill** n scierie f; ~**n-off**: ~**n-off shotgun** carabine f à canon scié

saxophone ['sæksəfəʊn] n saxophone m

say [seɪ] (pt, pp **said**) n: to have one's ~ dire ce qu'on a à dire ♦ vt dire; to have a or some ~ in sth avoir voix au chapitre; could you repeat that again? pourriez-vous répéter ce que vous venez de dire?; that goes without ~**ing** cela va sans dire, cela va de soi; ~**ing** n dicton m, proverbe m

scab [skæb] n croûte f; (pej) jaune m

scaffold ['skæfəʊld] n échafaud m; ~**ing** n échafaudage m

scald [skɔːld] n brûlure f ♦ vt ébouillanter

scale [skeɪl] n (of fish) écaille f

(MUS) gamme f; (of ruler, thermometer etc) graduation f, échelle (graduée); (of salaries, fees etc) barème m; (of map, also size, extent) échelle ♦ vt (mountain) escalader; ~s npl (for weighing) balance f; (also: bathroom ~) pèse-personne m inv; on a large ~ sur une grande échelle, en grand; ~ of charges tableau m des tarifs; ~ down vt réduire

scallop ['skɔləp] n coquille f Saint-Jacques; (SEWING) feston m

scalp [skælp] n cuir chevelu ♦ vt scalper

scamper ['skæmpə*] vi: to ~ away or off détaler

scampi ['skæmpi] npl langoustines (frites), scampi mpl

scan [skæn] vt scruter, examiner; (glance at quickly) parcourir; (TV, RADAR) balayer ♦ n (MED) scanographie f

scandal ['skændl] n scandale m; (gossip) ragots mpl

Scandinavian [skændɪ'neɪvɪən] adj scandinave

scant [skænt] adj insuffisant(e); ~y adj peu abondant(e), insuffisant(e); (underwear) minuscule

scapegoat ['skeɪpgəut] n bouc m émissaire

scar [skɑː*] n cicatrice f ♦ vt marquer (d'une cicatrice)

scarce ['skɛəs] adj rare, peu abondant(e); to make o.s. ~ (inf) se sauver; ~ly adv à peine; **scarcity** n manque m, pénurie f

scare ['skɛə*] n peur f, panique f ♦ vt effrayer, faire peur à; to ~ sb stiff faire une peur bleue à qn; bomb ~ alerte f à la bombe; ~ away vt faire fuir; ~ off vt = scare away; ~crow n épouvantail m; ~d adj: to be ~d avoir peur

scarf [skɑːf] (pl ~s or scarves) n (long) écharpe f; (square) foulard m

scarlet ['skɑːlət] adj écarlate; ~ **fever** n scarlatine f

scary ['skɛəri] (inf) adj effrayant(e)

scathing ['skeɪðɪŋ] adj cinglant(e),

acerbe

scatter ['skætə*] vt éparpiller, répandre; (crowd) disperser ♦ vi se disperser; ~**brained** adj écervelé(e), étourdi(e)

scavenger ['skævɪndʒə*] n (person: in bins etc) pilleur m de poubelles

scene [siːn] n scène f; (of crime, accident) lieu(x) m(pl); (sight, view) spectacle m, vue f; ~**ry** ['siːnəri] n (THEATRE) décor(s) m(pl); (landscape) paysage m; **scenic** ['siːnɪk] adj (picturesque) offrant de beaux paysages or panoramas

scent [sɛnt] n parfum m, odeur f; (track) piste f

sceptical ['skɛptɪkəl] (US **skeptical**) adj sceptique

schedule ['ʃɛdjuːl, (US) 'skɛdjuːl] n programme m, plan m; (of trains) horaire m; (of prices etc) barème m, tarif m ♦ vt prévoir; on ~ à l'heure (prévue); à la date prévue; to be ahead of/behind ~ avoir de l'avance/du retard; ~**d flight** n vol régulier

scheme [skiːm] n plan m, projet m; (dishonest plan, plot) complot m, combine f; (arrangement) arrangement m, classification f; (pension etc) régime m ♦ vi comploter, manigancer; **scheming** ['skiːmɪŋ] adj rusé(e), intrigant(e) ♦ n manigances fpl, intrigues fpl

scholar ['skɔlə*] n érudit(e); (pupil) boursier(ière); ~**ly** adj érudit(e), savant(e); ~**ship** n (knowledge) érudition f; (grant) bourse f (d'études)

school [skuːl] n école f; (secondary ~) collège m, lycée m; (US: university) université f; (in university) faculté f ♦ cpd scolaire; ~**book** n livre m scolaire or de classe; ~**boy** n écolier m; collégien m, lycéen m; ~**children** npl écoliers mpl; collégiens mpl, lycéens mpl; ~**days** npl années fpl de scolarité; ~**girl** n écolière f; collégienne f, lycéenne f; ~**ing** n instruction f, études fpl; ~**master** n (primary) instituteur m (secondary) professeur m; ~**mistress** n institutrice f; professeur m, ~**teacher** n instituteur(trice); professeur m

sciatica [saɪˈætɪkə] n sciatique f

science [ˈsaɪəns] n science f; ~ **fiction** n science-fiction f; **scientific** [saɪənˈtɪfɪk] adj scientifique; **scientist** [ˈsaɪəntɪst] n scientifique m/f; (eminent) savant m

scissors [ˈsɪzəz] npl ciseaux mpl

scoff [skɔf] vt (BRIT: inf: eat) avaler, bouffer ♦ vi: to ~ (at) (mock) se moquer (de)

scold [skəʊld] vt gronder

scone [skɒn] n sorte de petit pain rond au lait

scoop [sku:p] n pelle f (à main); (for ice cream) boule f à glace; (PRESS) scoop m; ~ **out** vt évider, creuser; ~ **up** vt ramasser

scooter [ˈsku:tə*] n (also: motor ~) scooter m; (toy) trottinette f

scope [skəʊp] n (capacity: of plan, undertaking) portée f, envergure f; (: of person) compétence f, capacités fpl; (opportunity) possibilités fpl; **within the ~ of** dans les limites de

scorch [skɔ:tʃ] vt (clothes) brûler (légèrement), roussir; (earth, grass) dessécher, brûler

score [skɔ:*] n score m, décompte m des points; (MUS) partition f; (twenty) vingt ♦ vt (goal, point) marquer; (success) remporter ♦ vi (FOOTBALL) marquer un but; (keep ~) compter les points; ~s **of** (very many) beaucoup de, un tas de (fam); **on that** ~ sur ce chapitre, à cet égard; **to ~ 6 out of 10** obtenir 6 sur 10; ~ **out** vt rayer, barrer, biffer; ~**board** n tableau m

scorn [skɔ:n] n mépris m, dédain m

Scorpio [ˈskɔ:pɪəʊ] n le Scorpion

Scot [skɒt] n Ecossais(e)

Scotch [skɒtʃ] n whisky m, scotch m

scotch vt (plan) faire échouer; (rumour) étouffer

scot-free [skɔtˈfri:] adv: **to get off ~** s'en tirer sans être puni(e)

Scotland [ˈskɒtlənd] n Ecosse f

Scots [skɒts] adj écossais(e); ~**man** (irreg) n Ecossais; ~**woman** (irreg) n Ecossaise f

Scottish [ˈskɒtɪʃ] adj écossais(e)

scoundrel [ˈskaʊndrəl] n vaurien m

scour [ˈskaʊə*] vt (search) battre, parcourir

scourge [skɜ:dʒ] n fléau m

scout [skaʊt] n (MIL) éclaireur m; (also: boy ~) scout m; **girl ~** (US) guide f; ~ **around** vi explorer, chercher

scowl [skaʊl] vi se renfrogner, avoir l'air maussade; **to ~ at** regarder de travers

scrabble [ˈskræbl] vi (also: ~ around: search) chercher à tâtons; (claw) for: ~ (at) gratter ♦ n: S~ ® Scrabble m (®)

scram [skræm] (inf) vi ficher le camp

scramble [ˈskræmbl] n (rush) bousculade f, ruée f ♦ vi: to ~ **up/down** grimper/descendre tant bien que mal; **to ~ out** sortir or descendre à toute vitesse; **to ~ through** se frayer un passage (à travers); **to ~ for** se bousculer or se disputer pour (avoir); ~**d eggs** npl œufs brouillés

scrap [skræp] n bout m, morceau m; (fight) bagarre f; (also: ~ iron) ferraille f ♦ vt jeter, mettre au rebut; (fig) abandonner, laisser tomber ♦ vi (fight) se bagarrer; ~s npl (waste) déchets mpl; ~**book** n album m; ~ **dealer** n marchand m de ferraille

scrape [skreɪp] vt, vi gratter, racler ♦ n: **to get into a ~** s'attirer des ennuis; **to ~ through** réussir de justesse; ~ **together** vt (money) racler ses fonds de tiroir pour réunir

scrap: ~ **heap** n (fig) au rancart or rebut; ~ **merchant** (BRIT) n marchand m de ferraille; ~ **paper** n papier m brouillon; ~**py** adj décousu(e)

scratch [skrætʃ] n égratignure f, rayure f; éraflure f; (from claw) coup m de griffe ♦ cpd: ~ **team** équipe de fortune or improvisée ♦ vt (rub) (se) gratter; (record) rayer;

(paint etc) érafler; *(with claw, nail)* griffer ♦ vi *(se)* gratter; **to start from** ~ partir de zéro; **to be up to** ~ être à la hauteur

scrawl [skrɔːl] vi gribouiller

scrawny ['skrɔːnɪ] adj décharné(e)

scream [skriːm] n cri perçant, hurlement m ♦ vi crier, hurler

screech [skriːtʃ] vi hurler; *(tyres)* crisser; *(brakes)* grincer

screen [skriːn] n écran m; *(in room)* paravent m; *(fig)* écran, rideau m ♦ vt *(conceal)* masquer, cacher; *(from the wind etc)* abriter, protéger; *(film)* projeter; *(candidates etc)* filtrer; **~ing** n *(MED)* test m *(or tests)* de dépistage; **~play** n scénario m

screw [skruː] n vis ♦ vt *(also:* ~ in*)* visser; **to** ~ **up** *(paper etc)* froisser; **to** ~ **up one's eyes** plisser les yeux; **~driver** n tournevis m

scribble ['skrɪbl] vi, vt gribouiller, griffonner

script [skrɪpt] n *(CINEMA etc)* scénario m, texte m; *(system of writing)* (écriture f) script m

Scripture(s) ['skrɪptʃə*(z)] n(pl) *(Christian)* Ecriture sainte; *(other religions)* écritures saintes

scroll [skrəʊl] n rouleau m

scrounge [skraʊndʒ] *(inf)* vt: **to** ~ **sth** *(off or from sb)* taper qn de qch; **~r** *(inf)* n parasite m

scrub [skrʌb] n *(land)* broussailles fpl ♦ vt *(floor)* nettoyer à la brosse; *(pan)* récurer; *(washing)* frotter; *(inf: cancel)* annuler

scruff [skrʌf] n: **by the** ~ **of the neck** par la peau du cou

scruffy ['skrʌfɪ] adj débraillé(e)

scrum(mage) ['skrʌm(ɪdʒ)] n *(RUGBY)* mêlée f

scruple ['skruːpl] n scrupule m

scrutiny ['skruːtɪnɪ] n examen minutieux

scuff [skʌf] vt érafler

scuffle ['skʌfl] n échauffourée f, rixe f

sculptor ['skʌlptə*] n sculpteur m

sculpture ['skʌlptʃə*] n sculpture f

scum [skʌm] n écume f, mousse f; *(pej: people)* rebut m, lie f

scurrilous ['skʌrɪləs] adj calomnieux(euse)

scurry ['skʌrɪ] vi filer à toute allure; **to** ~ **off** détaler, se sauver

scuttle ['skʌtl] n *(also:* coal ~*)* seau m *(à charbon)* ♦ vt *(ship)* saborder ♦ vi *(scamper)*: **to** ~ **away or off** détaler

scythe [saɪð] n faux f

sea [siː] n mer f ♦ cpd marin(e), de (la) mer; *(travel)* par mer, en bateau; **on the** ~ *(boat)* en mer; *(town)* au bord de la mer; **to be all at** ~ *(fig)* nager complètement; **out to** ~ au large; **(out) at** ~ en mer; **~board** n côte f; **~food** n fruits mpl de mer; **~front** n bord m de mer; **~going** adj *(ship)* de mer; **~gull** n mouette f

seal [siːl] n *(animal)* phoque m; *(stamp)* sceau m, cachet m ♦ vt sceller; *(envelope)* coller; *(: with seal)* cacheter; **~ off** vt *(forbid entry to)* interdire l'accès de

sea level n niveau m de la mer

sea lion n otarie f

seam [siːm] n couture f; *(of coal)* veine f, filon m

seaman ['siːmən] *(irreg)* n marin m

seance ['seɪɑːns] n séance f de spiritisme

seaplane ['siːpleɪn] n hydravion m

search [sɜːtʃ] n *(for person, thing, COMPUT)* recherche(s) f(pl); *(LAW: at sb's home)* perquisition f ♦ vt fouiller; *(examine)* examiner minutieusement; scruter ♦ vi: **to** ~ **for** chercher; **in** ~ **of** à la recherche de; ~ **through** vt fus fouiller; **~ing** adj pénétrant(e); **~light** n projecteur m; **~ party** n expédition f de secours; **~ warrant** n mandat m de perquisition

sea: **~shore** n rivage m, plage f, bord m de la mer; **~sick** ['siːsɪk] adj: **to be ~sick** avoir le mal de mer; **~side** n bord m de la mer; **~side resort** n station *f* balnéaire

season ['si:zn] *n* saison *f* ♦ *vt* assaisonner; relever; **to be in/out of ~** être/ne pas être de saison; **~al** *adj* (*work*) saisonnier(ère); **~ed** *adj* (*fig*) expérimenté(e); **~ ticket** *n* carte *f* d'abonnement

seat [si:t] *n* siège *m*; (*in bus, train: place*) place *f*; (*buttocks*) postérieur *m*; (*of trousers*) fond *m* ♦ *vt* faire asseoir, placer; (*have room for*) avoir des places assises pour, pouvoir accueillir; **~ belt** *n* ceinture *f* de sécurité

sea: **~ water** *n* eau *f* de mer; **~weed** ['si:wi:d] *n* algues *fpl*; **~worthy** ['si:wə:ði] *adj* en état de naviguer

sec. *abbr* = **second(s)**

secluded [sɪ'klu:dɪd] *adj* retiré(e), à l'écart

seclusion [sɪ'klu:ʒən] *n* solitude *f*

second¹ [sɪ'kɒnd] (*BRIT*) *vt* (*employee*) affecter provisoirement

second² ['sekənd] *adj* deuxième, second(e) ♦ *adv* (*in race etc*) en seconde position ♦ *n* (*unit of time*) seconde *f*; (*AUT: ~ gear*) seconde *f*; (*COMM: imperfect*) article *m* de second choix; (*BRIT: UNIV*) licence *f* avec mention ♦ *vt* (*motion*) appuyer; **~ary** *adj* secondaire; **~ary school** *n* collège *m*, lycée *m*; **~-class** *adj* de deuxième classe; (*RAIL*) de seconde (classe) (*POST*) au tarif réduit ♦ *adv* (*RAIL*) en seconde; (*POST*) au tarif réduit; **~-hand** *adj* d'occasion; de seconde main; **~ hand** *n* (*on clock*) trotteuse *f*; **~ly** *adv* deuxièmement; **~ment** [sɪ'kɒndmənt] (*BRIT*) *n* détachement *m*; **~-rate** *adj* de deuxième ordre, de qualité inférieure; **~ thoughts** *npl* doutes *mpl*; **on ~ thoughts** *or* (*US*) **~ thought** à la réflexion

secrecy ['si:krəsɪ] *n* secret *m*

secret ['si:krɪt] *adj* secret(ète) ♦ *n* secret *m*; **in ~** *adv* en secret, secrètement; en cachette

secretary ['sekrətrɪ] *n* secrétaire *m/*

f; (*COMM*) secrétaire général; **S~ of State (for)** (*BRIT: POL*) ministre *m* (de)

secretive ['si:krətɪv] *adj* dissimulé

sectarian [sek'tɛərɪən] *adj* sectaire

section ['sekʃən] *n* section *f*; (*of document*) section, article *m*, paragraphe *m*; (*cut*) coupe *f*

sector ['sektə*] *n* secteur *m*

secular ['sekjʊlə*] *adj* profane; laïque; séculier(ère)

secure [sɪ'kjʊə*] *adj* (*free from anxiety*) sans inquiétude, sécurisé(e); (*firmly fixed*) solide, bien attaché (*or* fermé(e)); (*in safe place*) en lieu sûr, en sûreté ♦ *vt* (*fix*) fixer, attacher; (*get*) obtenir, se procurer

security [sɪ'kjʊərɪtɪ] *n* sécurité *f*, mesures *fpl* de sécurité; (*for loan*) caution *f*, garantie *f*

sedan [sɪ'dæn] (*US*) *n* (*AUT*) berline *f*

sedate [sɪ'deɪt] *adj* calme; posé(e) ♦ *vt* (*MED*) donner des sédatifs à

sedative ['sedɪtɪv] *n* calmant *m*, sédatif *m*

seduce [sɪ'dju:s] *vt* séduire; **seduction** [sɪ'dʌkʃən] *n* séduction *f*; **seductive** [sɪ'dʌktɪv] *adj* séduisant(e); (*smile*) séducteur(trice); (*fig: offer*) alléchant(e)

see [si:] (*pt* **saw**, *pp* **seen**) *vt* voir; (*accompany*): **to ~ sb to the door** reconduire *or* raccompagner qn jusqu'à la porte ♦ *vi* voir ♦ *n* évêché *m*; **to ~ that** (*ensure*) veiller à ce que +*sub*, faire en sorte que +*sub*, s'assurer que; **~ you soon!** à bientôt!; **~ about** *vt fus* s'occuper de; **~ off** *vt* accompagner (à la gare *or* à l'aéroport *etc*); **~ through** *vt fus* mener à bonne fin ♦ *vt fus* voir clair dans; **~ to** *vt fus* s'occuper de, se charger de

seed [si:d] *n* graine *f*; (*sperm*) semence *f*; (*fig*) germe *m*; (*TENNIS*) tête *f* de série; **to go to ~** monter en graine; (*fig*) se laisser aller; **~ling** *n* jeune plant *m*, semis *m*; **~y** *adj* (*shabby*) minable, miteux(euse)

seeing ['siːɪŋ] conj: ~ (that) vu que, étant donné que

seek [siːk] (pt, pp sought) vt chercher, rechercher

seem [siːm] vi sembler, paraître; there ~s to be ... il semble qu'il y a ...; on dirait qu'il y a ...; ~ingly adv apparemment

seen [siːn] pp of see

seep [siːp] vi suinter, filtrer

seesaw ['siːsɔː] n bascule f

seethe [siːð] vi être en effervescence; to ~ with anger bouillir de colère

see-through ['siːθruː] adj transparent(e)

segment n segment m; (of orange) quartier m

segregate ['sɛɡrɪɡeɪt] vt séparer, isoler

seize [siːz] vt saisir, attraper; (take possession of) s'emparer de; (opportunity) saisir; ~ **up** vi (TECH) se gripper; ~ (**up**)**on** vt fus saisir, sauter sur

seizure ['siːʒə*] n (MED) crise f, attaque f; (of power) prise f

seldom ['sɛldəm] adv rarement

select [sɪ'lɛkt] adj choisi(e), d'élite ♦ vt sélectionner, choisir; ~**ion** n sélection f, choix m

self [sɛlf] (pl selves) n: the ~ le moi inv ♦ prefix auto-; ~**-assured** adj sûr(e) de soi; ~**-catering** (BRIT) adj avec cuisine, où l'on peut faire sa cuisine; ~**-centred** (US ~**-centered**) adj égocentrique; ~**-confidence** n confiance f en soi; ~**-conscious** adj timide, qui manque d'assurance; ~**-contained** (BRIT) adj (flat) avec entrée particulière, indépendant(e); ~**-control** n maîtrise f de soi; ~**-defence** (US ~**-defense**) n autodéfense f; (LAW) légitime défense f; ~**-discipline** n discipline personnelle; ~**-employed** adj qui travaille à son compte; ~**-evident** adj: to be ~-evident être évident(e), aller de soi; ~**-governing** adj autonome; ~**-indulgent** adj qui se refuse rien;

~**-interest** n intérêt personnel; ~**-ish** adj égoïste; ~**-ishness** n égoïsme m; ~**-less** adj désintéressé(e); ~**-pity** n apitoiement m sur soi-même; ~**-possessed** adj assuré(e); ~**-preservation** n instinct m de conservation; ~**-respect** n respect m de soi, amour-propre m; ~**-righteous** adj suffisant(e); ~**-sacrifice** n abnégation f; ~**-satisfied** adj content(e) de soi, suffisant(e); ~**-service** adj libre-service, self-service; ~**-sufficient** adj autosuffisant(e); (person: independent) indépendant(e); ~**-taught** adj (artist, pianist) qui a appris par lui-même

sell [sɛl] (pt, pp sold) vt vendre ♦ vi se vendre; to ~ at or for 10 F se vendre 10 F; ~ **off** vt liquider; ~ **out** vi: to ~ (of sth) (use up stock) vendre tout son stock (de qch); the tickets are all sold out il ne reste plus de billets; ~**-by date** n date f limite de vente; ~**er** n vendeur(euse), marchand(e); ~**ing price** n prix m de vente

Sellotape ['sɛləʊteɪp] (® BRIT) n papier collant m, scotch m (®)

selves [sɛlvz] npl of self

semblance ['sɛmbləns] n semblant m

semen ['siːmən] n sperme m

semester [sɪ'mɛstə*] n (esp US) n semestre m

semi ['sɛmɪ] prefix semi-, demi-; à demi, à moitié; ~**circle** n demi-cercle m; ~**colon** n point-virgule m; ~**detached (house)** (BRIT) n maison jumelée or jumelle; ~**final** n demi-finale f

seminar ['sɛmɪnɑː*] n séminaire m

seminary ['sɛmɪnərɪ] n (REL: for priests) séminaire m

semiskilled ['sɛmɪ'skɪld] adj: ~-worker ouvrier(ère) spécialisé(e)

senate ['sɛnɪt] n sénat m; **senator** n sénateur m

send [sɛnd] (pt, pp sent) vt envoyer; ~ **away** vt (letter, goods) envoyer; expédier; (unwelcome visitor) renvoyer; **~ away for** vt fus commander par correspondance, se faire envoyer; **~ back** vt renvoyer; **~ for** vt fus envoyer chercher; faire venir; **~ off** vt (goods) envoyer, expédier; (BRIT: SPORT: player) expulser ou renvoyer du terrain; **~ out** vt (invitation) envoyer (par la poste); (light, heat, signal) émettre; **~ up** vt faire monter; (BRIT: parody) mettre en boîte, parodier; **~er** n: expéditeur(trice); **~-off** n: a good **~-off** des adieux chaleureux

senior ['si:nɪə*] adj (high-ranking) de haut niveau; (of higher rank): to be **~ to sb** être le supérieur de qn ♦ n (older): **she is 15 years his ~** elle est son aînée de 15 ans, elle est plus âgée que lui de 15 ans; (in service) personne âgée; **~ citizen** n (in service) ancienne† f; **~ity** [si:nɪ'ɒrɪtɪ] n (in service) ancienneté f

sensation [sen'seɪʃən] n sensation f; **~al** adj qui fait sensation; (marvellous) sensationnel(le)

sense [sens] n sens m; (feeling) sentiment m; (meaning) sens, signification f; (wisdom) bon sens ♦ vt sentir, pressentir; **it makes ~** c'est logique; **~less** adj insensé(e), stupide; (unconscious) sans connaissance

sensible ['sensəbl] adj sensé(e), raisonnable; sage

sensitive ['sensɪtɪv] adj sensible

sensual ['sensjʊəl] adj sensuel(le)

sensuous ['sensjʊəs] adj voluptueux(euse), sensuel(le)

sent [sent] pt, pp de **send**

sentence ['sentəns] n (LING) phrase f; (LAW: judgment) condamnation f, sentence f; (: punishment) peine f ♦ vt: to **~ sb to death/to 5 years in prison** condamner qn à mort/à 5 ans de prison

sentiment ['sentɪmənt] n sentiment m; (opinion) opinion f, avis m; **~al** [sentɪ'mentl] adj sentimental(e)

sentry ['sentrɪ] n sentinelle f

separate [adj 'seprɪt, vb 'sepəreɪt] adj séparé(e), indépendant(e), différent(e) ♦ vt séparer; (make a dis-

tinction between) distinguer ♦ vi se séparer; **~ly** adv séparément; **~s** npl (clothes) coordonnés mpl; **separation** [sepə'reɪʃən] n séparation f

September [sep'tembə*] n septembre m

septic ['septɪk] adj (wound) infecté(e); **~ tank** n fosse f septique

sequel ['si:kwəl] n conséquence f; séquelles fpl; (of story) suite f

sequence ['si:kwəns] n ordre m, suite f; (film ~) séquence f; (dance ~) enchaînement m

sequin ['si:kwɪn] n paillette f

serene [sə'ri:n] adj serein(e), calme, paisible

sergeant ['sɑ:dʒənt] n sergent m; (POLICE) brigadier m

serial ['sɪərɪəl] n feuilleton m; **~ number** n numéro m de série

series ['sɪərɪz] n inv série f; (PUBLISHING) collection f

serious ['sɪərɪəs] adj sérieux(euse); (illness) grave; **~ly** adv sérieusement; (hurt) gravement

sermon ['sɜ:mən] n sermon m

serrated [se'reɪtɪd] adj en dents de scie

servant ['sɜ:vənt] n domestique m/f; (fig) serviteur/servante

serve [sɜ:v] vt (employer etc) servir, être au service de; (purpose) servir à; (customer, food, meal) servir; (subj: train) desservir; (apprenticeship) faire, accomplir; (prison term) purger ♦ vi servir; (be useful): to **~ as/for/to do** servir de/à/à faire ♦ n (TENNIS) service m; **it ~s him right** c'est bien fait pour lui; **~ out, ~ up** vt (food) servir

service ['sɜ:vɪs] n service m; (AUT: maintenance) révision f ♦ vt (car, washing machine) réviser; **the S~s** les forces armées; **to be of ~ to sb, to do sb a ~** rendre service à qn; **~able** adj pratique, commode; **~ charge** (BRIT) n service m; **~man** (irreg) n militaire m; **~ station** n station-service f

serviette [sɜ:vɪ'et] (BRIT) n serviette f (de table)

session ['sɛʃən] n séance f

set [sɛt] n (pt, pp set) n série f, assortiment m; (of tools etc) jeu m; (RADIO, TV) poste m; (TENNIS) set m; (group of people) cercle m, milieu m; (THEATRE: stage) scène f; (: scenery) décor m; (MATH) ensemble m; (HAIRDRESSING) mise f en plis ♦ adj (fixed) fixe, déterminé(e); (ready) prêt(e) ♦ vt (place) poser, placer; (fix, establish) fixer; (: record) établir; (adjust) régler; (decide: rules etc) fixer, choisir; (task) donner; (exam) composer ♦ vi (sun) se coucher; (jam, jelly, concrete) prendre; (bone) se ressouder; to ~ on doing être résolu à faire; to ~ the table mettre la table; to ~ to music mettre en musique; to ~ on fire mettre le feu à; to ~ free libérer; to ~ sth going déclencher qch; to ~ sail prendre la mer; to ~ about vt fus (task) entreprendre, se mettre à; ~ aside vt mettre de côté; (time) garder; ~ back vt (in time): to ~ sb back £5 coûter 5 livres à qn; (cost): to ~ back (by) retarder (de); ~ off vi se mettre en route, partir ♦ vt (bomb) faire exploser; (cause to start) déclencher; (show up well) mettre en valeur, faire valoir; ~ out vi se mettre en route, partir ♦ vt (arrange) disposer; (arguments) présenter, exposer; to ~ out to do entreprendre de faire, avoir pour but or intention de faire; ~ up vt (organization) fonder, créer; ~back n (hitch) revers m, contretemps m; ~ menu n menu m

settee [sɛ'ti:] n canapé m

setting ['sɛtɪŋ] n cadre m; (of jewel) monture f; (position: of controls) réglage m

settle ['sɛtl] vt (argument, matter, account) régler; (problem) résoudre; (MED: calm) calmer ♦ vi (bird, dust etc) se poser; (also: ~ down) s'installer, se fixer; (calm down) se calmer; to ~ for sth accepter qch, se contenter de qch; to ~ on sth op-

ter or se décider pour qch; ~ in vi s'installer; ~ up vi: to ~ up with sb régler (ce que l'on doit) à qn; ~ment n (payment) règlement m; (agreement) accord m; (village etc) établissement m; hameau m; ~r n colon m

setup ['sɛtʌp] n (arrangement) manière f dont les choses sont organisées; (situation) situation f

seven ['sɛvn] num sept; ~teen num dix-sept; ~th num septième; ~ty num soixante-dix

sever ['sɛvə*] vt couper, trancher; (relations) rompre

several ['sɛvrəl] adj, pron plusieurs m/fpl; ~ of us plusieurs d'entre nous

severance ['sɛvərəns] n (of relations) rupture f; ~ pay n indemnité f de licenciement

severe [sɪ'vɪə*] adj (stern) sévère, strict(e); (serious) grave, sérieux(euse); (plain) sévère, austère; **severity** [sɪ'vɛrɪtɪ] n sévérité f; gravité f; rigueur f

sew [səu] vt (pt sewed, pp sewn) vt, vi coudre; ~ up vt (re)coudre

sewage ['sju:ɪdʒ] n vidange(s) f(pl)

sewer ['sjuə*] n égout m

sewing ['səuɪŋ] n couture f; (item(s)) ouvrage m; ~ machine n machine f à coudre

sewn [səun] pp of sew

sex [sɛks] n sexe m; to have ~ with avoir des rapports (sexuels) avec; ~ist adj sexiste; ~ual ['sɛksjuəl] adj sexuel(le); ~y ['sɛksɪ] adj sexy inv

shabby ['ʃæbɪ] adj miteux(euse); (behaviour) mesquin(e), méprisable

shack [ʃæk] n cabane f, hutte f

shackles ['ʃæklz] npl chaînes fpl, entraves fpl

shade [ʃeɪd] n ombre f; (for lamp) abat-jour m inv; (of colour) nuance f, ton m ♦ vt abriter du soleil, ombrager; **in the** ~ à l'ombre; **a** ~ **too large/more** un tout petit peu trop grand(e)/plus

shadow ['ʃædəu] n ombre f ♦ vt (follow) filer; ~ **cabinet** (BRIT)

(POL) cabinet parallèle formé par l'Opposition; **~y** adj ombragé(e); (dim) vague, indistinct(e)

shady ['ʃeɪdɪ] adj ombragé(e); (fig: dishonest) louche, véreux(euse)

shaft [ʃɑːft] n (of arrow, spear) hampe f; (AUT, TECH) arbre m; (of mine) puits m; (of lift) cage f; (of light) rayon m, trait m

shaggy ['ʃægɪ] adj hirsute; en broussaille

shake [ʃeɪk] (pt shook, pp shaken) vt secouer; (bottle, cocktail) agiter; (house, confidence) ébranler ♦ vi trembler; **to ~ one's head** (in refusal) dire ou faire non de la tête; (in dismay) secouer la tête; **to ~ hands with sb** serrer la main à qn; **~ off** vt secouer; (pursuer) se débarrasser de; **~ up** vt secouer; **~n** ['ʃeɪkn] pp of shake; **shaky** ['ʃeɪkɪ] adj (hand, voice) tremblant(e); (building) branlant(e), peu solide

shall [ʃæl] aux vb: **I ~ go** j'irai; **~ I open the door?** j'ouvre la porte?; **I'll get the coffee, ~ I?** je vais chercher le café, d'accord?

shallow ['ʃæləʊ] adj peu profond(e); (fig) superficiel(le)

sham [ʃæm] n frime f ♦ vt simuler

shambles ['ʃæmblz] n (muddle) confusion f, pagaie f, fouillis m

shame [ʃeɪm] n honte f ♦ vt faire honte à; **it is a ~ (that/to do)** c'est dommage (que +sub/de faire); **what a ~!** quel dommage!; **~-faced** adj honteux(euse), penaud(e); **~ful** adj honteux(euse), scandaleux(euse); **~less** adj éhonté(e), effronté(e)

shampoo [ʃæm'puː] n shampooing m ♦ vt faire un shampooing à; **~ and set** n shampooing m (et) mise f en plis

shamrock ['ʃæmrɒk] n trèfle m (emblème de l'Irlande)

shandy ['ʃændɪ] n bière panachée

shan't [ʃɑːnt] = shall not

shanty town ['ʃæntɪ-] n bidonville m

shape [ʃeɪp] n forme f ♦ vt façonner,

modeler; (sb's ideas) former; (sb's life) déterminer ♦ vi (also: ~ up): (of events) prendre tournure; (: person) faire des progrès, s'en sortir; **to take ~** prendre forme ou tournure; **~-shaped** suffix: heart-shaped en forme de cœur; **~less** adj informe, sans forme; **~ly** adj bien proportionné(e), beau/belle

share [ʃɛə*] n part f; (COMM) action f ♦ vt partager; (have in common) avoir en commun; **~ out** vt partager; **~holder** n actionnaire m/f

shark [ʃɑːk] n requin m

sharp [ʃɑːp] adj (razor, knife) tranchant(e), bien aiguisé(e); (point, voice) aigu(guë); (nose, chin) pointu(e); (outline, increase) net(te); (cold, pain) vif(vive); (taste) piquant(e), âcre; (MUS) dièse; (person: quick-witted) vif(vive), éveillé(e); (: unscrupulous) malhonnête ♦ n (MUS) dièse m ♦ adv (precisely): **at 2 o'clock** à 2 heures pile ou précises; **~en** vt aiguiser; (pencil) tailler; **~ener** n (also: pencil ~ener) taille-crayon(s) m inv; **~-eyed** adj à qui rien n'échappe; **~ly** adv (turn, stop) brusquement; (stand out) nettement; (criticize, retort) sèchement, vertement

shatter ['ʃætə*] vt briser; (fig: upset) bouleverser; (: hopes) briser, ruiner ♦ vi voler en éclats, se briser

shave [ʃeɪv] vt raser ♦ vi se raser ♦ n: **to have a ~** se raser; **~r** n (also: electric ~r) rasoir m électrique

shaving ['ʃeɪvɪŋ] n (action) rasage m; **~s** npl (of wood etc) copeaux mpl; **~ brush** n blaireau m; **~ cream** n crème f à raser; **~ foam** n mousse f à raser

shawl [ʃɔːl] n châle m

she [ʃiː] pron elle ♦ prefix: **~-cat** chatte f; elephant n femelle

sheaf [ʃiːf] (pl sheaves) n gerbe f; (of papers) liasse f

shear [ʃɪə*] (pt **~ed**, pp **shorn**) vt (sheep) tondre; **~ off** vi (branch) partir, se détacher; ~s npl (for hedge) cisaille(s) f(pl)

sheath [ʃiːθ] n gaine f, fourreau m, étui m; (contraceptive) préservatif m

shed [ʃed] n remise f, resserre f ♦ vt (pt, pp **shed**) perdre; (tears) verser, répandre; (workers) congédier

she'd [ʃiːd] = she had; she would

sheen [ʃiːn] n lustre m

sheep [ʃiːp] n inv mouton m; ~**dog** n chien m de berger; ~**ish** adj penaud(e); ~**skin** n peau f de mouton

sheer [ʃɪə*] adj (utter) pur(e), pur et simple; (steep) à pic, abrupt(e); (almost transparent) extrêmement fin(e) ♦ adv à pic, abruptement

sheet [ʃiːt] n (on bed) drap m; (of paper) feuille f; (of glass, metal etc) feuille, plaque f

sheik(h) [ʃeɪk] n cheik m

shelf [ʃelf] n (pl **shelves**) étagère f, rayon m

shell [ʃel] n (on beach) coquillage m; (of egg, nut etc) coquille f; (explosive) obus m; (of building) carcasse f ♦ vt (peas) écosser; (MIL) bombarder (d'obus)

she'll [ʃiːl] = she will; she shall

shellfish [ʃelfɪʃ] n inv (crab etc) crustacé m; (scallop etc) coquillage m ♦ npl (as food) fruits mpl de mer

shell suit n survêtement m (en synthétique froissé)

shelter [ʃeltə*] n abri m, refuge m ♦ vt abriter, protéger; (give lodging to) donner asile à ♦ vi s'abriter, se mettre à l'abri; ~**ed housing** n foyers mpl (pour personnes âgées ou handicapées)

shelve [ʃelv] vt (fig) mettre en suspens or en sommeil; ~s npl of **shelf**

shepherd [ʃepəd] n berger m ♦ vt (guide) guider, escorter; ~'s **pie** (BRIT) n ≈ hachis m Parmentier

sheriff [ʃerɪf] (US) n shérif m

sherry [ʃerɪ] n xérès m, sherry m

she's [ʃiːz] = she is; she has

Shetland [ʃetlənd] n (also: the ~s, the ~ **Islands**) les îles fpl Shetland

shield [ʃiːld] n bouclier m; (protec-

tion) écran m de protection ♦ vt: to ~ (from) protéger (de or contre)

shift [ʃɪft] n (change) changement m; (work period) période f de travail; (of workers) équipe f, poste m ♦ vt déplacer, changer de place; (remove) enlever ♦ vi changer de place, bouger; ~**less** adj (person) fainéant(e); ~ **work** n travail m en équipe or par relais or par roulement; ~**y** adj sournois(e); (eyes) fuyant(e)

shilly-shally [ʃɪlɪʃælɪ] vi tergiverser, atermoyer

shimmer [ʃɪmə*] vi miroiter, chatoyer

shin [ʃɪn] n tibia m

shine [ʃaɪn] (pt, pp **shone**) n éclat m, brillant m ♦ vi briller ♦ vt (torch etc): to ~ **on** braquer sur; (polish: pt, pp ~**d**) faire briller or reluire

shingle [ʃɪŋgl] n (on beach) galets mpl; ~**s** n (MED) zona m

shiny [ʃaɪnɪ] adj brillant(e)

ship [ʃɪp] n bateau m; (large) navire m ♦ vt transporter (par mer); (send) expédier (par mer); ~**building** n construction navale; ~**ment** n cargaison f; ~**per** n affréteur m; ~**ping** n (ships) navires mpl; (the industry) industrie navale; (transport) transport m; ~**wreck** n (ship) épave f; (event) naufrage m ♦ vt: to be ~**wrecked** faire naufrage; ~**yard** n chantier naval

shire [ʃaɪə*] (BRIT) n comté m

shirk [ʃɜːk] vt esquiver, se dérober à

shirt [ʃɜːt] n (man's) chemise f; (woman's) chemisier m; **in (one's)** ~ **sleeves** en bras de chemise

shit [ʃɪt] (infl!) n, excl merde f (!)

shiver [ʃɪvə*] n frisson m ♦ vi frissonner

shoal [ʃəʊl] n (of fish) banc m; (fig: also: ~s) masse f, foule f

shock [ʃɒk] n choc m; (ELEC) secousse f; (MED) commotion f, choc ♦ vt (offend) choquer, scandaliser; (upset) bouleverser; ~ **absorber** n amortisseur m; ~**ing** adj (scandali-

zing) choquant(e), scandaleux(euse); (*appalling*) épouvantable

shod [ʃɔd] *pt, pp of* **shoe**

shoddy ['ʃɔdɪ] *adj* de mauvaise qualité, mal fait(e)

shoe [ʃuː] (*pt, pp* **shod**) *n* chaussure *f*, soulier *m*; (*also:* horse~) fer *m* à cheval ♦ *vt* (*horse*) ferrer; ~lace *n* lacet *m* (de soulier); ~ polish *n* cirage *m*; ~ shop *n* magasin *m* de chaussures; ~string *n* (*fig*): on a ~string avec un budget dérisoire

shone [ʃɔn] *pt, pp of* **shine**

shoo [ʃuː] *excl* ouste!

shook [ʃuk] *pt of* **shake**

shoot [ʃuːt] (*pt, pp* **shot**) *n* (*on branch, seedling*) pousse *f* ♦ *vt* (*game*) chasser; tirer; abattre; (*person*) blesser (*or* tuer) d'un coup de fusil (*or* de revolver); (*execute*) fusiller; (*arrow*) tirer; (*gun*) tirer un coup de; (*film*) tourner ♦ *vi* (*with gun, bow*): **to** ~ **(at)** tirer (sur); (FOOTBALL) shooter, tirer; ~ **down** *vt* (*plane*) abattre; ~ **in/out** entrer/sortir comme une flèche; ~ **up** *vi* (*fig*) monter en flèche; ~**ing** *n* (*shots*) coups *mpl* de feu, fusillade *f*; (HUNTING) chasse *f*; ~**ing star** *n* étoile filante

shop [ʃɔp] *n* magasin *m*; (*workshop*) atelier *m* ♦ *vi* (*also:* go ~ping) faire ses courses *or* ses achats; ~ **assistant** (BRIT) *n* vendeur(euse); ~ **floor** (BRIT) *n* (INDUSTRY: *fig*) ouvriers *mpl*; ~**keeper** *n* commerçant(e); ~**lifting** *n* vol *m* à l'étalage; ~**per** *n* personne *f* qui fait ses courses, acheteur(euse); ~**ping** *n* (*goods*) achats *mpl*, provisions *fpl*; ~**ping bag** *n* sac *m* (à provisions); ~**ping centre** (US ~**ping center**) *n* centre commercial; ~**soiled** *adj* défraîchi(e), qui a fait la vitrine; ~ **steward** (BRIT) *n* (INDUSTRY) délégué(e) syndical(e); ~ **window** *n* vitrine *f*

shore [ʃɔːr] *n* (*of sea, lake*) rivage *m*, rive *f* ♦ *vt*: **to** ~ **(up)** étayer; on

~ à terre

shorn [ʃɔːn] *pp of* **shear**

short [ʃɔːt] *adj* (*not long*) court(e); (*soon finished*) court, bref(brève); (*person, step*) petit(e); (*curt*) brusque, sec(sèche); (*insufficient*) insuffisant(e); **to be/run** ~ **of sth** être à court de *or* manquer de qch; **in** ~ bref, en bref; ~ **of doing ...** à moins de faire ...; **everything** ~ **of** tout sauf; **it is** ~ **for** c'est l'abréviation *or* le diminutif de; **to cut** ~ (*speech, visit*) abréger, écourter; **to fall** ~ **of** ne pas être à la hauteur de; **to run** ~ **of** arriver à court de, venir à manquer de; **to stop** ~ s'arrêter net; **to stop** ~ **of** ne pas aller jusqu'à; ~**age** *n* manque *m*, pénurie *f*; ~**bread** *n* ≈ sablé *m*; ~**change** *vt* ne pas rendre assez à; ~**circuit** *n* court-circuit *m*; ~**coming** *n* défaut *m*; ~**(crust) pastry** (BRIT) *n* pâte brisée; ~**cut** *n* raccourci *m*; ~**en** *vt* raccourcir; (*text, visit*) abréger; ~**fall** *n* déficit *m*; ~**hand** (BRIT) *n* sténographie *f*; ~**hand typist** (BRIT) *n* sténodactylo *m/f*; ~**list** (BRIT) *n* (*for job*) liste *f* des candidats sélectionnés; ~**lived** *adj* de courte durée; ~**ly** *adv* bientôt, sous peu; ~**s** *npl*: **(a pair of)** ~**s** un short; ~**sighted** *adj* (BRIT) myope; (*fig*) qui manque de clairvoyance; ~**staffed** *adj* à court de personnel; ~**story** *n* nouvelle *f*; ~**tempered** *adj* qui s'emporte facilement; ~**term** *adj* (*effect*) à court terme; ~**wave** *n* (RADIO) ondes courtes

shot [ʃɔt] *pt, pp of* **shoot** ♦ *n* coup *m* (de feu); (*try*) coup, essai *m*; (*injection*) piqûre *f*; (PHOT) photo *f*; **he's a good/poor** ~ il tire bien/mal; **like a** ~ comme une flèche; (*very readily*) sans hésiter; ~**gun** *n* fusil *m* de chasse

should [ʃud] *aux vb*: **I** ~ **go now** je devrais partir maintenant; **he** ~ **be there now** il devrait être arrivé maintenant; **I** ~ **go if I were you** je j'étais vous, j'irais; **I** ~ **like to**

j'aimerais bien, volontiers

shoulder ['ʃəʊldə*] n épaule f ♦ vt
(fig) endosser, se charger de; ~ **bag**
n sac m à bandoulière; ~ **blade** n
omoplate f; ~ **strap** n bretelle f

shouldn't ['ʃʊdnt] = should not

shout [ʃaʊt] n cri m ♦ vt crier ♦ vi
(also: ~ out) crier, pousser des cris;
~ **down** vt huer; ~**ing** n cris mpl

shove [ʃʌv] vt pousser; (inf: put) to
~ **sth in** fourrer ou ficher qch dans;
~ **off** (inf) vi ficher le camp

shovel ['ʃʌvl] n pelle f

show [ʃəʊ] (pt ~ed, pp shown) n
(of emotion) manifestation f, démonstration f; (semblance) semblant m,
apparence f; (exhibition) exposition
f, salon m; (THEATRE, TV) spectacle m ♦ vt montrer; (film) donner;
(courage etc) faire preuve de, manifester; (exhibit) exposer ♦ vi se voir,
être visible; **for** ~ pour l'effet; **on** ~
(exhibits etc) exposé(e); ~ **in** vt
(person) faire entrer; ~ **off** vi (pej)
crâner ♦ vt (display) faire valoir; ~
out vt (person) reconduire (jusqu'à
la porte); ~ **up** vi (stand out) ressortir; (inf: turn up) se montrer ♦ vt
(flaw) faire ressortir; ~ **business** n
le monde du spectacle; ~**down** n
épreuve f de force

shower ['ʃaʊə*] n (rain) averse f,
(of stones etc) pluie f, grêle f; (also:
~ **bath**) douche f ♦ vi prendre une
douche, se doucher ♦ vt: **to** ~ **sb**
with (gifts etc) combler qn de; **to**
have or **take a** ~ prendre une douche; ~**proof** adj imperméabilisé(e)

showing ['ʃəʊɪŋ] n (of film) projection f

show jumping n concours m hippique

shown [ʃəʊn] pp of **show**

show: ~-**off** ['ʃəʊɒf] (inf) n (person)
crâneur(euse), m'as-tu-vu(e); ~**piece**
n (of exhibition) trésor m; ~**room**
['ʃəʊrʊm] n magasin m or salle f
d'exposition

shrank [ʃræŋk] pt of **shrink**

shrapnel ['ʃræpnl] n éclats mpl
d'obus

shred [ʃred] n (gen pl) lambeau m,
petit morceau ♦ vt mettre en lambeaux, déchirer; (CULIN) râper;
couper en lanières; ~**der** n (for vegetables) râpeur m; (for documents)
déchiqueteuse f

shrewd [ʃru:d] adj astucieux(euse),
perspicace; (businessman) habile

shriek [ʃri:k] vi hurler, crier

shrill [ʃrɪl] adj perçant(e), aigu(guë),
strident(e)

shrimp [ʃrɪmp] n crevette f

shrine [ʃraɪn] n (place) lieu m de
pèlerinage

shrink [ʃrɪŋk] (pt shrank, pp
shrunk) vi rétrécir; (fig) se réduire,
diminuer; (move: also: ~ away) reculer ♦ vt (wool) (faire) rétrécir ♦ n
(inf: pej) psychiatre m/f, psy m/f; **to**
~ **from (doing) sth** reculer devant
(la pensée de) faire qch; ~**age** n ré-
trécissement m; ~**wrap** vt emballer
sous film plastique

shrivel ['ʃrɪvl] vt (also: ~ up) ratatiner, flétrir ♦ vi se ratatiner, se flétrir

shroud [ʃraʊd] n linceul m ♦ vt:
~**ed in mystery** enveloppé(e) de
mystère

Shrove Tuesday ['ʃrəʊv-] n (the)
Mardi gras

shrub [ʃrʌb] n arbuste m; ~**bery** n
massif m d'arbustes

shrug [ʃrʌg] n, vi, vi: **to** ~ (**one's**
shoulders) hausser les épaules; ~
off vt faire fi de

shrunk [ʃrʌŋk] pp of **shrink**

shudder ['ʃʌdə*] vi frissonner, frémir

shuffle ['ʃʌfl] vt (cards) battre ♦ vt,
vi: **to** ~ (**one's feet**) traîner les
pieds

shun [ʃʌn] vt éviter, fuir

shunt [ʃʌnt] vt (RAIL) aiguiller

shut [ʃʌt] (pt, pp shut) vt fermer ♦
vi (se) fermer; ~ **down** vt, vi fermer définitivement; ~ **off** vt couper,
arrêter; ~ **up** vi (inf: keep quiet) se
taire ♦ vt (close) fermer; (silence)
faire taire; ~**ter** n volet m; (PHOT)

obturateur m

shuttle ['ʃʌtl] n navette f; (also: ~ service) (service m de navette)

shuttlecock ['ʃʌtlkɔk] n volant m (de badminton)

shy [ʃai] adj timide

sibling ['sibliŋ] n: ~s enfants mpl de mêmes parents

Sicily ['sisili] n Sicile f

sick [sik] adj (ill) malade; (vomiting): **to be** ~ vomir; (humour) noir(e), macabre; **to feel** ~ avoir envie de vomir, avoir mal au cœur; **to be** ~ **of** (fig) en avoir assez de; ~**bay** n infirmerie f; ~ **en** vt écœurer; ~**ening** adj (fig) écœurant(e), dégoûtant(e)

sickle ['sikl] n faucille f

sick: ~ **leave** n congé m de maladie; ~**ly** adj maladif(ive), souffreteux(euse); (causing nausea) écœurant(e); ~**ness** n maladie f; (vomiting) vomissement(s) m(pl); ~ **pay** n indemnité f de maladie

side [said] n côté m; (of lake, road) bord m; (team) camp m, équipe f ♦ adj (door, entrance) latéral(e) ♦ vi: **to** ~ **with sb** prendre le parti de qn, se ranger du côté de qn; **by the** ~ **of** au bord de; ~ **by** ~ côte à côte; **from** ~ **to** ~ d'un côté à l'autre; **to take** ~**s (with)** prendre parti (pour); ~**board** n buffet m; ~**boards** (BRIT), ~**burns** (whiskers) npl favoris mpl; ~ **drum** n tambour plat; ~**effect** n effet m secondaire; ~**light** n (AUT) veilleuse f; ~**line** n (SPORT) ligne f de touche f; (fig) travail m secondaire; ~**long** adj oblique; ~**saddle** adv en amazone; ~**show** n attraction f; ~**step** n vt éluder; éviter; ~ **street** n (petite) rue transversale; ~**track** vt (fig) faire dévier de son sujet; ~**walk** (US) n trottoir m; ~**ways** adv de côté

siding ['saidiŋ] n (RAIL) voie f de garage

sidle ['saidl] vi: **to** ~ **up (to)** s'approcher furtivement (de)

siege [si:dʒ] n siège m

sieve [siv] n tamis m, passoire f

sift [sift] vt (fig: also: ~ through) passer en revue; (lit: flour etc) passer au tamis

sigh [sai] n soupir m ♦ vi soupirer, pousser un soupir

sight [sait] n (faculty) vue f; (spectacle) spectacle m; (on gun) mire f ♦ vt apercevoir; **in** ~ visible; **out of** ~ hors de vue; ~**seeing** n tourisme m; **to go** ~**seeing** faire du tourisme

sign [sain] n signe m; (with hand etc) signe, geste m; (notice) panneau m, écriteau m ♦ vt signer; ~ **on** vi (MIL) s'engager; (as unemployed) s'inscrire au chômage; (for course) s'inscrire ♦ vt (MIL) engager; (employee) embaucher; ~ **over** vt: **to sth over to sb** céder qch par écrit à qn; ~ **up** vi s'engager ♦ vt (MIL) s'engager; (for course) s'inscrire

signal ['signl] n signal m ♦ vi (AUT) mettre son clignotant ♦ vt (person) faire signe à; (message) communiquer par signaux; ~**man** n (irreg) n (RAIL) aiguilleur m

signature ['signətʃə*] n signature f; ~ **tune** n indicatif musical

signet ring ['signət-] n chevalière f

significance [sig'nifikəns] n signification f; importance f; **significant** [sig'nifikənt] adj significatif(ive); (important) important(e), considérable

signpost ['sainpəust] n poteau indicateur

silence ['sailəns] n silence m ♦ vt faire taire, réduire au silence; ~**r** n (on gun, BRIT: AUT) silencieux m

silent ['sailənt] adj silencieux(euse); (film) muet(te); **to remain** ~ garder le silence, ne rien dire; ~ **partner** n (COMM) bailleur m de fonds, commanditaire m

silhouette [silu:'et] n silhouette f

silicon chip ['silikən-] n puce f électronique

silk [silk] n soie f ♦ cpd de or en soie; ~**y** adj soyeux(euse)

silly ['sɪlɪ] *adj* stupide, sot(te), bête
silt [sɪlt] *n* vase *f*; limon *m*
silver ['sɪlvə*] *n* argent *m*; (*money*) monnaie *f* (en pièces d'argent); (*also:* ~*ware*) argenterie *f* ♦ *adj* d'argent, en argent; ~ **paper** (*BRIT*) *n* papier *m* d'argent or d'étain; ~-**plated** *adj* plaqué(e) argent; ~**smith** *n* orfèvre *m/f*; ~**y** *adj* argenté(e)
similar ['sɪmɪlə*] *adj:* ~ **(to)** semblable (à); ~**ly** *adv* de la même façon, de même
simile ['sɪmɪlɪ] *n* comparaison *f*
simmer ['sɪmə*] *vi* cuire à feu doux, mijoter
simple ['sɪmpl] *adj* simple; **simplicity** [sɪm'plɪsɪtɪ] *n* simplicité *f*; **simply** *adv* (*without fuss*) avec simplicité
simultaneous [sɪməl'teɪnɪəs] *adj* simultané(e)
sin [sɪn] *n* péché *m* ♦ *vi* pécher
since [sɪns] *adv, prep* depuis ♦ *conj* (*time*) depuis que; (*because*) puisque, étant donné que, comme; ~ **then, ever** ~ depuis ce moment-là
sincere [sɪn'sɪə*] *adj* sincère; ~**ly** *adv see* yours; **sincerity** [sɪn'serɪtɪ] *n* sincérité *f*
sinew ['sɪnjuː] *n* tendon *m*
sinful ['sɪnful] *adj* coupable; (*person*) pécheur(eresse)
sing [sɪŋ] (*pt* **sang**, *pp* **sung**) *vt, vi* chanter
singe [sɪndʒ] *vt* brûler légèrement; (*clothes*) roussir
singer ['sɪŋə*] *n* chanteur(euse)
singing ['sɪŋɪŋ] *n* chant *m*
single ['sɪŋgl] *adj* seul(e), unique; (*unmarried*) célibataire; (*not double*) simple ♦ *n* (*BRIT: also:* ~ **ticket**) aller *m* (simple); (*record*) 45 tours *m*; ~ **out** *vt* choisir; (*distinguish*) distinguer; ~-**breasted** *adj* droit(e); ~ **file** *n:* **in** ~ **file** en file indienne; ~-**handed** *adv* tout(e) seul(e), sans (aucune) aide; ~-**minded** *adj* résolu(e), tenace; ~ **room** *n* chambre *f* à un lit *or* pour une personne; ~**s** *n* (*TENNIS*) simple *m*; **singly** *adv* séparément

singular ['sɪŋgjʊlə*] *adj* singulier(ère), étrange; (*outstanding*) remarquable; (*LING*) (au) singulier, du singulier ♦ *n* singulier *m*
sinister ['sɪnɪstə*] *adj* sinistre
sink [sɪŋk] (*pt* **sank**, *pp* **sunk**) *n* évier *m* ♦ *vt* (*ship*) (faire) couler, faire sombrer; (*foundations*) creuser ♦ *vi* couler, sombrer; (*ground etc*) s'affaisser; (*also:* ~ **back, ~ down**) s'affaisser, se laisser retomber; **to ~ sth into** enfoncer qch dans; **my heart sank** j'ai complètement perdu courage; ~ **in** *vi* (*fig*) pénétrer, être compris(e)
sinner ['sɪnə*] *n* pécheur(eresse)
sinus ['saɪnəs] *n* sinus *m inv*
sip [sɪp] *n* gorgée *f* ♦ *vt* boire à petites gorgées
siphon ['saɪfən] *n* siphon *m*; ~ **off** *vt* siphonner; (*money: illegally*) détourner
sir [sə:*] *n* monsieur *m*; S~ **John Smith** sir John Smith; **yes** ~ oui, Monsieur
siren ['saɪərən] *n* sirène *f*
sirloin ['sə:lɔɪn] *n* (*also:* ~ **steak**) aloyau *m*
sissy ['sɪsɪ] (*inf*) *n* (*coward*) poule mouillée
sister ['sɪstə*] *n* sœur *f*; (*nun*) religieuse *f*, sœur; (*BRIT: nurse*) infirmière *f* en chef; ~-**in-law** *n* belle-sœur *f*
sit [sɪt] (*pt, pp* **sat**) *vi* s'asseoir; (*be sitting*) être assis(e); (*assembly*) être en séance, siéger; (*for painter*) poser ♦ *vt* (*exam*) passer, se présenter à; ~ **down** *vi* s'asseoir; ~ **in on** *vt fus* assister à; ~ **up** *vi* s'asseoir; (*straight*) se redresser; (*not go to bed*) rester debout, ne pas se coucher
sitcom ['sɪtkɔm] *n abbr* (= *situation comedy*) comédie *f* de situation
site [saɪt] *n* emplacement *m*, site *m*; (*also: building* ~) chantier *m* ♦ *vt* placer
sit-in ['sɪtɪn] *n* (*demonstration*) sit-in *m inv*, occupation *f* (de locaux)
sitting ['sɪtɪŋ] *n* (*of assembly etc*)

séance f; (in canteen) service m; ~ **room** n salon m

situated ['sɪtjʊeɪtɪd] adj situé(e)

situation [sɪtjʊ'eɪʃən] n situation f; "~**s vacant**" (BRIT) "offres d'emploi"

six [sɪks] num six; ~**teen** num seize; ~**th** num sixième; ~**ty** num soixante

size [saɪz] n taille f; (in shoes) pointure f; (of clothing) taille f; (of shoes) pointure f; (fig) ampleur f; (glue) colle f; ~ **up** vt juger, jauger; ~**able** adj assez grand(e); assez important(e)

sizzle ['sɪzl] vi grésiller

skate [skeɪt] n patin m; (fish: pl inv) raie f ♦ vi patiner; ~**board** n skateboard m, planche f à roulettes; ~**r** n patineur(euse); **skating** ['skeɪtɪŋ] n patinage m; **skating rink** n patinoire f

skeleton ['skɛlɪtn] n squelette m; (outline) schéma m; ~ **staff** n effectifs réduits

skeptical ['skɛptɪkl] (US) adj = **sceptical**

sketch [skɛtʃ] n (drawing) croquis m, esquisse f; (THEATRE) sketch m, saynète f ♦ vt esquisser, faire un croquis or une esquisse de; ~ **book** n carnet m à dessin; ~**y** adj incomplet(ète), fragmentaire

skewer ['skjuːə*] n brochette f

ski [skiː] n ski m ♦ vi skier, faire du ski; ~ **boot** n chaussure f de ski

skid [skɪd] vi déraper

ski: ~**er** ['skiːə*] n skieur(euse); ~**ing** ['skiːɪŋ] n ski m; ~ **jump** n saut m à skis

skilful ['skɪlfʊl] (US **skillful**) adj habile, adroit(e)

ski lift n remonte-pente m inv

skill [skɪl] n habileté f, adresse f, talent m; (requiring training: gen pl) compétences fpl; ~**ed** adj habile, adroit(e); (worker) qualifié(e)

skim [skɪm] vt (milk) écrémer; (glide over) raser; ♦ vi: to ~ **through** (fig) parcourir; ~**med milk** n lait écrémé

skimp [skɪmp] vt (also: ~ **on**: work)

bâcler, faire à la va-vite; (: cloth etc) lésiner sur; ~**y** adj maigre; (skirt) étriqué(e)

skin [skɪn] n peau f; (of fruit etc) éplucher; (animal) écorcher; ~ **cancer** n cancer m de la peau; ~-**deep** adj superficiel(le); ~-**diving** n plongée sous-marine; ~**ny** adj maigre, maigrichon(ne); ~**tight** adj (jeans etc) collant(e), ajusté(e)

skip [skɪp] n petit bond or saut; (BRIT: container) benne f ♦ vi gambader, sautiller; (with rope) sauter à la corde ♦ vt sauter

ski pants npl fuseau n (de ski)

ski pole n bâton m de ski

skipper ['skɪpə*] n capitaine m; (in race) skipper m

skipping rope ['skɪpɪŋ-] (BRIT) n corde f à sauter

skirmish ['skɜːmɪʃ] n escarmouche f, accrochage m

skirt [skɜːt] n jupe f ♦ vt longer, contourner; ~**ing board** (BRIT) n plinthe f

ski slope n piste f de ski

ski suit n combinaison f (de ski)

skittle ['skɪtl] n quille f; **skittles** (game) n (jeu m de) quilles fpl

skive [skaɪv] (BRIT: inf) vi tirer au flanc

skulk [skʌlk] vi rôder furtivement

skull [skʌl] n crâne m

skunk [skʌŋk] n mouffette f

sky [skaɪ] n ciel m; ~**light** n lucarne f; ~**scraper** n gratte-ciel m inv

slab [slæb] n (of stone) dalle f; (of food) grosse tranche

slack [slæk] adj (loose) lâche, desserré(e); (slow) stagnant(e); (careless) négligent(e), peu sérieux(euse) ou consciencieux(euse); ~ **s** npl (trousers) pantalon m; ~**en** vi ralentir, diminuer ♦ vt (speed) réduire; (grip) relâcher; (clothing) desserrer

slag heap [slæg-] n crassier m

slag off (BRIT: inf) vt dire du mal de

slain [sleɪn] pp of **slay**

slam [slæm] vt (door) (faire) cla-

slander   248   sling

quer; *(throw)* jeter violemment, flanquer *(fam)*; *(criticize)* démolir ♦ *vi* claquer

slander ['slɑːndə*] *n* calomnie *f*; diffamation *f*

slang [slæŋ] *n* argot *m*

slant [slɑːnt] *n* inclinaison *f*; *(fig)* angle *m*, point *m* de vue; **~ed** *adj* = **slanting**; **~ing** *adj* en pente, incliné(e); **~ing eyes** yeux bridés

slap [slæp] *n* claque *f*, gifle *f*; tape *f* ♦ *vt* donner une claque ou une gifle *or* une tape à; *(paint)* appliquer rapidement ♦ *adv* (*directly*) tout droit, en plein; **~dash** *adj* fait(e) sans soin *or* à la va-vite; *(person)* insouciant(e), négligent(e); **~stick** *n* (*comedy*) grosse farce, style *m* tarte à la crème; **~-up** (*BRIT*) *adj*: **a ~-up meal** un repas extra *or* fameux

slash [slæʃ] *vt* entailler, taillader; *(fig: prices)* casser

slat [slæt] *n* latte *f*, lame *f*

slate [sleɪt] *n* ardoise *f* ♦ *vt* (*fig: criticize*) éreinter, démolir

slaughter ['slɔːtə*] *n* carnage *m*, massacre *m* ♦ *vt* (*animal*) abattre; (*people*) massacrer; **~house** *n* abattoir *m*

slave [sleɪv] *n* esclave *m/f* ♦ *vi* (*also*: **~ away**) trimer, travailler comme un forçat; **~ry** *n* esclavage *m*; **slavish** *adj* servile

slay [sleɪ] (*pt* slew, *pp* slain) *vt* tuer

sleazy ['sliːzɪ] *adj* miteux(euse), minable

sledge [sledʒ] *n* luge *f*

sledgehammer *n* marteau *m* de forgeron

sleek [sliːk] *adj* (*hair, fur etc*) brillant(e), lisse; (*car, boat etc*) aux lignes pures *or* élégantes

sleep [sliːp] (*pt, pp* slept) *n* sommeil *m* ♦ *vi* dormir; (*spend night*) dormir, coucher; **to go to ~** s'endormir; **~ around** *vi* coucher à droite et à gauche; **~ in** *vi* (*over-*) se réveiller trop tard; **~er** *n* (*BRIT: RAIL: train*) train-couchettes *m*; (*RAIL: berth*) couchette *f*; **~ing bag** *n* sac *m* de

couchage; **~ing car** *n* (*RAIL*) wagon-lit *m*, voiture-lit *f*; **~ing partner** *n* (*BRIT*) = **silent partner**; **~ing pill** *n* somnifère *m*; **~less** *adj*: **a ~less night** une nuit blanche; **~walker** *n* somnambule *m/f*; **~y** *adj* qui a sommeil; *(fig)* endormi(e)

sleet [sliːt] *n* neige fondue

sleeve [sliːv] *n* manche *f*; *(of record)* pochette *f*

sleigh [sleɪ] *n* traîneau *m*

sleight [slaɪt] *n*: **~ of hand** tour *m* de passe-passe

slender ['slendə*] *adj* svelte, mince; *(fig)* faible, ténu(e)

slept [slept] *pt, pp of* **sleep**

slew [sluː] *vi* (*also*: **~ around**) virer, pivoter ♦ *pt of* **slay**

slice [slaɪs] *n* tranche *f*; *(round)* rondelle *f*; *(utensil)* spatule *f*, truelle *f* ♦ *vt* couper en tranches *or* en rondelles)

slick [slɪk] *adj* (*skilful*) brillant(e) (en apparence); *(salesman)* doué *m* à la bagout ♦ *n* (*also*: **oil ~**) nappe *f* de pétrole, marée noire

slide [slaɪd] (*pt, pp* slid) *n* (*in playground*) toboggan *m*; (*PHOT*) diapositive *f*; (*BRIT: also: hair ~*) barrette *f*; (*in prices*) chute *f*, baisse *f* ♦ *vt* (*faire*) glisser ♦ *vi* glisser; **sliding** ['slaɪdɪŋ] *adj* (*door*) coulissant(e); **sliding scale** *n* échelle *f* mobile

slight [slaɪt] *adj* (*slim*) mince, menu(e); (*frail*) frêle; (*trivial*) faible, insignifiant(e); (*small*) petit(e), léger(ère) (*before n*) ♦ *n* offense *f*, affront *m*; **not in the ~est** pas le moins du monde, pas du tout; **~ly** *adv* légèrement, un peu

slim [slɪm] *adj* mince ♦ *vi* maigrir; *(diet)* suivre un régime amaigrissant

slime [slaɪm] *n* (*mud*) vase *f*; *(other substance)* substance visqueuse

slimming ['slɪmɪŋ] *adj (foodstuff)* qui ne fait pas grossir

sling [slɪŋ] (*pt, pp* slung) *n* (*MED*) écharpe *f*; (*for baby*) porte-bébé *m*;

(weapon) fronde f, lance-pierre m ♦ vt lancer, jeter

slip [slɪp] n faux pas; (mistake) erreur f; étourderie f; bévue f; (underskirt) combinaison f; (of paper) petite feuille, fiche f ♦ vt (slide) glisser ♦ vi glisser; (decline) baisser; (move smoothly): to ~ into/out of se glisser or se faufiler dans/hors de; to ~ sth on/off enfiler/enlever qch; to give sb the ~ fausser compagnie à qn; a ~ of the tongue un lapsus; ~ away vi s'esquiver; ~ in vt glisser ♦ vi (errors) s'y glisser; ~ out vi sortir; ~ up vi faire une erreur, gaffer; ~ped disc n déplacement m de vertèbre

slipper ['slɪpə*] n pantoufle f

slippery ['slɪpərɪ] adj glissant(e)

slip road (BRIT) n (to motorway) bretelle f d'accès

slipshod ['slɪpʃɔd] adj négligé(e), peu soigné(e)

slip-up ['slɪpʌp] n bévue f

slipway ['slɪpweɪ] n cale f (de construction or de lancement)

slit [slɪt] (pt, pp slit) n fente f; (cut) incision f ♦ vt fendre; couper; inciser

slither ['slɪðə*] vi glisser; (snake) onduler

sliver ['slɪvə*] n (of glass, wood) éclat m; (of cheese etc) petit morceau, fine tranche

slob [slɔb] (inf) n rustaud(e)

slog [slɔg] (BRIT) vi travailler très dur ♦ n gros effort; tâche fastidieuse

slogan ['sləʊgən] n slogan m

slop [slɔp] vi (also: ~ over) se renverser; déborder ♦ vt répandre; renverser

slope [sləʊp] n pente f, côte f; (side of mountain) versant m; (slant) inclinaison f ♦ vi: to ~ down être en pente or descendre en pente; to ~ up monter; **sloping** adj en pente; (writing) penché(e)

sloppy ['slɔpɪ] adj (work) peu soigné(e), bâclé(e); (appearance) négligé(e), débraillé(e)

slot [slɔt] n fente f ♦ vt: to ~ sth into encastrer or insérer qch dans

sloth [sləʊθ] n (laziness) paresse f

slot machine n (BRIT: vending machine) distributeur m (automatique); (for gambling) machine f à sous

slouch [slaʊtʃ] vi avoir le dos rond, être voûté(e)

slovenly ['slʌvnlɪ] adj sale, débraillé(e); (work) négligé(e)

slow [sləʊ] adj lent(e); (watch): to be ~ retarder ♦ adv lentement ♦ vt, vi (also: ~ down, ~ up) ralentir; "~" (road sign) "ralentir"; ~**ly** adv lentement; ~ **motion** n: in ~ motion au ralenti

sludge [slʌdʒ] n boue f

slue [sluː] (US) vi = slew

slug [slʌg] n limace f; (bullet) balle f; **sluggish** ['slʌgɪʃ] adj (person) mou(molle), lent(e); (stream, engine, trading) lent

sluice [sluːs] n (also: ~ gate) vanne f

slum [slʌm] n (house) taudis m

slump [slʌmp] n baisse soudaine, effondrement m; (ECON) crise f ♦ vi s'effondrer, s'affaisser

slung [slʌŋ] pt, pp of **sling**

slur [slɜː*] n (fig: smear) ~ (on) atteinte f (à); insinuation f (contre) ♦ vt mal articuler

slush [slʌʃ] n neige fondue; ~ **fund** n caisse noire, fonds secrets

slut [slʌt] (pej) n souillon f

sly [slaɪ] adj (person) rusé(e); (smile, expression, remark) sournois(e)

smack [smæk] n tape f; (on face) gifle f ♦ vt donner une tape à; (on face) gifler; (on bottom) donner la fessée à ♦ vi: to ~ of avoir des relents de, sentir

small [smɔːl] adj petit(e); ~ **ads** (BRIT) npl petites annonces; ~ **change** n petite or menue monnaie; ~ **fry** n (fig) menu fretin; ~**holder** (BRIT) n petit cultivateur; ~ **hours** npl: in the ~ **hours** au petit matin; ~**pox** n variole f; ~ **talk** n menus propos

smart [smɑːt] adj (neat, fashionable) élégant(e), chic inv; (clever) intelligent(e), astucieux(euse), futé(e); (quick) rapide, vif(vive), prompt(e) ♦ vi faire mal, brûler; (fig) être piqué(e) au vif; **~en up** vi devenir plus élégant or se faire beau(belle) ♦ vt rendre plus élégant(e)

smash [smæʃ] n (also: **~up**) collision f, accident m; (: ~ hit) succès foudroyant ♦ vt casser, briser, fracasser; (opponent) écraser; (SPORT: record) pulvériser ♦ vi se briser, se fracasser; s'écraser; **~ing** (inf) adj formidable

smattering [ˈsmætərɪŋ] n: a ~ of quelques notions de

smear [smɪə*] n tache f, salissure f; trace f; (MED) frottis m ♦ vt enduire; (make dirty) salir; **~ campaign** n campagne f de diffamation

smell [smel] (pt, pp smelt or smelled) n odeur f; (sense) odorat m ♦ vt sentir ♦ vi (food etc) sentir; to ~ (of) sentir; (pej) sentir mauvais

smelly [ˈsmelɪ] adj qui sent mauvais, malodorant(e)

smile [smaɪl] n sourire m ♦ vi sourire

smirk [smɜːk] n petit sourire suffisant or affecté

smock [smɒk] n blouse f

smog [smɒg] n brouillard mêlé de fumée, smog m

smoke [sməuk] n fumée f ♦ vt, vi fumer; **~d** adj (bacon, glass) fumée(e); **~r** n (person) fumeur(euse); (RAIL) wagon m fumeurs; **~ screen** n rideau m or écran m de fumée; (fig) paravent m

smoking [ˈsməukɪŋ] n tabagisme m; "no smoking" (sign) "défense de fumer"; to give up smoking arrêter de fumer; **smoky** [ˈsməukɪ] adj enfumé(e); (taste) fumé(e)

smolder [ˈsməuldə*] (US) vi = smoulder

smooth [smuːð] adj lisse; (sauce) onctueux(euse); (flavour, whisky) moelleux(euse); (movement) régu-

lier(ère), sans à-coups or heurts; (pej: person) doucereux(euse), mielleux(euse) ♦ vt (also: ~ out: skirt, paper) lisser, défroisser; (: creases, difficulties) faire disparaître

smother [ˈsmʌðə*] vt étouffer

smoulder [ˈsməuldə*] (US **smolder**) vi couver

smudge [smʌdʒ] n tache f, bavure f ♦ vt salir, maculer

smug [smʌg] adj suffisant(e)

smuggle [ˈsmʌgl] vt passer en contrebande or en fraude; **~r** n contrebandier(ère); **smuggling** [ˈsmʌglɪŋ] n contrebande f

smutty [ˈsmʌtɪ] adj (fig) grossier(ère), obscène

snack [snæk] n casse-croûte m inv; **~ bar** n snack(-bar) m

snag [snæg] n inconvénient m, difficulté f

snail [sneɪl] n escargot m

snake [sneɪk] n serpent m

snap [snæp] n (sound) claquement m, bruit sec; (photograph) photo f, instantané m ♦ adj subite(e); fait(e) sans réflexion ♦ vt (break) casser net; (fingers) faire claquer ♦ vi se casser net or avec un bruit sec; (speak sharply) parler d'un ton brusque; to ~ shut se refermer brusquement; **~ at** vt fus (subj: dog) essayer de mordre; **~ off** vi (break) casser net; **~ up** vt sauter sur, saisir; **~py** (inf) adj prompt(e); (slogan) qui a du punch; **make it ~py!** (inf) grouille-toi!, et que ça saute!; **~shot** n photo f, instantané m

snare [snɛə*] n piège m

snarl [snɑːl] vi gronder

snatch [snætʃ] n (small amount): **~es of** des fragments mpl or bribes fpl ♦ vt saisir (d'un geste vif); (steal) voler

sneak [sniːk] (pt (US) also **snuck**) vi: to ~ in/out entrer/sortir furtivement or à la dérobée ♦ n (inf, pej: informer) faux jeton; to ~ up on sb s'approcher de qn sans faire de bruit; **~ers** [ˈsniːkəz] npl tennis mpl *or baskets* mpl

sneer [snɪə*] vi ricaner; **to ~ at** traiter avec mépris

sneeze [sniːz] vi éternuer

sniff [snɪf] vi renifler ♦ vt renifler, flairer; *(glue, drugs)* sniffer, respirer

snigger ['snɪgə*] vi pouffer de rire

snip [snɪp] n *(cut)* petit coup; *(BRIT: inf: bargain)* (bonne) occasion or affaire ♦ vt couper

sniper ['snaɪpə*] n tireur embusqué

snippet ['snɪpɪt] n bribe(s) f(pl)

snivelling ['snɪvlɪŋ] adj larmoyant(e), pleurnicheur(euse)

snob [snɔb] n snob m/f; **~bish** adj snob inv

snooker ['snuːkə*] n sorte de jeu de billard

snoop [snuːp] vi: **to ~ about** fureter

snooty ['snuːtɪ] adj snob inv

snooze [snuːz] n petit somme ♦ vi faire un petit somme

snore [snɔː*] vi ronfler

snorkel ['snɔːkl] n tuba m

snort [snɔːt] vi grogner; *(horse)* renâcler

snout [snaʊt] n museau m

snow [snəʊ] n neige f ♦ vi neiger; **~ball** n boule f de neige; **~bound** adj enneigé(e), bloqué(e) par la neige; **~drift** n congère f; **~drop** n perce-neige m or f; **~fall** n chute f de neige; **~flake** n flocon m de neige; **~man** (irreg) n bonhomme m de neige; **~plough** (US **~plow**) n chasse-neige m inv; **~shoe** n raquette f *(pour la neige)*; **~storm** n tempête f de neige

snub [snʌb] vt repousser, snober ♦ n rebuffade f; **~-nosed** adj au nez retroussé

snuff [snʌf] n tabac m à priser

snug [snʌg] adj douillet(te), confortable; *(person)* bien au chaud

snuggle ['snʌgl] vi: **to ~ up to sb** se serrer or se blottir contre qn

---

KEYWORD

so [səʊ] adv 1 *(thus, likewise)* ainsi;

if ~ si oui; ~ **do** or **have I** moi aussi; it's 5 o'clock - it is! il est 5 heures - en effet! or c'est vrai!; I hope/think ~ je l'espère/le crois; ~ **far** jusqu'ici, jusqu'à maintenant; *(in past)* jusque-là

2 *(in comparisons etc: to such a degree)* si, tellement; ~ **big (that)** si or tellement grand (que); **she's not** ~ **clever as her brother** elle n'est pas aussi intelligente que son frère

3: ~ **much** adj, adv tant (de); **I've got** ~ **much work** j'ai tant de travail; **I love you** ~ **much** je vous aime tant; ~ **many** tant (de)

4 *(phrases)*: 10 or ~ à peu près or environ 10; ~ **long!** *(inf: goodbye)* au revoir!, à un de ces jours!

♦ conj 1 *(expressing purpose)*: ~ **as to do** pour or afin de faire; ~ **(that)** pour que or afin que +sub

2 *(expressing result)* donc, par conséquent; ~ **that** si bien que, de (telle) sorte que

---

soak [səʊk] vt faire tremper; *(drench)* tremper ♦ vi tremper; ~ **in** vi être absorbé(e); ~ **up** vt absorber

soap [səʊp] n savon m; **~flakes** npl paillettes fpl de savon; **~ opera** n feuilleton télévisé; **~ powder** n lessive f; **~y** adj savonneux(euse)

soar [sɔː*] vi monter (en flèche), s'élancer; *(building)* s'élancer

sob [sɔb] n sanglot m ♦ vi sangloter

sober ['səʊbə*] adj qui n'est pas (or plus) ivre; *(serious)* sérieux(euse), sensé(e); *(colour, style)* sobre, discret(ète); ~ **up** vt dessoûler *(inf)* ♦ vi dessoûler

so-called ['səʊ'kɔːld] adj soi-disant inv

soccer ['sɔkə*] n football m

social ['səʊʃl] adj social(e); *(sociable)* sociable ♦ n (petite) fête; ~ **club** n amicale f, foyer m; ~ **ism** n socialisme m; ~ **ist** adj socialiste ♦ n socialiste m/f; ~ **ize** vi: **to** ~ **ize (with)** lier connaissance (avec); parler (avec); ~ **security** *(BRIT)* n aide sociale; ~ **work** n assistance sociale, travail social; ~ **worker** n assistant(e) social(e)

society [sə'saɪətɪ] n société f; (club) société, association f; (also: high ~) (haute) société, grand monde

sociology [səʊsɪ'ɒlədʒɪ] n sociologie f

sock [sɒk] n chaussette f

socket ['sɒkɪt] n cavité f; (BRIT: ELEC: also: wall ~) prise f de courant

soda ['səʊdə] n (CHEM) soude f; (also: ~ water) eau f de Seltz; (US: also: ~ pop) soda m

sodden ['sɒdn] adj trempé(e); détrempé(e)

sofa ['səʊfə] n sofa m, canapé m

soft [sɒft] adj (not rough) doux(douce); (not hard) doux; mou(molle); (not loud) doux, léger(ère); (kind) doux, gentil(le); ~ **drink** n boisson non alcoolisée; ~**en** ['sɒfn] vt ramollir; (fig) adoucir; atténuer ♦ vi se ramollir; s'adoucir; s'atténuer; ~**ly** adv doucement; gentiment; ~**ness** n douceur f; ~ **spot** n: to have a ~ spot for sb avoir un faible pour qn; ~**ware** ['sɒftwɛə*] n (COMPUT) logiciel m, software m

soggy ['sɒgɪ] adj trempé(e); détrempé(e)

soil [sɔɪl] n (earth) sol m, terre f ♦ vt salir; (fig) souiller

solace ['sɒləs] n consolation f

solar ['səʊlə*] adj solaire; ~ **panel** n panneau m solaire; ~ **power** n énergie solaire

sold [səʊld] pt, pp of **sell**

solder ['səʊldə*] vt souder (au fil à souder) ♦ n soudure f

soldier ['səʊldʒə*] n soldat m, militaire m

sole [səʊl] n (of foot) plante f; (of shoe) semelle f; (fish: pl inv) sole f ♦ adj seul(e), unique

solemn ['sɒləm] adj solennel(le); (person) sérieux(euse), grave

sole trader n (COMM) chef m d'entreprise individuelle

solicit [sə'lɪsɪt] vt (request) solliciter ♦ vi (prostitute) racoler

solicitor [sə'lɪsɪtə*] n (for wills etc) ≈ notaire m; (in court) ≈ avocat m

solid ['sɒlɪd] adj solide; (not hollow) plein(e), compact(e), massif(ive); (entire): 3 ~ hours 3 heures entières ♦ n solide m

solidarity [sɒlɪ'dærɪtɪ] n solidarité f

solitary ['sɒlɪtərɪ] adj solitaire; ~ **confinement** n (LAW) isolement m

solo ['səʊləʊ] n solo m ♦ adv (fly) en solitaire; ~**ist** n soliste m/f

soluble ['sɒljubl] adj soluble

solution [sə'luːʃən] n solution f

solve [sɒlv] vt résoudre

solvent ['sɒlvənt] adj (COMM) solvable ♦ n (CHEM) (dis)solvant m

---

KEYWORD

some [sʌm] adj 1 (a certain amount or number of): ~ tea/water/ice cream du thé/de l'eau/de la glace; ~ children/apples des enfants/pommes 2 (certain: in contrasts): ~ people say that ... il y a des gens qui disent que ...; ~ films were excellent, but most ... certains films étaient excellents, mais la plupart ... 3 (unspecified): ~ woman was asking for you il y avait une dame qui vous demandait; he was asking for ~ book (or other) il demandait un livre quelconque; ~ day un de ces jours; ~ day next week un jour la semaine prochaine
♦ pron 1 (a certain number) quelques-uns (f quelques-unes); I've got ~ (books etc) j'en ai (quelques-uns); ~ (of them) have been sold certains ont été vendus
2 (a certain amount) un peu; I've got ~ (money, milk) j'en ai un peu
♦ adv: ~ 10 people quelque 10 personnes, 10 personnes environ

---

some: ~**body** ['sʌmbədɪ] pron = someone; ~**how** ['sʌmhaʊ] adv d'une façon ou d'une autre; (for some reason) pour une raison ou une autre; ~one ['sʌmwʌn] pron quelqu'un; ~place ['sʌmpleɪs] (US) adv = somewhere

somersault ['sʌməsɔːlt] n culbute f, saut périlleux ♦ vi faire la culbute ou un saut périlleux; (car) faire un tonneau

something ['sʌmθɪŋ] pron quelque chose; ~ interesting quelque chose d'intéressant

sometime ['sʌmtaɪm] adv (in future) un de ces jours, un jour ou l'autre; (in past): ~ last month au cours du mois dernier

some: ~times ['sʌmtaɪmz] adv quelquefois, parfois; ~what ['sʌmwɔt] adv quelque peu, un peu; ~where ['sʌmwɛə*] adv quelque part

son [sʌn] n fils m

song [sɒŋ] n chanson f; (of bird) chant m

son-in-law ['sʌnɪnlɔː] n gendre m, beau-fils m

sonny ['sʌnɪ] (inf) n fiston m

soon [suːn] adv bientôt; (early) tôt; ~ afterwards peu après; see also as; ~er adv (time) plus tôt; (preference): I would ~er do j'aimerais autant or je préférerais faire; ~er or later tôt ou tard

soot [sut] n suie f

soothe [suːð] vt calmer, apaiser

sophisticated [sə'fɪstɪkeɪtɪd] adj raffiné(e); sophistiqué(e); (machinery) hautement perfectionné(e), très complexe

sophomore ['sɒfəmɔː*] (US) n étudiant(e) de seconde année

sopping ['sɒpɪŋ] adj (also: ~ wet) complètement trempé(e)

soppy ['sɒpɪ] (pej) adj sentimental(e)

soprano [sə'prɑːnəu] n (singer) soprano m/f

sorcerer ['sɔːsərə*] n sorcier m

sore [sɔː*] adj (painful) douloureux(euse), sensible ♦ n plaie f; ~ly adv (tempted) fortement

sorrow ['sɒrəu] n peine f, chagrin m

sorry ['sɒrɪ] adj désolé(e); (condition, excuse) triste, déplorable; ~! pardon!, excusez-moi!; ~? pardon?; to feel ~ for sb plaindre qn

sort [sɔːt] n genre m, espèce f, sorte f ♦ vt (also: ~ out) trier; classer; ranger; (: problems) résoudre, régler; ~ing office n bureau m de tri

SOS n abbr (= save our souls) S.O.S. m

so-so ['səu'səu] adv comme ci comme ça

sought [sɔːt] pt, pp of seek

soul [səul] n âme f; ~-destroying adj démoralisant(e); ~ful adj sentimental(e); (eyes) expressif(ive)

sound [saund] adj (healthy) en bonne santé, sain(e); (safe, not damaged) solide, en bon état; (reliable, not superficial) sérieux(euse), solide; (sensible) sensé(e) ♦ adv: ~ asleep profondément endormi(e) ♦ n son m; bruit m; (GEO) détroit m, bras m de mer ♦ vt (alarm) sonner ♦ vi sonner, retentir; (fig: seem) sembler (être); to ~ like ressembler à; ~ out vt sonder; ~ barrier n mur m du son; ~ effects npl bruitage m; ~ly adv (sleep) profondément; (beat) complètement, à plate couture; ~proof adj insonorisé(e); ~track n (of film) bande f sonore

soup [suːp] n soupe f, potage m; in the ~ (fig) dans le pétrin; ~ plate n assiette creuse or à soupe; ~spoon n cuiller f à soupe

sour ['sauə*] adj aigre; it's ~ grapes (fig) c'est du dépit

source [sɔːs] n source f

south [sauθ] n sud m ♦ adj sud inv, du sud ♦ adv au sud, vers le sud; S~ Africa n Afrique f du Sud; S~ African adj sud-africain(e) ♦ n Sud-Africain(e); S~ America n Amérique f du Sud; S~ American adj sud-américain(e) ♦ n Sud-Américain(e); ~-east n sud-est m; ~erly ['sʌðəlɪ] adj (du) sud; ~ern ['sʌðən] adj (du) sud; méridional(e); S~

Pole n Pôle m Sud; **~ward(s)** adv vers le sud; **~-west** n sud-ouest m

souvenir [suːvəˈnɪəʳ] n (objet) souvenir m

sovereign [ˈsɔvrɪn] n souverain(e)

soviet [ˈsəʊvɪət] adj soviétique; **the S~ Union** l'Union f soviétique

sow[1] [sau] n truie f

sow[2] [səʊ] (pt ~ed, pp sown) vt semer; **~n** [səʊn] pp of sow[2]

soya [ˈsɔɪə] (US soy) n: **~ bean** graine f de soja; **~ sauce** sauce f de soja

spa [spɑː] n (town) station thermale; (US: also: health ~) établissement m de cure de rajeunissement etc

space [speɪs] n (gen) espace m; (room) place f; espace; (length of time) laps m de temps ♦ cpd spatial(e) ♦ vt (also: ~ out) espacer; **~craft** n engin spatial; **~man** (irreg) n astronaute m, cosmonaute m; **~ship** n = spacecraft; **~woman** (irreg) n astronaute f, cosmonaute f; **spacing** n espacement m

spade [speɪd] n (tool) bêche f, pelle f; (child's) pelle; **~s** npl (CARDS) pique m

Spain [speɪn] n Espagne f

span [spæn] n (of bird, plane) envergure f; (of arch) portée f; (in time) espace m de temps, durée f ♦ vt enjamber, franchir; (fig) couvrir, embrasser

Spaniard [ˈspænjəd] n Espagnol(e)

spaniel [ˈspænjəl] n épagneul m

Spanish [ˈspænɪʃ] adj espagnol(e) ♦ n (LING) espagnol m; **the ~** npl les Espagnols mpl

spank [spæŋk] vt donner une fessée à

spanner [ˈspænəʳ] n (BRIT) clé f (de mécanicien)

spar [spɑːʳ] n espar m ♦ vi (BOXING) s'entraîner

spare [spɛəʳ] adj de réserve, de rechange; (surplus) de or en trop, de reste ♦ n (part) pièce f de rechange, pièce détachée ♦ vt (do without) se passer de; (afford to give) donner, accorder; (refrain from hurting)

épargner; **to ~** (surplus) en surplus, de trop; **~ part** n pièce f de rechange, pièce détachée; **~ time** n moments mpl de loisir, temps m libre; **~ wheel** n (AUT) roue f de secours; **sparing** [ˈspɛərɪŋ] adj: **to be sparing with** ménager; **sparingly** adv avec modération

spark [spɑːk] n étincelle f; **~(ing) plug** n bougie f

sparkle [ˈspɑːkl] n scintillement m, éclat m ♦ vi étinceler, scintiller; **sparkling** [ˈspɑːklɪŋ] adj (wine) mousseux(euse), pétillant(e); (water) pétillant(e); (fig: conversation, performance) étincelant(e), pétillant(e)

sparrow [ˈspærəʊ] n moineau m

sparse [spɑːs] adj clairsemé(e)

spartan [ˈspɑːtən] adj (fig) spartiate

spasm [ˈspæzəm] n (MED) spasme m; **~odic** [spæzˈmɔdɪk] adj (fig) intermittent(e)

spastic [ˈspæstɪk] n handicapé(e) moteur

spat [spæt] pt, pp of spit

spate [speɪt] n (fig): **a ~ of** une avalanche or un torrent de

spatter [ˈspætəʳ] vt éclabousser

spawn [spɔːn] vi frayer ♦ n frai m

speak [spiːk] (pt spoke, pp spoken) vt parler; (truth) dire ♦ vi parler; (make a speech) prendre la parole; **to ~ to sb/of** or **about sth** parler à qn/de qch; **~ up!** parle plus fort!; **~er** n (in public) orateur m; (also: loud~er) haut-parleur m; **the S~er** (BRIT POL) le président de la chambre des Communes; (US POL) le président de la chambre des Représentants

spear [spɪəʳ] n lance f ♦ vt transpercer; **~head** vt (attack etc) mener

spec [spek] (inf) n: **on ~** à tout hasard

special [ˈspeʃəl] adj spécial(e); **~ist** n spécialiste m/f; **~ity** n spécialité f; **~ize** vi: **to ~ize (in)** se spécialiser (dans); **~ly** adv spécialement, particulièrement; **~ty** n (esp US) = speciality

species ['spi:ʃi:z] *n inv* espèce *f*

specific [spə'sıfık] *adj* précis(e); particulier(ère); (BOT, CHEM *etc*) spécifique; ~ally *adv* expressément, explicitement; ~ation *n* (TECH) spécification *f*; (*requirement*) stipulation *f*

specimen ['spesımən] *n* spécimen *m*, échantillon *m*; (*of blood*) prélèvement *m*

speck [spek] *n* petite tache, petit point; (*particle*) grain *m*; ~ed ['spekld] *adj* tacheté(e), moucheté(e)

specs [speks] (*inf*) *npl* lunettes *fpl*

spectacle ['spektəkl] *n* spectacle *m*; ~s *npl* (*glasses*) lunettes *fpl*; **spectacular** [spek'tækjulə*] *adj* spectaculaire

spectator [spek'teıtə*] *n* spectateur(trice)

spectrum ['spektrəm] (*pl* spectra) *n* spectre *m*

speculation [spekju'leıʃən] *n* spéculation *f*

speech [spi:tʃ] *n* (*faculty*) parole *f*; (*talk*) discours *m*, allocution *f*; (*manner of speaking*) façon *f* de parler, langage *m*; (*enunciation*) élocution *f*; ~less *adj* muet(te)

speed [spi:d] *n* vitesse *f*; (*promptness*) rapidité *f* ♦ *vi*: to ~ along/past *etc* aller/passer *etc* à toute vitesse; at full *or* top ~ à toute vitesse *or* allure; ~ up *vi* aller plus vite, accélérer ♦ *vt* accélérer; ~boat *n* vedette *f*, hors-bord *m inv*; ~ily *adv* rapidement, promptement; ~ing *n* (AUT) excès *m* de vitesse; ~ limit *n* limitation *f* de vitesse, vitesse maximale permise; ~ometer [spı'dɒmıtə*] *n* compteur *m* (de vitesse); ~way *n* (SPORT: *also*: ~way racing) épreuve(s) *f(pl)* de vitesse de motos; ~y *adj* rapide, prompt(e)

spell [spel] (*pt, pp* spelt (BRIT) *or* ~ed) *n* (*also*: magic ~) sortilège *m*, charme *m*; (*period of time*) (courte) période *f* ♦ *vt* (*in writing*) écrire, orthographier; (*aloud*) épeler; (*fig*) signifier; to cast a ~ on sb jeter un

sort à qn; he can't ~ il fait des fautes d'orthographe; ~bound *adj* envoûté(e), subjugué(e); ~ing *n* orthographe *f*

spend [spend] (*pt, pp* spent) *vt* (*money*) dépenser; (*time, life*) passer; consacrer; ~thrift *n* dépensier(ère)

sperm [spɜ:m] *n* sperme *m*

spew [spju:] *vt* (*also*: ~ out) vomir

sphere [sfıə*] *n* sphère *f*

spice [spaıs] *n* épice *f*

spick-and-span ['spıkən'spæn] *adj* impeccable

spicy ['spaısı] *adj* épicé(e), relevé(e); (*fig*) piquant(e)

spider ['spaıdə*] *n* araignée *f*

spike [spaık] *n* pointe *f*; (BOT) épi *m*

spill [spıl] (*pt, pp* spilt *or* ~ed) *vt* renverser; répandre ♦ *vi* se répandre; ~ over *vi* déborder

spin [spın] (*pt* spun *or* span, *pp* spun) *n* (*revolution of wheel*) tour *m*; (AVIAT) (chute *f* en) vrille *f*; (*trip in car*) petit tour, balade *f* ♦ *vt* (*wool etc*) filer; (*wheel*) faire tourner ♦ *vi* filer; (*turn*) tourner, tournoyer; ~ out *vt* faire durer

spinach ['spınıtʃ] *n* épinard *m*; (*as food*) épinards

spinal ['spaınl] *adj* vertébral(e), spinal(e); ~ cord *n* moelle épinière

spindly ['spındlı] *adj* grêle, filiforme

spin-dryer ['spın'draıə*] *n* (BRIT) essoreuse *f*

spine [spaın] *n* colonne vertébrale; (*thorn*) épine *f*; ~less *adj* (*fig*) mou(molle)

spinning ['spınıŋ] *n* (*of thread*) filature *f*; ~ top *n* toupie *f*; ~ wheel *n* rouet *m*

spin-off ['spınɒf] *n* avantage inattendu; sous-produit *m*

spinster ['spınstə*] *n* célibataire *f*; vieille fille (*péj*)

spiral ['spaıərl] *n* spirale *f* ♦ *vi* (*fig*) monter en flèche; ~ staircase *n* escalier *m* en colimaçon

spire ['spaıə*] *n* flèche *f*, aiguille *f*

spirit ['spırıt] *n* esprit *m*; (*mood*) état *m* d'esprit; (*courage*) courage *m*, énergie *f*; ~s *npl* (drink) spiritueux *mpl*, alcool *m*; in good ~s de bonne humeur; ~ed *adj* vif(vive), fougueux(euse), plein(e) d'allant; ~ual ['spɪrɪtjuəl] *adj* spirituel(le); (religious) religieux(euse)

spit [spɪt] (*pt, pp* spat) *n* (for roasting) broche *f*; (saliva) salive *f* ♦ *vi* cracher; (sound) crépiter

spite [spaɪt] *n* rancune *f*, dépit *m* ♦ *vt* contrarier, vexer; in ~ of en dépit de, malgré; ~ful *adj* méchant(e), malveillant(e)

spittle ['spɪtl] *n* salive *f*; (of animal) bave *f*; (spat out) crachat *m*

splash [splæʃ] *n* (sound) plouf *m*; (fig: of colour) tache *f* ♦ *vt* éclabousser ♦ *vi* (also: ~ about) barboter, patauger

spleen [spliːn] *n* (ANAT) rate *f*

splendid ['splendɪd] *adj* splendide, superbe, magnifique

splint [splɪnt] *n* attelle *f*, éclisse *f*

splinter ['splɪntə*] *n* (in wood) écharde *f*; (glass) éclat *m* ♦ *vi* se briser, se fendre

split [splɪt] (*pt, pp* split) *n* fente *f*, déchirure *f*; (fig: POL) scission *f* ♦ *vt* diviser; (work, profits) partager, répartir ♦ *vi* (divide) se diviser; ~ up *vi* (couple) se séparer, rompre; (meeting) se disperser

splutter ['splʌtə*] *vi* bafouiller; (spit) postillonner

spoil [spɔɪl] (*pt, pp* spoilt *or* ~ed) *vt* (damage) abîmer; (mar) gâcher; (child) gâter; ~s *npl* butin *m*; (fig: profits) bénéfices *mpl*; ~sport *n* trouble-fête *m*, rabat-joie *m*

spoke [spəʊk] *pt of* speak ♦ *n* (of wheel) rayon *m*; ~n ['spəʊkn] *pp of* speak; ~sman ['spəʊksmən] (*irreg*) *n* porte-parole *m inv*; ~swoman ['spəʊkswʊmən] (*irreg*) *n* porte-parole *m inv*

sponge [spʌndʒ] *n* éponge *f*; (also: ~ cake) = biscuit de Savoie *m* ♦ *vt* éponger ♦ *vi*: to ~ off *or* on vivre aux crochets de; ~ bag (BRIT) *n* trousse *f* de toilette

sponsor ['spɒnsə*] *n* (RADIO, TV,

SPORT) sponsor *m*; (for application) parrain *m*, marraine *f*; (BRIT: for fund-raising event) donateur(trice) ♦ *vt* sponsoriser; parrainer; faire un don à; ~ship *n* sponsoring *m*; parrainage *m*; dons *mpl*

spontaneous [spɒn'teɪnɪəs] *adj* spontané(e)

spooky ['spuːkɪ] (*inf*) *adj* qui donne la chair de poule

spool [spuːl] *n* bobine *f*

spoon [spuːn] *n* cuiller *f*; ~-feed *vt* nourrir à la cuiller; (fig) mâcher le travail à; ~ful *n* cuillerée *f*

sport [spɔːt] *n* sport *m*; (person) chic type(fille) *f* ♦ *vt* arborer; ~ing *adj* sportif(ive); to give sb a ~ing chance donner sa chance à qn; ~s jacket (US) = sports jacket; ~s car *n* voiture *f* de sport; ~s jacket (BRIT) *n* veste *f* de sport; ~sman (*irreg*) *n* sportif *m*; ~smanship *n* esprit sportif, sportivité *f*; ~swear *n* vêtements *mpl* de sport; ~swoman (*irreg*) *n* sportive *f*; ~y *adj* sportif(ive)

spot [spɒt] *n* tache *f*; (dot: on pattern) pois *m*; (pimple) bouton *m*; (place) endroit *m*, coin *m*; (RADIO, TV: in programme: for person) numéro *m*; (: for activity) rubrique *f*; (small amount): a ~ of un peu de ♦ *vt* (notice) apercevoir, repérer; on the ~ sur place, sur les lieux; (immediately) sur-le-champ; (in difficulty) dans l'embarras; ~ check *n* sondage *m*, vérification ponctuelle; ~less *adj* immaculé(e); ~light *n* projecteur *m*; (AUT) phare *m* auxiliaire; ~ted *adj* (fabric) à pois; ~ty *adj* (face, person) boutonneux(euse)

spouse [spaʊz] *n* époux(épouse)

spout [spaʊt] *n* (of jug) bec *m*; (of pipe) orifice *m* ♦ *vi* jaillir

sprain [spreɪn] *n* entorse *f*, foulure *f* ♦ *vt*: to ~ one's ankle etc se fouler or se tordre la cheville etc

sprang [spræŋ] *pt of* spring

sprawl [sprɔːl] *vi* s'étaler

spray [spreɪ] *n* jet *m* (en fines gouttelettes); (from sea) embruns mpl; (container) vaporisateur m; (for garden) pulvérisateur m; (aerosol) bombe f; (of flowers) petit bouquet m ♦ vt vaporiser, pulvériser; (crops) traiter

spread [sprɛd] (pt, pp **spread**) n (distribution) répartition f; (CULIN) pâte f à tartiner; (inf: meal) festin m ♦ vt étendre, étaler; répandre; (wealth, workload) distribuer ♦ vi (disease, news) se propager; (also: ~ out: stain) s'étaler; ~ out vi (people) se disperser; ~-eagled ['sprɛːdiːgld] adj étendu(e) bras et jambes écartés; ~sheet n (COMPUT) tableur m

spree [spriː] n: to go on a ~ faire la fête

sprightly ['spraɪtlɪ] adj alerte

spring [sprɪŋ] (pt **sprang**, pp **sprung**) n (leap) bond m, saut m; (coiled metal) ressort m; (season) printemps m; (of water) source f ♦ vi (leap) bondir, sauter; in ~ au printemps; to ~ from provenir de; ~ up vi (problem) se présenter, surgir; (plant, buildings) surgir de terre; ~board n tremplin m; ~clean(ing) n grand nettoyage de printemps; ~time n printemps m

sprinkle ['sprɪŋkl] vt: to ~ water etc on, ~ with water etc asperger d'eau etc; to ~ sugar etc on, ~ with sugar etc saupoudrer de sucre etc; ~r ['sprɪŋklə*] n (for lawn) arroseur m; (to put out fire) diffuseur m d'extincteur automatique d'incendie

sprint [sprɪnt] n sprint m ♦ vi courir à toute vitesse; (SPORT) sprinter

sprout [spraʊt] vi germer, pousser; ~s npl (also: Brussels ~s) choux mpl de Bruxelles

spruce [spruːs] n inv épicéa m ♦ adj net(te), pimpant(e)

sprung [sprʌŋ] pp of spring

spry [spraɪ] adj alerte, vif(vive)

spun [spʌn] pt, pp of spin

spur [spəː*] n éperon m; (fig) aiguillon m ♦ vt (also: ~ on) éperonner; aiguillonner; on the ~ of the mo-

ment sous l'impulsion du moment

spurious ['spjʊərɪəs] adj faux(fausse)

spurn [spəːn] vt repousser avec mépris

spurt [spəːt] n (of blood) jaillissement m; (of energy) regain m, sursaut m ♦ vi jaillir, gicler

spy [spaɪ] n espion(ne) ♦ vi: to ~ on espionner, épier; (see) apercevoir; ~ing n espionnage m

sq. abbr = square

squabble ['skwɔbl] vi se chamailler

squad [skwɔd] n (MIL, POLICE) escouade f, groupe m; (FOOTBALL) contingent m

squadron ['skwɔdrən] n (MIL) escadron m; (AVIAT, NAUT) escadrille f

squalid ['skwɔlɪd] adj sordide

squall [skwɔːl] n rafale f, bourrasque f

squalor ['skwɔlə*] n conditions fpl sordides

squander ['skwɔndə*] vt gaspiller, dilapider

square [skwɛə*] n carré m; (in town) place f ♦ adj carré(e); (fig: ideas, tastes) vieux jeu inv ♦ vt (arrange) régler; arranger; (MATH) élever au carré ♦ vi (reconcile) concilier; all ~ quitte; à égalité; a ~ meal un repas convenable; 2 metres ~ (de) 2 mètres sur 2; 2 ~ metres 2 mètres carrés; ~ly adv carrément

squash [skwɔʃ] n (BRIT: drink): lemon/orange ~ citronnade f/ orangeade f; (US: marrow) courge f; (SPORT) squash m ♦ vt écraser

squat [skwɔt] adj petit(e) et épais(se), ramassé(e) ♦ vi (also: ~ down) s'accroupir; ~ter n squatter m

squawk [skwɔːk] vi pousser un or des gloussements

squeak [skwiːk] vi grincer, crier; (mouse) pousser un petit cri

squeal [skwiːl] vi pousser un or des cri(s) aigu(s) or perçant(s); (brakes) grincer

squeamish ['skwiːmɪʃ] *adj* facilement dégoûté(e)

squeeze [skwiːz] *n* pression *f*; (*ECON*) restrictions *fpl* de crédit ♦ *vt* presser; (*hand, arm*) serrer; ~ **out** *vt* exprimer

squelch [skwɛltʃ] *vi* faire un bruit de succion

squid [skwɪd] *n* calmar *m*

squiggle ['skwɪgl] *n* gribouillis *m*

squint [skwɪnt] *vi* loucher ♦ *n*: he has a ~ il louche, il souffre de strabisme

squirm [skwɜːm] *vi* se tortiller

squirrel ['skwɪrəl] *n* écureuil *m*

squirt [skwɜːt] *vi* jaillir, gicler

Sr *abbr* = **senior**

St *abbr* = **saint; street**

stab [stæb] *n* (*with knife etc*) coup *m* (de couteau *etc*); (*of pain*) lancée *f*; (*inf: try*): **to have a ~ at** (*doing*) **sth** s'essayer à (faire) qch ♦ *vt* poignarder

stable ['steɪbl] *n* écurie *f* ♦ *adj* stable

stack [stæk] *n* tas *m*, pile *f* ♦ *vt* (*also*: ~ **up**) empiler, entasser

stadium ['steɪdɪəm] (*pl* **stadia** *or* ~**s**) *n* stade *m*

staff [stɑːf] *n* (*workforce*) personnel *m*; (*BRIT: SCOL*) professeurs *mpl* ♦ *vt* pourvoir en personnel

stag [stæg] *n* cerf *m*

stage [steɪdʒ] *n* scène *f*; (*platform*) estrade *f* ♦ *n*; (*profession*): **the ~** le théâtre; (*point*) étape *f*, stade *m* ♦ *vt* (*play*) monter, mettre en scène; (*demonstration*) organiser; **in ~s** par étapes, par degrés; ~ **coach** *n* diligence *f*; ~ **manager** *n* régisseur *m*

stagger ['stægə*] *vi* chanceler, tituber ♦ *vt* (*person: amaze*) stupéfier; (*hours, holidays*) étaler, échelonner; ~**ing** (*amazing*) stupéfiant(e), renversant(e)

stagnate [stæg'neɪt] *vi* stagner, croupir

stag party *n* enterrement *m* de vie de garçon

staid [steɪd] *adj* posé(e), rassis(e)

stain [steɪn] *n* tache *f*; (*colouring*) colorant *m* ♦ *vt* tacher; (*wood*) teindre; ~**ed glass window** *n* vitrail *m*; ~**less steel** *n* acier *m* inoxydable, inox *m*; ~ **remover** *n* détachant *m*

stair [stɛə*] *n* (*step*) marche *f*; ~**s** *npl* (*flight of steps*) escalier *m*; ~**case** *n* escalier *m*; ~**way** *n* = **staircase**

stake [steɪk] *n* pieu *m*, poteau *m*; (*BETTING*) enjeu *m*; (*COMM: interest*) intérêts *mpl* ♦ *vt* risquer, jouer; **to be at ~** être en jeu; **to ~ one's claim** (*to*) revendiquer

stale [steɪl] *adj* (*bread*) rassis(e); (*food*) pas frais(fraîche); (*beer*) éventé(e); (*smell*) de renfermé; (*air*) confiné(e)

stalemate ['steɪlmeɪt] *n* (*CHESS*) pat *m*; (*fig*) impasse *f*

stalk [stɔːk] *n* tige *f* ♦ *vt* traquer ♦ *vi*: **to ~ out/off** sortir/partir d'un air digne

stall [stɔːl] *n* (*BRIT: in street, market etc*) éventaire *m*, étal *m*; (*in stable*) stalle *f* ♦ *vt* (*AUT*) caler; (*delay*) retarder ♦ *vi* (*AUT*) caler; (*fig*) essayer de gagner du temps; ~**s** *npl* (*BRIT: in cinema, theatre*) orchestre *m*

stallion ['stælɪən] *n* étalon *m* (cheval)

stalwart ['stɔːlwət] *adj* dévoué(e), fidèle

stamina ['stæmɪnə] *n* résistance *f*, endurance *f*

stammer ['stæmə*] *n* bégaiement *m* ♦ *vi* bégayer

stamp [stæmp] *n* timbre *m*; (*rubber* ~) tampon *m*; (*mark, also fig*) empreinte *f* ♦ *vi* (*also*: ~ **one's foot**) taper du pied ♦ *vt* (*letter*) timbrer; (*with rubber* ~) tamponner; ~ **album** *n* album *m* de timbres(-poste); ~ **collecting** *n* philatélie *f*

stampede [stæm'piːd] *n* ruée *f*

stance [stæns] *n* position *f*

stand [stænd] (*pt, pp* **stood**) *n* (*position*) position *f*; (*for taxis*) station *f* (de taxis); (*music* ~) pupitre *m* à musique; (*COMM*) étalage *m*, stand m; (SPORT) tribune f ♦ vi être or se tenir (debout); (rise) se lever, se mettre debout; (be placed) se trouver; (remain: offer etc) rester valable; (BRIT: in election) être candidat(e), se présenter ♦ vt (place) mettre, poser; (tolerate, withstand) supporter; (treat, invite to) offrir (treat, invite), payer; to make or take a ~ prendre position; to ~ at (score, value etc) être de; to ~ for parliament (BRIT) se présenter aux élections législatives; ~ by vi (be ready) se tenir prêt(e) ♦ vt fus (opinion) s'en tenir à; (person): ne pas abandonner, soutenir; ~ down vi (withdraw) se retirer; ~ for vt fus (signify) représenter, signifier; (tolerate) supporter, tolérer; ~ in for vt fus remplacer; ~ out vi (be prominent) ressortir; ~ up vi (rise) se lever, se mettre debout; ~ up for vt fus défendre; ~ up to vt fus tenir tête à, résister à

standard ['stændəd] n (level) niveau (voulu); (norm) norme f, étalon m; (criterion) critère m; (flag) étendard m ♦ adj (size etc) ordinaire, normal(e); (measure) courant(e); (text) de base; ~s npl (morals) morale f, principes mpl; ~ lamp (BRIT) n lampadaire m; ~ of living n niveau m de vie

stand-by ['stændbaɪ] n remplaçant(e); to be on ~ se tenir prêt(e) (à intervenir); être de garde; ~ ticket n (AVIAT) billet m stand-by

stand-in ['stændɪn] n remplaçant m

standing ['stændɪŋ] n debout inv; (permanent) permanent(e) ♦ n réputation f, rang m, standing m; of many years' ~ qui dure or existe depuis longtemps; ~ joke n vieux sujet de plaisanterie; ~ order (BRIT) n (at bank) virement m automatique, prélèvement m bancaire; ~ room n places fpl debout

standoffish [-'ɒfɪʃ] adj distant(e), froid(e)

standpoint ['stændpɔɪnt] n point m de vue

standstill ['stændstɪl] n: at a ~ paralysé(e); to come to a ~ s'immobiliser, s'arrêter

stank [stæŋk] pt of stink

staple ['steɪpl] n (for papers) agrafe f ♦ adj (food etc) de base ♦ vt agrafer; ~r n agrafeuse f

star [stɑ:*] n étoile f; (celebrity) vedette f ♦ vi: to ~ (in) être la vedette (de) ♦ vt (CINEMA etc) avoir pour vedette; the ~s npl l'horoscope m

starboard ['stɑ:bəd] n tribord m

starch [stɑ:tʃ] n amidon m; (in food) fécule f

stardom ['stɑ:dəm] n célébrité f

stare [stɛə*] n regard m fixe ♦ vi: to ~ at regarder fixement

starfish ['stɑ:fɪʃ] n étoile f de mer

stark [stɑ:k] adj (bleak) désolé(e), morne ♦ adv: ~ naked complètement nu(e)

starling ['stɑ:lɪŋ] n étourneau m

starry ['stɑ:rɪ] adj étoilé(e); ~-eyed adj (innocent) naïf(ïve)

start [stɑ:t] n commencement m, début m; (of race) départ m; (sudden movement) sursaut m; (advantage) avance f, avantage m ♦ vt commencer; (found) créer; (engine) mettre en marche ♦ vi partir, se mettre en route; (jump) sursauter; to ~ doing or to do sth se mettre à faire qch; ~ off vi commencer; (leave) partir; ~ up vi commencer; (car) démarrer ♦ vt (business) créer; (car) mettre en marche; ~er n (AUT) démarreur m; (SPORT: official) starter m; (BRIT: CULIN) entrée f; ~ing point n point m de départ

startle ['stɑ:tl] vt faire sursauter; donner un choc à; **startling** adj (news) surprenant(e)

starvation [stɑ:'veɪʃən] n faim f, famine f; **starve** [stɑ:v] vi mourir de faim; être affamé(e) ♦ vt affamer

state [steɪt] n état m; (POL) Etat ♦ vt déclarer, affirmer; the S~s (America) les Etats-Unis mpl; to be in a ~ être dans tous ses états; ~ly *adj* majestueux(euse), imposant(e); **~ment** *n* déclaration *f*; **~sman** (*irreg*) *n* homme *m* d'Etat

static ['stætɪk] *n* (*RADIO, TV*) parasites *mpl* ♦ *adj* statique

station ['steɪʃən] *n* gare *f*; (*police ~*) poste *m* de police ♦ *vt* placer, poster

stationary ['steɪʃənərɪ] *adj* à l'arrêt, immobile

stationer ['steɪʃənə*] *n* papetier(ère); **~'s (shop)** *n* papeterie *f*; **~y** *n* papier *m* à lettres, petit matériel de bureau

stationmaster ['steɪʃənmɑːstə*] *n* (*RAIL*) chef *m* de gare

station wagon (*US*) *n* break *m*

statistic [stə'tɪstɪk] *n* statistique *f*; **~s** *n* (*science*) statistique *f*

statue ['stætjuː] *n* statue *f*

status ['steɪtəs] *n* position *f*, situation *f*; (*official*) statut *m*; (*prestige*) prestige *m*; **~ symbol** *n* signe extérieur de richesse

statute ['stætjuːt] *n* loi *f*, statut *m*; **statutory** *adj* statutaire, prévu(e) par un article de loi

staunch [stɔːntʃ] *adj* sûr(e), loyal(e)

stave off [steɪv] *vt* (*attack*) parer; (*threat*) conjurer

stay [steɪ] *n* (*period of time*) séjour *m* ♦ *vi* rester; (*reside*) loger; (*spend some time*) séjourner; **to ~ put** ne pas bouger; **to ~ with friends** loger chez des amis; **to ~ the night** passer la nuit; **~ behind** *vi* rester en arrière; **~ in** *vi* (*at home*) rester à la maison; **~ on** *vi* rester; **~ out** *vi* (*of house*) ne pas rentrer; **~ up** *vi* (*at night*) ne pas se coucher; **~ing power** *n* endurance *f*

stead [stɛd] *n*: **in sb's ~** à la place de qn; **to stand sb in good ~** être très utile à qn

steadfast ['stɛdfɑːst] *adj* ferme, résolu(e)

steadily ['stɛdɪlɪ] *adv* (*regularly*) progressivement; (*firmly*) fermement; (: *walk*) d'un pas ferme; (*fixedly: look*) sans détourner les yeux

steady ['stɛdɪ] *adj* stable, solide, ferme; (*regular*) constant(e), régulier(ère); (*person*) calme, pondéré(e) ♦ *vt* stabiliser; (*nerves*) calmer; **a ~ boyfriend** un petit ami

steak [steɪk] *n* (*beef*) bifteck *m*, steak *m*; (*fish, pork*) tranche *f*

steal [stiːl] (*pt* **stole**, *pp* **stolen**) *vt* voler ♦ *vi* voler; (*move secretly*) se faufiler, se déplacer furtivement

stealth [stɛlθ] *n*: **by ~** furtivement

steam [stiːm] *n* vapeur *f* ♦ *vt* (*CULIN*) cuire à la vapeur ♦ *vi* fumer; **~ engine** *n* locomotive *f* à vapeur; **~er** *n* (*bateau m à*) vapeur *m*; **~ship** *n* = steamer; **~y** *adj* embué(e), humide

steel [stiːl] *n* acier *m* ♦ *adj* d'acier; **~works** *n* aciérie *f*

steep [stiːp] *adj* raide, escarpé(e); (*price*) excessif(ive)

steeple ['stiːpl] *n* clocher *m*

steer [stɪə*] *vt* diriger; (*boat*) gouverner; (*person*) guider, conduire ♦ *vi* tenir le gouvernail; **~ing** *n* (*AUT*) conduite *f*; **~ing wheel** *n* volant *m*

stem [stɛm] *n* (*of plant*) tige *f*; (*of glass*) pied *m* ♦ *vt* contenir, arrêter, juguler; **~ from** *vt fus* provenir de, découler de

stench [stɛntʃ] *n* puanteur *f*

stencil ['stɛnsl] *n* stencil *m*; (*pattern used*) pochoir *m* ♦ *vt* polycopier

stenographer [stɛ'nɔgrɑːfə*] (*US*) *n* sténographe *m/f*

step [stɛp] *n* pas *m*; (*stair*) marche *f*; (*action*) mesure *f*, disposition *f* ♦ *vi*: **to ~ forward/back** faire un pas en avant/arrière, avancer/reculer; **~s** *npl* (*BRIT*) = **stepladder**; **to be in/out of ~ (with)** (*fig*) aller dans le sens (de)/être déphasé(e) (par rapport à); **~ down** *vi* (*fig*) se retirer, se désister; **~ up** *vt* augmenter, intensifier; **~brother** *n* demi-frère *m*; **~daughter** *n* belle-fille *f*; **~father** *n* beau-père *m*; **~ladder** (*BRIT*) *n* escabeau *m*; **~mother** *n* belle-mère *f*; **~ping stone** *n* pierre *f* de gué; (*fig*) tremplin *m*; **~sister** *n* demi-sœur *f*;

~**son** n beau-fils m

stereo ['steriəυ] n (sound) stéréo f; (hi-fi) chaîne f stéréo inv ♦ adj (also: ~**phonic**) stéréo(phonique)

sterile ['sterail] adj stérile; **sterilize** ['sterilaiz] vt stériliser

sterling ['stɜ:liŋ] adj (silver) de bon aloi, fin(e) ♦ n (ECON) livres fpl sterling inv; **a pound** ~ une livre sterling

stern [stɜ:n] adj sévère ♦ n (NAUT) arrière m, poupe f

stew [stju:] n ragoût m ♦ vt, vi cuire (à la casserole)

steward ['stjuəd] n (on ship, plane, train) steward m; ~**ess** n hôtesse f (de l'air)

stick [stɪk] (pt, pp **stuck**) n (walking ~) canne f ♦ vt (glue) coller; (inf: put) mettre, fourrer; (: tolerate) supporter; (thrust): **to** ~ **sth into** planter or enfoncer qch dans ♦ vi (become attached) rester collé(e) or fixé(e); (be unmovable: wheels etc) se bloquer; (remain: hand) rester; ~ **out** vi dépasser, sortir; ~ **up** vi = stick out; ~ **up for** vt fus défendre; ~**er** n auto-collant m; ~**ing plaster** n sparadrap m, pansement adhésif

stickler ['stɪklə*] n: **to be a** ~ **for** être pointilleux(euse) sur

stick-up ['stɪkʌp] (inf) n braquage m, hold-up m inv

sticky ['stɪkɪ] adj poisseux(euse); (label) adhésif(ive); (situation) délicat(e)

stiff [stɪf] adj raide; rigide; dur(e); (difficult) difficile, ardu(e); (cold) froid(e), distant(e); (strong, high) fort(e), élevé(e) ♦ adv: **to be bored/scared/frozen** ~ s'ennuyer à mort/être mort(e) de peur/froid; ~**en** vi se raidir; ~ **neck** n torticolis m

stifle ['staifl] vt étouffer, réprimer

stigma ['stɪgmə] n stigmate m

stile [stail] n échalier m

stiletto [stɪ'letəυ] (BRIT) n (also: ~ **heel**) talon m aiguille

still [stɪl] adj immobile ♦ adv (up to this time) encore, toujours; (even) encore; (nonetheless) quand même, tout de même; (hi-fi) chaîne f stéréo inv né(e); ~ **life** n nature morte

stilt [stɪlt] n (for walking on) échasse f; (pile) pilotis m

stilted ['stɪltɪd] adj guindé(e), emprunté(e)

stimulate ['stɪmjυleɪt] vt stimuler

stimulus ['stɪmjυləs] (pl **stimuli**) n stimulant m; (BIOL, PSYCH) stimulus m

sting [stɪŋ] (pt, pp **stung**) n piqûre f; (organ) dard m ♦ vt, vi piquer

stingy ['stɪndʒɪ] adj avare, pingre

stink [stɪŋk] (pt **stank**, pp **stunk**) n puanteur f ♦ vi puer, empester; ~**ing** (inf) adj (fig) infect(e), vache; **a** ~**ing** ... un(e) foutu(e) ...

stint [stɪnt] n part f de travail ♦ vi: **to** ~ **on** lésiner sur, être chiche de

stir [stɜ:*] n agitation f, sensation f ♦ vt remuer ♦ vi remuer, bouger; ~ **up** vt (trouble) fomenter, provoquer

stirrup ['stɪrəp] n étrier m

stitch [stɪtʃ] n (SEWING) point m; (KNITTING) maille f; (MED) point de suture; (pain) point de côté ♦ vt coudre, piquer; (MED) suturer

stoat [stəυt] n hermine f (avec son pelage d'été)

stock [stɔk] n réserve f, provision f; (COMM) stock m; (AGR) cheptel m, bétail m; (CULIN) bouillon m; (descent, origin) souche f; (FINANCE) valeurs fpl, titres mpl ♦ adj (fig: reply etc) classique ♦ vt (have in ~) avoir, vendre; ~**s and shares** valeurs (mobilières), titres; **in/out of** ~ en stock or en magasin/épuisé(e); **to take** ~ **of** (fig) faire le point de; ~ **up** vi: **to** ~ **up (with)** s'approvisionner (en); ~**broker** ['stɔkbrəυkə*] n agent m de change; ~ **cube** n bouillon-cube m; ~ **exchange** n Bourse f

stocking ['stɔkiŋ] n bas m

stock: ~ **market** n Bourse f, marché financier; ~ **phrase** n cliché m; ~**pile** n stock m, réserve f ♦ vt stocker, accumuler; ~**taking** (BRIT)

(COMM) inventaire *m*

stocky ['stɔkɪ] *adj* trapu(e), râblé(e)

stodgy ['stɔdʒɪ] *adj* bourratif(ive), lourd(e)

stoke [stəʊk] *vt (fire)* garnir, entretenir; *(boiler)* chauffer

stole [stəʊl] *pt of* steal ♦ *n* étole *f*

stolen ['stəʊlən] *pp of* steal

stolid ['stɔlɪd] *adj* impassible, flegmatique

stomach ['stʌmək] *n* estomac *m*; *(abdomen)* ventre *m* ♦ *vt* digérer, supporter; **~ache** *n* mal *m* à l'estomac *or* au ventre

stone [stəʊn] *n* pierre *f*; *(pebble)* caillou *m*, galet *m*; *(in fruit)* noyau *m*; *(MED)* calcul *m*; *(BRIT: weight)* = 6,348 *kg* ♦ *adj* de *or* en pierre ♦ *vt (person)* lancer des pierres sur, lapider; **~-cold** *adj* complètement froid(e); **~-deaf** *adj* sourd(e) comme un pot; **~work** *n* maçonnerie *f*

stood [stʊd] *pt, pp of* stand

stool [stu:l] *n* tabouret *m*

stoop [stu:p] *vi (also: have a ~)* être voûté(e); (: *~ down: bend)* se baisser

stop [stɔp] *n* arrêt *m*; halte *f*; *(in punctuation: also: full ~)* point *m* ♦ *vt* arrêter, bloquer; *(break off)* interrompre; *(also: put a ~ to)* mettre fin à ♦ *vi* s'arrêter; *(rain, noise etc)* cesser, s'arrêter; **to ~ doing sth** cesser *or* arrêter de faire qch; **~ dead** *vi* s'arrêter net; **~ off** *vi* faire une courte halte; **~ up** *vt (hole)* boucher; **~gap** *n (person)* bouche-trou *m*; *(measure)* mesure *f* intérimaire; **~over** *n* halte *f*; *(AVIAT)* escale *f*; **~page** ['stɔpɪdʒ] *n (strike)* arrêt de travail; *(blockage)* obstruction *f*; **~per** ['stɔpə*] *n* bouchon *m*; **~ press** *n* nouvelles *fpl* de dernière heure; **~watch** ['stɔpwɔtʃ] *n* chronomètre *m*

storage ['stɔːrɪdʒ] *n* entreposage *m*; **~ heater** *n* radiateur *m* électrique par accumulation

store [stɔː*] *n (stock)* provision *f*, réserve *f*; *(depot)* entrepôt *m*; *(BRIT: large shop)* grand magasin *m*; *(US)*

magasin *m* ♦ *vt* emmagasiner; *(information)* enregistrer; **~s** *npl (food)* provisions; **in ~** en réserve; **~ up** *vt* mettre en réserve; accumuler; **~room** *n* réserve *f*, magasin *m*

storey ['stɔːrɪ] *(US* **story**) *n* étage *m*

stork [stɔːk] *n* cigogne *f*

storm [stɔːm] *n* tempête *f*; *(thunder~)* orage *m* ♦ *vi (fig)* fulminer ♦ *vt* prendre d'assaut; **~y** *adj* orageux(euse)

story ['stɔːrɪ] *n* histoire *f*; récit *m*; *(US)* = **storey**; **~book** *n* livre *m* d'histoires *or* de contes

stout [staʊt] *adj* solide; *(fat)* gros(se), corpulent(e) ♦ *n* bière brune

stove [stəʊv] *n (for cooking)* fourneau *m*; (: *small)* réchaud *m*; *(for heating)* poêle *m*

stow [stəʊ] *vt (also: ~ away)* ranger; **~away** *n* passager(ère) clandestin(e)

straddle ['strædl] *vt* enjamber, être à cheval sur

straggle ['strægl] *vi* être *(or* marcher*)* en désordre; *(houses)* être disséminé(e)

straight [streɪt] *adj* droit(e); *(hair)* raide; *(frank)* honnête, franc(franche); *(simple)* simple ♦ *adv* (tout) droit; *(drink)* sec, sans eau; **to put** *or* **get ~** *(fig)* mettre au clair; **~ away, ~ off** *(at once)* tout de suite; **~en** *vt* ajuster; **~en out** *vt (fig)* débrouiller; **~-faced** *adj* impassible; **~forward** *adj* simple; *(honest)* honnête, direct(e)

strain [streɪn] *n* tension *f*; pression *f*; *(physical)* effort *m*; *(mental)* tension *f* (nerveuse); *(breed)* race *f* ♦ *vt (stretch: resources etc)* mettre à rude épreuve, grever; *(hurt: back etc)* se faire mal à; *(vegetables)* égoutter; **~s** *npl (MUS)* accords *mpl*, accents *mpl*; **back ~** tour *m* de rein; **~ed** *adj (muscle)* froissé(e); *(laugh etc)* forcé(e), contraint(e); *(relations)* tendu(e); **~er** *n* passoire *f*

strait [streɪt] *n (GEO)* détroit *m*; **~s**

npl: **to be in dire ~s** avoir de sérieux ennuis (d'argent); (*of rope*) toron *m*; (*of hair*) mèche *f*; **~ed** *adj* en rade, en plan

strange [streɪndʒ] *adj* (*not known*) inconnu(e); (*odd*) étrange, bizarre; **~ly** *adv* étrangement, bizarrement; *see also* **enough**; **~r** *n* inconnu(e); (*from another area*) étranger/ère

strangle ['stræŋgl] *vt* étrangler; **~hold** *n* (*fig*) emprise totale, mainmise *f*

strap [stræp] *n* lanière *f*, courroie *f*, sangle *f*; (*of slip, dress*) bretelle *f*

strapping ['stræpɪŋ] *adj* costaud(e)

strategic [strə'tiːdʒɪk] *adj* stratégique; **strategy** ['strætədʒɪ] *n* stratégie *f*

straw [strɔː] *n* paille *f*; **that's the last ~!** ça, c'est le comble!

strawberry ['strɔːbərɪ] *n* fraise *f*

stray [streɪ] *adj* (*animal*) perdu(e), errant(e); (*scattered*) isolé(e) ♦ *vi* s'égarer; **~ bullet** *n* balle perdue

streak [striːk] *n* bande *f*, filet *m*; (*in hair*) raie *f* ♦ *vt* zébrer, strier ♦ *vi*: **to ~ past** passer à toute allure

stream [striːm] *n* ruisseau *m*, courant *m*, flot *m*; (*of people*) défilé ininterrompu, flot *f* ♦ *vt* (*SCOL*) répartir par niveau ♦ *vi* ruisseler; **to ~ in/out** entrer/sortir à flots; **~er** ['striːmə*] *n* serpentin *m*; (*banner*) banderole *f*; **~lined** *adj* aérodynamique; (*fig*) rationalisé(e)

street [striːt] *n* rue *f*; **~car** (*US*) *n* tramway *m*; **~ lamp** *n* réverbère *m*; **~ plan** *n* plan *m* (des rues); **~wise** (*inf*) *adj* futé(e), réaliste

strength [streŋθ] *n* force *f*; (*of girder, knot etc*) solidité *f*; **~en** *vt* fortifier; renforcer; consolider

strenuous ['strenjuəs] *adj* vigoureux(euse), énergique

stress [stres] *n* (*force, pressure*) pression *f*; (*mental strain*) tension (nerveuse), stress *m*; (*accent*) accent *m* ♦ *vt* insister sur, souligner

stretch [stretʃ] *n* (*of sand etc*) étendue *f* ♦ *vi* s'étirer; (*extend*): **to ~ to** *or* **as far as** s'étendre jusqu'à ♦ *vt* tendre, étirer; (*fig*) pousser (au maximum); **~ out** *vi* s'étendre ♦ *vt* (*arm etc*) allonger, tendre; (*spread*) étendre

stretcher ['stretʃə*] *n* brancard *m*, civière *f*

strewn [struːn] *adj*: **~ with** jonché(e) de

stricken ['strɪkən] *adj* (*person*) très éprouvé(e); (*city, industry etc*) dévasté(e); **~ with** (*disease etc*) frappé(e) or atteint(e) de

strict [strɪkt] *adj* strict(e)

stride [straɪd] (*pt* strode, *pp* stridden) *n* grand pas, enjambée *f* ♦ *vi* marcher à grands pas

strife [straɪf] *n* conflit *m*, dissensions *fpl*

strike [straɪk] (*pt, pp* struck) *n* grève *f*; (*of oil etc*) découverte *f*; (*attack*) raid *m* ♦ *vt* frapper; (*oil etc*) trouver, découvrir; (*deal*) conclure ♦ *vi* faire grève; (*attack*) attaquer; (*clock*) sonner; **on ~** (*workers*) en grève; **to ~ a match** frotter une allumette; **~ down** *vt* terrasser; **~ up** *vt* (*MUS*) se mettre à jouer; **to ~ up a friendship with** se lier d'amitié avec; **to ~ up a conversation (with)** engager une conversation (avec); **~r** *n* gréviste *m/f*; (*SPORT*) buteur *m*; **striking** ['straɪkɪŋ] *adj* frappant(e), saisissant(e); (*attractive*) éblouissant(e)

string [strɪŋ] (*pt, pp* strung) *n* ficelle *f*; (*row: of beads*) rang *m*; (: *of onions*) chapelet *m*; (*MUS*) corde *f* ♦ *vt*: **to ~ out** échelonner; **the ~s** *npl* (*MUS*) les instruments *mpl* à cordes; **to ~ together** enchaîner; **to pull ~s** (*fig*) faire jouer le piston; **~ bean** *n* haricot vert; **~(ed) instrument** *n* (*MUS*) instrument *m* à cordes

stringent ['strɪndʒənt] *adj* rigoureux(euse)

strip [strɪp] *n* bande *f* ♦ *vt* (*undress*) déshabiller; (*paint*) décaper; (*also:* ~ **down**: *machine*) démonter ♦ *vi* se déshabiller; ~ **cartoon** *n* bande dessinée

stripe [straɪp] *n* raie *f*, rayure *f*; (*MIL*) galon *m*; ~**d** *adj* rayé(e), à rayures

strip lighting (*BRIT*) *n* éclairage *m* au néon *or* fluorescent

stripper ['strɪpə*] *n* strip-teaseur(euse) *f*

strive [straɪv] (*pt* strove, *pp* striven) *vi*: to ~ to do/for sth s'efforcer de faire/d'obtenir qch

strode [strəud] *pt of* stride

stroke [strəuk] *n* coup *m*; (*SWIMMING*) nage *f*; (*MED*) attaque *f* ♦ *vt* caresser; at a ~ d'un (seul) coup

stroll [strəul] *n* petite promenade ♦ *vi* flâner, se promener nonchalamment; ~**er** (*US*) *n* (*pushchair*) poussette *f*

strong [strɒŋ] *adj* fort(e), vigoureux(euse); (*heart, nerves*) solide; they are 50 ~ ils sont au nombre de 50; ~**hold** *n* bastion *m*; ~**ly** *adv* fortement, avec force; vigoureusement; solidement; ~**room** *n* chambre forte

strove [strəuv] *pt of* strive

struck [strʌk] *pt, pp of* strike

structural ['strʌktʃərəl] *adj* structural(e); (*CONSTR*: *defect*) de construction; (*damage*) affectant les parties portantes

structure ['strʌktʃə*] *n* structure *f*; (*building*) construction *f*

struggle ['strʌgl] *n* lutte *f* ♦ *vi* lutter, se battre

strum [strʌm] *vt* (*guitar*) jouer (en sourdine)

strung [strʌŋ] *pt, pp of* string

strut [strʌt] *n* étai *m*, support *m* ♦ *vi* se pavaner

stub [stʌb] *n* (*of cigarette*) bout *m*, mégot *m*; (*of cheque etc*) talon *m* ♦ *vt*: to ~ one's toe se cogner le doigt de pied; ~ **out** *vt* écraser

stubble ['stʌbl] *n* chaume *m*; (*on chin*) barbe *f* de plusieurs jours

stubborn ['stʌbən] *adj* têtu(e), obstiné(e), opiniâtre

stuck [stʌk] *pt, pp of* stick ♦ *adj* (*jammed*) bloqué(e), coincé(e); ~-**up** (*inf*) *adj* prétentieux(euse)

stud [stʌd] *n* (*on boots etc*) clou *m*; (*on collar*) bouton *m* de col; (*earring*) petite boucle d'oreille; (*of horses:* also: ~ *farm*) écurie *f*, haras *m*; (*also:* ~ *horse*) étalon *m* ♦ *vt* (*fig*): ~**ded with** parsemé(e) *or* criblé(e) de

student ['stjuːdənt] *n* étudiant(e) ♦ *adj* estudiantin(e); d'étudiant; ~ **driver** (*US*) *n* (*conducteur(trice) débutant(e)

studio ['stjuːdɪəu] *n* studio *m*, atelier *m*; (*TV etc*) studio

studious ['stjuːdɪəs] *adj* studieux(euse), appliqué(e); (*attention*) soutenu(e); ~**ly** *adv* (*carefully*) soigneusement

study ['stʌdɪ] *n* étude *f*; (*room*) bureau *m* ♦ *vt* étudier; (*examine*) examiner ♦ *vi* étudier, faire ses études

stuff [stʌf] *n* chose(s) *f(pl)*; *affaires fpl*, trucs *mpl*; (*substance*) substance *f* ♦ *vt* rembourrer; (*CULIN*) farcir; (*inf*: *push*) fourrer; ~**ing** *n* bourre *f*, rembourrage *m*; (*CULIN*) farce *f*; ~**y** *adj* (*room*) mal ventilé(e) *or* aéré(e); (*ideas*) vieux jeu *inv*

stumble ['stʌmbl] *vi* trébucher; to ~ across *or* on (*fig*) tomber sur; **stumbling block** *n* pierre *f* d'achoppement

stump [stʌmp] *n* souche *f*; (*of limb*) moignon *m* ♦ *vt*: to be ~**ed** sécher, ne pas savoir que répondre

stun [stʌn] *vt* étourdir; abasourdir

stung [stʌŋ] *pt, pp of* sting

stunk [stʌŋk] *pp of* stink

stunning *adj* (*news etc*) stupéfiant(e); (*girl etc*) éblouissant(e)

stunt [stʌnt] *n* (*in film*) cascade *f*, acrobatie *f*; (*publicity*) ~ truc *m* publicitaire ♦ *vt* retarder, arrêter(r) ~**ed** *adj* rabougri(e); (*growth*) retardé(e); ~**man** (*irreg*) *n* cascadeur *m*

stupendous [stju'pendəs] adj prodigieux(euse), fantastique

stupid ['stju:pɪd] adj stupide, bête; **~ity** n stupidité f, bêtise f

sturdy ['stɜ:dɪ] adj robuste; solide

stutter ['stʌtə*] vi bégayer

sty [staɪ] n (for pigs) porcherie f

stye [staɪ] n (MED) orgelet m

style [staɪl] n style m; (distinction) allure f, cachet m, style; **stylish** ['staɪlɪʃ] adj élégant(e), chic inv

stylus ['staɪləs] (pl styli or ~es) n (of record player) pointe f de lecture

suave [swɑ:v] adj doucereux(euse), onctueux(euse)

sub... [sʌb] prefix sub..., sous-; **~conscious** adj subconscient(e); **~contract** vt sous-traiter

subdue [səb'dju:] vt subjuguer, soumettre; **~d** adj (light) tamisé(e); (person) qui a perdu de son entrain

subject [n 'sʌbdʒɪkt, vb səb'dʒɛkt] n sujet m; (SCOL) matière f ♦ vt: to ~ to soumettre à; exposer à; to be ~ to (law) être soumis(e) à; (disease) être sujet(te) à; **~ive** [səb'dʒɛktɪv] adj subjectif(ive); **~ matter** n (content) contenu m

sublet ['sʌb'lɛt] vt sous-louer

submarine [sʌbmə'ri:n] n sous-marin m

submerge [səb'mɜ:dʒ] vt submerger ♦ vi plonger

submission [səb'mɪʃən] n soumission f; **submissive** [səb'mɪsɪv] adj soumis(e)

submit [səb'mɪt] vt soumettre ♦ vi se soumettre

subnormal [sʌb'nɔ:məl] adj au-dessous de la normale

subordinate [sə'bɔ:dɪnət] adj subalterne ♦ n subordonné(e)

subpoena [səb'pi:nə] n (LAW) citation f, assignation f

subscribe [səb'skraɪb] vi cotiser; to ~ to (opinion, fund) souscrire à; (newspaper) s'abonner à; être abonné(e) à; **~r** n (to periodical, telephone) abonné(e); **subscription** [səb'skrɪpʃən] n (to magazine etc) abonne-

ment m

subsequent ['sʌbsɪkwənt] adj ultérieur(e), suivant(e); consécutif(ive); **~ly** adv par la suite

subside [səb'saɪd] vi (flood) baisser; (wind, feelings) tomber; **~nce** [səb'saɪdəns] n affaissement m

subsidiary [səb'sɪdɪərɪ] adj subsidiaire, accessoire ♦ n (also: ~ company) filiale f

subsidize ['sʌbsɪdaɪz] vt subventionner; **subsidy** ['sʌbsɪdɪ] n subvention f

substance ['sʌbstəns] n substance f

substantial [səb'stænʃəl] adj substantiel(le); (fig) important(e); **~ly** adv considérablement; (in essence) en grande partie

substantiate [səb'stænʃɪeɪt] vt étayer, fournir des preuves à l'appui de

substitute ['sʌbstɪtju:t] n (person) remplaçant(e); (thing) succédané m ♦ vt: to ~ sth/sb for substituer qch/qn à, remplacer par qch/qn

subterranean [sʌbtə'reɪnɪən] adj souterrain(e)

subtitle ['sʌbtaɪtl] n (CINEMA) sous-titre m

subtle ['sʌtl] adj subtil(e)

subtotal [sʌb'təʊtl] n total partiel

subtract [səb'trækt] vt soustraire, retrancher; **~ion** n soustraction f

suburb ['sʌbɜ:b] n faubourg m; the **~s** npl la banlieue; **~an** [sə'bɜ:bən] adj de banlieue, suburbain(e); **~ia** [sə'bɜ:bɪə] n la banlieue

subway ['sʌbweɪ] n (US: railway) métro m; (BRIT: underpass) passage souterrain

succeed [sək'si:d] vi réussir ♦ vt succéder à; to ~ in doing réussir à faire; **~ing** adj (following) suivant(e)

success [sək'sɛs] n succès m; réussite f; **~ful** adj (venture) couronné(e) de succès; to be **~ful** (in doing) réussir (à faire); **~fully** adv avec succès

succession [sək'sɛʃən] n succession f; 3 days in ~ 3 jours de suite

successive [sək'sɛsɪv] *adj* successif(ive); consécutif(ive)

such [sʌtʃ] *adj* tel(telle); (*of that kind*): ~ **a book** un livre de genre, un livre pareil, un tel livre; (*so much*): ~ **courage** un tel courage ♦ *adv* si; ~ **books** des livres de ce genre, des livres pareils, de tels livres; ~ **a long trip** un si long voyage; ~ **a lot of** tellement or tant de; ~ **as** (*like*) tel que, comme; **as** ~ en tant que tel, à proprement parler; **~-and-such** *adj* tel ou tel

suck [sʌk] *vt* sucer; (*breast, bottle*) téter; **~er** *n* ventouse *f*; (*inf*) poire *f*

suction [sʌkʃən] *n* succion *f*

sudden [sʌdn] *adj* soudain(e), subit(e); **all of a** ~ soudain, tout à coup; **~ly** *adv* brusquement, tout à coup, soudain

suds [sʌdz] *npl* eau savonneuse

sue [su:] *vt* poursuivre en justice, intenter un procès à

suede [sweɪd] *n* daim *m*

suet [suɪt] *n* graisse *f* de rognon

suffer [sʌfə*] *vt* souffrir, subir; (*bear*) tolérer, supporter ♦ *vi* souffrir; **~er** *n* (MED) malade *m/f*; **~ing** *n* souffrance(s) *f(pl)*

sufficient [sə'fɪʃənt] *adj* suffisant(e); ~ **money** suffisamment d'argent; **~ly** *adv* suffisamment, assez

suffocate [sʌfəkeɪt] *vi* suffoquer; étouffer

sugar [ʃʊgə*] *n* sucre *m* ♦ *vt* sucrer; ~ **beet** *n* betterave sucrière; ~ **cane** *n* canne *f* à sucre

suggest [sə'dʒɛst] *vt* suggérer, proposer; (*indicate*) dénoter; **~ion** *n* suggestion *f*

suicide [suɪsaɪd] *n* suicide *m*; *see also* commit

suit [su:t] *n* (*man's*) costume *m*, complet *m*; (*woman's*) tailleur *m*, ensemble *m*; (LAW) poursuite(s) *f(pl)*, procès *m*; (CARDS) couleur *f* ♦ *vt* aller à; convenir à; (*adapt*): **to** ~ **sth to** adapter or approprier qch à; **well ~ed** (*couple*) faits l'un pour l'autre, très bien assortis; **~able** *adj*

qui convient; approprié(e); **~ably** *adv* comme il se doit (or se devait etc), convenablement

suitcase [su:tkeɪs] *n* valise *f*

suite [swi:t] *n* (*of rooms, also* MUS) suite *f*; (*furniture*): **bedroom/dining room** ~ (ensemble *m* de) chambre *f* à coucher/salle *f* à manger

suitor [su:tə*] *n* soupirant *m*, prétendant *m*

sulfur [sʌlfə*] (US) *n* = sulphur

sulk [sʌlk] *vi* bouder; **~y** *adj* boudeur(euse), maussade

sullen [sʌlən] *adj* renfrogné(e), maussade

sulphur [sʌlfə*] (US **sulfur**) *n* soufre *m*

sultana [sʌl'tɑ:nə] *n* (CULIN) raisin (sec) de Smyrne

sultry [sʌltrɪ] *adj* étouffant(e)

sum [sʌm] *n* somme *f*; (SCOL etc) calcul *m*; ~ **up** *vt, vi* résumer

summarize [sʌməraɪz] *vt* résumer

summary [sʌmərɪ] *n* résumé *m*

summer [sʌmə*] *n* été *m* ♦ *adj* d'été, estival(e); **~house** *n* (*in garden*) pavillon *m*; **~time** *n* été *m*; **~time** *n* (*by clock*) heure *f* d'été

summit [sʌmɪt] *n* sommet *m*

summon [sʌmən] *vt* appeler, convoquer; ~ **up** *vt* rassembler, faire appel à; **~s** *n* citation *f*, assignation *f*

sump [sʌmp] (BRIT) *n* (AUT) carter *m*

sun [sʌn] *n* soleil *m*; **in the** ~ au soleil; **~bathe** *vi* prendre un bain de soleil; **~burn** *n* coup *m* de soleil; **~burned** *adj* = **sunburnt**; **~burnt** *adj* (*tanned*) bronzé(e)

Sunday [sʌndeɪ] *n* dimanche *m*; ~ **school** *n* catéchisme *m*

sundial [sʌndaɪəl] *n* cadran *m* solaire

sundown [sʌndaʊn] *n* coucher *m* du (or du) soleil

sundries [sʌndrɪz] *npl* articles divers

sundry [sʌndrɪ] *adj* divers(e), différent(e) ♦ *n*: **all and** ~ tout le monde, n'importe qui

sunflower ['sʌnflauə*] n tournesol m

sung [sʌŋ] pp of **sing**

sunglasses ['sʌnglɑ:sɪz] npl lunettes fpl de soleil

sunk [sʌŋk] pp of **sink**

sun: ~light ['sʌnlaɪt] n (lumière f du) soleil m; ~lit adj ensoleillé(e); ~ny adj ensoleillé(e); ~rise n lever m du (or de) soleil; ~ roof n (AUT) toit ouvrant; ~set n coucher m du (or de) soleil; ~shade n (over table) parasol m; ~shine n (lumière f du) soleil m; ~stroke n insolation f; ~tan n bronzage m; ~tan lotion n lotion f or huile f solaire; ~tan oil n huile f solaire

super ['su:pə*] (inf) adj formidable

superannuation ['su:pərænju'eɪʃən] n (contribution) cotisations fpl pour la pension

superb [su:'pɜ:b] adj superbe, magnifique

supercilious [su:pə'sɪlɪəs] adj hautain(e), dédaigneux(euse)

superficial [su:pə'fɪʃəl] adj superficiel(le)

superimpose [su:pərɪm'pəuz] vt superposer

superintendent [su:pərɪn'tendənt] n directeur(trice), (POLICE) ≈ commissaire m

superior [su'pɪərɪə*] adj, n supérieur(e); ~ity [supɪərɪ'ɒrɪtɪ] n supériorité f

superlative [su:'pɜ:lətɪv] n (LING) superlatif m

superman ['su:pəmæn] (irreg) n surhomme m

supermarket ['su:pəmɑ:kɪt] n supermarché m

supernatural [su:pə'nætʃərəl] adj surnaturel(le)

superpower ['su:pəpauə*] n (POL) superpuissance f

supersede [su:pə'si:d] vt remplacer, supplanter

superstitious [su:pə'stɪʃəs] adj superstitieux(euse)

supervise ['su:pəvaɪz] vt surveiller; diriger; **supervision** [su:pə'vɪʒən] n

surveillance f; contrôle m; **supervisor** n surveillant(e); (in shop) chef m de rayon

supine ['su:paɪn] adj couché(e) or étendu(e) sur le dos

supper ['sʌpə*] n dîner m; (late) souper m

supple ['sʌpl] adj souple

supplement [n 'sʌplɪmənt, vb sʌplɪ'ment] n supplément m ♦ vt compléter; ~ary [sʌplɪ'mentərɪ] adj supplémentaire; ~ary benefit (BRIT) n allocation f (supplémentaire) d'aide sociale

supplier [sə'plaɪə*] n fournisseur m

supply [sə'plaɪ] vt (provide) fournir; (equip): **to ~ (with)** approvisionner or ravitailler (en); fournir (en) provision f, réserve f; (~ing) approvisionnement m; supplies npl (food) vivres mpl; (MIL) subsistances fpl; ~ **teacher** (BRIT) n suppléant(e)

support [sə'pɔ:t] n (moral, financial etc) soutien m, appui m; (TECH) support m, soutien ♦ vt soutenir, supporter; (financially) subvenir aux besoins de; (uphold) être pour, être partisan de, appuyer; ~**er** n (POL etc) partisan(e); (SPORT) supporter m

suppose [sə'pəuz] vt supposer; imaginer; **to be ~d to do** être censé(e) faire; ~**dly** [sə'pəuzɪdlɪ] adv soi-disant; **supposing** [sə'pəuzɪŋ] conj si, à supposer que +sub

suppress [sə'pres] vt (revolt) réprimer; (information) supprimer; (yawn) étouffer; (feelings) refouler

supreme [su:'pri:m] adj suprême

surcharge ['sɜ:tʃɑ:dʒ] n surcharge f

sure [ʃuə*] adj sûr(e); (definite, convinced) sûr, certain(e); ~! (of course) bien sûr!; ~ **enough** effectivement; **to make ~ of sth** s'assurer de or vérifier qch; **to make ~ that** s'assurer or vérifier que; ~**ly** adv sûrement; certainement

surety ['ʃuərɪtɪ] n caution f

surf [sɜ:f] n (waves) ressac m

surface ['sɜ:fɪs] n surface f ♦ vt (road) poser un revêtement sur ♦

remonter à la surface; faire surface; ~ **mail** n courrier m par voie de terre (or maritime)

surfboard ['sɜːfbɔːd] n planche f de surf

surfeit ['sɜːfɪt] n: a ~ of un excès de; une indigestion de

surfing ['sɜːfɪŋ] n surf m

surge [sɜːdʒ] n vague f, montée f ♦ vi déferler

surgeon ['sɜːdʒən] n chirurgien m

surgery ['sɜːdʒərɪ] n chirurgie f; (BRIT: room) cabinet m (de consultation); (: also: ~ hours) heures fpl de consultation

surgical ['sɜːdʒɪkəl] adj chirurgical(e); ~ **spirit** (BRIT) n alcool m à 90°

surly ['sɜːlɪ] adj revêche, maussade

surname ['sɜːneɪm] n nom m de famille

surplus ['sɜːpləs] n surplus m, excédent m ♦ adj en surplus, de trop; (COMM) excédentaire

surprise [sə'praɪz] n surprise f; (astonishment) étonnement m ♦ vt surprendre; (astonish) étonner; **surprising** [sə'praɪzɪŋ] adj surprenant(e), étonnant(e); **surprisingly** adv (easy, helpful) étonnamment

surrender [sə'rendə*] n reddition f, capitulation f ♦ vi se rendre, capituler

surreptitious [sʌrəp'tɪʃəs] adj subreptice, furtif(ive)

surrogate ['sʌrəgeɪt] n substitut m; ~ **mother** n mère porteuse or de substitution

surround [sə'raund] vt entourer; (MIL etc) encercler; ~**ing** adj environnant(e); ~**ings** npl environs mpl, alentours mpl

surveillance [sɜː'veɪləns] n surveillance f

survey [n 'sɜːveɪ, vb sɜː'veɪ] n enquête f, étude f; (in housebuying etc) inspection f, (rapport m d')expertise f; (of land) levé m ♦ vt enquêter sur; inspecter; (look at) embrasser du regard; ~**or** [sə'veɪə*] n (of hou-

se) expert m; (of land) (arpenteur m) géomètre m

survival [sə'vaɪvl] n survie f; (relic) vestige m

survive [sə'vaɪv] vi survivre; (custom etc) subsister ♦ vt survivre à; **survivor** [sə'vaɪvə*] n survivant(e); (fig) battant(e)

susceptible [sə'sɛptəbl] adj: ~ (to) sensible (à); (disease) prédisposé(e) (à)

suspect [n, adj 'sʌspɛkt, vb səs'pɛkt] adj, n suspect(e) ♦ vt soupçonner, suspecter

suspend [səs'pɛnd] vt suspendre; ~**ed sentence** n condamnation f avec sursis; ~**er belt** n porte-jarretelles m inv; ~**ers** npl (BRIT) jarretelles fpl; (US) bretelles fpl

suspense [səs'pɛns] n attente f, incertitude f; (in film etc) suspense m

suspension [səs'pɛnʃən] n suspension f; (of driving licence) retrait m provisoire; ~ **bridge** n pont suspendu

suspicion [səs'pɪʃən] n soupçon(s) m(pl)

suspicious [səs'pɪʃəs] adj (suspecting) soupçonneux(euse), méfiant(e); (causing suspicion) suspect(e)

sustain [səs'teɪn] vt soutenir; (food etc) nourrir, donner des forces à; (suffer) subir; recevoir; ~**able** adj (development, growth etc) viable; ~**ed** adj (effort) soutenu(e), prolongé(e)

sustenance ['sʌstɪnəns] n nourriture f; (money) moyens mpl de subsistance

swab [swɔb] n (MED) tampon m

swagger ['swægə*] vi plastronner

swallow ['swɔləʊ] n (bird) hirondelle f ♦ vt avaler; ~ **up** vt engloutir

swam [swæm] pt of swim

swamp [swɔmp] n marais m, marécage m ♦ vt submerger

swan [swɔn] n cygne m

swap [swɔp] vt: to ~ (for) échanger (contre), troquer (contre)

swarm [swɔːm] n essaim m ♦ vi fourmiller, grouiller

swarthy ['swɔːðɪ] *adj* basané(e), bistré(e)

swastika ['swɒstɪkə] *n* croix gammée

swat [swɒt] *vt* écraser

sway [sweɪ] *vi* se balancer, osciller ♦ *vt* (*influence*) influencer

swear [swɛə*] (*pt* swore, *pp* sworn) *vt*, *vi* jurer; **~word** *n* juron *m*, gros mot

sweat [swɛt] *n* sueur *f*, transpiration *f* ♦ *vi* suer

sweater ['swɛtə*] *n* tricot *m*, pull *m*

sweaty ['swɛtɪ] *adj* en sueur, moite or mouillé(e) de sueur

Swede [swiːd] *n* Suédois(e)

swede [swiːd] (*BRIT*) *n* rutabaga *m*

Sweden ['swiːdn] *n* Suède *f*; **Swedish** ['swiːdɪʃ] *adj* suédois(e) ♦ *n* (*LING*) suédois *m*

sweep [swiːp] (*pt*, *pp* swept) *n* coup *m* de balai; (*also*: *chimney* ~) ramoneur *m* ♦ *vt* balayer; (*subj*: *current*) emporter ♦ *vi* (*hand*, *arm*) faire un mouvement; (*wind*) souffler; ~ **away** *vt* balayer; entraîner; emporter; ~ **past** *vi* passer majestueusement *or* rapidement; ~ **up** *vi* balayer; ~**ing** *adj* (*gesture*) large; circulaire; **a** ~**ing statement** une généralisation hâtive

sweet [swiːt] *n* (*candy*) bonbon *m*; (*BRIT*: *pudding*) dessert *m* ♦ *adj* doux(douce); (*not savoury*) sucré(e); (*fig*: *kind*) gentil(le); (*baby*) mignon(ne); ~**corn** *n* maïs *m*; ~**en** *vt* adoucir; (*with sugar*) sucrer; ~**heart** *n* amoureux(euse); ~**ness** *n* goût sucré; douceur *f*; ~**pea** *n* pois *m* de senteur

swell [swɛl] (*pt* swelled, *pp* swollen *or* ~ed) *n* (*of sea*) houle *f* ♦ *adj* (*US*: *inf*: *excellent*) chouette ♦ *vi* grossir, augmenter; (*sound*) s'enfler; (*MED*) enfler; ~**ing** *n* (*MED*) enflure *f*; (*lump*) grosseur *f*

sweltering ['swɛltərɪŋ] *adj* étouffant(e), oppressant(e)

swept [swɛpt] *pt*, *pp* of sweep

swerve [swɜːv] *vi* faire une embar-

dée *or* un écart; dévier

swift [swɪft] *n* (*bird*) martinet *m* ♦ *adj* rapide, prompt(e)

swig [swɪg] (*inf*) *n* (*drink*) lampée *f*

swill [swɪl] *n* (*also*: ~ *out*, ~ *down*) laver à grande eau

swim [swɪm] (*pt* swam, *pp* swum) *n*: **to go for a** ~ aller nager *or* se baigner ♦ *vi* nager; (*SPORT*) faire de la natation; (*head*, *room*) tourner ♦ *vt* traverser (à la nage); (*a length*) faire (à la nage); ~**mer** *n* nageur(euse); ~**ming** *n* natation *f*; ~**ming cap** *n* bonnet *m* de bain; ~**ming costume** (*BRIT*) *n* maillot *m* (de bain); ~**ming pool** *n* piscine *f*; ~**ming trunks** *npl* caleçon *m* or slip *m* de bain; ~**suit** *n* maillot *m* (de bain)

swindle ['swɪndl] *n* escroquerie *f*

swine [swaɪn] (*inf!*) *n inv* salaud *m* (!)

swing [swɪŋ] (*pt*, *pp* swung) *n* balançoire *f*; (*movement*) balancement *m*, oscillations *fpl*; (*MUS*: *also*: *rhythm*) rythme *m*; (*change*: *in opinion etc*) revirement *m* ♦ *vt* balancer, faire osciller; (*also*: ~ *round*) tourner, faire virer ♦ *vi* se balancer, osciller; (*also*: ~ *round*) virer, tourner; **to be in full** ~ battre son plein; ~ **bridge** *n* pont tournant; ~ **door** (*US* ~**ing door**) *n* porte battante

swingeing ['swɪndʒɪŋ] (*BRIT*) *adj* écrasant(e); (*cuts etc*) considérable

swipe [swaɪp] (*inf*) *vt* (*steal*) piquer

swirl [swɜːl] *vi* tourbillonner, tournoyer

swish [swɪʃ] *vi* (*tail*) remuer; (*clothes*) froufrouter

Swiss [swɪs] *adj* suisse ♦ *n inv* Suisse *m/f*

switch [swɪtʃ] *n* (*for light*, *radio etc*) bouton *m*; (*change*) changement *m*, revirement *m* ♦ *vt* changer; ~ **off** *vt* éteindre; (*engine*) arrêter; ~ **on** *vt* allumer; (*engine*, *machine*) mettre en marche; ~**board** *n* (*TEL*) standard *m*

Switzerland ['switsələnd] n Suisse f
swivel ['swivl] vi (also: ~ round) pivoter, tourner
swollen ['swəʊlən] pp of swell
swoon [swu:n] vi se pâmer
swoop [swu:p] n (by police) descente ♦ vi (also: ~ down) descendre en piqué, piquer
swop [swɔp] vt = swap
sword [sɔ:d] n épée f; ~**fish** n espadon m
swore [swɔ:ʳ] pt of swear
sworn [swɔ:n] pp of swear ♦ adj (statement, evidence) donné(e) sous serment
swot [swɔt] vi bûcher, potasser
swum [swʌm] pp of swim
swung [swʌŋ] pt, pp of swing
syllable ['sɪləbl] n syllabe f
syllabus ['sɪləbəs] n programme m
symbol ['sɪmbl] n symbole m
symmetry ['sɪmɪtrɪ] n symétrie f
sympathetic [sɪmpə'θɛtɪk] adj compatissant(e); bienveillant(e), compréhensif(ive); (likeable) sympathique; ~ **towards** bien disposé(e) envers
sympathize ['sɪmpəθaɪz] vi: to ~ **with sb** plaindre qn; (in grief) s'associer à la douleur de qn; to ~ **with sth** comprendre qch; ~**r** n (POL) sympathisant(e)
sympathy ['sɪmpəθɪ] n (pity) compassion f; **sympathies** npl (support) soutien m; **left-wing** etc **sympathies** penchants mpl à gauche etc; **in** ~ **with** (strike) en or par solidarité avec; **with our deepest** ~ en vous priant d'accepter nos sincères condoléances
symphony ['sɪmfənɪ] n symphonie f
symptom ['sɪmptəm] n symptôme m; indice m
syndicate ['sɪndɪkət] n syndicat m, coopérative f
synonym ['sɪnənɪm] n synonyme m
synopsis [sɪ'nɔpsɪs, pl -siːz] (pl synopses) n résumé m
syntax ['sɪntæks] n syntaxe f
synthetic [sɪn'θɛtɪk] adj synthétique
syphon ['saɪfən] n, vb = siphon

Syria ['sɪrɪə] n Syrie f
syringe [sɪ'rɪndʒ] n seringue f
syrup ['sɪrəp] n sirop m; (also: golden ~) mélasse raffinée
system ['sɪstəm] n système m; (ANAT) organisme m; ~**atic** [sɪstə'mætɪk] adj systématique; méthodique; ~ **disk** n (COMPUT) disque m système; ~**s analyst** n analyste fonctionnel(le)

T

ta [tɑː] (BRIT: inf) excl merci!
tab [tæb] n (label) étiquette f; (on drinks can etc) languette f; **to keep** ~**s on** (fig) surveiller
tabby ['tæbɪ] n (also: ~ **cat**) chat(te) tigré(e)
table ['teɪbl] n table f ♦ vt (BRIT: motion etc) présenter; **to lay** or **set the** ~ mettre le couvert or la table; ~**cloth** [-klɔθ] n nappe f; ~ **d'hôte** ['tɑːbl'dəʊt] adj (meal) à prix fixe; ~ **lamp** n lampe f de table; ~**mat** [-tɛɪblmæt] n (for plate) napperon m, set m; (for hot dish) dessous-de-plat m inv; ~ **of contents** n table f des matières; ~**spoon** ['teɪblspuːn] n cuiller f de service; (also: ~**spoonful**: as measurement) cuillerée f à soupe
tablet ['tæblɪt] n (MED) comprimé m; (of stone) plaque f
table tennis n ping-pong m ®, tennis m de table
table wine n vin m de table
tabloid ['tæblɔɪd] n quotidien m populaire
tabulate ['tæbjʊleɪt] vt (data, figures) présenter sous forme de table(s)
tack [tæk] n (nail) petit clou m; (fig) direction f; (BRIT: stitch) faufiler ♦ vi tirer un or des bord(s)
tackle ['tækl] n matériel m, équipement m; (for lifting) appareil m de levage; (RUGBY) plaquage m ♦ vt (difficulty, animal, burglar etc) s'attaquer à; (person: challenge) s'expli-

quer avec; (*RUGBY*) plaquer

tacky ['tækɪ] *adj* collant(e); (*pej: of poor quality*) miteux(euse)

tact [tækt] *n* tact *m*; **~ful** *adj* plein(e) de tact

tactical ['tæktɪkəl] *adj* tactique

tactics ['tæktɪks] *npl* tactique *f*

tactless ['tæktləs] *adj* qui manque de tact

tadpole ['tædpəʊl] *n* têtard *m*

taffy ['tæfɪ] (*US*) *n* (bonbon *m* au) caramel *m*

tag [tæg] *n* étiquette *f*; **~ along** *vi* suivre

tail [teɪl] *n* queue *f*; (*of shirt*) pan *m* ♦ *vt* (*follow*) suivre, filer; **~s** *npl* habit *m*; **~ away**, **~ off** *vi* (*in size, quality etc*) baisser peu à peu; **~back** (*BRIT*) *n* (*AUT*) bouchon *m*; **~ end** *n* bout *m*, fin *f*; **~gate** *n* (*AUT*) hayon *m* arrière

tailor ['teɪlə*] *n* tailleur *m*; **~ing** *n* (*cut*) coupe *f*; **~-made** *adj* fait(e) sur mesure; (*fig*) conçu(e) spécialement

tailwind ['teɪlwɪnd] *n* vent *m* arrière *inv*

tainted ['teɪntɪd] *adj* (*food*) gâté(e); (*water, air*) infecté(e); (*fig*) souillé(e)

take [teɪk] (*pt* **took**, *pp* **taken**) *vt* prendre; (*gain: prize*) remporter; (*require: effort, courage*) demander; (*tolerate*) accepter, supporter; (*hold: passengers etc*) contenir; (*accompany*) emmener, accompagner; (*bring, carry*) apporter, emporter; (*exam*) passer, se présenter à; **to ~ sth from** (*drawer etc*) prendre qch à; **I ~ it that ...** je suppose que ...; **~ after** *vt fus* ressembler à; **~ apart** *vt* démonter; **~ away** *vt* enlever; (*carry off*) emporter; **~ back** *vt* (*return*) rendre, rapporter; (*one's words*) retirer; **~ down** *vt* (*building*) démolir; (*letter etc*) prendre, écrire; **~ in** *vt* (*deceive*) tromper, rouler; (*understand*) comprendre, saisir; (*include*) comprendre, inclure; (*lodger*) prendre;

~ off *vi* (*AVIAT*) décoller ♦ *vt* (*go away*) s'en aller; (*remove*) enlever; **~ on** *vt* (*work*) accepter, se charger de; (*employee*) prendre, embaucher; (*opponent*) accepter de se battre contre; **~ out** *vt* (*invite*) emmener, sortir; (*remove*) enlever; **to ~ sth out of** (*drawer, pocket etc*) prendre qch dans, prendre qch à; **~ over** *vt* (*business*) reprendre ♦ *vi*: **to ~ over from sb** prendre la relève de qn; **to ~ to** (*person*) se prendre d'amitié pour; (*thing*) prendre goût à; **~ up** *vt* (*activity*) se mettre à; (*dress*) raccourcir; (*occupy: time, space*) prendre, occuper; **to ~ sb up on an offer** accepter la proposition de qn; **~away** (*BRIT*) *adj* (*food*) à emporter ♦ *n* (*shop, restaurant*) qui vend de plats à emporter; **~off** *n* (*AVIAT*) décollage *m*; **~over** *n* (*COMM*) rachat *m*; **takings** ['teɪkɪŋz] *npl* (*COMM*) recette *f*

talc [tælk] *n* (*also*: **~um powder**) talc *m*

tale [teɪl] *n* (*story*) conte *m*, histoire *f*; (*account*) récit *m*; **to tell ~s** (*fig*) rapporter

talent ['tælənt] *n* talent *m*, don *m*; **~ed** *adj* doué(e), plein(e) de talent

talk [tɔːk] *n* (*a speech*) causerie *f*, exposé *m*; (*conversation*) discussion *f*, entretien *m*; (*gossip*) racontars *mpl* ♦ *vi* parler; **~s** *npl* (*POL etc*) entretiens *mpl*; **to ~ about** parler de; **to ~ sb into/out of doing** persuader qn de faire/ne pas faire; **to ~ shop** parler métier *or* affaires; **~ over** *vt* discuter (de); **~ative** *adj* bavard(e); **~ show** *n* causerie (télévisée *or* radiodiffusée)

tall [tɔːl] *adj* (*person*) grand(e); (*building, tree*) haut(e); **to be 6 feet ~** ≈ mesurer 1 mètre 80; **~ story** *n* histoire *f* invraisemblable

tally ['tælɪ] *n* compte *m* ♦ *vi*: **to ~ (with)** correspondre (à)

talon ['tælən] *n* griffe *f*; (*of eagle*) serre *f*

tame [teɪm] *adj* apprivoisé(e); (*fig*:

story, style) insipide

tamper ['tæmpə*] *vi*: **to ~ with** toucher à

tampon ['tæmpɔn] *n* tampon *m* (hygiénique *or* périodique)

tan [tæn] *n (also: sun~)* bronzage *m*
♦ *vt, vi* bronzer ♦ *adj (colour)* brun roux *inv*

tang [tæŋ] *n* odeur *(or* saveur*)* piquante

tangent ['tændʒənt] *n (MATH)* tangente *f*; **to go off at a ~** *(fig)* changer de sujet

tangerine [tændʒə'riːn] *n* mandarine *f*

tangle ['tæŋgl] *n* enchevêtrement *m*; **to get in(to) a ~** s'embrouiller

tank [tæŋk] *n (water ~)* réservoir *m*; *(for fish)* aquarium *m*; *(MIL)* char *m* d'assaut, tank *m*

tanker ['tæŋkə*] *n (ship)* pétrolier *m*, tanker *m*; *(truck)* camion-citerne *m*

tantalizing ['tæntəlaɪzɪŋ] *adj (smell)* extrêmement appétissant(e); *(offer)* terriblement tentant(e)

tantamount ['tæntəmaʊnt] *adj*: **~ to** qui équivaut à

tantrum ['tæntrəm] *n* accès *m* de colère

tap [tæp] *n (on sink etc)* robinet *m*; *(gentle blow)* petite tape *f* ♦ *vt (hit gently)* frapper *or* taper légèrement; *(resources)* exploiter, utiliser; *(telephone)* mettre sur écoute; **on ~** *(fig: resources)* disponible; **~-dancing** ['tæpdɑːnsɪŋ] *n* claquettes *fpl*

tape [teɪp] *n* ruban *m*; *(also: magnetic ~)* bande *f* (magnétique); *(cassette)* cassette *f*; *(sticky)* scotch *m* ♦ *vt (record)* enregistrer; *(stick with ~)* coller avec du scotch; **~ deck** *n* platine *f* d'enregistrement; **~ measure** *n* mètre *m* à ruban

taper ['teɪpə*] *n* cierge *m* ♦ *vi* s'effiler

tape recorder *n* magnétophone *m*

tapestry ['tæpɪstrɪ] *n* tapisserie *f*

tar [tɑː*] *n* goudron *m*

target ['tɑːgɪt] *n* cible *f*; *(fig)* objectif *m*

tariff ['tærɪf] *n (COMM)* tarif *m*; *(taxes)* tarif douanier

tarmac ['tɑːmæk] *n (BRIT: on road)* macadam *m*; *(AVIAT)* piste *f*

tarnish ['tɑːnɪʃ] *vt* ternir

tarpaulin [tɑː'pɔːlɪn] *n* bâche (goudronnée)

tarragon ['tærəgən] *n* estragon *m*

tart [tɑːt] *n (CULIN)* tarte *f*; *(BRIT: inf: prostitute)* putain *f* ♦ *adj (flavour)* âpre, aigrelet(te); **~ up** *(BRIT: inf) vt (object)* retaper; **to o.s. up** se faire beau(belle), s'attifer *(pej)*

tartan ['tɑːtən] *n* tartan *m* ♦ *adj* écossais(e)

tartar ['tɑːtə*] *n (on teeth)* tartre *m*; **~(e) sauce** *n* sauce *f* tartare

task [tɑːsk] *n* tâche *f*; **to take sb to ~** prendre qn à partie; **~ force** *n* *(MIL, POLICE)* détachement spécial

tassel ['tæsəl] *n* gland *m*; pompon *m*

taste [teɪst] *n* goût *m*; *(fig: glimpse, idea)* idée *f*, aperçu *m* ♦ *vt* goûter ♦ *vi*: **to ~ of** *or* **like** *(fish etc)* avoir le *or* un goût de; **you can ~ the garlic (in it)** on sent bien l'ail; **can I have a ~ of this wine?** puis-je goûter un peu de ce vin?; **in good/bad ~** de bon/mauvais goût; **~ful** *adj* de bon goût; **~less** *adj (food)* fade; *(remark)* de mauvais goût; **tasty** ['teɪstɪ] *adj* savoureux(euse), délicieux(euse)

tatters ['tætəz] *npl*: **in ~** en lambeaux

tattoo [tə'tuː] *n* tatouage *m*; *(spectacle)* parade *f* militaire ♦ *vt* tatouer

tatty ['tætɪ] *(BRIT: inf) adj (clothes)* fripé(e); *(shop, area)* délabré(e)

taught [tɔːt] *pt, pp of* **teach**

taunt [tɔːnt] *n* raillerie *f* ♦ *vt* railler

Taurus ['tɔːrəs] *n* le Taureau

taut [tɔːt] *adj* tendu(e)

tax [tæks] *n (on goods etc)* taxe *f*; *(on income)* impôts *mpl*, contributions *fpl* ♦ *vt* taxer; imposer; *(fig: patience etc)* mettre à l'épreuve; **~able** *adj (income)* imposable; **~ation** [tæk'seɪʃən] *n* taxation *f*; impôts *mpl*

contributions fpl; **~ avoidance** n dégrèvement fiscal; **~ disc** (BRIT) n (AUT) vignette f (automobile); **~ evasion** n fraude fiscale; **~-free** adj exempt(e) d'impôts

taxi ['tæksɪ] n taxi m ♦ vi (AVIAT) rouler (lentement) au sol; **~ driver** n chauffeur m de taxi; **~ rank** (BRIT) n station f de taxis; **~ stand** n = taxi rank

tax: ~ payer n contribuable m/f; **~ relief** n dégrèvement fiscal; **~ return** n déclaration f d'impôts or de revenus

TB n abbr = tuberculosis

tea [tiː] n thé m; (BRIT: snack: for children) goûter m; **high ~** collation combinant goûter et dîner; **~ bag** n sachet m de thé; **~ break** (BRIT) n pause-thé f

teach [tiːtʃ] (pt, pp taught) vt: to **~ sb sth, ~ sth to sb** apprendre qch à qn; (in school etc) enseigner qch à qn ♦ vi enseigner; **~er** n (in secondary school) professeur m; (in primary school) instituteur(trice); **~ing** n enseignement m

tea cosy n cloche f à thé

teacup ['tiːkʌp] n tasse f à thé

teak [tiːk] n teck m

team [tiːm] n équipe f; (of animals) attelage m; **~work** n travail m d'équipe

teapot ['tiːpɒt] n théière f

tear¹ [tɛə*] (pt tore, pp torn) n déchirure f ♦ vt déchirer ♦ vi se déchirer; **~ along** vi (rush) aller à toute vitesse; **~ up** vt (sheet of paper etc) déchirer, mettre en morceaux or pièces

tear² [tɪə*] n larme f; **in ~s** en larmes; **~ful** adj larmoyant(e); **~ gas** n gaz m lacrymogène

tearoom ['tiːruːm] n salon m de thé

tease [tiːz] vt taquiner; (unkindly) tourmenter

tea set n service m à thé

teaspoon ['tiːspuːn] n petite cuiller; (also: **~ful:** as measurement) ≈ cuillerée f à café

teat [tiːt] n tétine f

teatime ['tiːtaɪm] n l'heure f du thé

tea towel (BRIT) n torchon m (à vaisselle)

technical ['tɛknɪkəl] adj technique; **~ity** [tɛknɪ'kælɪtɪ] n (detail) détail m technique; (point of law) vice m de forme; **~ly** adv techniquement; (strictly speaking) en théorie

technician [tɛk'nɪʃən] n technicien(ne)

technique [tɛk'niːk] n technique f

technological [tɛknə'lɒdʒɪkəl] adj technologique; **technology** [tɛk'nɒlədʒɪ] n technologie f

teddy (bear) ['tɛdɪ(bɛə*)] n ours m en peluche

tedious ['tiːdɪəs] adj fastidieux(euse)

tee [tiː] n (GOLF) tee m

teem [tiːm] vi: to **~ with** grouiller (de); it is **~ing (with rain)** il pleut à torrents

teenage ['tiːneɪdʒ] adj (fashions etc) pour jeunes, pour adolescents; (children) adolescent(e); **~r** n adolescent(e)

teens [tiːnz] npl: to be in one's **~** être adolescent(e)

tee-shirt ['tiːʃɜːt] n = T-shirt

teeter ['tiːtə*] vi chanceler, vaciller

teeth [tiːθ] npl of tooth

teethe [tiːð] vi percer ses dents

teething ring ['tiːðɪŋ-] n anneau pour bébé qui perce ses dents

teething troubles npl (fig) difficultés initiales

teetotal ['tiː'təʊtl] adj (person) qui ne boit jamais d'alcool

telegram ['tɛlɪgræm] n télégramme m

telegraph ['tɛlɪgrɑːf] n télégraphe m; **~ pole** n poteau m télégraphique

telephone ['tɛlɪfəʊn] n téléphone m ♦ vt (person) téléphoner à; (message) téléphoner; **on the ~** se téléphone; **to be on the ~** (BRIT: have a ~) avoir le téléphone; **~ booth**, **~ box** (BRIT) n cabine f téléphonique; **~ call** n coup m de téléphone, appel m téléphonique; ~ **directory** n annuaire m (du téléphone); ~ **number** n numéro m de téléphone; **telephonist** [təˈlɛfənɪst] (BRIT) n téléphoniste m/f

telescope ['tɛlɪskəʊp] n télescope m

television ['tɛlɪvɪʒən] n télévision f; **on** ~ à la télévision; ~ **set** n (poste f de) télévision m

telex ['tɛlɛks] n télex m

tell [tɛl] (pt, pp **told**) vt dire; (relate: story) raconter; (distinguish): **to** ~ **sth from** distinguer qch de ♦ vi (talk): **to** ~ (**of**) parler (de); (have effect) se faire sentir, se voir; **to** ~ **sb to do** dire à qn de faire; ~ **off** vt réprimander, gronder; ~**er** n (in bank) caissier(ère); ~**ing** adj (remark, detail) révélateur(trice); ~**tale** adj (sign) éloquent(e), révélateur(trice)

telly ['tɛlɪ] (BRIT) n abbr (= television) télé f

temp [tɛmp] n abbr (= temporary) (secrétaire f) intérimaire f

temper ['tɛmpə*] n (nature) caractère m; (mood) humeur f; (fit of anger) colère f ♦ vt (moderate) tempérer, adoucir; **to be in a** ~ être en colère; **to lose one's** ~ se mettre en colère

temperament ['tɛmprəmənt] n (nature) tempérament m; ~**al** [tɛmprəˈmɛntl] adj capricieux(euse)

temperate ['tɛmpərət] adj (climate, country) tempéré(e)

temperature ['tɛmprɪtʃə*] n température f; **to have** or **run a** ~ avoir de la fièvre

temple ['tɛmpl] n (building) temple m; (ANAT) tempe f

temporary ['tɛmpərərɪ] adj temporaire, provisoire; (job, worker) temporaire

tempt [tɛmpt] vt tenter; **to** ~ **sb into doing** persuader qn de faire; ~**ation** [tɛmptʃən] n tentation f

ten [tɛn] num dix

tenacity [təˈnæsɪtɪ] n ténacité f

tenancy ['tɛnənsɪ] n location f; état m de locataire

tenant ['tɛnənt] n locataire m/f

tend [tɛnd] vt s'occuper de ♦ vi: **to** ~ **to do** avoir tendance à faire

tendency ['tɛndənsɪ] n tendance f

tender ['tɛndə*] adj tendre; (delicate) délicat(e); (sore) sensible ♦ n (COMM: offer) soumission f ♦ vt offrir

tenement ['tɛnəmənt] n immeuble m

tenet ['tɛnət] n principe m

tennis ['tɛnɪs] n tennis m; ~ **ball** n balle f de tennis; ~ **court** n (court m de) tennis; ~ **player** n joueur(euse) de tennis; ~ **racket** n raquette f de tennis; ~ **shoes** npl (chaussures fpl de) tennis mpl

tenor ['tɛnə*] n (MUS) ténor m

tenpin bowling (BRIT) n bowling m (à dix quilles)

tense [tɛns] adj tendu(e) ♦ n (LING) temps m

tension ['tɛnʃən] n tension f

tent [tɛnt] n tente f

tentative ['tɛntətɪv] adj timide, hésitant(e); (conclusion) provisoire

tenterhooks ['tɛntəhʊks] npl: **on** ~ sur des charbons ardents

tenth [tɛnθ] num dixième

tent peg n piquet m de tente

tent pole n montant m de tente

tenuous ['tɛnjʊəs] adj ténu(e)

tenure ['tɛnjʊə*] n (of property) bail m; (of office) période f de jouissance

tepid ['tɛpɪd] adj tiède

term [tɜːm] n terme m; (SCOL) trimestre m ♦ vt appeler; ~**s** npl (conditions) conditions fpl; (COMM) tarif m; **in the short/long** ~ à court/long terme; **to come to** ~**s with** (problem) faire face à

terminal ['tɜːmɪnl] adj (disease) dans sa phase terminale; (patient) incurable ♦ n (ELEC) borne f; (for oil, ore etc, COMPUT) terminal m; (also: air ~) aérogare f; (BRIT: also: coach ~) gare routière

terminate ['tɜːmɪneɪt] vt mettre fin à; (pregnancy) interrompre

terminus ['tɜːmɪnəs] (pl **termini**) n

terminus m inv

terrace ['terəs] n terrasse f; (BRIT: row of houses) rangée f de maisons (attenantes); **the ~s** npl (: SPORT) les gradins mpl; **~d** adj (garden) en terrasses

terracotta ['terə'kɔtə] n terre cuite

terrain [te'reɪn] n terrain m (sol)

terrible ['terɪbl] adj terrible, atroce; (weather, conditions) affreux(euse), épouvantable; **terribly** ['terɪblɪ] adv terriblement; (very badly) affreusement mal

terrier ['terɪə*] n terrier m (chien)

terrific [tə'rɪfɪk] adj fantastique, incroyable, terrible; (wonderful) formidable, sensationnel(le)

terrify ['terɪfaɪ] vt terrifier

territory ['terɪtərɪ] n territoire m

terror ['terə*] n terreur f; **~ism** n terrorisme m; **~ist** n terroriste m/f

terse [tɜːs] adj (style) concis(e); (reply) sec(sèche)

Terylene ['terɪliːn] ® n tergal m ®

test [test] n (trial, check) essai m; (of courage etc) épreuve f; (MED) examen m; (CHEM) analyse f; (SCOL) interrogation f; (also: driving ~) (examen du) permis m de conduire ♦ vt essayer; mettre à l'épreuve; examiner; analyser; faire subir une interrogation à

testament ['testəmənt] n testament m; **the Old/New T~** l'Ancien/le Nouveau Testament

testicle ['testɪkl] n testicule m

testify ['testɪfaɪ] vi (LAW) témoigner, déposer; **to ~ to sth** attester qch

testimony ['testɪmənɪ] n témoignage m; (clear proof): **to be (a) ~ to** être la preuve de

test: **~ match** n (CRICKET, RUGBY) match international; **~ pilot** n pilote m d'essai; **~ tube** n éprouvette f

tetanus ['tetənəs] n tétanos m

tether ['teðə*] vt attacher ♦ n: **at the end of one's ~** à bout (de patience)

text [tekst] n texte m; **~book** n manuel m

textile n textile m

texture ['tekstʃə*] n texture f; (of skin, paper etc) grain m

Thames [temz] n: **the ~** la Tamise

than [ðæn, ðən] conj que; (with numerals): **more ~** 10/once plus de 10/d'une fois; **I have more/less ~ you** j'en ai plus/moins que toi; **she has more apples ~ pears** elle a plus de pommes que de poires

thank [θæŋk] vt remercier, dire merci à; **~s** npl (gratitude) remerciements mpl ♦ excl merci!; **~ you (very much)** merci (beaucoup); **~s to** grâce à; **~ God!** Dieu merci!; **~ful** adj: **~ful (for)** reconnaissant(e) (de); **~less** adj ingrat(e); **T~sgiving (Day)** n jour m d'action de grâce (fête américaine)

KEYWORD

that [ðæt] adj (demonstrative: pl those) ce, cet +vowel or h mute, f cette; **~ man/woman/book** cet homme/cette femme/ce livre; (not this) cet homme-là/cette femme-là/ce livre-là; **~ one** celui-là (celle-là)
♦ pron 1 (demonstrative: pl those) ce; (not this one) cela, ça; **who's ~?** qui est-ce?; **what's ~?** qu'est-ce que c'est?; **is ~ you?** c'est toi?; **I prefer this to ~** je préfère ceci à cela or ça; **~'s what he said** c'est or voilà ce qu'il a dit; **~ is (to say)** c'est-à-dire, à savoir
2 (relative: subject) qui; (: object) que; (: indirect) lequel(laquelle), lesquels(lesquelles) pl; **the book ~ I read** le livre que j'ai lu; **the books ~ are in the library** les livres qui sont dans la bibliothèque; **all ~ I have** tout ce que j'ai; **the box ~ I put it in** la boîte dans laquelle je l'ai mis; **the people ~ I spoke to** les gens auxquels or à qui je parlais
3 (relative: of time) où; **the day ~ he came** le jour où il est venu
♦ conj que; **he thought ~ I was ill**

il pensait que j'étais malade
♦ *adv* (*demonstrative*): **I can't
work** ~ **much** je ne peux pas travailler autant que cela; **I didn't
know it was** ~ **bad** je ne savais pas
que c'était si *or* aussi mauvais; **it's
about** ~ **high** c'est à peu près de
cette hauteur

thatched [θætʃt] *adj* (*roof*) de chaume; ~ **cottage** chaumière *f*

thaw [θɔː] *n* dégel *m* ♦ *vi* (*ice*) fondre; (*food*) dégeler ♦ *vt* (*also*: ~
out) (faire) dégeler

<hr>

KEYWORD

the [ðiː, ðə] *def art* **1** (*gen*) le, la *f*, l'
+*vowel or h mute*, les *pl*; ~ **boy/
girl/ink** le garçon/la fille/l'encre; ~
children les enfants; ~ **history of
the world** l'histoire du monde; **give
it to** ~ **postman** donne-le au facteur; **to play** ~ **piano/flute** jouer du
piano/de la flûte; ~ **rich and** ~ **poor**
les riches et les pauvres

2 (*in titles*): **Elizabeth** ~ **First** Elisabeth première; **Peter** ~ **Great**
Pierre le Grand

3 (*in comparisons*): ~ **more** ~
works, ~ **more he earns** plus il
travaille, plus il gagne de l'argent

theatre ['θɪətə*] *n* théâtre *m*; (*also*:
lecture ~) amphi(théâtre) *m*; (*MED*:
also: *operating* ~) salle *f* d'opération; ~**goer** *n* habitué(e) du théâtre;
theatrical [θɪ'ætrɪkəl] *adj* théâtral(e)

theft [θeft] *n* vol *m* (*larcin*)

their [ðɛə*] *adj* leur; (*pl*) leurs; *see
also* **my**; ~**s** *pron* (*sing*) le (la) leur; (*pl*)
les leurs; *see also* **mine**

them [ðɛm, ðəm] *pron* (*direct*) les;
(*indirect*) leur; (*stressed*, *after prep*)
eux(elles); *see also* **me**

theme [θiːm] *n* thème *m*; ~ **park** *n*
parc *m* d'(attraction) à thème; ~
song *n* chanson principale

themselves [ðəm'selvz] *pl pron* (*reflexive*) se; (*emphatic*, *after prep*)
eux-mêmes(elles-mêmes); *see also*

oneself

then [ðen] *adv* (*at that time*) alors, à
ce moment-là; (*next*) puis, ensuite
(*and also*) et puis ♦ *conj* (*therefore*)
alors, dans ce cas ♦ *adj*: **the** ~ **pre**-
sident le président d'alors *or* d
l'époque; **by** ~ (*past*) à ce momen▮
là; (*future*) d'ici là; **from** ~ **on** dè▮
lors

theology [θɪ'ɒlədʒɪ] *n* théologie *f*

theoretical [θɪə'rɛtɪkəl] *adj* théor▮
que

theorize ['θɪəraɪz] *vi* faire des théo▮
ries

theory ['θɪərɪ] *n* théorie *f*

therapy ['θerəpɪ] *n* thérapie *f*

<hr>

KEYWORD

there [ðɛə*] *adv* **1**: ~ **is**, ~ **are** il y ▮
a; ~ **are 3 of them** (*people, things*
il y en a 3; ~ **has been an accident**
il y a eu un accident

2 (*referring to place*) là, là-bas; **it'▮**
~ **c'est** là-(bas); **in/on/up/down** ~
là-dedans/là-dessus/là-haut/en bas; h▮
went ~ **on Friday** il y est allé ven▮
dredi; **I want that book** ~ je veu▮
ce livre-là; ~ **he is!** le voilà!

3: ~, ~ (*esp to child*) allons, allons!

thereabouts [ðɛərə'baʊts] *adv*
(*place*) par là, près de là; (*amount*
environ, à peu près

thereafter [ðɛər'uːftə*] *adv* par l▮
suite

thereby [ðɛə'baɪ] *adv* ainsi

therefore ['ðɛəfɔː*] *adv* donc, pa▮
conséquent

there's [ðɛəz] = there is; ther▮
has

thermal ['θəːml] *adj* (*springs*) the▮
mal(e); (*underwear*) en thermolact▮
(®); (*COMPUT*: *paper*) thermosens▮
ble; (: *printer*) thermos▮

thermometer [θə'mɒmɪtə*] *n*
momètre *m*

Thermos ['θəːməs] (®) *n* (*also*:
flask) thermos *m or f inv* (®)

thermostat ['θəːməʊstæt] *n* thermos▮
tat *m*

thesaurus [θɪˈsɔːrəs] n dictionnaire m des synonymes

these [ðiːz] pl adj ces; (not "those"): ~ books ces livres-ci ♦ pl pron ceux-ci(celles-ci)

thesis [ˈθiːsɪs] (pl theses) n thèse f

they [ðeɪ] pl pron ils(elles); (stressed) eux(elles); ~ **say that** ... (it is said that) on dit que ...; ~'**d** = they had; ~ **would**; ~'**ll** = they shall; ~ **will**; ~'**re** = they are; ~'**ve** = they have

thick [θɪk] adj épais(se); (stupid) bête, borné(e) ♦ n: **in the** ~ **of** au beau milieu de, en plein cœur de; **it's 20 cm** ~ il/elle a 20 cm d'épaisseur; ~**en** vi s'épaissir ♦ vt (sauce etc) épaissir; ~**ness** n épaisseur f; ~**set** adj trapu(e), costaud(e); ~**skinned** adj (fig) peu sensible

thief [θiːf] (pl **thieves**) n voleur(euse)

thigh [θaɪ] n cuisse f

thimble [ˈθɪmbl] n dé m (à coudre)

thin [θɪn] adj mince; (soup, sauce) peu épais(se); (hair, crowd) clairsemé(e) ♦ vt: to ~ (**down**) (sauce, paint) délayer

thing [θɪŋ] n chose f; (object) objet m; (contraption) truc m; (mania): **to have a** ~ **about** être obsédé(e) par; ~**s** npl (belongings) affaires fpl; **poor** ~! le(la) pauvre!; **the best** ~ **would be to** le mieux serait de; **how are** ~**s?** comment ça va?

think [θɪŋk] (pt, pp **thought**) vi penser, réfléchir; (believe) penser ♦ vt (imagine) imaginer; **what did you** ~ **of them?** qu'avez-vous pensé d'eux?; **to** ~ **about sth/sb** penser à qch/qn; **I'll** ~ **about it** je vais y réfléchir; **to** ~ **of doing** avoir l'idée de faire; **I** ~ **so/not** je crois or pense que oui/non; **to** ~ **well of** avoir une haute opinion de; ~ **over** vt bien réfléchir à; ~ **up** vt inventer, trouver; ~ **tank** n groupe m de réflexion

thinly adv (cut) en fines tranches; (spread) en une couche mince

third [θɜːd] num troisième ♦ n (fraction) tiers m; (AUT) troisième (vitesse) f; (BRIT: SCOL: degree) ≈ licence f sans mention; ~**ly** adv troisièmement; ~ **party insurance** (BRIT) n assurance f au tiers; ~**rate** adj de qualité médiocre; **the T~ World** n le tiers monde

thirst [θɜːst] n soif f; ~**y** adj (person) qui a soif, assoiffé(e); (work) qui donne soif; **to be** ~**y** avoir soif

thirteen [ˈθɜːˈtiːn] num treize

thirty [ˈθɜːtɪ] num trente

KEYWORD

this [ðɪs] adj (demonstrative: pl these) ce, cet +vowel or h mute, cette f; ~ **man/woman/book** cet homme/cette femme/ce livre; (not that) cet homme-ci/cette femme-ci/ce livre-ci; ~ **one** celui-ci(celle-ci)
♦ pron (demonstrative: pl these) ce; (not that one) celui-ci(celle-ci), ceci; **who's** ~? qui est-ce?; **what's** ~? qu'est-ce que c'est?; **I prefer** ~ **to that** je préfère ceci à cela; ~ **is what he said** voici ce qu'il a dit; ~ **is Mr Brown** (in introductions) je vous présente Mr Brown; (in photo) c'est Mr Brown; (on telephone) ici Mr Brown
♦ adv (demonstrative): **it was about** ~ **big** c'était à peu près de cette grandeur or grand comme ça; **I didn't know it was** ~ **bad** je ne savais pas que c'était si or aussi mauvais

thistle [ˈθɪsl] n chardon m

thorn [θɔːn] n épine f

thorough [ˈθʌrə] adj (search) minutieux(euse); (knowledge, research) approfondi(e); (work, person) consciencieux(euse); (cleaning) à fond; ~**bred** n (horse) pur-sang m inv; ~**fare** n route f; "**no** ~**fare**" "passage interdit"; ~**ly** adv minutieusement; en profondeur; à fond; (very) tout à fait

those [ðəʊz] pl adj ces; (not "these"): ~ **books** ces livres-là ♦ *pl pron* ceux-là/(celles-là)

though [ðəʊ] *conj* bien que +*sub*, quoique +*sub* ♦ *adv* pourtant

thought [θɔːt] *pt, pp of* **think** ♦ *n* pensée *f*; (*idea*) idée *f*; (*opinion*) avis *m*; ~**ful** *adj* (*deep in thought*) pensif(ive); (*serious*) réfléchi(e); (*considerate*) prévenant(e); ~**less** *adj* étourdi(e); qui manque de considération

thousand [ˈθaʊzənd] *num* mille; **two** ~ deux mille; ~**s of** des milliers de; ~**th** *num* millième

thrash [θræʃ] *vt* rouer de coups; donner une correction à; (*defeat*) battre à plate couture; ~ **about, ~ around** *vi* se débattre; ~ **out** *vt* débattre

thread [θrɛd] *n* fil *m*; (*of screw*) pas *m*, filetage *m* ♦ *vt* (*needle*) enfiler; ~**bare** *adj* râpé(e), élimé(e)

threat [θrɛt] *n* menace *f*; ~**en** *vi* menacer ♦ *vt*: to ~**en sb with sth/to do** menacer qn de qch/de faire

three [θriː] *num* trois; ~-**dimensional** *adj* à trois dimensions; ~-**piece suit** *n* complet *m* (avec gilet); ~-**piece suite** *n* salon *m* comprenant un canapé et deux fauteuils assortis; ~-**ply** *adj* (*wool*) trois fils *inv*

thresh [θrɛʃ] *vt* (*AGR*) battre

threshold [ˈθrɛʃhəʊld] *n* seuil *m*

threw [θruː] *pt of* **throw**

thrift [θrɪft] *n* économie *f*; ~**y** *adj* économe

thrill [θrɪl] *n* (*excitement*) émotion *f*, sensation forte; (*shudder*) frisson *m* ♦ *vt* (*audience*) électriser; to be ~**ed** (*with gift etc*) être ravi(e); ~**er** *n* film *m* (*or* roman *m or* pièce *f*) à suspense; ~**ing** *adj* saisissant(e), palpitant(e)

thrive [θraɪv] (*pt* ~**d,** **throve,** *pp* ~**d**) *vi* pousser, se développer; (*business*) prospérer; he ~**s on it** cela lui réussit; **thriving** *adj* (*business, community*) prospère

throat [θrəʊt] *n* gorge *f*; to have a **sore** ~ avoir mal à la gorge

throb [θrɒb] *vi* (*heart*) palpiter; (*engine*) vibrer; **my head is** ~**bing** j'ai des élancements dans la tête

throes [θrəʊz] *npl*: **in the** ~ **of** au beau milieu de

throne [θrəʊn] *n* trône *m*

throng [θrɒŋ] *n* foule *f* ♦ *vt* se presser dans

throttle [ˈθrɒtl] *n* (*AUT*) accélérateur *m* ♦ *vt* étrangler

through [θruː] *prep* à travers; (*time*) pendant, durant; (*by means of*) par, par l'intermédiaire de; (*owing to*) à cause de ♦ *adj* (*ticket, train, passage*) direct(e) ♦ *adv* à travers; to **put sb** ~ to **sb** (*BRIT: TEL*) passer qn à qn; to be ~ (*TEL*) avoir la communication; (*esp US: have finished*) avoir fini; to be ~ **with sb** (*relationship*) avoir rompu avec qn; **"no** ~ **road"** (*BRIT*) "impasse"; ~**out** [θruːˈaʊt] *prep* (*place*) partout dans; (*time*) durant tout(e) le(la) ♦ *adv* partout

throve [θrəʊv] *pt of* **thrive**

throw [θrəʊ] (*pt* **threw,** *pp* **thrown**) *n* jet *m*; (*SPORT*) lancer *m* ♦ *vt* lancer, jeter; (*SPORT*) lancer; (*rider*) désarçonner; (*fig*) décontenancer; to ~ **a party** donner une réception; ~ **away** *vt* jeter; ~ **off** *vt* se débarrasser de; ~ **out** *vt* jeter; (*reject*) rejeter; (*person*) mettre à la porte; ~ **up** *vi* vomir; ~**away** *adj* à jeter; (*remark*) fait(e) en passant; ~-**in** *n* (*SPORT*) remise *f* en jeu

thru [θruː] (*US*) = **through**

thrush [θrʌʃ] *n* (*bird*) grive *f*

thrust [θrʌst] (*pt, pp* **thrust**) *n* (*TECH*) poussée *f* ♦ *vt* pousser brusquement; (*push in*) enfoncer

thud [θʌd] *n* bruit sourd

thug [θʌg] *n* voyou *m*

thumb [θʌm] *n* (*ANAT*) pouce *m*, arrêter une voiture; to ~ **a lift** faire de l'auto-stop; ~ **through** *vt* (*book*) feuilleter; ~**tack** (*US*) *n* punaise *f* (*clou*)

thump [θʌmp] *n* grand coup; (*sound*) bruit sourd ♦ *vt* cogner sur

♦ vi cogner, battre fort

thunder ['θʌndə*] n tonnerre m ♦ vi tonner; (train etc): **to ~** past passer dans un grondement or un bruit de tonnerre; **~bolt** n foudre f; **~clap** n coup m de tonnerre; **~storm** n orage m; **~y** adj orageux(euse)

Thursday ['θə:zdeɪ] n jeudi m

thus [ðʌs] adv ainsi

thwart [θwɔ:t] vt contrecarrer

thyme [taɪm] n thym m

tiara [tɪ'ɑ:rə] n (woman's) diadème m

tick [tɪk] n (sound: of clock) tic-tac m; (mark) coche f; (ZOOL) tique f; (BRIT: inf): **in a ~** dans une seconde ♦ vi faire tic-tac ♦ vt (item on list) cocher; **~ off** vt (item on list) cocher; (person) réprimander, attraper; **~ over** vi (engine) tourner au ralenti; (fig) aller or marcher doucettement

ticket ['tɪkɪt] n billet m; (for bus, tube) ticket m; (in shop: on goods) étiquette f; (for library) carte f; (parking ~) papillon m, p.-v. m; **~ collector** n contrôleur(euse); **~ office** n guichet m, bureau m de vente des billets

tickle ['tɪkl] vt, vi chatouiller; **ticklish** adj (person) chatouilleux(euse); (problem) épineux(euse)

tidal ['taɪdl] adj (force) de la marée; (estuary) à marée; **~ wave** n raz-de-marée m inv

tidbit ['tɪdbɪt] (US) n = **titbit**

tiddlywinks ['tɪdlɪwɪŋks] n jeu m de puce

tide [taɪd] n marée f; (fig: of events) cours m ♦ vt: **to ~ sb over** dépanner qn; **high/low ~** marée haute/basse

tidy ['taɪdɪ] adj (room) bien rangé(e); (dress, work) net(te); (person) soigné(e); (person) ordonné(e), qui a de l'ordre ♦ vt (also: **~ up**) ranger

tie [taɪ] n (string etc) cordon m; (BRIT: also: **neck~**) cravate f; (fig: link) lien m; (SPORT: draw) égalité f de points; match nul ♦ vt (parcel)

attacher; (ribbon, shoelaces) nouer ♦ vi (SPORT) faire match nul; finir à égalité de points; **to ~ sth in a bow** faire un nœud à or avec qch; **to ~ a knot in sth** faire un nœud à qch; **~ down** vt (fig): **to ~ sb down (to)** contraindre qn (à accepter); **to be ~d down (by relationship)** se fixer; **~ up** vt (parcel) ficeler; (dog, boat) attacher; (prisoner) ligoter; (arrangements) conclure; **to be ~d up** (busy) être pris(e) or occupé(e)

tier [tɪə*] n gradin m; (of cake) étage m

tiger ['taɪgə*] n tigre m

tight [taɪt] adj (rope) tendu(e), raide; (clothes) étroit(e), très juste; (budget, programme, bend) serré(e); (control) strict(e), sévère; (inf: drunk) ivre, rond(e) ♦ adv (squeeze) très fort; (shut) hermétiquement, bien; **~en** vt (rope) tendre; (screw) resserrer; (control) renforcer ♦ vi tendre, se resserrer; **~fisted** adj avare; **~ly** adv (grasp) bien, très fort; **~rope** n corde f raide; **~s** (BRIT) npl collant m

tile [taɪl] n (on roof) tuile f; (on wall or floor) carreau m; **~d** adj en tuiles; carrelé(e)

till [tɪl] n caisse (enregistreuse) f ♦ vt (land) cultiver ♦ prep, conj = **until**

tiller ['tɪlə*] n (NAUT) barre f (du gouvernail)

tilt [tɪlt] vt pencher, incliner ♦ vi pencher, être incliné(e)

timber ['tɪmbə*] n (material) bois m (de construction); (trees) arbres mpl

time [taɪm] n temps m; (epoch: often pl) époque f, temps; (by clock) heure f; (moment) moment m; (occasion, also MATH) fois f; (MUS) mesure f ♦ vt (race) chronométrer; (programme) minuter; (visit) fixer; (remark etc) choisir le moment de; **a long ~** un long moment, longtemps; **for the ~ being** pour le moment; **4 at a ~** à 4 à la fois; **from ~ to ~** de temps en temps; **at ~s** parfois; **in ~** (soon enough) à temps; (after some avec le temps, à la longue; (MUS) en mesure; **in a week's ~** dans une semaine; **in no ~** en un rien de temps; **any ~** n'importe quand; **~ and again** de temps à autre; **for the ~ being** pour le moment ◆ vt (choose right moment for) choisir; (visit) fixer; (runners, race) chronométrer; (programme, operation) minuter; **a long ~ ago** il y a longtemps; **what ~ is it?** quelle heure est-il?; **to have a good ~** bien s'amuser; **~ bomb** n bombe f à retardement; **~ lag** (BRIT) n décalage m; (in travel) décalage horaire; **~less** adj éternel(le); **~ly** adj opportun(e); **~ off** n temps m libre; **~r** n (TECH) minuteur m; (in kitchen) compte-minutes m inv; **~scale** n délais mpl; **~share** n maison f ou appartement m en multipropriété; **~ switch** (BRIT) n minuteur m; (for lighting) minuterie f; **~table** n (RAIL) (indicateur m) horaire m; (SCOL) emploi m du temps; **~ zone** n fuseau m horaire

timid ['tɪmɪd] adj timide; (easily scared) peureux(euse)

timing ['taɪmɪŋ] n minutage m; chronométrage m; **the ~ of his resignation** le moment choisi pour sa démission

timpani ['tɪmpənɪ] npl timbales fpl

tin [tɪn] n étain m; (also: **~ plate**) fer-blanc m; (BRIT: can) boîte f (de conserve); (for storage) boîte f; **~foil** n papier m d'étain or aluminium

tinge [tɪndʒ] n nuance f ◆ vt: **~d with** teinté(e) de

tingle ['tɪŋgl] vi picoter; (person) avoir des picotements

tinker ['tɪŋkə*] n romanichel m; **~ with** vt fus bricoler, rafistoler

tinkle ['tɪŋkl] vi tinter

tinned [tɪnd] (BRIT) adj (food) en boîte, en conserve

tin opener [-'əʊpnə*] (BRIT) n ouvre-boîte m

tinsel ['tɪnsl] n guirlandes fpl de Noël (argentées)

tint [tɪnt] n teinte f; (for hair) shampooing colorant; **~ed** adj (hair) teinté(e); (spectacles, glass) teinté(e)

tiny ['taɪnɪ] adj minuscule

tip [tɪp] n (end) bout m; (gratuity)

pourboire m; (BRIT: for rubbish) décharge f; (advice) tuyau m ◆ vt (waiter) donner un pourboire à; (tilt) incliner; (overturn: also: **~ over**) renverser; (empty: also: **~ out**) déverser; **~-off** n (hint) tuyau m; **~ped** (BRIT) adj (cigarette) (à bout) filtre inv

tipsy ['tɪpsɪ] (inf) adj un peu ivre, éméché(e)

tiptoe ['tɪptəʊ] n: **on ~** sur la pointe des pieds

tiptop ['tɪp'tɒp] adj: **in ~ condition** en excellent état

tire ['taɪə*] n (US) = **tyre** ◆ vt fatiguer ◆ vi se fatiguer; **~d** adj fatigué(e); **to be ~d of** en avoir assez de, être las(lasse) de; **~less** adj (person) infatigable; (efforts) inlassable; **~some** adj ennuyeux(euse); **tiring** ['taɪərɪŋ] adj fatigant(e)

tissue ['tɪʃuː] n tissu m; (paper handkerchief) mouchoir m en papier, kleenex m (®); **~ paper** n papier m de soie

tit [tɪt] n (bird) mésange f; **to give ~ for tat** rendre la pareille

titbit ['tɪtbɪt] n (food) friandise f; (news) potin m

title ['taɪtl] n titre m; **~ deed** n (LAW) titre (constitutif) de propriété; **~ role** n rôle m titre

titter ['tɪtə*] vi rire (bêtement)

TM abbr = **trademark**

KEYWORD

to [tuː, tə] prep 1 (direction) à; **~ go France/Portugal/London/school** aller en France/au Portugal/à Londres/à l'école; **~ go ~ Claude's/the doctor's** aller chez Claude/le docteur; **the road ~ Edinburgh** la route d'Édimbourg

2 (as far as) (jusqu')à; **~ count ~ 10** compter jusqu'à 10; **from 40 ~ 50 people** de 40 à 50 personnes

3 (with expressions of time): **a quarter ~ 5** 5 heures moins le quart; **it's twenty ~ 3** il est 3 heures moins vingt

4 (for, of) de; **the key ~ the front door** la clé de la porte d'entrée; **a letter ~ his wife** une lettre (adressée) à sa femme

5 (expressing indirect object) à; **give sth ~ sb** donner qch à qn; **talk ~ sb** parler à qn

6 (in relation to) à; **3 goals ~ 2** 3 (buts) à 2; **30 miles ~ the gallon** ≈ 9,4 litres aux cent (km)

7 (purpose, result): **~ come ~ sb's aid** venir au secours de qn, porter secours à qn; **~ sentence sb ~ death** condamner qn à mort; **~ my surprise** à ma grande surprise

♦ **with vb 1** (simple infinitive): **~ go/eat** aller/manger

2 (following another vb): **want/try/start ~ do** vouloir/essayer de/commencer à faire

3 (with vb omitted): **I don't want ~** je ne veux pas

4 (purpose, result) pour; **I did it ~ help you** je l'ai fait pour vous aider

5 (equivalent to relative clause): **I have things ~ do** j'ai des choses à faire; **the main thing is ~ try** l'important est d'essayer

6 (after adjective etc): **ready ~ go** prêt(e) à partir; **too old/young ~ ...** trop vieux/jeune pour ...

♦ adv: **push/pull the door ~** tirez/poussez la porte

toad [təʊd] n crapaud m

toadstool n champignon (vénéneux)

toast [təʊst] n (CULIN) pain grillé, toast m; (drink, speech) toast m ♦ vt (CULIN) faire griller; (drink to) porter un toast à; **~er** n grille-pain m inv

tobacco [təˈbækəʊ] n tabac m; **~nist** [təˈbækənɪst] n marchand(e) de tabac; **~nist's (shop)** n (bureau m de) tabac m

toboggan [təˈbɒgən] n toboggan m; (child's) luge f

today [təˈdeɪ] adv (also fig) aujourd'hui ♦ n aujourd'hui m

toddler [ˈtɒdlə*] n enfant m/f qui

commence à marcher, bambin m

to-do [təˈduː] n (fuss) histoire f, affaire f

toe [təʊ] n doigt m de pied, orteil m; (of shoe) bout m ♦ vt: **to ~ the line** (fig) obéir, se conformer; **~nail** n ongle m du pied

toffee [ˈtɒfɪ] n caramel m; **~ apple** n (BRIT) pomme caramélisée

toga [ˈtəʊgə] n toge f

together [təˈgeðə*] adv ensemble; (at same time) en même temps; **~ with** avec

toil [tɔɪl] n dur travail, labeur m ♦ vi peiner

toilet [ˈtɔɪlət] n (BRIT: lavatory) toilettes fpl ♦ cpd (accessories etc) de toilette; **~ paper** n papier m hygiénique; **~ries** [ˈtɔɪlətrɪz] npl articles mpl de toilette; **~ roll** n rouleau m de papier hygiénique; **~ water** n eau f de toilette

token [ˈtəʊkən] n (sign) marque f, témoignage m; (metal disc) jeton m ♦ adj (strike, payment etc) symbolique; **book/record ~** (BRIT) chèque-livre/-disque m; **gift ~** bon-cadeau m

told [təʊld] pt, pp of **tell**

tolerable [ˈtɒlərəbl] adj (bearable) tolérable; (fairly good) passable

tolerant [ˈtɒlərənt] adj: **~ (of)** tolérant(e) (à l'égard de)

tolerate [ˈtɒləreɪt] vt supporter, tolérer

toll [təʊl] n (tax, charge) péage m ♦ vi (bell) sonner; **the accident ~ on the roads** le nombre des victimes de la route

tomato [təˈmɑːtəʊ] (pl **~es**) n tomate f

tomb [tuːm] n tombe f

tomboy [ˈtɒmbɔɪ] n garçon manqué

tombstone [ˈtuːmstəʊn] n pierre tombale

tomcat [ˈtɒmkæt] n matou m

tomorrow [təˈmɒrəʊ] adv (also fig) demain ♦ n demain m; **the day after ~** après-demain; **~ morning** demain matin

ton [tʌn] n tonne f (BRIT = 1016kg,

US = 907kg); (metric) tonne (= 1000 kg); ~s of (fig) des tas de

tone [təʊn] n ton m ♦ vi (also: ~ in) s'harmoniser; ~ **down** vt (colour, criticism) adoucir; (sound) baisser; ~ **up** vt (muscles) tonifier; ~-**deaf** adj qui n'a pas d'oreille

tongs [tɒŋz] npl (for coal) pincettes fpl; (for hair) fer à friser

tongue [tʌŋ] n langue f; ~ **in cheek** ironiquement; ~-**tied** adj (fig) muet(te); ~-**twister** n phrase f très difficile à prononcer

tonic [ˈtɒnɪk] n (MED) tonique m; (also: ~ water) tonic m, Schweppes m (®)

tonight [təˈnaɪt] adv, n cette nuit; (this evening) ce soir

tonsil [ˈtɒnsl] n amygdale f; ~**litis** n angine f

too [tuː] adv (excessively) trop; (also) aussi; ~ **much** adv trop de ♦ adj trop; ~ **many** trop de; ~ **bad!** tant pis!

took [tʊk] pt of **take**

tool [tuːl] n outil m; ~ **box** n boîte f à outils

toot [tuːt] n (of car horn) coup m de klaxon; (of whistle) coup de sifflet ♦ vi (with car horn) klaxonner

tooth [tuːθ] n (pl **teeth**) n (ANAT, TECH) dent f; ~**ache** n mal m de dents; ~**brush** n brosse f à dents; ~**paste** n (pâte f) dentifrice m; ~**pick** n cure-dent m

top [tɒp] n (of mountain, head) sommet m; (of page, ladder, garment) haut m; (of box, cupboard, table) dessus m; (lid: of box, jar) couvercle m; (: of bottle) bouchon m; (toy) toupie f ♦ adj du haut; (in rank) premier(ère); (best) meilleur(e) ♦ vt (exceed) dépasser; (be first in) être en tête de; **on** ~ **of** sur; (in addition to) en plus de; **from** ~ **to bottom** de fond en comble; ~ **up** (US ~ **off**) vt (bottle) remplir; (salary) compléter; ~ **floor** n dernier étage; ~ **hat** n haut-de-forme f; ~-**heavy** adj (object) trop lourd(e) du haut

topic [ˈtɒpɪk] n sujet m, thème m; ~**al** adj d'actualité

top: ~**less** [ˈtɒpləs] adj (bather etc) aux seins nus; ~-**level** [ˈtɒpˈlevl] adj (talks) au plus haut niveau; ~**most** [ˈtɒpməʊst] adj le(la) plus haut(e)

topple [ˈtɒpl] vt renverser, faire tomber ♦ vi basculer; tomber

top-secret [ˈtɒpˈsiːkrɪt] adj top secret(ète)

topsy-turvy [ˈtɒpsɪˈtɜːvɪ] adj, adv sens dessus dessous

torch [tɔːtʃ] n torche f; (BRIT: electric) lampe f de poche

tore [tɔː*] pt of **tear**[1]

torment [n ˈtɔːment, vb tɔːˈment] n tourment m ♦ vt tourmenter; (fig: annoy) harceler

torn [tɔːn] pp of **tear**[1]

tornado [tɔːˈneɪdəʊ] (pl ~**es**) n tornade f

torpedo [tɔːˈpiːdəʊ] (pl ~**es**) n torpille f

torrent [ˈtɒrənt] n torrent m

tortoise [ˈtɔːtəs] n tortue f; ~**shell** adj en écaille

torture [ˈtɔːtʃə*] n torture f ♦ vt torturer

Tory [ˈtɔːrɪ] (BRIT POL) adj tory, conservateur(trice) ♦ n tory m/f, conservateur(trice)

toss [tɒs] vt lancer, jeter; (pancake) faire sauter; (head) rejeter en arrière; to ~ **a coin** jouer à pile ou face; to ~ **up for** sth jouer qch à pile ou face; to ~ **and turn** (in bed) se tourner et se retourner

tot [tɒt] n (BRIT: drink) petit verre; (child) bambin m

total [ˈtəʊtl] adj total(e) ♦ n total m ♦ vt (add up) faire le total de, additionner; (amount to) s'élever à; ~**ly** [ˈtəʊtəlɪ] adv totalement

totter [ˈtɒtə*] vi chanceler

touch [tʌtʃ] n contact m, toucher m; (sense, also skill: of pianist etc) toucher ♦ vt toucher; (tamper with) toucher à; a ~ **of** (fig) une petit peu de; une touche de; to **get in** ~ **with** prendre contact avec; to **lose** ~

(friends) se perdre de vue; ~ **on** *vt fus (topic)* effleurer, aborder; ~ **down** *vi (paint)* retoucher; **~-and-go** *adj* incertain(e); **~line** *n* atterrissage *m; (on sea)* amerrissage *m; (US: FOOTBALL)* touché-en-but *m;* **~ed** *adj (moved)* touché(e); **~ing** *adj* touchant(e), attendrissant(e); **~line** *n (SPORT)* ligne *f* de touche *f;* **~y** *adj (person)* susceptible

tough [tʌf] *adj* dur(e); *(resistant)* résistant(e), solide; *(meat)* dur, coriace; *(firm)* inflexible; *(task)* dur, pénible; *(wear) vt (character)* endurcir; *(glass etc)* renforcer

toupee ['tuːpeɪ] *n* postiche *m*

tour [tʊə*] *n* voyage *m; (also: package)* ~ voyage organisé; *(of town, museum)* tour *m,* visite *f; (by artist)* tournée *f* ♦ *vt* visiter

tourism ['tʊərɪzm] *n* tourisme *m*

tourist ['tʊərɪst] *n* touriste *m/f* ♦ *cpd* touristique; ~ **office** *n* syndicat *m* d'initiative

tournament ['tʊənəmənt] *n* tournoi *m*

tousled ['taʊzld] *adj (hair)* ébouriffé(e)

tout [taʊt] *vi:* **to** ~ **for** essayer de raccrocher, racoler *(also:* **ticket** ~) revendeur *m* de billets

tow [təʊ] *vt* remorquer; *(caravan, trailer)* tracter; **"on** (BRIT) **or in** (US) ~" *(AUT)* "véhicule en remorque"

toward(s) [tə'wɔːd(z)] *prep* vers; *(of attitude)* envers, à l'égard de; *(of purpose)* pour

towel ['taʊəl] *n* serviette *f* (de toilette); **~ling** *n (fabric)* tissu éponge *m;* ~ **rail** (US ~ **rack**) *n* porte-serviettes *m inv*

tower ['taʊə*] *n* tour *f;* ~ **block** (BRIT) *n* tour *f* (d'habitation); **~ing** *adj* très haut(e), imposant(e)

town [taʊn] *n* ville *f;* **to go to** ~ aller en ville; *(fig)* y mettre le paquet; ~ **centre** *n* centre *m* de la ville, centre-ville *m;* ~ **council** *n* conseil municipal; ~ **hall** *n* ≈ mairie *f;* ~

plan *n* plan *m* de ville; ~ **planning** *n* urbanisme *m*

towrope ['təʊrəʊp] *n* (câble *m* de) remorque *f*

tow truck (US) *n* dépanneuse *f*

toy [tɔɪ] *n* jouet *m;* ~ **with** *vt fus* jouer avec; *(idea)* caresser

trace [treɪs] *n* trace *f* ♦ *vt (draw)* tracer, dessiner; *(follow)* suivre la trace de; *(locate)* retrouver; **tracing paper** *n* papier-calque *m*

track [træk] *n (mark)* trace *f; (path: gen)* chemin *m,* piste *f; (: of bullet etc)* trajectoire *f; (: of suspect, animal)* piste *f; (RAIL)* voie ferrée, rails *mpl; (on tape, SPORT)* piste; *(on record)* plage *f* ♦ *vt* suivre la trace ou la piste de; **to keep** ~ **of** suivre; ~ **down** *vt (prey)* trouver et capturer; *(sth lost)* finir par retrouver; **~suit** *n* survêtement *m*

tract [trækt] *n (GEO)* étendue *f,* zone *f; (pamphlet)* tract *m*

traction ['trækʃən] *n* traction *f; (MED):* **in** ~ en extension

tractor ['træktə*] *n* tracteur *m*

trade [treɪd] *n* commerce *m; (skill, job)* métier *m* ♦ *vi* faire du commerce ♦ *vt (exchange):* **to** ~ **sth** *(for sth)* échanger qch (contre qch); ~ **in** *(old car etc)* faire reprendre; ~ **fair** *n* foire-exposition *f* commerciale; **~-in price** *n* prix *m* à la reprise; **~mark** *n* marque *f* de fabrique; **~ name** *n* nom *m* de marque; **~r** *n* commerçant(e), négociant(e); **~sman** *(irreg) n (shopkeeper)* commerçant *m;* ~ **union** *n* syndicat *m;* **~ unionist** *n* syndicaliste *m/f*

tradition [trə'dɪʃən] *n* tradition *f;* **~al** *adj* traditionnel(le)

traffic ['træfɪk] *n* trafic *m; (cars)* circulation *f* ♦ *vi:* **to** ~ **in** *(pej: liquor, drugs)* faire le trafic de; ~ **circle** (US) *n* rond-point *m;* ~ **jam** *n* embouteillage *m;* ~ **lights** *npl* feux *mpl* (de signalisation); ~ **warden** *n* contractuel(le)

tragedy ['trædʒədɪ] *n* tragédie *f*

tragic ['trædʒɪk] *adj* tragique

trail [treɪl] *n (tracks)* trace *f,* piste *f*

(path) chemin m, piste; (of smoke etc) traînée f ♦ vt traîner, tirer; (follow) suivre ♦ vi traîner; (in game, contest) être en retard; ~ **behind** vi traîner, être à la traîne; ~**er** n (AUT) remorque f; (US) caravane f; (CINEMA) bande-annonce f; ~**er truck** (US) n (camion m) semi-remorque f

train [treɪn] n train m; (in underground) rame f; (of dress) traîne f ♦ vt (apprentice, doctor etc) former; (sportsman) entraîner; (dog) dresser; (memory) exercer; (point: gun etc): **to ~ sth on** braquer qch sur ♦ vi suivre une formation; (SPORT) s'entraîner; **one's ~ of thought** le fil de sa pensée; ~**ed** adj qualifié(e), qui a reçu une formation; (animal) dressé(e); ~**ee** n stagiaire m/f; (in trade) apprenti(e); ~**er** n (SPORT: coach) entraîneur(euse); (: shoe) chaussure f de sport; (of dogs etc) dresseur(euse); ~**ing** n formation f; entraînement m; **in ~ing** (SPORT) à l'entraînement; (fit) en forme; ~**ing college** n école professionnelle; (for teachers) = école normale; ~**ing shoes** npl chaussures fpl de sport

traipse [treɪps] vi: **to ~ in/out** entrer/sortir d'un pas traînant

trait [treɪ(t)] n trait m de caractère

traitor ['treɪtə*] n traître m

tram ['træm] (BRIT) n (also: ~**car**) tram(way) m

tramp [træmp] n (person) vagabond(e), clochard(e); (inf: pej: woman): **to be a ~** être coureuse ♦ vi marcher d'un pas lourd

trample ['træmpl] vt: **to ~ (underfoot)** piétiner

trampoline ['træmpəlin] n trampoline m

tranquil ['træŋkwɪl] adj tranquille; ~**izer** (US ~**izer**) n (MED) tranquillisant m

transact [træn'zækt] vt (business) traiter; ~**ion** n transaction f

transatlantic ['trænzət'læntɪk] adj transatlantique

transfer [n 'trænsfə*, vt træns'fə:*] n (gen, also SPORT) transfert m; (POL: of power) passation f; (picture, design) décalcomanie f; (: stickon) autocollant m ♦ vt transférer; passer; **to ~ the charges** (BRIT: TEL) téléphoner en P.C.V.

transform [træns'fɔːm] vt transformer

transfusion [træns'fjuːʒən] n transfusion f

transient ['trænzɪənt] adj transitoire, éphémère

transistor [træn'zɪstə*] n (ELEC, also: ~ **radio**) transistor m

transit ['trænzɪt] n: **in ~** en transit

transitive ['trænzɪtɪv] adj (LING) transitif(ive)

transit lounge n salle f de transit

translate [trænz'leɪt] vt traduire; **translation** [trænz'leɪʃən] n traduction f; **translator** [trænz'leɪtə*] n traducteur(trice)

transmission [trænz'mɪʃən] n transmission f

transmit [trænz'mɪt] vt transmettre; (RADIO, TV) émettre

transparency [træns'pærənsɪ] n (of glass etc) transparence f; (PHOT) diapositive f; **transparent** [træns'pærənt] adj transparent(e)

transpire [træns'paɪə*] vi (turn out): **it ~d that** ... on a appris que ...; (happen) arriver

transplant [vb træns'plɑːnt, n 'trænsplɑːnt] vt transplanter; (seedlings) repiquer ♦ n (MED) transplantation f

transport [n 'trænspɔːt, vb træns'pɔːt] n transport m; (car) moyen m de transport, voiture f ♦ vt transporter; ~**ation** [trænspɔː'teɪʃən] n transport m; (means of ~) moyen m de transport; ~ **café** (BRIT) n restaurant m de routiers

trap [træp] n (snare, trick) piège m; (carriage) cabriolet m ♦ vt prendre au piège; (confine) coincer; ~ **door** n trappe f

trapeze [trə'piːz] n trapèze m

trappings ['træpɪŋz] npl ornements mpl; attributs mpl

trash [træʃ] (pej) n (goods) camelote f; (nonsense) sottises fpl; ~ n (US) n poubelle f

trauma ['trɔːmə] n traumatisme m; ~tic adj traumatisant(e)

travel ['trævl] n voyage(s) m(pl) ♦ vi voyager; (news, sound) circuler, se propager ♦ vt (distance) parcourir; ~ agency n agence f de voyages; ~ agent n agent m de voyages; ~ler (US ~er) n voyageur(euse); ~ler's cheque (US ~er's check) n chèque m de voyage; ~ling (US ~ing) n voyage(s) m(pl); ~ sickness n mal m de la route (or de mer or de l'air)

travesty ['trævəstɪ] n parodie f

trawler ['trɔːlə*] n chalutier m

tray [treɪ] n (for carrying) plateau m; (on desk) corbeille f

treacherous adj (person, look) traître(esse); (ground, tide) dont il faut se méfier

treachery ['tretʃərɪ] n traîtrise f

treacle ['triːkl] n mélasse f

tread [tred] (pt trod, pp trodden) n pas m; (sound) bruit m de pas; (of tyre) chape f, bande f de roulement ♦ vi marcher; ~ on vt fus marcher sur

treason ['triːzn] n trahison f

treasure ['treʒə*] n trésor m ♦ vt (value) tenir beaucoup à

treasurer ['treʒərə*] n trésorier(ère)

treasury ['treʒərɪ] n: the T~, (US) the T~ Department n le ministère des Finances

treat [triːt] n petit cadeau, petite surprise ♦ vt traiter; to ~ sb to sth offrir qch à qn

treatment ['triːtmənt] n traitement m

treaty ['triːtɪ] n traité m

treble ['trebl] adj triple ♦ vt, vi tripler; ~ clef n (MUS) clé f de sol

tree [triː] n arbre m

trek [trek] n (long) voyage m; (on foot) (longue) marche, tirée f

tremble ['trembl] vi trembler

tremendous [trə'mendəs] adj (enormous) énorme, fantastique; (excellent) formidable

tremor ['tremə*] n tremblement m; (also: earth ~) secousse f sismique

trench [trentʃ] n tranchée f

trend [trend] n (tendency) tendance f; (of events) cours m; (fashion) mode f; ~y adj (idea, person) dans le vent; (clothes) dernier cri

trepidation [trepɪ'deɪʃən] n vive agitation or inquiétude f

trespass ['trespəs] vi: to ~ on s'introduire sans permission dans; "no ~ing" "propriété privée", "défense d'entrer"

trestle ['tresl] n tréteau m

trial ['traɪəl] n (LAW) procès m, jugement m; (test: of machine etc) essai m; ~s npl (unpleasant experiences) épreuves fpl; to be on ~ (LAW) passer en jugement; by ~ and error par tâtonnements; ~ period n période f d'essai

triangle ['traɪæŋgl] n (MATH, MUS) triangle m

tribe [traɪb] n tribu f; ~sman (irreg) n membre m d'une tribu

tribunal [traɪ'bjuːnl] n tribunal m

tributary ['trɪbjʊtərɪ] n (river) affluent m

tribute ['trɪbjuːt] n tribut m, hommage m; to pay ~ to rendre hommage à

trice [traɪs] n: in a ~ en un clin d'œil

trick [trɪk] n (magic ~) tour m; (joke, prank) tour, farce f; (skill, knack) astuce f, truc m; (CARDS) levée f ♦ vt attraper, rouler; to play a ~ on sb jouer un tour à qn; that should do the ~ ça devrait faire l'affaire; ~ery n ruse f

trickle ['trɪkl] n (of water etc) filet m ♦ vi couler en un filet or goutte à goutte

tricky ['trɪkɪ] adj difficile, délicat(e)

tricycle ['traɪsɪkl] n tricycle m

trifle ['traɪfl] n bagatelle f; (CULIN) ≈ diplomate m ♦ adv: a ~ long un peu long; **trifling** adj insignifiant(e)

trigger ['trɪgə*] n (of gun) gâchette f; ~ **off** vt déclencher

trim [trɪm] adj (house, garden) bien tenu(e); (figure) svelte ♦ n (haircut etc) légère coupe; (on car) garnitures fpl ♦ vt (cut) couper légèrement; (NAUT: sails) gréer; (decorate): to ~ (with) décorer (de); ~**mings** npl (CULIN) garniture f

trinket ['trɪŋkɪt] n bibelot m; (piece of jewellery) colifichet m

trip [trɪp] n voyage m; (excursion) excursion f; (stumble) faux pas ♦ vi (also: ~ up) trébucher, faire un faux pas; (go lightly) marcher d'un pas léger; on a ~ en voyage; ~ **up** vi trébucher ♦ vt faire un croc-en-jambe à

tripe [traɪp] n (CULIN) tripes fpl; (pej: rubbish) idioties fpl

triple ['trɪpl] adj triple; ~**ts** ['trɪplɪts] npl triplé(e)s; **triplicate** ['trɪplɪkɪt] n: **in triplicate** en trois exemplaires

tripod ['traɪpɔd] n trépied m

trite [traɪt] (pej) adj banal(e)

triumph ['traɪʌmf] n triomphe m ♦ vi: to ~ (over) triompher (de)

trivia ['trɪvɪə] (pej) npl futilités fpl

trivial ['trɪvɪəl] adj insignifiant(e); (commonplace) banal(e)

trod [trɔd] pt of **tread**

trodden ['trɔdn] pp of **tread**

trolley ['trɔlɪ] n chariot m

trombone [trɔm'bəʊn] n trombone m

troop [truːp] n bande f, groupe m ♦ vi: to ~ **in/out** entrer/sortir en groupe; ~**s** npl (MIL) troupes fpl; (: men) hommes mpl, soldats mpl; ~**ing the colour** (BRIT) n (ceremony) le salut au drapeau

trophy ['trəʊfɪ] n trophée m

tropic ['trɔpɪk] n tropique m; ~**al** adj tropical(e)

trot [trɔt] n trot m ♦ vi trotter; **on the** ~ (BRIT: fig) d'affilée

trouble ['trʌbl] n difficulté(s) f(pl), problème(s) m(pl); (worry) ennuis mpl, soucis mpl; (bother, effort) peine f; (POL) troubles mpl;

(MED): **stomach** etc ~ **troubles** gastriques etc ♦ vt (disturb) déranger, gêner; (worry) inquiéter ♦ vi: to ~ **to do** prendre la peine de faire; ~**s** npl (POL etc) troubles mpl; (personal) ennuis, soucis; to be in ~ avoir des ennuis; (ship, climber etc) être en difficulté; **what's the** ~? qu'est-ce qui ne va pas?; ~**d** adj (person) inquiet(ète); (epoch, life) agité(e); ~**maker** n élément perturbateur, fauteur m de troubles; ~**shooter** n (in conflict) médiateur m; ~**some** adj (child) fatigant(e), difficile; (cough etc) gênant(e)

trough [trɔf] n (also: **drinking** ~) abreuvoir m; (: **feeding** ~) auge f; (depression) creux m

trousers ['traʊzəz] npl pantalon m; **short** ~ culottes courtes

trout [traʊt] n inv truite f

trowel ['traʊəl] n truelle f; (garden tool) déplantoir m

truant ['trʊənt] (BRIT) n: to play ~ faire l'école buissonnière

truce [truːs] n trêve f

truck [trʌk] n camion m; (RAIL) wagon m à plate-forme; ~ **driver** n camionneur m; ~ **farm** (US) n jardin maraîcher

trudge [trʌdʒ] vi marcher lourdement, se traîner

true [truː] adj vrai(e); (accurate) exact(e); (genuine) vrai, véritable; (faithful) fidèle; to come ~ se réaliser

truffle ['trʌfl] n truffe f

truly ['truːlɪ] adv vraiment, réellement; (truthfully) sans mentir; see also **yours**

trump [trʌmp] n (also: ~ **card**) atout m; ~**ed up** adj inventé(e) (de toutes pièces)

trumpet ['trʌmpɪt] n trompette f

truncheon ['trʌntʃən] (BRIT) n bâton m (d'agent de police); matraque f

trundle ['trʌndl] vt, vi: to ~ **along** rouler lentement (et bruyamment)

trunk [trʌŋk] n (of tree, person)

truss [trʌs] n (MED) bandage m herniaire ♦ vt: to ~ (up) (CULIN) brider, trousser

trust [trʌst] n confiance f; (responsibility) charge f; (LAW) fidéicommis m ♦ vt (rely on) avoir confiance en; (hope) espérer; (entrust) to ~ sth to sb confier qch à qn; to take sth on ~ accepter qch les yeux fermés; ~ed adj en qui l'on a confiance; ~ee n (LAW) fidéicommissaire m/f; (of school etc) administrateur(trice); ~ful, ~ing adj confiant(e); ~worthy adj digne de confiance

truth [tru:θ, pl tru:ðz] n vérité f; ~ful adj (person) qui dit la vérité; (answer) sincère

try [traɪ] n essai m, tentative f; (RUGBY) essai m ♦ vt (attempt) essayer, tenter; (test: sth new: also: ~ out) essayer, tester; (LAW: person) juger; (strain) éprouver ♦ vi essayer; to have a ~ essayer; to ~ to do essayer de faire; (seek) chercher à faire; ~ on vt (clothes) essayer; ~ing adj pénible

T-shirt ['ti:ʃɜ:t] n tee-shirt m

T-square ['ti:skweə*] n équerre f en T, té m

tub [tʌb] n cuve f; (for washing clothes) baquet m; (bath) baignoire f

tubby ['tʌbɪ] adj rondelet(te)

tube [tju:b] n tube m; (BRIT: underground) métro m; (for tyre) chambre f à air

TUC n abbr (BRIT: = Trades Union Congress) confédération f des syndicats britanniques

tuck [tʌk] vt (put) mettre; ~ away vt cacher, ranger; ~ in vt rentrer; (child) border ♦ vi (eat) manger (de bon appétit); ~ up vt (child) border; ~ shop n boutique f à provisions (dans une école)

Tuesday ['tju:zdeɪ] n mardi m

tuft [tʌft] n touffe f

tug [tʌg] n (ship) remorqueur m ♦ vt tirer (sur); ~-of-war n lutte f à la corde; (fig) lutte acharnée

tuition [tju:'ɪʃən] n (BRIT) leçons fpl; (: private ~) cours particuliers; (US: school fees) frais mpl de scolarité

tulip ['tju:lɪp] n tulipe f

tumble ['tʌmbl] n (fall) chute f, culbute f ♦ vi tomber, dégringoler; to ~ to sth (inf) réaliser qch; ~down adj délabré(e); ~ dryer n (BRIT) ~ sé-choir m à air chaud

tumbler ['tʌmblə*] n (glass) verre (droit), gobelet m

tummy ['tʌmɪ] n (inf) ventre m

tumour ['tju:mə*] (US tumor) n tumeur f

tuna ['tju:nə] n inv (also: ~ fish) thon m

tune [tju:n] n (melody) air m ♦ vt (MUS) accorder; (RADIO, TV, AUT) régler; to be in/out of ~ (instrument) être accordé/désaccordé; (singer) chanter juste/faux; to be in/out of ~ with (fig) être en accord/désaccord avec; ~ in vi (RADIO, TV): to ~ in (to) se mettre à l'écoute (de); ~ up vi (musician) accorder son instrument; ~ful adj mélodieux(euse); ~r n: piano ~r accordeur m (de pianos)

tunic ['tju:nɪk] n tunique f

Tunisia [tju:'nɪzɪə] n Tunisie f

tunnel ['tʌnl] n tunnel m; (in mine) galerie f ♦ vi percer un tunnel

turbulence ['tɜ:bjʊləns] n (AVIAT) turbulence f

tureen [tju:'ri:n] n (for soup) soupière f; (for vegetables) légumier m

turf [tɜ:f] n gazon m; (clod) motte f (de gazon) ♦ vt gazonner; ~ out (inf) vt (person) jeter dehors

turgid ['tɜ:dʒɪd] adj (speech) pompeux(euse)

Turk [tɜ:k] n Turc(Turque) m(f)

Turkey ['tɜ:kɪ] n Turquie f

turkey ['tɜ:kɪ] n dindon m, dinde f

Turkish ['tɜ:kɪʃ] adj turc(turque) ♦ n (LING) turc m

turmoil ['tɜːmɔɪl] n trouble m, bouleversement m; **in ~** en émoi, en effervescence

turn [tɜːn] n tour m; (in road) tournant m; (of mind, events) tournure f; (performance) numéro m; (MED) crise f, attaque f ♦ vt tourner; (collar, steak) retourner; (change): **to ~ sth into** changer qch en ♦ vi (object, wind, milk) tourner; (person: look back) se (re)tourner; (reverse direction) faire demi-tour; (become) devenir; (age) atteindre; **to ~ into** se changer en; **a good ~** un service; **it gave me quite a ~** ça m'a fait un coup; **"no left ~"** (AUT) "défense de tourner à gauche"; **it's your ~** c'est (à) votre tour; **in ~** à son tour; **to .tour** de rôle; **to take ~s** (at) se relayer (pour or à); **~ away** vi (applicants) refuser; **~ back** vi revenir, faire demi-tour ♦ vt (person, vehicle) faire faire demi-tour à; (clock) reculer; **~ down** vt (refuse) rejeter, refuser; (reduce) baisser; (fold) rabattre; **~ in** vi (inf: go to bed) aller se coucher ♦ vt (fold) rentrer; **~ off** vi (from road) tourner ♦ vt (light, radio etc) éteindre; (tap) fermer; (engine) arrêter; **~ on** vt (light, radio etc) allumer; (tap) ouvrir; (engine) mettre en marche; **~ out** vt (light, gas) éteindre; (produce) produire ♦ vi (voters, troops etc) se présenter; **to ~ out to be** ... s'avérer ..., se révéler ...; **~ over** vi (person) se retourner ♦ vt (object) retourner; (page) tourner; **~ round** vi faire demi-tour; (rotate) tourner; **~ up** vi (person) arriver, se pointer (inf); (lost object) être retrouvé(e) ♦ vt (collar) remonter; (radio, heater) mettre plus fort; **~ing** n (in road) tournant m; **~ing point** n (fig) tournant m, moment décisif

turnip ['tɜːnɪp] n navet m

turnout ['tɜːnaʊt] n (of voters) taux m de participation

turnover ['tɜːnəʊvə*] n (COMM: amount of money) chiffre m d'affaires; (: of goods) roulement m; (of staff) renouvellement m, changement m

turnpike ['tɜːnpaɪk] (US) n autoroute f à péage

turnstile ['tɜːnstaɪl] n tourniquet m (d'entrée)

turntable ['tɜːnteɪbl] n (on record player) platine f

turn-up ['tɜːnʌp] (BRIT) n (on trousers) revers m

turpentine ['tɜːpəntaɪn] n (also: turps) (essence f de) térébenthine f

turquoise ['tɜːkwɔɪz] n (stone) turquoise f ♦ adj turquoise inv

turret ['tʌrɪt] n tourelle f

turtle ['tɜːtl] n tortue marine or d'eau douce; **~neck (sweater)** n (BRIT) pullover m à col montant; (US) pullover à col roulé

tusk [tʌsk] n défense f

tussle ['tʌsl] n bagarre f, mêlée f

tutor ['tjuːtə*] n (in college) directeur(trice) d'études; (private teacher) précepteur(trice); **~ial** [tjuːˈtɔːrɪəl] n (SCOL) (séance f de) travaux mpl pratiques

tuxedo [tʌkˈsiːdəʊ] (US) n smoking m

TV ['tiːˈviː] n abbr (= television) télé f

twang [twæŋ] n (of instrument) son vibrant; (of voice) ton nasillard

tweed [twiːd] n tweed m

tweezers ['twiːzəz] npl pince f à épiler

twelfth [twelfθ] num douzième

twelve [twelv] num douze; **at ~ (o'clock)** à midi; (midnight) à minuit

twentieth ['twentɪɪθ] num vingtième

twenty ['twentɪ] num vingt

twice [twaɪs] adv deux fois; **~ as much** deux fois plus

twiddle ['twɪdl] vt, vi: **to ~ (with) sth** tripoter qch; **to ~ one's thumbs** (fig) se tourner les pouces

twig [twɪg] n brindille f ♦ vi (inf) piger

twilight ['twaɪlaɪt] n crépuscule m

twin [twɪn] adj, n jumeau(elle) ♦ vt jumeler; **~(-bedded) room** n chambre f à deux lits

twine [twaɪn] n ficelle f ♦ vi (plant) s'enrouler

twinge [twɪndʒ] n (of pain) élancement m; **a ~ of conscience** un certain remords; **a ~ of regret** un pincement au cœur

twinkle ['twɪŋkl] vi scintiller; (eyes) pétiller

twirl [twɜːl] vt faire tournoyer ♦ vi tournoyer

twist [twɪst] n torsion f, tour m; (in road) virage m; (in wire, flex) tortillon m; (in story) coup m de théâtre ♦ vt tordre; (weave) entortiller; (roll around) enrouler; (fig) déformer ♦ vi (road, river) serpenter

twit [twɪt] (inf) n crétin/e

twitch [twɪtʃ] n (pull) coup sec, saccade f; (nervous) tic m ♦ vi se convulser; avoir un tic

two [tuː] num deux; **to put ~ and ~ together** (fig) faire le rapprochement; **~-door** adj (AUT) à deux portes; **~-faced** (pej) adj (person) faux(fausse); **~fold** adv: **to increase ~fold** doubler; **~-piece (suit)** n (man's) costume m (deux-pièces) (woman's) (tailleur m) deux-pièces m inv; **~-piece (swimsuit)** n (maillot m de bain) deux-pièces m inv; **~some** n (people) couple m; **~-way** adj (traffic) dans les deux sens

tycoon [taɪˈkuːn] n: **(business) ~** gros homme d'affaires

type [taɪp] n (category) type m, genre m, espèce f; (model, example) type m, modèle m; (TYP) type, caractère m ♦ vt (letter etc) taper (à la machine); **~-cast** adj (actor) condamné(e) à toujours jouer le même rôle; **~face** n (TYP) œil m de caractère; **~script** n texte dactylographié; **~writer** n machine f à écrire; **~written** adj dactylographié(e)

typhoid ['taɪfɔɪd] n typhoïde f

typical ['tɪpɪkl] adj typique, caractéristique

typing ['taɪpɪŋ] n dactylo(graphie) f

typist ['taɪpɪst] n dactylo m/f

tyrant ['taɪərnt] n tyran m

tyre [taɪə*] (US **tire**) n pneu m; **~ pressure** n pression f (de gonflage)

U

U-bend ['juːˈbend] n (in pipe) coude m

ubiquitous adj omniprésent(e)

udder ['ʌdə*] n pis m, mamelle f

UFO ['juːfəʊ] n abbr (= unidentified flying object) ovni m

Uganda [juːˈgændə] n Ouganda m

ugh [ɜːh] excl pouah!

ugly ['ʌglɪ] adj laid(e), vilain(e); (situation) inquiétant(e)

UK n abbr = **United Kingdom**

ulcer ['ʌlsə*] n ulcère m; (also: **mouth ~**) aphte f

Ulster ['ʌlstə*] n Ulster m; (inf: Northern Ireland) Irlande f du Nord

ulterior [ʌlˈtɪərɪə*] adj: **~ motive** arrière-pensée f

ultimate ['ʌltɪmət] adj ultime, final(e); (authority) suprême; **~ly** adv en fin de compte; finalement

ultrasound ['ʌltrəˈsaʊnd] n ultrason m

umbilical cord [ʌmˈbɪlɪkl-] n cordon ombilical

umbrella [ʌmˈbrelə] n parapluie m; (for sun) parasol m

umpire ['ʌmpaɪə*] n arbitre m

umpteen [ʌmpˈtiːn] adj je ne sais combien de; **~th** adj: **for the ~th time** pour la énième fois

UN n abbr = **United Nations**

unable [ʌnˈeɪbl] adj: **to be ~ to** ne pas pouvoir, être dans l'impossibilité de; (incapable) être incapable de

unaccompanied ['ʌnəˈkʌmpənɪd] adj (child, lady) non accompagné(e); (song) sans accompagnement

unaccountably ['ʌnəˈkaʊntəblɪ] adv inexplicablement

unaccustomed [ˈʌnəˈkʌstəmd] adj:
to be ~ to sth ne pas avoir l'habitude de qch

unanimous [juːˈnænɪməs] adj unanime; ~ly adv à l'unanimité

unarmed [ʌnˈɑːmd] adj (without a weapon) non armé(e); (combat) sans armes

unashamed [ʌnəˈʃeɪmd] adj effronté(e), impudent(e)

unassuming [ʌnəˈsjuːmɪŋ] adj modeste, sans prétentions

unattached [ʌnəˈtætʃt] adj libre, sans attaches; (part) non attaché(e), indépendant(e)

unattended [ˈʌnəˈtendɪd] adj (car, child, luggage) sans surveillance

unattractive [ʌnəˈtræktɪv] adj peu attrayant(e); (character) sans sympathie

unauthorized [ʌnˈɔːθəraɪzd] adj non autorisé(e), sans autorisation

unavoidable [ʌnəˈvɔɪdəbl] adj inévitable

unaware [ʌnəˈweə*] adj: to be ~ of ignorer, être inconscient(e) de; ~s adv à l'improviste, au dépourvu

unbalanced [ʌnˈbælənst] adj déséquilibré(e); (report) peu objectif(ive)

unbearable [ʌnˈbeərəbl] adj insupportable

unbeatable [ʌnˈbiːtəbl] adj imbattable

unbeknown(st) [ˈʌnbɪˈnəun(st)] adv: ~ to me/Peter à mon insu/à l'insu de Peter

unbelievable [ʌnbɪˈliːvəbl] adj incroyable

unbend [ʌnˈbend] (irreg) vi se détendre ♦ vt (wire) redresser, détordre

unbiased [ʌnˈbaɪəst] adj impartial(e)

unborn [ʌnˈbɔːn] adj à naître, qui n'est pas encore né(e)

unbreakable [ʌnˈbreɪkəbl] adj incassable

unbroken [ʌnˈbrəukən] adj intact(e); (fig) continu(e), ininterrom-

pu(e)

unbutton [ʌnˈbʌtn] vt déboutonner

uncalled-for [ʌnˈkɔːldfɔː*] adj déplacé(e), injustifié(e)

uncanny [ʌnˈkænɪ] adj étrange, troublant(e)

unceasing [ʌnˈsiːsɪŋ] adj incessant(e), continu(e)

unceremonious [ˈʌnserɪˈməuniəs] adj (abrupt, rude) brusque

uncertain [ʌnˈsɜːtn] adj incertain(e); (hesitant) hésitant(e); in no ~ terms sans équivoque possible; ~ty n incertitude f, doute(s) m(pl)

unchecked [ʌnˈtʃekt] adv sans contrôle or opposition

uncivilized [ʌnˈsɪvɪlaɪzd] adj (gen) non civilisé(e); (fig: behaviour etc) barbare; (hour) indu(e)

uncle [ˈʌŋkl] n oncle m

uncomfortable [ʌnˈkʌmfətəbl] adj inconfortable, peu confortable; (uneasy) mal à l'aise, gêné(e); (situation) désagréable

uncommon [ʌnˈkɔmən] adj rare, singulier(ère), peu commun(e)

uncompromising [ʌnˈkɔmprəmaɪzɪŋ] adj intransigeant(e), inflexible

unconcerned [ʌnkənˈsɜːnd] adj: to be ~ (about) ne pas s'inquiéter (de)

unconditional [ʌnkənˈdɪʃənl] adj sans conditions

unconscious [ʌnˈkɔnʃəs] adj sans connaissance, évanoui(e); (unaware): ~ of inconscient(e) de ♦ n: the ~ l'inconscient m; ~ly adv inconsciemment

uncontrollable [ʌnkənˈtrəuləbl] adj indiscipliné(e); (temper, laughter) irrépressible

unconventional [ʌnkənˈvenʃənl] adj peu conventionnel(le)

uncouth [ʌnˈkuːθ] adj grossier(ère), fruste

uncover [ʌnˈkʌvə*] vt découvrir

undecided [ˈʌndɪˈsaɪdɪd] adj indécis(e), irrésolu(e)

under [ˈʌndə*] prep sous; (less than) (de) moins de; au-dessous de; (ac-

cording to) selon, en vertu de ♦ *below*: au-dessous; ~ **there** là-dessous; ~ **repair** en (cours de) réparation

under: ~**age** *adj (person)* qui n'a pas l'âge réglementaire; ~**carriage** n *(AVIAT)* train *m* d'atterrissage; ~**charge** vt ne pas faire payer assez à; ~**coat** vt *n (paint)* couche *f* de fond; ~**cover** *adj* secret(ète), clandestin(e); ~**current** n courant ou sentiment sous-jacent; ~**cut** *(irreg)* vt vendre moins cher que; ~**dog** n opprimé(e); ~**done** *adj (CULIN)* saignant(e); *(pej)* pas assez cuit(e); ~**estimate** vt sous-estimer; ~**fed** *adj* sous-alimenté(e); ~**foot** *adv* sous les pieds; ~**go** *(irreg)* vt subir; *(treatment)* suivre; ~**graduate** n étudiant(e) *(qui prépare la licence)*; ~**ground** n *(BRIT: railway)* métro *m*; *(POL)* clandestinité *f* ♦ *adj* souterrain(e); *(fig)* clandestin(e) ♦ *adv* dans la clandestinité, clandestinement; ~**growth** n broussailles *fpl*, sous-bois *m*; ~**hand(ed)** *adj (fig: behaviour, method etc)* en dessous; ~**lie** *(irreg)* vt être à la base de; ~**line** vt souligner; ~**ling** *(pej)* n sous-fifre *m*, subalterne *m*; ~**mine** vt saper, miner; ~**neath** *adv* (en) dessous ♦ *prep* sous, au-dessous de; ~**paid** *adj* sous-payé(e); ~**pants** *npl* caleçon *m*, slip *m*; ~**pass** n *(BRIT)* passage souterrain; *(on motorway)* passage inférieur; ~**privileged** *adj* défavorisé(e), économiquement faible; ~**rate** vt sous-estimer; ~**shirt** *(US)* n tricot *m* de corps; ~**shorts** *(US)* npl caleçon *m*, slip *m*; ~**side** n dessous *m*; ~**skirt** *(BRIT)* n jupon *m*

understand [ʌndə'stænd] *(irreg: like stand)* vt, vi comprendre; **I** ~ **that ...** je me suis laissé dire que ...; **I crois comprendre que ...**; ~**able** *adj* compréhensible; ~**ing** *adj* compréhensif(ive) ♦ n compréhension *f*; *(agreement)* accord *m*

understatement ['ʌndəsteitmənt]

n: **that's an** ~ c'est (bien) peu dire, le terme est faible

understood [ʌndə'stud] *pt*, *pp* of **understand** ♦ *adj* entendu(e); *(implied)* sous-entendu(e)

understudy ['ʌndəstʌdɪ] n doublure *f*

undertake [ʌndə'teɪk] *(irreg)* vt entreprendre; se charger de; **to** ~ **to do sth** s'engager à faire qch

undertaker ['ʌndəteɪkə*] n entrepreneur *m* des pompes funèbres, croque-mort *m*

undertaking [ʌndə'teɪkɪŋ] n entreprise *f*; *(promise)* promesse *f*

undertone ['ʌndətəun] n: **in an** ~ à mi-voix

under: ~**water** [ʌndə'wɔːtə*] *adv* sous l'eau ♦ *adj* sous-marin(e); ~**wear** [ʌndəwɛə*] n sous-vêtements *mpl*; *(women's only)* dessous *mpl*; ~**world** ['ʌndəwəːld] n *(of crime)* milieu *m*, pègre *f*; ~**writer** ['ʌndəraitə*] n *(INSURANCE)* assureur *m*

undies ['ʌndɪz] *(inf)* npl dessous *mpl*, lingerie *f*

undiplomatic [ʌndɪplə'mætɪk] *adj* peu diplomatique

undo [ʌn'duː] *(irreg)* vt défaire; ~**ing** n ruine *f*, perte *f*

undoubted [ʌn'dautɪd] *adj* indubitable, certain(e); ~**ly** *adv* sans aucun doute

undress [ʌn'drɛs] vi se déshabiller

undue [ʌn'djuː] *adj* indu(e), excessif(ive)

undulating ['ʌndjuleɪtɪŋ] *adj* ondoyant(e), onduleux(euse)

unduly [ʌn'djuːlɪ] *adv* trop, excessivement

unearth [ʌn'əːθ] vt déterrer; *(fig)* dénicher

unearthly [ʌn'əːθlɪ] *adj (hour)* indu(e), impossible

uneasy [ʌn'iːzɪ] *adj* mal à l'aise, gêné(e); *(worried)* inquiet(ète); *(feeling)* désagréable; *(peace, truce)* fragile

uneconomic(al) [ʌniːkə'nɔmɪk(əl)] *adj* peu économique

uneducated [ʌn'ɛdjukeɪtɪd] adj (person) sans instruction

unemployed [ʌnɪm'plɔɪd] adj sans travail, en or au chômage ♦ n: the ~ les chômeurs mpl; **unemployment** [ʌnɪm'plɔɪmənt] n chômage m

unending [ʌn'ɛndɪŋ] adj interminable, sans fin

unerring [ʌn'ɜːrɪŋ] adj infaillible, sûr(e)

uneven [ʌn'iːvən] adj inégal(e); irrégulier(ère)

unexpected [ʌnɪk'spɛktɪd] adj inattendu(e), imprévu(e); **~ly** adv (arrive) à l'improviste; (succeed) contre toute attente

unfailing [ʌn'feɪlɪŋ] adj inépuisable, infaillible

unfair [ʌn'fɛə*] adj: ~ (to) injuste (envers)

unfaithful [ʌn'feɪθful] adj infidèle

unfamiliar [ʌnfə'mɪlɪə*] adj étrange, inconnu(e); **to be ~ with** mal connaître

unfashionable [ʌn'fæʃnəbl] adj (clothes) démodé(e); (place) peu chic inv

unfasten [ʌn'fɑːsn] vt défaire; détacher; (open) ouvrir

unfavourable [ʌn'feɪvərəbl] (US **unfavorable**) adj défavorable

unfeeling [ʌn'fiːlɪŋ] adj insensible, dur(e)

unfinished [ʌn'fɪnɪʃt] adj inachevé(e)

unfit [ʌn'fɪt] adj en mauvaise santé; pas en forme; (incompetent): ~ (for) impropre à; (work, service) inapte à

unfold [ʌn'fəuld] vt déplier ♦ vi se dérouler

unforeseen [ʌnfɔː'siːn] adj imprévu(e)

unforgettable [ʌnfə'gɛtəbl] adj inoubliable

unfortunate [ʌn'fɔːtʃnət] adj malheureux(euse); (event, remark) malencontreux(euse); **~ly** adv malheureusement

unfounded [ʌn'faundɪd] adj sans

fondement

unfriendly [ʌn'frɛndlɪ] adj inamical(e), peu aimable

ungainly [ʌn'geɪnlɪ] adj gauche, dégingandé(e)

ungodly [ʌn'gɒdlɪ] adj (hour) indu(e)

ungrateful [ʌn'greɪtful] adj ingrat(e)

unhappiness [ʌn'hæpɪnəs] n tristesse f, peine f

unhappy [ʌn'hæpɪ] adj triste, malheureux(euse); ~ **about** or **with** (arrangements etc) mécontent(e) de, peu satisfait(e) de

unharmed [ʌn'hɑːmd] adj indemne, sain(e) et sauf(sauve)

unhealthy [ʌn'hɛlθɪ] adj malsain(e); (person) maladif(ive)

unheard-of [ʌn'hɜːdɔv] adj inouï(e), sans précédent

unhurt [ʌn'hɜːt] adj indemne

unidentified [ʌnaɪ'dɛntɪfaɪd] adj non identifié(e); see also **UFO**

uniform ['juːnɪfɔːm] n uniforme m ♦ adj uniforme

uninhabited [ʌnɪn'hæbɪtɪd] adj inhabité(e)

unintentional [ʌnɪn'tɛnʃənəl] adj involontaire

union ['juːnjən] n union f; (also: trade ~) syndicat m ♦ cpd du syndicat, syndical(e); **U~ Jack** n drapeau du Royaume-Uni

unique [juː'niːk] adj unique

unison ['juːnɪsn] n: **in** ~ (sing) à l'unisson; (say) en chœur

unit ['juːnɪt] n unité f; (section: of furniture etc) élément m, bloc m; **kitchen** ~ élément de cuisine

unite [juː'naɪt] vt unir ♦ vi s'unir; **~d** adj uni(e); unifié(e); (effort) conjugué(e); **U~d Kingdom** n Royaume-Uni m; **U~d Nations (Organization)** n (Organisation f des) Nations unies; **U~d States (of America)** n Etats-Unis mpl

unit trust (BRIT) n fonds commun de placement

unity ['juːnɪtɪ] n unité f

universal [juːnɪ'vɜːsl] adj universel(le)

universe ['ju:nɪvɜːs] n univers m

university [ju:nɪ'vɜːsɪtɪ] n université f

unjust ['ʌn'dʒʌst] adj injuste

unkempt ['ʌn'kempt] adj négligé(e), débraillé(e); (hair) mal peigné(e).

unkind [ʌn'kaɪnd] adj peu gentil(le), méchant(e)

unknown [ʌn'nəʊn] adj inconnu(e)

unlawful [ʌn'lɔ:fʊl] adj illégal(e)

unleaded [ʌn'ledɪd] adj (petrol, fuel) sans plomb

unleash [ʌn'li:ʃ] vt (fig) déchaîner, déclencher

unless [ʌn'les] conj: ~ he leaves à moins qu'il ne parte

unlike [ʌn'laɪk] adj dissemblable, différent(e) ♦ prep contrairement à

unlikely [ʌn'laɪklɪ] adj improbable; invraisemblable

unlimited [ʌn'lɪmɪtɪd] adj illimité(e)

unlisted [ʌn'lɪstɪd] (US) adj (TEL) sur la liste rouge

unload ['ʌn'ləʊd] vt décharger

unlock [ʌn'lɒk] vt ouvrir

unlucky [ʌn'lʌkɪ] adj (person) malchanceux(euse); (object, number) qui porte malheur; to be ~ (person) ne pas avoir de chance

unmarried [ʌn'mærɪd] adj célibataire

unmistak(e)able [ʌnmɪs'teɪkəbl] adj indubitable; qu'on ne peut pas ne pas reconnaître

unmitigated [ʌn'mɪtɪgeɪtɪd] adj non mitigé(e), absolu(e), pur(e)

unnatural [ʌn'nætʃrəl] adj non naturel(le); (habit) contre nature

unnecessary [ʌn'nesəsərɪ] adj inutile, superflu(e)

unnoticed [ʌn'nəʊtɪst] adj: (to go or pass) ~ (passer) inaperçu(e)

UNO ['ju:nəʊ] n abbr = United Nations Organization

unobtainable ['ʌnəb'teɪnəbl] adj impossible à obtenir

unobtrusive [ʌnəb'tru:sɪv] adj discret(ète)

unofficial [ʌnə'fɪʃl] adj (news) offi-

cieux(euse); (strike) sauvage

unorthodox [ʌn'ɔ:θədɒks] adj peu orthodoxe; (REL) hétérodoxe

unpack ['ʌn'pæk] vi défaire sa valise ♦ vt (suitcase) défaire; (belongings) déballer

unpalatable [ʌn'pælətəbl] adj (meal) mauvais(e); (truth) désagréable (à entendre)

unparalleled [ʌn'pærəleld] adj incomparable, sans égal

unpleasant [ʌn'pleznt] adj déplaisant(e), désagréable

unplug ['ʌn'plʌg] vt débrancher

unpopular [ʌn'pɒpjʊlə*] adj impopulaire

unprecedented [ʌn'presɪdəntɪd] adj sans précédent

unpredictable [ʌnprɪ'dɪktəbl] adj imprévisible

unprofessional [ʌnprə'feʃənl] adj: ~ conduct manquement m aux devoirs de la profession

unqualified ['ʌn'kwɒlɪfaɪd] adj (teacher) non diplômé(e), sans titres; (success, disaster) sans réserve, total(e)

unquestionably [ʌn'kwestʃənəblɪ] adv incontestablement

unravel [ʌn'rævəl] vt démêler

unreal [ʌn'rɪəl] adj irréel(le); (extraordinary) incroyable; ~**istic** [ʌnrɪə'lɪstɪk] adj irréaliste; peu réaliste

unreasonable [ʌn'ri:znəbl] adj qui n'est pas raisonnable

unrelated [ʌnrɪ'leɪtɪd] adj sans rapport; sans lien de parenté

unrelenting [ʌnrɪ'lentɪŋ] adj implacable

unreliable [ʌnrɪ'laɪəbl] adj sur qui (or quoi) on ne peut pas compter, peu fiable

unremitting [ʌnrɪ'mɪtɪŋ] adj inlassable, infatigable, acharné(e)

unreservedly [ʌnrɪ'zɜːvɪdlɪ] adv sans réserve

unrest [ʌn'rest] n agitation f, troubles mpl

unroll [ʌn'rəʊl] vt dérouler

unruly [ʌnˈruːlɪ] *adj* indiscipliné(e)

unsafe [ʌnˈseɪf] *adj (in danger)* en danger; *(journey, car)* dangereux(euse)

unsaid [ʌnˈsed] *adj*: **to leave sth ~** passer qch sous silence

unsatisfactory ['ʌnsætɪsˈfæktərɪ] *adj* peu satisfaisant(e)

unsavoury [ʌnˈseɪvərɪ] (*US* **unsavory**) *adj (fig)* peu recommandable

unscathed [ʌnˈskeɪðd] *adj* indemne

unscrew [ʌnˈskruː] *vt* dévisser

unscrupulous [ʌnˈskruːpjʊləs] *adj* sans scrupules

unsettled [ʌnˈsetld] *adj* perturbé(e); instable

unshaven [ʌnˈʃeɪvn] *adj* non *or* mal rasé(e)

unsightly [ʌnˈsaɪtlɪ] *adj* disgracieux(euse), laid(e)

unskilled [ʌnˈskɪld] *adj*: **~ worker** manœuvre *m*

unspeakable [ʌnˈspiːkəbl] *adj* indicible; *(awful)* innommable

unstable [ʌnˈsteɪbl] *adj* instable

unsteady [ʌnˈstedɪ] *adj* mal assuré(e), chancelant(e), instable

unstuck [ʌnˈstʌk] *adj*: **to come ~** se décoller; *(plan)* tomber à l'eau

unsuccessful [ʌnsəkˈsesfʊl] *adj (attempt)* infructueux(euse), vain(e); *(writer, proposal)* qui n'a pas de succès; **to be ~ (in attempting sth)** ne pas réussir; ne pas avoir de succès; *(application)* ne pas être retenu(e)

unsuitable [ʌnˈsuːtəbl] *adj* qui ne convient pas, peu approprié(e); inopportun(e)

unsure [ʌnˈʃuə*] *adj* pas sûr(e); **to be ~ of o.s.** manquer de confiance en soi

unsuspecting [ʌnsəˈspektɪŋ] *adj* qui ne se doute de rien

unsympathetic ['ʌnsɪmpəˈθetɪk] *adj (person)* antipathique; *(attitude)* peu compatissant(e)

untapped ['ʌnˈtæpt] *adj (resources)* inexploité(e)

unthinkable [ʌnˈθɪŋkəbl] *adj* impensable, inconcevable

untidy [ʌnˈtaɪdɪ] *adj (room)* en désordre; *(appearance, person)* débraillé(e); *(person: in character)* sans ordre, désordonné

untie [ʌnˈtaɪ] *vt (knot, parcel)* défaire; *(prisoner, dog)* détacher

until [ənˈtɪl] *prep* jusqu'à; *(after negative)* avant ◆ *conj* jusqu'à ce que +*sub*; *(in past, after negative)* avant que +*sub*; **~ he comes** jusqu'à ce qu'il vienne, jusqu'à son arrivée; **~ now** jusqu'à présent, jusqu'ici; **~ then** jusque-là

untimely [ʌnˈtaɪmlɪ] *adj* inopportun(e); *(death)* prématuré(e)

untold [ʌnˈtəʊld] *adj (story)* jamais raconté(e); *(wealth)* incalculable; *(joy, suffering)* indescriptible

untoward [ʌntəˈwɔːd] *adj* fâcheux(euse), malencontreux(euse)

unused¹ [ʌnˈjuːzd] *adj (clothes)* neuf(euve)

unused² [ʌnˈjuːst] *adj*: **to be unused to sth/to doing sth** ne pas avoir l'habitude de qch/de faire qch

unusual [ʌnˈjuːʒʊəl] *adj* insolite, exceptionnel(le), rare

unveil [ʌnˈveɪl] *vt* dévoiler

unwanted [ʌnˈwɒntɪd] *adj (child, pregnancy)* non désiré(e); *(clothes etc)* à donner

unwelcome [ʌnˈwelkəm] *adj* importun(e); *(news)* fâcheux(euse)

unwell [ʌnˈwel] *adj* souffrant(e); **to feel ~** ne pas se sentir bien

unwieldy [ʌnˈwiːldɪ] *adj (object)* difficile à manier; *(system)* lourd(e)

unwilling [ʌnˈwɪlɪŋ] *adj*: **to be ~ to do** ne pas vouloir faire; **~ly** *adv* à contrecœur, contre son gré

unwind [ʌnˈwaɪnd] (*irreg*) *vt* dérouler ◆ *vi (relax)* se détendre

unwise [ʌnˈwaɪz] *adj* irréfléchi(e), imprudent(e)

unwitting [ʌnˈwɪtɪŋ] *adj* involontaire

unworkable [ʌnˈwɜːkəbl] *adj (plan)* impraticable

unworthy [ʌnˈwɜːðɪ] *adj* indigne

unwrap ['ʌnˈræp] *vt* défaire; ouvrir

unwritten [ʌnˈrɪtn] *adj (agreement)*

tacite

up [ʌp] *prep*: he went ~ the stairs/
the hill il a monté l'escalier/la colline; the cat was ~ a tree le chat
était dans un arbre; they live
further ~ the street ils habitent
plus haut dans la rue
♦ *adv* 1 (*upwards, higher*): ~ **in**
the sky/the mountains (là-haut) dans
le ciel/les montagnes; **put it a bit
higher** ~ mettez-le un peu plus haut;
~ **there** là-haut; ~ **above** au-dessus
2: **to be** ~ (*out of bed*) être
levé(e); (*prices*) avoir augmenté or
monté
3: ~ **to** (*as far as*) jusqu'à; ~ **to
now** jusqu'à présent
4: **to be** ~ **to** (*depending on*) c'est à
vous de décider; (*equal to*): **he's not**
~ **to it** (*job, task etc*) il n'en est pas
capable; (*inf: be doing*): **what is he**
~ **to?** qu'est-ce qu'il peut bien faire?
♦ *n*: ~**s and downs** hauts et bas
mpl

up-and-coming [ʌpənd'kʌmɪŋ] *adj*
plein(e) d'avenir *or* de promesses
upbringing ['ʌpbrɪŋɪŋ] *n* éducation *f*
update [ʌp'deɪt] *vt* mettre à jour
upgrade [ʌp'greɪd] *vt* (*house*) moderniser; (*job*) revaloriser; (*employee*) promouvoir
upheaval [ʌp'hiːvəl] *n* bouleversement *m*; branle-bas *m*; crise *f*
uphill [ʌp'hɪl] *adj* qui monte; (*fig:
task*) difficile, pénible ♦ *adv* (*face,
look*) en amont; **to go** ~ monter
uphold [ʌp'həʊld] (*irreg*) *vt* (*law,
decision*) maintenir
upholstery [ʌp'həʊlstərɪ] *n* rembourrage *m*; (*cover*) tissu *m* d'ameublement; (*of car*) garniture *f*
upkeep ['ʌpkiːp] *n* entretien *m*
upon [ə'pɒn] *prep* sur
upper ['ʌpər] *adj* supérieur(e); du
dessus ♦ *n* (*of shoe*) empeigne *f*; ~
class *adj* de la haute société, aristo-

cratique; ~ **hand** *n*: **to have the
hand** avoir le dessus; ~**most** *adj*
le(la) plus haut(e); **what was**
~**most in my mind** ce à quoi je
pensais surtout
upright ['ʌpraɪt] *adj* droit(e); verti-
cal(e); (*fig*) droit, honnête
uprising [ʌp'raɪzɪŋ] *n* soulèvement
m, insurrection *f*
uproar ['ʌprɔːr] *n* tumulte *m*; (*pro-
tests*) tempête *f* de protestations
uproot [ʌp'ruːt] *vt* déraciner
upset [*n* 'ʌpset, *vb. adj* ʌp'set]
(*irreg: like* set) *n* bouleversement
m; (*stomach*) indigestion *f* ♦ *vt*
(*glass etc*) renverser; (*plan*) déranger; (*person: offend*) contrarier; (:
grieve) faire de la peine à; bouleverser ♦ *adj* contrarié(e); peiné(e);
(*stomach*) dérangé(e)
upshot ['ʌpʃɒt] *n* résultat *m*
upside-down ['ʌpsaɪd'daʊn] *adv* à
l'envers; **to turn** ~ mettre sens dessus dessous
upstairs ['ʌp'steəz] *adv* en haut ♦
adj (*room*) du dessus, d'en haut ♦ *n*:
the ~ l'étage *m*
upstart ['ʌpstɑːt] *n* parvenu(e)
upstream ['ʌp'striːm] *adv* en amont
uptake ['ʌpteɪk] *n*: **to be quick/slow
on the** ~ comprendre vite/être lent à
comprendre
uptight ['ʌp'taɪt] (*inf*) *adj* très ten-
du(e), crispé(e)
up-to-date ['ʌptə'deɪt] *adj* moderne;
(*information*) très récent(e)
upturn ['ʌptɜːn] *n* (*in luck*) retourne-
ment *m*; (*COMM: in market*) hausse
f
upward ['ʌpwəd] *adj* ascendant(e);
vers le haut; ~**s** *adv* vers le haut;
(~**s**) **of 200** 200 et plus
urban ['ɜːbən] *adj* urbain(e); ~**e**
[ɜː'beɪn] *adj* urbain(e), courtois(e)
urchin ['ɜːtʃɪn] *n* polisson *m*
urge [ɜːdʒ] *n* besoin *m*; envie *f*; forte
envie, désir *m* ♦ *vt*: **to** ~ **sb to do**
exhorter qn à faire, pousser qn à faire; recommander vivement à qn de
faire

urgency ['ɜːdʒənsɪ] n urgence f; (of tone) insistance f

urgent ['ɜːdʒənt] adj urgent(e); (tone) instant(e), pressant(e)

urinal n urinoir m; (vessel) urinal m

urine ['jʊərɪn] n urine f

urn [ɜːn] n urne f; (also: tea ~) fontaine f à thé

US n abbr = United States

us [ʌs] pron nous; see also me

USA n abbr = United States of America

use [n juːs, vb juːz] n emploi m, utilisation f; usage m; (usefulness) utilité f ♦ vt se servir de, utiliser, employer; **in ~** en usage; **out of ~** hors d'usage; **to be of ~** servir, être utile; **it's no ~** ça ne sert à rien; **she ~d to do it** elle le faisait (autrefois), elle avait coutume de le faire; **~d to: to be ~d to** avoir l'habitude de, être habitué(e) à; **~ up** vt finir, épuiser; consommer; **~d** adj (car) d'occasion; **~ful** adj utile; **~fulness** n utilité f; **~less** adj inutile; (person: hopeless) nul(le); **~r** n utilisateur(trice), usager m; **~r-friendly** adj (computer) convivial(e), facile d'emploi

usher ['ʌʃəʳ] n (at wedding ceremony) placeur m; **~ette** [ʌʃə'rɛt] n (in cinema) ouvreuse f

usual ['juːʒʊəl] adj habituel(le); **as ~** comme d'habitude; **~ly** adv de l'habitude, d'ordinaire

utensil [juː'tɛnsl] n ustensile m

uterus ['juːtərəs] n utérus m

utility [juː'tɪlɪtɪ] n utilité f; (also: public ~) service public; **~ room** n buanderie f

utmost ['ʌtməʊst] adj extrême, le(la) plus grand(e) ♦ n: **to do one's ~** faire tout son possible

utter ['ʌtəʳ] adj total(e), complet(ète) ♦ vt (words) prononcer, proférer; (sounds) émettre; **~ance** n paroles fpl; **~ly** adv complètement, totalement

U-turn ['juː'tɜːn] n demi-tour m

V

v. abbr = verse; versus; volt; (= vide) voir

vacancy ['veɪkənsɪ] n (BRIT: job) poste vacant; (room) chambre f disponible

vacant ['veɪkənt] adj (seat etc) libre, disponible; (expression) distrait(e); **~ lot** (US) terrain inoccupé; (for sale) terrain à vendre

vacate [və'keɪt] vt quitter

vacation [və'keɪʃən] n vacances fpl

vaccinate ['væksɪneɪt] vt vacciner

vacuum ['vækjʊm] n vide m; **~ cleaner** n aspirateur m; **~-packed** adj emballé(e) sous vide

vagina [və'dʒaɪnə] n vagin m

vagrant ['veɪɡrənt] n vagabond(e)

vague [veɪɡ] adj vague, imprécis(e); (blurred: photo, outline) flou(e); **~ly** adv vaguement

vain [veɪn] adj (useless) vain(e); (conceited) vaniteux(euse); **in ~** en vain

valentine ['væləntaɪn] n (also: ~ card) carte f de la Saint-Valentin; (person) bien-aimé(e) (le jour de la Saint-Valentin)

valiant ['vælɪənt] adj vaillant(e)

valid ['vælɪd] adj valable; (document) valable, valide

valley ['vælɪ] n vallée f

valour ['væləʳ] (US **valor**) n courage m

valuable ['væljʊəbl] adj (jewel) de valeur; (time, help) précieux(euse); **~s** npl objets mpl de valeur

valuation [vælju'eɪʃən] n (price) estimation f; (quality) appréciation f

value ['væljuː] n valeur f ♦ vt (fix price) évaluer, expertiser; (appreciate) apprécier; **~ added tax** (BRIT) n taxe f à la valeur ajoutée; **~d** adj (person) estimé(e); (advice) précieux(euse)

valve [vælv] n (in machine) soupape f, valve f; (MED) valve, valvule f

van [væn] n (AUT) camionnette f

vandal ['vændl] n vandale m/f; **~ism** n vandalisme m; **~ize** ['vændalaɪz] vt saccager

vanguard ['vængɑːd] n (fig): **in the ~ of** à l'avant-garde de

vanilla [və'nɪlə] n vanille f

vanish ['vænɪʃ] vi disparaître

vanity ['vænɪtɪ] n vanité f

vantage point ['vɑːntɪdʒ-] n bonne position

vapour ['veɪpə*] (US vapor) n vapeur f; (on window) buée f

variable ['vɛərɪəbl] adj variable; (mood) changeant(e)

variance ['vɛərɪəns] n: **to be at ~ (with)** être en désaccord (avec); (facts) être en contradiction (avec)

varicose ['værɪkəus] adj: **~ veins** varices fpl

varied ['vɛərɪd] adj varié(e), divers(e)

variety [və'raɪətɪ] n variété f; (quantity) nombre m, quantité f; **~ show** n (spectacle m de) variétés fpl

various ['vɛərɪəs] adj divers(e), différent(e); (several) divers, plusieurs

varnish ['vɑːnɪʃ] n vernis m ♦ vt vernir

vary ['vɛərɪ] vt, vi varier, changer

vase [vɑːz] n vase m

Vaseline ['væsɪliːn] (®) n vaseline f

vast [vɑːst] adj vaste, immense; (amount, success) énorme

VAT [væt] n abbr (= value added tax) TVA f

vat [væt] n cuve f

vault [vɔːlt] n (of roof) voûte f; (tomb) caveau m; (in bank) salle f des coffres; chambre forte f ♦ vt (also: ~ over) sauter (d'un bond)

vaunted ['vɔːntɪd] adj: **much-vaunted** tant vanté(e)

VCR n abbr = video cassette recorder

VD n abbr = venereal disease

VDU n abbr = visual display unit

veal [viːl] n veau m

veer [vɪə*] vi tourner; virer

vegetable ['vedʒtəbl] n légume m ♦ adj végétal(e)

vegetarian [vedʒɪ'tɛərɪən] adj, n végétarien(ne)

vehement ['viːɪmənt] adj violent(e), impétueux(euse); (impassioned) ardent(e)

vehicle ['viːɪkl] n véhicule m

veil [veɪl] n voile m

vein [veɪn] n veine f; (on leaf) nervure f

velvet ['velvɪt] n velours m

vending machine ['vendɪŋ-] n distributeur m automatique

veneer [və'nɪə*] n (on furniture) placage m; (fig) vernis m

venereal [vɪ'nɪərɪəl] adj: **~ disease** maladie vénérienne

Venetian blind [vɪ'niːʃən-] n store vénitien

vengeance ['vendʒəns] n vengeance f; **with a ~** (fig) vraiment, pour de bon

venison ['venɪsn] n venaison f

venom ['venəm] n venin m

vent [vent] n conduit m d'aération; (in dress, jacket) fente f ♦ vt (fig: one's feelings) donner libre cours à

ventilator ['ventɪleɪtə*] n ventilateur m

ventriloquist [ven'trɪləkwɪst] n ventriloque m/f

venture ['ventʃə*] n entreprise f ♦ vt risquer, hasarder ♦ vi s'aventurer, se risquer

venue ['venjuː] n lieu m

verb [vɜːb] n verbe m; **~al** adj verbal(e); (translation) littéral(e)

verbatim [vɜː'beɪtɪm] adj, adv mot pour mot

verdict ['vɜːdɪkt] n verdict m

verge [vɜːdʒ] n (BRIT) bord m, bascôté m; **"soft ~s"** (: AUT) "accotement non stabilisé"; **on the ~ of doing** sur le point de faire; **~ on** vt fus approcher de

verify ['verɪfaɪ] vt vérifier; (confirm) confirmer

vermin ['vɜːmɪn] npl animaux mpl nuisibles; (insects) vermine f

vermouth ['vɜːməθ] n vermouth m

versatile ['vɜːsətaɪl] adj polyvalent(e)

verse [vɜːs] n (poetry) vers mpl; (stanza) strophe f; (in Bible) verset m

version ['vɜːʃən] n version f

versus ['vɜːsəs] prep contre

vertical ['vɜːtɪkəl] adj vertical(e) ♦ n verticale f

vertigo ['vɜːtɪgəu] n vertige m

verve [vɜːv] n brio m; enthousiasme m

very ['verɪ] adv très ♦ adj: the ~ book which le livre même que; the ~ last le tout dernier; at the ~ least tout au moins; ~ much beaucoup

vessel [vesl] n (ANAT, NAUT) vaisseau m; (container) récipient m

vest [vest] n (BRIT) tricot m de corps; (US: waistcoat) gilet m

vested interest ['vestɪd-] n (COMM) droits acquis

vet [vet] n abbr (BRIT: = veterinary surgeon) vétérinaire m/f ♦ vt examiner soigneusement

veteran ['vetərn] n vétéran m; (also: war ~) ancien combattant

veterinarian [vetrɪ'neərɪən] (US) n = veterinary surgeon

veterinary surgeon ['vetrɪnərɪ-] (BRIT) n vétérinaire m/f

veto ['viːtəu] (pl ~es) n veto m ♦ vt opposer son veto à

vex [veks] vt fâcher, contrarier; ~ed adj (question) controversé(e)

via ['vaɪə] prep par, via

viable ['vaɪəbl] adj viable

vibrate [var'breɪt] vi vibrer

vicar ['vɪkə*] n pasteur m (de l'Eglise anglicane); ~age n presbytère m

vicarious [vɪ'keərɪəs] adj indirect(e)

vice [vaɪs] n (evil) vice m; (TECH) étau m

vice- prefix vice-

vice squad n ≈ brigade mondaine

vice versa ['vaɪsɪ'vɜːsə] adv vice versa

vicinity [vɪ'sɪnɪtɪ] n environs mpl, alentours mpl

vicious ['vɪʃəs] adj (remark) cruel(le), méchant(e); (blow) brutal(e); (dog) méchant(e), dangereux(euse); (horse) vicieux(euse); ~ circle n cercle vicieux

victim ['vɪktɪm] n victime f

victor ['vɪktə*] n vainqueur m

Victorian [vɪk'tɔːrɪən] adj victorien(ne)

victory ['vɪktərɪ] n victoire f

video ['vɪdɪəu] cpd vidéo inv ♦ n (~ film) vidéo f; also: ~ cassette) vidéocassette f; (: ~ cassette recorder) magnétoscope m; ~ tape n bande f vidéo inv; (cassette) vidéocassette f

vie [vaɪ] vi: to ~ with rivaliser avec

Vienna [vɪ'enə] n Vienne

Vietnam [vjet'næm] n Viet-Nam m, Vietnam m; ~ese [vjetnə'miːz] adj vietnamien(ne) ♦ n inv Vietnamien(ne); (LING) vietnamien m

view [vjuː] n vue f; (opinion) avis m, vue f ♦ vt voir, regarder; (situation) considérer; (house) visiter; in full ~ of sous les yeux de; in ~ of the weather/the fact that étant donné le temps/que; in my ~ à mon avis; ~er n (TV) téléspectateur(trice); ~finder n viseur m; ~point n point m de vue

vigorous ['vɪgərəs] adj vigoureux(euse)

vile [vaɪl] adj (action) vil(e); (smell, food) abominable; (temper) massacrant(e)

villa ['vɪlə] n villa f

village ['vɪlɪdʒ] n village m; ~r n villageois(e)

villain ['vɪlən] n (scoundrel) scélérat m; (BRIT: criminal) bandit m; (in novel etc) traître m

vindicate ['vɪndɪkeɪt] vt (person) innocenter; (action) justifier

vindictive [vɪn'dɪktɪv] adj vindicatif(ive), rancunier(ère)

vine [vaɪn] n vigne f; (climbing plant) plante grimpante

vinegar ['vɪnɪgə*] n vinaigre m

vineyard ['vɪnjɑːd] n vignoble m

vintage ['vɪntɪdʒ] n (year) année f, millésime m; ~ **car** n voiture f d'époque; ~ **wine** n vin m de grand cru

viola [vɪ'əʊlə] n (MUS) alto m

violate ['vaɪəleɪt] vt violer

violence ['vaɪələns] n violence f

violent ['vaɪələnt] adj violent(e)

violet ['vaɪələt] adj violet(te) ♦ n (colour) violet m; (plant) violette f

violin [vaɪə'lɪn] n violon m; ~**ist** n violoniste m/f

VIP n abbr (= very important person) V.I.P. m

virgin ['vɜːdʒɪn] n vierge f ♦ adj vierge

Virgo ['vɜːɡəʊ] n la Vierge

virile ['vɪraɪl] adj viril(e)

virtually ['vɜːtjʊəlɪ] adv (almost) pratiquement

virtual reality n (COMPUT) réalité virtuelle

virtue ['vɜːtjuː] n vertu f; (advantage) mérite m, avantage m; **by** ~ **of** en vertu or en raison de; **virtuous** ['vɜːtjʊəs] adj vertueux(euse)

virus ['vaɪərəs] n (also: COMPUT) virus m

visa ['viːzə] n visa m

visibility [vɪzɪ'bɪlɪtɪ] n visibilité f

visible ['vɪzəbl] adj visible

vision ['vɪʒən] n (sight) vue f, vision f; (foresight, in dream) vision f

visit ['vɪzɪt] n visite f; (stay) séjour m ♦ vt (person) rendre visite à; (place) visiter; ~**ing hours** npl (in hospital etc) heures fpl de visite; ~**or** n visiteur(euse); (to one's house) visite f, invité(e)

visor ['vaɪzə*] n visière f

vista ['vɪstə] n vue f

visual ['vɪzjʊəl] adj visuel(le); ~ **aid** n support visuel; ~ **display unit** n console f de visualisation, visuel m; ~**ize** ['vɪzjʊəlaɪz] vt se représenter, s'imaginer

vital ['vaɪtl] adj vital(e); (person) plein(e) d'entrain; ~**ly** adv (important) absolument; ~ **statistics** npl (fig) mensurations fpl

vitamin ['vɪtəmɪn] n vitamine f

vivacious [vɪ'veɪʃəs] adj animé(e), qui a de la vivacité

vivid ['vɪvɪd] adj (account) vivant(e); (light, imagination) vif(vive); ~**ly** adv (describe) d'une manière vivante; (remember) de façon précise

V-neck ['viːnek] n décolleté m en V

vocabulary [vəʊ'kæbjʊlərɪ] n vocabulaire m

vocal ['vəʊkəl] adj vocal(e); (articulate) qui sait s'exprimer; ~ **cords** npl cordes vocales

vocation [vəʊ'keɪʃən] n vocation f; ~**al** adj professionnel(le)

vociferous [vəʊ'sɪfərəs] adj bruyant(e)

vodka ['vɒdkə] n vodka f

vogue [vəʊɡ] n: **in** ~ en vogue f

voice [vɔɪs] n voix f ♦ vt (opinion) exprimer, formuler

void [vɔɪd] n vide m ♦ adj nul(le); ~ **of** vide de, dépourvu(e) de

volatile ['vɒlətaɪl] adj volatil(e); (person) versatile; (situation) explosif(ive)

volcano [vɒl'keɪnəʊ] (pl ~es) n volcan m

volition [və'lɪʃən] n: **of one's own** ~ de son propre gré

volley ['vɒlɪ] n (of gunfire) salve f; (of stones etc) grêle f, volée f; (of questions) multitude f, série f; (TENNIS etc) volée f; ~**ball** n volley(-ball) m

volt [vəʊlt] n volt m; ~**age** n tension f, voltage m

volume ['vɒljuːm] n volume m

voluntarily ['vɒləntərɪlɪ] adv volontairement

voluntary ['vɒləntərɪ] adj volontaire; (unpaid) bénévole

volunteer [vɒlən'tɪə*] n volontaire m/f ♦ vt (information) fournir (spontanément) ♦ vi (MIL) s'engager comme volontaire; **to** ~ **to do** se proposer pour faire

vomit ['vɒmɪt] vt, vi vomir

vote [vəʊt] n vote m, suffrage m; (cast) voix f, vote; (franchise) droit m de vote ♦ vt (elect): **to be** ~

chairman *etc* être élu président *etc*; *(propose)*: to ~ that proposer que ♦ *vi* voter; ~ of thanks discours *m* de remerciement; ~r *n* électeur(trice).

voting ['vəutɪŋ] *n* scrutin *m*, vote *m*

voucher ['vautʃə*] *n (for meal, petrol, gift)* bon *m*

vouch for [vautʃ] *vt fus* se porter garant de

vow [vau] *n* vœu *m*, serment *m* ♦ *vi* jurer

vowel ['vauəl] *n* voyelle *f*

voyage ['vɔɪdʒ] *n* voyage *m* par mer, traversée *f*; *(by spacecraft)* voyage

vulgar ['vʌlgə*] *adj* vulgaire

vulnerable ['vʌlnərəbl] *adj* vulnérable

vulture ['vʌltʃə*] *n* vautour *m*

W

wad [wɔd] *n (of cotton wool, paper)* tampon *m*; *(of banknotes etc)* liasse *f*

waddle ['wɔdl] *vi* se dandiner

wade [weɪd] *vi*: to ~ through marcher dans, patauger dans; *(fig: book)* s'évertuer à lire

wafer ['weɪfə*] *n (CULIN)* gaufrette *f*

waffle ['wɔfl] *n (CULIN)* gaufre *f*; *(inf)* verbiage *m*, remplissage *m* ♦ *vi* parler pour ne rien dire, faire du remplissage

waft [wɔːft] *vt* porter ♦ *vi* flotter

wag [wæg] *vt* agiter, remuer ♦ *vi* remuer

wage [weɪdʒ] *n (also:* ~s) salaire *m*, paye *f* ♦ *vt*: to ~ war faire la guerre; ~ **earner** *n* salarié(e); ~ **packet** *n* (enveloppe *f* de) paye *f*

wager ['weɪdʒə*] *n* pari *m*.

waggle ['wægl] *vt*, *vi* remuer

wag(g)on ['wægən] *n (horse-drawn)* chariot *m*; *(BRIT: RAIL)* wagon *m* (de marchandises)

wail [weɪl] *vi* gémir; *(siren)* hurler

waist [weɪst] *n* taille *f*; ~**coat** *(BRIT)* *n* gilet *m*; ~**line** *n* (tour *m*

de) taille *f*

wait [weɪt] *n* attente *f* ♦ *vi* attendre; to keep sb ~ing faire attendre qn; to ~ for attendre; I can't ~ to ... *(fig)* je meurs d'envie de ...; ~ **behind** *vi* rester (à attendre); ~ **on** *vt fus* servir; ~**er** *n* garçon *m* (de café), serveur *m*; ~**ing**: "no ~**ing**" *(BRIT: AUT)* "stationnement interdit"; ~**ing list** *n* liste *f* d'attente; ~**ing room** *n* salle *f* d'attente; ~**ress** *n* serveuse *f*

waive [weɪv] *vt* renoncer à, abandonner

wake [weɪk] *(pt* woke, ~d, *pp* woken, ~d) *vt (also:* ~ up) réveiller ♦ *vi (also:* ~ up) se réveiller ♦ *n (for dead person)* veillée *f* mortuaire; *(NAUT)* sillage *m*

Wales [weɪlz] *n* pays *m* de Galles; **the Prince of** ~ le prince de Galles

walk [wɔːk] *n* promenade *f*; *(short)* petit tour; *(gait)* démarche *f*; *(path)* chemin *m*; *(in park etc)* allée *f* ♦ *vi* marcher; *(for pleasure, exercise)* se promener ♦ *vt (distance)* faire à pied; *(dog)* promener; **10 minutes'** ~ **from** à 10 minutes à pied de; **from all** ~**s of life** de toutes conditions sociales; ~ **out** *vi (audience)* sortir, quitter la salle; *(workers)* se mettre en grève; ~ **out on** *(inf) vt fus* quitter, plaquer; ~**er** *n (person)* marcheur(euse); ~**ie-talkie** *n* talkie-walkie *m*; ~**ing** *n* marche *f* à pied; ~**ing shoes** *npl* chaussures *fpl* de marche; ~**ing stick** *n* canne *f*; ~**out** *n (of workers)* grève-surprise *f*; ~**over** *(inf) n* victoire *f* ou examen *etc* facile; ~**way** *n* promenade *f*

wall [wɔːl] *n* mur *m*; *(of tunnel, cave etc)* paroi *f*; ~**ed** *adj (city)* fortifié(e); *(garden)* entouré(e) d'un mur, clos(e)

wallet ['wɔlɪt] *n* portefeuille *m*

wallflower ['wɔːlflauə*] *n* giroflée *f*; to be a ~ *(fig)* faire tapisserie

wallop ['wɔləp] *(BRIT: inf) vt* donner un grand coup à

wallow ['wɔləu] *vi* se vautrer

wallpaper ['wɔːlpeɪpə*] n papier peint ♦ vt tapisser

walnut ['wɔːlnʌt] n noix f; (tree, wood) noyer m

walrus ['wɔːlrəs] (pl ~ or ~es) n morse m

waltz [wɔːlts] n valse f ♦ vi valser

wan [wɒn] adj pâle; triste

wand [wɒnd] n (also: magic ~) baguette f (magique)

wander ['wɒndə*] vi (person) errer; (thoughts) vagabonder, errer ♦ vt errer dans

wane [weɪn] vi (moon) décroître; (reputation) décliner

wangle ['wæŋgl] (BRIT: inf) vt se débrouiller pour avoir; carotter

want [wɒnt] vt vouloir; (need) avoir besoin de ♦ n: for ~ of par manque de, faute de; ~s npl (needs) besoins mpl; to ~ to do vouloir faire; to ~ sb to do vouloir que qn fasse; ~ed adj (criminal) recherché(e) par la police; "cook ~ed" "on recherche un cuisinier"; ~ing adj: to be found ~ing ne pas être à la hauteur

wanton ['wɒntən] adj (gratuitous) gratuit(e); (promiscuous) dévergondé(e)

war [wɔː*] n guerre f; to make ~ (on) faire la guerre (à)

ward [wɔːd] n (in hospital) salle f; (POL) canton m; (LAW: child) pupille m/f; ~ off vt (attack, enemy) repousser, éviter

warden ['wɔːdən] n gardien(ne); (BRIT: of institution) directeur(trice); (: also: traffic ~) contractuel(le); (of youth hostel) père m or mère f aubergiste

warder ['wɔːdə*] (BRIT) n gardien m de prison

wardrobe ['wɔːdrəub] n (cupboard) armoire f, (clothes) garde-robe f, (THEATRE) costumes mpl

warehouse ['wɛəhaus] n entrepôt m

wares [wɛəz] npl marchandises fpl

warfare ['wɔːfɛə*] n guerre f

warhead ['wɔːhɛd] n (MIL) ogive f

warily ['wɛərɪlɪ] adv avec prudence

warm [wɔːm] adj chaud(e); (thanks, welcome, applause, person) chaleureux(euse); it's ~ il fait chaud; I'm ~ j'ai chaud; to ~ up vi (person, room) se réchauffer; (water) chauffer; (athlete) s'échauffer ♦ vt (food) (faire) réchauffer, (faire) chauffer; (engine) faire chauffer; ~-hearted adj affectueux(euse); ~ly adv chaudement; chaleureusement; ~th n chaleur f

warn [wɔːn] vt avertir, prévenir; to ~ sb (not) to do conseiller à qn de (ne pas) faire; ~ing n avertissement m; (notice) avis m; (signal) avertisseur m; ~ing light n avertisseur lumineux; ~ing triangle n (AUT) triangle m de présignalisation

warp [wɔːp] vi (wood) travailler, se déformer ♦ vt (fig: character) pervertir

warrant ['wɒrənt] n (guarantee) garantie f, (LAW: to arrest) mandat m d'arrêt; (: to search) mandat de perquisition

warranty ['wɒrəntɪ] n garantie f

warren ['wɒrən] n (of rabbits) terrier m; (fig: of streets etc) dédale m

warrior ['wɒrɪə*] n guerrier(ère)

Warsaw ['wɔːsɔː] n Varsovie

warship ['wɔːʃɪp] n navire m de guerre

wart [wɔːt] n verrue f

wartime ['wɔːtaɪm] n: in ~ en temps de guerre

wary ['wɛərɪ] adj prudent(e)

was [wɒz, wəz] pt of be

wash [wɒʃ] vt laver ♦ vi se laver; (sea): to ~ over/against sth inonder/baigner qch ♦ n (clothes) lessive f; (of ship) sillage m; (of船: of ship) sillage m; to have a ~ se laver, faire sa toilette; to give sth a ~ laver qch; ~ away vt (stain) enlever au lavage; (subj: river etc) emporter; ~ off vt partir au lavage; ~ up vi (BRIT) faire la vaisselle; (US) se débarbouiller; ~able adj lavable; ~basin (US ~bowl) n lavabo m; ~cloth (US) n gant m de toilette;

~er n (TECH) rondelle f, joint m; **~ing** n (dirty) linge m; (clean) lessive f; **~ing machine** n machine f à laver; **~ing powder** n (BRIT) lessive f (en poudre); **~ing-up** n vaisselle f; **~ing-up liquid** n produit m pour la vaisselle; **~-out** (inf) n désastre m; **~room** (US) n toilettes fpl

wasn't ['wɒznt] = **was not**

wasp [wɒsp] n guêpe f

wastage ['weɪstɪdʒ] n gaspillage m; (in manufacturing, transport etc) pertes fpl, déchets mpl; **natural ~** départs naturels

waste [weɪst] n gaspillage m; (of time) perte f; (rubbish) déchets mpl; (also: household ~) ordures fpl ♦ adj (leftover): **~ material** déchets mpl; (land, ground: in city) à l'abandon ♦ vt gaspiller; (time, opportunity) perdre; **~s** npl (area) étendue f désertique; **~ away** vi dépérir; **~ disposal unit** (BRIT) n broyeur m d'ordures; **~ful** adj gaspilleur(euse); (process) peu économique; **~ ground** (BRIT) n terrain m vague; **~paper basket** n corbeille f à papier; **~ pipe** n (tuyau m de) vidange f

watch [wɒtʃ] n montre f; (act of ~ing) surveillance f; guet m; (MIL: guards) garde f; (NAUT: guards, spell of duty) quart m ♦ vt (look at) observer; (: match, programme, TV) regarder; (spy on, guard) surveiller; (be careful of) faire attention à ♦ vi regarder; (keep guard) monter la garde; **~ out** vi faire attention; **~dog** n chien m de garde; (fig) garde(ne); **~ful** adj attentif(ive), vigilant(e); **~maker** n horloger(ère); **~man** (irreg) n see **night**; **~strap** n bracelet m de montre

water ['wɔːtə*] n eau f ♦ vt (plant, garden) arroser ♦ vi (eyes) larmoyer; (mouth): **it makes my mouth ~** j'en ai l'eau à la bouche; **in British ~s** dans les eaux territoriales britanniques; **~ down** vt (milk) couper d'eau; (fig: story)

édulcorer; **~colour** (US **~color**) n aquarelle f; **~cress** n cresson m (de fontaine); **~fall** n chute f d'eau; **~ heater** n chauffe-eau m; **~ing can** n arrosoir m; **~ lily** n nénuphar m; **~line** n (NAUT) ligne f de flottaison; **~logged** adj (ground) détrempé(e); **~ main** n canalisation f d'eau; **~melon** n pastèque f; **~proof** adj imperméable; **~shed** n (GEO) ligne f de partage des eaux; (fig) moment m critique, point décisif; **~-skiing** n ski m nautique; **~tight** adj étanche; **~way** n cours m d'eau navigable; **~works** n (building) station f hydraulique; **~y** adj (coffee, soup) faible; (eyes) humide, larmoyant(e)

watt [wɒt] n watt m

wave [weɪv] n vague f; (of hand) geste m, signe m; (RADIO) onde f; (in hair) ondulation f ♦ vi faire signe de la main; (flag) flotter au vent; (grass) ondoyer ♦ vt (handkerchief) agiter; (stick) brandir; **~length** n longueur f d'ondes

waver ['weɪvə*] vi vaciller; (voice) trembler; (person) hésiter

wavy ['weɪvɪ] adj ondulé(e); onduleux(euse)

wax [wæks] n cire f; (for skis) fart m ♦ vt cirer; (car) lustrer; (skis) farter ♦ vi (moon) croître; **~works** npl personnages mpl de cire ♦ n musée m de cire

way [weɪ] n chemin m, voie f; (distance) distance f; (direction) chemin, direction f; (manner) façon f, manière f; (habit) habitude f, façon; **which ~? - this ~** par où? - par ici; **on the ~** (en route) en route; **to be on one's ~** être en route; **to go out of one's ~ to do** (fig) se donner du mal pour faire; **to be in the ~** bloquer le passage; (fig) gêner; **to lose one's ~** perdre son chemin; **under ~** en cours; **in a ~** dans un sens, **in some ~s** à certains égards; **no ~!** (inf) pas question!; **by the ~ ...** à propos ...; **"~ in"** (BRIT) "entrée"; **"~ out"** (BRIT) "sortie"; **the ~**

back le chemin du retour; "give ~" (BRIT: AUT) "cédez le passage"; ~**lay** ['wer'ler] (irreg) vt attaquer

wayward ['werwəd] adj capricieux(euse), entêté(e)

we [wi:] pl pron nous

weak [wi:k] adj faible; (health) fragile; (beam etc) peu solide; ~**en** vi faiblir, décliner ♦ vt affaiblir; ~**ling** n (physically) gringalet m; (morally etc) faible m/f; ~**ness** n faiblesse f; (fault) point m faible; to have a ~**ness for** avoir un faible pour

wealth [wɛlθ] n (money, resources) richesse(s) f(pl); (of details) profusion f; ~**y** adj riche

wean [wi:n] vt sevrer

weapon ['wɛpən] n arme f

wear [wɛə*] (pt wore, pp worn) n (use) usage m; (deterioration through use) usure f; (clothing): sports/baby~ vêtements mpl de sport/pour bébés ♦ vt (clothes) porter; (put on) mettre; (damage: through use) user ♦ vi (last) faire de l'usage; (rub etc through) s'user; town/evening ~ tenue f de ville/soirée; ~ **away** vt user, ronger ♦ vi (inscription) s'effacer; ~ **down** vt user; (strength, person) épuiser; ~ **off** vi disparaître; ~ **out** vt user; (person, strength) épuiser; ~ **and tear** n usure f

weary ['wɪərɪ] adj (tired) épuisé(e); (dispirited) las(lasse), abattu(e) ♦ vi: to ~ of se lasser de

weasel ['wi:zl] n (ZOOL) belette f

weather ['wɛðə*] n temps m ♦ vt (tempest, crisis) essuyer, réchapper à, survivre à; (fig: ill) mal fichu(e); ~**-beaten** adj (person, face) hâlé(e); (building) dégradé(e) par les intempéries; ~**cock** n girouette f; ~ **forecast** n prévisions fpl météorologiques, météo f; ~ **man** (irreg: inf) n météorologue m; ~ **vane** n = ~**cock**

weave [wi:v] (pt wove, pp woven) vt (cloth) tisser; (basket) tresser; ~**r** n tisserand(e)

web [wɛb] n (of spider) toile f; (on foot) palmure f; (fabric, also fig) tissu m

wed [wɛd] (pt, pp wedded) vt épouser ♦ vi se marier

we'd [wi:d] = we had; we would

wedding ['wɛdɪŋ] n mariage m; silver/golden ~ (anniversary) noces fpl d'argent/d'or; ~ **day** n jour m du mariage; ~ **dress** n robe f de mariée; ~ **ring** n alliance f

Wednesday ['wɛnzdeɪ] n mercredi m

wee [wi:] adj (SCOTTISH) petit(e); tout(e) petit(e)

weed [wi:d] n mauvaise herbe ♦ vt désherber; ~**killer** n désherbant m; ~**y** adj (man) gringalet

week [wi:k] n semaine f; a ~ today/on Friday aujourd'hui/vendredi en huit; ~'s jour m de semaine; (COMM) jour ouvrable; ~**end** n week-end m; ~**ly** adv une fois par semaine, chaque semaine ♦ adj hebdomadaire ♦ n hebdomadaire m

weep [wi:p] (pt, pp wept) vi (person) pleurer; ~**ing willow** n saule pleureur

weigh [weɪ] vt, vi peser; to ~ anchor lever l'ancre; ~ **down** vt (person, animal) écraser; (fig: with worry) accabler; ~ **up** vt examiner

weight [weɪt] n poids m; to lose/put on ~ maigrir/grossir; ~**ing** n (allowance) indemnité f, allocation f; ~**-lifter** n haltérophile m; ~**y** adj lourd(e); (important) de poids, important(e)

weir [wɪə*] n barrage m

weird [wɪəd] adj bizarre

welcome ['wɛlkəm] adj bienvenu(e) ♦ n accueil m ♦ vt accueillir; (also: bid ~) souhaiter la bienvenue à; (be glad of) se réjouir de; thank you - you're ~! merci - de rien or il n'y a pas de quoi!

weld [weld] vt souder; **~er** n soudeur(euse)

welfare ['welfɛə*] n (well-being) bien-être m; (social aid) assistance sociale; **~ state** n Etat-providence m; **~ work** n travail social

well [wɛl] n puits m ♦ adv bien ♦ adj: **to be ~** aller bien ♦ excl eh bien!; bon!; enfin!; **as ~** aussi, également; **as ~ as** (in addition to) en plus de; **~ done!** bravo!; **get ~ soon** remets-toi vite!; **to do ~** bien réussir; (business) prospérer; **~ up** vi monter

we'll [wi:l] = we will; we shall

well-: **~-behaved** ['wɛlbɪ'heɪvd] adj sage, obéissant(e); **~-being** ['wɛlˈbiːŋ] n bien-être m; **~-built** ['wɛl'bɪlt] adj (person) bien bâti(e); **~ deserved** adj (rest) mérité(e); **~ dressed** adj bien habillé(e); **~ heeled** (inf) adj (wealthy) nanti(e)

wellingtons ['wɛlɪŋtənz] npl (also: wellington boots) bottes fpl de caoutchouc

well-: **~-known** ['wɛl'nəʊn] adj (person) bien connu(e); **~-mannered** ['wɛl'mænəd] adj bien élevé(e); **~ meaning** ['wɛl'miːnɪŋ] adj bien intentionné(e); **~-off** ['wɛl'ɒf] adj aisé(e); **~-read** ['wɛl'rɛd] adj cultivé(e); **~-to-do** ['wɛltə'duː] adj aisé(e); **~ wishers** ['wɛlwɪʃəz] npl amis mpl et admirateurs mpl; (friends) amis mpl

Welsh [wɛlʃ] adj gallois(e) ♦ n (LING) gallois m; **the ~** npl (people) les Gallois mpl; **~man** (irreg) n Gallois m; **~ rarebit** n toast m au fromage; **~woman** (irreg) n Galloise f

went [wɛnt] pt of go

wept [wɛpt] pt, pp of weep

were [wɜ:*] pt of be

we're [wɪə*] = we are

weren't [wɜ:nt] = were not

west [wɛst] n ouest m ♦ adj ouest inv, de or à l'ouest ♦ adv à or vers l'ouest; **the W~** n l'Occident m, l'Ouest m; **the W~ Country** (BRIT) n le sud-ouest de l'Angleterre; **~erly**

adj (wind) d'ouest; (point) à l'ouest; **~ern** adj occidental(e), de or à l'ouest ♦ n (CINEMA) western m; **W~ Indian** adj antillais(e) ♦ n Antillais(e); **W~ Indies** npl Antilles fpl; **~ward(s)** adv vers l'ouest

wet [wɛt] adj mouillé(e); (damp) humide; (soaked) trempé(e); (rainy) pluvieux(euse) ♦ n (BRIT: POL) modéré m du parti conservateur; **to get ~** se mouiller; **"~ paint"** "attention peinture fraîche"; **~ blanket** n (fig) rabat-joie m inv; **~ suit** n combinaison f de plongée

we've [wi:v] = we have

whack [wæk] vt donner un grand coup à

whale [weɪl] n (ZOOL) baleine f

wharf [wɔ:f] n (pl **wharves**) n quai m

KEYWORD

what [wɒt] adj quel(le); **~ size is he?** quelle taille fait-il?; **~ colour is it?** de quelle couleur est-ce?; **~ books do you need?** quels livres vous faut-il?; **~ a mess!** quel désordre!

♦ pron 1 (interrogative) que, prep +quoi; **~ are you doing?** que faites-vous?; qu'est-ce que vous faites?; **~ is happening?** qu'est-ce qui se passe? que se passe-t-il?; **~ are you talking about?** de quoi parlez-vous?; **~ is it called?** comment est-ce que ça s'appelle?; **~ about me?** et moi?; **~ about doing ...?** et si on faisait ...?

2 (relative: subject) ce qui; (: direct object) ce que; (: indirect object) ce +prep +quoi, ce dont; **I saw ~ you did/was on the table** j'ai vu ce que vous avez fait/ce qui était sur la table; **tell me ~ you remember** dites-moi ce dont vous souveniez

♦ excl (disbelieving) quoi!, comment!

whatever [wɒt'ɛvə*] adj: **~ book** quel que soit le livre que (or qui) +sub; n'importe quel livre ♦ pron:

do ~ is necessary faites (tout) ce qui est nécessaire; ~ happens quoi qu'il arrive; no reason ~ pas la moindre raison; nothing ~ rien du tout

whatsoever [wɒtˈsəʊevə*] adj = whatever

wheat [wiːt] n blé m, froment m

wheedle [ˈwiːdl] vt: to ~ sb into doing sth cajoler or enjôler qn pour qu'il fasse qch; to ~ sth out of sb obtenir qch de qn par des cajoleries

wheel [wiːl] n roue f; (also: steering ~) volant m; (NAUT) gouvernail m ♦ vt (pram etc) pousser ♦ vi (birds) tournoyer; (also: ~ round: person) virevolter; **~barrow** n brouette f; **~chair** n fauteuil roulant; **~ clamp** n (AUT) sabot m (de Denver)

wheeze [wiːz] vi respirer bruyamment

KEYWORD

when [wen] adv quand; ~ did he go? quand est-ce qu'il est parti?
♦ conj 1 (at, during, after the time that) quand, lorsque; she was reading ~ I came in elle lisait quand or lorsque je suis entré
2 (on, at which): on the day ~ I met him le jour où je l'ai rencontré
3 (whereas) alors que; I thought I was wrong ~ in fact I was right j'ai cru que j'avais tort alors qu'en fait j'avais raison

whenever [wenˈevə*] adv quand donc ♦ conj quand; (every time that) chaque fois que

where [wɛə*] adv, conj où; this is ~ c'est là que; **~abouts** [ˈwɛərəˈbaʊts] adv où ♦ n: nobody knows his ~abouts personne ne sait où il se trouve; **~as** [wɛərˈæz] conj alors que; **~by** adv par lequel (or laquelle etc); **~upon** adv sur quoi; **~ver** [wɛərˈevə*] adv où donc ♦ conj où que +sub; **~withal** [ˈwɛərwɪðɔːl] n moyens mpl

whet [wet] vt aiguiser

whether [ˈweðə*] conj si; I don't know ~ to accept or not je ne sais pas si je dois accepter ou non; it's doubtful ~ il est peu probable que +sub; ~ you go or not que vous y alliez ou non

KEYWORD

which [wɪtʃ] adj 1 (interrogative: direct, indirect) quel(le); ~ picture do you want? quel tableau voulez-vous?; ~ one? lequel(laquelle)?
2 in ~ case auquel cas
♦ pron 1 (interrogative) lequel(laquelle), lesquels(lesquelles) pl; I don't mind ~ peu importe lequel; ~ (of these) are yours? lesquels sont à vous?; tell me ~ you want dites-moi lesquels or ceux que vous voulez
2 (relative: subject) qui; (: object) que, prep +lequel(laquelle); the apple ~ you ate/~ is on the table la pomme que vous avez mangée/qui est sur la table; the chair on ~ you are sitting la chaise sur laquelle vous êtes assis; the book of ~ you spoke le livre dont vous avez parlé; he knew, ~ is true/I feared il le savait, ce qui est vrai/ce que je craignais; after ~ après quoi

whichever [wɪtʃˈevə*] adj: take ~ book you prefer prenez le livre que vous préférez, peu importe lequel; ~ book you take quel que soit le livre que vous preniez

whiff [wɪf] n bouffée f

while [waɪl] n moment m ♦ conj pendant que; (as long as) tant que; (whereas) alors que; bien que +sub; for a ~ pendant quelque temps; ~ away vt (time) (faire) passer

whim [wɪm] n caprice m

whimper [ˈwɪmpə*] vi geindre

whimsical [ˈwɪmzɪkəl] adj (person) capricieux(euse); (look, story) étrange

whine [waɪn] vi gémir, geindre

whip [wɪp] n fouet m; (for riding) cravache f; (POL: person) chef m de file assurant la discipline dans son groupe parlementaire ♦ vt fouetter; (eggs) battre; (move quickly) enlever (or sortir) brusquement; **~ped cream** n crème fouettée; **~round** (BRIT) n collecte f

whirl [wɜːl] vt faire tourbillonner; faire tournoyer ♦ vi tourbillonner; (dancers) tournoyer; **~pool** n tourbillon m; **~wind** n tornade f

whirr [wɜː] vi (motor etc) ronronner; (: louder) vrombir

whisk [wɪsk] n (CULIN) fouet m ♦ vt fouetter; (eggs) battre; to **~ sb away** or **off** emmener qn rapidement

whiskers ['wɪskəz] npl (of animal) moustaches fpl; (of man) favoris mpl

whisky ['wɪskɪ] (IRELAND, US **whiskey**) n whisky m

whisper ['wɪspə*] vt, vi chuchoter

whistle ['wɪsl] n (sound) sifflement m; (object) sifflet m ♦ vi siffler

white [waɪt] adj blanc(blanche); (with fear) blême ♦ n blanc m; (person) blanc(blanche); **~ coffee** (BRIT) n café m au lait, (café) crème m; **~-collar worker** n employé(e) de bureau; **~ elephant** n (fig) objet dispendieux et superflu; **~ lie** n pieux mensonge; **~ paper** n (POL) livre blanc; **~wash** n (paint) blanc m de chaux ♦ vt blanchir à la chaux; (fig) blanchir ♦ n (paint) blanc m de chaux

whiting ['waɪtɪŋ] n inv (fish) merlan m

Whitsun ['wɪtsn] n la Pentecôte

whittle ['wɪtl] vt: to **~ away**, **~ down** (costs) réduire

whizz [wɪz] vi: to **~ past** or **by** passer à toute vitesse; **~ kid** (inf) n petit prodige

who [huː] pron qui; **~dunit** [huː'dʌnɪt] (inf) n roman policier

whoever [huː'evə*] pron: **~ finds it** celui(celle) qui le trouve, qui que ce soit; quiconque le trouve; **ask ~ you like** demandez à qui vous vou-

lez; **~ he marries** quelle que soit la personne qu'il épouse; **~ told you that?** qui a bien pu vous dire ça?

whole [həʊl] adj (complete) entier(ère), tout(e); (not broken) intact(e), complet(ète) ♦ n (all): the **~ of** la totalité de, tout(e); the **~ of the town** la ville tout entière; **on the ~**, **as a ~** dans l'ensemble; **~food(s)** n(pl) aliments complets; **~hearted** adj sans réserve(s); **~meal** (BRIT) adj (bread, flour) complet(ète); **~sale** n (vente f en) gros m ♦ adj (price) de gros; (destruction) systématique ♦ adv en gros; **~saler** n grossiste m/f; **~wheat** adj = **~meal**; **wholly** ['həʊlɪ] adv entièrement, tout à fait

whom [huːm] pron 1 (interrogative) qui; **~ did you see?** qui avez-vous vu?; to **~ did you give it?** à qui l'avez-vous donné?

2 (relative) que, prep + qui; the **man ~ I saw**/to **~ I spoke** l'homme que j'ai vu/à qui j'ai parlé

whooping cough ['huːpɪŋ-] n coqueluche f

whore [hɔː*] n (inf: pej) n putain f

whose [huːz] adj 1 (possessive: interrogative): **~ book is this?** à qui est ce livre?; **~ pencil have you taken?** à qui est le crayon que vous avez pris?, c'est le crayon de qui que vous avez pris?; **~ daughter are you?** de qui êtes-vous la fille?

2 (possessive: relative): the **man ~** son you rescued l'homme dont or de qui vous avez sauvé le fils; the **girl ~ sister** you were speaking to la fille à la sœur de qui or de laquelle vous parliez; the **woman ~ car was stolen** la femme dont la voiture a été volée

♦ pron à qui; **~ is this?** à qui est

ceci?; **I know ~ it** is je sais à qui c'est

why [waɪ] adv pourquoi ♦ excl eh bien!; tiens!; **the reason ~** la raison pour laquelle; **tell me ~** dites-moi pourquoi; **~ not?** pourquoi pas?; **~ever** adv pourquoi donc, mais pourquoi

wicked ['wɪkɪd] adj mauvais(e), méchant(e); (crime) pervers(e); (mischievous) malicieux(euse)

wicket ['wɪkɪt] n (CRICKET) guichet m; terrain m (entre les deux guichets)

wide [waɪd] adj large; (area, knowledge) vaste, très étendu(e); (choice) grand(e) ♦ adv: **to open ~** ouvrir tout grand; **to shoot ~** tirer à côté; **~-angle lens** n objectif m grand angle; **~-awake** adj bien éveillé(e); **~ly** adv (differing) radicalement; (spaced) sur une grande étendue; (believed) généralement; (travel) beaucoup; **~n** vt élargir ♦ vi s'élargir; **~ open** adj grand(e) ouvert(e); **~spread** adj (belief etc) très répandu(e)

widow ['wɪdəu] n veuve f; **~ed** adj veuf(veuve); **~er** n veuf m

width [wɪdθ] n largeur f

wield [wiːld] vt (sword) manier; (power) exercer

wife [waɪf] (pl **wives**) n femme f, épouse f

wig [wɪg] n perruque f

wiggle ['wɪgl] vt agiter, remuer

wild [waɪld] adj sauvage; (sea) déchaîné(e); (idea, life) fou(folle); (behaviour) extravagant(e), déchaîné(e); **~s** npl (remote area) régions fpl sauvages; **to make a ~ guess** émettre une hypothèse à tout hasard; **~erness** ['wɪldənəs] n désert m, région f sauvage; **~-goose chase** n (fig) fausse piste; **~life** n (animals) faune f; **~ly** adv (behave) de manière déchaînée; (applaud) frénétiquement; (hit, guess) au hasard; (happy) follement

wilful ['wɪlful] (US **willful**) adj (person) obstiné(e); (action) délibéré(e)

KEYWORD

will [wɪl] (vt: pt, pp **willed**) aux vb **1** (forming future tense): **~ finish** it tomorrow je le finirai demain; **I ~ have finished it by tomorrow** je l'aurai fini d'ici demain; **~ you do it? - yes I ~/no I won't** le ferez-vous? - oui/non

2 (in conjectures, predictions): **he ~ or he'll be there by now** il doit être arrivé à l'heure qu'il est; **that ~ be the postman** ça doit être le facteur

3 (in commands, requests, offers): **~ you be quiet!** voulez-vous bien vous taire!; **~ you help me?** est-ce que vous pouvez m'aider?; **~ you have a cup of tea?** voulez-vous une tasse de thé?; **I won't put up with it!** je ne le tolérerai pas!

♦ vt: **to ~ sb to do** souhaiter ardemment que qn fasse; **he ~ed himself to go on** par un suprême effort de volonté, il continua

♦ n volonté f; testament m

willing ['wɪlɪŋ] adj de bonne volonté, serviable; **he's ~ to do it** il est disposé à le faire, il veut bien le faire; **~ly** adv volontiers; **~ness** n bonne volonté

willow ['wɪləu] n saule m

willpower ['wɪl'pauə*] n volonté f

willy-nilly ['wɪlɪ'nɪlɪ] adv bon gré mal gré

wilt [wɪlt] vi dépérir; (flower) se faner

wily ['waɪlɪ] adj rusé(e)

win [wɪn] (pt, pp **won**) n (in sports etc) victoire f ♦ vt gagner; (prize) remporter; (popularity) acquérir ♦ vi gagner; **~ over** vt convaincre; **~ round** (BRIT) vt = **~ over**

wince [wɪns] vi tressaillir

winch [wɪntʃ] n treuil m

wind¹ [wɪnd] n (also MED) vent m; (breath) souffle m ♦ vt (take breath) couper le souffle à

wind² [waɪnd] (*pt, pp* **wound**) *vt* enrouler; (*wrap*) envelopper; (*clock, toy*) remonter ♦ *vi* (*road, river*) serpenter; **wind up** *vt* (*clock*) remonter; (*debate*) terminer, clôturer

windfall ['wɪndfɔːl] *n* coup *m* de chance

winding ['waɪndɪŋ] *adj* (*road*) sinueux(euse); (*staircase*) tournant(e)

wind instrument *n* (MUS) instrument *m* à vent

windmill ['wɪndmɪl] *n* moulin *m* à vent

window ['wɪndəu] *n* fenêtre *f*; (*in car, train, also*: ~ **pane**) vitre *f*; (*in shop etc*) vitrine *f*; ~ **box** *n* jardinière *f*; ~ **cleaner** *n* (*person*) laveur(euse) de vitres; ~ **ledge** *n* rebord *m* de la fenêtre; ~ **pane** *n* vitre *f*, carreau *m*; ~**-shopping** *n*: **to go** ~**shopping** faire du lèche-vitrines; ~**sill** *n* (*inside*) appui *m* de la fenêtre; (*outside*) rebord *m* de la fenêtre

windpipe ['wɪndpaɪp] *n* trachée *f*

wind power *n* énergie éolienne

windscreen ['wɪndskriːn] *n* parebrise *m inv*; ~ **washer** *n* lave-glace *m inv*; ~ **wiper** *n* essuie-glace *m inv*

windshield ['wɪndʃiːld] (US) *n* = **windscreen**

windswept ['wɪndswept] *adj* balayé(e) par le vent; (*person*) ébouriffé(e)

windy ['wɪndɪ] *adj* venteux(euse); **it's** ~ **il y a du vent**

wine [waɪn] *n* vin *m*; ~ **bar** *n* bar *m* à vin; ~ **cellar** *n* cave *f* à vin; ~ **glass** *n* verre *m* à vin; ~ **list** *n* carte *f* des vins; ~ **waiter** *n* sommelier *m*

wing [wɪŋ] *n* aile *f*; ~**s** *npl* (THEATRE) coulisses *fpl*; ~**er** *n* (SPORT) ailier *m*

wink [wɪŋk] *n* clin *m* d'œil ♦ *vi* faire un clin d'œil; (*blink*) cligner des yeux

winner ['wɪnə*] *n* gagnant(e)

winning ['wɪnɪŋ] *adj* (*team*) ga-

gnant(e); (*goal*) décisif(ive); ~**s** *npl* gains *mpl*

winter ['wɪntə*] *n* hiver *m*; **in** ~ en hiver; ~ **sports** *npl* sports *mpl* d'hiver; **wintry** ['wɪntrɪ] *adj* hivernal(e)

wipe [waɪp] *n*: **to give sth a** ~ donner un coup de torchon (or de chiffon or d'éponge) à qch ♦ *vt* essuyer; (*erase: tape*) effacer; ~ **off** *vt* enlever; ~ **out** *vt* (*debt*) éteindre, amortir; (*memory*) effacer; (*destroy*) anéantir; ~ **up** *vt* essuyer

wire ['waɪə*] *n* fil *m* (de fer); (ELEC) fil électrique; (TEL) télégramme *m* ♦ *vt* (*house*) faire l'installation électrique de; (*also*: ~ **up**) brancher; (*person: send telegram to*) télégraphier à; ~**less** ['waɪəlɪs] (BRIT) *n* poste *m* de radio; **wiring** ['waɪərɪŋ] *n* installation *f* électrique

wiry ['waɪərɪ] *adj* noueux(euse), nerveux(euse); (*hair*) dru(e)

wisdom ['wɪzdəm] *n* sagesse *f*; (*of action*) prudence *f*; ~ **tooth** *n* dent *f* de sagesse

wise [waɪz] *adj* sage, prudent(e); (*remark*) judicieux(euse) ♦ *suffix*: ...**wise** *etc* en ce qui concerne le temps *etc*; ~**crack** *n* remarque *f* ironique

wish [wɪʃ] *n* (*desire*) désir *m*; (*specific desire*) souhait *m*, vœu *m* ♦ *vt* souhaiter, désirer, vouloir; **best** ~**es** (*on birthday etc*) meilleurs vœux; **with best** ~**es** (*in letter*) bien amicalement; **to** ~ **sb goodbye** dire au revoir à qn; **he** ~**ed me well** il m'a souhaité bonne chance; **to** ~ **to do/ sb to do** désirer or vouloir faire/que qn fasse; **to** ~ **for** souhaiter; ~**ful** *adj*: **it's** ~**ful thinking** c'est prendre ses désirs pour des réalités

wistful ['wɪstful] *adj* mélancolique

wit [wɪt] *n* (*gen pl*) intelligence *f*, esprit *m*; (*presence of mind*) présence *f* d'esprit; (*wittiness*) esprit; (*person*) homme/femme d'esprit

witch [wɪtʃ] *n* sorcière *f*; ~**craft** *n* sorcellerie *f*

---

with [wɪð, wɪθ] *prep* **1** (*in the company of*) avec; (*at the home of*) chez; we stayed ~ friends nous avons logé chez des amis; I'll be ~ you in a minute je suis à vous dans un instant
2 (*descriptive*): a room ~ a view une chambre avec vue; the man ~ the grey hat/blue eyes l'homme au chapeau gris/aux yeux bleus
3 (*indicating manner, means, cause*): ~ tears in her eyes les larmes aux yeux; to walk ~ a stick marcher avec une canne; red ~ anger rouge de colère; to shake ~ fear trembler de peur; to fill sth ~ water remplir qch d'eau
4: I'm ~ you (*I understand*) je vous suis; to be ~ it (*inf: up-to-date*) être dans le vent

withdraw [wɪðˈdrɔː] (*irreg*) *vt* retirer ♦ *vi* se retirer; ~al *n* retrait *m*; ~al symptoms *npl* (*MED*): to have ~al symptoms être en état de manque; ~n *adj* (*person*) renfermé(e)
wither [ˈwɪðəʳ] *vi* (*plant*) se faner
withhold [wɪðˈhəuld] (*irreg*) *vt* (*money*) retenir; to ~ (from) (*information*) cacher (à); (*permission*) refuser (à)
within [wɪðˈɪn] *prep* à l'intérieur de ♦ *adv* à l'intérieur; ~ his reach à sa portée; ~ sight of en vue de; ~ a kilometre of à moins d'un kilomètre de; ~ the week avant la fin de la semaine
without [wɪðˈaut] *prep* sans; ~ a coat sans manteau; ~ speaking sans parler; to go ~ sth se passer de qch
withstand [wɪðˈstænd] (*irreg*) *vt* résister à
witness [ˈwɪtnɪs] *n* (*person*) témoin *m* ♦ *vt* (*event*) être témoin de; (*document*) attester l'authenticité de; to bear ~ (to) (*fig*) attester; ~ box *n* barre *f* des témoins; ~ stand (*US*)

n = ~ box
witticism [ˈwɪtɪsɪzəm] *n* mot *m* d'esprit; **witty** [ˈwɪtɪ] *adj* spirituel(le), plein(e) d'esprit
wives [waɪvz] *npl of* **wife**
wizard [ˈwɪzəd] *n* magicien *m*
wk *abbr* = **week**
wobble [ˈwɒbl] *vi* trembler; (*chair*) branler
woe [wəu] *n* malheur *m*
woke [wəuk] *pt of* **wake**
woken [ˈwəukən] *pp of* **wake**
wolf [wulf, *pl* wulvz] (*pl* wolves) *n* loup *m*
woman [ˈwumən] (*pl* women) *n* femme *f*; ~ doctor *n* femme *f* médecin; ~ly *adj* féminin(e)
womb [wuːm] *n* (*ANAT*) utérus *m*
women [ˈwɪmɪn] *npl of* **woman**; ~'s lib (*inf*) *n* MLF *m*; W~'s (Liberation) Movement *n* mouvement *m* de libération de la femme
won [wʌn] *pt, pp of* **win**
wonder [ˈwʌndəʳ] *n* merveille *f*, miracle *m*; (*feeling*) émerveillement *m* ♦ *vi*: to ~ whether/why se demander si/pourquoi; to ~ at (*marvel*) s'émerveiller de; to ~ about songer à; it's no ~ (that) il n'est pas étonnant (que +*sub*); ~ful *adj* merveilleux(euse)
won't [wəunt] = **will not**
woo [wuː] *vt* (*woman*) faire la cour à; (*audience etc*) chercher à plaire à
wood [wud] *n* (*timber, forest*) bois *m*; ~ carving *n* sculpture *f* en ou sur bois; ~ed *adj* boisé(e); ~en *adj* en bois; (*fig*) raide, inexpressif(ive); ~pecker *n* pic *m* (*oiseau*); ~wind *n* (*MUS*): the ~wind les bois; ~work *n* menuiserie *f*; ~worm *n* ver *m* du bois
wool [wul] *n* laine *f*; to pull the ~ over sb's eyes (*fig*) en faire accroire à qn; ~len (*US* ~en) *adj* de *or* en laine; (*industry*) lainier(ère); ~lens *npl* (*clothes*) lainages *mpl*; ~ly (*US* ~y) *adj* laineux(euse); (*fig: ideas*) confus(e)
word [wɜːd] *n* mot *m*; (*promise*) pa-

role f; (news) nouvelles fpl ♦ vt rédiger, formuler; **in other ~s** en d'autres termes; **to break/keep one's ~** manquer à sa parole/tenir parole; **~ing** n termes mpl; libellé m; **~ processing** n traitement m de texte; **~ processor** n machine f de traitement de texte

wore [wɔː*] pt of wear

work [wɜːk] n travail m; (ART, LITERATURE) œuvre f ♦ vi travailler; (mechanism) marcher, fonctionner; (plan etc) marcher; (medicine) agir ♦ vt (clay, wood etc) travailler; (mine etc) exploiter; (machine) faire marcher ou fonctionner; (miracles, wonders etc) faire; **to be out of ~** être sans emploi; **to ~ loose** se défaire, se desserrer; **~ on** vt fus travailler à; (principle) se baser sur; (person) (essayer d')influencer; **~ out** vi (plans etc) marcher ♦ vt (problem) résoudre; (plan) élaborer; **it ~s out at £100** ça fait 100 livres; **~ up** vt: **to get ~ed up** se mettre dans tous ses états; **~able** adj (solution) réalisable; **~aholic** [wɜːkəˈhɒlɪk] n bourreau m de travail; **~er** n travailleur(euse), ouvrier(ère); **~force** n main-d'œuvre f; **~ing class** n classe ouvrière; **~ing-class** adj ouvrier(ère); **~ing order** n: **in ~ing order** en état de marche; **~man** (irreg) n ouvrier m; **~manship** n (skill) métier m, habileté f; **~s** n (BRIT: factory) usine f ♦ npl (of clock, machine) mécanisme m; **~sheet** n (COMPUT) feuille f de programmation; **~shop** n atelier m; **~station** n poste m de travail; **~to-rule** (BRIT) n grève f du zèle

world [wɜːld] n monde m ♦ cpd (champion) du monde; (power, war) mondial(e); **to think the ~ of sb** (fig) ne jurer que par qn; **~ly** adj de ce monde; (knowledgeable) qui a l'expérience du monde; **~wide** adj universel(le)

worm [wɜːm] n ver m

worn [wɔːn] pp of wear ♦ adj

usé(e); **~out** adj (object) complètement usé(e); (person) épuisé(e)

worried [ˈwʌrɪd] adj inquiet(ète)

worry [ˈwʌrɪ] n souci m ♦ vt inquiéter ♦ vi s'inquiéter, se faire du souci

worse [wɜːs] adj pire, plus mauvais(e) ♦ adv plus mal ♦ n pire m; **a change for the ~** une détérioration; **~n** vt, vi empirer; **~ off** adj, moins à l'aise financièrement; (fig): **you'll be ~ off this way** ça ira moins bien de cette façon

worship [ˈwɜːʃɪp] n culte m ♦ vt (God) rendre un culte à; (person) adorer; **Your W~** (BRIT: to mayor) Monsieur le maire; (: to judge) Monsieur le juge

worst [wɜːst] adj le(la) pire, le(la) plus mauvais(e) ♦ adv le plus mal ♦ n pire m; **at ~** au pis aller

worth [wɜːθ] n valeur f ♦ adj: **to be ~** valoir; **it's ~ it** cela en vaut la peine, ça vaut la peine; **it's ~ one's while (to do)** on gagne à (faire); **~less** adj qui ne vaut rien; **~while** adj (activity, cause) utile, louable

worthy [ˈwɜːðɪ] adj (person) digne; (motive) louable; **~ of** digne de

---
KEYWORD

---

would [wʊd] aux vb **1** (conditional tense): **if you asked him he ~ do it** si vous le lui demandiez, il le ferait; **if you had asked him he ~ have done it** si vous le lui aviez demandé, il l'aurait fait

2 (in offers, invitations, requests): **~ you like a biscuit?** voulez-vous ou voudriez-vous un biscuit?; **~ you close the door please?** voulez-vous fermer la porte, s'il vous plaît?

3 (in indirect speech): **I said I ~ do it** j'ai dit que je le ferais

4 (emphatic): **it WOULD have to snow today!** naturellement il se met à neiger aujourd'hui! or il fallait qu'il neige aujourd'hui!

5 (insistence): **she ~n't do it** elle n'a pas voulu or elle a refusé de le faire

6 (*conjecture*): it ~ have been midnight il devait être minuit
7 (*indicating habit*): he ~ go there on Mondays il y allait le lundi

would-be ['wudbi:] (*pej*) *adj* soi-disant

wouldn't ['wudnt] = would not

wound¹ [wu:nd] *n* blessure *f* ♦ *vt* blesser

wound² [waund] *pt, pp of* wind²

wove [wəuv] *pt of* weave

woven ['wəuvən] *pp of* weave

wrap [ræp] *vt* (*also:* ~ up) envelopper, emballer; (*wind*) enrouler; ~age
n (*BRIT: of book*) couverture *f*; (*on chocolate*) emballage *m*, papier *m*; ~ping paper *n* papier *m* d'emballage; (*for gift*) papier cadeau

wrath [rɔθ] *n* courroux *m*

wreak [ri:k] *vt*: to ~ havoc (on) avoir un effet désastreux (sur)

wreath [ri:θ, *pl* ri:ðz] (*pl* ~s) *n* couronne *f*

wreck [rɛk] *n* (*ship*) épave *f*; (*vehicle*) véhicule accidenté; (*pej: person*) loque humaine ♦ *vt* démolir; (*fig*) briser, ruiner; ~age *n* débris *mpl*; (*of building*) décombres *mpl*; (*of ship*) épave *f*

wren [rɛn] *n* (*ZOOL*) roitelet *m*

wrench [rɛntʃ] *n* (*TECH*) clé *f* (à écrous); (*tug*) violent mouvement de torsion; (*fig*) déchirement *m* ♦ *vt* tirer violemment sur, tordre; to ~ sth from arracher qch à *or* de

wrestle ['rɛsl] *vi*: to ~ (with sb) lutter (avec qn); ~r *n* lutteur(euse);
wrestling *n* lutte *f*; (*also: all-in wrestling*) catch *m*

wretched ['rɛtʃɪd] *adj* misérable;
(*inf*) maudit(e)

wriggle ['rɪgl] *vi* (*also:* ~ about) se tortiller

wring [rɪŋ] (*pt, pp* wrung) *vt* tordre; (*wet clothes*) essorer; (*fig*): to ~ sth out of sb arracher qch à qn

wrinkle ['rɪŋkl] *n* (*on skin*) ride *f*; (*on paper etc*) pli *m* ♦ *vt* plisser ♦ *vi* se plisser

wrist [rɪst] *n* poignet *m*; ~watch *n* montre-bracelet *f*

writ [rɪt] *n* acte *m* judiciaire

write [raɪt] (*pt* wrote, *pp* written) *vt, vi* écrire; (*prescription*) rédiger; ~ down *vt* noter; (*put in writing*) mettre par écrit; ~ off *vt* (*debt*) passer aux profits et pertes; (*project*) mettre une croix sur; ~ out *vt* écrire; ~ up *vt* rédiger; ~-off *n* perte totale; ~r *n* auteur *m*, écrivain *m*

writhe [raɪð] *vi* se tordre

writing ['raɪtɪŋ] *n* écriture *f*; (*of author*) œuvres *fpl*; **in** ~ par écrit;
~ paper *n* papier *m* à lettres

wrong [rɒŋ] *adj* (*incorrect*): answer, information) faux(fausse); (*inappropriate*: choice, action etc) mauvais(e); (*wicked*) mal; (*unfair*) injuste ♦ *adv* mal ♦ *n* tort *m* ♦ *vt* faire du tort à, léser; **you are** ~ to do it tu as tort de le faire; **you are** ~ about that, you've got it ~ tu te trompes; **what's** ~? qu'est-ce qui ne va pas?; **to go** ~ (*person*) se tromper; (*plan*) mal tourner; (*machine*) tomber en panne; **to be in the** ~ avoir tort; ~ful *adj* injustifié(e); ~ly *adv* mal, incorrectement; ~ side *n* (*of material*) envers *m*

wrote [rəut] *pt of* write

wrought [rɔ:t] *adj*: ~ iron fer forgé

wrung [rʌŋ] *pt, pp of* wring

wry [raɪ] *adj* désabusé(e)

wt. *abbr* = weight

X, Y, Z

Xmas ['ɛksməs] *n abbr* = Christmas

X-ray ['ɛks'reɪ] *n* (*ray*) rayon *m* X; (*photo*) radio(graphie) *f*

xylophone ['zaɪləfəun] *n* xylophone *m*

yacht [jɒt] *n* yacht *m*; voilier *m*; ~ing *n* yachting *m*, navigation *f* de plaisance; ~sman (*irreg*) *n* plaisancier *m*

Yank [jæŋk] (*pej*) *n* Amerloque *m/f*

Yankee ['jæŋkɪ] *n* = Yank

yap [jæp] vi (dog) japper

yard [jɑːd] n (of house etc) cour f; (measure) yard m (= 91,4 cm); **~stick** n (fig) mesure f, critères mpl

yarn [jɑːn] n fil m; (tale) longue histoire

yawn [jɔːn] n bâillement m ♦ vi bâiller; **~ing** adj (gap) béant(e)

yd. abbr = **yard(s)**

yeah [jɛə] (inf) adv ouais

year [jɪə*] n an m, année f; to be 8 ~s old avoir 8 ans; an eight-~-old child un enfant de huit ans; **~ly** adj annuel(le) ♦ adv annuellement

yearn [jɜːn] vi: to ~ for sth aspirer à qch, languir après qch; to ~ to do aspirer à faire

yeast [jiːst] n levure f

yell [jɛl] vi hurler

yellow [ˈjɛləʊ] adj jaune

yelp [jɛlp] vi japper; glapir

yeoman [ˈjəʊmən] (irreg) n: ~ of the guard hallebardier m de la garde royale

yes [jɛs] adv oui; (answering negative question) si ♦ n oui m; to say/answer ~ dire/répondre oui

yesterday [ˈjɛstədeɪ] adv hier ♦ n hier m; ~ **morning/evening** hier matin/soir; **all day** ~ toute la journée d'hier

yet [jɛt] adv encore; déjà ♦ conj pourtant, néanmoins; **it is not finished** ~ ce n'est pas encore fini or toujours pas fini; **the best** ~ le meilleur jusqu'ici or jusque-là; **as** ~ jusqu'ici, encore

yew [juː] n if m

yield [jiːld] n production f, rendement m; rapport m ♦ vt produire, rendre, rapporter; (surrender) céder ♦ vi céder; (US: AUT) céder la priorité

YMCA n abbr (= Young Men's Christian Association) YMCA m

yoghourt [ˈjɒgət] n yaourt m

yog(h)urt [ˈjɒgət] n = **yoghourt**

yoke [jəʊk] n joug m

yolk [jəʊk] n jaune m (d'œuf)

---

you [juː] pron 1 (subject) tu; (polite form) vous; (plural) vous; **French enjoy your food** vous autres Français, vous aimez bien manger; ~ **and I will go** toi et moi or vous et moi, nous irons

2 (object: direct, indirect) te, t' +vowel; vous; **I know** ~ je te or vous connais; **I gave it to** ~ je te or vous l'ai donné, je te l'ai donné

3 (stressed) toi; vous; **I told YOU to do it** c'est à toi or vous que j'ai dit de le faire

4 (after prep, in comparisons) toi; vous; **it's for** ~ c'est pour toi or vous; **she's younger than** ~ elle est plus jeune que toi or vous

5 (impersonal: one) on; **fresh air does** ~ **good** l'air frais fait du bien; ~ **never know** on ne sait jamais

---

you'd [juːd] = **you had**; **you would**

you'll [juːl] = **you will**; **you shall**

young [jʌŋ] adj jeune ♦ npl (of animal) petits mpl; (people) the ~ les jeunes, la jeunesse; **~er** adj (brother etc) cadet(te); **~ster** n jeune m (garçon m); (child) enfant m/f

your [ˈjɔː*] adj ton(ta), tes pl; (polite form, pl) votre, vos pl; see also **my**

you're [ˈjʊə*] = **you are**

yours [jɔːz] pron le(la) tien(ne), les tiens(tiennes); (polite form, pl) le(la) vôtre, les vôtres; ~ **sincerely/faithfully/truly** veuillez agréer l'expression de mes sentiments les meilleurs; see also **mine1**

yourself [jɔːˈsɛlf] pron (reflexive) te; (: polite form) vous; (after prep) toi; vous; (emphatic) toi-même; vous-même; see also **oneself**; **yourselves** pl pron vous; (emphatic) vous-mêmes

youth [juːθ, pl juːðz] n jeunesse f; (young man: pl youths) jeune homme m; ~ **club** n centre m de jeunes; **~ful** adj jeune; (enthusiasm) de jeunesse, juvénile; ~ **hostel** n auberge f de jeunesse

you've [ju:v] = **you have**

YTS (BRIT) n abbr (= Youth Training Scheme) ≈ TUC m

Yugoslav adj yougoslave ♦ n Yougoslave m/f; **~ia** n Yougoslavie f

yuppie ['jʌpɪ] (inf) n yuppie m/f

YWCA n abbr (= Young Women's Christian Association) YWCA m

zany ['zeɪnɪ] adj farfelu(e), loufoque

zap [zæp] vt (COMPUT) effacer

zeal [zi:l] n zèle m, ferveur f; empressement m

zebra ['zi:brə] n zèbre m; **~ crossing** (BRIT) n passage clouté or pour piétons

zero ['zɪərəʊ] n zéro m

zest [zest] n entrain m, élan m; (of

orange) zeste m

zigzag ['zɪgzæg] n zigzag m

Zimbabwe [zɪm'bɑːbwɪ] n Zimbabwe m

zinc [zɪŋk] n zinc m

zip [zɪp] n (also: ~ fastener) fermeture f éclair ® ♦ vt (: ~ up) fermer avec une fermeture éclair ®); **~ code** (US) n code postal; **~per** (US) n = **zip**

zodiac ['zəʊdɪæk] n zodiaque m

zone [zəʊn] n zone f

zoo [zu:] n zoo m

zoom [zu:m] vi: **to ~ past** passer en trombe; **~ lens** n zoom m

zucchini [zu:'ki:nɪ] (US) n(pl) courgette(s) f(pl)

VERB TABLES

1 Participe présent *2* Participe passé *3* Présent *4* Imparfait *5* Futur *6* Conditionnel *7* Subjonctif présent

acquérir *1* acquérant *2* acquis *3* acquiers, acquérons, acquièrent *5* acquérai *5* acquerrai *7* acquière

ALLER *1* allant *2* allé *3* vais, va, allons, allez, vont *4* allais *5* irai *6* irais *7* aille

asseoir *1* asseyant *2* assis *3* assieds, asseyons, asseyez, asseyent *4* asseyais *5* assiérai *7* asseye

atteindre *1* atteignant *2* atteint *3* atteins, atteignons *4* atteignais *7* atteigne

AVOIR *1* ayant *2* eu *3* ai, as, a, avons, avez, ont *4* avais *5* aurai *6* aurais *7* aie, aies, ait, ayons, ayez, aient

battre *1* battant *2* battu *3* bats, bat, battons *4* battais *7* batte

boire *1* buvant *2* bu *3* bois, buvons, boivent *4* buvais *7* boive

bouillir *1* bouillant *2* bouilli *3* bous, bouillons *4* bouillais *7* bouille

conclure *1* concluant *2* conclu *3* conclus, concluons *1* Rncluais *1*Rnclue

conduire *1* conduisant *2* conduit *3* conduis, conduisons *4* conduisais *7* conduise

connaître *1* connaissant *2* connu *3* connais, connaît, connaissons *4* connaissais *7* connaisse

coudre *1* cousant *2* cousu *3* couds, cousons, cousez, cousent *4* cousais *7* couse

courir *1* courant *2* couru *3* cours, ⸱⸱urons *4* courais *5* courrai *7*

coure

couvrir *1* couvrant *2* couvert *3* couvre, couvrons *4* couvrais *7* couvre

craindre *1* craignant *2* craint *3* crains, craignons *4* craignais *7* craigne

croire *1* croyant *2* cru *3* crois, croyons, croient *4* croyais *7* croie

croître *1* croissant *2* crû, crue, crus, crues *3* crois, croissons *4* croissais *7* croisse

cueillir *1* cueillant *2* cueilli *3* cueille, cueillons *4* cueillais *5* cueillerai *7* cueille

devoir *1* devant *2* dû, due, dus, dues *3* dois, devons, doivent *4* devais *5* devrai *7* doive

dire *1* disant *2* dit *3* dis, disons, dites, disent *4* disais *7* dise

dormir *1* dormant *2* dormi *3* dors, dormons *4* dormais *7* dorme

écrire *1* écrivant *2* écrit *3* écris, écrivons *4* écrivais *7* écrive

ÊTRE *1* étant *2* été *3* suis, es, est, sommes, êtes, sont *4* étais *5* serai *6* serais *7* sois, sois, soit, soyons, soyez, soient

FAIRE *1* faisant *2* fait *3* fais, fais, fait, faisons, faites, font *4* faisais *5* ferai *6* ferais *7* fasse

falloir *2* fallu *3* faut *4* fallait *5* faudra *7* faille

FINIR *1* finissant *2* fini *3* finis, finis, finit, finissons, finissez, finissent *4* finissais *5* finirai *6* finirais *7* finisse

fuir *1* fuyant *2* fui *3* fuis, fuyons,

fuient *4* fuyais *7* fuie

joindre *1* joignant *2* joint *3* joins, joignons *4* joignais *7* joigne

lire *1* lisant *2* lu *3* lis, lisons *4* lisais *7* lise

luire *1* luisant *7* lui *3* luis, luisons *4* luisais *7* luise

maudire *1* maudissant *2* maudit *3* maudis, maudissons *4* maudissait *7* maudisse

mentir *1* mentant *2* menti *3* mens, mentons *4* mentais *7* mente

mettre *1* mettant *2* mis *3* mets, mettons *4* mettais *7* mette

mourir *1* mourant *2* mort *3* meurs, mourons, meurent *4* mourais *5* mourrai *7* meure

naître *1* naissant *2* né *3* nais, naît, naissons *4* naissais *7* naisse

offrir *1* offrant *2* offert *3* offre, offrons *4* offrais *7* offre

PARLER *1* parlant *2* parlé *3* parle, parles, parle, parlons, parlez, parlent *4* parlais, parlais, parlait, parlions, parliez, parlaient *5* parlerai, parleras, parlera, parlerons, parlerez, parleront *6* parlerais, parlerais, parlerait, parlerions, parleriez, parleraient *7* parle, parles, parle, parlions, parliez, parlent *impératif* parle! parlez!

partir *1* partant *2* parti *3* pars, partons *4* partais *7* parte

plaire *1* plaisant *2* plu *3* plais, plaît, plaisons *4* plaisais *7* plaise

pleuvoir *1* pleuvant *2* plu *3* pleut, pleuvent *4* pleuvait *5* pleuvra *7* pleuve

pourvoir *1* pourvoyant *2* pourvu

3 pourvois, pourvoyons, pourvoient *4* pourvoyais *7* pourvoie

pouvoir *1* pouvant *2* pu *3* peux, peut, pouvons, peuvent *4* pouvais *5* pourrai *7* puisse

prendre *1* prenant *2* pris *3* prends, prenons, prennent *4* prenais *7* prenne

prévoir *like voir 5* prévoirai

RECEVOIR *1* recevant *2* reçu *3* reçois, reçois, reçoit, recevons, recevez, reçoivent *4* recevais *5* recevrai *7* reçoive

RENDRE *1* rendant *2* rendu *3* rends, rends, rend, rendons, rendez, rendent *4* rendais *5* rendrai *6* rendrais *7* rende

résoudre *1* résolvant *2* résolu *3* résous, résolvons *4* résolvais *7* résolve

rire *1* riant *2* ri *3* ris, rions *4* riais *7* rie

savoir *1* sachant *2* su *3* sais, savons, savent *4* savais *5* saurai *7* sache *impératif* sache, sachons, sachez

servir *1* servant *2* servi *3* sers, servons *4* servais *7* serve

sortir *1* sortant *2* sorti *3* sors, sortons *4* sortais *7* sorte

souffrir *1* souffrant *2* souffert *3* souffre, souffrons *4* souffrais *7* souffre

suffire *1* suffisant *2* suffi *3* suffis, suffisons *4* suffisais *7* suffise

suivre *1* suivant *2* suivi *3* suis, suivons *4* suivais *7* suive

taire *1* taisant *2* tu *3* tais, taisons *4* taisais *7* taise

tenir *1* tenant *2* tenu *3* tiens, tenons, tiennent *4* tenais *5* tiendrai *7* tienne

vaincre *1* vainquant *2* vaincu *3*

vaincs, vainc, vainquons 4
vainquais 7 vainque

valoir 1 valant 2 valu 3 vaux,
vaut, valons 4 valais 5 vaudrai
7 vaille

venir 1 venant 2 venu 3 viens,
venons, viennent 4 venais 5
viendrai   7   vienne

vivre 1 vivant 2 vécu 3 vis,
vivons 4 vivais 7 vive

voir 1 voyant 2 vu 3 vois, voyons,
voient 4 voyais 5 verrai 7 voie

vouloir 1 voulant 2 voulu 3 veux,
veut, voulons, veulent 4
voulais 5 voudrai 7 veuille *impératif* veuillez

VERBES IRRÉGULIERS

present	pt	pp	present	pt	pp
arise	arose	arisen	dig	dug	dug
awake	awoke	awaked	do (3rd	did	done
be (am, is,	was,	been	person;		
are;	were		he/she/it/		
being)			does)		
bear	bore	born(e)	draw	drew	drawn
beat	beat	beaten	dream	dreamed,	dreamed,
become	became	become		dreamt	dreamt
begin	began	begun	drink	drank	drunk
behold	beheld	beheld	drive	drove	driven
bend	bent	bent	dwell	dwelt	dwelt
beset	beset	beset	eat	ate	eaten
bet	bet, betted	bet,	fall	fell	fallen
		betted	feed	fed	fed
bid	bid,	bid,	feel	felt	felt
	bade	bidden	fight	fought	fought
bind	bound	bound	find	found	found
bite	bit	bitten	flee	fled	fled
bleed	bled	bled	fling	flung	flung
blow	blew	blown	fly (flies)	flew	flown
break	broke	broken	forbid	forbade	forbidden
breed	bred	bred	forecast	forecast	forecast
bring	brought	brought	forget	forgot	forgotten
build	built	built	forgive	forgave	forgiven
burn	burnt,	burnt,	forsake	forsook	forsaken
	burned	burned	freeze	froze	frozen
burst	burst	burst	get	got	got, (US)
buy	bought	bought			gotten
can	could	(been	give	gave	given
		able)	go (goes)	went	gone
cast	cast	cast	grind	ground	ground
catch	caught	caught	grow	grew	grown
choose	chose	chosen	hang	hung,	hung,
cling	clung	clung		hanged	hanged
come	came	come	have (has;	had	had
cost	cost	cost	having)		
creep	crept	crept	hear	heard	heard
cut	cut	cut	hide	hid	hidden
deal	dealt	dealt	hit	hit	hit

present	pt	pp	present	pt	pp
hold	held	held	sell	sold	sold
hurt	hurt	hurt	send	sent	sent
keep	kept	kept	set	set	set
kneel	knelt,	knelt,	shake	shook	shaken
	kneeled	kneeled	shall	should	—
know	knew	known	shear	sheared	shorn,
lay	laid	laid			sheared
lead	led	led	shed	shed	shed
lean	leant,	leant,	shine	shone	shone
	leaned	leaned	shoot	shot	shot
leap	leapt,	leapt,	show	showed	shown
	leaped	leaped	shrink	shrank	shrunk
learn	learnt,	learnt,	shut	shut	shut
	learned	learned	sing	sang	sung
leave	left	left	sink	sank	sunk
lend	lent	lent	sit	sat	sat
let	let	let	slay	slew	slain
lie (lying)	lay	lain	sleep	slept	slept
light	lit,	lit,	slide	slid	slid
	lighted	lighted	sling	slung	slung
			slit	slit	slit
lose	lost	lost	smell	smelt,	smelt,
make	made	made		smelled	smelled
may	might	—	sow	sowed	sown,
mean	meant	meant			sowed
meet	met	met	speak	spoke	spoken
mistake	mistook	mistaken	speed	sped,	sped,
mow	mowed	mown,		speeded	speeded
		mowed	spell	spelt,	spelt,
must	(had to)	(had to)		spelled	spelled
pay	paid	paid	spend	spent	spent
put	put	put	spill	spilt,	spilt,
quit	quit,	quit,		spilled	spilled
	quitted	quitted	spin	spun	spun
read	read	read	spit	spat	spat
rid	rid	rid	split	split	split
ride	rode	ridden	spoil	spoiled,	spoiled,
ring	rang	rung		spoilt	spoilt
rise	rose	risen	spread	spread	spread
run	ran	run	spring	sprang	sprung
saw	sawed	sawn	stand	stood	stood
say	said	said	steal	stole	stolen
see	saw	seen	stick	stuck	stuck
seek	sought	sought			

318

present	pt	pp	present	pt	pp
sting	stung	stung	think	thought	thought
stink	stank	stunk	throw	threw	thrown
stride	strode	stridden	thrust	thrust	thrust
strike	struck	struck, stricken	tread	trod	trodden
			wake	woke, waked	woken, waked
strive	strove	striven			
swear	swore	sworn	wear	wore	worn
sweep	swept	swept	weave	wove, weaved	woven, weaved
swell	swelled	swollen, swelled	wed	wedded, wed	wedded, wed
swim	swam	swum			
swing	swung	swung	weep	wept	wept
take	took	taken	win	won	won
teach	taught	taught	wind	wound	wound
tear	tore	torn	wring	wrung	wrung
tell	told	told	write	wrote	written

LES NOMBRES

NUMBERS

un (une)	1	one
deux	2	two
trois	3	three
quatre	4	four
cinq	5	five
six	6	six
sept	7	seven
huit	8	eight
neuf	9	nine
dix	10	ten
onze	11	eleven
douze	12	twelve
treize	13	thirteen
quatorze	14	fourteen
quinze	15	fifteen
seize	16	sixteen
dix-sept	17	seventeen
dix-huit	18	eighteen
dix-neuf	19	nineteen
vingt	20	twenty
vingt et un (une)	21	twenty-one
vingt-deux	22	twenty-two
trente	30	thirty
quarante	40	forty
cinquante	50	fifty
soixante	60	sixty
soixante-dix	70	seventy
soixante et onze	71	seventy-one
soixante-douze	72	seventy-two
quatre-vingts	80	eighty
quatre-vingt-un (-une)	81	eighty-one
quatre-vingt-dix	90	ninety
quatre-vingt-onze	91	ninety-one
cent	100	a hundred
cent un (une)	101	a hundred and one
trois cents	300	three hundred
trois cent un (une)	301	three hundred and one
mille	1 000	a thousand
un million	1 000 000	a million

premier (première), 1er	first, 1st
deuxième, 2e or 2ème	second, 2nd
troisième, 3e or 3ème	third, 3rd
quatrième	fourth, 4th
cinquième	fifth, 5th
sixième	sixth, 6th

LES NOMBRES

septième	seventh
huitième	eighth
neuvième	ninth
dixième	tenth
onzième	eleventh
douzième	twelfth
treizième	thirteenth
quatorzième	fourteenth
quinzième	fifteenth
seizième	sixteenth
dix-septième	seventeenth
dix-huitième	eighteenth
dix-neuvième	nineteenth
vingtième	twentieth
vingt-et-unième	twenty-first
vingt-deuxième	twenty-second
trentième	thirtieth
centième	hundredth
cent-unième	hundred-and-first
millième	thousandth

NUMBERS

Les Fractions etc

un demi	a half
un tiers	a third
deux tiers	two thirds
un quart	a quarter
un cinquième	a fifth
zéro virgule cinq, 0,5	(nought) point five, 0.5
trois virgule quatre, 3,4	three point four, 3.4
dix pour cent	ten per cent
cent pour cent	a hundred per cent

Fractions etc

Examples

il habite au dix	he lives at number 10
c'est au chapitre sept	it's in chapter 7
à la page sept	on page 7
il habite au septième (étage)	he lives on the 7th floor
il est arrivé (le) septième	he came in 7th
une part d'un septième	a share of one seventh
échelle au vingt-cinq millième	scale one to twenty-five thousand

Examples

L'HEURE	THE TIME
quelle heure est-il?	*what time is it?*
il est ...	*it's ...*
minuit	midnight, twelve p.m.
une heure (du matin)	one o'clock (in the morning), one (a.m.)
une heure cinq	five past one
une heure dix	ten past one
une heure et quart	a quarter past one, one fifteen
une heure vingt-cinq	twenty-five past one, one twenty-five
une heure et demie, une heure trente	half past one, one thirty
une heure trente-cinq, deux heures moins vingt-oinq	twenty-five to two, one thirty-five
deux heures moins vingt, une heure quarante	twenty to two, one forty
deux heures moins le quart, une heure quarante-cinq	a quarter to two, one forty-five
deux heures moins dix, une heure cinquante	ten to two, one fifty
midi	twelve o'clock, midday, noon
deux heures (de l'après-midi)	two o'clock (in the afternoon), two (p.m.)
sept heures (du soir)	seven o'clock (in the evening), seven (p.m.)
à quelle heure?	*at what time?*
à minuit	at midnight
à sept heures	at seven o'clock
dans vingt minutes	in twenty minutes
il y a quinze minutes	fifteen minutes ago